Christine

active MATHS 3

LEAVING CERTIFICATE MATHS ORDINARY LEVEL

Access your eBook

New eBook users

1. Scratch the foil below to reveal your unique licence code
2. Register on www.folenshive.ie with your code
3. A parent or legal guardian will have to give their consent for you to access our eBooks
4. Download the FolensHIVE app to your device or use the web platform
5. Login to access your eBook

Current FolensHIVE users can redeem additional eBooks through the app.

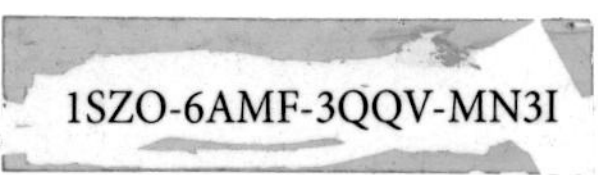

Teachers please go to FolensHIVE to login or register

FolensHIVE

First published in 2017 by Folens Publishers

Hibernian Industrial Estate, Greenhills Road, Tallaght, Dublin 24

Illustrations: Oxford Designers and Illustrators

ISBN 978-1-78090-701-7

Acknowledgements

Answers were checked by Jonathan Webley.

The authors and publisher are grateful to the following for permission to reproduce photographs: Alamy, iStock, Shutterstock and Thinkstock.

The publisher has made every effort to contact all copyright holders but if any have been overlooked, we will be pleased to make any necessary arrangements.

Contents

Paper 2

Paper 2

Easter - probability, statistics algebra
Trigonometry, The line

Authors and Advisors

Michael Keating teaches at Coláiste na Sceilge, Co. Kerry. He is an experienced examiner and in-service trainer and holds a Master's Degree in Curriculum Studies (Mathematics) from University College Cork.

Jim McElroy teaches at Castleknock College, Dublin. He holds a BA in Economics, a B.Sc. in Mathematics and an M.Sc. in Applied Mathematics and Theoretical Physics.

Derek Mulvany teaches at Castleknock College, Dublin. He has served as a committee member of the IMTA Dublin branch and is a former Dublin branch representative and vice-chairperson of the IMTA.

Oliver Murphy is the Principal of Castleknock College, Dublin. He is a committee member and a former chairperson of the IAMTA. He is also the bestselling author of *Fundamental Applied Maths* and the popular *Discovering Maths* series.

James O'Loughlin teaches at Castleknock College, Dublin. He is a member of the IMTA and holds a Master's Degree in Mathematics for Education.

Colin Townsend teaches at Castleknock College, Dublin. He is an experienced examiner and is an active member of the Dublin branch of the IMTA.

Introduction

Active Maths 3 (2nd edition) is a comprehensive single-volume revision of our existing, successful series covering the complete Leaving Certificate Ordinary Level course. This programme maintains all the benefits of the previous books, while introducing a range of new and improved features. This new single book covers all five strands of the Project Maths syllabus.

- Strand 1 Statistics and Probability: Chapters 11–14 (Paper 2)
- Strand 2 Geometry and Trigonometry: Chapters 15–19 (Paper 2)
- Strand 3 Number: Chapters 1, 3, 4, 7, 8, 10 (Paper 1)
- Strand 4 Algebra: Chapters 2 and 5 (Paper 1)
- Strand 5 Functions: Chapters 6 and 9 (Paper 1)

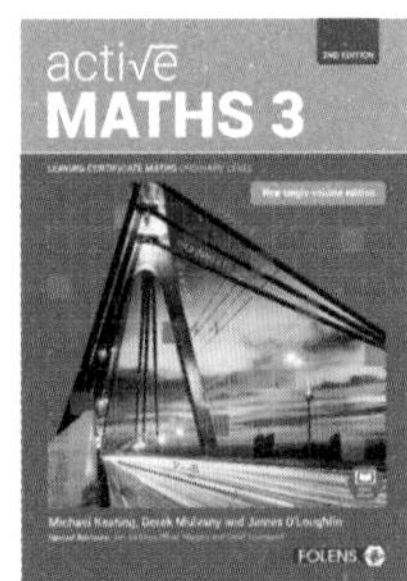

Active Maths 3, 2nd edition, allows teachers to meet the challenge of the Ordinary Level Maths syllabus, and encourages students to discover for themselves that maths can be enjoyable and relevant to everyday life while preparing for their exams.

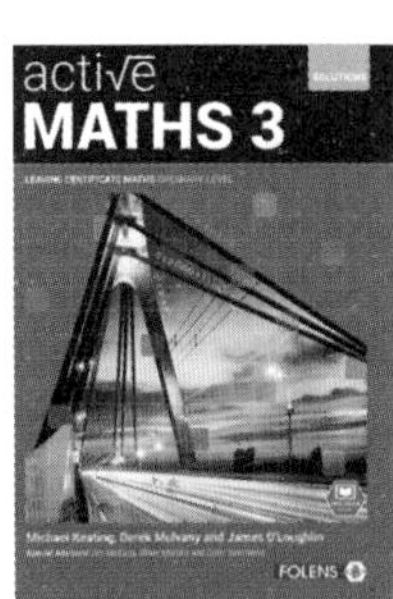

- Revised and current: Following a number of years of examination of Project Maths, additional worked examples, real-life examples, context questions and revised content reflect the reality of the curriculum.
- Exam-focused: End-of-chapter revision exercises, improved, better-graded questions and the inclusion of new past exam questions enable students to better prepare for the Leaving Certificate.
- Digital resources: An improved bank of interactive digital resources, including chapter summaries, topic PowerPoints and constructions, is available for use in the classroom, and for student revision.
- Differentiated learning: Comprehensive, carefully graded exercises facilitate progressive learning in mixed-ability classrooms.
- Improved layout: 'Handy Hints' boxes provide concept tips, and simplified, straightforward diagrams and graphs help students to learn effectively.
- Learning outcomes: A 'You Should Remember' section and a list of 'Key Words' are presented at the beginning of each chapter to inform students what they can expect to learn.

We believe we have improved the quality in this new edition and hope that those who use it will achieve the best mark possible in the Leaving Cert Maths examinations.

Michael Keating, Jim McElroy, Derek Mulvany, Oliver Murphy, James O'Loughlin and Colin Townsend

March 2017

Key to icons used in this book

 **Learning outcomes**

 **You should remember...**

 **Key words**

 **Formula**

 **Handy tips**

 **Digital resource available**

Arithmetic

In this chapter you will learn to:

- Calculate percentages
- Use the equivalence of fractions, decimals and percentages to compare proportions
- Consolidate understanding of the relationship between ratio and proportion
- Accumulate error (by addition or subtraction only)
- Make and justify estimates and approximations of calculations; calculate percentage error
- Calculate average rates of change (with respect to time)
- Solve problems that involve
  - Calculating cost price, selling price, loss, discount, mark-up (profit as a % of cost price), margin (profit as a % of selling price)
  - Compound interest, depreciation (reducing balance method), income tax and net pay (including other deductions)
  - Currency transactions
  - Costing: materials, labour and wastage
  - Metric system; change of units; everyday imperial units (conversion factors provided for imperial units)

You should remember...

- Calculation of percentages
- Fractions
- Cost price/selling price
- Income tax (standard rate)
- Decimals
- Percentages
- Discount

Key words

- Gross income
- Net/take-home income
- Statutory deductions
- Non-statutory deductions
- Income tax
- Pay-Related Social Insurance (PRSI)
- Universal social charge (USC)
- Standard rate of tax
- Standard rate cut-off point
- Tax credit
- Gross tax
- Tax payable
- VAT
- Compound interest
- Interest payable
- Investment interest
- Annual equivalent rate (AER)
- Annual percentage rate (APR)
- Depreciation
- Percentage error
- Tolerance
- Accumulated error

1.1 Proportional Parts – Dividing Quantities in a Given Ratio

Ratios are often used to divide or share quantities.

Worked Example 1.1

A pizza is cut into 14 equal slices and is shared between Alan, Brian and Ciara in the ratio 2 : 2 : 3, respectively.

How many slices does each person get?

Solution

Step 1 Write down the total number of parts. 2 + 2 + 3 = 7 parts

Step 2 Express each person's share as a fraction of the total number of parts.

Alan	Brian	Ciara
$\frac{2}{7}$	$\frac{2}{7}$	$\frac{3}{7}$

Step 3 Multiply each fraction by the amount to be shared.

Alan $\frac{2}{7} \times 14 = 4$ slices Brian $\frac{2}{7} \times 14 = 4$ slices Ciara $\frac{3}{7} \times 14 = 6$ slices

Worked Example 1.2

In making road grit, rock salt and sand are mixed together in the ratio 6 : 11, respectively. The amount of rock salt used is 312 kg. How many kilograms of sand are used?

Solution

Step 1 Rock salt = 6 parts = 312 kg

Step 2 Find what 1 part is.

$1 \text{ part} = \frac{312}{6} = 52 \text{ kg}$

Step 3 Find the amount of sand used.

$11 \text{ parts} = 52 \times 11 = 572$

$\therefore$ Sand used = 572 kg

Worked Example 1.3

Ben and Niall are the owners of a company. Ben has 30,000 shares and Niall has 20,000 shares. After taxes, the company has made a profit of €150,000 this year. The profit is divided between them in the ratio of their shareholdings.

(i) In what ratio will the profits be divided?

(ii) How much will Niall receive?

(iii) Who receives the bigger share of the profits?

Solution

(i) Ben : Niall

30,000 : 20,000

Write ratios as whole numbers in their simplest form.

Ratio = 3 : 2

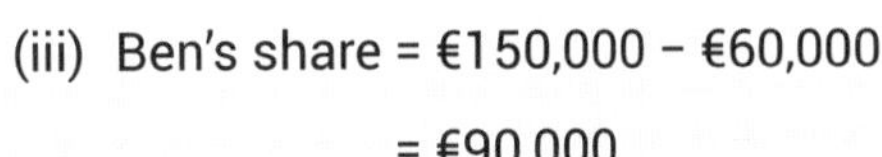

(ii) 3 + 2 = 5 parts

Niall receives $\frac{2}{5}$:

$\frac{2}{5} \times €150{,}000 = €60{,}000$

∴ Niall's share of the profits = €60,000

(iii) Ben's share = €150,000 − €60,000

= €90,000

∴ Ben receives the bigger share of the profits.

Exercise 1.1

1. Simplify each of the following ratios:

(i) 2 : 4

(ii) 20 : 15

(iii) 72 : 120

(iv) 14 : 28 : 42

(v) 27 : 63 : 108

(vi) $\frac{1}{2} : \frac{3}{4}$

(vii) $\frac{1}{3} : 1$

(viii) $\frac{1}{2} : \frac{1}{4} : 2$

(ix) $\frac{1}{2} : \frac{3}{4} : \frac{3}{8}$

(x) $\frac{1}{5} : \frac{3}{15} : \frac{2}{10}$

2. (i) Divide 450 g in the ratio 7 : 2.

(ii) Divide €132 in the ratio 7 : 4.

(iii) Divide 169 cm in the ratio 9 : 4.

(iv) Divide €4,500 in the ratio 6 : 9.

(v) Divide 156 kg in the ratio 8 : 5.

(vi) Divide 90 m in the ratio 1 : 2 : 3.

(vii) Divide 840 g in the ratio 5 : 1 : 1.

(viii) Divide €900 in the ratio 7 : 8 : 3.

(ix) Divide 221 g in the ratio 8 : 1 : 4.

(x) Divide 552 cm in the ratio 3 : 5 : 4.

3. (i) Divide 450 g in the ratio $1 : \frac{1}{2}$.

(ii) Divide €150 in the ratio $\frac{1}{2} : \frac{3}{4}$.

(iii) Divide 132 mm in the ratio $\frac{1}{3} : 1$.

(iv) Divide 4,400 g in the ratio $\frac{1}{2} : \frac{1}{4} : 2$.

(v) Divide 156 kg in the ratio $\frac{1}{2} : \frac{3}{4} : \frac{3}{8}$.

(vi) Divide 900 m in the ratio $\frac{1}{5} : \frac{3}{15} : \frac{2}{10}$.

(vii) Divide 444 g in the ratio $\frac{1}{2} : \frac{5}{6} : \frac{2}{3}$.

(viii) Divide €1,425 in the ratio $\frac{2}{3} : \frac{3}{4} : \frac{1}{6}$.

(ix) Divide 222 g in the ratio $\frac{1}{3} : \frac{2}{9} : \frac{3}{27}$.

(x) Divide 700 cm in the ratio $\frac{3}{14} : \frac{6}{7}$.

4. In a salad dressing, the ratio of oil to vinegar is 3 : 1. If James makes 200 ml of dressing, how many millilitres of vinegar are used?

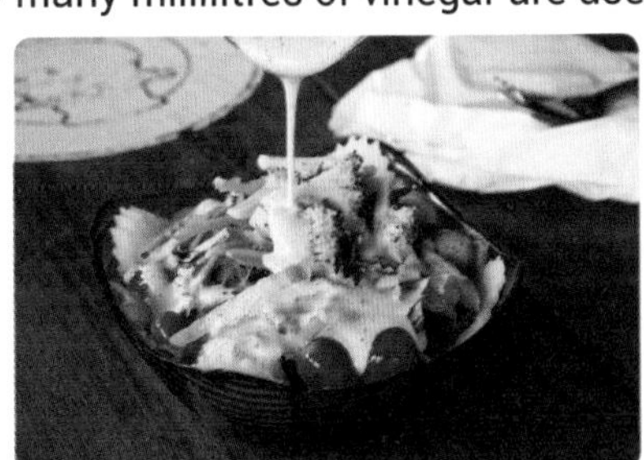

5. A school is given a grant of €4,800 for sports equipment for its volleyball and soccer teams. In the school, 184 students play volleyball and 296 play soccer. It is decided to divide the money in the ratio of players playing each sport.

   How much does each sport receive?

6. A teacher gives a prize of €24 to the three students who have made the biggest effort in her class. She decides to divide the money in the ratio of their results.

   If the results of the winners are 94%, 83% and 63%, how will the €24 be divided?

7. (i) A prize is divided betweeen Alan and Niall in the ratio $1 : \frac{1}{2}$. If Alan receives €400, what is the total prize?

   (ii) Two lengths of pipe are in the ratio $\frac{1}{2} : \frac{3}{4}$.
   If the longer piece is 45 cm, what length is the shorter piece of pipe?

   (iii) Colin has two children aged 9 years and 4 years. He won a sum of money playing the lottery and decided to divide it between his two children in the ratio of their ages. If his youngest child gets €340, how much did Colin win?

   (iv) Ross makes biscuits mixing sugar and flour in the ratio 6 : 9. If he uses 180 g of sugar, how much flour is used?

   (v) A piece of wood is cut in the ratio 5 : 2 : 1. If the shortest piece is 120 cm, what is the length of each of the other two pieces?

   (vi) A sum of money is divided between three people in the ratio 7 : 8 : 3.
   If the largest amount is €400, what is the smallest amount?

   (vii) Three people, Alan, Bilal and Cáit, eat a tin of sweets, each getting the following fraction: $\frac{1}{5}$, $\frac{7}{15}$ and $\frac{1}{3}$.
   If Alan gets 30 sweets, how many sweets do Bilal and Cáit each get?

8. 720 g of detergent is made up of bleach and soap in the ratio 3 : *k*.
   If there are 270 g of bleach in the detergent, what is the value of *k*?

9. Angie is reading a novel for school. She has read 160 pages and her teacher tells her that she has read $\frac{5}{8}$ of the book.

   How many pages are in the book?

10. Bryan and Niamh are given €70 to share. Bryan tells Niamh that her options are either to share the money in the ratio of their ages (19 and 16, respectively) or to share the money in the ratio $\frac{5}{9} : \frac{4}{9}$.

    What is the better option for Niamh?

1.2 Approximation and Percentage Error

Recall that:

- $9\% = \frac{9}{100}$, as a fraction
- $9\% = 0.09$, as a decimal

To write a fraction or a decimal as a percentage, multiply by 100 and add the % symbol.

Write $\frac{3}{5}$ as a percentage:

$\frac{3}{5} \times 100 = 60\%$

Write 0.58 as a percentage:

$0.58 \times 100 = 58\%$

Estimates and Approximations of Calculations

Sometimes it is necessary for us to make **estimates** and **approximations** of calculations. This can be to save time or money or simply for convenience. In performing rough calculations or estimates we sometimes round off numbers to make our calculations easier and quicker.

ARITHMETIC

If a hardware store was doing a stocktake (i.e. a count of all stock in the shop), it would be far too time consuming and costly for staff to count every single screw. Equally if a shop owner had a pick-and-mix stand for sweets, they would rarely count every sweet. They would simply make estimates.

Rounding is often used when we are estimating or approximating calculations.

Error

Humans are bound to make errors from time to time. These errors are sometimes unavoidable. Using estimates and approximations also leads to errors. To improve our precision, it is good practice to have an idea of how much we have possibly erred. Also, small errors left unchecked can grow over time. That is why we calculate **percentage error**.

Calculating Percentage Error

Step 1 Get the **observed value** and the **accurate value**.

Step 2 Subtract the observed value from the accurate value and take the 'absolute value' of this:

Error = |Accurate − Observed|

Step 3 Divide the error by the accurate value:

$$\text{Relative error} = \frac{\text{Error}}{\text{Accurate value}}$$

Step 4 Multiply by 100 to calculate the percentage error.

$$\text{Relative error} = \frac{\text{Error}}{\text{Accurate value}}$$

Percentage error = Relative error × 100

Worked Example 1.4

Find the percentage error in taking 1 cm for 0.8 cm.

Solution

Step 1 Observed value = 1 cm

Accurate value = 0.8 cm

Step 2 Error = |0.8 − 1|

= 0.2

Step 3 Relative error $= \frac{0.2}{0.8} = \frac{1}{4}$

Step 4 Percentage error $= \frac{1}{4} \times 100$

= 25%

Accumulated Error

Accumulated error is the collected inaccuracy that can occur when multiple errors are combined.

If the solution of a problem requires many arithmetic operations, each of which is performed using rounded numbers, the **accumulated error** may significantly affect the result.

Worked Example 1.5

ABC Ltd has a policy of rounding its invoices **to the nearest euro** when billing clients. If ABC had the following invoices in the last month, calculate the accumulated error.

Invoice 1 Amount before rounding = €1,560.46

Invoice 2 Amount before rounding = €950.32

Invoice 3 Amount before rounding = €144.52

Give all answers correct to the nearest cent when dealing with money.

Solution

Step 1 Calculate the actual amount billed.

Invoice 1 Rounded amount = €1,560

Invoice 2 Rounded amount = €950

Invoice 3 Rounded amount = €145

Amount billed = €2,655

Step 2 Calculate the amount that would be billed if rounding was not applied.

Total bill = 1,560.46 + 950.32 + 144.52

= €2,655.30

Step 3 Calculate the accumulated error.

Error = €2,655.30 − €2,655

= €0.30

Exercise 1.2

1. Copy and complete the table below.

	Accurate value	Observed value	Error	Relative error	% Error correct to two decimal places
(i)	150	149			
(ii)	36	36.9			
(iii)	180	183			
(iv)	4.8	5			
(v)	6.7	7			
(vi)	54.15	55			
(vii)	1.36	1.5			
(viii)	502	500			
(ix)	360	359			
(x)	58.6	60			

2. If 56 is taken as an approximation for 55.4, calculate to two decimal places the percentage error.

3. If 2.3 is taken as an approximation for 2.33, calculate to three significant figures the percentage error.

4. The mass of a bag of flour should be 1 kg. A quality control inspector misreads the weight of one bag and finds it to be 1,010 grams. What is the percentage error?

5. The depth of water in a reservoir is estimated to be 1.6 m. The true depth is 1.56 m. What is the percentage error, correct to one decimal place?

6. The value of $\dfrac{49.27 + 11.15}{15.24 - 3.06}$ was estimated to be 5. Calculate:

   (i) The error

   (ii) The percentage error, correct to one decimal place

ARITHMETIC

7. The value of $\frac{40.354}{\sqrt{16.45}}$ was estimated to be 10.

   Calculate:

   (i) The error

   (ii) The percentage error, correct to one decimal place

8. A statement arrives at an office showing four invoices that need to be paid:

Invoice 1	€245.45
Invoice 2	€364.78
Invoice 3	€1,445.12
Invoice 4	€4,500.25

   The office manager checks the statement quickly to make sure the final figure is accurate. She ignores the cent amount on each invoice.

   (i) What is the total that she arrives at?

   (ii) What is the correct amount owed?

   (iii) What is the accumulated error?

1.3 Income Tax

Income and Deductions

Employees expect to earn money for the work they carry out.

- If you are paid according to the number of hours worked or goods produced, this is called a **wage**.
- If you are paid the same amount regardless of the number of hours worked or goods produced, this is called a **salary**.

Most people cannot keep all the money they earn. Employees have several **deductions** made to their earnings before they receive their money.

Gross pay or **gross income** is money earned before deductions are made.

Net pay or **net income** is money received after all deductions have been made.

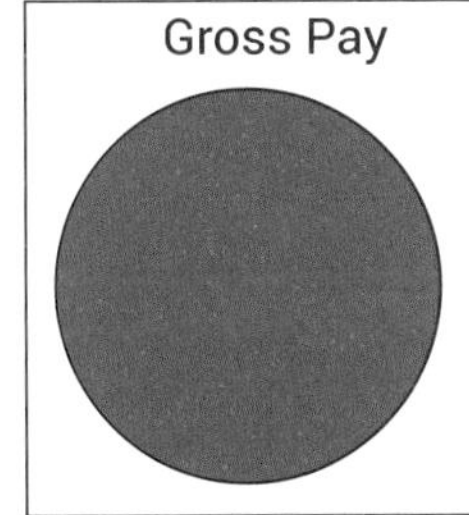

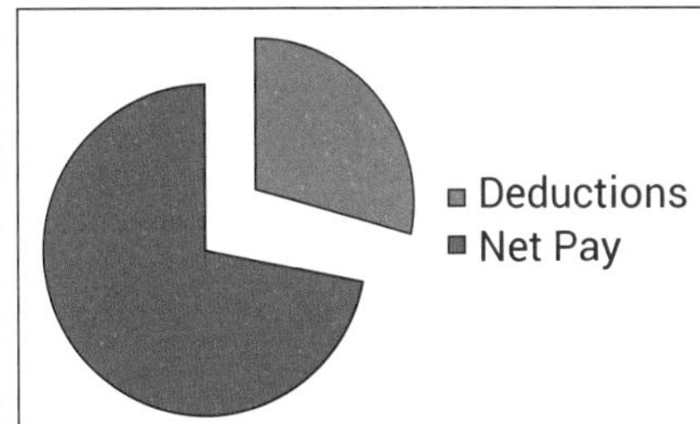

Statutory and Non-Statutory Deductions

Deductions can be **statutory** or **non-statutory**.

Statutory deduction	What is it used for?
Income tax (PAYE – Pay As You Earn)	Payment of public services, e.g. Gardaí, health care, education, etc.
Pay-Related Social Insurance (PRSI)	Old-age pensions, jobseeker's benefit, jobseeker's allowance, child benefit, etc.
Universal social charge (USC)	Income for the state

Statutory deductions are payments that **must** be made to the state. They are taken from gross pay by the employer.

The rates for the universal social charge (USC) are as follows (figures accurate for 2016):

- Zero, if total income is €13,000 or less

For people with an income of above €13,000, the rates will be:

Rate of USC	Charged on income from
1%	€0 to €12,012
3%	€12,012.01 to €18,668
5.5%	€18,668.01 to €70,044
8%	Income above €70,044
11%	Self-employed income in excess of €100,000.01

Non-statutory deductions are voluntary deductions. They are taken from gross pay by the employer at the request of the employee.

Income Tax

There are two rates of income tax in Ireland.

- The lower rate is called the **standard rate** of tax.
- The higher rate is called the **higher rate** of tax.

For example, the first €33,800 that a single person earns is taxed at 20%, and any income above this amount is taxed at 40% (figures accurate for 2016).

Every employee receives a **tax credit** certificate. This shows the employee's tax credit. This amount can change for individual employees.

Standard rate cut-off point → Taxed at 40% / Taxed at 20%

Tax payable is gross tax less the tax credit.

Note that these rates can vary from year to year.

The amount up to which an employee is taxed at the standard rate is called the standard rate cut-off point.

Gross tax is the amount of tax owed to the state before tax credits are deducted.

The tax credit is a sum deducted from the total amount (gross tax) a taxpayer owes to the state.

ARITHMETIC

Worked Example 1.6

Albert earns €27,000 a year. He pays tax at a rate of 20%. He has instructed his employer to pay his annual health insurance premium of €550 directly from his salary. He has a tax credit of €1,950. Find Albert's:

(i) Tax payable (ii) Total deductions (iii) Net pay

Solution

(i) Gross tax = €27,000 × 20%
= €27,000 × 0.20
= €5,400

Total payable = Gross tax − Tax credit
= €5,400 − €1,950
= €3,450

(ii) Total deductions = Tax payable + Other deductions
= €3,450 + €550
= €4,000

(iii) Net pay = Gross pay − Total deductions
= €27,000 − €4,000
= €23,000

Worked Example 1.7

Sanabel earns €50,000 per annum.
Calculate the amount that will be deducted from her pay for the universal social charge.

Rate of USC	Charged on income from
1%	€0 to €12,012
3%	€12,012.01 to €18,668
5.5%	€18,668.01 to €70,044
8%	Income above €70,044

Solution

Step 1

Break the salary down into the various threshold amounts.

€12,012 @ 1%

€18,668 - €12,012 = €6,656 @ 3%

€50,000 - €18,668 = €31,332 @ 5.5%

Step 2

Calculate the USC from each part.

First	Next	Remainder
€12,012	€6,656	€31,332
1%	3%	5.5%
€120.12	€199.68	€1,723.26

∴ The total USC = €120.12 + €199.68 + €1,723.26

= €2,043.06

Pay-Related Social Insurance (PRSI)

The amount of PRSI you pay depends on your earnings and the class under which you are insured.

For people in employment in Ireland, social insurance contributions are divided into different categories, known as classes or rates of contribution. The type of class and rate of contribution you pay is determined by the nature of your work.

There are 11 different classes of social insurance in Ireland. The majority of people fall into Class A.

The other classes are B, C, D, E, H, J, K, M, P and S. If you are insured under one of these classes, you are paying insurance at a lower rate than Class A contributors, which means that you are not entitled to the full range of social insurance payments.

PRSI is calculated on the employee's weekly or reckonable pay.

PRSI Contribution Rates from 1 January 2016

A class PRSI	Employee	Employer
Non cumulative weekly earning bands €	%	%
38 to 352	0	8.5
352.01 to 376	4	8.5
376 to 500	4	10.75
Over 500	4	10.75

A new weekly tapered PRSI credit of €12 is being introduced for employees insured at Class A whose earnings are between €352.01 and €424 in a week.

For the purposes of the questions in this text we will ignore this tax credit.

ARITHMETIC

Worked Example 1.8

Chloe earns €650 per week. She is in Class A1 for PRSI, which has the following rates:

Employee %	4
Employer %	10.75

Calculate:

(i) Her PRSI payment this week

(ii) Her employer's PRSI payment this week

(iii) The total amount of PRSI that will be paid this week

Solution

(i) €650 × 4% = €26

∴ Chloe's PRSI payment is €26.

(ii) €650 × 0.1075 = €69.875

≈ €69.88

∴ The PRSI payment by Chloe's employer is approximately €69.88.

(iii) Total PRSI payment = €26 + €69.88

= €95.88

Calculating Income Tax and Net Income

Worked Example 1.9

Derek has a gross annual income of €50,000. His standard rate cut-off point is €32,000. The standard rate of tax is 20%. The higher rate is 40%. His tax credit is €3,500. Derek is in Class A1 for PRSI. Assuming a 52-week year, calculate Derek's:

(i) Gross tax

(ii) Tax payable

(iii) Net income (ignoring PRSI)

(iv) PRSI payment

(v) Net income after PRSI has been paid

(vi) Weekly net income if he pays health insurance of €624 per annum

Solution

(i) Gross tax = Standard tax + Higher tax

Standard tax = Standard rate cut-off point × Standard rate

= €32,000 × 0.20

= €6,400

Higher tax = Income above standard rate cut-off point × Higher rate

Income above standard rate cut-off point = €50,000 − €32,000

= €18,000

Higher tax = €18,000 × 0.40

= €7,200

Gross tax = Standard tax + Higher tax

= €6,400 + €7,200

= €13,600

∴ The gross tax is €13,600.

(ii) Tax payable = Gross tax − Tax credit

= €13,600 − €3,500

= €10,100

∴ The tax payable is €10,100.

(iii) Net income = Gross income − Tax payable

= €50,000 − €10,100

= €39,900

∴ Derek's net income is €39,900.

(iv) PRSI payment

€50,000 × 0.04 = €2,000

∴ The PRSI payment is €2,000.

(v) Net income − PRSI

€39,900 − €2,000 = €37,900

∴ The net income after PRSI is paid is €37,900.

(vi) Net income − Insurance

€37,900 − €624 = €37,276

Weekly net income

€37,276 ÷ 52 = €716.85

Exercise 1.3

Ignore USC and PRSI unless asked to calculate.

If asked to calculate USC and/or PRSI, use the tables given earlier in this section to assist you.

1. Ian earns €37,000 a year. His standard rate cut-off point is €37,400. The standard rate of tax is 20%. His tax credit is €2,100. His union fees are €450 and his annual health insurance is €350. What is Ian's annual take-home pay?

2. Abdul earns €33,000 a year. His tax bill for the year is €6,930. What percentage of his income is paid in tax?

3. Neasa's tax bill for last year was €6,300. Her tax credit was €1,300. Her gross income was €38,000. She paid tax at the standard rate only.

(i) How much was her gross tax?

(ii) What rate did she pay tax at?

4. Lorraine and Ger had a net income of €60,400 last year. They paid tax at the standard rate, which amounted to €14,700. They had a combined tax credit of €3,600. Their non-statutory deductions were €2,000.

How much was their combined gross pay?

5. Sally earns €94,500 per annum. She has a standard rate cut-off point of €34,000. She pays tax at a standard rate of 20% and a higher rate of 40%. Her tax credit is €2,450.

Calculate:

(i) Her tax payable

(ii) Her net pay

6. Carol has a standard rate cut-off point of €36,400. The standard rate of tax is 20% and the higher rate is 40%. If Carol's gross tax is €10,396, what is her gross income?

7. Nicky earns €35,000 a year. What is her USC charge?

8. Conor has a gross income of €72,000. His standard rate cut-off point is €33,800. The standard rate of tax is 20% and the higher rate is 40%. He has a tax credit of €3,000. He is in the class A1 for PRSI.

(Assume a 52-week year.)

(i) What is his PRSI contribution per week (answer to two decimal places)?

(ii) What is his employer's PRSI contribution per week?

(iii) Calculate his USC payment for the year.

(iv) What is his weekly net income after all deductions?

9. (i) Sorcha has tax credits of €2,800 for the year and her standard rate cut-off point is €32,000. Her gross income is €45,000. The standard rate of income tax is 20% and the higher rate is 40%. Calculate her total tax payable.

(ii) Eoin pays tax at the same rate as Sorcha. Eoin's tax credits are €2,900 and he has the same standard rate cut-off point as Sorcha. His total tax payable amounts to €13,680. Calculate Eoin's gross income.

(iii) What is Eoin's and Sorcha's universal social charge, respectively?

1.4 VAT : Value-Added Tax

VAT is a tax charged by the state on spending.

For example, if you buy a computer game, you pay **VAT** on the game.

VAT is collected by the Revenue Commissioner. It is collected in stages, starting with the manufacturing stage and ending with the sale of the finished product to the consumer. VAT is collected at the following stages from the following people:

- Manufacturer
- Wholesaler
- Distributor
- Retailer
- Consumer

A tax is placed on the value added to the product or service at each stage, and this is where the name 'value-added tax' comes from.

VAT Rates

There are several different rates of VAT (figures accurate for 2016):

Standard rate	Applies to most goods and services	23%
Reduced rate	Applies to labour-intensive services, e.g. hairdressing	13.5%
Second reduced rate	Applies to restaurants	9%
Zero rate	Applies to many foods and medicines and to children's clothes	0%
Special rate	Applies to the sale of livestock	4.8%

Remember that these rates can change from year to year and country to country.

Rates of VAT vary depending on the product or service being purchased. For example, chocolate spread has a zero rate but chocolate biscuits have a 23% rate.

You can find which rate of VAT applies to different goods and services by checking the list available on the Revenue website at www.revenue.ie.

Worked Example 1.10

Claire sees a handbag in a shop window. The sign says '€250 + VAT @ 23%'.

How much will she pay for the bag?

€250 + VAT @ 23%

Solution

Method 1

Step 1 Find 23% of €250.

VAT = €250 × 0.23

∴ VAT = €57.50

Step 2 Find the total price.

Total price = €250 + VAT

= €250 + €57.50

∴ Price paid = €307.50

Method 2

Original price × 1.23

€250 × 1.23 = €307.50

Worked Example 1.11

Craig buys his boyfriend a birthday present that costs €215.65 including VAT @ 13.5%.

What was the original bill before VAT was added?

Solution

Original bill = 100%

Original bill + VAT = 113.5%

$$113.5\% = €215.65$$

$$\Rightarrow 1\% = \frac{€215.65}{113.5}$$

$$1\% = €1.90$$

$$100\% = €1.90 \times 100$$

$$= €190$$

$\therefore$ Original bill = €190

Worked Example 1.12

Una bought a new TV for €492. When she looked at the receipt, she noticed the amount of VAT charged was €92. What rate of VAT was charged?

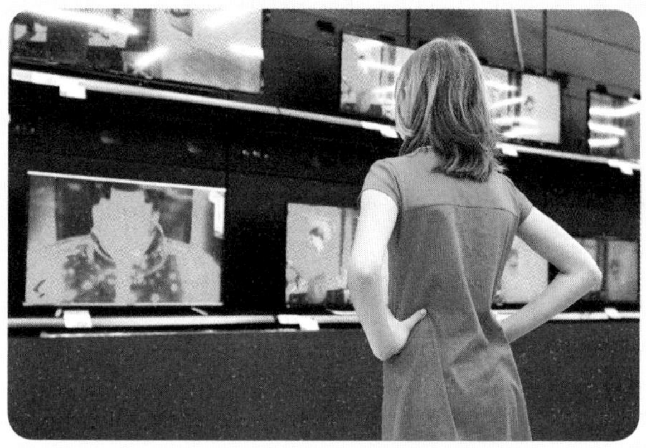

Solution

Step 1 Find the price before VAT.

Price before VAT = Final price − VAT

= €492 − €92

$\therefore$ Price before VAT = €400

Step 2 Express the VAT as a percentage of the original price.

$$\text{Rate of VAT} = \frac{\text{VAT}}{\text{Price before VAT}} \times \frac{100}{1}$$

Note that VAT is charged on the **original** cost figure.

$$= \frac{92}{400} \times \frac{100}{1}$$

$\therefore$ Rate of VAT = 23%

Exercise 1.4

Give all answers correct to the nearest cent where necessary.

1. If VAT charged on hairdressing is 13.5%, find the VAT to be charged on each of the following haircuts if the cost before VAT is:
   (i) €20 (ii) €14 (iii) €16 (iv) €12.50

2. The VAT charged on TVs is 21%. Find the **total price** of the following TVs if the price before VAT is:
   (i) €450 (ii) €190 (iii) €800 (iv) €899

3. Find the total price of ordering a pizza if the price of the pizza is €15 + VAT @ 21%.

4. The school canteen bought 600 bottles of fruit juice at €0.50 each + VAT @ 21%. Find the total cost of the fruit juice.

5. Conor buys two DVDs. The DVDs cost €18 and €12 excluding VAT. VAT is charged at 20%.

   What is the total cost of the DVDs?

6. Mohamed was shopping in a cash and carry. He didn't realise that all the prices stated were before VAT. When he got to the cash desk his bill came to €283.75.

   If VAT was charged at 13.5%, what was the cost of his bill before VAT?

7. The government of a particular country have decided to charge one standard rate of VAT @ 25%. If the price of a car (including VAT) is €9,000, how much of this price is VAT?

8. A laptop costs €990.99 and this includes VAT at 21%. How much of the selling price should be given to the Revenue Commissioner?

9. A sim free phone has a selling price inclusive of VAT of €600. If VAT is charged on this phone at $33\frac{1}{3}$%, what was the price before VAT was added?

10. The reduced rate of VAT is changed to 10%. A meal in a restaurant now costs €77. What was the price before VAT?

11. An auctioneer charges VAT at a rate of 21% on her fee. If the auctioneer is successful in selling a house, she charges a fee of 1.25% of the selling price.

    If she sells a house for €270,000, how much will her fee to the client be:

    (i) Before VAT (ii) After VAT

12. In a particular year's budget, the VAT rate falls from 13% to 12.5%. The price of a laptop drops by €3.50.

    (i) What was the price of the laptop before the change in VAT rate?

    (ii) What is the new VAT amount on the laptop?

    (iii) What is the total price of the laptop now?

    (iv) If the VAT rate had increased to 17%, how much would the laptop cost?

13. On which event does the state make more tax revenue?

    (i) The sale of a new car which sells for €19,750 after VAT at 23% has been charged.

    (ii) The sale of five thousand copies of a fitness magazine that costs €5.45 before VAT charged at 13.5%

14. Ed has his telephone service with Digicell. His monthly standing charge is €50. This includes 200 minutes of calls and 150 text messages. If he exceeds the number of minutes allowed, he is charged 15c per minute. Every additional text message costs 12c.

    During the month of December, Ed sends 160 text messages and the duration of all his calls is 220 minutes. VAT is charged at 21%. What is the total cost of his bill this month?

15. Study the following meter readings taken from electricity bills and calculate for **each** bill:

    (i) The number of units used

    (ii) The cost of electricity used if each unit costs 12 cent

	Present	Previous
Bill 1	9,625	9,556
Bill 2	11,455	10,004

    (iii) If the standing charge is €12 and VAT is charged at 13.5%, calculate the total cost of each bill in part (ii).

16. Michaela has the following bill pay option on her phone:

    - For €60 per month, she has unlimited calls to numbers within Ireland and 300 free text messages.
    - All calls to destinations outside of Ireland are charged at 45c per minute.

    Last month, she made an overseas call lasting 20 minutes. She did not exceed her quota for text messages.

    (i) How much did her overseas call cost?

    (ii) How much was her bill before VAT was added?

    (iii) If VAT is charged at 21%, what was the total of her bill?

1.5 Percentage Profit and Loss; Discounts (Allowed and Received)

Percentage Profit and Loss

If a product or service is sold for more than it cost to buy or produce, then the seller has made a profit.

If a product or service is sold for less than it cost to buy or produce, then the seller has made a loss.

The percentage profit mark-up is the profit expressed as a percentage of the cost price: $\frac{\text{Profit}}{\text{Cost price}} \times 100$.

If profit (loss) is made, the selling price is the cost price plus (minus) the profit (loss).

The percentage profit margin is the profit expressed as a percentage of the selling price: $\frac{\text{Profit}}{\text{Selling price}} \times 100$.

In practice, the profit margin and mark-up can also be given in euro, not just as a percentage.

Discounts

Discounts are offered for several reasons, e.g. to encourage customers to buy a product or to encourage a customer to pay for goods quickly or with cash.

A discount is a reduction in the price of a bill or charge.

Worked Example 1.13

Nick buys a DVD box set for €75 from an online retailer; he then sells it for €100.

What is:

(i) The cost price

(ii) The selling price

(iii) The profit or loss made

(iv) The percentage mark-up

(v) The percentage margin

Solution

(i) Cost price = €75 (the price Nick paid)

(ii) Selling price = €100 (the price Nick sells for)

(iii) Profit = Selling price - Cost price

= €100 − €75

∴ Profit = €25

(iv) Percentage mark-up $= \frac{\text{Profit}}{\text{Cost price}} \times \frac{100}{1}$

$= \frac{25}{75} \times \frac{100}{1}$

$= 33\frac{1}{3}\%$

(v) Percentage margin $= \frac{\text{Profit}}{\text{Selling price}} \times \frac{100}{1}$

$= \frac{25}{100} \times \frac{100}{1}$

= 25%

Worked Example 1.14

A company can manufacture a product for €120 and sell it, making a profit of 30%. What is the selling price?

Solution

Method 1

Profit = 120 × 0.30

∴ Profit = €36

Selling price = Cost + Profit

= €120 + €36

= €156

Method 2

120 × 1.30 = 156

Selling price = €156

Worked Example 1.15

Paula has a business selling farm supplies. The company's policy is sell all goods at cost plus 20% mark-up.

(i) If she sells fertiliser for €15, including a 20% mark-up, calculate the cost price of the fertiliser.

(ii) It is then decided to sell the goods at a 20% margin. Find the new selling price (to the nearest cent).

Solution

(i) Selling price = Cost + Profit

= 100% + 20%

∴ Selling price = 120% of cost price

Selling price = €15

∴ 120% = €15

$1\% = \frac{€15}{120}$

= €0.125

∴ 100% = €0.125 × 100

= €12.5

The cost price is €12.50.

(ii) Selling at a profit margin of 20% means that the profit is 20% of the selling price.

Therefore, the cost price must be 80% of the selling price.

Cost price = €12.50

80% = €12.50

$\therefore 1\% = \frac{€12.50}{80}$

= €0.15625

∴ 100% = €0.15625 × 100

= €15.625

The selling price is €15.63.

Worked Example 1.16

Matilda owns a clothes shop. She decides to sell off last season's stock at a loss of 10%. She sells a jacket for €18. How much did it cost her originally?

Solution

Selling price = Cost price – Loss

= 100% – 10%

∴ Selling price = 90% of cost price

90% = €18

$\therefore 1\% = \frac{€18}{90}$

= €0.20

∴ 100% = 0.20 × 100

= €20

The cost price is €20.

Worked Example 1.17

Asad receives an invoice for goods purchased. The total amount on the invoice is €500. If he pays within 21 days, he will receive a discount of 5%.

Calculate the amount that Asad must pay if he pays within 21 days.

Solution

From the invoice, Asad owes €500. As he is paying within 21 days, he will receive a 5% discount.

Method 1

Discount = €500 × 0.05

= €25

Price to pay = €500 – €25

= €475

Method 2

100% – 5% = 95%

500 × 0.95 = €475

Exercise 1.5

1. Jack imports jerseys for €10 and sells them at cost plus 12.5%. What is the selling price?

2. A retailer buys goods from a cash and carry outlet for €120. The recommended selling price is cost plus 15%.
   (i) How much should she sell the goods for?
   (ii) What is her percentage margin (to the nearest percent)?

3. Fill in the missing figures in the table below.

	Cost price (€)	Selling price (€)	Profit (€)	% Mark-up (2 d.p.)	% Margin (2 d.p.)
(i)	25.00	30.00	5.00		
(ii)	31.00	36.00			
(iii)	15.00	20.00			
(iv)	14.00		14.00		
(v)	12.00	18.00	6.00		
(vi)	18.00	18.90			
(vii)		4.00	3.00		
(viii)		2.80	0.70		
(ix)	10.00		2.00		
(x)	11.00		4.50		

4. Find the selling price of each of the following:

	Cost price (€)	% Mark-up
(i)	150.00	5.00
(ii)	1,020.00	6.00
(iii)	2,240.00	12.50
(iv)	6,450.00	21.50
(v)	23,250.00	16.00

5. Find the cost price of each of the following:

	Selling price (€)	% Margin
(i)	40	2
(ii)	85	5
(iii)	135	10
(iv)	100	0.5
(v)	1,565	3

6. Find the selling price of each of the following:

	Cost price (€)	% Loss
(i)	50	5.00
(ii)	1,250	15.00
(iii)	34,000	25.00
(iv)	12,800	37.50
(v)	14,400	12.00

7. A product costs a company €13,250 to produce. Find the percentage mark-up and percentage margin (2 d.p.) if the company sells the product for €15,900.

8. In each of the following, calculate:
   (a) The discount
   (b) The price after the discount

	Selling price (€)	% Discount
(i)	1,200	5
(ii)	1,600	15
(iii)	4,400	2
(iv)	1,460	37.50

9. In each of the following, calculate the percentage discount (2 d.p.):

	Selling price (€)	Discount (€)
(i)	150.00	25.00
(ii)	144.00	12.00
(iii)	270.00	30.00
(iv)	165.00	13.00
(v)	2,610.00	313.20

10. For the invoice below, calculate:

(i) The discount received if paid within 1 month

(ii) The price to be paid if paid within 1 month

Invoice no. 3546			
Terms: Discount 12% if paid within 1 month			
Quantity	**Description**	**Unit price (€)**	**Total ex. VAT (€)**
200	Decks of cards	2.00	400.00
120	Spinning tops	1.25	150.00
			550.00
		VAT 21%	115.50
		Total due	665.50

11. Henry owns an electrical store. He purchases 10 cameras at €25 each. The wholesaler offers him a trade discount of 15%. How much does Henry pay in total for the cameras?

12. Leona and Barbara were shopping in Mahon Point. Leona saw a sign on a shop window: '20% off'.

(i) Leona bought a camera for €120. What was the original price?

(ii) Barbara bought make-up for €25. What was the original price?

13. Elaine has a two-bed apartment in the city centre. She charges €750 rent per month. She tells her tenants that she will offer them a 2.5% discount if they pay the rent in cash before the last day of every month. How much rent will she receive if they pay before the last day of the month?

1.6 Compound Interest: Loans and Investments

Individuals and businesses do not always have enough cash to buy what they want or to pay their bills. It is sometimes necessary for them to borrow money. Equally, there are individuals and businesses that have large amounts of cash and so they decide to invest some of it.

If you borrow money from a bank or any financial institution, they will expect you to pay back the money you borrowed, but they will also charge you for the use of the money they loaned you. This is called **interest payable**.

In the case of loans and other forms of credit, there is a legal obligation to display the **annual percentage rate (APR)** prominently. APR is the rate at which the loan interest is calculated.

Annual Percentage Rate (APR) and Annual Equivalent Rate (AER)

The **annual percentage rate (APR)** is the annual interest rate (expressed as a percentage to at least one decimal place) that makes the present value of all future payments equal to the present value of the loan.

There are clear rules stated in legislation regarding how APR is to be calculated:

- All monies the customer will have to pay must be included in the calculation, i.e. loan repayments, set-up charges, etc.
- In calculating the present values, time is measured in years from the date the loan is drawn down (received).

When you invest money in an investment account or a financial institution, you are giving the people who run the account or institution the use of your money. So they must pay you for the use of this money. This is called **investment interest**.

In the case of investments, the rate of interest that is used to calculate the amount that is to be paid to the investor is called the **annual equivalent rate (AER)**.

In Ireland there are a number of different names for **annual equivalent rate (AER),** all of which mean the same thing: equivalent annual rate (EAR), compound annual return/compound annual rate (CAR).

- Rules governing AER are not as specific as those governing APR.
- Investments do not have a guaranteed return.
- Calculation of AER involves estimates of future interest/growth rates.

When a loan or an investment is paid back in full, the total amount is the sum borrowed or invested plus the interest that was paid.

Despite the difference in name (APR and AER), the method of calculation of both is exactly the same.

When dealing with interest, we use the following symbols:

F = Final value (amount borrowed/invested + interest)

P = Present value (amount borrowed/invested)

i = Rate of interest per unit time (usually years, always use decimal form)

t = Time (number of time periods you had the loan or investment)

$F = P(1 + i)^t$

This formula can be found on page 30 of *Formulae and Tables*.

The rate of interest that is used here, i, is the annual equivalent rate (AER) in the case of investments or annual percentage rate (APR) in the case of loans, as this formula assumes that compounding takes place once every year.
However, if compounding takes place more frequently, the respective AER/APR must be adjusted for this change in the compounding period.

Worked Example 1.18

Niall borrows €100 for three years at an APR of 2% compounded annually.
How much interest will he pay on the loan?

Solution

	Principal (€)	Rate of interest	Principal + interest	Amount at end of year (€)
Year 1	100	0.02	100(1.02)	102
Year 2	102	0.02	102(1.02)	104.04
Year 3	104.04	0.02	104.04(1.02)	106.12

Interest = €106.12 − €100 = €6.12

Worked Example 1.19

€10,000 is invested at 3% per annum. At the beginning of the second year, €1,450 is withdrawn from this amount. The interest rate for the second year rises to 3.5%.

Calculate:

(i) The value of the investment at the end of Year 1

(ii) The value of the investment at the end of Year 2

Solution

(i) Value of investment at end of Year 1:

$P = €10,000 \quad t = 1 \text{ year} \quad i = 0.03$

$F = P(1 + i)^t$

$F = 10,000(1 + 0.03)^1$

$= 10,000(1.03)^1$

$= 10,000(1.03)$

$\therefore F = 10,300$

The value of the investment at the end of Year 1 is €10,300.

ARITHMETIC

(ii) Value of investment at end of Year 2:

At the beginning of Year 2, €1,450 is withdrawn.

P = €10,300 − €1,450 = €8,850 $t = 1$ year $i = 0.035$

$F = P(1 + i)^t$

$F = 8{,}850(1 + 0.035)^1$

$= 8{,}850(1.035)^1$

$\therefore F = 9{,}159.75$

The value of the investment at the end of Year 2 is €9,159.75.

Worked Example 1.20

A sum of €100 is invested in a three-year savings bond with an annual equivalent rate (AER) of 3.23%. Find the value of the investment when it matures in three years' time (to the nearest euro).

Solution

$F = P(1 + i)^t$

P = €100 $t = 3$ years $i = 0.0323$

$F = 100(1 + 0.0323)^3$

$= 100(1.0323)^3$

$= 110.0064$

$\therefore F \approx$ €110

Worked Example 1.21

Aidan invested money in a 5.5-year bond when he started First Year. In the middle of Sixth Year, the bond matures and he has earned 21% interest in total. Calculate the AER for this bond.

Solution

Step 1 Write down the formula.

$F = P(1 + i)^t$

Step 2 Identify the parts that we are given in the question.

Final value (F) = Original amount + Interest

= 100% + 21%

= 121%

= 1.21

Principal (P) = Original amount

= 100%

= 1.00

Time in years (t) = 5.5

Step 3 Solve for the unknown value i.

$1.21 = 1.00(1 + i)^{5.5}$

$1.21 = (1 + i)^{5.5}$

$\sqrt[5.5]{1.21} = 1 + i$

$1.03526 = 1 + i$

$1.03526 - 1 = i$

$i = 0.03526$

$i = 3.53\%$

$\therefore$ The AER for this bond is 3.53%.

ARITHMETIC

Exercise 1.6

1. €22,500 was invested at 5% for three years. Calculate the final value.

2. €1,600 was invested at 3% for six years. Calculate the interest.

3. €102,000 was borrowed at 8% for four years. Calculate the final value.

4. €25,400 was borrowed at 3% for ten years. Calculate the interest.

5. €1,000,000 was invested at 10.5% for three and a half years. Calculate the final value.

6. €9,600 was borrowed at 2% for four years. Calculate the interest.

7. Find the amount, to the nearest cent, that needs to be invested at a rate of 5% to give €2,500 in five years' time.

8. How much would Louise need to invest, at a rate of 3.5%, to have €1,500 two years from now?

9. Haidir borrows €160,000 at 3%. At the end of Year 1, he repays €20,000. The rate of interest is then lowered to 2%.

   How much will he owe at the end of the second year?

10. A football club borrowed €15,000,000 to revamp their stadium. The rate for the first year was 3.5% and the rate for the second year was 4.2%.

    Calculate the amount owing at the end of the second year.

11. A business secures a three-year loan for €45,000 with the following conditions attached:

    - The loan must be repaid in full by the end of the third year.
    - The rate of interest is 3% for the first two years. Then it decreases by 0.5%.

    Calculate the total interest that will be paid on this loan (to the nearest euro).

12. A 10-year loan is drawn down for €350,000. The rate of interest is 5.2% per annum compound interest.

    (i) How much interest is charged in the first year?

    (ii) How much interest will have been charged after 10 years if no repayment is made in the 10 years (answer correct to the nearest cent)?

    (iii) If €60,000 is paid off at the end of Year 1, what will the interest charge be for Year 2?

13. A business is given a loan from a private bank of €50,000 for five years at a rate of 6% per annum. If the loan is repaid with interest in one lump sum at the end of five years, the lender will give a 15% discount.

    Alternatively, the business can repay €10,000 at the end of each of Years 1–4 and the balance at the end of Year 5.

    Which option will cost the business less?

    Show clearly how you arrived at your answer.

14. A sum of €6,000 is invested in an eight-year government bond with an annual equivalent rate (AER) of 6%.

    Find the value of the investment when it matures in eight years' time.

15. What AER would have to be earned each year so that compounded annually the gross return after six years would be 20%?

16. The National Treasury Management Agency offers a three-year savings bond with a return of 10%. Calculate the AER for this bond.

17. Calculate the AER offered on a bond offering 4.5% on a 15-month fixed term rate.

1.7 Depreciation (Reducing-Balance Method)

Depreciation is calculated in order to write off the value of an asset over its useful economic life.

Causes of Depreciation

Wear and tear	Assets that are used over a period of time eventually wear out.	Example: Vehicles
Obsolescence	An asset becomes out of date because of the development of a more efficient or less expensive alternative.	Example: Computers
Passage of time	Assets lose value as they near the end of their licence.	Example: Patents
Extraction	The value of an asset reduces as the asset is extracted.	Example: Mining

Types of Depreciation

There are two methods of calculating depreciation in practice:

- **Straight-line method:** The amount written off the asset is the same each year until the total value of the asset is written off or it is reduced to its residual value (the value of the asset after we are finished with it).
- **Reducing-balance method:** Rather than writing off a fixed amount every year, a (fixed) percentage of the remaining value of the asset is charged every year. Compared to straight-line depreciation, this method is more heavily weighted towards the early years.

For our syllabus, we will study the reducing-balance method only.

$F = P(1 - i)^t$

This formula appears on page 30 of *Formulae and Tables*.

F is called the **later value** in *Formulae and Tables* (page 30). In accounting, this is known as the **net book value (NBV)** of the asset.

Worked Example 1.22

U-Deliver Ltd bought a new delivery van for €25,000. It is company policy to depreciate delivery vans at a rate of 20% per annum using the reducing-balance method.

(i) What will be the net book value (NBV) of the asset after three years?

(ii) How much depreciation is written off the van in the first three years?

The net book value is the value of the asset after depreciation has been calculated.

Solution

(i) $F = P(1 - i)^t$

$= 25{,}000(1 - 0.20)^3$

$= 25{,}000(0.8)^3$

$= €12{,}800$

The NBV of the asset after three years will be €12,800.

(ii) Depreciation written off = Cost − Net book value

= €25,000 − €12,800

= €12,200

∴ Depreciation = €12,200

Worked Example 1.23

ABC Ltd purchased a delivery van costing €60,000. It is the policy of the company to depreciate all delivery vans at a rate of 20% using the reducing-balance method. What will be the value of the asset after five years?

Solution

Method 1 (Year by year)

Step 1 Calculate the depreciation for the first year.

Step 2 Calculate the net book value (NBV) of the asset at the end of Year 1.

NBV = Cost − Depreciation

Step 3 Repeat for Years 2 to 5.

	Cost	Rate of depreciation	Depreciation	NBV
Year 1	€60,000.00	0.2	€12,000.00	€48,000.00
Year 2	€48,000.00	0.2	€9,600.00	€38,400.00
Year 3	€38,400.00	0.2	€7,680.00	€30,720.00
Year 4	€30,720.00	0.2	€6,144.00	€24,576.00
Year 5	€24,576.00	0.2	€4,915.20	€19,660.80

The value of the asset at the end of five years will be €19,660.80.

Method 2 (Using formula)

$F = P(1 - i)^t$

$F = 60{,}000(1 - 0.20)^5$

$= 60{,}000(0.80)^5$

$= 19{,}660.80$

The value of the asset at the end of five years will be €19,660.80.

Worked Example 1.24

An accountant is auditing a set of books and sees that the net book value (NBV) of an asset four years after the date of purchase is €28,710.34. The policy of the company is to depreciate this asset at a rate of 15% using the reducing-balance method. What was the original cost of the asset to the nearest euro?

Solution

$F = P(1 - i)^t$

$28{,}710.34 = P(1 - 0.15)^4$

$28{,}710.34 = P(0.85)^4$

$$P = \frac{28{,}710.34}{(0.85)^4}$$

$P = 54{,}999.9928$

The original cost of the asset was approximately €55,000.

Exercise 1.7

1. Using the reducing-balance method of depreciation, calculate the value of the following assets after the given number of years (correct to the nearest euro):

	Asset cost (€)	Rate of depreciation (%)	Number of years	NBV (€)
(i)	200,000	10	1	
(ii)	1,500,000	15	4	
(iii)	60,600	3	8	
(iv)	21,000	3.5	2	

2. Using the reducing-balance method of depreciation, calculate the missing values in the table below, correct to two decimal places where necessary.

	Asset cost (€)	Rate of depreciation (%)	Number of years	NBV (€)
(i)	400,000		4	€208,802.50
(ii)	140,000	3	8	
(iii)	100,000		2	€93,122.50
(iv)	120,000		4	€37,968.75

3. How much will a €30,000 car be worth at the end of five years given a depreciation rate of 20% per annum (reducing balance)?

4. A coal mine is depleted at a rate of 15% per annum. If the initial volume of coal in the mine is 400,000 m^3, what volume of coal would there be in the mine after six years?

5. A car has an NBV of €19,660.80 at the end of five years, having been depreciated at a rate of 20% per annum (reducing balance).
   What was the initial cost of the car?

6. A building has an NBV of €800,000 at the end of 10 years, having been depreciated at a rate of 2% (reducing-balance method). What was the original cost of the building?
   Give your answer to the nearest €100.

7. A computer was purchased at the start of 2014 for €2,500. By the end of the year 2016, it is expected that the computer will be worth only €1,378.42.
   What is the rate of depreciation (reducing-balance method)?

8. A lorry was purchased for €150,000 at the end of 2011. At the start of 2016, the lorry was sold at its NBV of €49,152.
   What was the rate of depreciation charged (reducing-balance method) on the lorry?

9. A pharmaceutical company has just received a 10-year patent for its newest headache tablet. In keeping with company policy, the accountants for the firm decide to write off the patent using the reducing-balance method. The patent is currently estimated to be worth €15,000,000.
   What rate of depreciation should the firm's accountants apply to the patent in order to write it off (to 1 cent) over the 10-year period? Give your answer as a percentage, to two decimal places.

1.8 Average Rates of Change (with Respect to Time)

The most common rate of change with respect to time that we use is speed, the change in distance with respect to time. Rates of change are used in many other areas also; for example, the change in price with respect to time and the change in quantity produced with respect to time.

$$\text{Rate of change} = \frac{\text{Change in quantity}}{\text{Change in time}}$$

Worked Example 1.25

Rob completes a 10 km fun run in 1 hour 20 minutes. What is his average speed in kilometres per hour?

Solution

Step 1 Convert the time to hours.

$1 \text{ hr } 20 \text{ mins} = 1\frac{1}{3} \text{ hours}$

$= \frac{4}{3} \text{ hours}$ Leaving as a fraction avoids error created by rounding decimals.

Step 2 Calculate average speed.

$\text{Speed} = \frac{\text{Distance}}{\text{Time}}$

$= 10 \text{ km} \div \frac{4}{3} \text{ hr}$

$= 7.5 \text{ km h}^{-1}$

Worked Example 1.26

A TY student is selling bags of grit door-to-door during a cold spell of weather. He starts his door-to-door sales at 10 a.m., charging €5 for a bag of grit. He is surprised by the demand for the grit and so he puts his price up several times during the day. At 1 p.m. he is charging €8 per bag.

What is the rate of change of the price, per hour?

Solution

Step 1 Find the change in price.

€8 − €5 = €3

Step 2 Calculate the change in time.

1 p.m. = 13.00

10 a.m. = −10.00

3.00

Step 3 Calculate the rate of change.

$\text{Rate} = \frac{\text{Change in price}}{\text{Change in time}}$

$= \frac{€3}{3 \text{ hrs}}$

= €1 per hour.

The price he charges increases (on average) by €1 per hour.

Worked Example 1.27

A new HD television was launched with a selling price of €1,200.
Eighteen months later, the same television could be purchased for €900.

(i) What is the rate of change per month for the price of the television (correct to two decimal places)?

(ii) What does this rate of change mean?

Solution

(i) Change in price: €900 - €1200 = -€300

Change in time: 18 months

Rate of change in price: $\dfrac{-€300}{18 \text{ months}}$

= -€16.67 per month

(ii) This means the price has fallen, on average, by approximately €16.67 per month since the launch of the TV onto the market.

Exercise 1.8

1. Calculate the missing values in the table below.

	Time of departure	Time of arrival	Distance travelled (km)	Average speed (km h^{-1})
(i)	10:35	12:55	36	
(ii)	09:00	10:30	150	
(iii)	12:15	14:45		95
(iv)	08:02	14:47		108

2. Ian runs a marathon (26.2 miles) in 3 hours 45 mins.
Find his average speed in miles per hour.

3. A cyclist travelled 40 km. He started at 11:47 and arrived at his destination at 13:14.

Calculate his average speed to the nearest km h^{-1}.

4. Calculate the missing values in the table below.

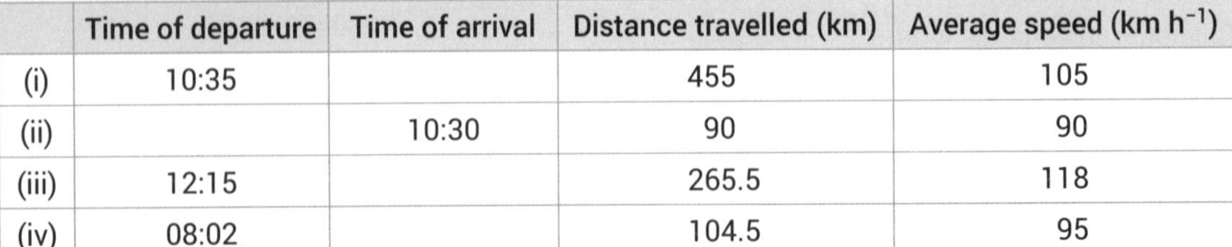

	Time of departure	Time of arrival	Distance travelled (km)	Average speed (km h^{-1})
(i)	10:35		455	105
(ii)		10:30	90	90
(iii)	12:15		265.5	118
(iv)	08:02		104.5	95

5. David commutes from his home to Limerick City, a distance of 85 km. His commute takes 1 hr 15 mins.

(i) Find his average speed in km h^{-1}.

(ii) His average speed was reduced to 35 km h^{-1} during heavy snow on his journey home. How long did the commute take, to the nearest minute?

(iii) What was his total commute time to and from the city that day?

6. A car journey of 560 km took 6 hrs 45 mins.
   (i) Calculate the average speed for this journey in km h^{-1}.
   (ii) Average diesel consumption was 7 km per litre. How many litres were consumed on the journey?
   (iii) If the cost of a litre of diesel is €1.48 per litre, inclusive of VAT at 21%, what is the cost of diesel excluding VAT?

7. During a housing boom, the price of houses increased steadily over an 18-month period. A house that cost €240,000 at the start of the period had a sale value of €276,000 at the end of the period. What was the average rate of change in the price per month?

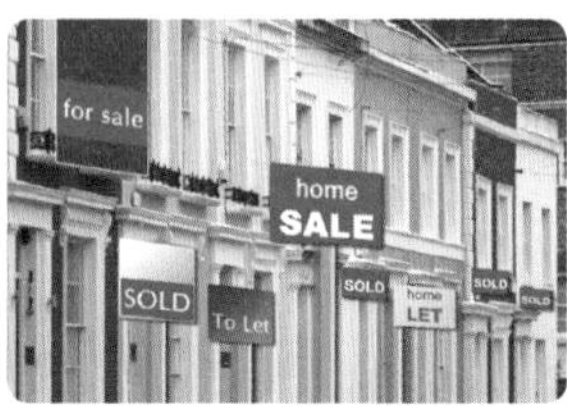

8. A new game costing €60 is released on 1 December. At the end of March, the same game costs €48.

   What is the rate of change in the price of this game over the period?

9. Management accountants for a firm forecast the following projections for sales over a six-month period: sales are expected to increase at a rate of 200 units per month. If sales at the start of the period are 240,000 units, what are the expected sales at the end of the period?

10. The price of a barrel of oil is expected to increase at an average rate of $0.50 per month over a 15-month period. A barrel costs $52 at present.
    (i) What is the expected price at the end of the 15-month period?
    (ii) Is an option to buy oil at $60 per barrel in 15 months' time a good deal? Why?

11. Two lorry drivers, Niall and John, are talking about their recent trips. Niall says he travelled 4,500 km over the past week, spending a total of 48 hours driving. John says, 'That is nothing. I travelled 4,000 km and spent a total of 33 hours driving.' Whose story is more believable? Justify your answer.

1.9 Costing: Materials, Labour and Wastage

Managers need to know the costs involved in getting their products to the market, for a number of reasons:

- **Planning** – Having an accurate cost of a product allows managers to set an accurate price.
- **Control** – By comparing the budgeted cost of a product with the actual cost of the product, managers can identify areas of the business that are underperforming or doing very well.
- **Stock valuation** – At the end of the financial year, all stocks need to be valued for accounting purposes. It is also important that businesses that manufacture their own products have a value for their goods for insurance purposes.

To get an accurate value, all the costs involved in getting the product to its finished state must be included in the valuation. The table below shows examples of both direct and indirect costs for a company manufacturing school desks.

Direct costs are costs linked directly to production.

Indirect costs are costs not linked directly to production, e.g. factory rent, rates, light and heat bills.

Variable costs are costs that vary directly with the level of output or activity, e.g. sales commission based on unit sales.

Fixed costs are costs that are not affected by the level of activity (within a given range of activity). For example, the rent for the factory is fixed regardless of the amount of product produced. If production exceeds the level the factory can cope with, additional space may need to be rented, causing the cost to rise.

Direct costs (costs directly linked to production)	Materials	Raw materials used in the manufacture of the product	Wood, metal frames
	Labour	Wages of those who work directly in the manufacture of the product	Saw operators who cut table tops, workers who assemble the desks, workers who spray the desk frames and varnish the table tops
	Direct expenses	Any expenses that may be attributed directly to the product	Hire of special equipment
Indirect costs (costs not directly linked to production)			Factory rent, rates, light and heat

Wastage

A manager will try to minimise wastage where possible in a business, as it reduces any profit that the company might make. However, there will inevitably be some wastage in almost all businesses because of human error, machine faults, inaccurate sales predictions and so on.

Worked Example 1.28

A company budgets to manufacture 5,000 units of its product.

The materials required are 50 kg per unit @ €0.50 per kg.

Each unit produced requires six hours of direct labour @ €7 per hour.

Indirect costs are €15,000.

Calculate:

(i) The cost of manufacture of the 5,000 units

(ii) The unit cost of manufacture

Unit cost = $\frac{\text{Total cost}}{\text{No. of units produced}}$

The unit cost is the cost of making one of the products.

Solution

(i)

Cost of manufacture (5,000 units)		
Direct materials	5,000 units @ 50 kg	250,000 kg
Cost per kg		€0.50
Cost of materials	250,000 × 0.50	**€125,000**
Direct labour	5,000 units × 6 hours	30,000 hrs
Cost per labour hour		€7
Total labour cost	30,000 × 7	**€210,000**
Indirect costs		**€15,000**
Total cost of manufacture	125,000 + 210,000 + 15,000	€350,000

(ii) The unit cost of manufacture = $\frac{350,000}{5,000}$

= €70

Worked Example 1.29

A confectionary company receives an order for 250 custom-made products for Christmas hampers. The production team has given the following breakdown for the product:

Material requirements	
Material *A*	25 g per unit
Material *B*	100 g per unit
Labour hours	0.05 per unit
Variable costs	€0.75 per unit
Fixed costs allocated to the product	€500
Cost material *A*	€0.01 per g
Cost material *B*	€0.05 per g
Labour rate	€7 per hour

(i) Find the total cost of the order and the cost per unit.

(ii) Find the price the company should charge per unit to make a profit on cost of 25% on each unit produced (assuming no wastage).

(iii) If on average 5% of the finished goods are damaged in the warehouse, how many units should the company produce to ensure the order is covered?

Solution

(i)

Costs		Cost (€)
Material *A*	25 g × 250 × €0.01	62.50
Material *B*	100 g × 250 × €0.05	1,250.00
Labour	0.05 × 250 × €7	87.50
Variable costs	250 × €0.75	187.50
Fixed costs		500.00
Total cost		**2,087.50**

The total cost of the order is €2,087.50.

$\therefore$ Unit cost $= \dfrac{€2{,}087.50}{250} = €8.35$

(ii) A profit on cost of 25%:

Profit: €8.35 × 0.25 = €2.0875

Selling price: €8.35 + €2.0875 = €10.4375

$\approx €10.44$

$\therefore$ The company should charge approximately €10.44 per unit to make a profit on cost of 25% on each unit produced.

(iii) On average 5% of goods are damaged.

So the 250 units represent 95% of the required production.

95% = 250 units

$$1\% = \frac{250}{95}$$

$$100\% = \frac{250}{95} \times 100$$

$$= 263.1579 \text{ units}$$

$\therefore$ The company should produce 264 units to ensure that there will be enough stock to meet the order.

ARITHMETIC

Exercise 1.9

1. Distinguish between:
   (i) Direct and indirect costs   (ii) Fixed and variable costs

2. Jimmy Jeans received an order from a retail outlet for a batch of 10,000 pairs of jeans. The following information relates to the production costs of the jeans:

	€
Direct materials	25,000
Factory rent	11,000
Wages of material cutters	4,000
Wages of machinists	€0.75 per unit produced
Factory overheads	20,000

   (i) Calculate the total manufacturing costs of the batch.
   (ii) Calculate the unit cost of a pair of jeans.

3. A deli recently received an order for 135 mini quiches.
   (i) If wastage of the finished product is assumed to be 10%, how many quiches should the deli prepare?

   The production costs of the quiches are as follows:

Direct materials	€250
Labour	€11 per hour
Labour hours required	4
Deli overheads allocated to this job	€100

   (ii) Calculate the cost of the batch (based on the number of units calculated in part (i)).
   (iii) Calculate the cost per unit.
   (iv) If the deli wishes to make a profit on cost of 20%, what price should it charge per quiche?

4. Townsend Ltd manufactures two products, *X* and *Y*. Both products use the same raw materials. The production costs are as follows:

	Product *X*	Product *Y*
Units produced	6,000	5,000
Materials in each product	8 kg	9 kg
Production time per unit	6 hours	5 hours
Wages	€5 per hour	
Cost of materials per kg	€3	

   (i) Calculate the quantity of materials required for the production of product *X*.
   (ii) Calculate the quantity of materials required for the production of product *Y*.
   (iii) Calculate the cost of materials for each of product *X* and product *Y*.
   (iv) Calculate the total cost of labour for products *X* and *Y*.

5. Nolan Plc is a boat manufacturing company. Two materials are used in the manufacture of the boat. An order is placed for 60 units.

The table below gives the production costs for one unit.

Material *A*	36 metres
Material *B*	108 metres
Expected price per metre	€7
Labour hours required	60
Labour rate	€7 per hour

There is approximate wastage of 10% on all materials used.

(i) How many metres of material *A* should be purchased to meet the requirements of the order?

(ii) How many metres of material *B* should be purchased to meet the requirements of the order?

(iii) Calculate the cost price of this order.

(iv) Calculate the selling price per unit this company should charge if they wish to make a profit on cost of 15%.

6. SIOAL Ltd manufactures two products, Primary and Superb.

It expects to sell Primary at €190 per unit and Superb at €230 per unit.

Sales demand is expected to be 6,000 units of Primary and 4,500 units of Superb.

Both products use the same raw materials and skilled labour but in different quantities per unit as follows:

	Primary	**Superb**
Material *W*	6 kg	5 kg
Material *X*	4 kg	7 kg
Skilled labour	7 hours	8 hours

The expected prices for raw materials during 2016 are:

- Material *W*: €3 per kg
- Material *X*: €5 per kg

The skilled labour rate is expected to be €11.00 per hour.

The company's production overhead costs are expected to be:

- Variable: €4.50 per skilled labour hour
- Fixed: €116,000 per annum

If SIOAL produces all units required for sales, find:

(i) The amount of material *W* needed

(ii) The total labour hours used in production

(iii) The total labour cost of production

(iv) The total cost of production (including variable and fixed costs)

(v) The total profit made if the company sells at the expected prices

(vi) The profit made if actual prices turn out to be 10% less than those expected

1.10 Currency Exchange

In the eurozone, the unit of currency is the euro. If you travel to any country within the eurozone, there is no need to change your money. However, if you travel to any country outside the eurozone, you will need to change your money. For example, if you travel to Japan, you will need to convert your money from euro into Japanese yen.

Worked Example 1.30

On a certain day, €1 = £0.84. Liam is travelling to London and wants to change €200 into sterling (£). How much sterling will he get?

Solution

€1 = £0.84

€1 × 200 = £0.84 × 200

€200 = £168

Liam will get £168.

Worked Example 1.31

On a particular day, €1 = $1.36. How much would you receive in euro in exchange for $129.20?

Solution

$\$1.36 = €1$

$\$1 = \dfrac{€1}{1.36}$

$\$1 \times 129.20 = \dfrac{€1}{1.36} \times 129.20$

$\$129.20 = €95$

You would receive €95.

Always arrange the exchange rate to have the currency you are looking for on the right-hand side.

Foreign currency can be bought and sold at a **bureau de change**. Many banks, building societies and department stores offer this service. However, they do not all offer the same exchange rates.

At a bureau de change you will see the following signs:

- If you are going on holiday and want to buy foreign currency, the bank is selling it to you. So use the 'WE SELL' exchange rate.
- If you have returned from holiday and want to sell back the currency you have left over, it is the 'WE BUY' rate that you must use.

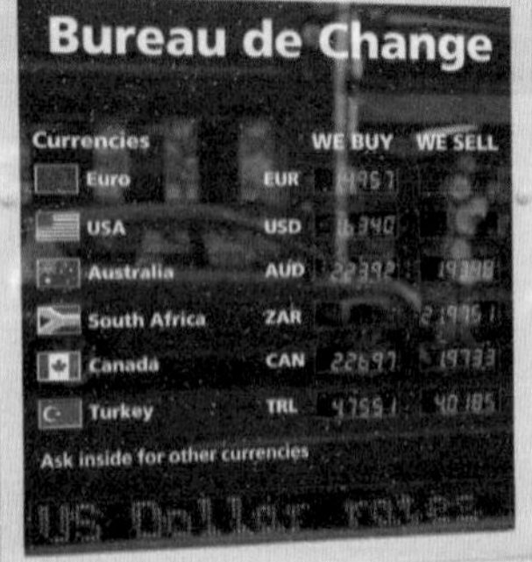

These two different rates are used in order for the operators of the bureau de change to make a profit. Another cost that you should consider is the **commission** the bureau de change will charge you. This is an extra charge for the service they have provided.

Worked Example 1.32

Carol is going on holiday to America. She wants to change €450 into dollars. She goes to her local bank. At the bureau de change counter, she sees a sign that says:

	We buy	We sell
US dollars	1.36	1.29

(i) How much will she get in dollars for €450?

(ii) If commission is charged at 2% of the euro value, how much will Carol pay in total?

Solution

(i) First ask the question: Is Carol buying or selling US dollars?

She is buying dollars – therefore, the bank is selling.

So, the exchange rate is €1 = $1.29 (the rate the bank sells at).

€1 = $1.29

€1 × 450 = $1.29 × 450

€450 = $580.50

Carol will get $580.50.

(ii) Commission is usually charged in addition to the cost of the currency.

Carol will pay €450 + 2% commission

Commission = €450 × 2%

= €9

∴ Total cost = €450 + €9

= €459

Exercise 1.10

1. If €1 = $1.48 (Australian dollars), €1= ¥116.84 (Japanese yen) and €1 = £0.89:
   (i) How many Australian dollars would you get for €560?
   (ii) How many Japanese yen would you get for €850?
   (iii) How many pounds would you get for €400?
   (iv) How many euro would you get for ¥67,122?
   (v) How many euro would you get for $106.50?
   (vi) Are you better off if you get ¥432,308 or £3,248.50?

2. Tickets to a gig at the O_2 in London are £38. Tickets to see the same artist at the 3Arena in Dublin are €48. If the exchange rate is €1 = £0.84, which ticket is cheaper?

3. A bank quotes the following exchange rates for euro:

	We buy	We sell
Sterling £	0.87	0.82
Yen ¥	111	108

   (a) Mark has €900 and wants to exchange it for sterling.
   (i) How much will he get?
   (ii) Commission is charged at €0.75 for every €200 or part thereof converted.
   How much will he pay in total for this transaction?
   (iii) What percentage of the total was the commission?

   (b) Alison has ¥5,994.
   (i) How much will she get in euro if no commission is charged?
   (ii) There is a bureau de change next to the bank that offers a buy rate of ¥108 but charges a €1.25 commssion. Which offer is better for Alison?

4. Ursula is importing wine for her restaurant. She is charged NZ$3.66 for each bottle of wine. There are 12 bottles in each case.
   If she imports 10 cases, how much will she pay in euro if €1 = $1.83?

5. A part for a computer costs €250 in Ireland. The same part costs $265 in the USA. If $1 = €0.78, is it cheaper to buy the part in the USA or Ireland? Ignore cost of delivery.

6. Mohamed buys IDR9,960,500 (Indonesian rupiah). The exchange rate is €1 = IDR12,450.50. Commission is charged on this transaction.
   (i) How much is the commission charge, in euro, if Mohamed pays €820?
   (ii) What is the rate of commission? Answer as a percentage to two significant figures.

7. An importer buys goods for £442 sterling when the exchange rate is €1 = £0.82. He sells the goods at cost price plus 20%.
   Calculate, in euro, the price at which he sells the goods.

1.11 Metric System – Imperial System

The metric system is an international decimalised system of measurement, first adopted by France in 1791. It is the common system of measuring units used by most of the world.

Since the 1960s the International System of Units ('Système International d'Unités' in French, hence SI) has been the internationally recognised standard metric system.

Metric units are universally used in scientific work and are widely used around the world for personal and commercial purposes.

The USA and UK still use the imperial system of measurement. All UK road signs must by law be shown in imperial measurement. It is often necessary for us to be able to convert from metric to imperial and from imperial to metric.

This conversion is done in a similar way to foreign exchange conversions.

Below is a table with some conversion rates.

Conversion factors					
From	*To*	*Multiply by*	*From*	*To*	*Multiply by*
Inches	Millimetres	25.4	Hectares	Acres	2.471
Millimetres	Inches	0.0394	Pints	Litres	0.5682
Inches	Centimetres	2.54	Litres	Pints	1.76
Centimetres	Inches	0.3937	Ounces	Grams	28.35
Feet	Metres	0.3048	Grams	Ounces	0.03527
Metres	Feet	3.281	Pounds	Grams	453.6
Yards	Metres	0.9144	Grams	Pounds	0.002205
Metres	Yards	1.094	Pounds	Kilograms	0.4536
Miles	Kilometres	1.609	Kilograms	Pounds	2.205
Kilometres	Miles	0.6214	Tonnes	Kilograms	1016.05
Acres	Hectares	0.4047	Kilograms	Tonnes	0.0009842

Worked Example 1.33

Convert 15 kg to pounds (lb), given 1 kg = 2.205 lb.

Solution

Step 1 Write down the conversion rate with the units needed on the right-hand side (RHS).

1 kg = 2.205 lb

Step 2 Multiply both sides of the equation by the number of kilograms that are to be converted.

(1 × 15) kg = (2.205 × 15) lb

∴ 15 kg = 33.075 lb

Worked Example 1.34

If Greg is 6 feet tall, what height is he in metres (correct to two decimal places), given 1 m = 3.281 feet?

Solution

Step 1 Write down the conversion rate with the desired units on the RHS.

3.281 feet = 1 m

Step 2 Find out what 1 foot is in metres by dividing both sides of the equation by 3.281.

$$\frac{3.281}{3.281}\text{ feet} = \frac{1}{3.281}\text{ m}$$

$$1\text{ foot} = \frac{1}{3.281}\text{ m}$$

Step 3 Calculate the height you are looking for by multiplying both sides of the equation.

$$(1 \times 6)\text{ feet} = \left(\frac{1}{3.281} \times 6\right)\text{ m}$$

$$6\text{ feet} = 1.8287\text{ m}$$

∴ Greg is approximately 1.8 m tall.

Exercise 1.11

1. Complete the conversions in the table below using the conversion rates provided at the start of this section (to two decimal places).

From	To
6 inches	cm
4.5 feet	m
5 miles	km
13 inches	mm
6 pints	litres
5 ounces	g
6 lbs	kg
3.5 tonnes	kg
22 yards	m
2 feet 3 inches	m

2. Jessie is making a cake in Home Economics class. The recipe says that 250 g of flour are needed. The weighing scale gives measurements in lbs. How many lbs, correct to two decimal places, will Jessie need, given that 1 lb = 453.6 g?

3. When a cyclist has travelled a distance of 12.6 km, she has completed $\frac{4}{7}$ of her journey.
   (i) What is her total journey length in kilometres?
   (ii) What is the length of her journey in miles, correct to two decimal places? (1 mile = 1.609 km)

Use the conversion rates given at the start of this section to answer the following questions.

4. Which is heavier, 10 tonnes of feathers or 10,200 kg of bricks?

5. Sailing rope is sold by the metre in a local marina shop. Eric needs a rope 20 feet long. What length of rope to the nearest metre must he buy to ensure he has enough rope?

6. There are two DIY stores in a business park. Both stores have a special offer on electrical wire.
   - Store A is selling wire at a reduced rate of €1.50 per metre.
   - Store B is selling the same type of wire at €1.25 per yard.

   Which store is offering the better deal?

Revision Exercises

Where necessary, use the tables for USC and PRSI given in Section 1.3.

1. The length and breadth of a rectangle are in the ratio 4 : 3, respectively. The length of the rectangle is 12.8 cm. Find the breadth of the rectangle.

2. Divide 714 g in the ratio $\frac{1}{2} : \frac{1}{4} : 1$. Convert the largest share to ounces (give your answer correct to one decimal place).

3. Conor and Dylan have a business together. Conor claims that he does 85% of the work and Dylan does the rest. Profits are shared on the basis of Conor's claim. If the business makes €6,500 this quarter, how much will Dylan receive (correct to two decimal places)?

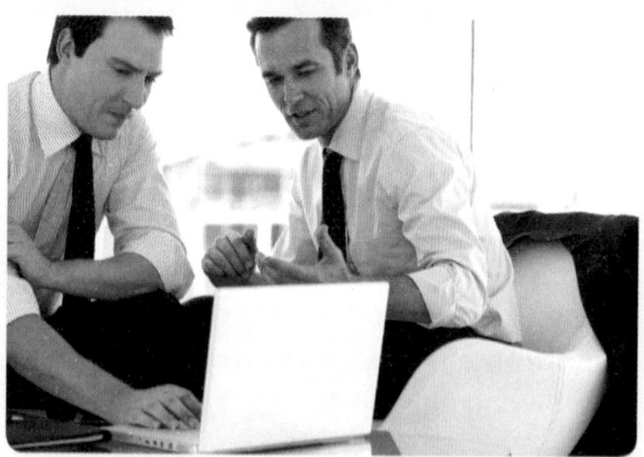

4. A grandfather gives his three grandchildren €150 to share. The children decide to share the money in the ratio of their ages. The six-year-old gets €30, the second child is 15 years old, and the third child gets €45. What age is the third child?

5. The value of $\frac{36.354}{\sqrt{4.45}}$ was estimated to be 18. Calculate:
   (i) The error
   (ii) The percentage error, correct to one decimal place

6. A statement arrives at an office showing three invoices that have to be paid.

Invoice 1	€2405.65
Invoice 2	€364.92
Invoice 3	€45.49

The office manager checks the statement quickly to make sure the final figure is accurate. She rounds each invoice to the nearest euro.
   (i) What is the total that she arrives at?
   (ii) What is the correct amount owed?
   (iii) What is the accumulated error?

7. Shane has an annual gross income of €60,000. He pays tax at 20% on the first €32,000 he earns and 40% on the remainder. His tax credit is €3,100. What is his tax payable?

8. Laura has a gross income of €45,000 a year. Her standard rate cut-off point is €33,000. The standard rate of tax is 20% and the higher rate is 40%. She has a tax credit of €2,400. She is in Class A1 for PRSI. (Assume a 52-week year.)
   (i) What is her PRSI contribution per week?
   (ii) What is her employer's PRSI contribution per week?
   (iii) Calculate her USC payment.
   (iv) What is her weekly net income after all deductions?

9. The standard rate of income tax is 20% and the higher rate is 42%. Eoin has tax credits of €1,493 for the year and a standard rate cut-off point of €30,000. He has a gross income of €31,650 for the year.
   (i) After tax is paid, what is Eoin's income for the year?
   (ii) What would Eoin's gross income for the year need to be in order for him to have an after-tax income of €29,379?

10. Calculate the VAT to be paid to the Revenue Commissioner on the following invoice:

20 Chairs @ €25 each
12 Tables @ €235 each
16 Stools @ €12 each
VAT is charged @ 13.5% on all items.

11. Nicki hears an ad on the radio:

New iPhone 5! €250, Pay as you go, 500 MB download, 100 minutes and 100 free text messages when you top up by €30 each month. Additional calls cost €0.13 per minute and texts cost €0.09 to any network.

Nicki avails of this deal. In the first month of her contract, she makes calls amounting to 124 minutes, sends 98 text messages and downloads 188 MB.

(i) What is her total cash outflow for the first month?

(ii) What is the cost of her calls and texts for the month?

(iii) How much credit has she left at the end of the month?

(iv) The €30 is inclusive of VAT at 21%. What is the cost exclusive of VAT?

12. Jackie pays a standing charge of €20 per month for her phone. Her calls cost €0.11 per minute. If Jackie does not want to spend more than €40 on her next phone bill, what is the maximum number of minutes she can use this month? (Ignore VAT.)

13. Aaron and Robbie are thinking of changing networks. Each researches the different networks.

Robbie says Network A will cost less and Aaron says Network B is the better option.

	Network A	Network B
Standing charge	€20	€15
Free minutes	100	100
Texts	10c per text	12c per text
Cost per minute for calls	15c	25c

(i) If Aaron and Robbie send text messages only, at what number of text messages will their bills be the same? (Assume that Aaron uses Network B and Robbie uses Network A, and that both send the same number of texts.)

(ii) If they make calls only, at what number of minutes will their bills be the same?

(iii) If both boys make calls for 120 minutes each month and send 150 text messages, which is the better network to choose?

14. A retailer buys in a product at €300 and sells the product on to customers at €1,000.

(i) Calculate the profit made on the sale of this product.

(ii) Calculate the mark-up in monetary terms.

(iii) Calculate the percentage mark-up.

(iv) Calculate the percentage margin.

(v) Explain why the percentage mark-up exceeds the percentage margin.

15. In a particular year's budget, the VAT rate falls from 13.5% to 12.5%. The price of a phone drops by €4.50.

(i) What was the price of the phone before the change in VAT rate?

(ii) What is the new VAT amount?

(iii) What is the price of the phone now?

(iv) If the VAT rate had increased to 15%, how much would the phone have cost?

16. A 15-year loan is drawn down for €250,000. The rate of interest is 5.3% per annum compound interest.

(i) How much interest is charged in Year 1?

(ii) How much interest will have been charged after 10 years if no repayment is made in the 10 years (to the nearest cent)?

(iii) If €55,000 is paid off at the end of Year 1, what will be the interest charge for Year 2?

17. A finance company offers a car loan package, the details of which are as follows:

Option 1	10-year loan	Total interest = 15%
Option 2	7-year loan	Total interest = 10%
Option 3	5-year loan	Total interest = 9%
Option 4	3-year loan	Total interest = 6%

(i) Calculate the annual percentage rate (APR) for each option.

(ii) Which option would you choose? Give a reason for your answer.

18. A sum of €15,000 is invested in an eight-year government bond with an annual equivalent rate (AER) of 3.5%. Find the value of the investment when it matures in eight years' time.

19. Molly hopes to take a year off before college to travel. She estimates that she will need €5,000 for expenses in case she cannot find work abroad. Her local bank are offering a savings account with the following conditions:
   - Invest for three years at a rate of 7% per annum compounded annually.
   - The initial sum must be invested as a lump sum.

   (i) How much would she need to invest to make the €5,000 she will need in three years' time?

   Her friend tells her about another offer.
   - Invest €4,000 now and earn 22.5% interest over three years.

   (ii) Calculate the annual equivalent rate (AER) for the second investment.

   (iii) Which investment will give Molly the best return?

20. Calculate the net book value (NBV) of each of the following:

Cost (€)	Rate of depreciation	Number of years of depreciation
25,000	10%	5
105,000	12.5%	6
1,600,000	2%	8
364,800	16%	4
2,460,000	22.5%	12

21. A building has an NBV of €160,000 at the end of five years, having been depreciated at a rate of 2% per annum (reducing-balance method). What was the original cost of the building?

22. A computer was purchased at the start of 2010 for €25,000. By the end of 2011, it is expected that it will only be worth €16,000.

   What is the rate of depreciation (reducing-balance method)?

23. At a recent board meeting, it was decided that all 100 Fifth Year students should have a laptop for their maths class. The board proposed that the laptops will be sold after three years and new laptops purchased.

   The cost of a laptop is €400 and the expected selling price in three years is €100.

   (i) What rate of depreciation should the school apply given the value placed on the laptops at the end of their useful life?

   (ii) What will be the depreciation charge in Year 1, Year 2 and Year 3?

24. James travelled from Dublin to London, a distance of approximately 460 km. If his flight time was 50 minutes:

   (i) What was the average speed of the plane in kilometres per hour?

   (ii) What was the distance travelled in miles? (Use the conversion factors given in this chapter.)

25. A gas meter reading for Alan's apartment is shown below.

Present	12,444 units
Previous	12,138 units
Conversion factor	11.3625
Unit rate	€0.035 per kWh used

   Calculate:

   (i) The number of units used

   (ii) The number of kilowatt hours used

   (iii) The cost of the gas used before VAT

   (iv) The total cost of the bill if VAT is charged at 13.5% (correct to two decimal places)

26. Heating oil is delivered to the Moore household. One litre costs 80c and VAT is charged at 13.5%. The total cost of the bill, inclusive of VAT, is €1,470.96.

   If there were 110 litres in the Moore's oil tank before the delivery, how many litres are there after the delivery?

27. A bank quotes the following exchange rates for euro:

	We buy	We sell
Sterling £	0.86	0.81
US dollar $	1.38	1.34
Yen ¥	191	111

(i) Jack has €950 and wants sterling. How much will he get in sterling?

(ii) Nico has ¥5884. How much will he get in euro if his bank charges a 2% commission?

(iii) Anna has £154 and she wants to change this sum to euro. How much will she receive in euro?

(iv) Henry has $1,200. How much will he get in euro in exchange if commission is set at €1.75 per €100 received or part thereof?

28. SVC Ltd has recently completed its sales forecasts for the year to 31 December 2016. It expects to sell two products:

Product 1 @ €125 and Product 2 @ €145.

Its budgeted sales for Product 1 are 12,000 units, and 5,000 units for Product 2.

Both products use the same materials but in different quantities per unit as follows:

	Product 1	Product 2
Material X	10 kg	5 kg
Material Y	5 kg	7 kg
Skilled labour	5 hours	4 hours

- Material X: €1.50 per kg
- Material Y: €3.50 per kg
- Skilled labour: paid at €7.50 per hour
- Variable costs: €7 per unit
- Fixed costs: €180,000

Calculate:

(i) The amount of material X needed

(ii) The amount of material Y needed

(iii) The total labour hours used in production

(iv) The total labour cost of production

(v) The total cost of production (including variable and fixed costs)

(vi) The profit made if the company sells at the expected prices

(vii) The profit made if the prices realised are 10% higher than expected

Exam Questions

1. Fiona earns a gross wage of €1550 every fortnight. She pays income tax, a Universal Social Charge (USC), and Pay Related Social Insurance (PRSI) on this wage.

(a) Each fortnight, Fiona pays income tax at the rate of 20% on the first €1300 she earns and 40% on the remainder. She has tax credits of €126 per fortnight.

Find how much income tax she pays per fortnight.

(b) Each fortnight, Fiona also pays USC on her gross wage. The rates are:

1% on the first €462 she earns, 3% on the next €214, and 5.5% on the balance.

Find the total amount of USC she pays each fortnight.

(c) (i) Fiona pays PRSI amounting to €18 each fortnight.

Find the sum of her fortnightly deductions.

(ii) Write the sum of her fortnightly deductions as a percentage of her gross wage.

Give your answer correct to one decimal place.

SEC Leaving Certificate Ordinary Level, Paper 1, 2016

2. Paul has €8000 that he wants to invest for a maximum of 3 years. His local bank is offering him two options, Option 1 and Option 2, as shown in the table below.

Option 1	Option 2
2% interest in Year 1	3.7% compound interest per year, for 3 years
3% interest in Year 2	
5% interest in Year 3	
Money can be taken out at the end of Year 1 or Year 2 without penalty	Money may not be taken out until the end of year 3

(a) Find the value of the investment at the end of 3 years if Paul chooses Option 1 and does not take any money out.

(b) Find the value of the investment at the end of 3 years if Paul chooses Option 2.

(c) Give one issue, other than the rate of interest earned, that Paul might take into account when deciding between Option 1 and Option 2.

(d) Paul would like his investment of €8000 to amount to €9000 after 3 years.

What annual rate of compound interest would be required for this to happen?

Give your answer as a percentage.

SEC Leaving Certificate Ordinary Level, Paper 1, 2016

3. Padraic works in America and travels between Ireland and America.

(a) In Ireland, he exchanged €2000 for US dollars when the exchange rate was €1 = $1.29.

Find how many US dollars he received.

(b) Padraic returned to Ireland and exchanged $21,000 for euro. He received €15,000. Write the exchange rate for this transaction in the form €1 = $□.□□.

(c) Padraic wants to exchange some dollars for sterling. On a day when the euro to dollar exchange rate is €1 = $1.24 and the euro to sterling exchange rate is €1 = £0.83, find the dollar to sterling exchange rate. Write your answer in the form $1 = £□.□□.

SEC Leaving Certificate Ordinary Level, Paper 1, 2015

4. John, Mary and Eileen bought a ticket in a draw. The ticket cost €50. John paid €25, Mary paid €15 and Elieen paid €10. The ticket won a prize of €20,000. The prize is divided in proportion to how much each paid. How much prize money does each person receive?

SEC Leaving Certificate Ordinary Level, Paper 1, 2015

5. A shopkeeper bought 25 school blazers at €30 each and 25 trousers at €20 each.

(a) Find the total cost to the shopkeeper.

(b) The shopkeeper sells a blazer and a trousers as a set for €89.95. Find her profit on this transaction.

(c) The shopkeeper sells 22 blazer and trouser sets at €89.95 each. She sells the remaining 3 sets at a discount of 20% on the selling price. Find her mark-up (profit as a percentage of cost price) on the total transaction.

SEC Leaving Certificate Ordinary Level, Paper 1, 2014

6. (a) Mary bought a new car for €20,000 on the 1st July 2010.

The value of the car depreciated at a compound rate of 15% each year.

Find the value of the car, correct to the nearest euro, on the 1st July 2014.

(b) Mary wishes to buy a new car, which costs €24,000, on the 1st July 2014.

(i) *Buy Right Car Sales* offers Mary €10,500 for her old car. She can borrow the balance for one year at a rate of 11.5%. How much would she repay on 1st July 2015?

(ii) *Bargain Deals Car Sales* offers Mary €10,000 for her old car and an interest free loan of the balance for six months. At the end of the six months Mary would make a payment of €4000 and would be charged interest at a compound rate of 1.5% per month for the next six months. How much would Mary repay on 1st July 2015?

(iii) Which of the above options should Mary choose if she wishes to pay the least amount?

Justify your answer by calculation.

SEC Leaving Certificate Ordinary Level, Paper 1, 2014

7. (a) A sum of €5,000 is invested in an eight-year government bond with an annual equivalent rate (AER) of 6%. Find the value of the investment when it matures in 8 years' time.

(b) A different investment bond gives 20% interest after 8 years.

Calculate the AER for this bond.

SEC Leaving Certificate Ordinary Level, Sample Paper 1, 2014

8. (a) Michael has a credit card with a credit limit of €1000. Interest is charged monthly at 1.5% of the amount owed. Michael gets a bill at the end of each month. At the start of January, Michael owes €800 on his credit card. If Michael makes no repayments and no more purchases, show that he will exceed his credit limit after 15 months.

(b) Michael buys an item costing £95 on the internet and pays with his credit card. If the exchange rate is €1 = £0.8473, calculate, correct to the nearest cent, the amount that will be included on Michael's credit card bill.

SEC Leaving Certificate Ordinary Level, Paper 1, 2013

9. Alan pays income tax, a universal social charge (USC) and pay-related social insurance (PRSI) on his gross wages. His gross weekly wages are €510.

(a) Alan pays income tax at the rate of 20%. He has weekly tax credits of €63. How much income tax does he pay?

(b) Alan pays the USC at the rate of 2% on the first €193, 4% on the next €115 and 7% on the balance. Calculate the amount of USC Alan pays.

(c) Alan also pays PRSI. His total weekly deductions amount to €76.92. How much PRSI does Alan pay?

SEC Leaving Certificate Ordinary Level, Paper 1, 2012

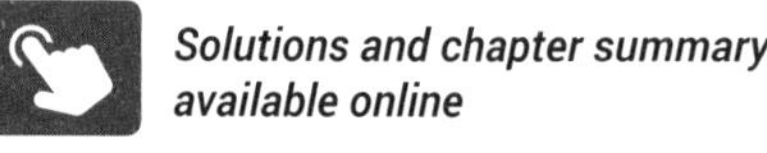

Solutions and chapter summary available online

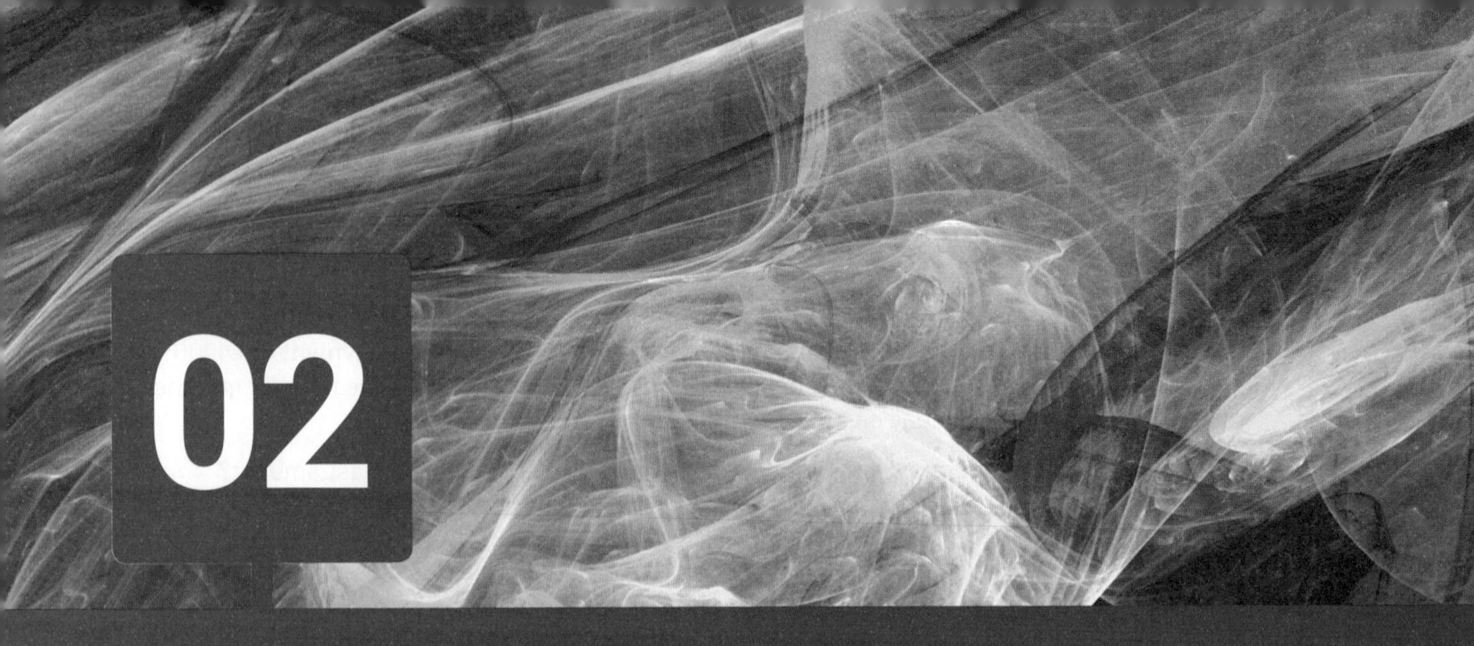

02

Algebra I

In this chapter you will learn to:

- Find the underlying formula written in words from which the data are derived (linear relationships)
- Evaluate expressions given the values of the variables
- Expand and re-group expressions
- Factorise expressions of order 2
- Add and subtract expressions of the form
  - $(ax + by + c) \pm \cdots \pm (dx + ey + f)$
  - $(ax^2 + bx + c) \pm \cdots \pm (dx^2 + ex + f)$
  - $\frac{ax + b}{c} \pm \frac{dx + e}{f}$
  - $\frac{a}{bx + c} \pm \frac{p}{qx + r}$

  where $a, b, c, d, e, f, p, q, r \in Z$
- Use the associative and distributive properties to simplify expressions of the form
  - $a(bx^2 + cx + d)$
  - $ax(bx^2 + c)$
  - $a(bx \pm cy \pm d) \pm \cdots \pm e(fx \pm gy \pm h)$

  where $a, b, c, d, e, f, g, h \in Z$
  - $(x \pm y)(w \pm z)$
- Divide expressions of the form: $(ax^2 + bx + c) \div (dx + e)$, where $a, b, c, d, e \in Z$
- Select and use suitable strategies (graphic, numeric, algebraic, mental) for finding solutions to equations of the form:
  - $f(x) = g(x)$, with $f(x) = ax + b$, $g(x) = cx + d$

  where $a, b, c, d \in Q$
- Select and use suitable strategies (graphic, numeric, algebraic, mental) for finding solutions to simultaneous linear equations with two unknowns and interpret the results
- Select and use suitable strategies (graphic, numeric, algebraic, mental) for finding solutions to inequalities of the form:
  - $g(x) \leqslant k$, $g(x) \geqslant k$
  - $g(x) < k$, $g(x) > k$

  where $g(x) = ax + b$ and $a, b, k \in Q$

You should remember...

- Order of operations
- How to add, subtract, multiply and divide integers
- How to simplify fractions
- Algebra from the Junior Certificate course
- Co-ordinate geometry

Key words

- Variable
- BIMDAS
- Term
- Constant
- Coefficient
- Expression
- Like terms
- Expand
- Lowest common denominator (LCD)
- Factors
- Highest common factor (HCF)
- Quadratic trinomials
- Manipulation
- Solve
- Unknown
- Linear
- Simultaneous
- Inequality
- Natural number
- Integer
- Real number

2.1 Expressions

Algebra has many uses, from the design of computer games to the modelling of weather patterns.

To be able to use algebra, we must first understand the rules involved in the basic operations of adding, subtracting, multiplying and dividing algebraic terms and expressions.

Notation in Algebra

A **variable** is a letter (usually x or y) that represents a number. This number may change or be unknown.

- In $5x$, the **variable** is x.
- In $20y$, the variable is y.

A **coefficient** is a number or symbol that is multiplying a variable.

- In $5x$, the **coefficient** is 5.
- In $20y$, the coefficient is 20.
- In x, the coefficient is 1.

A **constant** is a quantity that does not change in value, i.e. a number by itself.

In $10x + 2$, the **constant** is 2.

A **term** is a product of a constant and any number of variables, e.g. $7x^2y$.

$12x$ is an example of a **term**.

It means '12 times x'.

$x + 5y - 7$ contains three terms:

- x (a variable)
- $5y$ (a constant times a variable)
- -7 (a constant)

An **algebraic expression** is an expression that contains one or more numbers, one or more variables, and one or more arithmetic operations.

$5x + 2$ is an **expression**. Other examples of expressions include $x + 3y$, $8y^2$ and $4pr^3 - 7$.

ALGEBRA I

2.2 Substitution

One of the many cases where we encounter algebra is when we are given a formula and asked to substitute in certain values. This requires us to replace the variables with the numerical values given.

We must always remember to follow the correct **order of operations** (i.e. BIMDAS).

BIMDAS

These letters stand for Brackets, Indices, Multiplication, Division, Addition and Subtraction. We start at the top of the triangle and work down. Therefore, Brackets come first, then Indices (powers/roots), Multiplication/Division and finally Addition/Subtraction.

B, I, M D, A S

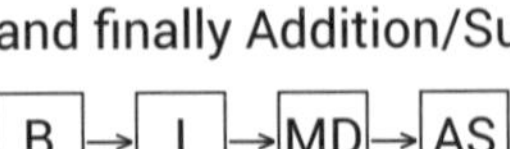

For MD and AS read left to right.

Consider the example where we are asked to find the value of $\sqrt{64} \div 4 \times (3 + 5) - 2$.

To ensure we find the correct value we must use BIMDAS.

$\sqrt{64} \div 4 \times (3 + 5) - 2$	
$= \sqrt{64} \div 4 \times 8 - 2$	(Brackets)
$= 8 \div 4 \times 8 - 2$	(Indices/powers)
$= 2 \times 8 - 2$	Division comes before multiplication.
$= 16 - 2$	(Multiplication)
$= 14$	(Addition/subtraction)

Worked Example 2.1

If $a = 2$, $b = 3$ and $c = -8$, find the value of the following expressions:

(i) $4a + 2b$ (ii) $3(a + b)$ (iii) $4ab$ (iv) $a^2 + ab + 2c$

Solution

Calculators can be of great help when evaluating expressions. We can input the expression with the correct numerical values directly into a calculator and the calculator will use BIMDAS to give us the answer.

(i) $4a + 2b$ — Write down the expression.
$= 4(2) + 2(3)$ — Rewrite the expression using brackets and replace a and b with their numerical values.
$= 8 + 6$
$= 14$

(ii) $3(a + b)$ — Write down the expression.
$= 3(2 + 3)$ — Insert the numerical values of a and b.
$= 3(5)$
$=15$

(iii) $4ab$ — Remember that ab means $a \times b$. This can also be written as $(a)(b)$.
$= 4(2)(3)$ — Insert the numerical values of a and b.
$= 24$

(iv) $a^2 + ab + 2c$ — Write down the expression.
$= (2)^2 + (2)(3) + 2(-8)$ — Insert the numerical values of a, b and c.
$= 4 + (2)(3) + 2(-8)$
$= 4 + 6 - 16$
$= 10 - 16$
$= -6$

Worked Example 2.2

If $x = 3$ and $y = -1$, evaluate the following expressions:

(i) $2x^2 - 2y^3$ (ii) $\frac{3x + 4y}{5x - 2y - 2}$ (iii) $\sqrt{2x + 3y^2}$

Solution

(i) $2x^2 - 2y^3$

$= 2(3)^2 - 2(-1)^3$

$= 2(9) - 2(-1)$

$= 18 + 2$

$= 20$

(ii) $\frac{3x + 4y}{5x - 2y - 2}$

As this is a fraction we can split the expression up into the top part (numerator) and the bottom part (denominator).

Top	Bottom
$3x + 4y$	$5x - 2y - 2$
$= 3(3) + 4(-1)$	$= 5(3) - 2(-1) - 2$
$= 9 - 4$	$= 15 + 2 - 2$
$= 5$	$= 15$

We now reform the fraction.

$\frac{\text{Top answer}}{\text{Bottom answer}} = \frac{5}{15} = \frac{1}{3}$

(iii) $\sqrt{2x + 3y^2}$

$= \sqrt{2(3) + 3(-1)^2}$

$= \sqrt{6 + 3(1)}$

$= \sqrt{6 + 3}$

$= \sqrt{9}$

$= 3$

Exercise 2.1

1. If $x = 1$ and $y = -3$, find the value of:

(i) $2x$ (vii) $3y^2$

(ii) $2y$ (viii) xy

(iii) $3(x + y)$ (ix) x^2y

(iv) $2(x - 2y) + 3x$ (x) x^2y^2

(v) x^3 (xi) xy^3

(vi) $4x^2$ (xii) x^2y^3

2. If $x = 2$, $y = 1$ and $z = -5$, find the value of:

(i) $3x + 4y$ (v) $12x + 2z - 8y$

(ii) $x + y + z$ (vi) $3y - 2x$

(iii) $2x + 6y + 4z$ (vii) $-6x + 2y - 4z$

(iv) $4x - 3z - 3y$ (viii) $-x - y - z$

3. If $a = 4$, $b = -2$ and $c = 6$, evaluate:

(i) abc (iv) $ab + bc$

(ii) $a^2 + b$ (v) $a^2b^2c^2$

(iii) $a^2 + 3b^3 - c^2$ (vi) $a^2b - c^3$

4. If $p = -1$, $q = 2$ and $r = 5$, find the value of:

(i) $2(p + q)$ (iii) $5(q + p) - 2r$

(ii) $4(q + r - p)$ (iv) $3(p - r)^2 - pq$

5. If $p = -1$, $q = 2$ and $r = 5$, find the value of:

(i) $\frac{3p + 1}{4q - r^2}$

(ii) $\frac{p}{5} - \frac{r}{2} - q$

(iii) $\frac{1}{5}r + \frac{1}{2}q + 2q$

(iv) $\sqrt{p + q}$

(v) $\sqrt{\frac{q^2 + (r + p)}{4q}}$

6. The volume of a cone can be found using the formula:

$$\text{Volume} = \frac{1}{3}\pi r^2 h$$

Work out the volume of each of the following cones:

Cone	π	r	h
1	3.14	5 cm	10 cm
2	3.14	4 m	5 m
3	$\frac{22}{7}$	56 mm	200 mm

ALGEBRA I

7. The surface area of a cuboid can be found using the formula:

Surface area = $2lb + 2lh + 2bh$

Work out the surface area of each of the following cuboids:

Cuboid	l	b	h
1	2 m	2 m	3 m
2	3.5 cm	12 cm	9 cm
3	8 m	9 m	12 m

8. The women's Heptathlon is a track and field seven-event contest where athletes are awarded points (P) based on their performance. The scores are calculated using a table and formulae.

A simplified version of the table is shown below.

Event	a	b	c
100 metres hurdles	9.2	27	1.8
High jump	1.8	75	1.3
Shot put	56	1.5	1.05
200 metres	4.9	43	1.8
Long jump	0.19	210	1.4
Javelin throw	16	3.8	1.04
800 metres	0.1	254	1.9

Running events (200 m, 800 m and 100 m hurdles):

$P = a(b - T)^c$

Jumping events (high jump and long jump):

$P = a(M - b)^c$

Throwing events (shot put and javelin):

$P = a(D - b)^c$

P = points (rounded **down** to the nearest whole number), T = time (in secs), M = height or length (in cm) and D = length (in m).

Katarina Johnson-Thompson's (GB) Rio 2016 results are shown.

Event	KJT's Results
100 metres hurdles	13.48 secs
High jump	1.98 m
Shot put	11.68 m
200 metres	23.26 secs
Long jump	6.51 m
Javelin throw	36.36 m
800 metres	2 min 10.47 secs

Calculate her points total for each event using the above table and formulae.

2.3 Adding and Subtracting Terms

When adding or subtracting algebraic terms we must always remember the following rules:

Algebra Rule: Only terms that have the exact same letter(s) raised to the same power(s) (**like terms**) can be added or subtracted.

Example: $5x + 6y + 4x - 3y = 9x + 3y$

Algebra Rule: When adding or subtracting like terms, the powers of the variables do not change, but the coefficients will change.

Example: $20y^2 + 8y^2 = 28y^2$

Worked Example 2.3

Simplify each of the following:

(i) $5a - 4b - 3 - a + 5b - 6$

(ii) $x^2 - 2x - 10 + 4 - 3x + 4x^2$

'Simplify' means to make the expression simpler by adding, subtracting, multiplying or dividing.

Solution

(i) $5a - 4b - 3 - a + 5b - 6$

$= 5a - a - 4b + 5b - 3 - 6$ — Put the like terms together. This is called grouping the terms

$= 4a + b - 9$ — Now add/subtract the like terms.

(ii) $x^2 - 2x - 10 + 4 - 3x + 4x^2$

$= x^2 + 4x^2 - 2x - 3x - 10 + 4$ — We usually put the like terms with the highest powers first, then the terms with the next highest power, etc. Remember, x^2 and x are **not** like terms.

$= 5x^2 - 5x - 6$

Exercise 2.2

Simplify each of the following:

1. (i) $a + a + a$
(ii) $2b + 5b + 4b$
(iii) $b - b - 2b$
(iv) $-d - 3d - 2d$
(v) $a + 5a - 10a$

2. (i) $4e - 3e - 6f + f$
(ii) $2g + 3g + 4h - 7$
(iii) $12j + 5j + 5k - 7k$
(iv) $7m - 7n + m$
(v) $2p - 4q - 3p + 2q$

3. (i) $2x + 3y + 4 + 4x + 2y + 8$
(ii) $14x + 5y - 3 - 10x - 3y + 11$
(iii) $2a + 2b - 2 + 5a - 7b - 5$
(iv) $-4p - 2q + 4 - 3p - 2q - 4$

4. (i) $2x^2 + 3x + 4 + x^2 + 4x + 1$
(ii) $5x^2 - 5x + 1 - x^2 + 2x - 6$
(iii) $3a^2 - 4a + 9 - 4a^2 + 4a - 5$
(iv) $-p^2 - 3p + 1 - 3p^2 - 2p - 4$

2.4 Multiplying Terms I

Unlike when adding or subtracting, in algebra any term may be multiplied by another term. When we multiply terms, we encounter another set of rules that are important to understand.

Commutative property (multiplication):

$2 \times 3 = 6$

$3 \times 2 = 6$

A change in the **order** of the numbers does not change the result.

Associative property (multiplication):

$(3 \times 4) \times 2 = 12 \times 2 = 24$

$3 \times (4 \times 2) = 3 \times 8 = 24$

A change in the **grouping** of the numbers does not change the result.

The same applies when multiplying terms in algebra.

Example: $(4x)(5y)$

$= (4)(x)(5)(y)$

$= (4)(5)(x)(y)$ (Commutative and associative)

$= 20xy$

Example: $(4x^3)(3x^5) = (4)(3)(x^3)(x^5)$

$= 12x^8$

Algebra Rule: To multiply terms: coefficient × coefficient, variable × variable.

Algebra Rule: When multiplying terms we **add** the powers or indices of that variable. This rule is also written as $a^p \cdot a^q = a^{p+q}$.

Worked Example 2.4

Simplify each of the following:

(i) $(2ab)(3a^2b^4)$ (ii) $(3x)^3$ (iii) $(3a^2b)^2$

Solution

Remember $a = a^1$, $b = b^1$, etc.

(i) $(2ab)(3a^2b^4)$

$= (2)(a)(b)(3)(a^2)(b^4)$ Remember $2ab = 2 \times a \times b$.

$= (2)(3)(a)(a^2)(b)(b^4)$ Reorder.

$= 6a^3b^5$ $(a)(a^2) = a^{1+2} = a^3$ and $(b)(b^4) = b^{1+4} = b^5$.

(ii) $(3x)^3$ Remember $x = x^1$.

$= (3x)(3x)(3x)$

$= (3)(3)(3)(x)(x)(x)$ Reorder.

$= 27x^3$ $(x)(x)(x) = (x^1)(x^1)(x^1) = x^{1+1+1} = x^3$

(iii) $(3a^2b)^2$

$= (3a^2b)(3a^2b)$

$= (3)(3)(a^2)(a^2)(b)(b)$

$= 9a^4b^2$

Exercise 2.3

Simplify each of the following:

1. (i) $(3a)(b)$ (ii) $(3b)(4)$ (iii) $(2a)(5a)$ (iv) $(4c)(2c)$ (v) $(2b)(-c)$ (vi) $(-d)(d)$ (vii) $(-5e)(-2e)$ (viii) $(-e)(-e)(f)$

2. (i) $(x^2)(x^2)$ (ii) $(x^3)(y^2)$ (iii) $(3x^5)(2x^2)$ (iv) $(x^5)(x^3)$ (v) $(2a^4)(3a^6)$ (vi) $(-y^2)(2y^3)$ (vii) $(-4y^2)(-5y^3)$ (viii) $(-b^{12})(-4b^3)$

3. (i) $(a)(ab)$ (ii) $(ab)(ab)$ (iii) $(2dc)(3d)$ (iv) $(a)(a^2b)$ (v) $(4xy)(xy^2)$ (vi) $(a)(-a)(-a)$ (vii) $(-3y)(y^2)(y^2)$ (viii) $(-5y)(-y)(2)$

4. (i) $(2xy)(4xy)(xy)$ (ii) $(-3y)(3x^2)(y^2)$ (iii) $(-5n)(-5n)(2m^2)$ (iv) $(3a^5)(4a^2)(-2a)$ (v) $(xy)(x^2y)(2)$ (vi) $(pq)(5p^2q)(2pq^2)$ (vii) $(-p^2q)(4p^2q)(2qp^4)$ (viii) $(2t^2p)(t^2p^2)(5t^3p)$

5. (i) $(b)^2$ (ii) $(2b)^2$ (iii) $(-3b)^2$ (iv) $(-3b)^3$ (v) $(4ab)^3$ (vi) $(-2ab)^2$ (vii) $(4x^2y)^2$ (viii) $(-2x^2y)^3$

6. (i) $(2a)(b) + (a)(3b)$

(ii) $(4p)(2q) - (2p)(q) + (4)(q)(p)$

(iii) $(3x)(x^2)(y) + (x)(xy) - (y)(xy^2)$

(iv) $(3ab)(-a) - (2a)(3b) + (4b)(a^2) - (5a^2)(b)$

(v) $(xy)^2 - 3(xy)(x) - (2x^2)(y)^2$

2.5 Multiplying Terms II

We may have to deal with multiplying an expression by a number or a term.

The distributive property of the real numbers is used to simplify expressions involving brackets.

$x(y + z) = xy + xz$, for $x, y, z \in R$ (Distributive property)

For example:

$2(4 + 3) = (2)(7) = 14$

However, we can use the fact that multiplication distributes over addition and subtraction to help find an alternative way to do this calculation.

$2(4 + 3)$

$= 2(4) + 2(3)$ (Distributive property)

$= 8 + 6$

$= 14$

In algebra, when asked to expand, we are being asked to remove the brackets using the correct method.

Worked Example 2.5

Expand and simplify the following:

(i) $6(x + 1) + 2(x + 2)$

(ii) $5(3a^2 + 4a + 5) - (a^2 + 3a - 2)$

(iii) $2x(x - 3)$

(iv) $2y(y + 2) - 5y(y - 1) + 3(y - 2)$

(v) $-3x(2x^2 - 3)$

Solution

(i) $6(x + 1) + 2(x + 2)$

$= 6(x) + 6(1) + 2(x) + 2(2)$ — Every term inside a set of brackets will be multiplied by the term outside the set of brackets.

$= 6x + 6 + 2x + 4$

$= 6x + 2x + 6 + 4$ — Group like terms.

$= 8x + 10$ — Simplify (add/subtract like terms).

(ii) $5(3a^2 + 4a + 5) - (a^2 + 3a - 2)$

$= 5(3a^2 + 4a + 5) - 1(a^2 + 3a - 2)$ — To help with the multiplication we put a 1 in front of the second bracket.

$= 15a^2 + 20a + 25 - 1a^2 - 3a + 2$ — We need to pay special attention to the signs.

$= 15a^2 - 1a^2 + 20a - 3a + 25 + 2$ — Group like terms.

$= 14a^2 + 17a + 27$ — Simplify (add/subtract like terms).

(iii) $2x(x - 3)$

$= 2x(x) + 2x(-3)$

$= 2x^2 - 6x$ — Remember $(x)(x) = x^1 . x^1 = x^{1+1} = x^2$.

(iv) $2y(y + 2) - 5y(y - 1) + 3(y - 2)$

$= 2y^2 + 4y - 5y^2 + 5y + 3y - 6$ Be careful with signs.

$= 2y^2 - 5y^2 + 4y + 5y + 3y - 6$ Group like terms.

$= -3y^2 + 12y - 6$ Simplify.

(v) $-3x(2x^2 - 3)$

$= -6x^3 + 9x$ Be careful with signs.

Exercise 2.4

In each part, remove the brackets and simplify:

1. (i) $3(a + 3)$
   (ii) $3(b - 3)$
   (iii) $-4(c - 4)$
   (iv) $5(x - 3y - 1)$

2. (i) $3(x + 2) + 4(x + 1)$
   (ii) $1(2a + 2) + 2(3a + 1)$
   (iii) $2(a - 4) - 5(a - 1)$
   (iv) $3(4b - 2) - 3(b - 4)$

3. (i) $2(a^2 - a + 1) + 2(a^2 + 5a + 4)$
   (ii) $-4(3a^2 + a - 1) - (4a^2 - 2a - 4)$
   (iii) $5(b^2 - 2b - 1) - 2(-2b - b^2 - 1)$

4. (i) $2x - y + 6 + (3x - y + 1) - (x - 2y - 2)$
   (ii) $x^2 + 3x + 5 + 3(2x^2 - 7x + 20) - 2(x^2 - 3x + 4)$
   (iii) $3(2a^2 - 3a - 1) - (3a^2 - 2a - 3) - 4(a^2 + 2a - 1)$

5. (i) $x(x + 3)$
   (ii) $y(y - 6)$
   (iii) $2a(2a + 1)$
   (iv) $4b(2b - 2)$
   (v) $2x(x^2 - 1)$
   (vi) $-5x(3x^2 - 7)$

6. (i) $a(a + 1) + a(a + 1)$
   (ii) $2x(3x - 7) - 2x(x - 5)$
   (iii) $3a(7a - 2) - 4a(3a + 1)$
   (iv) $3(x^2 - 3x + 1) + 5x(x + 3)$
   (v) $3y(2y - 3) - (y + 3)(2y)$

2.6 Algebraic Fractions I

When asked to add or subtract two algebraic fractions, we first must find the **lowest common denominator** (LCD).

We then apply a similar method to that of adding/subtracting numerical fractions.

For example, consider the case where we are asked to simplify $\frac{2}{3} + \frac{1}{5}$.

Step 1 The lowest common multiple (LCM) of 3 and 5 is 15.

15 is the smallest number that both 3 and 5 divide evenly into.

We now refer to 15 as the LCD.

Step 2 Now write as equivalent fractions using the LCD.

$$\frac{2}{3} + \frac{1}{5}$$

$$= \frac{10}{15} + \frac{3}{15}$$

Step 3 Add and simplify.

$$\frac{10 + 3}{15} = \frac{13}{15}$$

ALGEBRA I

Worked Example 2.6

Write as a single fraction: (i) $\frac{4x+3}{5}+\frac{3x-1}{2}$ (ii) $\frac{2x-3}{4}-\frac{x-5}{8}$

Solution

(i) **Step 1** The LCM of 5 and 2 is 10.

Step 2 Rewrite the expression as a single fraction with the LCD as the denominator.

5 into 10 goes 2 times.

2 into 10 goes 5 times.

$=\frac{2(4x+3)+5(3x-1)}{10}$

$=\frac{8x+6+15x-5}{10}$ Multiply out the brackets.

$=\frac{8x+15x+6-5}{10}$ Group like terms.

$=\frac{21x+1}{10}$ Add/subtract like terms.

(ii) **Step 1** The LCM of 4 and 8 is 8.

Step 2 Rewrite the expression as a single fraction with the LCD as the denominator.

4 into 8 goes 2 times.

8 into 8 goes 1 time.

$=\frac{2(2x-3)-1(x-5)}{8}$

$=\frac{4x-6-x+5}{8}$

$=\frac{4x-x-6+5}{8}$

$=\frac{3x-1}{8}$

Exercise 2.5

Simplify each of the following:

1. $\frac{x}{2}+\frac{x}{5}$
2. $\frac{y}{8}+\frac{y}{4}$
3. $\frac{a}{5}-\frac{a}{3}$
4. $\frac{3c}{2}-\frac{c}{4}$
5. $\frac{2x}{3}+\frac{4x}{7}$
6. $\frac{2a+1}{4}+\frac{a+5}{3}$
7. $\frac{4a+1}{5}+\frac{3a-1}{3}$
8. $\frac{2x-3}{4}+\frac{x-2}{8}$
9. $\frac{5x+3}{9}-\frac{x+2}{3}$
10. $\frac{3y-1}{8}-\frac{4y-5}{3}$
11. $\frac{4x-2}{12}-\frac{x-2}{24}-\frac{2}{3}$
12. $\frac{1}{3}(x+1)-\frac{3}{2}(3x-2)-\frac{5}{6}(x-3)$
13. $\frac{3}{5}(5x+1)-\frac{2}{3}(2x+3)+3\frac{1}{15}$

2.7 Expanding and Re-Grouping Expressions

Another type of algebra question involves the multiplication of two or more expressions.

For example: $(x+3)(x-4)$.

Again we can use numbers to explain the method used.

$(5+3)(5-4)=(8)(1)=8$

However.

$5(5-4)+3(5-4)$

$=5(5)+5(-4)+3(5)+3(-4)$ (Distributive property of multiplication over addition)

$=25-20+15-12$

$=8$

If we apply this method to our algebra question:

$(x + 3)(x - 4) = x(x - 4) + 3(x - 4)$

$= x(x) + x(-4) + 3(x) + 3(-4)$

$= x^2 - 4x + 3x - 12$

$= x^2 - x - 12$

Worked Example 2.7

Remove the brackets and simplify:

(i) $(x + 2)(x - 3)$ (ii) $(2y - 1)(y - 2)$ (iii) $(2a - 4)(a^2 - 4a - 1)$ (iv) $(5b - 2)^2$

Solution

(i) $(x + 2)(x - 3)$

$= x(x - 3) + 2(x - 3)$ First term by second bracket + second term by second bracket.

$= x(x) + x(-3) + 2(x) + 2(-3)$ (Distributive property)

$= x^2 - 3x + 2x - 6$ Multiply out the brackets.

$= x^2 - x - 6$ Add/subtract like terms.

(ii) $(2y - 1)(y - 2)$

$= 2y(y - 2) - 1(y - 2)$

$= 2y^2 - 4y - y + 2$

$= 2y^2 - 5y + 2$

(iii) $(2a - 4)(a^2 - 4a - 1)$

$= 2a(a^2 - 4a - 1) - 4(a^2 - 4a - 1)$

$= 2a^3 - 8a^2 - 2a - 4a^2 + 16a + 4$

$= 2a^3 - 8a^2 - 4a^2 - 2a + 16a + 4$

$= 2a^3 - 12a^2 + 14a + 4$

(iv) $(5b - 2)^2$

$= (5b - 2)(5b - 2)$

$= 5b(5b - 2) - 2(5b - 2)$

$= 25b^2 - 10b - 10b + 4$

$= 25b^2 - 20b + 4$

ALGEBRA I

We can also use the area model to multiply two expressions. When using the area model we calculate the areas of a collection of rectangles.

Worked Example 2.8

Simplify the following expressions:

(i) $(x + 3)(x + 5)$ (ii) $(x - 3)(x^2 + 4x - 5)$

Solution

(i) $(x + 3)(x + 5)$

We draw a rectangle with sides $x + 3$ and $x + 5$ and then work out the area of each of the smaller rectangles.

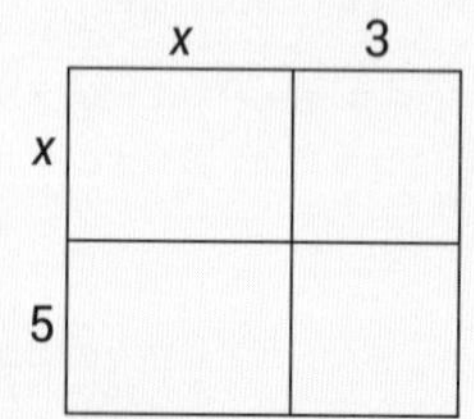

→

	x	3
x	$(x)(x) = x^2$	$(x)(3) = 3x$
5	$(5)(x) = 5x$	$(5)(3) = 15$

Area $= x^2 + 3x + 5x + 15$

$\therefore (x + 3)(x + 5) = x^2 + 8x + 15$

(ii) $(x - 3)(x^2 + 4x - 5)$

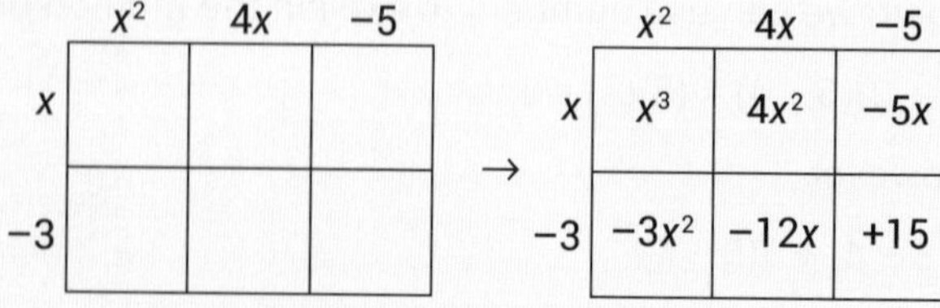

Area $= x^3 + 4x^2 - 5x - 3x^2 - 12x + 15$

$= x^3 + 4x^2 - 3x^2 - 5x - 12x + 15$

$\therefore (x - 3)(x^2 + 4x - 5) = x^3 + x^2 - 17x + 15$

Exercise 2.6

Expand and simplify:

1. (i) $(x + 3)(x + 2)$
   (ii) $(x + 4)(x + 1)$
   (iii) $(x - 7)(x + 3)$
   (iv) $(x - 1)(x + 5)$
   (v) $(y - 4)(y - 8)$
2. (i) $(4x + 1)(2x + 1)$
   (ii) $(2y - 4)(3y + 1)$
   (iii) $(3x - 3)(5x - 2)$
   (iv) $(6y - 3)(2y - 4)$
   (v) $(2 - 2b)(2b - 1)$
3. (i) $(x + y)(x + y)$
   (ii) $(p - q)(p + q)$
   (iii) $(m - n)(m - n)$
   (iv) $(2h - w)(2h - 3w)$
4. (i) $(x + 1)^2$
   (ii) $(x + 3)^2$
   (iii) $(x - 2)^2$
   (iv) $(x - 5)^2$
   (v) $(2y + 1)^2$
5. (i) $(x + 1)(x^2 + x + 1)$
   (ii) $(x - 3)(2x^2 + x - 1)$
   (iii) $(4x + 1)(4x^2 - 2x - 3)$
6. (i) $x(x + 3)(x + 4)$
   (ii) $h(10 - 2h)(10 - 2h)$
   (iii) $a(a - b)(a + b)$
7. (i) $(2x + 3)^3$
   (ii) $(y - 2)^3$
8. Use the area model to multiply:
   (i) $(2x + 3)(3x - 5)$
   (ii) $(x + 5)(x^2 - 5x + 25)$

2.8 Factorising I

Another important skill is that of finding the factors of an expression. This is called **factorising**.

To factorise an expression we rewrite the expression as a **product**, a product being two or more terms that when multiplied together will give the original expression.

Factorising is the reverse of expanding. We turn the given expression into a **product**.

For example, 5 and 7 are factors of 35 because 5 × 7 will give us 35.

If we consider the expression $5x + 10$, then 5 and $(x + 2)$ are factors as $5(x + 2) = 5x + 10$.

Remember to factorise each expression fully.

We met the following methods of factorising at Junior Certificate level:

- **Highest Common Factor**
  $x^2 - 3x = x(x - 3)$
- **Grouping**
  $ax - bx + ay - by$
  $= x(a - b) + y(a - b)$
  $= (x + y)(a - b)$
- **Difference of Two Squares**
  $x^2 - y^2 = (x + y)(x - y)$
- **Quadratic Trinomials**
  $x^2 + 8x + 15 = (x + 5)(x + 3)$

Worked Example 2.9

Factorise fully the following expressions:

(i) $y^2 + 4y$ (ii) $x^2 - 11x$

We can check our answer by multiplying out the factors. This is always a good idea in an exam setting.

Solution

(i) $y^2 + 4y$

y is the highest common factor for both terms.

$\therefore y^2 + 4y = y(y + 4)$

(ii) $x^2 - 11$

x is the highest common factor for both terms.

$= x(x - 11)$

Worked Example 2.10

Factorise fully the expressions:

(i) $mr - ms + nr - ns$ (ii) $ax - ay - cx + cy$

Solution

(i) $mr - ms + nr - ns$

$= m(r - s) + n(r - s)$ Remove the common factor from two pairs of terms. The two brackets must be the same.

$= (r - s)(m + n)$ Remove the common factor from the new expressions.

(ii) $ax - ay - cx + cy$

$= a(x - y) - c(x - y)$ Remember that the two brackets must be the same.

$=(x - y)(a - c)$

Worked Example 2.11

Factorise:

(i) $x^2 - 49$ (ii) $a^2 - 225$

Solution

(i) $x^2 - 49$

Write each term as a square.

$= (x)^2 - (7)^2$

$= (x - 7)(x + 7)$

(ii) $a^2 - 225$

$= (a)^2 - (15)^2$

$= (a - 15)(a + 15)$

Worked Example 2.12

Factorise:

$x^2 + 12x + 32$

Solution

$x^2 + 12x + 32$

Method 1

We are looking for the factors of +32 that add up to +12.

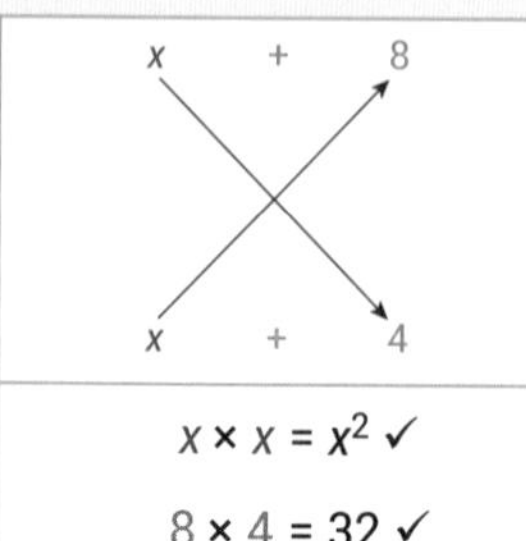

$x \times x = x^2$ ✓

$8 \times 4 = 32$ ✓

We now use the arrows:

$x \times 4 = +4x$

$x \times 8 = +8x$

$12x$ ✓

$\therefore x^2 + 12x + 32 = (x + 8)(x + 4).$

Method 2 (Guide Number)

Step 1 Multiply the coefficient of x^2 by the constant.

$1 \times 32 = 32$

Step 2 Find two factors that multiply to give 32 and add to give the coefficient of the middle term, i.e. +12.

4 and 8

Step 3 Use the answers from Step 2 to rewrite $x^2 + 12x + 32$ as follows:

$x^2 + 4x + 8x + 32$

$= x(x + 4) + 8(x + 4)$ Factorise by grouping.

$= (x + 4)(x + 8)$

Worked Example 2.13

Factorise:

(i) $x^2 + 5x - 14$ (ii) $x^2 - 11x + 30$

We must be very careful when dealing with expressions that have negative terms.

Solution

(i) $x^2 + 5x - 14$

Method 1

We are looking for factors of −14 (negative 14) that add to give us +5 (positive 5).

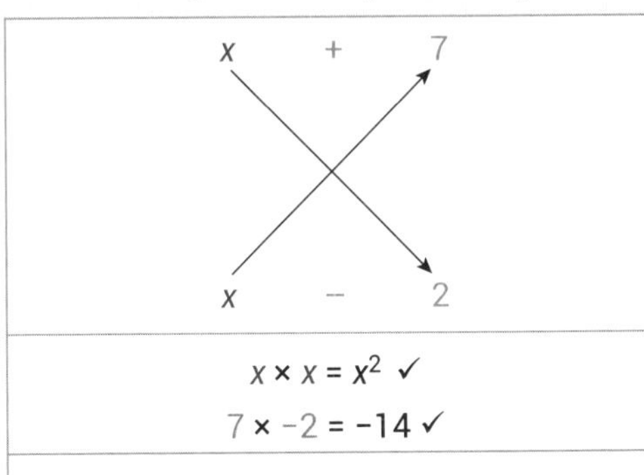

$x \times x = x^2$ ✓

$7 \times -2 = -14$ ✓

We now use the arrows:

$x \times -2 = -2x$

$x \times 7 = \underline{+7x}$

$5x$ ✓

$\therefore x^2 + 5x - 14 = (x + 7)(x - 2)$

Method 2 (Guide Number)

$x^2 + 5x - 14$

Step 1 Multiply the coefficient of x^2 by the constant.

$1 \times -14 = -14$

Step 2 Find two factors that multiply to give −14 and add to give the coefficient of the middle term, i.e. +5.

7 and −2

Step 3 Use the answers from Step 2 to rewrite $x^2 + 5x - 14$ as follows:

$x^2 + 7x - 2x - 14$

$= x(x + 7) - 2(x + 7)$ Factorise by grouping.

$= (x + 7)(x - 2)$

(ii) $x^2 - 11x + 30$

Method 1

We are looking for factors of +30 that add to give us −11.

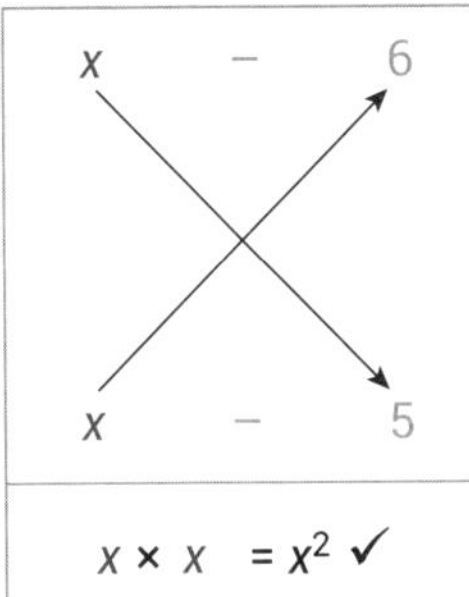

$x \times x = x^2$ ✓

$-6 \times -5 = 30$ ✓

We now use the arrows:

$x \times -5 = -5x$

$x \times -6 = \underline{-6x}$

$-11x$ ✓

$\therefore x^2 - 11x + 30 = (x - 6)(x - 5)$

Method 2 (Guide Number)

$x^2 - 11x + 30$

Step 1 Multiply the coefficient of x^2 by the constant.

$1 \times 30 = 30$

Step 2 Find two factors that multiply to give 30 and add to give the coefficient of the middle term, i.e. −11.

−6 and −5

Step 3 Use the answers from Step 2 to rewrite $x^2 - 11x + 30$ as follows:

$x^2 - 6x - 5x + 30$

$= x(x - 6) - 5(x - 6)$ Factorise by grouping.

$= (x - 6)(x - 5)$

- You can check your answer by expanding.

For quadratic trinomials:

- If the constant term is positive, then the signs in brackets are either both positive or both negative.
- If the constant term is negative, then one sign is positive and the other sign is negative.

Exercise 2.7

Factorise the following:

1. $x^2 + 5x$
2. $x^2 - 7x$
3. $x^2 - 2x$
4. $x^2 - 15x$
5. $a^2 - 11a$
6. $x^2 - 14x$
7. $ad + ae + cd + ce$
8. $ap + aq + bp + bq$
9. $mp - mq + np - nq$
10. $ac - ad - bc + bd$
11. $xy - y - 4x + 4$
12. $6ap - 3pe + 2ad - ae$
13. $2xr - rs - 10yx + 5ys$
14. $pm + nq + np + mq$
15. $x^2 - 16$
16. $x^2 - 9$
17. $x^2 - 100$
18. $x^2 - 4$
19. $b^2 - 25$
20. $y^2 - 121$
21. $x^2 - 225$
22. $x^2 + 6x + 9$
23. $x^2 + 8x + 7$
24. $x^2 + 13x + 36$
25. $x^2 + 4x + 4$
26. $x^2 - 12x + 27$
27. $x^2 + 5x - 14$
28. $x^2 - 5x - 14$
29. $x^2 - 12x + 32$
30. $x^2 - 16x + 64$
31. $x^2 - 3x - 4$
32. $x^2 + 7x - 18$
33. $x^2 - 2x - 63$
34. $x^2 - 2x - 24$
35. $x^2 - 15x + 56$
36. $b^2 - 361$
37. $pc + bd - bc - dp$
38. $x^2 + 3x - 70$
39. $x^2 - 10x - 39$
40. $x^2 + 15x + 56$
41. $x^2 - x - 90$
42. $9 - x^2$

2.9 Factorising II

In the previous section, when we factorised expressions in x of order 2, the x^2 term always had a coefficient of 1. We must also be able to factorise expressions where the coefficient of x^2 is not 1.

Worked Example 2.14

Factorise fully the following expressions:

(i) $5x^2 + 20x$ (ii) $2a^2 - 3a$

Solution

(i) $5x^2 + 20x$

The highest common factor of both terms is $5x$.

$\therefore\ 5x^2 + 20x = 5x(x + 4)$

(ii) $2a^2 - 3a$

In this case, the highest common factor of both terms is a.

$\therefore\ 2a^2 - 3a = a(2a - 3)$

Worked Example 2.15

Factorise:

(i) $4x^2 - 81$ (ii) $25a^2 - 144y^2$

Solution

(i) $4x^2 - 81$

Write each term as a square.

$= (2x)^2 - (9)^2$

$= (2x - 9)(2x + 9)$

(ii) $25a^2 - 144y^2$

$= (5a)^2 - (12y)^2$

$= (5a - 12y)(5a + 12y)$

Worked Example 2.16

Factorise:

(i) $2x^2 + 13x + 15$ (ii) $5y^2 - 16y + 3$ (iii) $4t^2 - 21t + 5$

Solution

(i) $2x^2 + 13x + 15$

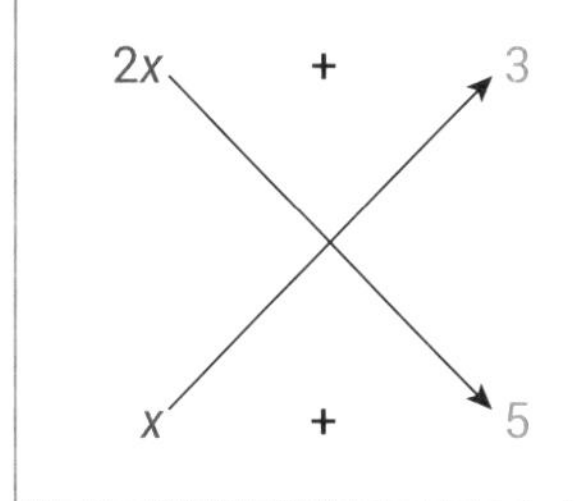

$2x \times x = 2x^2$ ✓

$3 \times 5 = 15$ ✓

We now use the arrows:

$2x \times 5 = 10x$

$x \times 3 = 3x$

$13x$ ✓

$\therefore\ 2x^2 + 13x + 15 = (2x + 3)(x + 5)$

(ii) $5y^2 - 16y + 3$ (Using the Guide Number method.)

Step 1 Multiply the coefficient of x^2 by the constant.

$5 \times 3 = 15$

Step 2 Find two factors that multiply to give 15 and add to give the coefficient of the middle term, i.e. -16.

-1 and -15

Step 3 $5y^2 - 16y + 3$

$= 5y^2 - y - 15y + 3$

$= y(5y - 1) - 3(5y - 1)$

$= (5y - 1)(y - 3)$

(iii) $4t^2 - 21t + 5$

4 has two pairs of factors that we must consider. 1, 4 **and** 2, 2.

$2t$ − 5 / $2t$ − 1	$4t$ − 5 / t − 1	$4t$ − 1 / t − 5
$2t \times 2t = 4t^2$ ✓ $-5 \times -1 = 5$ ✓	$4t \times t = 4t^2$ ✓ $-5 \times -1 = 5$ ✓	$4t \times t = 4t^2$ ✓ $-1 \times -5 = 5$ ✓
We now use the arrows: $2t \times -1 = -2t$ $2t \times -5 = -10t$ $-12t$ ✗	We now use the arrows: $4t \times -1 = -4t$ $t \times -5 = -5t$ $-9t$ ✗	We now use the arrows: $4t \times -5 = -20t$ $t \times -1 = -1t$ $-21t$ ✓

$\therefore 4t^2 - 21t + 5 = (4t - 1)(t - 5)$

Worked Example 2.17

Factorise fully $24x^2 + 92x - 16$.

Solution

Step 1 Take out the HCF.

$= 4(6x^2 + 23x - 4)$

Step 2 Now factorise $6x^2 + 23x - 4$.

$6x^2 + 23x - 4 = (6x - 1)(x + 4)$

Step 3 $\therefore 24x^2 + 92x - 16 = 4(6x - 1)(x + 4)$

Exercise 2.8

Factorise fully the following expressions:

1. $2x^2 + 6x$
2. $3x^2 + 21x$
3. $5y^2 - 25y$
4. $4x^2 - 16x$
5. $3a^2 - 39a$
6. $2b^2 + 3b$
7. $2a^2 - 15a$
8. $5x^2 + 2x$
9. $3x^2 + 7x$
10. $11p^2 - 3p$
11. $4x^2 - 16$
12. $9b^2 - 4$
13. $64x^2 - 49$
14. $25a^2 - 100$
15. $49b^2 - 36$
16. $121x^2 - 25$
17. $81y^2 - 196$
18. $169x^2 - 324$
19. $2x^2 + 5x + 3$
20. $5x^2 + 6x + 1$
21. $7p^2 + 15p + 2$
22. $5x^2 + 12x + 4$
23. $3q^2 + 8q + 4$
24. $3x^2 + 17x + 10$
25. $7x^2 + 2x - 5$
26. $3y^2 - 8y + 5$
27. $3x^2 - 4x - 7$

28. $2x^2 - x - 10$

29. $7a^2 + 2a - 5$

30. $5x^2 + 17x - 12$

31. $2b^2 - 13b + 15$

32. $5x^2 - 18x + 9$

33. $5p^2 + 28p - 49$

34. $11x^2 + 61x - 30$

35. $4x^2 - x - 5$

36. $8q^2 + 17q + 2$

37. $4x^2 + 5x - 21$

38. $900x^2 - 196$

39. $6x^2 + 10x + 4$

40. $3x^2 - 18x + 24$

2.10 Simplifying Algebraic Fractions

Simplifying algebraic fractions is very similar to simplifying numerical fractions. When we simplify an algebraic fraction, we need to divide the top (numerator) and bottom (denominator) by their HCF.

Consider if we were asked to simplify the fraction $\frac{16}{20}$.

$\frac{16}{20} = \frac{4(4)}{4(5)} = \frac{4}{5}$ Divide above and below by 4.

The fraction $\frac{12}{90}$ can be simplified so that

$$\frac{12}{90} = \frac{2.2.3}{2.3.3.5} = \frac{\overset{1}{\cancel{2}}.2.\overset{1}{\cancel{3}}}{\underset{1}{\cancel{2}}.\underset{1}{\cancel{3}}.3.5} = \frac{2}{15}$$

More easily we can divide the numerator and denominator by the HCF of 12 and 90, which is 6.

$\frac{12}{90} = \frac{6(2)}{6(15)} = \frac{2}{15}$ Divide above and below by 6.

Worked Example 2.18

Simplify:

(i) $\frac{20a^3b^5}{25a^2b^6}$ (ii) $\frac{10x + 20}{15}$ (iii) $\frac{6x^2 + 13x + 5}{2x + 1}$ (iv) $\frac{x - 3}{2x^2 - 11x + 15}$

Solution

(i) $\frac{20a^3b^5}{25a^2b^6}$ Divide above and below by $5a^2b^5$.

$= \frac{4a}{5b}$

(ii) $\frac{10x + 20}{15}$

$= \frac{5(2x + 4)}{5(3)}$ 5 is the HCF for the numerator and denominator.

$= \frac{2x + 4}{3}$ Divide above and below by 5.

(iii) $\frac{6x^2 + 13x + 5}{2x + 1}$

$= \frac{(2x + 1)(3x + 5)}{2x + 1}$ Factorise the numerator.

$= \frac{^1\cancel{(2x + 1)}(3x + 5)}{\cancel{2x + 1}_1}$ $2x + 1$ is the HCF. Divide above and below by $2x + 1$.

$= 3x + 5$

(iv) $\frac{x-3}{2x^2-11x+15}$

$= \frac{(x-3)}{(2x-5)(x-3)}$ Factorise the denominator.

$= \frac{\cancel{(x-3)}^1}{(2x-5)\cancel{(x-3)}_1}$ $x - 3$ is the HCF. Divide above and below by $x - 3$.

Remember that $(x - 3) \div (x - 3) = 1$.

$= \frac{1}{(2x-5)}$ Remember that the numerator is 1.

2.11 Long Division in Algebra

We can apply the method of long division from our primary school studies to help us understand how to do long division in algebra.

Example: Divide 1064 by 19.

Solution:

```
       5 6
19 | 1 0 6④
    -(9 5)↓
       1 1 4
     -(1 1 4)
           0
```

Steps:
- $106 \div 19 = 5$ (Write 5 on top.)
- Multiply 19 by 5 and subtract from 106. Remainder = 11.
- Bring down the 4.
- $114 \div 19 = 6$ (Write 6 on top.)
- Multiply 19 by 6 and subtract from 114. Remainder = 0.

$\therefore 1064 \div 19 = 56$

We can use similar steps when asked to do long division in algebra.

Worked Example 2.19

Divide $6x^2 + 13x + 5$ by $2x + 1$.

Solution

$$\begin{array}{r|l} & 3x+5 \\ 2x+1 & 6x^2+13x+5 \\ & -(6x^2+3x) \\ & \quad 10x+5 \\ & \quad -(10x+5) \\ & \quad\quad 0 \end{array}$$

Divide $6x^2$ by $2x$ to get $3x$.

Multiply $(2x + 1)$ by $3x$ to get $6x^2 + 3x$ and subtract to get $10x$.

Bring down the next term, which is 5. Divide $10x$ by $2x$ to get 5.

Multiply $(2x + 1)$ by 5 to get $10x + 5$ and subtract to get 0.

As the final remainder is 0, we know that $2x + 1$ divides 'evenly' into $6x^2 + 13x + 5$, i.e. $2x + 1$ is a factor of $6x^2 + 13x + 5$.

$\therefore$ Answer $= 3x + 5$

It is good practice to check your work by expanding.

ALGEBRA I

Exercise 2.9

Simplify each of the following algebraic fractions:

1. $\frac{a^{12}}{a^3}$
2. $\frac{16a^5}{2a^4}$
3. $\frac{15a^3b^2}{3ab}$
4. $\frac{25a^6b^3}{5ab^2}$
5. $\frac{-21x^{11}}{7x^7}$
6. $\frac{-22x^2y}{-11x}$
7. $\frac{42x^7y^6}{6x^3y^4}$
8. $\frac{64x^4y^5z^7}{8x^3y^2z^5}$
9. $\frac{5a+50}{5}$
10. $\frac{4b+2}{2}$
11. $\frac{2p-8}{2}$
12. $\frac{10x-5}{-5}$
13. $\frac{2x+9}{2x+9}$
14. $\frac{3x+1}{15x+5}$
15. $\frac{2x^2+10x}{x+5}$
16. $\frac{7x^2-14x}{x-2}$
17. $\frac{2x^2+4x-6}{2}$
18. $\frac{x^2-4x}{x-4}$
19. $\frac{x^2+7x+10}{x+2}$
20. $\frac{x^2-14x+48}{x-8}$
21. $\frac{4x^2+8x+3}{2x+1}$
22. $\frac{2x^2-13x+18}{2x-9}$
23. $\frac{8x^2-34x+35}{4x-7}$
24. $\frac{3}{3x^2-18x+24}$
25. $\frac{x-8}{x^2-64}$
26. $\frac{x+4}{x^2+6x+8}$
27. $\frac{2x+9}{2x^2+15x+27}$
28. $\frac{3x+5}{9x^2+18x+5}$
29. $\frac{8x+5}{16x^2-14x-15}$
30. $\frac{5x+9}{60x^2+83x-45}$
31. $\frac{25x^2-169}{5x-13}$

32. $g(x)$ is a function and $(11x-5) \times g(x) = 11x^2+61x-30$, for all $x \in R$. Find $g(x)$.

33. $f(x)\cdot h(x) = -6x^2+11x-4$ for all $x \in R$. If $f(x) = 3x-4$, find $h(x)$.

34. $f(x)$ is a function such that $f(x)\cdot g(x) = 10x^2+61x+91$ for all $x \in R$. If $g(x) = -2x-7$, find $f(x)$.

2.12 Algebraic Fractions II

Worked Example 2.20

Express as a single fraction in its simplest form:

$\frac{5}{x} + \frac{2}{5x-1}, x \neq 0, \frac{1}{5}$

$x \neq 0, \frac{1}{5}$ If $x = 0$ or $x = \frac{1}{5}$ then we would end up with 0 as a denominator. This means we would be trying to divide by zero, which is not possible.

Solution

$\frac{5}{x} + \frac{2}{5x-1}$

Step 1 The LCD is $(x)(5x-1)$.

Step 2 Rewrite the expression as a single fraction with the LCD as the denominator.

$$= \frac{5(5x-1)}{x(5x-1)} + \frac{2(x)}{x(5x-1)}$$

$$= \frac{5(5x-1)+2(x)}{x(5x-1)}$$

Step 3 Expand and simplify the numerator.

$$= \frac{25x-5+2x}{x(5x-1)}$$

$$= \frac{27x-5}{x(5x-1)}$$

We do not expand the denominator unless required to do so.

Worked Example 2.21

Express as a single fraction in its simplest form:

$\frac{2}{2x+1} - \frac{3}{x-4}, x \neq -\frac{1}{2}, 4$

Solution

Step 1 The LCD is $(2x+1)(x-4)$.

Step 2 Rewrite the expression as a single fraction with the LCD as the denominator.

$= \frac{2(x-4) - 3(2x+1)}{(2x+1)(x-4)}$

Step 3 Expand and simplify the numerator. Be careful with signs.

$= \frac{2x - 8 - 6x - 3}{(2x+1)(x-4)}$

$= \frac{-4x - 11}{(2x+1)(x-4)}$

Exercise 2.10

Express as single fractions in their simplest form:

1. $\frac{1}{x+2} + \frac{1}{x}, x \neq -2, 0$
2. $\frac{2}{x} + \frac{1}{x-2}, x \neq 0, 2$
3. $\frac{11}{2x-1} - \frac{3}{x}, x \neq \frac{1}{2}, 0$
4. $\frac{2}{x-3} + \frac{4}{x+2}, x \neq 3, -2$
5. $\frac{5}{2x+1} - \frac{3}{x+4}, x \neq -\frac{1}{2}, -4$
6. $\frac{2}{x-8} - \frac{3}{x+4}, x \neq 8, -4$
7. $\frac{1}{3x-1} - \frac{4}{2x-3}, x \neq \frac{1}{3}, \frac{3}{2}$
8. $\frac{7}{2x-1} - \frac{3}{1+2x}, x \neq \frac{1}{2}, -\frac{1}{2}$
9. $\frac{8}{2x+5} - \frac{1}{3}, x \neq -\frac{5}{2}$
10. $\frac{4}{x} + \frac{2}{3x}, x \neq 0$
11. $\frac{5}{2x} - \frac{1}{4x}, x \neq 0$
12. $\frac{5}{4x-3} + \frac{4}{3-4x}, x \neq \frac{3}{4}$

2.13 Solving Linear Equations

When solving an equation, we are being asked to find the value(s) of the unknown(s) that satisfy the equation. A linear equation is of the form $ax + b = 0, a \neq 0$.

There are numerous ways of solving a linear equation. This section will concentrate on using algebra.

When dealing with equations, we must remember certain rules.

Consider the equation $10 + 2 = 12$.

If we add 5 to the left hand side (LHS) of the equation, then

$$10 + 2 + 5 \neq 12$$

If we add 5 to **both sides** of the equation, then

$$10 + 2 + 5 = 12 + 5 \text{ as } 17 = 17$$

Algebra Rule: What you do to one side of the equation you must do to the other side as well. This is called **balancing** the equation.

ALGEBRA I

Worked Example 2.22

Solve $5x - 4 = 3x$ and verify your answer.

Solution

$5x - 4 = 3x$	
$5x - 3x - 4 = 3x - 3x$	To remove $3x$ from the RHS we subtract $3x$ from both sides.
$2x - 4 = 0$	Simplify both sides.
$2x - 4 + 4 = 0 + 4$	To remove -4 from the LHS, we add 4 to both sides.
$2x = 4$	Simplify both sides.
$\frac{2x}{2} = \frac{4}{2}$	Divide both sides by 2 (the coefficient of x).
$\therefore x = 2$	

Verify the answer.

This means checking to see if the answer is correct.

We substitute the value that we got for x back into the original equation.

LHS (left-hand side): $5x - 4$
$= 5(2) - 4$
$= 10 - 4$
$= 6$

RHS (right-hand side): $3x$
$= 3(2)$
$= 6$

LHS = RHS

$\therefore x = 2$ is correct.

Worked Example 2.23

Solve $2(x + 4) = 6(2x + 3)$.

Solution

$2(x + 4) = 6(2x + 3)$	
$2x + 8 = 12x + 18$	Multiply out the brackets.
$2x - 2x + 8 = 12x - 2x + 18$	To remove $2x$ from the LHS we subtract $2x$ from both sides.
$8 = 10x + 18$	Simplify both sides.
$8 - 18 = 10x + 18 - 18$	To remove 18 from the RHS we subtract 18 from both sides.
$-10 = 10x$	Simplify both sides.
$\frac{-10}{10} = \frac{10x}{10}$	Divide both sides by 10 (the coefficient of x).
$-1 = x$	
$\therefore x = -1$	

ALGEBRA I

Worked Example 2.24

Solve the following equation and verify your answer.

$3(2x - 3) - 4(x - 3) = 7x + 7$

Solution

Solve for x.

$3(2x - 3) - 4(x - 3) = 7x + 7$

$6x - 9 - 4x + 12 = 7x + 7$	Multiply out the brackets. Be careful with signs.
$2x + 3 = 7x + 7$	Simplify both sides.
$2x - 7x + 3 = 7$	Subtract $7x$ from both sides.
$-5x + 3 = 7$	Simplify.
$-5x = 7 - 3$	Subtract 3 from both sides.
$-5x = 4$	Simplify.
$\frac{-5x}{-5} = \frac{4}{-5}$	Divide both sides by -5.
$\therefore x = -0.8 \left(\text{or } x = -\frac{4}{5}\right)$	

Verify the answer.

LHS (left-hand side): $3(2x - 3) - 4(x - 3)$

$= 3(2(-0.8) - 3) - 4(-0.8 - 3)$

$= 3(-4.6) - 4(-3.8)$

$= -13.8 + 15.2$

$= 1.4$

RHS (right-hand side): $7x + 7$

$= 7(-0.8) + 7$

$= -5.6 + 7$

$= 1.4$

LHS = RHS

$\therefore x = -0.8$ is correct.

Exercise 2.11

Solve the following equations:

1. $5x = 15$
2. $3y = 6$
3. $2x + 4 = 12$
4. $3a + 7 = 34$
5. $3x - 6 = -9$
6. $7x + 8 = -13$
7. $5y - 3 = 17$
8. $3x - 10 = 2x - 3$
9. $4t - 2 = 5t - 5$
10. $x = -5x + 5$
11. $4x + 7 = -1$
12. $x + 5 = -x$
13. $2(x - 1) = 4x$
14. $4(x + 3) = 3(x + 2)$
15. $5(2y - 1) = 2(y - 1)$
16. $3(x + 1) = 2(x - 3) + 7$
17. $2(2x + 1) - 3(x - 1) = 9$
18. $5(7x + 3) = 2(3 - x) - 3 + x$
19. $2(2x - 4) = 12 - 3(2x - 1)$
20. $3(x - 6) + 15 = 4(x - 1) + 4$
21. $-3(4x - 2) = 2(3x - 1) + 18$
22. $11(a + 7) = 4 - 10(a - 1)$
23. $5(2x - 1) = 2(2x - 3) + 4x - 23$
24. $3(x - 2) = 7(x + 5) - 13$
25. $3(4x - 6) + 25(x + 2) = x - 4$
26. $11 = 7(x + 1) - 2(3 - 8x) - 3x$
27. Find the value of y that satisfies the equation $3(y - 1) = 1 + 4y$ and verify your solution.
28. Find the value of a that satisfies the equation $11a - 2 = 5(a - 2) - 2a$ and verify your solution.
29. Find the value of b that satisfies the equation $2(b + 3) - 4 = -(b + 2) - 3$ and verify your solution.

2.14 Solving Linear Equations with Fractions

When solving equations that contain fractions, we multiply both sides of the equation by the lowest common denominator (LCD). This eliminates all denominators.

Worked Example 2.25

Solve $\frac{x+1}{4} = \frac{3}{2}$.

Solution

The LCD of 4 and 2 is 4.

Multiply every term in the equation by 4.

$$\frac{4(x+1)}{4} = \frac{4(3)}{2}$$

$$\frac{{}^{1}\not{4}(x+1)}{\not{4}_1} = \frac{{}^{2}\not{4}(3)}{\not{2}_1} \quad \text{Simplify each term.}$$

$$1(x+1) = 2(3)$$

$$x + 1 = 6 \quad \text{Multiply out the brackets.}$$

$$x = 6 - 1 \quad \text{Subtract 1 from both sides.}$$

$$\therefore x = 5$$

Worked Example 2.26

Solve $\frac{8x-3}{3} - \frac{4x-2}{5} = 5$.

5 can be written as $\frac{5}{1}$.

Solution

The LCD of 3, 5 and 1 is 15.

Multiply every term in the equation by 15.

$$\frac{15(8x-3)}{3} - \frac{15(4x-2)}{5} = \frac{15(5)}{1}$$

$$\frac{{}^{5}\not{15}(8x-3)}{\not{3}_1} - \frac{{}^{3}\not{15}(4x-2)}{\not{5}_1} = 15(5)$$

$$5(8x-3) - 3(4x-2) = 75$$

$$40x - 15 - 12x + 6 = 75 \quad \text{Multiply out brackets. Be careful with signs.}$$

$$28x - 9 = 75 \quad \text{Simplify both sides.}$$

$$28x = 75 + 9 \quad \text{Add 9 to both sides.}$$

$$28x = 84$$

$$\frac{28x}{28} = \frac{84}{28} \quad \text{Divide both sides by 28.}$$

$$x = 3$$

Exercise 2.12

Solve the following equations:

1. $\frac{x+3}{5} = 1$
2. $\frac{x+4}{8} = 2$
3. $\frac{x+1}{3} = \frac{x}{2}$
4. $\frac{9x-4}{2} = 4$
5. $\frac{x}{6} - \frac{x}{2} = 5$
6. $\frac{x+1}{4} = \frac{x-1}{3}$
7. $\frac{2x-1}{3} = x - 4$
8. $\frac{5y-1}{8} + \frac{2y-4}{3} = 5$
9. $\frac{3x-2}{8} - \frac{x-1}{2} = 0$
10. $\frac{2x+2}{7} - \frac{4x-1}{3} = -3$
11. $\frac{t-3}{2} + \frac{2t+3}{4} = 3$
12. $\frac{x-2}{5} + \frac{x-3}{4} = \frac{11}{10}$

ALGEBRA I

13. $\dfrac{x+1}{3} + \dfrac{2x-9}{4} = \dfrac{17}{12}$

14. $\dfrac{4x+5}{5} - \dfrac{2x-3}{7} = \dfrac{32}{35}$

15. $\frac{1}{2}(x-4) - \frac{1}{3}(x-3) = 5$

16. $\dfrac{-x+2}{3} + \dfrac{5x+2}{6} = 1$

2.15 Manipulation of Formulae

Some countries measure temperature using the Fahrenheit scale (°F) instead of the Celsius scale (°C).

To convert degrees Fahrenheit (°F) into degrees Celsius (°C), we can use the following formula:

$$C = \frac{5(F-32)}{9}$$

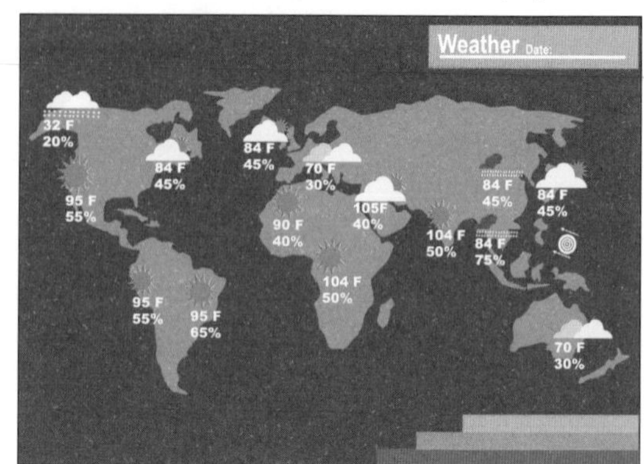

For example, if the temperature at a beach is 50 °F, we can use this formula to convert 50 °F into degrees Celsius (°C).

$$C = \frac{5(50-32)}{9} = 10\,°\text{C}$$

However, we may need to change degrees Celsius into degrees Fahrenheit.

The formula must be manipulated to do this.

$$F = \frac{9C}{5} + 32$$

To manipulate any formula, we follow a set of rules.

ALGEBRA I

Worked Example 2.27

Make x the subject of the formula when $y = mx + c$.

Solution

Making x the subject of the formula means that the final formula must be in the form $x = ...$, with all the other terms on the other side of the equal sign.

Rule: We move any variable (letter) we do **not** want to the **other side** of the equal sign. Make sure to follow correct mathematical procedure. This is SADMIB, which is BIMDAS in reverse.

$y = mx + c$

$\Rightarrow y - c = mx$ Subtract c from both sides.

$\dfrac{y-c}{m} = \dfrac{mx}{m}$ mx is in fact $(m) \times (x)$. So in order to isolate x, we must divide both sides of the equation by m.

$\therefore \dfrac{y-c}{m} = x$

Worked Example 2.28

Make a the subject of the formula if $\frac{a+b}{3} = \frac{c}{2}$.

Solution

The LCD of 3 and 2 is 6.

$\frac{6(a+b)}{3} = \frac{6(c)}{2}$ Multiply all the terms by the LCD.

$2(a+b) = 3c$

$2a + 2b = 3c$ Multiply out the brackets.

$2a = 3c - 2b$ Subtract $2b$ from both sides.

$\frac{2a}{2} = \frac{3c-2b}{2}$ Divide both sides by 2.

$\therefore a = \frac{3c-2b}{2}$

Worked Example 2.29

Express b in terms of a and c:

$2ab = 2a - 3bc$

Rule: Bring the terms that contain the desired variable to the same side.

Solution

$2ab = 2a - 3bc$

$2ab + 3bc = 2a$

Factorise using b as the common factor.

$b(2a + 3c) = 2a$

$\frac{b(2a+3c)}{2a+3c} = \frac{2a}{2a+3c}$ Divide both sides by $(2a + 3c)$.

$\therefore b = \frac{2a}{2a+3c}$

Worked Example 2.30

Express r in terms of p and q:

$\frac{1}{p} + \frac{1}{q} = \frac{1}{r}$

Solution

The LCD of p, q and r is pqr.

Multiply all terms by pqr.

$pqr\left(\frac{1}{p}\right) + pqr\left(\frac{1}{q}\right) = pqr\left(\frac{1}{r}\right)$

$\therefore qr + pr = pq$

Factorise $qr + pr$.

$r(q + p) = pq$

$\frac{r(q+p)}{(q+p)} = \frac{pq}{q+p}$ Divide both sides by $(q + p)$.

$\therefore r = \frac{pq}{q+p}$

Exercise 2.13

1. In each case, make the highlighted variable the subject of the formula.

(i) $3x = 9$ (ii) $4y = 16$ (iii) $4a + 3 = 7$ (iv) $2b - 9 = 5$ (v) $4y + x = 16$ (vi) $2b - 3c = 5$ (vii) $3r = r - 4t$ (viii) $-4a + 3 = 2a - 1$

In Questions 2–17, express the variable in the square brackets in terms of the other variables.

2. $A = lw$	[w]	**8.** $v = \sqrt{2gh}$	[g]	**13.** $\frac{1}{a} + \frac{1}{b} = \frac{1}{c}$	[b]
3. $K = \frac{1}{2}mv^2$	[m]	**9.** $s = \frac{a+b+c}{2}$	[b]	**14.** $pq = c + rq$	[q]
4. $E = mc^2$	[c]	**10.** $s = ut + \frac{1}{2}at^2$	[a]	**15.** $a + b = bx + x$	[b]
5. $a = b - 2c$	[c]	**11.** $x + \frac{y}{3} = 2z$	[y]	**16.** $T = 2\pi\sqrt{\frac{l}{g}}$	[l]
6. $F = \frac{mv^2}{r}$	[m]	**12.** $ab + bc = c$	[b]	**17.** $a = \frac{bc}{b+c}$	[b]
7. $a = \frac{b+c}{3}$	[c]				

18. The density of a substance ($g\,cm^{-3}$) is given by the formula $D = \frac{M}{V}$, where M is mass (in grams) and V is volume (in cm^3).

    (i) Express V in terms of the other variables.

    (ii) Find the volume of a substance which has a mass of 50 g and a density of $1.2\ g\,cm^{-3}$.

19. Given the formula $\frac{3x - y}{a + b} = k$:

    (i) Write y in terms of the other variables

    (ii) Write x in terms of the other variables

20. The formula for the volume of a cylinder is $V = \pi r^2 h$.

    (i) What is the volume of a cylinder with $h = 20$ cm, $r = 5$ cm and $\pi = 3.14$?

    (ii) Write h in terms of the other variables and hence find the height of a cylinder of $r = 10$ cm, $\pi = 3.14$ and $V = 3{,}768\ cm^3$.

    (iii) Write r in terms of the other variables and hence find the radius of a cylinder of $h = 2$ cm, $\pi = \frac{22}{7}$ and $V = 3{,}773\ cm^3$.

21. The time taken (T) for a simple pendulum to swing back and forth (period) is given by the formula $T = 2\pi\sqrt{\frac{l}{g}}$.

    l = length of pendulum in metres and g = acceleration due to gravity, $9.81\ ms^{-2}$.

    (i) What would be the period of a pendulum of length 2 m? (Take $\pi = 3.14$.) Give your answer correct to two decimal places.

    (ii) How long would the pendulum have to be in order to have a period of 3 seconds? (Take $\pi = 3.14$.) Give your answer correct to three significant figures.

2.16 Solving Simultaneous Linear Equations by Elimination or Substitution

Consider the following pair of simultaneous linear equations:

$2x - y = 4$

$5x - 3y = 1$

We are dealing with a pair of equations in two unknowns. When solving simultaneous equations, we are being asked to find the values of the unknowns that satisfy both equations.

We can use various methods to solve simultaneous linear equations with two unknowns. This section will deal with elimination and substitution methods.

Worked Example 2.31

Solve for x and y:

$2x + y = 7$

$x - 2y = 1$

Hence:

(i) Interpret the result (ii) Verify your answer

Solution

Make all x coefficients or all y coefficients the same in each equation.

$2x + y = 7 \quad \times 1 \quad \rightarrow 2x + y = 7$

$x - 2y = 1 \quad \times 2 \quad \rightarrow 2x - 4y = 2$

To make the x coefficients the same we need to multiply $x - 2y = 1$ by 2.

As the x terms are of the same sign, we will subtract.

$2x + y = 7$

$-(2x - 4y = 2)$

$5y = 5$

$\therefore y = 1$

Pick one of the original equations and substitute in $y = 1$.

$2x + y = 7$

$2x + (1) = 7$

$2x = 6$

$\therefore x = 3$

So our answer is: $x = 3, y = 1$.

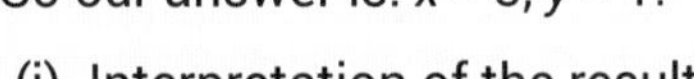

(i) Interpretation of the result:

$x = 3, y = 1$ are the only values for x and y that will satisfy both equations.

If we graph the lines $2x + y = 7$ and $x - 2y = 1$ we find that the point of intersection (POI) of the two lines is (3,1).

(ii) Verify your answer:

We let $x = 3$ and $y = 1$ in **both** equations.

$2x + y = 7$	$x - 2y = 1$
$2(3) + (1) = 7$	$3 - 2(1) = 1$
$6 + 1 = 7$	$3 - 2 = 1$
$7 = 7$	$1 = 1$
True	True

$\therefore x = 3$ and $y = 1$ is the correct solution.

Another method to use for solving simultaneous equations is that of substitution.

Worked Example 2.32

Solve for x and y: $2x + y = 7$

$x - 2y = 1$

Solution

We will pick either the x or y term and make it the subject of the formula for both equations.

$2x + y = 7$

$y = 7 - 2x$ Subtract $2x$ from both sides.

$x - 2y = 1$

$-2y = 1 - x$ Subtract x from both sides.

$y = -\frac{1}{2} + \frac{1}{2}x$ Divide both sides by -2.

We now have both equations with y as the subject.

$y = y$ Equate the y's.

$\Rightarrow 7 - 2x = -\frac{1}{2} + \frac{1}{2}x$

$-2x - \frac{1}{2}x = -\frac{1}{2} - 7$ Subtract $-\frac{1}{2}x$ from both sides.

$-2\frac{1}{2}x = -7\frac{1}{2}$

$x = 3$ Divide both sides of the equation by $-2\frac{1}{2}$.

Pick either equation, with y as the subject, and substitute in $x = 3$.

$y = 7 - 2x$

$y = 7 - 2(3)$

$y = 7 - 6$

$\therefore y = 1$

$\therefore x = 3, y = 1$

We may also encounter simultaneous equations that involve fractions or decimals or whose x-values and y-values are fractions or decimals.

Worked Example 2.33

Solve the following simultaneous equations:

$3x - 3 = -5y$ **Eq. I** $\frac{1}{2}x - \frac{2}{3}y = -\frac{1}{4}$ **Eq. II**

Solution

We need to ensure that both equations are in the same form i.e. $ax + by = c$.

Eq. I

$3x - 3 = -5y$

$3x + 5y = 3$ x and y terms on LHS, constant on RHS.

ALGEBRA I

Eq. II

$\frac{1}{2}x - \frac{2}{3}y = -\frac{1}{4}$ To make it easier we can multiply every term by the LCD, 12.

$12\left(\frac{1}{2}x\right) - 12\left(\frac{2}{3}\right)y = 12\left(-\frac{1}{4}\right)$ Multiply every term by 12.

$6x - 8y = -3$

We now proceed as normal.

$3x + 5y = 3 \quad \times 2 \quad \rightarrow 6x + 10y = 6$

$6x - 8y = -3 \quad \times 1 \quad \rightarrow 6x - 8y = -3$

$6x + 10y = 6$

$\underline{-(6x - 8y = -3)}$

$18y = 9$

$y = \frac{9}{18} = \frac{1}{2}$

If $y = \frac{1}{2}$, we can now find the value of x, using either of the original equations.

$3x + 5y = 3$

$3x + 5\left(\frac{1}{2}\right) = 3$

$3x + 2\frac{1}{2} = 3$

$3x = \frac{1}{2}$ Subtract $2\frac{1}{2}$ from both sides.

$\therefore x = \frac{1}{6}$ Divide both sides by 3.

So our answer is: $x = \frac{1}{6}, y = \frac{1}{2}$.

Exercise 2.14

Solve each of the following pairs of simultaneous equations. For the first five questions verify your solution and interpret the results.

1. $x + y = 7$
   $x - y = 1$
2. $x + y = 13$
   $x - y = 3$
3. $a + b = 4$
   $a - b = 10$
4. $4x + 3y = 10$
   $x + y = 3$
5. $p + 2q = 11$
   $2p + q = 10$
6. $2x + y = 9$
   $3x + y = 11$
7. $2a + 5b = -15$
   $4a + 3b = -9$
8. $3x + 5y = 17$
   $2x - 5y = -22$
9. $2x + 7y = 27$
   $3x + 5y = 13$
10. $4p + 3q = -21$
    $2p + 9q = -33$
11. $2x - 5y = 0$
    $x + 4y = 13$
12. $e - 3f - 5 = 0$
    $5e - f + 17 = 0$
13. $x - y + 1 = 0$
    $4x + 5y + 13 = 0$
14. $x + 11 = -3y$
    $y + 12 = -2x$
15. $\frac{5}{4}x - \frac{3}{4}y = 3$
    $3x + 2y = 11$
16. $\frac{x}{2} + y = 13$
    $\frac{x}{7} - \frac{y}{3} = 0$

2.17 Solving Simultaneous Linear Equations Graphically

Linear equations can also be solved using graphs. The equation of a line can be written in the form $y = mx + c$, where m is the slope and c is the y-intercept. So the line $y = 2x + 1$ has a slope of 2 and a y-intercept value of 1.

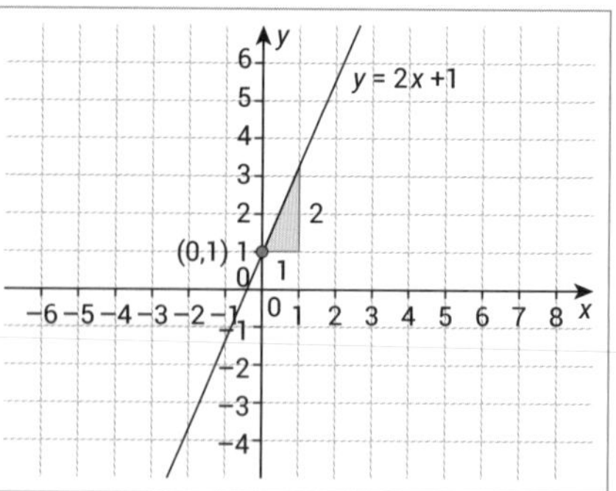

We can use this information to help us graph this line.

A slope $\left(= \frac{\text{rise}}{\text{run}}\right)$ of 2 $\left(= \frac{2}{1}\right)$ tells us that for every 1 unit across (from left to right) we move up 2 units.

A y-intercept of 1 means that the line $y = 2x + 1$ crosses the y-axis at the point (0,1).

Worked Example 2.34

(i) Graph the line $y = 3x + 6$.

(ii) Find the x-intercept.

(iii) Use algebra to solve $3x + 6 = 0$.

(iv) Explain the significance of the x-intercept.

Solution

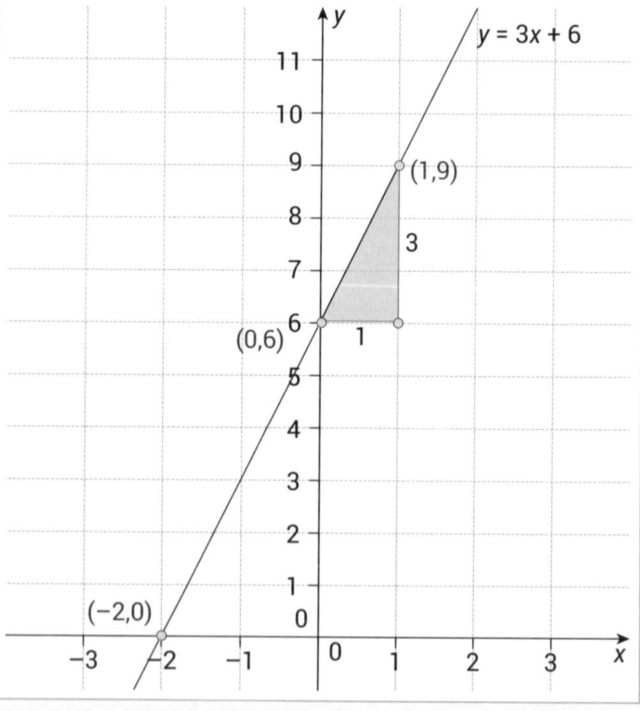

(i) $y = 3x + 6$.

As the line is in the form $y = mx + c$, the line has a slope of 3 and a y-intercept of 6.

We plot the point (0,6) as this is on the line.

The slope $\left(\frac{\text{rise}}{\text{run}}\right)$ is 3 $\left(\frac{3}{1}\right)$, so from the point (0,6) we move 1 unit across (from left to right) and 3 units up. This brings us to (1,9). We plot this point (1,9) as this point is also on the line.

We now can graph the line $y = 3x + 6$.

(ii) From the diagram, the line intersects the x-axis at the point (−2,0).

$\therefore$ The x-intercept value is −2.

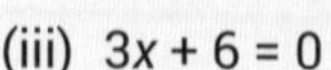

(iii) $3x + 6 = 0$

$3x = -6$ Subtract 6 from both sides.

$\therefore x = -2$ Divide by 3.

(iv) The x-intercept value is the solution (or root) of the equation $3x + 6 = 0$.

We can solve linear equations by graphing and finding the x-intercept.

Remember that solving a linear equation by graphing may only give an estimate and not the exact answer that is required.

Sometimes it is required that we find the point of intersection of two lines.

Worked Example 2.35

(a) Use the graph to solve the equation $4x - 2 = 2$ by:

(i) Graphing the lines $y = 4x - 2$ and $y = 2$

(ii) Finding the point of intersection of these two lines

(b) Explain the significance of this point of intersection.

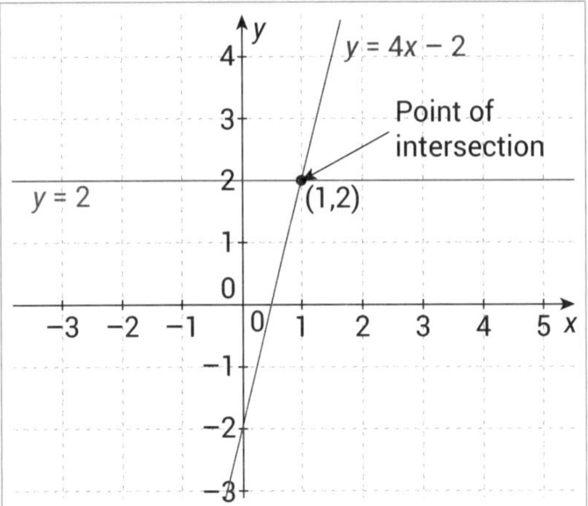

Solution

(a) (i) We graph the line $y = 4x - 2$.

This line has a slope of 4 and the y-intercept value is -2.

We also graph the line $y = 2$. This is a horizontal line 2 units above the x-axis.

(ii) The point of intersection of these two lines is (1,2).

So $x = 1$ is the solution to the equation $4x - 2 = 2$.

(b) (1,2), the point of intersection, is the only point that is common to both graphs. It satisfies both equations → $y = 4x - 2$ **and** $y = 2$.

Special Cases of Lines

Sometimes lines are in the form $y = a$ or $x = b$, $(a, b \in R)$.

For example, $y = 5$ is a line, drawn through the y-intercept value of 5, parallel to the x-axis. Every point on this line is 5 units above the x-axis.

For example, $x = -2$ is a line, drawn through the x-intercept value of -2, parallel to the y-axis. Every point on this line is 2 units to the left of the y-axis.

A line $y = 0$ would be a line, drawn parallel to the x-axis, through the y-intercept value of 0. So $y = 0$ represents the x-axis.

A line $x = 0$ would be a line, drawn parallel to the y-axis, through the x-intercept value of 0. So $x = 0$ represents the y-axis.

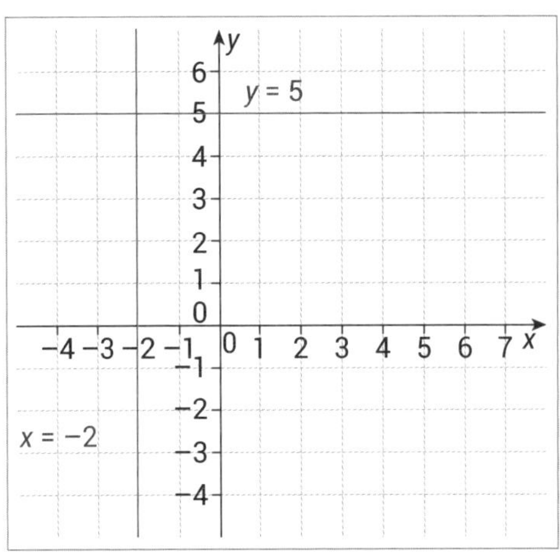

Worked Example 2.36

Solve the following simultaneous equations by graphing:

$x - y = 2 \qquad 2x + 3y = 24$

Solution

We plot both lines.

$x - y = 2$	
Let $x = 0$. $(0) - y = 2$ $-y = 2$ $\therefore y = -2$	Let $y = 0$. $x - (0) = 2$ $\therefore x = 2$
If $x = 0$, then $y = -2$.	If $y = 0$, then $x = 2$.
Point (0,−2)	Point (2,0)

$2x + 3y = 24$	
Let $x = 0$. $2(0) + 3y = 24$ $3y = 24$ $\therefore y = 8$	Let $y = 0$. $2x + 3(0) = 24$ $2x = 24$ $\therefore x = 12$
If $x = 0$, then $y = 8$.	If $y = 0$, then $x = 12$.
Point (0,8)	Point (12,0)

We draw these two lines and mark the point of intersection.

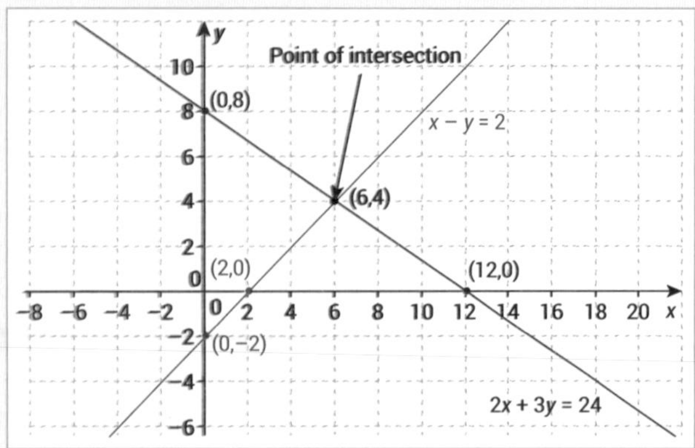

Reading from your graph, find where these two lines intersect. From our graph, the point of intersection is (6,4).

$\therefore$ $(x,y) = (6,4)$ is the required solution.

Exercise 2.15

1. Solve the following linear equations by graphing:
   (i) $3x + 2 = 0$
   (ii) $4x - 12 = 0$
   (iii) $3x + 10 = -5$
   (iv) $2x + 1 = x + 3$
   (v) $-(x - 3) = 10$

2. Solve the following pairs of simultaneous equations by graphing each line:
   (i) $2x + y = 6$
   $2x - y = 2$
   (ii) $2x + y = 4$
   $4x - 5y = 20$
   (iii) $x + 2y = 5$
   $3x - y = -6$
   (iv) $x - y = 4$
   $x + 5y = -2$

3. For each of the following:
   (a) Solve the simultaneous equations by graphing each line.
   (b) Verify your answer.
   (i) $2x - y = 2$
   $2x - 5y = -6$
   (ii) $x + 2y = 2$
   $6x - 2y = 5$

2.18 Linear Inequalities

Sometimes, when solving for an unknown, we are not asked for an exact value. Instead, our solution consists of a range of values.

An **inequality** gives a range of values.

$<$ means 'less than'

$\leqslant$ means 'less than or equal to'

$>$ means 'greater than'

$\geqslant$ means 'greater than or equal to'

Examples: $x < 3$ means 'x is less than 3'.

$x \geqslant 5$ means 'x is greater than or equal to 5'.

$x + 1 > 6$ means '$x + 1$ is greater than 6'.

We may be asked to graph a solution to an inequality. In such cases it is important that we distinguish between the different types of number we may be asked to graph.

You have dealt with different types of numbers in your Junior Cycle course.

Natural Numbers – N

A **natural number** is any positive whole number (i.e. any whole number greater than 0).

$N = \{1, 2, 3, 4, ...\}$

The set of naturals is denoted by the letter N.

If x is a natural number we can write $x \in N$. This means that x is an element of the set of natural numbers.

As natural numbers are whole numbers, to graph them on the number line we use shaded dots.

Arrows on a number line denote that the solution set continues indefinitely (forever) in that direction.

Integers – Z

An **integer** is any whole number; positive, negative or zero.

$Z = \{..., -3, -2, -1, 0, 1, 2, 3, ...\}$

The set of integers is denoted by the letter Z.

If x is an integer, we can write $x \in Z$.

As integers are also whole numbers, to graph them on the number line we use shaded dots.

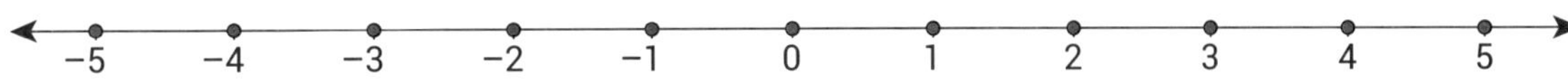

Real Numbers – R

A **real number** is any number that can be plotted on the number line.

The set of reals is denoted by the letter R.

If x is a real number, we can write $x \in R$.

Real numbers are any numbers that can be plotted on the number line. In order to show them on the number line we use solid continuous shading.

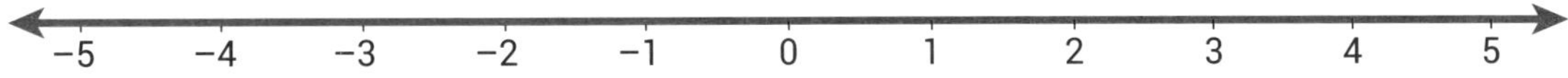

Types of number are explained in greater detail in Chapter 3.

Worked Example 2.37

Draw separate number lines to show the solution sets to the following inequalities:

(i) $x \geqslant 5, x \in Z$ (ii) $x < 4, x \in N$

Solution

(i) $x \geqslant 5, x \in Z$

As $x \in Z$, we use dots on the number line.

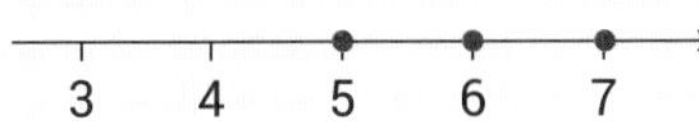

The next integer greater than 5 is 6, then 7, etc.

The arrow shows that the inequality continues past 7.

(ii) $x < 4, x \in N$

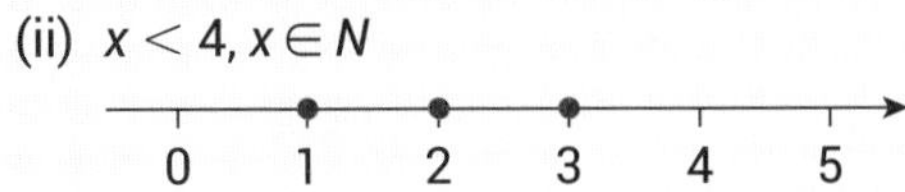

As there are no natural numbers smaller than 1, we do not use an arrow.

Worked Example 2.38

Draw separate number lines to represent the solution sets of the following inequalities:

(i) $x < -1, x \in R$ (ii) $x \geqslant -3, x \in R$

Solution

In both questions we are dealing with real numbers, so we use solid shading to denote our solution sets on the number line.

(i) $x < -1, x \in R$ means that x can take any value less than but **not including** -1.

An **empty disc** is used to help show this on the number line.

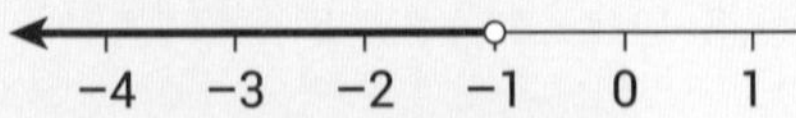

(ii) $x \geqslant -3, x \in R$ means that x can take any value greater than **and including** -3.

A **shaded disc** is used to show this on the number line.

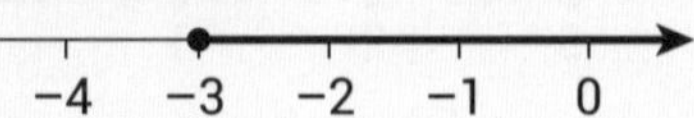

Exercise 2.16

1. Write down the first three values of the following inequalities:
   (i) $x > 7, x \in Z$
   (ii) $x > 5, x \in N$
   (iii) $x > -9, x \in Z$
   (iv) $x \leqslant 3, x \in N$
   (v) $x \geqslant -4, x \in Z$

2. Write down in your own words the meaning of each of the following inequalities:
   (i) $x > 4, x \in N$
   (ii) $x < -1, x \in Z$
   (iii) $x \leqslant 12, x \in R$
   (iv) $x < 2, x \in N$
   (v) $x \geqslant 3, x \in R$

3. Write an inequality, in terms of x, for each of the following statements:
   (i) A natural number whose value is greater than 9
   (ii) An integer whose value is greater than or equal to −1
   (iii) A real number whose value is at least 5
   (iv) A natural number whose value is less than 3
   (v) All the whole numbers greater than but not equal to −3
   (vi) All the numbers less than 2
   (vii) All the positive whole numbers less than 4
   (viii) All the numbers whose values are at most 19

4. Write the inequality shown on each of the following number lines:
   (i) 4 5 6 7, $x \in N$
   (ii) −8 −7 −6 −5, $x \in Z$
   (iii) 4 5 6 7, $x \in R$
   (iv) −5 −4 −3 −2, $x \in R$
   (v) −1 0 1 2, $x \in R$

5. Draw separate number lines to show the following inequalities.
   (i) $x \leqslant 3, x \in Z$
   (ii) $x < 5, x \in N$
   (iii) $x \geqslant -4, x \in R$
   (iv) $x > -1, x \in R$
   (v) $x < 2, x \in Z$
   (vi) $x < 0, x \in R$
   (vii) $x \geqslant -3, x \in R$
   (viii) $x < -4, x \in R$
   (ix) $x < 5, x \in Z$
   (x) $x < 3, x \in N$

2.19 Solving Inequalities

Solving an inequality is very similar to solving a linear equation.

When solving an inequality, we usually end up with a range of values for the unknown.

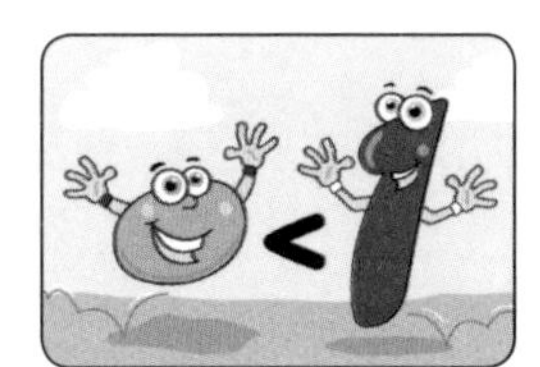

$3x > 9 \quad \Rightarrow x > 3$

This means the x can only have a value greater than 3. This range or set of values can be called the **solution set**.

Provided $x > 3$, the left-hand side of our inequality ($3x$) will always be greater than ($>$) the right-hand side (9).

$3(4) = 12 > 9$ True

$3(5) = 15 > 9$ True

If x is equal to or less than 3, the inequality will not hold true, i.e. $3x$ will not be > 9.

$3(2) = 6 > 9$ False

When solving an inequality, we generally move the variable to the left-hand side of the inequality.

Worked Example 2.39

Solve the inequality $4x + 5 < 1, x \in Z$, and show the solution set on the number line.

Solution

There are many different approaches that we can use.

Remember, when we are asked to solve an inequality we are being asked for a **range** of values.

Method 1 Trial and error

x	Is $4x + 5 < 1$?	True/False	
0	$4(0) + 5 = 5$	False	Answer too big
-1	$4(-1) + 5 = 1$	False	Answer equal to 1 but **not** less than 1
-2	$4(-2) + 5 = -3$	True	Answer is less than 1

Answer: $x < -1$

Method 2 Graphically

We can plot the lines $y = 4x + 5$ and $y = 1$.

$y = 4x + 5$ has a slope of 4 and a y-intercept value of 5.

$y = 1$ is a line, drawn through the y-intercept value of 1, parallel to the x-axis.

We are looking for the range of x-values for which $4x + 5 < 1$.

From our diagram, we can see that the line $y = 4x + 5$ is below (less than) the line $y = 1$ for $x < -1, x \in Z$.

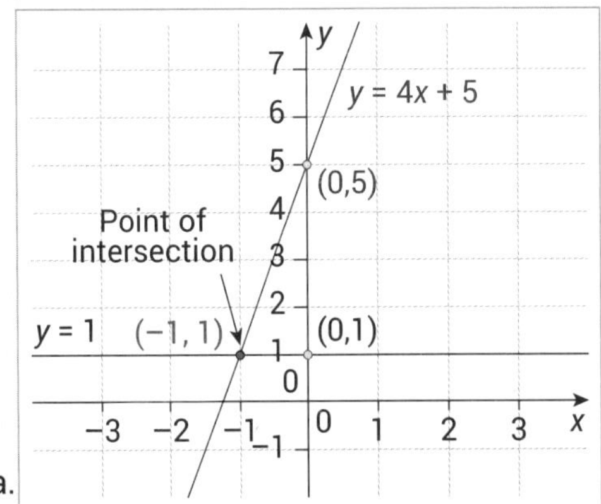

Generally, the easiest way to solve an inequality is by using algebra.

Method 3 Algebra (Generally the most accurate)

$4x + 5 < 1, x \in Z$

$4x < 1 - 5$ Subtract 5 from both sides.

$4x < -4$ Simplify the RHS.

$\therefore x < -1, x \in Z$ Divide both sides by 4.

Solution Set:

$x < -1, x \in Z$

Remember that we are plotting integers (Z) on the number line.

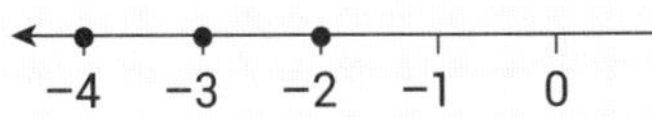

An Important Case: Multiplying/Dividing an Inequality by a Negative Number

Consider the following:

Is $3 > -2$? Yes	Is $3 \leqslant 6$? Yes
Now, multiply both sides by -1.	Now, divide both side by -3.
Is $-3 > 2$? No	Is $-1 \leqslant -2$? No

When solving an inequality, we may sometimes end up with a negative x term $(-x)$. A very specific rule applies when multiplying or dividing an inequality by a negative number.

When we multiply or divide both sides of an inequality by a negative number, we **flip** or **reverse** the inequality sign, as well as changing the signs of the terms.

Is $-3 < 2$? Yes	Is $1 \geqslant -2$? Yes
Consider the inequality:	$-5x \leqslant 10, x \in Z$.
Multiplying both sides by -1, we get:	$5x \geqslant -10, x \in Z$.
Dividing both sides by 5, we get:	$x \geqslant -2$.

Worked Example 2.40

Solve the following inequality and show the solution set on the number line:

$2(x-1) < 3x - 4, x \in R$

Solution

$2(x-1) < 3x - 4$

$2x - 2 < 3x - 4$ — Multiply out the brackets.

$2x - 3x < -4 + 2$ — Subtract $3x$ from both sides and add 2 to both sides.

$-x < -2$

Divide both sides by -1, so the signs change and the inequality is flipped.

$x > 2, x \in R$

1 2 3 4 5

As we are dealing with real numbers, we draw an empty disc at 2, with solid shading to the right and an arrow to the right.

Exercise 2.17

Solve each of the following inequalities and show each solution set on a number line:

1. $3x > 6, x \in N$
2. $4x - 4 \geqslant 8, x \in N$
3. $3x + 3 < 9, x \in N$
4. $5x + 3 \leqslant -2, x \in Z$
5. $7x + 8 \leqslant 1, x \in R$
6. $3x - 8 > 4, x \in R$
7. $\frac{x-5}{7} > -3, x \in Z$
8. $10x \leqslant 10 + 5x, x \in R$
9. $x + 3 > -4, x \in Z$
10. $2x + 1 \leqslant 3x + 2, x \in R$
11. $\frac{x+1}{2} < 5, x \in R$
12. $4x + 3 \geqslant 6x - 4, x \in N$
13. $\frac{5x-2}{2} > \frac{8x+10}{4}, x \in R$
14. $2(x+2) \leqslant 5x - 2, x \in R$
15. $3(2x+1) > 3(x-3), x \in R$
16. $\frac{-3(2x+3)}{2} \leqslant \frac{-4(x+4)}{3}, x \in Z$
17. $4(x-3) \geqslant -2(x+1) + 2, x \in R$
18. $4(3x+1) + 2(x-3) + 9 \geqslant 0, x \in Z$

2.20 Writing Expressions

One of the main uses of algebra is to solve problems. Information is given in a 'real life' context using words and/or diagrams. The student must then use the methods they have learnt to represent this information mathematically. This usually involves writing an algebraic equation (or equations) that is (are) then solved, giving us the answer(s) required.

When answering any problem-solving question we should always:

- Be careful of the units of measurements we have used in the question, especially that of our answer.
- Make sure that we have clearly defined the meanings of any letters (variables) that we have used.
- Check that our answer makes sense in the context of the question. For example, the length of a rectangle cannot be −8 cm.

Worked Example 2.41

Seán is x years old. Gavin is five years older than Seán. Abby is five times Seán's age.
Write down in terms of x an expression for: (i) Gavin's age (ii) Abby's age

Solution

(i) Seán is x years old.

Gavin is five years older than Seán.

$\therefore$ Gavin's age = $x + 5$

(ii) Abby is five times as old as Seán.

$\therefore$ Abby's age = $5x$

Worked Example 2.42

Susan buys nine shirts. If y shirts are blue, how many shirts are in other colours?

Solution

y = number of blue shirts

$\therefore$ number of other shirt colours = $9 - y$

Worked Example 2.43

How many months are there in:

(i) Four years and five months

(ii) n years and m months

Solution

(i) Four years and five months

$4(12) + 5 = 53$ months

(ii) n years and m months

$n(12) + m = (12n + m)$ months

Worked Example 2.44

A taxi fare is €4 plus 75 cents per extra km. Write a formula for the fare of an x km journey.

State the meaning of any letters used in your formula.

Solution

It is very important that we state the meaning of all the letters used in the formula.

We need to write down that

F = Taxi fare in euro

x = Distance travelled in km

The journey will cost €4 plus €0.75 per km travelled.

$\therefore F = 4 + 0.75x$ (euro)

So if $x = 1$, $F = 4 + 0.75(1)$

$= €4.75$

If $x = 2$, $F = 4 + 0.75(2)$

$= €5.5$

If $x = x$, $F = 4 + 0.75(x)$

$= €(4 + 0.75x)$

Exercise 2.18

1. (i) How many days are there in five weeks?
   (ii) How many days are there in seven weeks?
   (iii) How many days are there in n weeks?

2. (i) How many seconds are there in one minute?
   (ii) How many seconds are there in four minutes?
   (iii) How many seconds are there in t minutes?

3. (i) How many points does a hurling team get for 3 goals and 10 points?
   [1 goal = 3 points]
   (ii) How many points does a hurling team get for x goals and y points?

4. (i) Barry is 22 years old. How old will he be in 4 years' time?
   (ii) Carol is x years old. How old will she be in 4 years' time?

5. A car uses l litres of petrol per minute.
   (i) Write an expression for the total number of litres used during a 45-minute drive.
   Another car uses m litres of petrol per hour.
   (ii) Write an expression for how many litres this car would use on a 45-minute drive.

6. Bertie is x years old. Edna is n years older than Bertie.
   Write down an expression for Edna's age.

7. (i) 4 is a natural number. Write down the next five consecutive natural numbers.
   (ii) n is a natural number. Write down the next five consecutive natural numbers.

8. (i) 10 is an even number. Write down the next four consecutive even numbers.
   (ii) p is an even number. Write down the next four consecutive even numbers.

9. (i) 31 is an odd number. Write down the next three consecutive odd numbers.
   (ii) q is also an odd number. Write down the next three consecutive odd numbers.

10. (i) Harry is 80 years old. His son is half as old. How old was his son three years ago?
    (ii) Ivan is x years old. His son is half as old. How old was his son three years ago?

11. There is €100 in your wallet.
    (i) If you take out €50, how much is left in your wallet?
    (ii) If you take out €70, how much is left in your wallet?
    (iii) If you take out €x, how much is left in your wallet?

12. (i) There are 29 students in a class. If 17 of them are girls, how many are boys?
    (ii) There are 29 students in a class. If x of them are girls, how many are boys?

13. A garden has a length of $10x$ m and a width of $(4x - 1)$ m. Write down an expression for the perimeter of the garden.

14. A woman leaves €1,000 to her four children. €x is for the eldest. The rest is to be divided equally amongst the other three children. How much does each child get (in terms of x)?

15. An electrician charges €90 per hour plus a €60 call out fee. Write a formula that represents the cost in euro (C) of hiring the electrician for t hours.

16. A scientist is measuring how fast a plant grows. Initially the plant is 12 cm high. The plant grows 0.5 cm per day.
    Write a formula that represents the height of the plant after d days. State clearly the meaning of all variables used.

17. A gym has two methods of payment.
    Option 1: Pay €100 per year then €5 per visit
    Option 2: €15 per visit
    Write two formulae that show the cost of a person visiting the gym x times in a year.
    If you plan on making 12 visits in one year, which option will be better for you? Explain.

18. The following instructions are used to cook beef according to how it is going to be served to the customer.

Rare: 20 minutes per half a kilogram plus 20 minutes extra

Medium: 25 minutes per half a kilogram plus 20 minutes extra

Well done: 30 minutes per half a kilogram plus 30 minutes extra

How long will it take to cook beef that weighs x kg if it is to be served:

(i) Rare

(ii) Medium

(iii) Well done

19. Peter has €253 in his bank account at the start of January. He plans to deposit €x on the last day of every month into this account, except for December when he will deposit €50 less than he usually does. Write a formula for the total amount of money he will have in his bank account at the end of the year.

20. John has a base salary of €30,000 plus commission of 25% of the value of his total yearly sales. In a year he has sales worth €x.

(i) Write 25% as a decimal.

(ii) Write a formula for his yearly salary in terms of x.

2.21 Solving Problems Involving Linear Expressions

Using the techniques we learned in the previous section, we can now find the actual value of the unknown variable.

Worked Example 2.45

Amy is two years older than Ben. Carl is five years younger than Amy. The sum of their ages is 113.

Find the ages of all three.

Solution

When using algebra to solve such a problem, we generally follow these steps:

- Let x = the unknown value.
- Form a maths equation from the word equation.
- Solve for x.
- Remember to **answer** the question asked.
- Verify your solution.

It is usually better to start with the unknown that requires the fewest changes to be made.

Ben's age = x

Amy is two years older than Ben.

$\therefore$ Amy's age = $x + 2$

Carl is five years younger than Amy.

$\therefore$ Carl's age = $(x + 2) - 5$

$= x + 2 - 5$

$= x - 3$

Word equation: The sum of their ages is 113.

Amy's + Ben's + Carl's ages added together equals 113.

Maths equation: $(x + 2) + x + (x - 3) = 113$

$$x + x + 2 + x - 3 = 113$$

$$3x - 1 = 113$$

$$3x = 113 + 1$$

$$3x = 114$$

$$x = 38$$

We now must write down the ages of all three.

- Ben's age = x = 38 years
- Amy's age = $x + 2 = 38 + 2 = 40$ years
- Carl's age = $x - 3 = 38 - 3 = 35$ years

We can check our answer: 38 + 40 + 35 = 113.

Worked Example 2.46

A pet shop has hamsters and gerbils for sale. They have 30 in total for sale. They sell four hamsters. Two gerbils are also sold. The shop now has twice as many gerbils as hamsters.
How many of each type did the shop start with?

Solution

Start: Let x = Number of hamsters

$\therefore$ Number of gerbils = $30 - x$

Present: The shop sells four hamsters, so the number of hamsters is now $x - 4$.

Two gerbils are also sold, so the number of gerbils is now $30 - x - 2 = 28 - x$.

Word equation

The shop **now** has twice as many gerbils as hamsters.

Use 'Present' expressions to form the equation.

Twice the number of hamsters is equal to the number of gerbils.

Maths equation

$$2(x - 4) = 28 - x$$
$$2x - 8 = 28 - x$$
$$2x + x = 28 + 8$$
$$3x = 36$$
$$x = 12$$

- Number of hamsters = x = 12
- Number of gerbils = $30 - x = 30 - 12 = 18$

We now check our answer:

$12 + 18 = 30$ (total)

Also: $12 - 4 = 8$ hamsters

$18 - 2 = 16$ gerbils

$\therefore$ twice as many gerbils as hamsters

Exercise 2.19

1. Let x be equal to a number. The number is doubled and 17 is added.

   (i) Write an expression, in terms of x, for the resulting number.

   When the number is doubled and 17 is added the result is 35.

   (ii) Write an equation to show this information.

   (iii) Use this equation to find the number.

2. Let y be equal to a number. The number is trebled and 7 is taken away.

   (i) Write an expression, in terms of y, for the resulting number.

   When the number is trebled and 7 is taken away the result is 26.

   (ii) Write an equation to show this information.

   (iii) Solve this equation to find the number.

3. The diagram shows the angles of two triangles.

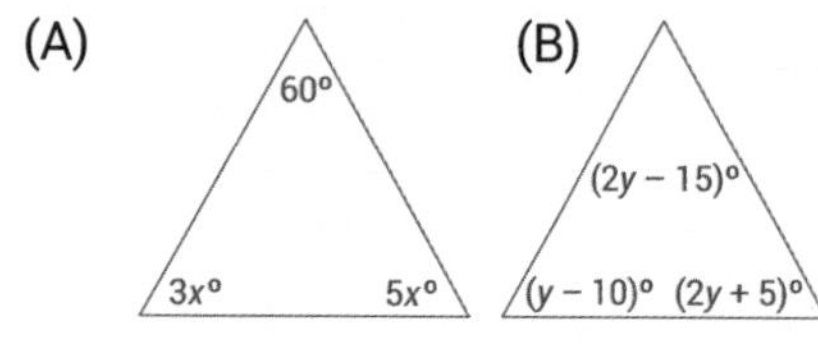

   (i) Write an expression, in terms of x, to show the sum of the angles in triangle A.

   (ii) Write an expression, in terms of y, to show the sum of the angles in triangle B.

   (iii) In each case, find the value of x and y, and hence find the value of the three angles.

4. Two rectangles are shown.

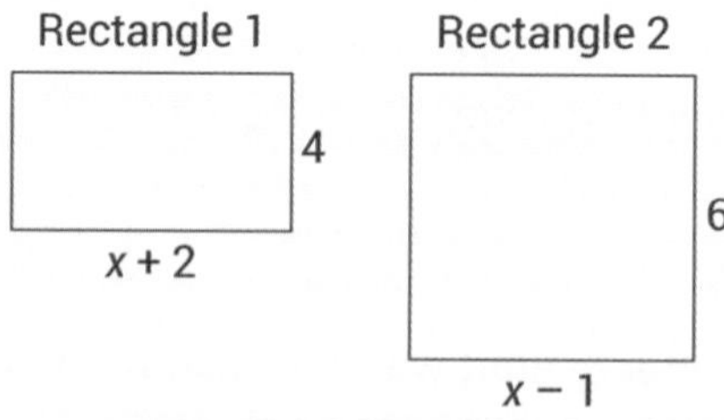

   (i) Write an expression, in terms of x, to show the area of rectangle 1.

   (ii) Write an expression, in terms of x, to show the area of rectangle 2.

   The two rectangles are of equal area.

   (iii) Write an equation to show this information.

   (iv) Hence, find all the dimensions of the rectangles.

5. Let n be equal to a natural number.
   (i) Write an expression, in terms of n, for the next consecutive natural number.
   (ii) Write an expression for the sum of the two consecutive natural numbers.

   The sum of the two consecutive natural numbers is 83.

   (iii) Write an equation to show this information.
   (iv) Use this equation to find the two consecutive natural numbers.

6. In a summer exam, the highest mark achieved was 37 marks higher than the lowest mark. The two marks added together give a total of 141 marks.

   Let x be the lowest mark.

   (i) Write an expression in x for the highest mark.
   (ii) Write an equation to represent the two marks totalling to 141.
   (iii) Solve this equation to find the two marks.

7. Annie is y years old. Her sister is twice as old as her.
   (i) Write an expression to show Annie's sister's age.

   Their mother is 25 years older than Annie's sister.

   (ii) Write an expression for Annie's mother's age.

   The total of all three ages is 80.

   (iii) Write an equation to show this information.
   (iv) Solve this equation to find Annie's age.

8. There are 100 seats in a theatre, all of which are standard or luxury.

   Let x represent the number of standard seats.

   (i) Write an expression in x for the number of luxury seats.

   Luxury seats cost €10 each and standard seats cost €5 each.

   (ii) Write an expression in x for the takings when the cinema is full.

   When the cinema is full, the takings come to a total of €650.

   (iii) How many of the seats are luxury?

9. Let n be an odd number.
   (i) Write an expression, in terms of n, for the next consecutive **odd** number.

   Seven times the first number is 12 more than five times the bigger number.

   (ii) Write an equation to represent this information.
   (iii) Find the two consecutive odd numbers.

10. Arthur has a certain number of euro. Barry has four and a half times as much money as Arthur. Ciara has €30 less than Arthur and Barry combined.

    Let x equal the amount of money, in euro, that Arthur has.

    Write an expression in x for:

    (i) Barry's money
    (ii) Ciara's money

    They have €432 altogether.

    (iii) Write an equation in x to represent that they have €432 altogether.
    (iv) Solve this equation to find how much money each one has.

11. The sum of two consecutive integers is at least -5.

    Let x equal the first integer.

    (i) Write an expression in x for the next consecutive integer.
    (ii) Write an inequality to represent this information.
    (iii) Solve this inequality to find the lowest possible consecutive integers.

12. At the close of business, a shopkeeper notices that she has $\frac{3}{4}$ as many candy bars as she has chocolate bars. She has 147 bars in total.

    Let y equal the number of chocolate bars.

    (i) Write an expression in y for the number of candy bars.
    (ii) Write an equation to represent the total number of bars the shopkeeper has.
    (iii) Solve this equation to find the number of each type of bar.

13. Jane works as a salesperson. She earns a basic salary of €18,000 per year plus commission of 12.5% of her sales amount for the year.

    (i) Write an expression for her salary if she had sales of €x in the year.

    She wants to know how much she will need to sell to earn a total salary of at least €60,000.

    (ii) Write an inequality to represent this information.

    (iii) Hence, solve this inequality to find how much she will need to sell to earn at least this salary.

14. Harry works at a restaurant during the summer and earns €12.50 per hour. Harry works x hours.

    (i) Write, in terms of x, Harry's gross wage.

    From his wage a total of 15% per hour is deducted for various taxes.

    (ii) Write, in terms of x, Harry's net wage.

    He is saving to buy a racing bike worth €2,395.90.

    (iii) Assuming he saves all his earnings, how many hours must he work to be able to afford the mountain bike?

15. An examination paper consists of 40 questions. For every correct answer, five marks are given.

    For every incorrect answer, three marks are deducted. A student answers all 40 questions, getting a total score for the examination of 112 marks.

    How many questions did the student answer incorrectly?

16. Amy gets €x as a prize. Brendan gets three times as much as Amy. Chloe gets half as much as Brendan. If the total money received is €550, how much does each person get?

17. Arthur owns 30% of a company. For every percent of the company he owns, he will normally get a salary of €x per month.

    - During January, the company pays as normal.
    - During February, the company pays out €500 less than normal.
    - Arthur then buys another 5% of the company.
    - During March, the company pays as normal.
    - On average, Arthur receives €2,050 per month for these three months.

    How much does the company pay out for each percentage owned?

18. A coach and a car leave a city at 11:00 and travel in opposite directions. The coach travels at an average speed of 55 km h^{-1} and the car travels at an average speed of 65 km h^{-1}.

    Let t equal the time taken for the journey in hours.

    (i) Write an expression in t for the distance travelled by the coach.

    (ii) Write an expression in t for the distance travelled by the car.

    (iii) Write an equation in t to show the time at which the bus and the car are 180 km apart.

    (iv) Solve for t.

    (v) If the coach and car had travelled in the same direction, at what time would the car be 75 km in front of the coach?

2.22 Solving Problems Using Simultaneous Equations

Sometimes we encounter algebra problems with two unknowns, x and y. These problems may be solved using simultaneous equations.

Worked Example 2.47

A set meal for five adults and three children costs €210 in a restaurant.
The next day it costs two adults and five children €160 to get the same set meal.

Find the cost of the meal per adult and per child.

Solution

Cost of adult meal = €x Cost of child meal = €y

Word equation (1): A set meal for five adults and three children costs €210.

Maths equation (1): $5x + 3y = 210$

Word equation (2): A set meal for two adults and five children costs €160.

Maths equation (2): $2x + 5y = 160$

Both equations **must** use the same units, in this case euros.

We now solve for x and y:

$5x + 3y = 210 \quad \times 2 \rightarrow 10x + 6y = 420$

$2x + 5y = 160 \quad \times 5 \rightarrow 10x + 25y = 800$

First we find the value of y:

$$10x + 6y = 420$$
$$-(10x + 25y = 800)$$
$$-19y = -380$$
$$\frac{-19y}{-19} = \frac{-380}{-19}$$
$$\therefore y = 20$$

If $y = 20$, we can now find the value of x:

$$2x + 5y = 160$$
$$2x + 5(20) = 160$$
$$2x + 100 = 160$$
$$2x = 160 - 100$$
$$2x = 60$$
$$\therefore x = 30$$

$\therefore$ Cost of adult meal = €x = €30

$\therefore$ Cost of child meal = €y = €20

Remember to answer the question asked.
Include the unit of measurement (€).

Worked Example 2.48

There are 62 animals on a farm. All of them are either cows or chickens.

Altogether, the animals have 192 legs. How many cows and how many chickens are on the farm?

Solution

Number of cows = x Number of chickens = y

Word equation (1): There are 62 animals on the farm.

Maths equation (1): $x + y = 62$

Word equation (2): Altogether, the animals have 192 legs.

Maths equation (2):

Cows have 4 legs $\Rightarrow 4x$

Chickens have 2 legs $\Rightarrow 2y$

$4x + 2y = 192$

$x + y = 62 \quad \times 4 \rightarrow 4x + 4y = 248$

$4x + 2y = 192 \quad \times 1 \rightarrow 4x + 2y = 192$

First we find the value of y:

$$4x + 4y = 248$$
$$-(4x + 2y = 192)$$
$$2y = 56$$
$$y = 28$$

$\therefore$ Number of chickens = y = 28

If $y = 28$, we can now find the value of x:

$$x + y = 62$$
$$x + 28 = 62$$
$$x = 62 - 28$$
$$x = 34$$

$\therefore$ Number of cows = x = 34

Exercise 2.20

1. The sum of two numbers is 25.

   Let x = the first number and y = the second number.

   (i) Write an equation in x and y to show this information.

   Twice the first number plus the second number is equal to 35.

   (ii) Write an equation in x and y to show this information.

   (iii) Hence, find the two numbers.

2. The sum of two numbers is 20.

   Let x = the first number and y = the second number.

   (i) Write an equation in x and y to show this information.

   The difference between the two numbers is 5.

   (ii) Write an equation in x and y to show this information.

   (iii) Hence, find the two numbers.

3. Let x = the cost of one soft drink and y = the cost of one bar.

   (i) Three soft drinks and six bars cost €9. Write an equation to represent this information.

   (ii) Five soft drinks and two bars cost €11. Write an equation to represent this information.

   (iii) Using your equations from parts (i) and (ii), find the cost of each item.

4. Let x = the price of one pen and y = the price of one pencil.

   (i) A pen and a pencil cost €1. Write an equation to represent this information.

   (ii) Four pens and two pencils cost €3.40. Write an equation to represent this information.

   (iii) Using your equations from parts (i) and (ii), find the cost of each item.

5. A rectangle is shown.

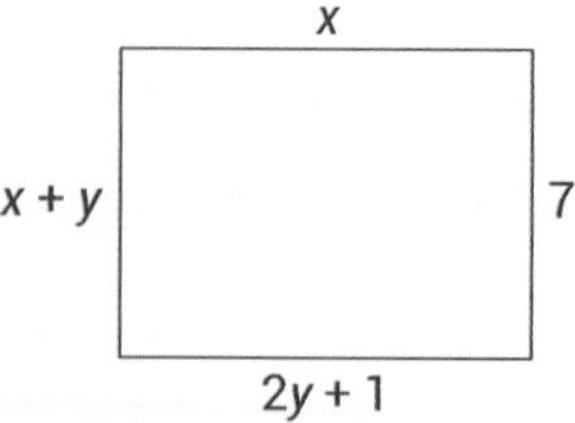

   Write down two equations in x and y and hence find their values.

6. In an election, the total number of votes cast for two candidates, Alan and Carol, was 735.

   Let x = the number of votes Alan received and y = the number of votes Carol received.

   (i) Write an equation in x and y to represent the above information.

   Alan received more votes than Carol. The difference between the number of votes cast for Alan and the number cast for Carol is 105.

   (ii) Write an equation in x and y to represent this information.

   (iii) How many votes did each candidate receive?

7. Let x = the number of goals and y = the number of points.

   (i) A Gaelic Football team scored on 11 occasions during a match (including goals and points). Write an equation in x and y to represent this information.

   (ii) At the end of the match their total score was worth 17 points. (A goal is worth 3 points.) Write an equation in x and y to represent this information.

   (iii) Hence find the number of goals and points the team scored.

8. A shop sells 50 sofas in a week. A leather sofa sells for €1,000 and a fabric sofa sells for €750. The shop sells €42,500 worth of these types of sofas.

   How many of each type does the shop sell?

ALGEBRA I

9. An entrance exam is worth 125 marks and contains 35 questions. Some of the questions are worth 3 marks and some are worth 5 marks.

   How many questions of each mark were on the exam?

10. Sheena spends €100 on a coat and bag. During a sale, the same coat and bag are sold at $\frac{3}{5}$ and $\frac{1}{4}$ the price that Sheena paid for them, respectively. She would have saved herself €54 if she had bought these items in the sale.

    How much did the coat and bag cost originally?

11. The first two sections of a race are x and y metres long respectively. Henry runs the first part of the race at 3 ms^{-1} and the second part at 6 ms^{-1}. George runs the same sections at 5 ms^{-1} and 3 ms^{-1}. It takes Henry half a minute to run these two sections, whereas it takes George 46 seconds to do the same distance.

    How long are these two sections of the race?

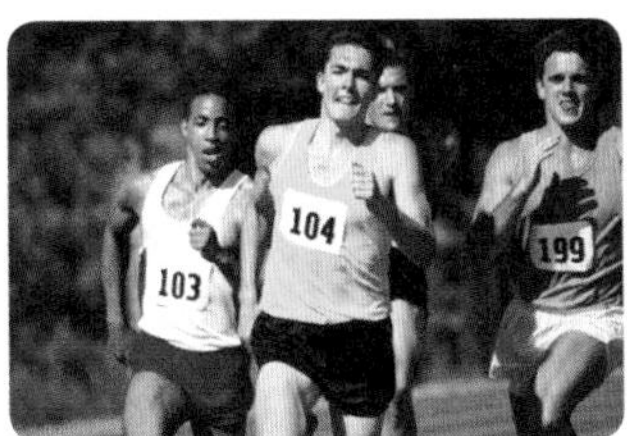

12. Karl's and Eddie's ages added together are equal to 65. Ten years ago, Karl was twice as old as Eddie. How old are they now?

13. Two runners run a race at steady speeds. After 2 hours they are 3 km apart. If they had run in opposite directions, they would have been 25.5 km apart after 3 hours.

    Let x and y represent the speed, in km h^{-1}, of the two runners.

    (i) Write an equation in x and y, when they are running in the same direction.

    (ii) Write an equation in x and y, when they are running in opposite directions.

    (iii) Hence, find the speeds of the two runners.

ALGEBRA I

Revision Exercises

1. (a) If $p = -2$ and $q = 3$, evaluate:

   (i) $p + q$ (ii) $p - q$ (iii) $q - p$ (iv) pq (v) $q^2 + pq - q$

   (b) (i) If $b = -3$, evaluate: $\frac{5b - 1}{b - 1}$ (ii) If $k = -7$, evaluate: $\frac{k^2 - 1}{k - 1}$ (iii) If $x = 8$, evaluate: $\sqrt{\frac{3x + 1}{2x}}$

   (c) The approximate time (t in seconds) taken for an object to fall from rest from a height of h metres is given by the following formula, where $g = 9.81$:

   $$t = \sqrt{\frac{2h}{g}}$$

   (i) Calculate the time taken for each object to fall from the given height. Give your answer in seconds correct to two decimal places.

Object	h
1	30 m
2	3,000 m
3	4,000 m
4	1 km
5	0.75 km

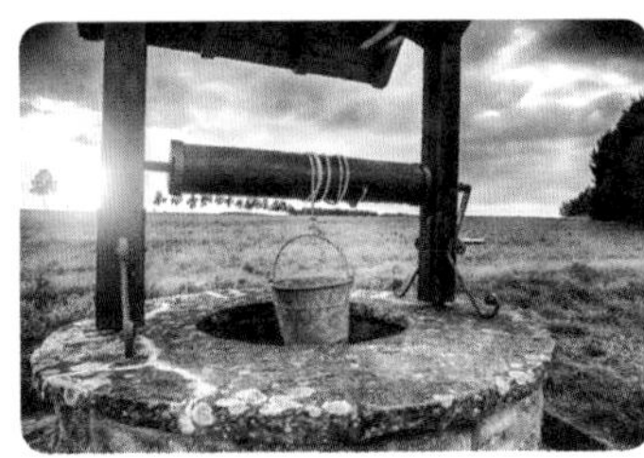

An archaeologist wishes to determine how deep the water level is in a well.

To ensure an accurate measurement, she drops 10 stones into the well and records the time taken for the stones to hit the water.

Her results are as shown.

Stone number	1	2	3	4	5	6	7	8	9	10
Time (secs)	2.0	2.1	1.9	1.8	2.1	2.1	1.9	2.0	2.1	1.8

(ii) What was the average time taken for the stone to hit the water?

(iii) Using this value for t, calculate the depth of water in the well to the nearest metre.

2. Simplify each of the following:

(a) (i) $3x + 2xy + 4x + 10xy$

(ii) $a + 8a^2 + 2a + 3a^2$

(iii) $9x^2 + x + 3x^2 + 10x$

(iv) $3y - 4 + 9y + 10$

(b) (i) $9x^2 + xy + 7 + 3x^2 + 10xy - 5$

(ii) $12x^2 + 5x - 8 - x^2 - 2x - 5$

(iii) $x^2 + 4x - 5 + 17x + x^2 - 11$

(iv) $3x^2 - 4x + 13 - x^2 - 15 + 11x$

(c) Multiply these terms:

(i) $(2a)(7a^2)$ (iv) $(2xy)(6xy^2)$

(ii) $(5c)(3c)(2c)$ (v) $(-2a)(-a)$

(iii) $(2ab)(10a^2b)$ (vi) $(-c)(-c)(-c)(-c)$

(d) Multiply out the following:

(i) $(11a)^2$ (iv) $(3m^2)^3$

(ii) $(5c)^3$ (v) $(-4b)^3$

(iii) $(-2b)^3$ (vi) $(-2k^2)^2$

3. Expand and simplify where possible:

(a) (i) $2(3a + 4b)$ (iii) $6(x + 2y + 3z)$

(ii) $3(4a + 10b)$ (iv) $-2(2x + 5y)$

(b) (i) $2(x + 3y) + 3(2x + y)$

(ii) $6(m + 3n) + 7(m + n)$

(iii) $3(x + 2y - 6) - 2(x - 10y - 7)$

(iv) $2(4x^2 + x + 3) + 3(x^2 - 4x - 7)$

(v) $4(2x^2 - x - 1) - 3(x^2 + 3x - 5)$

(c) (i) $2x(x - 8) + x(x - 7)$

(ii) $x(3x - 1) - (3x^2 - x - 11)$

(iii) $a(4a - 7b) - 2a(2a - 3b)$

(iv) $2x(3x^2 + x + 1) - x(5x^2 + x - 3)$

4. (a) Express each of the following as single fractions in their simplest form:

(i) $\frac{2}{x+1} + \frac{3}{x+7}, x \neq -1, -7$

(ii) $\frac{1}{x+5} + \frac{2}{x+6}, x \neq -5, -6$

(iii) $\frac{2}{2x+1} - \frac{3}{5x-1}, x \neq -\frac{1}{2}, \frac{1}{5}$

(iv) $\frac{12}{4x+1} - \frac{3}{x-7}, x \neq -\frac{1}{4}, 7$

(v) $\frac{3}{2x+1} - \frac{4}{2x-1}, x \neq \pm\frac{1}{2}$

(b) Expand the following and simplify:

(i) $(x + 1)(x + 5)$ (vi) $(2a + 4)(2a + 4)$

(ii) $(y + 2)(y + 7)$ (vii) $(3x - 1)(4x - 5)$

(iii) $(k + 1)(k - 7)$ (viii) $(3y + 2)^2$

(iv) $(x - 9)(x - 2)$ (ix) $(4y - 1)^2$

(v) $(2x + 1)(3x + 5)$ (x) $2x(x + 1)(x + 5)$

(c) Factorise fully the following expressions:

(i) $y^2 - 36$ (ix) $64y^2 - 16$

(ii) $x^2 - 50x$ (x) $12x^2 + 15x$

(iii) $x^2 - 81$ (xi) $8x^2 - 11x$

(iv) $x^2 + 6x + 5$ (xii) $2x^2 - 13x + 20$

(v) $x^2 - 7x + 12$ (xiii) $2x^2 - 30x + 108$

(vi) $x^2 + 3x - 10$ (xiv) $5x^2 + 34x - 7$

(vii) $2x^2 - 3x + 1$ (xv) $10x^2 + 5x - 5$

(viii) $5x^2 + 13x - 6$ (xvi) $4x^2 - 17x + 13$

5. Simplify the following:

(a) (i) $\frac{144xy^4z^5}{12xy^2z^5}$

(ii) $\frac{(3xy)(12x^2)}{6xy}$

(iii) $\frac{(12x^4y)(4xy^3)}{(2xy)^3}$

(iv) $\frac{(3p^4q^2)^2(10pq)}{(5pq)(3pq^2)}$

(b) (i) $\frac{x^2 + 8x + 15}{x + 5}$

(ii) $\frac{36x^3y}{6xy}$

(iii) $\frac{4x - 8}{2}$

(iv) $\frac{6x + 15}{3x}$

(v) $\frac{15x - 30}{5x - 10}$

6. (a) Solve these equations:

(i) $2x + 5 = 11$

(ii) $7x + 1 = 43$

(iii) $8x - 5 = 19$

(iv) $9x + 8 = 6x + 20$

(v) $2x + 1 = 8x - 53$

(vi) $5x + 7 = 9x - 5$

(b) Solve these equations:

(i) $5(x + 7) = 25(x - 1)$

(ii) $8(x + 3) = 5(x + 6)$

(iii) $9(2x - 3) = 25(x - 1) + 5$

(iv) $2(x + 7) - 5(x - 1) = 13$

(v) $5x - 1 - 2(x + 2) = x$

7. (a) Solve the following equations:

(i) $\frac{5x - 4}{3} = 2$

(ii) $\frac{a + 3}{4} = \frac{1}{2}$

(iii) $\frac{x + 2}{3} + \frac{x + 1}{4} = \frac{1}{3}$

(iv) $\frac{3x + 1}{5} - \frac{x - 1}{2} = 1$

(v) $\frac{5x - 1}{7} = \frac{x + 2}{2} + 1$

(b) In each case below, write the variable in the square brackets in terms of the other variables:

(i) $y = pq - t$ [q]

(ii) $p = tv$ [t]

(iii) $ax + by + c = 0$ [a]

(iv) $t = a + (n - 1)d$ [d]

(v) $A = 2\pi rh$ [r]

(c) In each case, write the variable in the square brackets in terms of the other variables:

(i) $ax = c - kx$ [x]

(ii) $r = 1 - rs + c$ [r]

(iii) $\frac{a - b}{k} = a$ [a]

(iv) $\frac{a - b}{b + 1} = c$ [b]

(v) $\frac{a - 5c}{c + 1} = d$ [c]

8. (a) Solve these simultaneous equations:

(i) $2x + y = 10$
$4x - y = 8$

(ii) $x + 3y = 2$
$2x + y = 9$

(iii) $x - 3y = 4$
$5x - 2y = 7$

(iv) $5x - 3y = 1$
$x - y = 0$

(b) Solve these simultaneous equations:

(i) $2x - 3y - 2 = 0$
$3x + 8y - 3 = 0$

(ii) $5x - 12y - 17 = 0$
$\frac{1}{9}(x + 2) - (y + 1) + \frac{3}{2} = 0$

9. (a) List the values of x that satisfy each inequality:

(i) $2x < 8, x \in N$

(ii) $x + 3 \leqslant 8, x \in N$

(iii) $2x + 1 \leqslant 7, x \in N$

(b) Show on the number line the solution set for each of the following:

(i) $4x + 1 > 13, x \in Z$

(ii) $2x - 1 \leqslant 13, x \in N$

(iii) $3 - 2x > 7, x \in R$

(c) Show on the number line the solution set for each of the following:

(i) $3 + 3x < x + 11, x \in R$

(ii) $8 - 2x \leqslant x - 7, x \in R$

(iii) $8(x - 3) > x + 4, x \in R$

(iv) $\frac{2}{5}x + \frac{1}{2} \leqslant \frac{9}{10}, x \in R$

10. (a) There are 44 people in a room. If n of them are adults, how many are children?
    (b) There are 53 people in a room. x of them are children. The adults are divided equally into male and female. Write down an expression for the number of female adults in the room.
    (c) There are n people in a town. Two-fifths of them are female. Two hundred males leave the town. How many males remain?
    (d) Let x be equal to a number. The number is multiplied by 4 and 37 is then added.
        (i) Write an expression, in terms of x, to show this information.

        When the number is multiplied by 4 and 37 is added the result is 325.

        (ii) Write an equation to show this information.
        (iii) Solve this equation to find the number.
    (e) Marie is x years old. Her brother, Ned, is 5 years older.
        (i) Write an expression for Ned's age.

        Oliver, their father, is three times as old as Ned.

        (ii) Write an expression for Oliver's age.

        The sum total of their three ages is 95.

        (iii) Write an equation to show this information.
        (iv) Use this equation to find Marie's age.

11. (a) I have 12 coins in my pocket. They are all either 10 cent or 5 cent coins.

        Let x = the number of 10 cent coins and y = the number of 5 cent coins.

        (i) Write an equation in x and y to represent the above information.

        The coins are worth €2.40.

        (ii) Write an equation in x and y to represent this information.
        (iii) Hence find the number of 10 cent coins and 5 cent coins.
    (b) 150 children have to go on a school tour. They can use minibuses, which carry x pupils each, or cars, which carry y pupils each. The Mathematics teacher works out that they could just manage with 10 minibuses and 6 cars, or with 5 minibuses and 18 cars.

        Write down two equations in x and y to represent this information and, hence, find the value of x and y.
    (c) A guesthouse has 10 rooms to let. Some of these sleep two people and some sleep three people. On a certain day all rooms are taken and full. There are 23 people in the guesthouse that day.

        How many of each kind of room are there?

Exam Questions

1. (a) Solve for x:

       $3(x - 7) + 5(x - 4) = 15$, where $x \in \mathbb{R}$.
   (b) Solve the equations below to find the value of a and the value of b:

       $$4a + 3b = -3$$
       $$5a = 25 + 2b.$$
   (c) List all the values of x that satisfy the inequality $2(2x - 3) + 6x < 25$, where $x \in \mathbb{N}$.

   SEC Leaving Certificate Ordinary Level, Paper 1, 2016

2. Emma works part time after school at the local takeaway. She is paid a rate per hour and also receives €2 for each delivery she makes.
   (a) One day, she works for 2 hours, makes 5 deliveries and is paid a total of €28.

       Find her hourly rate of pay.
   (b) One week, she works for h hours and makes d deliveries.

       Write a formula in h and d for the wage (w) she receives.
   (c) Another week, she works for 6 hours and makes 12 deliveries. She also works 5 hours on a Sunday, at time and a half, and makes some deliveries. In total, she receives €161.50 for that week. Find how many deliveries she makes on the Sunday.

   SEC Leaving Certificate Ordinary Level, Paper 1, 2016

3. (a) Simplify $3(4 - 5x) - 2(5 - 6x)$.

   (b) List all the values of x that satisfy the inequality $2 - 3x \geqslant -6, x \in N$.

   (c) $g(x)$ is a function and $(2 - 3x) \times g(x) = 15x^2 - 22x + 8$, for all $x \in R$. Find $g(x)$.

SEC Leaving Certificate Ordinary Level, Paper 1, 2015

4. (a) The length of the side of a square sheet of cardboard is 12 cm. Find the area of the sheet.

   (b) The diagram shows a square sheet of cardboard of side length 12 cm, from which four small squares, each of side length h, have been removed. The sheet can be folded to form an open rectangular box of height h.

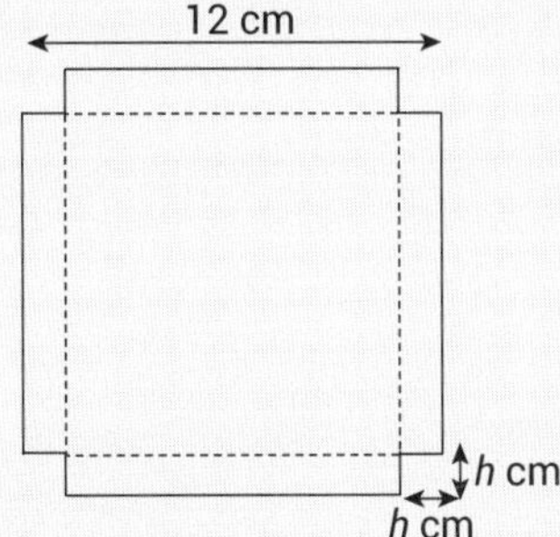

   Write the length and the width of the box in terms of h.

   (c) Show that the volume of the box, in terms of h, is $4h^3 - 48h^2 + 144h$.

SEC Leaving Certificate Ordinary Level, Paper 1, 2014

5. (i) Solve for x:

   $2(4 - 3x) + 12 = 7x - 5(2x - 7)$.

   (ii) Verify your answer to (i) above.

SEC Leaving Certificate Ordinary Level, Paper 1, 2014

6. Solve the equation $\frac{1}{2}(7x - 2) + 5 = 2x + 7$.

SEC Leaving Certificate Ordinary Level, Paper 1, 2012

7. Doctors sometimes need to work out how much medicine to give a child, based on the correct dose for an adult. There are different ways of doing this, based on the child's age, weight, height,or some other measure.

   (a) One rule for working out the child's dose from the adult dose is called *Clark's rule*. It is:

   $C = \left(\frac{W}{68}\right) \times A$

   where C is the child's dose, A is the adult's dose, and W is the child's weight in kilograms.

   The adult dose of a certain medicine is 125 mg per day. Calculate the correct dose for a child weighing 30 kg, using Clark's rule. Give the answer correct to the nearest 5 mg.

   (b) Another rule for working out the child's dose is called *Young's rule*. Below are three different descriptions of Young's rule, taken from the internet. In each case, write down a formula that *exactly* matches the description in words. State clearly the meaning of any letters you use in your formulae.

   (i) **Young's rule:** a mathematical expression used to determine a drug dosage for children. The correct dosage is calculated by dividing the child's age by an amount equal to the child's age plus 12 and then multiplying by the usual adult dose.

   Mosby's Dental Dictionary. 2nd edition.

   (ii) **Young's rule:** A rule for calculating the dose of medicine correct for a child by adding 12 to the child's age, dividing the sum by the child's age, then dividing the adult dose by the figure obtained.

   The American Heritage Medical Dictionary

   (iii) **Young's rule:** the dose of a drug for a child is obtained by multiplying the adult dose by the child's age in years and dividing the result by the sum of the child's age plus 12.

   Miller-Keane Encyclopedia and Dictionary of Medicine, Nursing, and Allied Health, Seventh Edition

   (c) Explain why the three formula in **(b)** above all give the same result.

   (d) The adult dose of a certain medicine is 150 mg per day. According to Young's rule, what is the correct dose for a six-year old child?

   (e) Young's rule results in a certain child being given one fifth of the adult dose of a medicine. How old is this child?

   (f) Another rule for working out a child's dose is based on 'body surface area' (BSA). The rule is:

   $$\text{child's dose} = \frac{\text{child's BSA in m}^2}{1.73} \times \text{adult dose}$$

BSA is difficult to measure directly, but an estimate can be calculated from a person's height and weight. The chart below allows you to read off the BSA for a given height and weight, by drawing a straight line from the height on the left scale to the weight on the right. For example, the dotted line shows that a person of height 100 cm and weight 16 kg has a BSA of 0.67 m^2.

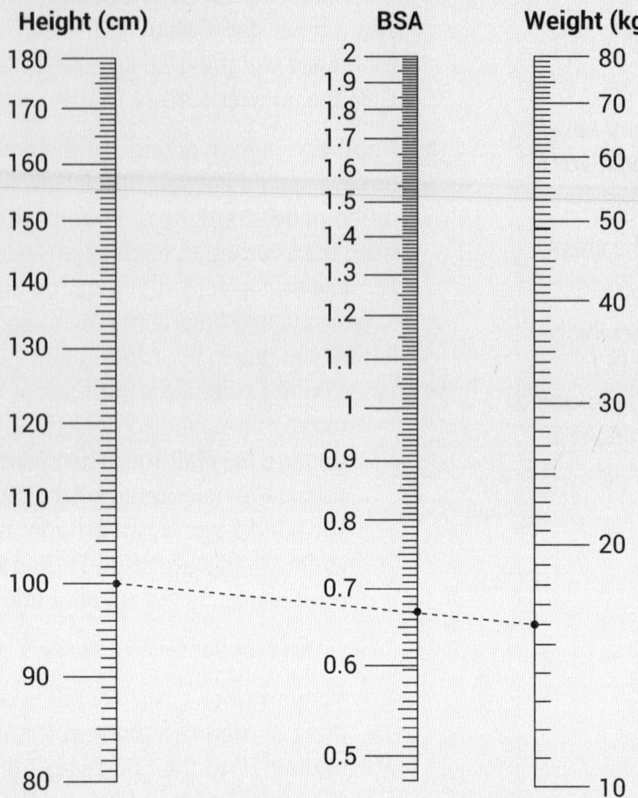

The correct adult dose of a certain medicine is 200 mg per day. Use the BSA rule to calculate the correct dose for a child of height 125 cm and weight 26 kg.

(g) The following apply in the case of a certain medicine and a certain child:

- the child is nine years old
- Clark's rule and Young's rule both give a dose of 90 mg per day
- the BSA rule gives a dose of 130 mg per day.

Find the weight and height of this child.

SEC Leaving Certificate Ordinary Level, Paper 1, 2012

8. (a) Solve the simultaneous equations:

$$2f + \frac{2}{3}g + 1 = 0$$

$$f + \frac{1}{2}g + 1 = 0$$

(b) Solve the following inequality, and show the solution set on the number line below.

$$5 - \frac{3}{4}x \leq \frac{19}{8}, x \in R$$

0

SEC Leaving Certificate Ordinary Level, Paper 1, 2011

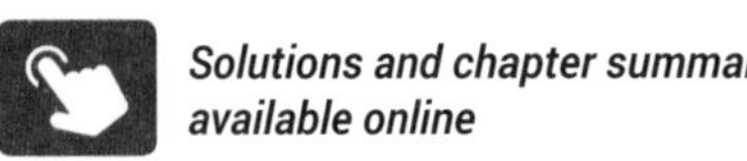

Solutions and chapter summary available online

ALGEBRA I

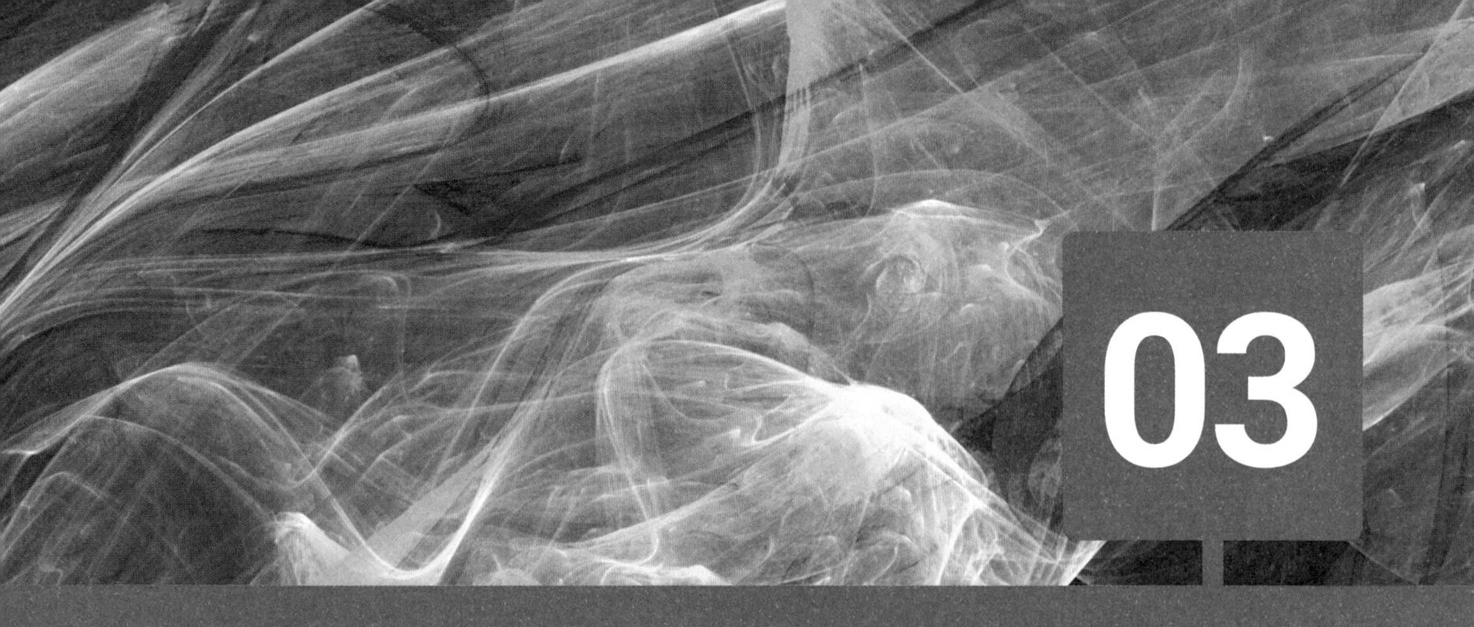

Real Numbers

In this chapter you will learn to:

- Recognise irrational numbers and appreciate that $R \neq Q$
- Work with irrational numbers
- Revisit the operations of addition, multiplication, subtraction and division in the following domains:
  - N of natural numbers
  - Z of integers
  - Q of rational numbers
  - R of real numbers

  and represent these numbers on a number line
- Develop decimals as special equivalent fractions strengthening the connection between these numbers and fraction and place-value understanding
- Consolidate your understanding of factors, multiples and prime numbers in N
- Express numbers in terms of their prime factors
- Express non-zero positive rational numbers in the form $a \times 10^n$, where $n \in Z$ and $1 \leq a < 10$ and perform arithmetic operations on numbers in this form
- Appreciate the order of operations, including brackets

You should remember...

- The commutative, associative and distributive properties of arithmetic
- Order of operations
- How to use the number line to order numbers in N, Z, and Q
- How to calculate percentages
- The relationship between ratio and proportion

Key words

- Natural number
- Factor
- Multiple
- Prime number
- HCF
- LCM
- Integer
- Rational number
- Terminating decimal
- Recurring decimal
- Reciprocal
- Irrational number
- Real number
- Number line
- Order of operations
- Scientific notation

3.1 Natural Numbers

The **natural numbers** are the ordinary counting numbers. The set of natural numbers is an **infinite** set. This means that the set is never-ending. The letter N is used to label the set of natural numbers.

$$N = \{1, 2, 3, 4, ...\}$$

The natural numbers are often represented on a number line:

0 1 2 3 4 5

3.2 Factors, Multiples and Prime Factors

Factors

A **factor** of a natural number is any natural number that divides evenly into the given number.

For example, the set of factors of 16 is {1, 2, 4, 8, 16}.

Every factor is part of a pair.

The number 16 has three **factor pairs**:

$1 \times 16 = 16$
$2 \times 8 = 16$
$4 \times 4 = 16$

⇒ Factor pairs are: 1 and 16
2 and 8
4 and 4

- 1 is a factor of every natural number.
- Every natural number is a factor of itself.

As you can see, 1 is a factor of 16, and 16 is a factor of 16.

Worked Example 3.1

List the factors of 24.

Solution

The factors of 24 are {1, 2, 3, 4, 6, 8, 12, 24}.

Worked Example 3.2

List the pairs of factors of 40.

Solution

The pairs of factors of 40 are

$1 \times 40, 2 \times 20, 4 \times 10, 5 \times 8$.

Multiples

A **multiple** of a natural number is itself a natural number into which the natural number divides, leaving no remainder.

The **multiples** of 6 are {6, 12, 18, 24, 30, 36, ...} because:

$6 \times 1 = 6$ $6 \times 2 = 12$ $6 \times 3 = 18$ $6 \times 4 = 24$ $6 \times 5 = 30$, and so on.

As you can see, the set of multiples of a natural number is an infinite set, i.e. it goes on forever.

Worked Example 3.3

List the first six multiples of 4.

Solution

$4 \times 1 = 4$ $4 \times 2 = 8$ $4 \times 3 = 12$ $4 \times 4 = 16$ $4 \times 5 = 20$ $4 \times 6 = 24$

The set of the first six multiples of 4 is {4, 8, 12, 16, 20, 24}.

Prime Numbers

Prime numbers are natural numbers that have exactly two factors.

- 7 is a **prime number**, as it has exactly two factors, 1 and 7.
- 2 is the only even prime number. Its two factors are 1 and 2.
- 11 is the first two-digit prime. Its two factors are 1 and 11.
- 1 is **not** a prime, as it has one factor only: itself.
- 0 is **not** a prime, as it is not a natural number.

Euclid (c. 365 BC–275 BC)

The Greek mathematician Euclid proved that the number of primes is infinite.

Natural numbers greater than 1 that are not prime are called composite numbers.
The first five composite numbers are 4, 6, 8, 9 and 10.

Worked Example 3.4

Consider the set A = {12, 13, 14, 15, 16, 17, 18}.

By writing out the set of factors for each number in A, determine which numbers in A are composite.

Solution

Factors of 12 = {1, 2, 3, 4, 6, 12}

Factors of 13 = {1, 13}

Factors of 14 = {1, 2, 7, 14}

Factors of 15 = {1, 3, 5, 15}

Factors of 16 = {1, 2, 4, 8, 16}

Factors of 17 = {1, 17}

Factors of 18 = {1, 2, 3, 6, 9, 18}

∴ 13 and 17 are prime as both numbers have exactly two factors.

∴ 12, 14, 15, 16 and 18 are composite.

Highest Common Factor (HCF)

The highest common factor of two natural numbers, n_1 and n_2, is the largest natural number that divides into both n_1 and n_2 leaving zero remainder.

The **highest common factor** of 12 and 20 is 4, as 4 is the largest natural number that divides into both 12 and 20 leaving zero remainder.

Lowest Common Multiple (LCM)

The lowest common multiple of two numbers is the smallest multiple that both numbers share.

The **lowest common multiple** of 3 and 4 is 12, as 12 is the smallest number that both 3 and 4 divide into leaving zero remainder.

Worked Example 3.5

What is the LCM of 6 and 15?

Solution

The multiples of 6 are {6, 12, 18, 24, (30), 36, ...}.

The multiples of 15 are {15, (30), 45, 60, 75, ...}.

$\therefore$ LCM = 30

The Greek mathematician Euclid discovered more than 2,000 years ago that every composite number could be written as a unique product of prime numbers. For example:

$30 = 2 \times 3 \times 5$

$36 = 2 \times 2 \times 3 \times 3 = 2^2 \times 3^2$

This fact is useful for finding HCFs and LCMs.

Worked Example 3.6

Write 48 and 80 as a product of primes. Hence, find the HCF of 48 and 80.

Solution

Divide using prime numbers, starting with the smallest possible prime that is a factor. Continue as shown, stopping when you get a quotient of 1.

(2)	48
(2)	24
(2)	12
(2)	6
3	3
	1

(2)	80
(2)	40
(2)	20
(2)	10
5	5
	1

$48 = (2) \times (2) \times (2) \times (2) \times 3$

$80 = (2) \times (2) \times (2) \times (2) \times 5$

2^4 is the highest common factor of 48 and 80.

$\therefore$ HCF = 2^4

HCF = 16

Worked Example 3.7

Find the LCM of 60 and 42.

Solution

2	60
2	30
3	15
5	5
	1

2	42
3	21
7	7
	1

$60 = 2 \times 2 \times 3 \times 5$

$42 = 2 \times 3 \times (7)$

$\Rightarrow 60 = (2^2) \times (3) \times (5)$

- 2^2 is the bigger of the factors 2 and 2^2.
- 3 is a common factor of both 60 and 42.
- 5 and 7 are the non-common factors.

$\therefore$ LCM = $2^2 \times 3 \times 5 \times 7$

LCM = 420

Exercise 3.1

1. Represent the following natural numbers on a number line:

   (i) 2 (ii) 4 (iii) 7 (iv) 11

2. Write down all the factors of each of the following natural numbers:

   (i) 40 (ii) 64 (iii) 28 (iv) 35 (v) 96 (vi) 48

3. List the first six multiples of each of the following natural numbers:

   (i) 4 (ii) 6 (iii) 8 (iv) 9 (v) 12 (vi) 14

4. Represent on a number line the prime numbers between 10 and 20.

5. By finding all the factors of each number, write down the HCF of each of the following:

   (i) 6 and 14 (iii) 12 and 36 (v) 16, 12 and 80

   (ii) 20 and 45 (iv) 3, 9 and 30 (vi) 9, 30 and 45

6. By writing out the first six multiples, write down the LCM of each of the following:

   (i) 4 and 6 (iii) 16 and 20 (v) 8, 10 and 20

   (ii) 10 and 12 (iv) 2, 3 and 4 (vi) 15, 18 and 30

7. (i) What is a prime number? (ii) What is a prime factor?

8. Write the following numbers as products of prime factors:

   (i) 64 (iii) 1,870 (v) 368

   (ii) 2,310 (iv) 102 (vi) 5,250

9. (a) Express each of the following pairs of numbers as the product of prime factors.

   (b) Hence, find the LCM and HCF for each pair.

   (i) 136 and 102 (ii) 117 and 130 (iii) 58 and 174 (iv) 102 and 170

10. 294 red pens, 252 green pens and 210 blue pens are distributed equally among some students (i.e. each student gets equal numbers of each colour).
    What is the largest possible number of students in the group?

11. Alice, Bob and Carl are jumping up a large flight of stairs. Alice jumps two steps at a time, Bob jumps four steps at a time, while Carl jumps five steps at a time.
    On which step will all three land together for the first time? (Assume they all begin at the foot of the stairs, i.e. on step 0.)

12. Find the value of $\frac{4n^2+1}{13}$ where $n \in \{17, 19, 21\}$.

n	$\frac{4n^2+1}{13}$
17	
19	
21	

    State which one of your answers is a natural number and why.

13. The Swiss mathematician and physicist, Euler, first noticed (in 1772) that the expression $n^2 - n + 41$ gives a prime number for all positive integer values of n less than 41.

    Explain why it does not give a prime number for $n = 41$.

3.3 Integers

The set of integers consists of zero (0), the natural numbers ({1, 2, 3, ...}) and the set of negative whole numbers ({..., −3, −2, −1}). The letter Z is used to label the set of integers.

$Z = \{..., -3, -2, -1, 0, 1, 2, ...\}$

The integers can also be represented on a number line.

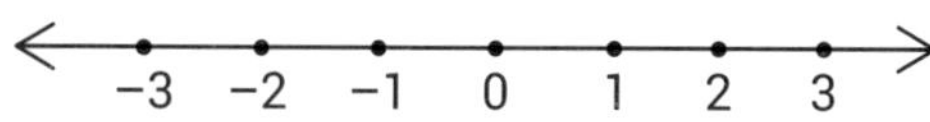

Multiplication and Division of Integers

Rules for Multiplication	Rules for Division
(i) positive × positive = positive (ii) positive × negative = negative (iii) negative × positive = negative (iv) negative × negative = positive	(i) positive ÷ positive = positive (ii) positive ÷ negative = negative (iii) negative ÷ positive = negative (iv) negative ÷ negative = positive

Note that division by 0 is **undefined**. For example, 8 ÷ 0 is undefined (math error on calculator).

Worked Example 3.8

Evaluate the following, without using a calculator:

(i) $3 \times (-12)$

(ii) $(-5)(-11)$

(iii) $60 \div (-30)$

(iv) $(-5)^3$

Solution

(i) $3 \times (-12) = -36$ (positive × negative = negative)

(ii) $(-5)(-11) = 55$ (negative × negative = positive)

(iii) $60 \div (-30) = -2$ (positive ÷ negative = negative)

(iv) $(-5)^3 = (-5)(-5)(-5) = (25)(-5) = -125$

REAL NUMBERS

Exercise 3.2

1. Evaluate each of the following, without using a calculator:

   (i) −3 − 9
   (ii) 8 − 1
   (iii) 2 − 12
   (iv) −5 − 10
   (v) −10 − 50
   (vi) 12 − 15

2. Evaluate each of the following:

   (i) 3 − 2 + 1
   (ii) 3 − 8 − 2
   (iii) 5 − 6 − 2 + 3
   (iv) 8 − 2 + 1 − 5
   (v) −7 − 4 − 3 − 4
   (vi) −3 + 4 − 1 + 2

3. On Sunday evening, Seán has €1,500 in his credit union account. The following week Seán visits his bank four times.

   (a) On Monday, he withdraws €700 from his account.
   (b) On Tuesday, he lodges €800 to his account.
   (c) On Thursday, he withdraws a further €700.
   (d) On Friday morning, he lodges €100.

   What is the balance in Seán's credit union account on Friday evening?

4. There are 10 questions on a multiple choice test. A correct answer is worth 5 marks. An incorrect answer incurs a penalty of −2 marks and an unanswered question is worth 1 mark. Alice, Bob and Kylie each take the test.

   (a) Alice answers four questions correctly, leaves two questions unanswered and gets the rest wrong.

   (b) Bob answers seven questions correctly and answers one incorrectly. He leaves the rest unanswered.

   (c) Kylie answers three questions incorrectly and leaves one unanswered. She gets the rest correct.

   How many marks did Alice, Bob and Kylie each get on the test?

5. Evaluate, without using a calculator, each of the following:

   (i) (10)(4)
   (ii) (−2)(16)
   (iii) (7)(−8)
   (iv) (−15)(−6)
   (v) (−5)(6)(−3)
   (vi) (−15)(−2)(−5)

6. Evaluate each of the following, without using a calculator:

   (i) −99 ÷ (−33)
   (ii) −66 ÷ 11
   (iii) 144 ÷ (−12)
   (iv) −16 ÷ (−8)
   (v) 121 ÷ (−11)
   (vi) (−72) ÷ 9

3.4 Rational Numbers

The letter Q is used to represent the set of rational numbers.

Rational numbers are also called fractions.

There are two parts to every fraction: the **numerator** (the top) and the **denominator** (the bottom).

Q = {any number that can be written in the form $\frac{a}{b}$, where $a, b \in Z, b \neq 0$}

Worked Example 3.9

Evaluate the following:

(i) $\frac{1}{3}+\frac{2}{5}$ (ii) $\frac{3}{4}-\frac{5}{8}$ (iii) $\frac{1}{5}\times\frac{2}{3}$ (iv) $\frac{3}{5}$ of $\frac{3}{4}$

Solution

(i) $\frac{1}{3}+\frac{2}{5}=\frac{5(1)+3(2)}{15}$

$=\frac{5+6}{15}$

$=\frac{11}{15}$

(ii) $\frac{3}{4}-\frac{5}{8}=\frac{2(3)-1(5)}{8}$

$=\frac{6-5}{8}$

$=\frac{1}{8}$

(iii) $\frac{1}{5}\times\frac{2}{3}=\frac{1\times 2}{5\times 3}$

$=\frac{2}{15}$

(iv) $\frac{3}{5}$ of $\frac{3}{4}=\frac{3}{5}\times\frac{3}{4}$

$=\frac{3\times 3}{5\times 4}$

$=\frac{9}{20}$

Worked Example 3.10

How many strips of ribbon, each $2\frac{1}{2}$ cm long, can be cut from a roll of ribbon $32\frac{1}{2}$ cm in length?

Solution

We need to find the number of $2\frac{1}{2}$ cm lengths in $32\frac{1}{2}$ cm, i.e. $32\frac{1}{2} \div 2\frac{1}{2}$.

Step 1

Find the reciprocal of the fraction by which you are dividing:

$2\frac{1}{2} = \frac{5}{2}$

The reciprocal of $\frac{5}{2}$ is $\frac{2}{5}$.

The reciprocal of a fraction is found by turning the fraction upside down.

For example, the reciprocal of $\frac{11}{12}$ is $\frac{12}{11}$.

Step 2

To divide by a fraction, we multiply by its reciprocal:

Therefore, $32\frac{1}{2} \div 2\frac{1}{2} = \frac{65}{2} \div \frac{5}{2}$

$= \frac{65}{2} \times \frac{2}{5}$

$= \frac{65 \times 2}{2 \times 5}$

$= \frac{130}{10}$

$= 13$

There are 13 strips.

Exercise 3.3

1. Evaluate each of the following, without using a calculator:
   (i) $\frac{2}{3} + \frac{5}{12}$
   (ii) $\frac{3}{5} - \frac{1}{10}$
   (iii) $\frac{2}{9} + \frac{7}{12}$
   (iv) $5\frac{3}{4} - 3\frac{1}{8}$
   (v) $5\frac{1}{6} + 6\frac{3}{8}$
   (vi) $3\frac{1}{2} - 1\frac{3}{4}$

2. Express each of the following as a single fraction in its simplest form:
   (i) $\frac{1}{5} \times \frac{2}{3}$
   (ii) $\frac{5}{6} \times \frac{1}{4}$
   (iii) $\frac{3}{5} \times \frac{3}{4}$
   (iv) $2\frac{3}{7} \times \frac{7}{15}$
   (v) $5\frac{1}{4} \times 1\frac{3}{7}$
   (vi) $2\frac{5}{8} \times 1\frac{1}{6}$

3. Evaluate each of the following and write the answer as a single fraction in its simplest form:
   (i) $\frac{1}{6} \div \frac{2}{3}$
   (ii) $3\frac{1}{9} \div 2\frac{1}{3}$
   (iii) $\frac{6}{25} \div \frac{9}{10}$
   (iv) $28\frac{1}{2} \div 2\frac{3}{8}$

4. A ball bearing weighs $1\frac{1}{4}$ g. How many ball bearings weigh a total of 35 g?

5. A householder burns $17\frac{3}{4}$ kg of coal every week during the winter months.
   (i) How much coal will he burn during the month of December? (31 days in December)
   (ii) How many weeks does it take to burn $97\frac{5}{8}$ kg of coal?

6. John was given $\frac{1}{3}$ of the 84 bars in a jar.
   He ate $\frac{3}{4}$ of the bars that he was given.
   How many bars did John eat?

7. Jenny has finished the third day of a six day hike. If she has completed $\frac{3}{7}$ of the hike's total distance of 336 km, how many kilometres per day must she average for the remainder of her trip?

8. Nessa is 120 cm tall.
   If John is $\frac{4}{3}$ of the height of Nessa and Paul is $\frac{5}{4}$ of the height of John, how tall is Paul?

3.5 Decimals and Irrational Numbers

Consider the decimal 0.352. This number is the sum of the fractions $\frac{3}{10} + \frac{5}{100} + \frac{2}{1{,}000}$.

Consider two types of decimal: terminating decimals and recurring decimals.

Terminating Decimals

A number such as 0.3456 is called a **terminating decimal**. It is called terminating because it terminates (or ends) after four decimal places. This number can be written as the sum $\frac{3}{10} + \frac{4}{100} + \frac{5}{1,000} + \frac{6}{10,000}$.

As you can see, all the denominators are powers of 10.

Examples of fractions that are terminating decimals are $\frac{2}{5}$, $\frac{3}{4}$ and $\frac{5}{16}$.

$\frac{2}{5} = 0.4$ $\qquad$ $\frac{3}{4} = 0.75$ $\qquad$ $\frac{5}{16} = 0.3125$

Worked Example 3.11

Write 0.8154 as the sum of four fractions.

Solution

$$0.8154 = \frac{8}{10} + \frac{1}{100} + \frac{5}{1,000} + \frac{4}{10,000}$$

Recurring Decimals

A decimal such as 0.353535..., which contains an infinite number of digits and where the digits form a pattern, is called a **recurring** or **repeating decimal**.

Any rational number whose denominator's prime factors are not just 2 or 5 are recurring decimals.

Examples of fractions that are recurring decimals are $\frac{1}{3}$, $\frac{2}{9}$ and $\frac{5}{13}$.

$\frac{1}{3} = 0.333333...$ $\qquad$ $\frac{2}{9} = 0.222222...$ $\qquad$ $\frac{5}{13} = 0.384615384615...$

The **dot notation** is often used to represent a recurring decimal. In the case where one digit repeats, just one dot is used. For example, 0.222... can be written as $0.\dot{2}$.

Otherwise, the dots go over the first digit of the block to be repeated and the last digit of the block to be repeated. For example, $0.8\dot{9}1\dot{7} = 0.8917917...$

All rational numbers are either recurring decimals or terminating decimals. You can use your calculator to convert rational numbers to decimals: simply divide the numerator by the denominator.

Examples: $\frac{7}{8} = 7 \div 8 = 0.875$ $\qquad$ $\frac{8}{15} = 8 \div 15 = 0.5333... = 0.5\dot{3}$

Rounding

Worked Example 3.12

Write the following correct to one decimal place: (i) 2.57 (ii) 39.32

Solution

(i) 2.57

When rounding to **one decimal place**, we look at the **second number after the decimal point**. If this number is 5 or greater, we will round up. With 2.57, as 7 is the second number after the decimal point, we round up to 2.6.

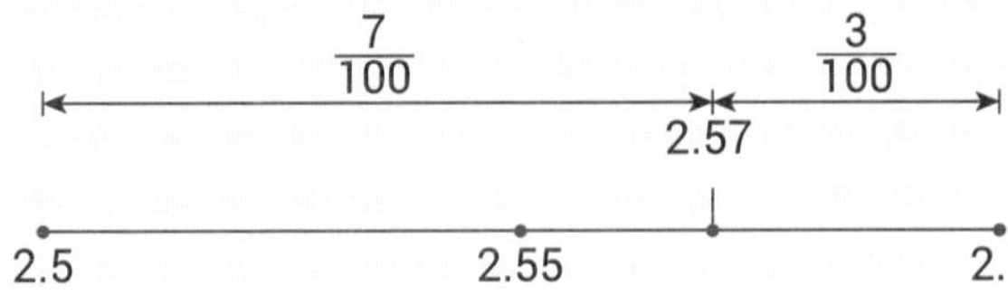

Answer = 2.6

As 2.57 is $\frac{3}{100}$ from 2.6 and $\frac{7}{100}$ from 2.5, we round up to 2.6 (it is nearer to 2.6 than 2.5).

(ii) 39.32

Here, the second number after the decimal point is 2, which is less than 5. Therefore, the number rounded to one decimal place is 39.3.

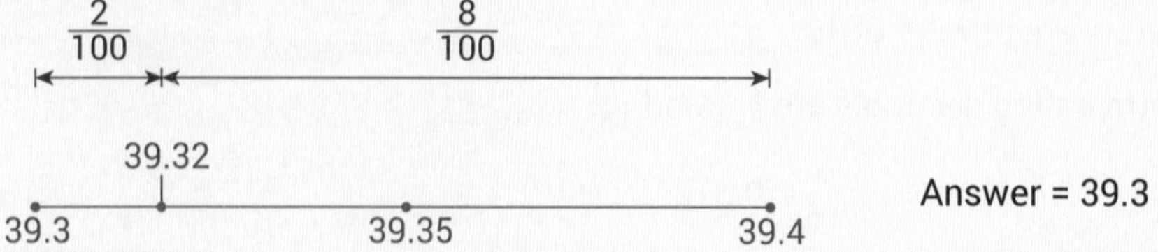

Answer = 39.3

As 39.32 is $\frac{2}{100}$ from 39.3 and $\frac{8}{100}$ from 39.4, we round down to 39.3 (it is nearer to 39.3 than 39.4).

Significant Figures

We do not always need detailed answers to problems. Sometimes an approximation is sufficient. One method of approximating answers is to round off using significant figures.

With the number 473,258, the 4 is the most significant figure, because it tells us that the number is 4 hundred thousand and something. It follows that the 7 is the next most significant and so on.

Worked Example 3.13

Correct the following numbers to two significant figures:

(i) 3.67765 (ii) 61,343 (iii) 0.00356

Solution

(i) 3.67765

The **first significant figure** in a number is the **first non-zero digit in the number**. In this number, 3 is the first significant figure. It tells us the number is 3 units and something. We need to correct to two significant figures, so we look at the third significant figure. If this number is 5 or greater, we round up the second figure. The third figure is 7, so the corrected number is 3.7.

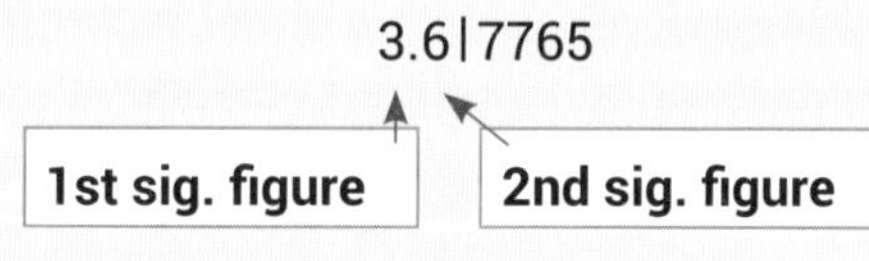

Answer = 3.7

(ii) 61,343

61,|343
1st sig. figure
2nd sig. figure

Here, the third figure is 3, which is less than 5. Therefore, the rounded number is 61,000.

Note that all other figures after the rounded figure change to zero.

Answer = 61,000

(iii) 0.00356

The first significant figure here is 3, telling us that the number is 3 thousandths and something.

The third significant figure is 6. Therefore, the rounded number is 0.0036.

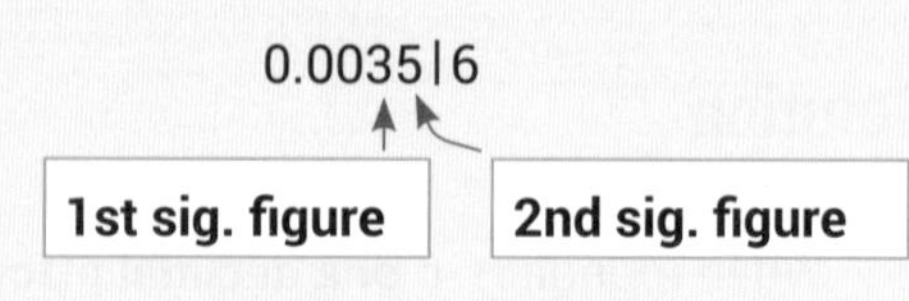

Answer = 0.0036

- Leading zeros are not significant figures. For example, 0.0053 has two significant figures, 5 and 3.
- Zeros that appear between two non-zero figures **are** significant. For example, 503.25 has five significant figures.

Worked Example 3.14

By rounding appropriately, estimate the value of the following expression:

$$\frac{\sqrt{85} \times 5.276}{1.01 \times 14.79}$$

Use your calculator to find the value of the expression to two decimal places.

Solution

$$\frac{\sqrt{85} \times 5.276}{1.01 \times 14.79} \approx \frac{\sqrt{81} \times 5}{1 \times 15}$$

$$= \frac{9 \times 5}{15}$$

$$= \frac{45}{15}$$

$\therefore$ Estimate = 3

On the calculator, the answer 3.2563... is displayed

≈ 3.26

Irrational Numbers

In the right-angled triangle shown, the value for x can be found using the theorem of Pythagoras. Here is the solution:

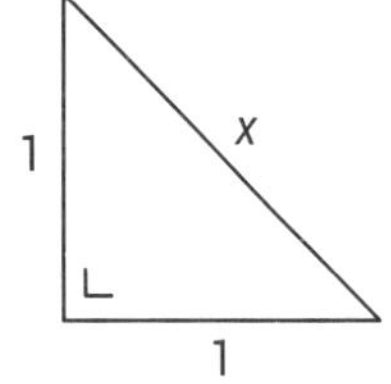

$$x^2 = 1^2 + 1^2$$

$$x^2 = 1 + 1$$

$$x^2 = 2$$

$$x = \sqrt{2} \quad (\text{as } x > 0)$$

Can $\sqrt{2}$ be written as a ratio of integers? This problem preoccupied the ancient Greek mathematicians for many years. Around 500 BC, Hippasus, a follower of Pythagoras, proved that $\sqrt{2}$ could not be written as a ratio of integers. Pythagoras, who believed that all numbers were rational, was so enraged by this proof that he supposedly had Hippasus thrown overboard from a ship and Hippasus subsequently drowned.

Hippasus, a follower of Pythagoras

Numbers that cannot be written as a ratio of integers are called **irrational numbers**. $\sqrt{2}$ was the first known irrational number.

An **irrational number** is a number that cannot be written in the form $\frac{a}{b}$, where a is an integer and b is a non-zero integer, i.e. an irrational number is a number that cannot be written as a ratio of integers.

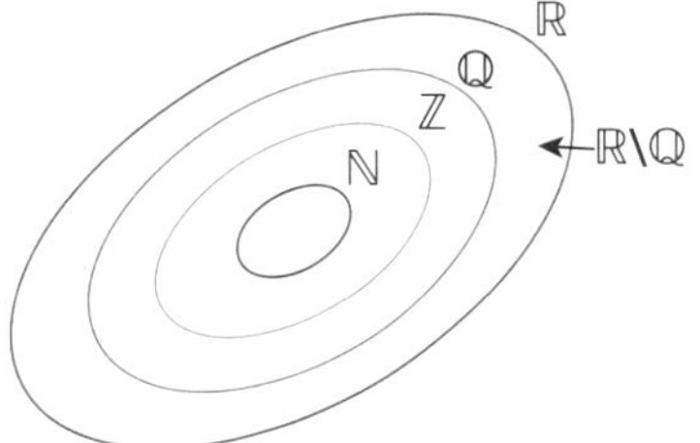

While $\sqrt{2}$ cannot be written as a fraction, it is possible to find an approximation for $\sqrt{2}$. A calculator gives the approximation $\sqrt{2} = 1.414213562$, but this decimal in fact goes on forever with no pattern or repetition. π is another example of an irrational number.

Any irrational number, when written as a decimal, is non-terminating and non-recurring.

The rational numbers together with the irrational numbers make up the **Real Number System**.

Since every real number is either rational (Q) or irrational, the set of irrationals is denoted by $R \backslash Q$.

Worked Example 3.15

Using a calculator, evaluate the following to four decimal places:

(i) $\sqrt{3}$ (ii) $\sqrt{14}$

Solution

(i) $\sqrt{3} = 1.7320508... \approx 1.7321$

(ii) $\sqrt{14} = 3.741657... \approx 3.7417$

Exercise 3.4

1. Using a calculator, evaluate the following to four decimal places:
   (i) $\sqrt{5}$ (iii) $\sqrt{17}$
   (ii) $\sqrt{8}$ (iv) $\sqrt{19}$

2. Evaluate, without the use of a calculator:
   (i) $(\sqrt{2})^2$ (iv) $(\sqrt{15})^2$
   (ii) $(\sqrt{11})^2$ (v) $(3\sqrt{5})^2$
   (iii) $(\sqrt{3})^2$ (vi) $(2\sqrt{13})^2$

3. Write each of the following correct to three decimal places:
   (i) $3 + \sqrt{2}$ (iii) $2\sqrt{7}$
   (ii) $5 - \sqrt{5}$ (iv) $8 - 3\sqrt{3}$

4. Write these numbers correct to one significant figure:
   (i) 45.28 (iv) 6,981
   (ii) 7.587 (v) 5,965
   (iii) 18,254 (vi) 9,987

5. Write these numbers correct to two significant figures:
   (i) 0.00894 (vi) 0.000048
   (ii) 0.0215 (vii) 957,444
   (iii) 0.0023 (viii) 0.238
   (iv) 0.000000852 (ix) 0.000912
   (v) 2.000045 (x) 0.00000008

6. (i) Write 4.78 correct to the nearest whole number.
   (ii) Write 6.19 correct to the nearest whole number.
   (iii) Write 10.31 correct to the nearest whole number.
   (iv) Using your answers from parts (i) to (iii), estimate the value of:
   $$\frac{4.78 \times 6.19}{10.31}$$
   (v) Calculate to four decimal places (using your calculator):
   $$\frac{4.78 \times 6.19}{10.31}$$

7. By rounding appropriately estimate:
   (i) $\dfrac{\sqrt{68} \times 15.2}{12.54}$
   (ii) $\dfrac{9.3 \times 2.6 \times 8.7}{\sqrt{10} \times \sqrt{15.8}}$
   (iii) $\dfrac{\sqrt{38} \times 5.2}{\sqrt{3.9} \times 15.34}$

8. Using your calculator, evaluate parts (i) to (iii) in Question 7 to four decimal places.

9. (i) Place the following numbers in order, starting with the smallest:
   $\frac{3}{2}$ 1.4 $\sqrt{2}$
   (ii) Which one of the following is **not** a rational number? Explain your answer.
   $3\frac{1}{7}$ 3.142 $\frac{22}{7}$ π

10. By putting the smallest number first, place the following numbers in order of magnitude:
    $\frac{10}{7}$ $\sqrt{2}$ $\frac{7}{2\sqrt{6}}$ $(1.19)^2$

11. (i) The columns in the table below represent the following sets of numbers: Natural numbers (N), Integers (Z), Rational numbers (Q), Irrational numbers ($R \backslash Q$) and Real numbers (R). Complete the table by writing either '**Yes**' or '**No**' into each box indicating whether each of the numbers
    $\sqrt{5}$, 8, −4, $3\frac{1}{2}$, $\frac{3\pi}{4}$
    is or is not an element of each.
    (One box has already been filled in. The '**Yes**' indicates that the number 8 is an element of the set of Real numbers, R).

Number/Set	N	Z	Q	$R \backslash Q$	R
$\sqrt{5}$					
8					**Yes**
−4					
$3\frac{1}{2}$					
$\frac{3\pi}{4}$					

    (ii) In the case of $\sqrt{5}$ explain your choice in relation to the set of Irrational numbers ($R \backslash Q$) (i.e. give a reason for writing either 'Yes' or 'No').

REAL NUMBERS

3.6 Scientific Notation

When doing calculations, scientists often use very large numbers or very small numbers. For example, the speed of light is about 300,000,000 metres per second, whilst the radius of a hydrogen atom is 0.0000000000529 metres.

Very large or very small numbers can be awkward to write down. So, scientists use **scientific notation** to write down these numbers.

A positive number written in **scientific notation** is of the form $a \times 10^n$, where $1 \leqslant a < 10$ and $n \in Z$.

Another name for scientific notation is **standard form**.

Worked Example 3.16

Write the following numbers in scientific notation:

(i) 725,000,000,000 (ii) 980,000 (iii) 0.0000056 (iv) 0.000000034

Solution

(i) First, note that dividing a number by 10^n, where $n \in N$, moves the decimal point n places to the left.

For example, $\frac{144.25}{10^2} = 1.4425$ (Decimal point moves two places to the left)

$$725{,}000{,}000{,}000 = \frac{725{,}000{,}000{,}000}{10^{11}} \times 10^{11}$$

$$= 7.25 \times 10^{11}$$

(ii) $980{,}000 = \frac{980{,}000}{10^5} \times 10^5 = 9.8 \times 10^5$

(iii) Note that dividing a number by 10^n, where n is a negative integer, moves the decimal point $-n$ places to the right.

For example, $\frac{0.00146}{10^{-3}} = 0.00146 \times \frac{1}{10^{-3}}$

$= 0.00146 \times 10^3$ (Rules of indices)

$= 1.46$ (Decimal point moves three places to the right)

$$0.0000056 = \frac{0.0000056}{10^{-6}} \times 10^{-6}$$

$$= 5.6 \times 10^{-6}$$

(iv) $0.000000034 = \frac{0.000000034}{10^{-8}} \times 10^{-8}$

$$= 3.4 \times 10^{-8}$$

Worked Example 3.17

According to scientists, the Earth's mass is 5.98×10^{24} kilograms. The mass of the Sun is 1.989×10^{30} kilograms.

(i) What is the difference between the mass of the Sun and the mass of the Earth? Give your answer in scientific notation and to six decimal places.

(ii) How many times greater is the mass of the Sun than the mass of the Earth? Answer to the nearest whole number.

Solution

(i) $1.989 \times 10^{30} - 5.98 \times 10^{24}$

$= 1{,}989{,}000 \times 10^{24} - 5.98 \times 10^{24}$

$= 1{,}988{,}994.02 \times 10^{24}$

$= 1.98894402 \times 10^{30}$ (Dividing 1,988,994 by 10^6 and multiplying 10^{24} by 10^6)

$= 1.988994 \times 10^{30}$ kg (To 6 d.p.)

Answer = 1.988994×10^{30} kg

(ii) $\dfrac{1.989 \times 10^{30}}{5.98 \times 10^{24}} = 332{,}609$ (To nearest whole number)

Answer = 332,609

So the mass of the Sun ≈ 332,609 × mass of the Earth.

Exercise 3.5

1. Write these numbers in scientific notation:

(i) 3,800
(ii) 75,000
(iii) 240
(iv) 848,000
(v) 5,376,000
(vi) 0.01
(vii) 0.001
(viii) 0.000032
(ix) 0.0001
(x) 0.0012
(xi) 0.00003
(xii) 532,600

2. Write these as decimal numbers:

(i) 2.65×10^2
(ii) 4.53×10^{-3}
(iii) 7.2×10^6
(iv) 1.7×10^{-5}
(v) 3×10^2
(vi) 4×10^{-2}
(vii) 2.64×10^7
(viii) 7.612×10^3
(ix) 2.76×10^8
(x) 3.02×10^{-9}

3. Write the following numbers in the form $a \times 10^n$, where $1 \leqslant a < 10$ and $n \in Z$:

(i) 0.000036 (ii) 0.0005613 (iii) 0.0345 (iv) 0.00063 (v) 0.0078

4. The following numbers are written in scientific notation. Rewrite the numbers in ordinary form.

(i) 1.5×10^{-3} (ii) 2.54×10^{-4} (iii) 3.5×10^{-5} (iv) 6.67×10^{-6} (v) 8.15×10^{-2}

5. The speed of light is 3×10^8 ms^{-1}. If the Sun is 1.5×10^{11} m from the Earth, how many seconds does it take light to reach the Earth? Express your answer in scientific notation.

6. One of the closest stars to our solar system is Alpha Centauri. It is 4.047×10^{13} km from Earth. A light year is the distance that light travels in one year, which is approximately 9.5×10^{12} km. How many light years from Earth is Alpha Centauri?

7. A computer is able to process 803,000 bits of data in 0.00000525 seconds. Find the rate of processing the data in bits/sec. Give your answer in scientific notation correct to 3 significant figures.

8. - The Earth has a diameter of 1.276×10^{7} m.
   - A plant cell has a diameter of 1.276×10^{-6} m.

   How many times bigger than the diameter of a plant cell is the diameter of the Earth?

3.7 Order of Operations

In maths, the order of operations is the order in which the arithmetic operations of addition, subtraction, multiplication and division are done. It is important to have order, otherwise answers will differ.

For example, is $2 + 3 \times 5 = 17$ or 25?

BIMDAS

We can use the guide shown to help us remember the order in which operations are carried out.

These letters stand for **B**rackets, **I**ndices, **M**ultiplication, **D**ivision, **A**ddition and **S**ubtraction. We start at the top of the triangle and work down.
Therefore, **B**rackets come first, then **I**ndices (powers and roots), **M**ultiplication/**D**ivision and finally **A**ddition/**S**ubtraction:

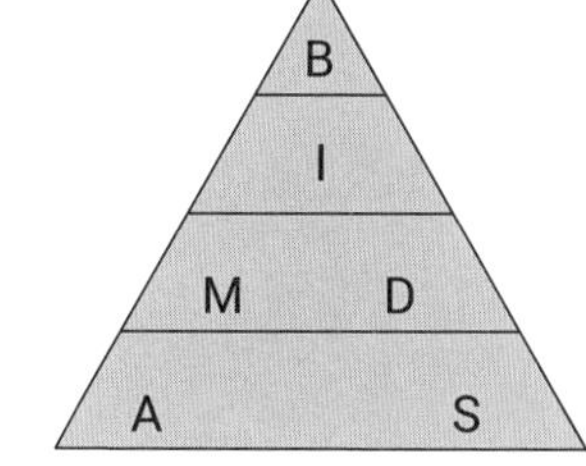

B → **I** → **MD** → **AS**

For MD and AS, read left to right.

Worked Example 3.18

Find the value of each of the following:

(i) $(2 + 5)^2 - 8 \div 2 + 3 \times 6$ (ii) $\left(2\frac{1}{3} + \frac{1}{6}\right)^2 - \frac{1}{2} \div \frac{3}{4} + \frac{5}{6} \times \frac{2}{3}$

Solution

(i) $(2 + 5)^2 - 8 \div 2 + 3 \times 6$

$= 7^2 - 8 \div 2 + 3 \times 6$ (Brackets)

$= 49 - 8 \div 2 + 3 \times 6$ (Indices)

$= 49 - 4 + 18$ (Multiplication/Division)

$= 63$ (Addition/Subtraction)

(ii) $\left(2\frac{1}{3} + \frac{1}{6}\right)^2 - \frac{1}{2} \div \frac{3}{4} + \frac{5}{6} \times \frac{2}{3}$

$\left(2\frac{1}{2}\right)^2 - \frac{1}{2} \times \frac{4}{3} + \frac{5}{6} \times \frac{2}{3}$ (Brackets)

$= \frac{25}{4} - \frac{1}{2} \times \frac{4}{3} + \frac{5}{6} \times \frac{2}{3}$ (Indices)

$= \frac{25}{4} - \frac{2}{3} + \frac{5}{9}$ (Multiplication/Division)

$= \frac{225}{36} - \frac{24}{36} + \frac{20}{36}$

$= \frac{221}{36}$

$= 6\frac{5}{36}$

Exercise 3.6

1. Calculate each of the following:
   (i) $5 + 5$
   (ii) $5 - 5$
   (iii) 5×5
   (iv) $5 \div 5$
   (v) 5^3

2. Calculate each of the following:
   (i) $12^2 + 13^2$
   (ii) $12^3 + 13^2$
   (iii) $13^2 + 14^2$
   (iv) $1^2 + 1^{10}$

3. Calculate each of the following:
   (i) $1^2 \times 3^2$
   (ii) $5^2 \times 2^2$
   (iii) $5^3 \div 5^2$
   (iv) $4^3 - 2^2$

4. Calculate each of the following:
   (i) $2\left(\frac{7}{9} - \frac{2}{3}\right)$
   (ii) $5\left(\frac{3}{4} + \frac{4}{9}\right) + 3\left(\frac{2}{7} + \frac{5}{9}\right)$
   (iii) $3\left(\frac{7}{4} - \frac{5}{12}\right)^2 + 5(5 - 2)^3$
   (iv) $2(5 - 2)^2 - 3\left(1\frac{1}{3} - \frac{2}{9}\right)^2$

5. Calculate each of the following:
   (i) $\frac{2 \times 4 + 3}{(6 + 5)}$
   (ii) $\frac{4 + 8 \times 3}{12 - 5}$
   (iii) $\frac{3(5 - 2)^2 - 3(4 \div 2)^2 + 5(3)^3}{(5 - 2)^2}$
   (iv) $\frac{7(6 - 2)^2 + 3(10 \div 2)^2 + 3}{(8 - 3)^2}$

Revision Exercises

1. (a) List the first six multiples of each of the following:
   (i) 5
   (ii) 2
   (iii) 12
   (iv) 13

   (b) Write down all the factors of each of the following:
   (i) 70
   (ii) 80
   (iii) 56
   (iv) 128

   (c) Write the following numbers as products of prime factors:
   (i) 128
   (ii) 204
   (iii) 748
   (iv) 2,652

2. Express each of the following numbers as the product of prime factors, and hence, or otherwise, find the LCM and HCF of each pair:
   (i) 68 and 102
   (ii) 69 and 123
   (iii) 104 and 351
   (iv) 123 and 615

3. Estimate the following expressions and then use your calculator to evaluate each expression correct to four decimal places:
   (i) $\frac{3.76 \times 7.21}{27.92}$
   (ii) $\frac{\sqrt{26} \times 5.2 + 7}{(1.8)^5}$
   (iii) $\frac{\sqrt{37} \times (3.8 + 0.98)}{\sqrt{4.1} \times 15.34}$

4. Write these numbers correct to two significant figures.
   (i) 852,233
   (ii) 0.134
   (iii) 2.00062
   (iv) 0.0000543
   (v) 652,494
   (vi) 0.000814

5. The table below shows the fraction by which the population of a particular town increased each year over a three-year period.

Year	Fractional increase
2015	$\frac{1}{10}$
2016	$\frac{1}{25}$
2017	$\frac{1}{50}$

At the start of the year 2015, the population of the town was 50,000.

(i) Find the population of the town at the end of the year 2017.

(ii) By what fraction did the population of the town increase over the period 2015–2017?

6. (a) (i) Find the values of the primes p and q, if $p^3 \times 13 \times q = 1{,}768$.

(ii) Find the values of the primes m and n, where $m < n$ and $24 \times m \times n = 3{,}192$.

(iii) Using your answers to parts (i) and (ii), find the HCF and LCM of 1,768 and 3,192.

(b) Evaluate the following, giving your answer in scientific notation:

$$\frac{3\frac{3}{7} \times \left(2\frac{2}{5} + 1\frac{1}{10}\right)}{3 \times 10^4}$$

7. Members of a club had two weeks to raise money for their club. The president of the club agreed to contribute an extra 5 cent for every euro raised by the members.

(i) In the first week, the members raised €2,700. How much did the president add to this in the first week?

(ii) In the second week, the total raised by the members and the president was €3,675. How much did the members raise in the second week?

8. John thinks that he has a method for finding **all** prime numbers.
He says that if he uses the formulae in the table below, he will generate the prime numbers.
He also says that these formulae will generate **only** the prime numbers.

(i) Complete the table.

p	$6p + 1$	$6p + 5$
0	1	5
1		
2		
3		
4		
5		

(ii) Give a reason why his first claim is not correct.

(iii) Give a reason why his second claim is not correct.

Exam Questions

1. (a) Explain what a *prime number* is.

(b) Express 2652 as a product of prime numbers.

(c) The number $2^{61} - 1$ is a prime number. Using your calculator, or otherwise, express its value, correct to two significant figures, in the form $a \times 10^n$, where $1 \leqslant a < 10$ and $n \in N$.

(d) Use your answer to part **(c)** to state how many digits there are in the exact value $2^{61} - 1$.

SEC Leaving Certificate Ordinary Level, Paper 1, 2011

2. Let $a = \sqrt{2}$.

(a) For each of the numbers in the table below, tick (✓) the correct box to say whether it is *rational* or *irrational*.

Number	Rational	Irrational
a		
$a - 1$		
$(-a)^2$		
$(a - 2)^2$		
$1 + a^2$		

(b) Show the following numbers on a number line.

$a, \quad -a, \quad \sqrt{a}, \quad a^{-2}$

SEC Leaving Certificate Ordinary Level, Paper 1, 2012

3. (a) The mean distance from the Earth to the Sun is 149,597,871 km. Write this number in the form $a \times 10^n$, where $1 \leqslant a < 10$ and $n \in Z$, correct to two significant figures.

(b) (i) Write each of the numbers below as a decimal correct to two decimal places.

	A	B	C	D	E	F	G
Number	2.1	$\sqrt{5}$	$\frac{243}{85}$	tan 70°	$\frac{3\pi}{4}$	250%	$\left(1+\frac{1}{10}\right)^{10}$
Decimal Number	2.10						

(ii) Mark 5 of the numbers in the table on the number line below and label each number clearly.

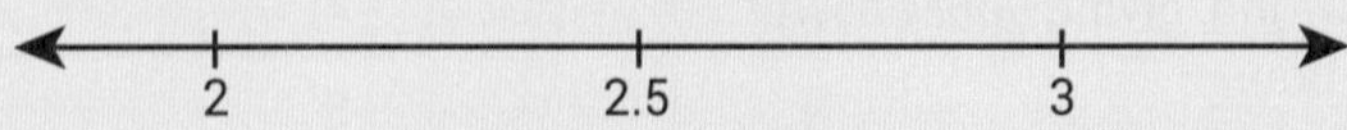

SEC Leaving Certificate Ordinary Level, Paper 1, 2013

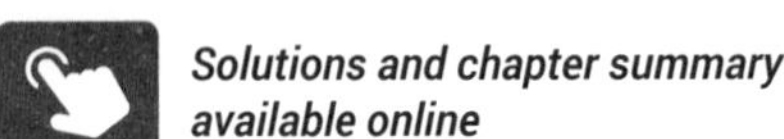

Solutions and chapter summary available online

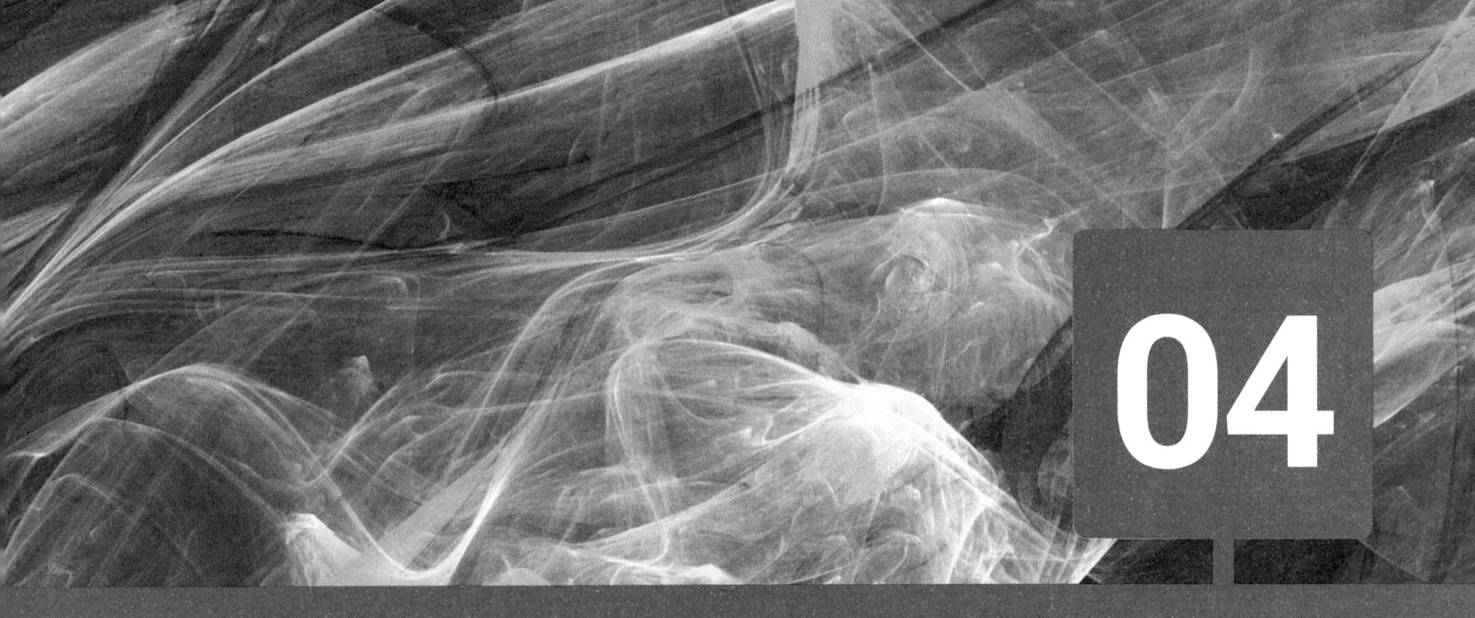

Indices

In this chapter you will learn about:

- The laws of indices
  - (1) $a^p \times a^q = a^{p+q}$
  - (2) $a^p \div a^q = a^{p-q}$
  - (3) $(a^p)^q = a^{pq}$
  - (4) $a^0 = 1$
  - (5) $a^{\frac{1}{q}} = \sqrt[q]{a}$
  - (6) $a^{\frac{p}{q}} = \sqrt[q]{a^p} = (\sqrt[q]{a})^p$
  - (7) $a^{-p} = \dfrac{1}{a^p}$
  - (8) $(ab)^p = a^p b^p$
  - (9) $\left(\dfrac{a}{b}\right)^p = \dfrac{a^p}{b^p}$
- Solving equations with x as an index
- The laws of surds
  - (1) $\sqrt{a}\sqrt{b} = \sqrt{ab}$
  - (2) $\dfrac{\sqrt{a}}{\sqrt{b}} = \sqrt{\dfrac{a}{b}}$

You should remember...

- Rules of signs for addition of integers
- Rules of signs for multiplication of integers

Key words

- Index
- Power
- Exponent
- Base
- Surd

4.1 Numbers in Index Form

Historians believe that the game of chess originated in India around the sixth century AD. There is an interesting fable from that time about the invention of the game.

The story goes that the inventor of the game was asked by the emperor to name his prize. The inventor told his master that he would like just one grain of rice on the first square of the chessboard, and double the number of grains on the first square to be placed on the second square. Then, double the number of grains on the second square to be placed on the third square, and so on.

This seemed to the emperor to be a modest request, so he called for his servants to bring the rice. How surprised he was to find that the rice quickly covered the chessboard and then filled the palace!

The table below shows the number of grains on each of the first 10 squares.

Square	1	2	3	4	5	6	7	8	9	10
Number of rice grains	1	2	4	8	16	32	64	128	256	512
Index form	2^0	2^1	2^2	2^3	2^4	2^5	2^6	2^7	2^8	2^9

How many grains of rice would be on the last square? In index form, there would be 2^{63} grains on the last square. This number contains 19 digits, so it is simpler to write it in index form.

A number in index form is of the form b^n. We call b the **base** and n the **index**, **power** or **exponent**.

Negative Bases to Even and Odd Powers

Consider the number $(-2)^3$. Is this a positive or a negative number?

$(-2)^3 = (-2) \times (-2) \times (-2) = -8$ (a negative number)

Is $(-2)^4$ positive or negative?

$(-2)^4 = (-2) \times (-2) \times (-2) \times (-2) = 16$ (a positive number)

Raising a negative number to a power requires careful use of brackets, i.e. in squaring −7 you need to write $(-7)^2$.
So $(-7)^2 = (-7)(-7) = 49$. On the other hand, $-7^2 = -(7)(7) = -49$.

4.2 Laws 1–4 of Indices

LAW 1 Multiplication

$2^3 \times 2^2 = (2 \times 2 \times 2) \times (2 \times 2)$

$= 2 \times 2 \times 2 \times 2 \times 2$

$= 2^5$

Similarly, $x^3 \times x^2 = x^5$ (Add the indices)

Law 1 $a^p \times a^q = a^{p+q}$

LAW 2 Division

$\dfrac{3^4}{3^2} = \dfrac{\overset{1}{\cancel{3}} \times \overset{1}{\cancel{3}} \times 3 \times 3}{\underset{1}{\cancel{3}} \times \underset{1}{\cancel{3}}}$

$= 3^2$

Similarly, $\dfrac{x^4}{x^2} = x^2$ (Subtract the indices)

Law 2 $\dfrac{a^p}{a^q} = a^{p-q}$

LAW 3 Index Raised to an Index

$(2^2)^3 = 2^2 \times 2^2 \times 2^2$

$= 2^4 \times 2^2$ (Law 1)

$= 2^6$ (Law 1)

Similarly, $(x^2)^3 = x^6$ (Multiply the indices)

Law 3 $(a^p)^q = a^{pq}$

LAW 4 Any Non-Zero Number to the Power of Zero

$\dfrac{5^6}{5^6} = 1$ and $\dfrac{5^6}{5^6} = 5^0$ (Law 2)

$\therefore 5^0 = 1$

Similarly, if $x \neq 0$, then $x^0 = 1$

Law 4 $a^0 = 1, a \neq 0$

Worked Example 4.1

Simplify the following, giving the answer in index notation:

(i) $(-2)^3$

(ii) $(-3)^4$

Solution

(i) $(-2)^3 = -2^3$ $\quad (-2 \times -2 \times -2 = -8 = -2^3)$

(ii) $(-3)^4 = 3^4$ $\quad (-3 \times -3 \times -3 \times -3 = 81 = 3^4)$

A negative number raised to an odd power gives a negative answer.

A negative number raised to an even power gives a positive answer.

Worked Example 4.2

Use the laws of indices to write each of the following in the form a^m, where a and $m \in N$:

(i) $3^4 \times 3^6$

(ii) $5^8 \div 5^3$

(iii) $(2^2)^5$

Solution

(i) $3^4 \times 3^6 = 3^{4+6}$ (Law 1)

$= 3^{10}$

(ii) $5^8 \div 5^3 = 5^{8-3}$ (Law 2)

$= 5^5$

(iii) $(2^2)^5 = 2^{10}$ (Law 3)

Worked Example 4.3

Simplify the following, giving each answer in index notation: (i) $\dfrac{3^3 \times 3^5}{3^4}$ (ii) $\dfrac{4^5(4^2)^3}{4^3}$

Solution

(i) $\dfrac{3^3 \times 3^5}{3^4} = \dfrac{3^{3+5}}{3^4}$ (Law 1)

$= \dfrac{3^8}{3^4}$

$= 3^{8-4}$ (Law 2)

$= 3^4$

(ii) $\dfrac{4^5(4^2)^3}{4^3} = \dfrac{4^5 \times 4^{2 \times 3}}{4^3}$ (Law 3)

$= \dfrac{4^5 \times 4^6}{4^3}$

$= \dfrac{4^{5+6}}{4^3}$ (Law 1)

$= \dfrac{4^{11}}{4^3}$

$= 4^{11-3}$ (Law 2)

$= 4^8$

Exercise 4.1

1. Without using a calculator, evaluate each of the following:

   (i) 5^2 (ii) 2^3 (iii) $(-5)^2$ (iv) $(-6)^3$ (v) $(-2)^4$ (vi) $(-3)^1$ (vii) $(-4)^2$ (viii) $(8)^0$

2. If $a^n = b$, find the values of a, b and n in each of the following cases:

   (i) a is the first odd prime number and n is the number of faces on a die.

   (ii) a is the only even prime number and b is the number of squares on a chessboard.

   (iii) b is the number of metres in a kilometre and n is the number of divisors of 4.

3. In the tables below, match each number in Column A with one number in Column B.

Column A
3^4
$(-2)^8$
$(-6)^8$
$-(-4)^4$
$-(6)^8$
$(-4)^4$
$-(-3)^3$
$(-5)^3$
$(-2)^4$

Column B
-4^4
-6^8
-125
27
6^8
16
81
4^4
256

4. Copy and complete the following tables:

(i)

Index notation	2	2^2	2^3	2^4	2^5	2^6	2^7
Whole number					32		

(ii)

Index notation	3	3^2	3^3	3^4	3^5	3^6
Whole number					243	

(iii)

Index notation	4	4^2	4^3	4^4	4^5	4^6
Whole number				256		

(iv)

Index notation	9	9^2	9^3	9^4	9^5	9^6
Whole number			729			

Using the tables above, find a value for x and a value for y in each of the following equations:

(a) $2^x = 4^y$ (b) $9^x = 3^y$

5. Use the law $a^p \times a^q = a^{p+q}$ to write the following in index notation:

(i) $5^3 \times 5^2$
(ii) $8^7 \times 8^3$
(iii) 6×6^2
(iv) $(-5)^3 \times (-5)^7$
(v) $(-2)^6 \times (-2)^3$
(vi) $\left(\frac{1}{2}\right)^7 \times \left(\frac{1}{2}\right)^5$
(vii) $\left(\frac{1}{4}\right)^6 \times \left(\frac{1}{4}\right)^5$
(viii) $\left(-\frac{1}{6}\right)^2 \times \left(-\frac{1}{6}\right)^3$
(ix) $(0.2)^3 \times (0.2)^2$
(x) $(2.4)^5 \times (2.4)^8$
(xi) $(-2.7)^4 \times (-2.7)^3$
(xii) $(-3.2)^{10} \times (-3.2)^5$

6. Use the law $\frac{a^p}{a^q} = a^{p-q}$ to write the following in index notation:

(i) $\frac{3^7}{3^6}$
(ii) $\frac{2^9}{2^3}$
(iii) $\frac{10^5}{10^2}$
(iv) $\frac{7^{12}}{7^5}$
(v) $\frac{(-12)^9}{(-12)^4}$
(vi) $\frac{(-2)^6}{(-2)^3}$
(vii) $\frac{4}{4}$
(viii) $\frac{8^3}{8^9}$
(ix) $\frac{7^2}{7^4}$
(x) $\frac{\left(-\frac{1}{2}\right)^{17}}{\left(-\frac{1}{2}\right)^{13}}$
(xi) $\frac{\left(-\frac{3}{5}\right)^{3}}{\left(-\frac{3}{5}\right)^{10}}$

7. Use the law $(a^p)^q = a^{pq}$ to simplify the following, giving each answer in index notation:

(i) $(3^3)^5$
(ii) $(6^4)^5$
(iii) $(10^5)^5$
(iv) $(4^5)^6$
(v) $(7^6)^7$
(vi) $(8^5)^3$
(vii) $(16^2)^3$
(viii) $(10^4)^9$
(ix) $(2^2)^2$
(x) $(13^9)^3$

8. Simplify the following giving each answer in index notation:

(i) $\frac{8^3 \times 8^5}{8^2}$
(ii) $\frac{7^3 \times 7^6}{7^4 \times 7^2}$
(iii) $\frac{5 \times (5^2)^4}{5^3}$
(iv) $\frac{6^3 \times (6^5)^6}{6^2 \times 6^9}$

9. Simplify the following giving each answer in index notation:

(i) $\frac{3^9 \times 3^2}{3^4}$
(ii) $\frac{4^5 \times 4^6}{4^3 \times 4^2}$
(iii) $\frac{5^9 \times 5^{12}}{(5^2)^3}$
(iv) $\frac{(5^2)^3 \times 5^6 \div 5^3}{(5^4)^2}$

4.3 Laws 5–9 of Indices

LAW 5 Roots and Fractional Indices

Consider $2^{\frac{1}{2}} \times 2^{\frac{1}{2}} = 2^{\frac{1}{2}+\frac{1}{2}}$ (Law 1)

$= 2^1$

$= 2$

So $2^{\frac{1}{2}}$ multiplied by itself gives an answer of 2.

Therefore, $\sqrt{2} = 2^{\frac{1}{2}}$

Similarly,

$5^{\frac{1}{3}} \times 5^{\frac{1}{3}} \times 5^{\frac{1}{3}} = 5^{\frac{1}{3}+\frac{1}{3}+\frac{1}{3}}$

$= 5^1$

$= 5$

So $5^{\frac{1}{3}}$ multiplied by itself three times gives an answer of 5.

Therefore, $\sqrt[3]{5} = 5^{\frac{1}{3}}$

In general $\sqrt[n]{x} = x^{\frac{1}{n}}$, where $n \in N$.

Law 5 $a^{\frac{1}{q}} = \sqrt[q]{a}$

$\sqrt[2]{a}$ is usually written as $\sqrt{a}$.

Worked Example 4.4

Use the laws of indices to evaluate each of the following:

(i) $\sqrt{25}$ (ii) $\sqrt[5]{32}$ (iii) $\sqrt[3]{1{,}000}$

Solution

(i) $\sqrt{25} = 25^{\frac{1}{2}}$ (Law 5)

$= (5^2)^{\frac{1}{2}}$

$= 5^1$ (Law 3)

$= 5$

(ii) $\sqrt[5]{32} = 32^{\frac{1}{5}}$ (Law 5)

$= (2^5)^{\frac{1}{5}}$

$= 2^1$ (Law 3)

$= 2$

(iii) $\sqrt[3]{1{,}000} = 1{,}000^{\frac{1}{3}}$ (Law 5)

$= (10^3)^{\frac{1}{3}}$

$= 10^1$ (Law 3)

$= 10$

LAW 6 Further Fractional Indices

Consider

$16^{\frac{3}{4}} = \left(16^{\frac{1}{4}}\right)^3$ (Law 3)

$= (\sqrt[4]{16})^3$ (Law 5)

$= 2^3$

$= 8$

Similarly, $x^{\frac{3}{4}} = (\sqrt[4]{x})^3$

The numerator in the power becomes the 'outside power'; the denominator in the power becomes the inside root.

Law 6 $a^{\frac{p}{q}} = \sqrt[q]{a^p} = (\sqrt[q]{a})^p$

Worked Example 4.5

Evaluate each of the following, using the law $a^{\frac{p}{q}} = \sqrt[q]{a^p} = (\sqrt[q]{a})^p$.

(i) $32^{\frac{4}{5}}$ (ii) $81^{\frac{5}{4}}$ (iii) $125^{\frac{2}{3}}$

Solution

(i) $32^{\frac{4}{5}} = (\sqrt[5]{32})^4$ (Law 6)

$= (2)^4$

$= 16$

(ii) $81^{\frac{5}{4}} = (\sqrt[4]{81})^5$ (Law 6)

$= (3)^5$

$= 243$

(iii) $125^{\frac{2}{3}} = (\sqrt[3]{125})^2$ (Law 6)

$= (5)^2$

$= 25$

LAW 7 Negative Indices

$$\frac{9^3}{9^5} = \frac{\cancel{9}^1 \times \cancel{9}^1 \times \cancel{9}^1}{\cancel{9}_1 \times \cancel{9}_1 \times \cancel{9}_1 \times 9 \times 9} = \frac{1}{9^2}$$

Also, $\frac{9^3}{9^5} = 9^{3-5}$ (Law 2)

$= 9^{-2}$

$\therefore \frac{1}{9^2} = 9^{-2}$

Similarly, $\frac{1}{x^2} = x^{-2}$

Law 7 $a^{-p} = \frac{1}{a^p}$

INDICES

Worked Example 4.6

Using the law $a^{-p} = \frac{1}{a^p}$, write each of the following in the form $\frac{1}{a^n}$, where $n \in N$:

(i) 2^{-5} (ii) 3^{-6} (iii) 4^{-2}

Solution

(i) $2^{-5} = \frac{1}{2^5}$ (ii) $3^{-6} = \frac{1}{3^6}$ (iii) $4^{-2} = \frac{1}{4^2}$

Worked Example 4.7

Evaluate each of the following:

(i) $64^{-\frac{4}{3}}$ (ii) $27^{-\frac{5}{3}}$

Solution

(i) $64^{-\frac{4}{3}} = \frac{1}{64^{\frac{4}{3}}}$ (Law 7)

$= \frac{1}{(\sqrt[3]{64})^4}$ (Law 6)

$= \frac{1}{(4)^4}$

$= \frac{1}{256}$

(ii) $27^{-\frac{5}{3}} = \frac{1}{27^{\frac{5}{3}}}$ (Law 7)

$= \frac{1}{(\sqrt[3]{27})^5}$ (Law 6)

$= \frac{1}{(3)^5}$

$= \frac{1}{243}$

LAW 8 A Product Raised to an Index

Consider

$(2 \times 3)^4 = 2 \times 3 \times 2 \times 3 \times 2 \times 3 \times 2 \times 3$

$= (2 \times 2 \times 2 \times 2) \times (3 \times 3 \times 3 \times 3)$

(Since multiplication is commutative and associative)

$\therefore (2 \times 3)^4 = 2^4 \times 3^4$

Similarly, $(xy)^4 = (x^4)(y^4)$

Law 8 $(ab)^p = a^p b^p$

LAW 9 A Quotient Raised to an Index

Consider

$\left(\frac{2}{3}\right)^4 = \frac{2}{3} \times \frac{2}{3} \times \frac{2}{3} \times \frac{2}{3}$

$= \frac{2 \times 2 \times 2 \times 2}{3 \times 3 \times 3 \times 3}$ (Rule for multiplication of fractions)

$\therefore \left(\frac{2}{3}\right)^4 = \frac{2^4}{3^4}$

Similarly, $\left(\frac{x}{y}\right)^4 = \frac{x^4}{y^4}$

Law 9 $\left(\frac{a}{b}\right)^p = \frac{a^p}{b^p}$

Worked Example 4.8

(i) Evaluate $\left(\frac{27}{1{,}000}\right)^{\frac{2}{3}}$. (ii) Hence, evaluate $\left(\frac{27}{1{,}000}\right)^{-\frac{2}{3}}$.

In each case you may not use a calculator.

Solution

(i) $\left(\frac{27}{1,000}\right)^{\frac{2}{3}} = \frac{27^{\frac{2}{3}}}{1,000^{\frac{2}{3}}}$ (Law 9)

$= \frac{(\sqrt[3]{27})^2}{(\sqrt[3]{1,000})^2}$ (Law 6)

$= \frac{3^2}{10^2}$

$= \frac{9}{100}$

(ii) $\left(\frac{27}{1,000}\right)^{-\frac{2}{3}} = \frac{1}{\left(\frac{27}{1,000}\right)^{\frac{2}{3}}}$ (Law 7)

$= \frac{1}{\left(\frac{9}{100}\right)}$ (From part (i))

$= \frac{100}{9}$ $\left(\text{Reciprocal of } \frac{9}{100}\right)$

Exercise 4.2

1. Copy and complete the following tables:

x	1	2	3	4	5	6	7	8	9	10
x^2			9						81	

x	1	4	9	16	25	36	49	64	81	100
$\sqrt{x}$						6				

2. Copy and complete the following tables:

x	1	2	3	4	5	6	7	8	9	10
x^3			27							1,000

x	1	8	27	64	125	216	343	512	729	1,000
$\sqrt[3]{x}$							7			

3. Using the law $a^{\frac{1}{q}} = \sqrt[q]{a}$ and the completed tables from Questions 1 and 2, evaluate each of the following:

(i) $100^{\frac{1}{2}}$ (iii) $216^{\frac{1}{3}}$ (v) $16^{\frac{1}{2}}$ (vii) $9^{\frac{1}{2}}$ (ix) $64^{\frac{1}{3}}$

(ii) $64^{\frac{1}{2}}$ (iv) $512^{\frac{1}{3}}$ (vi) $8^{\frac{1}{3}}$ (viii) $1,000^{\frac{1}{3}}$ (x) $36^{\frac{1}{2}}$

4. Using the law $a^{-p} = \frac{1}{a^p}$, write the following as fractions:

(i) 2^{-3} (iii) 9^{-3} (v) 6^{-2} (vii) 3^{-4} (ix) 4^{-3}

(ii) 4^{-2} (iv) 5^{-3} (vi) 7^{-2} (viii) 8^{-2} (x) 5^{-2}

5. Using the law $a^{-p} = \frac{1}{a^p}$, write the following as fractions in their simplest form:

(i) $2(5^{-3})$ (iii) $5(4^{-2})$ (v) $2(8^{-2})$ (vii) $4(2^{-4})$ (ix) $2(4^{-2})$

(ii) $3(8^{-2})$ (iv) $4(3^{-4})$ (vi) $3(7^{-2})$ (viii) $3(6^{-2})$ (x) $5(10^{-3})$

6. Without using a calculator, evaluate each of the following:

(i) $\sqrt{25}$ (ii) $\sqrt{49}$ (iii) $\sqrt[3]{27}$ (iv) $\sqrt[4]{16}$ (v) $\sqrt[5]{32}$ (vi) $\sqrt[10]{1}$ (vii) $\sqrt{36}$ (viii) $\sqrt[4]{81}$ (ix) $\sqrt[6]{64}$ (x) $\sqrt{121}$

7. Using the law $a^{\frac{p}{q}} = (\sqrt[q]{a})^p$, evaluate each of the following:

(i) $16^{\frac{1}{4}}$ (ii) $27^{\frac{2}{3}}$ (iii) $64^{\frac{2}{3}}$ (iv) $16^{\frac{3}{4}}$ (v) $100^{\frac{3}{2}}$ (vi) $125^{\frac{2}{3}}$ (vii) $16^{\frac{5}{4}}$ (viii) $81^{\frac{3}{4}}$ (ix) $9^{\frac{3}{2}}$ (x) $64^{\frac{4}{3}}$

8. Simplify the following:

(i) $(3x^2y)^3$ (ii) $(2t^{-3})^{-2}$

9. Using the laws $a^{-p} = \frac{1}{a^p}$ and $a^{\frac{p}{q}} = (\sqrt[q]{a})^p$, evaluate each of the following:

Write your answer in the form $\frac{1}{m}$, $m \in N$.

(i) $100^{-\frac{1}{2}}$ (ii) $36^{-\frac{1}{2}}$ (iii) $16^{-\frac{1}{4}}$ (iv) $9^{-\frac{3}{2}}$ (v) $81^{-\frac{3}{4}}$ (vi) $8^{-\frac{2}{3}}$ (vii) $9^{-\frac{5}{2}}$ (viii) $125^{-\frac{2}{3}}$ (ix) $16^{-\frac{5}{4}}$ (x) $100^{-\frac{5}{2}}$

10. Evaluate each of the following without using a calculator:

(i) $\left(\frac{1}{4}\right)^{\frac{1}{2}}$ (ii) $\left(\frac{1}{25}\right)^{\frac{1}{2}}$ (iii) $\left(\frac{4}{9}\right)^{\frac{1}{2}}$ (iv) $\left(\frac{81}{25}\right)^{\frac{1}{2}}$ (v) $\left(\frac{8}{27}\right)^{\frac{1}{3}}$ (vi) $\left(\frac{8}{125}\right)^{\frac{1}{3}}$ (vii) $\left(\frac{16}{81}\right)^{\frac{3}{4}}$ (viii) $\left(\frac{27}{64}\right)^{\frac{2}{3}}$

11. Use your calculator to evaluate each of the following:

(i) $\left(\frac{36}{25}\right)^{-\frac{1}{2}}$ (ii) $\left(\frac{4}{121}\right)^{-\frac{1}{2}}$ (iii) $\left(\frac{8}{125}\right)^{-\frac{1}{3}}$ (iv) $\left(\frac{27}{1{,}000}\right)^{-\frac{2}{3}}$ (v) $\left(\frac{125}{27}\right)^{-\frac{2}{3}}$ (vi) $\left(\frac{8}{125}\right)^{-\frac{2}{3}}$ (vii) $\left(\frac{4}{9}\right)^{-\frac{3}{2}}$ (viii) $\left(\frac{27}{64}\right)^{-\frac{2}{3}}$

12. Use your calculator to evaluate each of the following to two decimal places:

(i) $\sqrt{19}$ (ii) 2.75^4 (iii) $\sqrt[3]{28}$ (iv) $13^{\frac{1}{4}}$ (v) $39^{\frac{3}{4}}$ (vi) 3.42^{-3} (vii) $26^{\frac{3}{4}}$ (viii) $42^{-\frac{7}{8}}$ (ix) $\sqrt[5]{34}$ (x) $\sqrt[6]{100}$

13. Write each of the following in the form 2^p:

(i) 4 (ii) 8 (iii) 16 (iv) 32 (v) $\frac{1}{2}$ (vi) $\frac{1}{4}$ (vii) $\sqrt{2}$ (viii) $\sqrt[3]{2}$ (ix) $\frac{1}{\sqrt{2}}$

14. Write each of the following in the form 3^p:

(i) 1 (ii) 9 (iii) 27 (iv) 81 (v) $\frac{1}{3}$ (vi) $\frac{1}{9}$ (vii) $\sqrt{3}$ (viii) $\sqrt{27}$ (ix) $\frac{1}{\sqrt{3}}$

15. Write each of the following in the form 5^p:

(i) 25 (ii) 125 (iii) $\frac{1}{5}$ (iv) 1 (v) $\frac{1}{25}$ (vi) $\frac{1}{125}$ (vii) $\sqrt{5}$ (viii) $\sqrt[5]{5}$ (ix) $\frac{1}{\sqrt{5}}$

16. Write each of the following in the form 10^p:

(i) 100 (ii) 1,000 (iii) 0.01 (iv) 10,000 (v) $\frac{1}{10}$ (vi) $\frac{1}{1{,}000}$ (vii) $\sqrt{10}$ (viii) $\sqrt[100]{10}$ (ix) $\frac{1}{\sqrt{10}}$ (x) $\frac{\sqrt{10}}{\sqrt[3]{10}}$ (xi) $\sqrt{1{,}000}$ (xii) $\frac{100}{\sqrt{10}}$

17. Using the law $(ab)^p = a^pb^p$, verify that each of the following is true:

(i) $20^4 = 5^4 4^4$ (ii) $15^6 = 3^6 5^6$ (iii) $36^{\frac{1}{2}} = 9^{\frac{1}{2}} 4^{\frac{1}{2}}$ (iv) $216^{\frac{1}{3}} = 8^{\frac{1}{3}} 27^{\frac{1}{3}}$

18. Using the law $\left(\frac{a}{b}\right)^p = \left(\frac{a^p}{b^p}\right)$, verify that each of the following is true:

(i) $\left(\frac{3}{4}\right)^8 = \frac{6^8}{8^8}$ (ii) $\left(\frac{3}{5}\right)^9 = \frac{9^9}{15^9}$ (iii) $\left(\frac{9}{16}\right)^{\frac{1}{2}} = \frac{18^{\frac{1}{2}}}{32^{\frac{1}{2}}}$ (iv) $\left(\frac{25}{64}\right)^{-\frac{1}{2}} = \frac{75^{-\frac{1}{2}}}{192^{-\frac{1}{2}}}$

4.4 Equations with *x* as an Index

$2^x = 64$ is an example of an equation in which the unknown quantity x is an index or power. The laws of indices will help us to solve many equations where the unknown quantity is an index.

If $a^x = a^y$, and $a \neq -1, 0, 1$, then $x = y$.

For example, if $2^x = 2^5$, then $x = 5$.

Worked Example 4.9

Solve each of the following equations:

(i) $2^x = 2^5$ (ii) $3^y = 3^{-2}$ (iii) $\left(\frac{1}{2}\right)^z = \left(\frac{1}{2}\right)^{\frac{1}{4}}$

Solution

(i) $2^x = 2^5$

$\therefore x = 5$

(ii) $3^y = 3^{-2}$

$\therefore y = -2$

(iii) $\left(\frac{1}{2}\right)^z = \left(\frac{1}{2}\right)^{\frac{1}{4}}$

$\therefore z = \frac{1}{4}$

Worked Example 4.10

Solve each of the following equations:

(i) $2^x = 16$

(ii) $3^x = 27$

Solution

(i) $2^x = 16$

$2^x = 2^4$ (Express 16 as a power of 2)

$\therefore x = 4$

(ii) $3^x = 27$

$3^x = 3^3$ (Express 27 as a power of 3)

$\therefore x = 3$

Worked Example 4.11

Solve $4^x = \frac{8}{\sqrt{2}}, x \in Q$.

Solution

All numbers in the equation can be written as powers of 2.

$2 = 2^1$

$4 = 2^2$

$8 = 2^3$

The equation can now be written as:

$(2^2)^x = \frac{2^3}{\sqrt{2}}$

$2^{2x} = \frac{2^3}{2^{\frac{1}{2}}}$

$2^{2x} = 2^{2\frac{1}{2}}$

$\Rightarrow 2x = 2\frac{1}{2}$

$x = \frac{2\frac{1}{2}}{2}$

$\therefore x = 1\frac{1}{4}\left(\text{or } \frac{5}{4}\right)$

$(2^2)^x = 2^{2x}$ (Law 3)

$\sqrt{2} = 2^{\frac{1}{2}}$ (Law 5)

Exercise 4.3

1. Solve the following equations:
   (i) $2^x = 4$
   (ii) $3^x = 27$
   (iii) $5^x = 125$
   (iv) $10^x = 1{,}000$
   (v) $4^x = 64$
   (vi) $3^x = 81$
   (vii) $10^x = 10{,}000$
   (viii) $6^x = 216$
   (ix) $7^x = 49$
   (x) $3^x = 729$

2. Solve the following equations:
   (i) $9^x = 3^4$
   (ii) $4^x = 8^2$
   (iii) $5^x = 25^2$
   (iv) $10^x = 100^3$
   (v) $11^x = 121^5$
   (vi) $2^x = 16^5$
   (vii) $4^{2x} = 8^3$
   (viii) $3^{3x} = 27^2$
   (ix) $4^{5x} = 8^5$
   (x) $a^{2x} = (a^2)^3$

3. Write the following in the form 2^k, where $k \in Q$:
   (i) 16 (ii) 8 (iii) $\sqrt{8}$ (iv) $\frac{16}{\sqrt{8}}$
   Hence, solve the equation $2^{2x-1} = \left(\frac{16}{\sqrt{8}}\right)^3$.

4. Write the following in the form 3^k, where $k \in Q$:
   (i) 27 (ii) $\sqrt{3}$
   Hence, solve the equation $3^{3x-1} = \left(\frac{27}{\sqrt{3}}\right)^5$.

5. Write the following in the form 5^p, where $p \in Q$:
   (i) 25 (ii) $\sqrt{125}$ (iii) $\sqrt[3]{5}$
   Hence, solve the equation $25^x = \left(\frac{\sqrt{125}}{\sqrt[3]{5}}\right)^{12}$.

6. Write the following in the form 7^p, where $p \in Q$:
   (i) 49 (ii) $\sqrt[3]{7}$ (iii) $\sqrt{343}$
   Hence, solve the equation $49^{x-4} = \left(\frac{\sqrt{343}}{\sqrt[3]{7}}\right)^{2x}$.

7. (i) Evaluate $8^{\frac{1}{3}}$.
   (ii) Express $4^{\frac{1}{4}}$ in the form 2^k, $k \in Q$.
   (iii) Solve the equation:
   $\left(8^{\frac{1}{3}}\right)\left(4^{\frac{1}{4}}\right) = 2^{5-x}$

8. Find the prime factors of 75 and hence, solve the equation:
   $$\frac{5^x}{3} = \frac{5^6}{75}$$

9. Using the laws of indices, solve the following equations:
   (i) $2^x = 2^7\sqrt{2}$
   (ii) $2^x = \frac{2^7}{4}$
   (iii) $5^x = \frac{125}{\sqrt{5}}$
   (iv) $3^{x+1} = \frac{9}{\sqrt{3}}$
   (v) $10^{x-3} = \frac{\sqrt{10}}{100}$
   (vi) $7^x = \frac{49}{\sqrt[3]{7}}$
   (vii) $10^{2x-1} = \frac{\sqrt{1{,}000}}{10}$
   (viii) $4^x = \frac{32\sqrt{2}}{2}$

10. Solve the equation $\left(a^{\frac{1}{3}}\right)\left(b^{\frac{1}{3}}\right) = c^{5-x}$ if,
    (i) $a = 8$, $b = 4$ and $c = 2$
    (ii) $a = 27$, $b = 9$ and $c = 3$

11. (i) Copy and complete the table below. Answers in the second row must be in index form.

$2^2 - 2$	$2^3 - 2^2$	$2^4 - 2^3$	$2^5 - 2^4$	$2^6 - 2^5$	$2^7 - 2^6$
2	2^2				

    (ii) Hence, write $2^{p+1} - 2^p$ as a power of 2.
    (iii) Hence, or otherwise, solve for x:
    $\left(\frac{2^{12}}{16}\right) = 2^{x+1} - 2^x$

12. Solve each of the following equations for p:
    (i) $9^p = \frac{1}{\sqrt{3}}$ (ii) $2^{3p-7} = 2^6 - 2^5$

13. John is doing research on viral marketing. He sends a text message to 10 friends. The text message instructs each recipient to forward the message to 10 other people who each in turn forward it to 10 more people, and so on. Assuming that nobody receives the message more than once, complete the table below.

Level	0	1	2	3	4	5	6	7
Number of messages	1	10	100					

    (i) What is the total number of messages sent at level 7?
    (ii) How many messages will be received at level 10?

14. A population of ants grows according to the equation $p = 600(2^t)$, where p is the size of the population and t is time measured in months.

(i) How many ants are in the population after 2 months?

(ii) The population becomes extinct when its size exceeds 50,000. After how many months (to the nearest month) will the population exceed 50,000?

4.5 Surds

Suppose we wish to simplify $\sqrt{\frac{1}{25}}$. We can write it as $\frac{1}{5}$.
However, some numbers involving roots, such as $\sqrt{5}$, $\sqrt[3]{19}$, $\sqrt{\pi}$, cannot be written as fractions.
We call such numbers **surds**.

If $a, b > 0$, then:

Law 1 $\sqrt{a}\sqrt{b} = \sqrt{ab}$

Law 2 $\frac{\sqrt{a}}{\sqrt{b}} = \sqrt{\frac{a}{b}}$

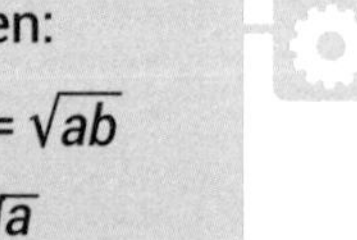

Any number of the form $\sqrt[n]{a}$, $n > 1, n \in N$, which cannot be written as a fraction, is called a **surd**.

Worked Example 4.12

Without using a calculator, evaluate each of the following:

(i) $\sqrt{25}\sqrt{25}$ (ii) $\sqrt{100}\sqrt{100}$ (iii) $\sqrt{169}\sqrt{169}$

Hence, for $a \geqslant 0$, write down what $\sqrt{a}\sqrt{a}$ is equal to.

Solution

(i) $\sqrt{25}\sqrt{25}$

$= 5(5)$

$= 25$

(ii) $\sqrt{100} \times \sqrt{100}$

$= 10(10)$

$= 100$

(iii) $\sqrt{169} \times \sqrt{169}$

$= 13(13)$

$= 169$

$\therefore \sqrt{a} \times \sqrt{a} = a$

Reducing Surds

Surds can be reduced or simplified if the number under the radical sign (square root sign) has a square number greater than 1 as a factor.

You should know the first few square numbers: 1, 4, 9, 16, 25, 36, 49, 64, 81, 100, 121, 144, 169, ...

Worked Example 4.13

Simplify $\sqrt{32}$, without using a calculator.

Solution

Step 1 Find the largest square number that is a factor of 32. 16 is the largest square number that is a factor of 32.

Step 2 $\sqrt{32} = \sqrt{16 \times 2}$

$= \sqrt{16}\sqrt{2}$ (Law 1 of Surds)

$= 4\sqrt{2}$

Worked Example 4.14

Simplify $\sqrt{50} + \sqrt{8} + \sqrt{32}$, without using a calculator.

Solution

$\sqrt{50} + \sqrt{8} + \sqrt{32} = \sqrt{25 \times 2} + \sqrt{4 \times 2} + \sqrt{16 \times 2}$

$= \sqrt{25}\sqrt{2} + \sqrt{4}\sqrt{2} + \sqrt{16}\sqrt{2}$

$= 5\sqrt{2} + 2\sqrt{2} + 4\sqrt{2}$

$= 11\sqrt{2}$

Exercise 4.4

1. Evaluate each of the following (no calculators allowed):
   (i) $(\sqrt{3})^2$ (ii) $(\sqrt{6})^2$ (iii) $(\sqrt{17})^2$ (iv) $(\sqrt{19})^2$ (v) $(\sqrt{30})^2$ (vi) $(2\sqrt{7})^2$ (vii) $(5\sqrt{10})^2$ (viii) $(2\sqrt{5})^2$ (ix) $(10\sqrt{2})^2$ (x) $(3\sqrt{15})^2$

2. Say if each of the following is true or false:
   (i) $\sqrt{3}+\sqrt{5}=\sqrt{8}$ (ii) $\sqrt{5}-\sqrt{3}=\sqrt{2}$ (iii) $\sqrt{5}\sqrt{3}=\sqrt{15}$ (iv) $\dfrac{\sqrt{35}}{\sqrt{5}}=\sqrt{7}$

3. Evaluate each of the following, without the use of a calculator:
   (i) $\sqrt{12}\sqrt{3}$ (ii) $\sqrt{20}\sqrt{5}$ (iii) $\sqrt{2}\sqrt{8}$ (iv) $\sqrt{2}\sqrt{32}$ (v) $\sqrt{50}\sqrt{2}$ (vi) $\dfrac{\sqrt{27}}{\sqrt{3}}$ (vii) $\dfrac{\sqrt{50}}{\sqrt{2}}$ (viii) $\dfrac{\sqrt{28}}{\sqrt{7}}$ (ix) $\dfrac{\sqrt{72}}{\sqrt{8}}$ (x) $\dfrac{\sqrt{200}}{\sqrt{8}}$

4. Simplify these surds:
   (i) $\sqrt{8}$ (ii) $\sqrt{45}$ (iii) $\sqrt{300}$ (iv) $\sqrt{12}$ (v) $\sqrt{32}$ (vi) $\sqrt{500}$ (vii) $\sqrt{27}$ (viii) $\sqrt{54}$ (ix) $\sqrt{75}$ (x) $\sqrt{98}$

5. Write $\sqrt{50}+\sqrt{8}$ in the form $k\sqrt{2}$, $k \in Q$.

6. Write $\sqrt{27}+\sqrt{12}$ in the form $k\sqrt{3}$, $k \in Q$.

7. Write $\sqrt{125}+\sqrt{20}$ in the form $k\sqrt{5}$, $k \in Q$.

8. If $\sqrt{44}+\sqrt{99}=n\sqrt{11}$, then find n where $n \in N$.

Revision Exercises

1. Use Laws 1 to 3 of indices to write the following in index notation:
   (i) $5^3 \times 5^8$ (ii) $\dfrac{8^7}{8^7}$ (iii) $(3^2)^3$ (iv) $\dfrac{16^9}{16^5}$

2. Use Laws 5 to 7 of indices to write the following in the form a^p, where $p \in Q$:
   (i) $\dfrac{1}{7^5}$ (ii) $\sqrt[8]{15}$ (iii) $\sqrt[5]{17^3}$ (iv) $\dfrac{5^3}{\sqrt{5^5}}$

3. Use the laws of indices to simplify each of the following. Leave your answer in index notation.
   (i) $((2^3)(2^5))^2$ (ii) $((7^6)(7^5))^2$ (iii) $\left(\dfrac{2^9}{2^5}\right)^6$ (iv) $\left(\dfrac{5^8}{5^3}\right)^7$

4. Use the laws of surds to simplify each of the following:
   (i) $\sqrt{125}$ (ii) $\sqrt{147}$ (iii) $\sqrt{128}$ (iv) $\sqrt{18}$

5. Write these in the form a^n:
   (i) $a^4 \times a^6$ (ii) $(a^4)^6$ (iii) $\sqrt[4]{a^6}$ (iv) $\sqrt[5]{a^3 \times a^7}$

6. Use the laws of surds to simplify each of the following:
   (i) $\sqrt{8}+\sqrt{98}+\sqrt{128}$
   (ii) $\sqrt{80}+\sqrt{245}+\sqrt{405}$

7. (i) Evaluate $25^{\frac{1}{2}}$.
   (ii) Write 9 and $\sqrt{3}$ as powers of 3 and hence, solve the equation $3^x = \dfrac{9}{\sqrt{3}}$.
   (iii) If $\sqrt{8}+\sqrt{50}-\sqrt{2}=n\sqrt{2}$, find n.

8. (i) Evaluate $64^{-\frac{1}{2}}$.
   (ii) Write 128 and $\sqrt{2}$ as a power of 2.
   Hence, solve the equation $2^{2x+1} = \dfrac{128}{\sqrt{2}}$.

9. (i) Evaluate $\left(\dfrac{4}{81}\right)^{-\frac{1}{2}}$.
   (ii) Write as a power of 7:
   (a) 343
   (b) $\sqrt{7}$
   Hence, solve the equation:
   $7^{2x+1} = \dfrac{343}{(\sqrt{7})^3}$

10. (i) Simplify $3a^5 + 6a^5$.
Hence, write $3(3^5) + 6(3^5)$ as a power of 3.

(ii) Write $20(3^8) + 7(3^8)$ as a power of 3.

(iii) Simplify $a^4 + a^4 + a^4 + a^4$.
Hence, write $2^4 + 2^4 + 2^4 + 2^4$ as a power of 2.

(iv) Write $2^{\frac{1}{4}} + 2^{\frac{1}{4}} + 2^{\frac{1}{4}} + 2^{\frac{1}{4}}$ as a power of 2.

11. For $y > 1$, write each of the following expressions in order of size, beginning with the expression with the least value:

$y^0, y^2, y, y^{-2}, y^{\frac{1}{2}}$

12. Simplify the following expressions:

(i) $\dfrac{x^2y^{-4}z^5}{xy^{-7}z^2}$ (iii) $(x^2y^{\frac{1}{2}}z^5)^3$

(ii) $\dfrac{xy^tz^{-\frac{2}{3}}}{x^2y^{-t}z^{-\frac{4}{5}}}$ (iv) $(x^4y^8z^{-6})^{-\frac{1}{2}}$

13. Complete the tables below.

n	$2^{\frac{1}{n}}$
1	
2	
5	
10	
100	

n	$\left(\frac{1}{2}\right)^{\frac{1}{n}}$
1	
2	
5	
10	
100	

(i) What happens to the nth root of 2 as n gets large?

(ii) What happens to the nth root of $\frac{1}{2}$ as n gets large?

Exam Questions

1. Solve the equation $27^{2x} = 3^{x+10}$.

SEC Leaving Certificate Ordinary Level, Paper 1, 2013

Solutions and chapter summary available online

05

Algebra II

In this chapter you will learn to:

- Find solutions, using algebraic methods, to equations of the form:
  - $f(x) = k$, $k \in Q$, with $f(x) = ax^2 + bx + c$ (and not necessarily factorisable) where $a, b, c \in Q$ and interpret the results
  - $f(x) = g(x)$, with $f(x) = \frac{a}{bx + c} \pm \frac{p}{qx + r}$, $g(x) = \frac{e}{f}$ where $a, b, c, e, f, p, q, r \in Z$
- Form quadratic equations given whole number roots
- Select and use suitable strategies (graphic, numeric, algebraic, mental) for finding solutions to one linear equation and one equation of order 2 with two unknowns (restricted to the case where either the coefficient of x or the coefficient of y is ± 1 in the linear equation) and interpret the results
- Solve problems involving quadratic equations

You should remember...

- How to solve linear equations
- How to find the factors of quadratic expressions
- How to plot and read graphs
- All content from Chapter 2, Algebra I

Key words

- Solve
- Verify
- Solution
- Roots
- Factors
- Highest common factor (HCF)
- Difference of two squares
- Quadratic trinomials
- Quadratic formula
- Co-ordinate plane

5.1 Solving Quadratic Equations by Factorising

Many problems that can be solved using algebra come down to one question. Can you find the value(s) of the unknown(s) when given in an equation (a set of equations)?

A quadratic equation in the unknown x is of the form $ax^2 + bx + c = 0$, $a \neq 0$. Solving quadratic equations means that we are finding the value(s) of x that will satisfy the equation.

One of the most common methods of solving a quadratic equation is to:

- Find the factors of the quadratic expression used.
- Use these factors to find values of the unknowns.

You have already encountered this approach at Junior Certificate level.

Quadratic equations come in a variety of forms. To solve any quadratic equation, we usually must ensure that:

- All the terms of the equation are on the same side of the equal sign, with zero on the other.
- The equation is written with powers in descending order (i.e. x^2 first, then x, then constant).
- The coefficient of x^2 is positive. (This makes our calculations easier.)

$\therefore$ The equation should be in the form $ax^2 + bx + c$, $a > 0$.

For convenience, we generally use the x variable in examples. However, other letters may be used instead. Commonly used other letters include t and y.

Worked Example 5.1

Solve $x^2 - 5x - 14 = 0$ and verify your answers.

Solution

This equation is a quadratic trinomial in x as it has an x^2 term, an x term and a constant.

We are looking for the factors of -14 that **add up** to -5.

$(-7)(2) = -14$

$(-7) + (2) = -5$

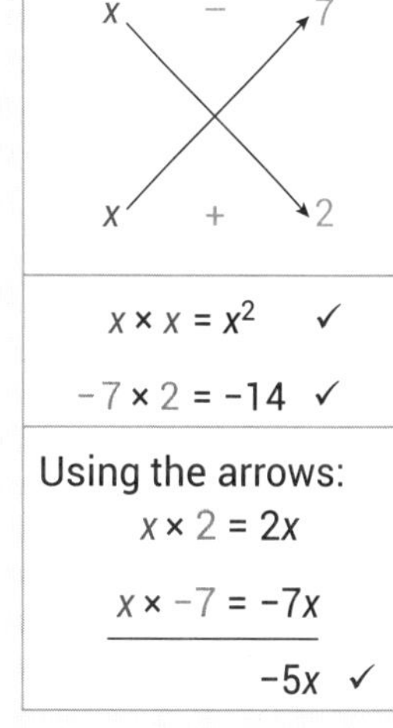

So our factors are $(x - 7)$ and $(x + 2)$.

$\Rightarrow (x - 7)(x + 2) = 0$

One of the factors must be zero, so we solve:

$x - 7 = 0$ **OR** $x + 2 = 0$

$\therefore x = 7$ **OR** $x = -2$

Verify:

$x = 7$ **OR** $x = -2$

Substitute $x = 7$ into the equation $x^2 - 5x - 14 = 0$.

$(7)^2 - 5(7) - 14 = 0$

$49 - 35 - 14 = 0$

$0 = 0$ True

$\therefore$ Verified for $x = 7$.

Substitute $x = -2$ into the equation $x^2 - 5x - 14 = 0$.

$(-2)^2 - 5(-2) - 14 = 0$

$4 + 10 - 14 = 0$

$0 = 0$ True

$\therefore$ Verified for $x = -2$.

Worked Example 5.2

Solve $x^2 + 5x = 0$ and verify your answers.

Solution

This equation has an x^2 term and an x term only. To solve this type of equation, we find the highest common factor.

x is the highest common factor for both terms.

$x(x + 5) = 0$

$x = 0$ **OR** $x + 5 = 0$

$x = 0$ **OR** $x = -5$

Verify:

Substitute $x = 0$ into the equation $x^2 + 5x = 0$.

$(0)^2 + 5(0) = 0$

$0 = 0$ True

$\therefore$ Verified for $x = 0$.

Substitute $x = -5$ into the equation $x^2 + 5x = 0$.

$(-5)^2 + 5(-5) = 0$

$25 - 25 = 0$

$0 = 0$ True

$\therefore$ Verified for $x = -5$.

Worked Example 5.3

Solve $q^2 - 49 = 0$

Solution

This equation has only an x^2 term and a constant. We will use two different methods to solve this type of equation.

Method 1	Method 2
$q^2 - 49 = 0$ $(q)^2 - (7)^2 = 0$ $(q - 7)(q + 7) = 0$	$q^2 - 49 = 0$ $q^2 = 49$
$q - 7 = 0$ **OR** $q + 7 = 0$	$q = \pm\sqrt{49}$
$q = 7$ **OR** $q = -7$	$q = \pm 7$

$x^2 - y^2$ is a difference of two squares. Factorised, $x^2 - y^2 = (x - y)(x + y)$.

Note: $\sqrt{\ }$ is defined as 'the non-negative root of'. For example, $(5)^2 = (-5)^2 = 25$. However $\sqrt{25} = 5$.

ALGEBRA II

Exercise 5.1

Solve the following equations. Verify your answers for each question.

1. $x^2 + 7x + 12 = 0$
2. $x^2 + 10x + 9 = 0$
3. $p^2 + 17p + 72 = 0$
4. $b^2 + 2b - 15 = 0$
5. $x^2 - 16 = 0$
6. $x^2 - x - 72 = 0$
7. $y^2 - 5y = 0$
8. $x^2 - 81 = 0$
9. $-x^2 - 7x - 10 = 0$
10. $2y^2 + 3y = 0$
11. $-x^2 - 12x = 0$
12. $-144 = -x^2$

Worked Example 5.4

Solve $3x^2 + 5x - 12 = 0$.

Solution

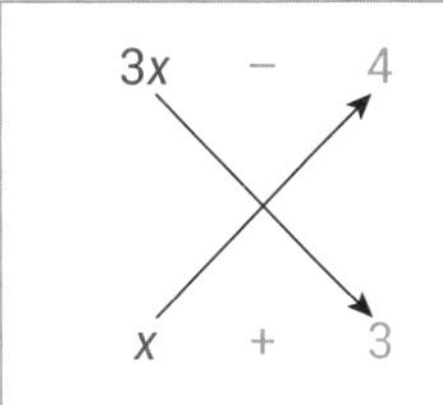

$3x \times x = 3x^2$ ✓

$-4 \times 3 = -12$ ✓

Using the arrows:

$3x \times 3 = 9x$

$x \times -4 = -4x$

$5x$ ✓

$(3x - 4)(x + 3) = 0$

Let both factors equal 0 and solve:

$3x - 4 = 0$ **OR** $x + 3 = 0$

$3x = 4$ **OR** $x = -3$

$\therefore x = \frac{4}{3}$ **OR** $x = -3$

Alternatively, we can use the **Guide number method**.

Step 1 Multiply the coefficient of x^2 by the constant:

$3x^2 + 5x - 12$

$3 \times -12 = -36$

Step 2 Find two factors of −36 that will multiply to −36 and add up to give 5, the coefficient of x.

−4 and 9

Step 3 Use the answers from Step 2 to rewrite $3x^2 + 5x - 12 = 0$ as follows:

$3x^2 - 4x + 9x - 12 = 0$

$x(3x - 4) + 3(3x - 4) = 0$ Factorise by grouping.

$(x + 3)(3x - 4) = 0$ (Distributive property)

$x + 3 = 0$ **OR** $3x - 4 = 0$

$x = -3$ **OR** $3x = 4$

$x = -3$ **OR** $x = \frac{4}{3}$

Worked Example 5.5

Solve $2y^2 - 6y = 0$.

Solution

$2y^2 - 6y = 0$

$y^2 - 3y = 0$ Divide all terms in the equation by 2.

$y(y - 3) = 0$

$y = 0$ **OR** $y - 3 = 0$

$\therefore y = 0$ **OR** $y = 3$

Worked Example 5.6

Solve $4p^2 - 25 = 0$.

Solution

Method 1	Method 2
$4p^2 - 25 = 0$	$4p^2 - 25 = 0$
$(2p)^2 - (5)^2 = 0$	$4p^2 = 25$
$(2p - 5)(2p + 5) = 0$	$p^2 = \frac{25}{4}$
$2p - 5 = 0$ **OR** $2p + 5 = 0$	
$2p = 5$ **OR** $2p = -5$	$p = \pm\sqrt{\frac{25}{4}}$
$\therefore p = \frac{5}{2}$ **OR** $p = -\frac{5}{2}$	$p = \pm\frac{5}{2}$

A calculator can help find the value of $\sqrt{\frac{25}{4}}$.

Worked Example 5.7

Solve $\frac{9}{2}x^2 - \frac{2}{5}x - \frac{1}{10} = 0$.

Solution

We have coefficients which are fractions in the equation. The fractions have a lowest common denominator of 10, so we will multiply each term in the equation by 10.

$$10\left(\frac{9}{2}x^2\right) - 10\left(\frac{2}{5}x\right) - 10\left(\frac{1}{10}\right) = 10(0)$$

$$45x^2 - 4x - 1 = 0$$

We now have an equation in the form $ax^2 + bx + c = 0$, where a, b and c are all whole numbers.

$45x^2 - 4x - 1 = 0$

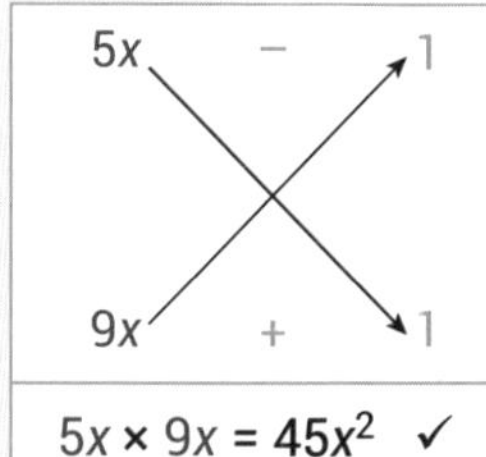

$5x \times 9x = 45x^2$ ✓

$-1 \times 1 = -1$ ✓

Using the arrows:

$5x \times 1 = 5x$

$9x \times -1 = -9x$

$-4x$ ✓

$(5x - 1)(9x + 1) = 0$

$5x - 1 = 0$ **OR** $9x + 1 = 0$

$5x = 1$ **OR** $9x = -1$

$\therefore x = \frac{1}{5}$ **OR** $x = -\frac{1}{9}$

Exercise 5.2

Solve the following equations. Verify your answers for questions 1 to 6.

1. $2x^2 + 13x - 45 = 0$
2. $2t^2 - 3t - 9 = 0$
3. $5x^2 + 19x + 12 = 0$
4. $7x^2 - 24x + 9 = 0$
5. $10x^2 - 7x = 0$
6. $49y^2 - 225 = 0$
7. $2x^2 - 8x - 10 = 0$
8. $7x^2 - 40x - 12 = 0$
9. $9x^2 - 9 = 0$
10. $12x^2 - 36x = 0$
11. $11x^2 - 121x = 0$
12. $x^2 - \frac{5}{2}x + 1 = 0$
13. $2x^2 - \frac{15}{2}x + \frac{9}{2} = 0$
14. $3y^2 = y$
15. $144x^2 = 16$
16. $-400 = -100x^2$
17. $6 - 31q = -5q^2$
18. $13x + 30 = 3x^2$
19. $(2x + 1)(x - 4) = 0$
20. $(2 + y)(8 - y) = 9$
21. $(x - 1)(x + 1) = 5x + 13$
22. $10x^2 = 3x + 4$
23. $6x^2 + 13x + 2 = 0$
24. $14p^2 + 15p - 9 = 0$
25. $\frac{e^2}{7} + \frac{e}{14} - \frac{3}{2} = 0$
26. $\frac{x^2}{4} + \frac{7}{20}x + \frac{1}{10} = 0$

5.2 Solving Quadratic Equations by Formula

There are alternative methods of solving quadratic equations. One approach is to use the quadratic formula.

We can use this formula instead of factorising an equation and then finding its roots.

Many quadratic equations are difficult or impossible to solve by factorisation. Using the quadratic formula will allow you to solve **any** quadratic equation.

When using the quadratic formula, it is important to note that in, for example, the equation $x^2 - 2x - 8 = 0$:

- $a = 1$ (the coefficient of x^2)
- $b = -2$ (the coefficient of x)
- $c = -8$ (the constant)

$ax^2 + bx + c = 0, \quad a \neq 0$

$$x = \frac{-b \pm \sqrt{b^2 - 4ac}}{2a}$$

a = coefficient of x^2

b = coefficient of x

c = constant term

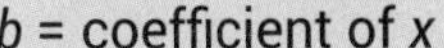

This formula appears on page 20 of *Formulae and Tables.*

To use the quadratic formula, we must ensure that the equation is written in the form $ax^2 + bx + c = 0$.

Worked Example 5.8

Solve $2x^2 + 5x - 12 = 0$.

Solution

Using the quadratic formula $x = \frac{-b \pm \sqrt{b^2 - 4ac}}{2a}$:

$a = 2 \qquad b = 5 \qquad c = -12$

$$x = \frac{-(5) \pm \sqrt{(5)^2 - 4(2)(-12)}}{2(2)}$$

$$x = \frac{-5 \pm \sqrt{25 + 96}}{4}$$

You can input this fraction directly into your calculator using the ▭/▭ or a/b buttons.

$x = \frac{-5 \pm \sqrt{121}}{4}$

$x = \frac{-5 \pm 11}{4}$

We now deal with the ± sign:

$x = \frac{-5 + 11}{4}$ **OR** $x = \frac{-5 - 11}{4}$

$x = \frac{6}{4}$ **OR** $x = \frac{-16}{4}$

$\therefore x = \frac{3}{2}$ **OR** $x = -4$

The symbol ± requires two procedures:

(i) Add $\sqrt{b^2 - 4ac}$ to $-b$ in the numerator.

(ii) Subtract $\sqrt{b^2 - 4ac}$ from $-b$ in the numerator.

Worked Example 5.9

Solve the equation $6t^2 - 7t = 24$.

Solution

$6t^2 - 7t = 24$

Write the equation in the form $at^2 + bt + c = 0, a > 0$.

$\Rightarrow 6t^2 - 7t - 24 = 0$

Using the quadratic formula $t = \frac{-b \pm \sqrt{b^2 - 4ac}}{2a}$:

$a = 6 \quad b = -7 \quad c = -24$

$t = \frac{-(-7) \pm \sqrt{(-7)^2 - 4(6)(-24)}}{2(6)}$

$t = \frac{7 \pm \sqrt{49 + 576}}{12}$

$t = \frac{7 \pm \sqrt{625}}{12}$

$t = \frac{7 \pm 25}{12}$

$t = \frac{7 + 25}{12}$ **OR** $t = \frac{7 - 25}{12}$

$t = \frac{32}{12}$ **OR** $t = \frac{-18}{12}$

$\therefore t = \frac{8}{3}$ **OR** $t = -\frac{3}{2}$

Exercise 5.3

Solve the following equations using the quadratic formula:

1. $x^2 + 6x + 5 = 0$
2. $x^2 - 7x + 12 = 0$
3. $x^2 + x - 12 = 0$
4. $2x^2 + 11x + 14 = 0$
5. $3y^2 + 2y - 5 = 0$
6. $7x^2 - 5x - 2 = 0$
7. $-3t^2 - 26t + 9 = 0$
8. $4y^2 + 5y - 26 = 0$
9. $5x^2 - 17x = 12$
10. $2x^2 = -39x - 85$
11. $2x^2 + \frac{8}{7}x + \frac{1}{14} = 0$
12. $\frac{5}{2}x^2 + \frac{11}{12}x = \frac{1}{6}$

One of the main reasons for using the quadratic formula instead of other methods is when the roots of the equation are decimals or surds.

Worked Example 5.10

Solve, to two decimal places, $8x^2 - x - 15 = 0$.

Solution

We know that we have to use the quadratic formula, as the question asks for the solution to be given to a certain number of decimal places.

Using the quadratic formula $x = \dfrac{-b \pm \sqrt{b^2 - 4ac}}{2a}$:

$a = 8 \qquad b = -1 \qquad c = -15$

$$x = \frac{-(-1) \pm \sqrt{(-1)^2 - 4(8)(-15)}}{2(8)}$$

Again we can use the calculator to input this information directly.

$$x = \frac{1 \pm \sqrt{481}}{16}$$

$$x = \frac{1 + \sqrt{481}}{16} \quad \textbf{OR} \quad x = \frac{1 - \sqrt{481}}{16}$$

Input each calculation separately into the calculator and use (in each case) the S⇔D or Change button to convert to decimals.

The calculator gives the following answers:

$x = 1.433232012$ **OR** $x = -1.308232012$

Rounding to two decimal places (as required) we get:

$\therefore x \approx 1.43$ **OR** $x \approx -1.31$

Worked Example 5.11

Solve the equation $2x^2 + 8x + 3 = 2$, leaving the answers in surd form.

Solution

Write the equation in the form $ax^2 + bx + c = 0, a > 0$.

$2x^2 + 8x + 3 - 2 = 0$

$2x^2 + 8x + 1 = 0$

Using the quadratic formula $x = \dfrac{-b \pm \sqrt{b^2 - 4ac}}{2a}$:

$a = 2 \qquad b = 8 \qquad c = 1$

$$x = \frac{-(8) \pm \sqrt{(8)^2 - 4(2)(1)}}{2(2)}$$

Again, we can input this information directly into the calculator.

$$x = \frac{-8 \pm \sqrt{56}}{4}$$

Our answer must be in surd form, so we need to simplify $\sqrt{56}$. The largest perfect square number that divides into 56 is 4 (as $56 = 4 \times 14$).

$\therefore \sqrt{56} = \sqrt{4 \times 14}$

$= \sqrt{4} \cdot \sqrt{14}$

$= 2\sqrt{14}$

$$\Rightarrow x = \frac{-8 \pm 2\sqrt{14}}{4}$$

You can input $\dfrac{-8 + \sqrt{56}}{4}$ directly into the calculator. The calculator will simplify the surd term. Likewise for $\dfrac{-8 - \sqrt{56}}{4}$.

This answer can then be simplified further as:

$$x = \frac{-4 \pm \sqrt{14}}{2}$$

$$\therefore x = \frac{-4 + \sqrt{14}}{2} \quad \textbf{OR} \quad x = \frac{-4 - \sqrt{14}}{2}$$

Exercise 5.4

Use the quadratic formula to solve each of the following equations.

1 d.p. = Answer to one decimal place.
2 d.p. = Answer to two decimal places.
3 d.p. = Answer to three decimal places.
4 d.p. = Answer to four decimal places.
surd = Answer in surd form.

1. $x^2 + 4x + 2 = 0$ (1 d.p.)
2. $x^2 + 9x + 6 = 0$ (1 d.p.)
3. $2x^2 + 9x + 1 = 0$ (2 d.p.)
4. $4a^2 + 2a - 21 = 0$ (2 d.p.)
5. $9x^2 + 6x + 1 = 0$ (3 d.p.)
6. $x^2 + 6x + 4 = 0$ (surd)
7. $x^2 - 8x + 9 = 0$ (surd)
8. $5b^2 + 2b - 25 = 0$ (surd)
9. $8y^2 + 8y - 3 = 0$ (surd)
10. $7x^2 + 4x - 4 = 0$ (surd)
11. $2q^2 - 3q - 23 = 0$ (2 d.p.)
12. $3x^2 - \frac{8}{3}x - \frac{7}{2} = 0$ (1 d.p.)
13. $6b^2 + 8b - 13 = 0$ (1 d.p.)
14. $3p^2 - p - 13 = 0$ (2 d.p.)
15. $4x^2 + \frac{1}{2}x - \frac{3}{7} = 0$ (3 d.p.)
16. $4x^2 = -x + 6$ (3 d.p.)
17. $17 - 9x^2 = 9$ (4 d.p.)
18. $5x^2 - \frac{10}{3}x + \frac{1}{9} = 0$ (surd)
19. $0 = 3x^2 + 6x - 10$ (surd)
20. $-\frac{4}{5}x^2 + \frac{3}{2}x = \frac{2}{3}$ (2 d.p.)

ALGEBRA II

5.3 Solving Quadratic Equations Involving Fractions

Worked Example 5.12

Solve $\frac{1}{y+1} + \frac{2}{2y-1} = 1, y \neq \frac{1}{2}, -1.$

Solution

$$\frac{1}{y+1} + \frac{2}{2y-1} = \frac{1}{1}$$

1 is the same as $\frac{1}{1}$.

This equation has three terms: $\frac{1}{y+1}, \frac{2}{2y-1}$ and $\frac{1}{1}$. The three denominators are $y + 1$, $2y - 1$, and 1.

None of these denominators can be factorised.

So the LCD of $y + 1$, $2y - 1$ and 1 is $(1)(y + 1)(2y - 1)$.

Multiply all terms in the equation by the LCD.

$$\frac{1(1)(y+1)(2y-1)}{y+1} + \frac{2(1)(y+1)(2y-1)}{2y-1} = \frac{1(1)(y+1)(2y-1)}{1}$$

$$\frac{1(1)\cancel{(y+1)}(2y-1)}{\cancel{y+1}} + \frac{2(1)(y+1)\cancel{(2y-1)}}{\cancel{2y-1}} = \frac{1\cancel{(1)}(y+1)(2y-1)}{\cancel{1}}$$

Common factors divide out.

$$(2y - 1) + 2(y + 1) = (y + 1)(2y - 1)$$
$$2y - 1 + 2y + 2 = 2y^2 - y + 2y - 1$$
$$4y + 1 = 2y^2 + y - 1 \quad \text{Simplify each side.}$$
$$2y^2 - 3y - 2 = 0 \quad \text{Gather terms on one side.}$$
$$(2y + 1)(y - 2) = 0 \quad \text{Factorise.}$$
$$2y + 1 = 0 \quad \textbf{OR} \quad y - 2 = 0$$
$$2y = -1 \quad \textbf{OR} \quad y = 2$$
$$\therefore y = -\frac{1}{2} \quad \textbf{OR} \quad y = 2$$

Worked Example 5.13

Solve, to two decimal places, $\frac{2}{3x - 1} - \frac{5}{x - 3} = \frac{2}{3}$, $x \neq \frac{1}{3}$, 3.

As we are asked to solve to two decimal places, we will need to use the quadratic formula.

Solution

$$\frac{2}{3x - 1} - \frac{5}{x - 3} = \frac{2}{3}$$

The three denominators are $3x - 1$, $x - 3$ and 3. None of these denominators can be factorised.

The LCD is $(3)(3x - 1)(x - 3)$.

Multiply all terms in the equation by the LCD.

$$\frac{2(3)(3x - 1)(x - 3)}{3x - 1} - \frac{5(3)(3x - 1)(x - 3)}{x - 3} = \frac{2(3)(3x - 1)(x - 3)}{3}$$

$$\frac{2(3)(\cancel{3x - 1})(x - 3)}{\cancel{3x - 1}} - \frac{5(3)(3x - 1)(\cancel{x - 3})}{\cancel{x - 3}} = \frac{2(\cancel{3})(3x - 1)(x - 3)}{\cancel{3}} \quad \text{Common factors divide out.}$$

$$2(3)(x - 3) - 5(3)(3x - 1) = 2(3x - 1)(x - 3)$$
$$6(x - 3) - 15(3x - 1) = 2(3x^2 - 9x - x + 3)$$
$$6x - 18 - 45x + 15 = 2(3x^2 - 10x + 3)$$
$$-39x - 3 = 6x^2 - 20x + 6 \quad \text{Simplify each side.}$$
$$6x^2 + 19x + 9 = 0 \quad \text{Gather terms on one side.}$$

Using the quadratic formula $x = \frac{-b \pm \sqrt{b^2 - 4ac}}{2a}$:

$a = 6 \quad b = 19 \quad c = 9$

$$x = \frac{-19 \pm \sqrt{(19)^2 - 4(6)(9)}}{2(6)}$$
$$x = \frac{-19 \pm \sqrt{361 - 216}}{12}$$
$$x = \frac{-19 \pm \sqrt{145}}{12}$$
$$x = \frac{-19 + \sqrt{145}}{12} \quad \textbf{OR} \quad x = \frac{-19 - \sqrt{145}}{12}$$
$$\therefore x \approx -0.58 \quad \textbf{OR} \quad x \approx -2.59 \quad \text{(Correct to two decimal places)}$$

ALGEBRA II

Exercise 5.5

Solve the following equations:

1. $\frac{1}{x}+\frac{9}{x+8}=1, x \neq 0, -8$
2. $\frac{1}{x+3}+\frac{1}{x}=\frac{7}{10}, x \neq -3, 0$
3. $\frac{1}{x+4}+\frac{1}{x+1}=\frac{1}{2}, x \neq -4, -1$
4. $\frac{5}{x+1}-\frac{3}{3x-1}=1, x \neq -1, \frac{1}{3}$
5. $x+\frac{1}{x}=2, x \neq 0$
6. $3x-5+\frac{2}{x}=0, x \neq 0$
7. $\frac{2}{x+1}+\frac{4}{2x-1}=2, x \neq -1, \frac{1}{2}$
8. $\frac{1}{x+1}+\frac{2}{x+3}=\frac{11}{15}, x \neq -1, -3$
9. $\frac{4}{2x-5}-\frac{3}{5x-1}=-3, x \neq \frac{5}{2}, \frac{1}{5}$
10. $10-\frac{5}{6x-1}=\frac{15}{2x+1}, x \neq \frac{1}{6}, -\frac{1}{2}$

Using the quadratic formula, solve the following equations to two decimal places:

11. $\frac{1}{x+3}+\frac{1}{x+4}=2, x \neq -3, -4$
12. $\frac{5}{2x-1}-\frac{3}{7x-2}=5, x \neq \frac{1}{2}, \frac{2}{7}$
13. $\frac{4}{x-5}-\frac{1}{2x+4}=\frac{1}{3}, x \neq 5, -2$
14. $\frac{1}{2x-3}=5-\frac{4}{3x}, x \neq 0, \frac{3}{2}$
15. $\frac{2}{x-3}+\frac{4}{x+2}=1, x \neq 3, -2$

5.4 Forming Quadratic Equations

If we are given the roots of a quadratic equation, it is possible to construct a quadratic equation with these roots. To form a quadratic equation when given the roots, we first change the roots into factors and then use these factors to form the equation.

Roots	→	Factors	→	Equation
$x = -2$ **OR** $x = -4$		$(x+2)$ and $(x+4)$		$(x+2)(x+4)=0$ $\Rightarrow x^2+6x+8=0$

Worked Example 5.14

Form a quadratic equation from each of the following pairs of roots:

(i) 3, 7 (ii) −5, 0

Solution

(i) 3, 7

State each root.	$x = 3$	$x = 7$
Find each factor by rearranging each formula.	$x - 3 = 0$	$x - 7 = 0$
Multiply the factors and set the product equal to 0.	$(x-3)(x-7)=0$ $x(x-7)-3(x-7)=0$ $x^2-7x-3x+21=0$	
This forms the equation:	$x^2-10x+21=0$	

(ii) −5, 0

State each root.	$x = -5$	$x = 0$
Find each factor by rearranging each formula.	$x + 5 = 0$	$x = 0$
Multiply the factors and set the product equal to 0.	$(x + 5)(x) = 0$ $x(x + 5) = 0$	
This forms the equation:	$x^2 + 5x = 0$	

Worked Example 5.15

The roots of a quadratic equation $x^2 + px + q = 0$ are 3 and −4. Find the values of p and q.

Solution

Method 1	Method 2
$x = 3$ **OR** $x = -4$	$x = 3$ **OR** $x = -4$
$x - 3 = 0$ **OR** $x + 4 = 0$	Substitute $x = 3$ into the equation $x^2 + px + q = 0$.
$(x - 3)(x + 4) = 0$	$(3)^2 + p(3) + q = 0$
$x(x + 4) - 3(x + 4) = 0$	$9 + 3p + q = 0$
$x^2 + 4x - 3x - 12 = 0$	$3p + q = -9$ **Eq. I**
$x^2 + x - 12 = 0$	Substitute $x = -4$ into the equation $x^2 + px + q = 0$.
We now compare this equation with the one from the question.	$(-4)^2 + p(-4) + q = 0$
	$16 - 4p + q = 0$
$x^2 + px + q = 0$	$-4p + q = -16$ **Eq. II**
$x^2 + x - 12 = 0$	Then solve the simultaneous equations.
$\therefore p = 1$ and $q = -12$	$-4p + q = -16$ $3p + q = -9$ **Eq. I**
	$-(3p + q = -9)$ $3(1) + q = -9$
	$-7p = -7$ $3 + q = -9$
	$p = 1$ $q = -12$

Exercise 5.6

Form a quadratic equation with the following pairs of roots:

1. 3, 4

2. 2, 5

3. −1, 2

4. 11, −1

5. −3, −3

6. 7, 0

7. −8, 8

8. 0, −4

9. ±3

10. p, $2p$

11. p, $-p$

12. p, q

13. The roots of a quadratic equation $x^2 + bx + c = 0$ are 5 and 3. Find the values of b and c.

14. The roots of a quadratic equation $x^2 + bx + c = 0$ are 0 and −6. Find the values of b and c.

15. The roots of a quadratic equation $x^2 + 8x + r = 0$ are the same. Find the value of r.

16. The roots of a quadratic equation $x^2 - 12x + c = 0$ are the same. Find the value of c.

5.5 Solving Simultaneous Equations: One Linear and One Non-Linear

In Chapter 2, Algebra I, we learned how to solve simultaneous linear equations by finding the point of intersection of two lines.

We may be asked to solve simultaneous equations where one of the equations is linear and the other is non-linear (but of order 2).

Solving simultaneously will give us the co-ordinates of the points of intersection between the line and the non-linear curve.

Worked Example 5.16

Solve for x and y:

$x + 4y = 17$

$x^2 + y^2 = 34$

If the equations being used are in the variables x and y, then:

- The *linear* equation will contain an x term and/or a y term.
- The *non-linear* equation will contain at least one of the following: an x^2 term, an xy term, a y^2 term.

Solution

Step 1 Linear equation	**Always start with the linear equation:** $x + 4y = 17$ We pick the variable that has a coefficient of ±1 and make this variable the subject of the formula. $x = 17 - 4y$
Step 2 Substitute into the non-linear equation. Always substitute from the linear into the non-linear equation.	Next we consider the non-linear equation: $x^2 + y^2 = 34$ We now know that $x = 17 - 4y$ and so we substitute this expression into the non-linear equation. $(17 - 4y)^2 + y^2 = 34$ $(17 - 4y)(17 - 4y) + y^2 = 34$ $(17 - 4y)^2 = (17 - 4y)(17 - 4y)$ $17(17 - 4y) - 4y(17 - 4y) + y^2 = 34$ Expand $(17 - 4y)(17 - 4y)$. $289 - 68y - 68y + 16y^2 + y^2 = 34$ $289 - 136y + 17y^2 = 34$ Simplify the LHS. $17y^2 - 136y + 289 = 34$ Rearrange LHS in descending powers. $17y^2 - 136y + 289 - 34 = 0$ Gather all terms on one side. $17y^2 - 136y + 255 = 0$ Simplify the LHS.
Step 3 Solve for one variable.	To make solving easier, divide all the terms by 17, as 17 is the HCF of 17, 136 and 255. $y^2 - 8y + 15 = 0$ y − 3 y − 5 $(y - 3)(y - 5) = 0$ $y - 3 = 0$ **OR** $y - 5 = 0$ $\therefore y = 3$ **OR** $y = 5$ Alternatively, use the quadratic formula. $17y^2 - 136y + 255 = 0$ $a = 17 \quad b = -136 \quad c = 255$ $y = \frac{-(-136) \pm \sqrt{(-136)^2 - 4(17)(255)}}{2(17)}$ $y = \frac{136 \pm \sqrt{1156}}{34}$ $y = \frac{136 + 34}{34}$ **OR** $y = \frac{136 - 34}{34}$ $\therefore y = 5$ **OR** $y = 3$

Step 4 Solve for the other variable using the linear equation.	As we know the two values of y, we can now find the corresponding values of x. $x = 17 - 4y$ Use the rearranged formula from Step 1. If $y = 3$: If $y = 5$: $x = 17 - 4(3)$ $x = 17 - 4(5)$ $x = 17 - 12$ $x = 17 - 20$ $x = 5$ $x = -3$
Step 5 Write answer(s) as ordered pairs.	$x = 5, y = 3$ **OR** $x = -3, y = 5$ Answer: $(x, y) = (5, 3)$ **OR** $(x, y) = (-3, 5)$
In this example we have found, using algebra, the points of intersection between a linear curve (the line $x + 4y = 17$) and a non-linear curve (the circle $x^2 + y^2 = 34$).	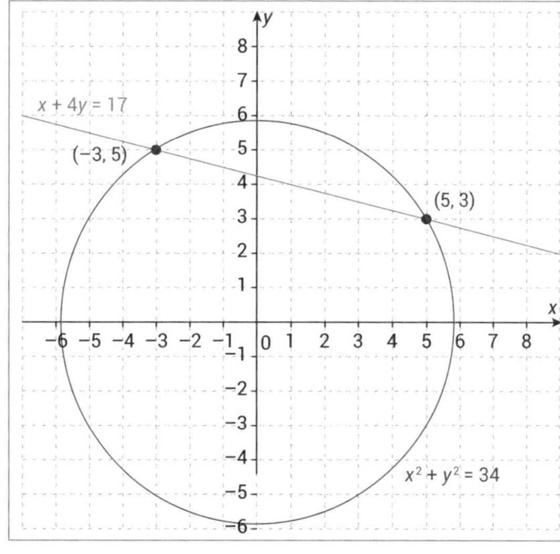 

Worked Example 5.17

Solve for a and b:

$2a - b = 0$

$a^2 - 2b^2 = -7$

Solution

Step 1 Linear equation	$2a - b = 0$ $2a = b$ $\therefore b = 2a$
Step 2 Substitute into the non-linear equation.	$a^2 - 2b^2 = -7$ $a^2 - 2(2a)^2 = -7$ $(2a)^2 = (2a)(2a)$ $a^2 - 2(2a)(2a) = -7$ Expand. $a^2 - 8a^2 = -7$ $-7a^2 = -7$ $7a^2 = 7$ $a^2 = 1$

Step 3 Solve for one variable.	$a^2 = 1$, $a = \pm 1$ **OR** $a^2 - 1 = 0$ $(a - 1)(a + 1) = 0$ $a - 1 = 0$ **OR** $a + 1 = 0$ $a = 1$ **OR** $a = -1$
Step 4 Solve for the other variable using the linear equation.	$b = 2a$ Use the rearranged formula from Step 1. If $a = 1$: $b = 2(1)$, $b = 2$ If $a = -1$: $b = 2(-1)$, $b = -2$
Step 5 Write answer(s) as ordered pairs.	$a = 1, b = 2$ **OR** $a = -1, b = -2$ Answer: $(a, b) = (1, 2)$ **OR** $(a, b) = (-1, -2)$

Exercise 5.7

Solve the following simultaneous equations:

1. $x = 5 - y$
   $x^2 + y^2 = 17$
2. $x = 1 + y$
   $x^2 + y^2 = 25$
3. $a + b = 4$
   $a^2 + b^2 = 16$
4. $p - q = 6$
   $p^2 + q^2 = 26$
5. $x - 2y = -5$
   $x^2 + y^2 = 10$
6. $4x - y = -3$
   $x^2 - y^2 = 0$
7. $5r - s = -13$
   $r^2 + s^2 = 13$
8. $x + 2y = 7$
   $x^2 + 3y^2 = 28$
9. $x = y$
   $x^2 + y^2 = 2$
10. $p = q$
    $p + 2q = 35$
11. $x + y = 7$
    $xy = 12$
12. $a + 2b = 11$
    $ab = 14$
13. $x - 2y + 1 = 0$
    $x^2 - xy = 10$
14. $y = -2x$
    $2x^2 - y^2 + xy = -16$
15. $2x = y + 3$
    $x^2 + y^2 - 3xy = -45$

5.6 Solving Problems Which Lead to a Quadratic Equation

Algebra can be used to solve a variety of problems. This section shows how to solve problems using quadratic equations.

Worked Example 5.18

One number is four more than another number. The sum of their squares is 10.

(i) If x is the smaller number, express the second number in terms of x.

(ii) Given that the sum of their squares is 10, form an equation in x.

(iii) By solving the equation in part (ii), find the two numbers.

(iv) Verify your answers.

Solution

(i) First number = x

One number is four more than another number.

$\therefore$ Second number = $x + 4$

(ii) **Word equation:** The sum of their squares is 10.

Maths equation: $x^2 + (x + 4)^2 = 10$

(iii) $x^2 + (x + 4)^2 = 10$

$x^2 + (x + 4)(x + 4) = 10$	$(x + 4)^2 = (x + 4)(x + 4)$
$x^2 + x^2 + 8x + 16 = 10$	Expand out.
$2x^2 + 8x + 16 = 10$	Simplify the LHS.
$2x^2 + 8x + 6 = 0$	Gather all terms on one side.
$x^2 + 4x + 3 = 0$	Divide the equation by 2.
$(x + 1)(x + 3) = 0$	Factorise.
$x + 1 = 0$ **OR** $x + 3 = 0$	Solve for x.
$x = -1$ **OR** $x = -3$	

x = First number

First number = -1	**OR**	First number = -3
Second number = $-1 + 4$		Second number = $-3 + 4$
$= 3$		$= 1$

(iv) Verify your answers. Remember the sum of the squares of the two numbers equals 10.

Using -1 and 3:	Using -3 and 1:
$(-1)^2 + (3)^2 = 10$	$(-3)^2 + (1)^2 = 10$
$1 + 9 = 10$	$9 + 1 = 10$
$10 = 10$ True	$10 = 10$ True
$\therefore$ Verified	$\therefore$ Verified

Make sure to verify both pairs of numbers.

Worked Example 5.19

An xy co-ordinate grid is used to represent the motion of a ship across a patch of open sea.

The linear path of the ship is given by the equation $2x + y = 6$.

The boundary of a reef is represented by the equation $x^2 + y^2 = 17$.

(i) At what two points will the ship cross the reef?

(ii) If each grid unit represents 2 km and the distance between two points (x_1, y_1) and (x_2, y_2) is $\sqrt{(x_2 - x_1)^2 + (y_2 - y_1)^2}$, calculate to the nearest metre the distance between the two crossing points.

Solution

(i) We have one linear and one non-linear equation.

Step 1 Linear equation	$2x + y = 6$ $y = 6 - 2x$	
Step 2 Substitute into the non-linear equation.	$x^2 + y^2 = 17$ $x^2 + (6 - 2x)^2 = 17$ $x^2 + (6 - 2x)(6 - 2x) = 17$ $x^2 + 36 - 24x + 4x^2 = 17$ $5x^2 - 24x + 36 = 17$ $5x^2 - 24x + 36 - 17 = 0$ $5x^2 - 24x + 19 = 0$	 $(6 - 2x)^2 = (6 - 2x)(6 - 2x)$ Expand out. Rearrange and simplify the LHS. Gather all terms on one side. Simplify the LHS.
Step 3 Solve for one variable.	**Method 1** $5x^2 - 24x + 19 = 0$ $5x$ – 19 x – 1 $(5x - 19)(x - 1) = 0$ $5x - 19 = 0$ **OR** $x - 1 = 0$ $5x = 19$ **OR** $x = 1$ $x = 3.8$ **OR** $x = 1$	**Method 2** $5x^2 - 24x + 19 = 0$ $a = 5 \quad b = -24 \quad c = 19$ $x = \dfrac{-(-24) \pm \sqrt{(-24)^2 - 4(5)(19)}}{2(5)}$ $x = \dfrac{24 \pm \sqrt{196}}{10}$ $x = \dfrac{24 + 14}{10}$ **OR** $x = \dfrac{24 - 14}{10}$ $x = 3.8$ **OR** $x = 1$
Step 4 Solve for the other variable using the linear equation.	$y = 6 - 2x$ If $x = 3.8$: $y = 6 - 2(3.8)$ $y = -1.6$	Use the formula from Step1. If $x = 1$: $y = 6 - 2(1)$ $y = 4$
Step 5 Write answer(s).	The ship crosses the reef at the co-ordinates $(x, y) = (3.8, -1.6)$ and $(x, y) = (1,4)$.	

(ii) Let $(x_1,y_1) = (1,4)$ and $(x_2,y_2) = (3.8,-1.6)$.

$$\text{Distance} = \sqrt{(3.8 - 1)^2 + (-1.6 - 4)^2}$$
$$= \sqrt{(2.8)^2 + (-5.6)^2}$$
$$= \sqrt{39.2}$$
$$= \frac{14\sqrt{5}}{5}$$
$$\text{Distance} = \frac{14\sqrt{5}}{5} \times 2 \text{ km}$$
$$= \frac{28\sqrt{5}}{5} \text{ km}$$
$$\approx 12.52198067 \text{ km}$$
$$\approx 12{,}522 \text{ m (Correct to nearest metre)}$$

Worked Example 5.20

The width of a rectangular office is 4 m less than the length. The area of the office is 221 m^2.

(i) If x is the length of the office, express the width of the office in terms of x.

(ii) Using your answer from part (i), write an equation to represent the area of the office.

(iii) Find the dimensions of the office.

Solution

(i) The width (w) of the office is 4 m less than its length (l).

If $l = x$, then $w = (x - 4)$ m.

(ii) Area of the office = 221 m^2 — Write out what we know.

$l \times w = 221$ — Use the appropriate formula (Area = $l \times w$).

$x(x - 4) = 221$ — Fill in the given values for l and w.

$x^2 - 4x = 221$ — Expand out.

$x^2 - 4x - 221 = 0$ — Gather all terms on one side.

(iii) Solve the equation, either by factorising or by using the quadratic formula.

Factorising	Quadratic formula
$x^2 - 4x - 221 = 0$ $(x - 17)(x + 13) = 0$ $x - 17 = 0$ **OR** $x + 13 = 0$ $x = 17$ **OR** ~~$x = -13$~~ (Reject, as x is a distance and so $x \geqslant 0$.)	$x^2 - 4x - 221 = 0$ $a = 1 \quad b = -4 \quad c = -221$ $x = \frac{-(-4) \pm \sqrt{(-4)^2 - 4(1)(-221)}}{2(1)}$ $x = \frac{4 \pm \sqrt{900}}{2}$ $x = \frac{4 + 30}{2}$ **OR** $x = \frac{4 - 30}{2}$ $x = 17$ **OR** ~~$x = -13$~~ (Reject, as x is a distance and so $x \geqslant 0$.)

In context questions we may need to reject some solutions. In this example, $x \neq -13$ (length cannot be negative). Therefore, accept $x = 17$ only.

Find the dimensions of the office.

$l = x$

$\Rightarrow$ length = 17 m

$w = x - 4$

$\Rightarrow$ width = 17 − 4 = 13 m

Don't forget the units in your answer(s).

Exercise 5.8

1. Let x be equal to a number.

(i) Write an expression for the square of this number.

(ii) Write an expression to show three times the number.

A number is squared and added to three times the number to give a total of 18.

(iii) Use your answers from parts (i) and (ii) to write an equation to show this information.

(iv) Use this equation to find all possible values for the number.

ALGEBRA II

2. Let x represent a number.
   (i) Write an expression for four times this number.
   (ii) Write an expression for five times the square of this number.

   The sum of five times the square of the number and four times the number is 28.
   (iii) Use your answers from parts (i) and (ii) to write an equation to show this information.
   (iv) Use this equation to find the two possible values for the number.

3. Let y represent a number. Another number is three more than this number.
   (i) Write an expression, in terms of y, for the larger number.

   The sum of the squares of these two numbers is 65.
   (ii) Write an equation to show this information.
   (iii) Use this equation to find the two pairs of numbers for which this is true.

4. Let n represent a natural number.
   (i) Write an expression, in terms of n, for the next consecutive natural number.
   (ii) Write an expression for the product of these two consecutive natural numbers.

   The product of two consecutive natural numbers is 56.
   (iii) Write an equation to show this information.
   (iv) Use this equation to find the two consecutive natural numbers.

5. $3n$ is an odd natural number.
   (i) Write an expression for the next consecutive odd natural number.

   $3n$ and the next consecutive odd natural number are multiplied.
   (ii) Write an expression for this product.

   The product of this number and the next consecutive odd natural number is 483.
   (iii) Write an equation to show this information.
   (iv) Use this equation to find the two consecutive odd natural numbers.

6. A child's age is x years. Her father's age is x^2 years.
   (i) Write an expression for the age of the father in 14 years' time.
   (ii) Write an expression for the age of the child in 14 years' time.

   In 14 years' time, the father's age will be two and a half times the age of his child.
   (iii) Write an equation to show this information.
   (iv) Find the child's age and her father's age now.

7. Amy is five years older than Bridget. Caroline is twice the age of Amy. Let x equal the age of Bridget.

   Write an expression for the age of:
   (i) Amy
   (ii) Caroline

   When Amy's and Caroline's ages are multiplied, the answer is 722.
   (iii) Write an equation to show this information and hence find all three ages.

8. The length of a rectangle is 5 m more than its width.
   (i) If x = the width, write down (in terms of x) an expression for the length.
   (ii) Write, in terms of x, an expression for the area of the rectangle.

   The area of the rectangle is 234 m^2.
   (iii) Write an equation to show this information.
   (iv) Use this equation to find the dimensions of the rectangle.

9. A garden has a lawn surrounded by a uniform path as shown. The dimensions of the rectangular lawn are 10 m by 12 m.

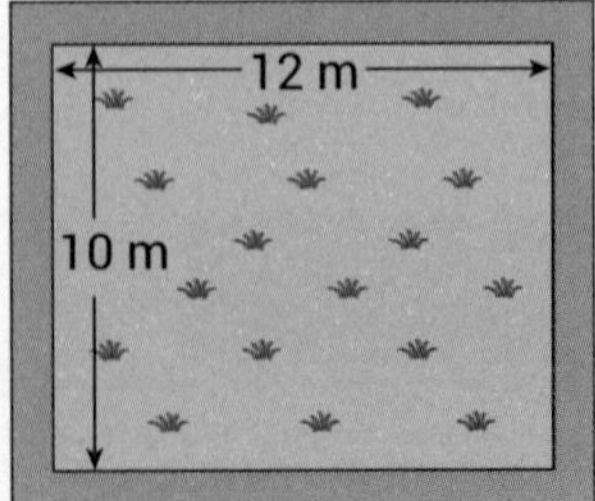

   Let x equal the width of the path that surrounds the lawn.

Write an expression, in terms of x, for the:

(i) Length of the garden

(ii) Width of the garden

(iii) Area of the garden

The uniform path has an area of 48 m^2.

(iv) Write an equation to show the area of the garden.

(v) Use this equation to find the width of the path.

10. A plot consists of a rectangular garden measuring 8 m by 10 m, surrounded by a path of constant width, as shown in the diagram. The total area of the plot (garden and path) is 143 m^2.

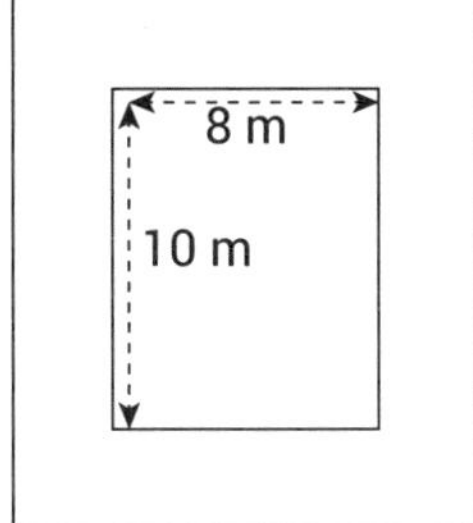

Three students, Kevin, Elaine and Tony, have been given the problem of trying to find the width of the path. Each of them is using a different method, but all of them are using x to represent the width of the path.

Kevin divides the path into eight pieces. He writes down the area of each piece in terms of x. He then forms an equation by setting the area of the path plus the area of the garden equal to the total area of the plot.

(i) Write, in terms of x, the area of each section in Kevin's diagram below.

(ii) Write down and simplify the equation that Kevin should get. Give your answer in the form $ax^2 + bx + c = 0$.

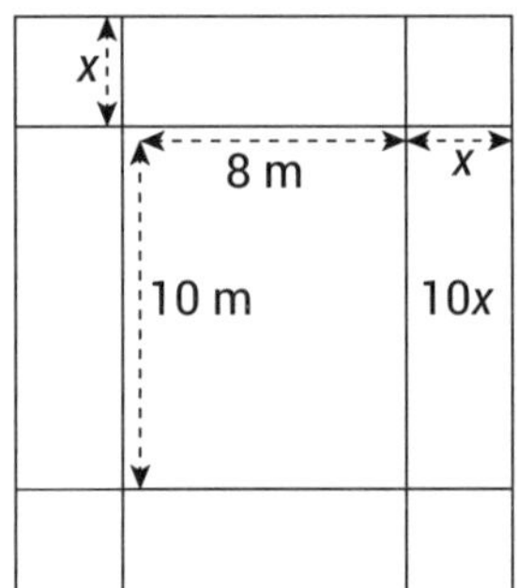

Kevin's diagram

Elaine writes down the length and width of the plot in terms of x.

She multiplies these and sets the answer equal to the total area of the plot.

(iii) Write, in terms of x, the length and the width of the plot in Elaine's diagram.

(iv) Write down and simplify the equation that Elaine should get. Give your answer in the form $ax^2 + bx + c = 0$.

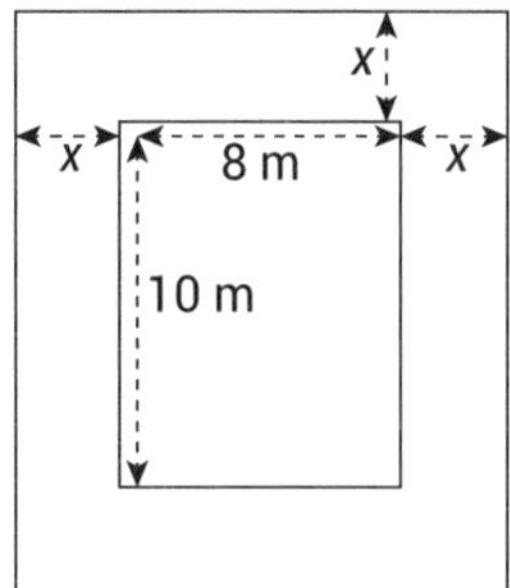

Elaine's diagram

(v) Solve an equation to find the width of the path.

(vi) Tony does not answer the problem by solving an equation. Instead, he does it by trying out different values for x. Show some calculations that Tony might have used to solve the problem.

(vii) Which of the three methods do you think is best? Give a reason for your answer.

11. A sheet of metal is 30 cm by 40 cm. A uniform strip of metal of width x cm is cut from around the edge of this sheet as shown.

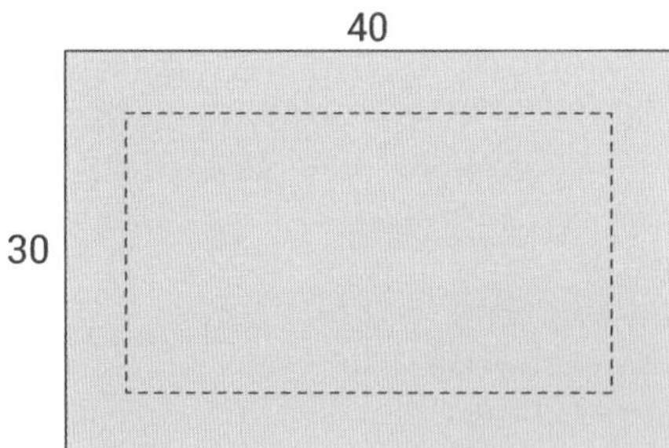

Write an expression in terms of x for the:

(i) Length

(ii) Width

(iii) Area

of the remaining rectangular piece of metal.

(iv) The strip of metal must be wide enough so as to leave half the area. Using your expression from part (iii), write an equation and use it to find the width of the strip of metal.

12. A net of an open rectangular box is shown.

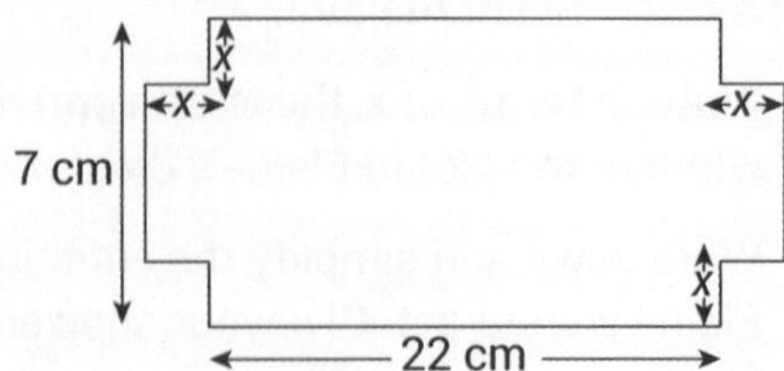

If 22 cm is the length of the box when formed, write an expression in terms of x for the:

(i) Width of the box when formed

(ii) Area of the box when formed

The area of the base of the box is 110 cm^2.

(iii) Write an equation to show this information.

(iv) Use this equation to find the value of x.

(v) Hence, find the volume of the box.

13. The sides of a right-angled triangle are shown. Using the theorem of Pythagoras, find the lengths of all three sides.

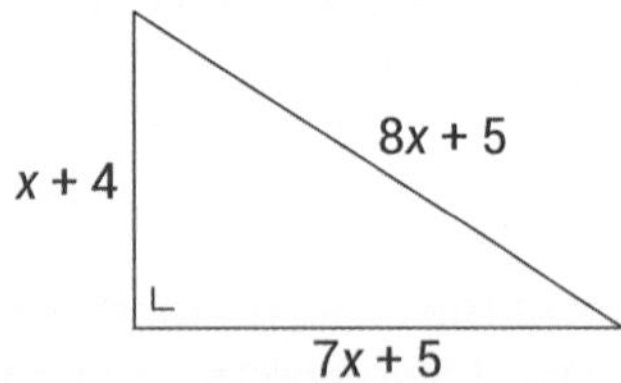

14. A woman walks a distance of 10 km from A to B at a speed of x km h^{-1}. She then walks 12 km from B to C at a speed of $(x - 1)$ km h^{-1}. The total time for the journey is 5 hours.

(i) Copy and complete the table below.

Journey	A to B	B to C
Distance (km)	10	12
Speed (km h^{-1})	x	$x - 1$
Time		

(ii) Solve for x.

15. The members of a lottery syndicate win a prize of €400. If two more people had joined the syndicate, each member would have received €10 less.

(i) Copy and complete the table below.

Total prize	€400	
Number of members	x	
Prize share per member		

(ii) Use the information given to write an equation in x.

(iii) How many members are in the syndicate?

16. Ann and Ben travel 45 km at steady speeds on their bikes. Ann travels 1 km h^{-1} faster than Ben. She finishes half an hour before Ben. Let x equal the speed that Ben travels.

(i) Copy and complete the table below.

	Ben	Ann
Distance (km)	45	
Speed (km h^{-1})	x	
Time		

(ii) Use the information given to write an equation in x.

(iii) Find their speeds on the journey.

17. An empty warehouse has a perimeter of 264 m. Let x equal the length and y equal the width of this warehouse.

(i) Write an equation, in terms of x and y, to show the perimeter of this warehouse.

(ii) Hence, show that the width of the warehouse, in metres, can be written as $y = (132 - x)$.

An extension increases the length by 12 m, the width by 6 m and the floor space to a total of 4,400 m^2.

(iii) Write an expression, in terms of x, for the extended width of the warehouse.

(iv) Show that the area of the extended warehouse, in square metres, can be written as $1{,}656 + 138x - x^2$.

(v) Write an equation to show the area of the extended warehouse.

(vi) Hence, find the dimensions of the original warehouse (two possible sets of dimensions).

18. Let x represent the length and y the width of a rectangular garden (in metres). The perimeter of this garden is 32 m.

(i) Write an equation, in terms of x and y, to represent the perimeter of the garden.

(ii) Hence, show that the width of the garden can be written as $y = (16 - x)$.

The area of the garden is 60 m^2.

(iii) Write an equation, in terms of x and y, to represent the area of the garden.

(iv) Hence, using your equations from parts (ii) and (iii), find the dimensions of the garden.

19. The length, width and height of a child's toy box are in the ratio 4 : 2 : 1.

It is decided to change the dimensions of the toy box, doubling the width, halving the height and keeping the length the same.

Calculate the percentage change in the toy box's:

(i) Volume (ii) Surface area

when compared to the original box.

20. The height (h) in metres of a firework above the ground, when fired from the top of a tower, is given by the formula $h(t) = 8 + 18t - 5t^2$ where t is the time in seconds after the firework is fired.

(i) What is the height of the firework after 2 seconds?

(ii) What is the height of the firework when fired?

(iii) How long will it take for the firework to hit the ground?

(iv) Bob says 'The firework never reaches a height of 30 m above the ground.' Show mathematically that Bob is right.

21. The linear flight path of an airplane is given by the equation $x + y = -3$. The airspace of a certain city is given by the equation $x^2 + y^2 = 29$.

(i) At what two points does the flight of this plane cross the boundary of the airspace of the city?

The airplane control tower is situated at the point (0,0), and the point (−2,4) is 2 km west and 4 km north of the tower.

(ii) Give the co-ordinates of each point of intersection as kilometres east/west and kilometres north/south.

(iii) How far are these two points from the tower? Give your answer (in km) in surd form.

22. A company has calculated that the daily cost (in euro) to produce x items is given by the production cost function $C(x) = 5x^2 + 750x + 3{,}000$. The total daily income from the sale of x items is given by the income function $I(x) = 1{,}200x$.

The company assumes that it will sell all the items it produces.

(i) If the company produces 20 items in one day, find the production cost and total income for the 20 items.

(ii) Find the profit the company makes on that day.

(iii) Find a general expression for the profit the company makes from the production if x items are produced that day.

(iv) Find the profit made when the company produces 45 items.

(v) The production costs on a particular day amount to €11,000. Find the number of items produced on that day.

Revision Exercises

1. (a) Solve:

(i) $x^2 + 3x = 0$

(ii) $x^2 - 2x - 8 = 0$

(iii) $x^2 - 12x + 20 = 0$

(iv) $x^2 + x - 6 = 0$

(v) $2a^2 + 7a = 0$

(vi) $x^2 - 100 = 0$

(vii) $2x^2 + 5x - 12 = 0$

(viii) $49x^2 = 100$

(b) Solve:

(i) $x^2 = 5x + 6$

(ii) $2x^2 = 4 - 7x$

(iii) $5x^2 - 18x + 9 = 0$

(iv) $6x^2 + 23x + 20 = 0$

(c) Solve:

(i) $(x + 1)(x - 1) = 24$

(ii) $x(2x - 1) = 3x$

(iii) $21x^2 = x^2 - 7x + 6$

2. (a) Use the quadratic formula to solve these equations, giving your answer to two decimal places:

(i) $x^2 + 2x - 5 = 0$

(ii) $-x^2 + 12x - 5 = 0$

(iii) $x^2 + x - 10 = 0$

(iv) $-x^2 + 3x + 20 = 0$

(v) $2x^2 + 2x - 1 = 0$

(b) Use the quadratic formula to solve these equations, giving your answers in surd form:

(i) $x^2 - 3x + 1 = 0$

(ii) $2x^2 - 12x + 1 = 0$

(iii) $-5x^2 + 14x - 4 = 0$

3. (a) Form the quadratic equations with these pairs of roots:

(i) 2 and 6

(ii) 11 and −2

(iii) −4 and 0

(iv) −5 and −7

(b) (i) The roots of $x^2 + px + q$ are both equal to −4. Find the values of p and q.

(ii) The roots of $x^2 + bx + c = 0$ are both equal to 10. Find the values of b and c.

(iii) The roots of $x^2 - 10x + k = 0$ are equal. Find the value of k.

4. Solve:

(i) $x = 1 + \frac{56}{x}, x \neq 0$

(ii) $\frac{18}{x} = x + 3, x \neq 0$

(iii) $\frac{3}{x-3} + \frac{2}{x-1} = 2, x \neq 3, 1$

(iv) $\frac{3}{x+1} + \frac{1}{x-1} = 1\frac{1}{4}, x \neq \pm 1$

5. (a) (i) Find two consecutive natural numbers whose squares add up to 61.

(ii) Two numbers differ by 3. Their product is 28. Find the numbers.

(b) Solve each of the following simultaneous equations:

(i) $x - y = 3$
$x^2 + y^2 = 17$

(ii) $x - 2y = 0$
$x^2 + y^2 = 5$

(iii) $2x - y = 7$
$xy = 15$

(iv) $x - 2y + 1 = 0$
$x^2 - xy = 10$

6. (a) Draw a sketch of a quadratic function that has:

(i) Two different roots

(ii) Two equal roots

(iii) No real roots

(b) Estimate from each graph the points of intersection of the linear and non-linear graphs.

(i)

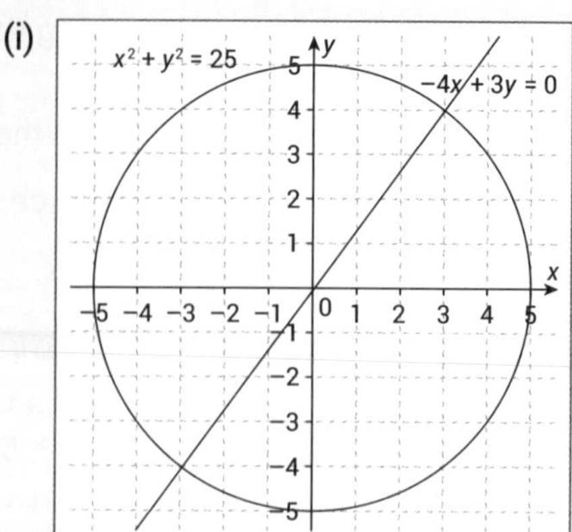

(ii)

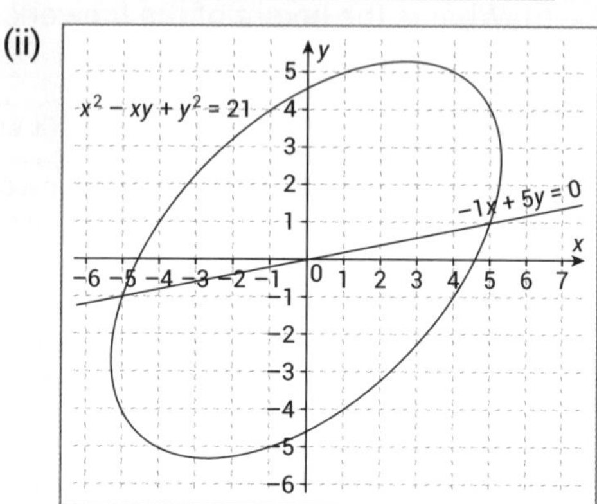

Check the answer to part (ii) by solving the simultaneous equations.

7. (a) Let x represent a number.

(i) Write an expression to show the square of this number.

(ii) Write an expression to show six times the number.

A number is squared and added to six times the number to give a sum of 55.

(iii) Use your answers from parts (i) and (ii) to write an equation to show this information.

(iv) Use this equation to find the two values for the number.

(b) Let y represent a natural number. A smaller natural number differs from this number by 3.

(i) Write an expression in y for this smaller number.

(ii) Write an expression in y for the product of the two numbers.

The product of these two numbers is 378.

(iii) Write an equation to represent this information.

(iv) Use this equation to find the two numbers.

(c) The perimeter of a rectangular room is 22 m. The area is 30 m^2. If x = the width and y = the length, in metres, write down two equations and, hence, find the dimensions of the room.

8. (a) A ball is launched straight up into the air. The height (h) of the ball after t seconds is given by the equation $h(t) = 40t - 5t^2$.

(i) What will the ball's height be after 2 seconds?

(ii) How long does it take the ball to reach its maximum height of 80 m?

(iii) How long will it take for the ball to return to the ground?

(b) A boat travels a distance of 30 km at a speed of x km h^{-1}. It then travels 20 km at a speed of $(x + 1)$ km h^{-1}.

(i) Copy and complete the table below.

	Journey *A*	Journey *B*
Distance (km)	30 km	
Speed (km h^{-1})		$x + 1$
Time		

(ii) If the total time for the two journeys is 15 hours, find the value of x.

(c) A student scores x marks in one test and y marks in another test. The combined score for the two tests is 27.

(i) Write an equation in x and y to show this information.

If the marks from both tests were squared and then subtracted, the difference between the two scores would be 81.

(ii) Write an equation in x and y to show this information.

(iii) Using your equations from parts (i) and (ii), find the student's results in each test.

Exam Questions

1. Solve the equation $-x^2 + 6x - 4 = 0$. Give each solution correct to one decimal place.

SEC Leaving Certificate Ordinary Level, Paper 1, 2015

2. (a) Solve the equation $x^2 - 6x - 23 = 0$. Give your answers in the form $a \pm b\sqrt{2}$ where $a, b \in Z$.

(b) Solve the simultaneous equations:

$2r - s = 10$

$rs - s^2 = 12$

SEC Leaving Certificate Ordinary Level, Sample Paper 1, 2014

3. Solve the simultaneous equations:

$x + y = 7$

$x^2 + y^2 = 25$

SEC Leaving Certificate Ordinary Level, Sample Paper 1, 2014

4. (a) Solve the equation $x^2 - x - 6 = 0$.

(b) The graphs of four quadratic functions are shown.

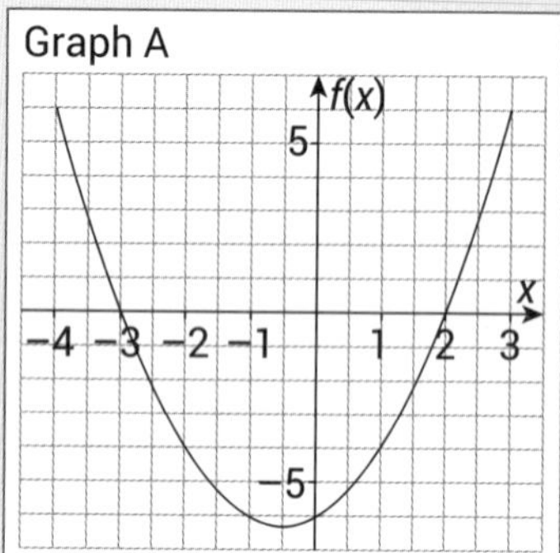

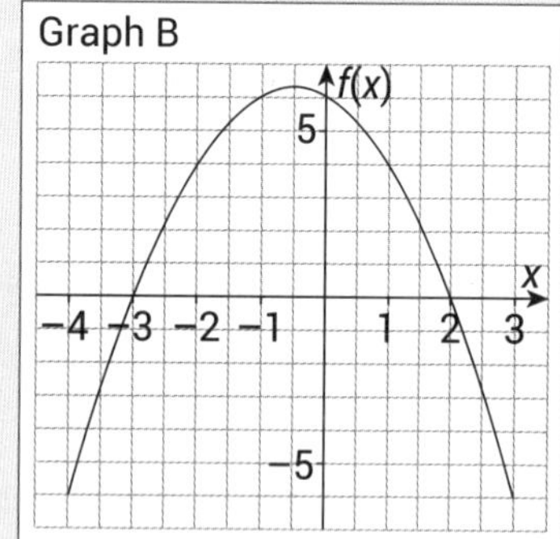

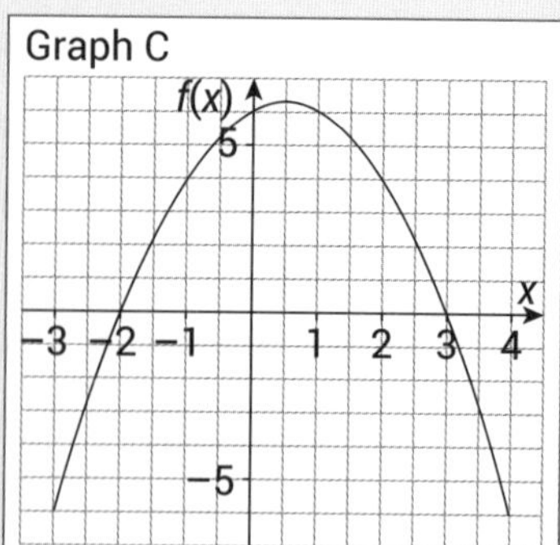

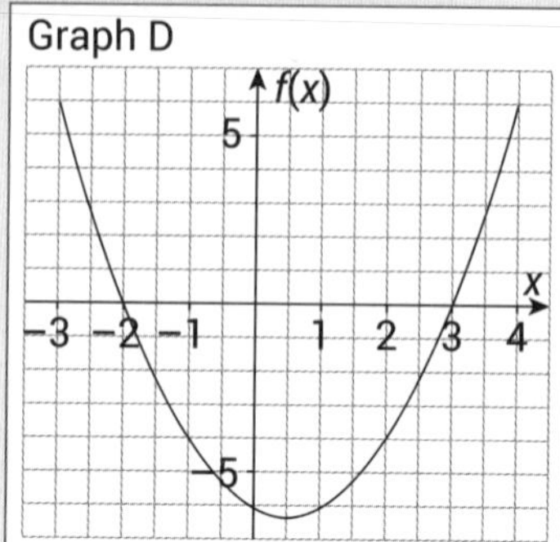

Which of the graphs above is that of the function $f: x \rightarrow x^2 - x - 6$, where $x \in R$?

SEC Leaving Certificate Ordinary Level, Paper 1, 2014

5. Solve the equation $\frac{2}{3x-4} - \frac{1}{2x+1} = \frac{1}{2}$ and give your answers correct to one decimal place.

SEC Leaving Certificate Ordinary Level, Paper 1, 2012

Solutions and chapter summary available online

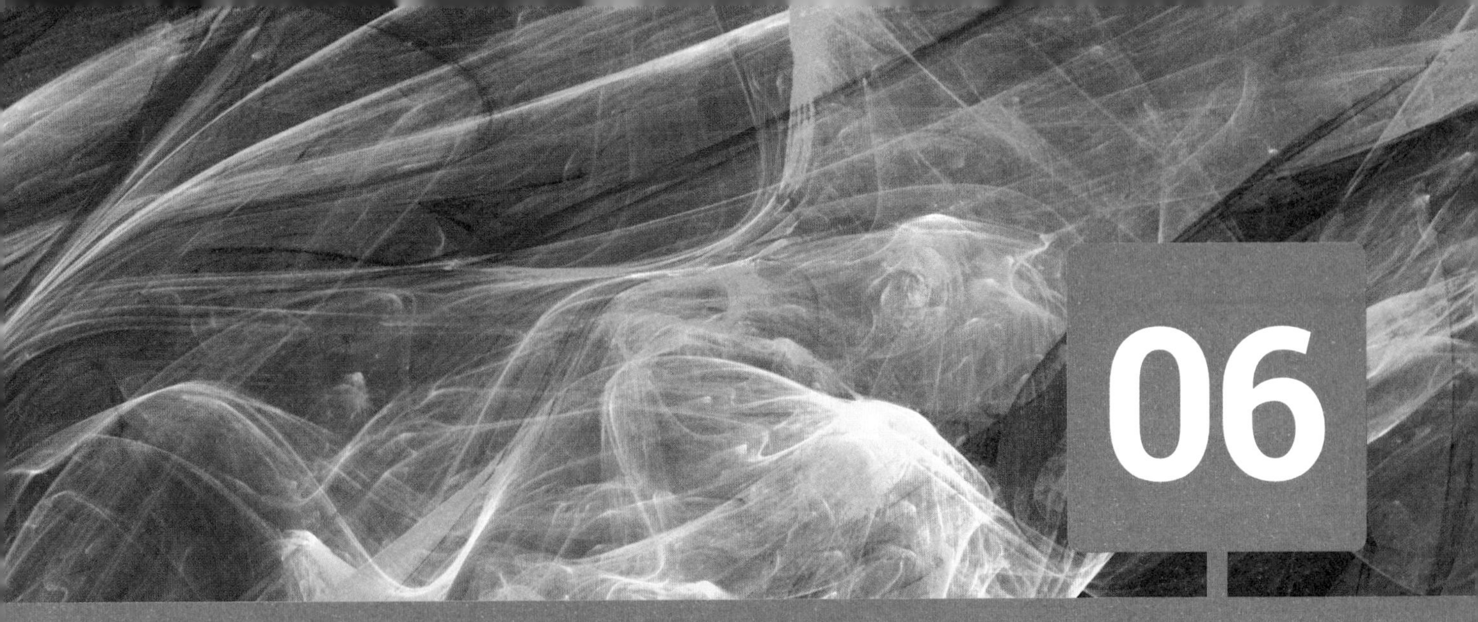

06

Functions

In this chapter you will learn to:

- Recognise that a function assigns a unique output to a given input
- Form composite functions
- Graph functions of the form:
    - $ax + b$, where $a, b \in Q, x \in R$
    - $ax^2 + bx + c$, where $a, b, c \in Z, x \in R$
    - $ax^3 + bx^2 + cx + d$, where $a, b, c, d \in Z, x \in R$
    - ab^x, where $a \in N, b, x \in R$
- Interpret equations of the form $f(x) = g(x)$ as a comparison of such functions
- Use graphical methods to find approximate solutions to:
    - $f(x) = 0$
    - $f(x) = k$
    - $f(x) = g(x)$

  where $f(x)$ and $g(x)$ are of the stated form, or where graphs of $f(x)$ and $g(x)$ are provided

You should remember...

- Substitution in algebra
- Solving equations
- Number patterns
- Input–output tables
- Domain, codomain, range
- Linear and quadratic functions

Key words

- Relation
- Function
- Input
- Output
- Composite function
- Mapping diagram
- Couples
- Ordered pairs
- Domain
- Codomain
- Range
- Transformation

6.1 Introduction

What is a Function?

A **function** is a rule that maps an input to a unique output.

Functions can be described as 'number machines' that transform one number into another. If we think of functions as machines, then something is put into the machine, something happens in the machine, and then something comes out of the machine.

Lowercase letters are used to name functions. *f* and *g* are often used, but remember any letter may be used to name/denote a function.

Functions in Everyday Life

You meet functions several times throughout your normal day.

Television remote controls are an example of functions at work. If you have programmed your television so that channel 103 is assigned to TV3 (for example), then when you key in 103 on your remote, TV3 appears on the television screen. Of course, you could also have TV3 pre-programmed for channel 104 (say), but you could not pre-programme two or more television stations for the same channel number. In other words, each input (channel number) is mapped to a unique output (television station).

Important Terms

- An **input** is an object that is put into the function.
- The **domain** is the set of all inputs for which a function is defined.
- An **output** is the object that comes out of the function.
- The **range** is the set of actual output values of a function.
- The **codomain** is the set of all possible output values of a function.

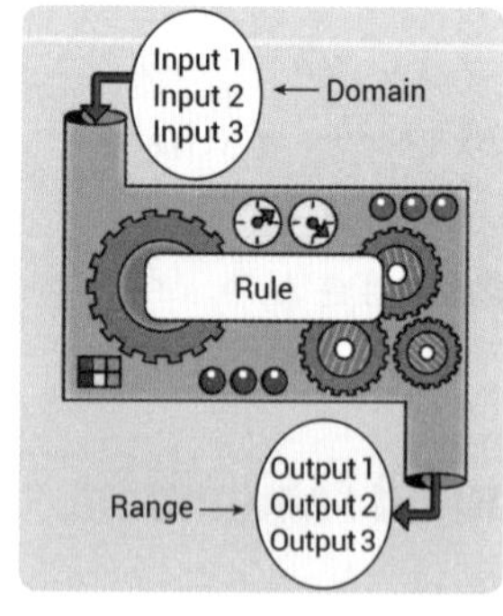

The following example illustrates the meanings of these terms:

Imagine a secondary school in which the Fifth Year classes are called 5.1, 5.2, 5.3 and 5.4. Each class is going on a class trip. They can choose from the following options:

cinema, ice-skating, go-karting, paint-balling or bowling

5.1 choose ice-skating, 5.2 choose go-karting, 5.3 choose ice-skating and 5.4 choose paint-balling. These choices can be represented by a function, as illustrated in the mapping diagram:

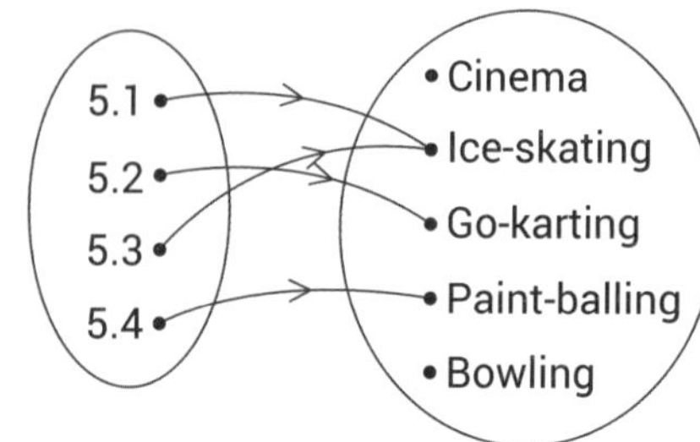

FUNCTIONS

- 5.1 is an example of an **input**.
- Ice-skating is an example of an **output**.
- The **domain** is the set of all Fifth Year classes: {5.1, 5.2, 5.3, 5.4}.
- The **range** is the set of the three chosen activities: {ice-skating, go-karting, paint-balling}.
- The **codomain** is the set of all five trip options: {cinema, ice-skating, go-karting, paint-balling, bowling}.

Examples of Functions

Suppose you write $f(x) = x^2$. You have just defined a rule for a function f that transforms any number into its square.

Consider the following inputs to this function: {−1, 0, 1, 2}.

The resulting outputs can be computed using an input–output table:

Input (x)	Application of function (x^2)	Output (y)
−1	$(-1)^2$	1
0	$(0)^2$	0
1	$(1)^2$	1
2	$(2)^2$	4

Here, y is the result of applying the rule (the function) to the input.

We can represent the rule for this function in a number of other ways.

Using function notation

$f(x) = x^2$

Pronounced '*f* of *x* equals *x*-squared'.

OR

Using alternative function notation

$f: x \rightarrow x^2$

Pronounced '*f* maps *x* to x^2'.

OR

As a set of couples/ordered pairs

$f = \{(-1,1), (0,0), (1,1), (2,4)\}$

For example, (2,4) tells us that if 2 is the input, then 4 is the output.

OR

Using a mapping diagram

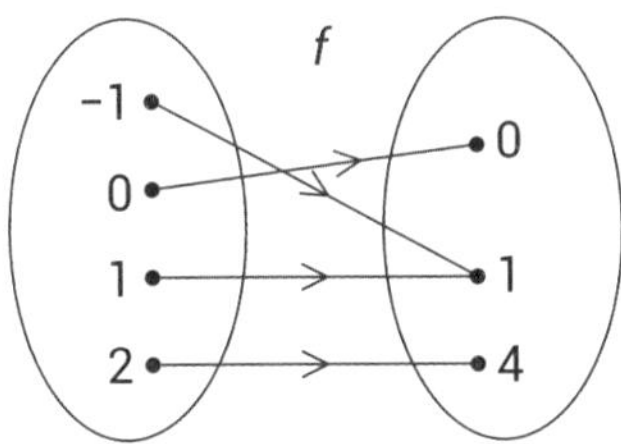

Points to Note: Inputs and Outputs

Look again at the function f defined as $f(x) = x^2$. You will note the following:

- An input can pass through the function and not change, i.e. the input 0 passes through the function and comes out as 0, giving the couple (0,0).
- Two inputs can result in the same output, i.e. the inputs −1 and 1 both result in the output 1.
- However, an input into a function will never result in two different outputs.

Worked Example 6.1

The function f is defined over the domain $\{0, 1, 2, 3, 4\}$, where $f(x) = 2x - 8$.

Calculate the range of this function.

Solution

x	$2x - 8$	y
0	$2(0) - 8$	-8
1	$2(1) - 8$	-6
2	$2(2) - 8$	-4
3	$2(3) - 8$	-2
4	$2(4) - 8$	0

Range = $\{-8, -6, -4, -2, 0\}$

Worked Example 6.2

The function j is defined such that $j(x)$ = the number of legs x has. The domain of j is {a healthy cat, a parrot with all its legs, a sheep, a three-legged dog}.

Find the range of j.

Solution

Remember that the range is the list of all actual outputs.

- j(a healthy cat) = 4
- j(a parrot with all its legs) = 2
- j(a sheep) = 4
- j(a three-legged dog) = 3

So the range is $\{2, 3, 4\}$.

Even though 4 appears twice, we list it only once in the range.

Worked Example 6.3

The function h can be represented by the following set of ordered pairs:

$\{(-4,16), (-3,9), (0,0), (1,1), (3,9), (5,25)\}$

Draw a mapping diagram to illustrate the function h.

Solution

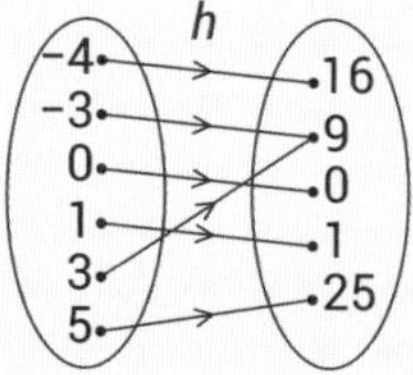

Worked Example 6.4

$f: x \rightarrow 6x - n$ is a function.

(i) If $f(-2) = -23$, find the value of n.

(ii) Find the value of x for which $f(x + 3) = -29$.

Solution

(i) $f(-2) = 6(-2) - n$

$= -12 - n$

$\Rightarrow -12 - n = -23$

$-n = -23 + 12$

$-n = -11$

$\therefore n = 11$

(ii) From part (i): $n = 11$

$\therefore f(x) = 6x - 11$

$\Rightarrow f(x + 3) = 6(x + 3) - 11$

$= 6x + 18 - 11$

$= 6x + 7$

$\Rightarrow 6x + 7 = -29$

$6x = -36$

$\therefore x = -6$

Worked Example 6.5

A function f is defined by the rule 'square the input and subtract 4'.

(i) Write an expression in x to represent this function.

(ii) Using this function, find the values of $f(4)$ and $f(-2)$.

Solution

(i) $f(x) = x^2 - 4$

(ii) $f(4) = (4)^2 - 4$

$= 16 - 4$

$= 12$

$f(-2) = (-2)^2 - 4$

$= 4 - 4$

$= 0$

Worked Example 6.6

The diagram shows part of the graph of the function g given by $g(x) = ax^2 + bx - 2, x \in R$.

Find the value of a and the value of b.

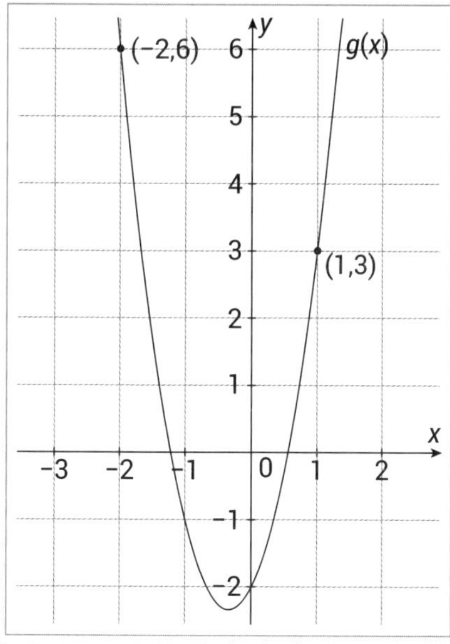

Solution

$(1,3) \in g$

$\Rightarrow a(1)^2 + b(1) - 2 = 3$

$a + b - 2 = 3$

$a + b = 5$ **Eq. I**

$(-2,6) \in g$

$\Rightarrow a(-2)^2 + b(-2) - 2 = 6$

$4a - 2b - 2 = 6$

$4a - 2b = 8$

$2a - b = 4$ **Eq. II**

Now solve the simultaneous equations Eq. I and Eq. II:

$a + b = 5$ Eq. I

$2a - b = 4$ Eq. II

$3a = 9$

$\therefore a = 3$

Substitute $a = 3$ into Eq. I:

$3 + b = 5$

$\therefore b = 2$

Answer: $a = 3, b = 2$

Exercise 6.1

1. Which of the following sets of ordered pairs represent functions?
   Give a reason for your answer.
   (i) {(1,4), (2,5), (3,6), (4,7)}
   (ii) {(1,2), (2,2), (3,4)}
   (iii) {(1,3), (3,5), (1,7), (4,9)}
   (iv) {(4,4), (3,4), (10,9)}
   (v) {(1,−3), (−3,1), (2,0), (3,0), (4,0)}

2. Which of the following mappings are functions?
   Give a reason for your answer.

(i)

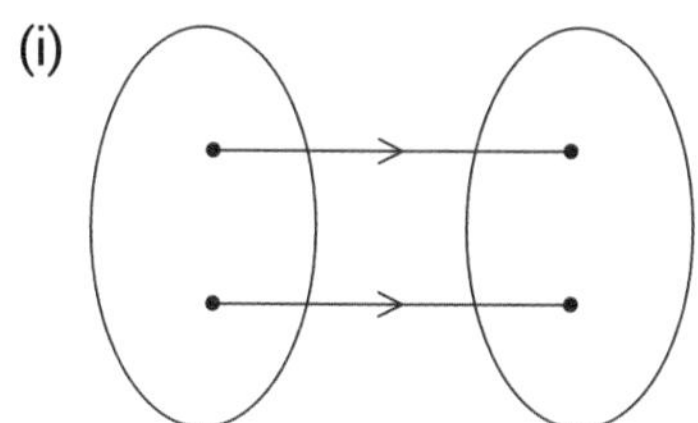

(ii)

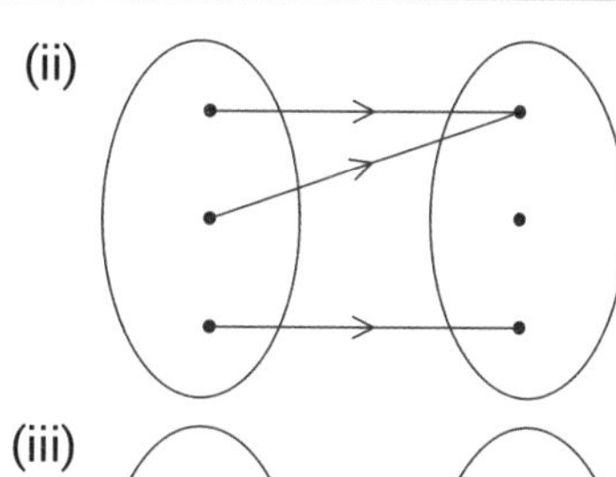

(iii)

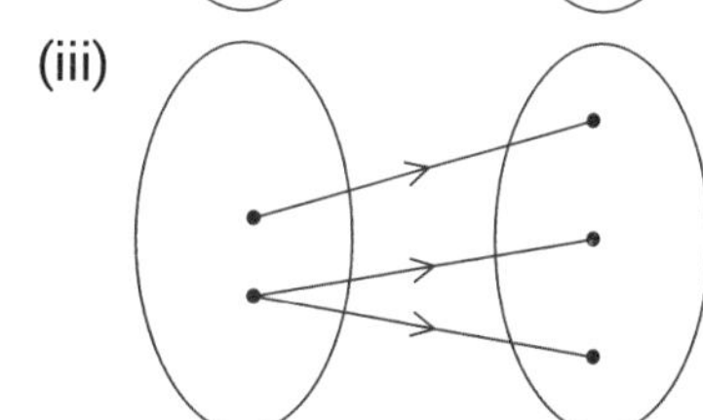

(iv)

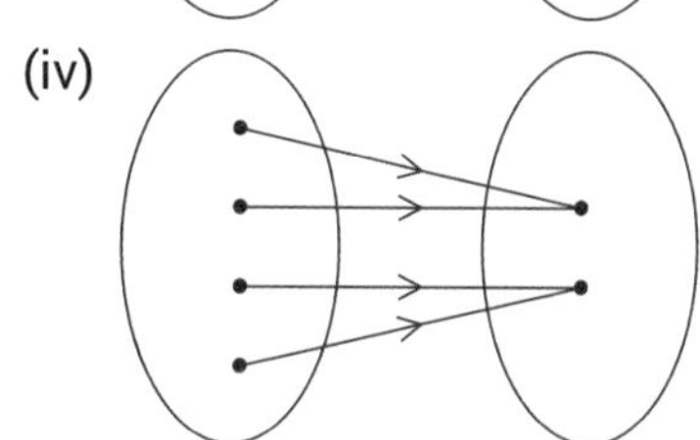

(v)

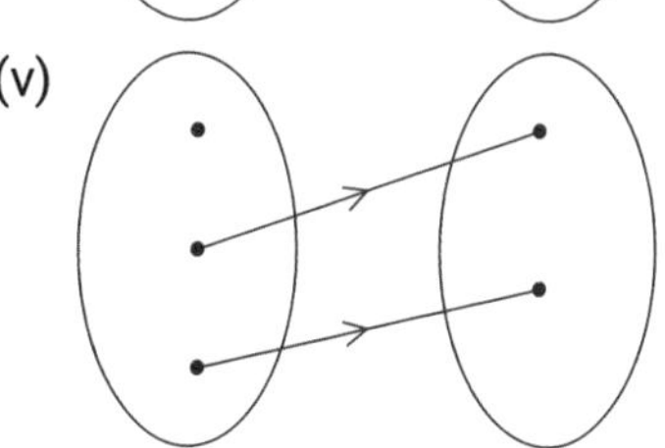

3. A function is defined by the following rule: 'Multiply the input by 4 and subtract 1'. The domain for this function is the set A = {1, 2, 3, 4, 5, 6}.

   List the elements of B, the range of this function.

4. A function is defined as 'square the input'.

   List the range of this function if the domain is:

   (i) {1, 2, 3, 5, 6}

   (ii) The first five prime numbers

   (iii) {−2, −1, 0, 1, 2, 3, 4}

5. Write down the domain, codomain and range of the following functions:

   (i)

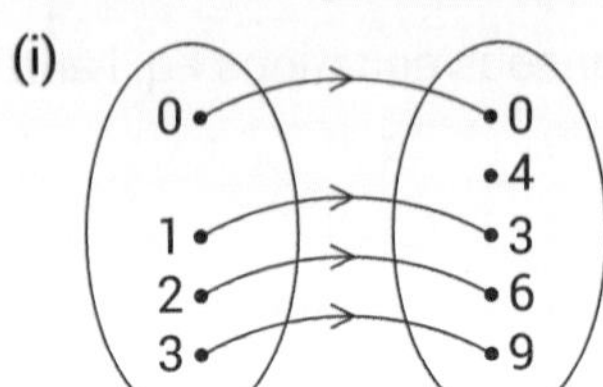

   (ii)

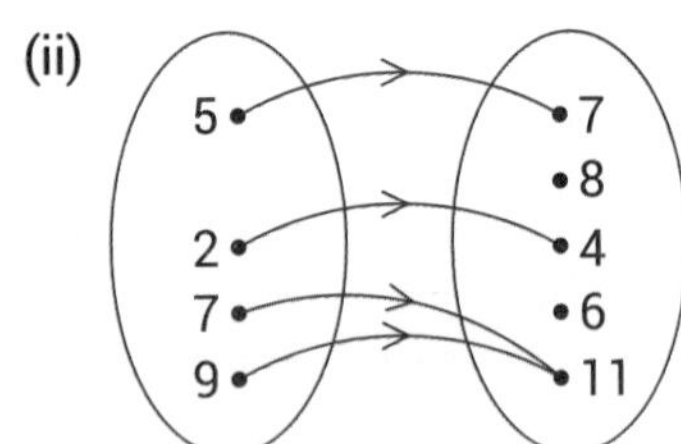

   (iii)

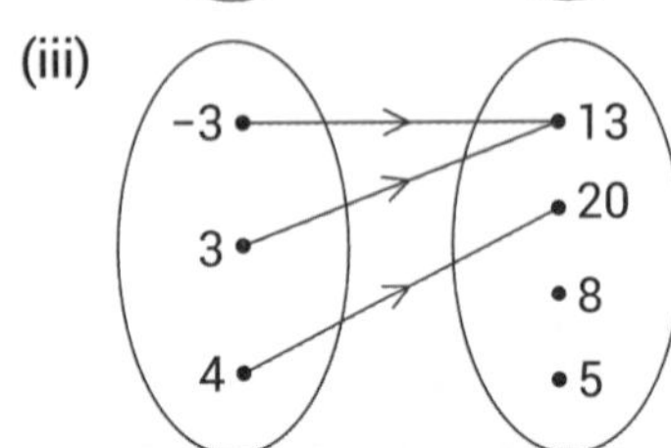

   (iv)

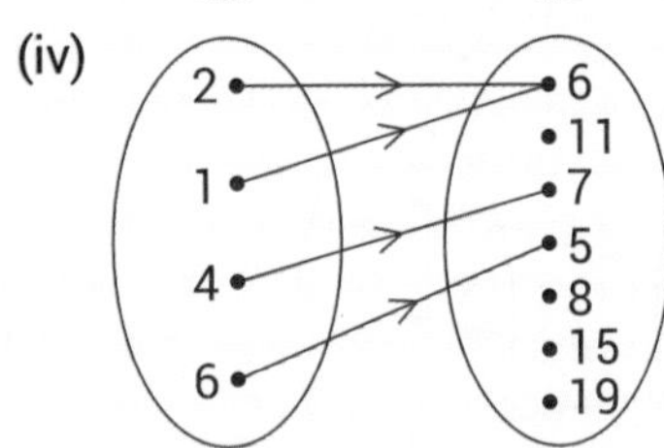

6. The following mapping is given:

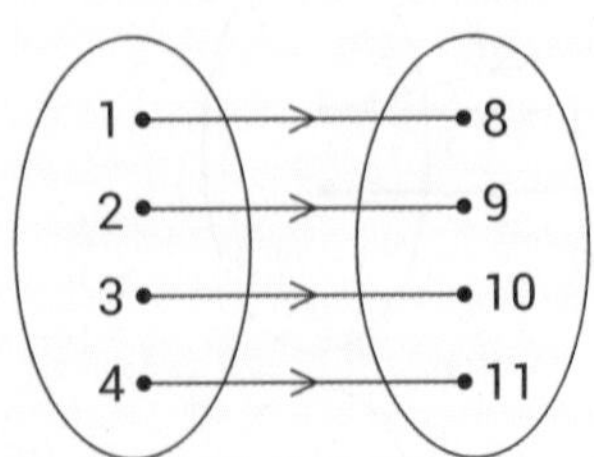

   (i) Is this mapping a function? Give a reason for your answer.

   (ii) Write out the domain and range of this mapping.

   (iii) Write an expression in terms of x for this mapping.

   (iv) Use this expression to find the input which maps to 77.

7. A function g is defined as $g(x)$ = the number of sides x has. Given the domain {triangle, hexagon, pentagon, rectangle, square, rhombus, octagon}, write out the range of this function.

8. A function f is defined by the rule 'Divide the input by 2 and add 3'.

   (i) Write an expression in x to represent this function.

   (ii) Using this expression, find the value of $f(4)$, $f(18)$ and $f(-6)$.

   (iii) For what value of x is $f(x) = 9$?

9. $f: x \to 2x + 6$ is a function. Find:

(i) $f(2)$	(iv) $f(-3)$
(ii) $f(-2)$	(v) $f(4)$
(iii) $f(0)$	(vi) $f(3.5)$

10. $f(x) = 2x^2 - 6x + 1$ is a function. Find:

(i) $f(0)$	(iv) $f(-3)$
(ii) $f(-2)$	(v) $f(4)$
(iii) $f(3)$	(vi) $f\left(\frac{1}{2}\right)$

11. A function g is defined as $g(t) = 6t - 4$.

   For what values of t are the following true:

(i) $g(t) = 8$	(iv) $g(t) = 14$
(ii) $g(t) = -2$	(v) $g(t) = 1$
(iii) $g(t) = -8$	(vi) $g(t) = 0$

12. $f: x \to 4x - 1$ defines a function. Find:

   (i) The value of $f(1)$

   (ii) The value of $f\left(\frac{1}{2}\right)$

   (iii) The value of k if $f(k) = 9$

   (iv) The value of p if $f(p) = p$

13. $f(x) = 2x + g$ defines a function.

   Find the value of g if $f(1) = 10$.

14. $g(x) = ax - 12$ defines a function.

   Find the value of a if $g(3) = 0$.

15. Given that $f(x) = \frac{x - 1}{x^2 + 2}$, find:

(i) $f(0)$ (iv) $f(2x)$

(ii) $f(-2)$ (v) $f\left(\frac{1}{x}\right)$

(iii) $f(3)$ (vi) $f(x + h)$

16. If $g(x) = 2x$, show that $g(x + 3) - g(x - 1) = 8$.

17. $f: x \rightarrow 2x + 11$ and $g: x \rightarrow x^2 - 4$ are two functions.

(i) Evaluate $f(4)$.

(ii) Evaluate $g(4)$.

(iii) Verify that $f(-3) = g(-3)$.

(iv) Find a value of k, other than -3, for which $f(k) = g(k)$.

18. The diagram shows part of the graph of the function $ax + by = 12$.

Find the value of a and the value of b.

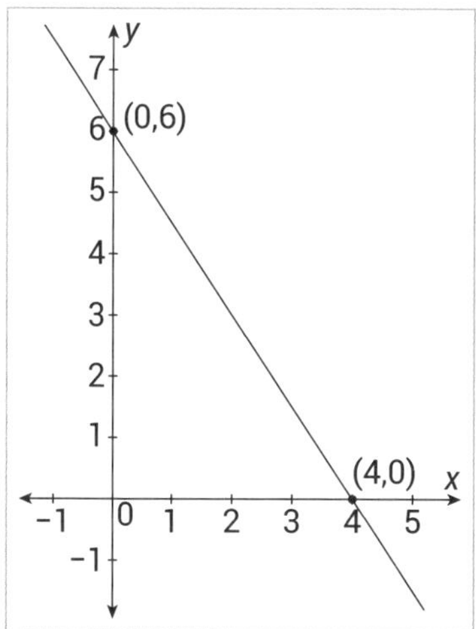

19. The diagram shows part of the graph of the function $y = ax + b$.

Find the value of a and the value of b.

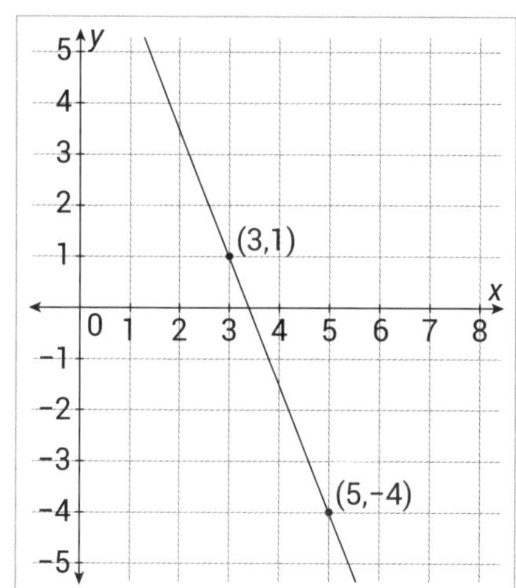

20. The diagram shows part of the graph of the function $f(x) = ax^2 + bx + 4$.

Find the value of a and the value of b.

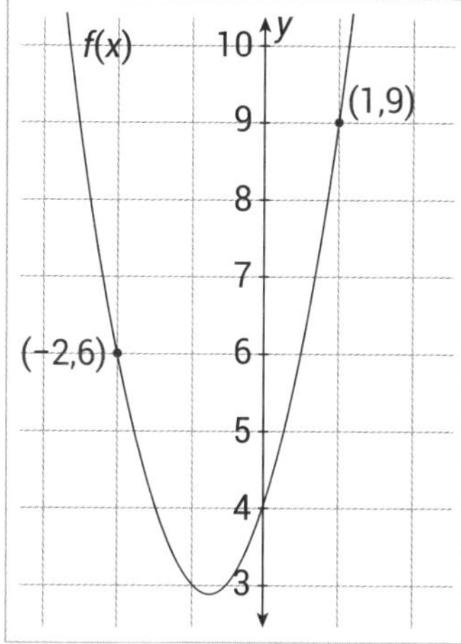

21. Find the value of a and b if $f(x) = x^2 + ax + b$, $f(2) = 0$ and $f(-2) = f(4)$.

22. Find the value of a and b if $f(x) = x^3 + ax^2 + bx - 8$, $f(-2) = 0$ and $f(1) = 0$.

23. Addy is decorating his Christmas tree. For every red bauble he puts on the tree, he puts on four gold baubles.

(i) Taking x as the number of red baubles and y as the number of gold baubles, define a function h such that $y = h(x)$.

(ii) Draw a sketch of the function.

(iii) If Addy puts 20 red baubles on the tree, how many gold baubles will be on the tree? How many baubles will there be on the tree in total?

(iv) If there are 125 baubles on the tree, how many are red?

24. Water empties out of a leaking tank. The amount of water in the tank at any instant is given by the rule 'Two hundred minus the input squared', where the input is the number of minutes for which the tank has been leaking (volume measured in litres).

(i) Define the function f such that $y = f(x)$, where y is the number of litres of water in the tank and x is the number of minutes passed.

(ii) How long will it take the tank to empty?

(iii) At what time will the tank be half empty?

6.2 Composite Functions

Let us say we have a function f given by $f(x) = x^2 + 1, x \in R$.
You can replace x with any real number.

For example: $f(1) = (1)^2 + 1 = 2$ $\quad f(-2) = (-2)^2 + 1 = 5$ $\quad f(x + h) = (x + h)^2 + 1$

Now consider the function p given by $p(x) = 3x^2 + 5$.

If we take an input value of 4, let us describe what we do to find $p(4)$:

- Square the input, 4 in this case. $(4)^2 = 16$
- Multiply the square of the input by 3. $3(16) = 48$
- Then add 5. $48 + 5 = 53$

We could break the function p into two separate functions here:

- Function 1 tells us to square the input.
- Function 2 tells us to multiply the output of Function 1 by 3 and then add 5.

We can understand this type of function more easily if we break p into two separate functions, g and h.

- The function g is defined as $g(x) = x^2, x \in R$.
- The function h is defined as $h(x) = 3x + 5, x \in R$.

We want to find $g(x)$ first and then use $g(x)$ as the input for our function h.

It means that we perform the function g first and then perform the function h.

If we perform function g first and then function h, we express this as:

This is read as 'the composition of h and g'. It is also read as 'h after g'.

$h \circ g(x)$ **OR** $(h \circ g)(x)$ **OR** $h(g(x))$ **OR** $hg(x)$

Note that the order in which we compose two functions is usually important.

For example, squaring 1 and adding 3 (= 4) is not the same as adding 3 to 1 and then squaring (= 16).

Worked Example 6.7

Consider the functions g and h defined as:

$g(x) = x^2$ and $h(x) = 3x + 5$

(i) Evaluate $h(g(3))$. (ii) Evaluate $g(h(3))$. (iii) Is $h(g(3)) = g(h(3))$?

Solution

(i) $h(g(3))$

First evaluate $g(3)$.

$g(3) = (3)^2$

$= 9$

Now evaluate $h(9)$.

$h(9) = 3(9) + 5$

$= 27 + 5$

$= 32$

$\therefore h(g(3)) = 32$

(ii) $g(h(3))$

First evaluate $h(3)$.

$h(3) = 3(3) + 5$

$= 9 + 5$

$= 14$

Now evaluate $g(14)$.

$g(14) = (14)^2$

$= 196$

$\therefore g(h(3)) = 196$

(iii) $h(g(3)) \neq g(h(3))$, as $32 \neq 196$.

Therefore, the order of composition is important.

In general, composition of functions is not commutative, i.e. $f \circ g(x) \neq g \circ f(x)$.

Worked Example 6.8

$f(x) = 6x + 2$ and $g(x) = x^3$, where both f and g are functions that map from R to R.

(i) Find the value of $f \circ g(2)$.

(ii) Find the value of $g \circ f(2)$.

(iii) Comment appropriately on your answers to parts (i) and (ii).

Solution

(i) $f \circ g(2)$

First find $g(2)$.

$g(2) = (2)^3$

$= 8$

Now find $f(8)$.

$f(8) = 6(8) + 2$

$= 48 + 2$

$= 50$

$\therefore f \circ g(2) = 50$

(ii) $g \circ f(2)$

First find $f(2)$.

$f(2) = 6(2) + 2$

$= 12 + 2$

$= 14$

Now find $g(14)$.

$g(14) = (14)^3$

$= 2{,}744$

$\therefore g \circ f(2) = 2{,}744$

(iii) $\left.\begin{array}{l} f \circ g(2) = 50 \\ g \circ f(2) = 2{,}744 \end{array}\right\} \Rightarrow f \circ g(2) \neq g \circ f(2)$

Exercise 6.2

1. A function is defined by $h(x) = 2x$.
A second function is defined by $g(x) = x^2$.

Find:

(i) $h \circ g(0)$ (v) $h \circ g(-1)$

(ii) $h \circ g(3)$ (vi) $h \circ g(-2)$

(iii) $h \circ g(4)$ (vii) $h \circ g(-3)$

(iv) $h \circ g(6)$ (viii) $h \circ g(-6)$

2. A function is defined by $h(x) = 2x + 4$.
A second function is defined by $g(x) = x^2 + 1$.

The function f is defined as $f = h \circ g$.

Find:

(i) $f(0)$ (v) $f(-1)$

(ii) $f(3)$ (vi) $f(-2)$

(iii) $f(4)$ (vii) $f(-3)$

(iv) $f(6)$ (viii) $f(-6)$

3. A function is defined by $h(x) = x + 1$.
A second function is defined by $g(x) = x^2$
and a third function is defined by $j(x) = x - 2$.

The function f is defined as $f = h \circ g \circ j$.

Find:

(i) $f(0)$ (v) $f(-1)$

(ii) $f(2)$ (vi) $f(-2)$

(iii) $f(-4)$ (vii) $f\left(\frac{3}{4}\right)$

(iv) $f(1)$ (viii) $f\left(\frac{5}{2}\right)$

4. The function f is defined as
$f(x) = 6x^2 + 3x + 6$, and the function h
is defined as $h(x) = 4x + 2$.

Evaluate:

(i) $f \circ h(1)$ (ii) $h \circ f(-1)$

5. Two functions are defined as $f(x) = 3x + 2$ and
$g(x) = x^2 + 2$.

Evaluate:

(i) $f \circ g(x)$ (ii) $g \circ f(x)$

6. The function g is defined as $g(x) = 4x + 3$.

(i) Write an expression for $g \circ g(x)$.

(ii) Evaluate $g \circ g(x)$ if $x = -2$.

6.3 Linear Functions

A **linear function** f in x is a function of the form $f(x) = ax + b$, where a and b are constants and x is a variable.

A constant is a value that does not vary.

A variable can change depending on the value we give it.

Variables are represented by letters.

Example: $f(x) = 2x + 1$. Here, x is the variable; 1 is the constant.

A graph is a pictorial representation of information showing how one quantity varies with another related quantity. The graph of a **linear function** is a straight line. The graph of $f(x) = 2x + 1$ is shown.

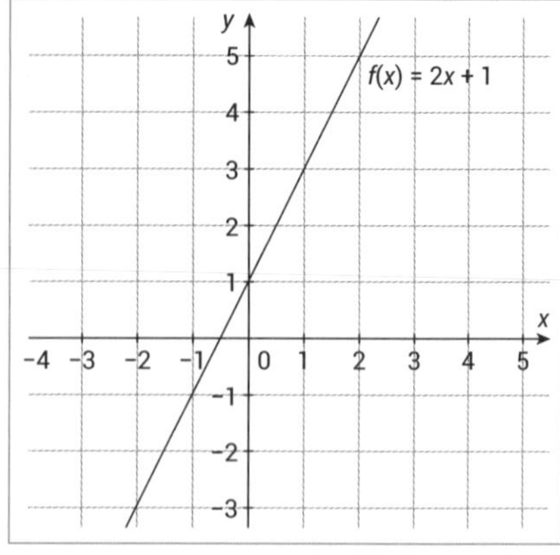

Worked Example 6.9

Draw the graph of the function $f(x) = 2x + 12$ for $0 \leqslant x \leqslant 10$, $x \in R$.

Solution

Step 1 Set up a table to show the input, the application of the rule (which performs the function) and the output.

Step 2 List the couples that will be graphed.

Step 3 Graph the couples and connect the plotted points with a straight line.

x (input)	$2x + 12$	y (output)	Couples to graph
0	2(0) + 12	12	(0,12)
1	2(1) + 12	14	(1,14)
2	2(2) + 12	16	(2,16)
3	2(3) + 12	18	(3,18)
4	2(4) + 12	20	(4,20)
5	2(5) + 12	22	(5,22)
6	2(6) + 12	24	(6,24)
7	2(7) + 12	26	(7,26)
8	2(8) + 12	28	(8,28)
9	2(9) + 12	30	(9,30)
10	2(10) + 12	32	(10,32)

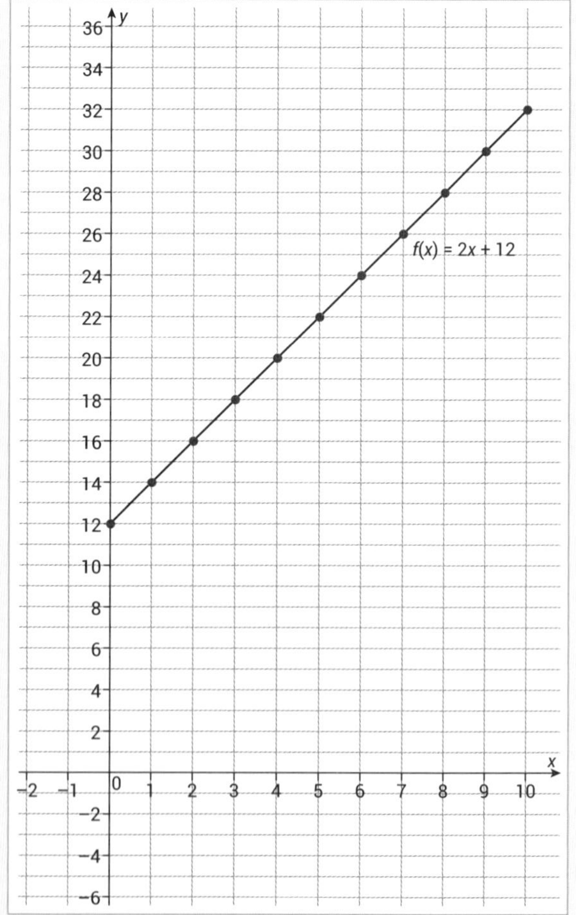

FUNCTIONS

Worked Example 6.10

The distances in metres that Rian and Eric are from school are given by the following functions:

Rian $r(t) = 250 - 1.3t$

Eric $e(t) = 325 - 2t$

where t is time in seconds.

(i) Graph the functions using the same axes and scales.

(ii) The bell for first class rings at $t = 0$.

How far are Rian and Eric from school at this time?

(iii) Use your graphs to estimate the time, to the nearest second, that each boy will arrive at school.

(iv) At what time will $r(t) = e(t)$ if the bell for first class rings at 8.40 a.m.? Explain what this means in the context of the question.

Solution

(i) Decide what domain to use. In setting up this solution, you could make an estimate of the latest you expect the boys to be for school, e.g. 4 minutes or 240 seconds.

As both functions are linear functions, it is not necessary to plot all points in the domain, so pick three t-values for each function: $t = 0$, $t = 120$ and $t = 240$.

Always pick the first and end value of the domain (if given). Pick a third value as a checking method.

Rian			
t	$250 - 1.3t$	$r(t)$	Couples to plot
0	250 − 1.3(0)	250	(0,250)
120	250 − 1.3(120)	94	(120,94)
240	250 − 1.3(240)	−62	(240,−62)

Eric			
t	$325 - 2t$	$e(t)$	Couples to plot
0	325 − 2(0)	325	(0,325)
120	325 − 2(120)	85	(120,85)
240	325 − 2(240)	−155	(240,−155)

(ii) Rian is 250 metres, and Eric is 325 metres, from the school.

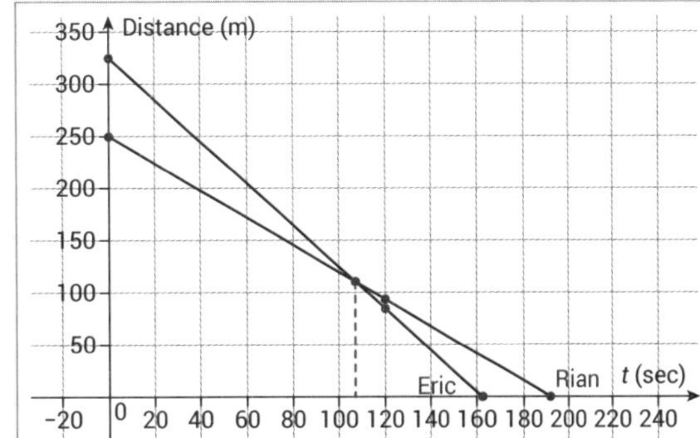

(iii) From the graph, you are looking for the values of t where the graphs cross the x-axis, i.e. they are 0 metres from the school.

Rian will arrive at approximately $t = 192$ seconds after the bell rings for first class.

Eric will arrive at approximately $t = 163$ seconds after the bell rings for first class.

Show your markings on the graph when you are asked to use the graph to answer.

(iv) $r(t) = e(t)$ at approximately $t = 107$ seconds.

This means that at approximately 8.41 and 47 seconds, Rian and Eric are the same distance from the school.

FUNCTIONS

6.4 Linear Functions Crossing the x-axis [$f(x) = 0$]

The graph of $f(x)$ crosses the x-axis when $y = 0$, i.e. $f(x) = 0$. Linear functions cross the x-axis at exactly one point.

Linear Functions Crossing Lines Parallel to the x-axis [$f(x) = k$]

Consider the line $y = 5$, which is parallel to the x-axis. Any linear function $f(x)$ crosses the line $y = 5$ at exactly one point, i.e. $f(x) = 5$.

Worked Example 6.11

The graph of the function $f: x \rightarrow 3x - 3$ in the domain $-3 \leqslant x \leqslant 4, x \in R$, is shown below.

Use the graph to estimate:

(i) The value of x for which $f(x) = 0$

(ii) The value of x for which $3x - 3 = 6$

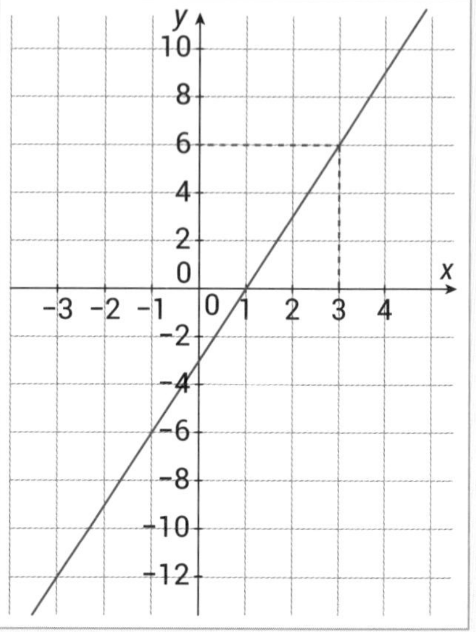

Solution

(i) $f(x) = 0$ means the output is neither positive (above the horizontal axis) nor negative (below the horizontal axis) but is zero. Therefore, we look for where the graph of the function f intersects the horizontal axis.

Answer: $x = 1$

(ii) $3x - 3 = 6$ can be rewritten as $f(x) = 6$. We want the output to be 6. Starting at the output axis (vertical axis) at a value of 6, we see that the required input is 3.

Answer: $x = 3$

The root of a function is the value of the input which makes the function equal to 0, i.e. where the function crosses the x-axis.

Exercise 6.3

1. Draw a graph of the following functions with the given domains:

	Function	Domain
(i)	$f(x) = 6x - 2$	$-2 \leqslant x \leqslant 2, x \in R$
(ii)	$g(x) = 2 - 4x$	$-3 \leqslant x \leqslant 1, x \in R$
(iii)	$h(x) = 2 - 3x$	$0 \leqslant x \leqslant 5, x \in R$
(iv)	$f: x \rightarrow x + 6$	$6 \leqslant x \leqslant 12, x \in R$
(v)	$g: x \rightarrow 2x + \frac{3}{4}$	$-8 \leqslant x \leqslant -2, x \in R$
(vi)	$h: x \rightarrow \frac{1}{5} - x$	$-2 \leqslant x \leqslant 2, x \in R$
(vii)	$h(x) = \frac{x}{2} + \frac{3}{2}$	$0 \leqslant x \leqslant 5, x \in R$
(viii)	$i(x) = 3x + \frac{1}{2}$	$6 \leqslant x \leqslant 12, x \in R$
(ix)	$f: x \rightarrow \frac{4}{5}x + \frac{1}{5}$	$-8 \leqslant x \leqslant -2, x \in R$
(x)	$g: x \rightarrow -0.2x$	$-2 \leqslant x \leqslant 2, x \in R$

2. Draw the graph of the linear function $f: x \rightarrow 3x - 1$ in the domain $-3 \leqslant x \leqslant 4$, $x \in R$.

Use your graph to estimate:

(i) $f(1.3)$

(ii) The value of x for which $f(x) = -6$

3. Draw the graph of the linear function $f: x \rightarrow 4x - 3$ in the domain $-3 \leqslant x \leqslant 4, x \in R$.

Use your graph to estimate:

(i) The value of $f(x)$ when $x = 2.5$

(ii) The value of x for which $4x - 3 = 6$

(iii) The value of x for which $4x - 3 = -7$

(iv) The range of values of x for which $f(x) \geqslant 1$

4. Using the same axes and scales, draw the two graphs $y = 2x - 2$ and $y = 8 - 4x$ in the domain $-1 \leqslant x \leqslant 4, x \in R$. What is the point of intersection of the two graphs?

5. A car passes a point P, after which its speed v (in ms^{-1}) is given by the function $v = 15 - 3t$, where t is the time in seconds.

   Draw a graph of v for $0 \leqslant t \leqslant 5$.
   Use your graph to estimate:

   (i) The speed of the car at $t = 2.3$

   (ii) The time at which the speed is $10\ ms^{-1}$

   (iii) The speed as the car passes P

   (iv) The time taken by the car to stop after it passes the point P

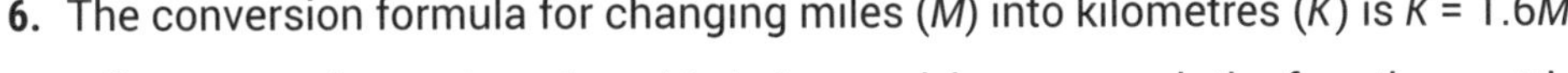

6. The conversion formula for changing miles (M) into kilometres (K) is $K = 1.6M$.

   (i) Copy and complete the table below and, hence, graph the function, putting miles on the horizontal axis.

Miles	0	10	20	30	40	50	60	70	80	90	100
Kilometres	0					80					

   (ii) Estimate from your graph the distance in kilometres if 75 miles have been travelled.

   (iii) Estimate from your graph the distance in miles if 140 km have been travelled.

   (iv) What is the range of distances in kilometres if a trip is said to be between 65 and 75 miles long?

7. The variable cost per unit of a product is €5. Fixed costs are €45,000 (these costs are incurred regardless of the quantity produced). [Use the same axes and scales in parts (i)–(iv).]

   (i) Graph the variable costs for this product for a range of production from 0 units to 50,000 units.

   (ii) Graph the fixed costs for this product for the same range of production.

   (iii) If total costs = fixed costs + variable costs, write a function in terms of x (quantity produced) to represent total costs.

   (iv) Graph the function for total costs.

   (v) If the selling price per unit is €6, write a function in terms of x to represent sales revenue for the same range of production (assuming all goods produced are sold).

   (vi) Graph this function on the same axes as in part (iv).

   (vii) The break-even point is the number of units at which sales revenue and total costs are equal – that is to say, neither a profit nor a loss is made. From your graphs, estimate what this level of production is.

6.5 Quadratic Functions

A **quadratic function** f in x involves an x^2 term and is of the form $f(x) = ax^2 + bx + c$, where a, b and c are constants ($a \neq 0$) and x is a variable.

The graph of a **quadratic function** takes the form of a curve known as a parabola. It can be drawn by making a table of values for x and finding the corresponding values for y. Then plot the resultant couples.

The graph can be ∩-shaped or ∪-shaped, depending on the coefficient of the squared variable.

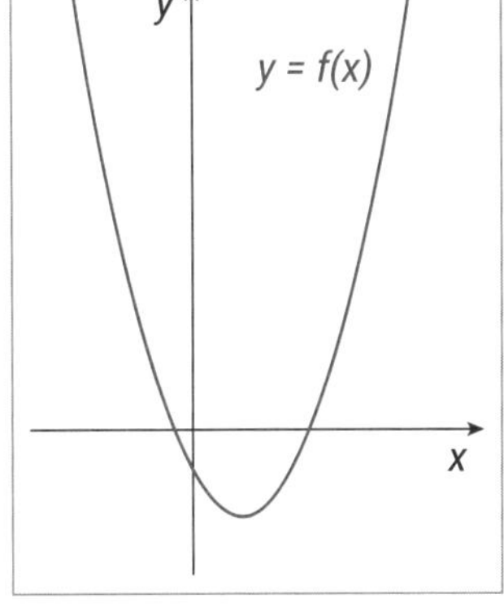

$f(x) = ax^2 + bx + c, x \in R$
Here, a is **positive**.

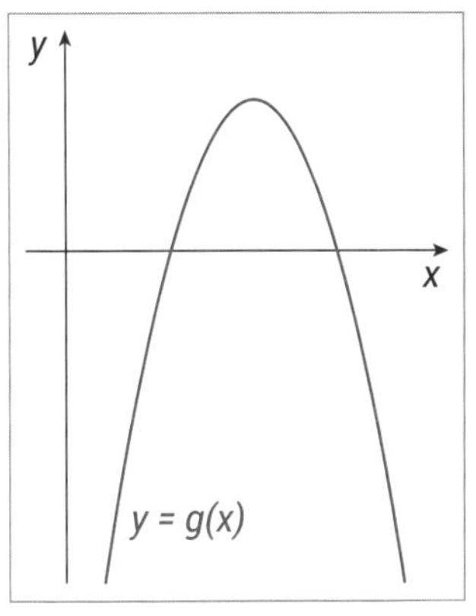

$g(x) = ax^2 + bx + c, x \in R$
Here, a is **negative**.

Worked Example 6.12

Graph the function $f: x \rightarrow 3x^2 - 2x - 7$ in the domain $-2 \leqslant x \leqslant 3, x \in R$.

Estimate from your graph:

(i) The value of $f(2.5)$

(ii) The values of x for which $f(x) = 3$

(iii) The minimum value of $f(x)$ and the x-value at which it occurs

(iv) The values of x for which $3x^2 - 2x - 7 \geqslant 0$

Solution

x (input)	$3x^2 - 2x - 7$	y (output)	Couples to graph
-2	$3(-2)^2 - 2(-2) - 7$	9	(-2,9)
-1	$3(-1)^2 - 2(-1) - 7$	-2	(-1,-2)
0	$3(0)^2 - 2(0) - 7$	-7	(0,-7)
1	$3(1)^2 - 2(1) - 7$	-6	(1,-6)
2	$3(2)^2 - 2(2) - 7$	1	(2,1)
3	$3(3)^2 - 2(3) - 7$	14	(3,14)

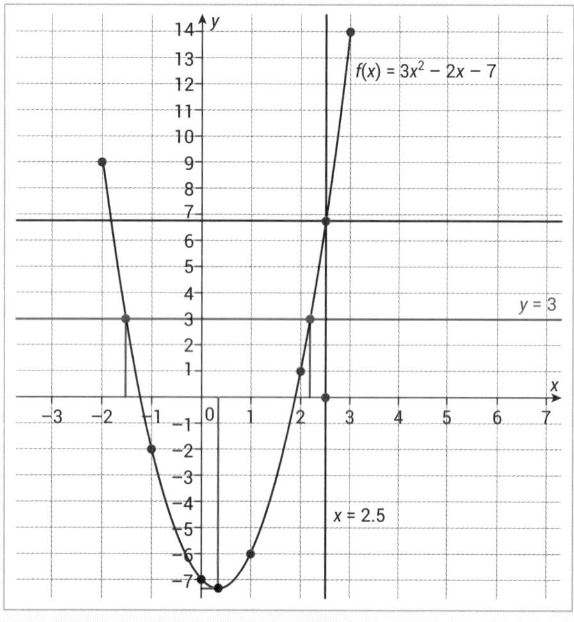

(i) Draw a line from $x = 2.5$ on the x-axis up to the graph. Then draw a line from here across to the y-axis. The reading is 6.75. Therefore, $f(2.5) \approx 6.75$.

(ii) Draw the line $y = 3$ (this is the horizontal red line on the diagram). Where this line cuts the graph of the function, drop perpendiculars to the x-axis.

This gives the corresponding x-values: $x \approx -1.6$ and $x \approx 2.2$.

(iii) The minimum value of $f(x)$ is approximately -7.3 at $x \approx 0.3$.

(iv) The values of x for which $3x^2 - 2x - 7 \geqslant 0$.

This means the values of x for which $f(x) \geqslant 0$, i.e. the values of x for which the graph is on or above the x-axis.

The graph is on the x-axis at $x \approx -1.2$ and $x \approx 1.9$.

$\therefore f(x) \geqslant 0$ for $-2 \leqslant x \leqslant -1.2$ or $1.9 \leqslant x \leqslant 3$.

Worked Example 6.13

Using the same scales and axes, graph the functions $g(x) = -x^2 + 6x$ and $h(x) = \frac{2}{3}x + 1$ in the domain $0 \leqslant x \leqslant 6, x \in R$.

Use your graph to estimate the values of x for which:

(i) $g(x) = 5.5$

(ii) $h(x) = 3.5$

(iii) $g(x) = h(x)$

(iv) $\frac{2}{3}x - 1 = 0$

Solution

Set up a table for each function to find the couples that need to be graphed.

$g(x)$			
x	$-x^2 + 6x$	y	(x,y)
0	$-0 + 0$	0	(0,0)
1	$-1 + 6$	5	(1,5)
2	$-4 + 12$	8	(2,8)
3	$-9 + 18$	9	(3,9)
4	$-16 + 24$	8	(4,8)
5	$-25 + 30$	5	(5,5)
6	$-36 + 36$	0	(6,0)

FUNCTIONS

$h(x) = \frac{2}{3}x + 1$ is a linear function, so three points will be sufficient to graph it.

Always pick the first and end value of the domain (if given). Pick a third value as a checking device.

$h(x)$			
x	$\frac{2}{3}x + 1$	y	(x,y)
0	$\frac{2}{3}(0) + 1$	1	(0,1)
3	$\frac{2}{3}(3) + 1$	3	(3,3)
6	$\frac{2}{3}(6) + 1$	5	(6,5)

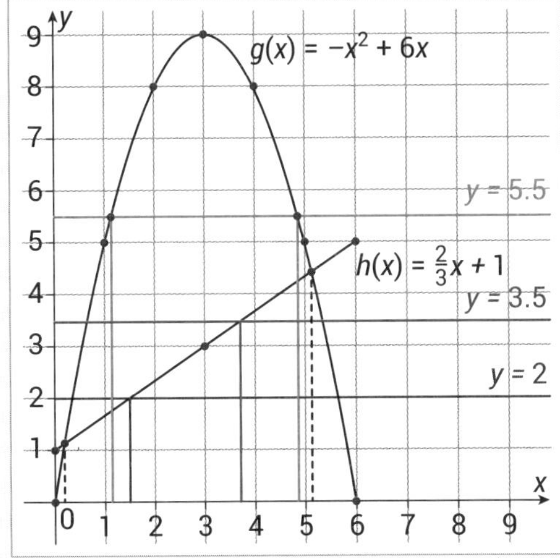

(i) Draw the line $y = 5.5$ (green line on graph). Where this line cuts the graph of $g(x)$, drop perpendiculars to the x-axis and read off the x-values: $x \approx 1.2$ and $x \approx 4.8$.

(ii) Draw the line $y = 3.5$ (red line on graph). Where this line cuts the graph of $h(x)$, drop a perpendicular to the x-axis and read off the x-value: $x \approx 3.7$.

(iii) Read off the two x-values where the graphs of the functions g and h intersect: $x \approx 0.2$ and $x \approx 5.2$.

(iv)
$$\frac{2}{3}x - 1 = 0$$
$$\Rightarrow \frac{2}{3}x + 1 - 2 = 0$$
$$\frac{2}{3}x + 1 = 2$$
$$\therefore h(x) = 2$$

Draw the line $y = 2$ (blue line on graph). Where the line cuts the graph of $h(x)$, drop a perpendicular to the x-axis and read off the x-value: $x \approx 1.5$.

Exercise 6.4

1. Match each of the following functions to the correct graph:

1	$x^2 - x - 6$
2	$x^2 + 2x + 1$
3	$-x^2 + x + 6$
4	$4 - 2x - x^2$

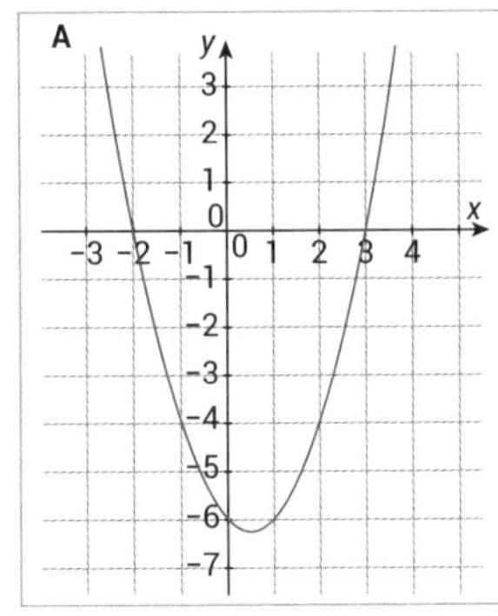

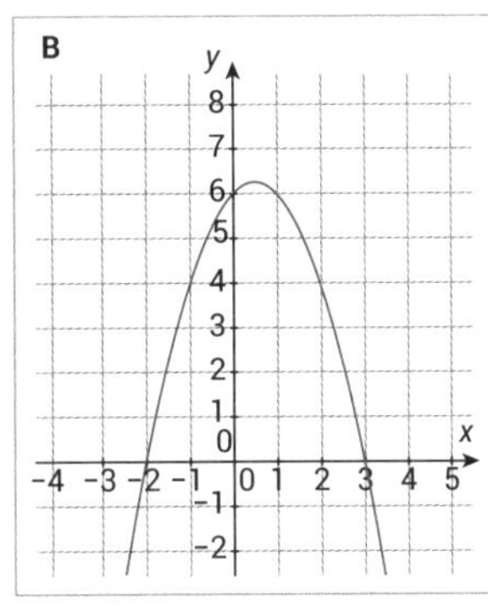

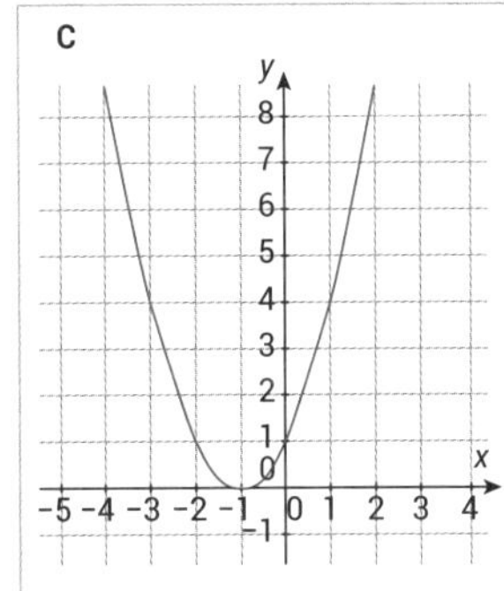

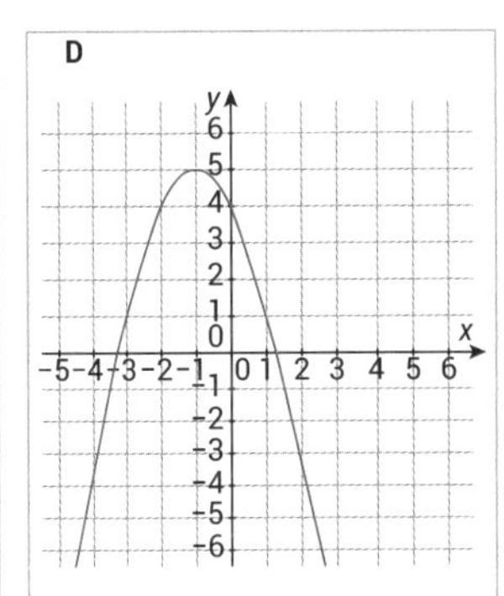

2. By completing the following input–output table, graph the function $f(x) = x^2 + 2x + 3$ in the domain $-3 \leqslant x \leqslant 2, x \in R$.

x	$x^2 + 2x + 3$	y	(x,y)
-3	$(-3)^2 + 2(-3) + 3$	6	
-2			
-1			
0			
1			
2			

3. Graph the following functions in the domain $-3 \leqslant x \leqslant 1, x \in R$:
   (i) $g(x) = x^2 + x + 2$
   (ii) $h(x) = 2x^2 + x - 2$
   (iii) $j(x) = 14 - 3x - 4x^2$
   (iv) $h: x \rightarrow x^2 + 2x + 12$
   (v) $f: x \rightarrow -x^2 - 3x + 7$

4. A tennis ball machine is malfunctioning and shoots out a tennis ball so that its height y (in metres) is given by the function $f(x) = 6x - x^2$, where x is the horizontal distance in metres travelled by the tennis ball.
   (i) Complete a table of values relating x to y for the domain $0 \leqslant x \leqslant 6, x \in R$.
   (ii) Draw the graph of y against x.
   (iii) What is the maximum height reached by the tennis ball?
   (iv) If the player hits the ball when it is at a height of 2 metres, estimate the two possible distances the ball has travelled.

5. Graph the function $f: x \rightarrow x^2 - 2x - 5$ in the domain $-2 \leqslant x \leqslant 4, x \in R$.

   Find from your graph:
   (i) The value of $f(2.2)$
   (ii) The values of x for which $x^2 - 2x - 5 = 0$
   (iii) The values of x for which $x^2 - 2x - 5 \leqslant 0$
   (iv) The minimum value of $f(x)$

6. Graph the function $f: x \rightarrow x^2 + 6x - 3$ in the domain $-8 \leqslant x \leqslant 2, x \in R$.

   Estimate from your graph:
   (i) The value of $f(x)$ if $x = -4.5$
   (ii) The values of x for which $x^2 + 6x - 3 = 0$
   (iii) The value of x for which $x^2 + 6x - 3 = 2$
   (iv) The values of x for which $x^2 + 6x - 8 = 0$
   (v) The minimum value of $f(x)$

7. Draw the graph of the function $f: x \rightarrow 2x^2 + 3x - 3$ in the domain $-2 \leqslant x \leqslant 2, x \in R$.

   Find from your graph:
   (i) The value of $f(1.5)$
   (ii) The value of x for which $2x^2 + 3x - 3 = 0$
   (iii) The value of x for which $2x^2 + 3x - 3 = 2$

8. The functions $f(x) = 8x - x^2$ and $g(x) = 0.5x + 4$ are graphed below.

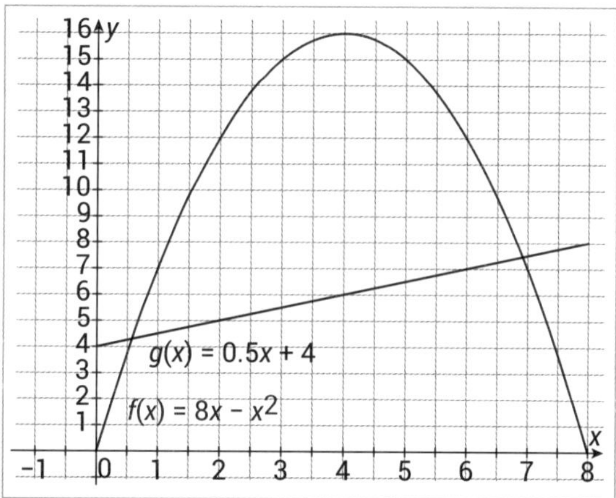

   (i) What is the maximum value of $f(x)$?
   (ii) Use the graph to estimate the values of x for which $f(x) = g(x)$.
   (iii) Use the graph to estimate the values of x for which $f(x) \geqslant g(x)$.
   (iv) Use the graph to estimate the values of x for which $f(x) \leqslant g(x)$.

9. Draw the graph of the function $g: x \rightarrow 2x^2 - 3x - 7$ in the domain $-2 \leqslant x \leqslant 3, x \in R$.

   Find from your graph:
   (i) The value of $g(2.5)$
   (ii) The values of x for which $2x^2 - 3x - 7 = 0$
   (iii) The values of x for which $2x^2 - 3x - 3 = 0$

10. The perimeter of a rectangular garden is 16 m. If the width of the garden is x metres:

(i) Show that the area of the garden is given by $8x - x^2$.

(ii) Draw a graph to represent the area of the garden for $0 \leqslant x \leqslant 8$.

(iii) From your graph, find the maximum area of the garden.

11. Draw the graph of the function $f{:}x \rightarrow 5 - 2x - x^2$ in the domain $-3 \leqslant x \leqslant 3, x \in R$.

Find from your graph:

(i) The value of $f(-1.5)$

(ii) The values of x for which $f(x) = 2$

(iii) The maximum value of $f(x)$

(iv) The range of values of k for which $5 - 2x - x^2 = k$ has two solutions, where $k \in R$

12. Use the same scales and axes to draw the graphs of the two functions $f(x) = 2 + 2x + x^2$ and $g(x) = 5 - 2x - x^2$ in the domain $-3 \leqslant x \leqslant 2, x \in R$.

(i) Use your graph to estimate the values of x for which $f(x) = g(x)$.

(ii) Use your graph to estimate the values of x for which $f(x) \geqslant g(x)$.

13. A missile is launched into the air following the trajectory mapped out by the quadratic function $h = 6t - t^2$, where h is the height in metres above the ground and t is the time in seconds.

(i) Graph the trajectory of the missile for 0–6 seconds.

(ii) At what times is the missile 8 metres above the ground?

A counter-attack missile is launched at the same time **from a height one metre above the ground**. The trajectory of this missile is given by the function $j = 1.2t$, where t is time in seconds.

(iii) Graph the trajectory of the counter-attack missile.

(iv) At what time will the two missiles collide?

(v) At what height will this collision take place?

14. The owner of a manufacturing company pays his workers on a piece rate basis. The owner uses a quadratic function to determine the pay each employee will receive each month. He has determined that above a certain level of production by each employee, he encounters a problem with wastage. To eliminate wastage, he has told his employees that above a given level of production, their pay will decline.

The quadratic function he uses for calculating pay is defined as $P = 10Q - Q^2$, where P is monthly pay in €100s and Q is quantity produced in 100s.

(i) Graph the function for pay, with quantity produced on the horizontal axis and monthly pay on the vertical axis. Use the domain $0 \leqslant Q \leqslant 10$.

(ii) What is the maximum monthly pay that an employee can receive?

(iii) How many units must the employee produce to earn this maximum monthly pay?

(iv) If a worker receives monthly pay of €2,400, what are the two possible levels of production she has reached?

(v) Is it more lucrative for an employee to produce 250 units or 725 units? Explain how you came to your decision.

(vi) Pay of €2,100 can be achieved at two different levels of production. Explain how P can still be a function if this is the case.

6.6 Cubic Functions

A **cubic function** f in x involves an x^3 term and is of the form $f(x) = ax^3 + bx^2 + cx + d$, where a, b, c and d are constants ($a \neq 0$) and x is a variable.

Examples of **cubic functions**:

$f(x) = x^3 - 6x^2 + 11x - 6$ $\quad$ $g(x) = 4x^3 + 5$ $\quad$ $h: x \to -x^3 + 9x$

The graph of any function of this form is called a **cubic graph**. The shape of the graph depends on whether a, the coefficient of x^3, is negative or positive (among other factors).

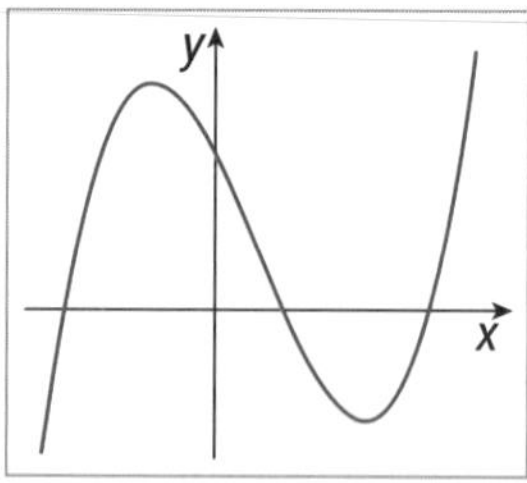

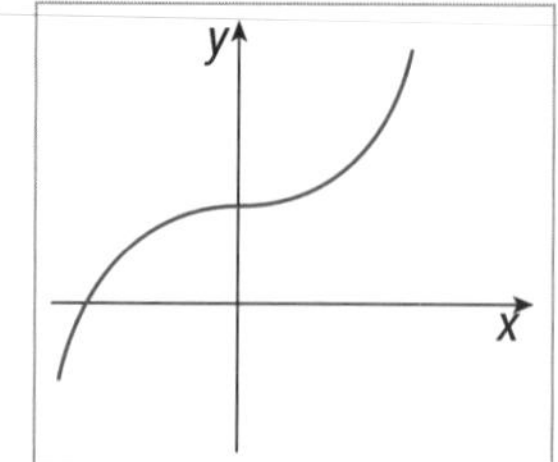

In these cases, a, the coefficient of x^3, is positive.

If the coefficient of x^3 is **positive**, the graph will **start low and end high**.

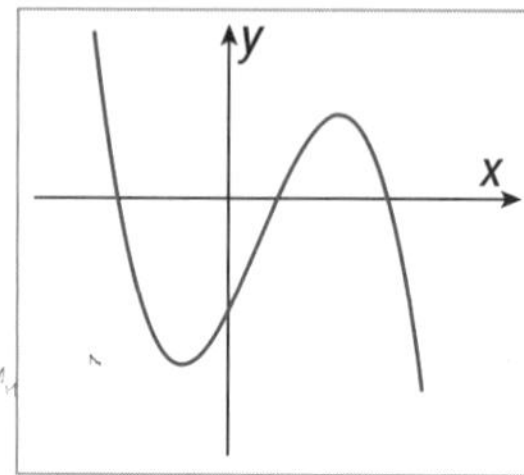

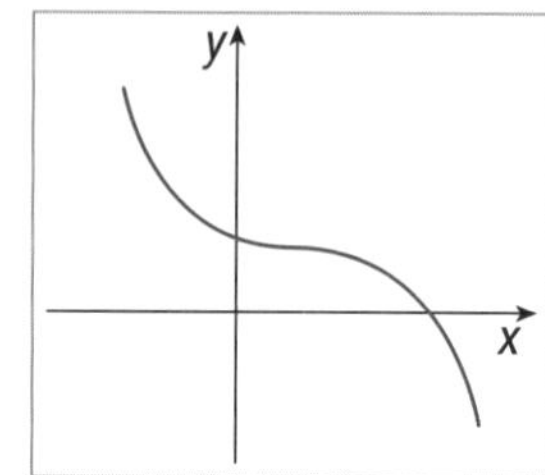

In these cases, a, the coefficient of x^3, is negative.

If the coefficient of x^3 is **negative**, the graph will **start high and end low**.

- A quadratic function may cross the x-axis at a maximum of two points. A cubic function may cross the x-axis at a maximum of three points.
- It is possible for the graph of a quadratic function not to touch or cross the x-axis, i.e. if the function has no real roots. However, this is **not** the case for a cubic function. There will always be at least one point where the graph of the cubic function will cross the x-axis.

Worked Example 6.14

Graph the function g, where $g(x) = x^3 - 6x^2 + 11x - 6$, in the domain $0.5 \leqslant x \leqslant 3.5$, $x \in R$.

Solution

Set up the input-output table.

x	$x^3 - 6x^2 + 11x - 6$	y	(x,y)
0.5	$(0.5)^3 - 6(0.5)^2 + 11(0.5) - 6$	−1.875	(0.5,−1.875)
1	$(1)^3 - 6(1)^2 + 11(1) - 6$	0	(1,0)
1.5	$(1.5)^3 - 6(1.5)^2 + 11(1.5) - 6$	0.375	(1.5,0.375)
2	$(2)^3 - 6(2)^2 + 11(2) - 6$	0	(2,0)
2.5	$(2.5)^3 - 6(2.5)^2 + 11(2.5) - 6$	−0.375	(2.5,−0.375)
3	$(3)^3 - 6(3)^2 + 11(3) - 6$	0	(3,0)
3.5	$(3.5)^3 - 6(3.5)^2 + 11(3.5) - 6$	1.875	(3.5,1.875)

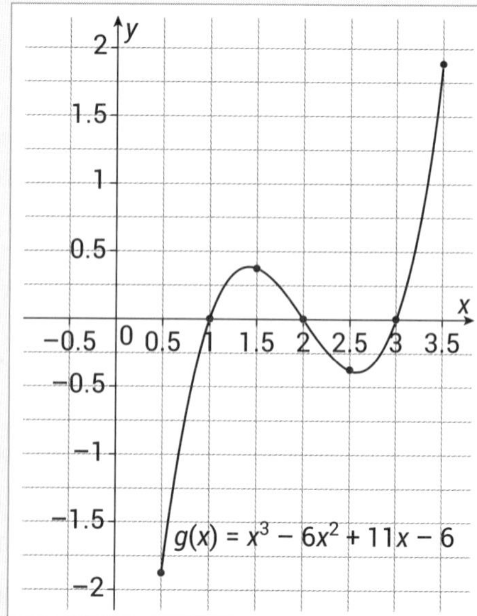

Graph the couples (x,y).

Points to note

- The graph starts low and finishes high.
  Reason: The coefficient of x^3 is positive (=1).
- The graph crosses the x-axis three times, at $x = 1$, $x = 2$ and $x = 3$.
  This indicates that the function has three real roots.

Worked Example 6.15

Graph the function $f: x \to x^3 - 5x^2 + 3x + 9$ in the domain $-1.5 \leqslant x \leqslant 4, x \in R$.

Use your graph to estimate:

(i) The values of x for which $f(x) = 0$

(ii) The value of $f(2.5)$

(iii) The minimum value of $f(x)$, where $x > 0$

(iv) The values of x for which $f(x)$ is decreasing

(v) The solutions of $x^3 - 5x^2 + 3x + 9 = 2$

(vi) The solutions of $x^3 - 5x^2 + 3x = -4$

Solution

x	$x^3 - 5x^2 + 3x + 9$	y	(x,y)
-1.5	$(-1.5)^3 - 5(-1.5)^2 + 3(-1.5) + 9$	-10.125	(-1.5,-10.125)
-1	$(-1)^3 - 5(-1)^2 + 3(-1) + 9$	0	(-1,0)
-0.5	$(-0.5)^3 - 5(-0.5)^2 + 3(-0.5) + 9$	6.125	(-0.5,6.125)
0	$(0)^3 - 5(0)^2 + 3(0) + 9$	9	(0,9)
0.5	$(0.5)^3 - 5(0.5)^2 + 3(0.5) + 9$	9.375	(0.5,9.375)
1	$(1)^3 - 5(1)^2 + 3(1) + 9$	8	(1,8)
1.5	$(1.5)^3 - 5(1.5)^2 + 3(1.5) + 9$	5.625	(1.5,5.625)
2	$(2)^3 - 5(2)^2 + 3(2) + 9$	3	(2,3)
2.5	$(2.5)^3 - 5(2.5)^2 + 3(2.5) + 9$	0.875	(2.5,0.875)
3	$(3)^3 - 5(3)^2 + 3(3) + 9$	0	(3,0)
3.5	$(3.5)^3 - 5(3.5)^2 + 3(3.5) + 9$	1.125	(3.5,1.125)
4	$(4)^3 - 5(4)^2 + 3(4) + 9$	5	(4,5)

(i) Using the graph, establish where the graph of the function crosses or touches the x-axis. This gives the values of x for which $f(x) = 0$.

$f(x) = 0$ at $x = -1$ or $x = 3$

(ii) Draw the vertical line $x = 2.5$ and read off the y-value where it crosses the graph of f, i.e. $y \approx 0.9$.

$\therefore f(2.5) \approx 0.9$

(iii) The minimum value of $f(x)$, where $x > 0$, is 0.

(iv) $f(x)$ is decreasing for $0.3 \leqslant x \leqslant 3, x \in R$.

(v) Draw the line $y = 2$ (green line). Where the line cuts the graph of f, drop perpendiculars to the x-axis and read off the x-values. $x \approx -0.8, 2.2$ or 3.7

(vi) $x^3 - 5x^2 + 3x = -4$

$\Rightarrow x^3 - 5x^2 + 3x + 9 = -4 + 9$

$\therefore f(x) = 5$

Draw the line $y = 5$.

This gives x-values of $x \approx -0.6, 1.6$ or 4.

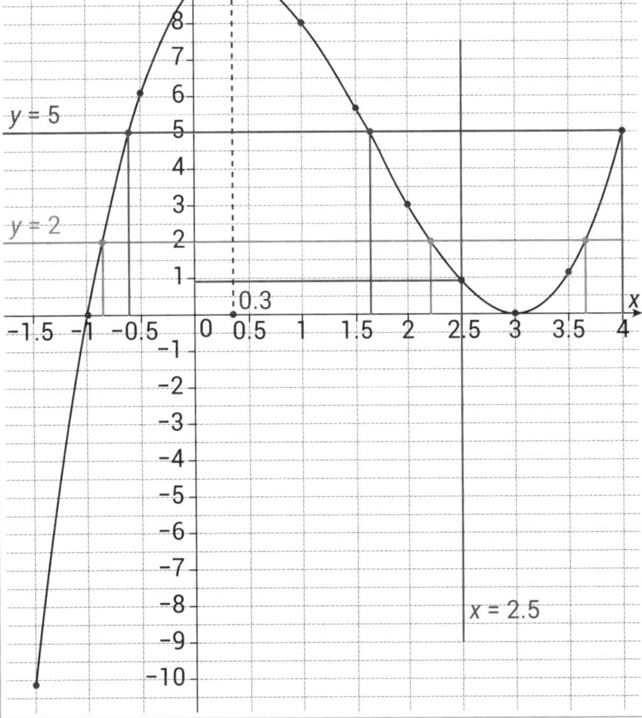

Answers to parts (ii), (iii), (iv), (v), and (vi) are estimates and depend on the accuracy of the graph drawn.

Worked Example 6.16

Graph the function $g: x \to 8 - 12x + 6x^2 - x^3$ in the domain $1 \leqslant x \leqslant 3, x \in R$.

Solution

x	$8 - 12x + 6x^2 - x^3$	y	(x,y)
1	$8 - 12(1) + 6(1)^2 - (1)^3$	1	(1,1)
1.5	$8 - 12(1.5) + 6(1.5)^2 - (1.5)^3$	0.125	(1.5,0.125)
2	$8 - 12(2) + 6(2)^2 - (2)^3$	0	(2,0)
2.5	$8 - 12(2.5) + 6(2.5)^2 - (2.5)^3$	-0.125	(2.5,−0.125)
3	$8 - 12(3) + 6(3)^2 - (3)^3$	-1	(3,−1)

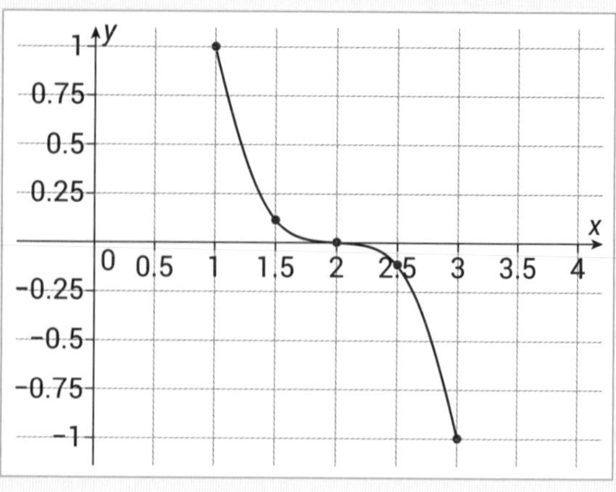

Points to note

- This function can be factorised to $g: x \to (2 - x)^3$.
- In this case, the function has three real roots. However, all three are the same ($x = 2$).
- In this case, the coefficient of x^3 is negative. Therefore, the graph starts high and finishes low.

Exercise 6.5

1. (a) Graph the following functions in the given domain.

   (b) Write down the roots of each function correct to one decimal place.

	Function	Domain
(i)	$x^3 - 4x^2 + x + 6$	$-3 \leqslant x \leqslant 4$
(ii)	$2x^3 + 3x^2 - 11x - 6$	$-3 \leqslant x \leqslant 2$
(iii)	$6 + 7x - x^3$	$-3 \leqslant x \leqslant 3$

2. (a)

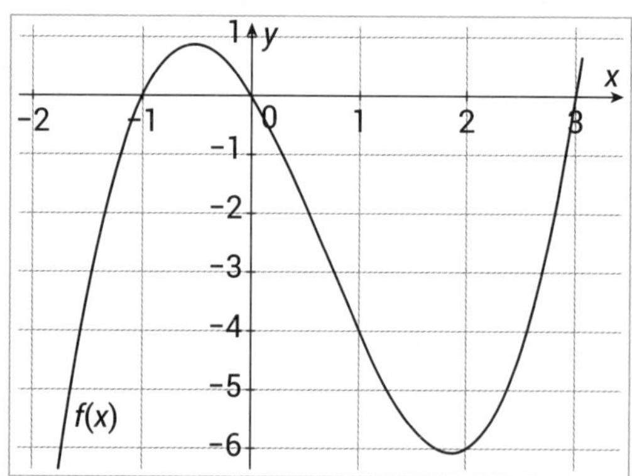

Using the graph above, estimate:

(i) The values of x for which $f(x) = 0$

(ii) The values of x for which $f(x) = -3$

(iii) The range of values of x for which $f(x)$ is decreasing

(b)

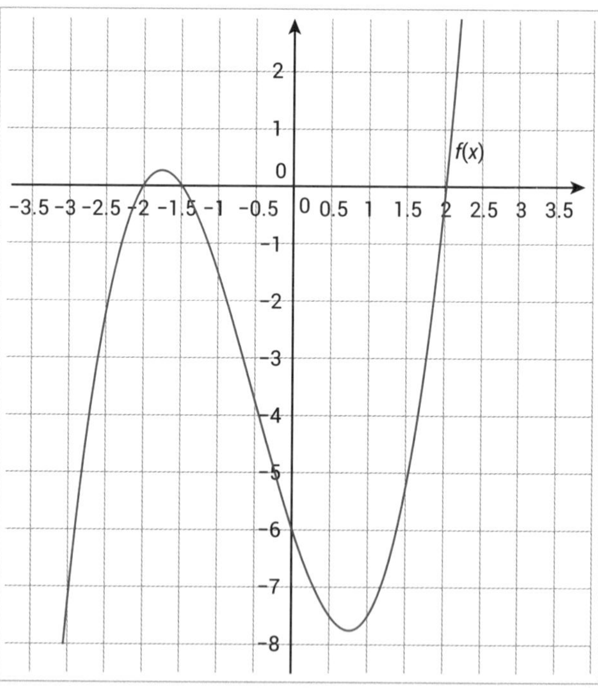

Using the graph above, estimate:

(i) The values of x for which $f(x) = 0$

(ii) The values of x for which $f(x) = 3$

(iii) The range of values of x for which $f(x)$ is decreasing

FUNCTIONS

(c)

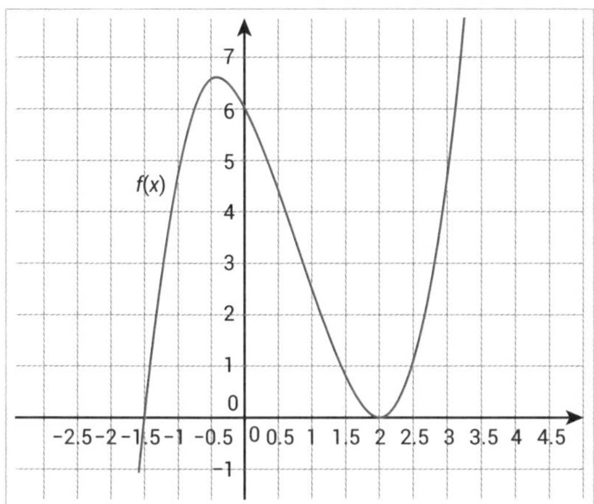

Using the graph above, estimate:

(i) The values of x for which $f(x) = 0$

(ii) The values of x for which $f(x) = -3$

(iii) The range of values of x for which $f(x)$ is decreasing

3. Draw the graph of the function $f: x \rightarrow 2x^3 + x^2 - 8x - 4$ in the domain $-2.5 \leqslant x \leqslant 2.5, x \in R$.

Estimate from your graph:

(i) The values of x for which $f(x) = 0$

(ii) The values of x for which $f(x) = 3$

4. Draw the graph of the function $f: x \rightarrow x^3 + 4x^2 + 3x - 4$ in the domain $-3 \leqslant x \leqslant 1, x \in R$.

Estimate from your graph:

(i) The value of x for which $f(x) = 0$

(ii) The values of x for which $f(x) = -3$

5. Draw the graph of the function $f: x \rightarrow x^3 + 3x^2 - x - 3$ in the domain $-4 \leqslant x \leqslant 2, x \in R$.

Estimate from your graph:

(i) The values of x for which $f(x) = 0$

(ii) The values of x for which $f(x)$ is decreasing

(iii) The value of x for which $x^3 + 3x^2 - x - 3 = 5$

6. The growth model used for a new product is given by the graph below.

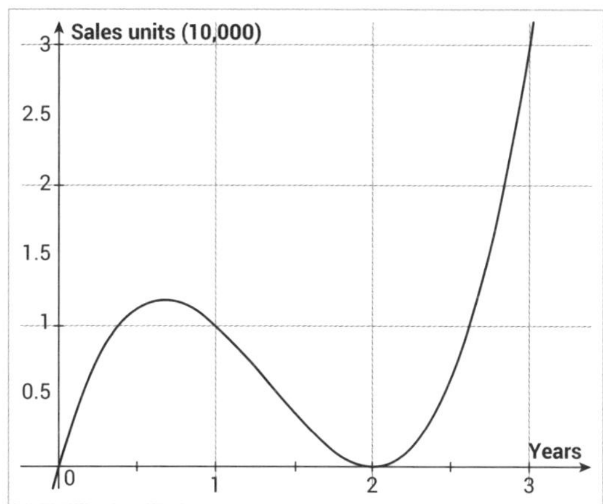

(i) What is the maximum level of sales reached in the first two years of the product's life cycle?

(ii) After approximately how many years is this maximum level reached?

(iii) Two aggressive marketing campaigns are undertaken during the product's life cycle. Estimate from the graph when these two campaigns took place. Explain your answer.

(iv) If the product has an expected life of three years, what is the maximum level of sales that the product can achieve?

7. The graphs of $f(x) = -5x^3 + 11x^2 - 3$ and $g(x) = 3x + 0.5$ for $-1 \leqslant x \leqslant 2, x \in R$, are shown.

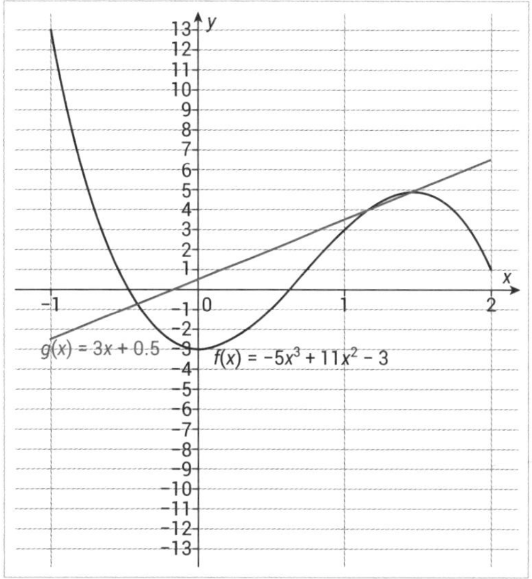

Use the graphs to find:

(i) The approximate value of $f(1.5)$

(ii) The approximate values of x for which $f(x) = 0$

(iii) The values of x for which $f(x) = g(x)$

8. The graph below models the temperature in degrees Celsius of a computer server over a four-minute period.

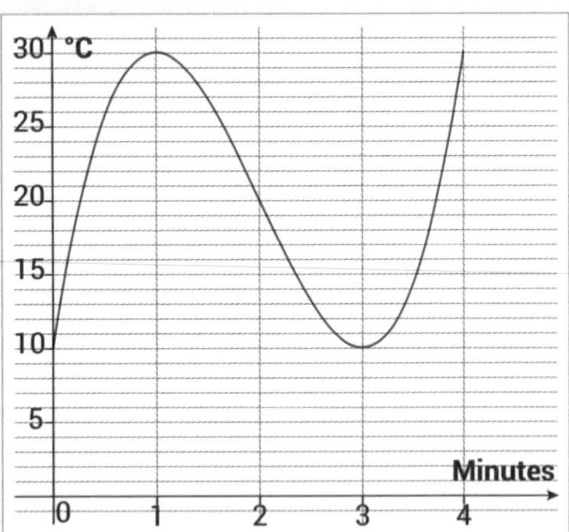

(i) What is the maximum temperature reached by the server?

(ii) At what times is this temperature recorded?

(iii) After 2.5 minutes, what is the temperature of the server?

(iv) It is recommended that the temperature of the server should not exceed 28°C.

Give the approximate time intervals for which the server is above the recommended temperature.

9. The graph below shows the sales cycle for a games console. The product will be removed from the market after 5.5 years.

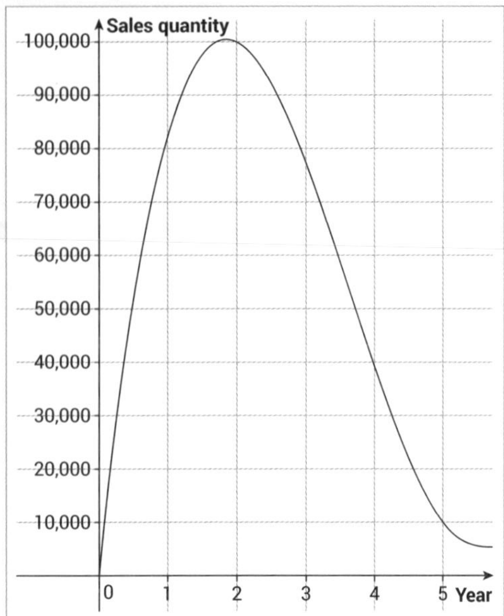

(i) At what time will sales quantity reach its peak?

(ii) At what two approximate times will sales quantity be 45,000 units?

(iii) The sales quantity can be represented by the cubic function $1{,}000(4x^3 - 44x^2 + 122x)$, where x is time in years. Using this function, investigate the accuracy of your answers to parts (i) and (ii).

6.7 Exponential Functions

Exponential functions are functions of the form $y = b^x$, where b is constant and x is the variable exponent or power.

When dealing with **exponential functions**, we take a number called the **base** and raise it to a power called the **exponent**.

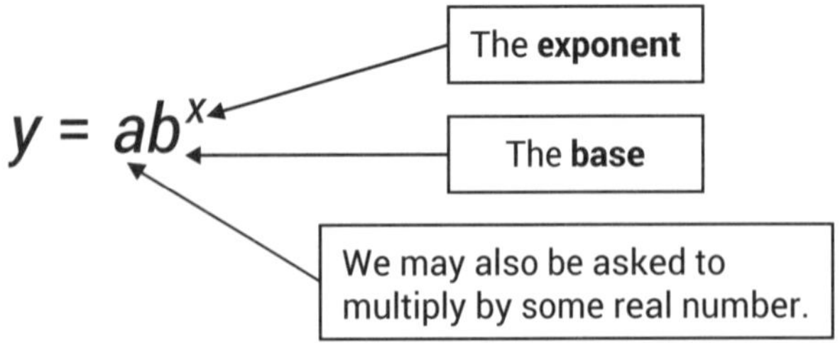

The base and exponent make up the exponential function.

Before dealing with exponential functions, it is essential that you know the rules for working with indices. Some key laws of indices are shown below.

Law 1 $a^p \times a^q = a^{p+q}$ **Law 3** $(a^p)^q = a^{pq}$

Law 2 $\frac{a^p}{a^q} = a^{p-q}$ **Law 4** $a^0 = 1, a \neq 0$

These formulae appear on page 21 of *Formulae and Tables.*

Graphs of Exponential Functions

The graph of an exponential function has a very distinctive shape.

The graph of the function $f(x) = ab^x$ will pass through the point $(0,a)$.

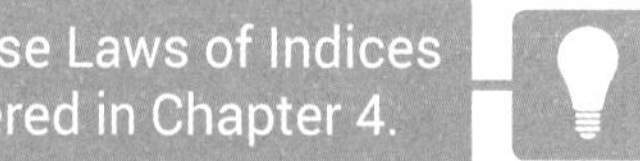

Revise Laws of Indices covered in Chapter 4.

Reason: At $x = 0$, $y = ab^0$

$= a(1)$

$= a$

The graph of an exponential function will never touch or cross the horizontal axis.

Worked Example 6.17

Graph the function $f(x) = 10^x$ in the domain $-2 \leqslant x \leqslant 1, x \in R$.

Solution

x	10^x	y	(x,y)
-2	10^{-2}	0.01	(-2,0.01)
-1	10^{-1}	0.1	(-1,0.1)
0	10^0	1	(0,1)
1	10^1	10	(1,10)

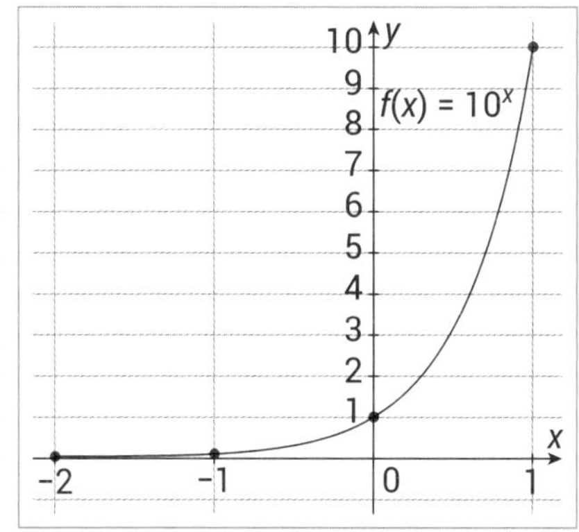

If the exponent is x and the base is greater than 1, the curve slopes upwards.

Worked Example 6.18

Graph the function $f(x) = 10^{-x}$ in the domain $-1 \leqslant x \leqslant 2, x \in R$.

Solution

x	10^{-x}	y	(x,y)
-1	$10^{-(-1)}$	10	(-1,10)
0	$10^{-(0)}$	1	(0,1)
1	10^{-1}	0.1	(1,0.1)
2	10^{-2}	0.01	(2,0.01)

10^{-x} can also be written as $\left(\frac{1}{10}\right)^x$ or 0.1^x.

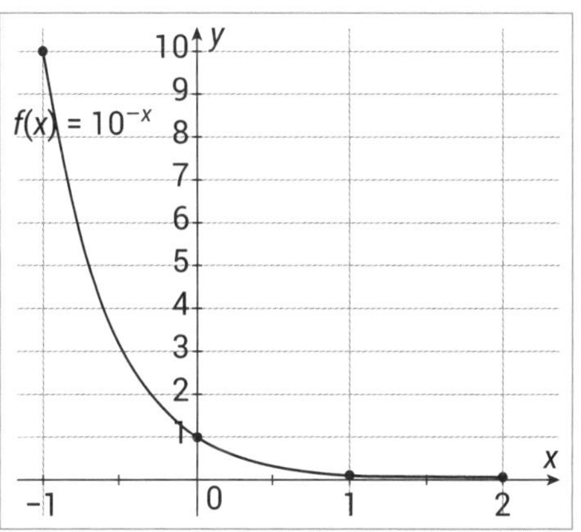

If the exponent is x and the base is positive and less than 1, the curve slopes downwards.

FUNCTIONS

Worked Example 6.19

Graph the function $f(x) = 2(3^x)$ in the domain $-2 \leqslant x \leqslant 2, x \in R$.

Solution

x	$2(3^x)$	y	(x,y)
-2	$2(3^{-2})$	$\frac{2}{9}$	$\left(-2,\frac{2}{9}\right)$
-1	$2(3^{-1})$	$\frac{2}{3}$	$\left(-1,\frac{2}{3}\right)$
0	$2(3^0)$	2	(0,2)
1	$2(3^1)$	6	(1,6)
2	$2(3^2)$	18	(2,18)

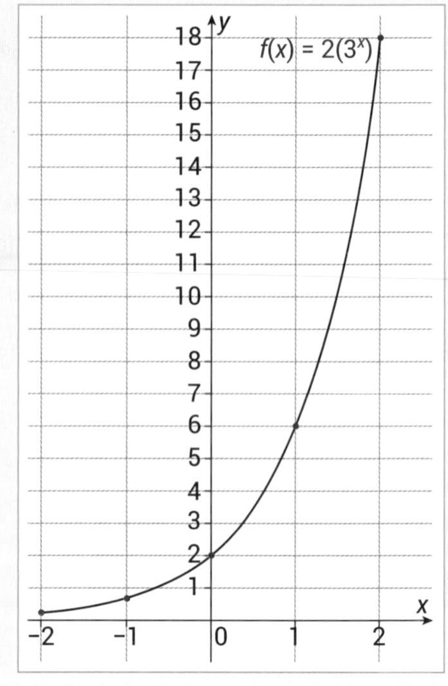

Worked Example 6.20

The growth of bacteria is modelled with an exponential function $y = 3(6^x)$, where x is time passed in seconds.

(i) Draw the graph of this function for the first 5 seconds of the bacteria's growth.

(ii) Use the graph to estimate the population of the bacteria after 3.5 seconds.

Solution

(i)

x	$3(6^x)$	y	(x,y)
0	$3(6^0)$	3	(0,3)
1	$3(6^1)$	18	(1,18)
2	$3(6^2)$	108	(2,108)
3	$3(6^3)$	648	(3,648)
4	$3(6^4)$	3888	(4,3888)
5	$3(6^5)$	23328	(5,23328)

(ii) Go to 3.5 on the x-axis. Draw a vertical line to meet the graph and then go across to the y-axis. Read off this value.
The population of the bacteria after 3.5 seconds is approximately 1,600.

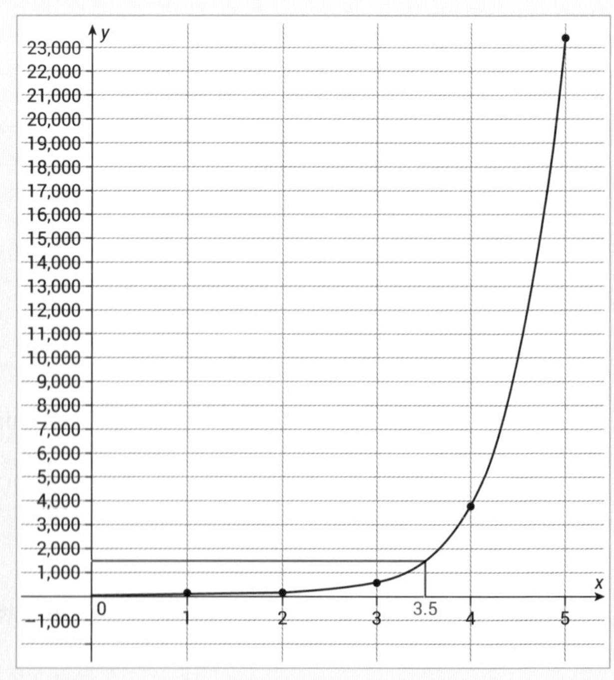

Exercise 6.6

In Questions 1–5, graph each function in the domain $-2 \leqslant x \leqslant 3, x \in R$.

1. $y = 2^x$
2. $y = 4^x$
3. $y = 3^x$
4. $y = \left(\frac{1}{5}\right)^x$
5. $y = \left(\frac{1}{3}\right)^x$

In Questions 6–12, graph each function in the domain $-2 \leqslant x \leqslant 2, x \in R$.

6. $y = 3(3^x)$
7. $y = 3(2^x)$
8. $y = 4(2^x)$
9. $y = 2(4^x)$
10. $y = 2(0.5^x)$
11. $y = 3(2^{-x})$
12. $y = 2(0.5^{-x})$

In Questions 13–17, identify the unknown values *a* and *b*.

13. $y = ab^x$

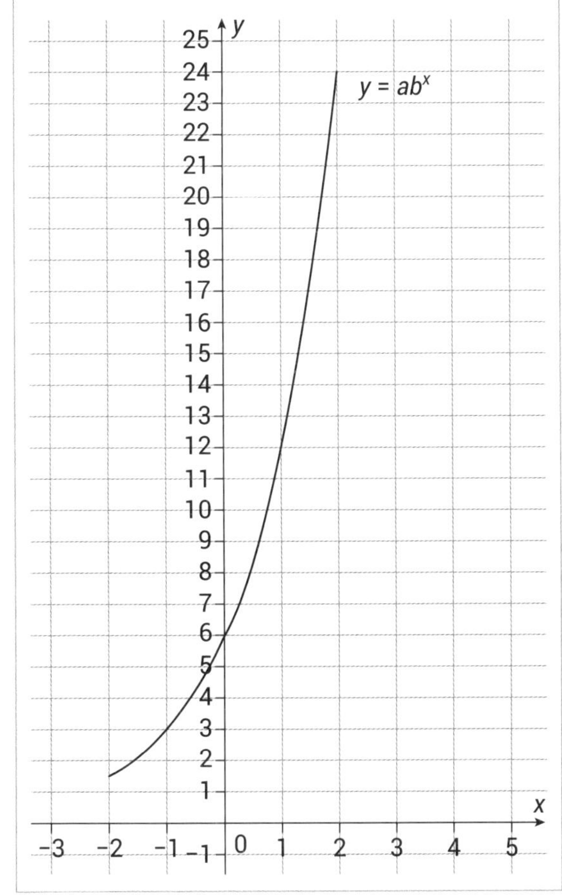

14. $y = ab^x$

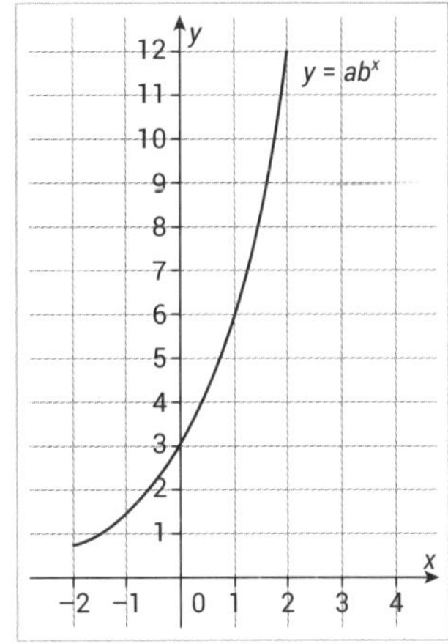

15. $y = ab^x$

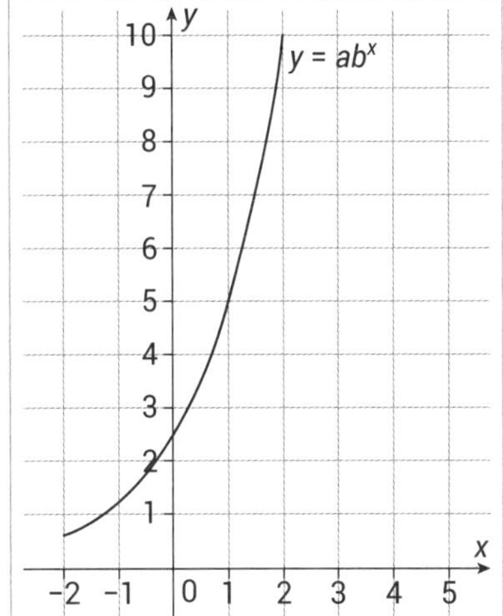

16. $y = ab^x$

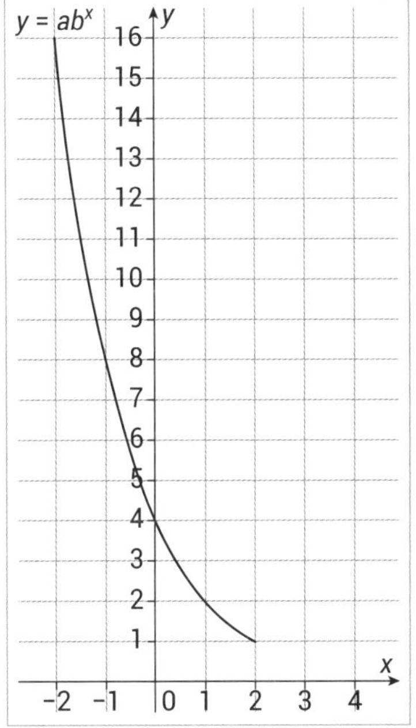

FUNCTIONS

17. $y = ab^x$

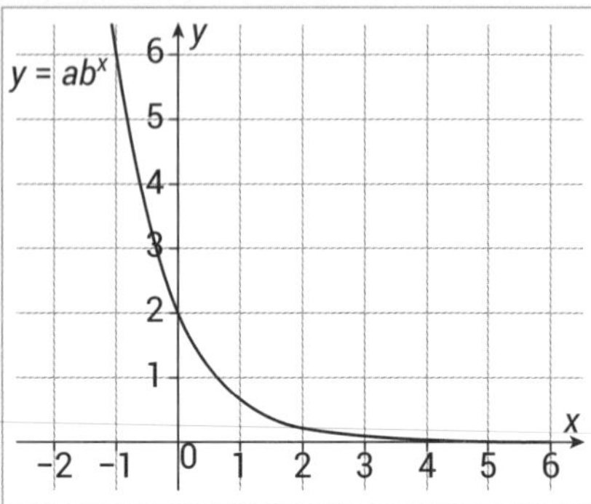

18. While making pizza dough in Home Economics class, the teacher points out that ideally the yeast mixture should be made about one hour before use. She points out that the mixture doubles in volume every hour.

Initially, Laura has 10 cm^3 of the mixture.

(i) Calculate the volume of the mixture each hour for the first four hours. (Use a table to display your results.)

(ii) Draw a graph to display this data.

(iii) Use your graph to estimate the volume of the mixture after 2.5 hours.

(iv) Use your graph to estimate how long it takes for the volume of the mixture to reach 100 cm^3 in size.

19. Since January 2000, the population of the city of Marville has grown according to the mathematical model $y = 720{,}500(1.022)^x$, where x is the number of years since January 2000.

(i) Explain what the numbers 720,500 and 1.022 represent in this model.

(ii) What would the population be in 2010 if the growth continued at the same rate?

(iii) Use this model to predict about when the population of Marville will first reach 1,000,000.

20. A population of 800 insects is growing each month at a rate of 5%.

(i) Write an equation that expresses the number of insects at time t.

(ii) About how many insects will there be in 8 months?

21. The populations of two ant hills vary with time t in days.

Ant hill A $P1 = 10 + 80t - t^3$ $0 \leqslant t \leqslant 6$

Ant hill B $P2 = 30(1.5^t)$ $0 \leqslant t \leqslant 6$

Both populations are in thousands.

(i) By completing the table below, plot the graphs of P1 and P2 against t on the same axes and scales.

t	1	2	3	4	5	6
P1						
P2						

(ii) Use your graph to find the time in days (correct to two decimal places) at which the two populations are the same.

22. ABC Ltd purchased a delivery van costing €60,000. It is the policy of the company to depreciate all delivery vans at a rate of 20% using the reducing-balance method.

(i) Complete the schedule of depreciation below for the first five years of the asset's useful economic life.

Year	Cost (€)/NBV	Rate of depreciation	Depreciation (€)	NBV (€)
1	60,000.00	0.2	12,000.00	48,000.00
2				
3				
4				
5				

(ii) Find the NBV at the end of Year 5 by using the formula for depreciation.

(iii) If F is the final value of the asset, write an exponential function in t (time passed in years) relating F (final value), P (initial cost of the asset), i (rate of depreciation) and t (time passed in years).

(iv) Graph the NBV against time passed, starting with the point (0,60000).

23. Mustafa bought a car for €5,000. He expects the car to have a useful life of three years, at the end of which it will be worth €3,645. He will depreciate the car at a rate of 10% per annum (reducing-balance method).

   (i) Using the formula for depreciation on page 30 of *Formulae and Tables*, identify the base and the exponent in the formula.

   (ii) Verify that Mustafa's residual value is in fact correct.

   (iii) Graph the net value of the car from the date of purchase to the date of disposal.

   (iv) From your graph, estimate the value of the car after 2.5 years.

   (v) Use the depreciation formula to find the value of the car after 2.5 years.

6.8 Transformations of Quadratic Functions

When we transform a quadratic function, the graph can:

(1) Narrow

For a quadratic function $f(x) = ax^2$, $a > 0$, as the value of a increases, the graph of $y = f(x)$ becomes narrower.

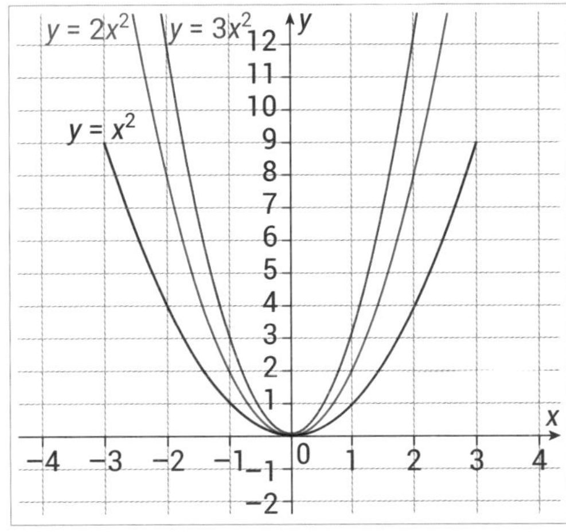

(2) Shift up or down

If b is positive, the graph of $f(x) = x^2 + b$ is the graph of $y = x^2$ shifted b units upwards.

If b is negative, the graph of $f(x) = x^2 + b$ is the graph of $y = x^2$ shifted $-b$ units downwards.

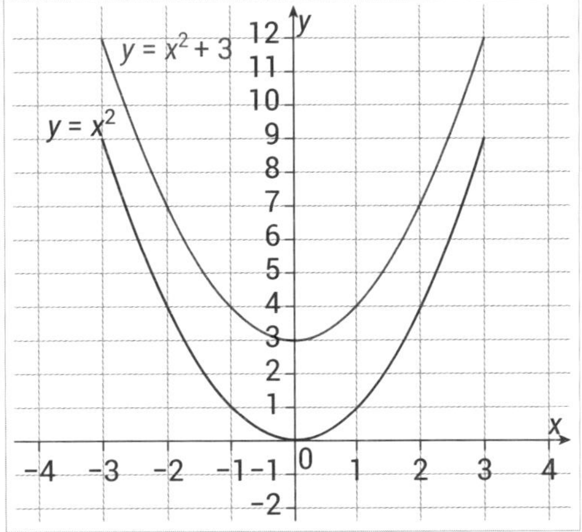

(3) Shift left or right

If b is positive, the graph of $f(x) = (x + b)^2$ is the graph of $y = x^2$ shifted b units to the left.

If b is negative, the graph of $f(x) = (x + b)^2$ is the graph of $y = x^2$ shifted $-b$ units to the right.

The y-intercept of the function $f(x) = (x + b)^2$ is $(0,(b)^2)$.

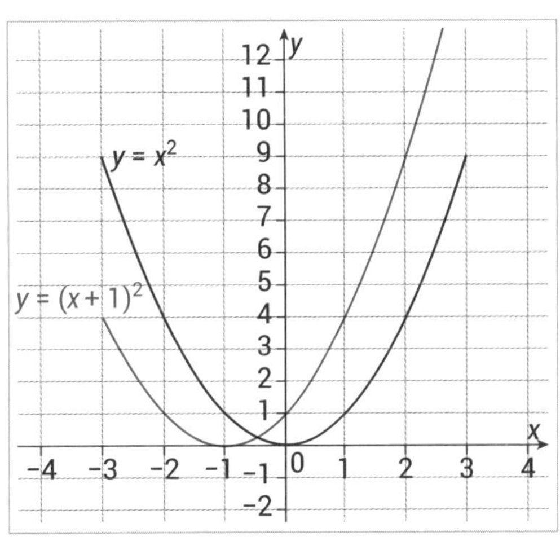

Worked Example 6.21

Graph the function $f(x) = (x + 2)^2$ in the domain $-5 \leqslant x \leqslant 1, x \in R$.

Use your graph to sketch the graphs of:

(i) $g(x) = (x - 1)^2$ (ii) $h(x) = (x + 2)^2 - 5$

Solution

We first draw the graph of the function $f(x) = (x + 2)^2$ in the domain $-5 \leqslant x \leqslant 1, x \in R$.

x	$(x + 2)^2$	y	(x,y)
-5	$(-5 + 2)^2$	9	(-5,9)
-4	$(-4 + 2)^2$	4	(-4,4)
-3	$(-3 + 2)^2$	1	(-3,1)
-2	$(-2 + 2)^2$	0	(-2,0)
-1	$(-1 + 2)^2$	1	(-1,1)
0	$(0 + 2)^2$	4	(0,4)
1	$(1 + 2)^2$	9	(1,9)

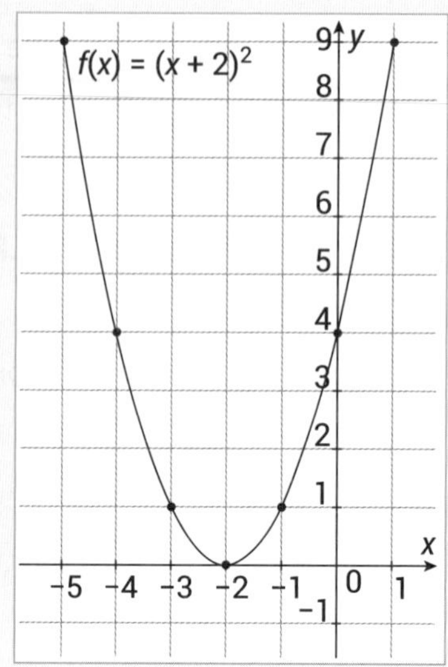

Couples: {(−5,9), (−4,4), (−3,1), (−2,0), (−1,1), (0,4), (1,9)}

(i) $g(x) = (x - 1)^2$

The graph touches the x-axis at (1,0).

The y-intercept is $(0,(-1)^2) = (0,1)$.

The graph of $g(x)$ is the graph of $f(x)$ shifted three units to the right.

Sketch the function through the point (1,0) and the point (0,1).

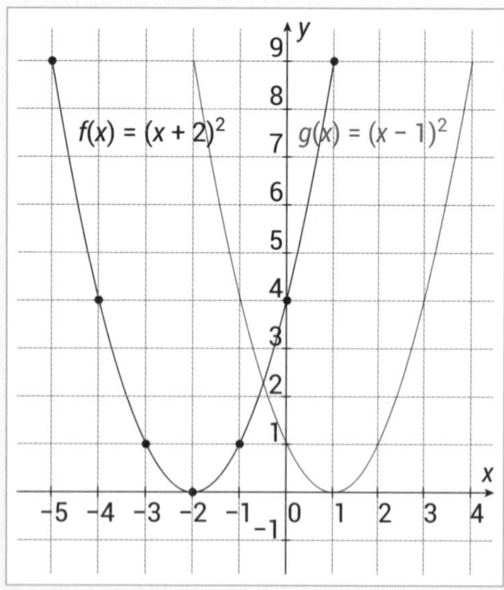

Here the graph is shifted to the right by 3.

(ii) $h(x) = (x + 2)^2 - 5$

The graph of $h(x)$ is the graph of $f(x)$ shifted downwards by five units.

∴ The lowest point is (−2,−5) and the y-intercept is (0,−1).

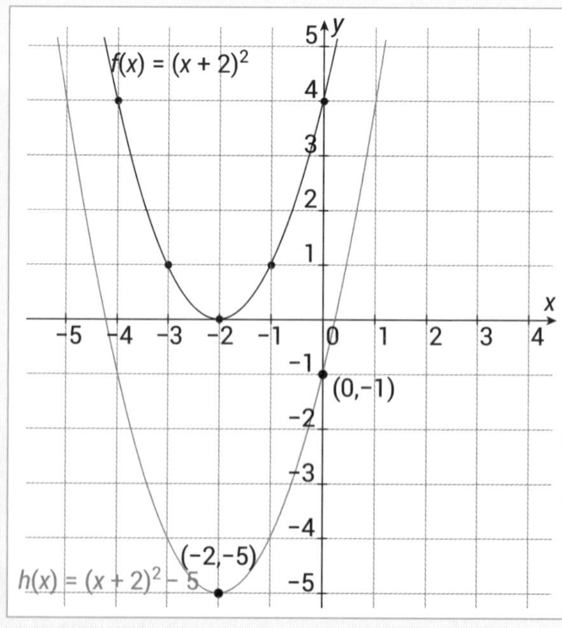

Here the graph is shifted down by 5.

Exercise 6.7

1. The graph of the function $y = x^2$ is shown. Use this graph to match the following functions with the functions shown on the graph:

   (i) $y = 3x^2$ (ii) $y = 5x^2$

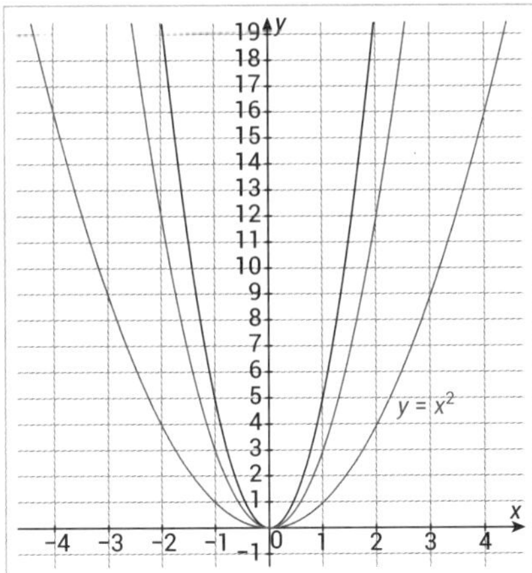

2. The graph of the function $y = x^2$ is shown. Use this graph to match the following functions with the functions shown on the graph:

   (i) $y = x^2 - 3$ (ii) $y = x^2 + 4$

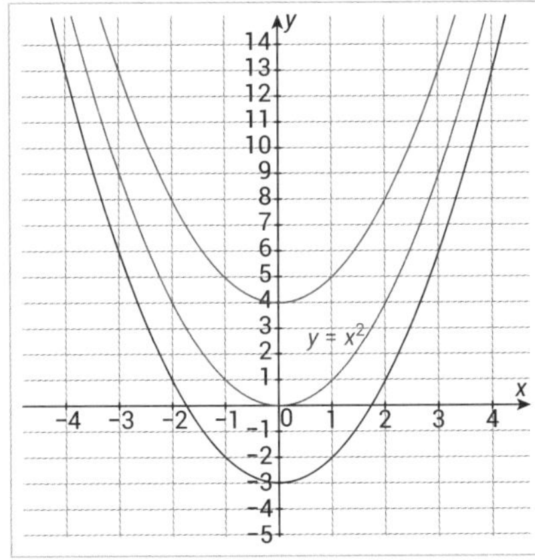

3. The graph of $f(x) = x^2 + x + 2$ is shown. Use this graph to match the following functions with the functions shown on the graph:

   (i) $g(x) = 3x^2 + 3x + 6$

   (ii) $h(x) = x^2 + x + 4$

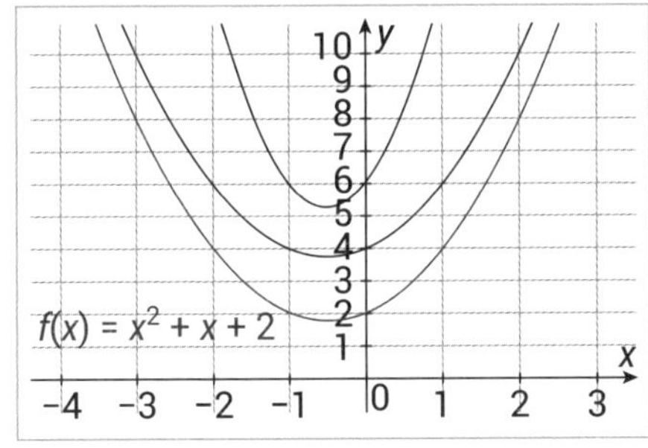

4. The graph of the function $y = x^2$ is shown. Use this graph to match the following functions with the functions shown on the graph:

   (i) $y = (x + 1)^2$ (ii) $y = (x - 5)^2$

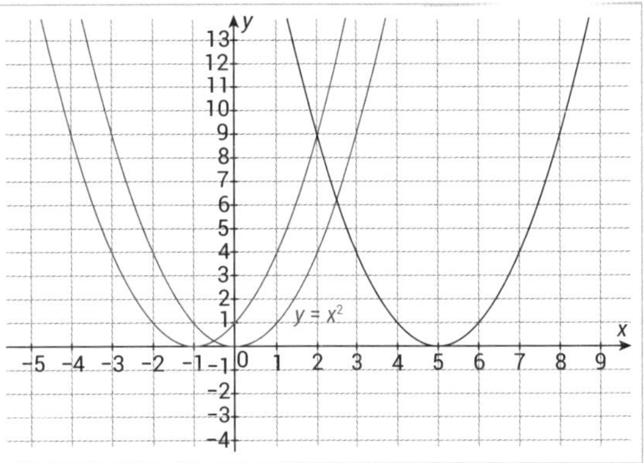

5. Graph the function $f(x) = x^2$ in the domain $-3 \leqslant x \leqslant 3, x \in R$.

   Hence, sketch the following functions:

   (i) $g(x) = 2x^2$ (ii) $h(x) = (x - 2)^2$

6. Graph the function $f(x) = 2x^2 + 4$ in the domain $-4 \leqslant x \leqslant 3, x \in R$.

   Hence, sketch the following functions:

   (i) $g(x) = f(x) - 3$ (ii) $h(x) = f(x) - 6$

7. The graph of the function $f(x) = (x - 3)^2$ is shown.

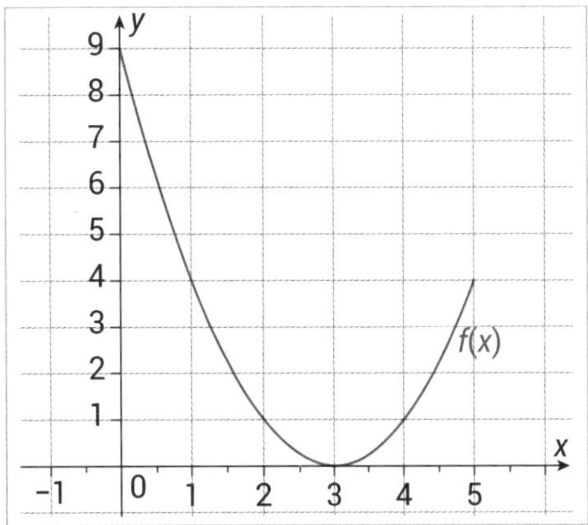

   Sketch the following functions:

   (i) $g(x) = (x - 3)^2 + 6$

   (ii) $h(x) = 2(x - 3)^2$

   (iii) $i(x) = (x - 2)^2$

FUNCTIONS

Revision Exercises

1. Which of the following are functions?
   Give a reason for your answer.
   (i) {(1,4), (3,5), (4,6), (5,7)}
   (ii) {(11,22), (22,32), (32,44)}
   (iii) {(1,3), (3,5), (1,8), (4,9)}
   (iv) {(4,4), (3,4), (5,9)}
   (v) {(2,−3), (−3,1), (2,0), (3,6), (4,8)}

2. Which of the following are functions?
   Give a reason for your answer.
   (i)
   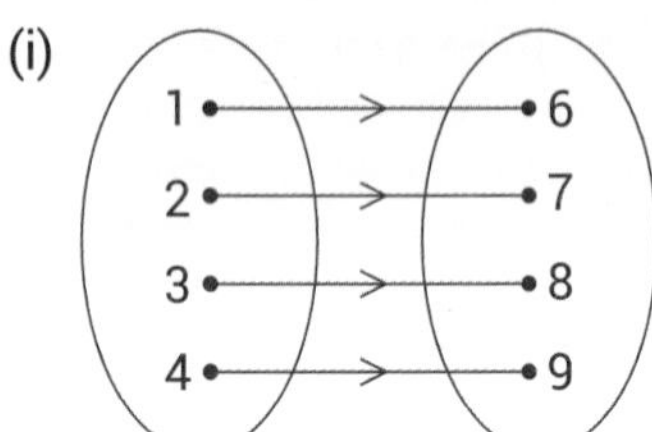
   (ii)
   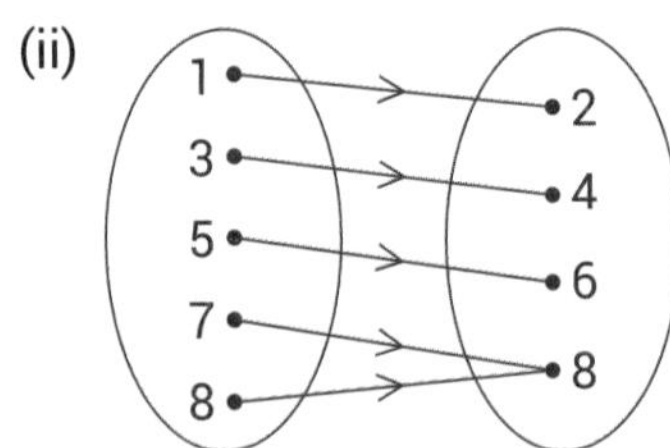
   (iii)
   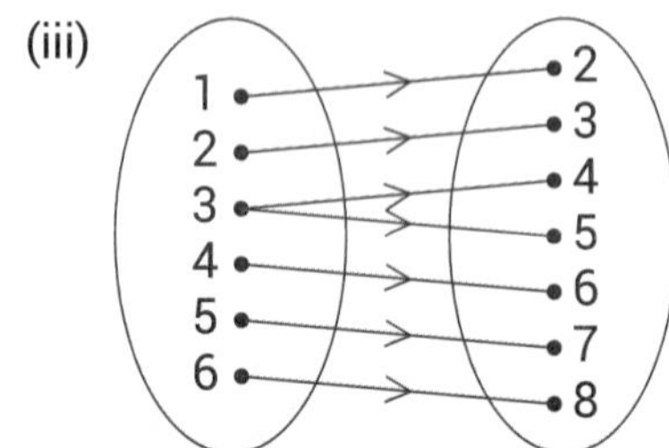
   (iv)
   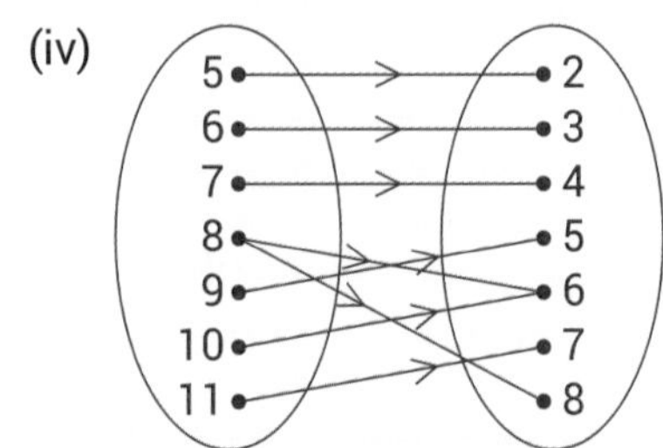

3. A function results in the following ordered pairs: (1,2), (2,4), (4,8), (8,16).
   List the following:
   (i) The domain of the function
   (ii) The range

4. The local Vincent de Paul society is selling tickets for a raffle. Ciara has 15 tickets to sell, and she sells each ticket for €5.
   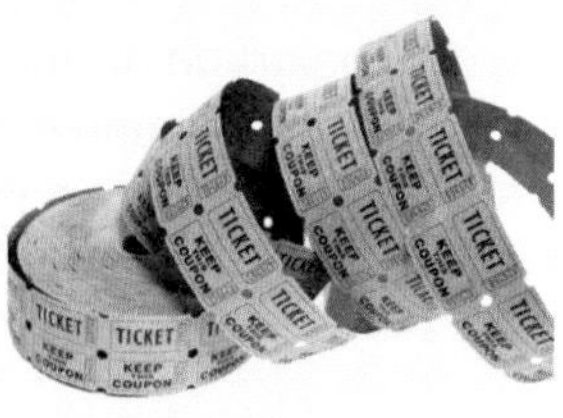
   She knows that the amount raised by her is a function of the number of tickets sold.
   (i) Define this function in terms of *x* and *y*, where *x* is the number of tickets sold and *y* is the amount of cash raised.
   (ii) What is the domain of this function?
   (iii) If Ciara sells 13 tickets, what amount does she raise?

5. $f(x) = 3x^2 - 5x + 4$ is a function.
   Find:
   (i) $f(1)$
   (ii) $f(-2)$
   (iii) $f(2)$
   (iv) $f(-3)$
   (v) $f(4)$

6. $f: x \to 4x^2 - 1$ is a function.
   Find:
   (i) The value of $f(1)$
   (ii) The value of $f\left(\frac{1}{2}\right)$
   (iii) The value of p if $f(2) = p$
   (iv) The values of k if $f(k) = 15$

7. $f(x) = 3x + g$ defines a function.
   Find the value of g if $f(3) = 12$.

8. $g(x) = ax - 12$ defines a function.
   Find the value of a if $g(4) = 0$.

9. A function is defined as 'square the input and subtract 1'.
   List the range of this function if the domain is:
   (i) {1, 2, 3, 5, 6}
   (ii) The first five prime numbers
   (iii) {−2, −1, 0, 1, 2, 3, 4}

10. A function is defined by:

$$f(x) = \frac{x^2 - 6}{x}, x \neq 0$$

(i) Evaluate $f(6)$.

(ii) Find the two values of x for which $f(x) = 1$.

(iii) Show that there is no value of x for which $f(x) = x$.

11. A function is defined by $h(x) = 3x - 2$.
A second function is defined by $g(x) = x^2 - 2$.
The function f is defined as $f = h \circ g$.

Find:

(i) $f(0)$

(ii) $f(3)$

(iii) $f(4)$

(iv) $f(6)$

(v) $f(-1)$

(vi) $f(-2)$

(vii) $f(-3)$

(viii) $f(-6)$

12. Draw a graph of the following functions with the given domains:

	Function	Domain
(i)	$f(x) = 3x - 4$	$-2 \leqslant x \leqslant 2, x \in R$
(ii)	$g(x) = 2 - 2.5x$	$-3 \leqslant x \leqslant 1, x \in R$
(iii)	$h(x) = 6 - 4x$	$0 \leqslant x \leqslant 5, x \in R$

13. Draw the graph of the linear function $f: x \rightarrow 3x - 2$ in the domain $-3 \leqslant x \leqslant 4, x \in R$.

Use your graph to estimate:

(i) The value of $f(x)$ when $x = 2.5$

(ii) The value of x for which $3x - 2 = 6$

(iii) The value of x for which $3x - 3 = -5$

(iv) The range of values of x for which $f(x) \geqslant 0$

14. Using the same axes and scales, draw the two graphs $f(x) = 3x - 8$ and $g(x) = 8 - 2x$ in the domain $-1 \leqslant x \leqslant 4, x \in R$.

What is the point of intersection of the two graphs?

15. A student suggests that the number of times a student goes out in a six-month period and the amount of weekly disposable income a student has over that period are given by a linear function $y = 1 + 0.2x$, where x represents the weekly disposable income in euro and y represents the number of times the student goes out.

(i) Copy and complete the table below, and hence draw the graph for the given domain.

Income (€)	10	20	30	40	50	60	70	80	90	100
Number of times to go out										

(ii) Estimate from your graph the number of times a student with a weekly income of €55 will go out in the six months.

(iii) Estimate from your graph the weekly income of a student who goes out 15 times in the six months.

(iv) Estimate from your graph the weekly income of a student who goes out at least eight times in the six months.

16. Draw the graph of the function $f: x \rightarrow x^2 - 3x - 4$ in the domain $-2 \leqslant x \leqslant 4, x \in R$.

Estimate from your graph:

(i) The value of $f(2.2)$

(ii) The values of x for which $x^2 - 3x - 4 \leqslant 0$

(iii) The minimum value of $f(x)$

(iv) The values of x for which $x^2 - 3x - 5 = 0$

17. Draw the graph of the function $f: x \rightarrow 6 - 3x - x^2$ in the domain $-5 \leqslant x \leqslant 3, x \in R$.

Find from your graph:

(i) The values of x for which $f(x) = 0$

(ii) The value of $f(-1.5)$

(iii) The values of x for which $y = 2$

(iv) The maximum value of $f(x)$

(v) The range of values of k for which $f(x) = k$ has two distinct real solutions

18. Use the same scales and axes to draw the graphs of the two functions $f(x) = 3 - 2x + x^2$ and $g(x) = 5 - 2x - x^2$ in the domain $-3 \leqslant x \leqslant 2$, $x \in R$.

(i) Use your graphs to estimate the values of x for which $f(x) = g(x)$.

(ii) Use your graphs to estimate the values of x for which $f(x) \geqslant g(x)$.

(iii) Use your graphs to estimate the values of x for which $f(x) < g(x)$.

19. The function graphed below is $f(x) = ax^2 + bx + c$. Find the values of a, b and c.

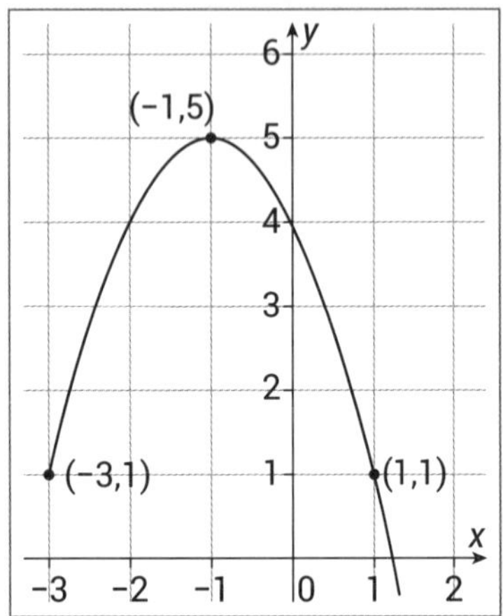

20. The diagram shows part of the graph of the function $y = ax^2 + bx + 2$.

Find the value of a and the value of b.

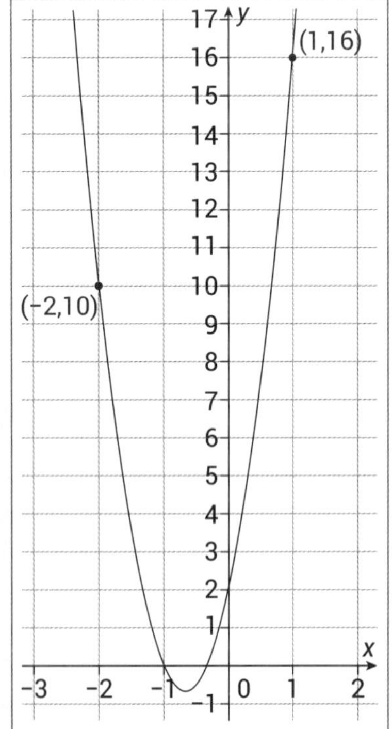

21. The diagram shows part of the graph of the function $y = ax^2 + bx - 3$.

Find the value of a and the value of b.

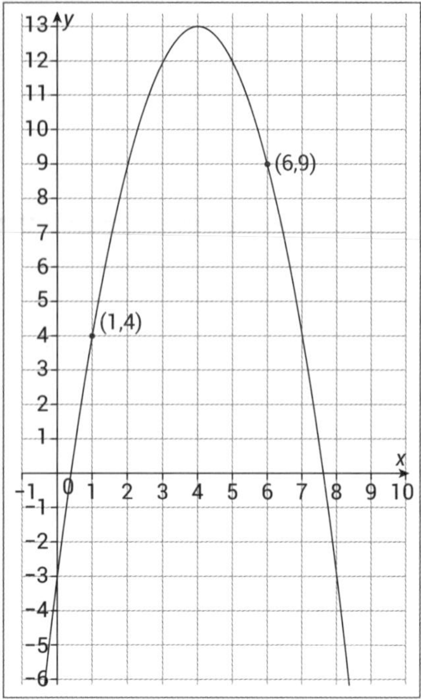

22. The diagram shows part of the graph of the function $y = ax^2 + bx + 17$.

Find the value of a and the value of b.

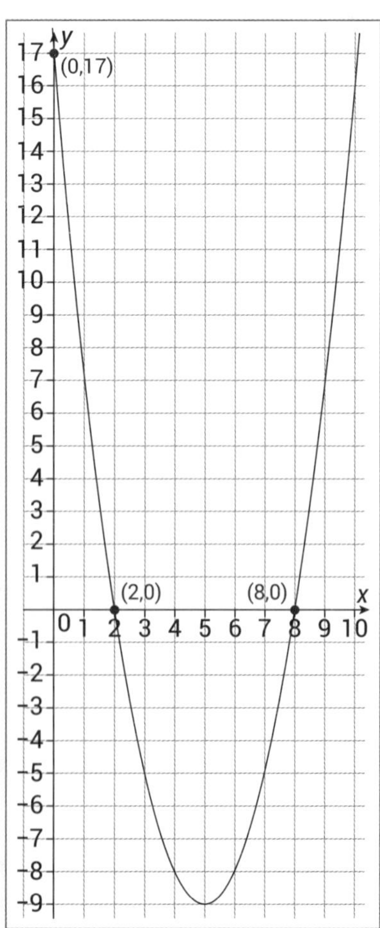

FUNCTIONS

23. Two fireworks were fired straight up in the air at $t = 0$ seconds.

The height, h metres, that each firework reached above the ground t seconds after it was fired is given by $h = 80t - 5t^2$.

The first firework exploded 5 seconds after it was fired.

(i) At what height was the first firework when it exploded?

(ii) What was the average speed of this firework?

The second firework failed to explode and it fell back to the ground.

(iii) At what two times was the firework at a height of 240 m?

24. Graph the function $f(x) = x^3 + x^2 - 3x + 1$ in the domain $-3 \leq x \leq 2, x \in R$.

Estimate from your graph:

(i) The value of x for which $f(x) = 0$

(ii) The value of x for which $f(x) = 2$

(iii) The number of real roots of the function

25. Draw the graph of the cubic function $f: x \rightarrow x^3 + 3x^2 + 2x - 3$ in the domain $-3 \leqslant x \leqslant 1, x \in R$.

Estimate from your graph:

(i) The value of x for which $f(x) = 0$

(ii) The values of x for which $f(x) = -3$

(iii) The number of real roots of the function

26. On the same axes and scales, graph the functions $f: x \rightarrow x^3 - 3x^2 + 2x + 3$ and $g: x \rightarrow 5 + 2x - x^2$ in the domain $-1 \leqslant x \leqslant 3, x \in R$.

Use your graph to approximate the value of x for which $f(x) = g(x)$.

27. Let $f(x) = x^3 + ax^2 + bx - 6$, where a and b are real numbers.

Given that $f(1) = 0$ and $f(2) = 0$, find the value of a and the value of b.

28. On the same axes and scales, graph the functions

$f: x \rightarrow \frac{1}{2}x + 2$

$g: x \rightarrow 2x^2 - 2x + 1$

in the domain $-2 \leqslant x \leqslant 3, x \in R$.

Using your graph, approximate the values of x for which $f(x) = g(x)$.

29.

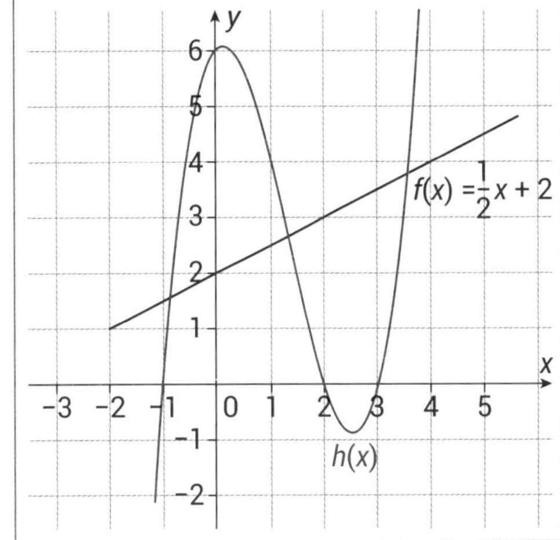

(i) Use the diagram to estimate the approximate value of $f(1.5)$.

(ii) Use the diagram to estimate the approximate value of x if $f(x) = 3.5$.

(iii) Use the diagram to estimate the values of x for which $f(x) = h(x)$.

30. Graph the following exponential functions in the domain $-3 \leqslant x \leqslant 2, x \in R$:

(i) $f(x) = 2(3^x)$

(ii) $g(x) = 2(1.5^x)$

(iii) $h(x) = 3(2^x)$

(iv) $p(x) = 3(0.5^x)$

31. Identify the value of a in the function $y = ab^x$ graphed below.

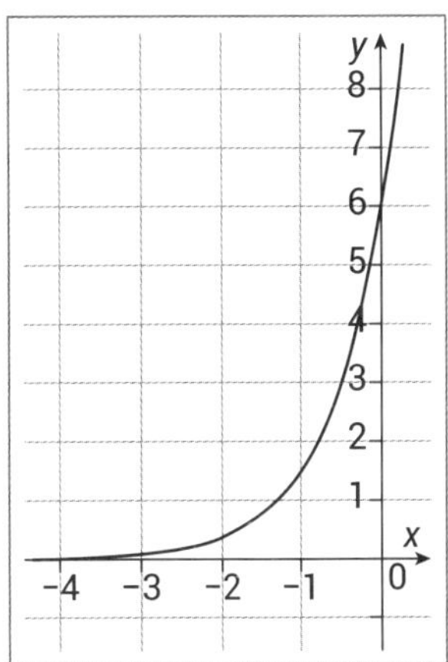

32. Identify the values of a and b in the function $y = ab^x$ graphed below.

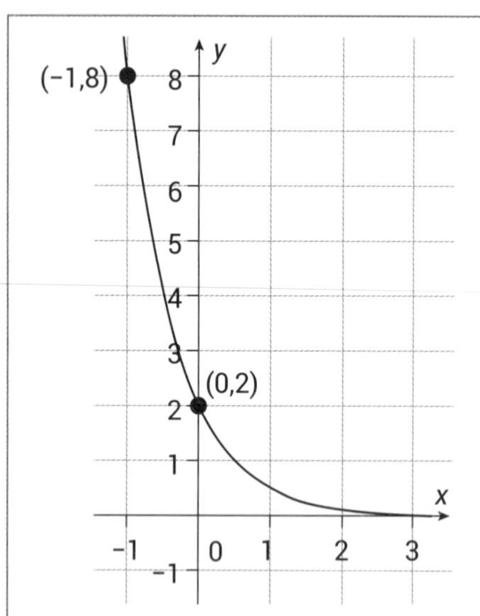

33. An investment follows the growth model $F = P(1 + i)^t$, where P is the initial amount invested, i is the rate of interest, and t is the length of time in years.

Consider an initial investment of €400 invested at 12% per annum for five years.

(i) Calculate the value of the investment at the end of each year for the first five years of the investment.

(ii) Using the number of years as the x-variable and the final value as the y-variable, graph the growth of the investment over a five-year period.

(iii) Clearly identify the base and the exponent in the formula $F = P(1 + i)^t$.

(iv) Use your graph to estimate the value of the investment after three years and three months.

34. A pension fund started to decline following an exponential decay model given by the function $y = 100{,}000(4^{-x})$, where x is years passed and y is value in euros.

(i) What was the initial value of the pension fund before the decline in value?

(ii) Graph the value of the pension fund over a five-year period.

(iii) How long does it take for the value of the fund to decay to €50,000?

(iv) Will the pension fund ever reach a value of €0?

35. Identify the colour of each function on the graph below.

(i) $f(x) = 2^x$

(ii) $g(x) = x^2 + 3x - 4$

(iii) $h(x) = x^3 - 2x^2 - 5x + 6$

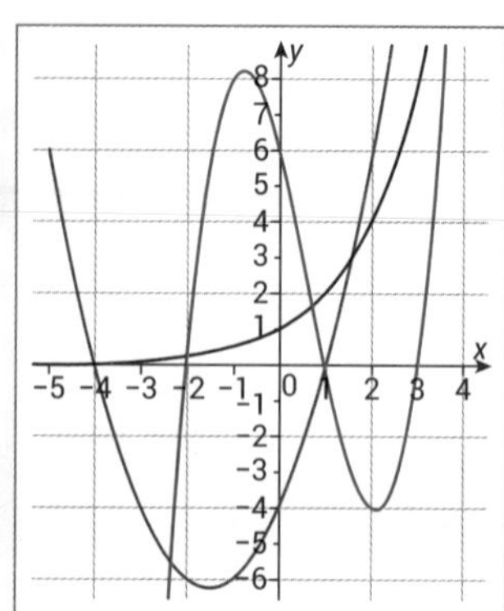

36. Two functions f and g are defined for $x \in R$ as follows:

$f: x \to 2^x$

$g: x \to 9x - 3x^2 - 1$

(i) Complete the table below, and use it to draw the graphs of f and g for $0 \leqslant x \leqslant 3$.

x	0	0.5	1	1.5	2	2.5	3
$f(x)$							
$g(x)$							

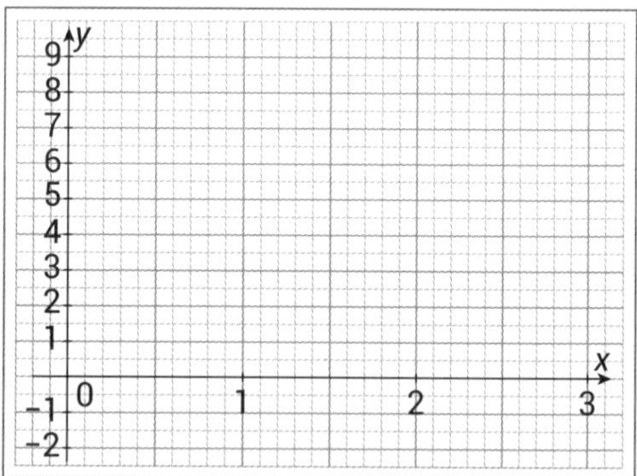

(ii) Use your graphs to estimate the value(s) of x for which $2^x + 3x^2 - 9x + 1 = 0$.

(iii) Let k be the number such that $2^k = 6$. Using your graph(s), or otherwise, estimate $g(k)$.

37. The graph of $f(x) = x^2 + 2x + 3$ is shown. Use this graph to match the following functions with the functions shown on the graph:

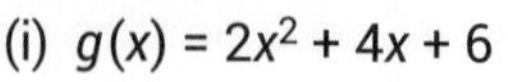
(i) $g(x) = 2x^2 + 4x + 6$

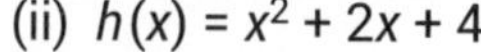
(ii) $h(x) = x^2 + 2x + 4$

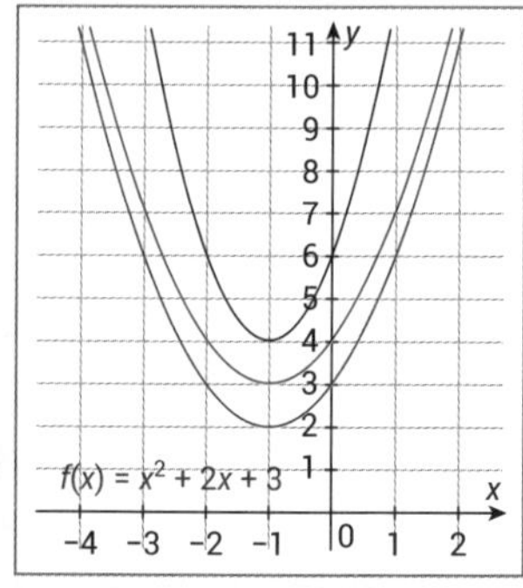

Exam Questions

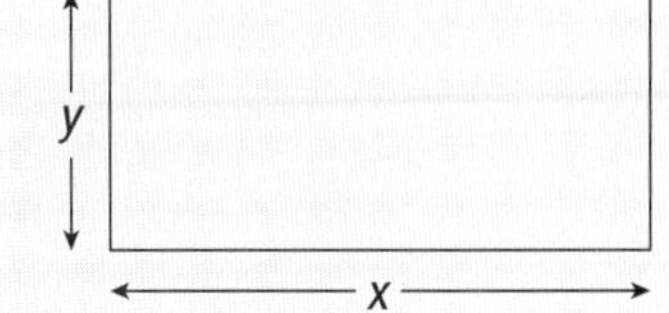

1. Kieran has 21 metres of fencing. He wants to enclose a vegetable garden in a rectangular shape as shown.

(a) By writing an expression for the perimeter of the vegetable garden in terms of x (length in metres) and y (width in metres), show that $y = 10.5 - x$.

(b) (i) Complete the table below to show the values of y and A (the area of the garden) for each given value of x.

x (m)	0	1	2	3	4	5	6	7	8	9	10
y (m)					6.5						
A (m²)					26						

(ii) Use the values of x and A from the table to plot the graph of A on the grid below.

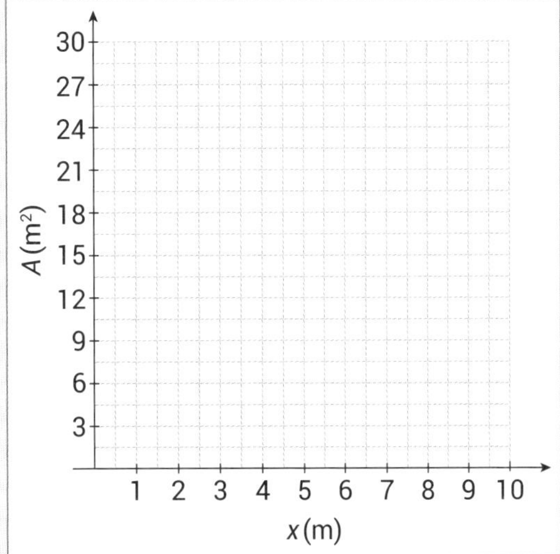

(c) Use your graph to estimate the maximum value of A and write the corresponding length and width.

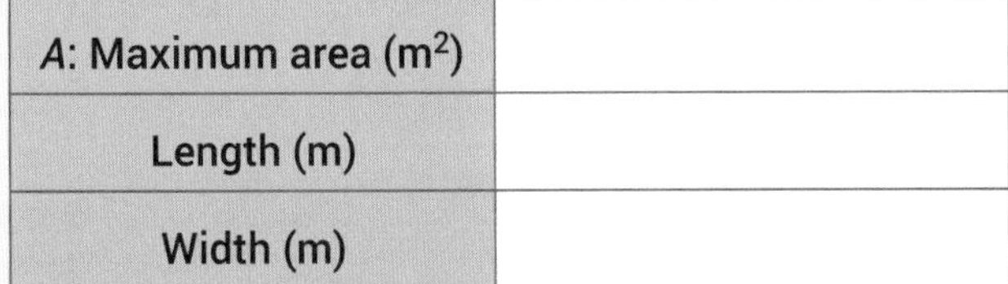

A: Maximum area (m²)	
Length (m)	
Width (m)	

SEC Leaving Certificate Ordinary Level, Paper 1, 2016

2. Company A uses the following formula to charge a customer for a job:

$$A(h) = 30 + 9.5h,$$

where $A(h)$ is the cost of the job, in euro, and h is the length of time that the job takes in hours.

Company B uses the following formula to charge a customer for the same job:

$$B(h) = 10(1.74)^h$$

where $B(h)$ is the cost of the job, in euro, and h is again the length of time that the job takes in hours.

(a) (i) Complete the table below to show what Company A charges and what Company B charges for jobs that take up to 5 hours. Where necessary give the charge correct to the nearest cent.

Time (hours)	0	1	2	3	4	5
$A(h)$ (€)					68	
$B(h)$ (€)					91.66	

(ii) On a copy of the grid below draw separate graphs to show the charge for Company A and the charge for Company B. Label each graph clearly.

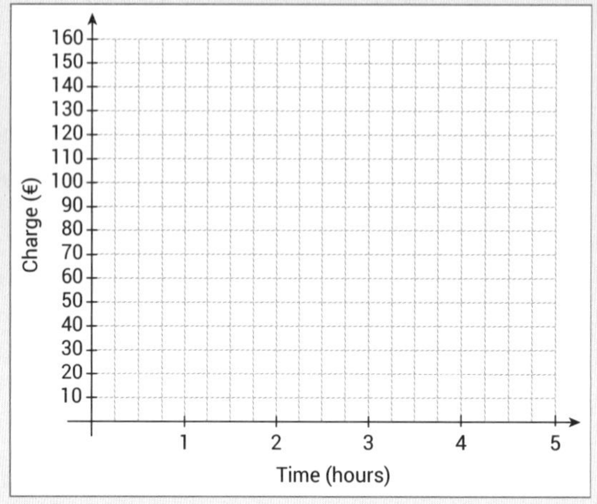

(b) Which company would charge least for a job that takes $2\frac{1}{2}$ hours to complete?

Give a reason for your answer.

(c) Use your graphs to estimate the value of h for which the charge is the same for both companies.

(d) Find the difference in cost for a job that takes 6 hours to complete.

SEC Leaving Certificate Ordinary Level, Paper 1, 2016

3. The diagram shows the graph of the function $f(x) = 5x - x^2$ in the domain $0 \leqslant x \leqslant 5, x \in R$.

(a) The function g is $g(x) = x + 3, x \in R$. The points $A(1,k)$ and B are the points of intersection of f and g. Find the co-ordinates of A and of B.

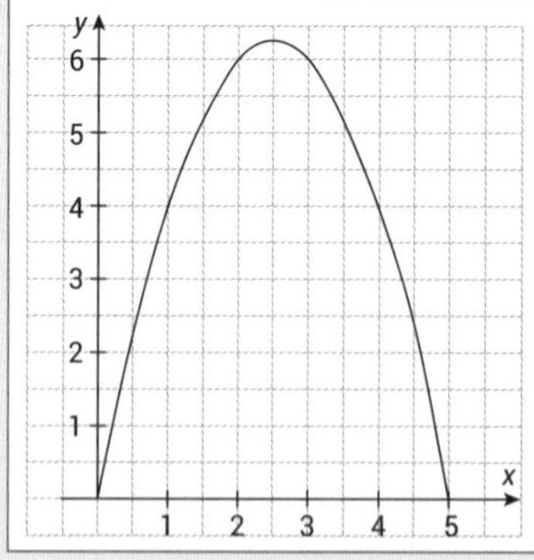

(b) The points $O(0,0)$ and $C(5,0)$ are on the graph of f.

(i) Draw the quadrilateral $OCBA$ on a copy of the diagram.

(ii) Find the area of the quadrilateral $OCBA$.

SEC Leaving Certificate Ordinary Level, Paper 1, 2015

FUNCTIONS

4. (a) Solve the equation $x^2 - x - 6 = 0$.

(b) The graphs of four quadratic functions are shown below.

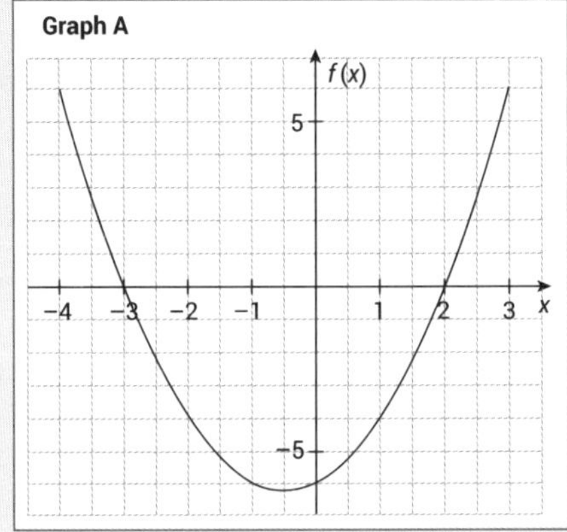

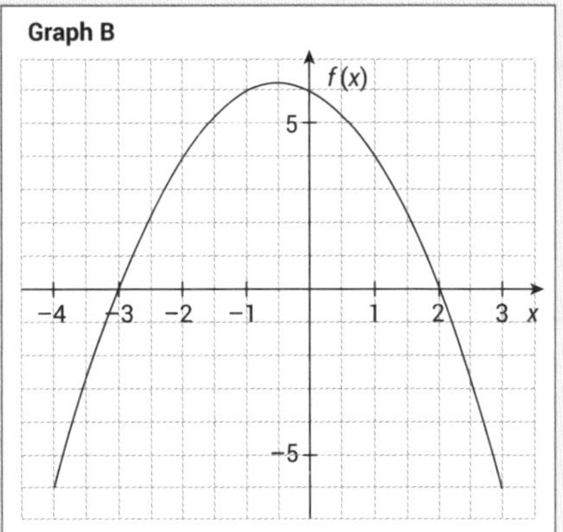

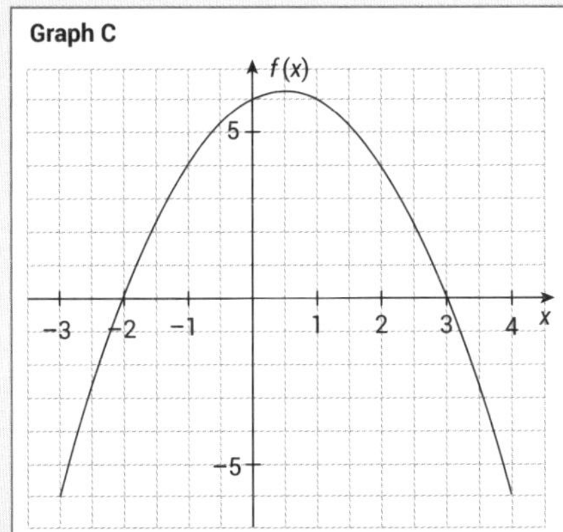

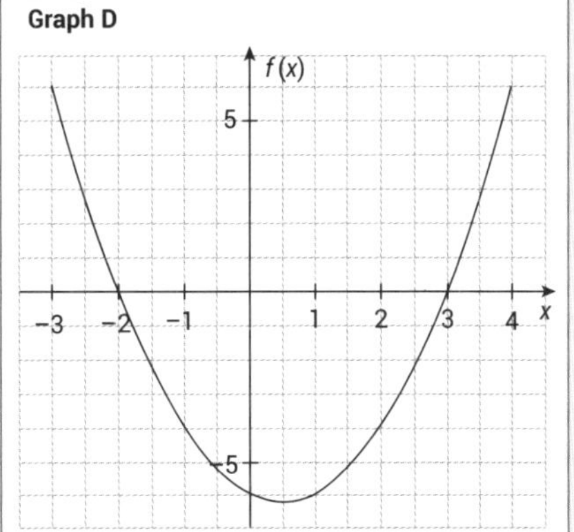

Which of the graphs above is that of the function $f: x \rightarrow x^2 - x - 6$, where $x \in R$?

(c) The graph of $g(x) = x^2 - 2x$, where $x \in R$, is shown on the diagram below. On a copy of the diagram, sketch the graph of each of the functions:

(i) $h(x) = g(x) + 2$

(ii) $k(x) = g(x + 2)$

Label each sketch clearly.

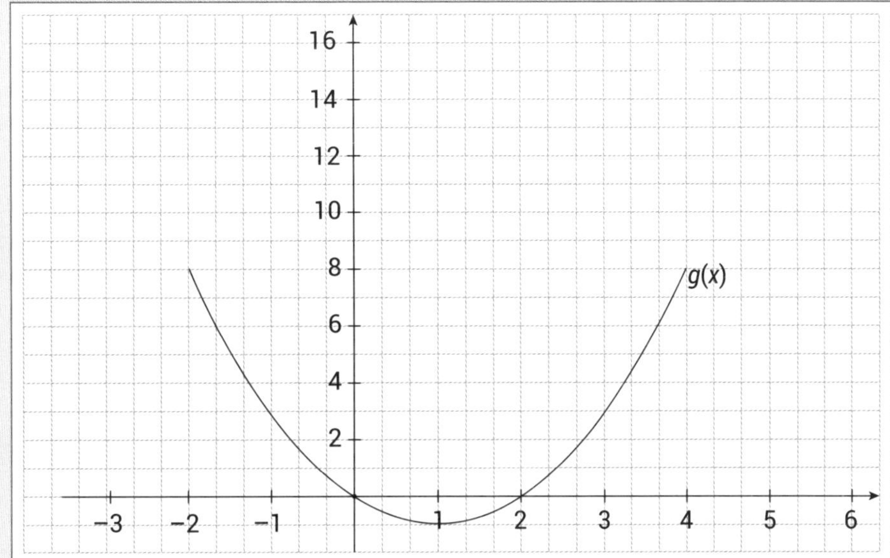

SEC Leaving Certificate Ordinary Level, Paper 1, 2014

5. A small rocket is fired into the air from a fixed position on the ground. Its flight lasts ten seconds. The height, in metres, of the rocket above the ground after *t* seconds is given by

$$h = 10t - t^2.$$

(a) Complete the table below.

Time, *t*	0	1	2	3	4	5	6	7	8	9	10
Height, *h*						25	24	21	16		

(b) Draw a graph to represent the height of the rocket during the ten seconds.

(c) Use your graph to estimate:

(i) The height of the rocket after 2.5 seconds

(ii) The time when the rocket will again be at this height

(iii) The co-ordinates of the highest point reached by the rocket

(d) (i) Find the slope of the line joining the points (6,24) and (7,21).

(ii) Would you expect the line joining the points (7,21) and (8,16) to be steeper than the line joining (6,24) and (7,21) or not? Give a reason for your answer.

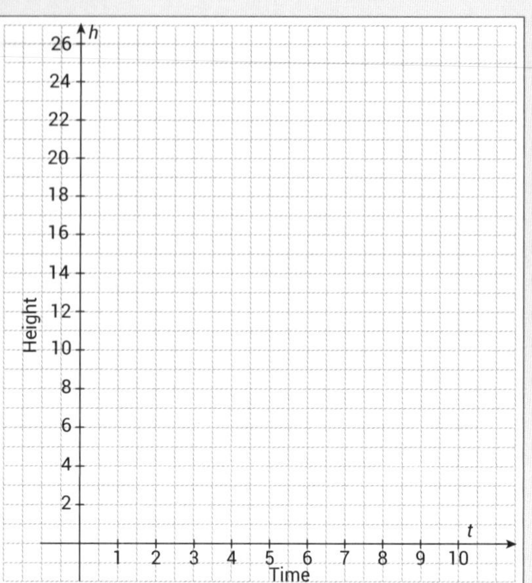

SEC Leaving Certificate Ordinary Level, Paper 1, 2014

6. Two functions *f* and *g* are defined for $x \in R$ as follows:

$$f : x \rightarrow 2^x$$

$$g : x \rightarrow 9x - 3x^2 - 1.$$

(a) Complete the table below, and use it to draw the graphs of *f* and *g* for $0 \leqslant x \leqslant 3$.

x	0	0.5	1	1.5	2	2.5	3
f(*x*)							
g(*x*)							

(b) Use your graphs to estimate the value(s) of *x* for which $2^x + 3x^2 - 9x + 1 = 0$.

(c) Let *k* be the number such that $2^k = 6$.
Using your graph(s), or otherwise, estimate $g(k)$.

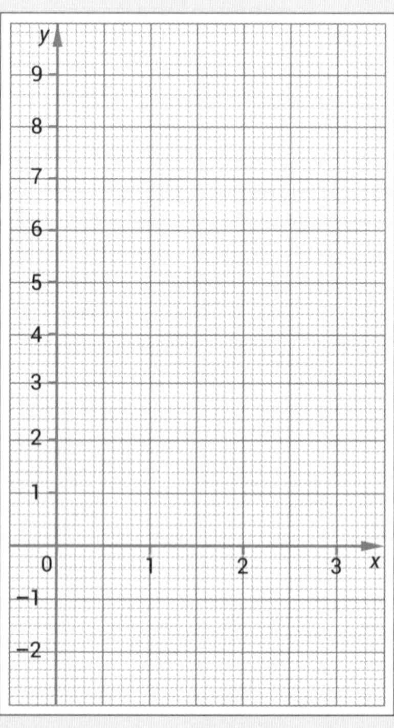

SEC Leaving Certificate Ordinary Level, Sample Paper 1, 2014

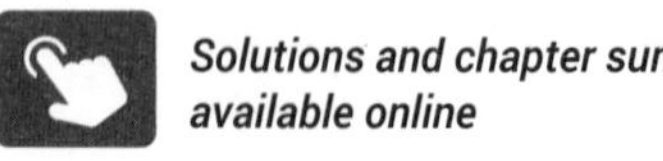

Solutions and chapter summary available online

Number Patterns

In this chapter you will learn to:

- Appreciate that patterns can generate sequences of numbers or objects
- Investigate patterns among these sequences
- Use patterns to continue the sequence
- Generalise and explain patterns and relationships in algebraic form
- Recognise whether a pattern is arithmetic, geometric or neither
- Find the sum to *n* terms of an arithmetic series

You should remember...

- How to graph straight lines
- How to graph non-linear functions

Key words

- Pattern
- Sequence
- Arithmetic sequence
- First difference
- Second difference
- General term (T_n)
- Arithmetic series
- Sum to *n* terms (S_n)
- Non-linear sequence
- Quadratic sequence
- Geometric sequence

7.1 Patterns

Patterns appear all around us: a **recurring** theme or motif in a piece of music, a **repeating** decimal such as 0.232323..., or the passage of the seasons over time. In many respects, mathematics is the study of patterns.

The word 'pattern' comes from the French word *patron*. In the 14th century, when the word 'pattern' first appeared, a patron was somebody who paid for work (like the construction of a sword or a piece of pottery) to be done, often by giving an example to the workman to copy.

This leads us to the following definition:

A **pattern** is a set of numbers, objects or diagrams that repeat in a particular manner.

Here are some examples of **patterns**:

(a)

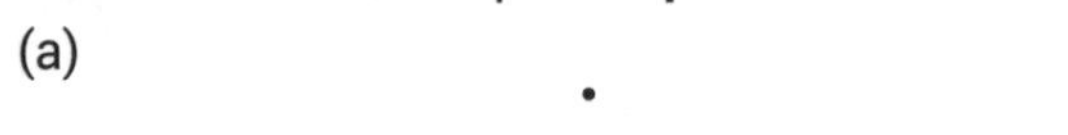

(b)

(c) 1, 1, 2, 3, 5, 8, ... (the **Fibonacci pattern**; the first two terms are 1 and each successive term is the sum of the two previous terms)

(d) 101, 1,001, 10,001, 100,001, 1,000,001, ...

We call each distinct object, number or diagram in a pattern a **term** of the pattern.

The first **term** of a pattern is called T_1, the second term T_2, and so on. To predict what will come next in a pattern, we must find a rule that links one number, object or diagram in the pattern with the next.

Worked Example 7.1

A four-tile repeating pattern is made up of the shapes shown.

(i) Draw the next two shapes in the pattern.

(ii) What is the shape of the 100th tile?

(iii) What is the shape of the 253rd tile?

Solution

(i)

As the pattern repeats every four tiles, the fifth and sixth tiles will be the same as the first and second tiles.

(ii) We can draw a table, like the one on the right, to help us.

We can see that the pattern repeats itself every four tiles.

100 ÷ 4 = 25, with a remainder of 0.
So the first 100 tiles are made of 25 blocks of 4.

If we consider our table, we see that the last tile in each block of 4 is a hexagon.

∴ The 100th tile is a hexagon.

Tile	Shape
1	Triangle
2	Square
3	Pentagon
4	Hexagon
5	Triangle
6	Square
7	Pentagon
8	Hexagon
9	Triangle

(iii) $\frac{253}{4}$ = 63 with remainder 1.

So the first 253 tiles are made up of 63 blocks of 4 and the first tile from the next block of 4.
The first tile in each block of 4 is the triangle.

∴ The 253rd tile is a triangle.

Worked Example 7.2

The pattern below begins with the integer 101. Each successive term is found by inserting an extra 0 immediately to the left of the units digit of the previous term.

101 1,001 10,001 100,001 1,000,001 10,000,001

(i) Write down the next two terms of the pattern.

(ii) How many zeros are in the 12th term?

(iii) How many zeros are in the nth term?

Solution

(i) 100,000,001 and 1,000,000,001

(ii) The number of zeros in each term is equal to the number of the term.

∴ There are 12 zeros in the 12th term.

(iii) The number of zeros in each term is equal to the number of the term.

∴ There are n zeros in the nth term.

Exercise 7.1

1. Find the next shape in each of the following patterns:

   (i) □◆♥□◆♥□ (repeats every three)

   (ii) ÷ ≠ ≡ ≈ ÷ ≠ ≡ ≈ (repeats every four)

   (iii) ∠ ∇ ® © ∠ ∇ ® © (repeats every four)

   (iv) ⮜⮞⮝⮟⮜⮞⮝⮟⮜ (repeats every four)

   (v) ⭘☙⌗⭘❧❋▪☙❋⭘☙ (repeats every nine)

2. A coloured pattern is shown. In each case, after the last block shown, the pattern repeats. Identify the colour of the next three blocks.

   (i) 

   (iii) 

   (ii) 

   (iv) 

3. A coloured pattern is shown. In each case, after the last block shown, the pattern repeats. Identify:

   (a) The colours of the next three blocks

   (b) The colours of the 50th block, the 100th block and the 150th block

   (i)

   (ii)

   (iii)

   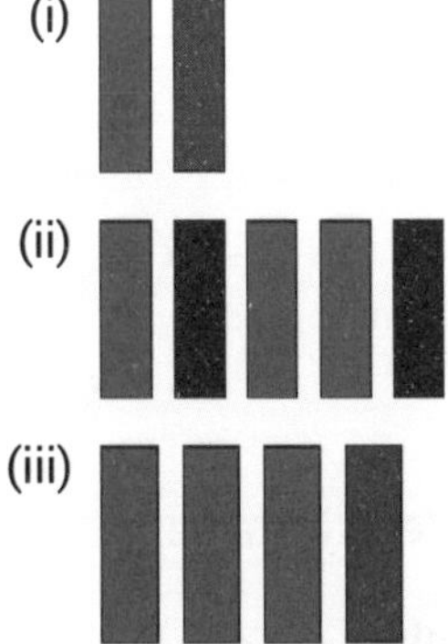

   (iv) 

   (v) 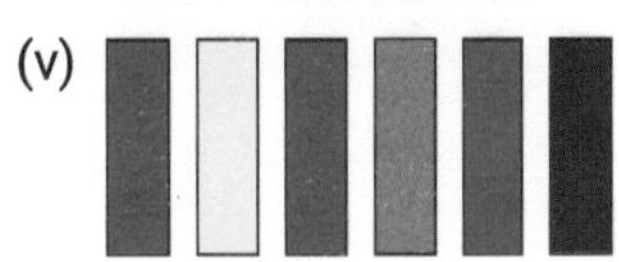

4. A two-tile repeating pattern consisting of a triangle and a hexagon is shown.

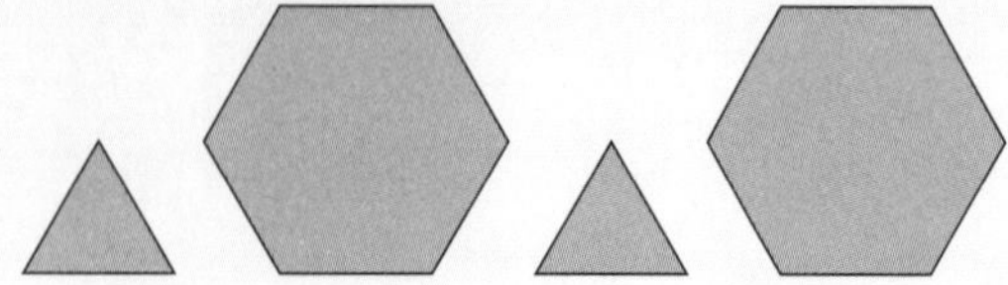

(i) What is the shape of the 50th tile?

(ii) What is the shape of the 93rd tile?

(iii) What is the shape of the *n*th tile if *n* is an even number?

(iv) What is the shape of the *n*th tile if *n* is an odd number?

5. A three-tile repeating pattern is shown.

(i) What is the shape of the 30th tile?

(ii) What is the shape of the 40th tile?

(iii) What is the shape of the 53rd tile?

6. A four-tile repeating pattern is shown.

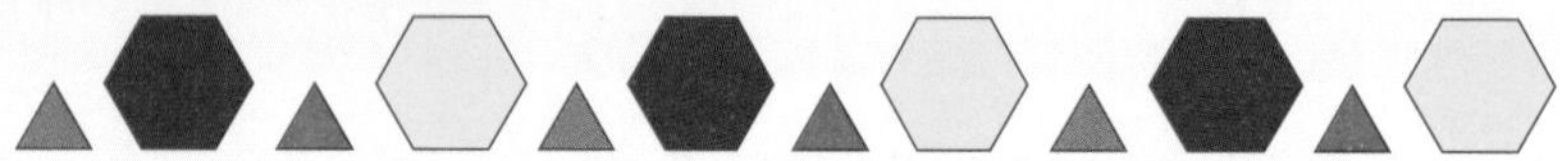

(i) What is the shape of the 15th tile?

(ii) What is the shape of the 94th tile?

(iii) What colour is the 100th tile?

(iv) Copy and complete the following sentence:

If *n* is even, then the *n*th term will always be a __________ -shaped tile, whereas if *n* is odd, the *n*th term will always be a __________ -shaped tile.

7. Consider the pattern shown below.

Identify the colours of the next nine squares. Explain your reasoning.

8. To predict what will come next in a pattern, we must find a rule that will link one number or diagram with the next.

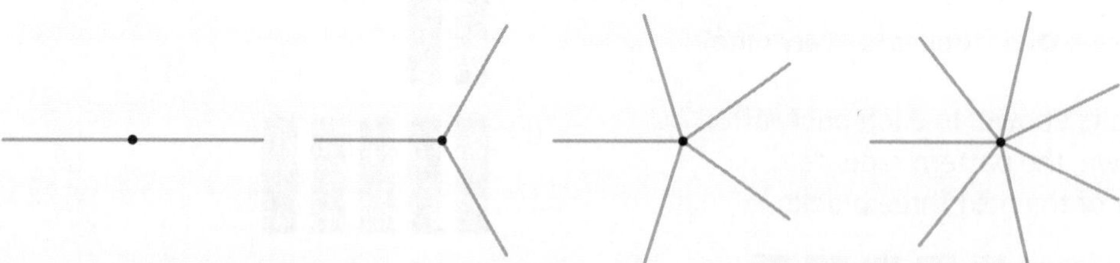

(i) Copy and complete the table below.

Pattern number	1	2	3	4	5	6
No. of sticks	2	3	5	7		

(ii) Explain the rule that you have used to complete the table.

7.2 Arithmetic Sequences

Arithmetic sequences can be used to predict real-life situations. For example, a taxi fare moves in an arithmetic sequence as the distance travelled increases.

A **sequence** is a set of terms, in a definite order, where the terms are obtained by some rule.
A **number sequence** is an ordered set of numbers, with a rule to find every number in the sequence.

2, 6, 10, 14, 18, ... is an example of a **number sequence**. The first term is 2 ($T_1 = 2$). The rule for finding a particular term is to add 4 to the previous term.

In an **arithmetic (linear) sequence** the difference or change between one term and the next is always the same number. This means that the change in an arithmetic sequence is always constant.
An arithmetic sequence is sometimes called an **arithmetic progression**.

In the **arithmetic sequence** 2, 6, 10, 14, 18, ... the difference between consecutive terms is 4.

The difference, $T_n - T_{n-1}$, between consecutive terms in any sequence is referred to as the **first difference**. (It is also known as the **first change**.)

The difference between consecutive terms in an arithmetic sequence can also be referred to as the **common difference**. The letter d is used to represent the common difference.

The two sequences shown below are arithmetic. The first sequence has first term, or start term, 11 and first difference 7. The second sequence has first term, or start term, 2 and first difference −3.

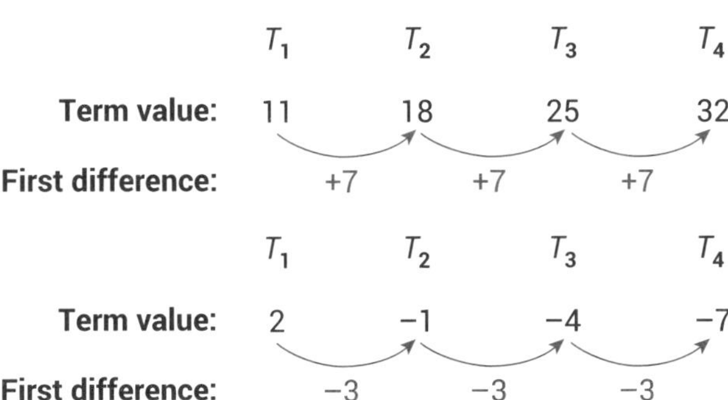

When we graph the terms of an arithmetic sequence against the term number, the plotted points lie on a straight line, hence the name 'linear sequence'. The first six terms of the arithmetic sequence 2, 5, 8, 11, 14, 17, ... are graphed below.

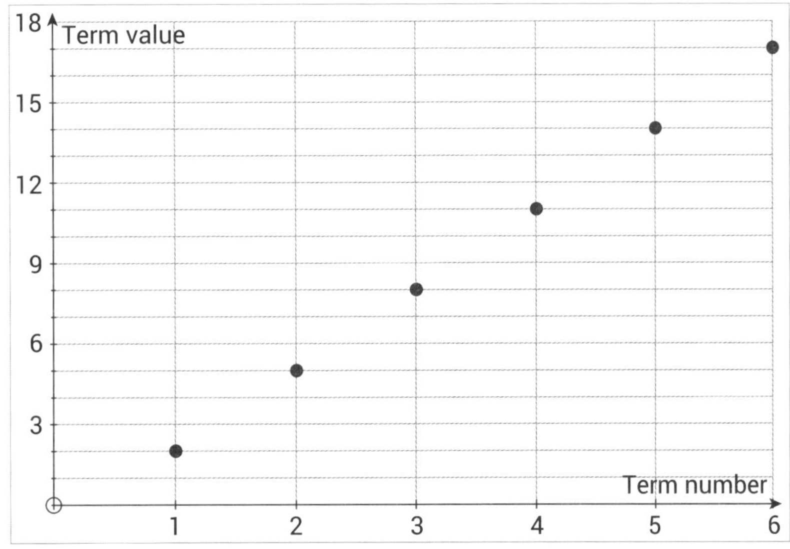

NUMBER PATTERNS

Worked Example 7.3

For each of the following arithmetic sequences, write down:

(a) T_1, the first term of the sequence

(b) d, the common difference

(c) The next three terms

(i) 1, 5, 9, 13, ... (ii) 3, 1, −1, −3, ...

Solution

(i) 1, 5, 9, 13, ...

(a) $T_1 = 1$

(b) $d = T_2 - T_1$

$= 5 - 1$

$\therefore d = 4$

(c) 17, 21, 25

(ii) 3, 1, −1, −3, ...

(a) $T_1 = 3$

(b) $d = T_2 - T_1$

$= 1 - 3$

$\therefore d = -2$

(c) −5, −7, −9

Worked Example 7.4

The first three terms of a pattern are shown.

$T_1 =$ $T_2 =$ $T_3 =$

(i) Draw the next two terms of the pattern.

(ii) Count the number of dots in each of the first five terms and display the results in a table.

(iii) Describe the sequence of numbers generated by the pattern.

(iv) How many dots are there in T_7, the seventh term?

(v) How many dots are there in T_n, the nth term?

Solution

(i) $T_4 =$ $T_5 =$

(ii)

Term	T_1	T_2	T_3	T_4	T_5
Number of dots	6	8	10	12	14

(iii) The sequence is arithmetic, with first term 6 and common difference 2.

(iv)

T_1	T_2	T_3	T_4	T_5	T_6	T_7
6	8	10	12	14	16	18

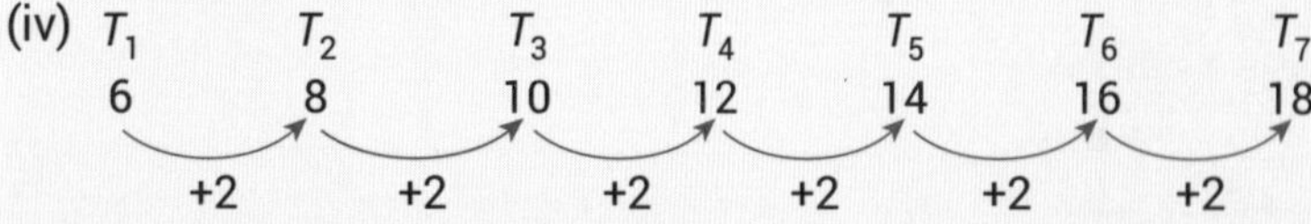

From the diagram, it is clear that $T_7 = 6 + (6)2 = 18$.

(v) Using the same reasoning as in part (iv), $T_n = 6 + (n - 1)2$

$= 6 + 2n - 2$

$= 4 + 2n$

$\therefore T_n = 4 + 2n$

Worked Example 7.5

x, $2x + 1$ and $5x - 4$ are the first three terms of an arithmetic sequence. Find:

(i) The value of x

(ii) The fourth term of the sequence

Solution

(i) Since the sequence is arithmetic, the difference between any two consecutive terms is a constant.

$T_2 - T_1 = T_3 - T_2$

$\therefore (2x + 1) - x = (5x - 4) - (2x + 1)$

$2x + 1 - x = 5x - 4 - 2x - 1$ (Distributive property)

$x + 1 = 3x - 5$ (Adding 'like' terms)

$-2x = -6$ (Subtracting 1 from both sides)

$2x = 6$ (Multiplying both sides by −1)

$\therefore x = 3$ (Dividing both sides by 2)

(ii) If $x = 3$, then the sequence is $3, 2(3) + 1, 5(3) - 4, \ldots$
This gives the sequence 3, 7, 11, ... The common difference is 4.

$\therefore T_4 = 11 + 4 = 15$

Exercise 7.2

Remember: In an arithmetic (linear) sequence, the first difference is a constant.

1. State, giving a reason, whether or not the following sequences are arithmetic:

(i) 3, 5, 7, 9, ...

(ii) 2, 4, 6, 8, 10, ...

(iii) 1, 2, 4, 8, 16, ...

(iv) 1, 1, 2, 3, 5, 8, ...

(v) 25, 20, 15, 10, ...

(vi) 2, 2.5, 3, 3.5, 4, ...

(vii) 12, 15, 18, 21, ...

(viii) $\frac{1}{2}, \frac{1}{3}, \frac{1}{4}, \frac{1}{5}, \frac{1}{6}, \ldots$

(ix) −5, −1, 3, 7, 11, ...

(x) 20, 21, 22, 23, ...

2. For each of the following arithmetic sequences, write down:

(a) T_1, the first term of the sequence

(b) d, the common difference

(c) The next three terms

(i) 2, 6, 10, ...

(ii) 5, 7, 9, 11, ...

(iii) 19, 16, 13, ...

(iv) 100, 90, 80, ...

(v) 13, 20, 27, ...

(vi) −5, −3, −1, ...

(vii) 5.5, 6, 6.5, ...

(viii) $1, 1\frac{1}{4}, 1\frac{1}{2}, \ldots$

(ix) 72, 61, 50, ...

(x) $\frac{1}{6}, \frac{1}{3}, \frac{1}{2}, \ldots$

3. For each of these arithmetic sequences, write down:

(a) The value of d, the common difference

(b) The next three terms

(i) $-6, -9, \ldots$ (iv) $-4, 0, \ldots$ (vii) $11, 13\frac{3}{4}, 16\frac{1}{2}, \ldots$ (x) $\frac{7}{8}, \frac{3}{4}, \ldots$

(ii) $210, 160, 110, \ldots$ (v) $-10, -7\frac{1}{2}, \ldots$ (viii) $-5.4, -1, \ldots$

(iii) $4.4, 6, 7.6, \ldots$ (vi) $15\frac{1}{2}, 14, \ldots$ (ix) $\frac{1}{10}, \frac{1}{5}, \ldots$

4. For each of the following graphs of arithmetic sequences, identify:

(a) T_1, the first term (b) d, the common difference (c) T_4, the fourth term

(i)

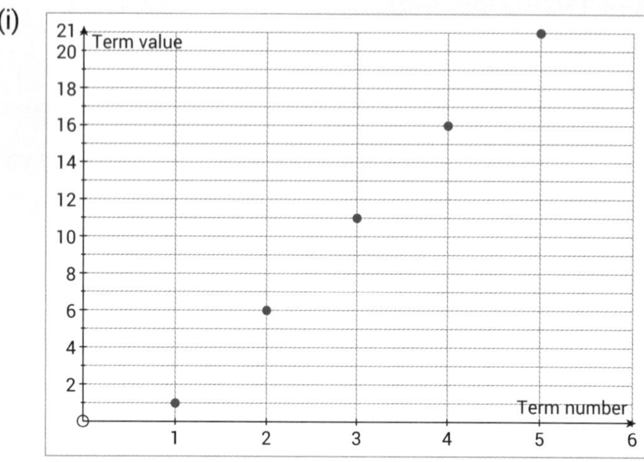

(ii)

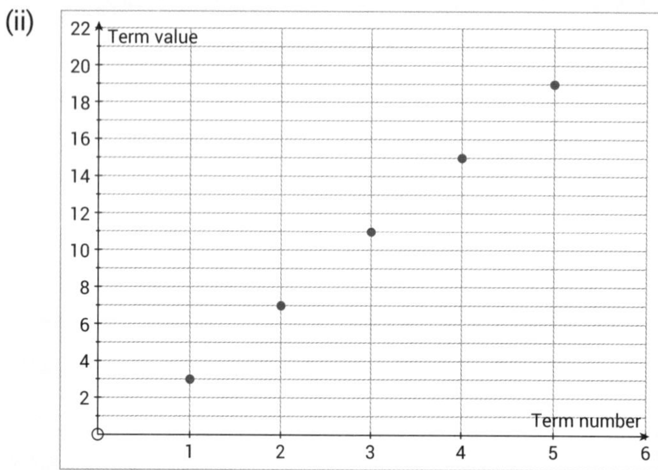

(iii)

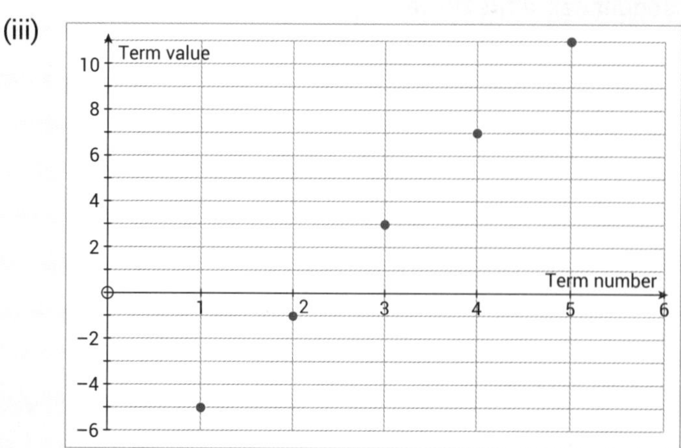

NUMBER PATTERNS

(iv)

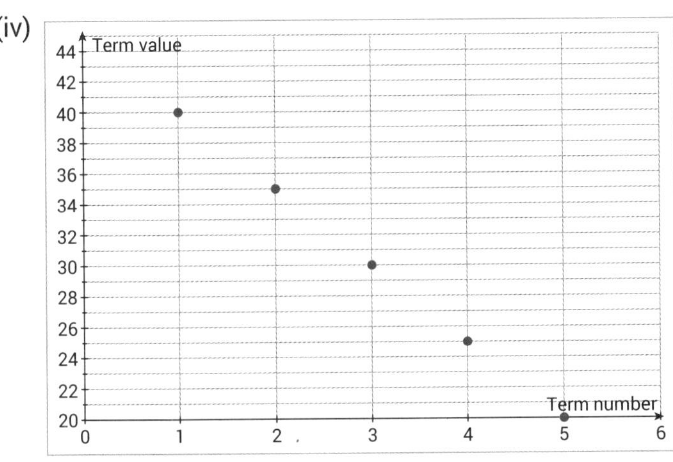

(v)

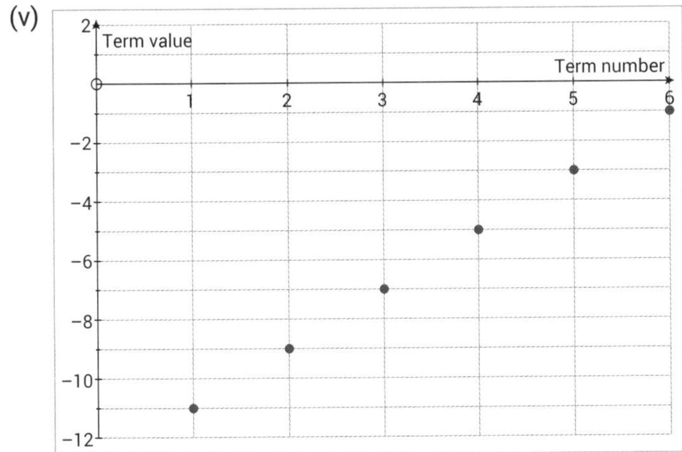

5. The first three terms of a linear pattern are shown.

T_1 = T_2 = T_3 =

(i) Draw the next two terms of the pattern.

(ii) Copy and complete the table below.

Term	T_1	T_2	T_3	T_4	T_5
No. of dots	6	9			

(iii) Describe the sequence of numbers generated by the pattern.

(iv) How many dots are there in T_8, the eighth term?

6. The first three terms of a pattern are shown.

(i) Draw the next two terms of the pattern.

(ii) Count the number of dots in each of the first five terms and display the results in a table.

(iii) Describe the sequence of numbers generated by the pattern.

(iv) How many dots are there in T_9, the ninth term?

7. The first three terms of a pattern are shown.
   (i) Draw the next two terms of the pattern.
   (ii) Count the number of red squares in each of the first five terms and display the results in a table.
   (iii) Describe the sequence of numbers generated by the pattern.
   (iv) How many red squares are there in T_7, the seventh term?
   (v) How many white squares are in T_9, the ninth term?

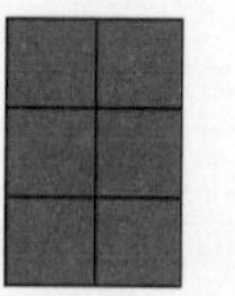
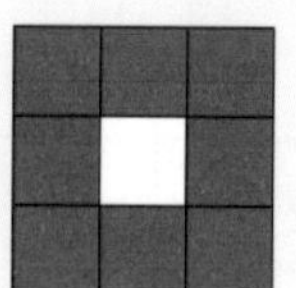
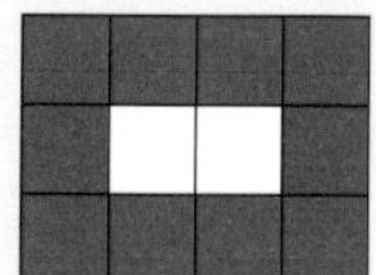

8. The first three terms of a pattern are shown.
   (i) Draw the next two terms of the pattern.
   (ii) Count the number of red squares in each of the first five terms and display the results in a table.
   (iii) Describe the sequence of numbers generated by the pattern.
   (iv) How many red squares are there in T_7, the seventh term?

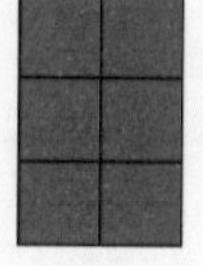
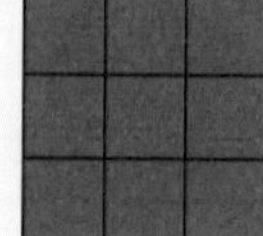

9. The graphs of three sequences are shown. Lines and curves are included for clarity.
   (i) Write down the first three terms of each of the sequences.
   (ii) Identify the arithmetic sequence.
   (iii) What is d, the common difference, in the arithmetic sequence?

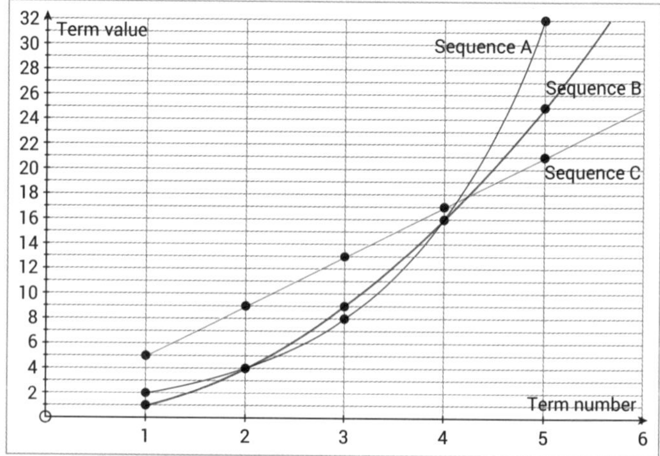

10. The graphs of three sequences are shown. Lines and curves are included for clarity.
   (i) Write down the first three terms of each of the sequences.
   (ii) Identify the arithmetic sequence.
   (iii) What is d, the common difference, in the arithmetic sequence?

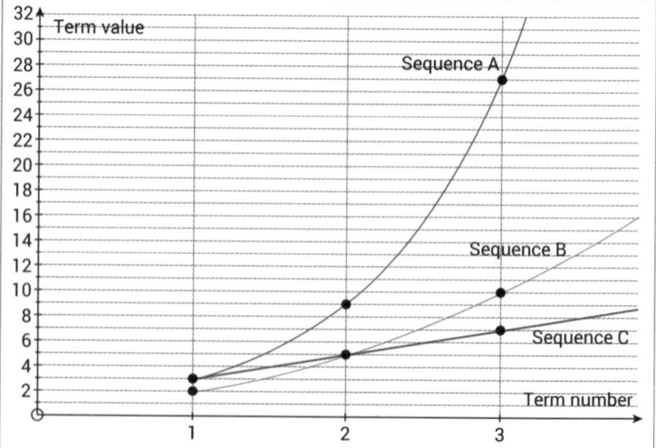

NUMBER PATTERNS

11. The graphs of three sequences are shown. Lines are included for clarity.

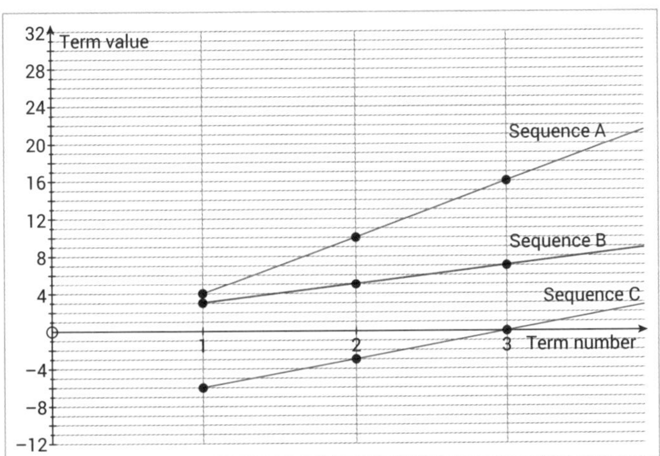

(i) Find the common differences, d_A, d_B and d_C, for each of the three sequences.

(ii) Find m_A, m_B and m_C, the slopes of each of the three lines associated with each sequence.

(iii) What is the connection between the common differences and the slopes?

12. $x + 3$, $3x - 1$ and $4x - 1$ are the first three terms of an arithmetic sequence. Solve for x.

13. $x + 1$, $3x$ and $2x + 8$ are the first three terms of an arithmetic sequence. Solve for x.

14. $3x + 2$, 20 and $2x + 3$ are the first three terms of an arithmetic sequence. Find:

(i) The value of x

(ii) The value of d, the common difference

(iii) The fourth term, T_4

15. $3x - 2$, $2x + 1$ and $18 - x$ are the first three terms of an arithmetic sequence. Find:

(i) The value of x

(ii) The value of d, the common difference

(iii) The fourth and fifth terms (T_4 and T_5)

7.3 The General Term of an Arithmetic Sequence

Let a be the first term of an arithmetic sequence and d be the common difference. The table below shows the first five terms of the sequence.

T_1	T_2	T_3	T_4	T_5
a	$a + d$	$a + 2d$	$a + 3d$	$a + 4d$

What is T_n, the nth term of the sequence?

Continuing the pattern, $T_n = a + (n - 1)d$.

The **general term** for any arithmetic sequence is $T_n = a + (n - 1)d$, where a is the first term and d is the common difference.

If the first term of an arithmetic sequence is labelled T_0, then the general term of the sequence is $T_n = a + nd$, where a is the first term and d the common difference.

This formula appears on page 22 of *Formulae and Tables*.

Worked Example 7.6

For the arithmetic sequence 5, 15, 25, 35, ... find the following:

(i) T_n, the nth term (ii) The 20th term (iii) The first term that is greater than 450

Solution

(i) $d = T_2 - T_1$

$= 15 - 5$

$\therefore d = 10 \qquad a = 5$

$T_n = a + (n - 1)d$

$= 5 + (n - 1)10$

$= 5 + 10n - 10$

$\therefore T_n = 10n - 5$

(ii) $T_{20} = 10(20) - 5$

$\therefore T_{20} = 195$

(iii) $T_n > 450$

$10n - 5 > 450$

$10n > 455$

$n > 45.5$

$\therefore$ The first term greater than 450 is the 46th term (as $n \in N$).

Worked Example 7.7

A number sequence has general term $T_n = 5 - 3n$.

Prove that the sequence has a common difference.

Solution

$T_n = 5 - 3n$

$T_{n-1} = 5 - 3(n - 1)$

$= 5 - 3n + 3$

$= 8 - 3n$

$T_n - T_{n-1} = (5 - 3n) - (8 - 3n)$

$= 5 - 3n - 8 + 3n$

$= -3$ (A constant)

$\therefore$ The sequence has a common difference. (In other words the sequence is arithmetic.)

To prove a sequence is arithmetic show that $T_n - T_{n-1}$ = a constant.

Worked Example 7.8

How many terms of the arithmetic sequence 45, 43, 41, ... are positive?

Solution

$a = 45 \qquad d = 43 - 45 = -2$

We need to find the largest value of n, for which $T_n > 0$.

$T_n = a + (n - 1)d$

$T_n = 45 + (n - 1)(-2)$

$= 45 - 2n + 2$

$\therefore T_n = 47 - 2n$

$T_n > 0$

$\Rightarrow 47 - 2n > 0$

$-2n > -47$

$2n < 47$ Change inequality sign.

$n < 23.5$

$\Rightarrow n = 23$ n must be a whole number.

$\therefore$ 23 terms of the sequence are positive.

Worked Example 7.9

In an arithmetic sequence the twelfth term, $T_{12} = 41$ and the thirtieth term, $T_{30} = 95$.

(i) If a is the first term of the sequence and d is the common difference, then find a and d.

(ii) Find T_n, the general term of the arithmetic sequence.

Solution

(i) $T_n = a + (n - 1)d$

$T_{12} = a + (12 - 1)d$

$= a + 11d$

$\therefore a + 11d = 41$ ... **Eq. I**

$T_{30} = a + (30 - 1)d$

$= a + 29d$

$\therefore a + 29d = 95$ ... **Eq. II**

Now solve Eq. I and Eq. II simultaneously for a and d.

$a + 29d = 95$

$a + 11d = 41 \quad \times -1$

$a + 29d = 95$

$-a - 11d = -41$

$18d = 54$

$d = \frac{54}{18}$

$d = 3$

$a + 11(3) = 41$

$a + 33 = 41$

$a = 41 - 33$

$a = 8$

(ii) $T_n = a + (n - 1)d$

$T_n = 8 + (n - 1)3$

$T_n = 8 + 3n - 3$

$T_n = 3n + 5$

Exercise 7.3

1. In each of the following arithmetic sequences, find:

(a) The first term

(b) The common difference

(c) The nth term (general term)

(i) 5, 7, 9, 11, ...

(ii) 4, 7, 10, 13, ...

(iii) 1, 5, 9, 13, ...

(iv) 13, 20, 27, 34, ...

(v) 59, 57, 55, ...

(vi) −12, −7, −2, ...

(vii) 43, 40, 37, 34, ...

(viii) −16, −20, −24, ...

(ix) 75, 84, 93, ...

(x) −20, −17, −14, ...

2. −11, −15, −19, ... is an arithmetic sequence.

(i) Find the nth term of the sequence.

(ii) Hence, write down the 55th term.

3. 10, 22, 34, ... is an arithmetic sequence.

(i) Find the nth term of the sequence.

(ii) Hence, write down the 64th term.

4. 0, 7, 14, 21, 28, ... is an arithmetic sequence.

(i) Find the nth term of the sequence.

(ii) Hence, write down the 85th term.

5. 7, 13, 19, ... is an arithmetic sequence.

(i) Find the nth term of the sequence.

(ii) Hence, write down the 33rd term.

6. 3, 11, 19, ... is an arithmetic sequence.

(i) Find the nth term of the sequence.

(ii) Hence, write down the 96th term.

7. 31, 25, 19, ... is an arithmetic sequence.
   (i) Find the nth term of the sequence.
   (ii) Hence, write down the 21st term.

8. 5, 9, 13, ... is an arithmetic sequence.
   (i) Find the nth term of the sequence.
   (ii) Hence, write down the 55th term.

9. 116 is the nth term of the arithmetic sequence 14, 17, 20, ...
   Find the value of n.

10. How many terms of the arithmetic sequence 91, 89, 87, ... are positive?

11. How many terms of the arithmetic sequence 17, 21, 25, ... are less than 100?

12. How many terms of the sequence 100, 97, 94, ... are positive?

13. The first three terms of an arithmetic sequence are 200, 193, 186, ...
   (i) Find T_n, the nth term of the sequence.
   (ii) How many terms of the sequence are positive?
   (iii) What is the first negative term in the sequence?

14. The nth term of some sequences are given below.
   (a) Write down the first four terms of each sequence.
   (b) By considering $T_n - T_{n-1}$, decide whether the sequence is arithmetic or not.
   (i) $T_n = 2n + 1$ (ii) $T_n = 3n - 1$ (iii) $T_n = n^2 + 3$ (iv) $T_n = 12 - 2n$ (v) $T_n = \frac{1}{n}$

15. The nth term of some sequences are given below.
   (a) Write down the first four terms of each sequence.
   (b) By considering $T_n - T_{n-1}$, decide whether the sequence is arithmetic or not.
   (i) $T_n = 4n + 1$ (ii) $T_n = 13 - 3n$ (iii) $T_n = 2n^2 + 3$ (iv) $T_n = 10 - 3n$ (v) $T_n = 4^n$

16. The 19th term of an arithmetic sequence is 150. If T_1, the first term, is 6, then find d, the common difference.

17. In an arithmetic sequence the eleventh term, $T_{11} = 17$ and the fiftieth term, $T_{50} = 95$.
   (i) If a is the first term of the sequence and d its common difference, then find a and d.
   (ii) Find T_n, the general term of the arithmetic sequence.

18. The 51st term of an arithmetic sequence is 248. If d, the common difference, is 15, then find a, the first term.

19. In an arithmetic sequence the fourth term $T_4 = 14$, and the tenth term, T_{10}, is four times the second term, T_2. If a is the first term of the sequence and d its common difference, then find:
   (i) T_2 in terms of a and d
   (ii) T_4 in terms of a and d
   (iii) T_{10} in terms of a and d
   (iv) Two simultaneous equations in a and d
   Solve the simultaneous equations to find a and d.

20. The natural numbers greater than 1 are arranged as shown in the chart below.

	A	B	C	D	E
Row 1			2	3	4
Row 2	7	6	5		
Row 3			8	9	10
Row 4	13	12	11		
Row 5			14	15	16
Row 6					
Row 7					
Row 8					
Row 9					

(i) Copy and complete the pattern for rows 6 to 9.

(ii) What number will appear in Row 100 of Column A?

(iii) What number will appear in Row 99 of Column E?

(iv) Determine the position of the integer 2,011.

7.4 Arithmetic Series

An **arithmetic series** is the sum of all the terms in an arithmetic sequence.

Carl Friedrich Gauss

Carl Friedrich Gauss (1777–1855) was a German mathematician who made significant contributions to many fields, including number theory, statistics, calculus, geometry and physics. He has been called 'the greatest mathematician since antiquity'.

Gauss was a child prodigy. When he was in primary school, he was punished by his teacher for misbehaviour. His punishment was to add all the whole numbers from 1 to 100. To the amazement of his teacher, he calculated the sum in a matter of seconds. How did he do it?

Gauss's Method

It is most likely that the young Gauss employed the following method to sum the first 100 natural numbers:

Step 1: Write the series in ascending order from 1 to 100.

$1 + 2 + 3 + 4 + \dots + 97 + 98 + 99 + 100$

Step 2: Write the series in descending order from 100 to 1.

$100 + 99 + 98 + 97 + \dots + 4 + 3 + 2 + 1$

Step 3: Add together both representations of the series.

$$\begin{array}{r} 1 + \ \ 2 + \ \ 3 + \ \ 4 + \dots + \ 97 + \ 98 + \ 99 + 100 \\ 100 + \ 99 + \ 98 + \ 97 + \dots + \ \ 4 + \ \ 3 + \ \ 2 + \ \ 1 \\ \hline 101 + 101 + 101 + 101 + \dots + 101 + 101 + 101 + 101 \end{array}$$

This gives $100(101) = 10{,}100$.

This is the sum of two series. Therefore, the sum of one series is $\frac{1}{2}(10{,}100) = 5{,}050$.

$1 + 2 + 3 + 4 + \dots + 97 + 98 + 99 + 100 = 5{,}050$

The sum of the first n terms of an arithmetic series is given by the formula

$S_n = \frac{n}{2}[2a + (n - 1)d]$.

This formula appears on page 22 of *Formulae and Tables*.

- a is the first term.
- d is the common difference.

Worked Example 7.10

Find the sum of the first 100 terms of the arithmetic series 7 + 10 + 13 + ...

Solution

$a = 7, \quad d = 3, \quad n = 100$

$$S_n = \frac{n}{2}[2a + (n - 1)d]$$

$$S_{100} = \frac{100}{2}[2(7) + (100 - 1)3]$$

$$= 50[14 + 99(3)]$$

$$= 50[311]$$

$$\therefore S_{100} = 15{,}550$$

Worked Example 7.11

Find the sum of all the terms in the arithmetic series 11 + 13 + 15 + ... + 51.

Solution

Step 1

We need to know how many terms there are in the series.

Let n = the number of terms. Therefore, $T_n = 51$.

$a = 11 \quad d = 2$

$T_n = a + (n - 1)d$

$\therefore T_n = 11 + (n - 1)2$

$= 11 + 2n - 2$

$\Rightarrow T_n = 2n + 9$

$2n + 9 = 51$

$2n = 51 - 9$

$2n = 42$

$\therefore n = 21$

There are 21 terms.

Step 2

Next we must find the sum of these 21 terms.

$$S_n = \frac{n}{2}[2a + (n - 1)d]$$

$a = 11, \quad d = 2, \quad n = 21$

$$S_{21} = \frac{21}{2}[2(11) + (21 - 1)2]$$

$$= 10.5[22 + 20(2)]$$

$$= 10.5[62]$$

$$\therefore S_{21} = 651$$

$\Rightarrow 11 + 13 + 15 + ... + 51 = 651$

Worked Example 7.12

In an arithmetic sequence the fourth term, $T_4 = 24$ and the sum of the first ten terms, $S_{10} = 285$. If a is the first term and d is the common difference, then find the value of:

(i) a (iv) S_n

(ii) d (v) T_{20}

(iii) T_n (vi) S_{20}

Solution

(i) $T_n = a + (n - 1)d$

$T_4 = a + (4 - 1)d$

$\therefore a + 3d = 24$ ... **Eq. I**

$$S_n = \frac{n}{2}[2a + (n - 1)d]$$

$$S_{10} = \frac{10}{2}[2a + (10 - 1)d]$$

$$= 5[2a + 9d]$$

$\therefore 10a + 45d = 285$ ... **Eq. II**

Now, solve simultaneously to find a and d.

$$10a + 30d = 240 \quad \text{(Eq. I × 10)}$$
$$-10a - 45d = -285 \quad \text{(Eq. II × −1)}$$
$$-15d = -45$$
$$d = \frac{45}{15}$$
$$d = 3$$

$$a + 3(3) = 24 \quad \text{(Substituting into Eq. I)}$$
$$a + 9 = 24$$
$$a = 24 - 9$$
$$a = 15$$

(ii) $d = 3$

(iii) $T_n = a + (n - 1)d$

$T_n = 15 + (n - 1)3$

$T_n = 15 + 3n - 3$

$T_n = 3n + 12$

(iv) $S_n = \frac{n}{2}[2(15) + (n - 1)3]$

$S_n = \frac{n}{2}[30 + 3n - 3]$

$S_n = \frac{n}{2}[3n + 27]$

$S_n = \dfrac{3n^2 + 27n}{2}$

(v) $T_{20} = 3(20) + 12$

$= 60 + 12$

$= 72$

(vi) $S_{20} = \dfrac{3(20)^2 + 27(20)}{2}$

$= 870$

Worked Example 7.13

On 1 January 2017, Caitlin opened a bank account and deposited €200 in the account. On 1 February 2017, she deposited €210 in the account. She plans to make deposits on the first of every month, increasing the amount deposited by €10 each month.

(i) How much will Caitlin deposit on 1 December 2022?

(ii) In total, how much will Caitlin have deposited by the end of December 2022?

Solution

(i) Consider the first six deposits Caitlin makes.

200, 210, 220, 230, 240, 250

The deposits form an arithmetic sequence.

Now find the total number of deposits made.

There are 12 deposits made each year for six years. This gives a total of 72 deposits.

Therefore, the 72nd term of the sequence 200, 210, 220, 230, ... gives the amount that Caitlin deposited on 1 December 2022.

$a = 200 \qquad d = 10$

$T_n = a + (n - 1)d$

$T_{72} = 200 + (72 - 1)10$

$= 200 + 710$

$= 910$

Caitlin deposits €910 on 1 December 2022.

(ii) We need to sum 72 terms of the series 200 + 210 + 220 + ...

$S_n = \frac{n}{2}[2a + (n - 1)d]$

$a = 200, \qquad d = 10, \qquad n = 72$

$S_{72} = \frac{72}{2}[2(200) + (72 - 1)10]$

$= 36[400 + 710]$

$= 36[1,110]$

$= 39,960$

Caitlin will have deposited €39,960 by the end of December 2022.

Exercise 7.4

1. Find the sum of the first 20 terms of each of the following arithmetic series:
   (i) $11 + 22 + 33 + ...$
   (ii) $5 + 7 + 9 + ...$
   (iii) $43 + 40 + 37 + ...$
   (iv) $1 + 5 + 9 + ...$
   (v) $13 + 20 + 27 + ...$

2. Find the sum of the first 30 terms of each of the following arithmetic series:
   (i) $4 + 7 + 10 + ...$
   (ii) $3 + 8 + 13 + ...$
   (iii) $-5 + 2 + 9 + ...$
   (iv) $35 + 33 + 31 + ...$
   (v) $20 + 19 + 18 + ...$

3. Find the sum of the first 10 terms of each of the following series:
   (i) $-11 + 1 + 13 + ...$
   (ii) $-8 - 2 + 4 + ...$
   (iii) $4 - 2 - 8 - ...$
   (iv) $-8 - 10 - 12 - ...$
   (v) $-4 - 2 - 0 + ...$

4. $S_{80} = 1 + 2 + 3 + 4 + ... + 79 + 80$ is the sum of the first 80 natural numbers. Find S_{80}.

5. Find the sum of the first 30 odd natural numbers: $1 + 3 + 5 + ... + 59$.

6. How many terms are there in the arithmetic series $2 + 4 + 6 + ... + 80$? Find their sum.

7. Given the arithmetic series $1 + 7 + 13 + 19 + ...$
   (i) Find the sum of the first 10 terms.
   (ii) Find the sum of the first 20 terms.
   (iii) Hence, find the sum of the second 10 terms.

8. Given the arithmetic series $2 + 10 + 18 + ...$
   (i) Find the sum of the first 20 terms.
   (ii) Find the sum of the first 40 terms.
   (iii) Hence, find the sum of the second 20 terms.

9. Find the sum of the following arithmetic series:
   (i) $2 + 5 + 8 + ... + 65$
   (ii) $11 + 22 + 33 + ... + 319$
   (iii) $88 + 86 + 84 + ... + 8$
   (iv) $55 + 51 + ... + 11$
   (v) $3 + 6 + 9 + ... + 99$

10. 5, 9, 13, ... is an arithmetic sequence.
    (i) Find the nth term of the sequence.
    (ii) Hence, write down the 55th term.
    (iii) Find S_{50}, the sum of the first 50 terms.

11. On 1 January 2017, Fergal opened a bank account and deposited €100 in the account. On 1 February 2017, he deposited €105 in the account. He plans to make deposits on the first of every month, increasing the amount deposited by €5 each month.
    (i) How much will Fergal deposit on 1 December 2021?
    (ii) In total, how much will Fergal have deposited by the end of December 2021?

12. In an arithmetic sequence the third term, $T_3 = 21$ and the sum of the first seven terms, $S_7 = 175$. Find T_1, the first term and the common difference.

13. In an arithmetic sequence the fifth term, $T_5 = 13$ and the sum of the first four terms, $S_4 = 32$. If a is the first term and d is the common difference, then find:
    (i) a
    (ii) d
    (iii) T_n
    (iv) S_n
    (v) T_{20}
    (vi) S_{30}

14. For each of the following arithmetic sequences, find:
    (a) T_1, the first term
    (b) The common difference
    (c) S_5, the sum of the first five terms
    (i) $T_7 = 15, S_3 = 15$
    (ii) $T_3 = 4, S_7 = 49$
    (iii) $T_4 = 17, S_3 = 27$
    (iv) $T_2 = 14, S_6 = 57$

15. The terms in an arithmetic sequence are given by the formula

$$T_n = 38 - 4n, \text{ for } n = 1, 2, 3, 4, \ldots$$

(i) Write out the first three terms in the sequence.

(ii) What is the first negative term in the sequence?

(iii) Find the sum of the first 15 terms of the sequence.

(iv) Find the value of n for which the sum of the first n terms of the sequence is 0.

16. Two brothers, Eoin and Peter, began work in 2005 on starting salaries of €20,000 and €17,000 per annum, respectively. Eoin's salary increased by €500 per annum and Peter's salary increased by €1,250 per annum. This salary pattern will continue.

(a) Complete the table, showing the annual salary of each brother for the years 2005 to 2010.

Year	1	2	3	4	5	6
Eoin's salary (€)	20,000					
Peter's salary (€)	17,000					

(b) In what year will both brothers earn the same amount?

(c) Eoin claims that their salaries over the years can be represented by an arithmetic sequence.

(i) Explain what an arithmetic sequence is.

(ii) Do you agree with Eoin? Explain your answer.

(d) Find, in terms of n, a formula that gives Eoin's salary in the nth year of the pattern.

(e) Using your formula, or otherwise, find Eoin's salary in 2015.

(f) Find, in terms of n, a formula that gives the total amount earned by Peter from the first to the nth year of the pattern.

(g) Using your formula, or otherwise, find the total amount earned by Peter from the start of 2005 up to the end 2015.

(h) Give one reason why the graph below is not an accurate way to represent Peter's salary over the period 2005 to 2011.

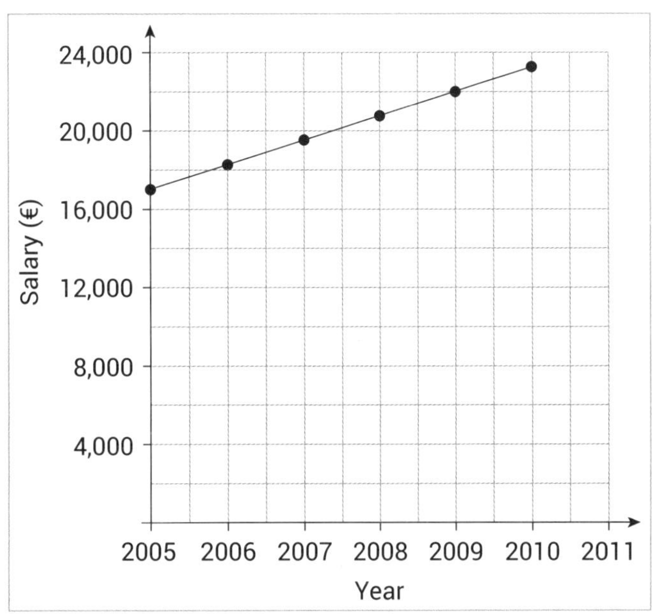

NUMBER PATTERNS

17. A football stadium has a section of red seating in one of its stands.

The first and second rows contain two red seats each. The third and fourth rows contain three red seats each. This pattern continues for all other rows in the section. There are 100 rows in the section. The table below gives the pattern for the first nine rows.

Row number	1	2	3	4	5	6	7	8	9
Number of red seats	2	2	3	3	4	4	5	5	6

(i) How many red seats are in the 51st row?

(ii) How many red seats are in the 98th row?

(iii) How many red seats in total are in the section?

7.5 Some Non-Linear Sequences

In arithmetic (linear) sequences, the difference between consecutive terms, also called the first difference, is always constant. If the difference between consecutive terms is **not constant**, then we say that the sequence is **non-linear**.

> In non-linear sequences, the first difference changes between each pair of consecutive terms.

The sequence 1, 8, 27, 64, ... is non-linear.

> A quadratic sequence is a sequence where the nth term is of the form $T_n = an^2 + bn + c$, $a, b, c \in R$, $a \neq 0$.
>
> The second difference is a non-zero constant. It is also known as the second change.

Quadratic Sequences

Consider the non-linear sequence 2, 5, 10, 17, ...

We can see that the first difference between each term is **not** the same.

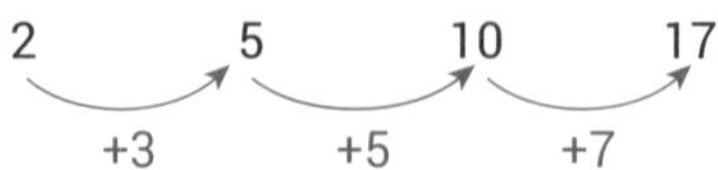

When we look at the **second difference**, i.e. the difference between the first differences, we see that the second difference is the same non-zero constant each time.

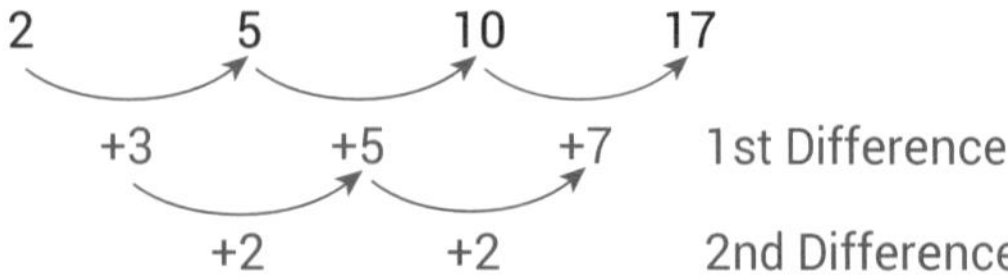

In this case, the pattern is referred to as a **quadratic pattern**.

The graph of a quadratic pattern will be in the shape of a parabolic **curve** and **not** a straight line.

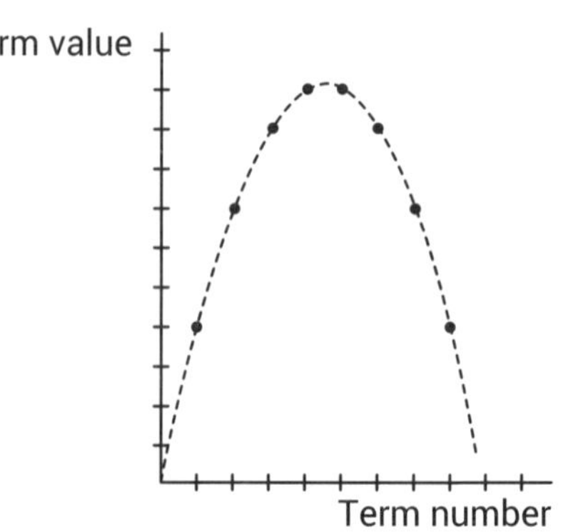

Quadratic sequences have many real-life applications. Consider a ball kicked from a point, p, on level ground, which hits the ground again after 10 seconds at a point q. The vertical heights of the ball above the ground at equally spaced points in time ($t = 1$, $t = 2$, ...) form a quadratic sequence.

Worked Example 7.14

Show that the sequence 1, 6, 15, 28, 45, ... is quadratic.

Solution

Term	Sequence	First difference	Second difference
T_1	1		
T_2	6	5	
T_3	15	9	4
T_4	28	13	4
T_5	45	17	4

We see that the second difference is constant. Therefore, the sequence is quadratic.

Worked Example 7.15

The first three terms of a pattern are shown.

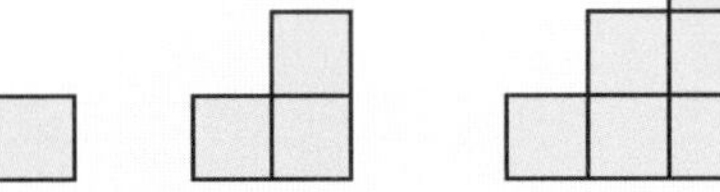

(i) Draw the next term of the pattern.

(ii) Count the number of squares in each of the first four terms and display the results in a table.

(iii) What type of sequence is the sequence of numbers generated by the pattern?

(iv) How many squares are there in T_7, the seventh term?

Solution

(i)

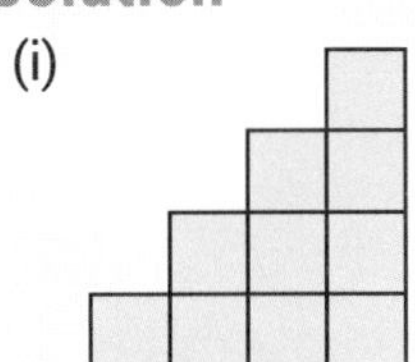

(ii)

Term	Number of squares
1	1
2	3
3	6
4	10

(iii)

Term	Number of squares	First difference	Second difference
1	1		
2	3	2	
3	6	3	1
4	10	4	1

The sequence is quadratic, as the second differences are all 1, a non-zero constant.

(iv) The second difference is a constant of 1.

Therefore, the first difference will increase by 1 each term.

Use a table to help find T_7.

$T_1 = 1$
$T_2 = 1 + 2 = 3$
$T_3 = 3 + 3 = 6$
$T_4 = 6 + 4 = 10$
$T_5 = 10 + 5 = 15$
$T_6 = 15 + 6 = 21$
$T_7 = 21 + 7 = 28$

$\therefore$ T_7 has 28 squares.

NUMBER PATTERNS

Geometric Sequences

A **geometric sequence** is a sequence of numbers where each term after the first is found by multiplying the previous term by a fixed non-zero real number called the **common ratio**.

The sequence 2, 8, 32, 128, ... is a **geometric sequence** with first term 2 and **common ratio** 4.

The sequence 40, 20, 10, 5, ... is a geometric sequence with first term 40 and common ratio $\frac{1}{2}$.

In a geometric sequence, $\frac{T_2}{T_1} = \frac{T_3}{T_2}$

Worked Example 7.16

Find the first term and the common ratio of each of the following geometric sequences:

(i) 3, 27, 243, ...

(ii) 1, 4, 16, 64, ...

Solution

(i) First term = 3

$$\text{Common ratio} = \frac{T_2}{T_1} = \frac{27}{3} = 9$$

(ii) First term = 1

$$\text{Common ratio} = \frac{T_2}{T_1} = \frac{4}{1} = 4$$

Worked Example 7.17

Decide which of the following sequences are arithmetic, geometric, quadratic or none of these:

(i) 10, 100, 1,000, 10,000, ...

(ii) 2, 5, 10, 17, ...

(iii) 50, 60, 70, 80, ...

(iv) 1, 1, 2, 3, 5, ...

Solution

(i) $\frac{T_2}{T_1} = \frac{100}{10} = 10$

$\frac{T_3}{T_2} = \frac{1,000}{100} = 10$

$\frac{T_4}{T_3} = \frac{10,000}{1,000} = 10$

$\frac{T_2}{T_1} = \frac{T_3}{T_2} = \frac{T_4}{T_3}$

$\therefore$ Geometric

(ii) The second difference is a non-zero constant, 2.

$\therefore$ Quadratic

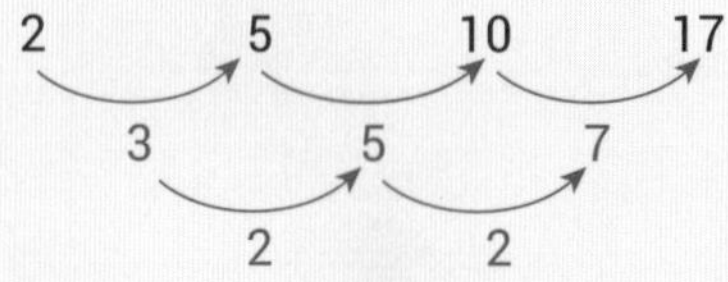

(iii) $T_2 - T_1 = 60 - 50 = 10$

$T_3 - T_2 = 70 - 60 = 10$

$T_4 - T_3 = 80 - 70 = 10$

$\therefore T_2 - T_1 = T_3 - T_2 = T_4 - T_3$

$\therefore$ Arithmetic

(iv) None, as it doesn't satisfy conditions necessary for arithmetic, geometric or quadratic sequences.

(In fact, the sequence 1, 1, 2, 3, 5, ... is the Fibonacci sequence.)

Exercise 7.5

Remember: Linear sequence ⇒ 1st difference is a non-zero constant
Quadratic sequence ⇒ 2nd difference is a non-zero constant

1. The first four terms of a pattern are shown.

   (i) Draw the next two terms of the pattern.

   (ii) Copy and complete the table below.

Term	1	2	3	4	5
No. of dots	1	3			

   (iii) Describe the sequence of numbers generated by the pattern.

   (iv) How many dots are there in T_7, the seventh term?

2. The first four terms of a pattern are shown.

   (i) Draw the next two terms of the pattern.

   (ii) Count the number of dots in each of the first five terms and display the results in a table.

   (iii) Describe the sequence of numbers generated by the pattern.

   (iv) How many red dots are there in T_8, the eighth term?

   (v) Find a formula for L_n, the number of dots on the base of the nth square.

   (vi) Find a formula for H_n, the number of dots on the height of the nth square.

   (vii) Hence, find a formula for T_n, the number of dots in the nth square.

3. Determine whether the following sequences are arithmetic, quadratic or geometric.
   In each case give a reason for your answer.

   (i) −1, 2, 9, 20, ...

   (ii) 2, 4, 8, 16, ...

   (iii) 1, 5, 11, 19, ...

   (iv) 5, 20, 45, 80, ...

   (v) 5, 10, 15, 20, ...

   (vi) 3, 9, 27, 81, ...

   (vii) 3, 6, 13, 24, ...

   (viii) 6, 8, 10 ,12, ...

   (ix) 5, 10, 20, 40, ...

   (x) 4, 12, 36, 108, ...

4. For each of the following quadratic sequences, find:

   (a) *a*, the first term

   (b) The first and second differences

   (c) The next three terms

   (i) 8, 14, 24, 38, ...

   (ii) 1, 3, 6, 10, ...

   (iii) 7, 16, 31, 52, ...

   (iv) 3, 13, 27, 45, ...

   (v) 15, 23, 39, 63, ...

   (vi) 8, 12, 14, 14, 12, ...

   (vii) 5, 7, 5, −1, −11, ...

   (viii) 1, −2, −2, 1, ...

   (ix) 10, 4, 1, 1, 4, ...

5. For each geometric sequence:

   (a) Determine whether it doubles or triples.

   (b) Find the next three terms.

   (i) 8, 16, 32, 64, 128, ...

   (ii) 6, 18, 54, 162, 486, ...

   (iii) 33, 99, 297, 891, ...

   (iv) 13, 26, 52, 104, 208, ...

   (v) −5, −15, −45, −135, −405, ...

6. The first four terms in a quadratic pattern are given in the table below.

Term	u_1	u_2	u_3	u_4	u_5	u_6	u_7
Number	3	7	13	21			

(i) Follow the pattern of the first four terms to complete the table.

(ii) If $u_n = n^2 + bn + c$, then find u_1 and u_2 in terms of b and c.

(iii) Show, by setting the expressions for u_1 and u_2 in part (ii) equal to the values for u_1 and u_2 in the table, that we obtain the following equations:

$b + c = 2$

$2b + c = 3$

(iv) Solve the equations in part (iii) to find the value of b and the value of c.

(v) Hence, find u_{15}.

7. The first four terms in a quadratic pattern are given in the table below.

Term	u_1	u_2	u_3	u_4	u_5	u_6	u_7	u_8
Number	6	11	18	27				

(i) Follow the pattern of the first four terms to complete the table.

(ii) If $u_n = n^2 + pn + q$, then find u_1 and u_2 in terms of p and q.

(iii) Show, by setting the expressions for u_1 and u_2 in part (ii) equal to the values for u_1 and u_2 in the table, that we obtain the following equations:

$p + q = 5$

$2p + q = 7$

(iv) Solve the equations in part (iii) to find the value of p and the value of q.

(v) Hence, find u_{25}.

8. The first three terms of a pattern are shown.

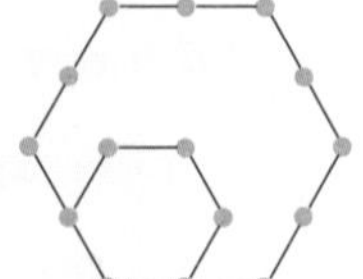

(i) Draw the next shape in the pattern.

(ii) Copy and complete the table to show the number of dots for each given term:

Term	1	2	3	4
No. of dots	1			

(iii) How many dots are there in terms 5 and 6?

(iv) What type of sequence is this? Give a reason for your answer.

Revision Exercises

1. The first three terms of a pattern are shown.

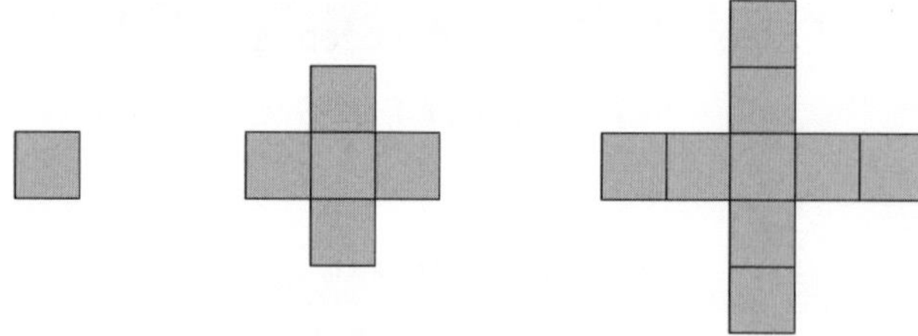

(i) Draw the fourth pattern.

(ii) How many squares are there in the nth term?

(iii) How many squares are there in the 50th term?

(iv) Which term has 237 squares?

2. A pattern of triangles is built up from matchsticks as follows:

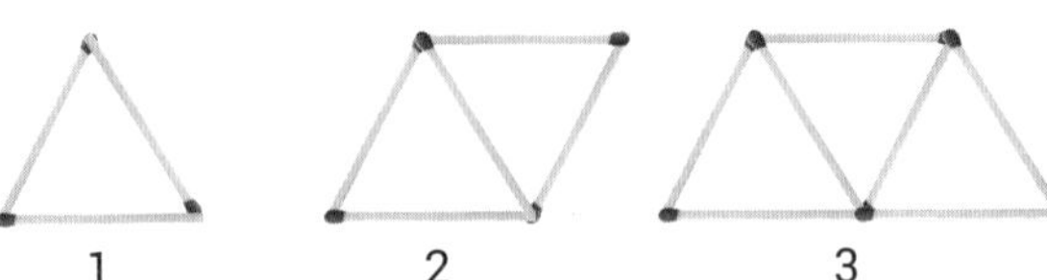

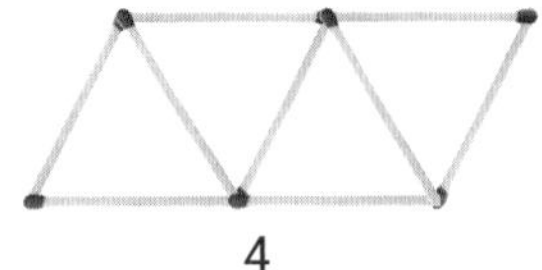

(i) Draw the next set of triangles in the pattern.

(ii) How many matchsticks are needed for the nth set of triangles?

(iii) Using your result from part (ii), find the number of matchsticks needed to make the 50th set of triangles.

(iv) If there are only 200 matchsticks, which is the largest set of triangles that could be made?

---

3. The first three terms of a pattern are shown.

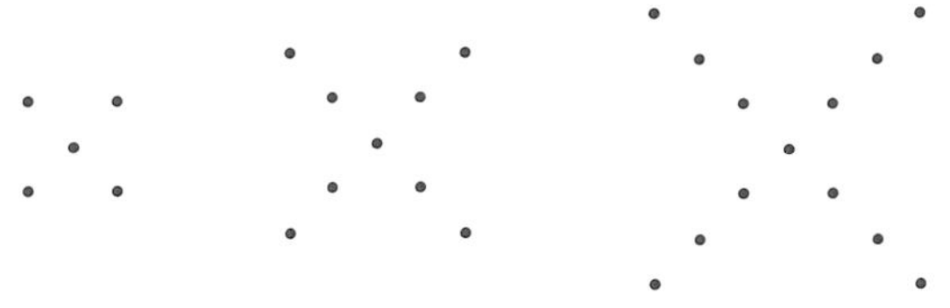

(i) Draw the next two terms of the pattern.

(ii) Copy and complete the table below.

Term	1	2	3	4
No. of dots	5	9		

(iii) Describe the sequence of numbers generated by the pattern.

(iv) How many dots are there in T_n, the nth term?

(v) How many dots are there in T_8, the eighth term?

4. The nth term of an arithmetic sequence is given by $T_n = 5n + 1$.

(i) Find the value of a, the first term.

(ii) Find the value of d, the common difference.

(iii) Find the value of n for which $T_n = 156$.

(iv) Find the sum of the first 12 terms of the sequence.

5. For each sequence, state if it is arithmetic, geometric, or neither.

(i) 1, 3, 6, 10, 15, ...

(ii) 40, 43, 46, 49, 52, ...

(iii) $4, \frac{13}{3}, \frac{14}{3}, 5, \frac{16}{3}, \ldots$

(iv) −4, 12, −36, 108, −324, ...

(v) 4, 16, 36, 64, 100, ...

(vi) −29, −34, −39, −44, −49, ...

(vii) 1, 5, 25, 125, 625, ...

(viii) 1, 4, 9, 16, 25, ...

6. For each of the following quadratic sequences, find:

(a) The first term

(b) The first and second differences

(c) T_7, the 7th term of the sequence

(i) 16, 17, 19, 22, ...

(ii) 1, 3, 6, 10, ...

(iii) 12, 14, 17, 21, ...

(iv) 1, 6, 15, 28, 45, ...

(v) 8, 9, 8, 5, ...

7. Copy the pattern shown.

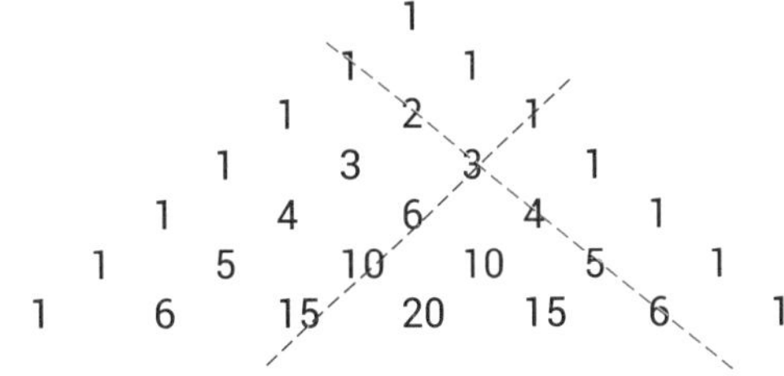

(i) Draw the next two rows of the pattern.

(ii) Identify the type of sequence along the diagonal marked with a broken red line and find its nth term.

(iii) Identify the type of sequence along the diagonal marked with a broken blue line.

(iv) Show that $T_n = \frac{1}{2}n^2 + \frac{1}{2}n$ generates the first five terms in the sequence in part (iii).

8. The first four numbers in a pattern of numbers are given in the table below.

Term	u_1	u_2	u_3	u_4	u_5	u_6	u_7
Number	3	12	29	54			

(i) Follow the pattern of the first four terms to complete the table.

(ii) Use the data in the table to show that the pattern is quadratic.

(iii) $u_n = 4n^2 + bn + c$, where $b, c, \in Z$. Find the value of b and the value of c.

(iv) Hence, find u_{20}.

Exam Questions

1. The first three patterns in a sequence of patterns are shown below.

1

2

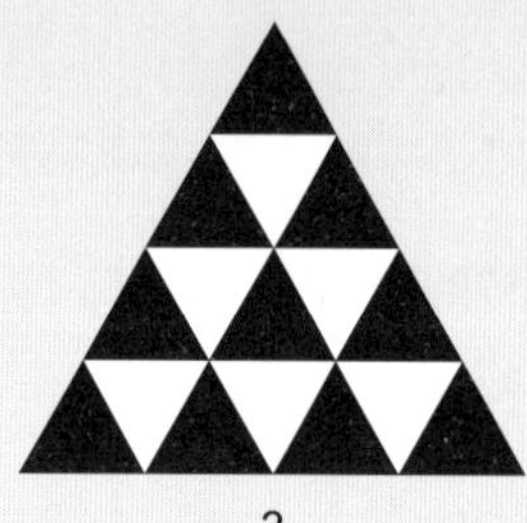

3

(a) Draw the fourth pattern in the sequence.

(b) Complete the table below.

	Number of black triangles	Number of white triangles	Total number of small triangles
Pattern 1	3	1	$T_1 = 4$
Pattern 2			$T_2 =$
Pattern 3			$T_3 =$
Pattern 4			$T_4 =$
Pattern 5			$T_5 =$

(c) Show that the number of **black** triangles form a quadratic sequence.

(d) (i) How many **black** triangles are in the 9th pattern?

(ii) How many **white** triangles are in the 9th pattern?

(iii) How many small triangles, in total, are in the 9th pattern?

(e) Write an expression in n for the total number of triangles in the nth pattern.

(f) The number of **black** triangles in the nth pattern is given by the formula $B_n = \frac{1}{2}n^2 + \frac{3}{2}n + c$.

Find the value of c.

(g) Use your answer to parts **(e)** and **(f)** above to find a formula for the number of **white** triangles in the nth pattern.

(h) One particular pattern has a total of 625 triangles. Find the number of black triangles and the number of white triangles in that pattern.

SEC Leaving Certificate Ordinary Level, Paper 1, 2015

2. Lucy is arranging 1 cent and 5 cent coins in rows. The pattern of coins in each row is as shown below.

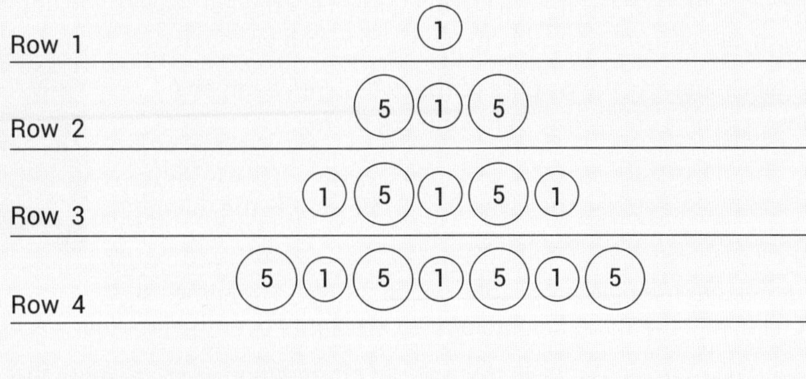

(a) Draw the next row of coins above, continuing the same pattern.

(b) The table below gives the number of coins and the total value of the coins in each row. Complete the table for rows 4 to 7.

Row number n	Number of 1 cent coins	Number of 5 cent coins	Total number of coins in the row	Total value of the coins in the row
1	1	0	1	1
2	1	2	3	11
3	3	2	5	13
4				
5				
6				
7				

(c) Complete the following sentences to state, in terms of n, the number of 1 cent and 5 cent coins in row n.

(i) If n is odd, row n has ______ 1 cent coins and ______ 5 cent coins.

(ii) If n is even, row n has ______ 1 cent coins and ______ 5 cent coins.

(d) Find the total number of coins in the 40th row.

(e) Find the total value of the coins in the 40th row.

(f) Which row has coins with a total value of 337 cent?

(g) Find the total value of the coins in the first 40 rows.

SEC Leaving Certificate Ordinary Level, Paper 1, 2012

3. The general term of an arithmetic sequence is $T_n = 15 - 2n$, where $n \in N$.

(a) (i) Write down the first three terms of the sequence.

(ii) Find the first negative term of the sequence.

(b) (i) Find $S_n = T_1 + T_2 + ... + T_n$, the sum of the first n terms of the series, in terms of n.

(ii) Find the value of n for which the sum of the first n terms of the series is 0.

SEC Leaving Certificate Ordinary Level, Paper 1, 2014

NUMBER PATTERNS

4. John is given two sunflower plants. One plant is 16 cm high and the other is 24 cm high. John measures the height of each plant at the same time every day for a week. He notes that the 16 cm plant grows 4 cm each day, and the 24 cm plant grows 3.5 cm each day.

   (a) Draw up a table showing the heights of the two plants each day for the week, starting on the day that John got them.

   (b) Write down two formulae – one for each plant – to represent the heights of the two plants on any given day. State clearly the meaning of any letters used in your formulae.

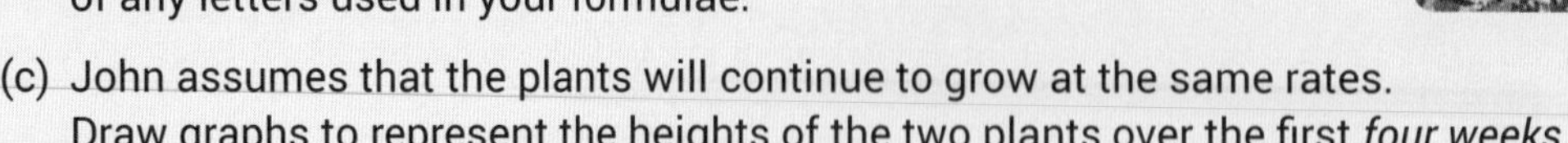

   (c) John assumes that the plants will continue to grow at the same rates. Draw graphs to represent the heights of the two plants over the first *four weeks*.

   (d) (i) From your diagram, write down the point of intersection of the two graphs.

   (ii) Explain what the point of intersection means, with respect to the two plants. Your answer should refer to the meaning of *both* co-ordinates.

   (e) Check your answer to part (d)(i) using your formulae from part (b).

   (f) The point of intersection can be found either by reading the graph or by using algebra. State one advantage of finding it using algebra.

   (g) John's model for the growth of the plants might not be correct. State one limitation of the model that might affect the point of intersection and its interpretation.

SEC Leaving Certificate Ordinary Level, Sample Paper 1, 2014

5. The first five numbers in a pattern of numbers are given in the table below.

Term	Number
U_1	13
U_2	15
U_3	19
U_4	25
U_5	33
U_6	
U_7	
U_8	

   (a) (i) Follow the pattern in the table above to write the next three numbers into the table.

   (ii) Use the data in the table to show that the pattern is quadratic.

   (b) $U_n = n^2 + bn + c$ where $b, c \in Z$. Find the value of b and the value of c.

SEC Leaving Certificate Ordinary Level, Paper 1, 2016

Solutions and chapter summary available online

Complex Numbers

In this chapter you will learn to:

- Investigate the operations of addition, multiplication, subtraction and division with complex numbers *C* in rectangular form $a + ib$
- Illustrate complex numbers on an Argand diagram
- Interpret the modulus as distance from the origin on an Argand diagram and calculate the complex conjugate

You should remember...

- The rules of indices and surds
- The commutative, associative and distributive properties of the real numbers
- Pythagoras' theorem
- How to plot points on a Cartesian plane

Key words

- Complex number
- Imaginary number
- Argand diagram
- Real part
- Imaginary part
- Translation
- Dilation
- Modulus
- Conjugate
- Rotation

8.1 Introduction

The Italian mathematicians Gerolamo Cardano (1501–1576) and Niccolò Tartaglia (1500–1557) were the first to encounter complex numbers.

Gerolamo Cardano | Niccolò Tartaglia

While working on the solutions to cubic equations, they came upon some unusual solutions involving the square root of −1. Today we call such solutions **complex** solutions.

Complex numbers have been introduced to allow for the solutions of certain equations that have no real solutions.

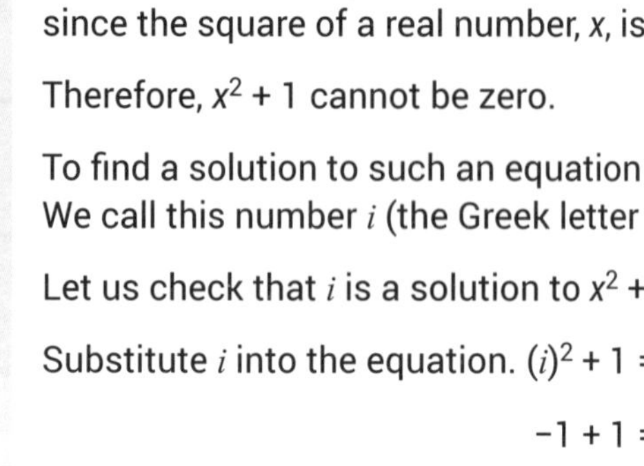

For example, the equation $x^2 + 1 = 0$ has no real solution, since the square of a real number, x, is either 0 or positive.

Therefore, $x^2 + 1$ cannot be zero.

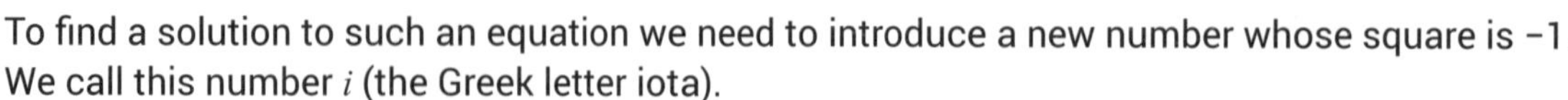

To find a solution to such an equation we need to introduce a new number whose square is −1. We call this number i (the Greek letter iota).

Let us check that i is a solution to $x^2 + 1 = 0$.

Substitute i into the equation. $(i)^2 + 1 = 0$

$$-1 + 1 = 0$$

$$0 = 0$$

$\therefore$ i is a solution.

$i^2 = -1$

Also written as $i = \sqrt{-1}$

The product, $\sqrt{9}\sqrt{4}$ can be evaluated as follows: $\sqrt{9}\sqrt{4} = (3)(2)$

$$= 6$$

We can arrive at the same answer as follows: $\sqrt{9}\sqrt{4} = \sqrt{(9)(4)}$

$$= \sqrt{36}$$

$$= 6$$

More generally, as long as at least one of a and b is greater than or equal to zero ($a, b \in R$) then,

$\sqrt{a}\sqrt{b} = \sqrt{ab}$

For example, $\sqrt{-9} = \sqrt{(9)(-1)}$

$$= \sqrt{9}\sqrt{-1}$$

$$= 3i$$

Numbers of the form bi, where $b \in R$ and $i^2 = -1$, are called imaginary numbers.

Positive Integer Powers of i

Positive integer powers of i always simplify to one of the numbers in the set $\{1, -1, i, -i\}$. For example,

$i^3 = (i^2)(i) = (-1)(i) = -i$

$i^4 = (i^2)(i^2) = (-1)(-1) = 1$

As $i^4 = 1$, any power of i that is a multiple of 4 is also 1.

In fact, the powers of i form a cycle (repeating pattern) of order (size) four.

$i = i$	$i^5 = i$	$i^9 = i$
$i^2 = -1$	$i^6 = -1$	$i^{10} = -1$
$i^3 = -i$	$i^7 = -i$	$i^{11} = -i$
$i^4 = 1$	$i^8 = 1$	$i^{12} = 1$

Worked Example 8.1

Express each of the following in terms of i, where $i^2 = -1$:

(i) $\sqrt{-4}$ (ii) $\sqrt{-72}$ (iii) $\sqrt{-48} + \sqrt{-27}$

Solution

(i) $\sqrt{-4} = \sqrt{4}\sqrt{-1}$

$= 2i$

(ii) $\sqrt{-72} = \sqrt{72}\sqrt{-1}$

$= \sqrt{36}\sqrt{2}\sqrt{-1}$

$= 6\sqrt{2}i$

(iii) $\sqrt{-48} + \sqrt{-27}$

$= \sqrt{48}\sqrt{-1} + \sqrt{27}\sqrt{-1}$

$= \sqrt{16 \times 3}i + \sqrt{9 \times 3}i$

$= 4\sqrt{3}i + 3\sqrt{3}i$

$= 7\sqrt{3}i$

In order to write $\sqrt{72}$ in its simplest form, we look for the largest square number that is a factor of 72, i.e. 36. So, 72 = (36)(2).

Worked Example 8.2

Simplify the following:

(i) i^3 (ii) i^4 (iii) i^{49}

Solution

(i) $i^3 = (i^2)(i)$

$= (-1)(i)$

$\therefore i^3 = -i$

(ii) $i^4 = (i^2)^2$

$= (-1)^2$

$\therefore i^4 = 1$

OR $i^4 = (i^3)(i)$

$= (-i)(i)$

$= -i^2$

$= -(-1)$

$\therefore i^4 = 1$

(iii) $i^{49} = (i^{48})(i)$

$= (i^2)^{24}(i)$

$= (-1)^{24}(i)$

$= (1)i$

$\therefore i^{49} = i$

OR $i^{49} = i^{48}i$

$= (i^4)^{12}(i)$

$= (1)^{12}(i)$

$= (1)i$

$= i$

$\therefore i^{49} = i$

Exercise 8.1

1. Write the following in the form ki, $k \in R$, $i^2 = -1$:

(i) $\sqrt{-100}$ (ii) $\sqrt{-81}$ (iii) $\sqrt{-25}$ (iv) $\sqrt{-36}$ (v) $\sqrt{-121}$ (vi) $\sqrt{-49}$ (vii) $\sqrt{-64}$ (viii) $\sqrt{-169}$ (ix) $\sqrt{-144}$ (x) $\sqrt{-16}$

2. Write the following in the form pi, $p \in R$, $i^2 = -1$:

(i) $\sqrt{-17}$ (ii) $\sqrt{-31}$ (iii) $\sqrt{-14}$ (iv) $\sqrt{-19}$ (v) $\sqrt{-21}$ (vi) $\sqrt{-23}$ (vii) $\sqrt{-29}$ (viii) $\sqrt{-43}$ (ix) $\sqrt{-5}$ (x) $\sqrt{-3}$

3. Write the following in the form $a\sqrt{b}i$, where $a, b \in R, \sqrt{b}$ is in its simplest form and $i^2 = -1$:

   (i) $\sqrt{-8}$ (vi) $\sqrt{-32}$

   (ii) $\sqrt{-98}$ (vii) $\sqrt{-500}$

   (iii) $\sqrt{-45}$ (viii) $\sqrt{-54}$

   (iv) $\sqrt{-300}$ (ix) $\sqrt{-27}$

   (v) $\sqrt{-12}$ (x) $\sqrt{-125}$

4. Simplify the following in the form $a\sqrt{b}i$, where $a, b \in R, \sqrt{b}$ is in its simplest form and $i^2 = -1$:

   (i) $\sqrt{-50} + \sqrt{-8}$ (iii) $\sqrt{-125} + \sqrt{-20}$

   (ii) $\sqrt{-27} - \sqrt{-12}$ (iv) $\sqrt{-44} + \sqrt{-99}$

5. Simplify each of the following ($i^2 = -1$):

   (i) i^3 (iii) i^5 (v) i^{13}

   (ii) i^6 (iv) i^{12} (vi) i^{45}

6. Simplify the following, giving your answer in the form $pi, p \in N, i^2 = -1$:

   (i) $(3i)^3$ (iv) $(4i)^5$

   (ii) $(5i)^3$ (v) $(2i)^7$

   (iii) $(5i)^4$ (vi) $(2i)^8$

7. Match each number in Column A with one number in Column B.

A	B
i^4	$1 - i$
$2i^3$	-3
$i^8 + i^3$	$-128i$
i^{98}	$1 + i$
$3(i)^2$	0
$i^4 - i^8$	$-64i$
$(2i)^7$	1
$i^4 - i^7$	$9i$
$(4i)^3$	$-2i$
$5i + 4i$	-1

8. A spinner has eight equal sectors and on each sector is a different power of i.

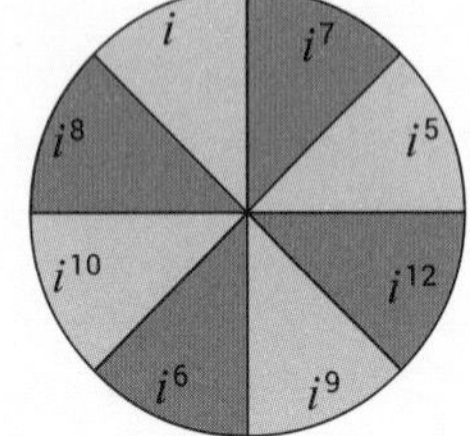

i	-1	$-i$	1
- €5	€2	€10	€2

The table gives possible winnings or losses for one spin of the spinner. By simplifying the powers of i on the spinner, find the probability of:

   (i) Winning €10 on one spin

   (ii) Losing €5 on one spin

8.2 Complex Numbers and the Argand Diagram

A **complex number**, z, is any number of the form $z = a + bi,\ a, b \in R,\ i^2 = -1$.

a is called the **real part** of z, which is written as Re(z), and b is called the **imaginary part** of z, which is written as Im(z).

C is used to denote the set of complex numbers.

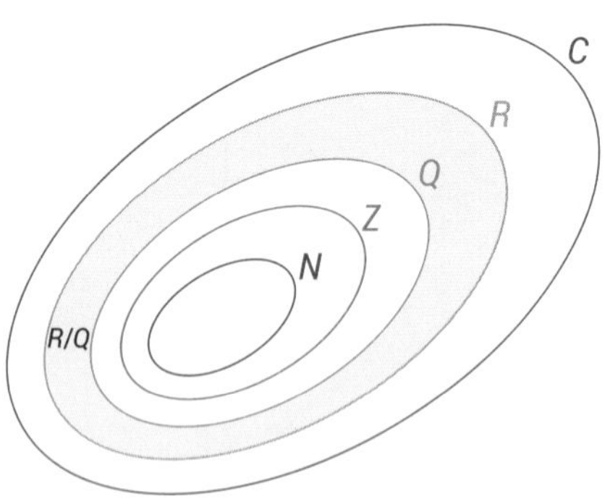

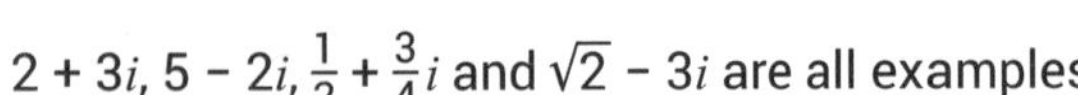

$2 + 3i$, $5 - 2i$, $\frac{1}{2} + \frac{3}{4}i$ and $\sqrt{2} - 3i$ are all examples of **complex numbers**.

7 is another example since it can be written as $7 + 0i$.
In fact, all real numbers are complex.

The set of real numbers is a subset of the set of complex numbers.

Worked Example 8.3

$z = 7 - 8i$ is a complex number. Write down Re(z) and Im(z).

Solution

Re(z) = 7 and Im(z) = −8

Do not include i in Im(z).

The Argand Diagram

Just as a real number can be represented on a real number line, a complex number can be represented on a diagram called the **Argand diagram**, also known as the **complex plane**. The Argand diagram is a two-dimensional plane with two perpendicular axes. The horizontal axis is the real axis and the vertical axis is the imaginary axis. The complex number $3 + 2i$ is represented on the Argand diagram on the right.

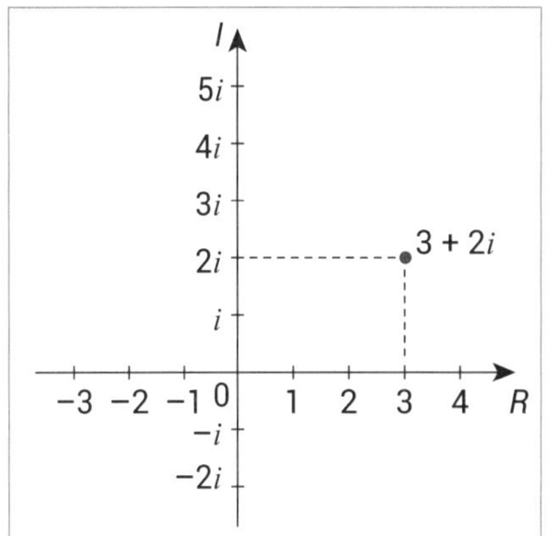

The Argand diagram was devised by the Swiss mathematician, Jean-Robert Argand (1768–1822).

Worked Example 8.4

Represent the following numbers on an Argand diagram:

(i) $-1 + 2i$ (ii) $2 + 3i$ (iii) $-3 - 2i$ (iv) $3 - i$

Solution

(i) $-1 + 2i$ is one step left of $0 + 0i$ and then two steps up.

(ii) $2 + 3i$ is two steps right of $0 + 0i$ and three steps up.

(iii) $-3 - 2i$ is three steps left of $0 + 0i$ and then two steps down.

(iv) $3 - i$ is three steps right of $0 + 0i$ and one step down.

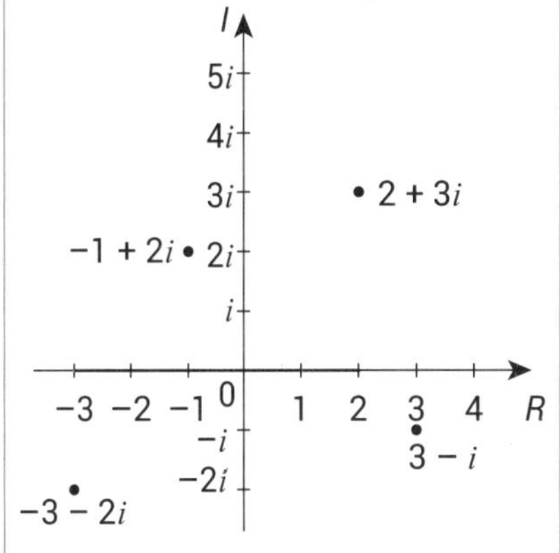

You should always clearly label each complex number on an Argand diagram.

Exercise 8.2

1. For each of the following complex numbers (z), write down Re(z) and Im(z), the real and imaginary parts of the complex number z:

   (i) $\frac{1}{2} - \frac{3}{2}i$ (ii) $\sqrt{2} - 3i$ (iii) $\frac{22}{7} - 3.14i$ (iv) $3 - \frac{1}{\sqrt{3}}i$ (v) $-\frac{5}{6} + 3i$

2. Plot the following complex numbers on an Argand diagram:

   (i) $3 + 2i$ (ii) $5 - 2i$ (iii) $-6 + 2i$ (iv) $-3 - 2i$ (v) $2 - 3i$ (vi) $4 + i$

3. Show the following complex numbers on the complex plane:

   (i) -2 (ii) $3i$ (iii) 4 (iv) $-5i$ (v) $2 + 0i$ (vi) i

4. Say whether the following numbers lie on the real axis or the imaginary axis:

(i) 2
(ii) $3i$
(iii) $-2i$
(iv) -4
(v) $0 + 2i$
(vi) $-1 + 0i$
(vii) i^2
(viii) i^3
(ix) i^4
(x) $(2i)^4$

5. Plot the following numbers on an Argand diagram:

(i) $3 + \sqrt{-4}$
(ii) $5 + \sqrt{-49}$
(iii) $-4 + \sqrt{-9}$
(iv) $8 - \sqrt{-25}$
(v) $10 - \sqrt{-36}$
(vi) $-2 + \sqrt{-1}$
(vii) $1 - \sqrt{-144}$
(viii) $-4 - \sqrt{-1}$
(ix) $7 - \sqrt{-81}$

6. Using the data in the box below, form six different complex numbers in the form $a + bi$, where a and b are non-zero integers and $a \neq \pm b$.

3, 2, i, +, −

For example: $-3 + 2i$

Then plot these complex numbers on an Argand diagram.

7. Using the data in the box below, form 12 different complex numbers in the form $a + bi$ where a and b are integers and $a \neq \pm b$.

0, 3, 4, 5, i, +, −

For example: $4 + 5i$

Plot these complex numbers on an Argand diagram.

8.3 Addition and Subtraction of Complex Numbers; Multiplication by a Real Number

To add, subtract, multiply and divide complex numbers, we follow certain well-defined steps.

Addition and Subtraction of Complex Numbers

To add two complex numbers we add the real parts to the real parts and the imaginary parts to the imaginary parts. If $z_1 = a + bi$ and $z_2 = c + di$, where $a, b, c, d \in R$, then $z_1 + z_2 = (a + c) + (b + d)i$.

If z_1 and z_2 are two complex numbers, then $z_1 + z_2 = (\text{Re}(z_1) + \text{Re}(z_2)) + (\text{Im}(z_1) + \text{Im}(z_2))i$.
Add the real parts and add the imaginary parts.

Worked Example 8.5

$z_1 = 2 + 3i$ and $z_2 = 1 + 5i$. Evaluate $z_1 + z_2$.

We use z_1 and z_2 to distinguish between different complex numbers.

Solution

$z_1 + z_2 = (2 + 3i) + (1 + 5i)$
$= (2 + 1) + (3 + 5i)i$
$\therefore z_1 + z_2 = 3 + 8i$

OR

$z_1 + z_2 = (2 + 3i) + (1 + 5i)$
$= 2 + 3i + 1 + 5i$
$= 2 + 1 + 3i + 5i$
$= 3 + 8i$

If $z_1 = a + bi$ and $z_2 = c + di$, where $a, b, c, d \in R$, then $z_1 - z_2 = (a - c) + (b - d)i$.

If z_1 and z_2 are two complex numbers, then $z_1 - z_2 = (\text{Re}(z_1) - \text{Re}(z_2)) + (\text{Im}(z_1) - \text{Im}(z_2))i$.

Worked Example 8.6

$z_1 = 8 + 6i$ and $z_2 = 4 + 2i$. Find $z_1 - z_2$.

Solution

$z_1 - z_2 = (8 + 6i) - (4 + 2i)$ **OR** $z_1 - z_2 = 8 + 6i - 4 - 2i$

$= (8 - 4) + (6 - 2)i$ $= 8 - 4 + 6i - 2i$

$\therefore z_1 - z_2 = 4 + 4i$ $= 4 + 4i$

Multiplying a Complex Number by a Real Number

While this section focuses on addition and subtraction, we will also deal with multiplying a complex number by a real number.

If z is a complex number and a is a real number, then $az = a\,\text{Re}(z) + a\,\text{Im}(z)i$.

Worked Example 8.7

If $z = 4 + 2i$, find:

(i) $3z$

(ii) $-5z$

Solution

(i) $3z = 3(4 + 2i)$

$= 3(4) + 3(2i)$

$\therefore 3z = 12 + 6i$

(ii) $-5z = -5(4 + 2i)$

$= -5(4) - 5(2i)$

$\therefore -5z = -20 - 10i$

Transformations I: Translation and Dilation

Addition of complex numbers is the equivalent of a **translation** on the complex plane. Multiplication by a real number is the equivalent of a **dilation** (stretching, contraction) on the complex plane.

Worked Example 8.8

$z_1 = 2 + 4i$, $z_2 = 2 + 3i$, $z_3 = -1 + 2i$ and $\omega = 1 + i$.

(i) Plot z_1, z_2, and z_3 on an Argand diagram.

(ii) Evaluate $z_1 + \omega$, $z_2 + \omega$, and $z_3 + \omega$.

(iii) Plot the answers to part (ii) on an Argand diagram.

(iv) Describe the transformation that is the addition of ω.

Solution

(i)

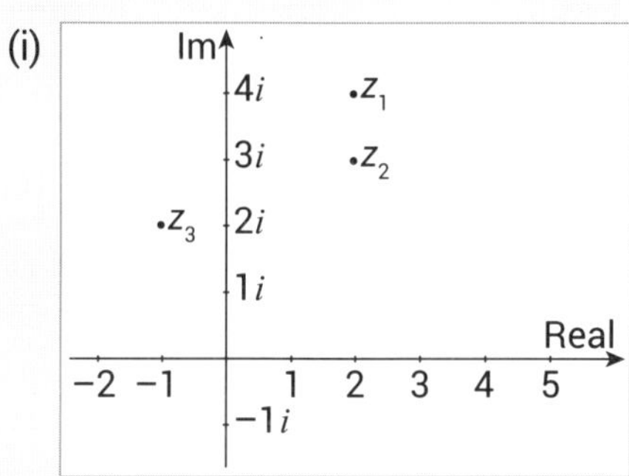

(ii) $z_1 + \omega = (2 + 4i) + (1 + i)$

$= 3 + 5i$

$z_2 + \omega = (2 + 3i) + (1 + i)$

$= 3 + 4i$

$z_3 + \omega = (-1 + 2i) + (1 + i)$

$= 0 + 3i$

(iii)

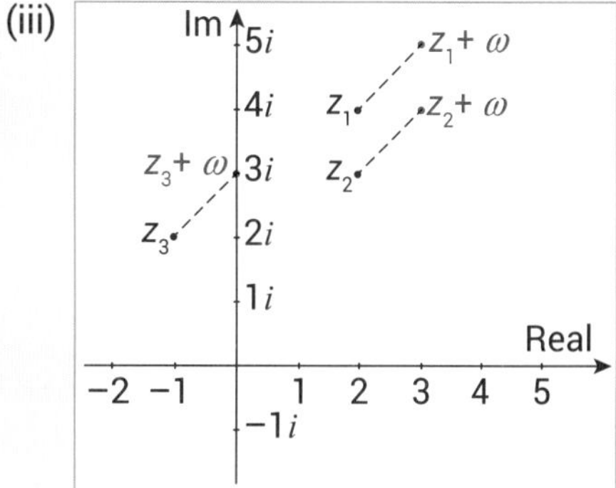

(iv) From the Argand diagram, the numbers z_1, z_2 and z_3 are moved the same distance and in the same direction. The numbers are transformed one unit to the right and then one unit up. We call such a transformation a translation.

Worked Example 8.9

$z_1 = 2 + 4i$, $z_2 = 2 + 3i$, $z_3 = -1 + 2i$ and $a = 2$.

(i) Plot z_1, z_2 and z_3 on an Argand diagram.

(ii) Evaluate az_1, az_2 and az_3.

(iii) Plot the answers to part (ii) on an Argand diagram.

(iv) Describe the transformation that is multiplication by a.

Solution

(i)

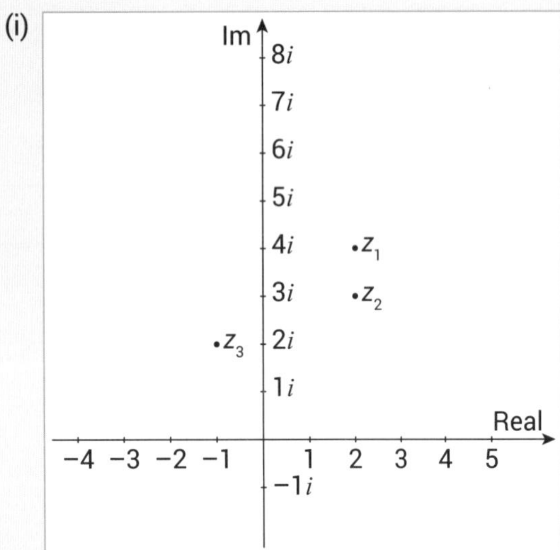

(ii) $az_1 = 2(2 + 4i)$

$= 4 + 8i$

$az_2 = 2(2 + 3i)$

$= 4 + 6i$

$az_3 = 2(-1 + 2i)$

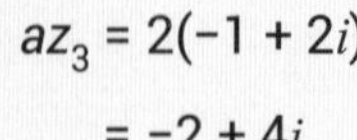

$= -2 + 4i$

(iii)

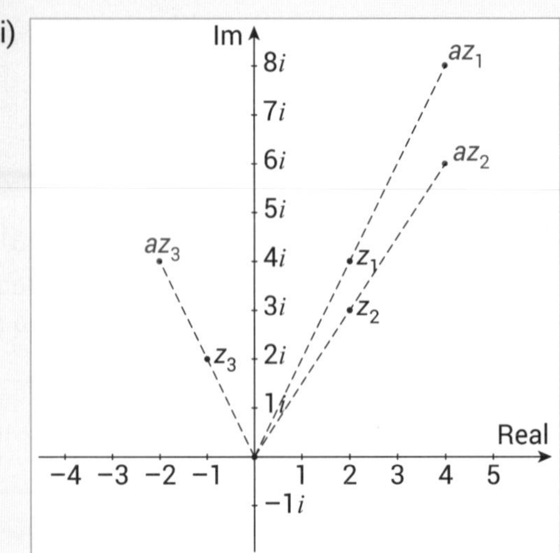

(iv) From the diagram we see that all the points are moved further from the origin by a factor of 2. We call such a transformation a dilation by a factor of 2.

- If F is the dilation factor and if $F > 1$ or $F < -1$, the dilation is sometimes referred to as a **stretching** on the complex plane.
- If $-1 < F < 1$, the dilation is sometimes referred to as a **contracting** on the complex plane.

Worked Example 8.10

z_1, z_2, z_3, z_4 and z_5 are the complex numbers shown in the diagram on the right. Using the following information, label the complex numbers:

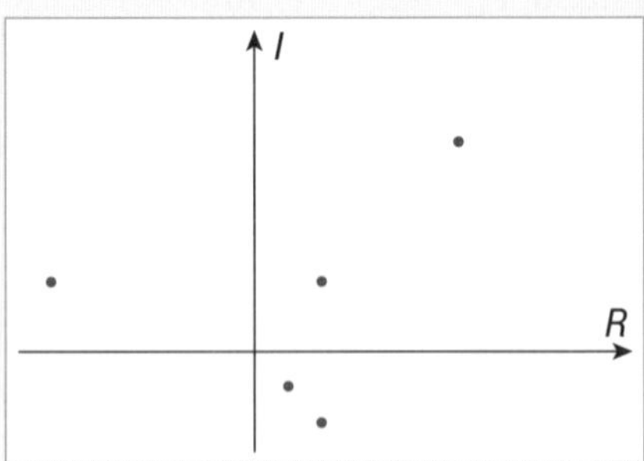

(i) $z_4 = 3z_1$

(ii) $\text{Re}(z_5) < 0$

(iii) $z_2 = \frac{1}{2}z_3$

Solution

(i) z_4 is three times the distance from the origin as is z_1 and z_4 will lie along the ray $0z_1$, where 0 is the origin.

(ii) If $\text{Re}(z_5) < 0$, then this implies that z_5 lies somewhere to left of the imaginary axis.

(iii) z_2 is half the distance from the origin as is z_3 and z_2 will lie along the ray $0z_3$, where 0 is the origin.

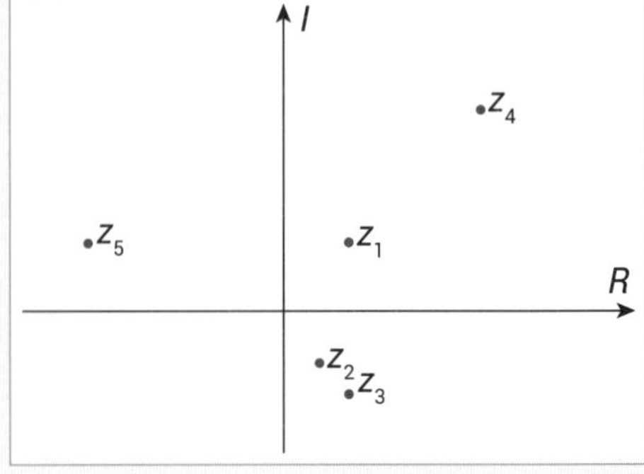

Exercise 8.3

1. Let $z_1 = 7 + 5i$ and $z_2 = 2 + i$.
Evaluate each of the following:
   (i) $z_1 + z_2$ (iii) $3z_1 + 2z_2$
   (ii) $z_1 - z_2$ (iv) $2z_1 - 3z_2$

2. Let $z_1 = 3 - 2i$ and $z_2 = 2 + 4i$.
Evaluate each of the following:
   (i) $z_1 + z_2$ (iii) $z_1 + 3z_2$
   (ii) $z_1 - z_2$ (iv) $2z_1 - 5z_2$

3. Let $z_1 = -1 + 2i$ and $z_2 = 2 + 3i$.
Evaluate each of the following:
   (i) $2z_1 + z_2$ (iii) $2z_2 - 3z_1$
   (ii) $2z_1 - z_2$ (iv) $z_2 - z_1$

4. Let $z = 2 + i$. Find:
   (i) $z + 3$ (iii) $z - 3z$ (v) $2z + 3 - 3i$
   (ii) $z + 3i$ (iv) $2z + 5z$

5. Let $z = 2 - 3i$.
Show the following on an Argand diagram:
   (i) $z + 3$ (iii) $1 - z$
   (ii) $2z + 6i$ (iv) $\frac{1}{2}(z + i)$

6. Let $z = 1 + i$.
   (a) Show the following on an Argand diagram:
      (i) z (iii) $3z$ (v) $5z$
      (ii) $2z$ (iv) $4z$
   (b) Describe the transformation of z in parts (ii) to (v) above.

7. Let $z = -1 + i$.
   (a) Show the following on an Argand diagram:
      (i) z (iii) $3z$ (v) $5z$
      (ii) $2z$ (iv) $4z$
   (b) Describe the transformation of z in parts (ii) to (v) above.

8. Let $z = -24 + 48i$.
   (a) Show the following on an Argand diagram:
      (i) z (iii) $\frac{1}{3}z$ (v) $\frac{1}{6}z$
      (ii) $\frac{1}{2}z$ (iv) $\frac{1}{4}z$
   (b) Describe the transformation of z in parts (ii) to (v) above.

9. $z_1 = 2 + 3i$, $z_2 = -2 + 5i$, $z_3 = -1 + 4i$ and $\omega = 1 + i$.
   (i) Plot z_1, z_2 and z_3 on an Argand diagram.
   (ii) Evaluate $z_1 + \omega$, $z_2 + \omega$ and $z_3 + \omega$.
   (iii) Plot the answers to part (ii) on an Argand diagram.
   (iv) Describe the transformation that is the addition of ω.

10. $z_1 = 3 + 2i$, $z_2 = -1 + 4i$, $z_3 = -3 + 5i$ and $\omega = 1 - i$.
   (i) Plot z_1, z_2 and z_3 on an Argand diagram.
   (ii) Evaluate $z_1 + \omega$, $z_2 + \omega$ and $z_3 + \omega$.
   (iii) Plot the answers to part (ii) on an Argand diagram.
   (iv) Describe the transformation that is the addition of ω.

11. Copy the Argand diagram and label the complex numbers z_1, z_2, z_3, z_4 and z_5, using the information given below.

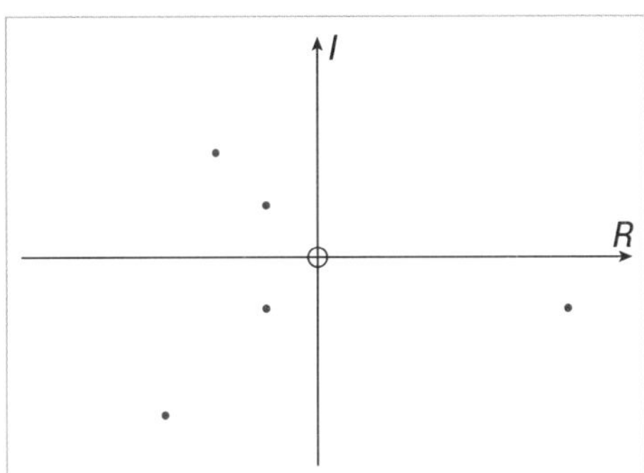

   (i) $z_1 = 2z_2$ (iii) $\text{Re}(z_5) > 0$
   (ii) $z_4 = \frac{1}{3}z_3$

12. Copy the Argand diagram and label the complex numbers z_1, z_2, z_3 and z_4, using the information given below.

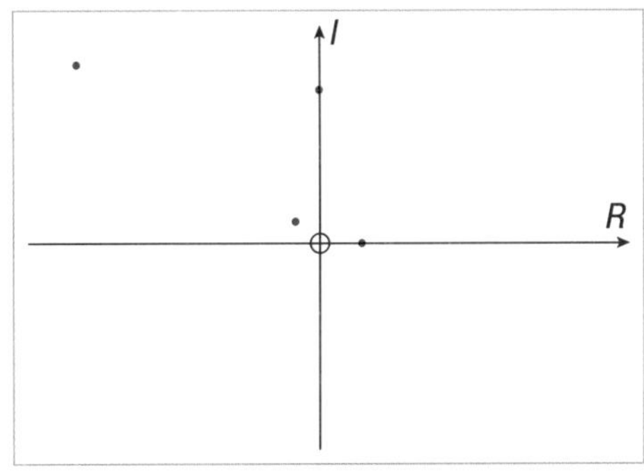

   (i) $\text{Im}(z_1) > 0$ (iii) $\text{Re}(z_3) = 0$
   (ii) $z_2 = 10z_1$ (iv) $\text{Im}(z_4) = 0$

8.4 Modulus of a Complex Number

The **modulus** of a complex number, $a + bi$, is its distance from the origin.

We can use the theorem of Pythagoras to find the distance, x, from the origin to $a + bi$.

$a^2 + b^2 = x^2$

$\therefore x = \sqrt{a^2 + b^2}$

If $z = a + bi$, $a, b \in R$ and $i^2 = -1$, then $|z| = |a + bi| = \sqrt{a^2 + b^2}$.

The modulus of $a + bi$ is written $|a + bi|$.

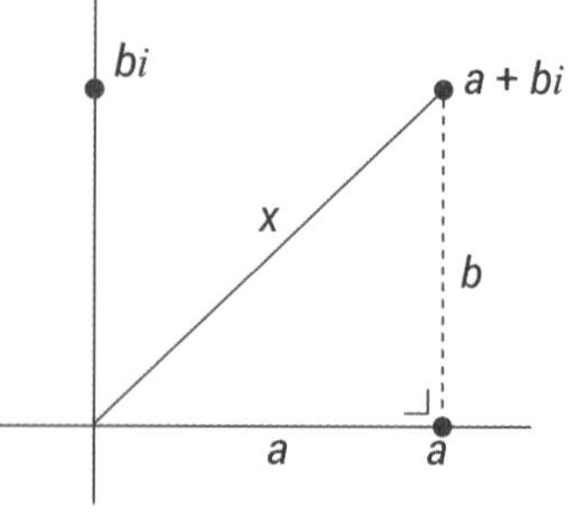

Worked Example 8.11

$z_1 = 12 + 16i$ and $z_2 = -12 + 5i$. Find:

(i) $|z_1|$ (ii) $|z_2|$ (iii) $|z_1 + z_2|$ (iv) Hence, show that $|z_1 + z_2| < |z_1| + |z_2|$.

Solution

(i) $|z_1| = |12 + 16i|$

$= \sqrt{(12)^2 + (16)^2}$

$= \sqrt{144 + 256}$

$= \sqrt{400}$

$\therefore |z_1| = 20$

Do not use i in the square root.

(ii) $|z_2| = |-12 + 5i|$

$= \sqrt{(-12)^2 + (5)^2}$

$= \sqrt{144 + 25}$

$= \sqrt{169}$

$\therefore |z_2| = 13$

(iii) $|z_1 + z_2| = |(12 + 16i) + (-12 + 5i)|$

$= |0 + 21i|$

$= \sqrt{(0)^2 + (21)^2}$

$= \sqrt{441}$

$\therefore |z_1 + z_2| = 21$

(iv) $|z_1| + |z_2| = 20 + 13 = 33$ (From parts (i) and (ii))

$|z_1 + z_2| = 21$

$21 < 33$

$\therefore |z_1 + z_2| < |z_1| + |z_2|$

Worked Example 8.12

$z_1 = 8 - i$ and $z_2 = 7 + ki$ are two complex numbers.

(i) Find $|z_1|$. (ii) Express $|z_2|$ in terms of k. (iii) If $|z_1| = |z_2|$, find two possible values for k.

Solution

(i) $|z_1| = |8 - i|$

$= \sqrt{(8)^2 + (-1)^2}$

$= \sqrt{64 + 1}$

$\therefore |z_1| = \sqrt{65}$

(ii) $|z_2| = |7 + ki|$

$= \sqrt{(7)^2 + (k)^2}$

$\therefore |z_2| = \sqrt{49 + k^2}$

(iii) If $|z_1| = |z_2|$, then:

$\sqrt{65} = \sqrt{49 + k^2}$

Square both sides:

$65 = 49 + k^2$

$65 - 49 = k^2$

$16 = k^2$

$\therefore \pm 4 = k$

Worked Example 8.13

Evaluate each of the following, giving the answer in simplest surd form:

(i) $|2 + 2i|$ (ii) $|3 - 3i|$

Solution

(i) $|2 + 2i| = \sqrt{(2)^2 + (2)^2}$
$= \sqrt{4 + 4}$
$= \sqrt{8}$
$= \sqrt{4}\sqrt{2}$
$= 2\sqrt{2}$

(ii) $|3 - 3i| = \sqrt{(3)^2 + (-3)^2}$
$= \sqrt{9 + 9}$
$= \sqrt{18}$
$= \sqrt{9}\sqrt{2}$
$= 3\sqrt{2}$

Exercise 8.4

1. Evaluate each of the following:
   (i) $|8 - 6i|$
   (ii) $|5 - 12i|$
   (iii) $|7 - 24i|$
   (iv) $|8 + 15i|$
   (v) $|9 - 40i|$
   (vi) $|-3 + 4i|$

2. Evaluate each of the following:
   (i) $|11 + 60i|$
   (ii) $|3 - 4i|$
   (iii) $|12 + 35i|$
   (iv) $|13 - 84i|$
   (v) $|-33 + 56i|$
   (vi) $|6 - 8i|$

3. Evaluate each of the following.
   Give your answer in simplest surd form.
   (i) $|1 + 2i|$
   (ii) $|2 + 2i|$
   (iii) $|3 - i|$
   (iv) $|1 - i|$
   (v) $|3 - 10i|$
   (vi) $|-7 + 3i|$

4. Evaluate each of the following:
   (i) $|3 + \sqrt{2}i|$
   (ii) $|1 + \sqrt{8}i|$
   (iii) $|3 + 2\sqrt{10}i|$
   (iv) $|-3 - \sqrt{7}i|$
   (v) $|2\sqrt{6} - i|$
   (vi) $|7 - 2\sqrt{5}i|$

5. If $z_1 = 12 + 5i$ and $z_2 = 3 - 4i$, then verify that:
   (i) $|z_1 - z_2| = |z_2 - z_1|$
   (ii) $2|z_1| = |2z_1|$

6. If $z_1 = 10 + 8i$ and $z_2 = 8 - 15i$, then verify that:
   (i) $5|z_1| = |5z_1|$
   (ii) $|z_1 - z_2| = |z_2 - z_1|$

7. If $z_1 = 2 + 3i$ and $z_2 = -2 + 5i$, then verify that $|z_1 + z_2| < |z_1| + |z_2|$.

8. Show that $|3 + 4i| = |0 + 5i|$.

9. If $|11 + 2i| = |10 + ki|$, then find two possible values of k, where $k \in R$.

10. If $|8 + ki| = 10$, then find two possible values of k, where $k \in R$.

11. If $|p + pi| = |7 - i|$, then find two possible values of p, where $p \in R$.

8.5 Multiplying Complex Numbers 

First we will look at multiplication of a complex number whose real part is zero, i.e. a number of the form qi, $q \in R$, by a second complex number.

Worked Example 8.14

If $z = 4 + i$, find iz.

Solution

$iz = i(4 + i)$
$= 4i + i^2$
$= 4i - 1$ (as $i^2 = -1$)
$\therefore iz = -1 + 4i$ It is important to write the complex number in the form $a + bi$.

Transformations II: Rotation

Multiplication of a complex number by i is the equivalent of rotating the complex number **anti-clockwise** through 90° about the origin. Multiplication by $-i$ is the equivalent of rotating the complex number **clockwise** through 90° about the origin.

Worked Example 8.15

$z_1 = 2 + i$

(i) Find z_2, if $z_2 = iz_1$.

(ii) Plot z_1 and z_2 on an Argand diagram.

(iii) Describe the transformation that maps z_1 onto z_2.

Solution

(i) $z_2 = i(2 + i)$

$= 2i + i^2$

$= 2i - 1$ (As $i^2 = -1$)

$\therefore z_2 = -1 + 2i$

(ii)

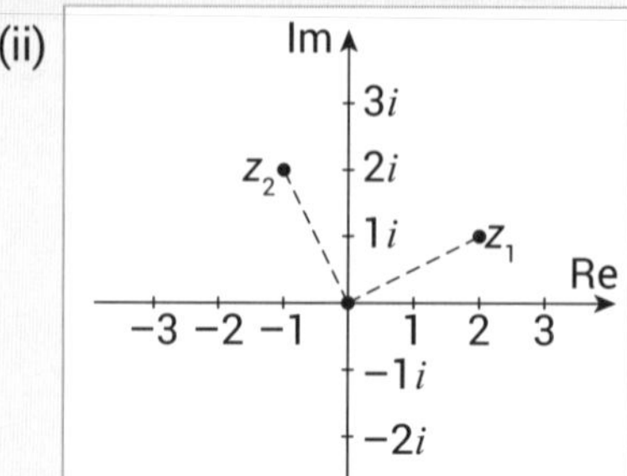

(iii) z_1 is mapped onto z_2 by an anti-clockwise rotation of 90° about the origin. Multiplication by i rotates the complex number anti-clockwise through 90°.

Worked Example 8.16

$z_1 = 2 - 7i, \quad z_2 = 3 + 7i, \quad z_3 = \frac{1}{2} - \frac{3}{2}i$ and $z_4 = 4 + 6i$.

Find: (i) z_1z_2 (ii) z_3z_4

Solution

(i) $z_1z_2 = (2 - 7i)(3 + 7i)$

$= 2(3 + 7i) - 7i(3 + 7i)$ (Distributive property)

$= 6 + 14i - 21i - 49i^2$

$= 6 - 7i - 49(-1)$

$= 6 - 7i + 49$

$\therefore z_1z_2 = 55 - 7i$

(ii) $z_3z_4 = \left(\frac{1}{2} - \frac{3}{2}i\right)(4 + 6i)$

$= \frac{1}{2}(4 + 6i) - \frac{3}{2}i(4 + 6i)$

$= 2 + 3i - 6i - 9i^2$

$= 2 - 3i - 9(-1)$

$= 2 - 3i + 9$

$\therefore z_3z_4 = 11 - 3i$

Multiplication of complex numbers is a closed operation, i.e. the product of two complex numbers is itself a complex number.

Worked Example 8.17

Evaluate: (i) $(\sqrt{5} - 3i)(\sqrt{5} + 3i)$ (ii) $(\sqrt{2} + \sqrt{3}i)(\sqrt{2} - \sqrt{3}i)$

Solution

(i) $(\sqrt{5} - 3i)(\sqrt{5} + 3i)$

$= \sqrt{5}(\sqrt{5} + 3i) - 3i(\sqrt{5} + 3i)$

$= 5 + 3\sqrt{5}i - 3\sqrt{5}i - 9i^2$

$= 5 - 9(-1)$

$= 5 + 9$

$= 14$

(ii) $(\sqrt{2} + \sqrt{3}i)(\sqrt{2} - \sqrt{3}i)$

$= \sqrt{2}(\sqrt{2} - \sqrt{3}i) + \sqrt{3}i(\sqrt{2} - \sqrt{3}i)$

$= 2 - \sqrt{6}i + \sqrt{6}i - 3i^2$

$= 2 - 3(-1)$

$= 2 + 3$

$= 5$

Worked Example 8.18

$z_1 = 3 + 4i$ and $z_2 = 5 + 12i$.

(i) Find $|z_1|$ and $|z_2|$.

(ii) Evaluate z_1z_2.

(iii) Find $|z_1z_2|$.

(iv) How are $|z_1||z_2|$ and $|z_1z_2|$ related?

Solution

(i) $|z_1| = |3 + 4i|$

$= \sqrt{(3)^2 + (4)^2}$

$= \sqrt{9 + 16}$

$= \sqrt{25}$

$\therefore |z_1| = 5$

$|z_2| = |5 + 12i|$

$= \sqrt{(5)^2 + (12)^2}$

$= \sqrt{25 + 144}$

$= \sqrt{169}$

$\therefore |z_2| = 13$

(ii) $z_1z_2 = (3 + 4i)(5 + 12i)$

$= 3(5 + 12i) + 4i(5 + 12i)$

$= 15 + 36i + 20i + 48i^2$

$= 15 + 56i + 48(-1)$

$= 15 + 56i - 48$

$\therefore z_1z_2 = -33 + 56i$

(iii) $|z_1z_2| = |-33 + 56i|$

$= \sqrt{(-33)^2 + (56)^2}$

$= \sqrt{1{,}089 + 3{,}136}$

$= \sqrt{4{,}225}$

$\therefore |z_1z_2| = 65$

(iv) $|z_1||z_2| = (5)(13)$ (From part (i))

$= 65$

$= |z_1z_2|$

Therefore, $|z_1||z_2| = |z_1z_2|$.

Exercise 8.5

1. $z_1 = 3 + i$

(i) Find z_2 if $z_2 = iz_1$.

(ii) Plot z_1 and z_2 on an Argand diagram.

(iii) Describe the transformation that maps z_1 onto z_2.

2. $z_1 = -3 + 2i$

(i) Find z_2 if $z_2 = iz_1$.

(ii) Plot z_1 and z_2 on an Argand diagram.

(iii) Describe the transformation that maps z_1 onto z_2.

3. $z_1 = -3 + 4i$

(i) Find z_2 if $z_2 = -iz_1$.

(ii) Plot z_1 and z_2 on an Argand diagram.

(iii) Describe the transformation that maps z_1 onto z_2.

4. $z_1 = -2 - 3i$

(i) Find z_2 if $z_2 = -iz_1$.

(ii) Plot z_1 and z_2 on an Argand diagram.

(iii) Describe the transformation that maps z_1 onto z_2.

5. Evaluate the following products:

(i) $7i(3 + 5i)$ (iii) $2(7 + i)$ (v) $7(2 - i)$

(ii) $i(3 - i)$ (iv) $3(1 + 5i)$ (vi) $-2(4 + i)$

6. Write the following products in the form $a + bi$:

(i) $(2 + 7i)(3 - 5i)$ (vi) $(1 + i)(7 - 3i)$

(ii) $(1 + 4i)(2 + 5i)$ (vii) $(1 - i)(1 + i)$

(iii) $(6 + i)(-2 + 3i)$ (viii) $(-2 - 2i)(-2 + 2i)$

(iv) $(2 + 3i)(2 - 3i)$ (ix) $(7 + 5i)(2 + i)$

(v) $(3 + 4i)(3 - 4i)$ (x) $(3 - 2i)(7i)$

7. Write the following products in the form $a + bi$:

(i) $\left(\frac{1}{2} + \frac{3}{2}i\right)\left(\frac{1}{2} - \frac{1}{4}i\right)$ (iv) $(\sqrt{3} + 2i)(\sqrt{3} - 2i)$

(ii) $\left(\frac{1}{5} + \frac{3}{5}i\right)\left(\frac{1}{5} - \frac{3}{5}i\right)$ (v) $(3\sqrt{7} + 5i)(3\sqrt{7} - 5i)$

(iii) $\left(\frac{3}{8} + \frac{2}{11}i\right)\left(\frac{1}{4} - \frac{2}{5}i\right)$ (vi) $(\sqrt{2} + \sqrt{3}i)(\sqrt{8} - \sqrt{3}i)$

8. $z_1 = 3 + 4i$ and $z_2 = 10 - 24i$.

(i) Write, in the form $a + bi$, the product z_1z_2.

(ii) Evaluate $|z_1|$, $|z_2|$ and $|z_1z_2|$.

(iii) Show that $|z_1||z_2| = |z_1z_2|$.

9. Copy the diagram below.

(i) Multiply each complex number on the diagram by i.

(ii) Plot your answers from part (i).

(iii) Describe the transformation of the shape.

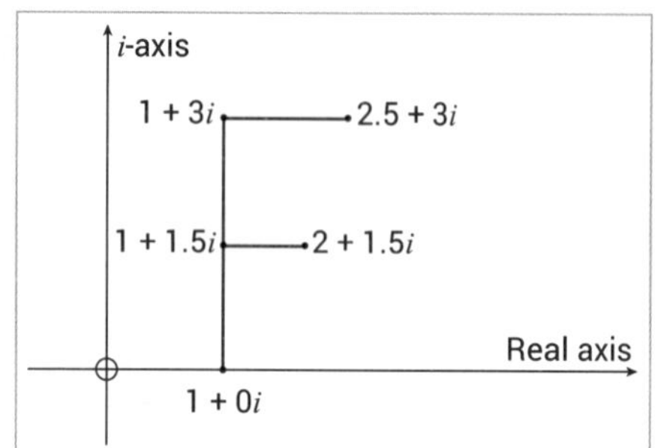

10. Copy the diagram below.

(i) Multiply each complex number on the diagram by $-i$.

(ii) Plot your answers from part (i).

(iii) Describe the transformation of the shape.

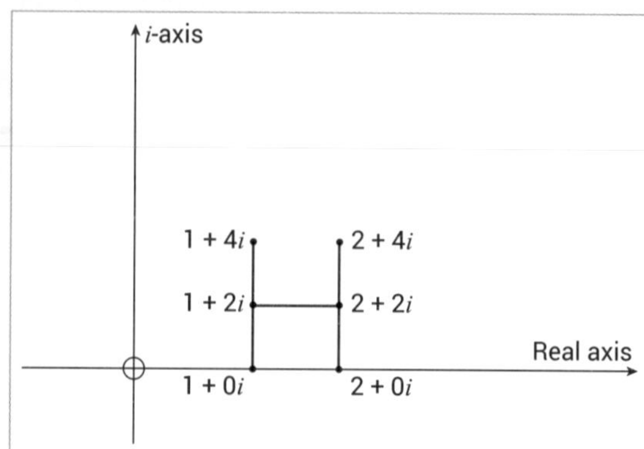

8.6 Conjugate of a Complex Number

If $z = a + bi$, $a, b \in R$ and $i^2 = -1$, then the **conjugate** of z is denoted $\bar{z}$ and is defined as $\bar{z} = a - bi$.

Worked Example 8.19

$z = -2 + 3i$. Find $\bar{z}$.

Solution

$\bar{z} = -2 - 3i$

Rule: Change the sign of the imaginary part.

Worked Example 8.20

$z_1 = 2 - 2i$, $z_2 = -4i$, and $z_3 = 5$.

(i) Find $\bar{z}_1$. (ii) Find $\bar{z}_2$. (iii) Find $\bar{z}_3$. (iv) Plot z_1 and $\bar{z}_1$ on the Argand diagram.

Solution

(i) $\bar{z}_1 = 2 + 2i$

(ii) $z_2 = 0 - 4i$

$\therefore \bar{z}_2 = 0 + 4i$

$= 4i$

(iii) $z_3 = 5 + 0i$

$\therefore \bar{z}_3 = 5 - 0i$

$= 5$

(iv)

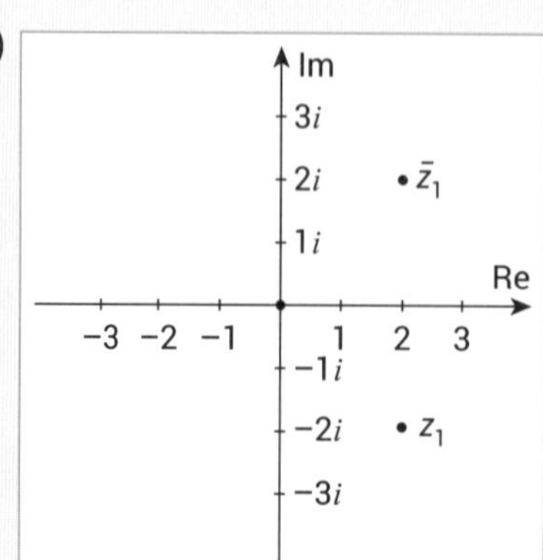

$\bar{z}$ is the image of z by an axial symmetry in the real axis.

Worked Example 8.21

$z = 1 + 2i$

(a) Find:

(i) $\bar{z}$ (iii) $z - \bar{z}$

(ii) $z + \bar{z}$ (iv) $z\bar{z}$

(b) Plot each solution in (a) on an Argand diagram.

(c) Describe how z is transformed by each operation in (a).

Solution

(a) (i) $\bar{z} = 1 - 2i$

(ii) $z + \bar{z} = (1 + 2i) + (1 - 2i)$

$= 2$ (A real number)

(iii) $z - \bar{z} = (1 + 2i) - (1 - 2i)$

$= 1 + 2i - 1 + 2i$

$= 4i$

(iv) $z\bar{z} = (1 + 2i)(1 - 2i)$

$= 1(1 - 2i) + 2i(1 - 2i)$

$= 1 - 2i + 2i - 4i^2$

$= 1 - 4(-1)$

$= 1 + 4$

$= 5$ (A real number)

(b)

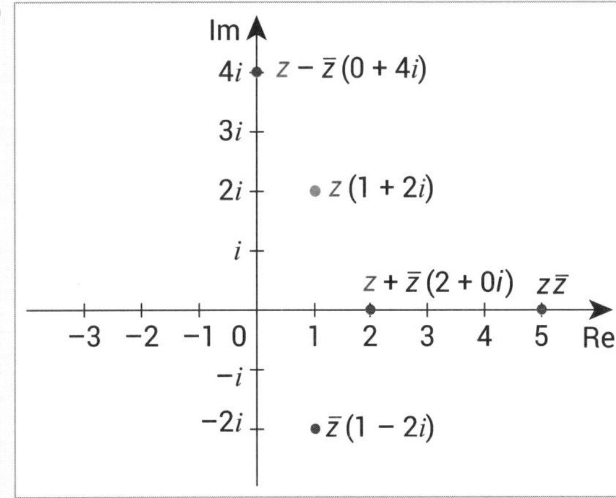

(c) (i) $\bar{z}$ is a reflection of z in the real axis.

(ii) $z + \bar{z}$ is a vertical projection of z onto the real axis followed by a translation of one unit to the right.

(iii) $z - \bar{z}$ is a horizontal projection of z onto the imaginary axis followed by a translation of two units upwards.

(iv) $z\bar{z}$ is a projection of z onto the real axis followed by a translation of four units to the right.

Exercise 8.6

1. Calculate the conjugate of each of these complex numbers:

(i) $1 + 2i$ (viii) $3 - 2i$

(ii) $3 + 6i$ (ix) $\frac{1}{2} - \frac{3}{4}i$

(iii) $-2 + 7i$ (x) $10 + 0i$

(iv) $-10 + 3i$ (xi) 3

(v) $-2 - 4i$ (xii) $0 + 3i$

(vi) $-3 - 5i$ (xiii) $-4i$

(vii) $-4 - i$ (xiv) $5i$

2. $z_1 = 7 + 5i$ and $z_2 = 2 + i$. Find:

(i) $\bar{z}_1$ (iii) $z_1 + \bar{z}_1$

(ii) $\bar{z}_2$ (iv) $z_2 + \bar{z}_2$

3. $z_1 = 5 + 2i$ and $z_2 = 3 - 4i$. Find:

(i) $\bar{z}_1$ (iv) $z_1 + z_2$

(ii) $\bar{z}_2$ (v) $\overline{z_1 + z_2}$

(iii) $\bar{z}_1 + \bar{z}_2$

4. $z_1 = -1 + 2i$ and $z_2 = 2 + 3i$. Find:

(i) $\bar{z}_1$ (iii) $\bar{z}_1 + \bar{z}_2$ (v) $\overline{z_1 + z_2}$

(ii) $\bar{z}_2$ (iv) $z_1 + z_2$

5. $z_1 = 5 + 6i$ and $z_2 = 3 - i$. Find:

(i) $\bar{z}_1$ (iii) z_1z_2 (v) $\bar{z}_1\bar{z}_2$

(ii) $\bar{z}_2$ (iv) $\overline{z_1z_2}$

6. Identify z_1, z_2, z_3, z_4 and z_5 on the Argand diagram using the following information:

(i) $z_1 = \bar{z}_2$ (iii) $z_4 = \text{Im}(z_3)$

(ii) $z_3 = 2z_2$ (iv) $z_5 = z_1 + \bar{z}_1$

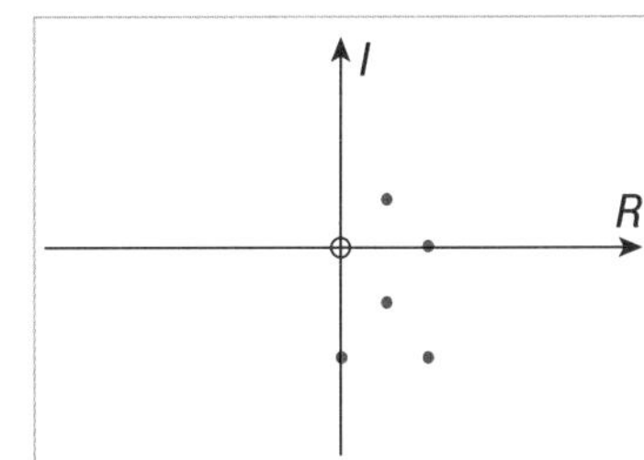

8.7 Dividing Complex Numbers 

In the real number system, if $\frac{a}{b} = c$, then $a = b \times c$, where $a, b, c \in R$.

Similarly, in the complex number system, if $\frac{a}{b} = c$, then $a = b \times c$, where $a, b, c \in C$.

However, in the complex number system, we need to follow certain well-defined steps to divide one complex number by another.

Worked Example 8.22

Calculate $\frac{15 + 10i}{5}$.

Solution

When we multiply a complex number z by a real number a, we multiply a by Re(z) and a by Im(z). Similarly, when we divide a complex number by a real number a, we divide Re(z) by a and Im(z) by a.

$$\frac{15 + 10i}{5} = \frac{15}{5} + \frac{10}{5}i$$
$$= 3 + 2i$$

Worked Example 8.23

Calculate $\frac{2 + 11i}{2 + i}$.

Solution

In this question we are dividing a complex number by a complex number. If we could reduce the denominator to a real number, then our task would be much easier, as we know how to divide a complex number by a real number. If we multiply a complex number by its conjugate, the result is a real number.

Step 1

Write down the conjugate of the denominator:
$\overline{2 + i} = 2 - i$

Step 2

Multiply the denominator by $2 - i$.

$$(2 + i)(2 - i) = 2(2 - i) + i(2 - i)$$
$$= 4 - 2i + 2i - i^2$$
$$= 4 - (-1)$$
$$= 4 + 1$$
$$= 5$$

Step 3

Multiply the numerator by $2 - i$.

$$(2 + 11i)(2 - i) = 2(2 - i) + 11i(2 - i)$$
$$= 4 - 2i + 22i - 11i^2$$
$$= 4 + 20i - 11(-1)$$
$$= 4 + 20i + 11$$
$$= 15 + 20i$$

Step 4

$$\frac{2 + 11i}{2 + i} = \frac{(2 + 11i)(2 - i)}{(2 + i)(2 - i)}$$
$$= \frac{15 + 20i}{5}$$
$$= \frac{15}{5} + \frac{20}{5}i$$
$$= 3 + 4i$$

Multiplying above and below by $(2 - i)$ is equivalent to multiplying the original quotient by 1, which does not change its value.

When dealing with division by a complex number, multiply both the numerator and the denominator by the conjugate of the denominator.

Worked Example 8.24

Write $\frac{15}{i}$ in the form $p + qi$, $p, q \in Q$ and $i^2 = -1$.

Solution

Step 1

Write down the conjugate of the denominator.

$\bar{i} = \overline{0 + i}$

$= 0 - i$

$\therefore \bar{i} = -i$

Step 2

Multiply the denominator by $-i$.

$(i)(-i) = -i^2$

$= -(-1)$

$= 1$

Step 3

Multiply the numerator by $-i$.

$15(-i) = -15i$

Step 4

$\frac{15}{i} = \frac{15(-i)}{i(-i)}$

$= \frac{-15i}{1}$

$= -15i$

$= 0 - 15i$

Exercise 8.7

1. Write the following in the form $p + qi$, $p, q \in Q$:

(i) $\frac{6 + 3i}{2}$ (ii) $\frac{15 - 20i}{5}$ (iii) $\frac{16 - 8i}{8}$ (iv) $\frac{5 + 12i}{7}$

2. Write the following in the form $p + qi$, $p, q \in R$:

(i) $\frac{5 + 5i}{1 + 2i}$ (ii) $\frac{1 - 5i}{1 - i}$ (iii) $\frac{5}{1 + 2i}$ (iv) $\frac{1 + 3i}{1 + i}$

3. Write the following in the form $p + qi$, $p, q \in R$:

(i) $\frac{5 - 5i}{2 + i}$ (ii) $\frac{6}{1 - i}$ (iii) $\frac{1 + 5i}{i}$ (iv) $\frac{6 + 8i}{2i}$ (v) $\frac{-7 + 24i}{3 + 4i}$

4. Write the following in the form $p + qi$, $p, q \in Q$:

(i) $\frac{1}{1 + i}$ (ii) $\frac{1 + 2i}{1 + 3i}$ (iii) $\frac{1 + 5i}{2 - i}$ (iv) $\frac{11 + 10i}{2(2 + 3i)}$ (v) $\frac{1 - 9i}{2i}$

5. Write the following in the form $p + qi$, $p, q \in Q$:

(i) $\frac{2 + i}{i}$ (ii) $\frac{8 - 4i}{2i}$ (iii) $\frac{27 - 18i}{3i}$ (iv) $\frac{-16 + 48i}{-4i}$ (v) $\frac{1 + i}{5i}$

6. Write in the form $p + qi$, $p, q \in Q$:

(i) $\frac{16}{i}$ (ii) $\frac{10}{2i}$ (iii) $\frac{25}{3i}$ (iv) $\frac{17}{5i}$ (v) $\frac{33}{12i}$

7. If $z = 1 - 3i$, write $\frac{\bar{z}}{z}$ in the form $a + bi$, $a, b \in Q$.

8. Let $z_1 = -1 + 5i$ and let $z_2 = 2 + 3i$.

Investigate whether $\overline{\left(\frac{z_1}{z_2}\right)} = \frac{\bar{z}_1}{\bar{z}_2}$.

9. Let $z_1 = -15 + 16i$ and let $z_2 = 6 + i$.

Investigate whether $\overline{\left(\frac{z_1}{z_2}\right)} = \frac{\bar{z}_1}{\bar{z}_2}$.

10. Let $z_1 = 11 - 10i$ and let $z_2 = 4 + i$.

(i) Find $\frac{z_1}{z_2}$.

(ii) Calculate $|z_1|$ and $|z_2|$.

(iii) Investigate whether $\left|\frac{z_1}{z_2}\right| = \frac{|z_1|}{|z_2|}$.

Revision Exercises

1. $z_1 = 3 + i$ and $z_2 = 4 - 2i$. Evaluate:
   (i) $z_1 + z_2$ (ii) $z_1 - z_2$ (iii) z_1z_2 (iv) $\bar{z}_2$ (v) $\frac{z_1}{z_2}$ (vi) $|z_2|$
2. $z_1 = 7 + i$ and $z_2 = -5 - 4i$. Evaluate:
   (i) $z_1 + z_2$ (ii) $z_1 - z_2$ (iii) z_1z_2 (iv) $\bar{z}_2$ (v) $\frac{z_1}{z_2}$ (vi) $|z_1 z_2|$
3. $z_1 = 2 + i$ and $z_2 = 11 + 9i$. Evaluate:
   (i) $z_1 - z_2$ (ii) $\frac{z_1}{z_2}$ (iii) $|z_1|$ (iv) $|z_2|$ (v) $\left|\frac{z_1}{z_2}\right|$ (vi) $\overline{z_1z_2}$
4. $z_1 = 21 + 28i$ and $z_2 = 9 - 40i$. Evaluate:
   (i) z_1z_2 (ii) $\overline{z_1z_2}$ (iii) $\bar{z}_1$ (iv) $\bar{z}_2$ (v) $\bar{z}_1\bar{z}_2$ (vi) $3z_1 - 2z_2$
5. $z_1 = 48 + 14i$ and $z_2 = 33 + 56i$. Evaluate:
   (i) z_1z_2 (ii) $|z_1z_2|$ (iii) $|z_1|$ (iv) $|z_2|$ (v) $|z_1||z_2|$ (vi) $-2z_1 + 3z_2$
6. $z_1 = 16 - 63i$ and $z_2 = 39 + 52i$. Evaluate:
   (i) $\frac{z_1}{z_2}$ (ii) $\frac{z_2}{z_1}$ (iii) $|z_2|$ (iv) $|z_1|$ (v) $2z_1 - z_2$ (vi) $2(z_1 - z_2)$
   Show that $\left|\frac{z_1}{z_2}\right| = \left|\frac{z_2}{z_1}\right|$.
7. $\omega = 1 - i$, $z_1 = 2 + i$, $z_2 = 3 - i$ and $z_3 = -2 - 4i$.
   (i) Plot z_1, z_2 and z_3 on an Argand diagram.
   (ii) Evaluate $\omega + z_1$, $\omega + z_2$, $\omega + z_3$ and plot your answers on the Argand diagram.
   (iii) Describe the transformation that is the addition of ω.
8. If $z_1 = -3 - i$ and $z_2 = 1 - i$, write the following in the form $a + bi$, $a, b \in R$:
   (i) $3z_1 - z_2$ (ii) $\bar{z}_2$ (iii) $\frac{z_1}{z_2}$
9. Evaluate the following:
   (i) i^5 (ii) i^6 (iii) i^7
   Hence, show that $z = i$ is a solution to the equation $4z^7 - 6z^6 + 4z^5 - 6 = 0$.

Exam Questions

1. Let $z_1 = 5 - i$ and $z_2 = 4 + 3i$, where $i^2 = -1$.
   (a) (i) Find $z_1 - z_2$.
   (ii) Verify that $|z_1 - z_2| = |z_2 - z_1|$.
   (iii) Give a reason why $|z - w| = |w - z|$ will always be true, for any complex numbers z and w.
   (b) Find a complex number z_3 such that $z_1 = \frac{z_2}{z_3}$.
   Give your answer in the form $a + bi$, where $a, b \in R$.

SEC Leaving Certificate Ordinary Level, Project Maths Paper 1, 2014

2. The complex number $z = 1 - 4i$, where $i^2 = -1$.
   (a) Plot z and $-2z$ on the Argand diagram.
   (b) Show that $2|z| = |-2z|$.
   (c) What does part **(b)** tell you about the points you plotted in part **(a)**?
   (d) Let k be a real number such that $|z + k| = 5$.
   Find the two possible values of k.

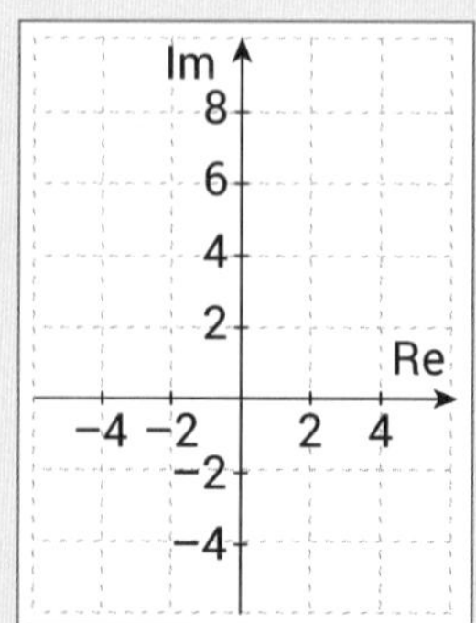

SEC Leaving Certificate Ordinary Level, Project Maths Paper 1, 2012

3. Let $z_1 = 3 - 4i$ and $z_2 = 1 + 2i$, where $i^2 = -1$.

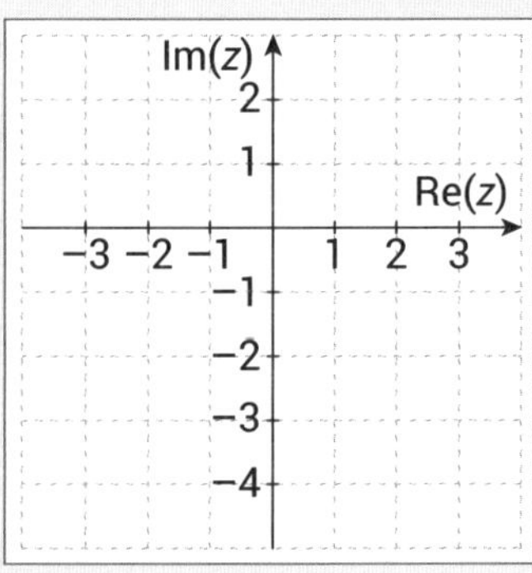

(a) Plot z_1 and z_2 on the Argand diagram above.

(b) From your diagram, is it possible to say that $|z_1| > |z_2|$?
Give the reason for your answer.

(c) Verify algebraically that $|z_1| > |z_2|$.

(d) Find $\frac{z_1}{z_2}$ in the form $x + yi$, where $x, y \in R$.

SEC Leaving Certificate Ordinary Level, Paper 1, 2013

4. $z_1 = 1 + 3i$ and $z_2 = 2 - i$, where $i^2 = -1$, are two complex numbers.

(a) Let $z_3 = z_1 + 2z_2$. Find z_3 in the form $a + bi$ where $a, b \in Z$.

(b) Plot z_1, z_2 and z_3 on an Argand diagram and label each point clearly.

(c) Investigate if $|z_2 - z_3| = |z_1 + z_2|$.

(d) Find the complex number w, such that $w = \frac{z_1}{z_2}$.
Give your answer in the form $a + bi$, where $a, b \in R$.

SEC Leaving Certificate Ordinary Level, Paper 1, 2016

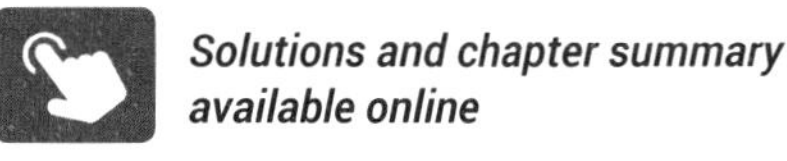

Solutions and chapter summary available online

Calculus

In this chapter you will learn to:

- Investigate the concept of the limit of a function
- Find first and second derivatives of linear, quadratic and cubic functions by rule
- Associate derivatives with slopes and tangent lines
- Apply differentiation to
  - rates of change
  - maxima and minima
  - curve sketching

You should remember...

- How to solve linear and quadratic equations
- How to find the equation of a line

Key words

- Derivative
- Slope
- Constant
- First derivative
- Second derivative
- Stationary points
- Maximum value
- Minimum value

9.1 Calculus

The discovery of calculus is often attributed to two men, Isaac Newton (1642–1727) and Gottfried Leibniz (1646–1716). They independently developed its foundations.

Newton was an English physicist, mathematician, astronomer and theologian.

Leibniz was a German philosopher and mathematician. He wrote in many languages, including Latin, French and German.

Isaac Newton (1642–1727)

Gottfried Leibniz (1646–1716)

9.2 Limits

The concept of the limit of a function was central to the development of calculus.

The distance–time graph shows the distance travelled by a particle from a fixed point 0 during the time interval [0 s, 4 s].

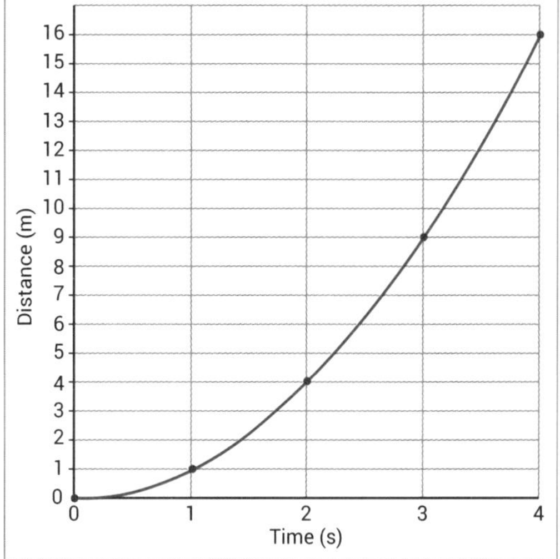

The distance travelled by the particle can be modelled by the function, $f(t) = t^2$. The table below gives the average speed of the particle over smaller and smaller time intervals that get closer and closer to 1 second.

Time interval $[1, t]$	Distance travelled $f(t) - f(1)$	Time taken	Average speed
[1, 4]	15 m	3 s	$\frac{15}{3} = 5 \text{ ms}^{-1}$
[1, 3]	8 m	2 s	$\frac{8}{2} = 4 \text{ ms}^{-1}$
[1, 2]	3 m	1 s	$\frac{3}{1} = 3 \text{ ms}^{-1}$
[1, 1.5]	1.25 m	0.5 s	$\frac{1.25}{0.5} = 2.5 \text{ ms}^{-1}$
[1, 1.25]	0.5625 m	0.25 s	$\frac{0.5625}{0.25} = 2.25 \text{ ms}^{-1}$

As the time intervals get smaller, the average speed over the intervals gets smaller. From the table, we see that the average speed approaches 2 ms^{-1} as the time intervals get smaller.

- Each time interval is of the form $[1, 1 + h]$.
  e.g. first time interval is $[1, 1 + 3] = [1, 4]$
- The time taken to travel over each interval is $(1 + h) - 1 = h$ seconds.
  e.g. time taken over first interval is $(1 + 3) - 1 = 3$ seconds
- The distance travelled over each interval is $f(1 + h) - f(1)$.
  e.g. distance travelled over first interval is $f(4) - f(1) = 16 - 1 = 15$ m
- Average speed over each interval is $v = \dfrac{f(1+h) - f(1)}{h}$.

As h gets smaller and smaller (i.e. approaches zero), then the average speed approaches 2 ms^{-1}.

We say, $\lim\limits_{h \to 0} v = 2 \text{ ms}^{-1}$.

Worked Example 9.1

The function $f(x) = 2x - 8$ is defined for all $x \in R$.
By drawing a graph of the function for values of x close to 5, find $\lim_{x \to 5} f(x)$.

Solution

We will graph the function in the domain $4 \leqslant x \leqslant 6$, as 5 is contained in this domain.

f(x)			
x	$2x - 8$	y	(x,y)
4	2(4) − 8	0	(4,0)
5	2(5) − 8	2	(5,2)
6	2(6) − 8	4	(6,4)

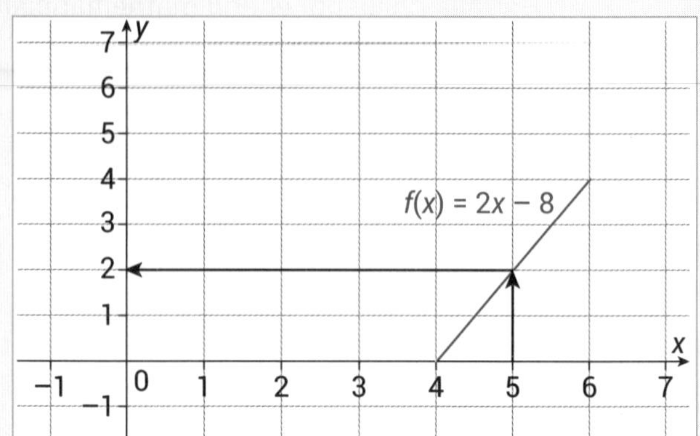

From the graph, we can see that as x approaches 5, $f(x)$ approaches 2.

We say, $\lim_{x \to 5} f(x) = 2$.

Exercise 9.1

1. The function $f(x) = 2x - 4$ is defined for all $x \in R$.
   (i) Copy and complete the following table:

x	$f(x)$	x	$f(x)$
1.0	−2	3.0	2
1.5		2.5	
1.8	−0.4	2.2	
1.9		2.1	0.2
1.95		2.05	
1.99		2.01	
1.995		2.005	
1.999		2.001	

   (ii) Hence, find $\lim_{x \to 2} f(x)$.

2. The function $g(x) = 2x^2 - 4$ is defined for all $x \in R$.
   (i) Copy and complete the following table:

x	$g(x)$	x	$g(x)$
4.0	28	6.0	68
4.5		5.5	
4.8	42.08	5.2	
4.9		5.1	48.02
4.95		5.05	
4.99		5.01	
4.995		5.005	
4.999		5.001	

   (ii) Hence, find $\lim_{x \to 5} g(x)$.

3. Use the graph of each function to find the required limit.
   (i) $\lim_{x \to 2} f(x)$

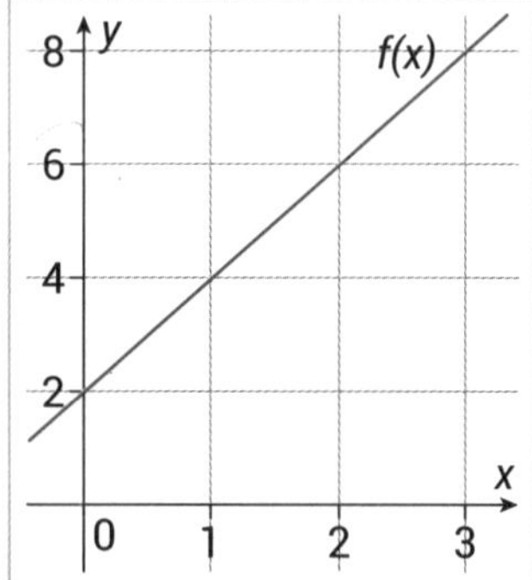

   (ii) $\lim_{x \to 0} m(x)$

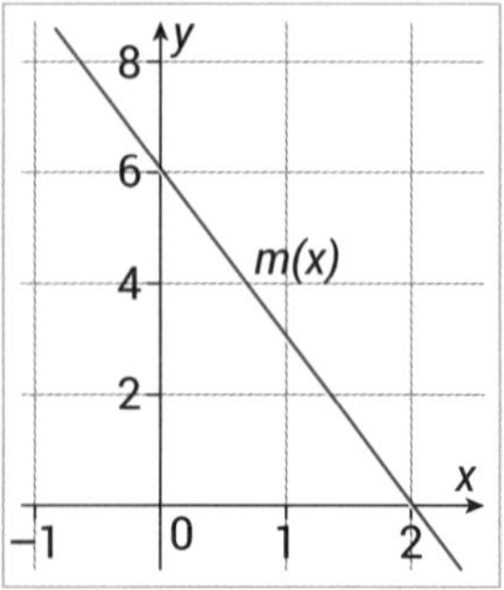

(iii) $\lim_{x \to 3} g(x)$

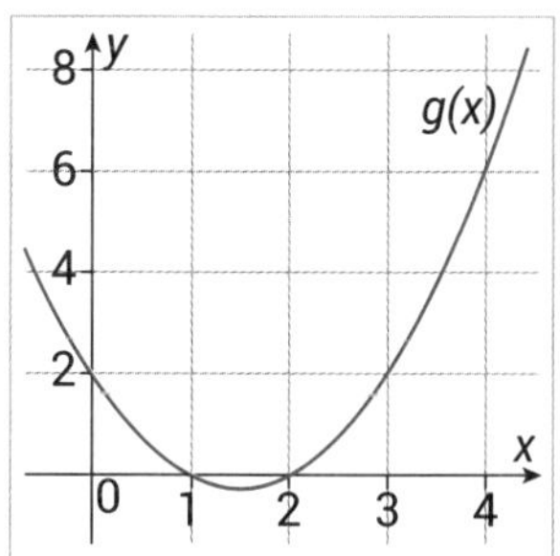

(iv) $\lim_{x \to 2} h(x)$

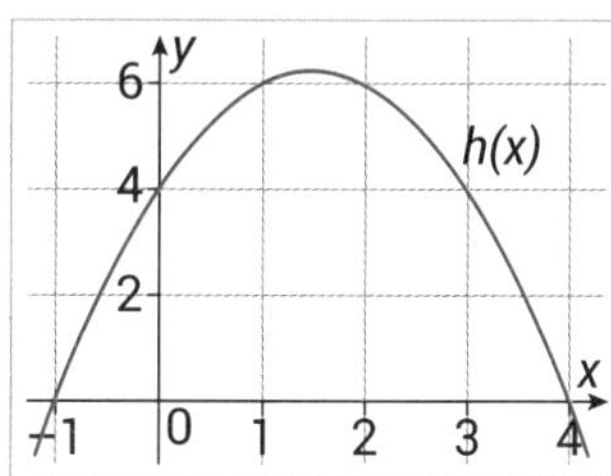

(v) $\lim_{x \to 3} p(x)$

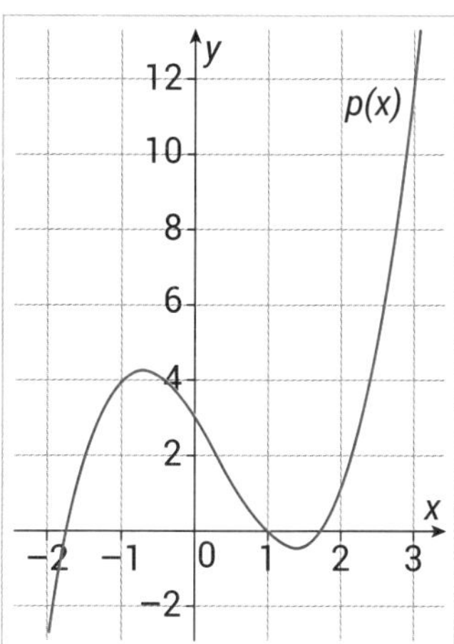

(vi) $\lim_{x \to 0} k(x)$

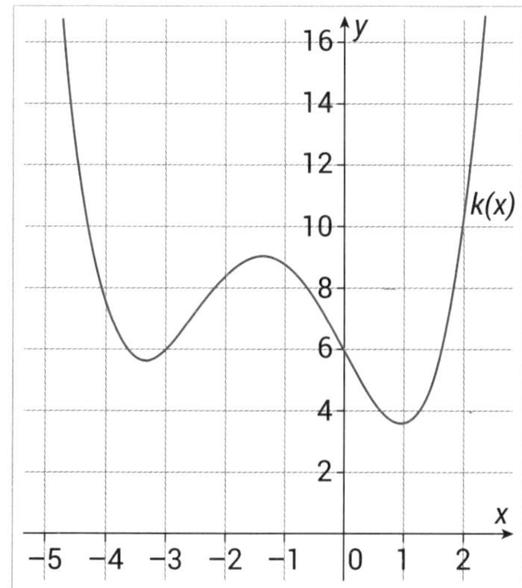

4. Evaluate each of the following limits:

(i) $\lim_{x \to 3} (x + 4)$

(ii) $\lim_{x \to 1} (2x - 3)$

(iii) $\lim_{x \to 2} (x^2)$

(iv) $\lim_{x \to 1} (x^2 - 2x + 4)$

(v) $\lim_{x \to 5} (x^3)$

(vi) $\lim_{x \to 3} (2x + 3)$

(vii) $\lim_{x \to -1} (2 - 3x)$

(viii) $\lim_{x \to 2} (5x^2)$

(ix) $\lim_{x \to 1} (5 - 6x - x^2)$

(x) $\lim_{x \to 3} (x^3 - 1)$

5. $f(x) = \frac{x^2 - 9}{x - 3}$, $x \in R$, $x \neq 3$

(i) Simplify $\frac{x^2 - 9}{x - 3}$ for $x \neq 3$.

(ii) Hence or otherwise, find $\lim_{x \to 3} f(x)$.

6. $f(x) = \frac{x^2 - 16}{x + 4}$, $x \in R$, $x \neq -4$

(i) Simplify $\frac{x^2 - 16}{x + 4}$ for $x \neq -4$.

(ii) Hence or otherwise, find $\lim_{x \to -4} f(x)$.

7. $f(x) = \frac{x^2 - 2x - 8}{x - 4}$, $x \in R$, $x \neq 4$

(i) Simplify $\frac{x^2 - 2x - 8}{x - 4}$ for $x \neq 4$.

(ii) Hence or otherwise, find $\lim_{x \to 4} f(x)$.

9.3 First Derivatives

Calculus is **the study of rates of change** and has applications in all the natural sciences, as well as in engineering, finance, economics and medicine.

In mathematics, we can use graphs to illustrate the rate at which things grow or decay. Graph A shows the growth of bacteria in a culture over a short interval of time. The graph indicates that the rate of growth is relatively small at the beginning but increases as time goes by.

Calculus enables us to find the growth rate at any instant in time. The growth rate at a particular time, t, is the slope of the tangent to the graph at t (Graph B).

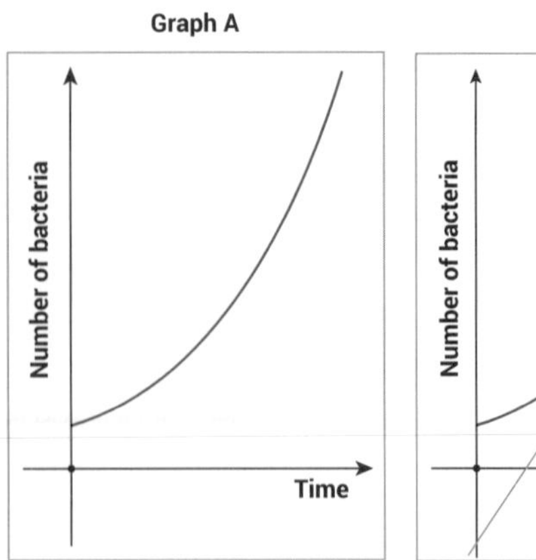

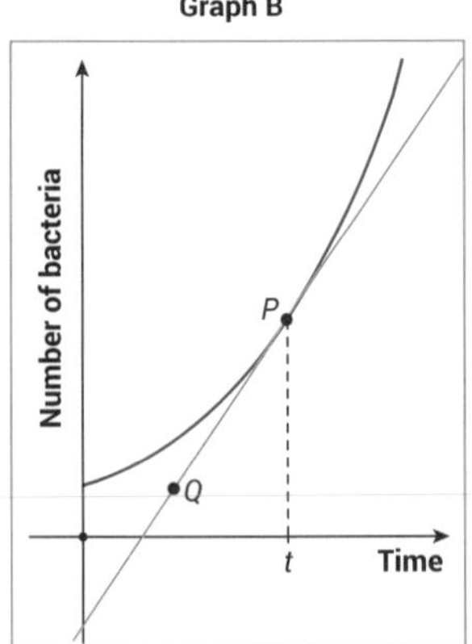

If a tangent is drawn at a point P on a curve, then the slope of this tangent is said to be the **slope of the curve** at P. In Graph B, the slope of the curve at P is equal to the slope of the tangent PQ.

The process of finding a general expression for the slope of a curve at any point is known as **differentiation**.

The expression for the slope of a curve $y = f(x)$ is itself a function, so it is called the slope function. In practice, it is more often called the **derived function** or the **derivative**.

For any curve $y = f(x)$, $\frac{dy}{dx}$ is the notation used for the slope.

$\frac{dy}{dx}$ represents the slope of the curve, i.e. the rate of change of y with respect to x.

The slope of the tangent to a curve $y = f(x)$ at any point $(x, f(x))$ on the curve is denoted by $\frac{dy}{dx}$ or $f'(x)$.

- $\frac{dy}{dx}$ is read as 'dee y dee x'.
- $f'(x)$ is read as 'f prime of x'.

Use the following rules to differentiate linear, quadratic and cubic functions.

Rule 1

If $y = ax$, where $x \in R$ and a is any constant, then $\frac{dy}{dx} = a$.

[Also written as $f'(x) = a$]

Rule 2

If $y = ax^2$, where $x \in R$ and a is any constant, then $\frac{dy}{dx} = 2ax$.

[Also written as $f'(x) = 2ax$]

Rule 3

If $y = ax^3$, where $x \in R$ and a is any constant, then $\frac{dy}{dx} = 3ax^2$.

[Also written as $f'(x) = 3ax^2$]

Rule 4

If $y = a$, where a is any constant, then $\frac{dy}{dx} = 0$.

Rule 5

If $y = f(x) + g(x)$, then $\frac{dy}{dx} = \frac{df}{dx} + \frac{dg}{dx}$.

[Differentiate both functions and add the resultant answers.]

If $y = x^n \Rightarrow \frac{dy}{dx} = nx^{n-1}$

See page 25 of *Formulae and Tables*.

CALCULUS

Worked Example 9.2

The distance–time graph shows the journey of a cyclist who leaves home at 12 noon and returns at 12.15.

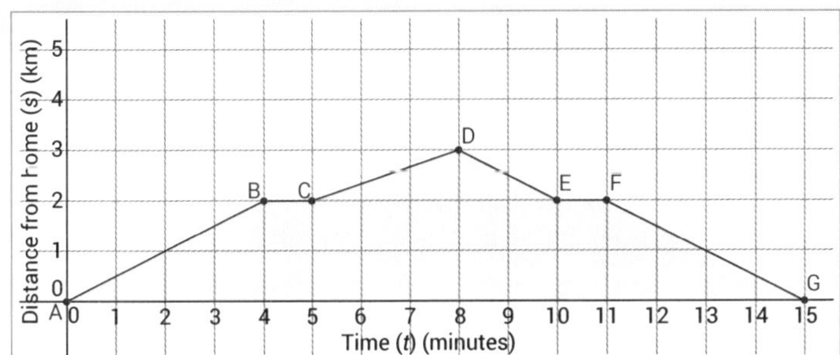

(i) Using the graph, explain why the cyclist does not accelerate during any stage of the journey.

(ii) At what time does the cyclist first stop?

(iii) At what time does the cyclist begin his return journey home?

(iv) What is the cyclist's speed between time A and time B?

(v) Find $\frac{ds}{dt}$ at $t = 13$.

(vi) What is the cyclist's average speed for the whole journey?

Solution

(i) The graph of the journey is made up of a series of linear functions. Therefore, for each of the time intervals [A, B], [B, C], [C, D], [D, E], [E, F] and [F, G] the speed is constant.

(ii) 12.04

(iii) 12.08

(iv) His speed is constant between time A (12 noon) and time B (12.04).

$$\text{Speed} = \frac{\text{Distance}}{\text{Time}}$$

$$\text{Speed} = \frac{2}{4}$$

$$= 0.5 \text{ km/min}$$

(v) Because the graph is linear between F and G, the cyclist's speed is constant during this interval.

$\frac{ds}{dt}$ represents the velocity of the cyclist, and as the slope of the function is $\frac{ds}{dt}$ we have

$$\frac{ds}{dt} = -\frac{2}{4}$$

$$= -0.5$$

So at $t = 13$, $\frac{ds}{dt} = -0.5$ km/min.

The velocity is negative, as the cyclist has changed direction and is now travelling in the opposite direction.

(vi) Average speed = $\frac{\text{Total distance}}{\text{Total time}}$

Total distance: From the graph, the cyclist cycles a distance of 3 km away from home and then returns home. He cycles a total of $2 \times 3 = 6$ km.

$$\text{Average speed} = \frac{6}{15}$$

$$= \frac{2}{5}$$

$$= 0.4 \text{ km/min}$$

Worked Example 9.3

Differentiate the following with respect to x:

(i) $f(x) = x^2$

(ii) $f(x) = 2x$

(iii) $f(x) = 4$

(iv) $f(x) = x^2 - 2x + 5$

(v) $f(x) = x^3 + 4x^2$

Solution

(i) $f'(x) = 2x$ (Rule 2)

(ii) $f'(x) = 2$ (Rule 1)

(iii) $f'(x) = 0$ (Rule 4)

(iv) $f'(x) = 2x - 2$ (Rules 1, 2, 4 and 5)

(v) $f'(x) = 3x^2 + 8x$ (Rules 2, 3 and 5)

Worked Example 9.4

If $y = x^2 - 3x + 8$, find $\frac{dy}{dx}$ when $x = -1$.

Solution

$\frac{dy}{dx} = 2x - 3$ (Differentiation)

At $x = -1$:

$\frac{dy}{dx} = 2(-1) - 3$ (Substitution)

$= -5$

Another way of asking this question is to find $f'(-1)$, given that $f(x) = x^2 - 3x + 8$.

Exercise 9.2

1.

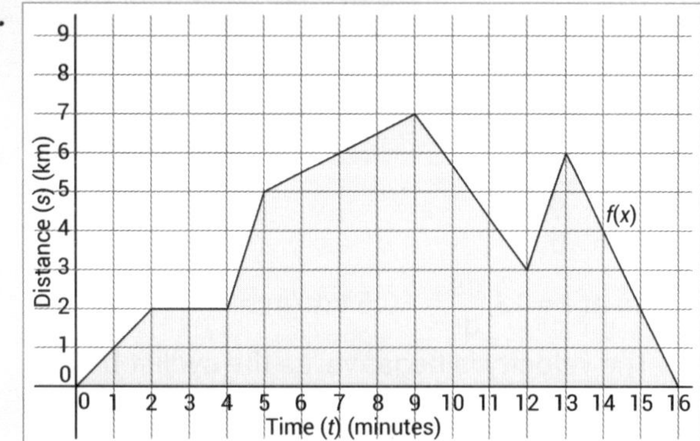

Use the graph of the function $f(x)$ to find $f'(x)$ for each of the following values of x.

(i) $x = 1$ (iv) $x = 11$

(ii) $x = 3$ (v) $x = 15$

(iii) $x = 8$

2. Differentiate with respect to x:

(i) $y = x^3$ (iv) $y = -8x$

(ii) $y = 3x^2$ (v) $y = -16x$

(iii) $y = 2x^3$ (vi) $y = \frac{1}{2}x^2$

3. For each of the following, find $\frac{ds}{dt}$:

(i) $s = 2t$ (iv) $s = \frac{1}{3}t^3$

(ii) $s = 3t^2$ (v) $s = \frac{1}{2}t^2$

(iii) $s = 5t^3$ (vi) $s = -15t$

4. Differentiate with respect to x:

(i) $y = 4$ (iv) $y = \sqrt{2}$

(ii) $y = -8$ (v) $y = 0.25$

(iii) $y = \frac{1}{2}$ (vi) $y = 12.25$

5. Find $\frac{dy}{dx}$ when:

(i) $y = 3x$ (iv) $y = 12 - 15x$

(ii) $y = 5 - 2x$ (v) $y = 2 - x$

(iii) $y = 17x + 12$ (vi) $y = x^2 - 3x - 6$

6. Differentiate the following with respect to the letter in brackets.

Note that you can differentiate with respect to any variable.
For example, $\frac{ds}{dt}$, $\frac{dA}{dr}$.

(i) $y = \frac{1}{2}x^2$ [x] (iv) $A = \frac{1}{2}\pi r^2$ [r]

(ii) $s = \frac{1}{3}t^3$ [t] (v) $C = 2\pi r$ [r]

(iii) $A = \pi r^2$ [r] (vi) $V = x^3$ [x]

7. Differentiate the following with respect to x:

(i) $y = 4x^2 + 2x + 6$ (iv) $y = 3x^3 + 4x^2 - 3x + 8$

(ii) $y = 3x^2 + 10x + 2$ (v) $y = 3x^2 + 4$

(iii) $y = x^2 + 9x + 12$

8. Find $f'(x)$ when:

(i) $f(x) = x^3 + x^2 + x$

(ii) $f(x) = x^3 - x$

(iii) $f(x) = x^3 + x$

(iv) $f(x) = 10x^3 + 11x^2$

(v) $f(x) = 9x^3 - 8x^2$

(vi) $f(x) = x^3 + 6x^2 - 3x + 8$

CALCULUS

9. Find $\frac{dy}{dx}$ when:
   (i) $y = x^3 + x^2 - x + 1$
   (ii) $y = 3x^3 + 2x^2 - x + 1$

10. $f(x) = x^2 - 2x + 12$
   (i) Find $f'(x)$. (ii) Evaluate $f'(100)$.

11. $f(x) = x^3 - x^2 + 4$
   (i) Find $f'(x)$. (ii) Evaluate $f'(-5)$.

12. $y = x^3 - 3x^2 + 2x - 8$
   (i) Find $\frac{dy}{dx}$.
   (ii) Evaluate $\frac{dy}{dx}$ when $x = 3$.

13. $y = 2x^3 + 3x^2 - 2x + 7$
   (i) Find $\frac{dy}{dx}$. (ii) Evaluate $\frac{dy}{dx}$ when $x = -1$.

14. $y = 5x^3 - 2x^2 - 12x + 10$
   (i) Find $\frac{dy}{dx}$. (ii) Evaluate $\frac{dy}{dx}$ when $x = 0$.

15. $f(x) = (x - 3)(x + 4)$, $x \in R$.
   (i) Write $f(x)$ in the form $f(x) = x^2 + mx + n$, $m, n \in Z$.
   (ii) Hence, find $f'(x)$.
   (iii) Evaluate $f(1)$.
   (iv) Evaluate $f'(1)$.

9.4 Second Derivatives

When a function $y = f(x)$ is differentiated with respect to x, the derivative is written as $\frac{dy}{dx}$ or $f'(x)$.

If the function is differentiated again, the second derivative is obtained and is written as $\frac{d^2y}{dx^2}$ or $f''(x)$.

$\frac{d^2y}{dx^2}$ is read as 'dee squared *y* dee *x* squared'.

$f''(x)$ is read as '*f* double prime of *x*'.

Worked Example 9.5

For each of the following functions, find the second derivative:

(i) $y = 5x^2 + 2x - 6$ (ii) $f(x) = 8x^3 + 10x$

Solution

(i) $y = 5x^2 + 2x - 6$

$\frac{dy}{dx} = 10x + 2$ Differentiate once.

$\frac{d^2y}{dx^2} = 10$ Differentiate a second time.

(ii) $f(x) = 8x^3 + 10x$

$f'(x) = 24x^2 + 10$ Differentiate once.

$f''(x) = 48x$ Differentiate a second time.

Worked Example 9.6

If $s(t) = 10t + 20t^2 - t^3$, show that $s''(5) = 10$.

Solution

$s(t) = 10t + 20t^2 - t^3$

$s'(t) = 10 + 40t - 3t^2$ Differentiate once.

$s''(t) = 40 - 6t$ Differentiate a second time.

$s''(5) = 40 - 6(5)$ Substitute.

$= 40 - 30$

$= 10$

Exercise 9.3

1. For each of the following functions, find the second derivative:
   (i) $y = 12x^2 - 2x - 6$
   (ii) $y = 8x^2 + 10x + 2$
   (iii) $y = 9x^2 + 9x + 12$
   (iv) $y = 23x^3 + 2x^2 - 3x - 9$
   (v) $y = 33x^2 + 4$

2. For each of the following functions, find $f''(x)$ at $x = -3$:
   (i) $f(x) = x^3 + x$
   (ii) $f(x) = x^2 - x$
   (iii) $f(x) = x^3 + x^2 + x$
   (iv) $f(x) = 10x^3 + 11x^2$
   (v) $f(x) = 9x^2 - 8x^3$

3. For each of the following, find $\frac{d^2s}{dt^2}$:
   (i) $s = 4.9t^2$
   (ii) $s = 5t - 4.9t^2$
   (iii) $s = t^3 + t^2 - 5t$
   (iv) $s = t^4 - t^2$

4. Find the second derivative of each of the following functions:
   (i) $f(x) = x^3$
   (ii) $f(x) = x^3 - 3x^2$
   (iii) $g(t) = -4t^2$
   (iv) $A(r) = \pi r^2$

5. The function $f(x) = 3x^3 - 9x + 2$ is defined for all real values of x.
   (i) Find $f''(x)$, the second derivative of $f(x)$.
   (ii) Hence, find $f''(2)$.

6. The function $f(x) = x^3 + 3x + 2$ is defined for all real values of x.
   (i) Find $f''(x)$, the second derivative of $f(x)$.
   (ii) Hence, find the value of x for which $f''(x) = f'(x)$.

CALCULUS

9.5 Slopes of Tangents

We have already seen that the slope of the tangent to a curve $y = f(x)$ at any point $(x, f(x))$ on the curve is given by:

$$\frac{dy}{dx} \quad \textbf{OR} \quad f'(x)$$

Worked Example 9.7

A graph of the cubic function $f(x) = 2x^3 + 5x^2 + x - 3$ is shown. The tangent t to $f(x)$ at the point (0,−3) is also shown on the diagram.

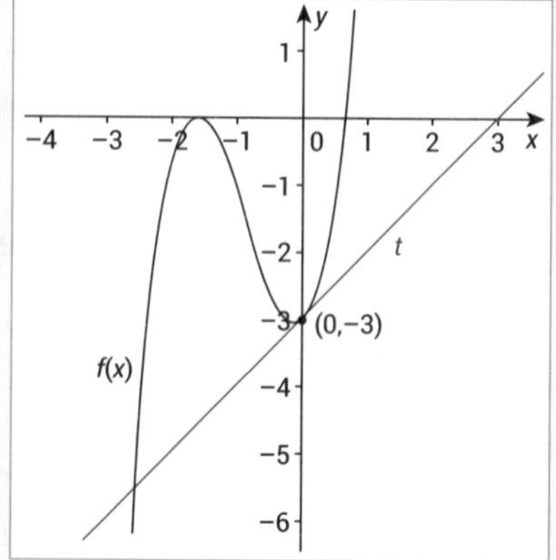

(i) Write down $f'(x)$, the derivative of $f(x)$.
(ii) Hence, find the slope of the tangent to $f(x)$ at (0,−3).
(iii) Find the equation of this tangent line.

Solution

(i) $f(x) = 2x^3 + 5x^2 + x - 3$

$\Rightarrow f'(x) = 6x^2 + 10x + 1$

(ii) To find the slope of the tangent at a particular point, substitute the x co-ordinate of the point into the derived function.

We need to find the slope of the tangent at (0,−3).

$\therefore f'(0) = 6(0)^2 + 10(0) + 1$

$\Rightarrow f'(0) = 1$

Therefore, the slope of the tangent to the curve at $x = 0$ is 1.

(iii) $y - y_1 = m(x - x_1)$ Point: (0,−3), $m = 1$

$y - (-3) = 1(x - 0)$

$\therefore y + 3 = 1(x - 0)$

$y + 3 = x$

$\therefore y = x - 3$ (Equation of tangent)

See Finding the equation of a line in Chapter 18.

If asked for the equation in the form, $ax + by + c = 0$:

$y = x - 3$

$0 = x - y - 3$

$\therefore x - y - 3 = 0$

Worked Example 9.8

Find a point on the curve $y = x^2 - 8x + 21$ where the tangent to the curve has a slope of 4.

Solution

$y = x^2 - 8x + 21$

$\Rightarrow \frac{dy}{dx} = 2x - 8$ (Slope of all tangents to the curve)

The slope of the required tangent to the curve is 4.

Set $2x - 8 = 4$

$2x = 12$

$\therefore x = 6$

We must now find the y co-ordinate when $x = 6$.

$y = x^2 - 8x + 21$

Let $x = 6$.

$y = (6)^2 - 8(6) + 21$

$\Rightarrow y = 9$

Therefore, the required point is (6,9).

Exercise 9.4

1. The diagram shows a tangent to the curve $f(x) = x^2 + 2x + 1$ at the point (0,1).

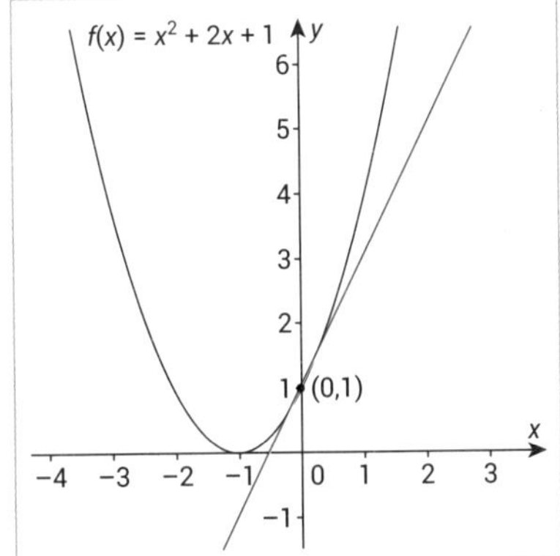

(i) Write down $f'(x)$, the derivative of $f(x)$.

(ii) Hence, find the slope of the tangent to $f(x)$ at (0,1).

(iii) Find the equation of the tangent to the curve at (0,1).

2. Below is a diagram showing a tangent to the curve $f(x) = 5 + 3x - x^2$ at the point (4,1).

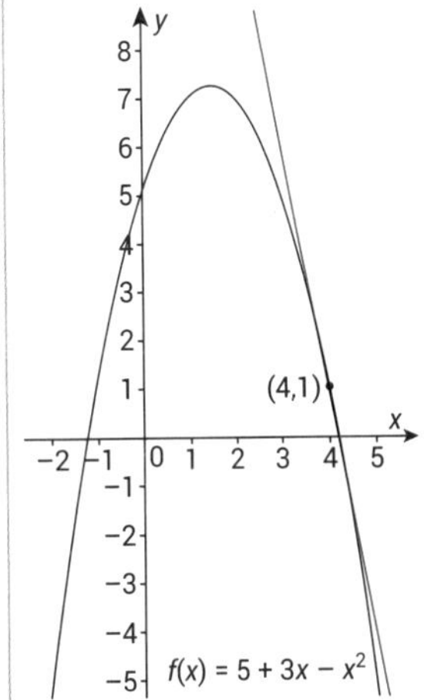

(i) Write down $f'(x)$, the derivative of $f(x)$.

(ii) Find the equation of the tangent to $f(x)$ at (4,1).

3. Show that the tangent to the curve $y = x^2 - 2x + 5$ at the point (1,4) has a slope of zero.

4. Find the point on the curve $y = x^2 - 2x + 11$ where the slope is equal to 6.

5. Find the point on the curve $f(x) = x^2 - 6x + 11$ where the tangent is parallel to the x-axis.

6. The function $f(x) = x^2 - 2x + 9$ is defined for all real values of x.
   (i) Find the value of x for which $f'(x) = 8$.
   (ii) Hence, find the equation of the tangent to the curve of $f(x)$ that has a slope of 8.

7. A graph of the cubic function $f(x) = 1 + 2x + 3x^2 - x^3$ is shown.
   The tangent to $f(x)$ at the point (0,1) is also shown on the diagram.

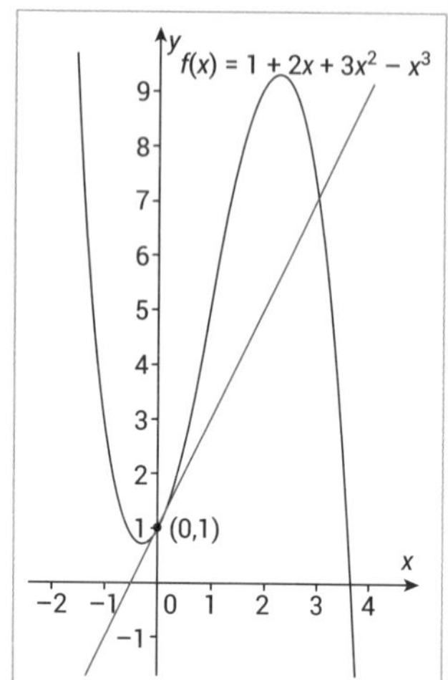

   (i) Write down $f'(x)$, the derivative of $f(x)$.
   (ii) Hence, find the slope of the tangent to $f(x)$ at (0,1).
   (iii) Find the equation of the tangent to the curve at (0,1).
   (iv) Find the co-ordinates of the points where the tangent intersects the x-axis and the y-axis.
   (v) Hence, calculate the area enclosed between the tangent, the x-axis and the y-axis.
   (vi) Show that the tangent intersects the curve at the point (3,7).

9.6 Increasing and Decreasing Functions

A function $f(x)$ **increases** on an interval, I, if $f(b) \geqslant f(a)$ for all $b > a$, where $a, b \in I$.

If $f(b) > f(a)$ for all $b > a$, the function is said to be **strictly increasing** on the interval I.

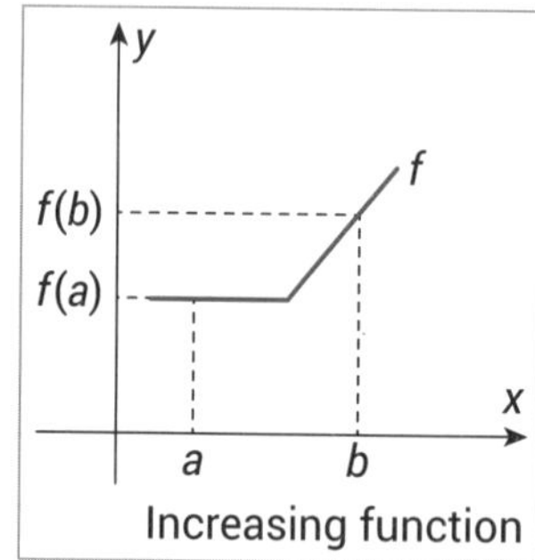

Increasing function

Strictly increasing function

A function $f(x)$ **decreases** on an interval, I, if $f(b) \leqslant f(a)$ for all $b > a$, where $a, b \in I$.

If $f(b) < f(a)$ for all $b > a$, the function is said to be **strictly decreasing** on the interval I.

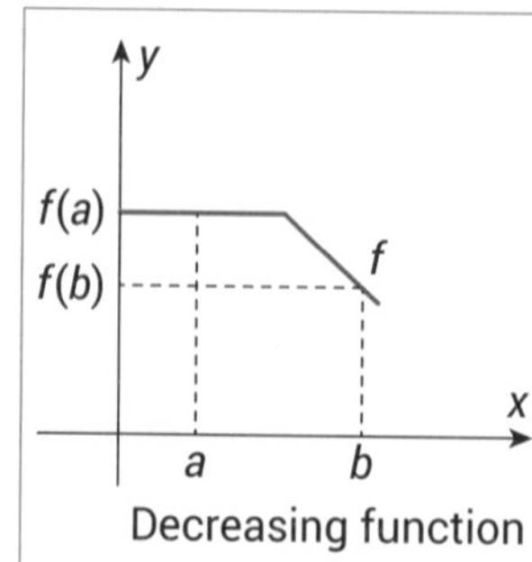

Decreasing function

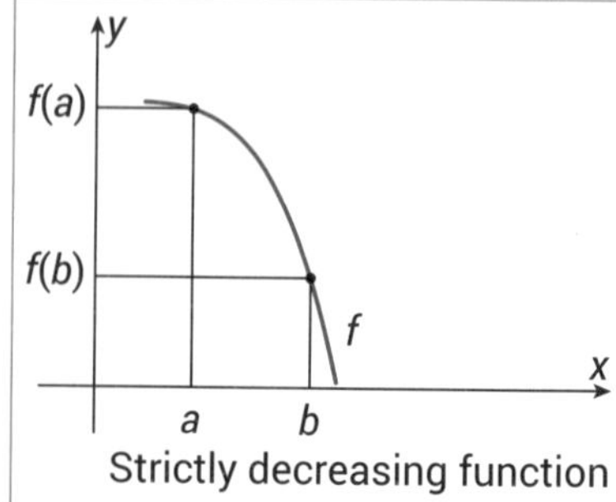

Strictly decreasing function

Worked Example 9.9

$f(x) = x^3 - 3x^2 + 1, x \in R$.

(i) Write down $f'(x)$, the derivative of $f(x)$.

(ii) Hence, find the range of values of x for which $f(x)$ is increasing.

Solution

(i) $f(x) = x^3 - 3x^2 + 1$

$\Rightarrow f'(x) = 3x^2 - 6x$

(ii) $f(x)$ increases when $f'(x) \geqslant 0$.

A sketch of the graph of $f'(x)$ will show us the x-values for which $f'(x) \geqslant 0$.

$f'(x) = 3x^2 - 6x$

$= 3x(x - 2)$

To find the x-intercepts:

Let $f'(x) = 0$.

$3x(x - 2) = 0$

$3x = 0$ **OR** $x - 2 = 0$

$x = 0$ **OR** $x = 2$

The coefficient of x^2 in $f'(x)$ is positive, therefore the graph is U-shaped.

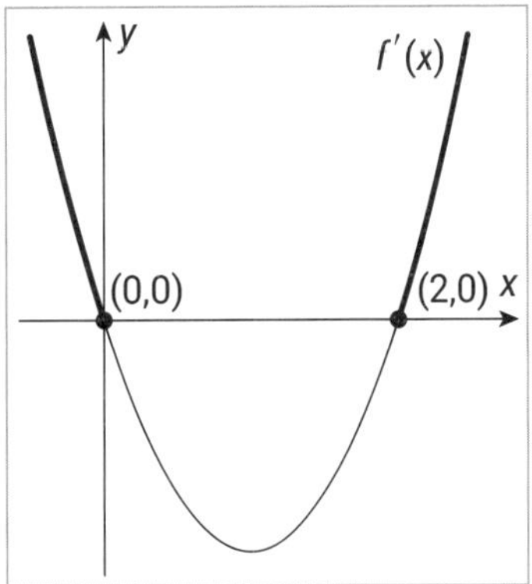

Reading from the graph, $f'(x) \geqslant 0$ when $x \leqslant 0$ or $x \geqslant 2$.

Therefore, $f(x)$ is increasing when $x \leqslant 0$ or $x \geqslant 2$.

Worked Example 9.10

The graph of a cubic function f is shown on the right.

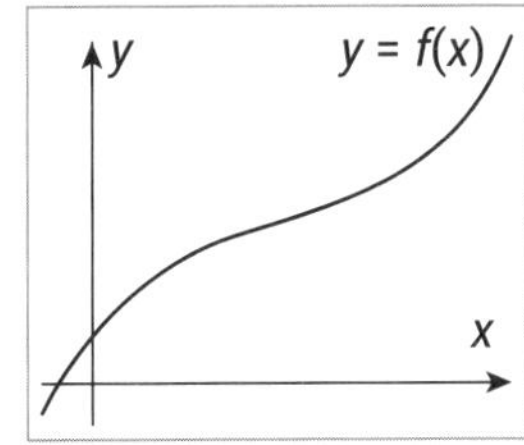

One of the four diagrams **A**, **B**, **C**, **D** below shows the graph of the derivative of f.

State which one it is, and justify your answer.

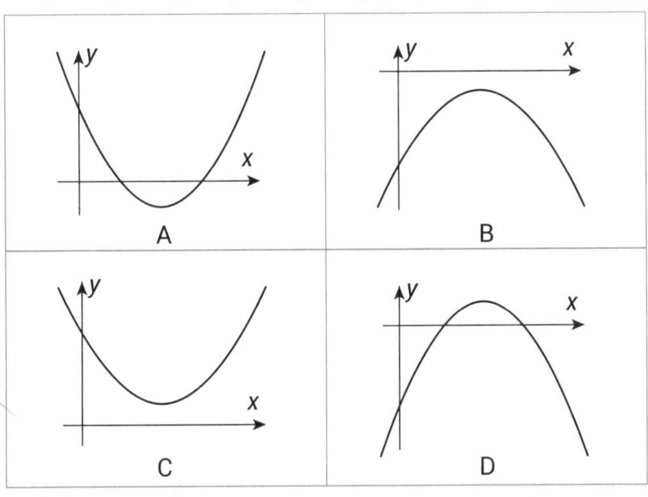

Solution

The cubic function f is strictly increasing, therefore its derivative is positive for all values of x.

Diagram C is the graph of the derivative of f because it is positive for all values of x. We know it is positive for all values of x since it is always above the x-axis.

Exercise 9.5

1. The diagrams below show the graphs of two cubic functions. For each function, write down the range of values of x for which the function is:
(a) decreasing (b) increasing

(i)

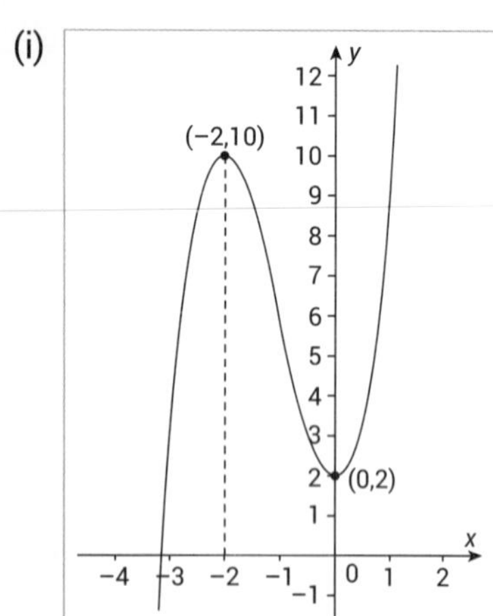

(ii)

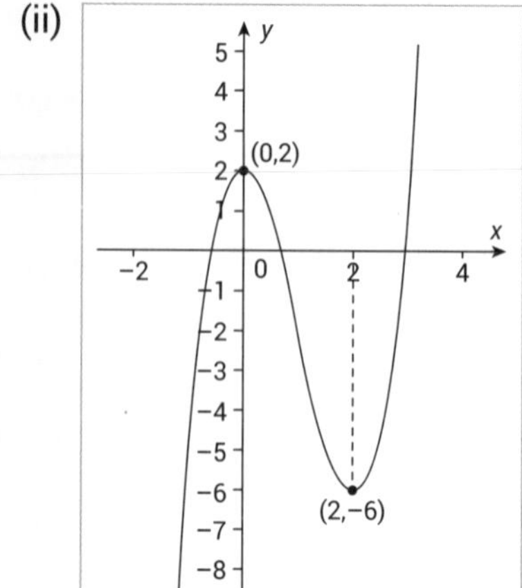

2. Find the range of values of x for which the following functions are increasing ($x \in R$):

(i) $f(x) = x^2 - 2x - 8$

(ii) $f(x) = x^2 + 3x - 5$

(iii) $f(x) = 2x^3 - 9x^2 + 12x - 5$

(iv) $f(x) = -27x + x^3$

(v) $f(x) = x^3 - x$

(vi) $f(x) = 18x - 15x^2 - 4x^3$

3. The graph of a quadratic function h is shown.

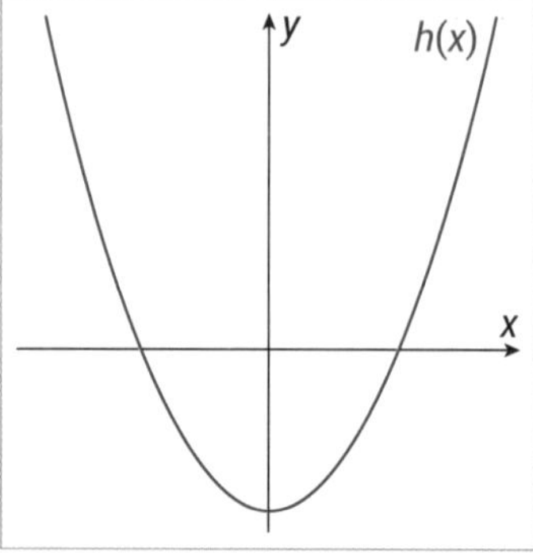

One of the two diagrams A and B below shows the graph of the derivative of h. State which one it is and justify your answer.

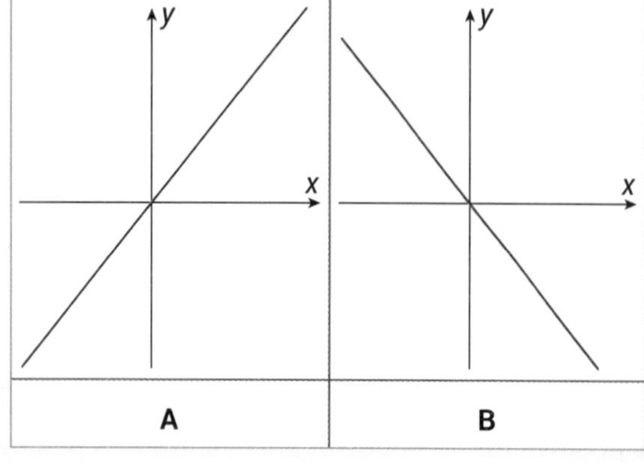

4. The graph of a quadratic function g is shown.

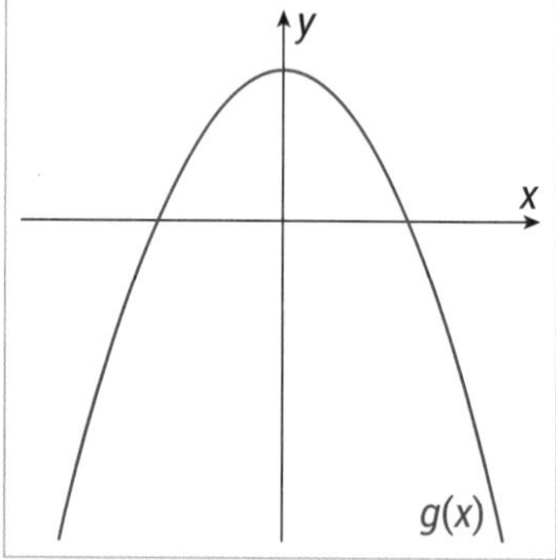

One of the two diagrams A and B below shows the graph of the derivative of g. State which one it is and justify your answer.

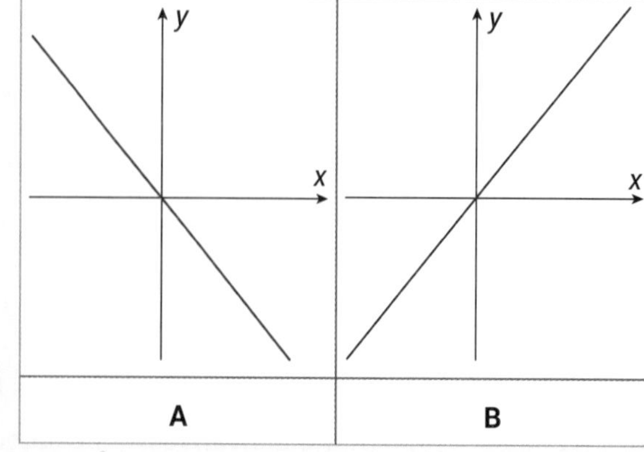

5. The graph of a cubic function f is shown.

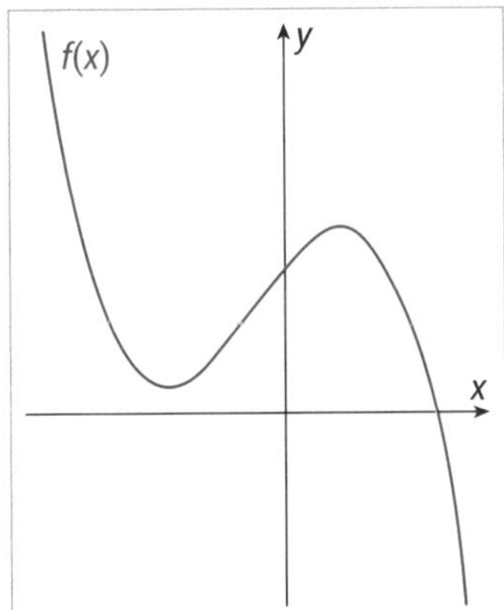

One of the four diagrams A, B, C and D shows the graph of the derivative of f. State which one it is and justify your answer.

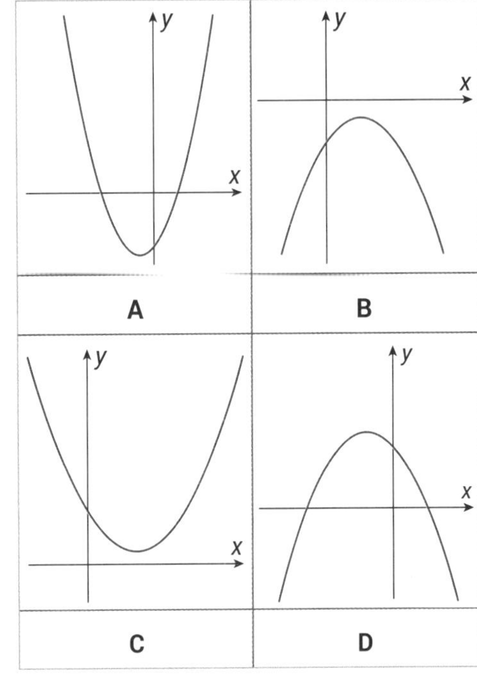

9.7 Maxima and Minima

At a stationary point on a curve, the slope is zero. For our course, we will look at two types of stationary points called **local maximum** and **local minimum** points. These are also called **turning points** because the graph turns at these points.

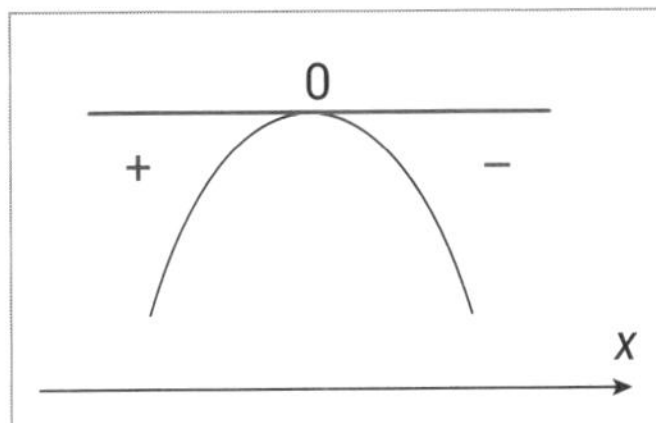

Maximum points – 'humps'

As x increases, the slope goes positive → 0 → negative.

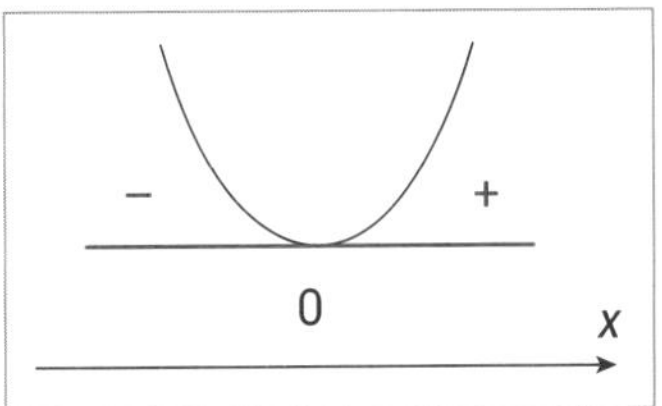

Minimum points – 'troughs'

As x increases, the slope goes negative → 0 → positive.

At a **stationary point** on a curve, the slope is zero,

i.e. $\frac{dy}{dx} = 0$.

If $f(x) = ax^2 + bx + c$ (i.e. f is a quadratic function) then,

(i) If $a > 0$, the turning point is a **local minimum**.

(ii) If $a < 0$, the turning point is a **local maximum**.

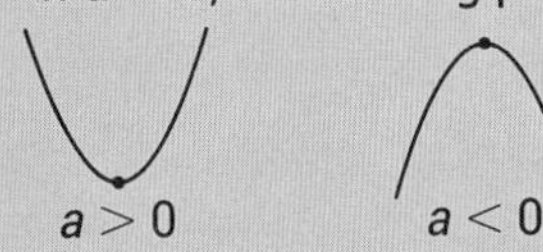

If $f(x) = ax^3 + bx^2 + cx + d$ is a cubic function with turning points, then such functions are of the following shapes:

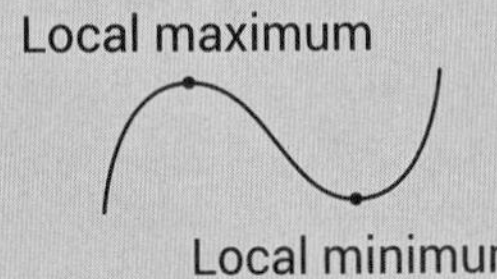

Local maximum

Local minimum

Such functions have two turning points.

The turning point with the larger y co-ordinate is the local maximum. The other one is the local minimum.

Worked Example 9.11

Let $f(x) = 2 - 9x + 6x^2 - x^3$ for $x \in R$.

(i) Find $f'(x)$, the derivative of $f(x)$.

(ii) Find the co-ordinates of the stationary points of $f(x)$.

(iii) Determine the nature of the stationary points.

(iv) At what point does the graph of $f(x)$ intersect the y-axis?

(v) Hence, sketch a graph of $f(x)$ in the domain $-1 \leqslant x \leqslant 5, x \in R$.

Solution

(i) $f(x) = 2 - 9x + 6x^2 - x^3$

$\Rightarrow f'(x) = -9 + 12x - 3x^2$

(ii) $f'(x) = 0$ for a stationary point.

Let $-9 + 12x - 3x^2 = 0$

$-3x^2 + 12x - 9 = 0$ (Reordering)

$3x^2 - 12x + 9 = 0$ (Change all signs)

$x^2 - 4x + 3 = 0$ (Divide by 3)

$(x - 3)(x - 1) = 0$ (Factorise)

$x = 3$ **OR** $x = 1$ (Solve for x)

We need to find the corresponding y-values.

Make sure that you use the original function.

$x = 1 \Rightarrow y = 2 - 9(1) + 6(1)^2 - (1)^3$

$\therefore y = -2$

$x = 3 \Rightarrow y = 2 - 9(3) + 6(3)^2 - (3)^3$

$\therefore y = 2$

Therefore, the stationary points are (1,−2) and (3,2).

(iii) Compare the y co-ordinates in (1,−2) and (3,2).

The co-ordinates of the local minimum are (1,−2) and the co-ordinates of the local maximum are (3,2).

(iv) Let $x = 0$ in $f(x)$, the original function.

$y = 2 - 9(0) + 6(0)^2 - (0)^3$

$y = 2$

Therefore, (0,2) is the y-intercept.

(v) $f(x) = 2 - 9x + 6x^2 - x^3$

We are required to sketch a graph for $-1 \leqslant x \leqslant 5$.

Therefore, we should find $f(-1)$ and $f(5)$.

$f(-1) = 2 - 9(-1) + 6(-1)^2 - (-1)^3$

$= 2 + 9 + 6 + 1$

$= 18$

(−1,18) is a point on the graph.

$f(5) = 2 - 9(5) + 6(5)^2 - (5)^3$

$= 2 - 45 + 150 - 125$

$= -18$

(5,−18) is a point on the graph.

Important points to plot:

- Turning points (1,−2) and (3,2)
- End points: (−1,18) and (5,−18)
- y-intercept: (0,2)

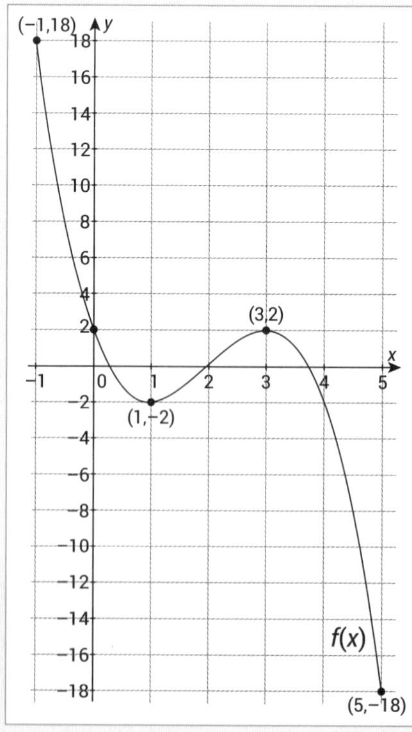

Exercise 9.6

1. Let $f(x) = x^3 - 3x + 1, x \in R$. The graph of $f(x)$ is shown.
   x_1 and x_2 are the x-values of the turning points of the curve of $f(x)$.

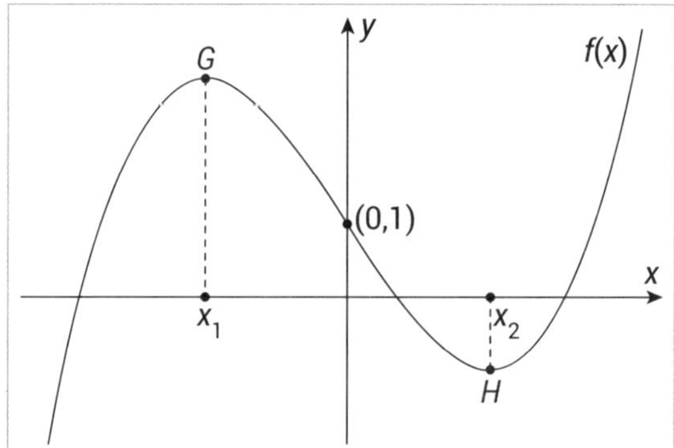

   (i) Solve the quadratic equation $f'(x) = 0$.
   (ii) Explain why the solutions to $f'(x) = 0$ are x_1 and x_2.
   (iii) Find the co-ordinates of G and H.

2. Find the co-ordinates of the turning point on the curve $y = x^2 + 2x - 8$. Determine the nature of the turning point.

3. Find the co-ordinates of the turning point on the curve $y = -x^2 + 9x - 14$. Determine the nature of the turning point.

4. Find the co-ordinates of the local maximum point and the local minimum point on the curve $y = 2x^3 - 3x^2 - 36x + 10$.

5. Find the co-ordinates of the local maximum point and the local minimum point on the curve $y = 10 + 15x + 6x^2 - x^3$.

6. Let $f(x) = (x + 1)^2(2 - x), x \in R$.
   (i) Write $f(x)$ in the form, $f(x) = ax^3 + bx^2 + cx + d$.
   (ii) Find the co-ordinates of the local maximum point and the local minimum point on the curve of $f(x)$.
   (iii) Find the co-ordinates of the points where the curve intersects the x-axis and y-axis.
   (iv) Draw a rough sketch of the curve.
   (v) Hence, write down the range of values of x for which $f(x)$ is increasing.

7. Let $f(x) = x^3 - 3x^2 - 24x, x \in R$.
   (i) Find the co-ordinates of the local maximum point and the local minimum point on the curve of $f(x)$.
   (ii) Show that the curve of $f(x)$ intersects the x-axis at $x = 0$.
   (iii) Draw a rough sketch of the curve, given that its negative x-intercept lies between -4 and -3 and its positive x-intercept lies between 6 and 7.

9.8 Maximum and Minimum Problems

Calculus is an important tool in solving maximum–minimum problems. We can use the analysis of stationary points to solve these real-life problems.

Worked Example 9.12

The diagram shows a square sheet of cardboard of side length 30 cm, from which four small squares, each of side length x, have been removed. The sheet can be folded to form an open rectangular box of height x.

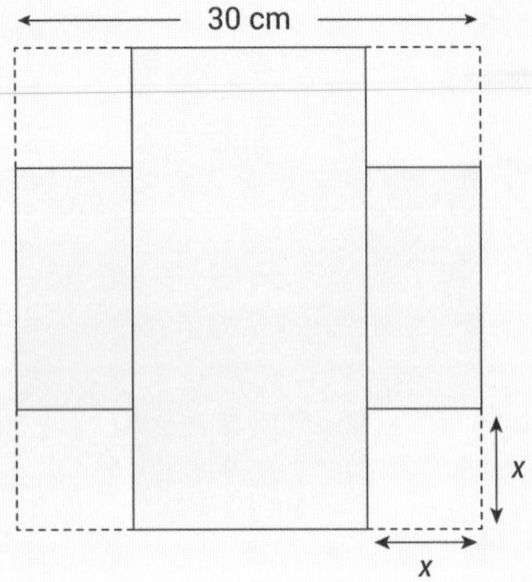

(i) Write down the length and width of the box in terms of x.

(ii) Show that the volume of the box, in terms of x, is $4x^3 - 120x^2 + 900x$.

(iii) Find the value of x which gives the maximum volume of the box.

(iv) Find the maximum volume of the box.

Solution

(i) Length = $30 - 2x$, width = $30 - 2x$

(ii)

x

$30 - 2x$ $30 - 2x$

$\therefore$ Volume $(V) = (30 - 2x)(30 - 2x)(x)$

$= (900 - 120x + 4x^2)(x)$

$\therefore V = 900x - 120x^2 + 4x^3$

OR

$V = 4x^3 - 120x^2 + 900x$ (Rearranging)

(iii) $\frac{dV}{dx} = 12x^2 - 240x + 900$

Let $\frac{dV}{dx} = 0$ and solve to find the stationary points.

$12x^2 - 240x + 900 = 0$

$x^2 - 20x + 75 = 0$ Divide by 12.

$(x - 15)(x - 5) = 0$ Factorise.

$x = 15$ **OR** $x = 5$ Solve for x.

$V(15) = 4(15)^3 - 120(15)^2 + 900(15)$

$= 0$

$V(5) = 4(5)^3 - 120(5)^2 + 900(5)$

$= 2{,}000$

$2{,}000 > 0$

$\therefore x = 5$ gives the maximum volume of the box.

(iv) Maximum volume of box = $20 \times 20 \times 5$

$= 2{,}000 \text{ cm}^3$

Exercise 9.7

1. A chicken coop is enclosed using 40 m of fencing. The enclosure is rectangular.

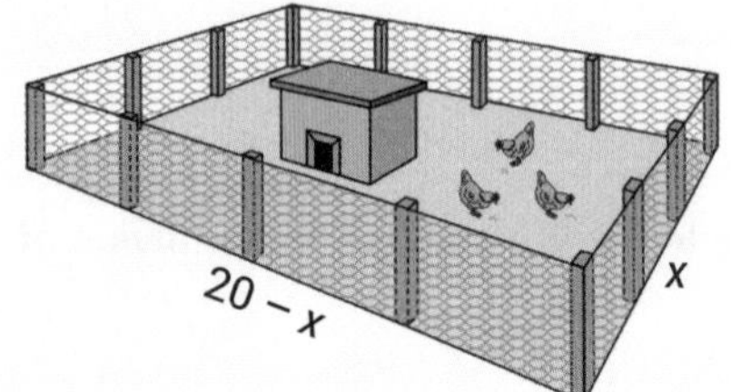

(i) If one side of the enclosure is x metres long, explain why the adjacent side is $(20 - x)$ metres long.

(ii) Find, in terms of x, the area of the enclosure.

(iii) Find the value of x that maximises the area of the enclosure.

(iv) What is the maximum area of the enclosure?

2. A wealthy businessman has a property on the shores of a quiet inlet. He wishes to enclose a rectangular swimming area in the inlet. He has purchased 300 m of pontoon with which to construct the swimming area.

(i) If one side of the enclosure is x metres long, explain why the adjacent side is $(150 - x)$ metres long.

(ii) Find, in terms of x, the area of the enclosure.

(iii) Find the value of x that maximises the area of the enclosure.

(iv) What is the maximum area of the enclosure?

3. A rectangle has a perimeter of 100 cm.

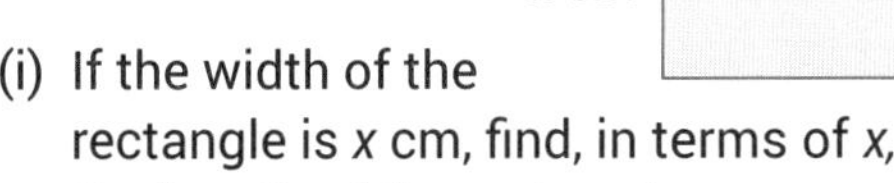

(i) If the width of the rectangle is x cm, find, in terms of x, the length of the rectangle.

(ii) Show that the area of the rectangle is given by $A = 50x - x^2$.

(iii) Find the value of x that maximises the area of the rectangle.

(iv) Find the maximum area of the rectangle.

4. An enclosure is in the shape of a rectangle. One side of the enclosure is fenced in by a building. 100 m of fencing is available to fence the other three sides.

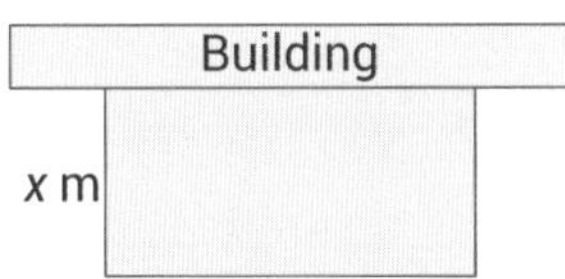

(i) If the width of the enclosure is x m, find, in terms of x, the length of the enclosure.

(ii) Show that the area of the enclosure is given by $A = 100x - 2x^2$.

(iii) Find the value of x that maximises the area of the enclosure.

(iv) Find the maximum area of the enclosure.

5. The speed v of a car (in metres/second) is related to time t (in seconds) by the equation $v = 3 + 12t - 3t^2$.

Determine the maximum speed of the car in kilometres/hour.

6. A lifeguard needs to rope off a rectangular swimming area in front of a beach, using 200 m of rope and floats. The beach will form one side of the swimming area.

(i) The left- and right-hand sides of the swimming area are each x metres long. Find the length of the adjacent side in terms of x.

(ii) Find, in terms of x, the area of the enclosure.

(iii) Find the value of x that maximises the area of the enclosure.

(iv) What is the maximum area of the enclosure?

7. A farmer wants to enclose two rectangular paddocks, which are equal in area. A river runs along the side of both paddocks. The farmer has 300 m of fencing.

(i) If x represents the length (from the river bank) of each paddock and y represents the width, show that $y = 150 - \frac{3}{2}x$.

(ii) Find, in terms of x, the area of one of the paddocks.

(iii) Find the value of x that maximises the area of each paddock.

(iv) What is the maximum area of the enclosure?

8. A sports area is to be designed in the form of a rectangular field with a semicircular area at each end. The perimeter of the sports area is to be 1,400 m.

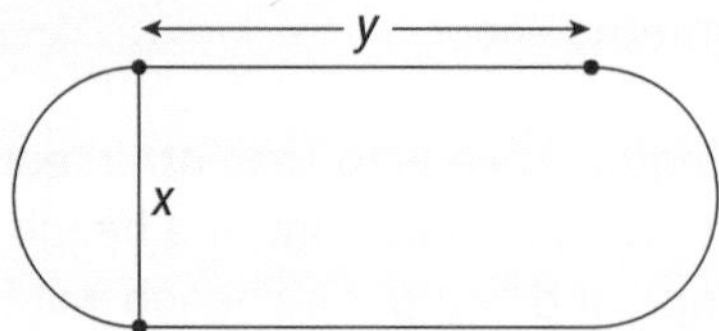

(i) Write the perimeter in terms of x and y.

(ii) Express y in terms of x.

(iii) What should the dimensions of the sports area be if the rectangular field is to have as large an area as possible? Give your answers in metres correct to one decimal place.

9. From a 50 cm × 50 cm sheet of aluminium, square corners are cut out so that the sides are folded up to make a box.

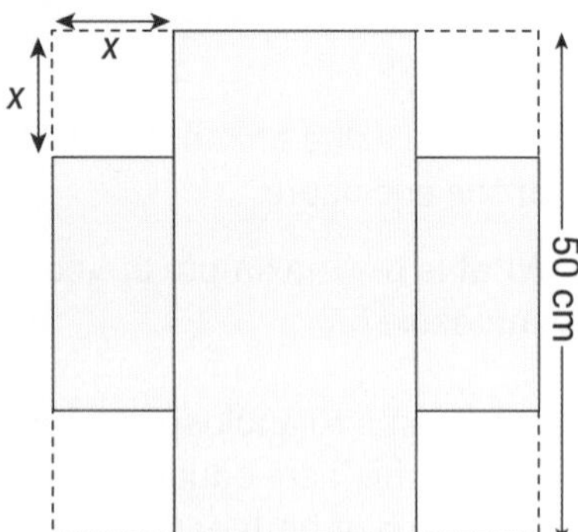

(i) Write the length and width of the box in terms of x.

(ii) Show that the volume of the box, in terms of x, is $4x^3 - 200x^2 + 2{,}500$.

(iii) Find the value of x which gives the maximum volume of the box.

(iv) Find the maximum volume of the box.

10. Liffey Appliances is marketing a new washing machine. It determines that in order to sell x machines, the price per machine (in euro) must be $440 - 0.3x$.

It also determines that the cost of producing x washing machines is given by $C(x) = 6{,}000 + 0.5x^2$.

(i) If x machines are sold, find $R(x)$, the total revenue received. Your answer will be a quadratic expression in x.

(ii) Find $P(x)$, the profit function, if x machines are sold. $[P(x) = R(x) - C(x)]$

(iii) How many machines must be produced to maximise profit?

(iv) What is the maximum profit?

11. A company has calculated that the daily cost (in euro) to produce x items is given by the production cost function $C(x) = 5x^2 + 750x + 3{,}000$. The total daily income from the sale of items is given by the revenue function $R(x) = 1{,}200x$. The company assumes that it will sell all the items it produces.

(i) The company produces 20 items in one day. Find the production cost and total income for the 20 items.

(ii) Find the profit the company makes on that day.

(iii) Find a general expression for the profit the company makes from the production of x items.

(iv) How many of these items will the company have to produce and sell in order to make a maximum profit?

(v) Find the maximum profit the company can make.

(vi) The production costs on a particular day amount to €11,000. Find the number of items produced on that day.

9.9 Rates of Change

We have already learned that $\frac{dy}{dx}$ represents the rate at which y changes with respect to x.

For example, if $\frac{dy}{dx} = 3$, then this implies that y is changing three times as fast as x or that y is increasing by 3 units for every 1 unit that x increases.

If a function is written in terms of t, where t is in terms of some unit of time (seconds, minutes, hours etc.), then the rate at which the function changes over time is simply known as the rate of change of the function. Therefore, we can use differentiation to calculate the rate at which the function is growing or declining.

Worked Example 9.13

Investments can increase or decrease in value. The value of a particular investment of €100 was found to fit the following model:

$$V = 100 + 45t - 1.5t^2$$

where V is the value of the investment in euro, and t is the time in months after the investment was made.

(i) Find the rate at which the value of the investment was changing after 6 months.

(ii) State whether the value of the investment was increasing or decreasing after 18 months. Justify your answer.

(iii) The investment was cashed in at the end of 24 months. How much was it worth at that time?

(iv) How much was the investment worth when it had its maximum value?

Solution

(i) $V = 100 + 45t - 1.5t^2$

$\frac{dV}{dt} = 45 - 3t$ (Rate of change of investment at time t)

Let $t = 6$.

$\frac{dV}{dt} = 45 - 3(6)$ (Rate of change of the investment after 6 months)

$= 45 - 18$

$=$ €27 per month

Always ensure that your answer is expressed using the correct units, in this case € per month.

(ii) $\frac{dV}{dt} = 45 - 3t$

Let $t = 18$.

$\frac{dV}{dt} = 45 - 3(18)$

$= 45 - 54$

$= -9$

After 18 months the investment is **decreasing** at a rate of €9 per month.

(iii) $V = 100 + 45t - 1.5t^2$ (Value of the investment after t months)

Let $t = 24$.

$V = 100 + 45(24) - 1.5(24)^2$

$=$ €316

(iv) $\frac{dV}{dt} = 45 - 3t$

Set $45 - 3t = 0$.

$3t = 45$

$t = 15$ months (Investment will have its maximum value at $t = 15$)

$V(15) = 100 + 45(15) - 1.5(15)^2$

$=$ €437.50

The maximum value of the investment is €437.50.

Distance, Velocity and Acceleration

When a body moves in a horizontal straight line, away from a fixed point, than usually

s = the body's displacement from the fixed point

t = time

v = velocity

a = acceleration.

Velocity is the rate of change of displacement.

$$v = \frac{ds}{dt}$$

Acceleration is the rate of change of velocity.

$$a = \frac{dv}{dt}$$

When a body moves in a vertical straight line away from a fixed point, then usually

h = height of the body above the surface

t = time

v = velocity

a = acceleration.

$$v = \frac{dh}{dt} \quad \text{and} \quad a = \frac{d^2h}{dt^2}$$

Worked Example 9.14

From a point 1.2 m above ground level, a ball is thrown vertically upwards.

The height, h metres, of the ball above ground level at time t seconds is given by

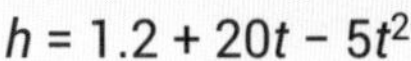

$h = 1.2 + 20t - 5t^2$

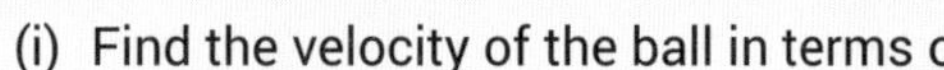

(i) Find the velocity of the ball in terms of t.

(ii) Find the rate at which the ball is decelerating.

(iii) What is the velocity of the ball when it reaches its maximum height?

(iv) After how many seconds does the ball reach its maximum height?

(v) What is the maximum height above ground level reached by the ball?

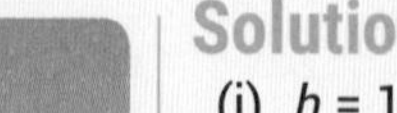

Solution

(i) $h = 1.2 + 20t - 5t^2$

$\frac{dh}{dt} = 20 - 10t$ (Velocity of the ball at time t)

(ii) $\frac{d^2h}{dt^2} = -10$ (Acceleration of the ball)

$\therefore$ The ball is decelerating at a rate of 10 ms^{-2}.

(iii) When it reaches its maximum height the ball will have zero velocity.

(iv) Set velocity equal to zero.

$20 - 10t = 0$

$10t = 20$

$t = 2$ seconds

(v) $h = 1.2 + 20(2) - 5(2)^2$

$h = 21.2$ m (Maximum height)

Exercise 9.8

1. A loaf of bread has just been taken out of the oven and is cooling off before being eaten. The temperature T of the bread (measured in degrees Celsius) is a function of t (measured in minutes), the length of time the bread has been out of the oven. Therefore, we have $T = f(t)$.

(i) What is the meaning of $f(5)$?

(ii) Is $f'(t)$ positive or negative? Explain.

(iii) What are the units for $f'(t)$?

2. The weight W of an infant in kilograms is a function of its age, m (measured in months), so $W = f(m)$.

(i) Would you expect $f'(m)$ to be positive or negative? Explain.

(ii) What does $f(7) = 7.65$ tell you?

(iii) What are the units of $f'(m)$?

3. A car accelerates in a straight line so that its distance s (in metres) from its starting point p after t seconds is given by the function $s(t) = t^2$. Find:

(i) The distance of the car from p after 4 seconds

(ii) The distance of the car from p after 5 seconds

(iii) The speed of the car in terms of t

(iv) The speed of the car after 4 seconds

4. A ball is thrown straight up into the air. The height h (measured in metres) of the ball after t seconds is given by the function $h(t) = 40t - 5t^2$.

(i) Find the height of the ball after 1 second.

(ii) Explain why $h'(t)$ represents the speed of the ball after t seconds.

CALCULUS

(iii) Find the speed of the ball after t seconds.

(iv) What is the speed of the ball when it reaches its maximum height?

(v) Find the time at which the ball reaches its maximum height.

(vi) Find the maximum height reached.

5. The temperature T of a patient during an illness is given by $T(t) = -0.6t^2 + 0.67t + 37$, where T is the temperature (in degrees Celsius) at time t (in days).

(Time is measured from the onset of the illness.)

(i) Find $T'(t)$, the rate at which the temperature is changing with respect to time.

(ii) Find the rate at which the temperature is changing at $t = 3$ days.

(iii) When will the patient's temperature begin to fall? Answer correct to the nearest hour.

6. A marble is dropped from the top of a fifteen-storey building. The height of the marble above the ground, in metres, after t seconds is given by the formula:

$$h(t) = 44.1 - 4.9t^2$$

Find the speed at which the marble hits the ground.

Give your answer in:

(i) ms^{-1}

(ii) km h^{-1}

7. A farmer is growing winter wheat. The amount of wheat he will get per hectare depends on, among other things, the amount of nitrogen fertiliser that he uses. For his particular farm, the amount of wheat depends on the nitrogen in the following way:

$$Y = 7{,}000 + 32N - 0.1N^2$$

where Y is the amount of wheat produced, in kg per hectare, and N is the amount of nitrogen added, in kg per hectare.

(i) How much wheat will he get per hectare if he uses 100 kg of nitrogen per hectare?

(ii) Find the amount of nitrogen that he must use in order to maximise the amount of wheat produced.

(iii) What is the maximum possible amount of wheat produced per hectare?

(iv) The farmer's total costs for producing the wheat are €1,300 per hectare. He can sell the wheat for €160 per tonne. He can also get €75 per hectare for the leftover straw. If he achieves the maximum amount of wheat, what is his profit per hectare?

8. A particle moves in a straight line from a fixed point O. Its distance s in metres from O is given by $s = -33t + 12t^2 - t^3$.

Find:

(i) The velocity of the particle in terms of t

(ii) The acceleration of the particle in terms of t

(iii) The time when the particle comes to rest

(iv) The particle's acceleration after 4 seconds

9. As soon as it touches down, an aeroplane applies its brakes. The distance s which the plane has travelled along the runway at any subsequent time t is given by the function $s(t) = 200t - 4t^2$, where s is measured in metres and t in seconds.

Find:

(i) The distance travelled after 10 seconds

(ii) The plane's speed at any time t

(iii) The speed of the plane at $t = 10$

(iv) The plane's speed as it touches down

(v) The time at which the plane comes to rest

(vi) The distance that the plane has travelled along the runway when it stops

Revision Exercises

1. Differentiate the following with respect to x:
   (i) $y = 2x^2 + 12x + 16$
   (ii) $y = 15x^2 + 10x - 12$
   (iii) $y = x^3 - 19x + 120$
   (iv) $y = 3x^3 - 12x^2 - 4x + 12$
   (v) $y = 4x^3 + 4$

2. Differentiate the following functions with respect to the letter in brackets:
   (i) $f(t) = (t^2 - 1)(t + 2)$ [t]
   (ii) $A(y) = (y + 2)(y^2 - y + 3)$ [y]
   (iii) $g(x) = (x - 4)(x + 4)$ [x]
   (iv) $h(t) = \frac{1}{2}(10t - 9.8t^2)$ [t]

3. A graph of the cubic function $f(x) = x^3 - 3x + 2$ is shown. The tangent to $f(x)$ at the point (1.5,0.875) is also shown on the diagram.

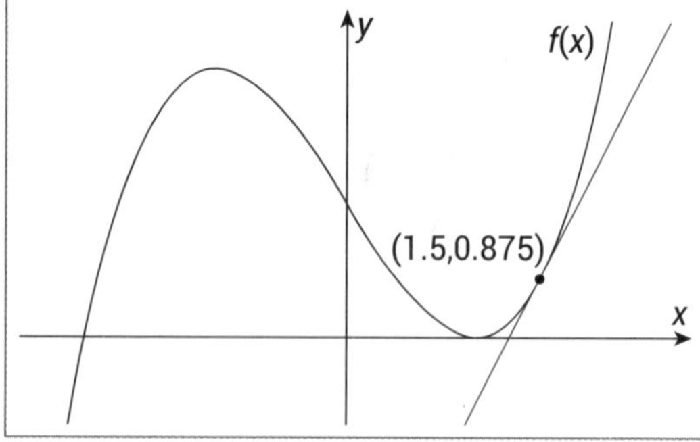

   (i) Write down $f'(x)$, the derivative of $f(x)$.
   (ii) Hence, find the slope of the tangent to $f(x)$ at (1.5,0.875).
   (iii) Find the equation of the tangent to the curve at this point.
   (iv) Find the co-ordinates of the points where the tangent intersects the x-axis and the y-axis.
   (v) Hence, calculate the area enclosed between the tangent, the x-axis and the y-axis.

4. Evaluate each of the following limits:
   (i) $\lim_{x\to 8}(x + 9)$
   (ii) $\lim_{x\to 2}(x^2 - 2x + 4)$
   (iii) $\lim_{x\to 1}\left(\frac{x^2 - 2x + 1}{x - 1}\right)$
   (iv) $\lim_{x\to 7}\left(\frac{x^2 - 49}{x - 7}\right)$

5. A graph of the cubic function $f(x) = x^3 - 3x^2 - 10x + 24$ is shown. The tangent to $f(x)$ at the point (3.5, − 4.875) is also shown on the diagram.

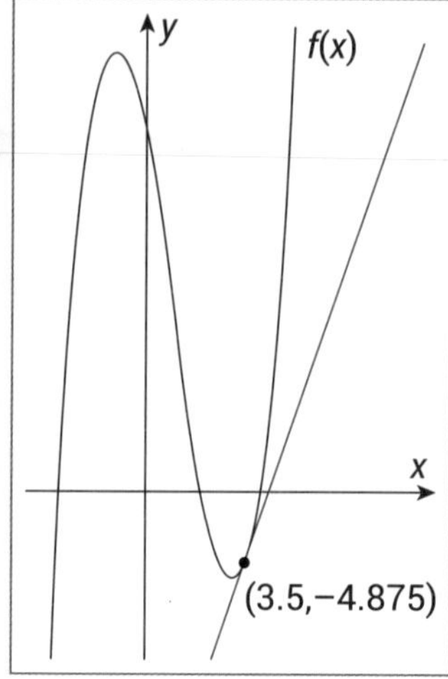

   (i) Write down $f'(x)$, the derivative of $f(x)$.
   (ii) Hence, find the slope of the tangent to $f(x)$ at $x = 3.5$.
   (iii) Find the equation of the tangent to the curve at this point.

6. For each of the following functions, find $f''(x)$ and, hence, $f''(-3)$:
   (i) $f(x) = 3x^3 + 2x^2 + x$
   (ii) $f(x) = 5x^3 - 12x$
   (iii) $f(x) = -3x^3 + 5x$

7. Let $f(x) = x^3 - 3x^2$, $x \in R$.
   (i) Find the co-ordinates of the local maximum point and the local minimum point on the curve of $f(x)$.
   (ii) Find the co-ordinates of the points where the curve intersects the x-axis and the y-axis.
   (iii) Draw a rough sketch of the curve.
   (iv) Hence, write down the range of values of x for which $f(x)$ is increasing.

8. The weight W (measured in kilograms) of a young calf is a function of its age, m (measured in months), so $W = f(m)$.
   (i) What are the units of $f'(m)$?
   (ii) Interpret the meaning of $f'(3) = 4$.

CALCULUS

9. The function $f(x) = 2x^3 + 4x + 2$ is defined for all values of x.

(i) Find the values of x for which $f'(x) = 10$.

(ii) Find $f''(8)$.

10. A particle moves in a straight line so that its distance s from a fixed point O at any subsequent time t is given by $s(t) = t^3 - 2t^2 + t$, where s is measured in metres and t is measured in seconds.

Find:

(i) The distance of the particle from O after 2 seconds

(ii) The particle's speed after 2 seconds

(iii) The times at which the particle is at rest

11. Let $f(x) = 3x^3 - 16x^2 + 5$.

(i) Write down $f'(x)$, the derivative of $f(x)$.

(ii) Hence, find the range of values of x for which $f(x)$ is increasing.

12. Consider the beaker with red liquid in the picture shown.

It consists of a roughly spherical bottom part and a roughly cylindrical top part as shown.

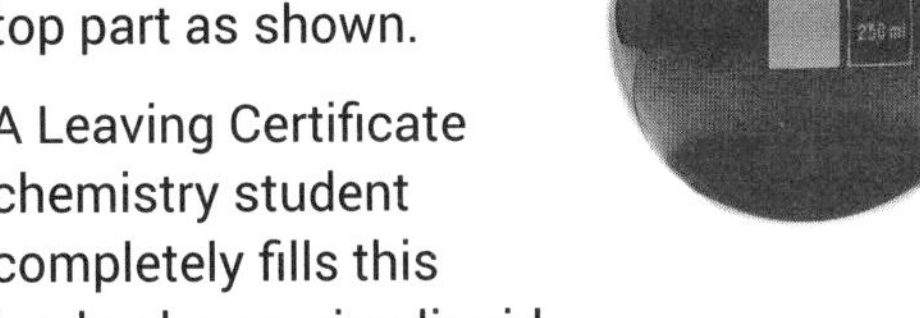

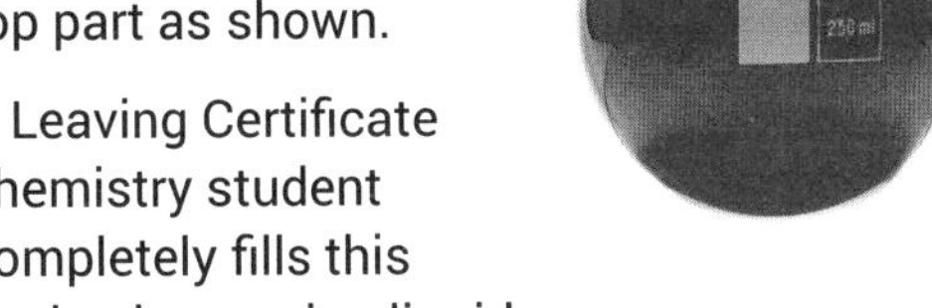

A Leaving Certificate chemistry student completely fills this beaker by pouring liquid into it at a constant rate.

(a) Assuming that the beaker was empty to begin with, draw a graph that relates the *height* of liquid in the beaker to the *time* that the student spends pouring liquid into the beaker.

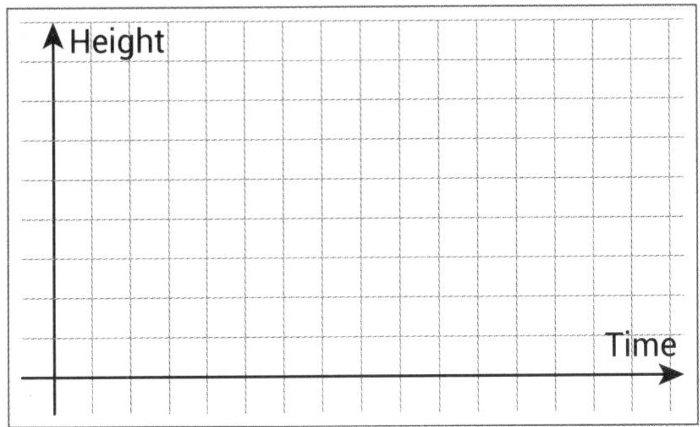

(b) Describe, in your own words, how the rate at which the height was increasing changed over time.

(c) A different beaker is filled with a liquid at a constant rate. Initially the height of liquid in the beaker is 2 cm.

Below is a graph of the height of liquid in the beaker against time spent filling the beaker.

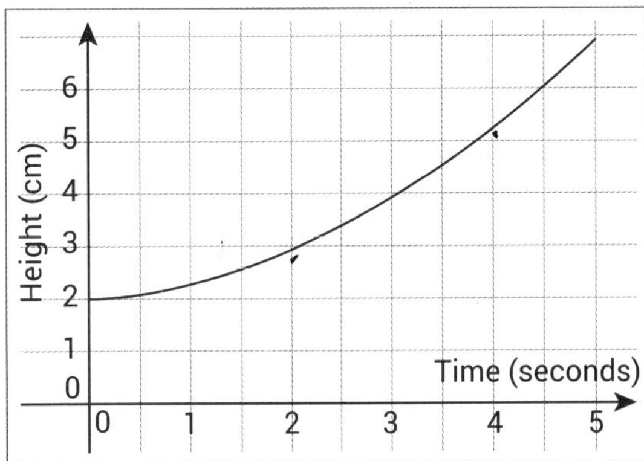

Use your graph to estimate the following:

(i) The rate of change in height between 2 seconds and 4 seconds

(ii) The rate of change in height between 2 seconds and 3 seconds

(iii) The rate of change in height between 0 seconds and 2 seconds

(iv) The rate of change in height between 1 second and 2 seconds

(d) Can you guess what the **instantaneous** rate of change in height is at 2 seconds?

(e) The relationship between height (h) and time (t) in the diagram above is actually given by the formula $h = 0.2t^2 + 2$.

By calculating the derivative $\frac{dh}{dt}$ at $t = 2$, verify your answer to part (iv).

13. The diagram shows a rectangle of perimeter 12 cm.

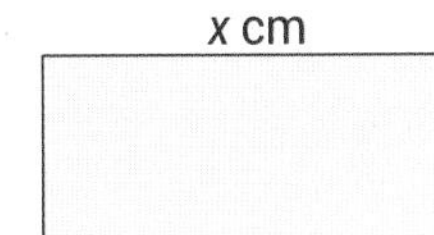

The length of the rectangle is x cm.

(i) Write the width of the rectangle in terms of x.

(ii) Show that the area of the rectangle is $6x - x^2$.

(iii) Find the value of x which gives the maximum area of the rectangle.

(iv) Find this maximum area.

Exam Questions

1. The function $f: x \mapsto x^3 + x^2 - 2x + 7$ is defined for $x \in R$.
   (a) Find the co-ordinates of the point at which the graph of f cuts the y-axis.
   (b) Verify, using algebra, that the point $A(1,7)$ is on the graph of f.
   (c) (i) Find $f'(x)$, the derivative of $f(x)$.
   Hence, find the slope of the tangent to the graph of f when $x = 1$.
   (ii) Hence, find the equation of the tangent to the graph of f at the point $A(1,7)$.

SEC Leaving Certificate Ordinary Level, Paper 1, 2016

2. A small rocket is fired into the air from a fixed position on the ground. Its fight lasts ten seconds. The height, in metres, of the rocket above the ground after t seconds is given by $h = 10t - t^2$.
   (a) Complete the table below.

Time, t	0	1	2	3	4	5	6	7	8	9	10
Height, h						25	24	21	16		

   (b) Draw a graph to represent the height of the rocket during the ten seconds.
   (c) Use your graph to estimate:
   (i) The height of the rocket after 2.5 seconds
   (ii) The time when the rocket will again be at this height
   (iii) The co-ordinates of the highest point reached by the rocket
   (d) (i) Find the slope of the line joining the points (6,24) and (7,21).
   (ii) Would you expect the line joining the points (7,21) and (8,16) to be steeper than the line joining (6,24) and (7,21) or not? Give a reason for your answer.
   (e) (i) Find $\frac{dh}{dt}$.
   (ii) Hence, find the maximum height reached by the rocket.
   (iii) Find the speed of the rocket after 3 seconds.
   (iv) Find the co-ordinates of the point at which the slope of the tangent to the graph is 2.

SEC Leaving Certificate Ordinary Level, Paper 1, 2014

3. Kieran has 21 metres of fencing. He wants to enclose a vegetable garden in a rectangular shape as shown.

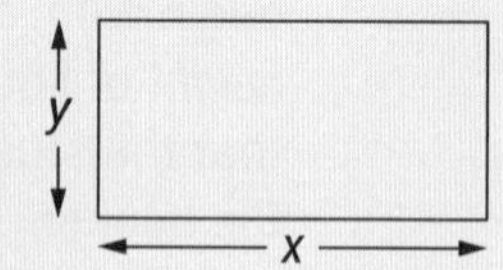

   (a) By writing an expression for the perimeter of the vegetable garden in terms of x (length in metres) and y (width in metres), show that $y = 10.5 - x$.
   (b) (i) Complete the table below to show the values of y and A (the area of the garden) for each given value of x.

x (m)	0	1	2	3	4	5	6	7	8	9	10
y (m)					6.5						
A (m^2)					26						

   (ii) Use the values of x and A from the table to plot the graph of A.

CALCULUS

(c) Use your graph to estimate the maximum value of A and write the corresponding length and width.

(d) (i) Show that the area of the rectangle can be written as $A = 10.5x - x^2$.

(ii) Find $\frac{dA}{dx}$.

(iii) Hence, find the value of x which will give the maximum area.

(iv) Find this maximum area.

SEC Leaving Certificate Ordinary Level, Paper 1, 2016

Solutions and chapter summary available online

CALCULUS

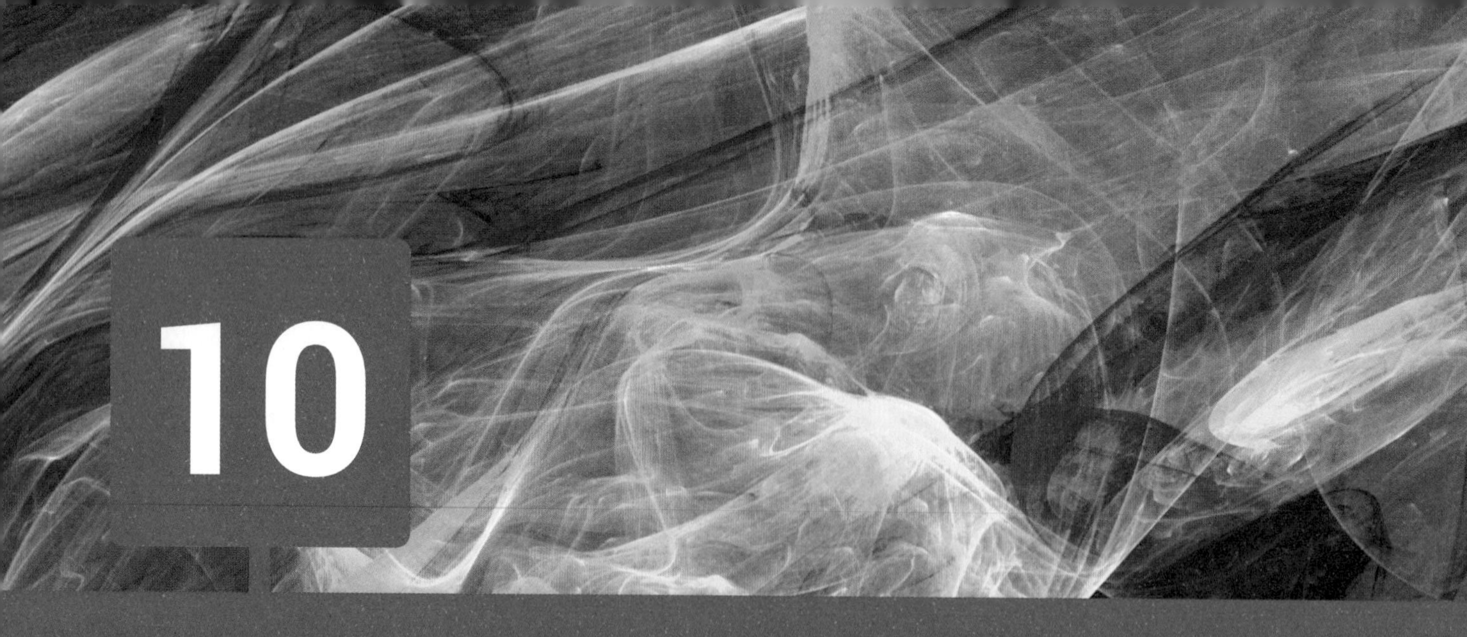

Applied Measure

In this chapter you will learn to:

- Investigate the nets of prisms, cylinders and cones
- Solve problems involving the length of the perimeter and the area of plane figures: disc, triangle, rectangle, square, parallelogram, trapezium, sectors of discs, and figures made from combinations of these
- Solve problems involving surface area and volume of the following solid figures: rectangular block, cylinder, right cone, triangular-based prism (right angle, isosceles and equilateral), sphere, hemisphere, and solids made from combinations of these
- Use the trapezoidal rule to approximate area

You should remember...

- Length, area and volume from your Junior Certificate course
- The theorem of Pythagoras

Key words

- Triangle
- Rectangle
- Square
- Parallelogram
- Trapezium
- Disc (circle)
- Sector of a disc
- Rectangular block
- Cylinder
- Right cone
- Right prism
- Sphere
- Hemisphere
- Trapezoidal rule
- Perimeter
- Area
- Volume
- Surface area

10.1 Area and Perimeter of Triangles and Quadrilaterals

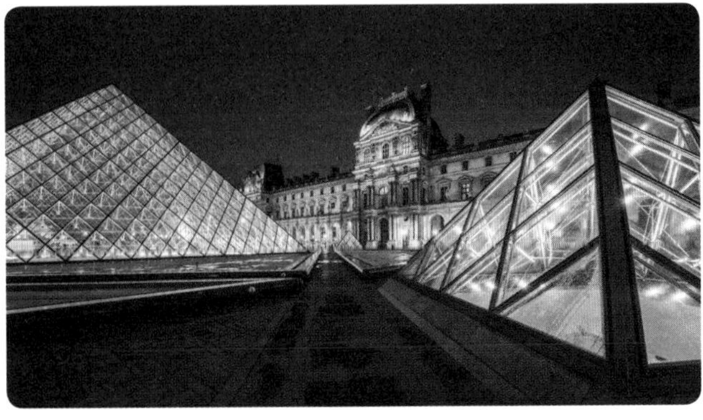

Area is the amount of flat space that a shape occupies.
Perimeter is the sum of the length of all the sides of a shape.

The units of **area** will always be units^2, for example: mm^2, cm^2, m^2, km^2, etc. The units of **perimeter** will not be squared, as calculating perimeter involves addition. When finding the area or perimeter of a shape, make sure that you use the **same** units: mm × mm, cm × cm, m + m, etc.

Rectangle	**Square**
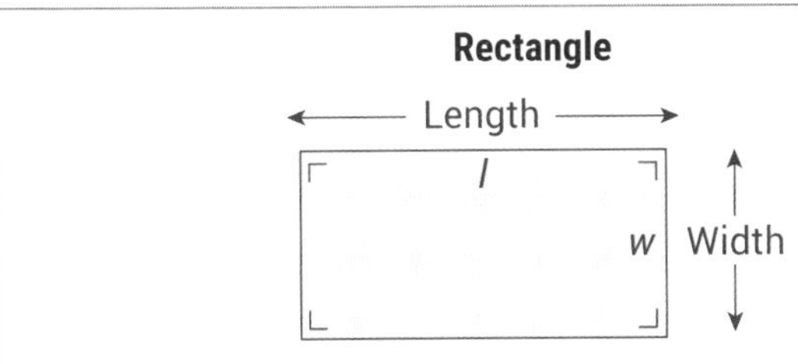 Area = (length × width) = lw Perimeter = $2l + 2w$ **or** $2(l + w)$	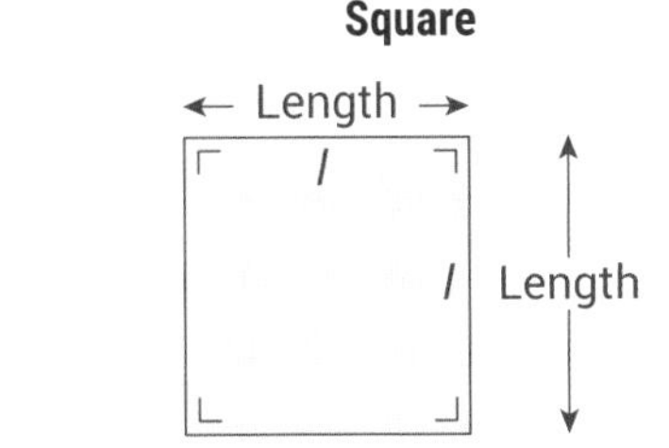 Area = (length)^2 = l^2 Perimeter = $4l$
Triangle	**Parallelogram**
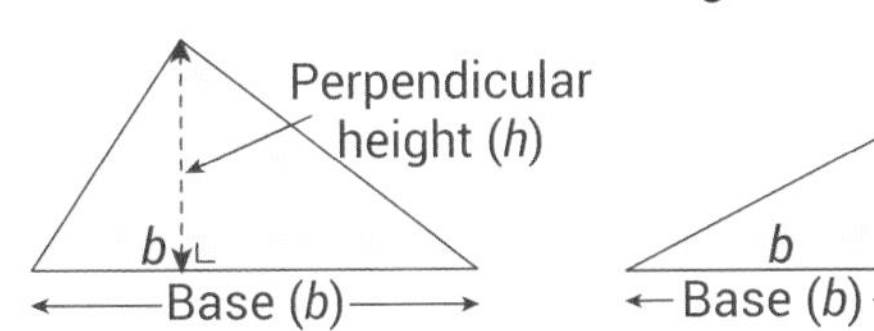 Area = $\frac{1}{2}$ × base × perpendicular height $= \frac{1}{2}bh$	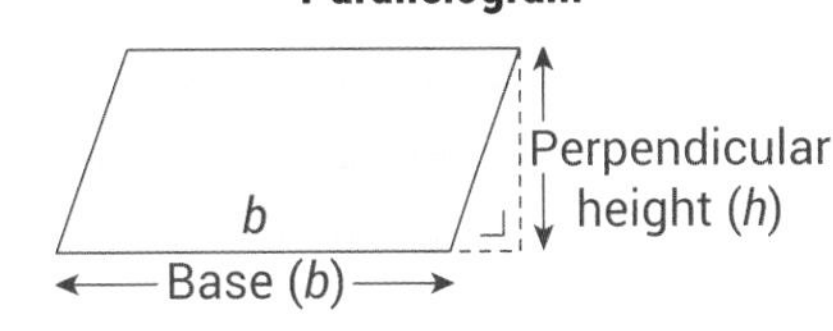 Area = base × perpendicular height $= bh$

Trapezium

A **trapezium** or trapezoid is a quadrilateral (four-sided figure) that has one pair of parallel sides.

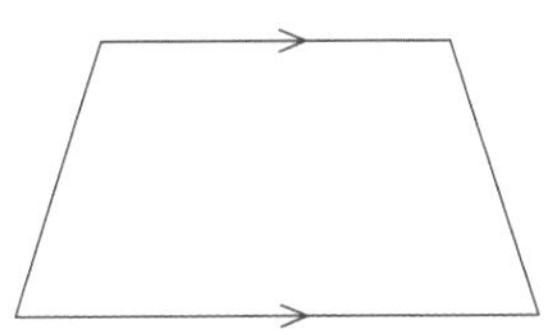

Trapezium	
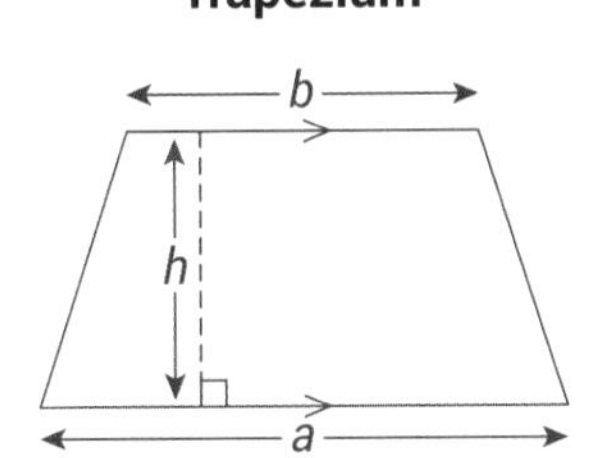	Area = $\frac{1}{2}$ × sum of parallel bases × perpendicular height Area = $\frac{1}{2}(a + b)h$ **or** Area = $\left(\frac{a+b}{2}\right)h$  This formula appears on page 8 of *Formulae and Tables*.

APPLIED MEASURE

The theorem of Pythagoras can be useful when dealing with 2D shapes.

Theorem 14: The Theorem of Pythagoras
In a right-angled triangle, the square on the hypotenuse is equal to the sum of the squares on the other two sides.

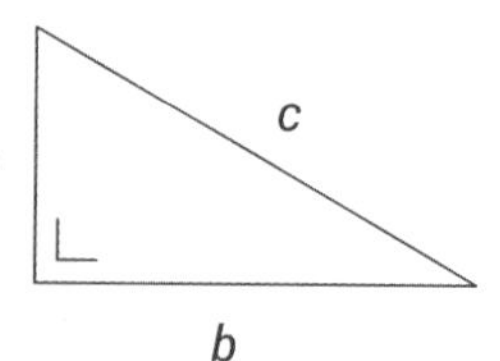

The hypotenuse is the longest side in a right-angled triangle. Therefore, the hypotenuse is the side opposite the largest angle (the 90° angle).

$c^2 = a^2 + b^2$

Worked Example 10.1

Find the area of each of the following shapes:

(i)

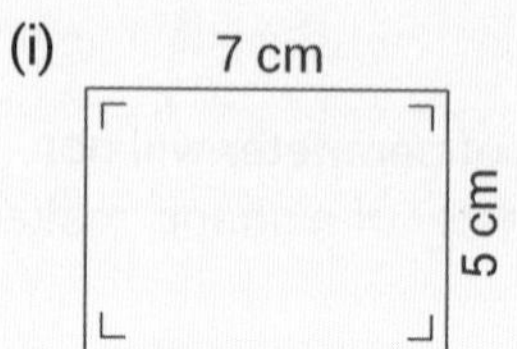

(ii)

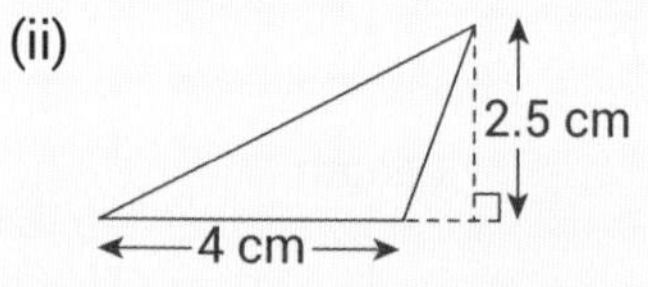

(iii)

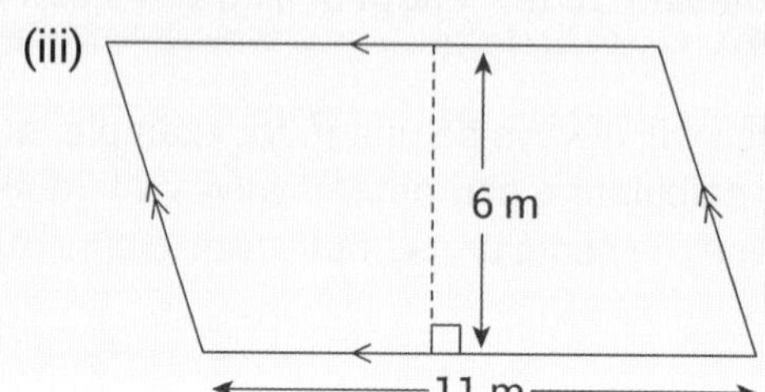

(iv)

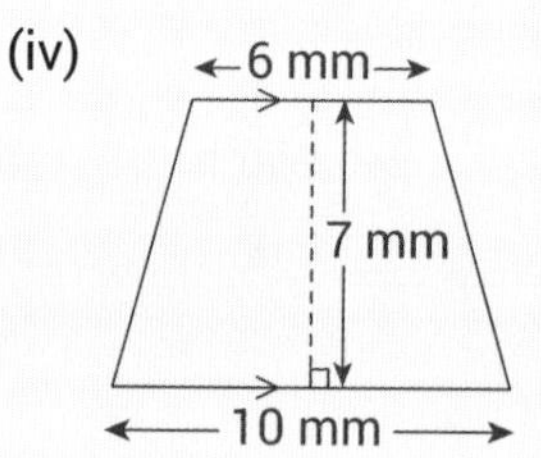

Solution

(i) This shape is a rectangle.

$\therefore$ Area $= l \times w = 7 \times 5 = 35$ cm^2

(ii) This shape is a triangle.

$\therefore$ Area $= \frac{1}{2}bh = \frac{1}{2} \times 4 \times 2.5 = 5$ cm^2

(iii) This shape is a parallelogram.

$\therefore$ Area $= bh = 11 \times 6 = 66$ m^2

(iv) This shape is a trapezium.

$\therefore$ Area $= \frac{1}{2}(a + b)h = \frac{1}{2}(10 + 6)(7)$

$= \frac{1}{2}(16)(7) = 56$ mm^2

Worked Example 10.2

A shape consists of a trapezium with a triangle cut out of it. Calculate the shaded area of this shape.

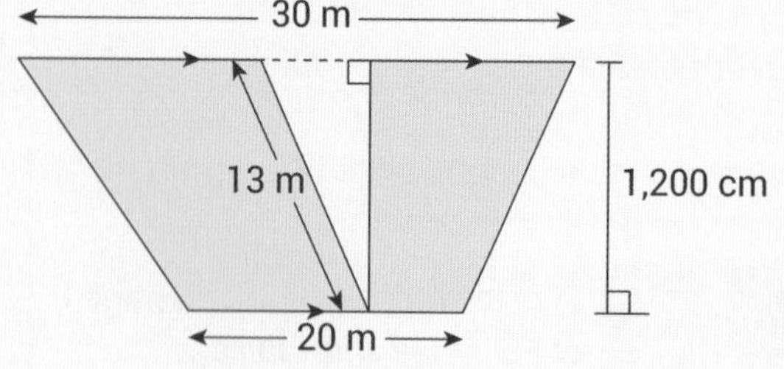

Solution

Step 1 Find the area of the unshaded triangle first.

It is important to ensure that all the measurements used in our calculations are in the same units.

1,200 cm = 12 m

Use the theorem of Pythagoras to find the length of the triangle's base.

$$c^2 = a^2 + b^2$$
$$(13)^2 = (12)^2 + b^2$$
$$169 = 144 + b^2$$
$$169 - 144 = b^2$$
$$25 = b^2$$
$$5 = b$$
$$\therefore \text{ Area of triangle} = \frac{1}{2}bh = \frac{1}{2}(5)(12) = 30 \text{ m}^2$$

Step 2 We can now find the area of the whole shape, which is a trapezium.

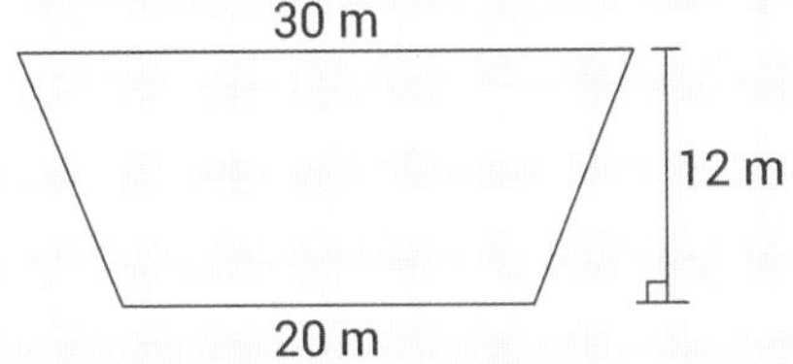

$$\text{Area} = \frac{1}{2}(a + b)h$$
$$= \frac{1}{2}(20 + 30)(12)$$
$$= \frac{1}{2}(50)(12)$$
$$= 300 \text{ m}^2$$

Step 3

$$\text{Shaded area} = \text{total area} - \text{unshaded area}$$
$$\therefore \text{ Shaded area} = 300 \text{ m}^2 - 30 \text{ m}^2$$
$$= 270 \text{ m}^2$$

Take care.

1 m = 100 cm

$1 \text{ m}^2 = 1 \text{ m} \times 1 \text{ m} = 100 \text{ cm} \times 100 \text{ cm} = 10{,}000 \text{ cm}^2$

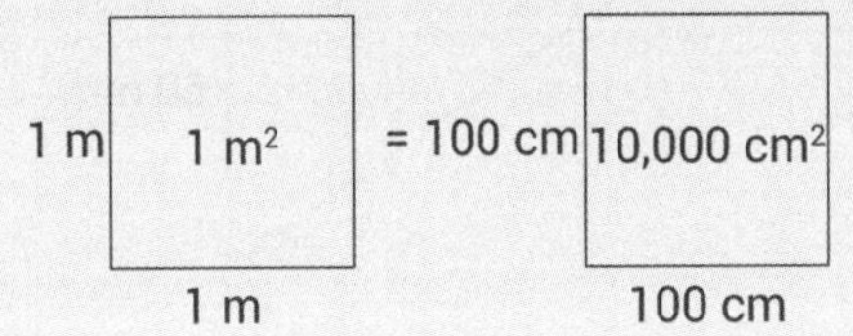

Similarly,

$1 \text{ cm}^2 = 1 \text{ cm} \times 1 \text{ cm} = 10 \text{ mm} \times 10 \text{ mm} = 100 \text{ mm}^2$.

Exercise 10.1

1. Find the area of each of the following shapes:

(i)

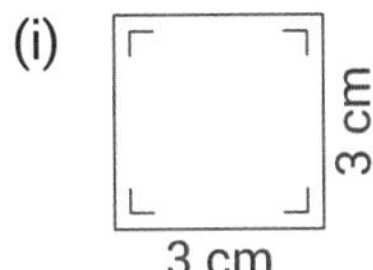

(ii)

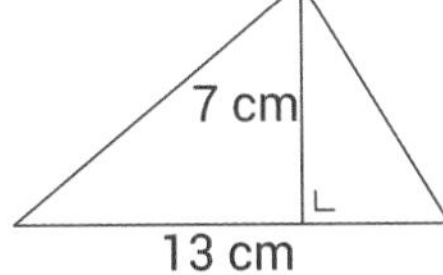

(iii)

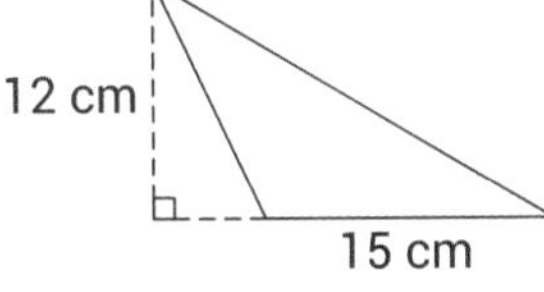

(iv)

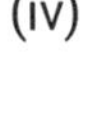

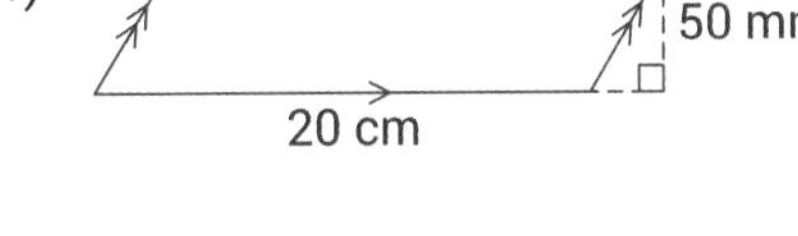

(v)

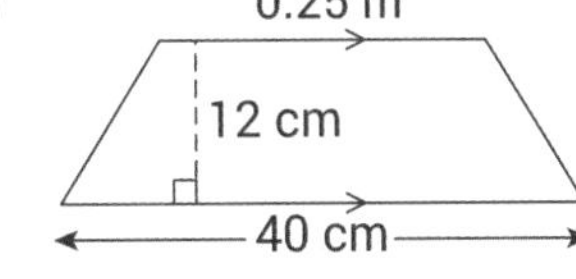

(vi)

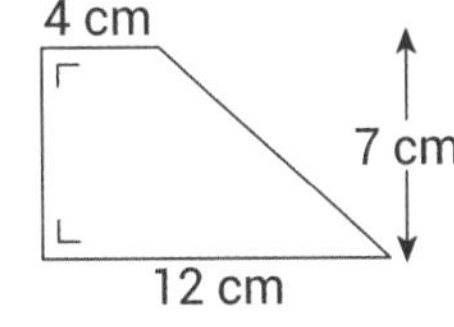

(vii)

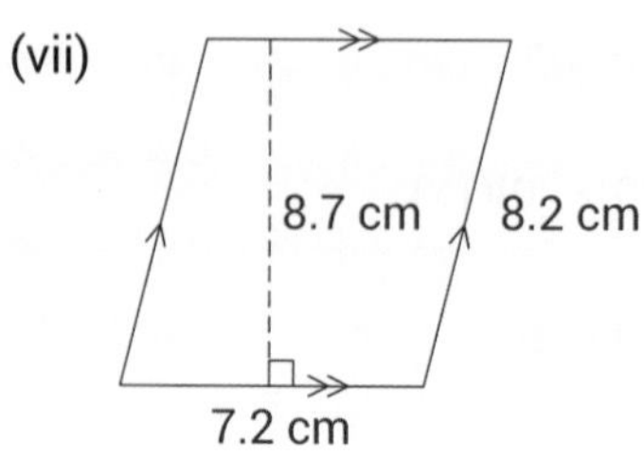

(viii)

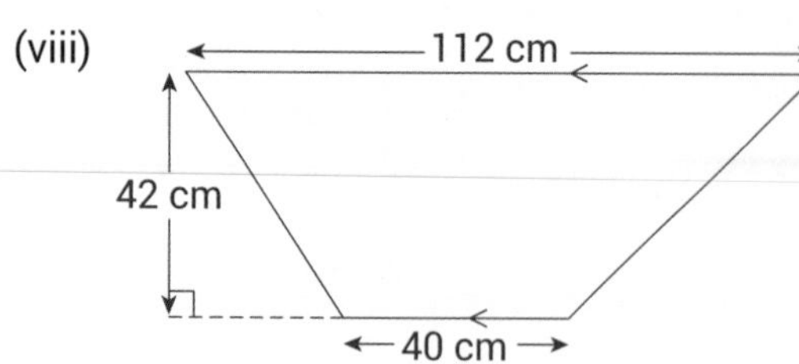

(ix)

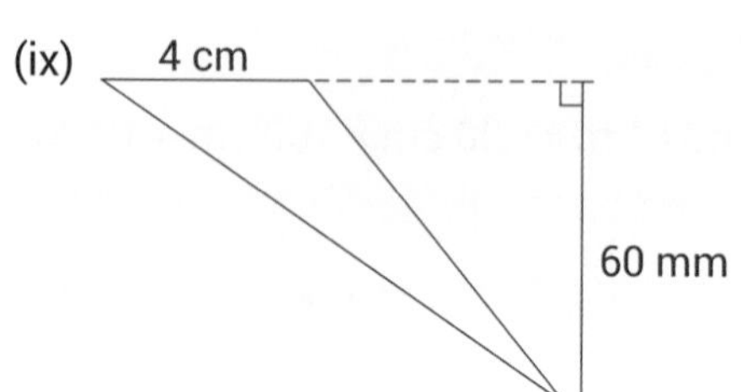

(x)

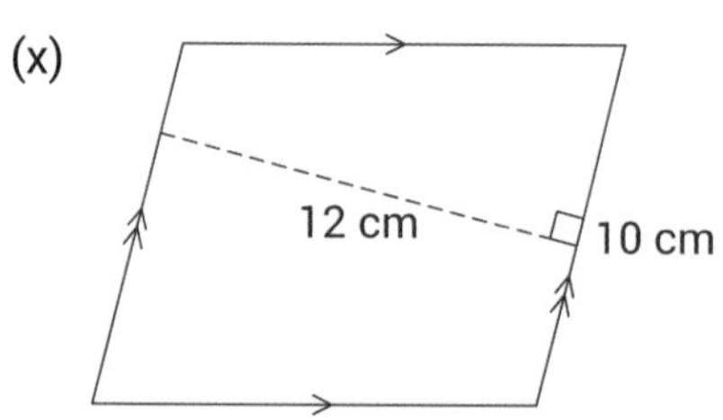

2. Find the area and perimeter of each of the following compound shapes:

(i)

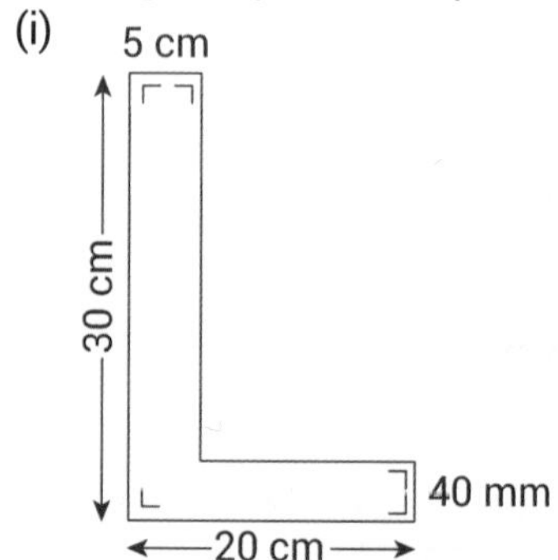

(ii)

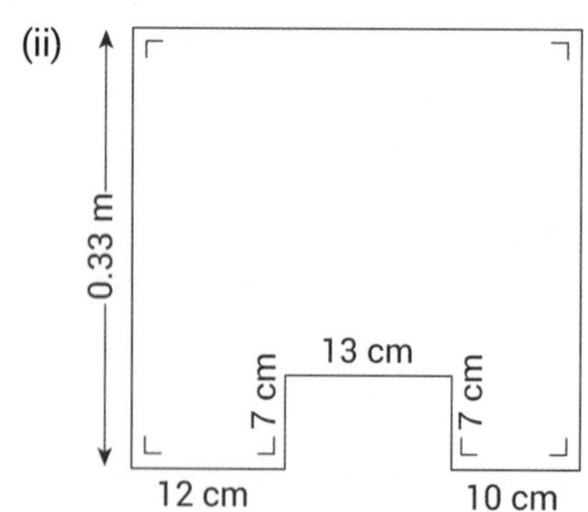

(iii)

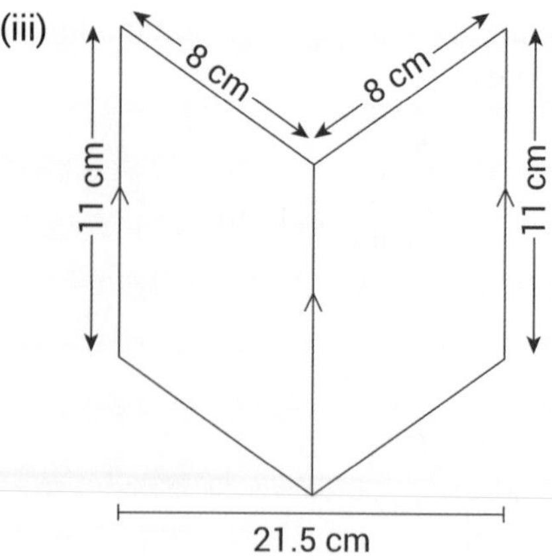

(iv)

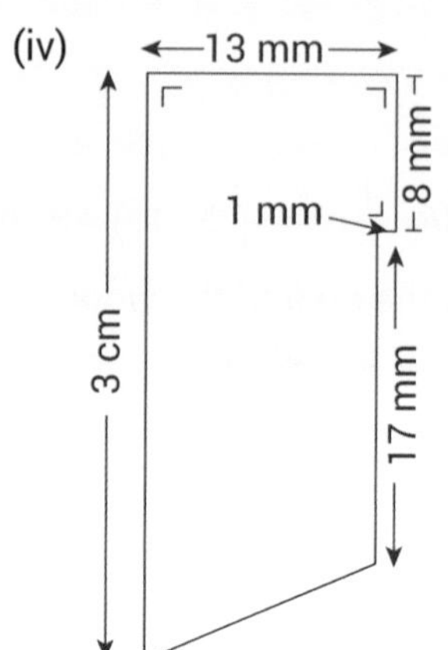

(v)

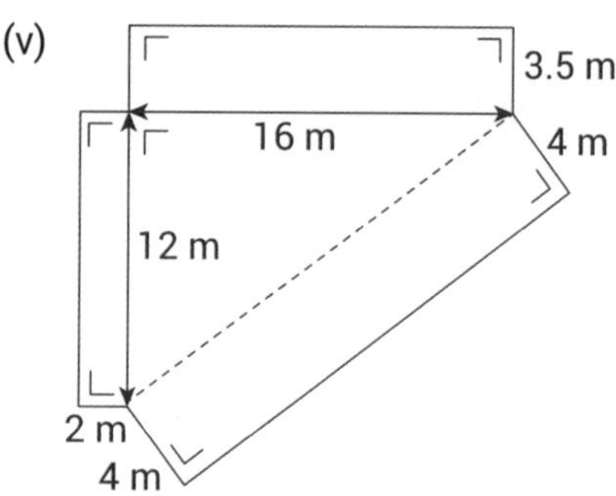

3. A rectangular tile is shaded as shown.

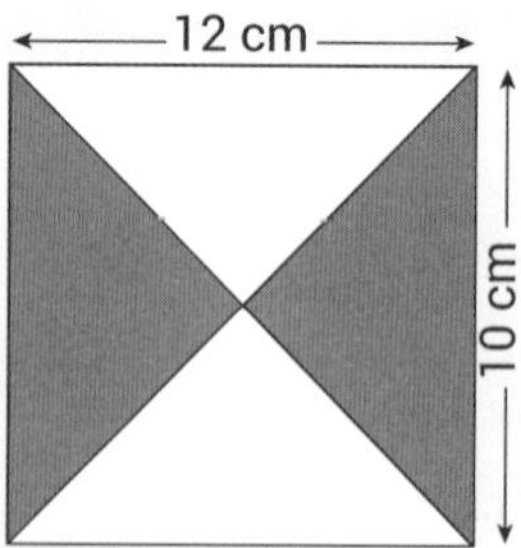

(i) Calculate the area covered by the pink part of the tile.

(ii) To the nearest tile, how many tiles will be needed to tile a room measuring 5 m × 4 m?

(iii) What area of this floor will be white?

APPLIED MEASURE

4. A panel from a stained glass window is shown.

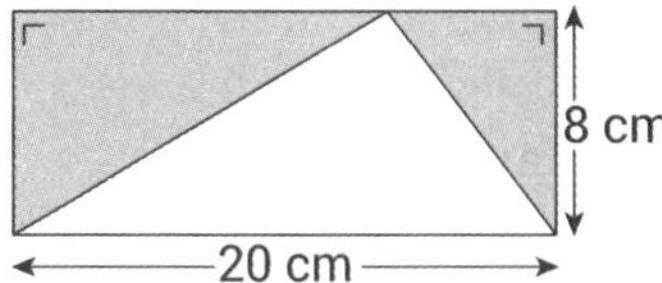

It costs 50c per cm^2 to manufacture the clear glass portion of the panel. The blue glass costs 20c per cm^2 to produce.

(i) Find the cost of producing the panel shown.

(ii) How many of these panels would be needed if the blue window glass used covers an area of 4.48 m^2?

5. There is a path 3 metres wide around a small park as shown.

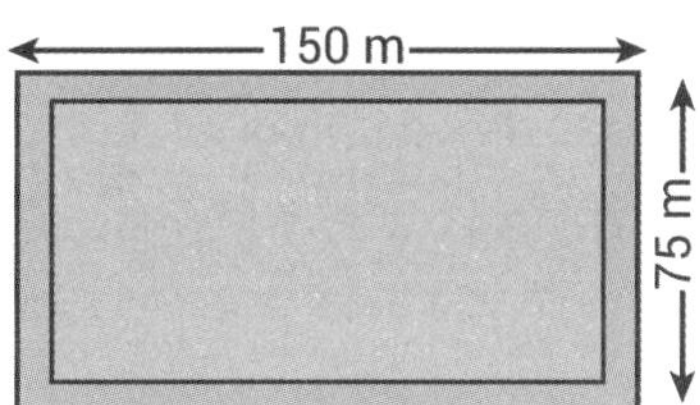

Find:

(i) The area of the park

(ii) The area of the path

(iii) The cost of replacing the path if each 2 m^2 of path cost €5.25

6. A garden design in the shape of a square is shown. The green areas represent shrubs and the remainder is covered with patio slabs.

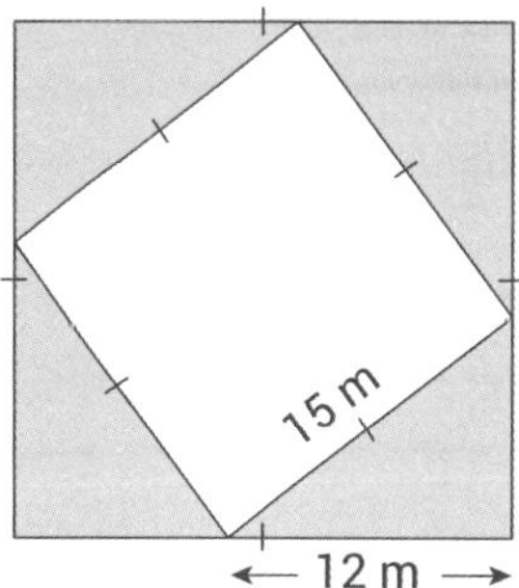

(a) Calculate the area of the garden covered by:

(i) Shrubs

(ii) Patio slabs

(b) It will cost on average €19 per m^2 to build this garden.

A breakdown of the cost (excluding labour) is given:

- Patio slabs: €10 per m^2 + VAT @ 21%
- Shrubbery: €1.50 per m^2 + VAT @ 21%
- Ground preparation for the whole garden: €5 per m^2

What were the builder's labour costs, to the nearest euro?

10.2 Circle

Another 2D shape is the circle or disc. When dealing with questions associated with circles we encounter some terms we need to be familiar with.

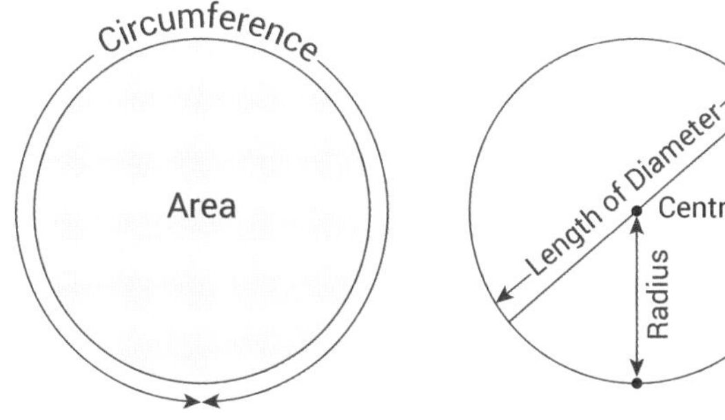

Circumference – the perimeter or length of the circle.

Radius – the line segment from the centre of the circle to any point on the circle.

Diameter – a chord that passes through the centre of a circle. The diameter is twice the radius in length. The diameter is the longest chord of a circle.

The **circumference** of any circle divided by the length of its **diameter** is always the same. This ratio is π (pronounced 'pi'). We use π to help calculate the area and circumference (length) of a circle or sector of a circle.

$$\pi = \frac{\text{Circumference of a circle}}{\text{Length of diameter}}$$

π is an irrational number. To eight decimal places, $\pi = 3.14159265$. As π is an infinite non-recurring decimal, we often use approximations of π in our calculations. In calculating the area or circumference of a circle, we may be told to use one of the following values for π:

- $\pi = 3.14$
- $\pi = \frac{22}{7}$
- The value of π from the calculator 

We may also be asked to leave our answer in terms of π.

Area and Circumference of a Circle 

Area of a circle = $\pi \times r^2$, usually written as πr^2. 

Circumference of a circle = $2 \times \pi \times r$, usually written as $2\pi r$. 

These formulae appear on page 8 of *Formulae and Tables*.

In maths, a circle refers to the curve, while a disc refers to the area within the curve. We find the area of a disc and the circumference of a circle. Commonly, it is acceptable to say that we find the area of a circle.

Worked Example 10.3

Find the area and circumference of a circle of radius 15 cm.

(i) Answer in terms of π.

(ii) Take $\pi = 3.14$.

(iii) Take $\pi = \frac{22}{7}$.

(iv) Use the π button on the calculator.

Remember that the circumference of a circle is also known as the length or perimeter of a circle.

Solution

(i) In terms of π

Area of circle $= \pi \times r^2$
$= \pi \times (15)^2$
$= 225\pi \text{ cm}^2$

Circumference of circle $= 2 \times \pi \times r$
$= 2 \times \pi \times 15$
$= 30\pi \text{ cm}$

(ii) $\pi = 3.14$

Area of circle $= \pi \times r^2$
$= 3.14 \times (15)^2$
$= 706.5 \text{ cm}^2$

Circumference of circle $= 2 \times \pi \times r$
$= 2 \times 3.14 \times 15$
$= 94.2 \text{ cm}$

(iii) $\pi = \frac{22}{7}$

Area of circle $= \pi \times r^2$
$= \frac{22}{7} \times (15)^2$
$= 707\frac{1}{7} \text{ cm}^2$

Circumference of circle $= 2 \times \pi \times r$
$= 2 \times \frac{22}{7} \times 15$
$= 94\frac{2}{7} \text{ cm}$

(iv) π button on the calculator

Area of circle $= \pi \times r^2$
$= \pi \times (15)^2$
$= 225\pi$
$\approx 706.8583471 \text{ cm}^2$

Circumference of circle $= 2 \times \pi \times r$
$= 2 \times \pi \times 15$
$= 30\pi$
$\approx 94.24777961 \text{ cm}$

To convert our answer we use the 'change' button on the calculator.

Remember that when we let $\pi = 3.14$ or $\frac{22}{7}$ we are using an approximation (estimate) for π. A more accurate answer can be obtained when we use the π button on the calculator or when we express our answer in terms of π.

Sectors

A **sector** is a specific slice of a circle (a pie-shaped part).

A sector of a circle is the portion of a circle bounded by two radii and the included arc.

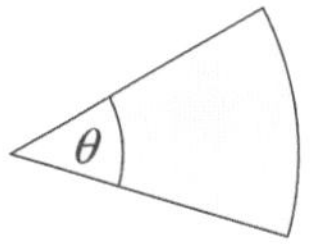

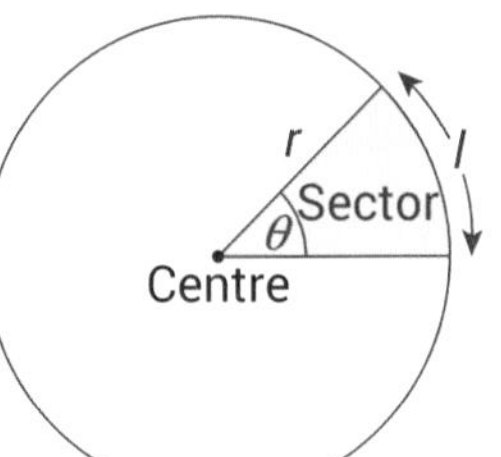

The sector angle, usually referred to as θ (theta), is needed to work out the area and length of arc of the sector.

Area of sector $= \pi r^2\left(\frac{\theta}{360°}\right)$

Length of arc (circumference of arc)
$l = 2\pi r\left(\frac{\theta}{360°}\right)$

These formulae appear on page 9 of *Formulae and Tables*.

θ must be in degrees.

Worked Example 10.4

Find the area, length of arc and perimeter of the following sector of a circle ($\pi = 3.14$).

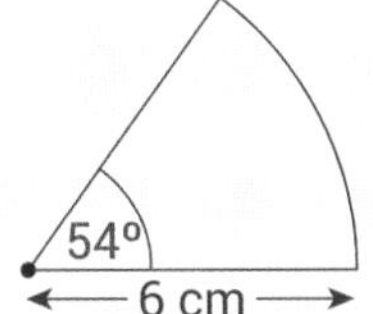

Solution

Area of sector

$\pi r^2\left(\frac{\theta}{360°}\right) = 3.14 \times (6)^2 \times \frac{54}{360}$

$= 16.956 \text{ cm}^2$

Length of arc

$l = 2\pi r\left(\frac{\theta}{360°}\right)$

$l = 2 \times 3.14 \times 6 \times \frac{54}{360}$

$l = 5.652$ cm

Perimeter

Length of arc = 5.652 cm

Length of two radii = 6 × 2 = 12 cm

$\therefore$ Perimeter = 5.652 + 12 = 17.652 cm

Worked Example 10.5

A part for a machine is shown. Find the total area of the machine part. ($\pi = 3.14$)

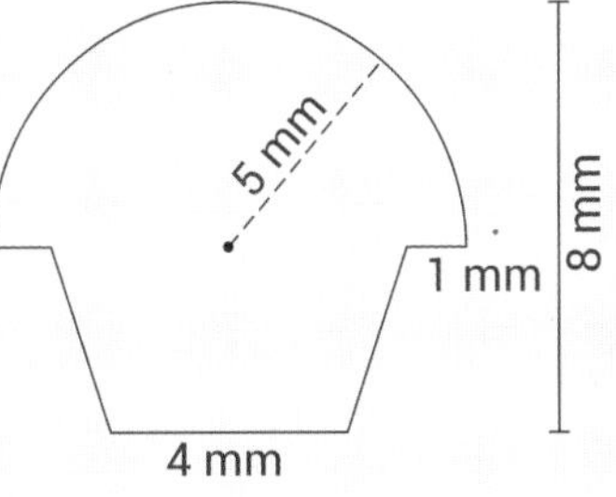

Solution

We work out all the relevant dimensions.

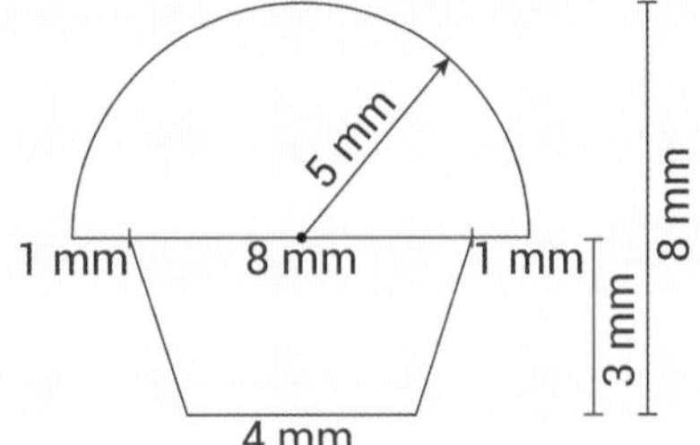

Step 1

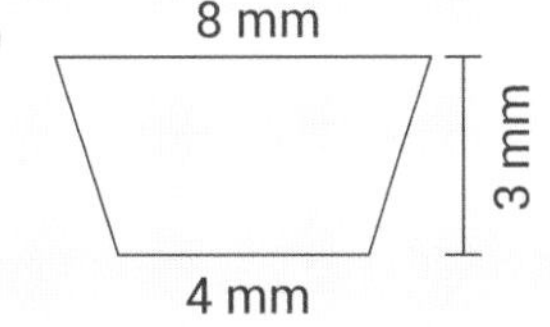

Area of trapezium $= \frac{1}{2}(a + b)h = \frac{1}{2}(4 + 8)3$

$= \frac{1}{2}(12)(3) = 18 \text{ mm}^2$

Step 2

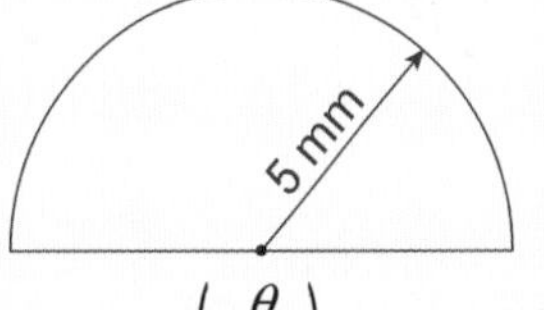

Area of semicircle $= \pi r^2\left(\frac{\theta}{360}\right) = 3.14 \times (5)^2 \times \frac{180}{360}$

$= 39.25 \text{ mm}^2$

Step 3

The area is $18 \text{ mm}^2 + 39.25 \text{ mm}^2 = 57.25 \text{ mm}^2$.

APPLIED MEASURE

Exercise 10.2

1. Taking $\pi = 3.14$, find the area and circumference of each of the following circles:
   (i) Radius = 10 cm
   (ii) Radius = 120 mm
   (iii) Diameter length = 320 cm

2. Taking $\pi = \frac{22}{7}$, find the area and circumference of each of the following circles:
   (i) Radius = 140 cm
   (ii) Radius = 89 cm
   (iii) Diameter length = $11\frac{1}{5}$ cm

3. Find the area and circumference of each of the the following circles, in terms of π:
   (i) Radius = 10 cm
   (ii) Radius = 12 m
   (iii) Diameter length = 0.5 cm

4. Find the area, length of arc and perimeter of each of the following sectors:

   (i) $\pi = 3.14$

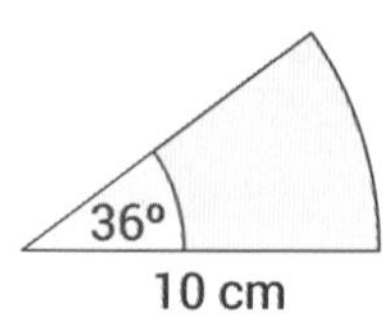

   (iii) $\pi = \frac{22}{7}$

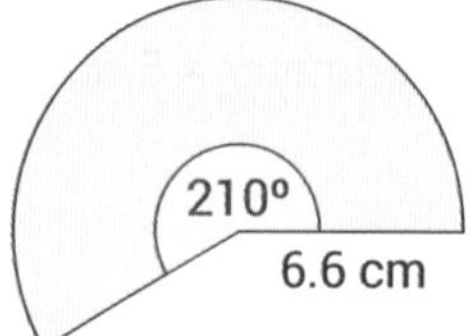

   (ii) $\pi = 3.14$

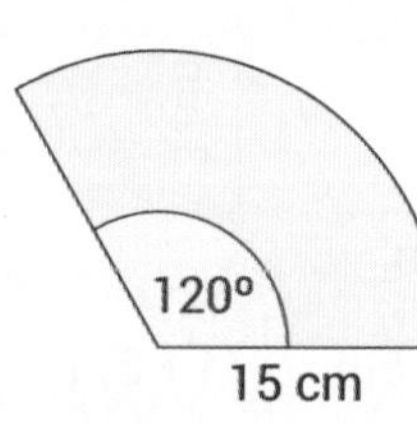

   (iv) $\pi = \frac{22}{7}$

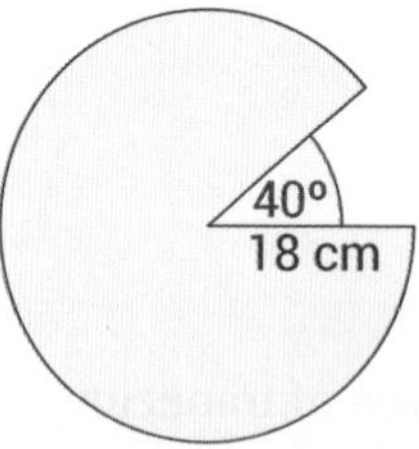

5. Find the area and perimeter of each of the following compound shapes ($\pi = 3.14$):

   (i)

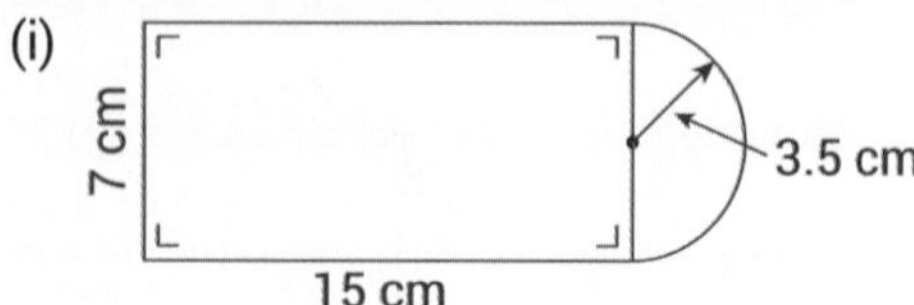

   (ii)

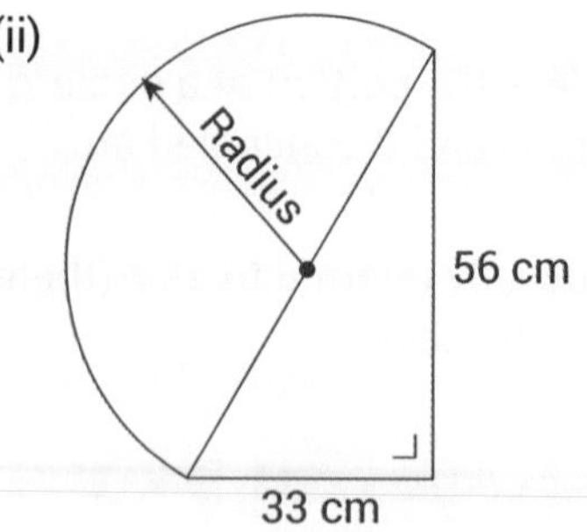

   (iii)

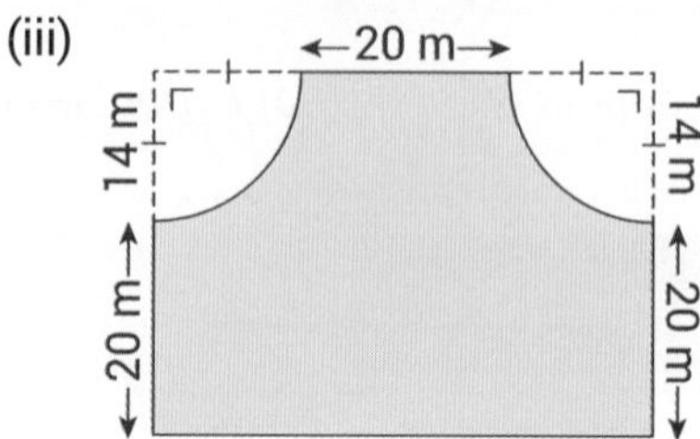

6. A satellite orbits a planet of radius 3,000 km as shown in the diagram.

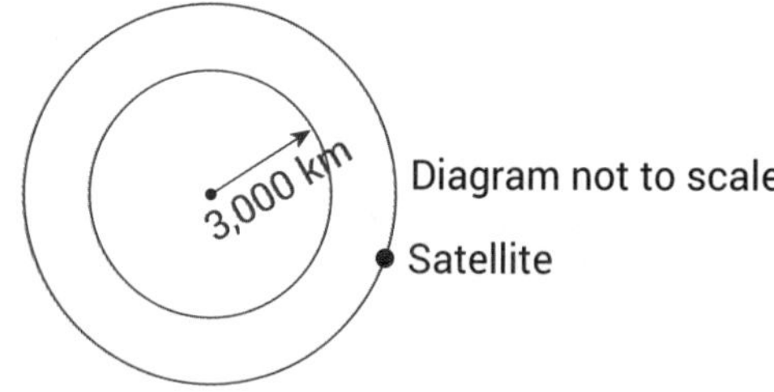

   The satellite orbits the planet at a height of 100 km and a speed of 6,000 ms^{-1}. How long, to the nearest minute, does it take the satellite to complete one full orbit? ($\pi = 3.14$)

7. A circular swimming pool has a radius of 15 m. It is surrounded by a path of width 1.5 m. Taking $\pi = \frac{22}{7}$, find:
   (i) The area of the path
   (ii) The cost of paving the path if paving costs €5.50 per square metre

8. The radii of two circles are 4 cm and 16 cm respectively. Find the ratio of:
   (i) Their circumferences
   (ii) Their areas

9. In a carnival a game is played where, if a dart hits the shaded region of a square board, a prize is given.

Which board would you pick to have the best chance of winning?

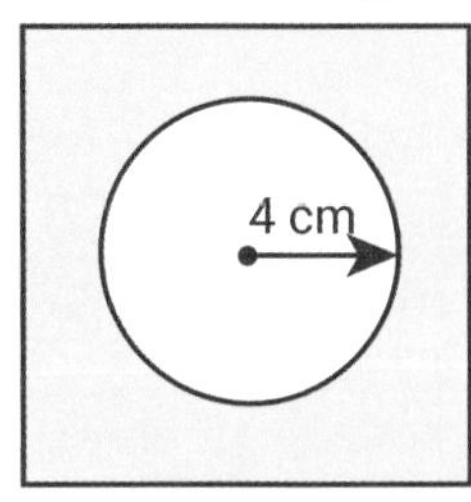

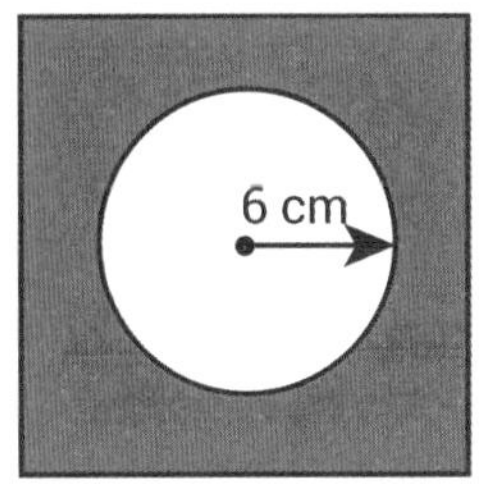

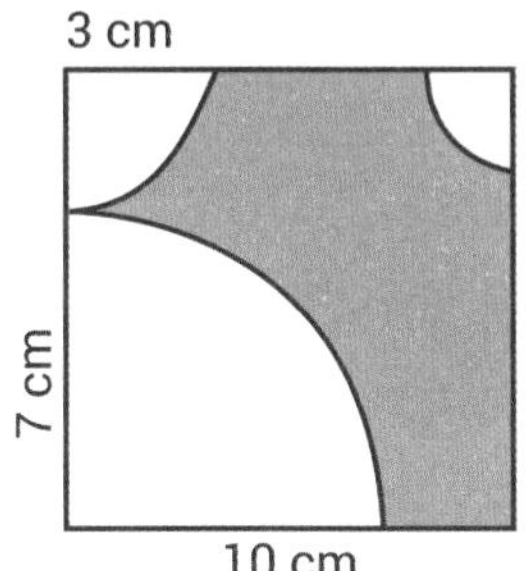

Diagrams are not drawn to scale.

10. Two race tracks with semicircular ends have the same perimeter.

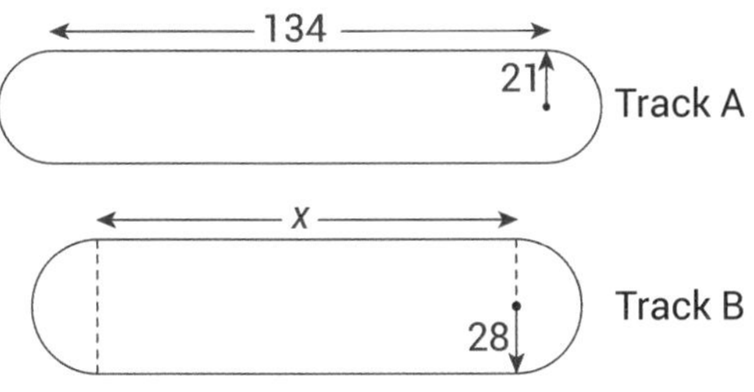

Taking $\pi = \frac{22}{7}$, find:

(i) The perimeter of track A

(ii) The length of the straight part of Track B

(All dimensions are in metres. Give answers to one decimal place.)

11. A metal part of a machine is shown. The arcs shown are semicircles.

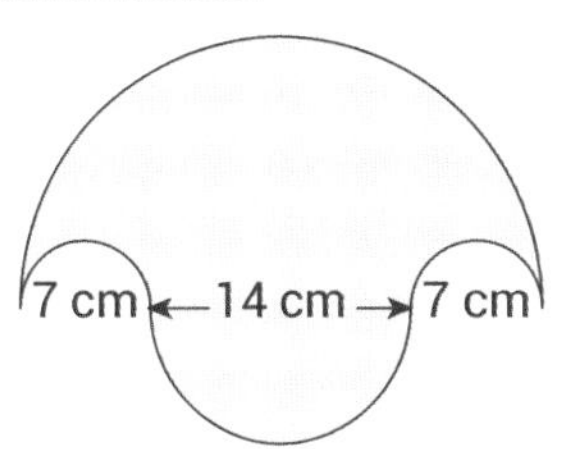

(i) Find, taking $\pi = 3.14$, the total area of the machine part.

This part is made by cutting from a rectangular sheet of metal 5 m by 3 m. The part is cut from the metal sheet as shown.

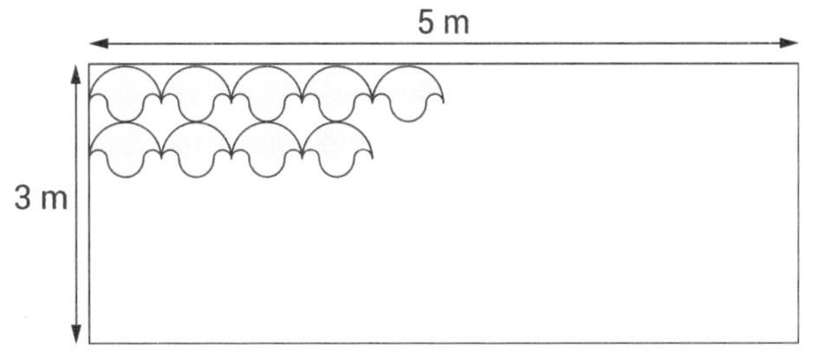

(ii) Find the number of complete parts that can be made from one such sheet of metal.

10.3 Finding Dimensions When Given Area or Perimeter

Sometimes we may be given the area or perimeter of a shape and have to work backwards to find an unknown length. To do this, we follow certain steps.

Worked Example 10.6

The area of this triangle is 20 cm^2. Find the perpendicular height of the triangle.

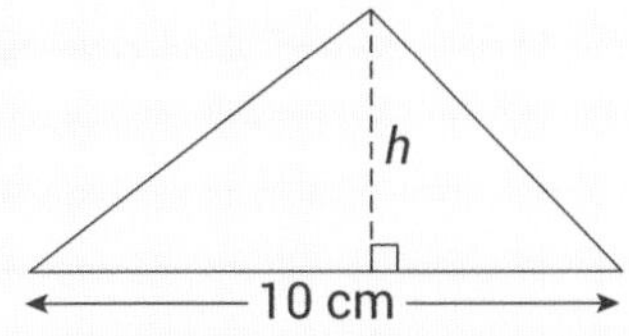

Don't forget the units of measurement in your answer.

Solution

Write down what we are given.	Area of triangle = 20
Write down formula.	$\frac{1}{2}bh = 20$
Fill in given dimensions.	$\frac{1}{2}(10)(h) = 20$ $5h = 20$
Solve.	$h = 4$ cm

APPLIED MEASURE

Worked Example 10.7

The area of a circle is 153.86 cm^2. Calculate the radius of the circle (π = 3.14).

Solution

Write down what we are given.	Area of circle = 153.86
Write down formula.	$\pi r^2 = 153.86$
Fill in given dimensions.	$(3.14)(r)^2 = 153.86$ $3.14r^2 = 153.86$
Solve.	$r^2 = \frac{153.86}{3.14} = 49$ $r = \sqrt{49}$ (as $r > 0$) $r = 7$ cm

Don't forget the units of measurement in your answer.

Worked Example 10.8

The circumference of a circle is 22π mm. Find the length of the radius of the circle.

Solution

The circumference of the circle is given in terms of π.

Write down what we are given.	Circumference of circle = 22π
Write down formula.	$2\pi r = 22\pi$
Solve. As **both** sides of the equation contain π, we can divide both sides by π.	$2\pi r = 22\pi$ $2r = 22$ $r = 11$ mm

Worked Example 10.9

The area of a rectangular lawn is 50 m^2. The length of the lawn is twice its width. Find the perimeter of the lawn.

Solution

The length of the lawn is twice its width. If the width (w) = x, then the length (l) = $2x$.

A diagram can help us visualise the problem.

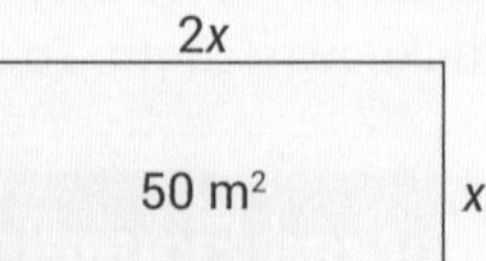

Write down what we are given.	Area of lawn = 50 m^2	
Write down formula.	$lw = 50$ m^2	
Fill in given dimensions.	$(2x)(x) = 50$ $2x^2 = 50$	
Solve.	$x^2 = 25$ $\therefore x = 5$ (as $x > 0$)	
Find perimeter.	Width (w) = x = 5 Length (l) = $2x$ = 2(5) = 10 Perimeter = $2(l) + 2(w)$ = 2(5) + 2(10) $\therefore$ Perimeter = 30 m	Width = 5 m Length = 10 m

Exercise 10.3

1. By using the information from each diagram below, find the value of x.
Diagrams are not to scale.

(i)

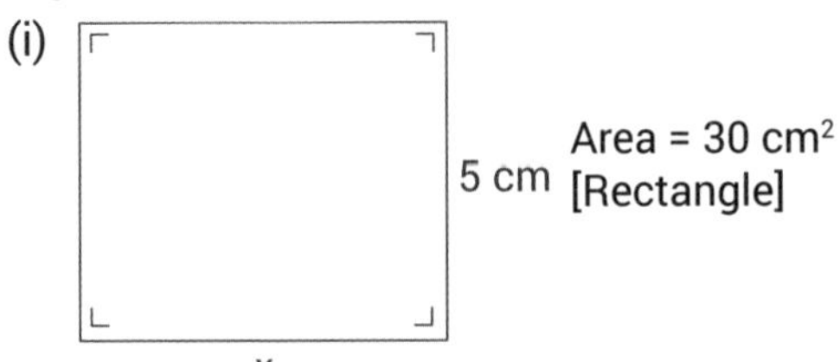

(ii)

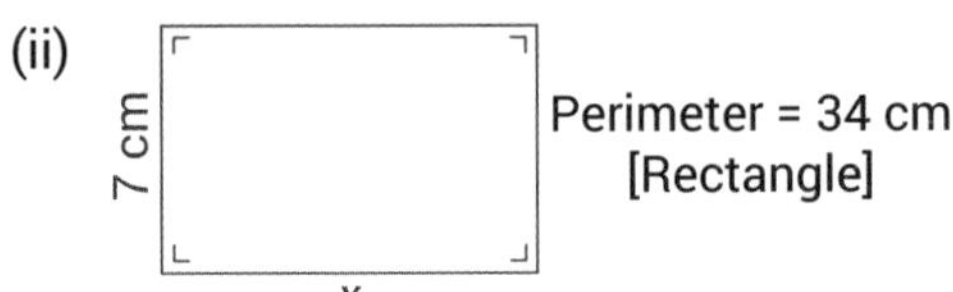

(iii)

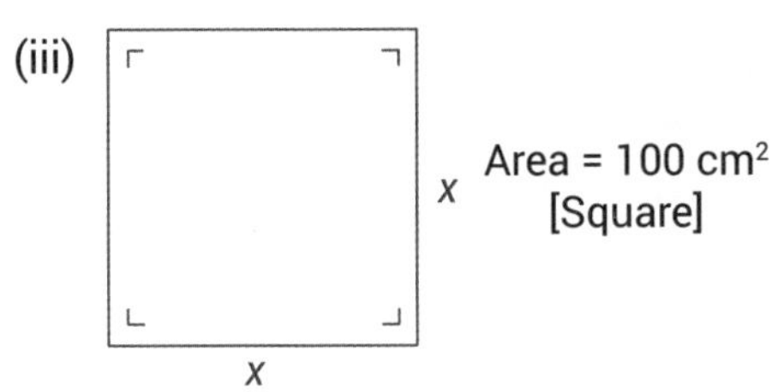

(iv)

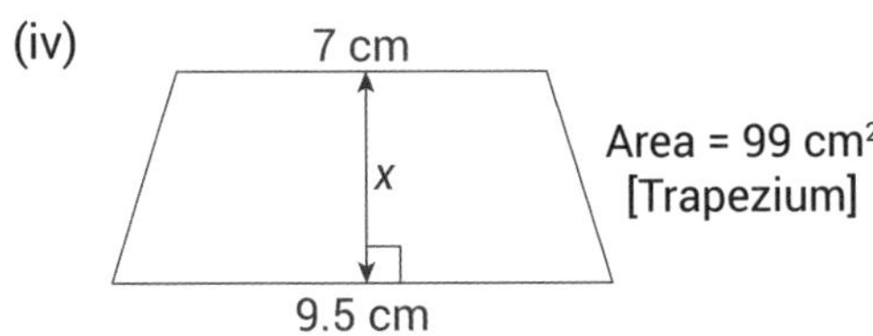

(v)

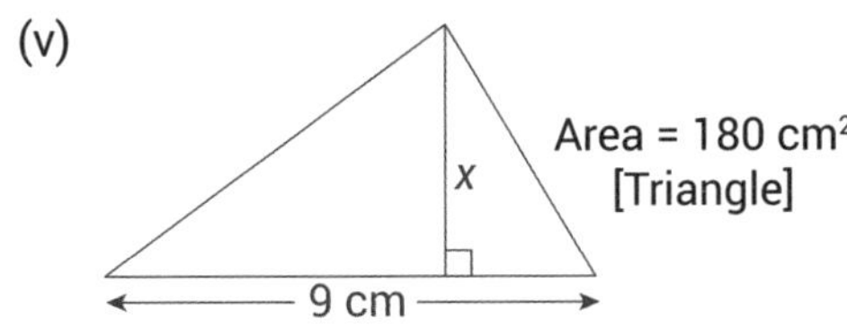

(vi) Area rectangle + Area triangle = 133 cm²

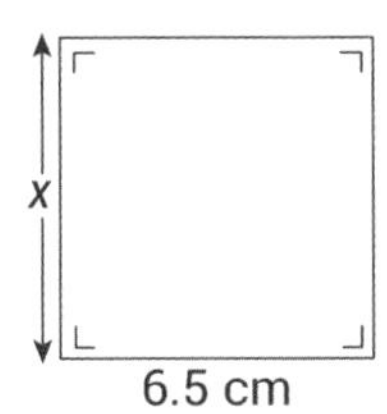

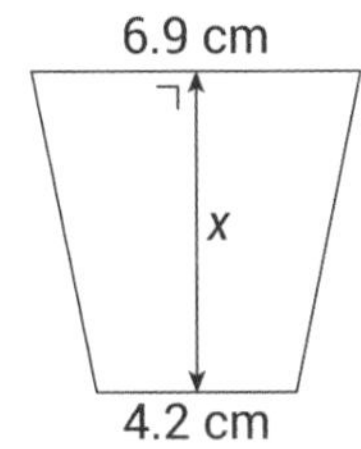

(vii) Area rectangle + Area trapezium = 51.815 cm²

2. Fill in the table below by first finding the radius of each of the circles.

π	r	Area	Circumference
π		49π	
3.14			43.96
$\frac{22}{7}$		2,464	
π			70π
3.14		803.84	
$\frac{22}{7}$			$100\frac{4}{7}$
3.14		28.26	
π		$\frac{1}{81}\pi$	

3. Using the information given, find the measure of the unknown radius or the angle of each of the following sectors:

(i) Length of arc $= 7\pi$ cm

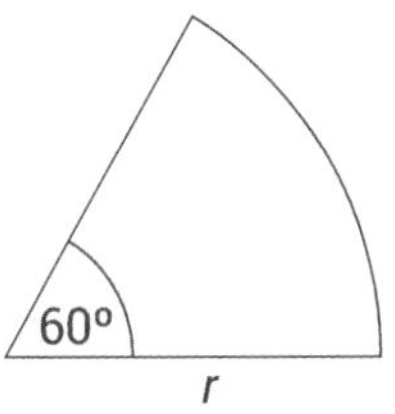

(ii) Area = 1,413 cm² ($\pi = 3.14$)

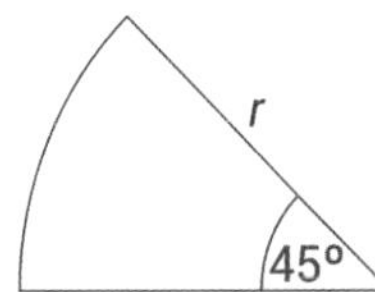

(iii) Area $= 78\frac{4}{7}$ cm² $\left(\pi = \frac{22}{7}\right)$

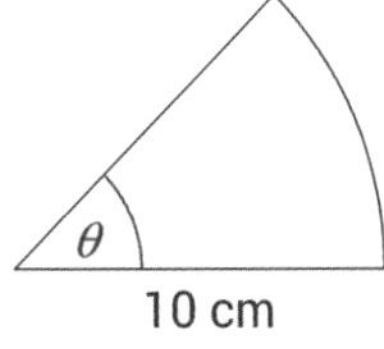

(iv) Length of arc $= 23.8\pi$ cm

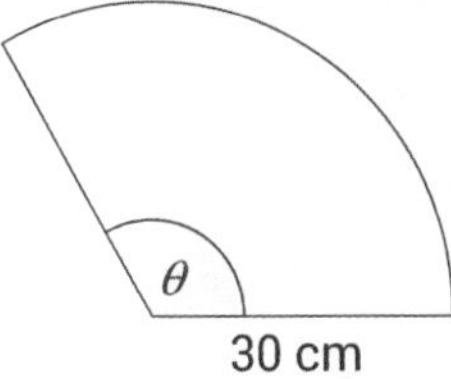

(v) Area = 841.52 cm^2 (π = 3.14)

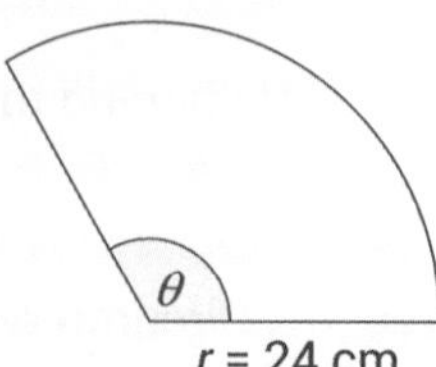

4. The area of a rectangular room is 12 m^2. Its length is 4 m. Find:
   (i) Its width
   (ii) The length of a diagonal

5. The perimeter of a rectangular garden is 34 m. Its length is 12 m. Calculate:
   (i) Its width
   (ii) The length of a diagonal

6. The length of a rectangular page is 10 cm greater than its width. The perimeter is 1 m. Find the area of one page in square centimetres.

7. A wheel has a circumference of 308 cm.
   (i) Taking $\pi = \frac{22}{7}$, find the radius of the wheel.
   (ii) This wheel must be checked every 10,000 revolutions. How far would the wheel travel in km?

8. The area of a circle is 225π m^2. Find:
   (i) Its radius
   (ii) Its circumference (to one decimal place)

9. A landscaping firm charges €7.50 per m^2. Landscaping the garden shown costs €10,026. The owner decides to erect a fence to surround the garden. How many metres of fence will be needed? (π = 3.14)

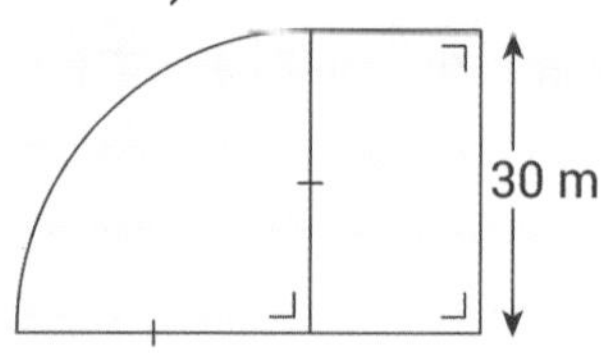

10. A square is inscribed in a circle of radius 5 cm as shown. Find:
    (i) The area of the square
    (ii) The area of the shaded region to the nearest cm^2

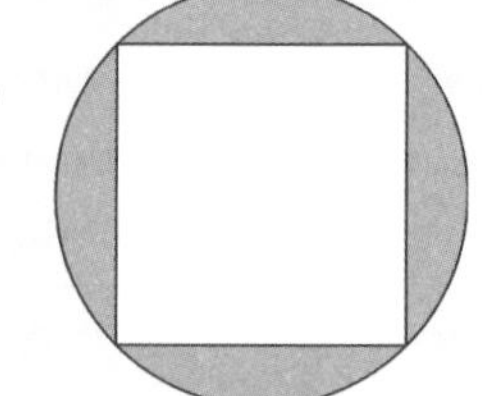

11. The area of a circular swimming pool is 64π m^2. A protective circular tarpaulin to cover this pool needs to be bought.

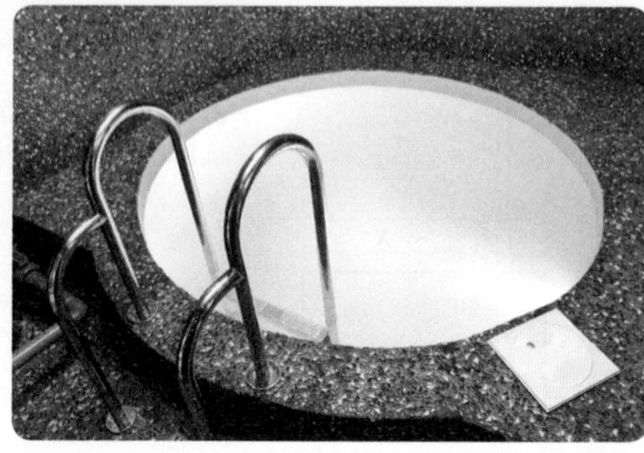

    (i) The tarpaulin must have a radius of 50 cm greater than the radius of the pool in order to cover the pool correctly.
    Find the radius of the tarpaulin needed.
    (ii) After buying the tarpaulin, it is discovered that the incorrect size was bought. The diameter of this tarpaulin cover is 20 m. It is then decided to cut the tarpaulin so as to fit the pool correctly.
    Calculate the area of the cover that must be removed. (π = 3.14)

12. The diagram shows six circles with the same centre, each a distance x width apart.
    The diameter of the centre circle also measures x units.
    Which has the greater area: the inner red shaded region or the outer blue shaded region?

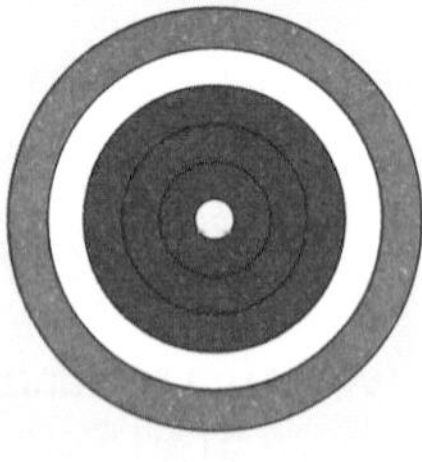

10.4 Rectangular Solids

APPLIED MEASURE

Rectangular Solids

One type of 3D object is the rectangular solid. To find the amount of space (**volume**) that a rectangular solid (**cuboid**) occupies, we multiply out the three dimensions given.

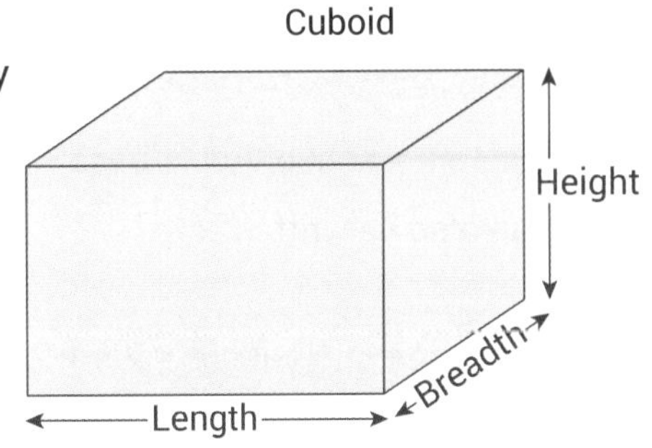

Volume of a cuboid = length × breadth × height
$\therefore$ Volume = lbh

Volume (capacity) is the amount of space an object occupies.

When measuring volume, the units of measurement will always be units^3, for example: mm^3, cm^3, m^3, km^3, etc.

If all sides of the rectangular solid are equal in length, then it can be referred to as a **cube**.

Volume of a cube = length × length × length
$\therefore$ Volume = l^3

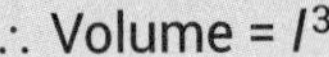

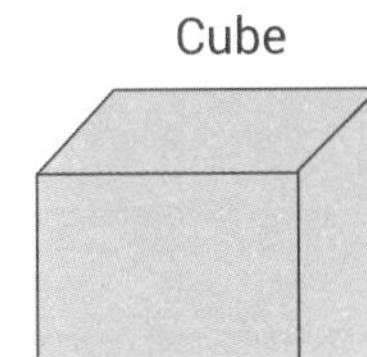

Take care.

1 m = 100 cm

1 m^3 = 1 m × 1 m × 1 m = 100 cm × 100 cm × 100 cm = 1,000,000 cm^3

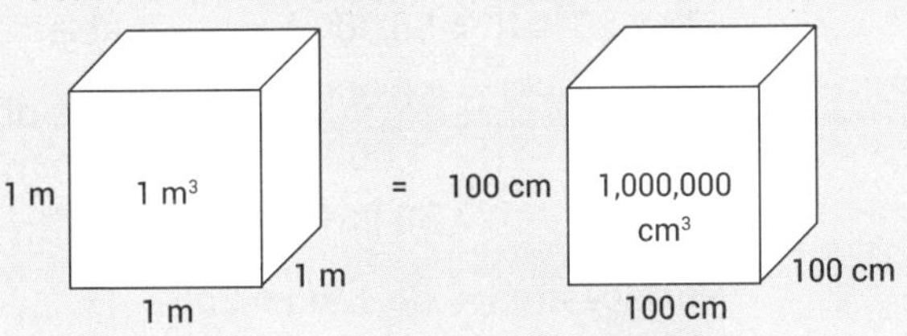

Surface Area and Nets

A cube or cuboid has six flat sides or faces.

The line where two faces meet is called an **edge**.

The corner where three edges meet is called a **vertex**.

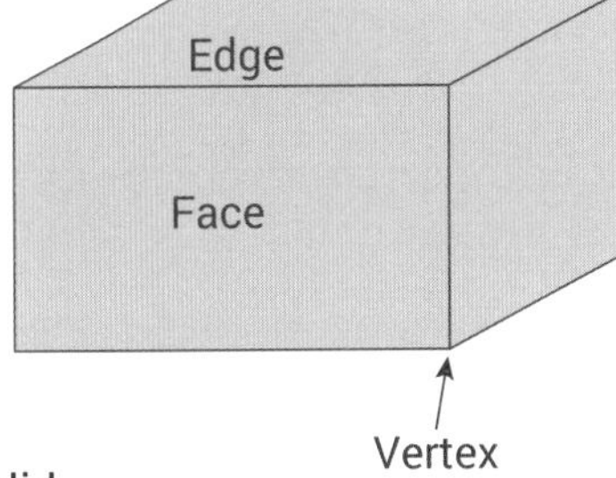

If we cut along the edges of a rectangular solid, we can create a **net** of that solid.

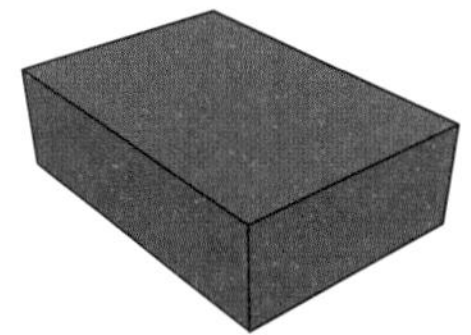

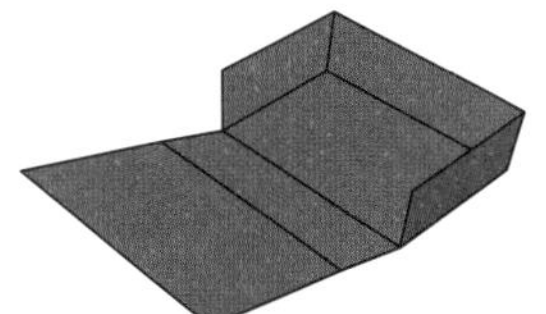

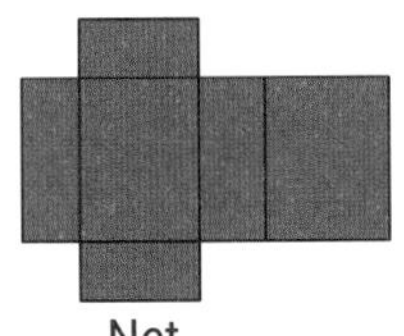

A **net** is a 2D (flat) shape that folds up along its edges to make a 3D solid.

There can be many different nets for one rectangular solid. These are two possible nets for a cube. In total there are 11 possible nets for a cube. (Check this out online.)

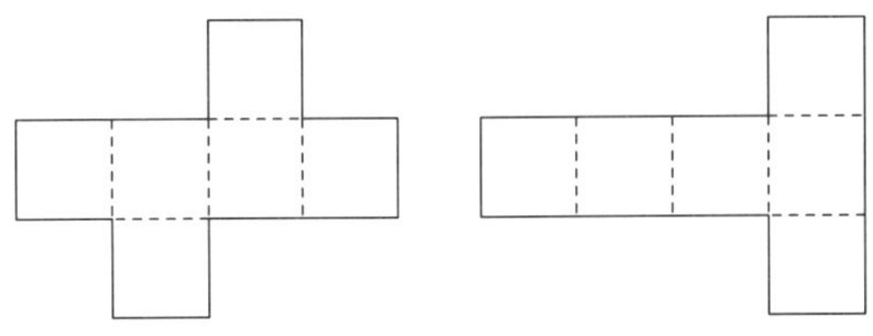

APPLIED MEASURE

Nets can be used to help determine the **surface area** of a 3D solid.

Surface area of a cuboid = the sum of the area of all six faces of its net.

Surface area = area of (top + base + front + back + side + side).

This can also be written as:

Surface area of a cuboid = $2lb + 2lh + 2bh$

Surface area of a cube = $6(\text{length})^2$ or $6l^2$

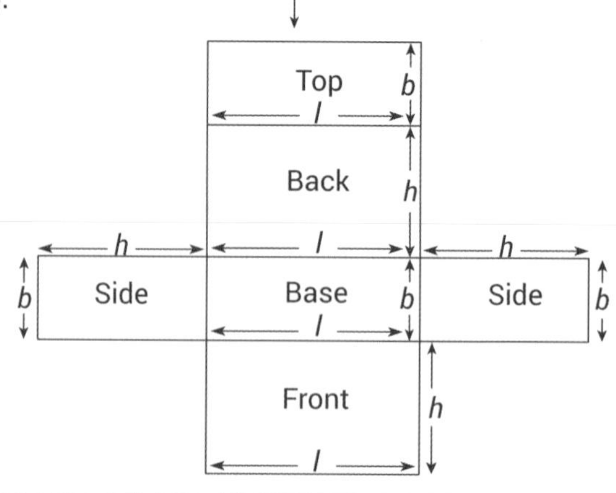

Worked Example 10.10

Find the volume (in litres) and the surface area (in cm²) of the cuboid shown below.

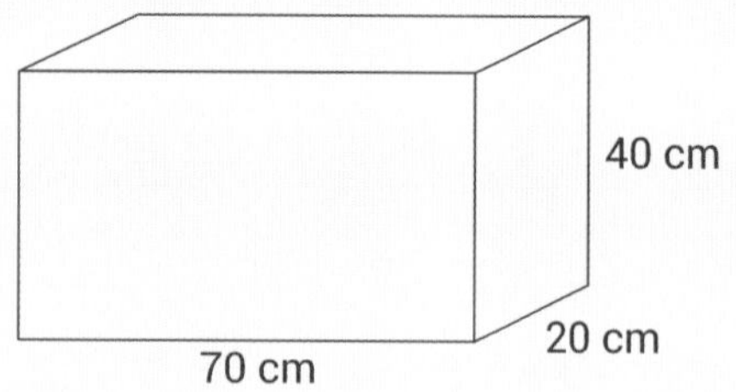

Solution

Volume = lbh = length × breadth × height

$70 \times 20 \times 40 = 56{,}000 \text{ cm}^3$

$= \dfrac{56{,}000}{1{,}000}$

$= 56$ litres

1 litre = 1,000 cm³

∴ We divide by 1,000 to convert cm³ into litres.

Surface area = $2lb + 2lh + 2bh$

$= 2(70)(20) + 2(70)(40) + 2(20)(40)$

$= 2{,}800 + 5{,}600 + 1{,}600$

$= 10{,}000 \text{ cm}^2$

It is important to ensure that all the measurements used in our calculations are in the same units.

Worked Example 10.11

The net of an open rectangular box is shown. Find the volume and surface area of this solid.

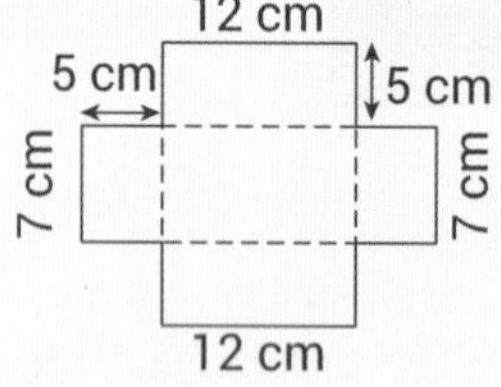

Solution

Volume

From the net drawing, we can work out the dimensions of the box.

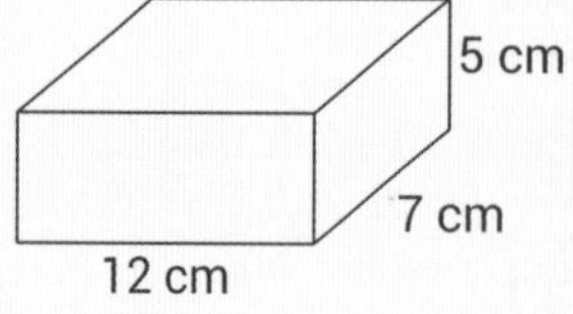

Length = 12 cm, breadth = 7 cm, height = 5 cm

Volume = $lbh = 12 \times 7 \times 5 = 420 \text{ cm}^3$

Surface area

Use the net of the shape to calculate the surface area.

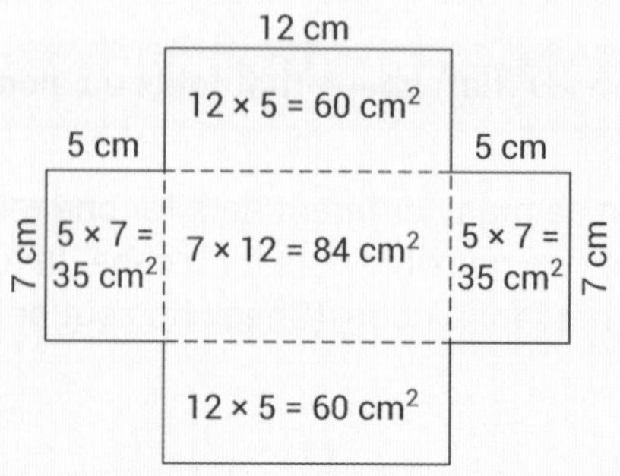

$35 + 35 + 60 + 60 + 84 = 274 \text{ cm}^2$

APPLIED MEASURE

Exercise 10.4

1. Find the volume and surface area of each of the following rectangular solids:

(i)

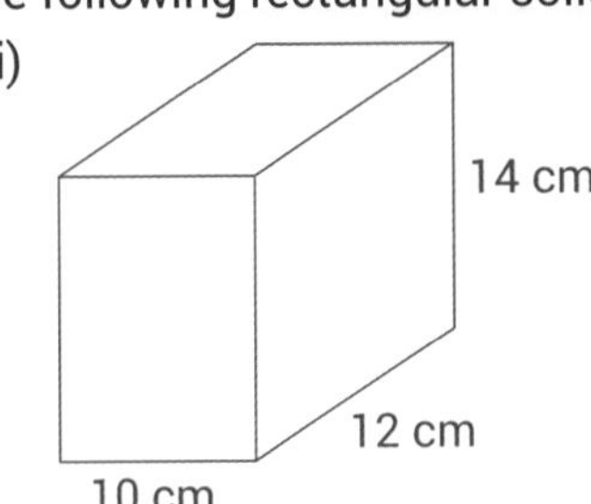

(ii)

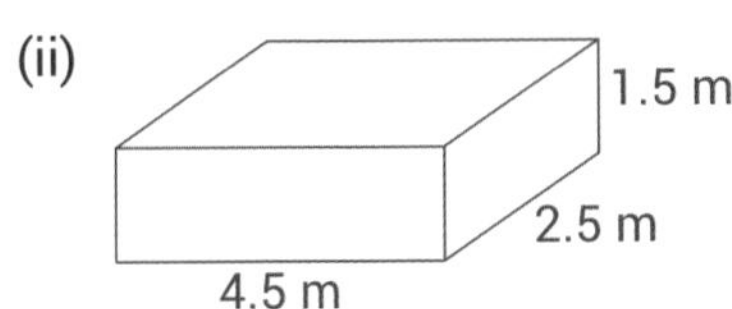

(iii)

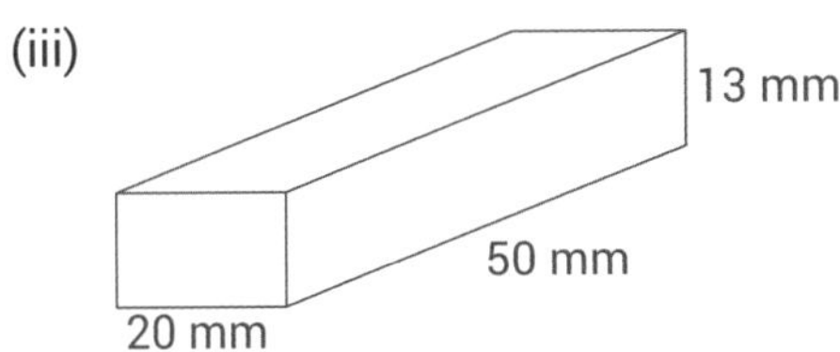

(iv)

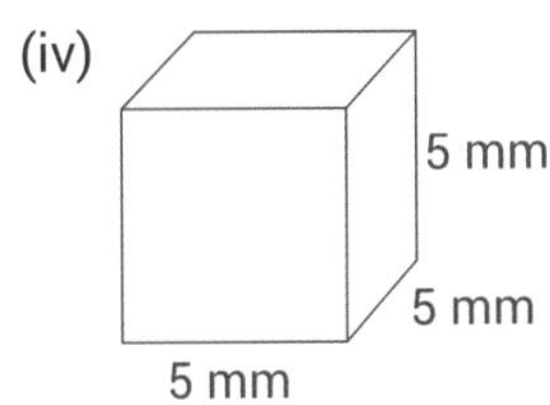

2. Use the nets of the following rectangular solids to find their volumes and surface areas:

(i)

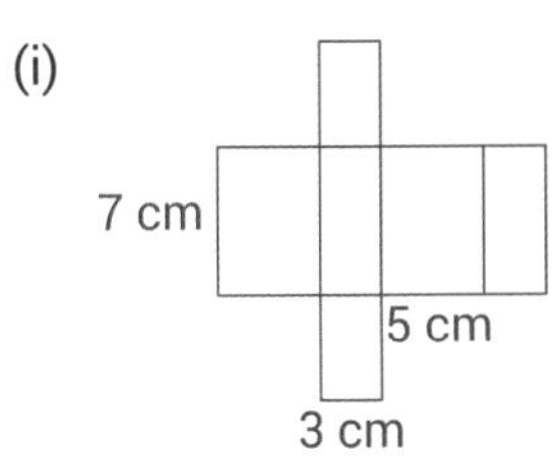

(ii)

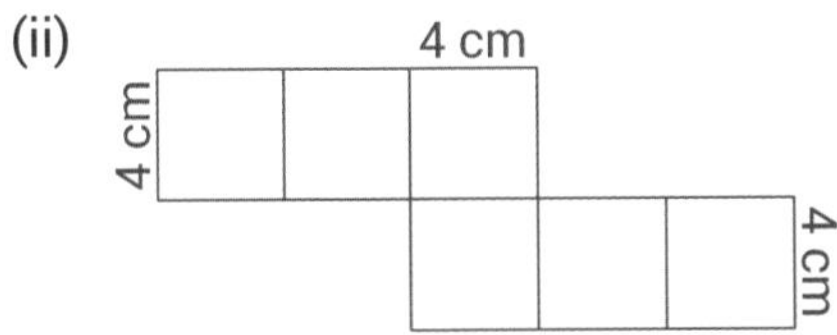

(iii)

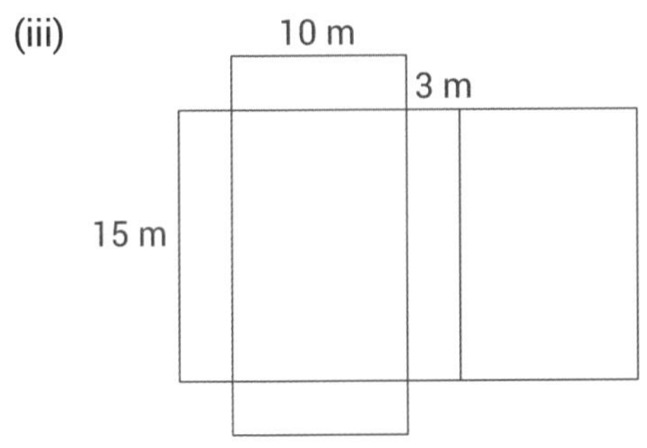

3. Draw nets of the following solids (include dimensions of at least three faces).

   (i) A cube with sides of 4 cm.

   (ii) A cuboid with labelled sides of 10 cm, 7 cm and 4 cm.

4. (i) Which one of the following nets will not fold to make a cube?

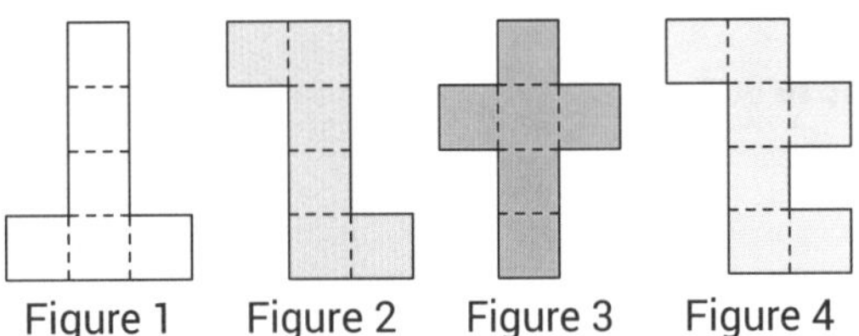

   (ii) Draw two more different nets for a cube.

5. The net of a cardboard rectangular solid is shown.

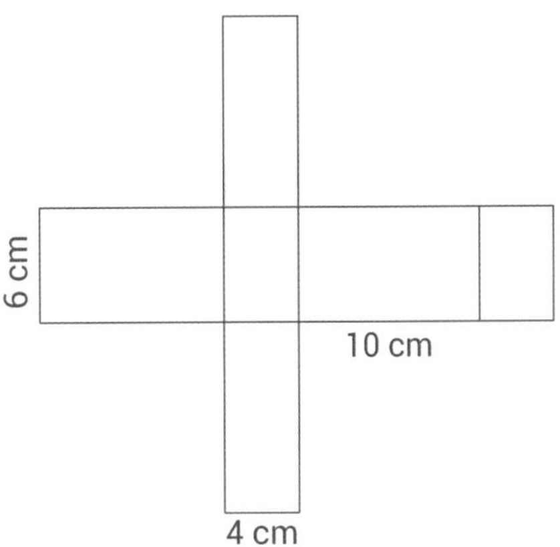

   (i) Calculate the surface area of the solid.

   (ii) How many cubes of side 2 cm can be formed from this solid?

6. A rectangular water tank is 55 cm long, 36 cm wide and 10 cm high. Find:

   (i) The volume of water in the tank if the tank is half full, giving your answer in litres (note: 1 litre = 1,000 cm^3)

   (ii) The surface area in cm^2, if the tank has no lid

10.5 Prisms

A **prism** is a 3D solid that has parallel congruent bases that are both polygons.

A **right prism** is a prism in which one of the bases is directly above the other. Its side faces are therefore rectangles.

The volume of a **right prism** is the area of its base multiplied by the prism's length.

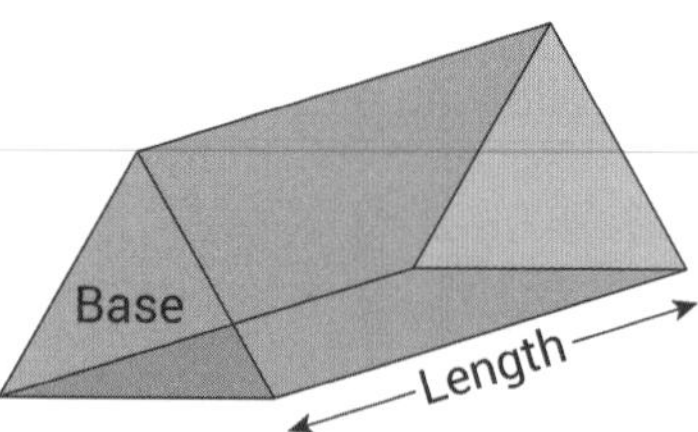

The surface area of a prism can be found by using nets.

Volume of a prism = area of base × length

Worked Example 10.12

Find the volume and surface area of the following prism.

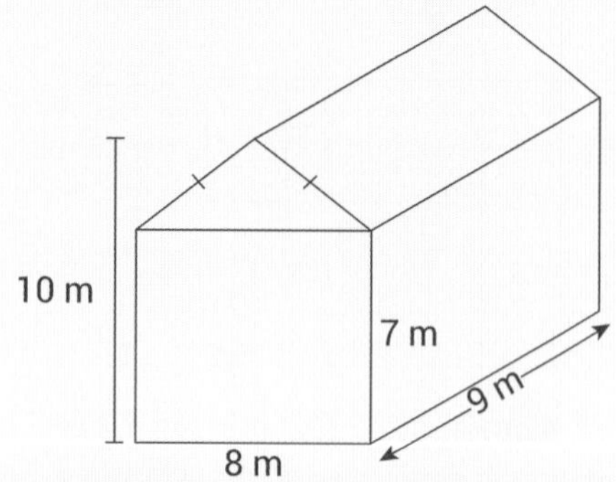

Solution

Volume

We work out the area of the base (front face) of the solid.

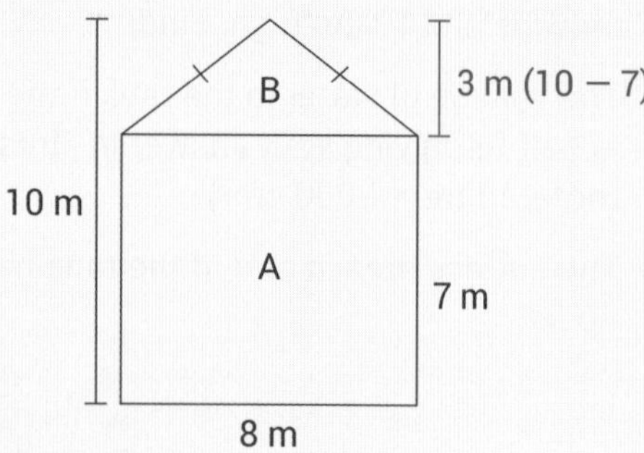

Area of A (rectangle) = (8)(7) = 56 m^2

Area of B (triangle) = $\frac{1}{2}(8)(3) = 12\ m^2$

Total area = 68 m^2

Volume = area of cross-section × length

= (68)(9)

= 612 m^3

Surface area

We draw the net of the prism.

$h^2 = 4^2 + 3^2$

$h^2 = 25$

$\therefore h = 5$ m

Work out the area of each face.

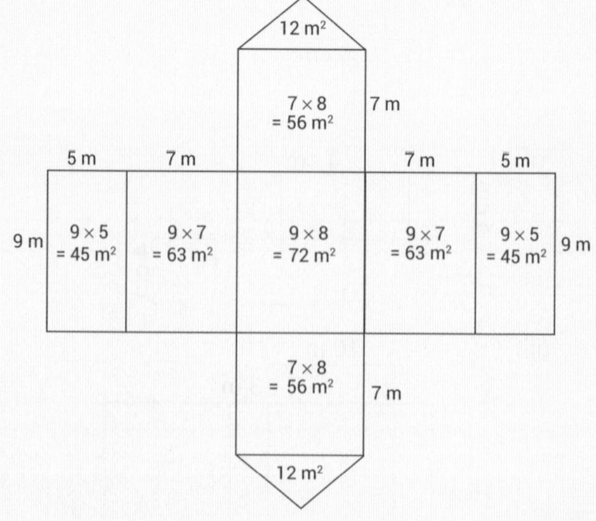

Surface area = 2(45) + 2(63) + 2(56) + 2(12) + 72

= 424 m^2

Exercise 10.5

1. Find the volume and surface area of the following right prisms:

(i)

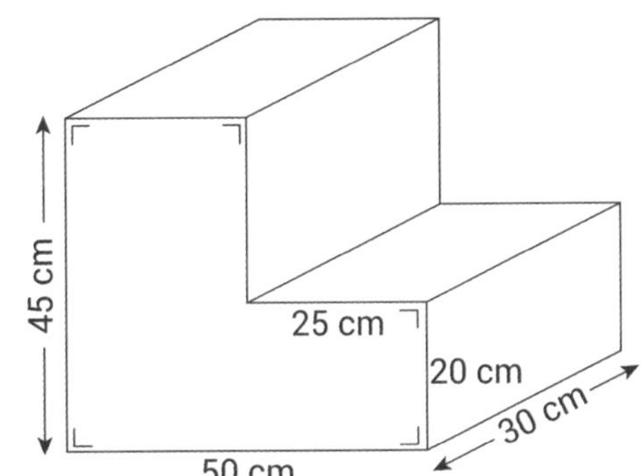

(ii)

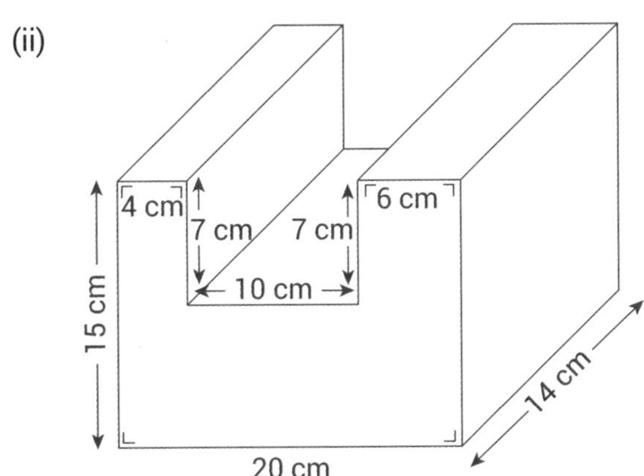

(iii)

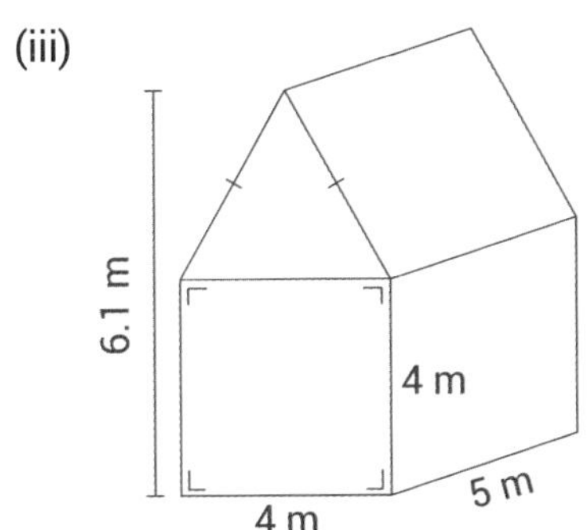

2. Draw a net for each of the following solids:

(i)

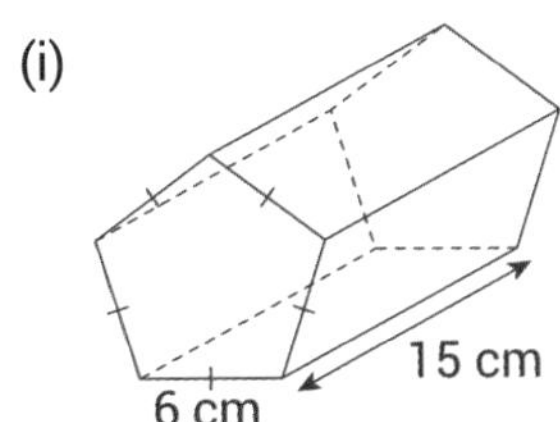

(ii)

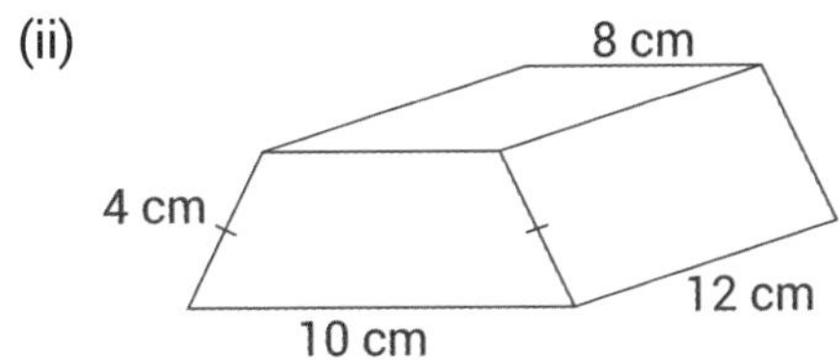

(iii)

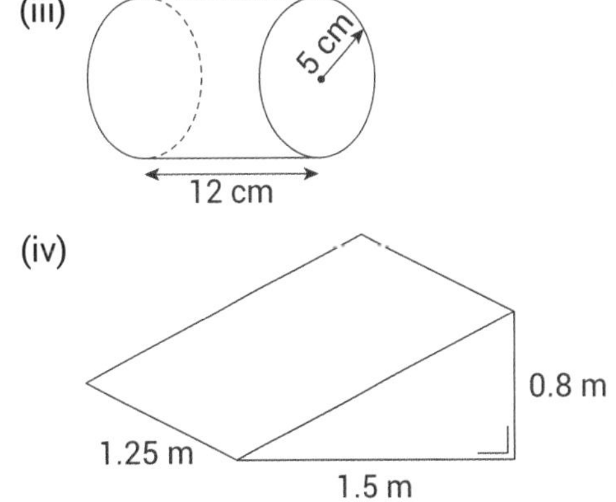

(iv)

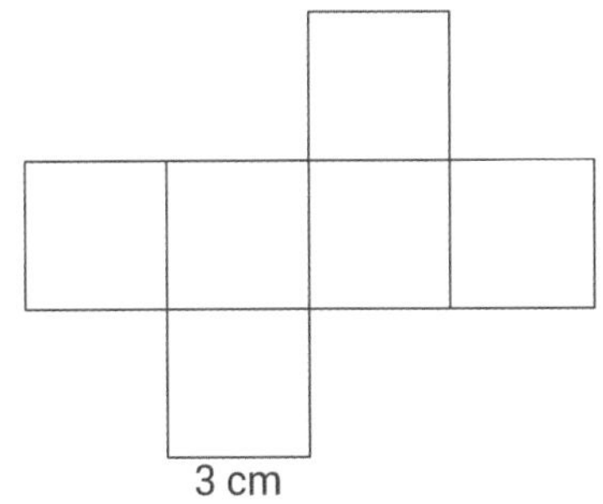

3. Find the volume and surface area of the right prisms whose nets are shown below.

(i) Cube

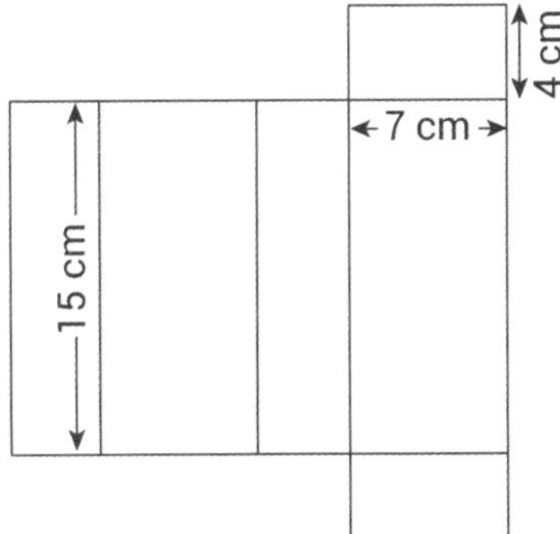

(ii) Cuboid

(iii) Right prism

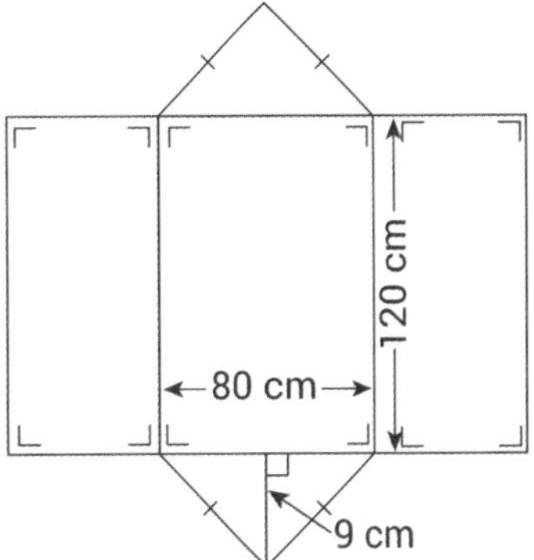

4. The length of a Toblerone packet is 8 cm. The length of the base is 2 cm. The perpendicular height is also 2 cm. Find the volume of the Toblerone packet.

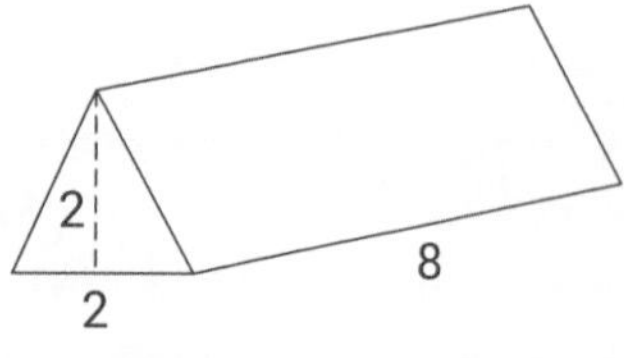

5. A diagram for the construction of a shed is shown.

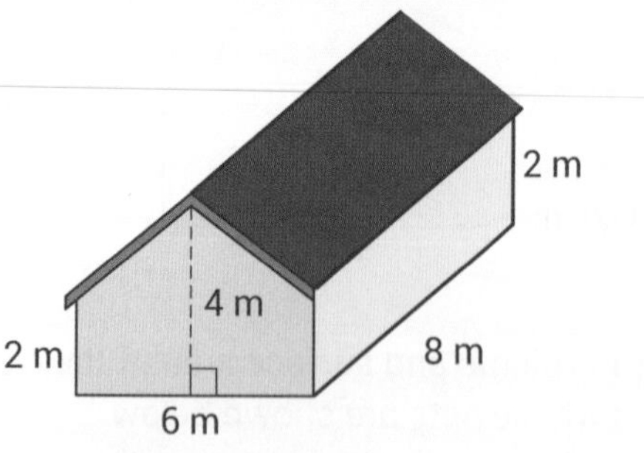

   (i) Find the area of the shaded side of the shed.

   (ii) Find the total volume of the interior of the shed.

6. A pair of steps is made out of concrete as shown.

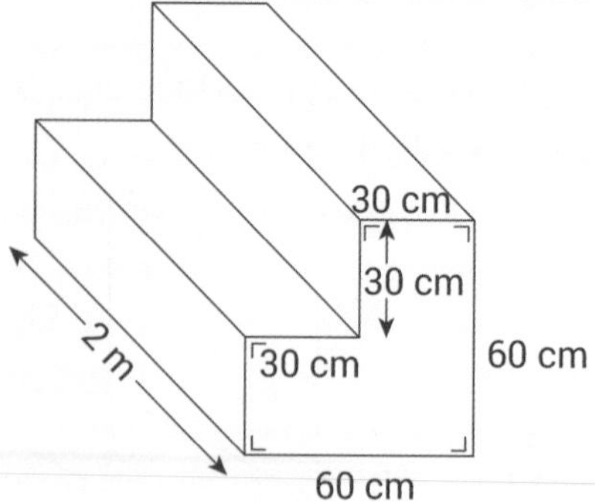

Find:

(i) The volume of the concrete contained in the steps (in cubic metres)

(ii) The cost of making the steps if concrete costs €88 per cubic metre

10.6 Cylinders 

Volume of cylinder = $\pi \times (\text{radius})^2 \times$ height
$\therefore$ Volume = $\pi r^2 h$

This formula appears on page 10 of *Formulae and Tables*.

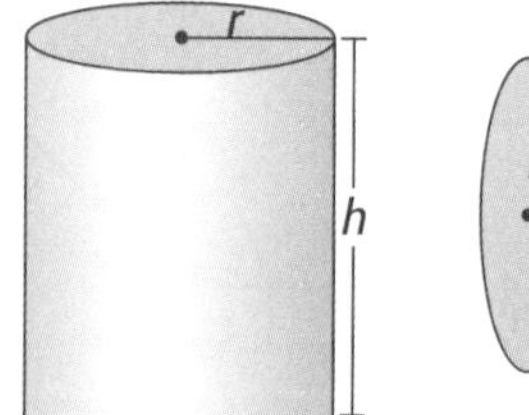

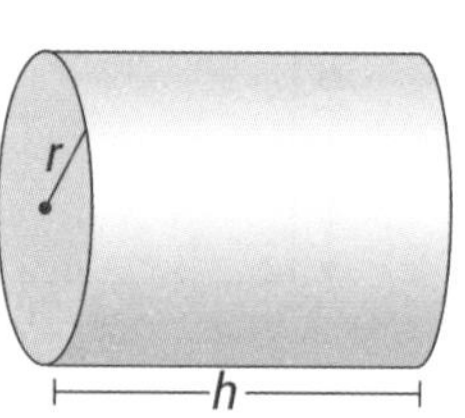

Surface Area of a Cylinder

We can use a net to show how to calculate the two types of surface area of a cylinder.

Curved Surface Area (CSA) of a cylinder

This is the area of just the curved part of the cylinder.

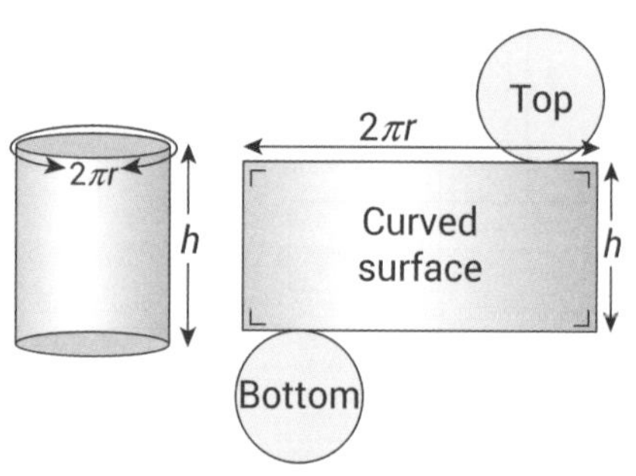

Curved surface area (CSA) of cylinder = $2\pi rh$

This formula appears on page 10 of *Formulae and Tables*.

Total Surface Area (TSA) of a cylinder

There are three cases that must be considered:

Cylinder open at both ends

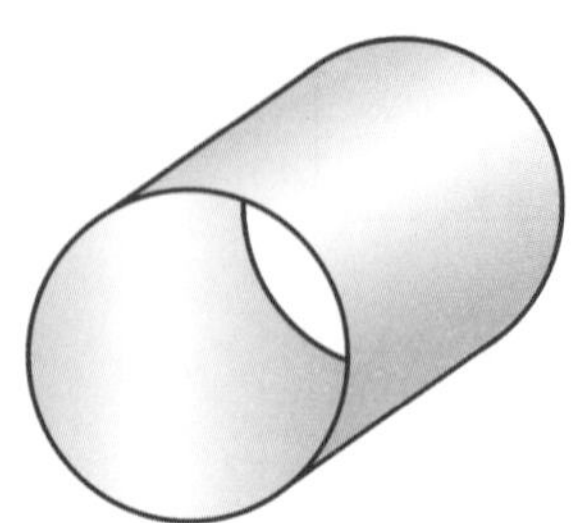

TSA = CSA
$\therefore$ TSA = $2\pi rh$

Cylinder closed at one end

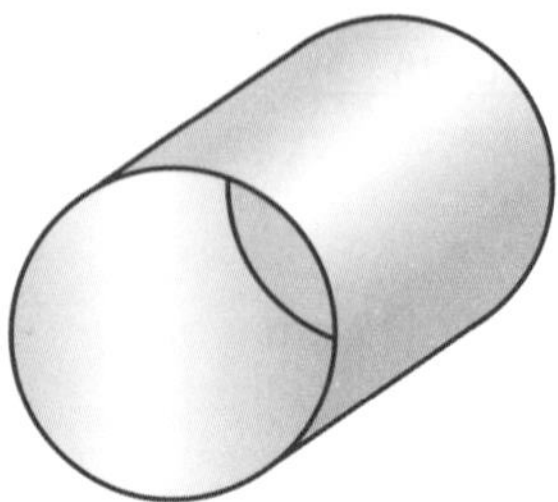

TSA = CSA + πr^2
$\therefore$ TSA = $2\pi rh + \pi r^2$

Cylinder closed at both ends (solid cylinder)

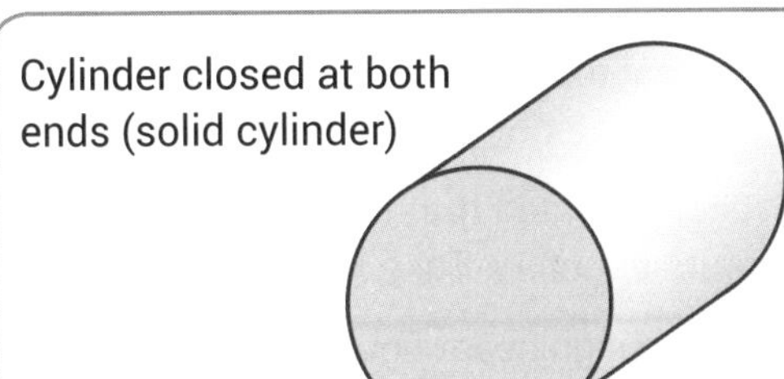

TSA = CSA + $2\pi r^2$
$\therefore$ TSA = $2\pi rh + 2\pi r^2$

Total surface area (TSA) of solid cylinder = CSA + $2\pi r^2$
$\therefore$ TSA = $2\pi rh + 2\pi r^2$ or $2\pi r(h + r)$

Worked Example 10.13

Find the volume, curved surface area (CSA) and total surface area (TSA) of a solid cylinder with a radius of 5 cm and a height of 6 cm:

(i) In terms of π (ii) Taking $\pi = 3.14$

Solution

(i) In terms of π

Volume = $\pi r^2 h$
= $\pi \times (5)^2 \times 6$
= 150π cm^3

Curved surface area
CSA = $2\pi rh$
= $2 \times \pi \times 5 \times 6$
= 60π cm^2

Total surface area
TSA = $2\pi rh + 2\pi r^2$
= $60\pi + 2 \times \pi \times (5)^2$
= $60\pi + 2 \times \pi \times 25$
= $60\pi + 50\pi$
= 110π cm^2

(ii) Taking $\pi = 3.14$

Volume = $\pi r^2 h$
= $3.14 \times (5)^2 \times 6$
= 471 cm^3

Curved surface area
CSA = $2\pi rh$
= $2 \times 3.14 \times 5 \times 6$
= 188.4 cm^2

Total surface area
TSA = $2\pi rh + 2\pi r^2$
= $188.4 + 2 \times 3.14 \times (5)^2$
= $188.4 + 2 \times 3.14 \times 25$
= $188.4 + 157$
= 345.4 cm^2

Exercise 10.6

1. Find the volume of each of the following cylinders:
   (i) $r = 10$ cm, $h = 10$ cm ($\pi = 3.14$)
   (ii) $r = 1.2$ cm, $h = 4$ cm $\left(\pi = \frac{22}{7}\right)$
   (iii) $r = 9$ m, $h = 8$ m (in terms of π)
   (iv) $r = 25$ m, $h = 21$ m $\left(\pi = \frac{22}{7}\right)$
   (v) $r = 5$ mm, $h = 14$ mm ($\pi = 3.14$)

2. Find the curved surface area and the total surface area of each of the following solid cylinders:
   (i) $r = 0.25$ m, $h = 2$ m ($\pi = 3.14$)
   (ii) $r = 3$ cm, $h = 5$ cm (in terms of π)
   (iii) $r = 5$ cm, $h = 11$ cm ($\pi = 3.14$)
   (iv) $r = 22$ cm, $h = 44$ cm $\left(\pi = \frac{22}{7}\right)$

3. Find the volume and total surface area of each of the following solid cylinders:
   (i) $r = 14$ mm, $h = 2$ mm $\left(\pi = \frac{22}{7}\right)$
   (ii) $r = 2.25$ mm, $h = 0.5$ cm (in terms of π)

4. Find the total surface area of each of the following cylinders:
   (i) $r = 11$ m, $h = 22$ m ($\pi = 3.14$, open at both ends)
   (ii) $r = 8$ cm, $h = 14$ cm ($\pi = \frac{22}{7}$, open at one end)

5. A cylindrical tin of paint has a radius of 14 cm and a height of 22 cm. Taking π as 3.14, find:

   (i) The volume of paint in a full tin (give answer in litres to two decimal places)

   (ii) The area of sheet metal needed to make the tin

6. Two cylinders have a height of 10 cm, but have radii of 16 and 8 cm, respectively. Find:

   (i) Their volumes in terms of π

   (ii) The ratio of their volumes

7. An above ground cylindrical swimming pool is shown.

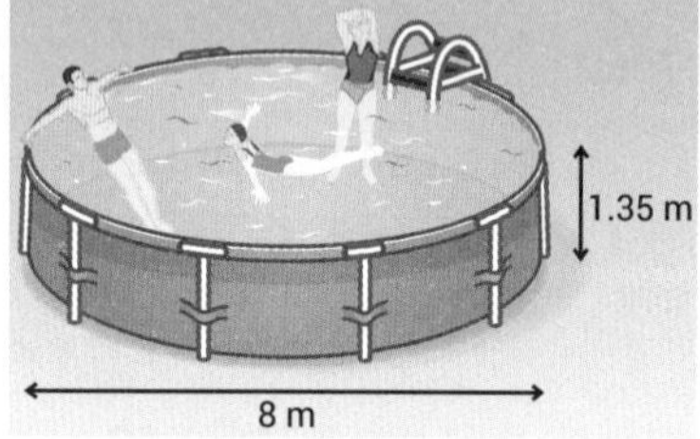

The internal diameter of the pool measures 8 m and the height of the pool is 1.35 m.

It is recommended that the pool is filled to 95% of its capacity. Take π = 3.14.

   (i) Find, to two significant figures, the maximum volume (in litres) that the pool is allowed to hold.

   (ii) The pool's side walls and base are made from PVC. Find the minimum surface area of PVC needed to build this pool.

8. A cylindrical storage tank is filled with a liquid chemical to be used in food production. The tank has a height of 3 m and a diameter of 75 cm. One ml of this liquid weighs 1.035 g. The storage tank is made from a metal alloy that weighs 2.5 g per cm^2. (Assume the metal alloy is of negligible thickness.)

   Find the combined weight of the tank and the chemical.

   (π = 3.14. Give your answer in kg correct to two decimal places.)

10.7 Right Circular Cones

A **right circular cone** has an apex (top) directly above the centre of a circular base.

Volume of a Cone

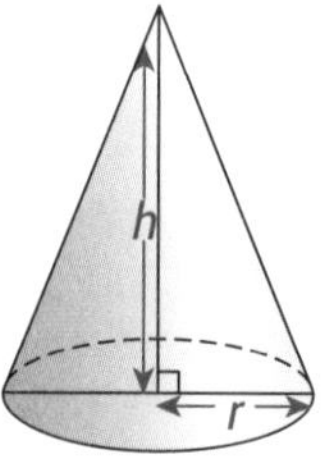

Volume of cone = $\frac{1}{3} \times \pi \times (\text{radius})^2 \times \text{height}$

$\therefore$ Volume = $\frac{1}{3}\pi r^2 h$

This formula appears on page 10 of *Formulae and Tables*.

Worked Example 10.14

Find the volume of the following cones:

(i) $r = 7.5$ m, $h = 11$ m (π = 3.14)

(ii) $r = 4$ mm, $h = 15$ mm (in terms of π)

Solution

(i) Volume $= \frac{1}{3}\pi r^2 h$

$= \frac{1}{3} \times 3.14 \times (7.5)^2 \times 11$

$= 647.625$ m^3

(ii) Volume $= \frac{1}{3}\pi r^2 h$

$= \frac{1}{3} \times \pi \times (4)^2 \times 15$

$= 80\pi$ mm^3

Surface Area of a Cone

There are two types of surface area of a cone.

Curved Surface Area (CSA) of a Cone

This is the area of the curved part of the cone.

Curved surface area (CSA) of cone = πrl

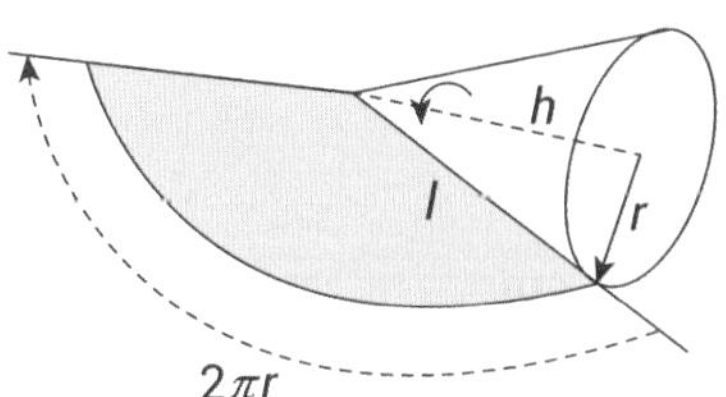

This formula appears on page 10 of *Formulae and Tables*.

The shaded region on the diagram indicates a net of the curved surface area of a cone.

To calculate the CSA, we must have the slant height (l) of the cone.

Using Pythagoras' theorem, we can state that $l^2 = h^2 + r^2$.

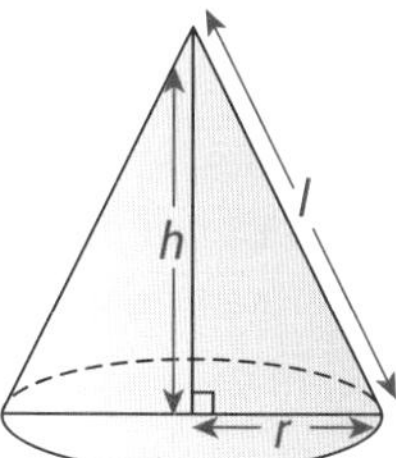

l in the formula refers to the slant height of the cone. This is the distance from any point on the circular base to the top (apex) of the cone.

h is the perpendicular height (altitude) of the cone.

r is the radius of the circular base.

$l^2 = h^2 + r^2$

Total Surface Area (TSA) of a Cone

This is the area of the curved part of the cone **plus** the circular base.

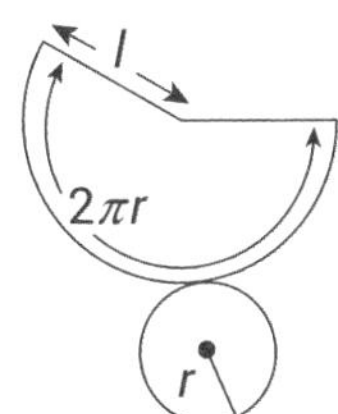

Net of a cone

Total surface area (TSA) of cone = CSA + πr^2

$\therefore$ TSA $= \pi rl + \pi r^2$ or $\pi r(l + r)$

Worked Example 10.15

Calculate the curved surface area and the total surface area of the cone shown.

Give your answers in terms of π.

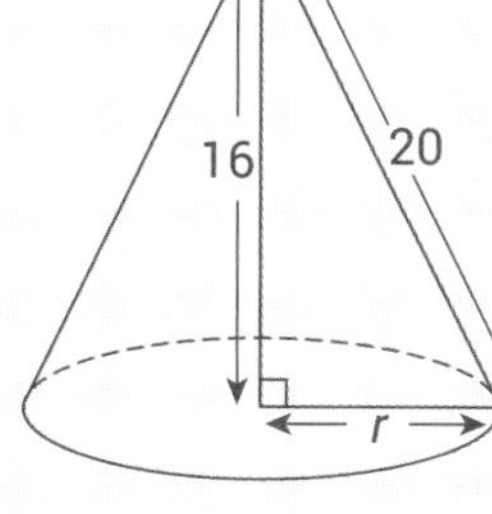

Solution

To find the surface area of a cone we must know the slant height and radius (r).

Step 1

$l^2 = h^2 + r^2$

$(20)^2 = (16)^2 + r^2$

$400 = 256 + r^2$

$400 - 256 = r^2$

$144 = r^2$

$12 = r$

Step 2

CSA $= \pi rl$

$= \pi \times 12 \times 20$

$\therefore$ CSA $= 240\pi$ units^2

Step 3

TSA = CSA + πr^2

$= 240\pi + \pi(12)^2$

$= 240\pi + 144\pi$

$= 384\pi$ units^2

Exercise 10.7

1. Find the volume of each of the following cones:
   (i) $r = 2$ cm, $h = 4$ cm (in terms of π)
   (ii) $r = 40$ mm, $h = 21$ mm $\left(\pi = \frac{22}{7}\right)$
   (iii) $r = 400$ mm, $h = 30$ mm ($\pi = 3.14$)
   (iv) $r = 1.5$ m, $h = 2.5$ mm ($\pi = 3.14$)
   (v) $r = 25$ cm, $h = 14$ cm $\left(\pi = \frac{22}{7}\right)$
   (vi) Diameter = 10 cm, $h = 16$ cm ($\pi = 3.14$)

2. Find the curved surface area and the total surface area of each of the following cones:
   (i) $r = 11$ cm, $l = 61$ cm ($\pi = 3.14$)
   (ii) $r = 6$ m, $h = 8$ m (in terms of π)
   (iii) $l = 35$ mm, $h = 21$ mm $\left(\pi = \frac{22}{7}\right)$
   (iv) $r = 30$ cm, $l = 500$ mm (in terms of π)

3. Find the volume and total surface area of each of the following cones to two decimal places:
   (i) $r = 20$ cm, $h = 20$ cm
   (ii) $r = 1.8$ m, $h = 2.6$ m

4. Diagrams of two conical storage silos are shown.

A

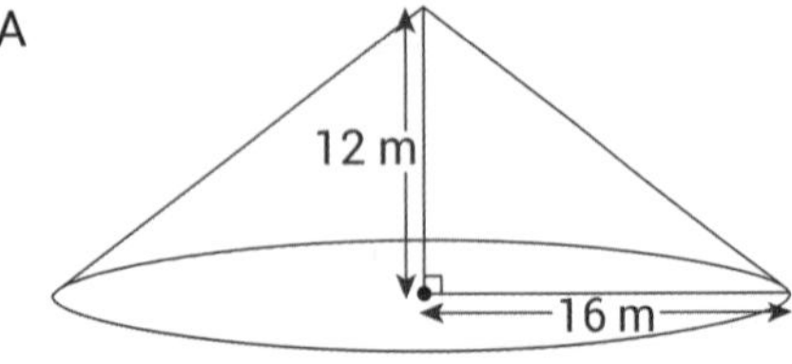

B

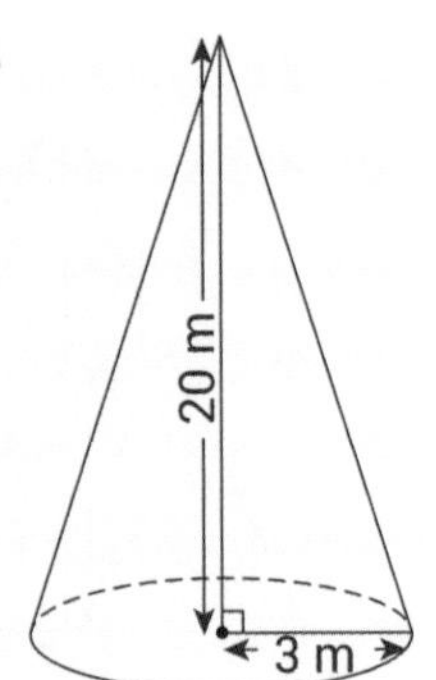

   (i) Calculate the volume (in litres) of each silo.
   (ii) Find the surface area (in m^2) of each silo.

5. An ornament in the shape of a cone is to be **electroplated**.

> Electroplating is the process of coating metal onto an object's surface using electricity.

Find the cost of electroplating this ornament if it costs €5 per cm^2. (Take $\pi = 3.14$)

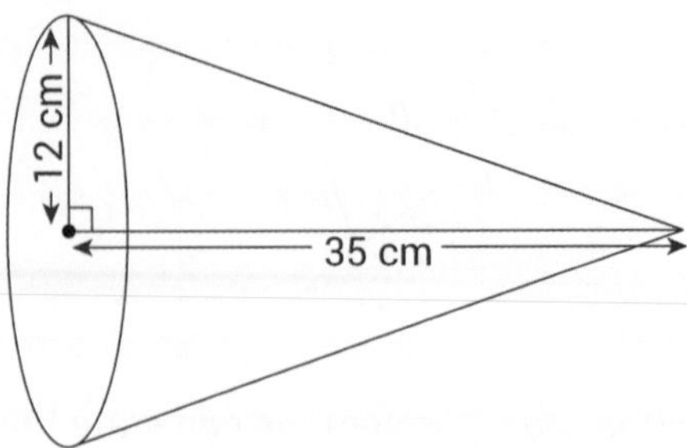

6. A space module consists of a cone on top of a cylinder. The radius of both is 4 m. The height of the cylindrical part is 8 m; the slant height of the conical part is 5 m.

Find, in terms of π, the total volume of the module.

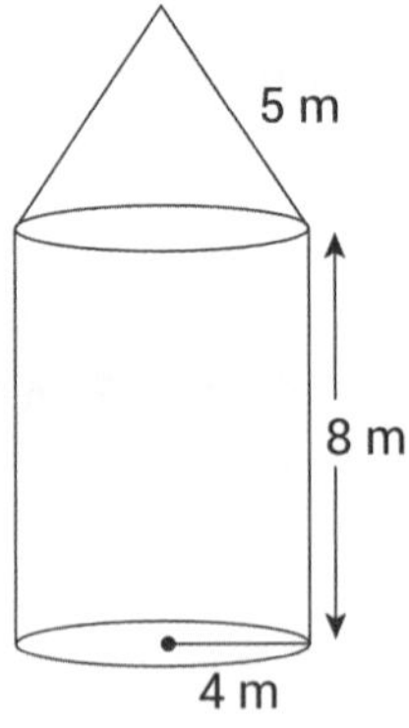

7. The diagram shows a solid cylinder of diameter 30 cm and height 50 cm.

A cone, of the same diameter but a height of 45 cm, is cut from inside the cylinder.

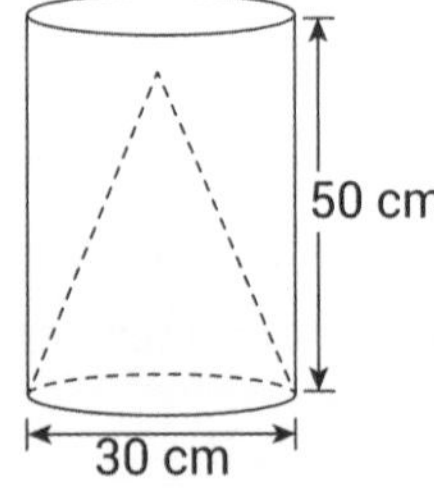

(a) (i) Calculate the volume of the cylinder. Give your answer in terms of π.
   (ii) Calculate the volume of the cone. Give your answer in terms of π.
   (iii) What fraction of the cylinder remains after the cone is removed?

(b) Calculate, to three significant figures, the surface area of the remaining solid. ($\pi = 3.14$)

10.8 Spheres

Volume of a Sphere

Volume of sphere = $\frac{4}{3} \times \pi \times (\text{radius})^3$

$\therefore$ Volume = $\frac{4}{3}\pi r^3$

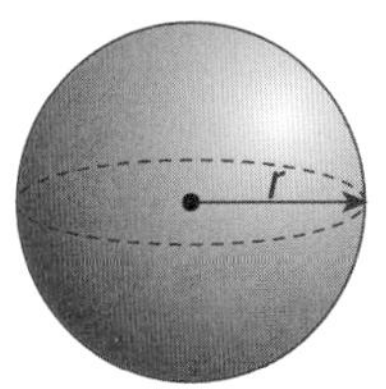

Surface Area of a Sphere

A sphere has no flat parts, so we can only have one type of surface area.

Surface area of sphere = $4\pi r^2$

These formulae appear on page 10 of *Formulae and Tables*.

Volume of a Hemisphere

A hemisphere is **half** a sphere.

Volume of hemisphere = $\frac{2}{3}\pi r^3$

Surface Area of a Hemisphere

A hemisphere has a flat circular part, so two types of surface area can be found.

Curved Surface Area (CSA) of a Hemisphere

The area of the curved part of the hemisphere is **half** that of the surface area of a sphere.

Curved surface area (CSA) of hemisphere = $2\pi r^2$

Total Surface Area (TSA) of a Hemisphere

This is the area of the curved part of the hemisphere **plus** the circular top.

Total surface area (TSA) of hemisphere = CSA + πr^2

$\therefore$ TSA = $2\pi r^2 + \pi r^2 = 3\pi r^2$

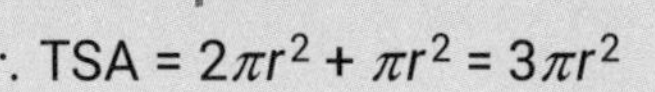

Worked Example 10.16

Find the volume and surface area of the sphere shown below, in terms of π.

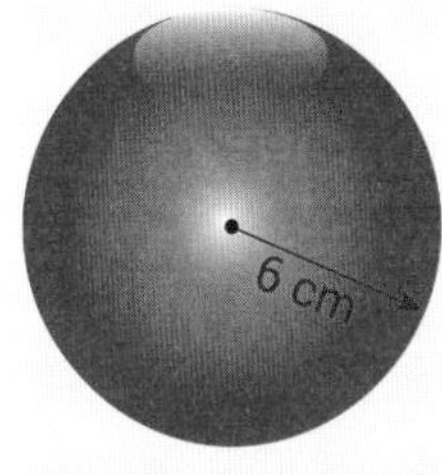

Solution

Volume = $\frac{4}{3}\pi r^3$

$= \frac{4}{3} \times \pi \times (6)^3$

$= 288\pi$ cm^3

Surface area = $4\pi r^2$

$= 4 \times \pi \times (6)^2$

$= 144\pi$ cm^2

Worked Example 10.17

Find the curved surface area and the total surface area of a hemisphere of radius 10 cm (π = 3.14).

Solution

CSA

$2\pi r^2 = 2 \times 3.14 \times (10)^2$

$= 628$ cm^2

TSA

CSA + $\pi r^2 = 3\pi r^2$

$= 3 \times 3.14 \times (10)^2$

$= 942$ cm^2

Exercise 10.8

1. Find the volume of each of the following spheres:
   (i) Radius = 9 cm (in terms of π)
   (ii) Radius = 12 cm $\left(\pi = \frac{22}{7}\right)$
   (iii) Radius = 5 mm (π = 3.14)
   (iv) Diameter length = 21 cm $\left(\pi = \frac{22}{7}\right)$

2. Find the volume of each of the following hemispheres:
   (i) Radius = 13 cm $\left(\pi = \frac{22}{7}\right)$
   (ii) Diameter length = 0.12 m (in terms of π)
   (iii) Radius = 1.5 m (π = 3.14)
   (iv) Radius = 20 mm (in terms of π)

3. Find the surface area of each of the following spheres:
   (i) r = 9 cm (in terms of π)
   (ii) r = 12 m $\left(\pi = \frac{22}{7}\right)$

4. Find the total surface area of each of the following hemispheres:
   (i) r = 5 mm (π = 3.14)
   (ii) r = 100 km $\left(\pi = \frac{22}{7}\right)$

5. Find the curved surface area and the total surface area (where applicable) of each of the following spheres or hemispheres:
   (i) Sphere: r = 20 mm (in terms of π)
   (ii) Hemisphere: r = 15 m (π = 3.14)
   (iii) Hemisphere: r = 27 cm (π = 3.14)
   (iv) Sphere: $r = 14\frac{1}{4}$ cm $\left(\pi = \frac{22}{7}\right)$

6. A spherical ball is made from a sheet of plastic. The diameter of the ball is 21.6 cm.Taking π as 3.14, find, to the nearest whole number:
   (i) The area of plastic material used to make the ball
   (ii) The volume of air inside the ball

7. A solid sphere of chocolate fits exactly into a cubic box. The radius of the sphere is 7 cm. Taking π as $\frac{22}{7}$, find:

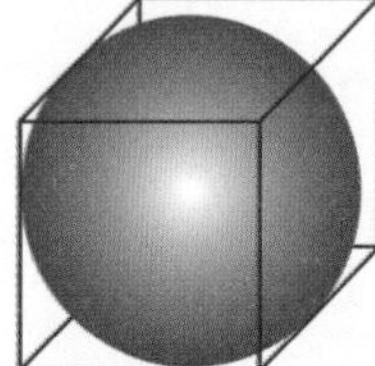

   (i) The volume of the sphere
   (ii) The volume of the box
   (iii) The volume of the box not occupied by the sphere, written as a percentage (correct to one decimal place)

8. A cylindrical part of an engine has a height of 14 cm and a radius of 6 cm. A spherical ball bearing of radius 4.5 cm is placed in the cylinder and oil is then poured into the cylinder until it is full. Taking π as $\frac{22}{7}$, find:
   (i) The capacity of the cylinder
   (ii) The volume of the ball bearing
   (iii) The volume of the oil used

9. A spinning top consists of a solid cone on a solid hemisphere. The radius of both is 3.5 cm and the height of the cone is 6 cm. Find the total volume of the spinning top to the nearest cubic centimetre.
   Take $\pi = \frac{22}{7}$.

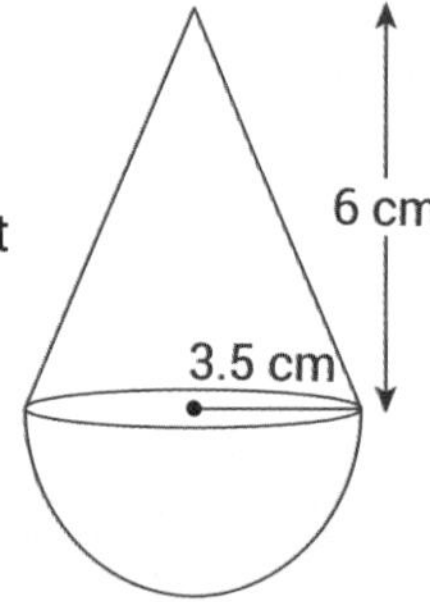

10. A tennis ball has a radius of 3.5 cm. Calculate, correct to two decimal places:
   (i) The volume of the tennis ball
   Three tennis balls fit exactly into a cylindrical tube. Calculate:

   (ii) The height of the tube
   (iii) The radius of the tube
   (iv) The volume of the tube
   (v) The fraction of the volume of the tube taken up by the three tennis balls

11. A golf-ball manufacturer produces golf balls with a diameter of 4 cm. It costs the manufacturer €0.12 to manufacture each cm^3 of golf ball. Each ball is then painted with one coat of paint. Each cm^2 of golf ball costs 0.723 cents to paint.
   Find the costs to the manufacturer of producing an order of 10,000 golf balls. (Take π = 3.14.)

10.9 Finding Dimensions When Given Volume or Surface Area

We may encounter problems where we must work backwards from the volume or surface area to find a missing length.

Worked Example 10.18

The volume of a cylinder is 847π cm^3. If it has a radius of 11 cm, find its height.

Solution

Write down what we are given.	Volume = 847π	
Write down formula.	$\pi r^2 h = 847\pi$	
Fill in given dimensions.	$\pi(11)^2(h) = 847\pi$	
Solve.	$121\pi h = 847\pi$ $121h = 847$ $h = 7$ cm	Divide both sides by π.

Worked Example 10.19

The volume of a sphere is $3{,}054\frac{6}{7}$ mm^3.
Taking $\pi = \frac{22}{7}$, find the radius of the sphere.

Solution

Write down what we are given.	Volume = $3{,}054\frac{6}{7}$	
Write down formula.	$\frac{4}{3}\pi r^3 = 3{,}054\frac{6}{7}$	
Fill in given dimensions.	$\frac{4}{3}\left(\frac{22}{7}\right)(r)^3 = 3{,}054\frac{6}{7}$ $\frac{88r^3}{21} = \frac{21{,}384}{7}$	
Solve.	$88r^3 = 64{,}152$ $r^3 = 729$ $r = \sqrt[3]{729}$ $r = 9$ mm	Multiply both sides by LCD, 21.

Worked Example 10.20

The total surface area of a cone is 373.66 cm^2. Find the slant height of the cone if its radius is 7 cm ($\pi = 3.14$).

Solution

Write down what we are given.	TSA = 373.66
Write down formula.	$\pi rl + \pi r^2 = 373.66$
Fill in given dimensions.	$(3.14)(7)(l) + (3.14)(7)^2 = 373.66$ $21.98l + 153.86 = 373.66$
Solve.	$21.98l = 373.66 - 153.86$ $21.98l = 219.8$ $l = \frac{219.8}{21.98}$ $l = 10$ cm

Worked Example 10.21

An experiment to measure the volume of a metal spherical ball is conducted. The ball is lowered into a cylinder of water. The cylinder has a radius of 5 cm and a height of 9 cm and is half full of water. When the ball is lowered into the cylinder, and is completely submerged in the water, the water level rises by 4 cm.

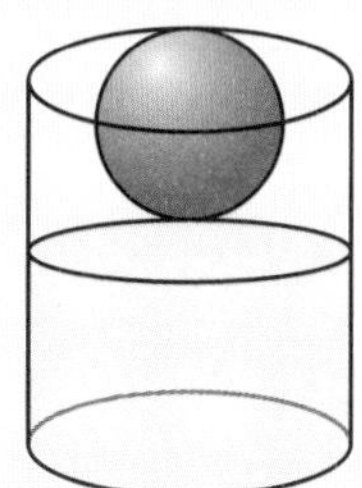

Find the radius of the metal spherical ball in cm correct to one decimal place.

APPLIED MEASURE

Solution

When the ball is lowered into the water, the water level rises by 4 cm.

The volume of the sphere is equal to the volume of the displaced water.

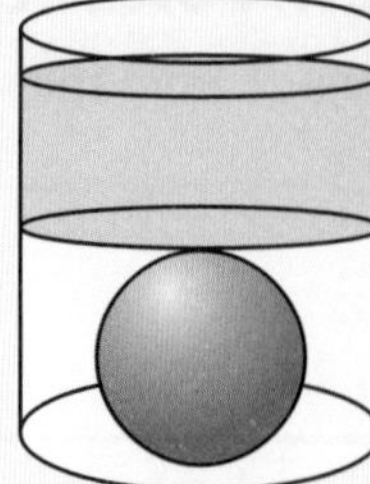

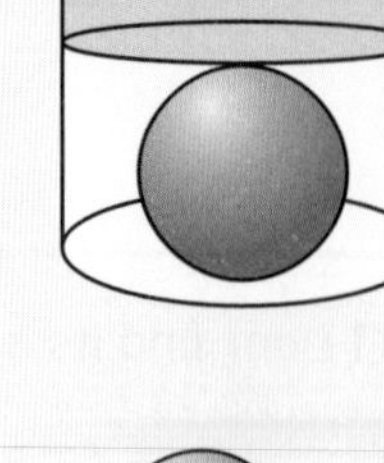

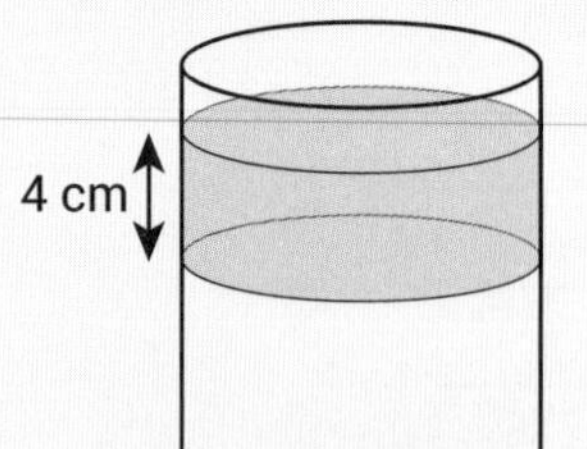

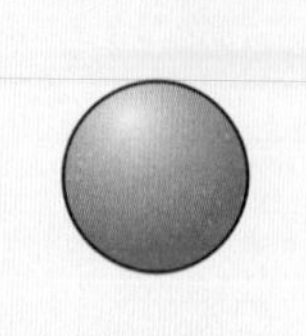

Volume of displaced water $= \pi r^2 h$

$= \pi \times (5)^2 \times 4$

$= 100\pi \text{ cm}^3$

$\therefore$ Volume of sphere $= 100\pi \text{ cm}^3$

$\frac{4}{3}\pi r^3 = 100\pi$

$\frac{4}{3}r^3 = 100$

$r^3 = 75$ Dividing both sides by $\frac{4}{3}$.

$\Rightarrow r = \sqrt[3]{75}$

$\Rightarrow r = 4.2172...$

$\therefore r \approx 4.2$ cm (to one decimal place)

Exercise 10.9

1. Fill in the tables below. Make sure you show all your work.

(i) Rectangular solids

Length (cm)	Breadth (cm)	Height (cm)	Volume (cm^3)	Surface area (cm^2)
4	5		180	
2		3	6	
	7.5	2	210	

(ii) Cylinders

π	r (cm)	h (cm)	Volume (cm^3)	CSA (cm^2)	TSA (cm^2)
π	5		100π		
3.14		11	2,797.74		
$\frac{22}{7}$		14		616	

(iii) Cones

π	r (cm)	h (cm)	l (cm)	Volume (cm^3)	CSA (cm^2)	TSA (cm^2)
π	4			16π		
3.14			41		1,158.66	
$\frac{22}{7}$		99		$41{,}485\frac{5}{7}$		

(iv) Spheres/hemispheres

(a) Spheres

π	r (cm)	Volume (cm^3)	TSA (cm^2)
π		$166\frac{2}{3}\pi$	
$\frac{22}{7}$			$50\frac{2}{7}$
3.14		3,052.08	

(b) Hemispheres

π	r (cm)	Volume (cm^3)	TSA (cm^2)	CSA (cm^2)
π		$83\frac{1}{3}\pi$		
$\frac{22}{7}$			$37\frac{5}{7}$	
3.140				508.68

2. A cuboid has a volume of 2,700 cm^3. It has a length of 10 cm and a width of 15 cm.

Find its height.

3. A rectangular solid has a surface area of 5,900 cm^2.

Find its width, if it has a length of 25 cm and a height of 40 cm.

4. A solid metal sphere of radius 6 cm is melted down and remoulded into a solid cone of radius 3 cm.

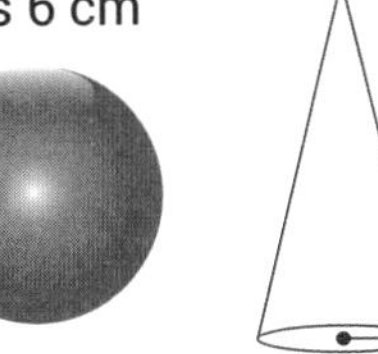

Find:

(i) The volume of the sphere in terms of π

(ii) The height of the cone

5. A solid sphere of diameter 18 cm is made of plasticine. It is remoulded to form a cone of height 81 cm. Find the radius of the cone.

6. A cone of radius 10 cm has the same volume as a cylinder with height 8 cm and radius 4 cm. Find the height of the cone to the nearest millimetre.

7. A toy consists of a solid hemisphere surmounted by a solid cone.

The toy fits exactly into a cylindrical container, as shown.

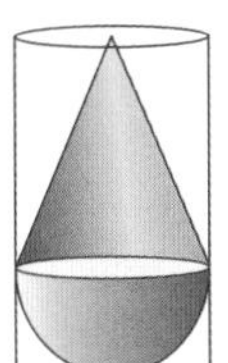

(a) The radius of the cone is of length 6 cm. The volume of the cone is one third of the volume of the hemisphere.

Find:

(i) The volume of the hemisphere in terms of π

(ii) The height of the cone

(iii) The overall height of the toy

(b) Does the toy take up more than half of the capacity of the container? Show clearly how you arrived at your answer.

8. A candle is in the shape of a cone on top of a cylinder. The cylinder has radius 4 cm. The slant height of the cone is 5 cm.

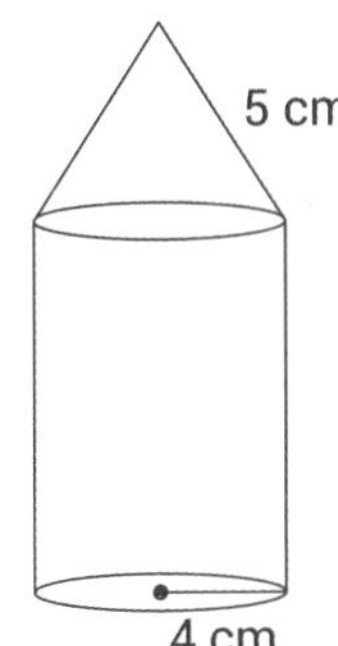

Find:

(i) The height, h, of the cone

(ii) The volume of the cone in terms of π

(iii) The height of the cylinder, given that its volume is ten times the volume of the cone

9. A cuboid has three dimensions in the ratio 1 : 2 : 3. Find all three lengths if its volume is 10,368 cm^3.

10. A cylindrical tank of radius 12 cm is partly filled with water. A sphere of radius 6 cm is completely immersed in the water. By how much will the water rise?

11. A cylindrical tank of radius 4 cm is partly filled with water. A cone of radius 2 cm and height 3 cm is completely immersed in the water.

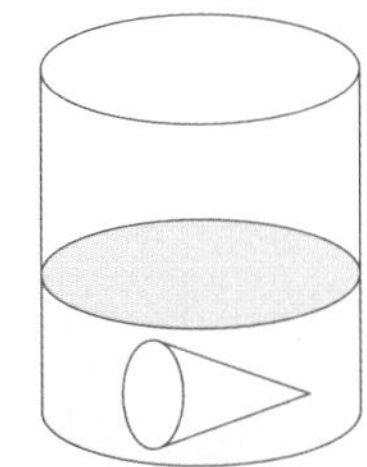

By how much will the water rise?

12. A closed plastic container is in the shape of a hollow cylinder on a hollow hemisphere, both of radius-length 3 cm. The container is partly filled with water, to a depth of 10 cm.

3 cm

10 cm

(i) Find the volume of the water, in terms of π.

(ii) If the container is turned upside down, what will the depth of the water be in the cylindrical part?

APPLIED MEASURE

13. Water flows through a cylindrical pipe at a rate of 10 cm per second. The diameter of the pipe is 7 cm. The water is poured into an empty rectangular tank of length 55 cm and width 20 cm.

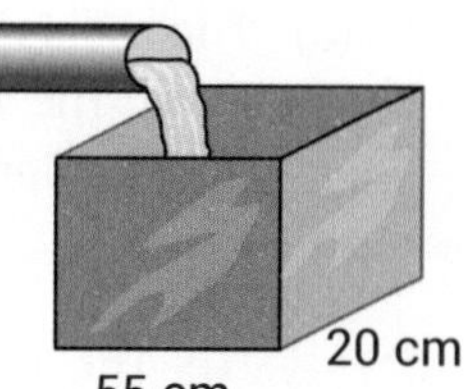

What is the depth of the water in the tank after one minute? ($\pi = 3.14$. Give answer correct to nearest cm.)

14. Water flows through a cylindrical pipe at a rate of 35 cm per second. The pipe has diameter 4 cm. How long would it take to pour out 22 litres of water?
(Take $\pi = \frac{22}{7}$. 1 litre = 1,000 cm^3.)

15. A ladle is in the shape of a hemisphere of diameter 3 cm. It is used to remove soup from a cylindrical container of radius 6 cm.

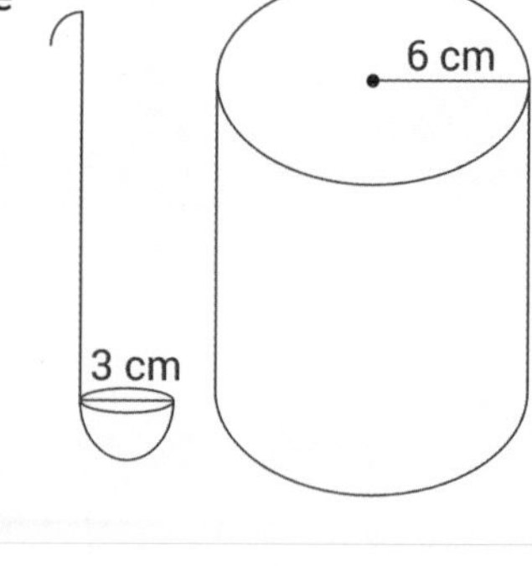

(i) Find the volume of one ladleful in terms of π.

(ii) How far will the depth of the soup drop if 24 ladlefuls of soup are removed?

(iii) If the depth of the soup is now $2\frac{1}{2}$ cm, how many more ladlefuls could still be removed?

10.10 Trapezoidal Rule

It is difficult to measure the exact area of an irregular shape and therefore we generally approximate the area.

The **trapezoidal (trapezium) rule** is used to estimate the area under a curve.

The area under the curve is approximated by trapezoids of equal width.

Worked Example 10.22

The curve $y = x^2 + 1$, in the domain $0 \leqslant x \leqslant 4$, is shown. Using the trapeziums given, estimate the area underneath the curve.

Solution

Area of a trapezoid $= \frac{1}{2}(a + b)h$

Trapezoid	A	B	C	D
a	1	2	5	10
b	2	5	10	17
h	1	1	1	1
Area	$= \frac{1}{2}(1 + 2)(1)$	$= \frac{1}{2}(2 + 5)(1)$	$= \frac{1}{2}(5 + 10)(1)$	$= \frac{1}{2}(10 + 17)(1)$

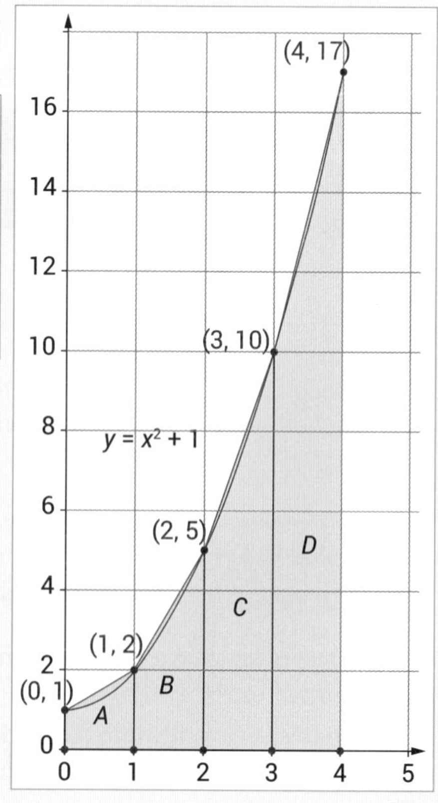

We can then find the sum of the areas of the trapezoids.

Sum of areas $= \frac{1}{2}(1 + 2)(1) + \frac{1}{2}(2 + 5)(1) + \frac{1}{2}(5 + 10)(1) + \frac{1}{2}(10 + 17)(1)$

$= \frac{1}{2}(1)[1 + 2 + 2 + 5 + 5 + 10 + 10 + 17]$

$= \frac{1}{2}[1 + 17 + 2(2 + 5 + 10)]$

Area underneath the curve $y = x^2 + 1$, in the domain $0 \leqslant x \leqslant 4$

$= \frac{1}{2}[52]$

$= 26$ units^2

APPLIED MEASURE

From this we can derive the formula:

Area $\approx \frac{h}{2}$[first height + last height + 2 (the sum of the rest of the heights)]

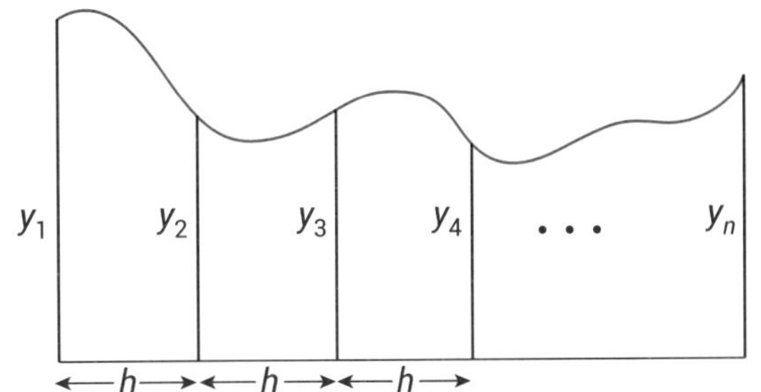

This can be generalised to the case with $(n-1)$ trapezoids:

Sum of areas = $\frac{h}{2}[y_1 + y_n + 2(y_2 + y_3 + \dots + y_{n-1})]$

When we use this rule, the shape to be measured must be divided into **segments or strips of equal width**. We then need to measure the height at the boundaries of each of these segments.

In the diagram shown, h is the equal width, and $y_1, y_2, \dots, y_n$ are the heights.

When using the trapezoidal rule, the smaller the width of each segment, the more accurate the approximation of the area will be.

Area $\approx \frac{h}{2}[y_1 + y_n + 2(y_2 + y_3 + y_4 + \dots + y_{n-1})]$

Here, y_{n-1} refers to the second-last height.

This formula appears on page 12 of *Formulae and Tables*.

Worked Example 10.23

Estimate the area of the piece of land shown below. (Measurements are in metres.)

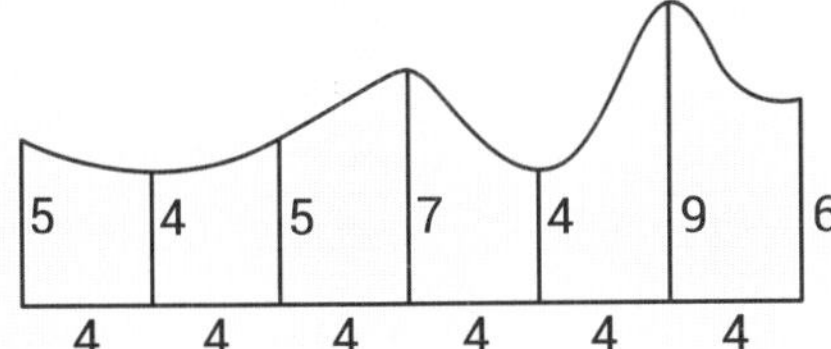

Solution

$h = 4$ m

First height = 5 m

Last height = 6 m

Area $\approx \frac{4}{2}[5 + 6 + 2(4 + 5 + 7 + 4 + 9)]$

$= 2[11 + 2(29)]$

$= 2[69]$

$= 138$ m^2

Worked Example 10.24

Estimate the area of the shape shown below. (Measurements are in metres.)

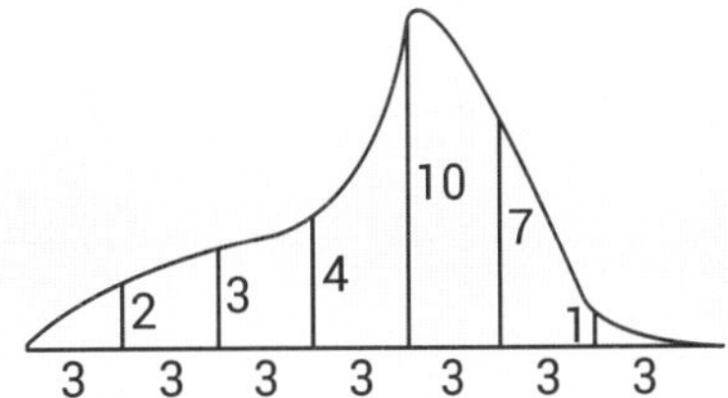

Solution

$h = 3$ m

First height = 0 m

Last height = 0 m

Area $\approx \frac{3}{2}[0 + 0 + 2(2 + 3 + 4 + 10 + 7 + 1)]$

$= \frac{3}{2}[0 + 2(27)]$

$= \frac{3}{2}[54]$

$= 81$ m^2

Worked Example 10.25

The area of the following shape was estimated to be 800 cm^2 using the trapezoidal rule. Find the width of each segment.

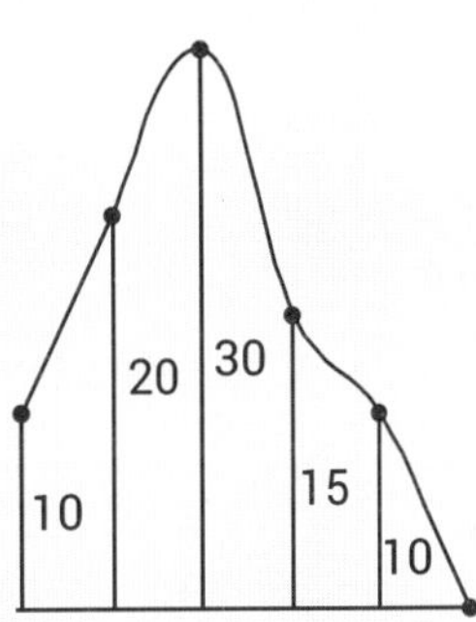

Solution

Area = 800

$= \frac{h}{2}[10 + 0 + 2(20 + 30 + 15 + 10)]$

$\frac{h}{2}[10 + 2(75)] = 800$

$\frac{h}{2}[160] = 800$

$80h = 800$

$\therefore h = 10$ cm

APPLIED MEASURE

Exercise 10.10

1. Use the trapezoidal rule to estimate the area of each of the following (all measurements are in metres):

(i)

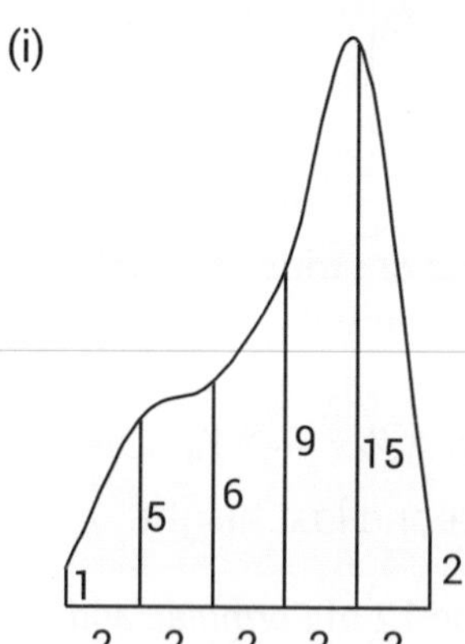

(ii)

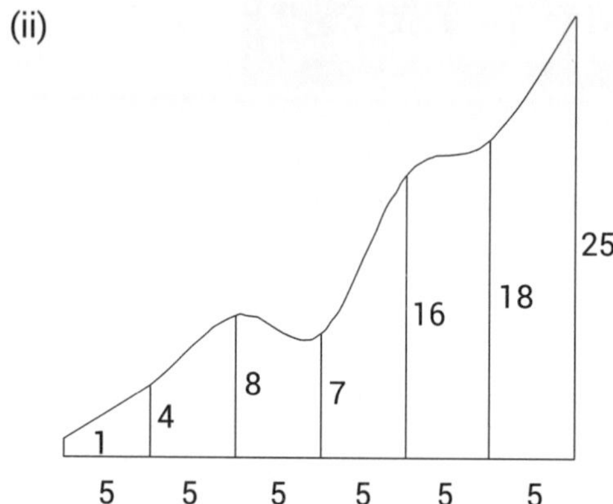

(iii)

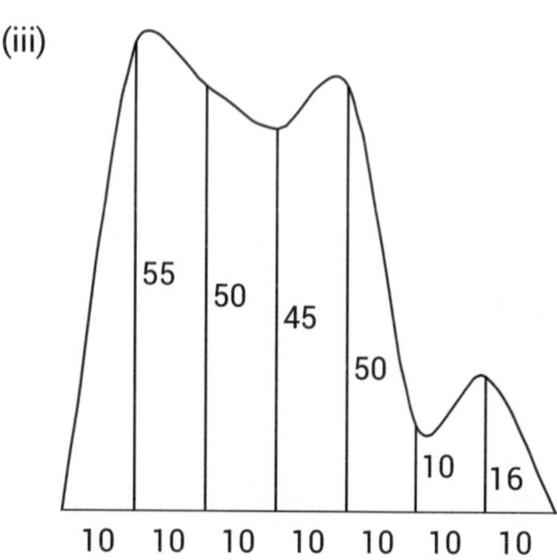

(iv)

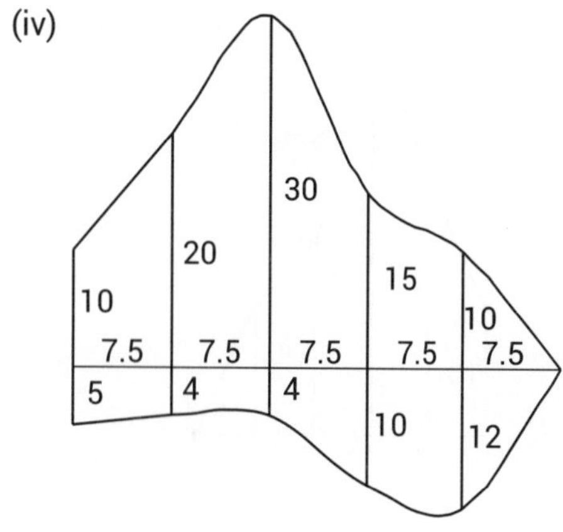

(v)

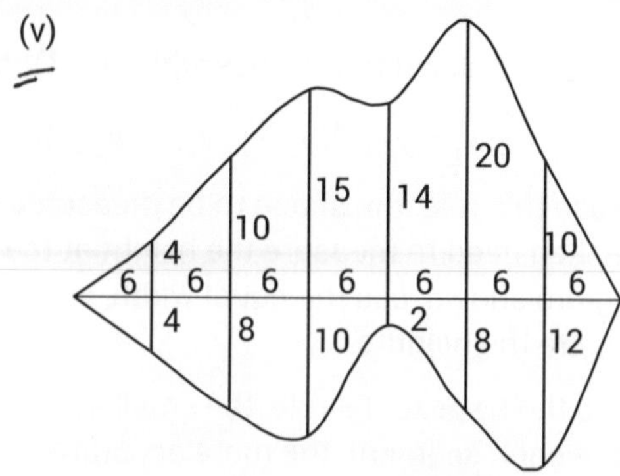

2. The area of this irregular shape is approximately 230 square units. Find the value of x.

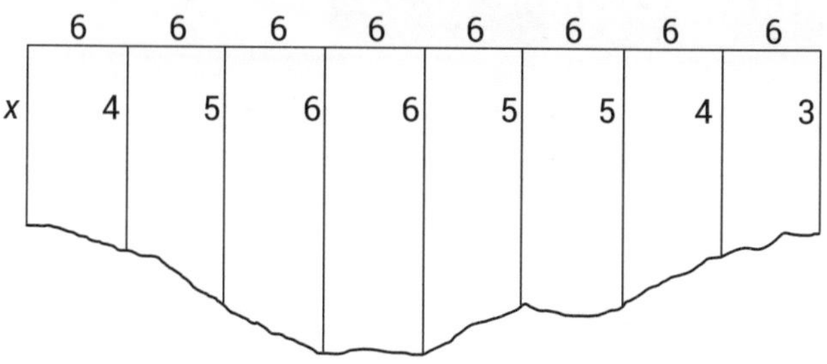

3. The area between the curve and the line was estimated to be 40 units^2 using the trapezoidal rule. Calculate the value of x.

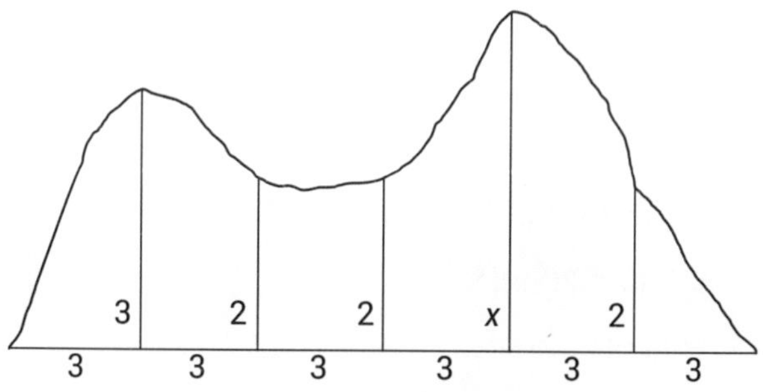

4. The area of this field is approximately 1.5 hectares. Find the value of h. Measurements are in metres. (1 hectare = 10,000 square metres)

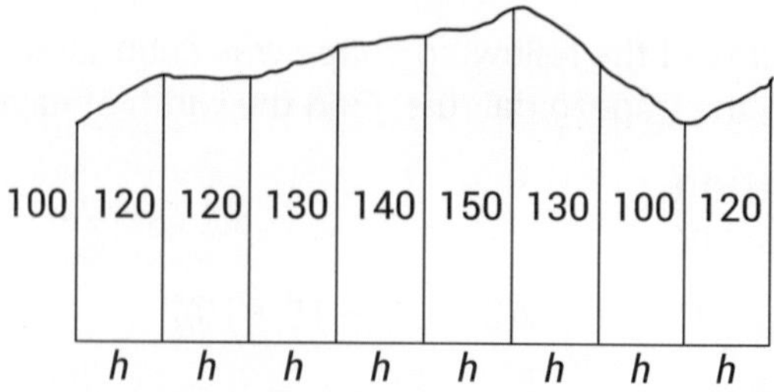

Revision Exercises

1. (a) Find the area of each of the following shapes:

(i)

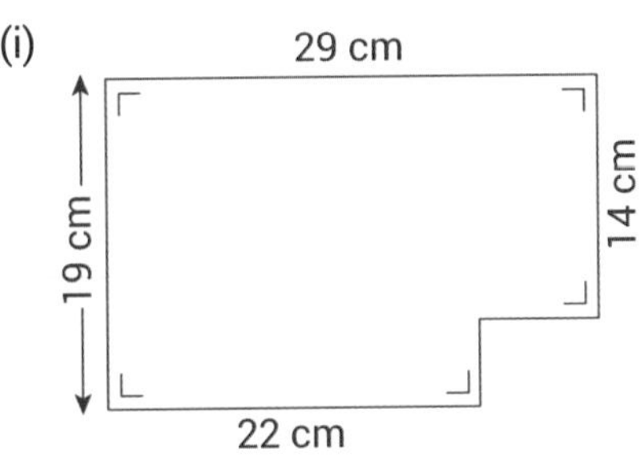

(ii)

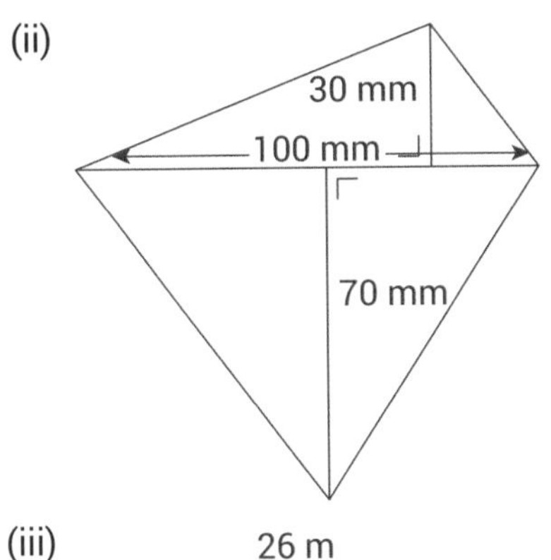

(iii)

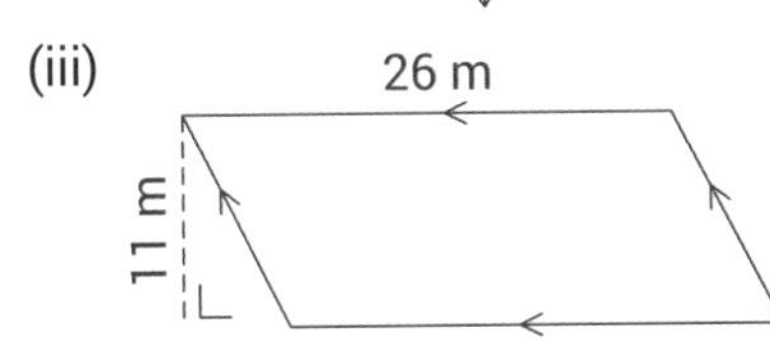

(b) Find the area and perimeter of each of the following circles:

(i) Radius = 25 cm (in terms of π)

(ii) Radius = 18 cm ($\pi = 3.14$)

(iii) Diameter = 0.5 mm $\left(\pi = \frac{22}{7}\right)$

2. (a) Find the area of the shaded region in each of the following shapes:

(i)

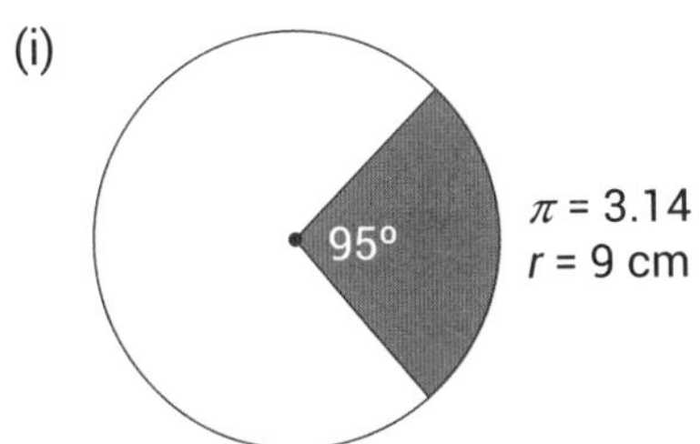

(ii)

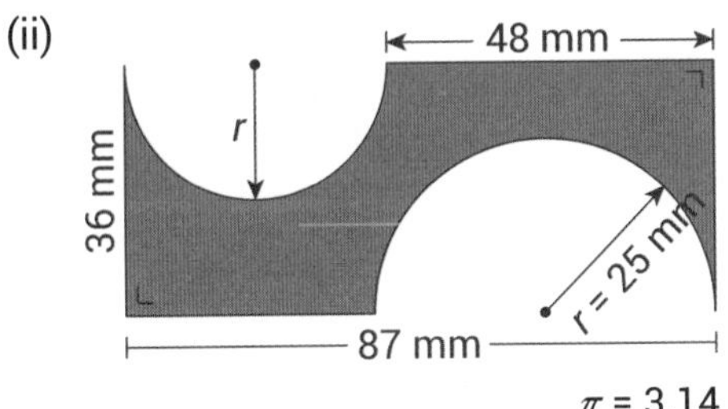

$\pi = 3.14$

(b) By using the information from each diagram below, find the value of x.

(i)

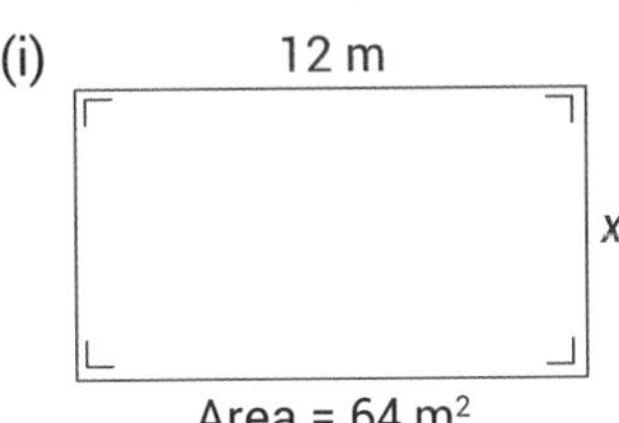

(ii)

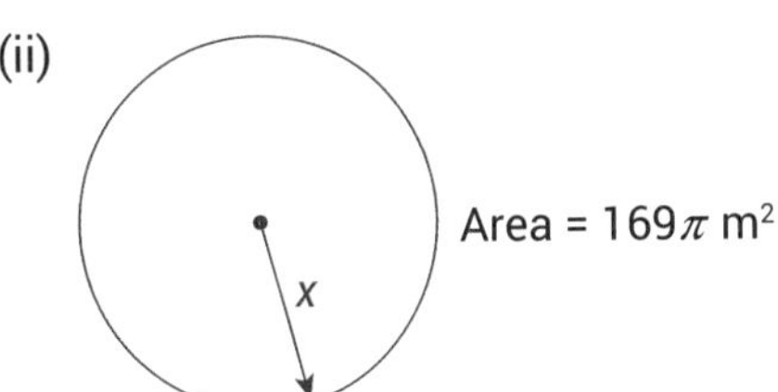

(iii)

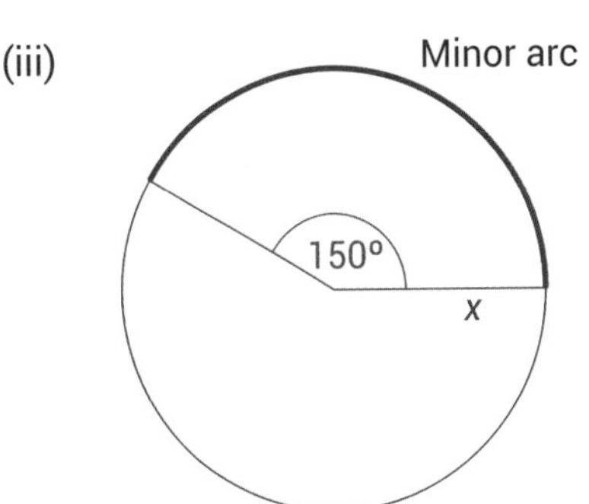

Length of minor arc = 110 mm

$\pi = \frac{22}{7}$

(iv)

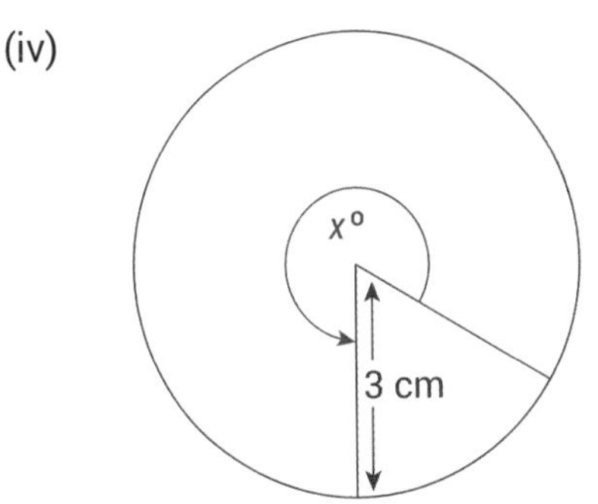

Area of shaded region = 5.495 cm²

$\pi = 3.14$

3. (a) The slant height of a cone is 17 cm. The height is 15 cm.

Find:

(i) The radius length

(ii) The volume of the cone in terms of π

APPLIED MEASURE

(b) The propellers of a wind turbine are shown.

On a certain day, the propellers complete 20 revolutions per minute and have a speed at their tip of 45 ms^{-1}.

Calculate the radius of a propeller to one decimal place. ($\pi = 3.14$)

4. (a) Use the trapezoidal rule to estimate the area of each of the following (measurements are in metres):

(i)

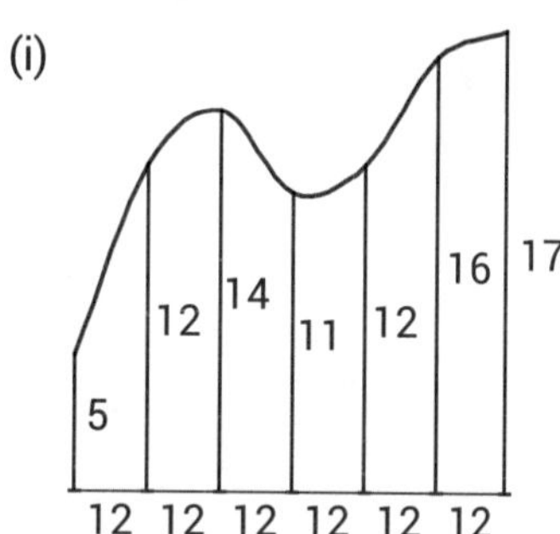

(ii)

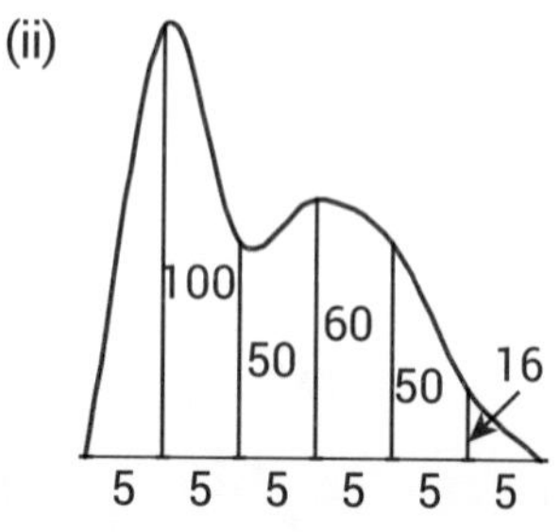

(iii)

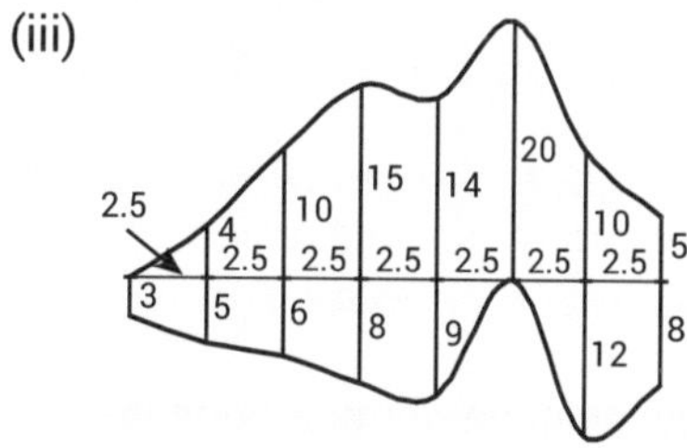

(b) (i) The area of this irregular shape is 3,395 square units. Find the value of x.

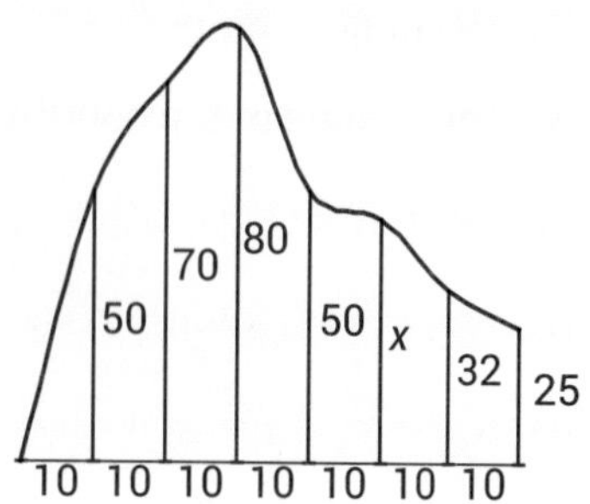

(ii) The area of this shape is estimated using the trapezoidal rule as 820 square units. Calculate the width of each strip.

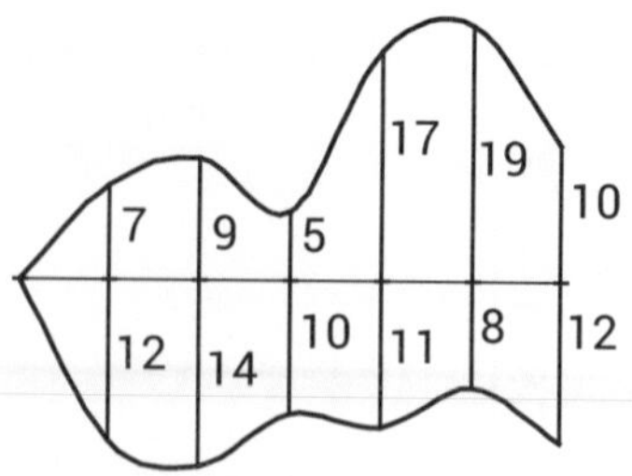

5. Find the volume and surface area of the following prisms (to two decimal places):

(i)

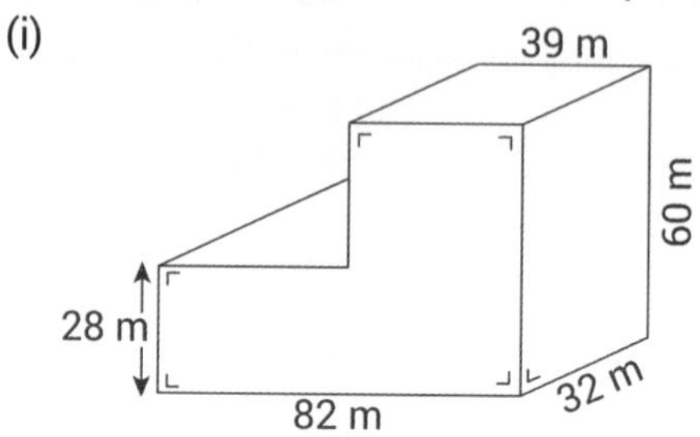

(ii)

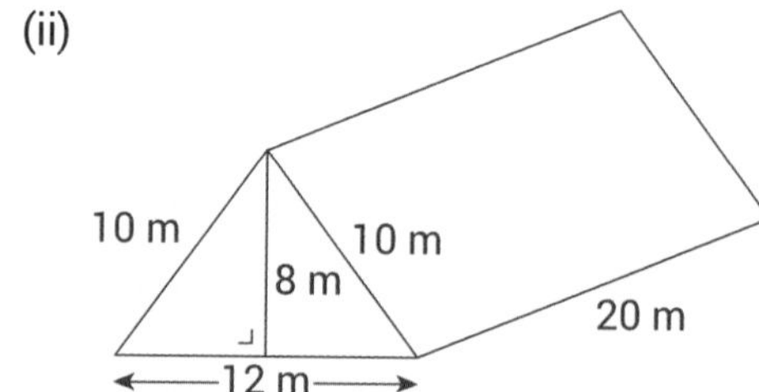

6. (i) Find the area of this sector, using $\pi = 3.14$:

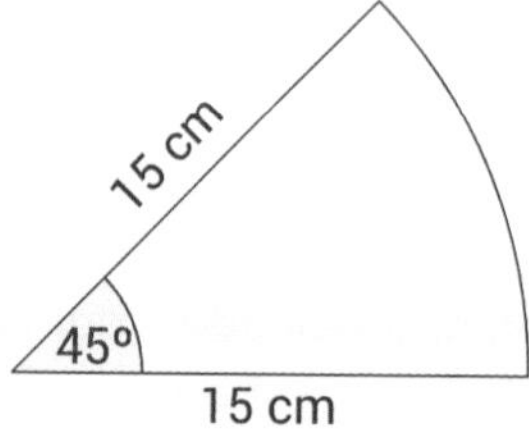

(ii) A solid metal sphere of radius 4 cm is melted and recast into a cone of radius 8 cm. Find the height of the cone.

7. (i) A hollow cylindrical pipe has inner radius 3 cm and outer radius 4 cm. The height is 50 cm. Using $\pi = \frac{22}{7}$, find the volume of material needed to make this pipe.

(ii) A rectangular box is 1 m by 150 cm by 80 cm. Another rectangular box is to be built that will hold 4 times as much as the first. The length, height and width of this box are all different.

Give one set of possible values for the dimensions of the box.

8. Water is kept cool in a cylindrical container of diameter 28 cm and height 30 cm.

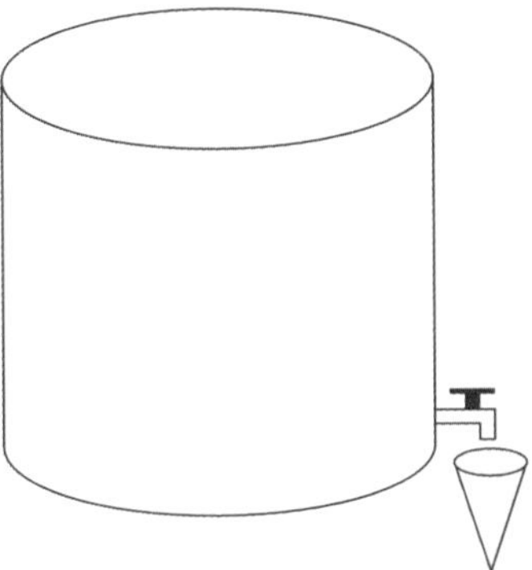

The water is poured into small conical cups, each of diameter 3 cm and height 3.5 cm.

When the cooler is full, how many cupfuls does it contain?

9. (a) Find the area and perimeter of this sector, using $\pi = 3.14$:

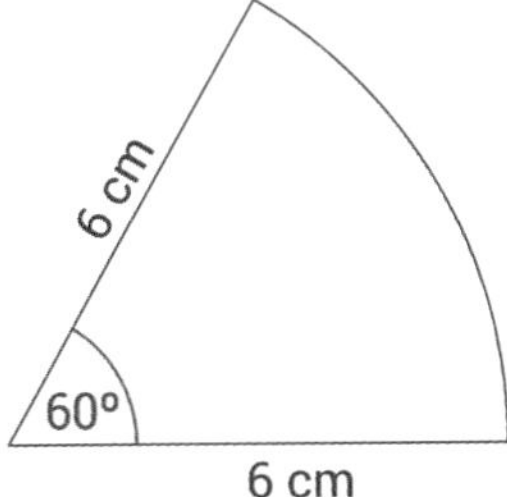

(b) (i) A soup ladle is in the shape of a hemisphere of diameter 9 cm, with a handle attached. Find the volume of one ladleful in terms of π.

(ii) This ladle is used to remove soup from a cylindrical container of diameter 36 cm.

Find the drop in the level of the soup when 24 ladlefuls are removed.

(iii) If the remaining soup has a depth of 6 cm, how many more ladlefuls can be removed?

10. (a) Two spheres have radii in the ratio 3 : 1. What is the ratio of their volumes?

(b) (i) The diagram shows the plan of a lake. Use the trapezoidal rule to estimate the area of the lake, given that the offsets are a distance 10 m apart, and all measurements are in metres.

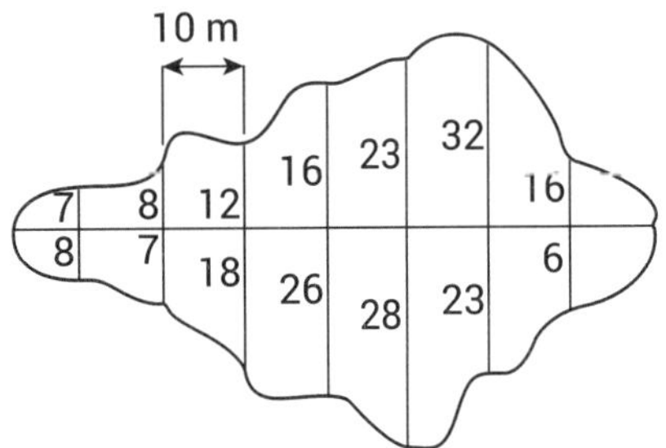

(ii) If the average depth of the lake is 7 m, estimate the volume of water in the lake.

(c) A rectangular block has height 6 cm, length 11 cm and width 8 cm.

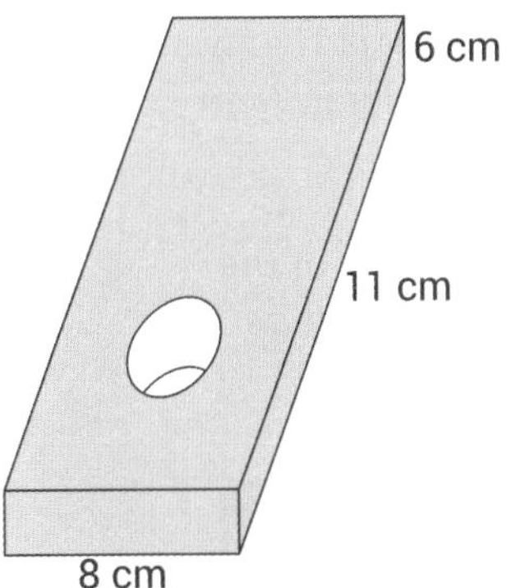

(i) Find its volume.

(ii) A vertical cylindrical hole of radius r centimetres is drilled in the block, as shown. The volume of the remaining piece is $87\frac{1}{2}\%$ of the original volume. Find r, correct to one decimal place. (Take $\pi = \frac{22}{7}$.)

11. (a) Water flows through a cylindrical pipe of diameter 3.5 cm into a rectangular tank of length 1.1 metres, width 1.4 metres and height 1.5 metres. The tank is filled in 40 minutes.

Find $\left(\text{using } \pi = \frac{22}{7}\right)$ the rate at which the water flows through the pipe (in cms^{-1}).

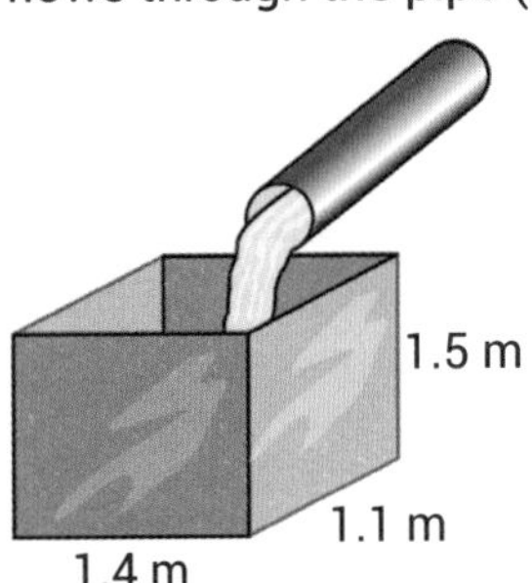

APPLIED MEASURE

(b) A cone has radius 2 cm and height $\frac{27}{8}$ cm. It is totally immersed in water inside a cylindrical tank of radius 6 cm.

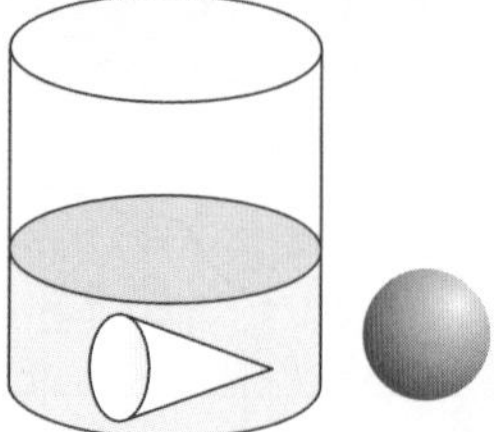

(i) When the cone is removed, calculate the drop in the depth of the water in the tank.

(ii) A sphere of radius r cm is then immersed in the water, which returns to its previous level. Find the value of r.

12. (a) A closed container consists of a cylinder joined to a cone. The height of the cylinder is 10 cm and its diameter is 7 cm.

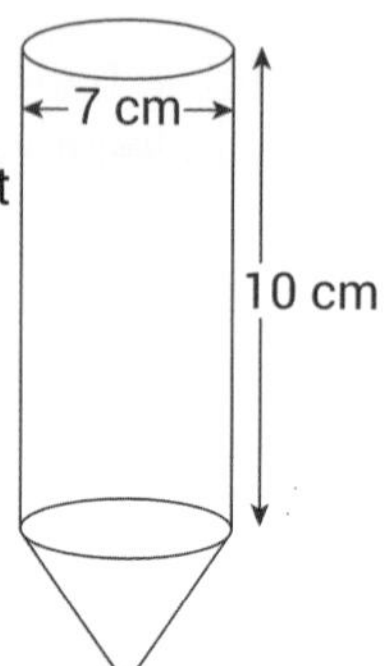
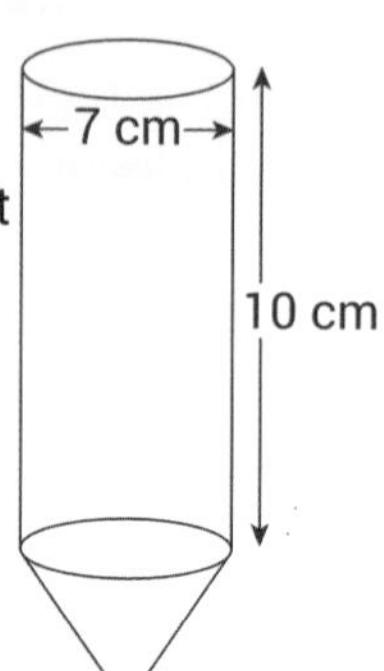

Calculate:

(i) The capacity of the cylindrical part in terms of π

(ii) The vertical height of the cone, given that its capacity is one-fifth of the capacity of the cylinder

(iii) The volume of the water (in terms of π) in the container when its depth is 13 cm and the height of the water in the cylinder if this container is inverted.

(b) Water pours through a pipe of radius 3 cm at a rate of 15 cm per second. It flows into a conical tank of height 0.9 metres and radius 0.6 metres.

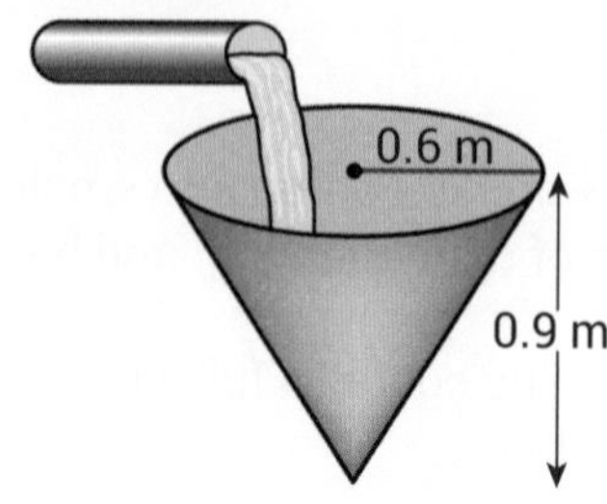

How long will it take to fill the tank?

Exam Questions

1. The Atomium in Brussels is one of Belgium's most famous landmarks.

It consists of 9 identical spheres joined by two types of cylindrical pipes.

(a) The diameter of each sphere in the Atomium is 18 metres.

(i) Find the radius of each sphere.

(ii) Find the volume of each sphere, correct to two decimal places.

(b) Find the combined surface area of all 9 spheres in the Atomium, correct to the nearest m^2.

(c) Each of the 8 cylindrical pipes extending from the centre sphere has a radius of 1.65 m and a length of 23 m.

(i) Find the sum of the curved surface areas of all 8 pipes, correct to the nearest m^2.

(ii) The other 12 cylindrical pipes connect the outer spheres to each other. Each pipe has a radius of 1.45 m. All 12 pipes are equal in length. The sum of the curved surface areas of the 12 pipes is 3,170 m^2. Find the length of one pipe.

Give your answer correct to the nearest metre.

(iii) The curved surfaces of the 20 pipes and 9 spheres are covered in stainless steel. Stainless steel costs €70 per square metre. Use the areas you have calculated or have been given above to find the approximate cost of the stainless steel required to resurface the Atomium.

SEC Leaving Certificate Ordinary Level, Paper 2, 2016

2. (a) A company has a spherical storage tank. The diameter of the tank is 12 m.

(i) Write down the radius of the tank.

(ii) Find the volume of the tank, correct to the nearest m^3.

(b) The company paints the outside curved surface of the spherical tank.

(i) Find the curved surface area of the tank, correct to one decimal place.

(ii) The curved surface is painted with a special paint. One litre of paint will cover $3.5\ m^2$. Find how many litres of paint are used, correct to the nearest litre.

(iii) The paint is sold in 25 litre tins. Each tin costs €180. Find the total cost of the paint.

(c) At another site the company has a differently-shaped tank with the same volume. This tank has hemispherical ends and a cylindrical mid-section of length h m, as shown. The radius of each hemispherical end is 4.5 m.

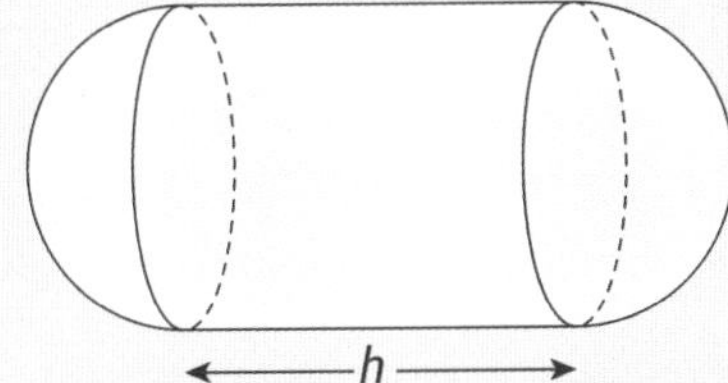

(i) Find the volume of one hemispherical end, correct to the nearest m^3.

(ii) Find the length, h, of the cylindrical section, correct to one decimal place.

SEC Leaving Certificate Ordinary Level, Paper 2, 2015

3. (a) The square $ABCD$ has an area of $81\ cm^2$. Find $|AD|$.

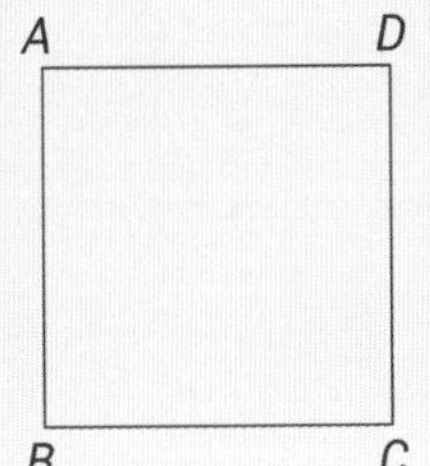

(b) A sector of a circle, centre B and radius $|BC|$, is drawn inside $ABCD$ as shown by the shaded region.

(i) Find the area of the sector, correct to one decimal place.

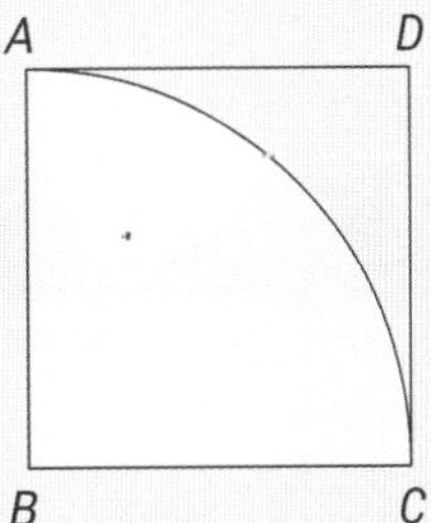

(ii) A second sector of a circle, centre D and radius $|DA|$, is drawn. Find the area of the shaded region (the overlap of the two sectors), correct to one decimal place.

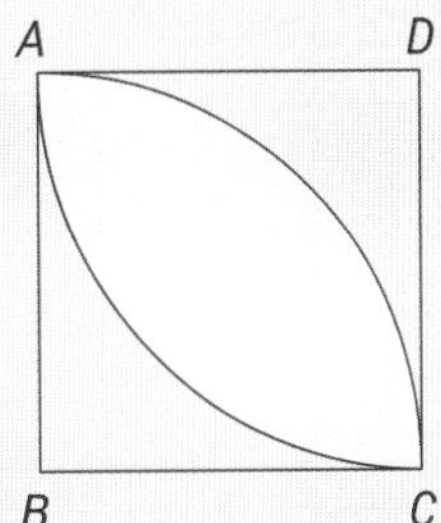

(c) The point P is on the arc of the sector DAC, as shown. The triangle APC is isosceles. Find the area of the triangle APC, correct to one decimal place.

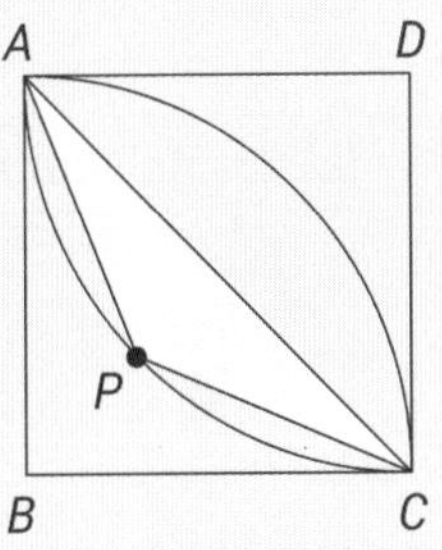

SEC Leaving Certificate Ordinary Level, Paper 2, 2014

4. A solid cylinder has a radius of 10 mm and a height of 45 mm.

(a) Draw a sketch of the net of the surface of the cylinder and write its dimensions on the sketch.

(b) Calculate the volume of the cylinder. Give your answer in terms of π.

(c) A sphere has the same volume as the cylinder.

Find the surface area of the sphere. Give your answer in terms of π.

SEC Leaving Certificate Ordinary Level, Paper 2, 2013

5. The diagram below is a scale drawing of a hopper tank used to store grain. An estimate is needed of the capacity (volume) of the tank. The figure of the man standing beside the tank allows the scale of the drawing to be estimated.

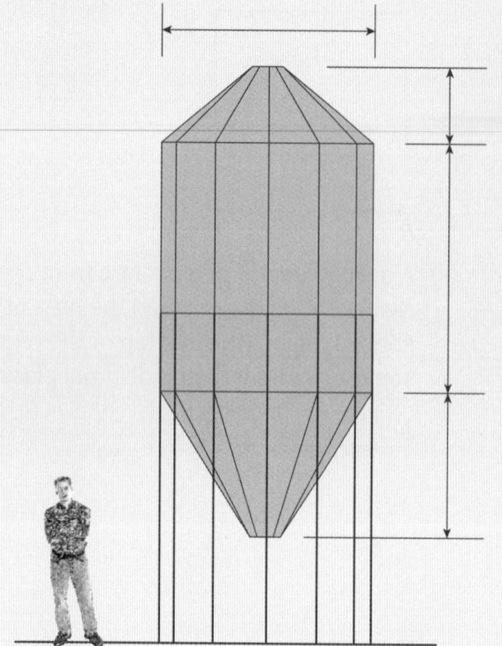

(a) Give an estimate, in metres, of the height of an average adult man.

(b) Using your answer to part **(a)**, estimate the dimensions of the hopper tank.

(c) Taking the tank to be a cylinder with a cone above and below, find an estimate for the capacity of the tank, in cubic metres.

SEC Leaving Certificate Ordinary Level, Sample Paper 2, 2014

6. (a) The diagram shows a circle inscribed in a square.

The area of the square is 16 cm^2.

(i) Find the radius length of the circle.

(ii) Find the area of the shaded region, in cm^2, correct to one decimal place.

(b) A solid wax candle is in the shape of a cylinder with a cone on top, as shown in the diagram.

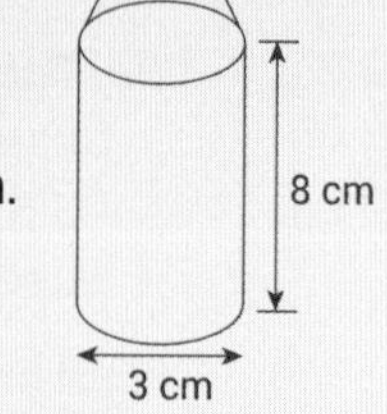

The diameter of the base of the cylinder is 3 cm and the height of the cylinder is 8 cm.

The volume of the wax in the candle is 21π cm^3.

(i) Find the height of the candle.

(ii) Nine of these candles fit into a rectangular box. The base of the box is a square. Find the volume of the smallest rectangular box that the candles will fit into.

SEC Leaving Certificate Ordinary Level, Paper 2, 2014

7. The diagram below shows a shape with two straight edges and one irregular edge. By dividing the edge [*AB*] into five equal intervals, use the trapezoidal rule to estimate the area of the shape.

Record your constructions and measurements on the diagram. Give your answer correct to the nearest cm^2.

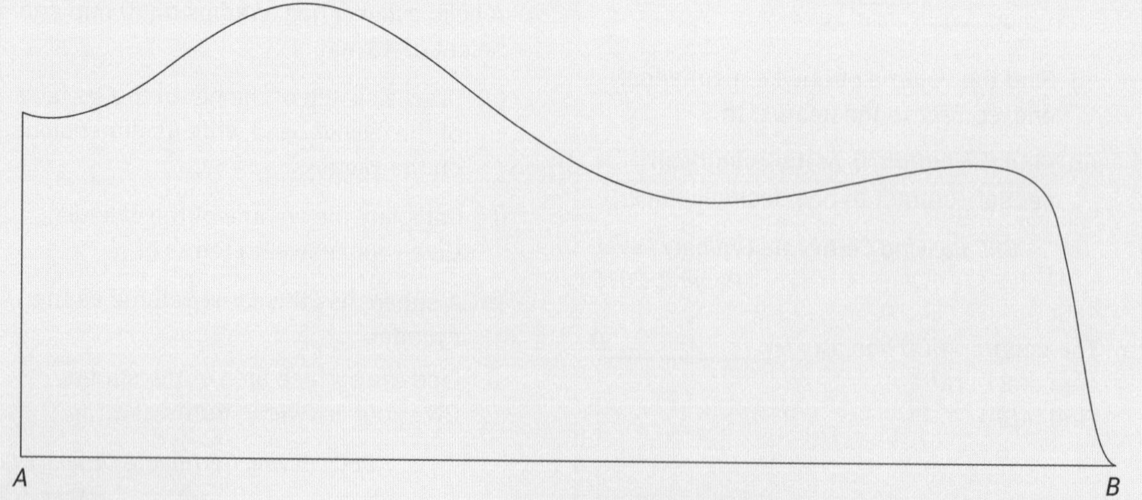

SEC Leaving Certificate Ordinary Level, Sample Paper 2, 2014

Solutions and chapter summary available online

APPLIED MEASURE

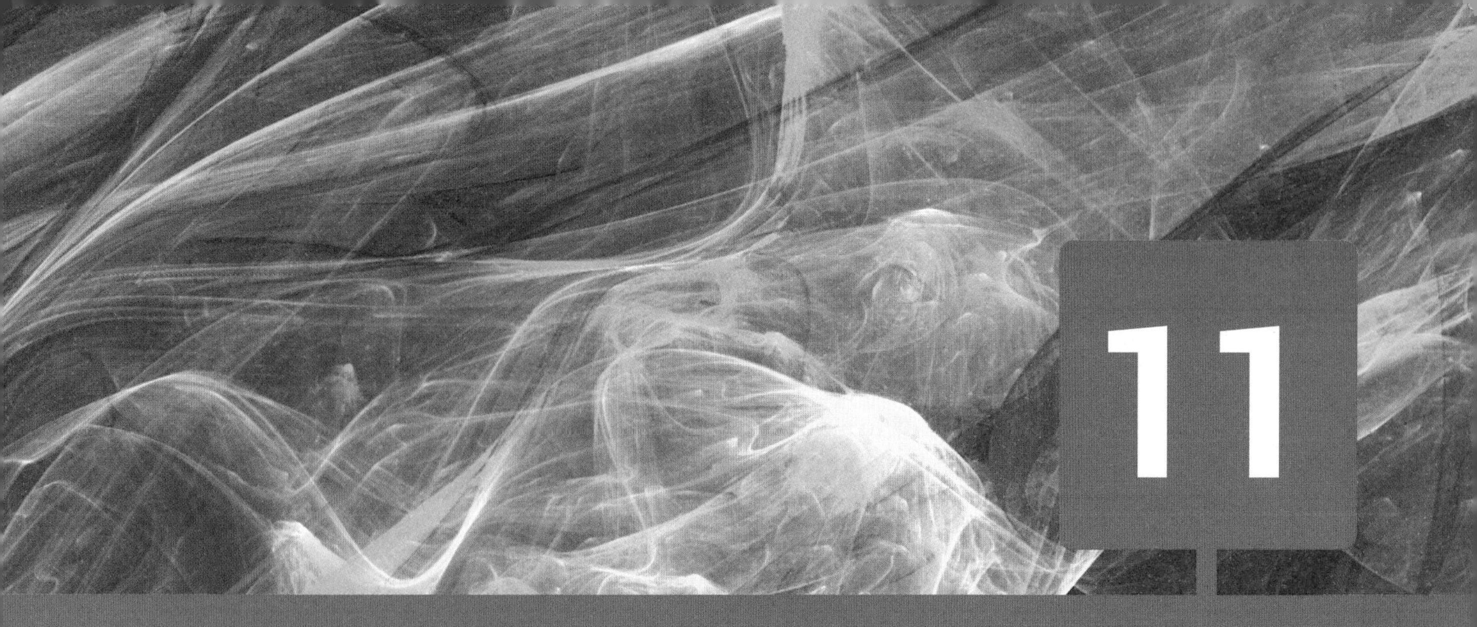

Counting and Permutations

In this chapter you will learn to:

- List all possible outcomes of an experiment using:
  - Systematic listing
  - Two-way tables
  - Tree diagrams
- Apply the Fundamental Principle of Counting
- Count the arrangements of n distinct objects ($n!$)
- Count the number of ways of arranging r objects from n distinct objects

You should remember...

- How to list outcomes in an ordered way
- Different methods of listing outcomes

Key words

- Sample space
- Systematic listing
- Two-way table
- Tree diagram
- Fundamental Principle of Counting
- Arrangements
- Permutations
- Factorial

11.1 Listing Outcomes

In mathematics and in everyday life it is important to be able to list all the possible **outcomes** that can occur in real-life situations or in **experiments**.

We encounter many common terms that have special meanings we must be aware of.

A trial is the act of doing an experiment.
An experiment is an action that leads to a well-defined result.
An outcome is one of the possible results of the trial.
The set of all possible outcomes is referred to as the sample space.

When listing all the outcomes (the elements of the **sample space**), three main methods can be used:

- Systematic listing

Systematic listing involves writing down all the possible outcomes.

For example, the possible outcomes of rolling one die are: {1, 2, 3, 4, 5, 6}.

- Two-way tables

Two-way tables are used to write down all the possible outcomes when there are two sets of options (i.e. two experiments combined).

- Tree diagrams

The branches of tree diagrams are used to show all the possible outcomes when there are two or more sets of options (i.e. two or more experiments combined).

Systematic Listing

This method involves writing down all the possible outcomes.

Two-Way Tables

Systematic listing can be difficult and can take a long time if there are many outcomes in the sample space. Two-way tables are a much more convenient way of showing numerous possible outcomes. They are used when there are **two** sets of options.

Worked Example 11.1

Harry has a choice of three types of bread (pitta, rye or white) and four fillings (beef, chicken, ham or turkey). How many different sandwiches can Harry order?

Solution

We put the outcomes of Harry's choice of bread on the side of the two-way table and the outcomes of his choice of fillings on the top of the table. We use letters to represent each of Harry's choices.

Bread		Fillings			
		Beef (B)	Chicken (C)	Ham (H)	Turkey (T)
	Pitta (P)	PB	PC	PH	PT
	Rye (R)	RB	RC	RH	RT
	White (W)	WB	WC	WH	WT

So PB represents a pitta beef sandwich, for example.

It is now a simple matter of using the table to list all the outcomes. It is clear from the table that there are $4 \times 3 = 12$ choices.

Tree Diagrams

A tree diagram is another method of listing outcomes. Its name comes from the fact that, when completed, the diagram looks like the branches of a tree.

The tree diagram method is useful when listing all of the possible outcomes when there are two or more sets of options.

Worked Example 11.2

A motorist drives through two sets of traffic lights. List all the possible sequences of colours of traffic lights that she could encounter.

Solution

At the first set of traffic lights, the outcomes (red, amber and green) can be drawn on the tree diagram as follows:

1st traffic light

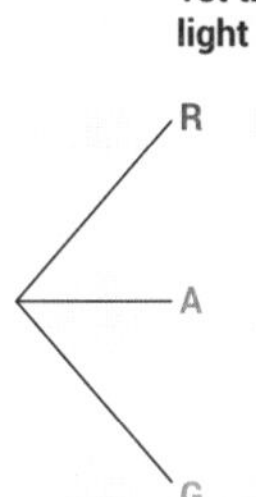

At the second set of traffic lights, the driver could meet the following outcomes:

1st traffic light | 2nd traffic light

R — R, A, G
A — R, A, G
G — R, A, G

If we follow each branch, we can fill in all the outcomes.

1st traffic light	2nd traffic light	Outcomes
R	R	RR
	A	RA
	G	RG
A	R	AR
	A	AA
	G	AG
G	R	GR
	A	GA
	G	GG

Exercise 11.1

In the following questions, use the most appropriate method unless stated otherwise.

Methods	Systematic listing	Two-way tables	Tree diagrams

1. A spinner with 10 equal sectors numbered 20 to 29 is spun once. What are all the possible outcomes?

2. This is a pack or deck of cards (excluding Jokers).

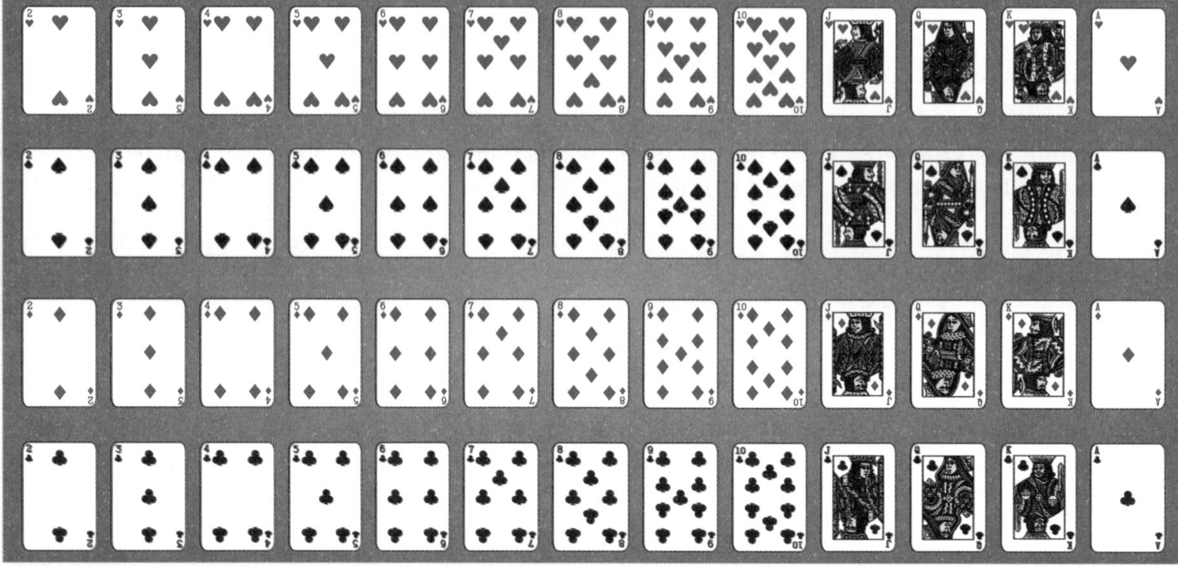

   (i) How many cards are there in a pack of cards?

   (ii) The pack is divided up into four different types called suits. Name the four suits.

   (iii) How many cards are there in each suit?

   The card shown on the right is called a picture card.

   (iv) Name this card.

   (v) How many picture cards in total are there in a deck of cards?

3. The number system we use has 10 digits: 0, 1, 2, 3, 4, 5, 6, 7, 8 and 9.

   The number 3,557 is a four-digit number.

   How many digits are there in each of the numbers in the table?

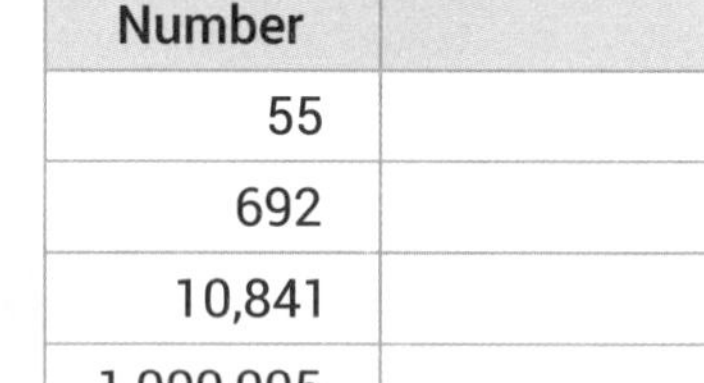

Number	
55	
692	
10,841	
1,000,005	

4. John throws a six-sided die and flips a coin.

   List all the possible outcomes.

   How many outcomes are possible?

5. Customers at a fast-food restaurant can choose a medium or large meal size, and they can choose chicken, a hamburger or a vegetarian option for their meal.

   Show all the possible combinations of meals and sizes.

6. In a certain deck of cards there are two types of cards: numbered and pictured. Each card can also be a Heart, a Club, a Spade or a Diamond. Use a tree diagram to show all the possible outcomes when a single card is picked at random. (Aces can be considered numbered cards for this question.)

7. Two dice are thrown. Copy and complete the two-way table below to show all the outcomes.

First die	Second die					
	1	2	3	4	5	6
1		1, 2				
2			2, 3			
3						
4						
5						
6	6, 1					6, 6

(i) How many outcomes are there?

(ii) What other method could you use to count the number of outcomes?

(iii) How many outcomes have the same digits, for example (2, 2)?

(iv) Is the outcome (1, 3) the same as the outcome (3, 1)? Explain your answer.

8. A spinner lettered A, B, C and D is spun. Another spinner numbered 1 to 5 is then spun.

(i) Copy the two-way table to list all the outcomes.

(ii) How many different outcomes are there?

(iii) How many outcomes have an odd number?

(iv) How many outcomes have an even number?

(v) How many outcomes have a vowel AND an even number?

(vi) How many outcomes have a vowel OR an even number?

First spinner	Second spinner				
	1	2	3	4	5
A					
B					
C			C3		
D					

9. A bag contains a number of red, yellow and orange balls. Two balls are taken from the bag and the colours are noted. What are the possible outcomes?

10. A fair spinner numbered from 1 to 3 is spun, and another spinner numbered 10 and 11 is spun. The scores from each spin are added together.

(i) Draw a two-way table to show all the outcomes.

(ii) How many of these outcomes add up to an even number?

11. Two dice are thrown. A score is obtained by subtracting the lower number from the higher number (this is done to ensure that there are no negative numbers).

First die	Second die					
	1	2	3	4	5	6
1		2 − 1 = 1				
2						
3						
4						
5						
6	6 − 1 = 5					

(i) Complete the table to show all the outcomes. (Some have been filled in for you.)

(ii) What is the most common outcome?

(iii) What is the least common outcome?

(iv) How many outcomes total to an odd number?

(v) How many outcomes total to an even number?

(vi) How many outcomes total to a prime number?

12. An unbiased coin is flipped three times.
    (i) Use a tree diagram to list all the possible outcomes.
    (ii) How many outcomes contain:
        (a) Three tails
        (b) Exactly two tails
        (c) At least two tails
        (d) At least one tail

13. A marble is picked from each of three bags, A, B and C.

    Bag A contains red and yellow marbles.

    Bag B contains red and green marbles.

    Bag C contains red, yellow and blue marbles.

    (i) Use a tree diagram to list all the possible outcomes.
    (ii) How many outcomes are possible?
    (iii) How many outcomes contain:
        (a) No red marbles
        (b) A yellow marble
        (c) Exactly two marbles of the same colour
        (d) All different coloured marbles

11.2 The Fundamental Principle of Counting

The Fundamental Principle of Counting is a quick and easy way to determine the number of outcomes of two or more experiments combined.

Worked Example 11.3

A normal die is rolled and a spinner numbered 1, 2, 3 is spun.
How many different outcomes are possible?

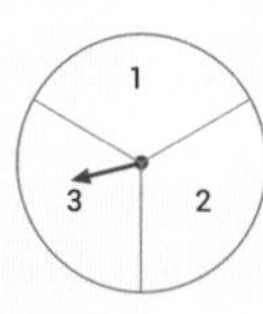

Solution

The **number of outcomes** for the first experiment – the die being rolled – is 6: {1, 2, 3, 4, 5, 6}.

The **number of outcomes** for the second experiment – the spinner being spun – is 3: {1, 2, 3}.

The total possible number of outcomes is $6 \times 3 = 18$.

Number of outcomes from die roll — Number of outcomes from spinner spin

Fundamental Principle of Counting

If one experiment has m possible outcomes and a second experiment has n possible outcomes, then the total number of possible outcomes is $m \times n$.

Remember that it is the **number of outcomes** that we multiply each time.

Worked Example 11.4

A spinner numbered 1, 3, 5, 7 and 9 is spun twice, and a coin is flipped once. How many different outcomes are possible?

Solution

- The number of outcomes for the first experiment is 5: {1, 3, 5, 7, 9}.
- The number of outcomes for the second experiment is 5: {1, 3, 5, 7, 9}.
- The number of outcomes for the third experiment is 2: {Head, Tail}.

The total possible number of outcomes is $5 \times 5 \times 2 = 50$.

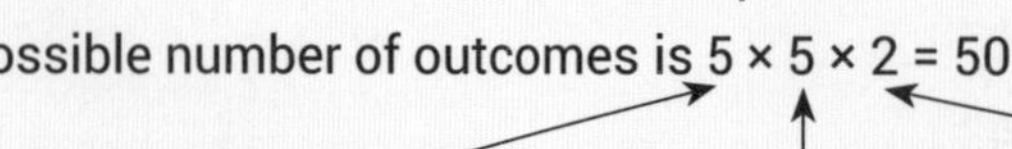

Number of outcomes from first spin — Number of outcomes from second spin — Number of outcomes from coin flip

Worked Example 11.5

A customer wishes to place an order in a pizzeria and is given the following choices for a meal.

Starter	Pizza	Drink	Dessert
Potato wedges	Margherita	Cola	Ice-cream
Garlic bread	Ham & pineapple	Juice	Apple tart
Chicken wings	Pepperoni	Water	
Ciabatta			

If the customer chooses a starter, pizza, drink and dessert, how many different meals can be ordered?

Solution

Number of outcomes = $4 \times 3 \times 3 \times 2 = 72$

Number of starter options, Number of pizza options, Number of drink options, Number of dessert options

Exercise 11.2

1. A furniture shop has five different types of sofa in four different colours. How many different sofas can a customer order?

2. A cinema has 10 films showing. Each film can be viewed in standard format or in 3D. How many choices of film are there?

3. Andrea is choosing a new pair of shoes. The shoes come in sizes 5, 5½, 6, 6½ and 7. They also come in five different colours and three different styles. How many different choices of shoes are possible?

4. In a restaurant, there are four choices for the starter, six choices for the main course and five choices for dessert. How many possible three-course meals are there?

5. A town decides to introduce registration plates for bicycles. Each registration plate has a single capital letter followed by a single digit (for example, J7, L8, Z0, etc.). How many different registration plates are possible?

6. How many three-letter passwords (lower case only) can be created if no letter can be used more than once?

7. A card is drawn from a pack of 52 cards, a coin is flipped and a six-sided die is rolled?
   (i) How many outcomes are possible?
   (ii) Name one possible outcome.

8. A six-sided die is rolled five times.
   (i) How many outcomes are possible?
   (ii) Name one possible outcome.

9. A coin is flipped 10 times. How many possible outcomes are there?

10. An online test consists of 12 questions, each with four choices. In how many ways can this test be filled out if all the questions are answered?

11. Eight people are in a race. How many ways can gold, silver and bronze medals be awarded if there are no dead heats?

12. An ID badge is made up of four capital letters. How many different ID badges are possible if no letter can be used more than once? An example is shown below.

    BRSV

13. A college has ten candidates for a rugby scholarship, twelve candidates for a soccer scholarship and seven candidates for an athletic scholarship.
    In how many ways can these scholarships be awarded?

14. In a school, all Fifth Year students have to choose one subject from each of the following options:

    Option A {French, German, Italian or Spanish}

    Option B {Business, Economics or Art}

    Option C {Biology, Chemistry, Geography, History or Physics}

    Oliver is a Fifth Year student at the school. He has to choose his three subjects.

    (i) In how many different ways can Oliver choose his three subjects?

    (ii) Oliver cannot decide which language to choose. He definitely will not pick Italian. In how many ways can he now pick his subjects?

    (iii) If Oliver decides that he will take French, in how many ways can he pick his other subjects?

    The school realises that students should have been allowed to pick two subjects from Option C to give a total of four subjects.

    (iv) In how many ways can a student now pick their four subjects?

15. A code is made up of two letters of the English alphabet (lower case) followed by three digits. Find the total number of codes possible when:

    (i) No letter may be used more than once

    (ii) No digit may be used more than once

    (iii) No letter or digit may be used more than once

11.3 Permutations

When using the Fundamental Principle of Counting we often multiply a list of numbers in descending order, for example, 5 × 4 × 3 × 2 × 1. In mathematics, a shorter way of writing this list is to use the factorial symbol, which is the exclamation mark. So 5 × 4 × 3 × 2 × 1 is written as 5! (pronounced '5 factorial').

The factorial $n!$ is defined for a non-negative integer n as $n! = n(n-1)(n-2) \dots 3.2.1$

Worked Example 11.6

Calculate

(i) 10!

(ii) 6!

(iii) 2(5!)

Solution

(i) $10! = 10 \times 9 \times 8 \times 7 \times 6 \times 5 \times 4 \times 3 \times 2 \times 1$

$= 3{,}628{,}800$

We can use the factorial button $n!$ or $x!$ on the calculator. This is generally a second function operator. Press 10 followed by $n!$, which should give you an answer of 3,628,800.

(ii) $6! = 6 \times 5 \times 4 \times 3 \times 2 \times 1 = 720$

(iii) $2(5!) = 2 \times 5 \times 4 \times 3 \times 2 \times 1 = 240$

Factorials can be useful when we are using the Fundamental Principle of Counting and outcomes have to be arranged in a particular order or position.

Worked Example 11.7

Find how many ways the letters of the word LEAVING can be arranged in each of the following cases:

(i) If there are no restrictions

(ii) If the arrangements must begin with a V

(iii) If the arrangements must **not** begin with a V

(iv) If the arrangements must begin and end with a vowel

(v) If the three vowels must be together

You have been asked to arrange LEAVING, so no letter may be used more than once.

An **arrangement** is the arranging of a set of items in a certain order.

Solution

(i) If there are no restrictions

- We note that there are seven letters in the word LEAVING.
- For the first letter of the arrangement, we have a choice of seven letters.
- For the second letter of the arrangement, we now have a choice of six letters, as one letter has already been used. This continues until we come to our last letter, where there is only one choice left.

Letter	1st		2nd		3rd		4th		5th		6th		7th	
Number of choices	7	×	6	×	5	×	4	×	3	×	2	×	1	= 7! = 5,040

(ii) If the arrangements must begin with a V

- The first letter must be a V (there is only one V, so there is only one choice).
- This means that we now have six letters to choose from for our second letter, and so on.

Letter	1st		2nd		3rd		4th		5th		6th		7th	
Number of choices	1	×	6	×	5	×	4	×	3	×	2	×	1	= 1 × 6! = 720

(iii) If the arrangements must **not** begin with a V

- There are a total of 5,040 different ways to arrange the seven letters of the word LEAVING, and 720 of these arrangements start with the letter V.
- The rest of the arrangements must not start with the letter V. The number of arrangements that do not start with the letter V is:

  5,040 – 720 = 4,320

(iv) If the arrangements must begin and end with a vowel

- The **first letter** must be a vowel. There are only three vowels (A, E, I), so there are three choices.
- The **last letter** must also be a vowel. As we have already picked one vowel for the first letter, we now have two choices left.
- Then the arrangements must be filled with the remaining five letters.

Letter	1st		2nd		3rd		4th		5th		6th		7th	
Number of choices	3	×	5	×	4	×	3	×	2	×	1	×	2	= 720

Note that because the question asked for the arrangement to begin and end with a vowel, those are the choices that we filled in first.

In general, we first fill in the choices that have restrictions placed on them.

(v) If the three vowels must be together

The three vowels can be placed anywhere in the arrangement as long as they are all together. For example

A I E L V N G

or

V L E A I G N

- We treat the three vowels as **one** letter, taking into account that the three vowels can be arranged in any order, AEI, EIA,... etc. There are 3! ways in which they can be arranged.
- There are now **five** letters to be arranged: L, V, N, G, AIE. There are 5! ways of arranging these letters.

∴ The answer is 3! × 5! = 720.

^nP_r: The Number of Ways of Arranging r Objects from n Distinct Objects

Worked Example 11.8

In how many ways can the letters of the word IRELAND be arranged, taking them three at a time? No repetitions are allowed.

Solution

There are seven choices for the first letter, six choices for the next letter and five choices for the last letter.

Letter	1st		2nd		3rd	
Number of choices	7	×	6	×	5	= 210 ways

In the above example we are trying to arrange a population of seven, taking three at a time.

In general, if you have a population of n distinct items, and you want to arrange r of them in order, then the number of possible **permutations** (or arrangements) is called ^nP_r and is defined as follows:

- n is the total number of distinct objects or items to choose from.
- r is the total number of objects or items we have to arrange in order.

$$^nP_r = \frac{n!}{(n-r)!}$$

We can use a calculator to apply this formula by using the nPr button.

On the calculator, we would press:

The answer 210 comes up on the screen.

Note that the buttons used on individual calculators may differ.

So, $^7P_3 = \frac{7!}{(7-3)!} = \frac{7!}{4!} = \frac{7 \times 6 \times 5 \times 4 \times 3 \times 2 \times 1}{4 \times 3 \times 2 \times 1} = 7 \times 6 \times 5 = 210$

A **permutation** is all the possible arrangements of a set of items, in a certain order.

Worked Example 11.9

(i) How many different four-digit numbers can be made using the digits 1, 2, 4, 6, 7 and 8 if no digit may be used more than once?

How many of these four-digit numbers are:

(ii) Even (iii) Odd (iv) Greater than 7,000

Solution

(i) If there are no restrictions:

- It will be a four-digit number.
- For our first digit we have six numbers to choose from. It is important to realise that we fill in our number of choices, not the actual number.
- For our second digit we have five numbers to choose from, and so on.

Digit	1st		2nd		3rd		4th	
Number of choices	6	×	5	×	4	×	3	= 360

- Alternatively, we could use $^6P_4 = 360$.

COUNTING AND PERMUTATIONS

(ii) If the number must be even:

- Even numbers are determined by their last digit being even (e.g. 4,876).
- The last digit must be even; therefore there are four choices for this last digit (2, 4, 6 or 8).
- Once this choice has been filled in, we can return to the first digit. For the first digit we now have five numbers to choose from (one number has already been used for the last digit).

Digit	1st		2nd		3rd		4th	
Number of choices	5	×	4	×	3	×	4	= 240

- Alternatively, we could use ${}^5P_3 \times 4 = 240$.

(iii) If the number must be odd:

- A total of 360 different four-digit numbers can be made from the digits 1, 2, 4, 6, 7 and 8. Of these four-digit numbers, 240 are even.
- Therefore, the remaining numbers must be odd: 360 – 240 = 120.
- Alternatively, we could represent our choices as $\boxed{5} \times \boxed{4} \times \boxed{3} \times \boxed{2} = 120$ (i.e. ${}^5P_3 \times 2 = 120$).

(iv) If the arrangements must be greater than 7,000:

- If the number is greater than 7,000, then its first digit must be a 7 or an 8. For the first digit, we therefore have two choices.
- For the next digit, we have five choices (one number has already been used), and so on.

Digit	1st		2nd		3rd		4th	
Number of choices	2	×	5	×	4	×	3	= 120

- Alternatively, we could use $2 \times {}^5P_3 = 120$.

Exercise 11.3

1. Investigate if:

   (i) $4! + 5! = 9!$ (ii) $3! \times 4! = 12!$

2. List all the possible four-digit numbers that can be made from the digits 1, 2, 3 and 4, using each digit only once to make up your number.

   (i) How many outcomes are there?
   (ii) How many of these numbers are even?
   (iii) How many of these numbers are odd?
   (iv) How many are greater than 3,400?
   (v) How many are less than 3,400?
   (vi) How many start with a 4?

3. Write down all the possible arrangements of the letters G, A, M, E, S that begin with a vowel and end with a vowel. For example, AGMSE.

   (i) How many arrangements did you get?
   (ii) How many have M in the middle?
   (iii) How many arrangements end with E?
   (iv) In how many does G appear before S?
   (v) In how many does S appear before G?
   (vi) In how many are M and G side by side?
   (vii) In how many are M and G not side by side?

4. There are five finalists in a school music contest. In how many different ways can a winner and a runner-up be chosen?

5. How many five-digit numbers can be formed by rearranging the digits in the number 38,621?

6. A company has 20 members on its board of directors. In how many different ways can the members elect a president, vice-president, secretary and treasurer?

7. Six greyhounds (A, B, C, D, E and F) enter a race. A special betting slip must be filled out in which you must predict which greyhound will come first, which second and which third. In how many different ways can the betting slip be filled?

Placement	Greyhound
1st	
2nd	
3rd	

8. A baby presses six of the ten numbers (0 to 9) on a phone dial pad once each. How many different number sequences could she have dialled?

9. In how many different ways can the letters of the word SQUARE be arranged:
   (i) Taking the letters six at a time
   (ii) Taking the letters five at a time
   (iii) Taking the letters two at a time

10. A company wishes to introduce an identification number for each employee. Every number consists of four digits, the first digit of which is never zero. How many different numbers are there if the digits may be repeated?

11. A church has seven different bells in its bell tower. Before each church service, five different bells are rung in sequence.
    How many possible sequences are there?

12. (i) In how many ways can the letters of the word MODAL be arranged?
    (ii) How many of these arrangements begin with L?
    (iii) How many do not begin with L?
    (iv) How many end with M?

13. Seven horses (A, B, C, D, E, F and G) take part in a race. (Assume no dead heats, and all horses finish.)
    (i) In how many different orders can they finish the race?
    (ii) If A wins, how many orders are possible?
    (iii) If A wins and B comes last, how many different orders are possible?
    (iv) In how many ways can the first four horses come in?

14. Karen has to study seven subjects for her Christmas exams: Maths, French, Irish, CSPE, English, History and Geography. She decides to study four of these subjects on a particular day. Find the number of different orders in which she can study her four subjects:
    (i) If there are no restrictions
    (ii) If she must start with Maths
    (iii) If she must **not** start with Maths
    (iv) If she must start with a language
    (v) If she must **not** start with a language

15. How many three-digit numbers can be made using any of the digits 2, 3, 4 and 5:
    (i) If repetitions are not allowed (e.g. 233 and 555 are **not** allowed)
    (ii) If repetitions are allowed

    If repetitions are not allowed, how many of these numbers are:
    (iii) Odd (iv) Even

16. A password for a computer system consists of three different digits followed by two different capital letters.
    (i) How many different passwords are possible?

    Ian forgets his password but knows that the first number is 5 and the last letter is A.
    (ii) How many different passwords match this description?

17. How many three-digit numbers can be made from the digits 5, 7, 8 and 9 (no digit may be repeated):
    (i) If there are no restrictions
    (ii) If the number is even
    (iii) If the number is odd
    (iv) If the number is over 700

18. In how many ways can the letters of the word TRIANGLE be arranged:
    (i) If there are no restrictions
    (ii) If the arrangements must begin with N
    (iii) If they must begin with a vowel
    (iv) If the three vowels must come at the start

19. Three girls (Aoife, Betty and Carol) and two boys (Darren and Eoin) are to line up for a photograph. How many different ways are there of arranging them in a straight line:
    (i) If they may line up in any order
    (ii) If they must be girl–boy–girl–boy–girl

20. In how many different ways can the letters of the word PIGLET be arranged:
    (i) If there are no restrictions
    (ii) If the arrangements must begin with a vowel
    (iii) If the arrangements must begin with a vowel and end with T
    (iv) If the two vowels must be together at the start
    (v) If the two vowels must be together
    (vi) If the two vowels must be apart

21. How many three-digit numbers can be made using any of the digits 0, 1, 2, 3, 4 and 5 (no digit may be repeated):
    (i) If there are no restrictions
    (ii) If the number must be even
    (iii) If the number must be odd
    (iv) If the number must be greater than 300
    (v) If the number must be greater than 300 and odd
    (vi) If zero must be included

22. (i) How many different numbers with three digits or less can be formed from the digits 4, 5, 6, 7 and 8?
    No repetitions are allowed.
    (ii) How many of the above numbers are odd?

Revision Exercises

1. An electrical store has numerous televisions for sale. A television can have a large, medium or small screen size, and it can have a plasma or LCD screen.
    (i) Show all possible different types of television using a two-way table.
    (ii) Find the number of different types of television a customer can purchase.

2. A factory produces a range of shirts. They can be short-sleeved or long-sleeved; black, white or blue; and medium or large size.
    Use a tree diagram to show all the different types of shirts that this factory produces.

3. There are three horses in a race: A, B and C.
    (i) Use a tree diagram to show the different orders in which they can finish the race.
    (ii) If B comes first, how many different orders are possible?
    (iii) If B comes first and A last, how many different orders are possible?

4. A spinner numbered 1, 2 and 3 and a spinner numbered 1, 2, 3, 4 and 5 are spun. The score from the first spinner is added to the score from the second spinner.
    (i) Use a two-way table to show all the possible outcomes.
    (ii) How many outcomes are:
        (a) Odd numbers
        (b) Prime numbers
        (c) Divisible by 2
        (d) Divisible by 3

5. A spinner numbered 2, 3 and 6 is spun once and a coin is flipped twice.
    (i) Use a tree diagram to list all the possible outcomes.
    (ii) How many outcomes are possible?
    (iii) Give an example of one such outcome.
    (iv) How many outcomes contain a prime number?

6. In a restaurant, there are three choices of starter, ten choices of main course and four choices of dessert. How many different three course meals could be eaten at this restaurant?

7. John is going to a festival for the weekend. Each outfit he can wear consists of a pair of jeans, a shirt, a jumper and a pair of shoes. He has packed:

   3 pairs of jeans (black, navy and blue)

   4 shirts (white, green, yellow and red)

   2 jumpers (black and brown)

   3 pairs of shoes (boots, sandals and flip-flops)

   (i) Write down two examples of different outfits John could select to wear.

   (ii) How many different possible outfits can John wear over the weekend?

8. Reading City FC has two jerseys, blue and green, from which to select. They can also select from five different colours of shorts (blue, red, green, orange and white) and three different colours of socks (red, blue and green).

   (i) How many different kits (jerseys, shorts and socks) can Reading City have?

   Reading City are due to play Colchester Forest, who play in an all red kit. It is decided that Reading City FC can't select red for any part of their kit.

   (ii) Calculate how many different kits Reading City FC can select.

9. How many ways are there of arranging the letters of QUARTZ if the letters are taken:

   (i) Three at a time

   (ii) Four at a time

   (iii) Six at a time

   (iv) Two at a time

10. A lock has a four-digit code, for example, 5091. How many different codes are possible:

    (i) If a digit can be used only once

    (ii) If a digit can be used more than once

    (iii) If the code has to end with a prime digit

11. The letters of the word POWERS are arranged in as many different ways as possible.

    (i) In how many ways can this be done?

    (ii) How many of these arrangements begin with a vowel?

    (iii) How many of these arrangements begin with a vowel and end with a vowel?

12. The five letters A, B, C, D and E are arranged in a row.

    (i) In how many ways can this be done?

    (ii) How many of these arrangements begin with B?

    (iii) How many arrangements begin with a vowel?

    (iv) How many arrangements begin with a consonant?

13. (i) How many four-digit numbers can be made using the four digits 1, 3, 5 and 7:

    (a) If repetitions are not allowed (e.g. 7,333 and 5,155 are **not** allowed)

    (b) If repetitions are allowed

    (ii) How many different numbers between 3,000 and 9,000 can be made using only the digits 1, 3, 5 and 7, if no digit may be repeated?

14. (i) How many ways are there of arranging the letters of the word WINTER?

    (ii) How many arrangements begin with a vowel?

    (iii) How many arrangements begin with a vowel and end with a consonant?

    (iv) How many arrangements end with the two vowels side by side?

    (v) How many arrangements have the two vowels beside each other?

15. A family of two adults and three children is seated in a row. In how many different ways can they be seated if:

    (i) There are no restrictions on the order of seating

    (ii) A child must be seated at the beginning of the row

    (iii) A child must be seated at the beginning of the row and an adult at the end of the row

    (iv) The two adults must be seated beside each other

16. (i) How many different four-digit numbers can be made from the digits 2, 3, 4 and 5 (if no digit may be used more than once)?

    How many of these numbers are:

    (ii) Less than 3,000

    (iii) Even

    (iv) Divisible by 5

    (v) Divisible by 5 and less than 3,000

17. (i) How many ways are there of arranging the letters of the word JOSHUA, taking them four at a time?

    How many of these arrangements:

    (ii) Begin with A

    (iii) Do **not** begin with A

    (iv) Have the three vowels together

18. (i) How many ways are there of arranging the letters of the word MICROBES?

    How many of these arrangements:

    (ii) Begin with R

    (iii) Begin with a vowel

    (iv) Have the three vowels as the first three letters

    (v) Have the three vowels together

19. Nine students (four girls and five boys) are to be lined up for a photo.

    (i) How many arrangements are possible?

    (ii) How many arrangements are possible if all the boys stand on the left and all the girls on the right?

    (iii) How many arrangements are possible if no two boys may stand side by side?

20. (i) How many different five-digit numbers can be formed from the digits 3, 4, 5, 6 and 8 (if no digit may be used more than once)?

    (ii) How many of the numbers are less than 40,000?

    (iii) How many of the numbers are divisible by 2?

    (iv) How many of the numbers are less than 40,000 and divisible by 2?

Exam Questions

1. Mandy wants to buy a ticket to the theatre. She can choose a ticket in the Balcony (B) or the Stalls (S). Mandy can go on Monday (M), Wednesday (W) or Friday (F). For an extra charge she can choose a VIP ticket (V) where she will meet the band or she can choose the show only (O).

   Complete the tree diagram, and hence or otherwise, find the probability that Mandy chooses a VIP ticket on a Wednesday.

   You may assume that all choices are equally likely.

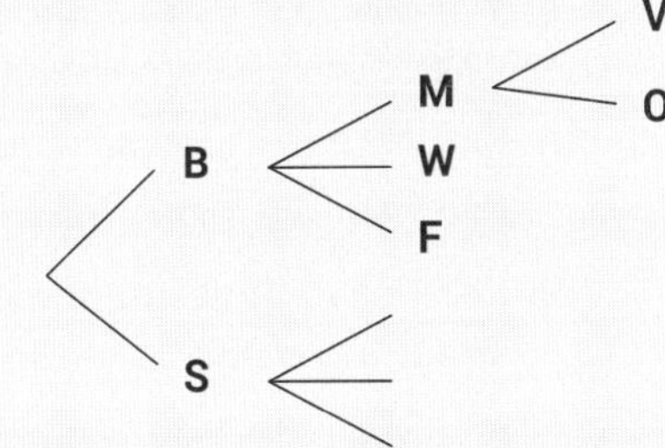

SEC Leaving Certificate Ordinary Level, Paper 2, 2016

2. A bank issues a unique six-digit password to each of its online customers. The password may contain any of the numbers 0 to 9 in any position and numbers may be repeated. For example, the following is a valid password.

0	7	1	7	3	7

   (a) How many different passwords are possible?

   (b) (i) How many different passwords do **not** contain **any** zero?

   (ii) One password is selected at random from all the possible passwords. What is the probability that this password contains at least one zero?

(c) John is issued with one such password from the bank. Each time John wants to access his account online, the bank's website requires him to input three of his password digits into the boxes provided. For example, he may be asked for the 2nd, 4th and 5th digits, as shown below.

In how many different ways can the bank select the three required boxes?

SEC Leaving Certificate Ordinary Level, Paper 2, 2015

3. (a) State the *fundamental principle of counting.*

(b) How many different ways are there to arrange five distinct objects in a row?

(c) Peter is arranging books on a shelf. He has five novels and three poetry books. He wants to keep the five novels together and the three poetry books together. In how many different ways can he arrange the books?

SEC Leaving Certificate Ordinary Level, Sample Paper 2, 2014

4. An unbiased circular spinner has a movable pointer and five equal sectors, two coloured green and three coloured red.

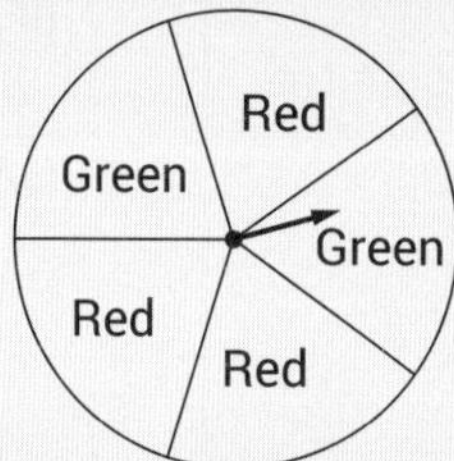

List all the possible outcomes of 3 successive spins of the spinner.

SEC Leaving Certificate Ordinary Level, Paper 2, 2013

5. Peter and Niamh go to a large school. One morning, they arrive early. While they are waiting, they decide to guess whether each of the next three students to come in the door will be a boy or a girl.

(a) Write out the sample space showing all the possible outcomes. For example, BGG is one outcome, representing Boy, Girl, Girl.

(b) Peter says these outcomes are equally likely. Niamh says they are not. What do you need to know about the students in the school to decide which of them is correct?

(c) If all the outcomes are equally likely, what is the probability that the three students will be two girls followed by a boy?

(d) Niamh guesses that there will be at least one girl among the next three students. Peter guesses that the next three students will be either three boys or two boys and a girl. Who is more likely to be correct, assuming all outcomes are equally likely? Justify your answer.

SEC Leaving Certificate Ordinary Level, Paper 2, 2012

Solutions and chapter summary available online

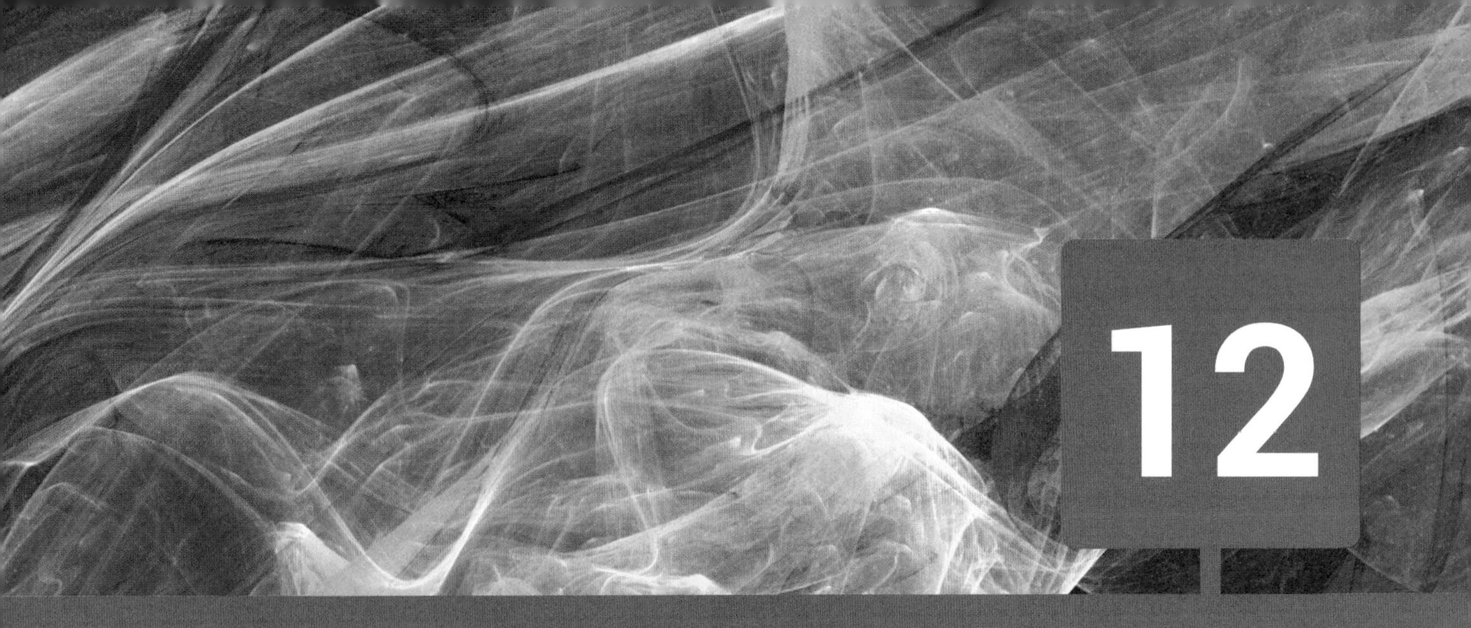

12

Probability

In this chapter you will learn to:

- Use set theory to discuss experiments, outcomes, sample spaces
- Discuss basic rules of probability (AND/OR, mutually exclusive) through the use of Venn diagrams
- Calculate expected value and understand that this does not need to be one of the outcomes
- Recognise the role of expected value in decision making and explore the issue of fair games
- Understand the meaning of independent events
- Find the probability that two independent events both occur
- Apply an understanding of Bernoulli trials
- Solve problems involving up to three Bernoulli trials
- Calculate the probability that the first success occurs on the *n*th Bernoulli trial, where *n* is specified

You should remember...

- How to work with fractions
- How to work with decimals
- How to work with percentages
- Two-way tables
- Tree diagrams
- How to work with sets
- The cards in a normal pack

Key words

- Probability scale
- Likelihood scale
- Trial
- Outcome
- Sample space
- Event
- Relative frequency
- Expected frequency
- Fairness
- Equally likely
- Theoretical probability
- Set theory
- Mutually exclusive events
- AND/OR events
- Two-way table
- Tree diagram
- Independent events
- Bernoulli trial
- Expected value

12.1 Introducing Probability

Probability is a branch of mathematics that studies the chance or likelihood of something occurring.

We encounter probability in some form or another in everyday life, from the chance of a horse winning a race to the chance of rain the following day.

Probability is also involved in determining car insurance premiums and forecasting the weather.

In probability we encounter many common terms that have special meanings we must be aware of.

A **trial** is the act of doing an experiment in probability.

The flipping of a coin is an example of a **trial**.

An **outcome** is one of the possible results of the trial.

When flipping a coin, the **outcomes** are that you could flip a head or a tail.

Head

Tail

The set or list of all possible outcomes in a trial is called the **sample space**.

For a coin, the **sample space** is {head, tail}.

An **event** is the occurrence of one or more **specific outcomes**.

The flipped coin landing on a head would be the **event**.

Likelihood Scale

We use the likelihood scale when we use words to describe the probability of an event. We use words such as:

Impossible — Unlikely — Evens — Likely — Certain

Using words to describe the probability of an event can be problematic. Saying an event is 'unlikely' is open to many different interpretations.

Probability Scale

Probability is a numerical measure of the chance of an event happening.

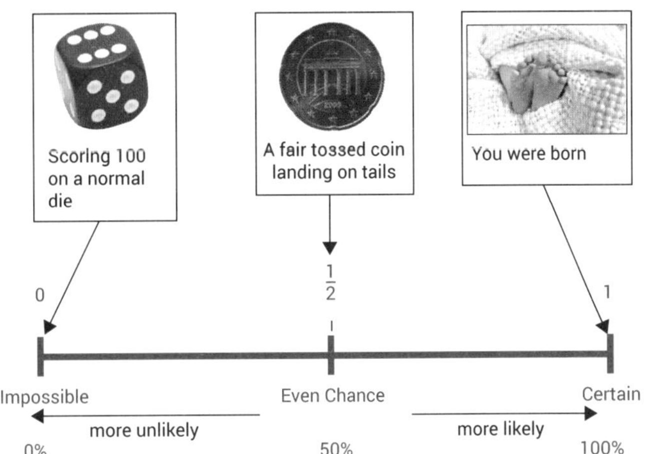

A probability scale using percentages ranges from 0% (impossible) to 100% (certain).

A probability scale using decimals ranges from 0 (impossible) to 1 (certain).

It is also important to remember that the probabilities of **all** outcomes of a particular experiment will add up to 1.

A **fair** coin is one where the chance of landing on a head or a tail is equally likely. 

Loaded dice are unfair dice that have been altered to give a more predictable outcome. 

Remember that there are four suits (Clubs, Diamonds, Hearts and Spades) in a standard pack of 52 cards. Each suit contains an Ace, a King, a Queen and a Jack, as well as numbered cards from 2 to 10.

Worked Example 12.1

For each event below, mark on the probability scale an estimate of its probability.

A: You will get Maths homework today.

B: A normal die will land on an even number.

C: A normal die will land on a 6.

D: You will pick a Jack from a standard deck of cards.

Solution

A: As this is Maths, homework is a near certainty.

B: Three {2, 4, 6} out of a total of six outcomes {1, 2, 3, 4, 5, 6} are even on a normal die.

C: One {6} out of a total of six outcomes {1, 2, 3, 4, 5, 6} is a 6 on a normal die.

D: There are four Jacks in a standard deck of 52 playing cards.

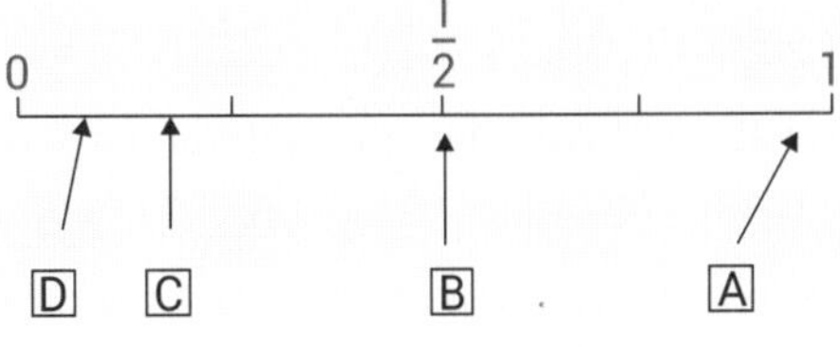

Exercise 12.1

Describe each of the following events as: impossible, unlikely, evens, likely or certain to occur.

1. A fair coin will land on a head.
2. Roll a normal die once and get a 5.
3. The sun will set today.
4. A card chosen from a standard pack of 52 cards will be red.
5. It will rain next August in Ireland.
6. Roll an odd number on a single throw of a fair die.
7. A card chosen from a standard pack of cards will be a Diamond.
8. The next baby born in Ireland will be a girl.
9. Roll a normal die and get a prime number.
10. Roll a 7 on a single throw of a fair die.
11. The probabilities of five events are shown on the probability scale below.

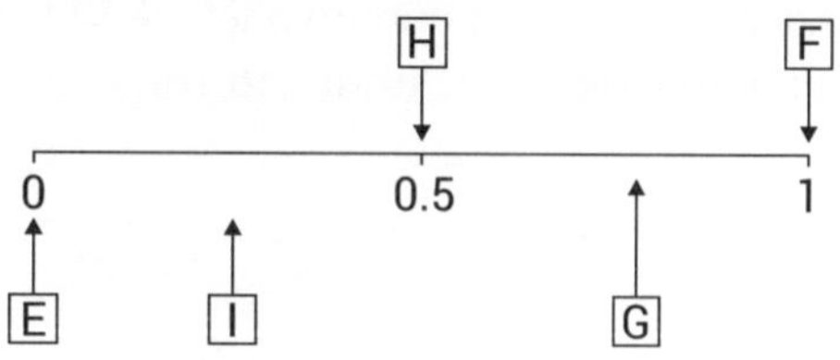

   (i) Which event is impossible?
   (ii) Which event is more than likely going to occur?
   (iii) Which event is unlikely to happen?
   (iv) Which event is certain to occur?
   (v) Which event has a 50–50 chance of happening?

12. Draw a probability scale. Mark each event with its letter on the scale.
   A: It will be sunny in Spain tomorrow.
   B: You will get a 10 on a single throw of a fair die.
   C: A fair coin will land on tails on a single flip.
   D: You will read a book on the weekend.

13. Draw a probability scale. Mark each event with its letter on the scale.
   A: You will pick a number divisible by two when selecting at random a number from the set {1, 2, 3, ...,10}.
   B: The Atlantic Ocean will disappear tomorrow.
   C: You will go home after school.
   D: You will get a 1 or a 2 on a single roll of a fair die.

14. Mark the probability of each event on a probability scale, when a single card is drawn at random from a standard pack of cards:
   (i) A Diamond, Heart, Club or Spade
   (ii) A red card
   (iii) A Diamond
   (iv) A Diamond picture card
   (v) The King of Diamonds

15. Explain what is wrong with each of the following statements:
   (i) The probability of rain today is 1.5.
   (ii) The chance of winning a lottery is −1.
   (iii) The probability of rolling a 1, 2, 3, 4, 5 or 6 on a normal die is 0.9.

12.2 Relative Frequency (Experimental Probability), Fairness and Expected Frequency

The probability of an event occurring can be estimated from statistical data derived from experiments or observations.

The question of whether your school team will win their next match can be used as an example. You can look at the team's recent results in order to estimate the likelihood of them winning their next match.

This is referred to as **relative frequency** or **experimental probability**.

Relative frequency is an estimate of the probability of an event.

$$\text{Relative frequency} = \frac{\text{frequency or number of times the event happens in trials}}{\text{total number of trials}}$$

In comparison, **theoretical probability** is the number of ways that a desirable outcome can occur divided by the number of all possible outcomes.

Worked Example 12.2

A coin was flipped 1,000 times. It landed on tails 450 times. Find the relative frequency of getting a tail.

Solution

$$\text{Relative frequency} = \frac{\text{number of times a tail was flipped}}{\text{number of times coin was flipped}}$$

$$= \frac{450}{1{,}000}$$

$$= \frac{9}{20} \text{ or } 0.45 \text{ (or 45\%)}$$

John Kerrich was interned in Denmark during the Second World War. He wanted to see if a coin was fair (unbiased). He tossed a coin 10,000 times and recorded his results.

Heads	Tails
5,067	4,933

He then worked out the relative frequency for both results:

$$\text{Relative frequency for heads} = \frac{5{,}067}{10{,}000} = 0.5067$$

$$\text{Relative frequency for tails} = \frac{4{,}933}{10{,}000} = 0.4933$$

While not exactly 50–50, they were so close to the theoretical probabilities for a fair coin that he concluded that the coin was fair or unbiased.

It is important to note that, in general, as the number of trials carried out increases, the relative frequency of an event tends towards the theoretical probability of that event.

Worked Example 12.3

An experiment is conducted to show how the number of trials improves the accuracy of the relative frequency.

Mick rolls a fair die and notes the number of times a 1 is rolled.
He records his results for every six throws of the die. (Note: 2 d.p. = two decimal places.)

	Total times 1 is rolled	Relative frequency (2 d.p.)
6 throws	0	0
12 throws	1	0.08
18 throws	2	0.11
24 throws	5	0.21
30 throws	5	0.17
36 throws	6	0.17
42 throws	8	0.19
48 throws	9	0.19
54 throws	9	0.17
60 throws	11	0.18

Mick then plots his results on a graph.

Show Mick's results on a graph and comment on the overall trend.

PROBABILITY

Solution

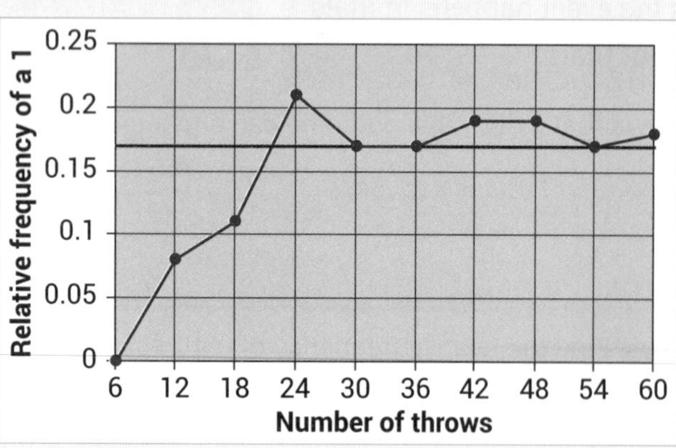

As the experiment is repeated, the relative frequency tends towards the theoretical probability (in this case $\frac{1}{6}$ or 0.17 to two decimal places).

Expected Frequency

If we know the relative frequency or theoretical probability of an event, we can then estimate how many times that event would be expected to happen over a certain number of trials. This is called the **expected frequency**.

Expected frequency = number of trials × relative frequency or theoretical probability

Worked Example 12.4

A fair die is rolled 900 times. How many times would you expect to roll a 1?

Solution

The probability of rolling a 1 on a fair die: $P(1) = \frac{1}{6}$

Number of times a 1 would be expected to appear after rolling a die 900 times:

$900 \times \frac{1}{6} = 150$

Worked Example 12.5

A random and large survey of shoppers was carried out in a supermarket. It was found that the relative frequency of a shopper buying the supermarket's own toilet paper brand is 28%. If the supermarket has 1,500 customers on a particular day, what is the expected number who will buy the supermarket's own toilet paper brand?

Solution

$1{,}500 \times \frac{28}{100} = 420$ shoppers

Fairness

A fair coin, as there are only two outcomes, should land on tails around 50% of the time and on heads around 50% of the time. A game played with a fair coin where the player wins by flipping the coin and getting a tail would be considered a fair game. This is because the player is equally likely to win as to lose the game.

If an object (e.g. die, coin, spinner) or game is said to be **fair** or **unbiased**, then all outcomes are equally likely to occur.

Worked Example 12.6

A spinner is made from a pentagon. Its sectors are labelled 1, 2, 3, 4 and 5. The spinner is spun and the number of the sector it lands on is noted after each spin. The results are recorded and shown in this table.

Number on spinner	Results
1	20
2	45
3	20
4	21
5	14

Is the spinner fair?

Solution

Total number of spins = 20 + 45 + 20 + 21 +14 = 120

Relative frequency of landing on 2 = $\frac{45}{120}$ = 0.375

If the spinner were fair, we would expect a relative frequency close to $\frac{1}{5}$ or 0.2.

Conclusion: The spinner is not fair, as the relative frequency is not close to the theoretical probability (assuming fairness) even after 120 trials.

Exercise 12.2

1. A die is rolled 100 times. The number 1 shows 25 times. What is the relative frequency of rolling a 1?

2. A coin is flipped 1,000 times. It lands on heads 350 times. What is the experimental probability of the coin landing on:

   (i) Heads (ii) Tails

3. A deli sells 75 lunches in one day. Ten of these lunches are vegetarian. What is the relative frequency of selling a non-vegetarian lunch?

4. In a survey of 570 people, it was found that 190 people had a college degree. What is the relative frequency that a person does not have a college degree?

5. 55,000 students sit a Maths exam. Ten thousand of these students get an O3 grade. What is the relative frequency of a student getting an O3 grade?

6. A spinner is spun and the number of times it lands on each of its five sectors is recorded as shown:

Spinner sector	A	B	C	D	E
Frequency	5	10	12	10	13

   Find the relative frequency of the spinner landing on each sector. Write each answer as a percentage.

7. A die is rolled and the relative frequency for each possible outcome is recorded in the table below.

Number on die	1	2	3	4	5	6
Relative frequency	0.1	0.15	0.2	0.18	0.12	

   (i) Work out the relative frequency of rolling a 6 on the die.
   (ii) What outcome occurred the least often?
   (iii) What outcome occurred the most often?
   (iv) How many times did the die show a 4 if the die was rolled 200 times in total?
   (v) Given the results above, do you think the die is fair? Explain your answer.

8. The results of games played by three children are shown in the table.

Child	Games won	Games lost	Games drawn
Megan	5	1	4
Alex	2	2	3
Jack	0	1	1

(i) What is the experimental probability of a win for each child?

(ii) Who, according to their experimental probabilities, is the best player?

(iii) Explain what might be wrong in deciding who is the best player on the basis of the calculated experimental probabilities of wins.

9. A bag contains tokens of three different colours. A token is picked at random from the bag, its colour noted and then returned to the bag. This experiment is done 100 times. Every 20th time, the relative frequency of picking a pink token is calculated. The graph of the results is shown below.

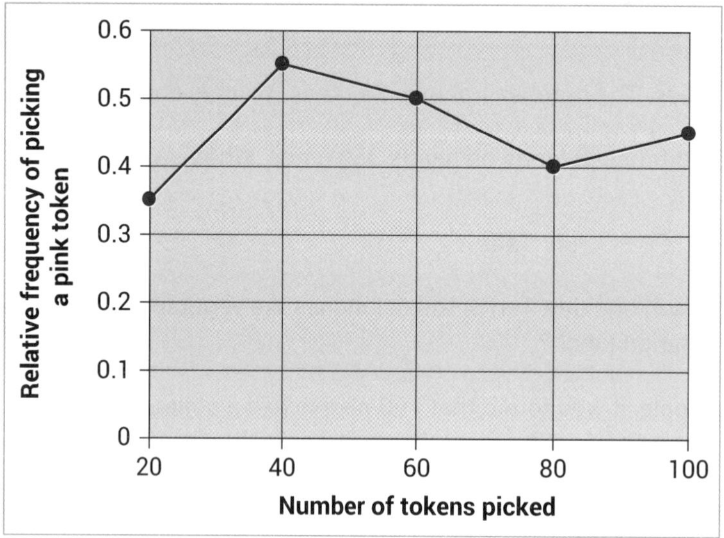

(i) Estimate how many times a pink token was picked after 20 trials.

(ii) Estimate how many times a pink token was picked after 40 trials.

(iii) Estimate how many times a pink token was picked after 80 trials.

(iv) In your opinion, is there an equal number of each coloured token in the bag? Give a reason for your answer.

10. A spinner is spun 500 times and shows red 75 times. How many times would you expect it to show red after 1,000 spins?

11. A card is drawn from a pack of cards and replaced. This is done 260 times. How many times would you expect to get:

(i) A black card

(ii) A picture card

(iii) The King of Clubs

(iv) A red Ace

12. Decide if each of the following games is fair and give a reason for your answer.

(i) A game won on rolling an even number on a single throw of a die

(ii) A game won on rolling a 1, 3, 5 or 6 on a single throw of a die

(iii) A game won on rolling a prime number on a single throw of a die

13. A die is rolled 400 times and lands on a 5 40 times. In your opinion, is the die fair? Give a reason for your answer.

PROBABILITY

14. A coin is flipped 100 times. It lands on tails 30 times.

(i) Do you think the coin is biased? Explain the reasons for your answer.

(ii) If the coin was flipped another 20 times, how many of the 120 times would you expect it to land on tails?

15. An unfair die is rolled a number of times and the relative frequency that it lands on 3 is calculated to be 0.28. Estimate the number of times the die will land on a 3 if it is rolled 600 times.

16. The experimental probability of scoring from a penalty in the World Cup is 0.77.

If 46 penalties are awarded during the next World Cup, how many (to the nearest whole number) would you expect to be missed?

17. A company determines that the probability of a television developing a fault is 0.05% over a period of one year. If the company sells 50,000 televisions, how many would you expect to develop a fault over the first year?

18. Global Car Breakdown Assistance (GCBA) wishes to study how the time of year affects the number of car breakdowns. It has a total of 13,450 customers. The results are shown below.

Month	Number of breakdowns per month
January	540
February	677
March	496

What is the experimental probability, as a percentage to two decimal places, of breakdowns per month?

19. Phones for All is a company that sells mobile phones directly to its customers. It records the number of faulty phones returned for the year versus the number sold as shown.

Model	Number sold	Number returned
A	650	30
B	7,320	367
C	8,999	449
D	15,200	609

If the relative frequency of faulty phones returned exceeds 5%, the company will refuse to stock that model of phone the following year.

Determine, using relative frequency, which if any make of phones should not be stocked for next year.

20. A random survey of 50 adults is carried out, asking what mode of transport they use to go to work in a certain town. The results are shown below.

Mode	Walk	Car	Bus
Number	10	25	15

If there are 5,000 adults working in the town, how many would we expect to use each mode of transport listed to get to work?

21. A bag contains a number of discs lettered A, B, C and D. An experiment is conducted in which a disc is taken from the bag, its letter is recorded, and it is then returned to the bag. Two students conduct the experiment and record their results.

Letter on disc	A	B	C	D
Mark	50	10	20	40
Gayle	16	3	5	13

(i) Mark says that the experimental probability of choosing D is approximately 33%, while Gayle says it is approximately 35%. Mark argues that Gayle's calculated probabilities are not as reliable as his own. State, giving a reason, whether you agree with Mark.

(ii) Using Mark's results, find the relative frequency for each lettered disc.

(iii) Does the bag contain the same number of each lettered disc? Explain.

(iv) How might the results in the table above be used to best calculate the theoretical probability for each lettered disc?

(v) Use your answer to (iv) above to calculate the number of times you would expect a disc labelled B to be picked following 500 trials.

12.3 Theoretical Probability

When an experiment takes place and **all outcomes are equally likely**, the probability of a certain event, E, taking place is written as P(E), and is defined by:

$$\text{Probability (Event)} = P(E) = \frac{\text{number of desirable outcomes}}{\text{total number of all possible outcomes}} = \frac{\#D}{\#S}$$

S is the sample space, the set of all possible outcomes.

# denotes the cardinal number, which is the number of elements in the set.

Worked Example 12.7

A bag contains 5 red and 10 blue marbles. One marble is picked at random from the bag. What is the probability that it is blue?

Solution

There are 10 blue marbles, ∴ the number of desirable outcomes = 10.

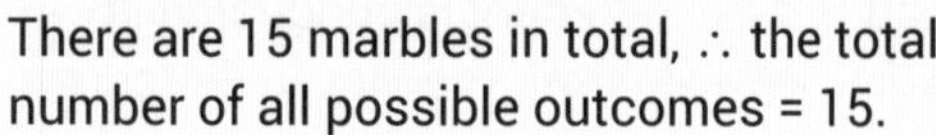

There are 15 marbles in total, ∴ the total number of all possible outcomes = 15.

$$P(\text{blue}) = \frac{\text{number of blue marbles}}{\text{total number of marbles}} = \frac{10}{15} = \frac{2}{3}$$

Always ensure that you fully simplify your answer if it is written in fraction form.

Worked Example 12.8

A fair six-sided die is thrown.

What is the probability of rolling an even number?

Solution

The set of all desirable outcomes is {2, 4, 6}.

The set of all possible outcomes (sample space) is {1, 2, 3, 4, 5, 6}.

desirable outcomes = 3

sample space = 6

$$P(\text{even}) = \frac{\#\text{ desirable outcomes}}{\#\text{ sample space}} = \frac{3}{6} = \frac{1}{2}$$

Worked Example 12.9

(a) A card is drawn at random from a standard pack of 52 cards. What is the probability that the card drawn is:

(i) A Jack (ii) A Heart (iii) A picture card

(b) A card is picked at random from all the red cards. What is the probability that it is a King?

Solution

(a) (i) A Jack

$$P(\text{Jack}) = \frac{\text{number of cards that are Jacks}}{\text{total number of cards in the pack}} = \frac{4}{52} = \frac{1}{13}$$

(ii) A Heart

$$P(\text{Heart}) = \frac{\text{number of cards that are Hearts}}{\text{total number of cards in the pack}} = \frac{13}{52} = \frac{1}{4}$$

(iii) A picture card

$$P(\text{picture card}) = \frac{\text{number of picture cards}}{\text{total number of cards in the pack}} = \frac{12}{52} = \frac{3}{13}$$

(b) It is important to note that we are selecting a card out of all the red cards in a pack of cards.

The sample space is the set of all red cards.

$$P(\text{King}) = \frac{\text{number of } \textbf{red} \text{ Kings}}{\text{total number of } \textbf{red} \text{ cards in the pack}} = \frac{2}{26} = \frac{1}{13}$$

If the probability of an event happening is $x\%$, then the probability of that event **not** happening is $(100 - x)\%$. For example, if there is an 80% chance that it will rain tomorrow then there is a 20% chance that it will not rain tomorrow.

P(not event) = 1 – P(event)

Worked Example 12.10

A card is drawn at random from a standard pack of 52 cards. What is the probability that the card drawn is not a Club?

Solution

$P(\text{Club}) = \frac{1}{4}$

$P(\text{not a Club}) = 1 - \frac{1}{4}$

$= \frac{3}{4}$

Exercise 12.3

1. A fair coin is flipped once. Calculate the probability of getting:
   (i) A head
   (ii) A tail

2. In a Maths class there are eight boys and seven girls. A student is chosen at random. What is the probability that this student will be:
   (i) A boy
   (ii) A girl

3. If the probability that it will rain tomorrow in Athlone is 0.75, what is the probability that it will not rain in Athlone tomorrow?

4. The following cards are put into a hat.

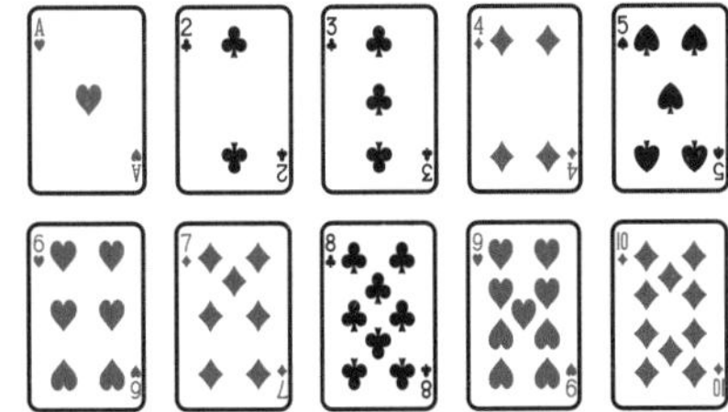

The Ace in this example counts as the number 1.

(a) A card is chosen at random. What is the probability that it will be:
   (i) the six of Hearts
   (ii) a red card

(iii) not a red card

(iv) a card showing an odd number

(b) A red card is chosen at random. What is the probability that it will be:

(i) the six of Hearts

(ii) not the six of Hearts

(iii) a card showing a prime number

(iv) a card showing an odd number

(v) a picture card

5. A fair die is rolled once. Work out the probability that you roll:

(i) 5

(ii) 1

(iii) 20

(iv) 1, 2, 3, 4, 5 or 6

(v) An even number

(vi) An odd number

(vii) A number less than 4

6. A bag contains 15 white marbles, 6 black marbles and 4 blue marbles. A marble is taken from the bag at random.

Calculate the probability (as a percentage) that this marble will be:

(i) White

(ii) Black

(iii) Blue

(iv) Not blue

(v) White or black

7. A card is selected at random from a pack of 52 playing cards.

Calculate the probability that it is:

(i) A red card

(ii) A black card

(iii) The Ace of Spades

(iv) A black King

(v) The King of Clubs

8. A spinner with 20 equal sectors numbered 1–20 is spun. Calculate the probability that it lands on:

(i) 10

(ii) 5

(iii) 20

(iv) An even number

(v) A prime number

(vi) A composite number

9. Eight Scrabble tiles are placed in a bag. They are P, A, R, A, L, L, E, L. One tile is drawn out at random.

Work out the probability that the selected tile is:

(i) The letter L

(ii) The letter P

(iii) The letter A

(iv) A vowel

10. The fair spinner shown is spun once.

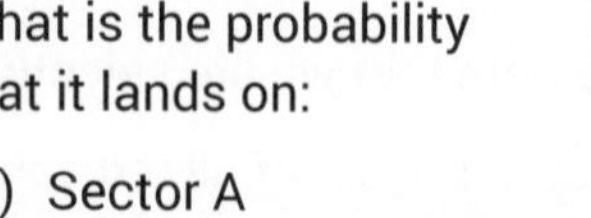

What is the probability that it lands on:

(i) Sector A

(ii) Sector B

(iii) A sector showing a vowel

11. There are 20 students in a class. This table shows the number who are girls or boys and how many are left-handed or right-handed:

	Left-handed	Right-handed
Girls	2	10
Boys	3	5

A student is picked at random from the class. Find the probability that this student will be:

(i) A girl

(ii) A boy

(iii) A right-handed girl

(iv) A left-handed boy

A boy is picked at random from the class. Find the probability that this boy will be:

(v) Left-handed

12. A person is stopped in the street at random and asked on what day of the week they were born. What is the probability that the person was born on:

(i) A Sunday

(ii) Not a Sunday

(iii) A Saturday or Sunday

(iv) A weekday (Monday to Friday)

(v) A day beginning with the letter T

13. The following coins are in a money box: two 5c coins, ten 20c coins, five €1 coins and three €2 coins. A single coin is taken at random from the box. What is the probability that it is:

(i) A 5c coin

(ii) A 20c or 5c coin

(iii) A €2 or €1 coin

(iv) Not a €2 or €1 coin

14. In a pencil case there are a number of pens: one red, three blue, two black and one green. If a student picks a pen at random, find the probability that the pen is:

(i) A blue pen

(ii) A red pen

(iii) A red or a blue pen

(iv) A green or a black pen

(v) Not a green or a black pen

15. A bag contains one red token, four blue tokens and five yellow tokens.

A token is taken out of the bag at random. What is the probability that it is:

(i) Red

(ii) Blue

(iii) Yellow

(iv) Red or blue

(v) Blue or yellow

(vi) Red or yellow

16. A spinner has two red sectors, one of size 45° and the other of size 90°.

(i) Calculate the probability that the spinner does not land on a red sector.

(ii) The angle size of the bigger red sector is changed so that the probability of landing on a red sector is now 70%.

What angle size is this new red sector?

17. A drop of water lands randomly on a rectangular counter 0.5 m wide and 1 m long. A bowl of radius 10 cm is placed on this counter.

(i) Calculate, to two decimal places, the probability that the drop lands in the bowl.

(ii) What's the smallest number of bowls that would be needed in order to have at least an evens chance of the drop landing in a bowl?

18. A bag contains 13 tokens: three red, four blue and the remainder white. If one token is drawn at random from the bag, what is the probability that it is:

(i) Blue

(ii) Not blue

A number of blue and white tokens are added, so that the probability of getting a red token is $\frac{1}{8}$.

(iii) How many tokens are added?

12.4 Set Theory and Probability

Set theory is very useful when trying to solve questions involving probability.

Consider the following example where we are asked to draw a Venn diagram to represent the outcomes of a die roll.

U = {1, 2, 3, 4, 5, 6} A = {1, 2} B = {5, 6}

There are two ways we could represent the above situation with a Venn diagram.

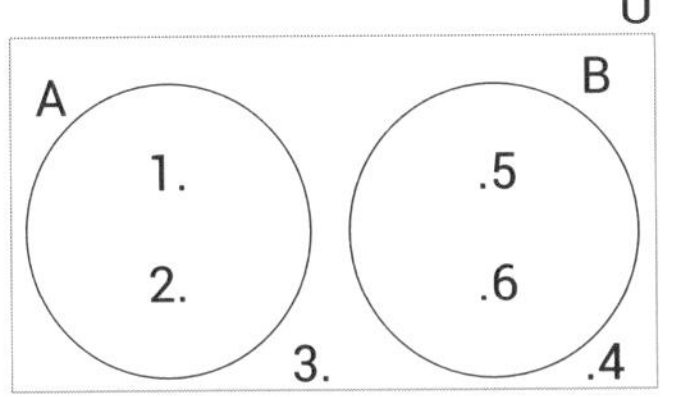

OR

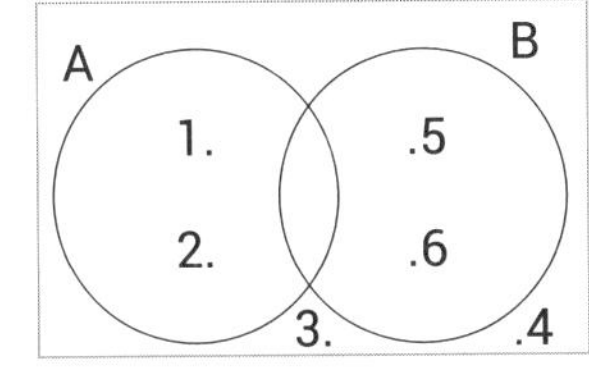

U is the universal set (the set of all elements under consideration) and is represented by a rectangle. The universal set represents the sample space of the experiment.

Notice how the sets have no elements in common. ∴ These sets are **mutually exclusive**.

Mutually exclusive events have no elements or outcomes in common. This means that the events cannot occur at the same time. Two events are mutually exclusive if their intersection is empty.

Now consider the example where a Venn diagram shows the preference of 50 adults for a certain brand, A or B, of chocolate.

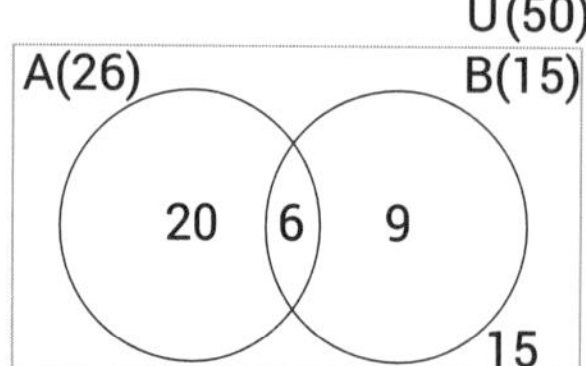

From this Venn diagram we can determine (among other things) how many adults liked:

(i) Brand A and Brand B

(ii) Brand A or Brand B

(iii) Not Brand A

(iv) Brand B only

(v) Neither brand

(i) Brand A and Brand B (written as $A \cap B$)

6 adults liked Brand A and Brand B.

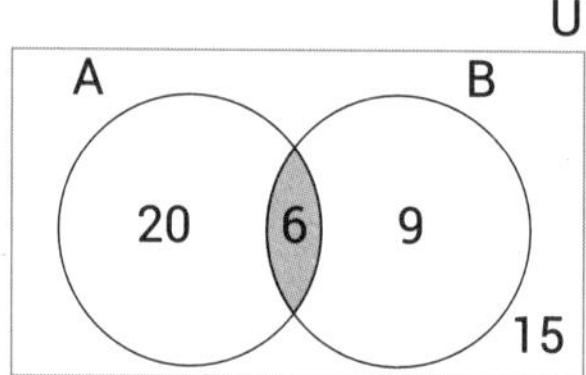

(ii) Brand A or Brand B (written as $A \cup B$)

These are adults who like Brand A **or** Brand B **or both brands.**

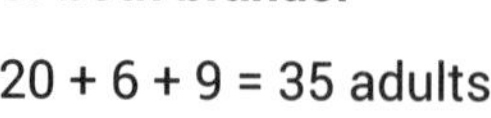

20 + 6 + 9 = 35 adults

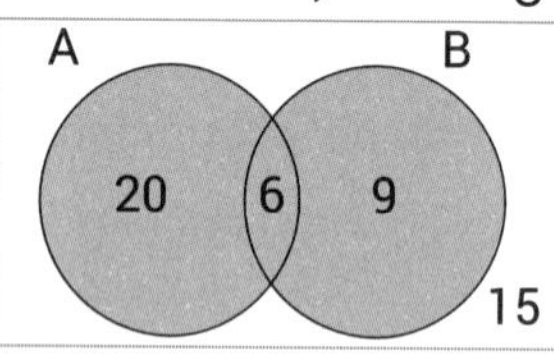

(iii) Not Brand A (written as A')

9 + 15 = 24 adults

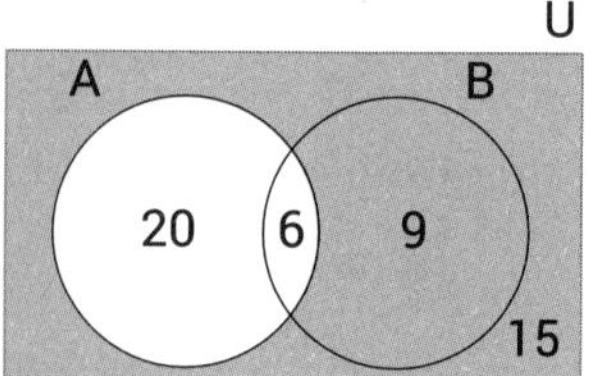

(iv) Brand B only (written as $B \backslash A$)

9 adults

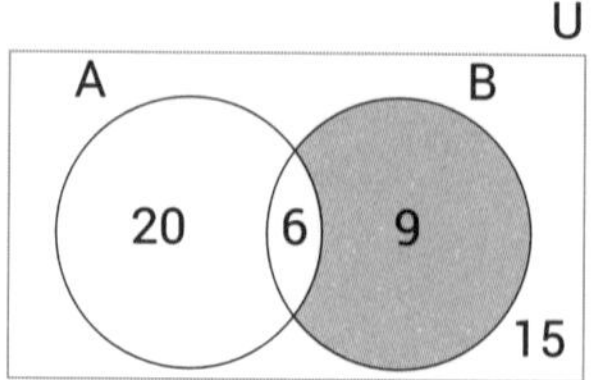

(v) Neither brand

These are the elements that are in neither Set A nor Set B (written $(A \cup B)'$).

15 adults

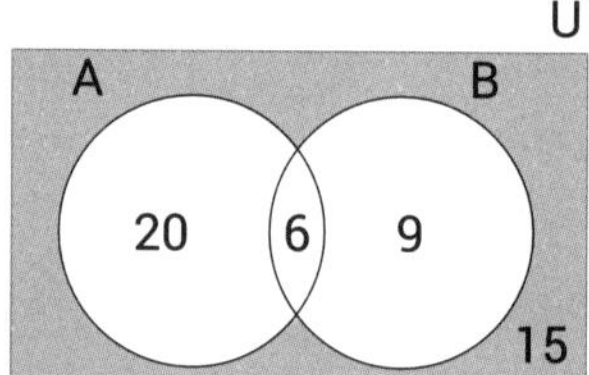

Worked Example 12.11

This Venn diagram shows the teenagers in a group who like tea OR coffee.

What is the probability that a teenager chosen at random:

(i) Likes tea (ii) Likes tea or coffee (iii) Likes tea and coffee

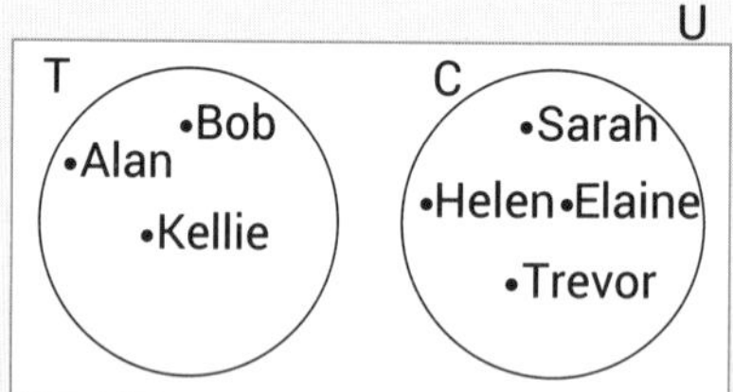

Solution

(i) The number of teenagers in Set T is 3. The number of teenagers in the universal set is 7.

$$P(T) = \frac{3}{7}$$

(ii) This is the union of the two sets.

$$P(T \text{ or } C) = \frac{7}{7} = 1$$

The next solution shows an example of **mutually exclusive** events.

(iii) This is the intersection of the two sets. As this is empty:

$$P(T \text{ and } C) = \frac{0}{7} = 0$$

PROBABILITY

Worked Example 12.12

Thirty students in a college were asked if they studied Art or Biology. The Venn diagram below shows the results of the survey.

What is the probability that a student chosen at random:

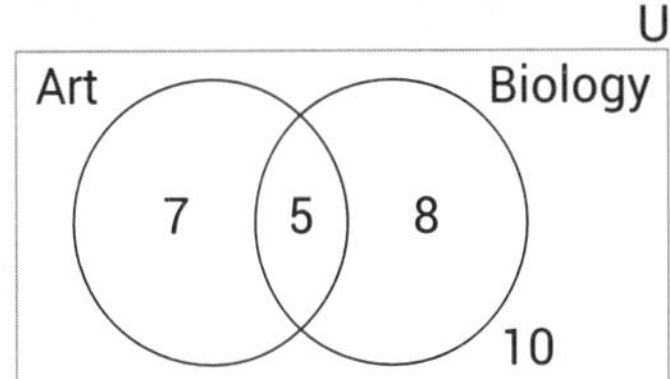

(i) Studies Art

(ii) Studies Biology

(iii) Studies Art and Biology

(iv) Studies Art or Biology

(v) Studies Art only

(vi) Studies neither subject

Solution

(i) What is the probability that a student studies Art?

$$P(A) = \frac{\#A}{\#U} = \frac{7+5}{30} = \frac{12}{30} = \frac{2}{5}$$

(ii) What is the probability that a student studies Biology?

$$P(B) = \frac{\#B}{\#U} = \frac{5+8}{30} = \frac{13}{30}$$

(iii) What is the probability that a student studies Art and Biology?

$$P(A \cap B) = \frac{\#(A \cap B)}{\#U} = \frac{5}{30} = \frac{1}{6}$$

(iv) What is the probability that a student studies Art or Biology?

$$P(A \cup B) = \frac{\#(A \cup B)}{\#U} = \frac{7+5+8}{30} = \frac{20}{30} = \frac{2}{3}$$

(v) What is the probability that a student studies Art only?

$$P(A \backslash B) = \frac{\#(A \backslash B)}{\#U} = \frac{7}{30}$$

(vi) What is the probability that a student studies neither subject?

$$P(A \cup B)' = \frac{\#(A \cup B)'}{\#U} = \frac{10}{30} = \frac{1}{3}$$

We may sometimes encounter set questions on probability in which we are given the actual probabilities of certain events.

Worked Example 12.13

Kerrie conducts a survey to discover how many students in her college participate in either soccer or Gaelic football. She discovers that the probability that a student plays soccer is 0.25 and the probability that a student plays Gaelic football is 0.4. The probability that they play neither of these sports is 0.45.

(i) Draw a Venn diagram to show this data.

A student is picked at random.

(ii) Find the probability that the student plays both soccer and Gaelic football.

(iii) Find the probability that the student plays soccer only.

Solution

(i) The probabilities should all add up to 1.

$0.25 + 0.4 + 0.45 = 1.1$

$1.1 - 1 = 0.1$

0.1 is the probability that a student plays both sports.

Soccer only = $0.25 - 0.1 = 0.15$

Gaelic football only = $0.4 - 0.1 = 0.3$

We can now draw the Venn diagram.

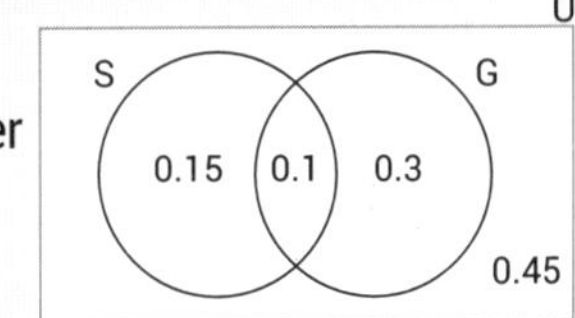

(ii) The probability that the student plays both soccer and Gaelic football = 0.1.

(iii) The probability that the student plays soccer only = 0.15.

In many cases, probability deals with a single event where one outcome **OR** another outcome is desirable. We can use set theory, sample spaces and counting outcomes to help explain what happens in these cases.

Worked Example 12.14

What is the probability of getting a King **OR** a Queen when selecting a single playing card from a normal deck?

Solution: Using a Venn Diagram

The number of Kings or Queens is #(K ∪ Q) = 8.

U		
K: 4	Q: 4	44

P(King or Queen) = $\frac{8}{52} = \frac{2}{13}$

It is clear that if we pick **one** card and get a King there is no possibility this card could also be a Queen. The two events are mutually exclusive; they have no outcomes in common.

Solution: Using Sample Space Diagrams or Listing Outcomes

We can list all the cards in a normal deck. We are looking for a King or a Queen, so we highlight both types of cards.

♥ Heart	♦ Diamond	♣ Club	♠ Spade
Ace	Ace	Ace	Ace
King	King	King	King
Queen	Queen	Queen	Queen
Jack	Jack	Jack	Jack
10	10	10	10
9	9	9	9
8	8	8	8
7	7	7	7
6	6	6	6
5	5	5	5
4	4	4	4
3	3	3	3
2	2	2	2

We have highlighted eight cards out of a possible 52.

P(King or Queen) = $\frac{8}{52} = \frac{2}{13}$

Solution: By Counting Outcomes

Another method is to count the number of outcomes that would give us a King or a Queen.

- King: 4 outcomes
- Queen: 4 outcomes

P(King or Queen) = $\frac{8}{52} = \frac{2}{13}$

Solution: By Formula

For events that are mutually exclusive, when dealing with OR events, we simply add the probabilities of the two events.

P(King) = $\frac{4}{52}$ P(Queen) = $\frac{4}{52}$

For mutually exclusive events P(A or B) = P(A ∪ B) = P(A) + (B).

P(King or Queen) = $\frac{4}{52} + \frac{4}{52} = \frac{8}{52} = \frac{2}{13}$

Of course, we may deal with problems that are not mutually exclusive, i.e. they have events in common.

Worked Example 12.15

What is the probability of getting a King or a Club when selecting a single playing card from a normal deck?

Solution: Using a Venn Diagram

We must pay attention to the intersection, as we have one card that is the King of Clubs. We must not count this card twice (this is referred to as double counting).

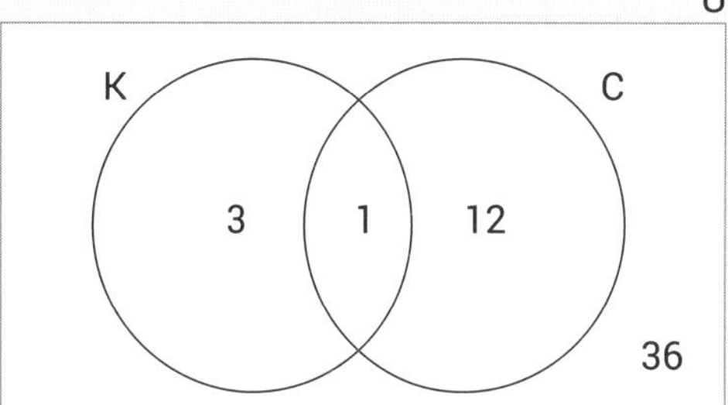

From the Venn diagram, the number of Kings or Clubs is $\#(K \cup C) = 16$.

P(King or a Club) $= \frac{16}{52} = \frac{4}{13}$

Solution: Using Sample Space Diagrams

We can list all the cards in a normal deck.

We are looking for a King or a Club, so we highlight both types of cards.

♥ Heart	♦ Diamond	♣ Club	♠ Spade
Ace	Ace	Ace	Ace
King	King	King	King
Queen	Queen	Queen	Queen
Jack	Jack	Jack	Jack
10	10	10	10
9	9	9	9
8	8	8	8
7	7	7	7
6	6	6	6
5	5	5	5
4	4	4	4
3	3	3	3
2	2	2	2

We have highlighted 16 cards out of a possible 52.

P(King or a Club) $= \frac{16}{52} = \frac{4}{13}$

Solution: By Counting Outcomes

We can count the number of outcomes that would give us a King or a Club.

- King: 4 outcomes
- Club: 13 outcomes
- King of Clubs: 1 outcome (we must subtract this from our total so as not to double count)

The total number of desirable outcomes is 16 [13 Clubs + 4 Kings – 1 King of Clubs].

The total number of possible outcomes is 52.

P(King or a Club) $= \frac{16}{52} = \frac{4}{13}$

PROBABILITY

Solution: By Formula

In this example, when we pick **one** card we could get a King that is also a Club, the King of Clubs. The two events are NOT mutually exclusive; they have an outcome in common. We must therefore subtract the probability of this outcome (King of Clubs) after we have added the two probabilities.

> $P(A \text{ or } B) = P(A \cup B) = P(A) + P(B) - P(A \cap B)$
> The probability of A or B happening is the probability of A added to the probability of B minus the probability of A and B.

$P(\text{King}) = \frac{4}{52}$ $\quad$ $P(\text{Club}) = \frac{13}{52}$ $\quad$ $P(\text{King AND Club}) = \frac{1}{52}$

$P(\text{King or Club}) = \frac{4}{52} + \frac{13}{52} - \frac{1}{52} = \frac{16}{52} = \frac{4}{13}$

Exercise 12.4

1. A B

A: 2. 1. 3. 4.

B: 5. 6. 7.

(i) List the elements of Set A.

(ii) List the elements of Set B.

A student picks a number at random from the numbers 1 to 7 inclusive. Find the probability that this number is in:

(iii) Set A

(iv) Set B

2. A Venn diagram is shown below.

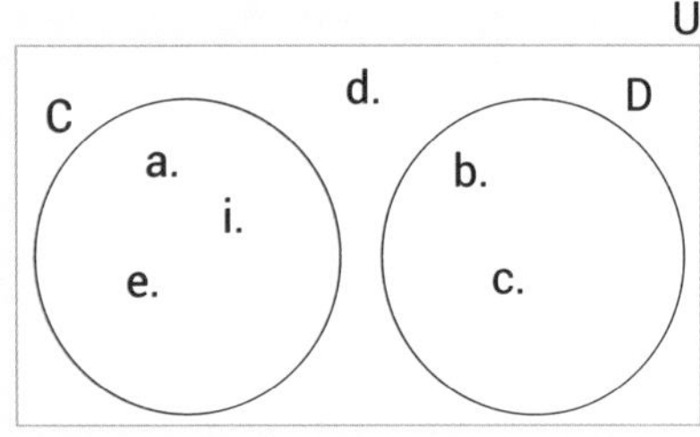

(i) List the elements of Set C.

(ii) List the elements of Set D.

(iii) What name is given to sets that have no elements in common?

(iv) Find the probability of picking a letter from Set C in a single pick.

(v) Find the probability of picking a letter from Set D in a single pick.

3. A Venn diagram is shown below.

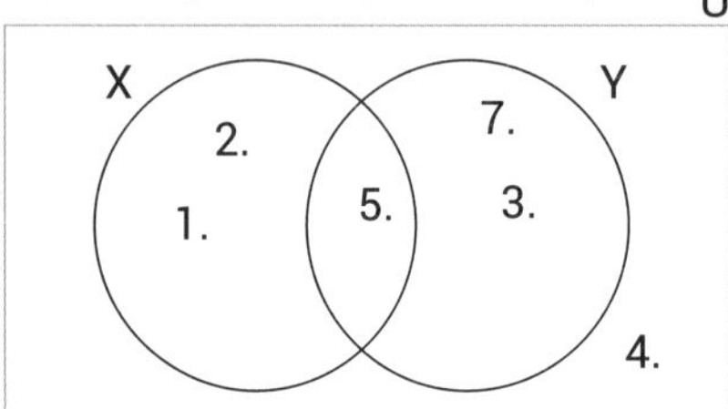

(i) Write down #X.

(ii) Write down #Y.

(iii) Find the probability of picking a number from Set X in a single pick.

(iv) Find the probability of picking a number from Set X or Set Y in a single pick.

(v) Find the probability of picking a number from Set X and Set Y in a single pick.

4. A Venn diagram is shown below. The number of elements in each region is given.

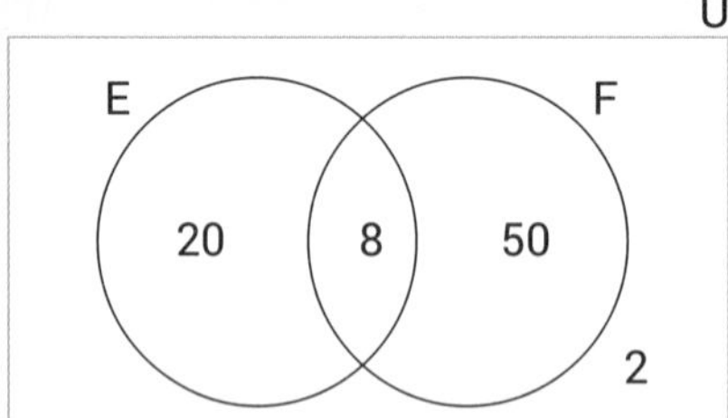

One element is selected at random.

(i) Find the probability of picking an element from Set E.

(ii) Find the probability of picking an element from Set E or Set F.

(iii) Find the probability of picking an element from Set E and Set F.

5. For each of the Venn diagrams below, find the probability of randomly selecting in a single pick an element from:

(i) $P \cup Q$ (iii) $P \setminus Q$

(ii) $P \cap Q$ (iv) $(P \cup Q)'$

(a)

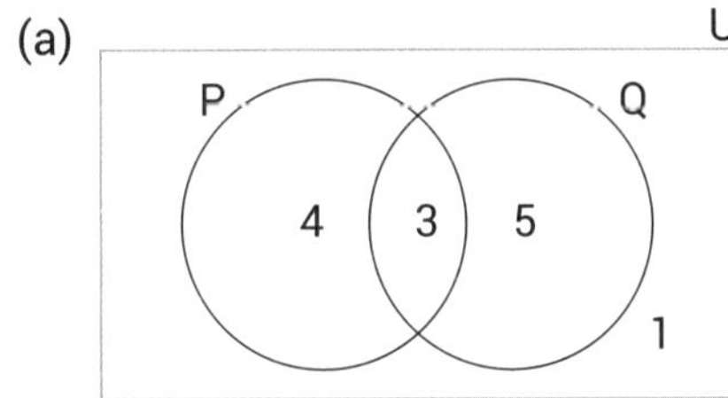

(b)

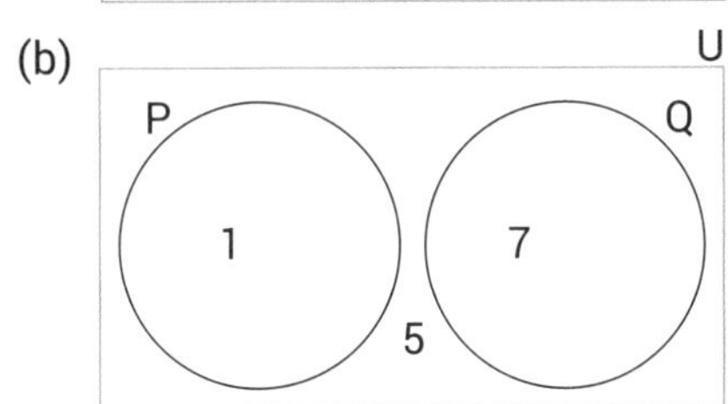

6. The Venn diagram below shows the response to a survey carried out in a supermarket. Customers were asked what coffee brand they had purchased.

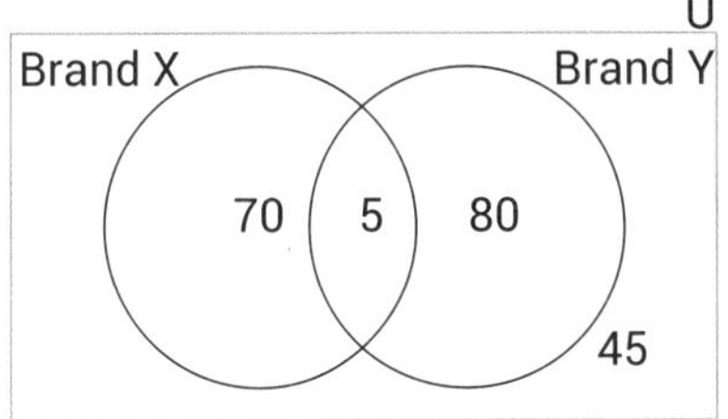

A customer is selected at random. What is the probability that:

(i) The customer purchased Brand X

(ii) The customer did not purchase Brand X

(iii) The customer did not purchase either brand

7. Students are asked which paper of the Maths syllabus they like. The Venn diagram shows the results.

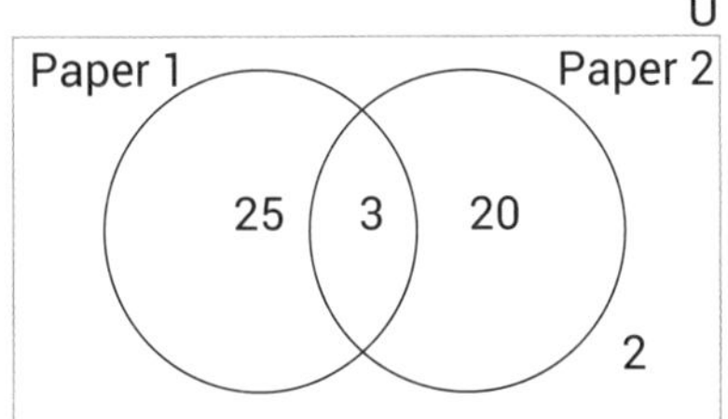

What is the probability that a student selected at random likes:

(i) Paper 1

(ii) Paper 1 and Paper 2

(iii) Paper 1 or Paper 2

(iv) Neither of the papers

8. In a survey the probability that a household has a dog for a pet is 0.6. The probability that a household has a cat for a pet is 0.3. The probability that the households surveyed did not have a dog or a cat is 0.35.

(i) Draw a Venn diagram to show this data.

(ii) Find the probability that a household has a cat and a dog.

(iii) Find the probability that a household has a cat or a dog.

(iv) Find the probability that a household has a cat only.

9. Thirty per cent of the students at a school have a part-time job. Ten per cent of students have a part-time job and attend evening study in school. Twenty-five per cent of students do neither.

(i) Draw a Venn diagram to show this data.

Find the probability that a student selected at random:

(ii) Attends evening study or has a part-time job

(iii) Attends evening study but does not have a part-time job

10. On a museum tour, the probability that a visitor visits the Egyptian exhibit only is $\frac{1}{5}$. The probability that they visit the African exhibit only is $\frac{1}{3}$. The probability that they visit neither exhibit is $\frac{1}{10}$.

(i) Draw a Venn diagram to show this data.

A visitor is selected at random. What is the probability that they:

(ii) Visited both exhibits

(iii) Visited the African exhibit

(iv) Visited the Egyptian exhibit

(v) Visited one exhibit only

(vi) Visited at least one exhibit

11. Twenty people in a club were asked what they did the previous week for entertainment. Ten went to a movie and seven went to a concert. Four did neither. A person is selected at random from the club. What is the probability that the person selected:

(i) Went to a movie and a concert

(ii) Went to a movie or a concert

(iii) Went to a movie only

12. Thirty students in a class were asked whether they watched a film or documentary on television the previous day. 16 watched the film, 10 watched the documentary and 3 watched both. A person is selected at random from the class. What is the probability that the student selected watched:

(i) The film

(ii) The documentary

(iii) The film or the documentary

13. In group of 50 girls, 15 play Gaelic football, 12 play camogie and 7 play both sports. A girl is selected at random from the group. What is the probability that the girl selected plays:

(i) Gaelic football

(ii) Camogie

(iii) Gaelic football or camogie

14. First Year students in a school were asked what types of calculator they owned. Of the 100 students surveyed, 60 owned a Casio, 45 owned a Sharp and 20 owned both. What is the probability that a student selected at random:

(i) Does not own a calculator

(ii) Owns a Casio only

(iii) Owns at least one of these calculators

15. Out of 40 students, 14 are taking Music and 29 are taking Chemistry.

(i) If five students are in both classes, how many students are in neither class?

What is the probability that a randomly chosen student from this group is taking:

(ii) Music or Chemistry class

(iii) the Chemistry class only

16. A teacher gave two Maths problems to a class of 30 students. The next day 25 students said they had got the first question right and 10 had got the second question right. Five students said they got both questions wrong. A student is selected at random from the class. What is the probability that the student:

(i) Got both questions right

(ii) Got only the second question right

(iii) Got at least one question right

17. A fair six-sided die is rolled once. What is the probability that you obtain:

(i) 3 (ii) 3 or 5

(iii) An even number

(iv) An even number or an odd number

(v) A number that is prime and even

(vi) A number that is odd and divisible by 3

18. A spinner with 20 equal sectors numbered 1–20 is spun. What is the probability that it lands on:

(i) 5 or 11 (ii) 12 or an odd number

(iii) A single-digit number or an even number

(iv) A single-digit number and an even number

(v) A prime number or a number greater than 15

(vi) A prime number and a number greater than 15

(vii) A number that is even or divisible by 5

12.5 Combined Events 

When dealing with more complicated questions involving probability, it can be advisable to use a two-way table or a tree diagram. This is especially the case when dealing with the probability of **combined events**.

A **combined event** is where two or more experiments occur and their outcomes are combined together.

Worked Example 12.16

Two fair dice are thrown and the scores are added together.

(a) Draw a two-way table to show all possible outcomes.

(b) Find the probability that the sum of the scores on the two dice is:

(i) 7
(ii) Less than 5
(iii) 5 or greater
(iv) Even **OR** divisible by 3
(v) Even **AND** divisible by 3

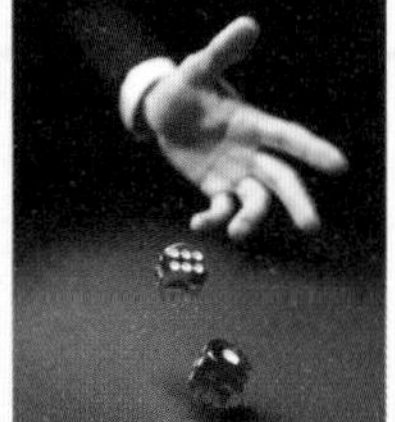

Solution

(a) We must first draw a two-way table (or sample space diagram) to show all the outcomes.

Put the outcomes of the first die along the side, from top to bottom.

Put the outcomes of the second die along the top, from left to right.

Find all possible outcomes by adding the two scores, e.g. 6 + 5 = 11.

First die \ Second die	1	2	3	4	5	6
1	2	3	4	5	6	7
2	3	4	5	6	7	8
3	4	5	6	7	8	9
4	5	6	7	8	9	10
5	6	7	8	9	10	11
6	7	8	9	10	11	12

Then count the total number of possible outcomes, which in this case is 36.

(b) (i) Probability of a score of 7:

A total of six outcomes add up to 7 (coloured green).

First die \ Second die	1	2	3	4	5	6
1	2	3	4	5	6	7
2	3	4	5	6	7	8
3	4	5	6	7	8	9
4	5	6	7	8	9	10
5	6	7	8	9	10	11
6	7	8	9	10	11	12

The probability of a score of 7

$= \frac{\text{number of outcomes that total 7}}{\text{total number of possible outcomes}} = \frac{6}{36} = \frac{1}{6}$

(ii) Probability of a score less than 5:

A total of six outcomes are of a score less than 5 (coloured red).

First die \ Second die	1	2	3	4	5	6
1	2	3	4	5	6	7
2	3	4	5	6	7	8
3	4	5	6	7	8	9
4	5	6	7	8	9	10
5	6	7	8	9	10	11
6	7	8	9	10	11	12

The probability of a score less than 5

$= \frac{\text{number of outcomes that are less than 5}}{\text{total number of possible outcomes}}$

$= \frac{6}{36} = \frac{1}{6}$

(iii) Probability of a score of 5 or greater:

Six outcomes are less than 5 and there are 36 possible outcomes. Therefore, the number of outcomes that will give us a score of 5 or greater is 36 – 6 = 30.

The probability of a score of 5 or greater

$= \frac{\text{number of outcomes that total 5 or more}}{\text{total number of possible outcomes}}$

$= \frac{30}{36} = \frac{5}{6}$

(Alternatively, we could count the outcomes in the two-way table.)

(iv) Probability of a score that is even **OR** divisible by 3:

A total of 24 outcomes are either even or divisible by 3 or both (coloured orange).

First die	Second die					
	1	**2**	**3**	**4**	**5**	**6**
1	2	3	4	5	6	7
2	3	4	5	6	7	8
3	4	5	6	7	8	9
4	5	6	7	8	9	10
5	6	7	8	9	10	11
6	7	8	9	10	11	12

The probability of a score that is even or divisible by 3

$= \frac{\text{number of outcomes even or divisible by 3}}{\text{total number of possible outcomes}}$

$= \frac{24}{36} = \frac{2}{3}$

(v) Probability of a score that is even **AND** divisible by 3:

A total of six outcomes are even and divisible by 3 (coloured blue).

First die	Second die					
	1	**2**	**3**	**4**	**5**	**6**
1	2	3	4	5	6	7
2	3	4	5	6	7	8
3	4	5	6	7	8	9
4	5	6	7	8	9	10
5	6	7	8	9	10	11
6	7	8	9	10	11	12

The probability of a score that is even and divisible by 3

$= \frac{\text{number of outcomes even and divisible by 3}}{\text{total number of possible outcomes}}$

$= \frac{6}{36} = \frac{1}{6}$

Worked Example 12.17

A spinner as shown is spun three times. Using a tree diagram, determine the probability of the spinner landing on:

(i) Three red sectors

(ii) A red sector followed by two green sectors

(iii) A red and two green sectors in any order

(iv) At least one green sector

Solution

We first draw a tree diagram to show all our outcomes.

We can count that there are eight possible outcomes.

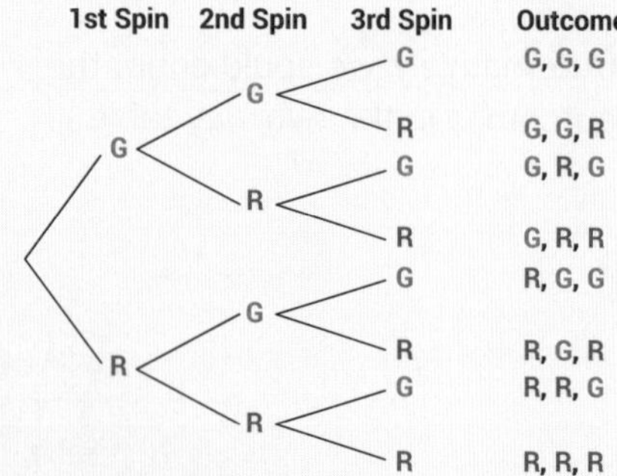

(i) Probability of getting three red sectors:

Red, Red, Red appears only once as an outcome:

$P(R, R, R) = \frac{1}{8}$

(ii) Probability of a red sector followed by two green sectors:

Red, Green, Green appears only once as an outcome:

$P(R, G, G) = \frac{1}{8}$

(iii) Probability of a red and two green sectors in any order:

We count how many times Red, Green, Green appears in the outcomes, ignoring order. There are three outcomes out of eight in which this occurs:

$P(R, G, G \text{ in any order}) = \frac{3}{8}$

(iv) Probability of at least one green sector:

'At least one' means one or more.

We count how many outcomes have one or more green in them. There are seven such outcomes:

$P(\text{at least one G}) = \frac{7}{8}$

Alternatively, this could have been found as:

P(at least one Green) = 1 − P(no Green)

= 1 − P(all Red)

$= 1 - \frac{1}{8}$

$= \frac{7}{8}$

P(at least one) = 1 − P(none)

Exercise 12.5

1. A fair coin is flipped and a fair die is rolled. Use a two-way table to show all possible outcomes.

		Die					
		1	2	3	4	5	6
Coin	H		H2				
	T					T5	

What is the probability of getting:

(i) A head and a 1

(ii) A tail and an even number

(iii) A head and an even number

(iv) A head or an even number

2. A game is played with a spinner with four quarters labelled A, B, C and D. The spinner is spun twice and a point is scored if the spinner lands on the same letter twice. Complete the following two-way table to show all possible outcomes:

		Second spin			
		A	B	C	D
First spin	A	AA			
	B			BC	
	C				
	D				

Find the probability that:

(i) The spinner lands on the same letter twice

(ii) A point will not be scored

3. A fair coin is flipped twice.

(i) Complete the following tree diagram:

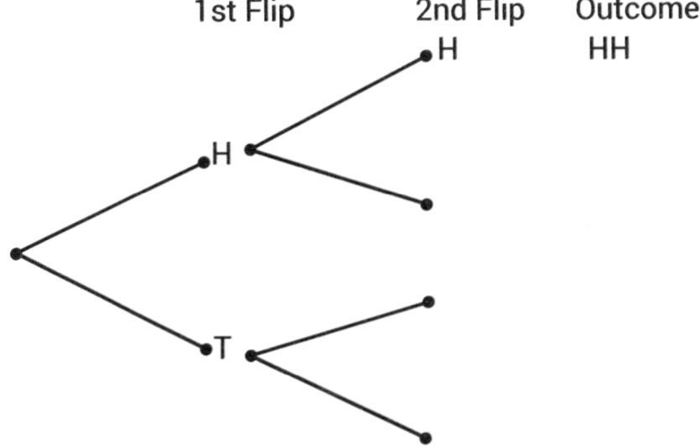

Find the probability that:

(ii) The coin will land on heads twice

(iii) The coin will land on heads and then tails

(iv) The coin will land on heads and tails in any order

(v) The coin will land on tails at least once

4. A die is rolled twice. Complete the following two-way table:

		Second roll					
		1	2	3	4	5	6
First roll	1	(1, 1)					
	2						
	3					(3, 5)	
	4			(4, 3)			
	5						
	6						

What is the probability that:

(i) An even number is obtained on both rolls of the die

(ii) An odd number is obtained on both rolls of the die

(iii) The same number is obtained on both rolls of the die

(iv) A different number is obtained on each roll of the die

5. Two dice, one coloured red and the other black, are thrown. The score from the red die is added to the score from the black die. Use a two-way table to show all the possible outcomes.

		Black die					
		1	2	3	4	5	6
Red die	1	2					
	2						
	3						
	4						
	5					10	
	6		8				

What is the probability that the score on the two dice will add up to:

(i) 5

(ii) An even number

(iii) A number divisible by 5 or even

(iv) A number divisible by 5 and even

(v) A number that is greater than 10 and odd

6. Two dice are thrown. The score on the second die is subtracted from the score on the first die. Complete the following two-way table:

		Second die					
		1	2	3	4	5	6
First die	1	0					
	2	1		−1			
	3					−2	
	4						
	5						
	6						

Find the probability that the final score on the two dice is:

(i) 1

(ii) A negative number

(iii) An integer

(iv) A natural number

(v) A number greater than 5

7. A spinner as shown is spun three times.

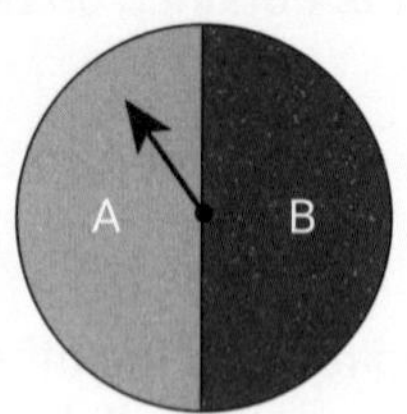

(i) Copy and fill in all the possible outcomes using the tree diagram below.

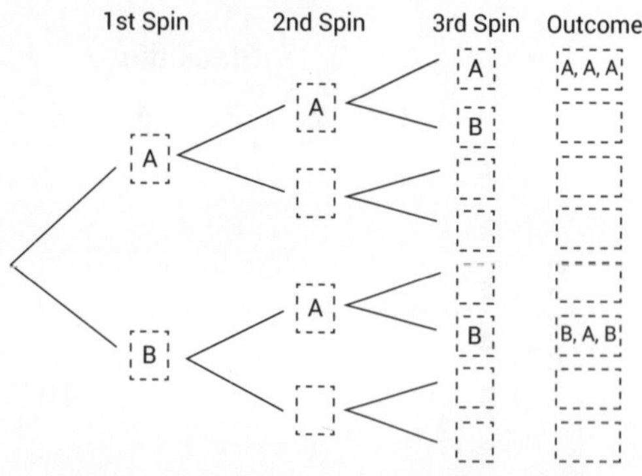

(ii) How many outcomes are there?

(iii) How many outcomes have three As?

(iv) Find the probability of getting three As.

(v) How many outcomes have an A on the first spin and a B on the second and third spins?

(vi) What is the probability of getting an A on the first spin and a B on the second and third spins?

(vii) How many outcomes have at least one B?

(viii) What is the probability of getting at least one B?

(ix) What is the probability of getting the same letter on all three spins?

(x) What is the probability of getting two As and one B?

8. A spinner with three equal sectors of red, blue and green is spun three times. Use a tree diagram to show all possible outcomes.

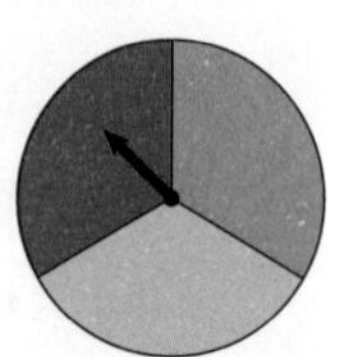

What is the probability that:

(i) The spinner lands on red three times

(ii) The spinner lands on green, blue and red in that order

(iii) The spinner lands on green, blue and red in any order

(iv) The spinner doesn't land on red

(v) The spinner lands on red only once

9. In a year of 100 students, each student studies one of the following subjects: Art, Biology or Technical graphics.

(a) Complete the following two-way table:

	Art	Biology	Tech. graphics	Total
Boy		12		33
Girl			15	
Total	30		23	100

(b) A student is selected at random. What is the probability that the student:

(i) Is a boy

(ii) Studies Art

(iii) Is a girl studying Biology

(iv) Does not study Biology

A girl is selected at random. What is the probability that she:

(v) Studies Art

(vi) Does not study Technical graphics

10. A four-sided die and a six-sided die are rolled. The outcomes for the first die are 1, 2, 3 or 4. The outcomes for the second die can be 1, 2, 3, 4, 5 or 6. After rolling the dice, a student calculates the product of the two outcomes (by multiplying them). Complete the following table, by working out the products each time:

		Second die					
		1	2	3	4	5	6
First die	1	1					
	2		4				
	3					15	
	4						

What is the probability that the product of the outcomes will be:

(i) Even

(ii) A prime number

(iii) Odd and a prime number

(iv) Divisible by both 2 and 5

(v) Less than 7 and even

11. An unbiased coin is flipped three times. Use a tree diagram to list all the possible outcomes. Find the probability that:

(i) The coin will land on a tail three times

(ii) The coin will land on a tail exactly twice

(iii) The coin will land on a tail at least twice

(iv) The coin will not land on a tail

12. The blood groups of 150 patients in a hospital are as follows:

- Twenty patients have blood group A.
- Twenty-five female patients have blood group B.
- Thirty male patients have blood group O.

$\frac{4}{5}$ of all patients with blood group A are women. There are a total of 60 male patients in the hospital.

(a) Complete the following table:

	A	B	O	Total
Male				
Female				
Total				

(b) A patient is selected at random. What is the probability that this patient:

(i) Belongs to blood group A

(ii) Belongs to blood group B or O

(iii) Is male and belongs to blood group B

(iv) Is female and belongs to blood group A or B

A male patient is selected at random. What is the probability that this patient:

(v) Belongs to blood group O

A female patient is selected at random. What is the probability that this patient:

(vi) Does not belong to blood group O

13. A fair die is rolled and a fair coloured spinner is spun. The die is numbered 1, 1, 2, 2, 2, 6 and the spinner has three equal sectors of green, white and orange as shown.

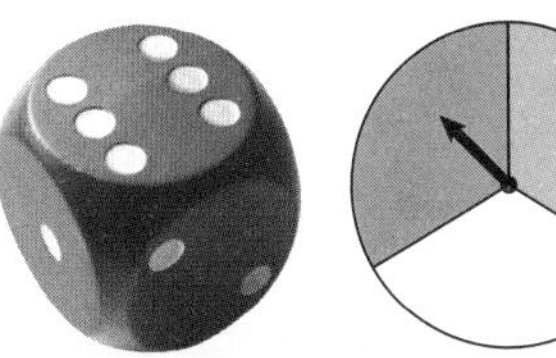

(a) Draw a two-way table to show all possible outcomes.

(b) What is the probability of getting:

(i) 1 and any colour

(ii) An even number or orange colour

(iii) An even number and orange colour

(iv) An odd number and white colour

14. A table-tennis tournament has eight players taking part. There are two groups. Alan, Barbara, Claire and Declan are in Group 1. Eric, Fred, Gerry and Holly are in Group 2. Every player has an equal chance of winning their group. The winner from each group plays in the final.

(i) Draw a two-way table to show the possible outcomes for the final.

(ii) What is the probability that Alan plays Holly in the final?

(iii) What is the probability that Fred does not play in the final?

(iv) What is the probability that Gerry plays in the final?

(v) What is the probability that Gerry or Holly plays in the final?

15. A library does a survey of all its books out on loan on a particular day. For the purpose of the survey, it divides its books into the following categories: fiction, non-fiction or children's books, and hardback or paperback books.

The survey showed that on that particular day:

- 1,250 books were out on loan.
- 56% of all books on loan were paperback.
- $\frac{3}{5}$ of the paperback books on loan were fiction. This was $\frac{2}{3}$ of the total number of fiction books out on loan for that day.
- $\frac{1}{5}$ of all hardback books on loan were in the children's category.
- A total of 200 non-fiction paperback books were out on loan.

(a) Complete the following table:

	Hardback	Paperback	Totals
Fiction			
Non-fiction			
Children's books			
Total			

(b) A library record for a book on loan is chosen at random.

Calculate the probability that the book chosen is:

(i) Non-fiction

(ii) Hardback

(iii) Children's paperback

(iv) Fiction hardback or non-fiction paperback

(c) How many of the first 300 books taken out on loan the following day would you expect to be non-fiction paperbacks?

12.6 AND/OR: Multiple Events

When finding the probability of two or more events, we can also calculate probabilities without having to use two-way tables or tree diagrams.

Consider a game with two trials: rolling a die and flipping a coin. What is the probability that the coin will land on a tail and the die will roll a 1?

$P(\text{tails}) = \frac{1}{2} \qquad P(1) = \frac{1}{6}$

We play the game 600 times.

We would expect the coin to land on tails 300 times $\left(\frac{1}{2} \times 600\right)$. Out of these 300 tails, we would expect to roll a 1 on a die 50 times $\left(\frac{1}{6} \times 300\right)$.

The probability of getting a Tail AND a one $= \frac{\text{number of outcomes that have a tail and a 1}}{\text{total number of outcomes}} = \frac{50}{600} = \frac{1}{12}$

$\therefore P(T, 1) = \frac{1}{2} \times \frac{1}{6} = \frac{1}{12}$

Worked Example 12.18

A fair six-sided die is rolled twice. What is the probability that a score of 1 will show on the die both times?

Solution

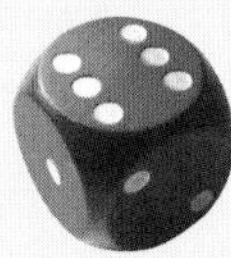

It is important to think of this as getting a 1 on the first roll AND getting a 1 on the second roll.

The probability of getting a 1 on the first roll is $\frac{1}{6}$.

The probability of getting a 1 on the second roll is also $\frac{1}{6}$.

We know from the Fundamental Principle of Counting that we multiply when we encounter the word AND.

First roll		Second roll	
P(1)		P(1)	
$\frac{1}{6}$	×	$\frac{1}{6}$	$= \frac{1}{36}$

Independent events are events in which the outcome of the first trial does not affect the outcome of the second trial.

These types of events are called **independent events.** The score on the second roll is not affected by the score on the first roll.

Independent event ⇒ P(A and B) = P(A) × P(B)

Worked Example 12.19

A bag contains 15 marbles: six blue marbles and nine yellow marbles. A player picks a marble at random out of the bag, its colour is noted and the marble is returned to the bag. Another marble is then picked at random.

Find the probability of getting:

(i) Two blue marbles

(ii) A blue marble and then a yellow marble

(iii) A blue marble and a yellow marble in any order

(iv) At least one blue marble

(v) Two marbles that are both the same colour

Solution

After each trial, the marble is returned. This means that the outcome of the first trial does not affect the outcome of the second trial. This is another example of **independent events**.

P (blue marble) → $\frac{6}{15} = \frac{2}{5}$ or 0.4

P (yellow marble) → $\frac{9}{15} = \frac{3}{5}$ or 0.6

(i) Two blue marbles:

P (B, B) = 0.4 × 0.4 = 0.16

(ii) A blue marble and then a yellow marble:

P (B, Y) = 0.4 × 0.6 = 0.24

(iii) A blue marble and a yellow marble in any order:

This means we could have Blue, Yellow OR Yellow, Blue as our outcomes:

P (B, Y OR Y, B) = P(B, Y) + P(Y, B)

= (0.4 × 0.6) + (0.6 × 0.4)

= 0.24 + 0.24 = 0.48

Remember that OR means to add.

(iv) At least one blue marble (one OR more blue marbles):

We add the probabilities of the outcomes that have one or more blue marbles:

$$P(B, B \text{ OR } B, Y \text{ OR } Y, B)$$
$$= P(B, B) + P(B, Y) + P(Y, B)$$
$$= 0.16 + 0.24 + 0.24 = 0.64$$

(v) Two marbles that are both the same colour:

The marbles picked could be Blue, Blue OR Yellow, Yellow:

$$P(B, B \text{ OR } Y, Y)$$
$$= P(B, B) + P(Y, Y)$$
$$= 0.16 + 0.36 = 0.52$$

We could also use the other method:

$$P(Y, Y) = 0.6 \times 0.6$$
$$= 0.36$$

$$P(\text{at least one blue}) = 1 - P(\text{none blue})$$
$$= 1 - P(Y, Y)$$
$$= 1 - 0.36$$
$$= 0.64$$

Worked Example 12.20

Two cards are drawn at random from a deck of cards. The first card is drawn, recorded and replaced back into the deck. A second card is then drawn.

What is the probability that the two cards are:

(i) Both red

(ii) A King and then a Club

(iii) A King and a Club in any order

Solution

(i) Both red:

First card		Second card	
Red		Red	
$\frac{26}{52}$	$\times$	$\frac{26}{52}$	$= \frac{1}{4}$

(ii) A King and then a Club:

First card		Second card	
King		Club	
$\frac{4}{52}$	$\times$	$\frac{13}{52}$	$= \frac{1}{52}$

(iii) A King and a Club in any order:

King	AND	Club	OR	Club	AND	King
$\frac{4}{52}$	×	$\frac{13}{52}$	+	$\frac{13}{52}$	×	$\frac{4}{52}$
	$\frac{1}{52}$		+		$\frac{1}{52}$	

$$= \frac{2}{52}$$

$$= \frac{1}{26}$$

Exercise 12.6

1. A spinner has 10 sectors numbered 1 to 10 as shown.

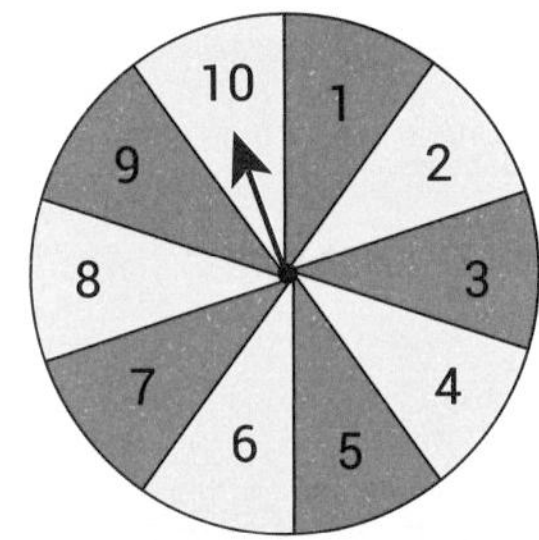

(a) The spinner is spun twice. The number the spinner lands on is noted each time. For example, (1, 2) is an outcome. Using the Fundamental Principle of Counting, calculate:

(i) The number of possible outcomes

(ii) The number of outcomes that will give an even number on both spins

(iii) The number of outcomes that will give a prime number on both spins

(b) What is the probability of getting:

(i) an even number on both spins

(ii) a prime number on both spins

(iii) a 5 on each spin

2. A bag contains 12 blue balls and 5 white balls. A student picks a ball at random out of the bag. She then returns the ball to the bag and picks another ball at random. What is the probability that she picks a blue ball on her first pick and a white ball on her second pick?

3. A fair spinner numbered 1–10 is spun three times. What is the probability that it lands on a 3 each time?

4. Two bags containing marbles are shown.

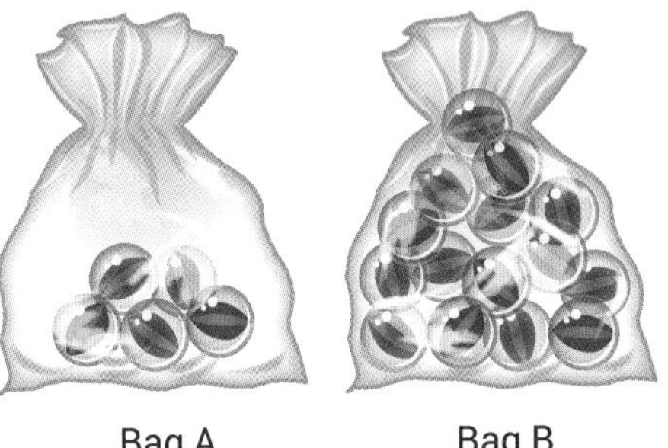

Bag A contains 2 red and 3 blue marbles. Bag B contains 5 red and 10 blue marbles.

A student picks a marble at random out of bag A. He then picks a marble at random out of bag B.

Copy and fill out the following tree diagram, showing all the probabilities:

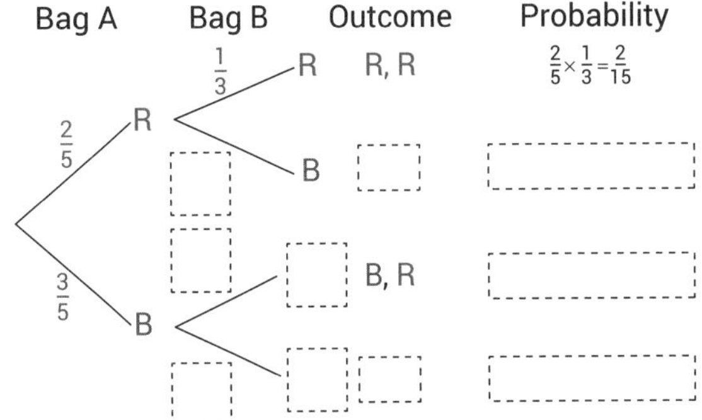

What is the probability that the marbles picked will be:

(i) Both red

(ii) Both blue

(iii) Red first and then blue

(iv) Red and blue (in any order)

(v) At least one blue

5. An urn contains 10 red tokens and 12 green tokens. A token is selected at random and its colour is noted. It is then replaced and another token is selected and its colour is noted.

   Find the probability of:

   (i) Picking two red tokens
   (ii) Picking a red token and then a green token
   (iii) Picking a red and a green token in any order

6. Two cards are drawn at random from a pack of cards. The first card is removed and recorded and then replaced. A second card is then removed. What is the probability that the two cards are:

   (i) Both red
   (ii) Both Spades
   (iii) A Queen and then a King
   (iv) A Queen and a King

7. A bag contains 10 red tokens and 8 black tokens. A token is picked at random from the bag and then returned. A second token is then picked at random.

   What is the probability of picking:

   (i) A black token followed by a red token
   (ii) A red token followed by a black token
   (iii) Two red tokens
   (iv) Two tokens of the same colour
   (v) Two tokens of different colour

8. A student plays two snooker matches. The probability that he wins the first match is 0.35 and his probability of winning the second match is 0.25.

   What is the probability that he:

   (i) Wins the first match and loses the second match
   (ii) Loses the first match and wins the second match
   (iii) Wins one match and loses another match
   (iv) Wins at least one match

9. Two people are chosen at random and say in what month their birthday lies. Taking each month as equally likely, find the probability that:

   (i) Both were born in December
   (ii) Both were born in the same month
   (iii) They were not born in the same month

10. Zoe sits two exams. The probability that Zoe will pass the first exam is 0.8. If she passes the first exam the probability that Zoe will pass the second exam is 0.9. If Zoe fails her first exam, the probability that she will pass the second exam is 0.65.

    (i) Copy and complete the following tree diagram, showing all the probabilities:

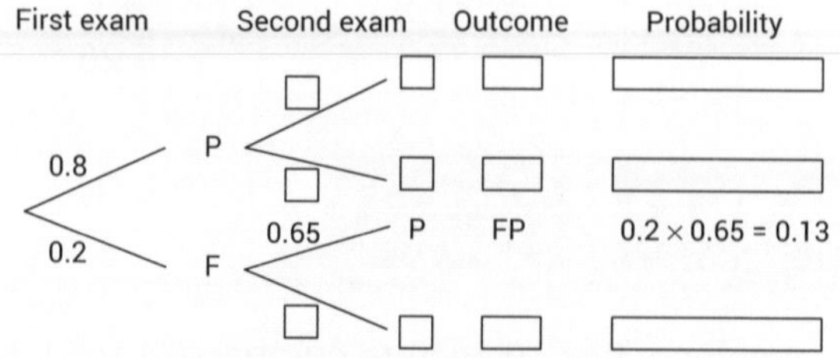

    What is the probability that Zoe:

    (ii) Passes both exams
    (iii) Fails both exams
    (iv) Passes the first exam then fails the second exam
    (v) Fails one exam
    (vi) Passes at least one exam

11. A scooter manufacturer wishes to determine how many of their scooters are defective. According to their research the two main defects of their scooters are broken bolts and loose wheels. Their survey indicates that the probability of a scooter having broken bolts is 0.05. A scooter that has broken bolts has a probability of 0.7 of having loose wheels. A scooter that doesn't have broken bolts has a probability of 0.08 of having loose wheels.

    A scooter is chosen at random from the assembly line. Find the probability that the scooter has:

    (i) Broken bolts only
    (ii) Loose wheels only
    (iii) One of these defects
    (iv) Both of these defects
    (v) At least one of these defects

12. For a medical study, volunteers are divided up into their respective blood groups.

    The number of each type is shown in the table below.

Type	O	A	B	AB
Number	46	39	12	3

A volunteer's name is picked at random from a hat and a blood sample is taken. The volunteer's name is then put back into the hat and another volunteer's name is picked.

(i) Draw a tree diagram to show all the possible outcomes.

Find the probability that:

(ii) Both volunteers picked have blood type A

(iii) The first volunteer picked has blood type O and the second volunteer picked has blood type AB

(iv) The first volunteer picked has blood type B and the second volunteer has a different blood type

(v) Both volunteers picked have the same blood type

(vi) Both volunteers picked have different blood types

(vii) At least one volunteer picked has the blood group AB.

13. Three friends agree to meet up for a meal. Chloe has a 90% chance of being on time, Siobhan has a 80% chance and Ayesha has a 70% chance of being on time.

Find the probability, given as a percentage, that:

(i) All three will be on time

(ii) All three will be late

(iii) Siobhan is the only one late

(iv) Only one of the friends will be late

(v) Exactly two of the friends will be late

14. How many ways are there of arranging the letters of the word SEAT using each letter only once:

(i) If there are no restrictions

(ii) If the first letter is a T

(iii) If the first letter is a T and the last letter is a vowel

(iv) If the two vowels are together

The letters of the word SEAT are picked at random. What is the probability that:

(v) The first letter is a T

(vi) The first letter is a T and the last letter is a vowel

(vii) The two vowels are together

15. A country has a car licence plate system made up of three randomly generated capital letters followed by a randomly generated natural number of up to three digits.

(a) How many licence plates are possible:

(i) If letters may be used more than once, for example AAA

(ii) If no letter may be used more than once

(b) If letters may be used more than once, what is the probaibility that a licence plate:

(i) Starts with an A

(ii) Ends with the digits 23

12.7 Bernoulli Trials

In real life, we deal with many examples where we are interested only in the probability of two outcomes: success or failure.

When dealing with experiments whose outcomes are random and have two possible outcomes – success or failure – we are dealing with a type of trial called a **Bernoulli trial**.

The properties of a Bernoulli trial are:

- Two possible outcomes: success or failure, hit or miss, yes or no.
- The trials are independent of each other. The outcome of one trial has no effect on the outcome of another trial.
- The probability of success or failure does not change from one trial to another.
- There is a fixed number of trials.

Examples of Bernoulli trials include:

- Flipping a coin where getting a tails is a success
- Rolling a die where it landing on a 3 is a success

Worked Example 12.21

A game is played with 10 marbles in a bag: seven blue marbles and three yellow marbles.
A player picks a marble at random out of the bag. If a yellow marble is picked, the player wins the game. If a blue marble is picked, it is returned to the bag (replaced) and the player tries again.
What is the probability, in percentages, that the player wins the game on the:

(i) Second go (ii) Third go

Solution

(i) Second go:

For the player to win on their second go, they must have picked a blue marble first. The outcome we are looking for is Blue, Yellow (B, Y).

We calculate our probabilities for the two outcomes:

A blue marble → $\frac{7}{10}$ or 0.7

A yellow marble → $\frac{3}{10}$ or 0.3

P(B, Y) = 0.7 × 0.3 = 0.21 or 21%

(ii) Third go:

For the player to win on the third go, they must have picked a blue marble on their first and second goes. The outcome we are looking for is Blue, Blue, Yellow (B, B, Y).

P(B, B, Y) = 0.7 × 0.7 × 0.3

= 0.147 or 14.7%

Worked Example 12.22

A car drives through three sets of traffic lights. The probability of a set of traffic lights showing a red light is $\frac{1}{5}$.

(a) What is the probability that the car will first meet a red light at the:

(i) First set of lights

(ii) Second set of lights

(iii) Third set of lights

(b) What is the probability that as the car passes the three sets of traffic lights it will meet exactly two red lights?

Solution

We fill in our probabilities for the two events:

Success or Red (R): $\frac{1}{5}$

Failure or Not red (F): $1 - \frac{1}{5} = \frac{4}{5}$

(a) (i) First lights (R)

We are looking for a Red as an outcome.

The probability of stopping at the first light = $\frac{1}{5}$.

(ii) Second lights (F, R)

The desired outcome is Not red, Red.

$P(F, R) = \frac{4}{5} \times \frac{1}{5} = \frac{4}{25}$

(iii) Third lights (F, F, R)

The desired outcome is Not red, Not red, Red.

$P(F, F, R) = \frac{4}{5} \times \frac{4}{5} \times \frac{1}{5} = \frac{16}{125}$

(b) This can happen a number of ways.

Red, Red, Not Red	OR	Red, Not Red, Red	OR	Not Red, Red, Red
P(R, R, F)	+	P(R, F, R)	+	P(F, R, R)
$\frac{1}{5} \times \frac{1}{5} \times \frac{4}{5}$	+	$\frac{1}{5} \times \frac{4}{5} \times \frac{1}{5}$	+	$\frac{4}{5} \times \frac{1}{5} \times \frac{1}{5}$
$\frac{4}{125}$	+	$\frac{4}{125}$	+	$\frac{4}{125}$
		$= \frac{12}{125}$		

Exercise 12.7

1. Consider whether each of the following probability problems are Bernoulli trials. If not, give a reason why:
   (i) Asking a hundred people if they voted for Fine Gael in the last election
   (ii) Taking a survey of 200 people; asking whether they like, dislike or have no opinion about a certain brand of tea
   (iii) Rolling a die 100 times and counting how many times you get a 5
   (iv) Counting the number of people who have brown shoes that pass by a shop
   (v) Checking a shipment of 1000 phones to see whether they're defective or not
   (vi) Taking five consecutive penalty kicks where the chances of missing increase after each kick

2. A spinner with equal sectors numbered 1 to 5 is spun. What is the probability that it lands on an odd number for the first time on the:
   (i) First spin (ii) Second spin (iii) Third spin

3. A coin is flipped three times. A player wins if the coin lands on a tail. What is the probability that the player wins for the first time on the:
   (i) First flip (ii) Second flip (iii) Third flip

4. A fair die is rolled up to three times. A player wins if a roll of 5 is scored. What is the probability that the player wins on the:
   (i) First turn (ii) Second turn (iii) Third turn

   What is the probability that the player doesn't win?

5. A game is played with a deck of cards. A card is picked at random from the deck, recorded and then put back into the deck. The game is won when a player picks an Ace card. The player has up to three goes to try and win the game. What is the probability that the player wins on the:
   (i) First card (ii) Second card (iii) Third card

   What is the probability that the player doesn't win?

6. A die is rolled three times. Find the probability of getting exactly one six.

7. A student is sitting an exam. She is allowed up to three attempts to pass the exam. The probability that she will pass the exam on any attempt is 45%. What is the probability that she will:
   (i) Pass the exam on the second attempt
   (ii) Pass the exam on the third attempt
   (iii) Not pass the exam

8. A student enters a spelling competition and reaches the final. The final consists of three rounds. In each round he is asked to spell a word correctly. If he spells all three words correctly he wins; if he misspells any word he will be knocked out of the final. He calculates that on average the probability of him misspelling a word is 0.09. What is the probability, written as a percentage to the nearest whole number:
   (i) That he gets knocked out of the final on the second round
   (ii) That he gets knocked out of the final on the third round
   (iii) That he wins the spelling competition

9. The probability that an Olympic archer hits a target is 0.6. She fires three arrows at the target. What is the probability that she:
   (i) Hits the target for the first time on her third arrow
   (ii) Misses the target on all three arrows
   (iii) Hits the target exactly twice

10. The probability that Liam will be on time for school on any given day is 0.85.
    (a) (i) What is the probability that he will be late for school?
    What is the probability that Liam will be late for the first time on:
    (ii) The second of two days
    (iii) The third of three days
    (b) To the nearest percent, what is the probability that Liam will be late exactly once over three days?

11. A game is played with an unfair coin. The coin is biased so that the probability of getting heads is 0.8 and the probability of getting tails is 0.2. The game is won if the player gets two tails. What is the probability of winning the game on the third flip of the coin?

12. A motorist drives through three sets of traffic lights on her way to work each day. The probability that she has to stop at the first light is 0.25. The probability that she will have to stop at the second light is 0.35. The probability that she will have to stop at the third light is 0.5. What is the probability that the car will first stop at the:

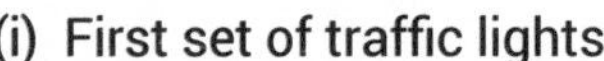

    (i) First set of traffic lights

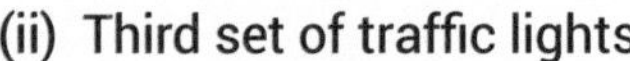

    (ii) Third set of traffic lights
    What is the probability that the driver has to stop at:
    (iii) All sets of traffic lights
    (iv) No set of traffic lights
    If the driver makes this journey 300 times a year, how many times would she expect to stop at at least one of these sets of traffic lights?

13. A bag contains four balls: three yellow balls and one orange ball. A ball is drawn from the bag at random, its colour is noted and it is then replaced. If an orange ball is drawn, the person wins a prize and the game is over.
    (a) What is the probability that a prize is first won:
        (i) On the second go
        (ii) On the third go
    (b) Five more yellow and two more orange balls are added. Does a person have a better chance of winning a prize now? Explain your answer.
    (c) The rules of the game are then changed so that a game continues for three turns and the player wins a prize every time an orange ball is drawn. What is the probability that a player wins:
        (i) Exactly two prizes
        (ii) At least two prizes

14. The probability that a person hits a target with a dart is 20%. If he throws three successive darts, what is the probability that he will:
    (i) Not hit the target once
    (ii) Hit the target one or more times

12.8 Expected Value

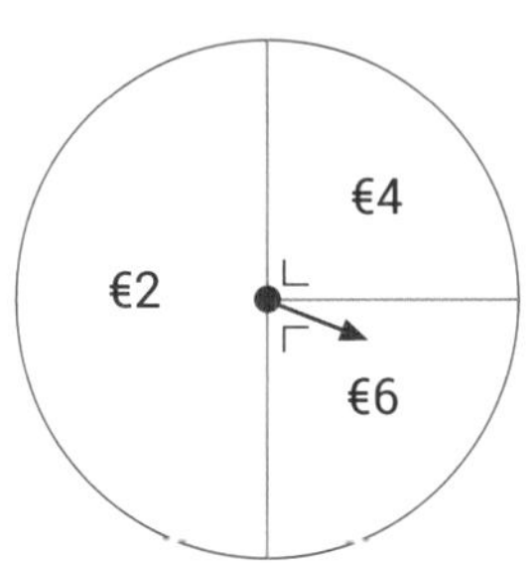

Here is a spinner. You bet €5, then spin the wheel and you win whatever amount the arrow is pointing to. Is this a good or a bad bet? We can decide mathematically by calculating the **expected value** (or mean). The expected value $E(x)$ is defined as $E(x) = \sum x \cdot P(x)$ (where $\sum$ means 'the sum of'). In this case, the probability of getting €2 is $\frac{1}{2}$, of getting €4 is $\frac{1}{4}$ and of getting €6 is $\frac{1}{4}$.

The expected return = $E(x) = \sum x \cdot P(x)$

$$\therefore E(x) = 2\left(\frac{1}{2}\right) + 4\left(\frac{1}{4}\right) + 6\left(\frac{1}{4}\right)$$

$$= 1 + 1 + 1.5$$

$$= 3.5$$

$\therefore E(x) =$ €3.50 (in money)

$E(x) = \sum x \cdot P(x)$

Expected value — Sum — Outcome — Probability of outcome

But you paid out €5, so the expected value of the transaction is:

€(3.50 − 5) = −€1.50

This means that you expect to lose €1.50. It is therefore a bad bet.

When we say, 'you expect to lose €1.50', we mean that if you played this spinning game over and over, the mean outcome would be a loss of €1.50 per game. For this reason, it is a bad bet.

Fair, Good and Bad Bets

If the expected return from a bet is zero [$E(x) = 0$], then the bet is said to be a **fair bet**.
If the expected return is greater than zero [$E(x) > 0$], then the bet is a **good bet**.
If the expected return is less than zero [$E(x) < 0$], then the bet is a **bad bet**.

Worked Example 12.23

A single card is picked from a deck of cards numbered 1 to 4. A probability distribution table is shown.

(i) Find the probability of picking a card which is numbered 4.

(ii) Find the expected value.

Card number	1	2	3	4
Probability	0.1	0.3	0.4	

Solution

(i) The total probabilities of the experiment will add to 1.

$1 - 0.1 - 0.3 - 0.4 = 0.2$

$P(4) = 0.2$

The expected value does not have to be an actual outcome. In this example, $E(x) = 2.7$ but the outcomes are 1, 2, 3 or 4.

(ii)

Outcome		Probability		
1	×	0.1	=	0.1
2	×	0.3	=	0.6
3	×	0.4	=	1.2
4	×	0.2	=	0.8
			Total	2.7

$E(x) = 2.7$

PROBABILITY

Worked Example 12.24

A game is played where you have to pick a card at random from the hand shown.

Whatever card you pick you win that amount of money. For example, picking the two of Spades will win you €2. If the game costs €5 to play, would you advise a person that this game is worth playing?

Solution

We can use the expected value of this game to help us determine if this game is worth playing.

To work out the expected value we multiply each outcome value by its probability.

Outcome		Probability		
€10	×	0.2	=	€2
€5	×	0.2	=	€1
€3	×	0.2	=	€0.60
€2	×	0.4	=	€0.80
			Total	€4.40

If the game cost nothing to play we would have an expected value of €4.40 for this game. In other words, if we played this game over and over, the average (mean) amount of money won per game would be €4.40.

However, the game costs €5 per play.

Expected value or $E(x) = 4.40 - 5$

$$E(x) = -€0.60$$

You would expect to lose €0.60 per game on average.

Therefore, you would advise the person not to play the game.

Worked Example 12.25

A fair six-sided die is rolled.

(i) Calculate the expected value of the die roll.

(ii) Consider a game where you win in euro what the die rolls. What are the expected winnings per game?

(iii) How much should the game cost to play to make it fair?

Solution

(i)

Outcome		Probability		
1	×	$\frac{1}{6}$	=	$\frac{1}{6}$
2	×	$\frac{1}{6}$	=	$\frac{2}{6}$
3	×	$\frac{1}{6}$	=	$\frac{3}{6}$
4	×	$\frac{1}{6}$	=	$\frac{4}{6}$
5	×	$\frac{1}{6}$	=	$\frac{5}{6}$
6	×	$\frac{1}{6}$	=	$\frac{6}{6}$

Adding these values together gives us the expected value $E(x)$:

$$E(x) = \frac{1}{6} + \frac{2}{6} + \frac{3}{6} + \frac{4}{6} + \frac{5}{6} + \frac{6}{6} = 3.5$$

The expected value of a die roll is 3.5.

The expected value does not have to be an actual outcome.

(ii) We would expect to win (on average) €3.50 per game.

(iii) To make the game fair, the expected value would be equal to zero. We would have to charge €3.50 to make the game fair.

Worked Example 12.26

A game is played by rolling a fair six-sided die. It costs €2 to play the game. The winnings for each outcome are shown below.

Die roll	Outcome
1	Win €9
2, 3 or 4	Money back
5 or 6	Lose. Nothing back.

(i) Find the expected value of the game.

(ii) Explain what this value represents.

Solution

(i) We fill in the following table:

Die roll	Outcome		Probability		€
1	€9	×	$\frac{1}{6}$	=	1.50
2, 3 or 4	€2	×	$\frac{3}{6}$	=	1.00
5 or 6	€0	×	$\frac{2}{6}$	=	0
			Total	=	2.50

We put in an outcome of 0 when we lose, as we have won nothing.

We must now factor in the cost of the game.

$E(x) = €2.50 - €2.00$

$\therefore E(x) = €0.50$

The expected value of this game is 50 cents.

(ii) On average, a player would expect to win 50 cents per game, so this is a good bet.

Exercise 12.8

1. Find the expected value when this spinner is spun. Each sector is of equal size.

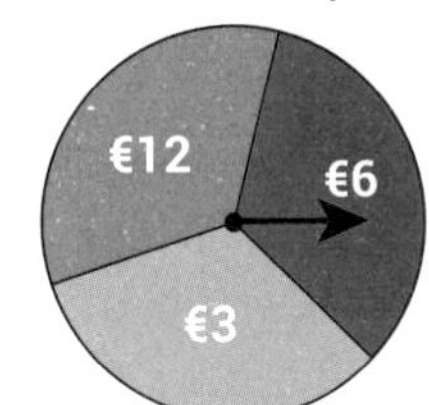

2.

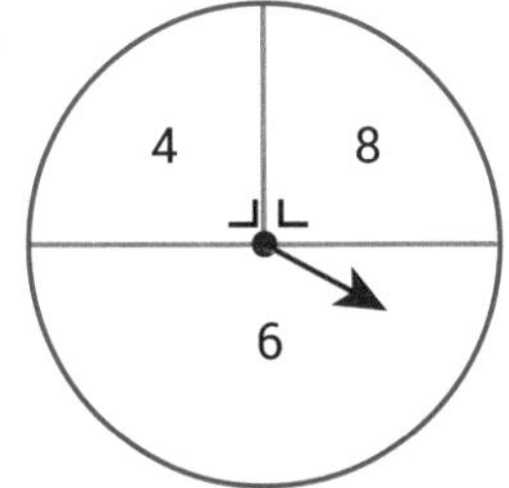

Find the expected value when this spinner is spun.

3. The spinner shown is used to play a game.

The game costs €5 to play. A player wins whatever amount the spinner lands on.

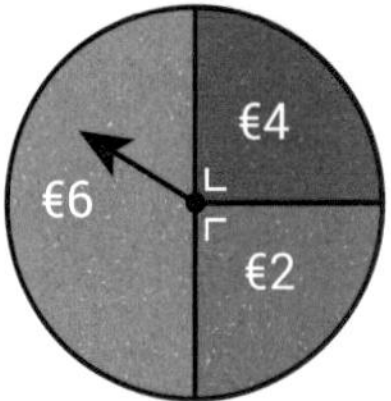

(i) Calculate the expected value.

(ii) Would you advise a person to play this game? Justify your answer.

4. A game with a spinner as shown is played.

If the spinner lands on red, you lose €3.

If the spinner lands on blue, you win €8.

(i) Calculate the expected value for this game.

(ii) Is this game fair? Explain your answer.

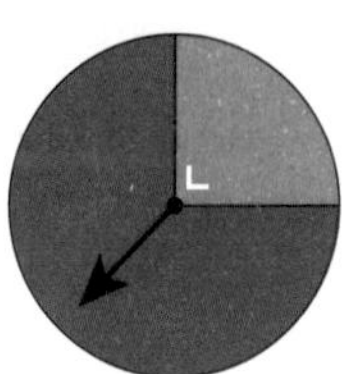

5. A card is drawn from a normal pack of cards. If an Ace is drawn, €20 is won; if a picture card is drawn, €5 is won. It costs €3 to draw a card. One prize only may be won. Is it worthwhile to play this game? Explain your answer with reference to the expected value.

6. Five thousand tickets are sold for a raffle at €10 each for a single prize of €20,000. What is the expected value if a person purchases one ticket? Is this good value?

7. A die is rolled and the winnings for each outcome are as follows:

- Roll a 6: Win €5
- Roll a 3: Win €1
- Roll any other number: Win nothing

(i) Calculate to the nearest cent the expected value for this game.

It is then decided to charge €5 per game.

(ii) Calculate the expected value for this game.

8. For €5, the following spinner is spun and the amount it lands on is won.

Is this a fair game? Give a reason, using the expected value in your answer.

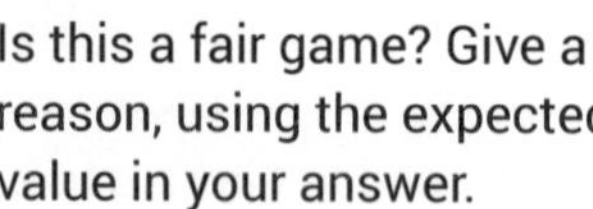

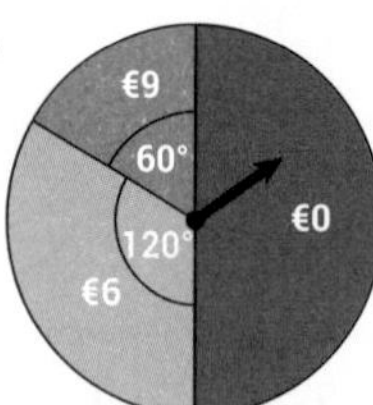

9. A friend offers to play a game by picking a card from a pack of cards at random. The rules of the game are as follows:

- It costs €1 to play.
- If you pick a numbered Heart card, you get your €1 back.
- If you pick a King, you win €2.
- If you pick the Ace of Spades, you win €13.

Is this a fair game? Explain your answer.

10. A €50, a €20, a €10 and a €5 note are placed in a bag. A person draws a note at random and wins that amount.

(i) What is the expected value for this game?

(ii) Six more €5 notes are placed in the bag. A person draws a note at random and wins that amount.

What is the expected value for this game?

11. Shane and Jackie play a game where a die is rolled and the winner is decided by referring to the following table:

Number on die	Result
1	Jackie gives Shane €4
2	Shane gives Jackie €2
3	No one wins or loses
4	Jackie gives Shane €1
5	Jackie gives Shane €2
6	Shane gives Jackie €10

Which person will expect to win more per game: Shane or Jackie?

12. John and Caroline decide to play a game to divide up a bag of sweets. A single die is rolled and the sweets are divided up as follows:

Roll a 1: John gets five sweets.

Roll a 2: Both get no sweets.

Roll a 3: Caroline gets eight sweets.

Roll a 4: John gets five sweets.

Roll a 5: Caroline gets two sweets.

Roll a 6: Caroline gets one sweet.

(i) Who would expect to get the most sweets?

(ii) Give one example of how you would change the rules to make this a fair game.

13. It costs €10 to play a game in which a coin is flipped four times. If the coin lands on heads four times, the player wins €100. Otherwise the player wins nothing.

(i) Find the expected value for this game.

(ii) The game is played again but with new rules.

- It costs €10 to play.
- If the coin lands on heads at least twice in the four flips, €50 will be paid.
- Otherwise the player wins nothing.

Is this a fair game to play?

(iii) If a person played this game 20 times, how much would they expect to win or lose, to the nearest cent?

PROBABILITY

14. Ten thousand tickets are to be sold for a prize draw. There is a first prize of €1,000, a second prize of €250 and a third prize of €50. A winning ticket will not be put back for the next draw.

(i) Vera buys one ticket. What is the probability that she wins a prize?

(ii) What price do you think that Vera would be willing to pay for her ticket?

Explain your answer, making sure to refer to expected value.

Revision Exercises

1. (a) The events A, B, C and D have probabilities as shown on this probability scale:

(i) Which event is the most likely to happen?

(ii) Which event is the least likely to happen?

(b) Match each term to its correct definition.

Term	Definition
Relative frequency	One of the possible results of the trial
Fairness	The act of doing an experiment in probability
Trial	All outcomes are equally likely to occur
Sample space	The occurrence of one or more specific outcomes
Event	An estimate of the probability of an event
Outcome	The set or list of all possible outcomes in a trial

(c) A card is drawn at random from a normal deck of cards. Find the probability that the card is:

(i) The Ace of Clubs

(ii) An Ace

(iii) A King

(iv) A King or a Heart

2. (a) A bag contains one blue token, two red tokens, three black tokens and four yellow tokens.
One token is taken at random from the bag.
What is the probability that the token drawn is:

(i) Blue

(ii) Red

(iii) Yellow

(iv) Not yellow

(v) Blue or black

(vi) Red or yellow

(vii) Not red or yellow

(viii) Green

(b) A fair coin is flipped and a fair die is rolled.

(i) Draw a two-way table to show all possible outcomes.

Find the probability of obtaining:

(ii) A tail on the coin and a 5 on the die

(iii) A head on the coin and a 1 on the die

(iv) A tail on the coin and an odd number on the die

(v) A tail on the coin and a number less than 4 on the die

3. (a) Give an example of each of the following events and show them on a likelihood scale:

(i) Impossible (ii) Certain (iii) Likely (iv) Unlikely (v) Evens

(b) What is meant by the term 'mutually exclusive events'?
In each case below, state whether the events are mutually exclusive.

Event 1	Event 2
Picking a student who is a girl	Picking a student who is a boy
Picking a red top	Picking a cotton top
Rolling a die and getting an odd number	Rolling a die and getting a prime number
Flipping a coin and getting a head	Flipping a coin and getting a tail
Picking a Spade from a deck of cards	Picking a Heart from a deck of cards
Picking a King from a deck of cards	Picking a Diamond from a deck of cards

(c) What is meant by the term 'independent events'?
In each case below, state whether the events are independent of each other.

(i) A die being rolled and a coin being flipped

(ii) Two tokens taken from a bag, one after another with replacement

(iii) Two tokens taken from a bag, one after another without replacement

(iv) Checking six smoke alarms to see if any are defective

4. (a) A student plays a game of chess and a game of draughts. The probability that she wins the game of chess is 0.5. The probability that she wins the game of draughts is 0.3. The probability that she wins both games is 0.15.

(i) Draw a Venn diagram to show this data.

(ii) Find the probability that she wins only at draughts.

(iii) Find the probability that she loses both games.

(b) A game is played with two dice. A player wins if the scores on both dice are the same.

(i) Draw a two-way table for the outcomes of rolling two dice.

(ii) Megan suggests that this is not a fair game. Do you agree? Explain your answer.

(iii) Jack suggests a rule to make the game fair. Give an example of such a rule and refer to the two-way table to explain how this rule would make the game fair.

5. (a) A game is played in which a die is rolled. If an odd number is rolled, you lose the amount on the die. If an even number is rolled, you gain the amount on the die.

(i) Find the expected value.

(ii) Is this a fair game?

(iii) Would you play this game given the opportunity? Explain.

(b) A game is played by rolling a fair six-sided die three times. A player wins if the die rolls a 1 on any of the rolls.

(i) Find the probability that a player wins on the first roll of the die.

(ii) Find the probability that a player wins on the third roll of the die.

(iii) Find the probability that a player doesn't win.

(iv) It is decided to change the rules so the player wins only if he rolls a 1 twice.

If the die is rolled three times, find the probability that a player wins.

6. (a) Two cards are drawn at random from a normal deck of cards. The first card is drawn, recorded and then replaced. A second card is then chosen. Find the probability that:

(i) The first card is a Club and the second card is a Diamond

(ii) Both cards are Hearts

(iii) Neither card is a Heart

(iv) Neither card is a picture card (Jack, King or Queen)

(v) At least one card is a King

(b) A courier firm delivers 80% of all packages the next day. Two packages are posted. The deliveries are independent of each other.

(i) Explain what the term 'independent' means in this context.

(ii) Draw a tree diagram to show all the possible outcomes.

Find the probability that:

(iii) Both packages are delivered the next day

(iv) Neither package is delivered the next day

(v) One package only is delivered the next day

7. (a) A game involves rolling two dice. The scores from the two dice are added together.

(i) Draw a two-way table to show all possible outcomes.

A score of 2, 3, 9, 10, 11 or 12 will win €10. A roll of anything else will cost you €10.

(ii) With reference to expected value, explain why this game is not fair.

(iii) Explain one rule change that would make this game fair.

(b) Laura works in a factory, checking to see if a component the factory makes is faulty or not. The probability that any one component is faulty is $\frac{1}{20}$. She checks three components in a row.

(i) Draw a tree diagram to show all the possible outcomes.

Calculate the probability that:

(ii) The first component only is faulty

(iii) No component is faulty

(iv) At least one component is faulty

Laura checks 10,000 components in a week. How many of these would you expect not to have a fault?

8. (a) A person is selected at random. If there is an equal likelihood of being born on any day of the week, what is the probability that the person selected:

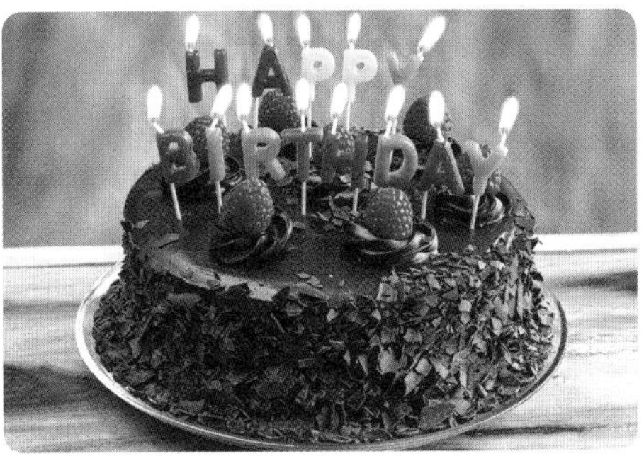

(i) Was born on a Monday

(ii) Was **not** born on a Monday

Two people are selected at random. What is the probability that:

(iii) Both were born on a Monday

(iv) Only one of them was born on a Monday

(v) They were born on different days of the week

(b) A container contains 1,000 light bulbs, of which 200 are broken. A light bulb is chosen at random from the container, checked and then put back. A second bulb is then chosen. What is the probability of selecting:

(i) Two broken lights bulbs

(ii) Two working light bulbs

(iii) One broken and one working light bulb

9. (a) The independent probabilities that three different species of animal – A, B and C – will be extinct in 100 years are 0.8, 0.1 and 0.2, respectively. Calculate the probability that in 100 years' time:

(i) All three species will be extinct

(ii) All three species will survive

(iii) Species A will be extinct, but species B and C will still survive

(iv) Only one species will survive

(v) At least one species will survive

(b) In how many ways can the letters of the word CASTLE be arranged if:

(i) There are no restrictions

(ii) The arrangements must begin with the letter T

(iii) The first two letters are vowels

(iv) The vowels are beside each other

The letters of the word CASTLE are randomly arranged in a row. What is the probability that:

(v) The letter T will come first

(vi) The vowels will be beside each other

Exam Questions

1. An unbiased circular spinner has a movable pointer and five equal sectors, two coloured green and three coloured red.

(a) (i) Find the probability that the pointer stops on green for one spin of the spinner.

(ii) List all the possible outcomes of 3 successive spins of the spinner.

(b) A game consists of spinning the spinner 3 times. Each time the spinner stops on green the player wins €1; otherwise the player wins nothing. For example, if the outcome of one game is 'green, red, green' the player wins €2.

Complete the following table:

Player wins	€0	€1	€2	€3
Required outcomes				

(c) Is one spin of the spinner above an example of a Bernoulli trial?

Explain what a Bernoulli trial is.

SEC Leaving Certificate Ordinary Level, Paper 2, 2013

2. A survey of 168 people was carried out. Participants were asked whether they owned a cat or a dog. Some of the results are recorded in the Venn diagram.

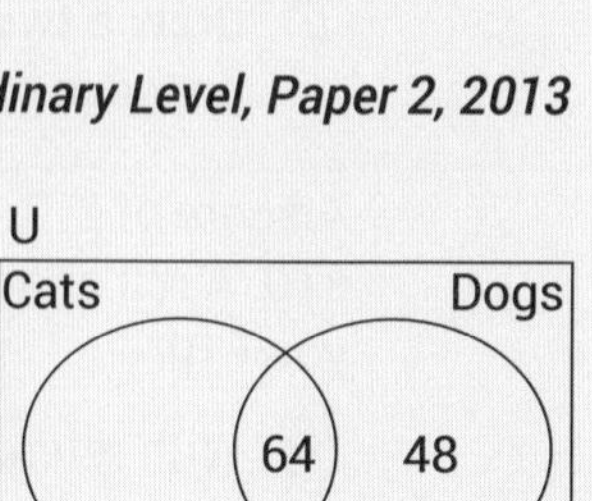

(i) Of those surveyed, 19 people did not own either a cat or a dog. Complete the diagram.

(ii) A person is chosen at random from those surveyed.

What is the probability that the person owned both a cat and a dog?

(iii) What percentage of the people surveyed owned one animal only?

Give your answer correct to one decimal place.

SEC Leaving Certificate Ordinary Level, Paper 2, 2016

3. A garage has 5 black cars, 9 red cars and 10 silver cars for sale.

   (a) A car is selected at random. What is the probability that:

      (i) The car is black

      (ii) The car is black or red

   (b) Three of the black cars, two of the red cars and four of the silver cars have diesel engines. One car from the garage is again selected at random. What is the probability that it is a red car or a diesel car?

SEC Leaving Certificate Ordinary Level, Paper 2, 2014

4. When taking a penalty kick, the probability that Kevin scores is always $\frac{3}{4}$.

   (a) Kevin takes a penalty. What is the probability that he does not score?

   (b) Kevin takes two penalties. What is the probability that he scores both?

   (c) Kevin takes three penalties. What is the probability that he scores exactly twice?

   (d) Kevin takes five penalties. What is the probability that he scores for the first time on his fifth penalty?

SEC Leaving Certificate Ordinary Level, Paper 2, 2014

5. A biased die is used in a game. The probabilities of getting the six different numbers on the die are shown in the table below.

Number	1	2	3	4	5	6
Probability	0.25	0.25	0.15	0.15	0.1	0.1

   (a) Find the expected value of the random variable X, where X is the number thrown.

   (b) There is a game at a funfair. It costs €3 to play the game. The player rolls a die once and wins back the number of euro shown on the die. The sentence below describes the difference between using the above biased die and using a fair (unbiased) die when playing this game. By doing the calculations required, complete the sentence.

   'If you play the game many times with a fair die, you will win an average of ________ per game, but if you play with the biased die you will lose an average of ________ per game.'

SEC Leaving Certificate Ordinary Level, Sample Paper 2, 2014

6. Katie tossed a coin 200 times and threw 109 heads. Joe tossed the same coin 400 times and threw 238 heads. Lucy tossed the same coin 500 times and threw 291 heads. Katie, Joe and Lucy now think the coin may be biased.

   (a) Give a reason why they think that the coin may be biased.

   (b) Lucy uses all the above data and calculates that the best estimate of the probability of throwing a head with this coin is 0.58. Show how Lucy might have calculated this probability.

   (c) Joe agrees with Lucy's estimate of 0.58 as the probability of throwing a head with this coin. He claims that the probability of throwing 3 successive heads with this coin is less than the probability of throwing 2 successive tails. Calculate the probability of each event and state whether Joe's claim is true or not.

SEC Leaving Certificate Ordinary Level, Paper 2, 2013

7. The 2006 census shows that the number of males living in Ireland is about the same as the number of females.

(a) If a person is selected at random, write down the probability that the person is male.

(b) Four people are chosen at random. We are interested in whether they are male or female.

(i) Complete the sample space below showing the sixteen equally likely outcomes.

M M M M

M M M F

(ii) Hence, or otherwise, complete the table of probabilities below.

four males	three males; one female	two males; two females	one male; three females	four females
$\frac{1}{16}$				

(c) A person states the following: 'If you pick four people at random, it's **more likely than not** that you'll get two males and two females.'

Is this statement correct? Justify your answer using the answer(s) to part **(b)**.

SEC Leaving Certificate Ordinary Level, Sample Paper 2, 2012

8. (a) In the Venn diagram below, the universal set is a normal deck of 52 playing cards. The two sets shown represent Clubs and picture cards (Kings, Queens and Jacks).

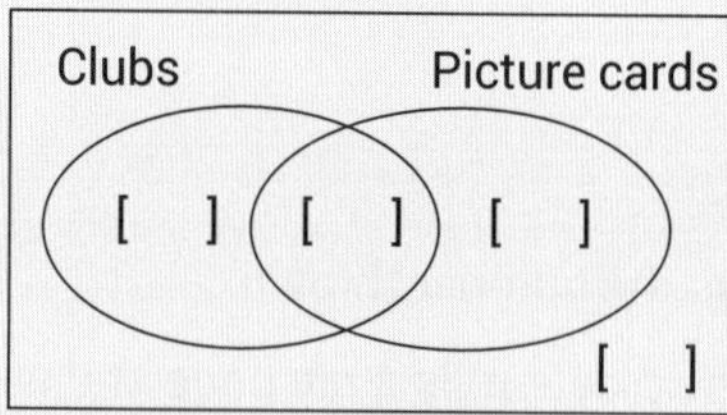

Show on the diagram the number of elements in each region.

(b) (i) A card is drawn from a pack of 52 cards.

Find the probability that the card drawn is the King of Clubs.

(ii) A card is drawn from a pack of 52 cards.

Find the probability that the card drawn is a Club or a picture card.

(iii) Two cards are drawn from a pack of 52 cards. Find the probability that neither of them is a Club or a picture card. Give your answer correct to two decimal places.

SEC Leaving Certificate Ordinary Level, Paper 2, 2012

9. A plastic toy is in the shape of a hemisphere. When it falls on the ground, there are two possible outcomes: it can land with the flat side facing down or with the flat side facing up. Two groups of students are trying to find the probability that it will land with the flat side down.

(a) Explain why, even though there are two outcomes, the answer is not necessarily equal to $\frac{1}{2}$.

(b) The students estimate the probability by experiment. Group A drops the toy 100 times. From this, they estimate that it lands flat side down with probability 0.76. Group B drops the toy 500 times. From this, they estimate that it lands flat side down with probability 0.812.

(i) Which group's estimate is likely to be better, and why?

(ii) How many times did the toy land flat side down for Group B?

(iii) Using the data from the two groups, what is the best estimate of the probability that the toy lands flat side down?

SEC Leaving Certificate Ordinary Level, Paper 2, 2011

10. The table below gives motor insurance information for fully licensed, 17 to 20-year-old drivers in Ireland in 2007. All drivers who had their own insurance policy are included.

	Number of drivers	Number of claims	Average cost per claim
Male	9634	977	€6108
Female	6743	581	€6051

(Source: adapted from: Financial Regulator. Private Motor Insurance Statistics 2007.)

Questions **(a)** to **(e)** below refer to drivers in the table above only.

(a) What is the probability that a randomly selected **male** driver made a claim during the year? Give your answer correct to three decimal places.

(b) What is the probability that a randomly selected **female** driver made a claim during the year? Give your answer correct to three decimal places.

(c) What is the *expected value* of the cost of claims on a male driver's policy?

(d) What is the *expected value* of the cost of claims on a female driver's policy?

(e) The male drivers were paying an average of €1,688 for insurance in 2007 and the female drivers were paying an average of €1,024. Calculate the average surplus for each group, and comment on your answer.

(Note: the *surplus* is the amount paid for the policy minus the expected cost of claims.)

(f) A 40-year-old female driver with a full license has a probability of 0.07 of making a claim during the year. The average cost of such claims is €3,900. How much should a company charge such drivers for insurance in order to show a surplus of €175 per policy?

SEC Leaving Certificate Ordinary Level, Paper 2, 2010

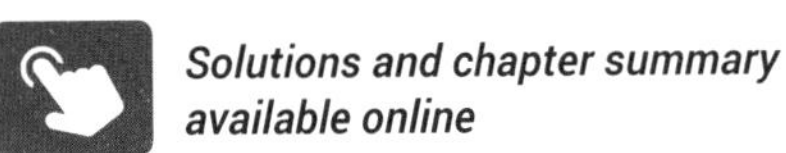

Solutions and chapter summary available online

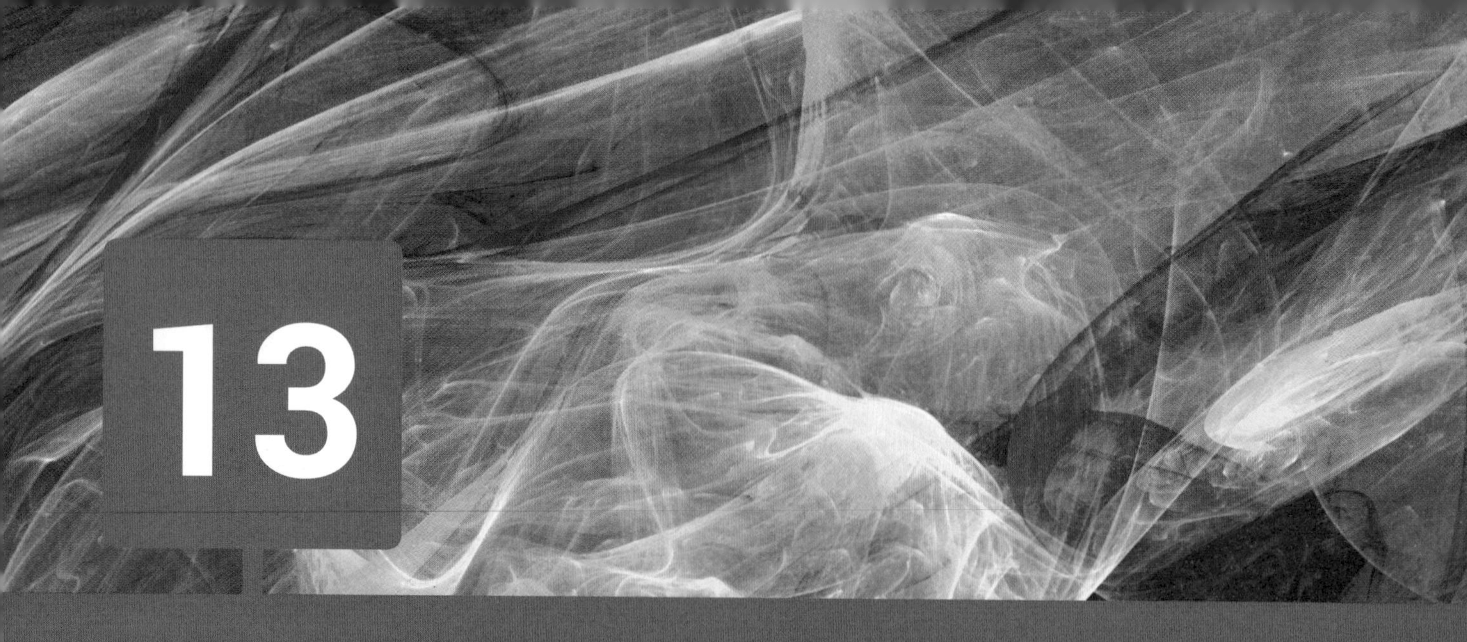

13

Statistics I

In this chapter you will learn how to:

- Discuss populations and samples
- Decide to what extent conclusions can be generalised
- Work with different types of bivariate data
- Select a sample (Simple Random Sample)
- Recognise the importance of representativeness so as to avoid biased samples
- Discuss different types of studies: sample surveys, observational studies and designed experiments
- Design a plan and collect data on the basis of above knowledge
- Describe the sample (both univariate and bivariate data) by selecting appropriate graphical or numerical methods
- Explore the distribution of data, including concepts of symmetry and skewness
- Compare data sets using appropriate displays, including back-to-back stem-and-leaf plots
- Determine the relationship between variables using scatterplots
- Recognise that correlation is a value from −1 to +1 and it measures the extent of the linear relationship between two variables
- Match correlation coefficient values to appropriate scatterplots
- Understand that correlation does not imply causality
- Interpret a histogram in terms of distribution of data

You should remember...

- How to construct a bar chart
- How to construct a line plot
- How to construct a stem-and-leaf plot
- How to construct a pie chart
- How to construct a histogram

Key words

- Numerical data
- Categorical data
- Primary data
- Secondary data
- Population
- Sample
- Survey
- Designed experiment
- Questionnaire
- Stem-and-leaf diagram
- Scatter graph
- Correlation
- Histogram
- Skewed (right or left)

Nowadays, numbers appear all around us. Making sense of numbers is the purpose of statistics. Open a newspaper or watch TV, and you will come across **statistics** in news reports, sports reports, advertisements and documentaries.

The word **statistics** comes from the Latin word *status* (meaning 'state').

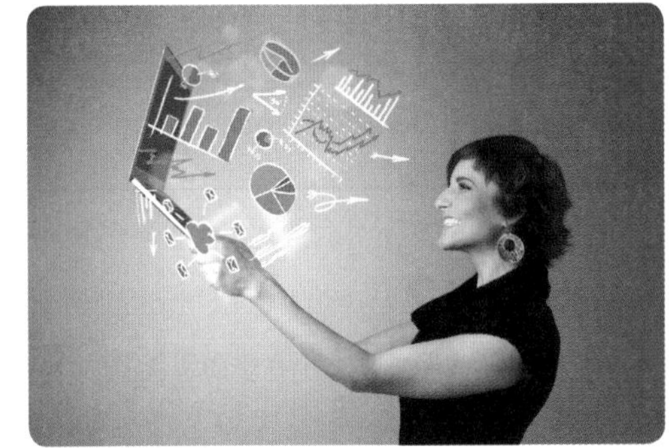

Statistics play a very important part in understanding the world in which we live. When we turn on our TVs, browse the Internet or open a newspaper, we encounter numbers, charts, tables, graphs and other statistical results.

13.1 Statistics in Today's World

Statistics are used in many different areas. Here are just a few examples:

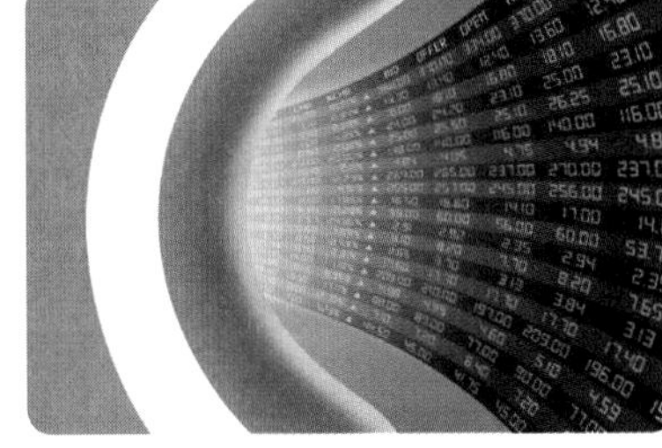

- Weather reports
- Stock market reports
- Football league tables
- Music charts
- Summaries of road traffic deaths
- Elections

This list is not exhaustive. Can you think of any other areas in which statistics are used?

13.2 Statistical Investigations

Statistical investigations are an integral part of the work of many professionals. Economists, scientists and engineers use statistical investigations to analyse numerous problems. Research students use statistical investigations to prove many of their theories. Newspapers often conduct statistical investigations to gauge the public mood on various issues. In lots of ways, modern societies are dependent on the information provided by statistical investigations.

A large part of any statistical investigation is the production of **data**.

We collect data by asking questions, taking measurements, observing what is happening or doing experiments. The characteristic we record is called a **variable**.

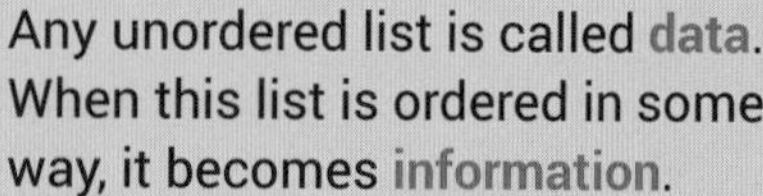

Any unordered list is called data. When this list is ordered in some way, it becomes information.

A statistical investigation on the heights of students in your class will produce data in the form of measurements. In this case, height is the variable being measured.

When we study one variable at a time, the data we work with is called univariate data.

Types of Data

All data is either **categorical** data or **numerical** data.

Categorical Data

Questions that **cannot be** answered with **numbers** provide categorical data. The following are examples of such questions:

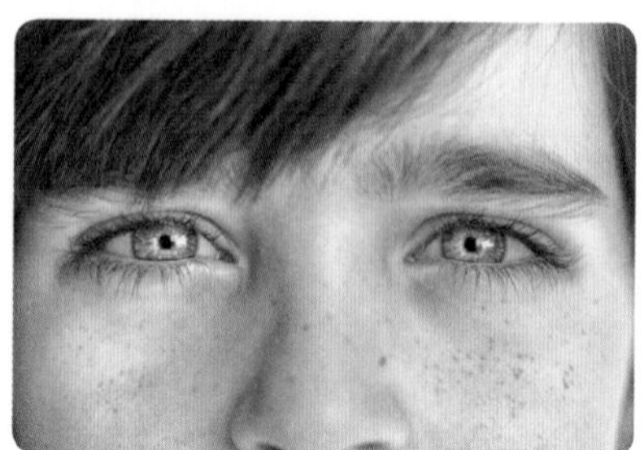

- What films have you seen in the last year?
- What colour are your eyes?
- What is your favourite soccer team?
- What make of car do you drive?
- What grade did you get in Junior Certificate maths?

There are two types of categorical data, **ordinal** and **nominal**:

Ordinal categorical data **can be ordered** in some way.

Examples include exam results (A, B, C, D, E, F, NG), stress levels (low, medium, high) and social class (lower, middle, upper).

Nominal categorical data **cannot be ordered**.

Examples include hair colour, phone type and favourite band.

Ordinal categorical data can be ordered in some way.

Nominal categorical data cannot be ordered.

Numerical Data

Questions that **can be** answered with **numbers** provide numerical data:

- How many people in the EU are employed in agriculture?
- How many Irish people emigrated in 2016?
- How many houses were built in Ireland in 2016?
- What was the the temperature in Dubai at midday on 5 June 1998?

There are two types of numerical data, **continuous** and **discrete**:

The greatest annual total rainfall recorded in this country was at Ballaghbeema Gap, Co. Kerry. The year was 1960, and the amount of rainfall recorded for the year was 3964.9 mm. Of course, this measurement could have been 3964.89764 mm, but Met Éireann give rainfall measurements corrected to one decimal place. Rainfall measurements are an example of **continuous numerical data**, as rainfall measurements for a particular region can be any one of an infinite number of values within a given range.

Numbers or measurements that can only have certain values, for example, shoe size and family size, are called **discrete numerical data**. Your family size must be a number such as 3, 4, 5, etc. It cannot be 3.5.

- If numerical data can have any value inside some range, then the data is continuous numerical data.
- If numerical data can only take values that move in steps, then it is discrete numerical data.

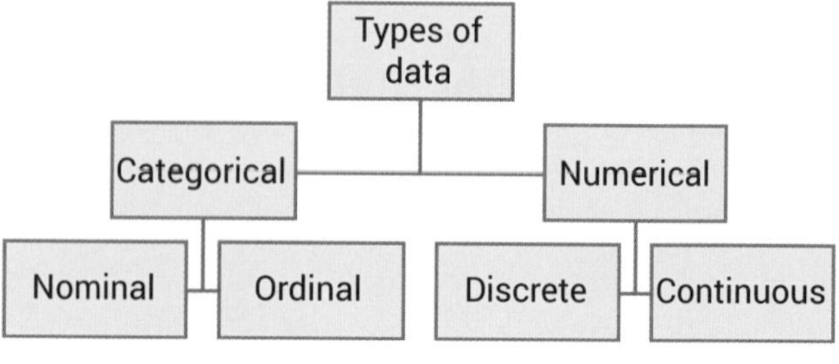

STATISTICS I

Worked Example 13.1

State whether the following are:

(a) continuous numerical data
(b) discrete numerical data
(c) nominal categorical data
(d) ordinal categorical data

(i) The number of aeroplanes flying out of Shannon every day
(ii) The heights of basketball players
(iii) The blood group of 50 blood donors
(iv) A randomly selected group of adults being categorised as either heavy, moderate, light or non smoker
(v) The time taken by each student in your class to run 100 metres

Solution

(i) The number of aeroplanes flying out of Shannon every day is **discrete numerical** data. This data can only have certain values, i.e. 0 and the positive whole numbers.

(ii) The heights of basketball players is **continuous numerical** data. Heights can be any one of an infinite number of values within a given range.

(iii) This is **nominal categorical** data, as the data is not numerical and it can not be ordered in a meaningful way.

(iv) The data is **ordinal categorical** data, as it is not numerical and it can be ordered from heavy to non smoker.

(v) The times taken by students to run 100 metres is **continuous numerical** data. Times can take on any value within a given range.

Populations and Samples

Suppose that you wish to do a study on the TV viewing habits of students in your school. You realise that it is impractical to interview everybody, so instead you decide to interview 80 out of the 1,000 students in the school. In this case, the group of all 1,000 students is called the **population**.

The **population** is the entire group that is being studied.

The group of 80 students is called a **sample**. It is very important that a sample is representative of the population. For example, the sample of 80 students mentioned above would not be representative of the whole school if they were all First Year students.

A **sample** is a group that is selected from the population.

Choosing a Simple Random Sample

Imagine you are asked to generate a simple random sample of size 20 from a population of 500 students. You need to generate the sample in such a way that every possible sample of size 20 has the same chance of being selected. To do this you could assign each student in the population a different whole number from 1 to 500. Your calculator could then be used to generate (randomly) twenty whole numbers from 1 to 500. This sample is a **simple random sample**.

It may be necessary to generate more than the required random sample number in case of repetition (some random number appearing more than once).

A random sample of size n is a **simple random sample** if every possible sample of size n within the population has an equal chance of being selected. In a simple random sample, every member of the population has an equal chance of being selected.

Reliability of Data

When choosing a sample from a population, it is important to ensure that:

- The sample is large enough. For large populations, i.e. populations greater than 100,000, a sample size of at least 400 should be selected. Many statisticians would choose a sample size of 1,000 from such a population. For smaller populations, the sample size as a proportion of the population needs to be quite large. In fact, for populations as small as 2,000, statisticians would still pick a sample size of 400.
- The sample is a random selection from the population.
- Everybody has an equal chance of being selected.
- The response rate is as high as possible.

If sample data is not collected in an appropriate way, then the data may be completely useless.

Bias in Sampling

Samples that are not representative are called **biased samples**. If there is a tendency for a particular group in a population to be omitted from a sample, then the sample is biased. To minimise bias, samples should be randomly selected.

Primary and Secondary Data

Primary data is collected by or for the person who is going to use it. Therefore, the person collecting the data must organise a study to collect the data. There are different types of studies for which primary data is collected. We will look at two of them:

- Observational studies
- Designed experiments

In an **observational study**, the researcher collects the information of interest but does not influence events. A study into the TV viewing habits of teenagers, in which data is collected by means of a questionnaire, is an example of an observational study.

In a **designed experiment**, the researcher sets up an experiment and investigates the effects of the experiment, e.g. a pharmaceutical company testing the effects of a drug. In this case, the drug or drug dosage is called an **explanatory variable** and the effect of the drug is called a **response variable**.

Very often, it is not possible to collect data from everybody. In such cases, a sample is chosen and data is collected from the sample. This is known as a **sample survey**.

Secondary data is **not** collected by the person who is going to use it. Sources for secondary data include *The Guinness Book of Records*, the Census of Population or Internet-based sources such CensusAtSchools. If you are using data from a secondary source, there are some important questions you should ask before you believe the results:

- Who carried out the survey?
- How was the sample chosen?
- What was the population?
- What size was the sample?
- What was the response rate?

Steps in a Statistical Investigation

All statistical investigations begin with a question. Here are the steps in a statistical investigation:

- Pose a question.
- Collect data.
- Present the data.
- Analyse the data.
- Interpret the results.

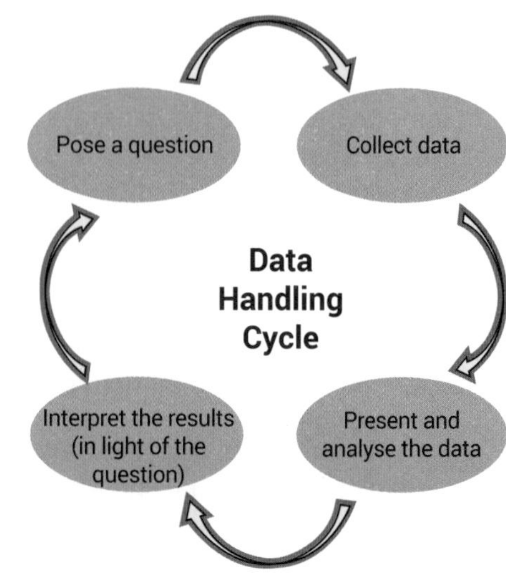

13.3 Collecting Data

Statistical data can be collected in different ways. The most common way of collecting data is by **survey**. There are several ways to carry out a survey:

- Face-to-face interview
- Questionnaire that is available online
- Questionnaire that is sent out by post
- Telephone interview
- Observation

Here are the advantages and disadvantages of each type of survey:

Survey	Advantages	Disadvantages
Face-to-face interview	• Questions can be explained to the interviewee.	• Not random • Expensive to carry out
Telephone interview	• It is possible to select a sample from almost the entire adult population. • Questions can be explained to the interviewee.	• Expensive in comparison to postal and online surveys
Postal questionnaire	• Inexpensive	• People do not always reply to postal surveys and those who reply may not be representative of the whole population.
Online questionnaire	• Very low cost • Anonymity of respondents ensures more honest answers to sensitive questions.	• Not representative of the whole population. Only those who go online and do online surveys are represented.
Observation	• Low cost • Easy to administer	• Not suitable for many surveys • Questions cannot be explained.

Designing a Questionnaire

A **questionnaire** is an important method of collecting data.

A **questionnaire** is a set of questions designed to obtain data from a population.

Here are some important points to note when designing questionnaires.

Questionnaires should:

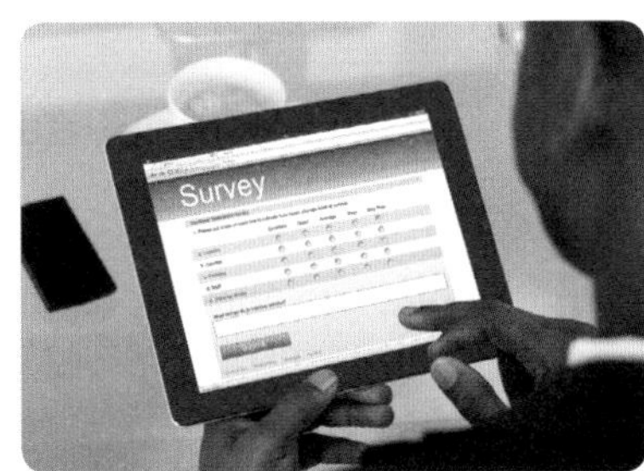

- Be useful and relevant to the survey you are undertaking.
- Use clear and simple language.
- Be as brief as possible.
- Begin with simple questions to encourage people to complete the questionnaire.
- Accommodate all possible answers.
- Be clear where answers should be recorded.
- Have no leading questions, which give a clue as to how you would like the person to respond. For example, 'Manchester United are losing a lot of games this season. Do you think their manager should resign?'
- **Not** ask for a response to more than one topic. For example, 'Do you think the government spends too much money on sport and should be voted out of office in the next election?'

13.4 Frequency Tables

When data is collected, it is often convenient to display it in a frequency table. Frequency tables show you how frequently each piece of data occurs. It is good practice to include a tally row in your table. Tallies are marks to help you keep track of counts. The marks are bunched in groups of five.

Worked Example 13.2

A class sits a Mathematics test. Their marks out of 10 are as follows:

7	8	9	7	9	10
8	8	6	9	7	5
9	6	4	8	6	9
7	8	9	7	9	10
9	7	5	9	8	8

(i) Sort the data into a frequency table. Include a tally row in your table.

(ii) How many students sat the test?

(iii) What percentage of students scored 9 or better?

Solution

(i)

Mark	4	5	6	7	8	9	10
Tally	|	||	|||	~~||||~~ |	~~||||~~ ||	~~||||~~ ||||	||
Frequency	1	2	3	6	7	9	2

(ii) $1 + 2 + 3 + 6 + 7 + 9 + 2 = 30$ students

(iii) The number of students who scored 9 or 10 marks is $9 + 2 = 11$ students.

$\therefore$ Percentage $= \frac{11}{30} \times \frac{100}{1} = 36\frac{2}{3}\%$

Exercise 13.1

1. What is categorical data?
   Give four examples of categorical data.

2. What are the two types of categorical data?
   Explain each one, giving a relevant example.

3. What is numerical data? Give four examples.

4. What are the two types of numerical data?
   Explain each one, giving a relevant example.

5. Explain the terms 'population' and 'sample'.

6. List two sources of secondary data.

7. Formulate two questions that can be answered with numerical data.

8. Formulate two questions that can be answered with categorical data.

9. Write a brief note on each of the following, giving an appropriate example in each case:
   (i) Observational studies
   (ii) Designed experiments
   (iii) Sample surveys

10. Explain the terms 'explanatory variable' and 'response variable'.

11. Alan would like to predict the winning time for the men's 100 m final in the next Olympic Games. He gathers data from past editions of *The Guinness Book of Records*. Explain why the data collected by Alan is secondary data.

12. What questions should you ask about a secondary source to determine whether the data is reliable?

13. Shauna rolls a die 50 times. Her scores are listed below.

5	3	3	3	5	1	2	5	1	5
1	3	3	6	4	6	1	2	1	1
1	6	5	6	3	4	2	2	5	2
4	6	5	1	2	6	1	1	6	2
2	6	2	5	2	3	4	4	6	6

(i) Sort the data in a frequency table that includes a tally row.

Outcome	1	2	3	4	5	6
Tally						
Frequency						

(ii) How many times did Shauna roll a 6?

(iii) How many times did Shauna roll a 1?

(iv) What percentage of the rolls were 4s?

14. Below is some data selected at random from the CensusAtSchools database. The data gives the different modes of transport a group of students uses to go to school.

Walk	Bus	Walk	Walk	Walk
Bus	Walk	Car	Car	Bus
Walk	Bus	Car	Walk	Walk
Car	Rail	Bus	Walk	Rail

(i) Sort the data into a frequency table.

(ii) What is the most popular mode of transport?

(iii) What is the least popular mode of transport?

(iv) What type of data has been selected?

15. A survey is made of the number of goals scored in a series of soccer matches. The findings are as follows:

2	0	1	2	2	1	3
1	1	4	0	1	3	4
0	2	0	4	2	0	4
3	1	2	4	2	2	0
1	1	2	1	2	2	0

(i) Sort the data into a frequency table.

(ii) What type of data is given?

(iii) How many soccer matches were played?

(iv) How many scoreless draws were there?

(v) What is the maximum number of games that could have been drawn?

(vi) What is the minimum number of games that could have been drawn?

16. John takes three coins from his pocket and flips the three coins together. He repeats this experiment 25 times and records his results as follows:

TTT	TTH	HTT	THT	HHH
HTH	THH	HHT	HHH	HTT
TTH	HHT	TTT	THH	HHH
THT	HTH	HTH	HTH	THH
THT	TTH	HHT	HTH	HTT

(i) Describe the type of data used in this question.

(ii) Copy and complete the frequency table.

Result	3 Heads	2 Heads	1 Head	0 Head
Tally				
Frequency				

(iii) What percentage of the throws revealed one head only?

13.5 Graphing Data: Stem-and-Leaf Diagrams

In this section, we look at important methods of graphing sets of data. Data that is graphed is always easier to analyse and interpret. In your Junior Certificate maths course, you learned how to graph data using line plots, bar charts and pie charts. You will still need to construct bar charts and pie charts to display discrete data. Another way to display discrete data is to construct a stem-and-leaf diagram.

Florence Nightingale (1820–1910), regarded by many as the founder of the nursing profession, compiled massive amounts of data in an attempt to convince the British Parliament to invest in supplying nursing and medical care to soldiers in the field. Included in her presentation was the first 'pie chart'.

Florence Nightingale (1820–1910)

Stem-and-Leaf Diagrams

Stem-and-leaf diagrams represent data in a similar way to bar charts.
A stem-and-leaf diagram represents data by separating each value into two parts: the stem and the leaf (the final digit). This allows you to show the distribution in the same way as a bar chart.

It is important to arrange the data in ascending order when drawing the stem-and-leaf diagram. All diagrams should have a key.

Worked Example 13.3

Twenty people from the audience of a TV programme are randomly selected and each person is asked his/her age. Their ages are shown here:

15	14	25	23	33
45	13	51	62	48
19	57	47	56	44
11	38	46	21	16

(i) Represent the data on a stem-and-leaf diagram.

(ii) How many people in their fifties are in the audience?

Solution

(i) **Step 1** Begin by writing out the stems:

Stem
1
2
3
4
5
6

Step 2 Write each leaf on the proper stem:

Stem	Leaf
1	5, 4, 3, 9, 1, 6
2	5, 3, 1
3	3, 8
4	5, 8, 7, 4, 6
5	1, 7, 6
6	2

Step 3 Arrange the leaves in ascending order and write the key:

Stem	Leaf
1	1, 3, 4, 5, 6, 9
2	1, 3, 5
3	3, 8
4	4, 5, 6, 7, 8
5	1, 6, 7
6	2 Key: 1|4 = 14 years

(ii) Reading from the stem-and-leaf diagram, we see that there are three people in their fifties in the audience. Their ages are 51, 56 and 57.

Back-to-Back Stem-and-Leaf Diagrams

A back-to-back stem-and-leaf diagram is a useful way of comparing data from two different groups. The leaves on each side are ordered out from the common stem in ascending order.

Worked Example 13.4

Here is a back-to-back stem-and-leaf diagram showing the marks obtained by 30 girls and 30 boys in a Physics test. The girls' marks are on the left-hand side of the diagram.

Leaf (Girls)	Stem	Leaf (Boys)
6	0	9
9, 7, 2	1	3, 4, 5
	2	9
6, 6	3	5, 7
8, 6, 6, 6, 4, 2, 2	4	3, 4, 4, 9
9, 8, 6, 4	5	2, 2, 3, 5, 7, 7
8, 2	6	1, 2, 5, 8, 8, 9
9, 6, 5, 4	7	3, 4, 5, 9
5, 2, 0	8	4, 7
Key: 2|6| = 62 marks 9, 8, 4, 3	9	1 Key: |3|5 = 35 marks

(i) How many girls scored more than 80?

(ii) How many boys scored more than 80?

(iii) If 50 is the pass mark, did more boys than girls pass the test?

Solution

(i) Six girls scored more than 80. Their scores are 82, 85, 93, 94, 98 and 99.

(ii) Three boys scored more than 80. Their scores are 84, 87 and 91.

(iii) Yes – 19 boys passed and 17 girls passed.

Exercise 13.2

1. Here are the marks obtained by 20 students in an English test. The test was marked out of 100.

30	86	90	52	62
57	69	86	55	40
54	61	70	76	62
77	45	86	60	48

(i) Copy and complete the stem-and-leaf diagram.

Stem	Leaf
3	0
4	
5	
6	
7	0, 6, 7
8	
9	Key:

(ii) What percentage of students achieved a mark higher than 50?

2. John measures the heights (in centimetres) of all students in his class. Here are his results:

160	155	166	154	150
158	170	175	156	153
140	168	170	149	145
157	160	165	180	181
165	153	139	183	160

(i) Copy and complete the stem-and-leaf diagram.

Stem	Leaf
13	9
14	
15	
16	
17	
18	Key: 13|9 = 139 cm

(ii) How many students are in the class?

(iii) John's height is 166 cm. What fraction of the class is taller than him?

3. A class has to elect two representatives to the student council. An election is held and the results are as follows:

Student	Rachel	Alan	Tom	Tanya	Joe
Votes	7	4	5	9	6

(i) Draw a line plot to illustrate the data.

(ii) Which students were elected?

4. Fifteen plants are randomly selected and their heights (in centimetres) are measured.

49	27	44	37	43
32	40	46	45	32
38	27	40	37	45

(i) Show the results on a stem-and-leaf diagram. Include a key.

(ii) What was the smallest height recorded?

(iii) What was the tallest plant in the sample?

(iv) What fraction of the sample had heights greater than 43 cm?

5. The ordered stem-and-leaf diagram below shows the number of box sets owned by a group of 12 students. The diagram contains three different errors. Describe each error.

2	1, 2, 2
3	2, 4
4	1, 4, 3
5	1, 5
6	8

6. A PE teacher carried out a survey into the participation of teenagers in sport. He selected a sample of 50 students in his school and asked them the question: 'How many sports do you play?'
The data he collected is given in the table below.

1	3	5	2	3	2	2	4	2	2
0	3	3	3	5	2	2	5	0	3
1	1	1	4	3	4	4	2	2	0
2	2	2	1	2	1	2	4	1	0
1	1	1	3	2	2	2	2	1	5

(i) Copy and complete the frequency table:

No. of sports	0	1	2	3	4	5
Frequency						

(ii) Display the data on a line plot.

7. The table below shows the modes of transport used by a group of students to travel to school.

Mode of transport	Walk	Bus	Cycle	Car	Train
No. of students	6	15	5	2	1

(i) How many students are there in the group?

(ii) What is the most popular mode of transport?

(iii) Represent the data on a bar chart.

(iv) Represent the data on a line plot.

(v) State one difference and one similarity between the line plot and the bar chart.

8. The back-to-back stem-and-leaf diagram below compares the pulse rates of 25 people immediately before and immediately after a 5 km run.

Before run		After run
7, 5, 2	5	
8, 6, 4, 2, 1, 1, 0	6	
8, 8, 8, 8, 6, 5, 3, 3, 1	7	
3, 2, 1	8	
8, 5	9	
9	10	0, 2, 5
	11	8, 6
	12	0, 0, 1, 5, 6, 6, 8, 9
	13	1, 2, 2, 6, 9
	14	7, 8, 8
	15	0, 1, 7
Key: 1|8 = 81 beats/min	16	2 Key: 11|8 = 118 beats/min

(i) How many people had pulse rates of 100 or more beats per minute after the run?

(ii) How many people had pulse rates of 100 or more beats per minute before the run?

(iii) What conclusions can you draw from the stem-and-leaf diagram?

9. The following table shows the heights (in centimetres) of a group of men and a group of women.

Men	179, 183, 181, 186, 185, 175, 191, 171, 174, 176, 179, 184, 159, 160, 166, 170, 178, 175, 170, 161, 168, 174, 183
Women	157, 155, 148, 171, 151, 157, 167, 162, 174, 166, 165, 149, 169, 178, 158, 154, 153, 152, 155, 150, 161, 158, 163

(i) Copy and complete the back-to-back stem-and-leaf diagram to compare their heights.

Men	Stem	Women
	14	
	15	
	16	
	17	
	18	
	19	

(ii) What conclusion can be drawn from this diagram?

10. In a class of 20 students, 5 are girls and 15 are boys.
    (i) Draw a pie chart to represent this data.
    (ii) What percentage of the class consists of boys?
    (iii) Draw a bar chart to represent the data.
    (iv) You are asked to find the approximate fraction of the class that is female by referring to one of the charts you have drawn. Which chart would you select? Explain your choice.

11. The air we breathe is made up of 78% nitrogen, 21% oxygen and 1% other gases.
    Draw a pie chart to represent this information.

13.6 Graphing Data: Histograms

If you wish to graph height, foot length or arm span, then you could use a histogram. Histograms are used to represent continuous data.

Histograms are similar to bar charts. In a bar chart, the height of the bar represents the frequency. In a histogram, the area of the bar represents the frequency. However, in our course we will deal only with histograms in which the bars have a width of 1. Therefore, the **area** of the bar will have the same value as the **height** of the bar.

Worked Example 13.5

The following frequency table shows the times, in minutes, spent by a group of girls in a clothes shop. Draw a histogram of the distribution.

Time	0–10	10–20	20–30	30–40	40–50
Number	1	4	8	7	9

Note: 10–20 means 10 or more but less than 20, and so on.

Solution

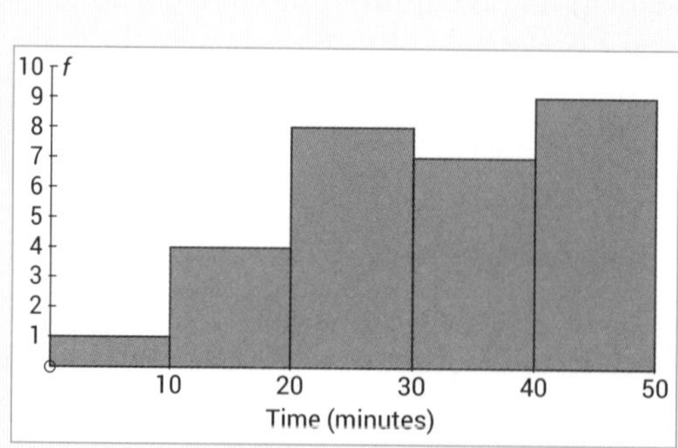

13.7 Distribution of Data

Here are the times (in minutes) taken by a group of 14 students to complete a Maths problem.

1	1.5	2	2.5	3	4	4.5
5.5	5.7	6	7	7.5	8.5	9.5

While it may not be obvious from the list, many of the times are between 4 minutes and 6 minutes. Also, few people had very low times or very high times. A histogram shows this distribution very well.

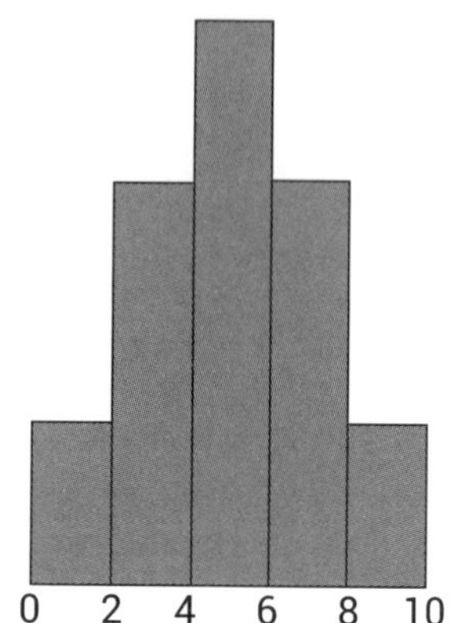

We call this distribution a **symmetric distribution.**

In a symmetric distribution, the left half of the histogram is roughly a mirror image of its right half.

Here are the times (in minutes) taken by another group of 21 students to complete the same Maths problem.

1.5	2	2.4	3.8	4	4.2	4.5
5.7	5.8	6.1	6.3	6.4	7	7.2
8.2	8.3	8.5	8.8	9	9.2	9.5

In this distribution, many students took a relatively long time to complete the problem. Here is the histogram for this distribution, which tails off towards the lower numbers on the left.

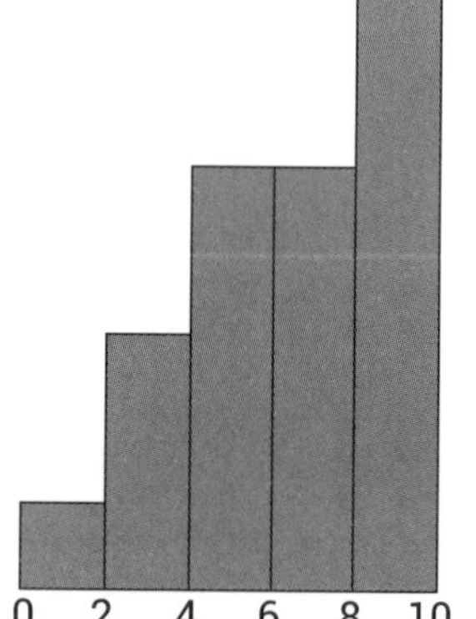

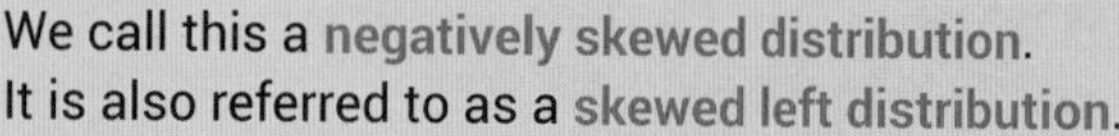

We call this a **negatively skewed distribution.**
It is also referred to as a **skewed left distribution.**

The following are the times of another group of 25 students who also took the Maths problem.

0.9	1.1	1.2	1.3	1.3	1.6	1.6	1.9	2	2
3.1	3.2	3.6	3.9	4.1	4.5	5.1	5.8	5.8	6
7.1	7.5	7.9	8	9					

In this distribution, many students solved the problem in a short time. Here is the histogram for this distribution, which tails off towards the higher numbers on the right.

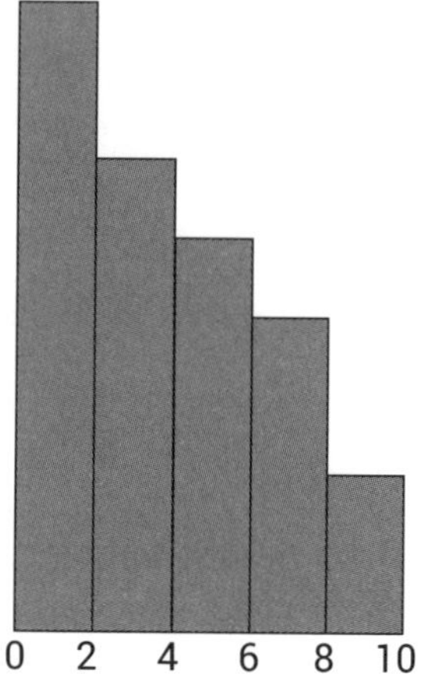

We call this a **positively skewed distribution.**
It is also referred to as a **skewed right distribution.**

STATISTICS I

Exercise 13.3

1. For each of the following distributions, identify whether the distributions are skewed left, skewed right, symmetric or roughly symmetric.

(i)

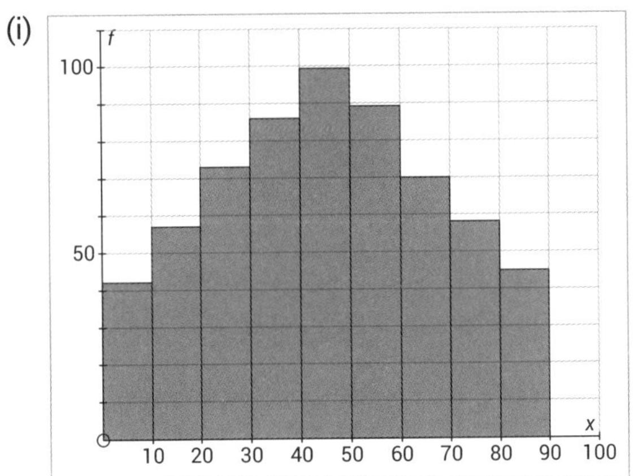

(iii)

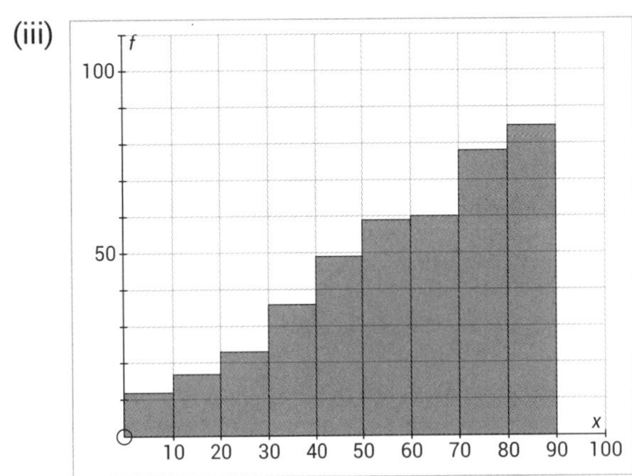

(ii)

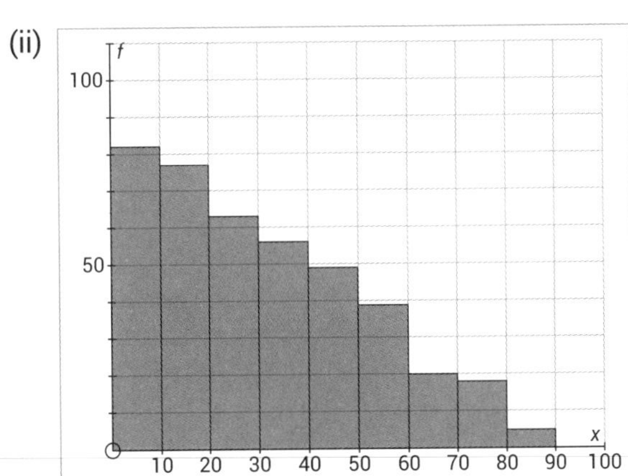

(iv)

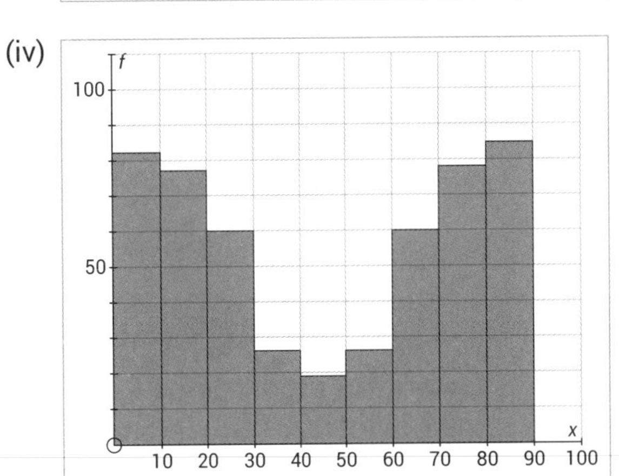

2. Display the following data sets on a stem-and-leaf plot and then identify whether the distributions are skewed left, skewed right, symmetric or roughly symmetric.

   (i) {12, 21, 34, 41, 52, 13, 22, 35, 41, 52, 14, 22, 36, 42, 54, 15, 23, 37, 43, 54, 15, 24, 44, 55, 16, 16, 55, 56}

   (ii) {31, 42, 56, 63, 71, 32, 43, 58, 62, 33, 43, 58, 61, 34, 44, 58, 36, 45, 37, 37, 38}

   (iii) {19, 28, 29, 33, 34, 35, 36, 42, 43, 44, 44, 45, 45, 52, 52, 52, 53, 55, 57, 59, 59}

   (iv) {42, 53, 61, 77, 82, 83, 78, 62, 54, 43, 55, 62, 79, 79, 63, 68, 69}

3. The histogram shows the distances, in kilometres, that some students have to travel to school.

   (i) Complete the following table:

Distance (km)	0-2	2-4	4-6	6-8	8-10
Number					

   (ii) Is this distribution symmetric, positively skewed or negatively skewed?

4. The ages (in years) of a group of people at a party were recorded. The results are shown in the table.

   Draw a histogram to represent the data.

Age	15-20	20-25	25-30	30-35	35-40
Frequency	4	8	16	12	4

Note: 15-20 means 15 or more but less than 20.

5. The time, in minutes, taken by each member of a group of students to solve a problem is represented in the histogram.

   (i) Copy and complete the following table:

Time (min)	0–1	1–2	2–3	3–4	4–5
Number					

   Note: 0–1 means 0 or more but less than 1, and so on.

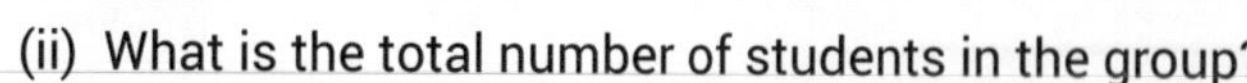

   (ii) What is the total number of students in the group?

   (iii) How many students solved the problem in less than 3 minutes?

   (iv) What percentage of students solved it in less than a minute? (Give your answer correct to two decimal places.)

6. The number of hours' sleep taken by 50 people on a certain night was tabled as follows:

Time (hours)	0–3	3–6	6–9	9–12
Number	4	11	20	15

   Note: 0–3 means 0 or more but less than 3, and so on.

   (i) Draw a histogram that will represent the data.

   (ii) What is the highest possible number of people who had more than 8 hours' sleep?

   (iii) What is the least possible number of people who had more than 8 hours' sleep?

7. The stem-and-leaf diagram shows the time (in seconds) it took contestants to answer a general knowledge question. All contestants answered in less than 7 seconds.

2	1, 2, 2
3	2, 4, 8, 9
4	1, 3, 4, 6, 7
5	1, 5
6	8

   Key: 5|1 = 5.1 seconds

   (i) Describe the distribution (left-skewed, right-skewed, symmetric or roughly symmetric).

   (ii) Copy and complete the table.

Time (sec)	2–3	3–4	4–5	5–6	6–7
Number		4			

   Note: 2–3 means 2 or more but less than 3, and so on.

   (iii) Draw a histogram to represent the data.

8. The table below shows some of the data gathered by a company on average water usage in homes.

Activity	Percentage used	Angle (degrees)
WC flushing	30%	
Personal washing – baths and taps	21%	
Personal washing – showers	12%	
Clothes washing	13%	46.8°
Other		

   (a) Find the percentage used for the 'Other' activity and write it in the table.

   (b) A pie chart representing the data is to be drawn.

      (i) The size of the angle representing 'Clothes washing' on the pie chart is 46.8°. Complete the table to show the remaining angles in the pie chart.

      (ii) Draw a pie chart to represent the data. Label the sector corresponding to each activity and write the size of the angle in each sector.

STATISTICS I

(c) John compiled a table showing the amount of water used in his own household over the course of a week. He recorded the number of litres required for each activity and the number of times each activity was undertaken.

The data is shown in the table below.

		John's weekly household water usage	
Activity	**Water required per activity**	**Frequency**	**Number of litres used**
One bath	80 litres	3 baths	240
One shower	125 litres	20 showers	
Brushing teeth with tap running	6 litres per minute	32 minutes	
One WC flush	6 litres	60 flushes	
One use of washing machine	45 litres	8 uses	
One use of dishwasher	20 litres	7 uses	
Washing one car with a bucket	10 litres	1 wash	
Hosepipe	9 litres per minute	15 minutes	
		Total number of litres used	

(i) Complete the table to show the number of litres used for the various activities and the total number of litres used in the week.

(ii) If water were charged at €1.85 per 1,000 litres, find what John's household would pay for the water used **in one year** if the household uses the same amount of water each week.

(iii) Find John's total bill for this water if VAT were to be included at a rate of 13.5%.

(d) John would like to reduce his water bill to €260 per year.

If water were charged at €1.85 plus VAT at 13.5% per 1,000 litres, find the number of litres of water he could purchase for €260.

9. (i) Give one example of a data set you would expect to have a symmetric (or roughly symmetric) distribution.

Clearly explain why you would expect this distribution to be symmetric.

(ii) Give one example of a data set you would expect to have a skewed left distribution.

Clearly explain why you would expect this distribution to be skewed left.

(iii) Give one example of a data set you would expect to have a skewed right distribution.

Clearly explain why you would expect this distribution to be skewed right.

10. A group of 50 Sixth Year Ordinary Level Maths students sat a mock Leaving Certificate Maths exam. Their results are shown in the table.

12%	17%	29%	36%	36%	37%	39%	44%	44%	46%
47%	49%	50%	50%	53%	55%	56%	59%	59%	61%
61%	61%	67%	67%	67%	68%	69%	69%	69%	71%
72%	74%	74%	77%	78%	78%	79%	79%	79%	81%
81%	83%	85%	85%	88%	88%	90%	90%	91%	93%

(a) Represent this data with a stem-and-leaf plot.

(b) Represent this data with a histogram.

STATISTICS I

(c) From 2017 onwards, the grading system at Leaving Certificate Ordinary Level is:

Percentage mark	Grade
90–100	01
80–89	02
70–79	03
60–69	04
50–59	05
40–49	06
30–39	07
0–29	08

Complete the frequency table below for the group of 50 Maths students and their results.

Grade	08	07	06	05	04	03	02	01
Frequency								

(d) For the categorical data in part (c), represent this data with:

(i) A line plot (ii) A bar chart (iii) A pie chart

11. In studying earthquake patterns in Southern California, a team of seismologists from the United States Geological Survey (USGS) take a random sample of earthquakes from all recorded earthquakes with epicentres within a 200 km radius of downtown San Diego, over the period 1997 to 2016 inclusive. The sample data is shown in the table.

Magnitude				
4.3	5.7	4.9	5.1	6.2
6.0	3.7	4.9	4.8	7.1
5.3	5.1	2.5	2.3	2.9
3.4	4.7	5.3	4.6	6.5

(a) What is the sample size?

(b) What is the population from which the sample is selected?

(c) How might the USGS team have selected this random sample?

(d) Why would they have selected a **random** sample?

(e) What type of data is being studied by the USGS team?

(f) Represent the sampled earthquake data with:

(i) A stem-and-leaf plot

(ii) A histogram

(g) The USGS team decide to **categorise** the sample data as follows:

Magnitude	Category
< 3	Background
$3 \leqslant$ Mag. < 4.5	Mild
$4.5 \leqslant$ Mag. < 6.5	Moderate
$\geqslant 6.5$	Severe

Complete the following frequency table for the sampled data:

Category	Background	Mild	Moderate	Severe
Frequency				

(h) Represent the categorical data from part (g) above with:

(i) A bar chart (ii) A pie chart (iii) A line plot

(j) The USGS team randomly sample similar earthquake data from Ireland for the same 1997 to 2016 period. The sample of data is presented in the **unordered** stem-and-leaf plot below:

Stem	Leaf
1	3, 6, 1, 4, 9
2	7, 7, 7, 0, 9, 5, 2
3	3, 1, 3, 6, 9, 0
4	0, 0
	Key: 2|0 = Mag. 2.0

Complete the back-to-back stem-and-leaf plot below for the Irish and Californian data.

Ireland	Stem	California
	0	
4, 3, 1	1	
	2	
	3	
	4	
	5	
	6	0, 2, 5
	7	
Key: 3|1 = Mag. 13		Key: 6|2 = Mag. 6.2

(k) By comparing the two data sets in part (j) above, or otherwise, what conclusions can you reach about the type of seismic activity in Ireland versus California over the 1997 to 2016 period?

12. A newspaper report in October 2013 stated that 90% of homeowners who were liable for property tax had registered for it. The total number of properties liable for the tax was estimated at 1.9 million.

(a) (i) Estimate the number of properties that were registered.

(ii) Suggest one reason why some properties were not registered.

(b) Homeowners who registered were required to value their property in one of a number of given Valuation Bands. The percentage who had valued their properties in each Valuation Band is given in the table below.

Valuation Band	€0– €100,000	€100,001– €150,000	€150,001– €200,000	€200,001– €250,000	€250,001– €300,000	Over €300,000
Percentage of registered homeowners	24.9	28.6	21.9	10.4	4.9	9.3

Represent the data on the table using a pie chart. Label each sector you create and show the angle in each sector clearly.

(c) (i) Use the data in the table above and your answer to part (a) (i) above to complete the following table:

Valuation Band	Tax per property	Number of properties	Total tax due (€)
€0–€100,000	€45	425,790	19,160,550
€100,001–€150,000	€112	489,060	
€150,001–€200,000	€157		
€200,001–€250,000	€202		
€250,001–€300,000	€247		
Over €300,000	NA		NA

NA = Not Available

(ii) Find the total tax due on those properties, registered by October 2013, with a valuation up to €300,000.

(iii) The total tax due on all the properties that were registered was estimated at €241 million. Find the total tax due on those properties with a valuation over €300,000.

(iv) Some homeowners may under-value their property in order to pay less tax. For example, one estimate stated that 20% of properties in the €100,001–€150,000 band should have been valued in the €150,001–€200,000 band. Based on this estimate, find the amount of extra tax that would be raised if these properties were registered in the correct Valuation Band.

13.8 Scatter Graphs and Correlation

Scatter graphs are used to investigate relationships between two sets of numerical data.

On our course we will investigate the linear relationship, if any, between two sets of numerical data.

If the points on a scatter graph are vertically close to a straight line, then we say there is a strong **linear correlation** between the two sets of data.

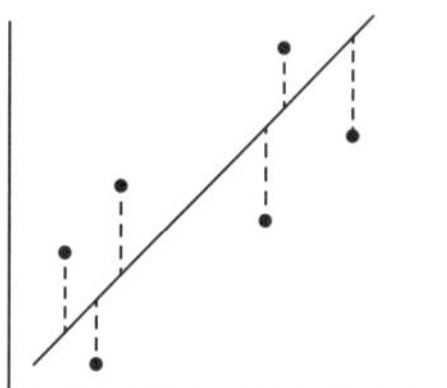

Correlation is not strong

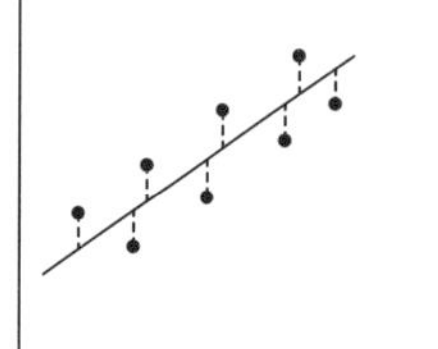

Correlation is strong

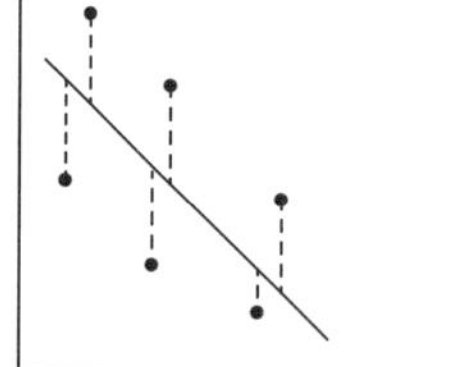

Correlation is not strong

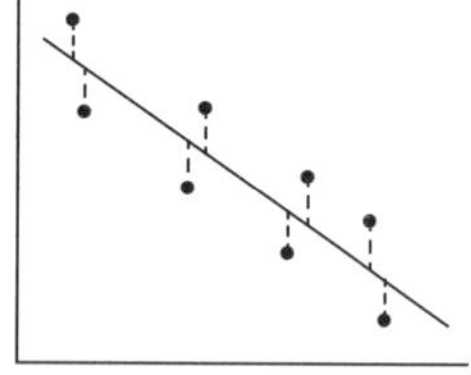

Correlation is strong

Suppose you measure the arm span and height of all students in your class. For each height measurement, there is a corresponding arm span measurement, so the data can be **paired**.

Data that can be paired is known as paired data or bivariate data.

The following tables show the height and arm span measurements of a group of students. All measurements are in centimetres.

Height (cm)	160	170	165	159	161	163	165	166
Arm span (cm)	159	168	162	161	162	164	164	164

Height (cm)	166	167	167	169	170	171	171	177
Arm span (cm)	165	166	167	171	169	169	170	175

Each height measurement and corresponding arm span measurement form a couple. Here are the couples for the data above:

(160, 159), (170, 168), (165, 162), (159, 161), (161, 162), (163, 164), (165, 164), (166, 164), (166, 165), (167, 166), (167, 167), (169, 171), (170, 169), (171, 169), (171, 170), (177, 175)

Always put the **explanatory variable**, if there is one, on the horizontal (x) axis. If there is no explanatory variable, then either variable can go on the horizontal axis.

A **response variable** is the quantity that we ask a question about in our study.
An **explanatory variable** is any factor that can influence the response variable.

Here is the scatter graph for the data:

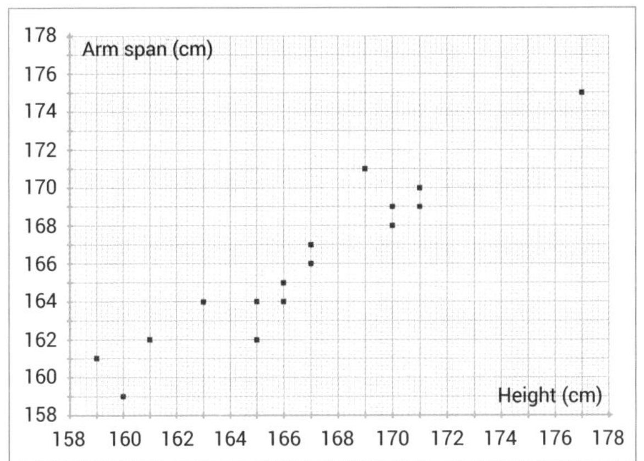

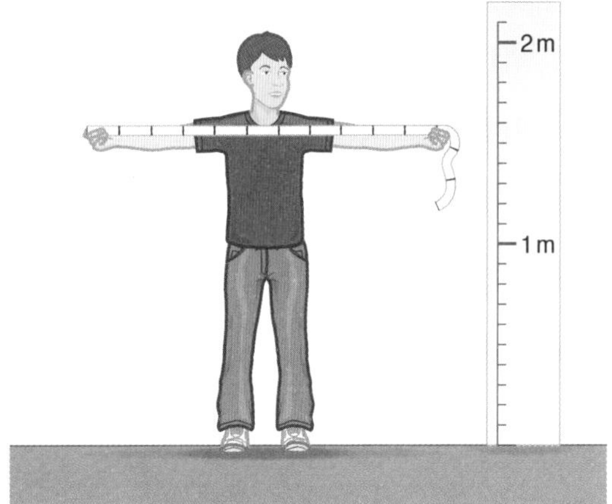

You can see from the graph that the points lie reasonably close to a straight line. We can, in this case, conclude that there is a relationship between arm span and height. In general, the greater the height, the greater the arm span.

Worked Example 13.6

The table below gives the marks obtained by 10 students taking a Maths test and a Physics test. Both tests are marked out of 50.

Maths mark	40	43	28	49	34	31	32	40	38	39
Physics mark	43	46	32	47	39	36	38	45	43	42

(i) Draw a scatter graph for the data.

(ii) Is there a correlation between the two sets?

Solution

(i)

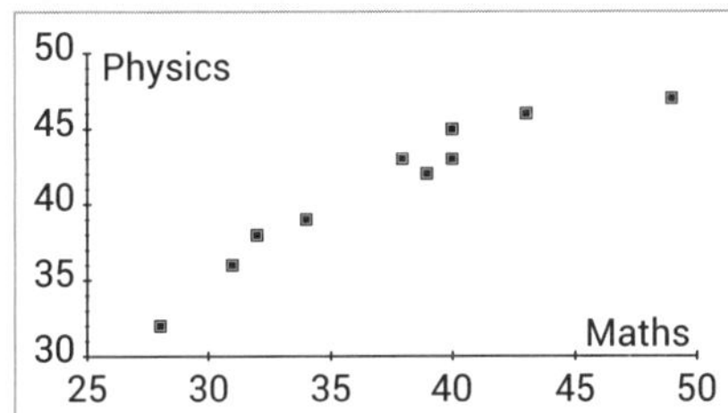

(ii) The points are reasonably close to a straight line, so we can say that a correlation exists between the sets. We cannot say that a student who scores highly in Maths will definitely score highly in Physics. We can only conclude that, **in general**, the better you are at Maths, the more likely you are to do well in Physics.

The Correlation Coefficient

The **correlation coefficient**, r, is a number in the following range: $-1 \leqslant r \leqslant 1$.

The correlation coefficient is a measure of the strength of the linear relationship between two sets of data. It has a value between −1 and 1.

- If r is close to 1, then there is a **strong positive correlation** between two sets of data.
- If r is close to −1, we say there is a **strong negative correlation** between the two sets.
- If r is close to 0, then there is **no correlation** between the two sets.

Types of Correlation

It is important that you state both the **direction** (positive or negative) and the **strength** of a correlation when asked for the type of correlation.

(i) Strong positive correlation

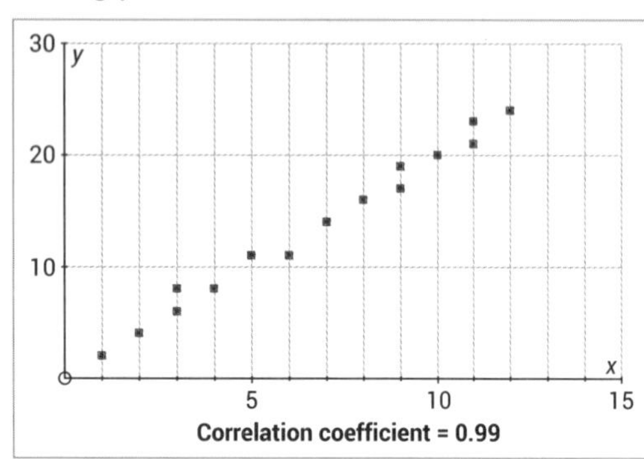

Correlation coefficient = 0.99

(ii) Strong negative correlation

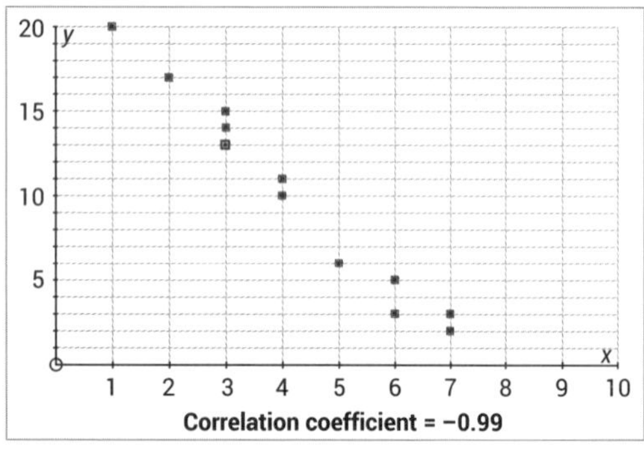

Correlation coefficient = −0.99

(iii) Weak positive correlation

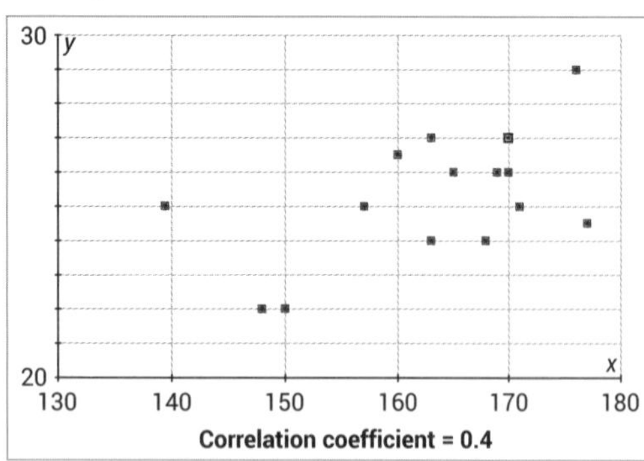

Correlation coefficient = 0.4

For our course, we will not be asked to evaluate r.

(iv) Weak negative correlation

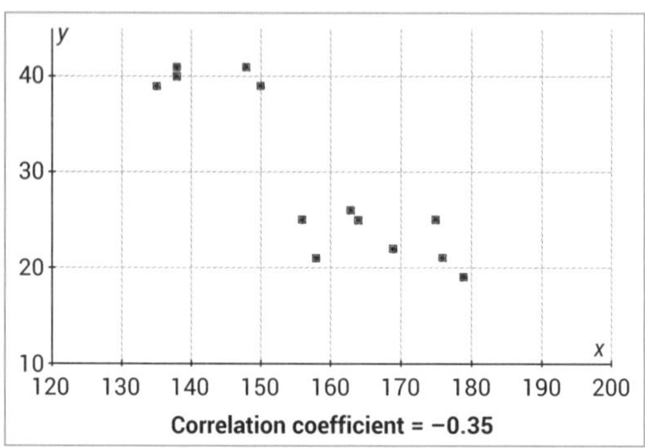

Correlation coefficient = −0.35

(v) No correlation

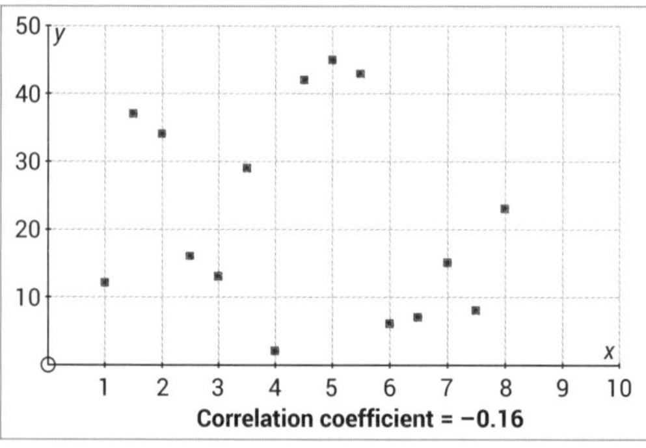

Correlation coefficient = −0.16

r-value	Correlation
$r = 1$	Perfect positive
$0.8 \leqslant r < 1$	Strong positive
$0.5 \leqslant r < 0.8$	Moderate positive
$0 < r < 0.5$	Weak positive
$r = 0$	Zero
$-0.5 < r < 0$	Weak negative
$-0.8 < r \leqslant -0.5$	Moderate negative
$-1 < r \leqslant -0.8$	Strong negative
$r = -1$	Perfect negative

Worked Example 13.7

At the end of a marathon, eight athletes are randomly selected. All of the athletes are asked to give their age and their time (in minutes) for the race. The results are given in the table below.

Age	33	33	31	26	26	25	30	29
Time	132.6	132.1	133.1	134.0	134.1	134.6	133	133.5

(i) Draw a scatter graph of the data.

(ii) What is the type of correlation between the two sets of data?

(iii) Describe the correlation between age and time.

(iv) Explain why the correlation described in part (iii) will probably not apply for athletes in the 54–64 age bracket.

Solution

(i)

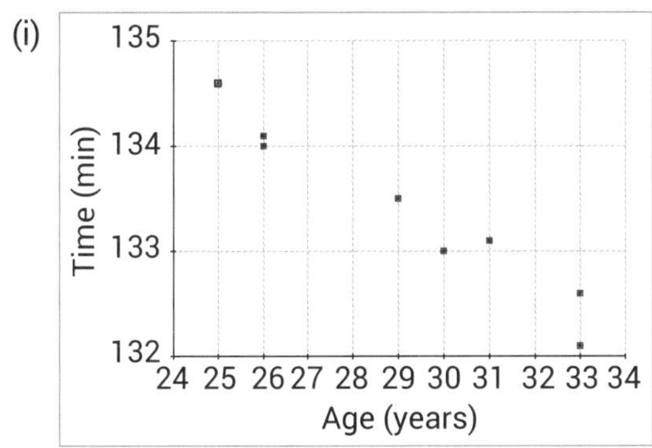

(ii) There is a strong negative correlation between the two sets of data.

(iii) As age increases, the times, in general, decrease.

(iv) In the 54–64 age bracket, one would expect marathon times to increase as athletes get older. In the 24–34 age bracket, times improve as the athletes get older, as marathon athletes generally achieve their best times in their early thirties. Therefore, it is important that we are careful when making predictions that are outside the range of the sample data.

Correlation Versus Causality

In general, the amount of fuel burned by a car depends on the size of its engine, since bigger engines burn more fuel. We say there is a **causal relationship** between the size of the car's engine and the amount of fuel used.

If we find a statistical relationship between two variables, then we cannot always conclude that one of the variables affects the other, i.e. **correlation does not always imply causality**.

During the period 1980–1999, there was a large increase in the sale of calculators and the sale of computers. As the sale of calculators increased, the sale of computers also increased, i.e. there was a strong positive correlation between the sale of calculators and the sale of computers. Did the increase in the sale of calculators cause an increase in the sale of computers? Of course, the answer is no. During this 20-year period, the cost of producing both of these technologies decreased dramatically, leading to an increase in sales. A third variable, the cost of production, was responsible for the increase in the other variables. We call this third variable a **lurking variable**.

Worked Example 13.8

(a) Explain the term causality.

(b) In the following situations, is there likely to be a correlation between the variables and, if so, does the correlation imply causality?

(i) The number of loaves of bread baked and the amount of flour used

(ii) The number of letter boxes and the number of shops in a town

(iii) The time spent exercising and the number of calories burned

Solution

(a) Casuality is when a change in one quantity (variable) causes a change in a second quantity (variable).

(b) (i) There is a positive correlation: as the number of loaves of bread increases, the amount of flour used increases. Correlation does imply causality as the number of loaves baked causes the amount of flour used to increase.

(ii) There is a positive correlation: as the population of the town increases, so too does the number of letter boxes and the number of shops. However, installing more letter boxes will not cause the number of shops to increase. Therefore, correlation does not imply causality.

(iii) There is a positive correlation: as the time spent exercising increases, the number of calories burned also increases. Correlation does imply causality.

Exercise 13.4

1. Four scatter graphs are shown.

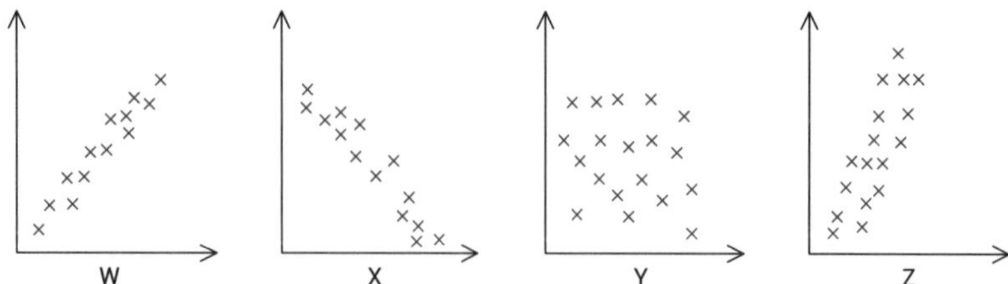

(i) Identify the graphs with positive correlation.

(ii) Which graph has negative correlation?

(iii) Which graph has the correlation coefficient that is closest to zero?

2. Four scatter graphs are shown below.

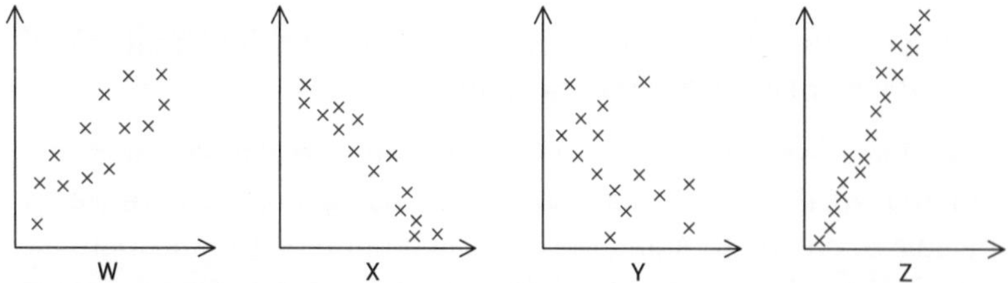

(i) Identify the graph with the strongest positive correlation.

(ii) Identify the graph with the weakest negative correlation.

(iii) Which graph has the strongest correlation?

3. The heights (in centimetres) and ages (in years) of 10 girls are tabled as follows:

Age	8	9	9	10	11	12	12	13	14	15
Height	145	139	140	142	147	154	153	158	160	162

(i) Using suitable scales, plot the scatter diagram for these results.

(ii) Describe the correlation between age and height.

4. The marks obtained by eight candidates in two tests – Maths and Science – are as follows:

Maths	48	87	56	90	59	82	62	78
Science	50	82	58	80	65	70	80	76

(i) Plot the marks on a scatter diagram.

(ii) How are scores in Maths tests correlated with scores in Science tests?

5. A teacher decides to investigate the connection between progress at school and the number of hours of TV watched per week. He collects data from 10 randomly selected students. The data includes the number of hours of TV watched by each student and his/her mean mark across all subjects in a recent end-of-term test.

TV hours	21	4	9	11	12	7	13	5	25	14
Average mark	47	76	70	55	65	68	50	70	40	55

(i) Represent the data on a scatter graph.

(ii) Using your graph, estimate the correlation coefficient.

(iii) Describe the correlation between number of hours of TV watched and the mean mark obtained.

(iv) Explain the term 'bivariate data'.

6. For each of the diagrams below, describe the correlation.

(i)

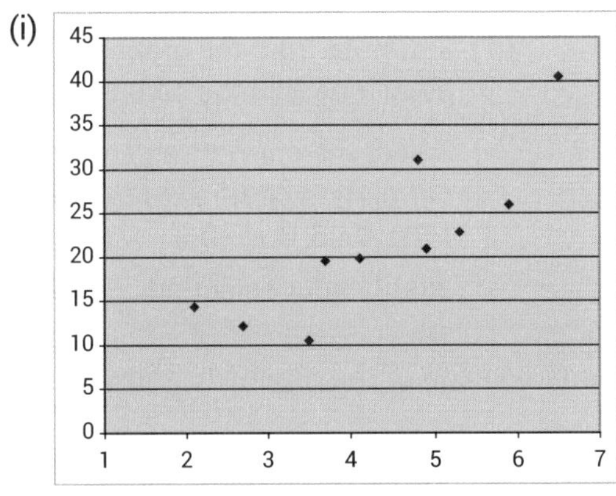

(ii)

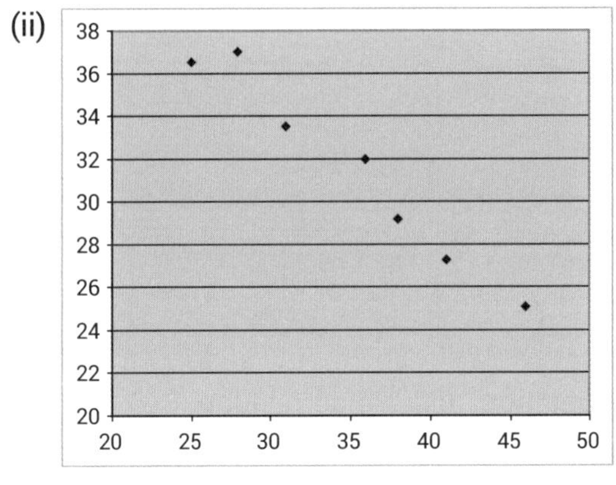

(iii)

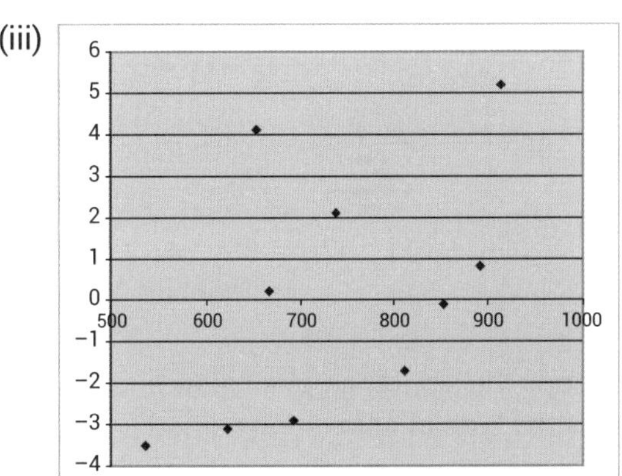

(iv)

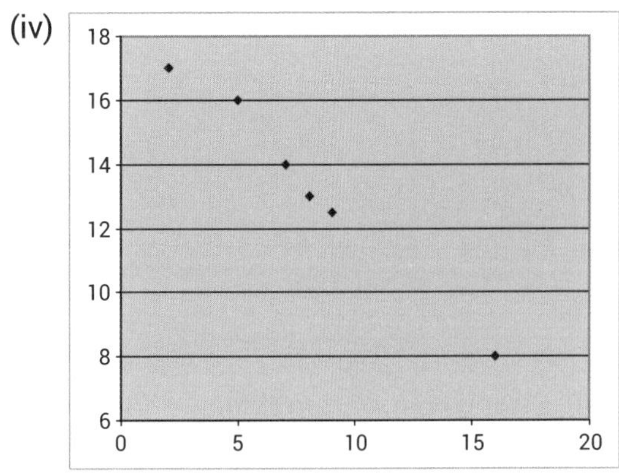

(v)

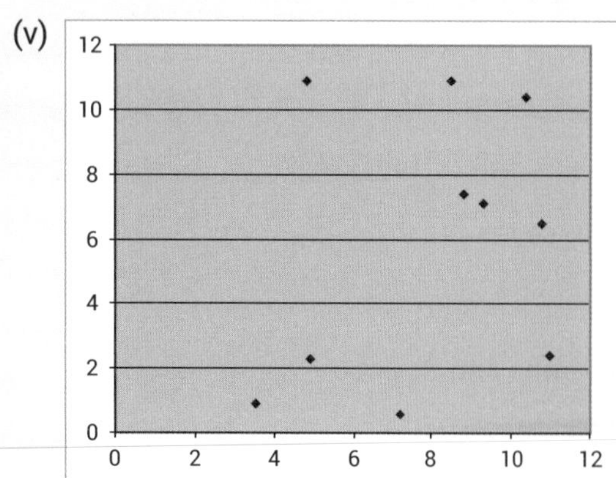

(vi)

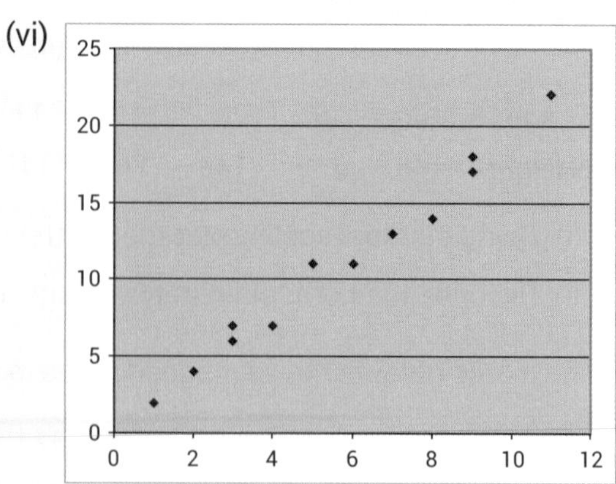

7. Consider the following situations. State whether the variables are correlated and, if so, does the correlation imply causality.

(a) Ice cream sales and the number of shark attacks on swimmers

(b) Shoe size and reading age in primary school children

(c) The amount you pay for a house and the amount you pay for a car

(d) Burning fossil fuels and increased global warming

(e) Sugar consumption and the area of sea ice cover in the Arctic

8. The petal width and petal length of a random sample of 150 irises are plotted on the scatter graph below. Three different classes of iris are included in the sample. All measurements are in centimetres.

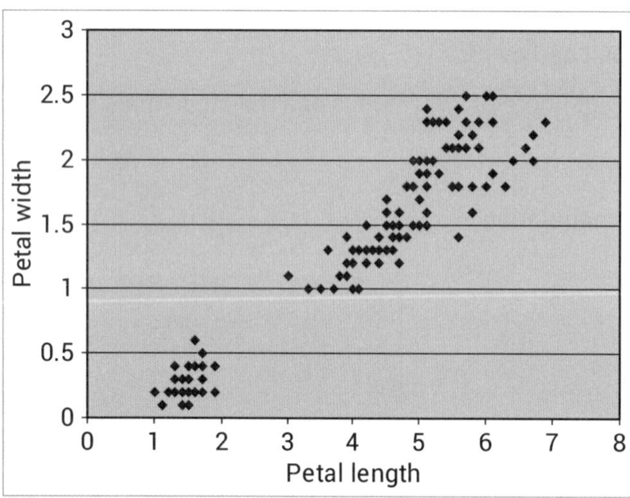

(i) Describe the correlation between petal length and petal width.

(ii) How many irises in the sample had a petal width of 2.5 cm?

(iii) How many irises in the sample had a petal length of 2.5 cm?

(iv) Estimate from the graph the longest petal length in the sample.

(v) Select the correct value of the correlation coefficient from this list: −0.2, 0.96, 0.1, −0.8.
Justify your selection.

9. Copy the scatter graphs below and mark **ten or more** points on each of the graphs to show an example of the type of correlation named under each graph.

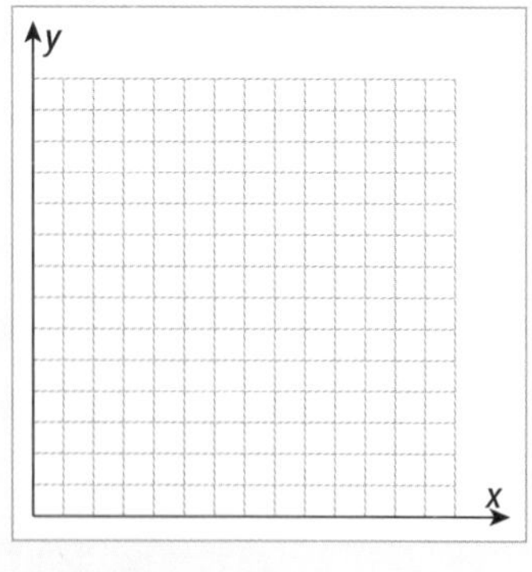

(i) Strong positive correlation

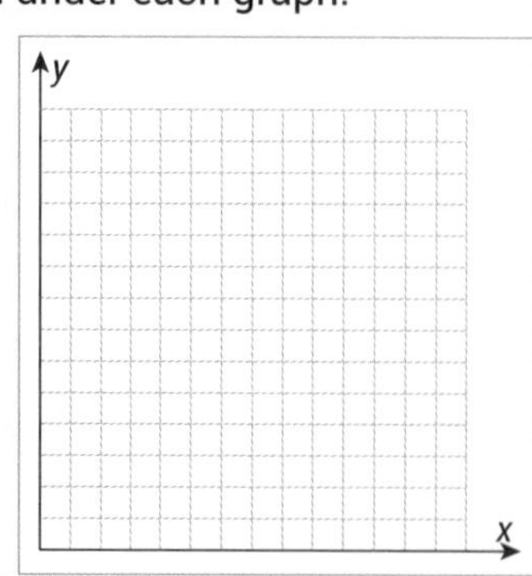

(ii) Strong negative correlation

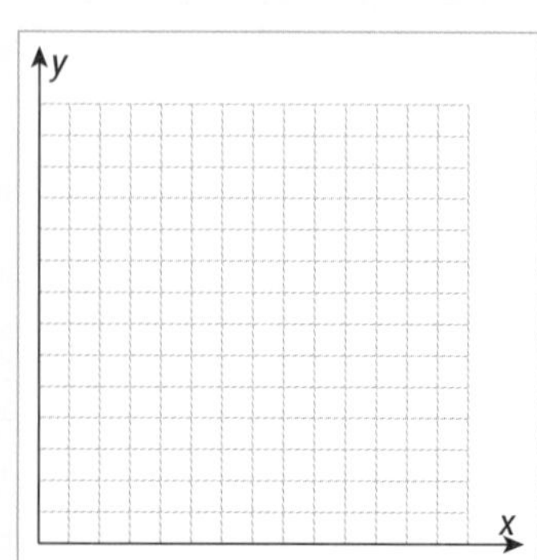

(iii) No correlation

10. The *King of the Hill* triathlon race in Kinsale consists of a 750-metre swim, followed by a 20-kilometre cycle, followed by a 5-kilometre run.

The questions below are based on data from 224 athletes who completed this triathlon in 2010.

Máire is analysing data from the race, using statistical software. She has a data file with each competitor's time for each part of the race, along with various other details of the competitors.

Máire produces histograms of the times for the three events. Here are the three histograms.

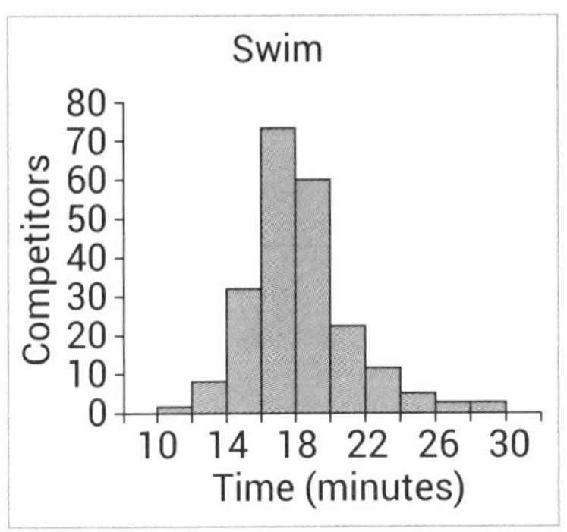

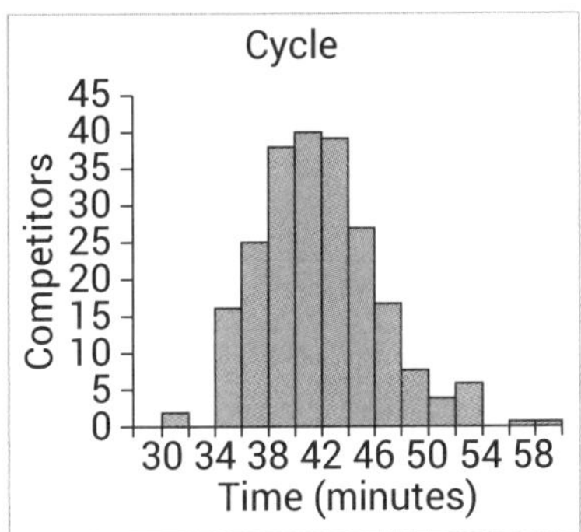

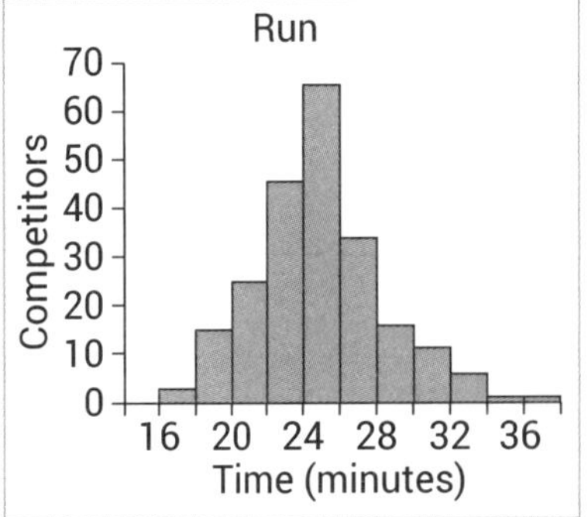

(a) Máire is interested in the relationship between the athletes' performance in the run and in the cycle. She produces the following scatter diagram.

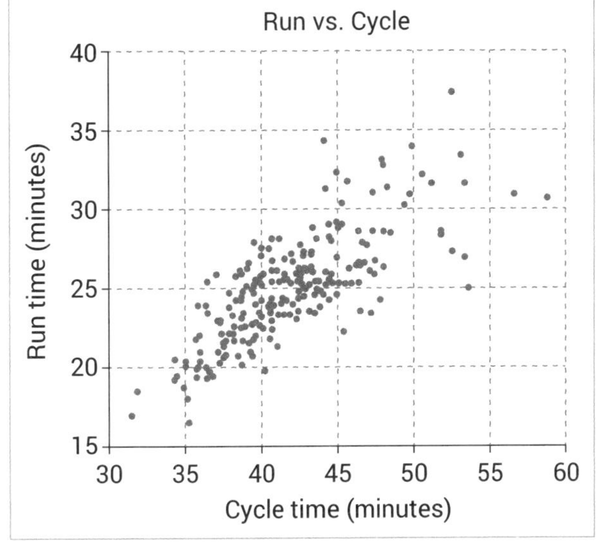

(i) The correlation coefficient between the times for these two events is one of the numbers below. Which is the correct answer?

A. 0.95 **B.** 0.77 **C.** 0.13 **D.** −0.13 **E.** −0.77 **F.** −0.95

(ii) Frank was the slowest person in the run. How many people took longer to complete the cycle than Frank did?

(iii) Brian did not enter this race. Suppose that he had, and suppose that he completed the cycle in 52 minutes and the run in 18 minutes.

Explain why this performance would have been very unusual.

(b) Máire knows already that the male athletes tend to be slightly faster than the female athletes. She also knows that athletes can get slower as they get older. She thinks that male athletes in their forties might be about the same as female athletes in their thirties. She decides to draw a back-to-back stem-and-leaf diagram of the times of these two groups for the swim. There were 28 females in their thirties and 32 males in their forties. Here is the diagram:

Female, 30–39 years		Male, 40–49 years
4	13	
	14	9
1 0	15	1 3 4 5 6
9 8 8 7 3 2 2	16	3 4 6 7 7 8
6 4 3 2	17	6 7 7
1	18	0 1 3 8 9
9 6 3 1 0 0	19	0 0 1 2 3 4
	20	3 9 9
3 3 2	21	2 2
4	22	
	23	0
8	24	
	25	
5	26	
	27	
	28	
7	29	

Key: 1|18 = 18.1 minutes Key: 14|9 = 14.9 minutes

(i) Describe what differences, if any, there are between the two distributions above.

(ii) Máire drew the diagram because she thought that these two groups would be about the same. Do you think that the diagram would cause Máire to confirm her belief or change it? Give reasons for your answer.

Revision Exercises

1. A random sample of 90 workers revealed that the car was the most popular mode of transport for getting to work. The results of the survey are given in the table below.

Mode	Car	Bus	Bike	Walk
Number	40	20	15	15

(i) Represent the data using a pie chart.

(ii) Is this an example of categorical data or numerical data? Explain.

(iii) What percentage of the group walked to work?

2. The following data was downloaded from the CensusAtSchools database:

Right-handed	Right-handed	Right-handed	Right-handed	Right-handed
Ambidextrous	Right-handed	Left-handed	Right-handed	Right-handed

(i) Show the data on a frequency table.

(ii) Represent the information on a pie chart.

(iii) You would like to collect this data from your class. What question should you pose?

(iv) Using your question from (iii), collect the data from your class.

(v) Represent the information on a pie chart.

(vi) Find the percentage of students that are right-handed in the CensusAtSchools sample.

(vii) Find the percentage of students in your class that are right-handed.

3. The marks, out of 5, in a Maths quiz for a class of 20 pupils are as follows:

4	2	3	5	4
1	1	2	3	5
4	3	1	5	3
3	1	3	5	3

(i) Show the data on a frequency table.

(ii) Represent the data on a line plot.

(iii) If 2 is the mark needed to pass the test, then how many students failed the test?

(iv) What percentage of students passed the test?

(v) Represent the data on a pie chart.

(vi) If you wanted to find the number of students who got a mark of 3, would you consult the line plot or the pie chart? Why?

4. A company has been asked to design and market a magazine for teenagers. Explain what primary data sources and secondary data sources the company might use in its research.

5. In 'The Effects of Temperature on Marathon Runners' Performance' by David Martin and John Buoncristiani (*Chance*, 2012), high temperatures and times (in minutes) were given for women who won the New York City marathon in recent years. The results are shown in the table below.

Temp. (°F)	55	61	49	62	70	73	51	57
Time (min)	145.28	148.72	148.30	148.10	147.62	146.40	144.67	147.53

(i) Represent the data on a scatter graph.

(ii) Select the correct value of the correlation coefficient from this list: –0.94, –0.12, 0.18, 0.94.

(iii) Does it appear that winning times are affected by temperature? Explain your answer.

6. A sample of young people was asked how many songs were downloaded on their phones. Here are the results:

401	412	422	430	424
425	440	412	402	472
426	457	458	438	472
464	402	409	482	467

(i) How many young people were surveyed?

(ii) Represent the data on a stem-and-leaf diagram.

(iii) What percentage of those surveyed had fewer than 450 songs?

(iv) You decide to carry out a similar survey in your school. Outline the method you would use to select a sample.

STATISTICS I

7. Comment on the reliability of the following ways of finding a sample.
Suggest a more reliable method where necessary.
   (i) Find out how many people have computers in their home by interviewing people outside a computer shop.
   (ii) Find out whether the potatoes are cooked by testing one with a fork.
   (iii) Find out the most popular make of car by counting 100 cars in a five-star hotel car park.
   (iv) You decide to do a survey on the amount of pocket money received by students in your school. You use your phone and ring 15 of your friends. All respond to the survey.

8. The manager of a company relies on travelling salespeople to sell the company's products. She wishes to investigate the relationship between sales and the amount of time spent with customers. She collects data from 10 salespeople. This data includes the sales for the month (in euro) and the time (in hours) spent with customers. The results are given in the table below.

Time (hours)	3.1	4.5	3.8	5.2	6.0	4.1	5.5	5.2	5.0	7.0
Sales	1,648	2,000	1,800	2,440	2,860	2,000	2,440	2,400	2,280	3,200

   (i) Represent the data on a scatter graph.
   (ii) Select the correct value of the correlation coefficient from this list: –0.98, –0.4, 0.5, 0.99.
   (iii) Describe the correlation between sales and time spent with customers.

9. The ages of all the teachers in a school are as follows:

21, 21, 22, 23, 23, 25, 27, 28, 30, 31 32, 34, 34, 35, 37, 38, 39, 40, 40, 41, 42, 42, 43, 44, 44, 44, 45, 46, 46, 47, 49, 49, 50, 50, 50, 54, 55, 57, 57, 58, 59, 59, 60, 60, 63, 63, 64

   (i) Copy and complete the frequency table below.

Age (years)	20–30	30–40	40–50	50–60	60–70
Frequency					

   Note: 20–30 means 20 or more but less than 30, and so on.
   (ii) Construct a histogram to represent the data.
   (iii) Describe the distribution.

10. A random sample of 500 households in Dublin is selected and several questions are asked of the householders. Which of the following statements are **not** correct?
   (a) Total household income is ordinal categorical data.
   (b) The number of persons in the household is discrete data.
   (c) Socioeconomic status is coded as 1 = low income, 2 = middle income and 3 = high income, and is nominal categorical data.
   (d) The primary language used at home is nominal categorical data.

   Now correct the incorrect statements.

Exam Questions

1. The heights of a random sample of 1,000 students were collected and recorded.

   (a) Tick one box from the table below to indicate how you would categorise the type of data collected. Explain your choice.

Categorical Nominal	
Categorical Ordinal	
Numerical Discrete	
Numerical Continuous	

   (b) The sample of 1,000 students was made up of 500 boys and 500 girls. The data from the 500 girls was used to create the information shown in Table 1.

   (i) Use the data in Table 1 to complete Table 2 by finding the percentage of girls in each of the height categories.

Table 1 (Girls)								
Height (cm)	145–150	150–155	155–160	160–165	165–170	170–175	175–180	180–185
Number of girls	15	48	80	112	125	81	29	10

Table 2 (Girls, %)								
Height (cm)	145–150	150–155	155–160	160–165	165–170	170–175	175–180	180–185
Percentage of girls				22.4	25			

   (ii) Use the data in Table 2 to draw a histogram showing the percentage of girls in each height category.

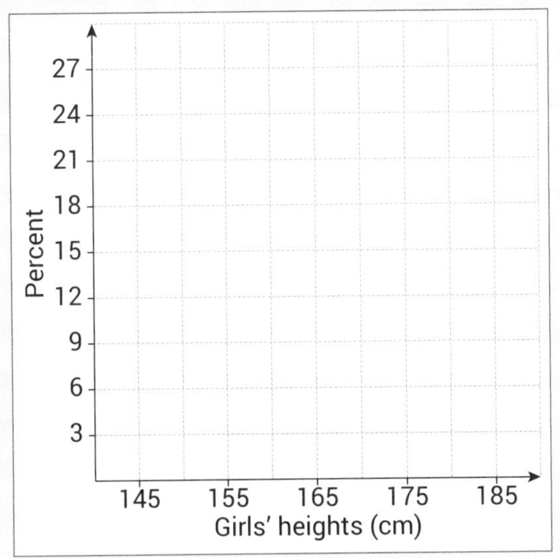

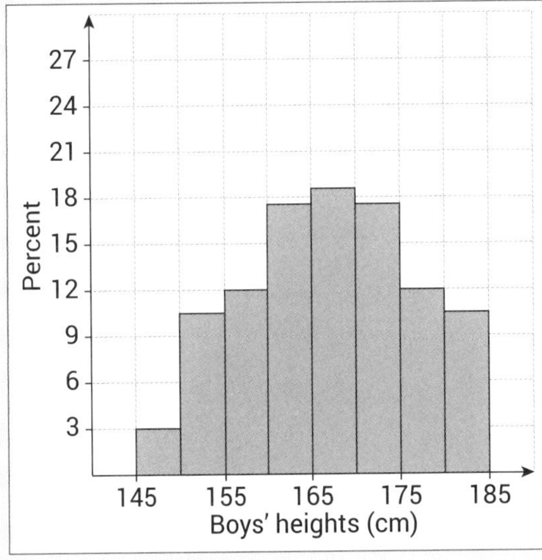

   (iii) A histogram showing the percentage of boys in each height category is given above. John examines both histograms and comments that 'There are roughly twice as many boys as girls in the 175 to 180 cm category'. Do the histograms support his claim? Explain your answer.

   (iv) Mary examines both histograms and comments that 'I see that there are more tall girls than tall boys'. Do the two histograms support her claim? Explain your answer.

SEC Leaving Certificate Ordinary Level, Paper 2, 2015

2. One of the items of information gathered in a census is the *size* of every household. The size of the household is the number of people living in it. The following table shows the number of 'Permanent Private Households' of each size in Ireland, according to the census held in various years from 1926 to 2006. For the purposes of this question, you should ignore the fact that there are also other types of household in Ireland.

	1 person	2 people	3 people	4 people	5 people	6 people	7 people	8 people	9 people	⩾10 people	All sizes
1926	51,537	98,437	102,664	96,241	82,324	65,310	48,418	33,297	21,089	23,361	622,678
1946	68,881	118,738	116,401	103,423	84,437	62,955	44,028	28,503	17,970	17,318	662,654
1966	88,989	139,541	114,436	97,058	79,320	61,068	42,512	27,098	16,550	20,732	687,304
1986	176,017	195,647	143,142	155,534	127,336	83,657	44,139	23,088	8,438	7,884	964,882
2006	326,134	413,786	264,438	243,303	136,979	54,618	15,141	5,050	1,719	1,128	1,462,296

Source: Central Statistics Office, http://www.cso.ie/statistics/HousingandHouseholds.htm

(a) Use the information in the table to answer the following:

(i) In 1966, how many households had exactly 8 people living in them?

(ii) In 1986, how many **people** lived in households of exactly 7 people?

(b) Conor, Fiona and Ray were each asked, separately, to make a presentation about the patterns they could see in the data. They each spoke for one minute and showed one slide. The slides they made are shown below. By considering the slides, state the main point or points that each of them was trying to make.

Conor's slide

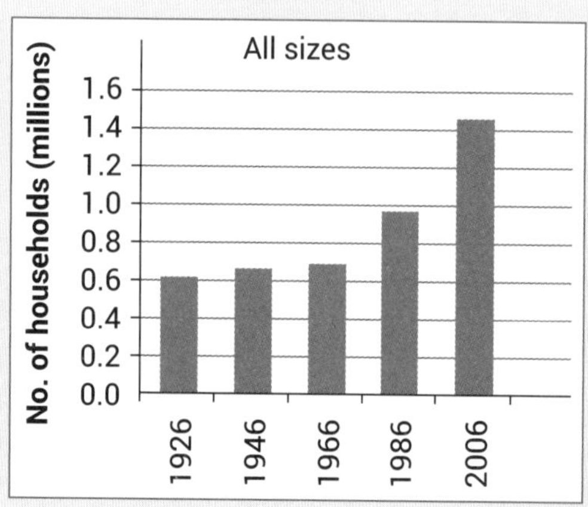

Fiona's slide

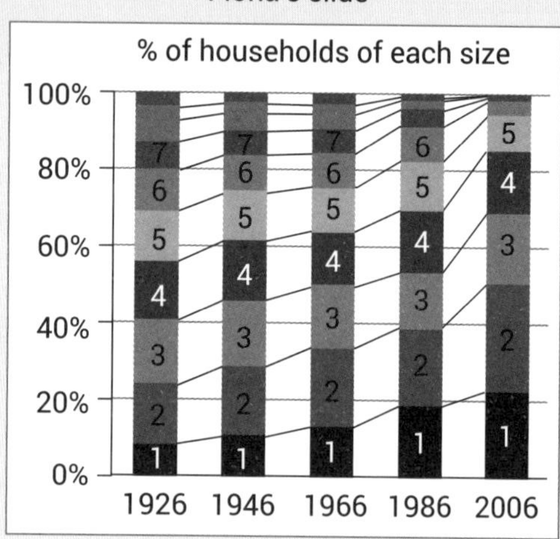

Ray's slide

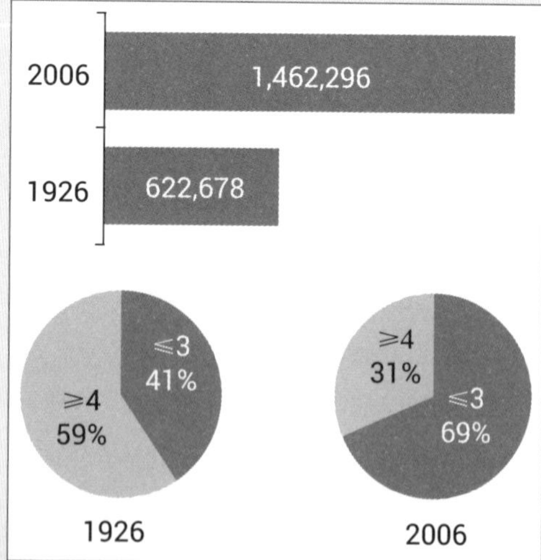

(c) A household is randomly selected from among all the households in 2006. What is the probability that it has seven or eight people?

(d) Mary wonders whether there are differences in size between the households in South Dublin and those in Dublin City. She gets the relevant data for 2006 and makes the following charts.

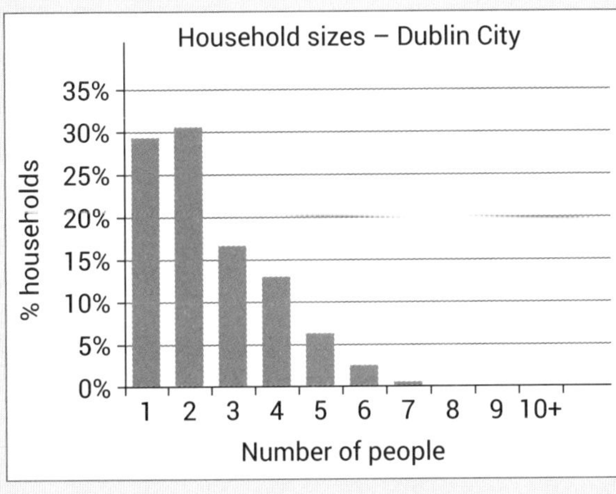

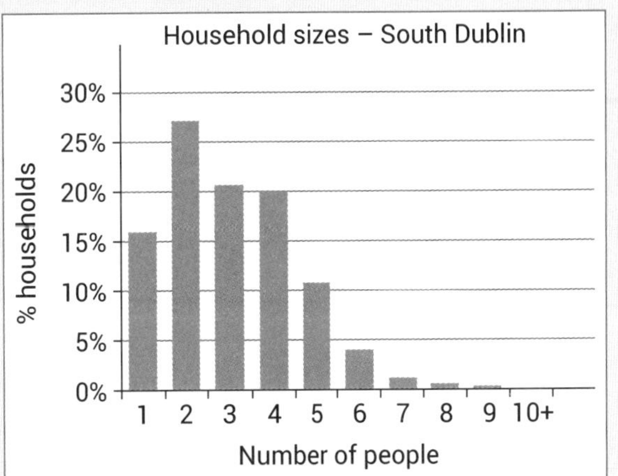

(i) Describe what differences there are, if any, between the two distributions above.

(ii) There are approximately 81,000 households in South Dublin. Approximately how many people live in 4-person households in South Dublin?

(iii) A person is selected at random from among all those living in Dublin City. Which is more likely: that the person lives alone, or that the person lives in a three-person household? Explain your answer.

SEC Leaving Certificate Ordinary Level, Paper 2, 2011

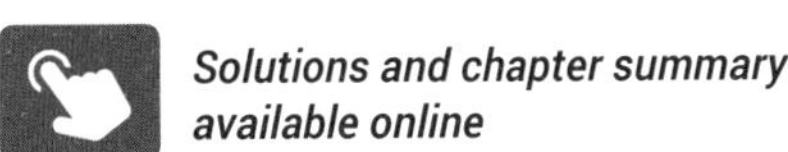

Solutions and chapter summary available online

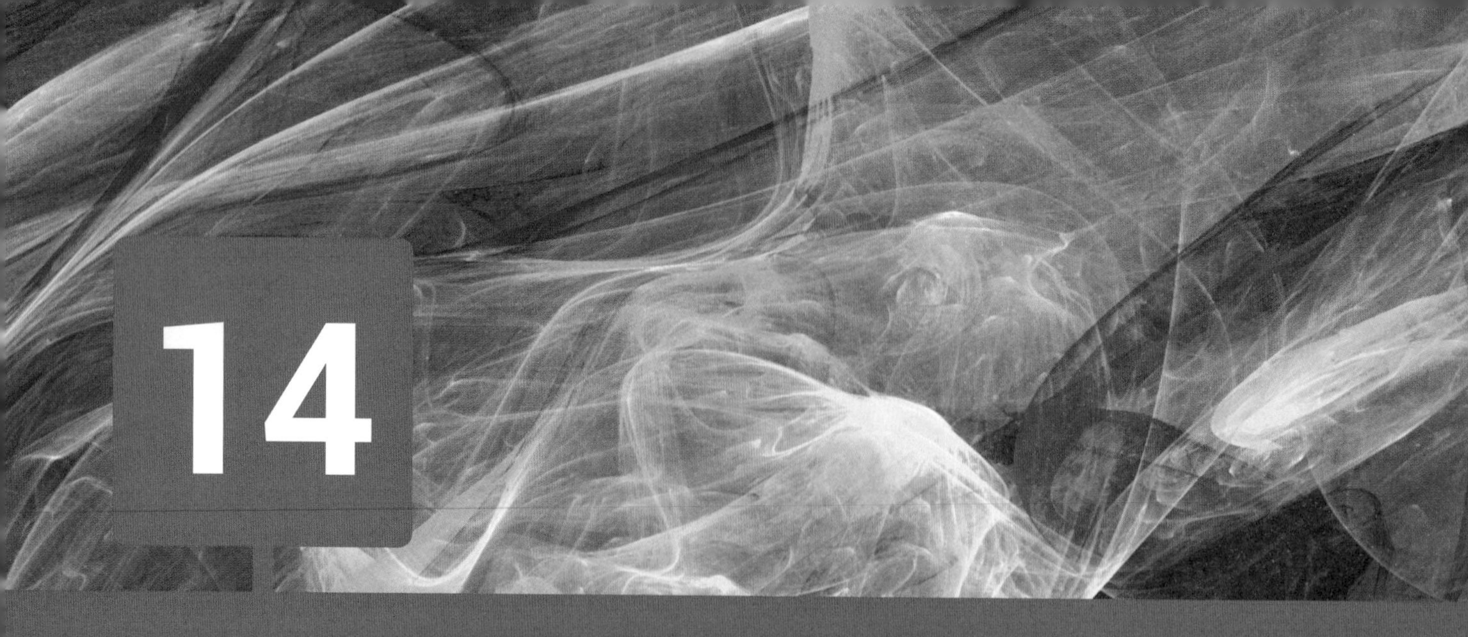

14

Statistics II

In this chapter you will learn how to:

- Engage in discussions about the purpose of statistics and recognise misconceptions and misuses of statistics
- Use a variety of summary statistics to describe data: central tendency – mean, median and mode; variability – range
- Recognise standard deviation and interquartile range as measures of variability
- Use a calculator to calculate standard deviation
- Find quartiles and the interquartile range
- Use the interquartile range appropriately when analysing data
- Recognise the existence of outliers
- Recognise how sampling variability influences the use of sample information to make statements about the population
- Use appropriate tools to describe variability drawing inferences about the population from the sample
- Interpret the analysis and relate the interpretation to the original question
- Make decisions based on the empirical rule
- Recognise the concept of an hypothesis test
- Calculate the margin of error, $\left(\frac{1}{\sqrt{n}}\right)$ for a population proportion
- Conduct an hypothesis test on a population proportion using the margin of error

You should remember...

- How to represent data graphically in a variety of ways
- How to calculate percentage error
- All content presented in Chapter 13 Statistics I

Key words

- Mean, median and mode
- Range
- Quartiles
- Interquartile range
- Standard deviation
- Mid-interval values
- The normal distribution
- The empirical rule
- Margin of error
- Population proportion
- Hypothesis testing
- Sampling variability

14.1 Measures of Central Tendency: Mean, Mode and Median

When statisticians describe and compare data sets, they often look for one number to represent each data set. This number is known as an **average** or a **measure of centre**. Measures of centre are sometimes called **measures of location**. There are different ways of working out the average. We will look at three averages: the mean, the mode and the median.

The Mean

The **mean** of a set of values is the sum of all the values divided by the number of values.

The **mean** uses all values in the data set.

For example, the mean of the set {2, 2, 3, 5, 9, 9} is:

$$\text{Mean} = \frac{2+2+3+5+9+9}{6} = \frac{30}{6} = 5$$

The mean can be used with numerical data.

The Mode

The **mode** of a data set is the data point that has the greatest frequency (occurs the most often).

For example, the **mode** of the set {2, 2, 2, 3, 3, 3, 3, 5, 5} is 3.

The mode can be used with numerical data, but can also be used with categorical data. For example, the mode of the set {red, red, green} is red.

Sometimes a data set has more than one mode (for example, {1, 1, 2, 2, 3}) or no mode (for example, {2, 3, 5, 6, 11}).

The Median

The **median** of a set of data points is the middle value when the data points are arranged in order.

The **median** is the value that divides an ordered data set into two equal parts.

The first step in finding the median is to arrange the data in order of increasing magnitude. This is called ranking the data. Suppose we want to find the median of the following set:

{4, 7, 11, 9, 12, 10, 8, 11, 14, 2, 6}

Ranking the set gives:

{2, 4, 6, 7, 8, ⑨, 10, 11, 11, 12, 14}

The number in the middle of the ranked set is called the median, which in this case equals 9. There are five values greater than 9 and five values less than 9; therefore 9 has divided the data set into two equal parts.

STATISTICS II

What happens if the set contains an even number of values?
For example, the set {2, 1, 4, 3} contains an even number of values.

First, ranking the set gives {1, 2, 3, 4}. As there are two middle values, the median is the mean of these two numbers. In this case, we sum the two middle numbers, 2 and 3, and divide our result by 2:

$$\text{Median} = \frac{2+3}{2} = \frac{5}{2} = 2.5$$

Worked Example 14.1

A golfer keeps a record of his scores in competitions during 2016.

Score	75	76	77	78	79
Frequency	4	3	4	7	2

Find:

(i) His mean score for 2016 (ii) His modal score for 2016 (iii) His median score for 2016

Solution

(i)
$$\text{Mean} = \frac{\text{Total of all scores}}{\text{Total number of competitions}}$$
$$= \frac{4(75) + 3(76) + 4(77) + 7(78) + 2(79)}{4+3+4+7+2}$$
$$= \frac{1,540}{20}$$
$\therefore$ Mean score = 77

(ii) Mode = most common score = 78
(78 has the highest frequency)

(iii) There are 20 scores. The middle two numbers of the ranked data are the 10th and 11th numbers. Both these numbers are 77.

$$\text{Median} = \frac{77+77}{2} \Rightarrow \text{Median score} = 77$$

Worked Example 14.2

The stem-and-leaf diagram below displays the predicted high-water tides at the North Wall, Dublin, for 15 consecutive days in April 2017.

Find the median predicted high-water mark at the North Wall during this period.

Stem	Leaf
32	7, 7
33	6, 9
34	9
35	7
36	1
37	0, 3, 7
38	1, 5, 6
39	6
40	1

Key: 33|6 = 3.36 m

Solution

To find the median, cross out the smallest and the largest number (3.27 and 4.01), then the second largest and the second smallest, and so on until you are left with the number in the middle. This number is the median.

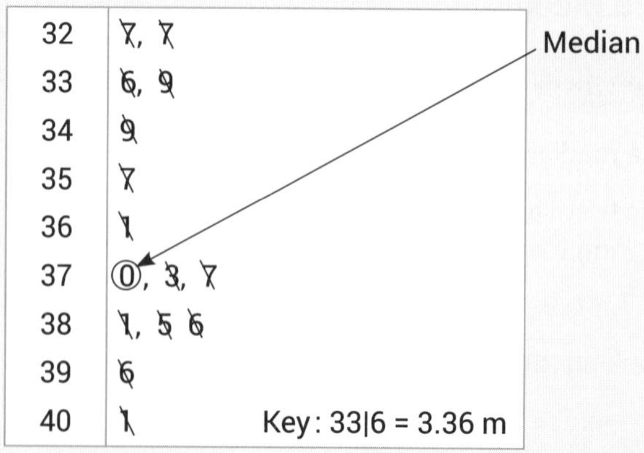

The median predicted high-water mark is 3.70 m.

Mean of a Grouped Frequency Distribution

Consider the grouped frequency table below. The table summarises the resting pulse rates of 82 adults in beats per minute.

Pulse rate	60–70	70–80	80–90	90–100	100–110	110–120
Frequency	5	8	22	29	13	5

Note: 60–70 means that 60 is included but 70 is not, and so on.

We can see from the table that five people had a pulse rate of 60–70 beats per minute. However, the table does not tell us the exact pulse rates of each person. In order to estimate the mean resting pulse rate, we must assign each person a resting pulse rate. We choose the mid-interval values as the rate for each group.

Here is how we calculate the mid-interval values (M.I.V.):

M.I.V.	$\frac{60+70}{2}$	$\frac{70+80}{2}$	$\frac{80+90}{2}$	$\frac{90+100}{2}$	$\frac{100+110}{2}$	$\frac{110+120}{2}$
Frequency	5	8	22	29	13	5

We can now continue and estimate the mean:

M.I.V.	65	75	85	95	105	115
Frequency	5	8	22	29	13	5

$$\text{Mean} = \frac{(65)(5) + (75)(8) + (85)(22) + (95)(29) + (105)(13) + (115)(5)}{5 + 8 + 22 + 29 + 13 + 5} = \frac{7{,}490}{82}$$

≈ 91 beats per minute

This answer is correct to the nearest beat.

Exercise 14.1

1. Find the mean of these sets of numbers:

(i) {3, 4, 8, 9, 9}

(ii) {7, 8, 9, 10, 11, 12, 13}

(iii) {5, 8, 6, 4, 5, 3, 4}

(iv) {8.2, 7.9, 8.1, 7.8}

(v) {0, 1, 0, 1, 0, 1, 0, 1, 0, 1}

(vi) {−1, −2, −3, −8, −8}

2. Find the median and mode of these sets:

(i) {6, 7, 7, 4, 5, 6, 7}

(ii) {3, 5, 7, 3, 4, 9, 10}

(iii) {6, 2, 2, 2, 6}

(iv) {6, 7, 8, 6, 7, 8, 9, 6, 7, 8, 9, 10}

(v) {0, 0, 0}

3. Aoife is doing a study on the relationship between time (in minutes per day) spent playing computer games and success in exams. She surveys a random sample of students in her school. One question on her survey generated the following data:

Stem	Leaf
2	1, 2, 4, 5, 5, 5, 5, 6, 7, 7, 8
3	0, 0, 1, 1, 1, 2, 2, 3, 3, 6, 7, 8, 8
4	1, 1, 1, 2, 2, 3, 3, 4, 8, 9
5	0, 1, 1, 2, 7, 7
6	1, 2, 2, 6, 6

Key 4|1 = 41 min

(i) Suggest a question that generated this data.

(ii) What is the size of the sample?

(iii) Find the mode of the data.

(iv) Find the median of the data.

STATISTICS II

4. The table below shows mean monthly sea temperatures, in degrees Celsius, at Malin Head, Co. Donegal, for the year 2009. Mean monthly readings for the period 1961–1990 are also given.

Month	2009	1961–1990
January	7.3	7.3
February	6.9	6.7
March	7.6	7
April	8.8	8.1
May	10.4	9.9
June	12.4	12
July	14.3	13.8
August	15.3	14.6
September	14.4	14
October	13.0	12.4
November	11.1	10.2
December	8.8	8.5

Source: http://www.met.ie/marine/marine_climatology.asp

(i) Using the mean monthly readings, estimate the mean annual sea temperature at Malin Head for 2009. (Give your answer correct to two decimal places.)

(ii) Using the mean monthly readings, estimate the mean annual sea temperature at Malin Head for the period 1961 to 1990. (Give your answer correct to two decimal places.)

(iii) Comment on the difference between the 2009 mean figure and the 1961–1990 mean figure.

(iv) Is the comparison made in part (iii) a fair comparison? Explain.

5. A teacher marks a test for 20 students and summarises the results in a stem-and-leaf diagram.

Stem	Leaf
0	6
1	3
2	1
3	6, 7
4	3, 3, 3, 5, 5
5	3, 8, 9
6	3, 7
7	7, 8
8	2, 5
9	9 Key 6|3 = 63%

(i) Find the mode of the data.

(ii) Find the median of the data.

(iii) How many students scored higher than the median?

(iv) Explain how the median of a data set divides the set.

6. The foot lengths (to the nearest centimetre) of a group of students is given below.

20, 22, 23, 25, 26, 25, 22, 25, 24, 25, 25, 24, 22, 24, 23, 25

(i) Find the mode of the data.

(ii) Rank the data.

(iii) Find the median.

(iv) Find the mean.

7. The stem-and-leaf diagram below displays the weights, in kilograms, of 10-week-old babies.

Stem	Leaf
3	7, 9
4	2, 4, 7, 8, 8, 8
5	0, 1, 3, 6, 7, 7, 9
6	0, 1, 2, 3, 5
7	1, 2 Key 4|2 = 4.2 kg

(i) Find the mode of the data.

(ii) Find the median.

(iii) Find the mean.

8. The table below gives the number of vehicles registered in Ireland for the first time from 2006 to 2015.

Year	2006	2007	2008	2009	2010
New Vehicles	316,140	333,996	282,557	149,389	160,418
Year	2011	2012	2013	2014	2015
New Vehicles	160,777	145,033	164,043	187,920	216,523

Source: http://www.cso.ie/

(i) In what year was the highest number of vehicles registered?

(ii) In what year was the lowest number of vehicles registered?

(iii) What was the mean number of vehicles registered for the first time during these 10 years?

(iv) What was the median number of vehicles registered for the first time during these 10 years?

9. The frequency table below shows the grades achieved by a Fifth Year Maths class in an end-of-term test.

Grade	O1	O2	O3	O4	O5
Number	3	8	7	2	1

(i) What is the mode of this distribution?

(ii) Explain why you cannot write down the mean of this distribution.

10. The length (in minutes) of 20 phone calls made to a school switchboard is shown in the grouped frequency distribution below.

Length (min)	0–2	2–4	4–6	6–8	8–10
Frequency	3	5	6	4	2

Note: 0–2 means 0 is included but 2 is not, etc.

(i) Using mid-interval values, estimate the mean length of a phone call.

(ii) What is the maximum number of calls that could have been longer than 6.2 minutes?

11. The following frequency distribution shows the time (in minutes) taken by a group of 74 people to complete an 8 km run:

Time (min)	30–35	35–40	40–45	45–50	50–55
Frequency	13	13	24		4

Note: 30–35 means 30 is included but 35 is not, etc.

(i) Complete the grouped frequency table.

(ii) Using mid-interval values, estimate the mean time taken to complete the 8 km run.

(iii) What is the maximum number of people who could have completed the run in less than 37 minutes?

12. The frequency distribution below shows the ages of people living in a street.

Age (years)	0–20	20–30	30–50	50–80
Frequency	24	16	41	15

Note: 0–20 means 0 is included but 20 is not, etc.

(i) How many people are living in the street?

(ii) Estimate the mean age.

(iii) What percentage of the people are less than 20 years old?

13. The heights (in centimetres) of a random sample of 1,000 women are given in the frequency distribution below.

Height (cm)	140–145	145–150	150–155	155–160	160–165	165–170	170–175	175–180
Frequency	9	65		325	253	133	31	7

Note: 140–145 means 140 is included but 145 is not, etc.

(i) Complete the grouped frequency table.

(ii) Estimate the mean height.

(iii) Construct a histogram to represent the data.

14. Alice removes all the Aces and picture cards from a deck of playing cards. She then **deals out six** cards. She **reveals four** of the cards to her audience. The four cards revealed are the 3 of Clubs, the 3 of Hearts, the 3 of Spades and the 3 of Diamonds.

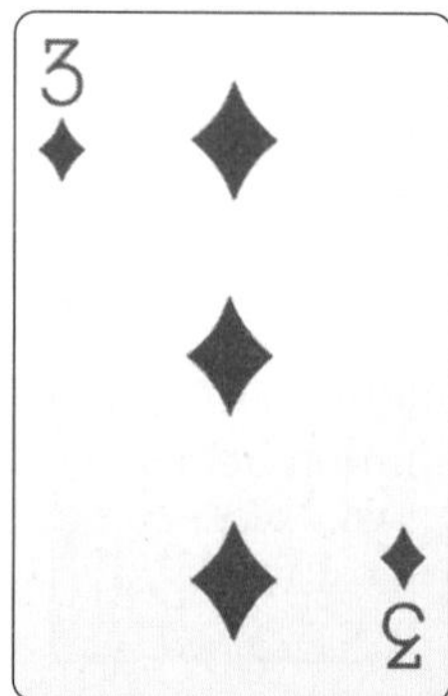

(a) Is it possible for Alice's audience to give:

(i) The median of the six numbers on the cards

(ii) The mode of the six numbers

(iii) The mean of the six numbers

Explain your reasoning in each case.

(b) Alice then reveals that the number on one of the hidden cards is less than 3 and the number on the other hidden card is greater than 3.

(i) What is the smallest possible mean of the six numbers?

(ii) What is the largest possible mean of the six numbers?

(iii) If the mean of the six numbers is 4, find the numbers on the hidden cards.

15. Four girls and six boys received text messages. The mean number of messages received by the four girls was 42, and the mean number of messages received by the six boys was 40.

(i) How many messages in total were received by the girls?

(ii) How many messages in total were received by the boys?

(iii) What was the mean number of messages received by the entire group (girls and boys)?

(iv) Is it possible to say with certainty that a girl must have received the most messages? Explain.

14.2 Deciding Which Average to Use

The mean, median and mode of a set of data are all averages, but each one has a different meaning. The average, or measure of central tendency, that we choose depends on the characteristics of the data set we are studying. The following table will help you decide when to use the mean, the median or the mode.

Average	When to use	Advantages/Disadvantages
Mode	• If data is **categorical**, then the mode is the only sensible measure of centre to use. Therefore, for data on hair colour, eye colour, gender, etc., use only the mode. • The mode can also be used with **numerical** data.	*Advantages* • It can be used with any type of data. • It is easy to find. • It is not affected by extreme values. *Disadvantages* • There is not always a mode, or there are several modes. • For sets of numerical data, the mode can be very different to the mean or median.
Median	• Used with **numerical** data and **ordinal categorical** data. • If there are **outliers** in the data set, or if the distribution is **skewed**, then use the median.	*Advantages* • It is easy to calculate. • It is not affected by outliers or skews.
Mean	• Used **only** with **numerical** data. • If there are **no outliers** and the distribution is **not skewed**, then use the mean.	*Advantage* • It uses all the data. *Disadvantage* • It is affected by outliers and skews.

An **outlier** is an observation that lies an abnormal distance from other values in a data set.

Worked Example 14.3

Eight European professional soccer players are selected at random. They are asked the following question: 'What is the most money any club has paid for you in transfer fees?' Below is the data generated by the question. All amounts are in sterling.

£3 million	£80 million	£5.8 million	£18.25 million
£3.5 million	£3.7 million	£8 million	£7 million

(i) Find the mean transfer fee for the sample (correct to two decimal places).

(ii) Find the median transfer fee.

(iii) Which of the above averages is the most typical of transfer fees?

Solution

(i) Mean $= \dfrac{3 + 80 + 5.8 + 18.25 + 3.5 + 3.7 + 8 + 7}{8}$

$= \dfrac{129.25}{8} \approx$ £16.16 million

(ii) Median = {~~3~~, ~~3.5~~, ~~3.7~~, **5.8**, **7**, ~~8~~, ~~18.25~~, ~~80~~}

$= \dfrac{5.8 + 7}{2} =$ £6.4 million

(iii) The median is the most typical. The extreme value of £80 million drags the mean up and makes it an unrepresentative measure of centre.

In fact, of the eight amounts given, six are less than the mean fee of £16.16 million.

STATISTICS II

Exercise 14.2

1. Decide which average is best for each of the following. Give a reason for your answer.
   (i) The average height of students in your class
   (ii) The average eye colour of all teachers in the school
   (iii) The average mark in a maths exam
   (iv) The average colour of all cars in the school car park
   (v) The average wage of 100 workers in a company, given that 90 of the workers earn between €30,000 and €40,000 per annum, five workers earn between €60,000 and €80,000, and the remaining five workers earn over €600,000 per annum

2. Match the type of average given in Column A with the description given in Column B.

A	B
Median	This average uses all values of numerical data.
Mean	This average is used with categorical data.
Mode	This average is useful with data that contains extreme values.

3. Below is some data selected at random from the CensusAtSchools database. The data gives the different modes of transport a group uses to go to school.

Walk	Bus	Walk	Walk	Walk
Bus	Walk	Car	Car	Bus
Walk	Bus	Car	Walk	Walk
Car	Rail	Bus	Walk	Rail

   (i) What type of data is contained in this sample?
   (ii) What average are you using when you refer to the most popular mode of transport used by these students?

4. Rex has just been given the result of his last Maths test. He does not know the results his classmates received, but would like to know how his result compares with those of his friends. The teacher has given the class the modal mark, the mean mark and the median mark for the test.
   (i) Which average tells Rex whether he is in the top half or the bottom half of the class?
   (ii) Is the modal mark useful to Rex? Explain.
   (iii) Which average tells Rex how well he has done in comparison to everyone else?

5. Find the mean, median and mode of the following set of numbers:

   1, 2, 12, 12, 18, 19, 20, 24, 188

   Which average would you use to describe these numbers? Give a reason for your answer.

6. The number of hours per day that the secretary of a construction firm spends on the phone is recorded. The following data shows the number of hours per day over a 30-day period:

4.21	1.12	0.33	1.1	3.3	3.2	5.2	1.5	3.1	0.5
1.22	2.51	0.8	0.7	1.8	6	1.2	2.5	5.2	1.6
4	1.4	0.9	2.8	5	0.2	1.9	2.3	1.79	4

   (i) Is this data discrete or continuous? Explain.
   (ii) Complete the frequency table below.

Hours	0–1	1–2	2–3	3–4	4–5	5–6	6–7
Tally							
No. of days							

Note: 0–1 means 0 is included but 1 is not, etc.

(iii) Draw a histogram of the distribution.

(iv) Describe the distribution.

(v) Rank the raw data and find the median.

(vi) Using mid-interval values, estimate the mean of the distribution.

(vii) Now, using the raw data, calculate the mean. Answer correct to three significant figures.

(viii) What is the percentage error in the estimated mean? Answer correct to two decimal places.

(ix) Which is the better measure of centre, the mean or the median? Explain.

7. The following are the daily maximum temperatures in Dubai for the month of June (in degrees Celsius):

29.2	29.4	34.1	36.3	36.5	32.1	32.0	35.7	35.6	34.9
36.2	32.3	32.6	36.5	33.8	32.1	32.2	38.8	36.5	35.7
31.1	33.9	34.7	34.3	37.3	40	33.8	32.2	40	34.2

(i) Is this data discrete or continuous? Explain.

(ii) Complete the frequency table below.

Max. temp.	29–31	31–33	33–35	35–37	37–39	39–41
Tally						
No. of days						

Note: 29–31 means 29 is included but 31 is not, etc.

(iii) Draw a histogram of the distribution.

(iv) Describe the distribution.

(v) Rank the raw data and find the median.

(vi) Using mid-interval values, estimate the mean of the distribution.

(vii) Now, using the raw data, calculate the mean.

(viii) What is the percentage error in the estimated mean?

14.3 Measures of Variation I: Range and Interquartile Range

Measures of centre supply us with one number to describe a set of data. However, such numbers give no indication of data variation or data spread (dispersion).

Consider the sets A = {8, 8, 9, 11, 14} and B = {1, 3, 8, 17, 21}.

- The mean of set A = $\frac{8+8+9+11+14}{5} = \frac{50}{5} = 10$.
- The mean of set B = $\frac{1+3+8+17+21}{5} = \frac{50}{5} = 10$.

Both sets have the same mean, but the members of set A are more tightly bunched around the mean than the members of set B. To measure the spread of values, we could use the **range**.

The **range** of a set of numerical data is the difference between the maximum value and the minimum value in the data set.

Range = Maximum value − Minimum value

$\text{Range}_A = 14 - 8 = 6$ $\text{Range}_B = 21 - 1 = 20$

This indicates that the elements of set B have a greater spread of values.

Quartiles and the Interquartile Range

Quartiles divide a data set into four parts. There are three quartiles: the lower quartile, the median and the upper quartile. The **interquartile range** is the difference between the first, or lower, quartile (Q_1) and the third, or upper, quartile (Q_3). The interquartile range (or IQR) is more reliable than the range as a measure of spread, as it is not affected by extreme values (outliers). The IQR tells us how spread out the middle 50% of the data is.

Q_1, the **lower quartile** of a ranked set of data, is a value such that one-quarter of the values are less than or equal to it.
Q_2, the **second quartile**, is the median of the data.
Q_3, the **upper quartile** of a ranked set of data, is a value such that three-quarters of the values are less than or equal to it.
The **interquartile range** = $Q_3 - Q_1$.

Different acceptable methods exist for finding the interquartile range (IQR). Depending on the method used, answers may vary slightly. Two different methods for finding the interquartile range of the data set {7, 5, 1, 27, 2, 6, 19, 9, 12, 18, 15} are outlined below.

Interquartile range = $Q_3 - Q_1$

Method 1

Step 1

Rank the data.

{1, 2, 5, 6, 7, 9, 12, 15, 18, 19, 27}

Step 2

Find the median of the data set.

{~~1~~, ~~2~~, ~~5~~, ~~6~~, ~~7~~, (9) ~~12~~, ~~15~~, ~~18~~, ~~19~~, ~~27~~}

Median = 9

Step 3

If the data set contains an odd number of data points, then find the median of the set containing all data points less than the median. If the data set contains an even number of data points, then find the median of the set containing all data points less than or equal to the median.

Find the median of the set {~~1~~, ~~2~~, 5, ~~6~~, ~~7~~}.
[Set of numbers below the median in the original data set]

$Q_1 = 5$ (Lower quartile)

Find the median of the set {~~12~~, ~~15~~, 18, ~~19~~, ~~27~~}.
[Set of numbers above the median in the original data set]

If the original set contains an even number of data points, then include the median in this set.

$Q_3 = 18$ (Upper quartile)

Step 4

Subtract Q_1 from Q_3 to find the interquartile range.

IQR = 18 − 5
= 13

Method 2

Step 1

Rank the data.

{1, 2, 5, 6, 7, 9, 12, 15, 18, 19, 27}

Step 2

Count the number of data points in the set.
There are 11 data points in the set.

Step 3

Find $\frac{1}{4}$ of 11, which is 2.75. As this is not a whole number, round up to the nearest whole number (always round up), which is 3. The third value in the data set is Q_1, the lower quartile.

$Q_1 = 5$

Step 4

Find $\frac{3}{4}$ of 11, which is 8.25. Round up to the nearest whole number, which is 9. The ninth value in the data set is Q_3, the upper quartile.

$Q_3 = 18$

Step 5

Subtract Q_1 from Q_3 to find the interquartile range.

IQR = 18 − 5
= 13

Worked Example 14.4

The stem-and-leaf plot below gives the ages of 31 people attending a meeting about a government proposal not to grant medical cards to all people over the age of 70.

Calculate:

(i) Q_1, the lower quartile

(ii) Q_3, the upper quartile

(iii) The interquartile range (IQR)

(iv) Explain the meaning of the IQR in the context of this question.

Stem	Leaf
5	1, 4, 4, 4
5	5, 9, 9, 9, 9
6	3, 3, 3, 4
6	5, 6, 6, 7, 7, 8, 8, 9
7	1, 1, 2, 3, 3, 3, 3, 3, 4
7	5 Key: 6|6 = 66 years

Solution

Lower quartile

Stem	Leaf
5	1, 4, 4, 4
5	5, 9, 9, (9), 9
6	3, 3, 3, 4, 5
6	6, 6, 7, 7, 8, 8, 9
7	1, 1, (2), 3, 3, 3, 3, 3, 4
7	5 Key: 6|6 = 66 years

Upper quartile

(i) **Step 1**

Count the number of leaves on the stem-and-leaf plot. There are 31 leaves in total.

Step 2

Find $\frac{1}{4}$ of 31, which is 7.75. As this is not a whole number, we round up to the nearest whole number (always round up), which is 8. We then find the eighth value in the plot, which is 59. This is the lower quartile.

Q_1 = 59 years

(ii) Find $\frac{3}{4}$ of 31, which is 23.25. As this is not a whole number, round up to the nearest whole number, which is 24. We then find the 24th value in the plot, which is 72. This is the upper quartile.

Q_3 = 72 years

(iii) The interquartile range is $Q_3 - Q_1 = 72 - 59 = 13$ years.

(iv) Approximately 50% of attendees are between 59 and 72 years of age.

Alternative method for finding the IQR

Step 1

Find the median of the data. In this case the median is 66.

Step 2

List all the data less than the median.

{51,54,54,54,55,59,59,(59),59,63,63,63,64,65,66}

The lower quartile is the median of this set.

$\therefore Q_1 = 59$

Step 3

List all data greater than the median.

{67,67,68,68,69,71,71,(72),73,73,73,73,73,74,75}

The upper quartile is the median of this set.

$\therefore Q_3 = 72$

Step 4

$\therefore \text{IQR} = Q_3 - Q_1$

$= 72 - 59$

$= 13$ years

Worked Example 14.5

The stem-and-leaf plot below compares the average daily temperature in Austin, Texas, and Seattle, Washington, for ten days in January.

Austin		Seattle
9	4	0, 0, 2, 4, 5, 7
9, 6, 6, 3, 1	5	1, 2, 4, 6
7, 4, 2, 1	6	
Key: 1|6| = 61°F		Key: |5|1 = 51°F

(i) What is the range of the temperatures in Austin?

(ii) What is the range of the temperatures in Seattle?

(iii) Find Q_1, the lower quartile, and Q_3, the upper quartile, for both Austin and Seattle.

(iv) What is the IQR for both sets of data?

Solution

(i) $\text{Range}_{\text{Austin}} = 67 - 49 = 18$ °F

(ii) $\text{Range}_{\text{Seattle}} = 56 - 40 = 16$ °F

(iii) **Austin**

$Q_2 = \dfrac{56 + 59}{2}$

$= 57.5$ °F

Data less than or equal to the median:

{49, 51, 53, 56, 56, 57.5}

So, $Q_1 = \dfrac{53 + 56}{2} = 54.5$ °F.

Data greater than or equal to the median:

{57.5, 59, 61, 62, 64, 67}

So, $Q_3 = \dfrac{61 + 62}{2} = 61.5$ °F.

Seattle

$Q_2 = \dfrac{45 + 47}{2}$

$= 46$ °F

Data less than or equal to the median:

{40, 40, 42, 44, 45, 46}

So, $Q_1 = \dfrac{42 + 44}{2} = 43$ °F.

Data greater than or equal to the median:

{46, 47, 51, 52, 54, 56}

So, $Q_3 = \dfrac{51 + 52}{2}$

$= \dfrac{103}{2} = 51.5$ °F.

(iv) $\text{IQR}_{\text{Austin}} = 61.5 - 54.5$

$= 7$ °F

$\text{IQR}_{\text{Seattle}} = 51.5 - 43$

$= 8.5$ °F

Exercise 14.3

1. Find the lower quartile, Q_1, the upper quartile, Q_3, and the interquartile range, IQR, for the following sets:

Note: You should first rank the data.

(i) {2, 5, 7, 3, 3, 2, 8}

(ii) {5, 8, 6, 4, 5, 3, 4, 12}

(iii) {8, 7, 6, 5, 4, 3, 2, 1}

(iv) {8, 7, 8, 7, 6, 5, 6, 5, 4, 3, 4, 3}

(v) {−3, −2, −1, 0, 1, 2, 3}

(vi) {1, 2, −3, 8, 7, −5, −2}

2. Twenty people attend a fancy dress party. Their ages are shown in the following stem-and-leaf diagram:

Calculate:

(i) The range

(ii) Q_1, the lower quartile

(iii) Q_3, the upper quartile

(iv) The interquartile range

Stem	Leaf
1	1, 3, 4, 5, 6, 9
2	1, 3, 5
3	3, 8
4	4, 5, 6, 7, 8
5	1, 6, 7
6	2 Key: 1|4 = 14 years

3. The stem-and-leaf diagram shows the time (in seconds) it took contestants to answer a general knowledge question. All contestants answered in less than 7 seconds.

Calculate:

(i) The range

(ii) Q_1, the lower quartile

(iii) Q_3, the upper quartile

(iv) The interquartile range

Stem	Leaf
2	1, 2, 2
3	2, 4, 8, 9
4	1, 3, 4, 6, 7
5	1, 5
6	8 Key: 3|2 = 3.2 seconds

4. Here is a back-to-back stem-and-leaf diagram showing the marks obtained by 30 girls and 30 boys in the same Maths test. The girls' marks are on the left-hand side of the diagram.

Calculate for both sets:

(i) The median mark

(ii) Q_1, the lower quartile

(iii) Q_3, the upper quartile

(iv) The interquartile range

(v) Interpret the IQR in the context of this question.

Leaf (Girls)	Stem	Leaf (Boys)
9	0	7, 9
7, 2	1	3, 4
8	2	9
9, 6, 6	3	5, 7, 9
8, 8, 6, 6, 6, 4, 2, 2	4	3, 4, 4
8, 6, 4	5	2, 2, 3, 5, 7, 7, 8
8, 2	6	1, 2, 5, 8, 9
9, 6, 4	7	3, 4, 5, 9
8, 5, 2, 0	8	4, 7
Key: 3|9 = 93% 9, 8, 3	9	1 Key: 3|7 = 37%

5. Here are the IQ scores for a group of Sixth Year students:

100	113	126	110	99	106	109	117	121	116
97	108	103	115	119	125	132	93	87	130
88	116	102	119	130	110	123	109	119	132

(i) Draw a stem-and-leaf diagram to illustrate the data.

(ii) Describe the distribution.

(iii) Find the range.

(iv) Find the median.

(v) Find the interquartile range.

6. The magnitude of numerous tremors felt off the coast of Iceland is recorded. The following data indicates the magnitude of 30 such tremors:

4.2	1.1	0.3	1.1	3.3	3.2	5.2	1.5	3.1	0.5
1.2	2.5	0.8	0.7	1.8	6	1.2	2.5	5.2	1.6
4	1.4	0.9	2.8	5	0.2	1.9	2.3	1.7	4

(i) Draw a stem-and-leaf diagram to illustrate the data.

(ii) Describe the distribution.

(iii) Find the range.

(iv) Find the median.

(v) Find the interquartile range.

7. John has done a survey of the cost of bed-and-breakfast in his town. The results are summarised in the following stem-and-leaf diagram:

Stem	Leaf
2	1, 2, 2, 2, 2, 2, 6, 6, 7, 8, 9
3	0, 0, 0, 0, 0, 5, 5, 5, 5, 5, 5, 8, 8
4	0, 0, 0, 0, 0, 0, 5, 5, 5, 5, 9, 9, 9, 9
5	0, 0, 0, 0, 0, 0, 0, 5, 5
6	2, 3, 8, 8, 8, 8, 8
7	5, 5, 9, 9, 9 Key: 6|2 = €62

(i) Write down the median of these costs.

(ii) The mean of the data is 44.59. Why is the mean greater than the median?

(iii) Calculate the range of costs.

(iv) Find the lower and upper quartiles.

(v) Find the interquartile range.

(vi) Which measure of spread is most appropriate in the context of this question? Explain.

14.4 Measures of Variation II: Standard Deviation

Standard deviation measures the **average deviation or spread from the mean of all values in a set**. It is a reliable measure of spread, as it takes account of all values in the set, unlike the range or interquartile range. However, if there are extreme values in the data set, it is best to use the interquartile range as a measure of spread.

$$\sigma = \sqrt{\frac{\sum(x-\mu)^2}{n}}$$

See page 33 of *Formulae and Tables*.

σ is the standard deviation.
$\sum$ means 'sum of'.
x is the variable.
μ is the mean.
n is the number of variables.

Worked Example 14.6

Set A = {8, 8, 9, 11, 14} and set B = {1, 5, 9, 14, 21}

(i) Show that A and B have the same mean.

(ii) Find the range of A and the range of B.

(iii) Comment on the range as a measure of spread in the context of this question.

(iv) Why is the standard deviation a better measure of spread than the range?

(v) Calculate the standard deviation from the mean of both sets.

Solution

(i) The mean of set A, $\mu_A = \frac{8+8+9+11+14}{5} = \frac{50}{5} = 10.$

The mean of set B, $\mu_B = \frac{1+5+9+14+21}{5} = \frac{50}{5} = 10.$

(ii) $\text{Range}_A = 14 - 8 = 6$ $\text{Range}_B = 21 - 1 = 20$

(iii) The range indicates that set B has a greater spread than set A. However, as a measure of spread, it is limited to just two values in the set, the maximum value and the minimum value. If an outlier or extreme value exists in the data, then this will distort the true measure of spread.

(iv) The standard deviation uses all values in the set to calculate the spread and is therefore a much better measure. The standard deviation is a measure of the average spread of the data from the mean.

(v) We can calculate the standard deviation using the formula $\sigma = \sqrt{\frac{\sum(x-\mu)^2}{n}}$.

The work can be summarised in the following tables:

Set A			
x	μ	d	d^2
8	10	-2	4
8	10	-2	4
9	10	-1	1
11	10	1	1
14	10	4	16
			26

Set B			
x	μ	d	d^2
1	10	-9	81
5	10	-5	25
9	10	-1	1
14	10	4	16
21	10	11	121
			244

Note: $d = x - \mu$

$\sigma_A = \sqrt{\frac{26}{5}}$ $\sigma_B = \sqrt{\frac{244}{5}}$

$\sigma_A = \sqrt{5.2}$ $\sigma_B = \sqrt{48.8}$

$\sigma_A \approx 2.28$ $\sigma_B \approx 6.99$

The statistics functions on your calculator can also be used to find standard deviation. Here are the keystrokes for finding σ_A in the example above.

Individual calculators may differ and it is important that you know how to calculate the standard deviation on your own calculator.

Worked Example 14.7

One hundred students are given a Maths problem to solve. The times taken to solve the problem are tabled as follows:

Time (minutes)	10–14	14–18	18–22	22–26	26–30
Number of students	13	28	26	21	12

Note: 14–18 means 14 is included and 18 is not, etc.

Using mid-interval values, estimate the mean of the distribution, and hence, estimate the standard deviation from the mean. Give your answers to two decimal places.

Solution

	$\frac{10+14}{2}$	$\frac{14+18}{2}$	$\frac{18+22}{2}$	$\frac{22+26}{2}$	$\frac{26+30}{2}$
MIV	12	16	20	24	28
No. of students	13	28	26	21	12

$$\text{Estimated mean} = \frac{(12)(13) + (16)(28) + (20)(26) + (24)(21) + (28)(12)}{13 + 28 + 26 + 21 + 12} = 19.64 \text{ minutes}$$

The statistics functions on your calculator can now be used to find standard deviation. Here are the keystrokes for this problem. Note that individual calculators may differ.

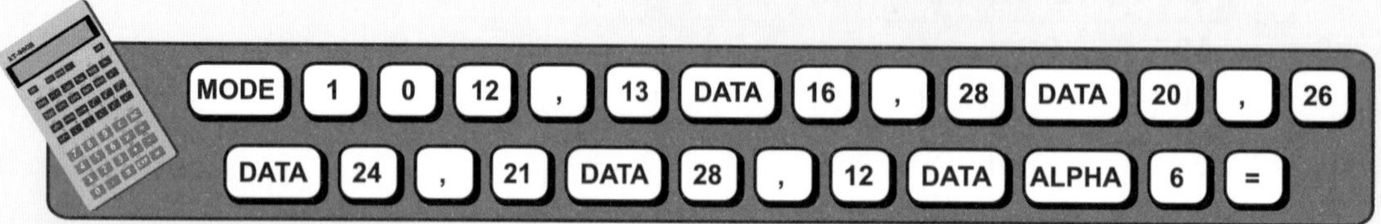

Standard deviation $\sigma = \approx 4.87$

Note: It is not required to calculate the standard deviation manually. Using a calculator is acceptable.

Exercise 14.4

1. Find, correct to one decimal place, the standard deviation of the following sets of numbers:
   (i) {5, 8, 9, 10}
   (ii) {1, 0, 2, 5, 7}
   (iii) {3, 5, 6, 8, 8}
   (iv) {9, 13, 14, 4, 7}
   (v) {3.1, 3.2, 3.3, 3.4}

2. A = {0, 1, 3, 4, 7, 15}
   (i) Verify that A has a mean of 5.
   (ii) Verify that the standard deviation is 5.

3. A = {4, 5, 5, 6, 10} B = {1, 2, 7, 9, 11}
   (i) Verify that sets A and B have a mean of 6.
   (ii) Find the standard deviation in each case, correct to one decimal place.

4. The ages of children in a crèche were tabled as follows:

Age (years)	1	3	4	5
Frequency	1	2	2	5

   Show that 4 is the mean age, and calculate the standard deviation, correct to two decimal places.

5. Twenty households were asked the number of pets they kept. Their responses were tabled as follows:

Number	0	1	2	3	4
Frequency	2	4	8	4	2

   Calculate the standard deviation of the data, correct to two significant figures.

6. The grouped frequency table below refers to the number of minutes it took 20 people to solve a problem.

Time (min)	2–4	4–8	8–10	10–16
Frequency	2	7	8	3

   Note: 2–4 means 2 is included and 4 is not, and so on.
   (i) Using mid-interval values, estimate the mean of the distribution.
   (ii) Hence, estimate the standard deviation. Answer correct to one decimal place.

STATISTICS II

7. The following frequency distribution shows the pocket money of 100 students:

Pocket money (€)	0–1	1–2	2–5	5–10
Frequency	4	23	42	31

Note: 0–1 means 0 is included and 1 is not, and so on.

(i) Estimate the mean pocket money.

(ii) Estimate the standard deviation from the mean.

8. Twenty students were asked how many minutes they spent watching television on a particular day. The following frequency distribution summarises their replies:

Time (min)	0–40	40–60	60–80	80–100	100–120
Frequency	2	6	5	3	4

Note: 0–40 means 0 is included and 40 is not, and so on.

(i) Estimate the mean time spent watching television.

(ii) Hence estimate, to the nearest minute, the standard deviation from the mean.

9. Consider the data displayed in the back-to-back stem-and-leaf plot below.

Set A		Set B
6, 1	2	1, 1, 4, 5, 8, 9
4, 3, 2, 1	3	2, 5, 6, 8
5, 4, 3, 2	4	1, 2
7, 2	5	6
Key: 2|5 = 52		Key: 5|6 = 56

(i) Describe the shape of each distribution.

(ii) Calculate the mean of set A and the median of set B.

(iii) Explain why the mean is an appropriate measure of centre for set A, while the median is an appropriate measure of centre for set B.

(iv) Find the IQR for set B.

(v) Calculate the standard deviation for set A.

(vi) Explain why the standard deviation is a more appropriate measure of spread for set A, while the IQR is a more appropriate measure of spread for set B.

14.5 The Normal Distribution and the Empirical Rule

In nature, there are many continuous distributions that are symmetric. For example, if we measure the heights of all adult males in Ireland, we will find a high proportion of the adult male population with heights close to the mean height of the population. As measurements increase or decrease away from the mean, the proportion of the population with these heights begins to decrease. This results in a **symmetric distribution**.

If the distribution is very large and we allow the class intervals (base widths of the rectangles) to become small enough, the distribution forms a smooth, symmetrical, bell-shaped curve called the **normal distribution curve**.

In any normal distribution:

(i) Approximately 68% of the population lies within one standard deviation of the mean, i.e. 68% lies within the range $[\mu - \sigma, \mu + \sigma]$.

(ii) Approximately 95% of the population lies within the range $[\mu - 2\sigma, \mu + 2\sigma]$.

(iii) Approximately 99.7% of the population lies within the range $[\mu - 3\sigma, \mu + 3\sigma]$.

This is known as the **Empirical Rule** or '68–95–99.7 Rule'.

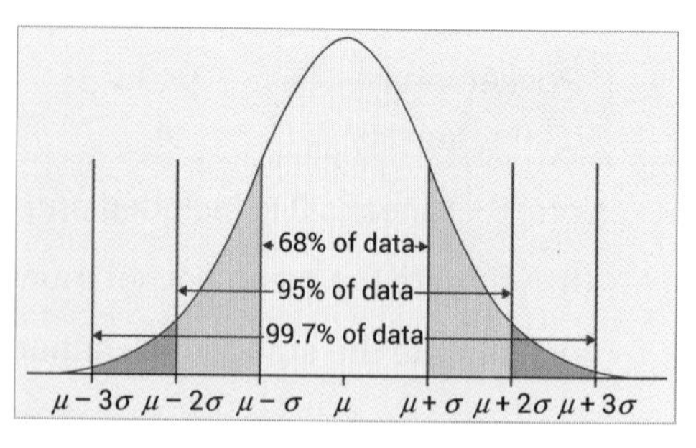

Worked Example 14.8

The frequency table below shows the number of hits a website received each day during a particular week.

Day	Mon	Tue	Wed	Thu	Fri
Number of hits	50	80	120	40	20

(i) Calculate μ, the mean number of hits per day during that week.

(ii) Calculate σ, the standard deviation from the mean. Answer correct to two decimal places.

(iii) Calculate $\mu - \sigma$.

(iv) Calculate $\mu + \sigma$.

(v) Now find the range $[\mu - \sigma, \mu + \sigma]$.

Solution

(i) $\mu = \dfrac{50 + 80 + 120 + 40 + 20}{5} = \dfrac{310}{5} = 62$ hits

(ii) Using a calculator, $\sigma \approx 34.87$.

(iii) $\mu - \sigma = 62 - 34.87 = 27.13$

(iv) $\mu + \sigma = 62 + 34.87 = 96.87$

(v) $[\mu - \sigma, \mu + \sigma] = [27.13, 96.87]$

Worked Example 14.9

The distribution of heights of a large group of students is normal, with a mean of 158 cm and a standard deviation from the mean of 10 cm. The empirical rule says that approximately 68% of a normally distributed population lies within one standard deviation of the mean.

(i) Using the empirical rule, find the range of heights within which 68% of this population lies.

(ii) If a student is chosen at random from the population, find the probability that the student has a height between 148 cm and 168 cm.

Solution

(i) Range $= [\mu - \sigma, \mu + \sigma]$

$= [158 - 10, 158 + 10]$

$= [148 \text{ cm}, 168 \text{ cm}]$

(ii) From part (i), we know that 68% of the population have heights in the range [148 cm, 168 cm]. Therefore, the probability that the student has a height between 148 cm and 168 cm is 68% or 0.68.

Worked Example 14.10

Washers are produced so that their inside diameter is normally distributed with a mean of 1.25 cm.
If 95% of the diameters are between 1.2375 cm and 1.2625 cm, then what is the approximate standard deviation from the mean?

Solution

The empirical rule tells us that approximately 95% of the diameters will be in the range $[1.25 - 2\sigma, 1.25 + 2\sigma]$.

$\therefore 1.25 - 2\sigma = 1.2375$

$-2\sigma = 1.2375 - 1.25$

$-2\sigma = -0.0125$

$\sigma = 0.00625$ cm

Worked Example 14.11

Two hundred senior students were asked how long they had to wait in the canteen line for lunch. Their responses were found to be normally distributed, with a mean of 15 minutes and a standard deviation of 3.5 minutes. How many students would you expect to wait more than 18.5 minutes?

Solution

Using the empirical rule, 68% of the population lie in the range $[15 - 3.5, 15 + 3.5] = [11.5, 18.5]$.

$\therefore$ The percentage lying in the tails of the distribution is $100 - 68 = 32\%$.

Since the distribution is symmetrical, 16% of the students would expect to wait for more than 18.5 minutes.

16% of 200 = 32 students

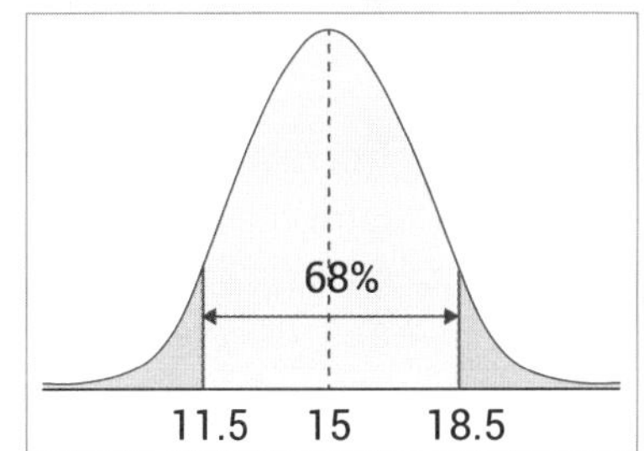

Exercise 14.5

1. In a normal distribution:
   (i) Approximately what proportion of observations lies within one standard deviation of the mean?
   (ii) Approximately what proportion of observations lies within two standard deviations of the mean?
   (iii) Approximately what proportion of observations lies within three standard deviations of the mean?

2. The principal of Fermat High School records the number of pupils absent each day during a week in December. The results are displayed in the table below.

Day	Monday	Tuesday	Wednesday	Thursday	Friday
Number	12	19	17	25	20

   (i) Calculate μ, the mean number of students absent per day during that week.
   (ii) Calculate σ, the standard deviation from the mean. Answer correct to one decimal place.
   (iii) Now find the range $[\mu - \sigma, \mu + \sigma]$.

3. In each of the following, the mean (μ) and the standard deviation (σ) of the normal distributions are given. For each distribution, find the range within which 68% of the distribution lies.
   (i) $\mu = 200, \sigma = 25$ (ii) $\mu = 100, \sigma = 20$ (iii) $\mu = 20, \sigma = 2$ (iv) $\mu = 25, \sigma = 2.5$

4. In each of the following, the mean (μ) and the standard deviation (σ) of the normal distributions are given. For each distribution, find the range within which 95% of the distribution lies.

   (i) $\mu = 280, \sigma = 35$ (iii) $\mu = 25, \sigma = 2$

   (ii) $\mu = 120, \sigma = 30$ (iv) $\mu = 35, \sigma = 5.5$

5. In each of the following, the mean (μ) and the standard deviation (σ) of the normal distributions are given. For each distribution, find the range within which 99.7% of the distribution lies.

   (i) $\mu = 150, \sigma = 25$ (iii) $\mu = 20, \sigma = 2$

   (ii) $\mu = 300, \sigma = 15$ (iv) $\mu = 100, \sigma = 5$

6. IQ scores are normally distributed with a mean of 100 and a standard deviation of 15. Isaac has taken an IQ test and scored 132. His friend Eoin has remarked that Isaac's score is in the top 5% of all IQ scores. Isaac disagrees and says that he is in the top 2.5%. Is Eoin's remark correct? Explain your reasoning.

7. Men's heights in a particular country are normally distributed with a mean of 172.5 cm and a standard deviation from the mean of 7 cm. Séamus, the statistician, has designed a house with doorways high enough to allow all men, except the tallest 2.5%, to pass through without stooping. What doorway height has Séamus used?

8. Human body temperatures are normally distributed with a mean of 36.8 °C and a standard deviation from the mean of 0.4 °C. Rita has a body temperature of 38.8 °C. Should Rita be concerned? Explain your reasoning using statistics.

9. Birth weights in Ireland are normally distributed with a mean of 3.42 kg and a standard deviation of 0.5 kg. What percentage of babies born will weigh between 2.92 kg and 3.92 kg? Explain your answer.

10. The lifetime of a certain type of tube light is normally distributed. The mean life is 300 hours and the standard deviation is 50 hours. For a group of 1,000 tube lights, how many are expected to last between 250 hours and 350 hours?

11. The mean height of an adult male in the Netherlands is 186.5 cm with a standard deviation of 6.3 cm. How tall is a Dutch man who is just in the top 2.5% of the population?

14.6 Sampling Variability

Suppose the mean height of all 16-year-old males in the country is 176 cm. (In a real problem, of course, you would never know exactly this value.) Then, suppose you take a random sample from this population and compute the mean height of the sample. Will it be exactly 176 cm? Probably not. Most likely it will be close to 176 cm, especially if the sample size is large. If another sample is taken, will the mean height of the new sample be exactly the same as the mean of the original sample? Again, probably not.

Sampling variability refers to the difference between sample statistics from different samples (e.g. the difference between one sample mean and another sample mean).

The difference between the mean height of a sample and the mean of the population is known as the **sampling error**. In practice we never know the sampling error, as we never know the mean of the population. (After all, we are looking for an estimate of the mean of the population.)

Reducing the amount of sampling error helps us make more accurate generalisations about the whole population when using sample data. One way in which this can often be done is by increasing the sample size.

Sampling error refers to the difference between a sample statistic and a true population parameter (e.g. the difference between a sample mean and the true population mean).

Worked Example 14.12

A group of five boys measured each other's heights in centimetres. The results are: 168, 175, 178, 182, 190.

The boys are investigating the concept of sampling variability. They decide to select all possible samples of size 3 from the five measurements. Their results are shown in the table below.

Sample 1	168	175	178
Sample 2	168	175	182
Sample 3	168	175	190
Sample 4	168	178	182
Sample 5	168	178	190
Sample 6	168	182	190
Sample 7	175	178	182
Sample 8	175	178	190
Sample 9	175	182	190
Sample 10	178	182	190

(i) Calculate the mean height of the five boys.

(ii) Calculate each sample mean height (correct to two decimal places where necessary).

(iii) Calculate the mean value of the sample means. What do you notice?

(iv) What is the probability of selecting a random sample of size 3 whose mean is within 1 cm of the true mean?

(v) What is the probability of selecting a random sample of size 3 whose mean is greater than 1 cm but less than 2 cm from the true mean?

Solution

(i) Mean $= \dfrac{168 + 175 + 178 + 182 + 190}{5} = 178.6$ cm

(ii)

				Mean (cm)
Sample 1	168	175	178	173.67
Sample 2	168	175	182	175
Sample 3	168	175	190	177.67
Sample 4	168	178	182	176
Sample 5	168	178	190	178.67
Sample 6	168	182	190	180
Sample 7	175	178	182	178.33
Sample 8	175	178	190	181
Sample 9	175	182	190	182.33
Sample 10	178	182	190	183.33

(iii) Mean $= \dfrac{173.67 + 175 + 177.67 + 176 + 178.67 + 180 + 178.33 + 181 + 182.33 + 183.33}{10}$

$= 178.6$ cm

Therefore, the mean of the sample means is equal to the mean of the population.

(iv) There are three samples whose mean is within 1 cm of the true mean (Samples 3, 5 and 7). Therefore, the probability of selecting a sample within 1 cm of the true mean is $\frac{3}{10} = 0.3$.

(v) There is just one sample (Sample 6) whose mean is greater than 1 cm but less than 2 cm from the true mean. Therefore, the probability of selecting a sample whose mean is greater than 1 cm but less than 2 cm from the true mean is $\frac{1}{10} = 0.1$.

Exercise 14.6

1. A shop sells shoes. Use the most appropriate words from the list below to complete the sentences.

   sample ordered discrete numerical continuous categorical nominal

   (i) The number of pairs of shoes sold by the shop is ______________ data.

   (ii) The colour of the shoes is ______________ data.

   (iii) The weight of the shoes is ______________.

   (iv) A selection of shoes chosen from the back of the shop is called a ______________.

2. The manager of a factory wants to carry out a survey to find out the workers' views on the sale of overalls at the factory. There are 1,800 workers in the factory.

   (i) Give two reasons why the manager would take a sample rather than a census to find out the workers' views.

   (ii) The manager has decided to use a questionnaire to find out the workers' views on the sale of overalls at the factory. One of the questions on the questionnaire is shown below.

Give one reason why you support the idea of having overalls sold at the factory.

   Write down one criticism of this question.

   (iii) The manager's assistant distributes the questionnaire to the first 30 workers to arrive at the factory on a particular morning. Will the assistant's sample be representative of all workers, or will it be biased? Explain your answer in detail.

3. Dublin Bus wishes to obtain opinions on the quality of its service.

   (i) Explain why a sample of its customers should be taken, rather than a census.

   (ii) The general manager of Dublin Bus suggests that everyone on the 46A bus on Monday morning should be surveyed. Give two possible sources of bias in this sample.

   (iii) An afternoon radio programme asks listeners to call in with their views on the quality of the Dublin Bus company's services. Why might the views of those calling into the programme not be representative of all Dublin Bus customers? Give two possible reasons.

   (iv) Describe a suitable way in which Dublin Bus might select a representative sample of its customers.

4. Eoin wants to choose a sample of size 8 from his class. He writes down all the students' names on pieces of paper, puts all the boys' names in one bag and all the girls' names in another bag. He then chooses, without looking, four pieces of paper from each bag.

   (i) Explain why Eoin's sample is random.

   (ii) Explain why Eoin's sample is not a simple random sample.

   (iii) Explain how Eoin could obtain a simple random sample of eight students from his class.

5. Here is an extract from a table of random numbers.

86	13	84	10	7	30	39	5	97	96	88	7	37	26	4	89	13	48	19	20
60	78	48	12	99	47	9	46	91	33	17	21	3	94	79	0	8	50	40	16
78	48	6	37	82	26	1	6	64	65	94	41	17	26	74	66	61	93	14	97

   (i) Starting from the first line and the fifth column with the number 7, and reading across the table, from left to right, write down ten random numbers betweeen 0 and 69.

   (ii) Explain how you could use the above table of random numbers to select a sample of 12 students from 80 students.

6. Thomas is investigating if distance from a polling station affects whether people usually vote in his town. He decides to select a simple random sample of 50 people from the register of electors, use the telephone directory to find the telephone numbers of the people in the sample and then carry out a telephone survey.

   (i) Define the population for this survey.

   (ii) What obstacles could Thomas encounter in carrying out this survey?

   (iii) One question he uses is, 'What is the distance from your house to the polling station?' Give one criticism of this question.

7. Bob wants to find out what is the most popular PlayStation game in his school. He randomly selects a group of First Year boys and asks them to name their favourite PlayStation game. Using his results, he concludes that *Call of Duty* is the most popular game in the school.

   (i) Define the population for this survey.

   (ii) Why is the sample that Bob uses non-representative of the school population?

   (iii) Describe an improved way in which Bob could select a suitable sample for his study.

8. A researcher determines that she needs results from at least 400 subjects to conduct a study. To compensate for low return rates, she mails the survey to 5,000 subjects. She receives 750 responses. Is the sample of 750 responses a good sample for her to use? Explain.

9. Give one example of each of the following:

   (i) A non-random sample

   (ii) A simple random sample

   (iii) A random sample that is not a simple random sample

10. Using stopwatches, a group of five girls asked each other to estimate 80 seconds. The results (in seconds) are: 68, 75, 78, 82, 87.

    The girls are investigating the concept of sampling variability. They decide to select all possible samples of size 3 from the five estimates. Their results are shown in the table below.

Sample 1	68	75	78
Sample 2	68	75	82
Sample 3	68	75	87
Sample 4	68	78	82
Sample 5	68	78	87
Sample 6	68	82	87
Sample 7	75	78	82
Sample 8	75	78	87
Sample 9	75	82	87
Sample 10	78	82	87

    (i) Calculate the mean estimated time for the five girls.

    (ii) Calculate the mean estimated time of each sample.

    (iii) Calculate the mean value of the sample means. What do you notice?

    (iv) What is the probability of selecting a random sample of size 3 whose mean is within 1 second of the true mean?

    (v) What is the probability of selecting a random sample of size 3 whose mean is greater than 1 second but less than 2 seconds from the true mean?

11. A company making light bulbs advertises that less than 1% of its bulbs have defects. To guarantee this claim, the company tests a percentage of bulbs produced every day.

    There are three different testing methods currently in use to check daily production.

    Method 1: Test every 400th bulb produced.

    Method 2: Test 200 randomly selected bulbs at the end of the day. A computer program selects the bulbs at random by batch number. Each bulb has a unique batch number.

    Method 3: Test every bulb produced between 12:59 and 13:00 that day.

(i) Complete the table below.

	Method 1	Method 2	Method 3
Number of bulbs tested			292
Number of defects	3		4
Proportion of defects		$\frac{2}{200}$ (= 1%)	
Total daily production		140,000	

(ii) Does any method of testing provide some evidence that contradicts the company's claim? Say which method(s) and explain the evidence.

(iii) Which of the three methods is the only method that involves simple random sampling? Give reasons for your answer.

(iv) In your opinion, which method is most likely to generate a biased sample of daily production? Explain your answer.

(v) Excluding the method you outlined in part (iv) above, which of the remaining two methods would you choose as the most suitable method of testing to use? Why?

(vi) How could you adjust the method of testing you outlined in part (v) above, so that the company's claim could be accepted/rejected with more certainty?

(vii) What disadvantages could such an adjustment lead to?

14.7 Margin of Error and Hypothesis Testing

In this section, we begin working with **inferential statistics**, as we use sample data to make inferences (draw conclusions) about populations.

The two main applications of inferential statistics that we will study involve the use of sample data to:

1. Estimate the value of a population proportion
2. Test some claim (hypothesis) about a population proportion

To begin, you will need to know what statisticians mean by a **population proportion** and a **sample proportion**. Suppose you want to know the percentage of Leaving Certificate students in Ireland who have applied to study Medicine next year. To find out, you decide to survey your class and use the result to infer the percentage of students for the whole country. (Not a great sample! Why?)

Suppose the survey reveals that 5 out of the 30 students in your class have applied to study Medicine next year. Then $\frac{5}{30}$ or $0.1\dot{6}$ is the sample proportion. We use the symbol $\hat{p}$ (pronounced 'p hat') to denote the sample proportion.

The population proportion is the proportion of the whole population (in this case, this year's Leaving Certificate students) who will go on to third-level education. We use p to denote the population proportion.

We can never find the exact value of p from $\hat{p}$. We can only estimate p.

Margin of Error

To understand the margin of error, we need to know about confidence intervals.

Out of 50 randomly selected students in an all girls school, 15 said they liked rock music, i.e. the sample proportion $\hat{p}$ is $\frac{15}{50} = 0.3$. The school population is 500. Using only information from the sample, can we give the exact proportion of girls in the school who like rock music? The answer is no, but we can give a range within which we can state, with a certain degree of confidence, the proportion of students who like rock music lie.

STATISTICS II

A statistician might say, 'I can say with a confidence level of 95% that the proportion of girls in this school who like rock music lies in the interval $0.1586 < p < 0.4414$.' This interval is called a **confidence interval**. How does the statistician determine the interval and what does he mean by 'a confidence level of 95%'?

First, we calculate the margin of error using the formula shown, where n is the size of the sample. There are other ways of calculating the **margin of error**, but we will use this formula on our course.

The **margin of error** is the maximum likely difference between the sample proportion, $\hat{p}$, and the population proportion, p.

Margin of error

$$E = \frac{1}{\sqrt{n}}$$

In this example, $n = 50$, so $E = \frac{1}{\sqrt{50}} \approx 0.1414$.

This means that we would expect the population proportion p will differ from the sample proportion $\hat{p}$ by at most 0.1414, 95% of the time. In other words, if we were to take 100 random samples of size 50 from any population, we would expect 95 of the samples would have proportions that would differ from the population proportion by at most 0.1414. When we use this formula, our level of confidence is always 95%.

The confidence interval for the proportion is:

$$\hat{p} - \frac{1}{\sqrt{n}} < p < \hat{p} + \frac{1}{\sqrt{n}}$$

Worked Example 14.13

A company wishes to estimate the proportion, p, of its employees who went on sick leave during the past year. A random sample of 20 employees was taken. Nine of the sample went on sick leave during the past year. Construct a 95% confidence interval for p.

Solution

Step 1 Calculate the sample proportion, $\hat{p}$.

$$\hat{p} = \frac{9}{20} = 0.45$$

Step 2 Find E, the margin of error.

$$E = \frac{1}{\sqrt{20}} \approx 0.2236$$

Step 3 Construct the confidence interval.

$$0.45 - 0.2236 < p < 0.45 + 0.2236$$

$$0.2264 < p < 0.6736$$

The margin of error in Worked Example 14.13 is quite big, 0.2236 or 22.36%. Margins of error that are this big are of little use. However, we can reduce the margin of error by increasing the size of our sample.

Worked Example 14.14

What size sample is required to have a margin of error of 0.04 or 4%?

Solution

Let n be the sample size.

$$\frac{1}{\sqrt{n}} = 0.04$$

$$\frac{1}{\sqrt{n}} = \frac{1}{25}$$

$$\sqrt{n} = 25$$

$$(\sqrt{n})^2 = 25^2$$

$$\therefore n = 625$$

STATISTICS II

Hypothesis Testing 

Hypothesis testing is an important aspect of statistics.

An **hypothesis** is a claim or statement about a property of a population.

An **hypothesis test** is a procedure for testing a claim about a population.

The following statement is an example of an hypothesis about a population: '65% of all heavy smokers will contract a serious lung or heart ailment by the age of 60.' To accept or reject this statement, you must collect a random sample of medical records of heavy smokers at age 60 and find the proportion of the sample who have contracted serious heart or lung ailments. Then you must set up an hypothesis test to prove or disprove the claim. In our course, we will only test claims about a population proportion.

Procedure for hypothesis testing for a population proportion

Step 1 State clearly the **null hypothesis**, H_0, and the alternative hypothesis, H_1.

For example, H_0: '65% of all heavy smokers will contract a serious lung or heart ailment by age 60.'

H_0, the **null hypothesis**, is a statement which describes the population proportion.

Step 2 Calculate $\hat{p}$, the sample proportion.

Step 3 Calculate $\frac{1}{\sqrt{n}}$, the margin of error.

Step 4 Set up a confidence interval for p, the population proportion.

- If the population proportion stated in the null hypothesis is within the confidence interval, then fail to reject H_0, the null hypothesis.
- If the population proportion stated in the null hypothesis is outside the confidence interval, then reject the null hypothesis in favour of H_1.

Note that we say, 'Fail to reject the null hypothesis'. You should not say, 'Accept the null hypothesis'.

Worked Example 14.15

A local newspaper is investigating a claim made by the CEO of a large multinational company. The CEO claimed that 80% of the company's 500,000 customers are satisfied with the service they receive. Using simple random sampling, the newspaper surveyed 200 customers. Among the sampled customers, 146 said they were satisfied with the company's service. Based on these findings, can we reject the CEO's claim that 80% of customers are satisfied with the company's service?

Solution

Step 1 H_0 – The company's satisfaction rating is 80%. So, H_0: $p = 0.8$.

H_1 – The company's satisfaction rating is **not** 80%. So, H_1: $p \neq 0.8$.

Step 2 Sample proportion $\hat{p} = \frac{146}{200} = 0.73$ or 73%.

Step 3 Margin of error $E = \frac{1}{\sqrt{200}} \approx 0.0707$.

Step 4 Confidence Interval (CI) for the population proportion is $0.73 - 0.0707 < p < 0.73 + 0.0707$.

CI: $0.6593 < p < 0.8007$

CI: $[0.6593, 0.8007]$

The population proportion under the null hypothesis is within the confidence interval. Therefore, we fail to reject the null hypothesis that the satisfaction rating is 80%, and hence, we are not rejecting the CEO's claim.

Worked Example 14.16

In a survey of 1,000 randomly selected households, 600 households had two or more cars. A recent report stated that 80% of all households in the country had two or more cars.

(i) Find a 95% confidence interval estimate of the proportion of households that had two or more cars.

(ii) Are the survey results consistent with the report?

Solution

(i) **Step 1** H_0: $p = 80\%$ (The proportion of households having two or more cars is 80%.)

H_1: $p \neq 80\%$ (The proportion of households having two or more cars is not 80%.)

Step 2 Sample proportion $\hat{p} = \frac{600}{1{,}000} = 0.6$ or 60%.

Step 3 Margin of error $E = \frac{1}{\sqrt{1{,}000}} \approx 0.03162$.

Step 4 CI for the population proportion is $0.6 - 0.03162 < p < 0.6 + 0.03162$.

CI: $0.56838 < p < 0.63162$

(ii) The population proportion under the null hypothesis is not within the confidence interval. Therefore, we reject the null hypothesis that the proportion of households having two or more cars is 80%.

Exercise 14.7

1. A manufacturer of computer components wishes to estimate the proportion, p, of its present stock of components that are defective. A random sample of 500 components is selected and 10 are found to be defective.

   Construct a 95% confidence interval for p, the proportion of all components that are defective.

2. A bank randomly selected 120 customers with savings accounts and found that 90 of them also had cheque accounts.

   Construct a 95% confidence interval for the true proportion of savings-account customers who also have cheque accounts.

3. In a survey of 1,000 people, 740 said that they voted in a recent general election. Voting records show that 71% of eligible voters actually did vote.

   (i) Find a 95% confidence interval estimate of the proportion of people who voted.

   (ii) Are the survey results consistent with the actual voter turnout? Explain.

4. In a recent poll, 1,000 randomly selected adults were surveyed and 27% of them said that they use the Internet for shopping at least once a year. Construct a 95% confidence interval for the true proportion of adults who shop on the Internet.

5. A company wishes to estimate the proportion of its employees who would accept an extra week of holidays instead of the annual rise in salary.

   If the maximum margin of error the company will accept for the proportion is 5%, then find the necessary sample size at the 95% level.

6. In a study of 10,000 car crashes, it was found that 5,550 of them occurred within 10 kilometres of the driver's home. Car safety experts believe that 50% of car crashes occur within 10 kilometres of home. They wish to test this hypothesis.

   (i) Clearly state H_0, the null hypothesis.

   (ii) Clearly state H_1, the alternative hypothesis.

   (iii) Carry out the appropriate hypothesis test, at a 95% confidence level, stating your conclusion clearly.

7. A coin is tossed 100 times and heads occurs 57 times. Test the hypothesis that the coin is fair by:

   (i) Clearly stating H_0, the null hypothesis

   (ii) Clearly stating H_1, the alternative hypothesis

   (iii) Carrying out the appropriate hypothesis test, at a 95% confidence level, stating your conclusion clearly

8. A six-sided die is thrown 180 times and a 6 occurs 40 times. Can we conclude that the die is biased? (Hint: Let the null hypothesis be that the die is fair.)

9. A pharmaceutical company is replacing one of its pain-killing drugs with another drug that the company has developed and tested. The company's records show that the old drug provided relief for 70% of all patients who were administered it. A random sample of 625 patients was administered the new drug, and 450 of these claimed that the new drug provided relief.

   Test the hypothesis that the new drug is as effective as its old counterpart.

14.8 Misuses of Statistics

Statistics presented in newspapers, on TV, on websites and in other media can sometimes be misleading. It is important that we, as consumers, are able to spot errors and exaggerations in such statistics. The following is a list of possible errors and exaggerations that may mislead the consumer:

1. *Arithmetic errors or omissions.* Always check that everything adds up. Do all percentages add up to 100? Does the number in each group add up to the total number surveyed?
2. *Sample size.* Many advertisements or newspaper articles contain statements such as 'Four out of five owners said their cats preferred KAT food.' How many cat owners were surveyed? If only 10 cat owners were surveyed and 8 said that their cats preferred KAT, we cannot say that this number is representative of all cat owners, as the number surveyed is too small.
3. *Misleading comparisons.* Newspaper articles and TV reports sometimes make misleading comparisons. For example:

   The unemployment situation in the country at present is twice as bad as it was in the 1980s. There are twice as many unemployed now as at any time in the 1980s.

   However, there is a larger workforce now than in the 1980s. Unemployment figures should always be given as a percentage of the workforce. This is an example of a misleading comparison.
4. *Sources.* Always check the source of the information. Surveys are sometimes sponsored by companies with vested interests to promote. Very often, the sponsor can gain financially from the results of the survey.
5. *Misleading graphs.* The chart below summarises the results of 500 throws of a die. Do you think the die is biased?

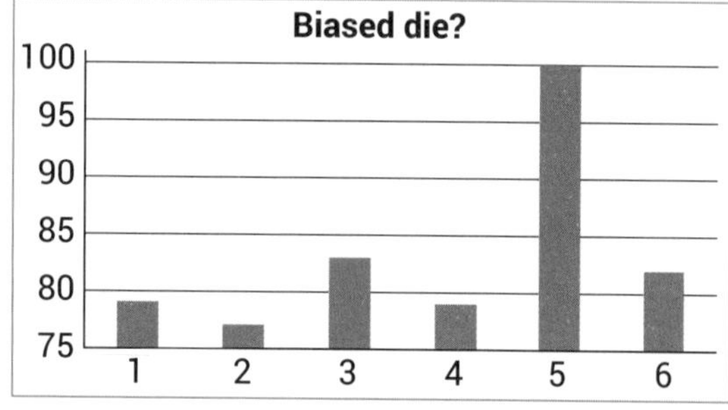

What makes the chart exaggerate the difference between the number of times a 5 was thrown and the number of times a 3 was thrown?

Now look at a different chart that summarises the same results:

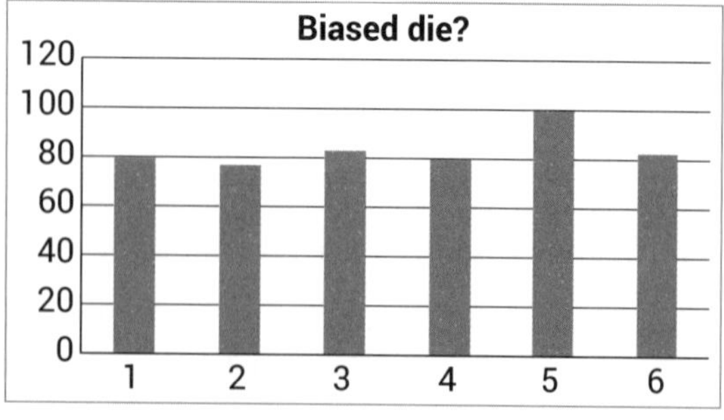

The second graph is more correct, as it starts with zero at the bottom of each bar.

6. *Non-representative samples*. A sample should always be representative of the population from which it is taken, otherwise the results will be misleading. For example, suppose you want to find the mean height of 16-year-olds in your school, and you wish to do it by taking a sample. You decide to choose thirty 16-year-olds at random. However, you limit your sample to girls only. This is not a representative sample, as boys have been deliberately omitted from the sample. This will lead to misleading results.
7. *Response bias*. This occurs when people can choose whether or not to take part in a survey. For example, a television show might ask people to call in and vote on some issue. First, the people who watch that particular show may not be representative of the overall population; second, people who do phone in might be more likely or less likely to vote 'Yes' than people who don't phone in. In other words self-selection may lead to over-representation of certain opinions.

Revision Exercises

1. The following are the pulse rates (beats per minutes) of a group of 30 adults:

68	64	86	72	64	72	66	86	76	56
64	60	87	72	56	64	60	64	86	74
74	72	64	60	56	56	64	56	86	84

(i) Is this data discrete or continuous? Explain.

(ii) Complete the frequency table below.

No. of beats	56–59	60–63	64–67	68–71	72–75	76–79	80–83	84–87
Tally								
Frequency								

(iii) Draw a bar chart of the distribution.

(iv) Rank the raw data and find the median.

(v) Using mid-interval values, estimate the mean of the distribution.

(vi) Now, using the raw data, calculate the mean. Answer correct to two decimal places.

(vii) Hence, calculate the percentage error in the estimated mean.

(viii) Using the raw data, find the standard deviation from the mean, correct to two decimal places.

2. A class was asked to estimate the height of a tall building adjacent to the school. The following table gives their estimates. All estimates are in metres.

36	41	60	53	75	83
43	54	64	79	86	47
56	64	49	48	58	66
58	59	38	79	52	31
21	22				

(i) Is this data categorical data or numerical data? Explain.

(ii) How many students are in the class?

(iii) Represent the data on a stem-and-leaf plot.

(iv) Describe the shape of the distribution.

(v) What is the median estimate?

(vi) Calculate the mean estimate.

(vii) What is the difference between the mean and median estimates?

(viii) Explain why the difference between the mean and the median is small.

3. The following frequency table shows the time spent by a group of students on a difficult Maths problem:

Time (min)	0–4	4–8	8–12	12–16
Number	8	12	10	7

Note: 0–4 means 0 is included but 4 is not, etc.

(i) How many students worked on the problem?

(ii) Construct a histogram for the data.

(iii) Describe the shape of the distribution.

(iv) Using mid-interval values, calculate the mean time taken to solve the problem. Answer correct to two decimal places.

(v) Using mid-interval values, find the standard deviation from the mean. Answer correct to two decimal places.

4. Twenty people attend a meeting on healthy diets. Their ages are summarised in the following stem-and-leaf diagram.

Using the stem-and-leaf diagram, calculate:

(i) The median age

(ii) Q_1, the lower quartile

(iii) Q_3, the upper quartile

(iv) The interquartile range

(v) The range

(vi) The mean age

Stem	Leaf
1	1, 1, 1, 4, 5
2	1, 3, 5
3	3, 8
4	4, 5, 6, 7, 8
5	9, 9
6	8, 9, 9 Key: 1|4 = 14 years

5. There are 15 boys and 13 girls in a Maths class. The mean time spent on homework each week for the boys is 5.5 hours. The mean time spent on homework for the girls is 7.2 hours.

(i) Find the mean time spent on homework for all students in the class. Answer correct to the nearest minute.

(ii) 'All girls spend more time on homework than all boys.' Is this a true statement based on the given information? Explain your answer.

(iii) Can we conclude that girls will do better in exams than boys based on the mean time spent on homework? Explain.

6. The table below shows the monthly salaries (in euro) of 20 families living in a particular neighbourhood.

2,451	2,580	2,595	2,635
2,635	2,530	2,550	2,680
2,654	2,520	2,560	2,575
2,462	2,540	2,690	2,740
2,635	2,635	2,673	2,480

(i) Complete the grouped frequency distribution below.

Salary (€)	2,450–2,500	2,500–2,550	2,550–2,600	2,600–2,650	2,650–2,700	2,700–2,750
Number						

Note: 2,450–2,500 includes 2,450 but excludes 2,500, etc.

(ii) Draw a histogram to represent the distribution.

(iii) Comment on the shape of the histogram.

(iv) Using the original table, calculate the mean and the median salary.

(v) Estimate the mean salary from the grouped frequency distribution.

(vi) Find the lower quartile, upper quartile and interquartile range for the above data.

Another family have moved into the neighbourhood. One member of the family is a very successful writer and earns €10,000 a month.

(vii) Comment on how this will affect the mean salary for the neighbourhood.

(viii) Which average will now be more representative of salaries for the neighbourhood? Explain.

(ix) Will the interquartile range be affected? Explain.

7. In 1798 Henry Cavendish, using a piece of equipment known as a torsion balance, obtained measurements for the density of the Earth. A random sample of the measurements is given below. Measurements are in g cm^{-3}.

5.10	5.30	5.42	5.53
5.26	5.34	5.44	5.55
5.27	5.34	5.46	5.57
5.29	5.36	5.47	5.58
5.29	5.39	5.50	5.61

(i) Display the data on a stem-and-leaf diagram.

(ii) Comment on the shape of the distribution.

(iii) Find the mean and median measurements.

(iv) Find the lower quartile, upper quartile and interquartile range for the above data.

8. The size, mean and standard deviation from the mean of four different data sets are given below.

	A	B	C	D
Size	500	100	50	20
Mean	50	120	5	34
Standard deviation	15	10	7	3

Complete the sentences below by inserting the relevant letter in each space.

(i) The biggest data set is ____________ and the smallest data set is ____________.

(ii) In general, the data in set ________ is the biggest and the data in set ________ is the smallest.

(iii) The data in set ____________ is more spread out than the data in the other sets.

(iv) Set ____________ must contain some negative numbers.

9. Women's heights in a particular country are normally distributed with a mean of 159 cm and a standard deviation from the mean of 6.25 cm. Find the range of heights within which:

(i) Approximately 99.7% of the female population lie

(ii) Approximately 68% of the female population lie

(iii) Approximately 95% of the female population lie

10. (a) The following chart shows the points accumulated by the top three Premiership teams in the 2008–2009 season:

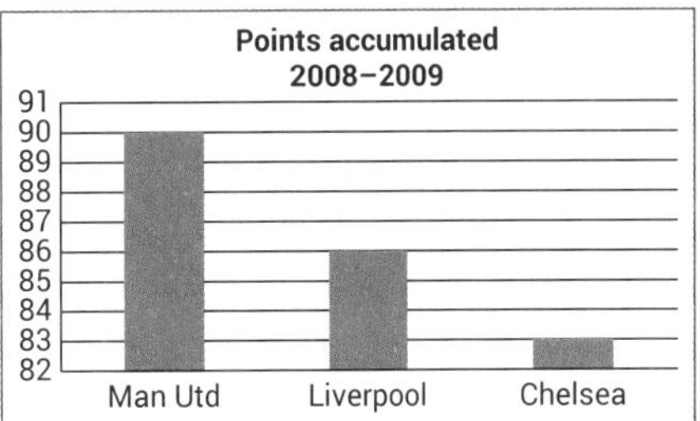

(i) What are your first impressions upon viewing the graph?

What conclusions did you draw?

(ii) How is this graph misleading?

(iii) Present the data on a chart that doesn't mislead.

(b) 'Should people who work in the home be entitled to financial support from the state?' This question was put to listeners of a morning radio show. There was a large response to the survey, and 87% of listeners said that people who work at home should be entitled to state support. Give two reasons why this is misleading.

(c) After studying the heights of boys and girls who play basketball, a student comes to the conclusion that exercise from playing basketball makes people grow taller. Comment on the student's reasoning.

(d) John believes he has found the cure for the common cold. His cure is one teaspoon of honey taken every morning for a period of two weeks. He randomly selects 10 students from all students in the school suffering from the cold. In two weeks, all 10 students had recovered. He concludes that he has made a major discovery. Comment on John's reasoning.

Exam Questions

1. A few days before the Scottish Independence Referendum in September 2014 a *YouGov* poll estimated the support for the 'No' campaign to be 54%.
   (a) If *YouGov* sampled 1,000 people, find the margin of error. Write your answer as a percentage, correct to one decimal place.
   (b) Create a 95% confidence interval for the level of support for the 'No' campaign in the population.

   SEC Leaving Certificate Ordinary Level, Paper 2, 2015

2. The table below shows the rates of births, marriages and deaths in Ireland from 1990 to 2010. The rates are per 10,000 of the estimated population.

Numbers of Births, Marriages and Deaths in Ireland (per 10,000 of the estimated population)			
Year	Births	Marriages	Deaths
1990	151	51	90
1991	150	49	89
1992	144	47	87
1993	138	47	90
1994	135	46	86
1995	135	43	90
1996	140	45	87
1997	144	43	86
1998	146	45	85
1999	144	50	87
2000	145	51	83
2001	150	50	79
2002	155	52	76
2003	155	51	73
2004	153	52	71
2005	148	52	68
2006	154	52	67
2007	163	52	64
2008	168	50	63
2009	167	48	63
2010	165	46	61

Source: Central Statistics Office. http://www.cso.ie

   (a) Complete the back-to-back stem-and-leaf plot below to show the marriage rate and death rate in Ireland during the period covered in the table above.

Marriage rate		Death rate
	4	
	5	
	6	
	7	
	8	
	9	
		Key:

   (b) State one difference that can be observed between the distributions of the marriage rate and the death rate in your plot.
   (c) Find the median and interquartile range of the yearly marriage rates in Ireland from 1990 to 2010.

STATISTICS II

(d) (i) Find the mean of the death rate in Ireland from 1990 to 2010. Give your answer correct to one decimal place.

(ii) The standard deviation of the death rates in the table over is 10.3. List all of the death rates that are within 1 standard deviation of the mean.

(e) In 2010, the number of children born in Ireland was 75,174. Use this number to estimate the total population of Ireland in 2010.

(f) Use your answer to **(e)** to estimate the number of people who died in Ireland in 2010.

(g) 'More children were born in Ireland in 1990 than in 2000.' Give a reason, based on the data, why this statement is not necessarily true.

(h) Find the ratio, Birth rate : Death rate, for the two years 1990 and 2010. Based on your answers for the two years, what would you predict about the population of Ireland in future years? Give a reason for your answer.

(i) The birth rate and death rate over the 21 years are plotted against each other in the scatter plot below. The correlation coefficient between the two sets of data is −0.85. Describe the relationship between the two sets of data and suggest a reason why this might be the case.

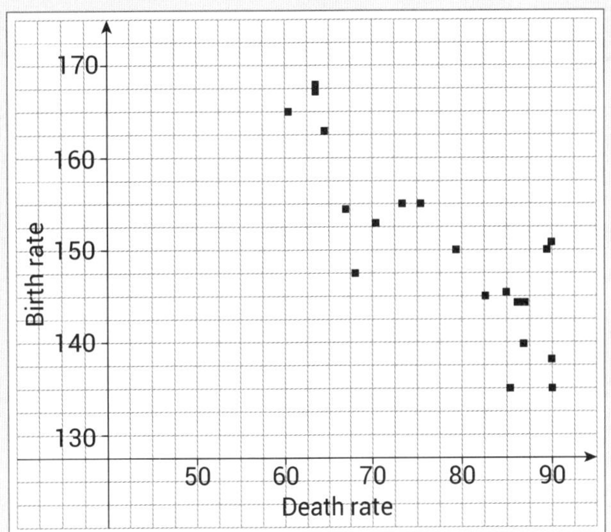

SEC Leaving Certificate Ordinary Level, Paper 2, 2013

3. The waiting times, in minutes, for 16 patients at dentist's surgery are recorded for a particular week **(Week 1)** on the following stem-and-leaf plot:

Week 2		Week 1
	0	5, 8
	1	2, 2, 2, 3
	2	0, 4, 5, 7
	3	0, 1, 2, 4, 4
	4	4
		Key: 1|3 = 13 minutes

(a) Find the mode and the median of the data.

(b) Find the mean waiting time for **Week 1**, correct to 1 decimal place.

(c) The waiting times were recorded again the following week. The results were:

27, 23, 6, 15, 18, 29, 16, 17, 15, 18, 40, 32, 16, 12, 28, 9

Show these results on the plot above (under **Week 2**), creating a back-to-back stem-and-leaf plot to display the data.

SEC Leaving Certificate Ordinary Level, Paper 2, 2016

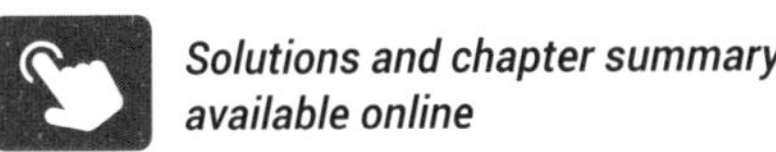

Solutions and chapter summary available online

15

Geometry

Theorems and corollaries have been marked throughout this chapter with a digital icon. They are contained within the Chapter 15 Review PowerPoint file on folens.ie.

In this chapter you will learn:

- The basic concepts of geometry and geometry notation
- What an axiom is and how to use axioms to solve problems
- The following terms related to logic and deductive reasoning: *theorem; proof; axiom; corollary; converse; implies; is equivalent to; if and only if; proof by contradiction*
- To review geometry studied at JCOL
- Theorem 7. In a triangle, the angle opposite the greater of two sides is greater than the angle opposite the lesser side. Conversely, the side opposite the greater of two angles is greater than the side opposite the lesser angle
- Theorem 8. Two sides of a triangle are together greater than the third
- Theorem 11. If three parallel lines cut off equal segments on some transversal line, then they will cut off equal segments on any other transversal
- Theorem 12. Let ABC be a triangle. If a line l is parallel to BC and cuts $[AB]$ in the ratio $m:n$, then it also cuts $[AC]$ in the same ratio
- Theorem 13. If two triangles are similar, then their sides are proportional, in order
- Theorem 16. For a triangle, base times height does not depend on the choice of base
- Theorem 17. A diagonal of a parallelogram bisects the area
- Theorem 18. The area of a parallelogram is the base times the height
- Theorem 20. Each tangent is perpendicular to the radius that goes to the point of contact. If P lies on s, and a line l is perpendicular to the radius to P, then l is a tangent to s
- Corollary 6. If two circles intersect at one point only, then the two centres and the point of contact are collinear
- Theorem 21. (i) The perpendicular from the centre to a chord bisects the chord. (ii) The perpendicular bisector of a chord passes through the centre

You should remember...

- Geometry notation
- Types of angles
- Types of triangles
- Types of quadrilaterals
- Parallel
- Perpendicular
- Junior Certificate geometry theorems
- How to deal with fractions

Key words

- Plane
- Axiom
- Theorem
- Corollary
- Converse
- Implies
- Polygon
- Quadrilateral
- Parallelogram
- Pythagoras
- Proportional
- Similar triangles
- Congruent triangles
- Area
- Circle
- Radius
- Perpendicular
- Tangent

15.1 Introduction

Geometry comes from the Greek word meaning 'earth measurement' (*γεωμετρία*; *geo* = earth, *metria* = measure). It is the study of figures and their properties in two- and three-dimensional space.

Geometry has applications from laying tiles on a floor to building a space station.

15.2 Basic Concepts

The Plane

A **plane** is a flat two-dimensional surface. It has length and width, but it has no thickness.

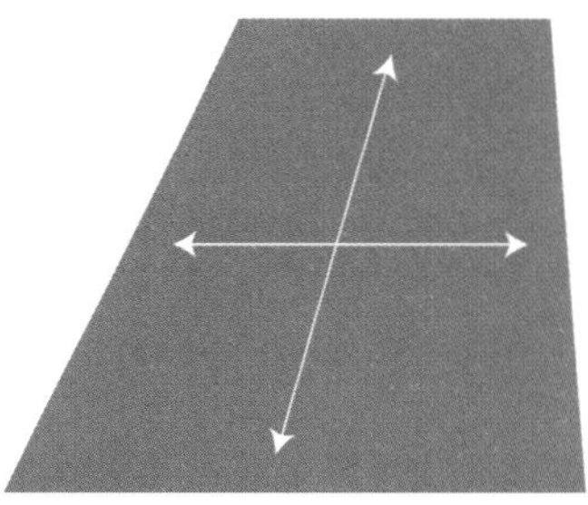

A **plane** stretches on to infinity. Points and lines are shown on a plane.

Points on the Plane

A **point** is a position on a plane. It has no dimensions.

A **point** is denoted by a capital letter and a dot.

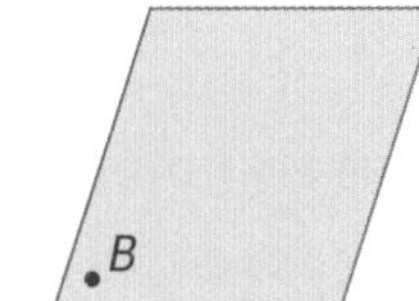

This is the point B.

If points lie on the same plane they are said to be **coplanar**.

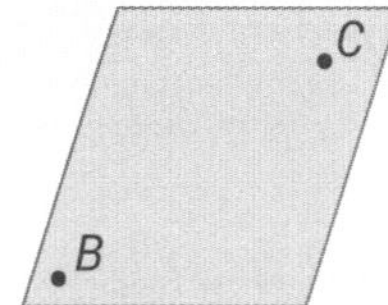

Here, B and C are **coplanar**.

Lines

A **line** is a straight, infinitely thin one-dimensional figure that continues forever in both directions; it has no endpoints.

A **line** can be named by any two points on the line or by a lower-case letter. It has an infinite number of points on it.

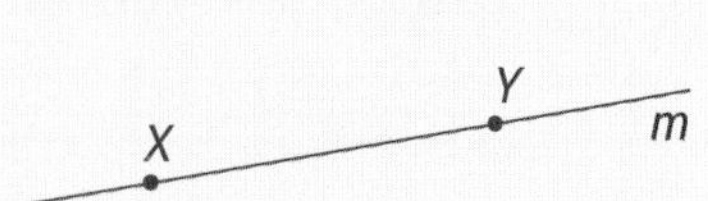

The line *XY* or the line *m*.

Points that lie on the same line are called collinear points.

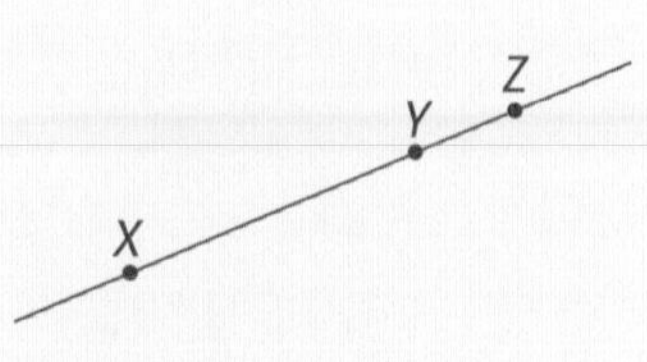

The points *X*, *Y* and *Z* are **collinear**.

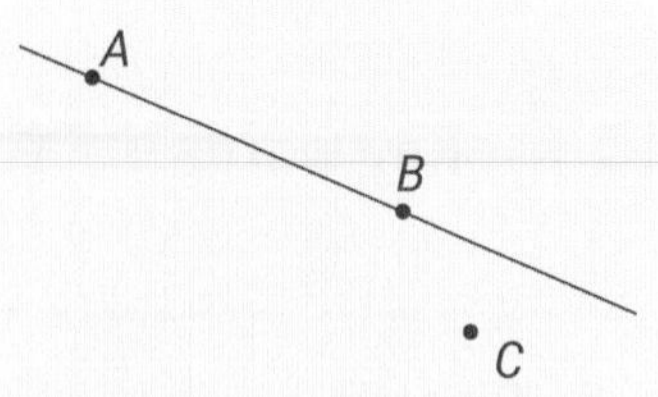

The points *A*, *B* and *C* are not collinear.

Perpendicular and Parallel Lines

The line *a* is **perpendicular** to the line *b*.

Perpendicular lines are lines that are at right angles or 90° to each other.

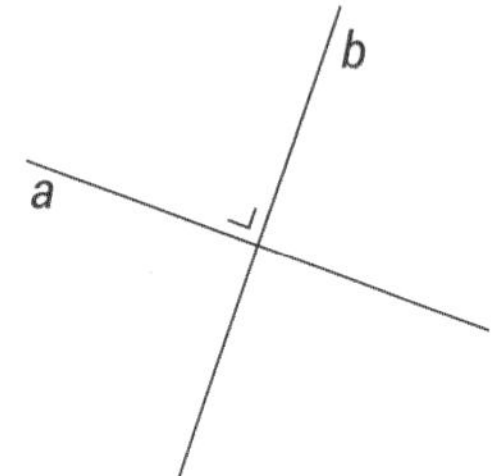

We denote this as $a \perp b$.

The line *d* is **parallel** to the line *e*.

Parallel lines are lines that are the same distance apart. They never meet.

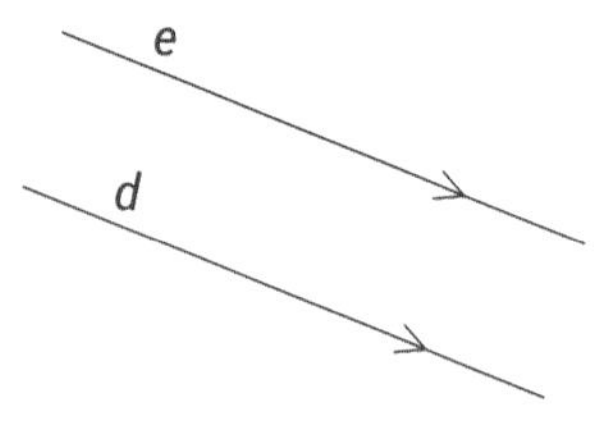

We denote this as $d \parallel e$.

Line Segment

The **line segment** shown has one endpoint *A* and another endpoint *B*.

A line segment is part of a straight line. It has two endpoints and can be measured using a ruler.

A B

This is the line segment [*AB*] or [*BA*].

When we write an actual measurement, we use the | | symbols to show this.

A 5 cm B

$|AB| = 5$ cm

Ray

A ray is part of a line that originates at a point and goes on forever in only one direction. A ray is sometimes called a half-line.

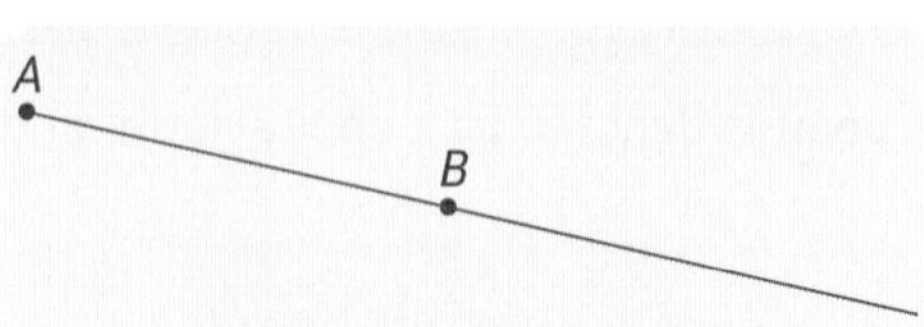

This is the **ray** [*AB*. It can also be called *BA*]

A single square bracket is used to denote from where the ray originates.

When two rays meet at a point called the vertex, they make an angle.

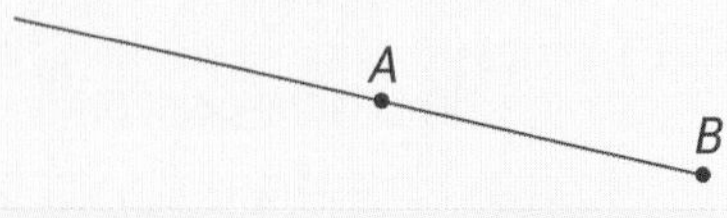

This is the ray [*BA*. It can also be called *AB*]

15.3 Angles

Angle Notation

There are many different ways to label an angle.

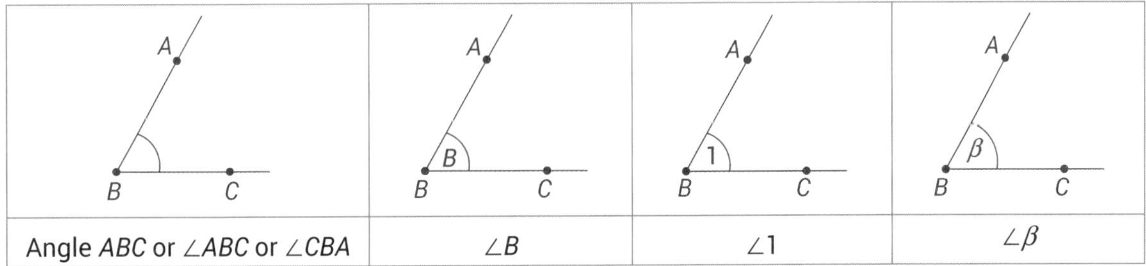

Angle ABC or $\angle ABC$ or $\angle CBA$	$\angle B$	$\angle 1$	$\angle \beta$

Identifying Different Types of Angles

Angles can be divided into many different types.

Null angle	**Acute angle**	**Right angle**
Angle = 0°	An angle that measures more than 0° but less than 90°	Angle = 90°
Obtuse angle	**Straight angle**	**Reflex angle**
An angle that measures more than 90° but less than 180°	180° Angle = 180°	An angle that measures more than 180° but less than 360°
Full angle	**Ordinary angle**	**Supplementary angles**
360° Full rotation, angle = 360°	An angle that measures more than 0° but less than 180°	1 2 Two angles whose measures add up to 180° $\vert\angle 1\vert + \vert\angle 2\vert = 180°$

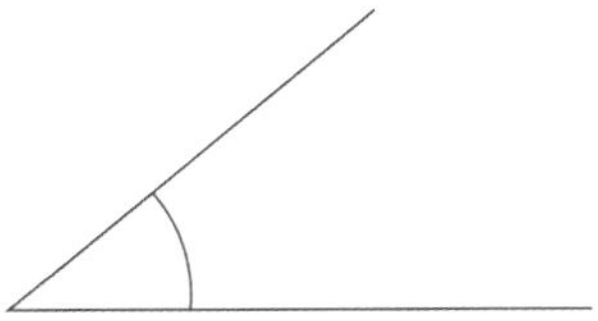

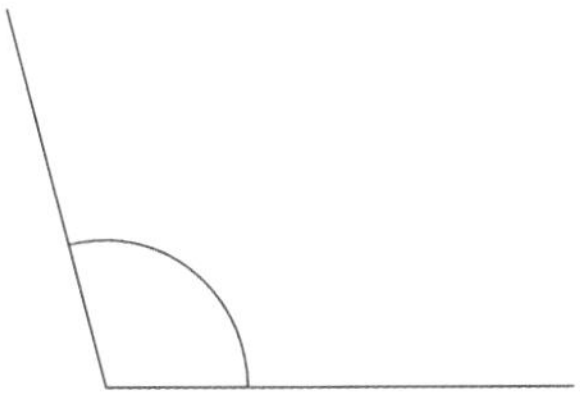

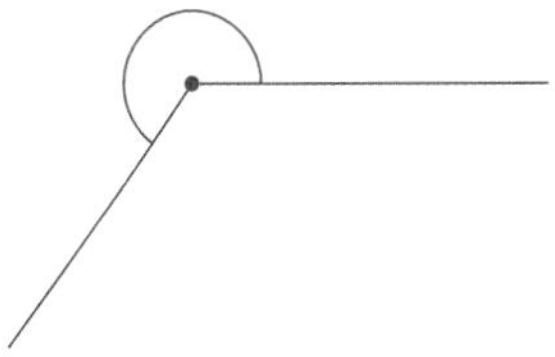

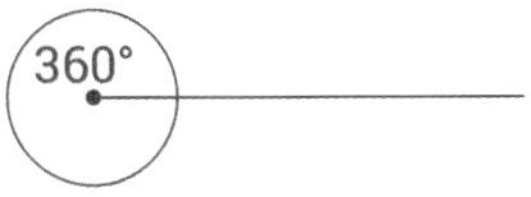

Supplementary angles do not need to be beside or adjacent to each other.

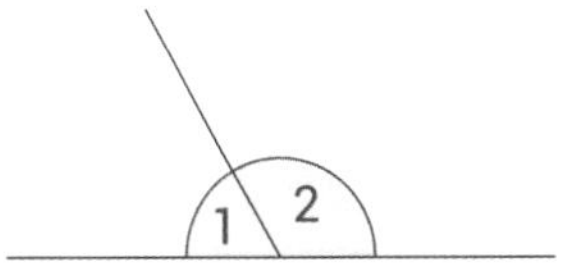

For example, the two angles shown are supplementary.

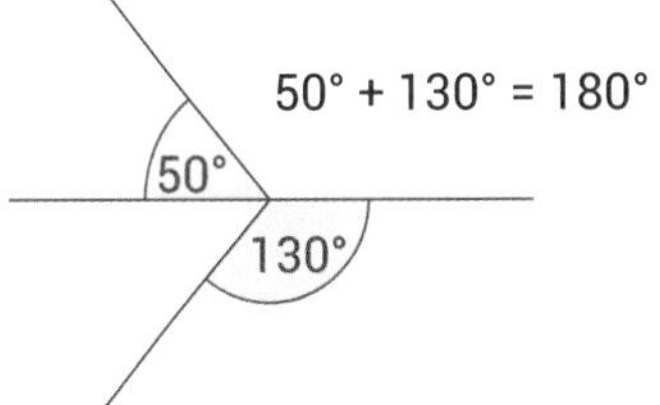

Measuring Angles

Angles on our course are measured in degrees.

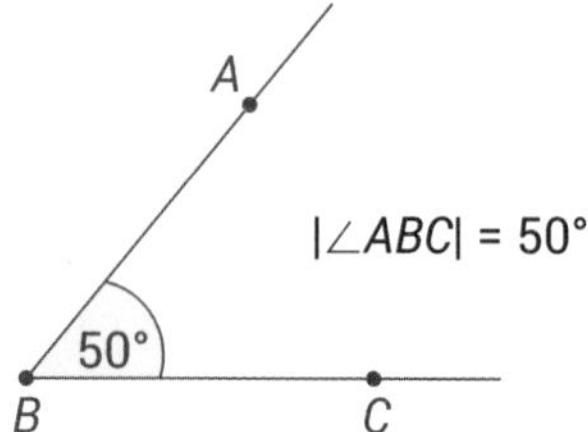

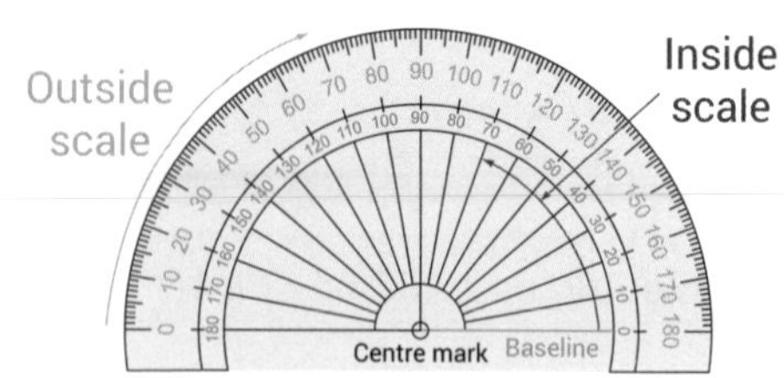

We use a protractor to measure angles accurately.
A protractor has two scales, a centre point and a baseline.

15.4 Axioms

An axiom is a statement that we accept **without any proof**. Knowing axioms is essential to understanding geometry and proving geometry theorems.

Axiom 1 (Two Points Axiom)
There is exactly one line through any two given points.

We can draw only one line through the points A and B.

Axiom 2 (Ruler Axiom)
The properties of the distance between points.

1. Distance is never a negative number.
2. $|AB| = |BA|$
3. If C lies on AB, between A and B, then $|AB| = |AC| + |CB|$.

4. Given any ray from the point X and a distance $d \geqslant 0$, there is exactly one point Y on the ray whose distance from X is d. This property means that we can mark off a distance of, say, 4 cm on a ray from a point X and call this point Y.
The length of the line segment $[XY]$ will also be 4 cm.

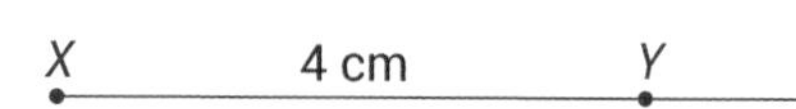

Axiom 3 (Protractor Axiom)
The properties of the degree measure of an angle.

The number of degrees in an angle is always a number between 0 and 360. This axiom has the following properties:

1. A straight angle has 180°.

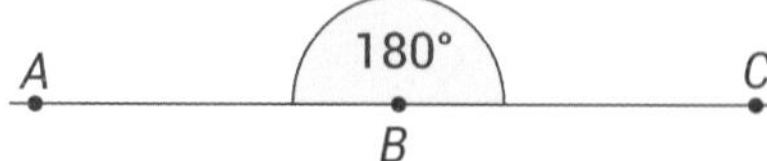

All the angles at a point add up to 360°.

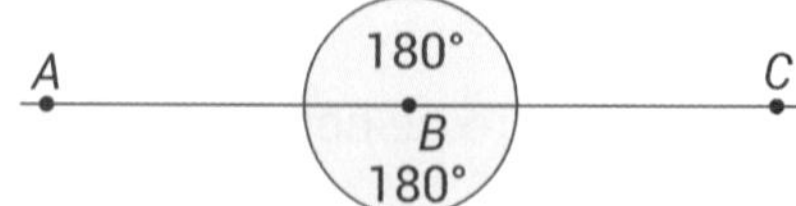

2. Given a ray $[AB$ and a number between 0 and 180, there is exactly one ray from A, on each side of the line AB, that makes an (ordinary) angle having d degrees with the ray $[AB$.
This property of the protractor axiom means that there is, for example, only one 60° angle on each side of the line AB.

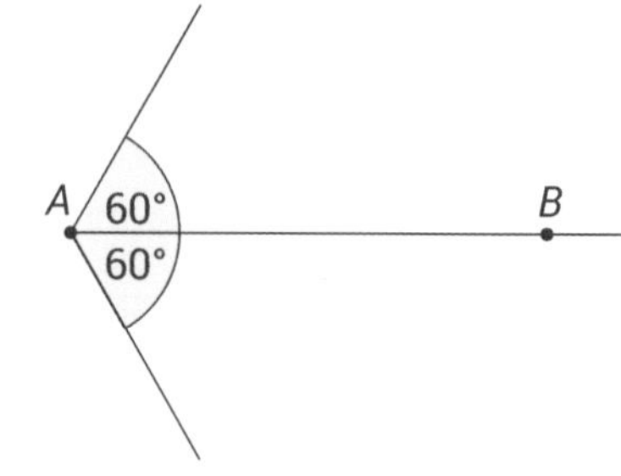

3. If an angle is divided into two smaller angles, then these two angles add up to the original angle.

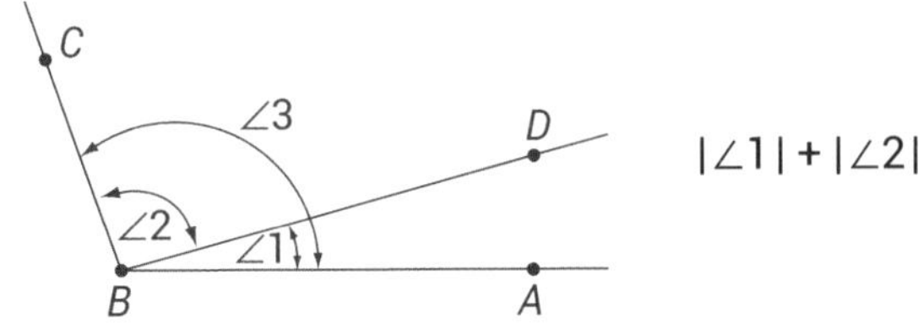

$|\angle 1| + |\angle 2| = |\angle 3|$

Axiom 5 (Axiom of Parallels)
Given any line *l* and a point *P*, there is exactly one line through *P* that is parallel to *l*.

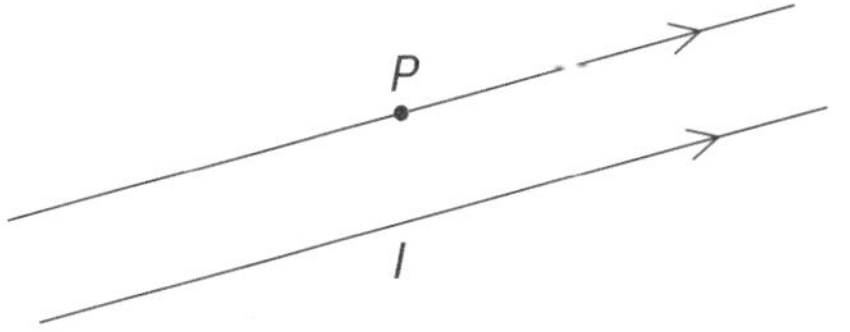

Only one line can be drawn through the point *P* that is parallel to the line *l*.

Worked Example 15.1

Solve for *x* in the following diagram, given that *AB* is a straight line:

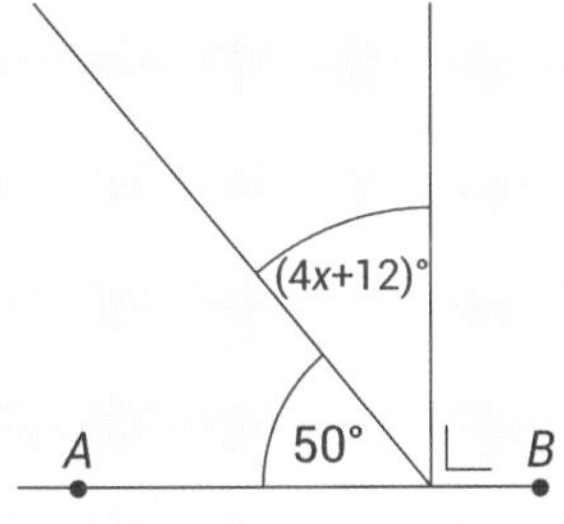

Note any symbols and their meaning. The symbol ∟ denotes an angle measuring 90°.

Solution

$50° + (4x + 12)° + 90° = 180°$ (Straight angle)

$\Rightarrow \quad 4x + 152° = 180°$

$\Rightarrow \quad 4x = 180° - 152°$

$\Rightarrow \quad 4x = 28°$

$\therefore \quad x = 7°$

Remember to show as much work as possible.

Remember also to give reasons for your workings.

Worked Example 15.2

Without measuring, find the measure of $\angle ABC$.

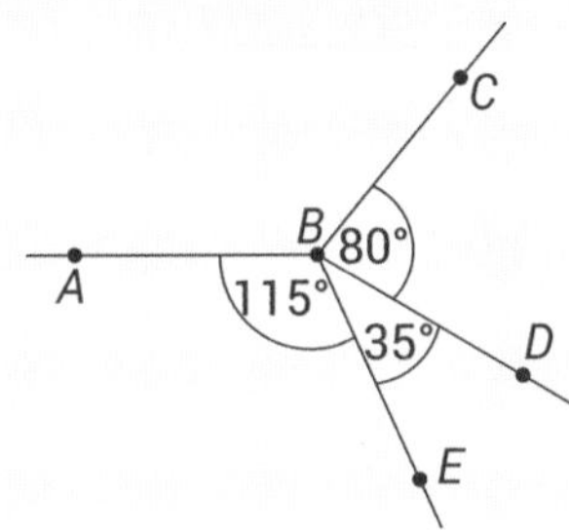

Solution

$115° + 35° + 80° + |\angle ABC| = 360°$ (Full angle)

$|\angle ABC| + 230° = 360°$

$\Rightarrow |\angle ABC| = 360° - 230°$

$\therefore |\angle ABC| = 130°$

GEOMETRY

Exercise 15.1

1. Identify in the following figure:

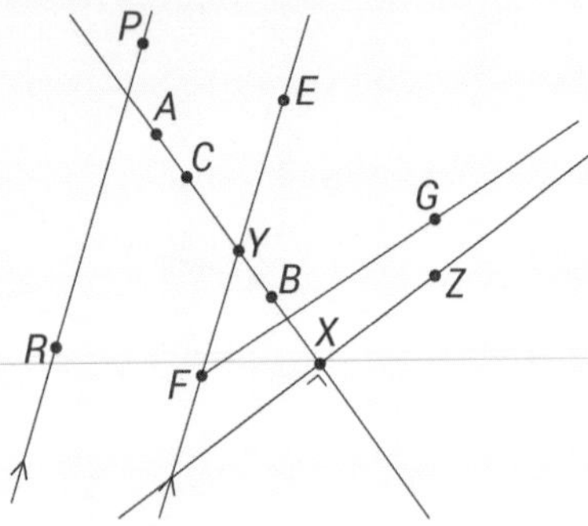

   (i) A point
   (ii) A line
   (iii) A ray
   (iv) A pair of parallel lines
   (v) A pair of perpendicular lines
   (vi) Four collinear points
   (vii) A point of intersection of two lines

2. Explain each of the following terms used in geometry. Use diagrams if necessary.

   (i) Obtuse angle
   (ii) Right angle
   (iii) Acute angle
   (iv) Straight angle
   (v) Reflex angle
   (vi) Null angle

3. Use a protractor to measure the following angles. In each case, name and identify the type of angle.

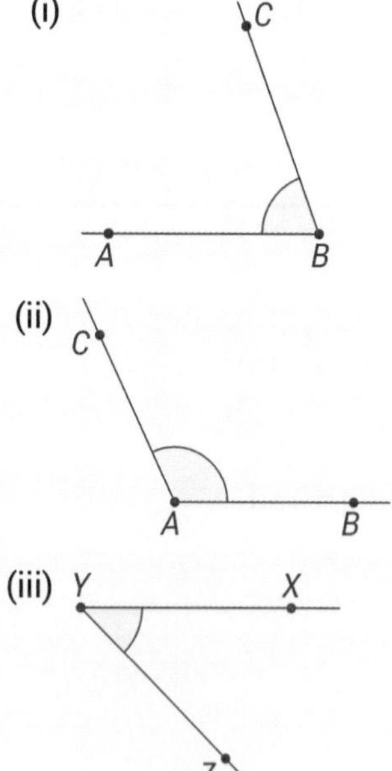

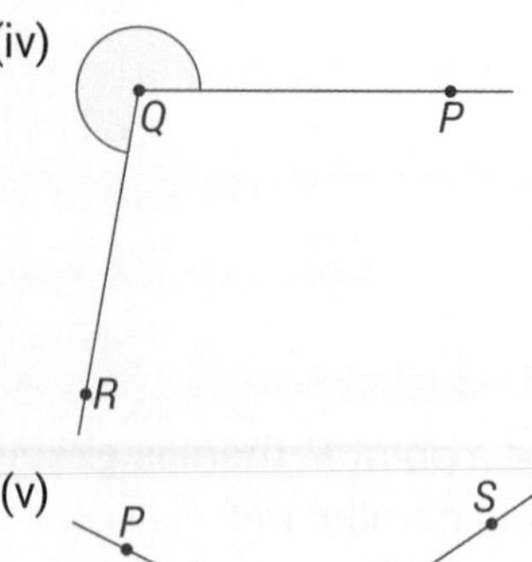

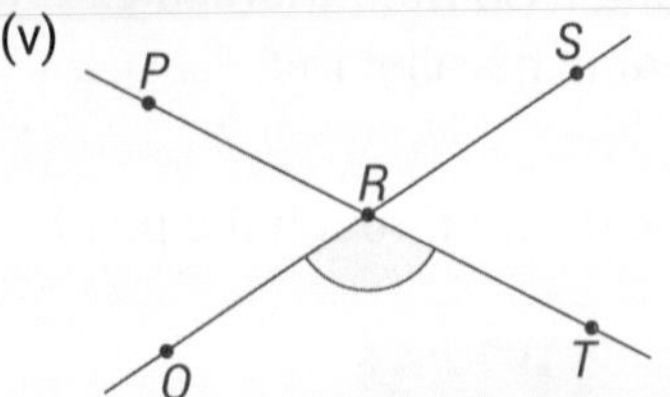

4. Use a protractor to draw the following angles:

   (i) 65°
   (ii) 135°
   (iii) 210°
   (iv) 335°
   (v) 90°
   (vi) 172°

5. Consider the following angles:

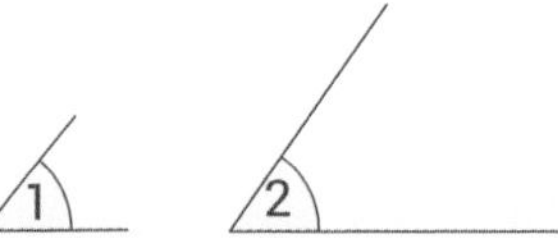

   (i) Estimate which angle is the smallest.
   (ii) Explain how you estimated your answer.
   (iii) Check your answer using a protractor.
   (iv) Does the length of the arm of the angle affect the measure of the angle? Give a reason for your answer.

6. Find the measure of each of the unknown angles without measuring them, given that *l* is a straight line (where shown).

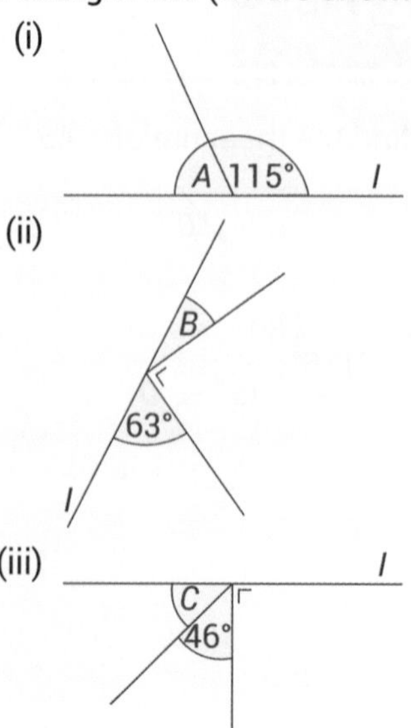

(iv)

(v)

(vi)

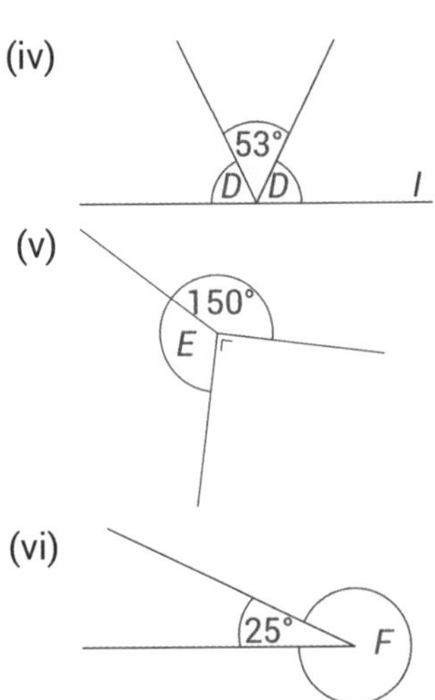

(vii)

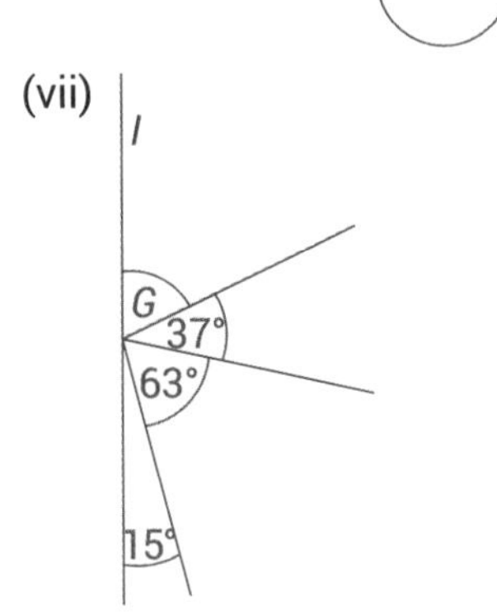

7. Solve for x in each of the following diagrams, given that l is a straight line:

(i)

(ii)

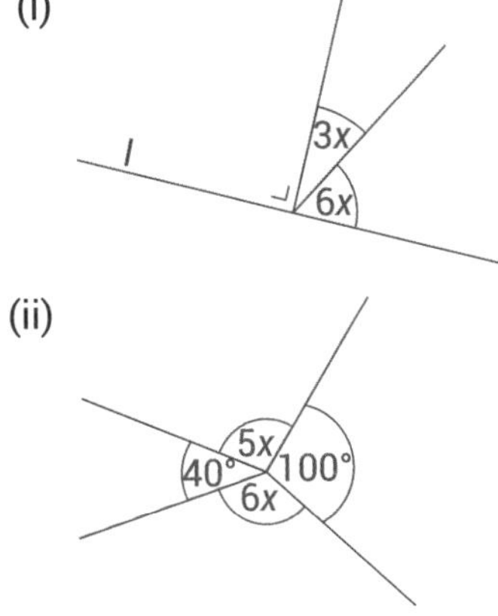

(iii)

(iv)

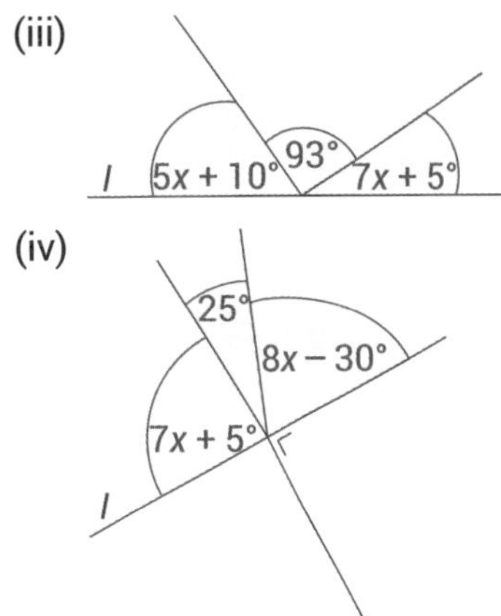

8. Solve for x and y in each of the following diagrams, given that l is a straight line:

(i)

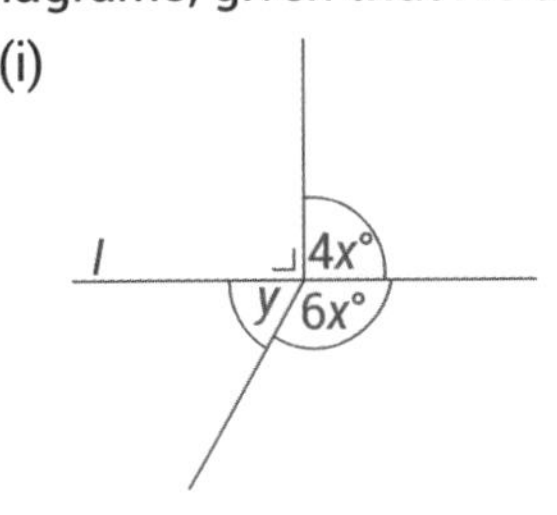

(ii)

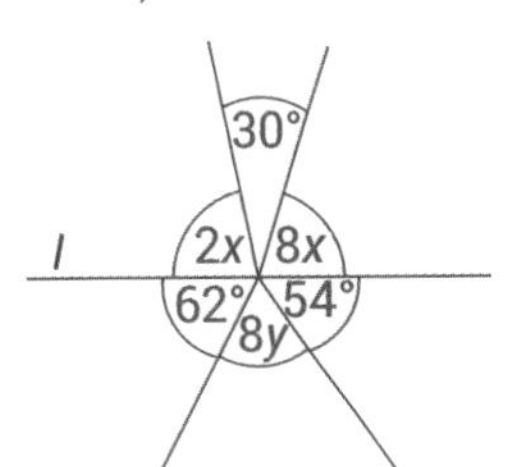

15.5 Theorem Terms

When dealing specifically with **theorems**, there are some terms that we need to understand.

A **proposition** is a mathematical statement. It may be true or false.
A **proof** is a series of logical steps that we use to prove a proposition.

To help us in writing a **proof**, we need to know the meaning of certain terms.

Basic Geometric Terms

An **axiom** is a rule or statement that we accept without any proof.

For example: There is exactly one line through any two given points.

GEOMETRY

A **theorem** is a statement that may be proved by following a certain number of logical steps. These steps may use previously proven theorems or axioms.

For example: 'A diagonal of a parallelogram bisects the area' is a theorem.

A **corollary** is a statement that follows readily from a previous theorem.

For example: Each angle in a semicircle is a right angle.

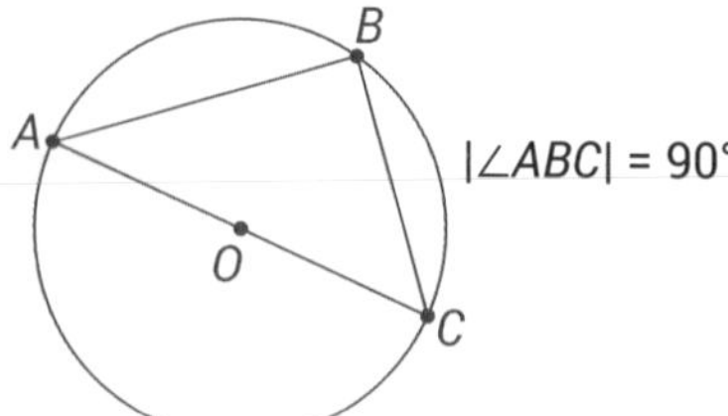

Most geometry theorems begin with a statement (hypothesis), which leads to a conclusion.

The **converse** of a theorem is formed by swapping the order of the hypothesis and conclusion. The conditional statement 'if A, then B' has a hypothesis (A) and a conclusion (B). In general, the converse of 'if A, then B' is 'if B, then A'. Converses may or may not be true.

For example:

Statement: If a transversal makes equal alternate angles on two lines, then the lines are parallel.

Converse: If two lines are parallel, then any transversal will make equal alternate angles with them.

This converse is true.

Another example of a statement with a true converse would be:

Statement: In an isosceles triangle the angles opposite the equal sides are equal in measure.

Converse: If two angles in a triangle are equal in measure, then the triangle is isosceles.

A converse of a statement may not be true. For example:

Statement: If a quadrilateral is a square, then opposite sides are equal in length (True).

Converse: If opposite sides in a quadrilateral are equal in length, then the quadrilateral is a square (False).

Implies is a term we use in a proof when we can write down a fact we have proved from our previous statements. The symbol for implies is $\Rightarrow$.

For example, consider the triangle ABC shown.

The angles in triangle ABC are all equal.

$\Rightarrow$ Triangle ABC is equilateral.

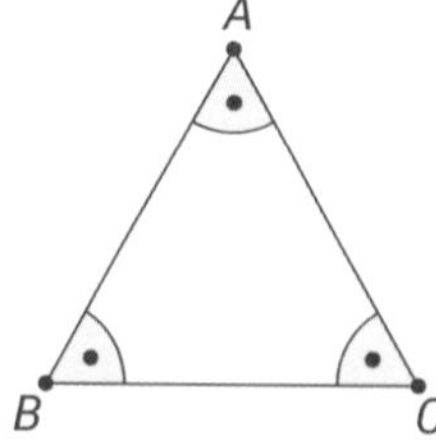

GEOMETRY

Exercise 15.2

1. Write down, in your own words, an explanation for the following terms. Use diagrams where necessary and give an example in each case.

   (i) Proposition (ii) Proof (iii) Axiom (iv) Theorem (v) Corollary (vi) Converse (vii) Implies

2. (i) Complete the table below. One has been done for you.

Statement	True/False	Converse	True/False
The diagonals of a parallelogram bisect one another.	True	If the diagonals of a quadrilateral bisect one another, then the quadrilateral is a parallelogram.	True
If a person is in Cork then they are in Munster.			
In a right-angled triangle, the square on the hypotenuse is equal to the sum of the squares of the other two sides.			
If a triangle is equilateral, then it is also isosceles.			
If $x = 5$ then $x^2 = 25$.			
If today is Monday then yesterday was Sunday.			

(ii) Without using the statements in part (i), give an example of:

(a) A statement that is true, of which the converse is also true

(b) A statement that is true, of which the converse is false

15.6 Angles and Lines

In the previous sections, we looked at the different concepts, types of angle and axioms from our geometry course. We can now investigate certain properties, rules or theorems associated with various geometrical shapes.

Let us begin by investigating the relationships between angles and certain lines.

Given two intersecting lines, **vertically opposite angles** are angles that have the same vertex and are not adjacent to each other.

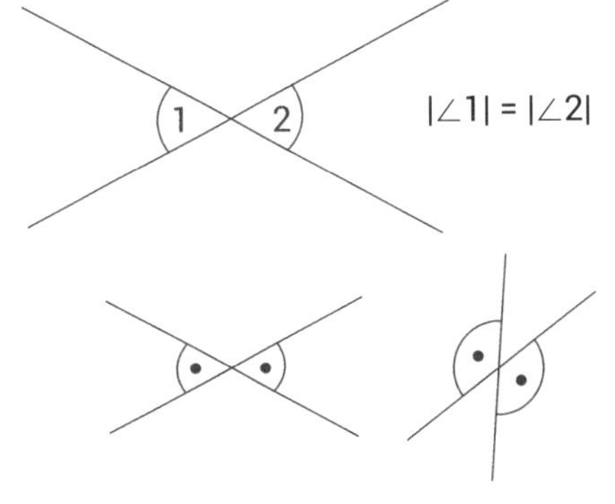

Theorem 1
Vertically opposite angles are equal in measure.

To spot **vertically opposite angles,** we look for the **X shape**.

Worked Example 15.3

Two lines, *AD* and *CE*, intersect at *B*. Find the measure of the angle *ABC* and the angle *DBC*.

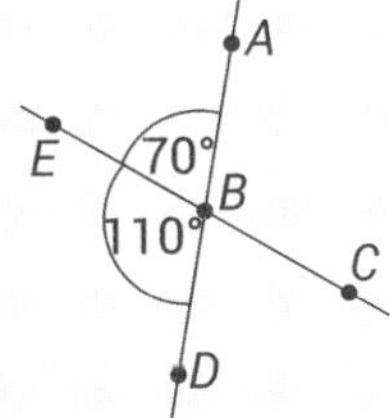

Solution

$|\angle ABC| = 110°$ Angle vertically opposite is 110°.

$|\angle DBC| = 70°$ Angle vertically opposite is 70°.

When a line cuts across two or more other lines, certain angles are formed.

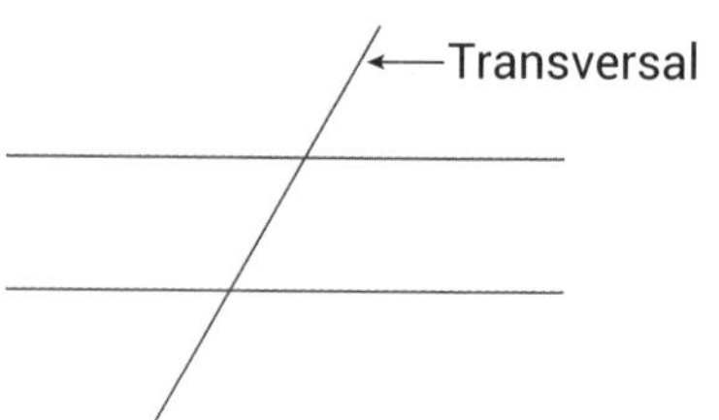

A line that cuts two or more lines is called a **transversal**.

Alternate angles are on opposite sides of the transversal that cuts two lines but are between the two lines.

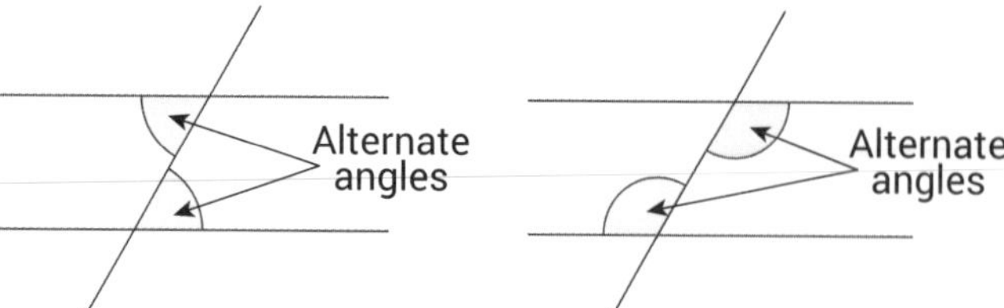

Remember to look for the **Z shape**.

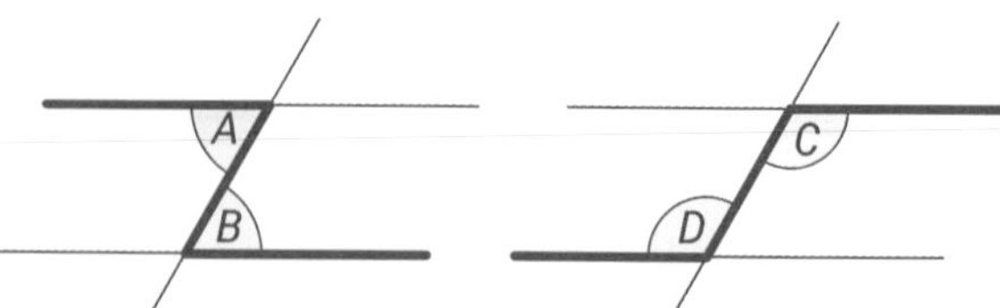

If we have two **parallel lines**, then the alternate angles formed by a transversal are **equal**.

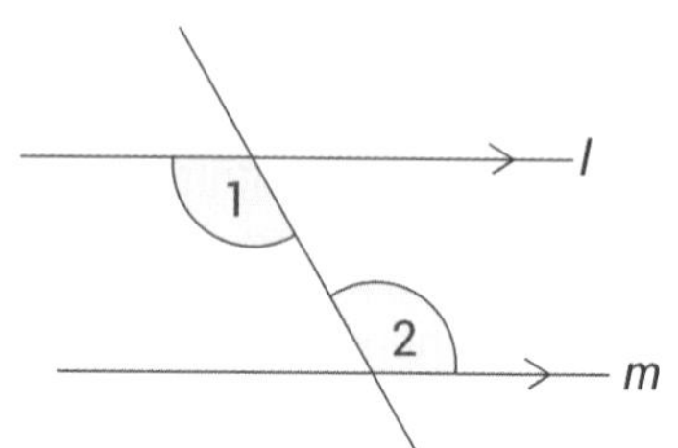

$l \parallel m \Rightarrow |\angle 1| = |\angle 2|$

The converse (reverse) of this statement also applies:

If the alternate angles are **equal**, the transversal has cut two **parallel lines**.

Remember that alternate angles are formed when a traversal cuts two or more lines. The alternate angles are equal only if the lines the transversal cuts are parallel.

Theorem 3

If a transversal makes equal alternate angles on two lines then the lines are parallel (and converse).

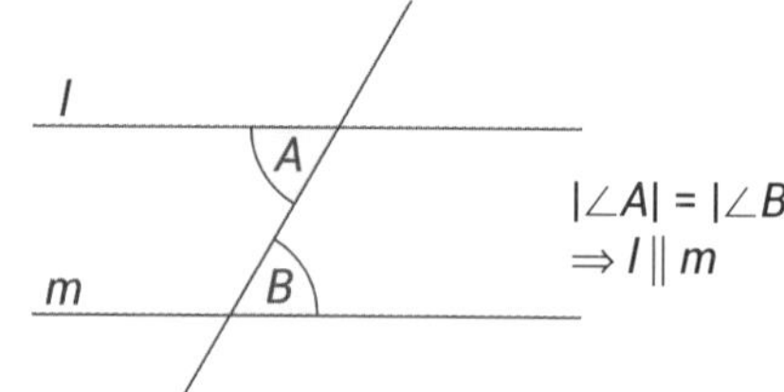

$|\angle A| = |\angle B|$
$\Rightarrow l \parallel m$

Corresponding angles are on the same side of the transversal that cuts two lines. One angle is between the lines, and the other angle is outside the lines.

Remember to look for the **F shape**.

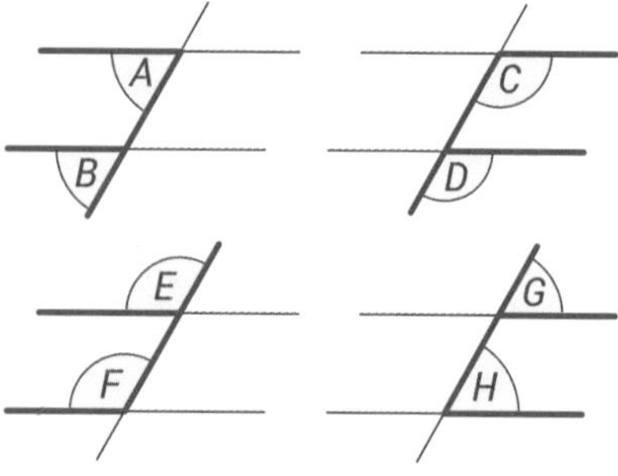

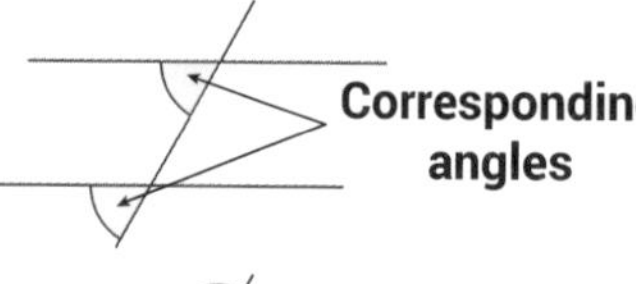

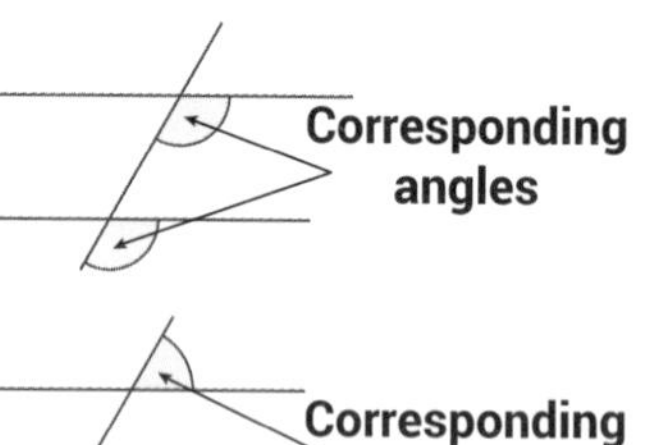

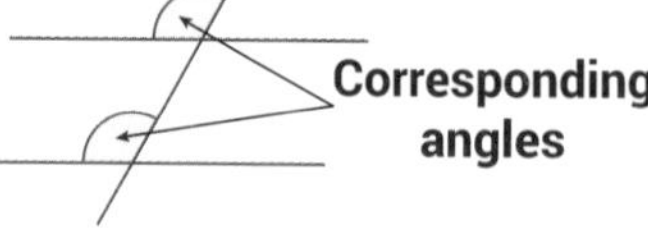

If we have two **parallel lines**, then the corresponding angles formed by a transversal are **equal**.

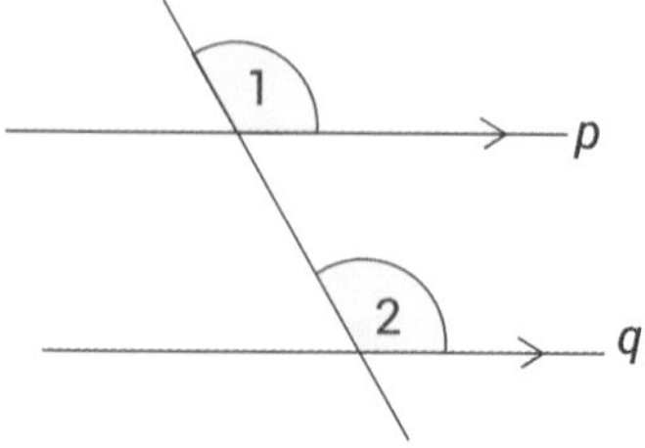

$p \parallel q \Rightarrow |\angle 1| = |\angle 2|$

The converse (reverse) of this statement is also true.

If the corresponding angles are **equal**, the transversal has cut two **parallel lines**.

$|\angle 1| = |\angle 2| \Rightarrow p \parallel q$

Theorem 5

Two lines are parallel if, and only if, for any transversal, the corresponding angles are equal.

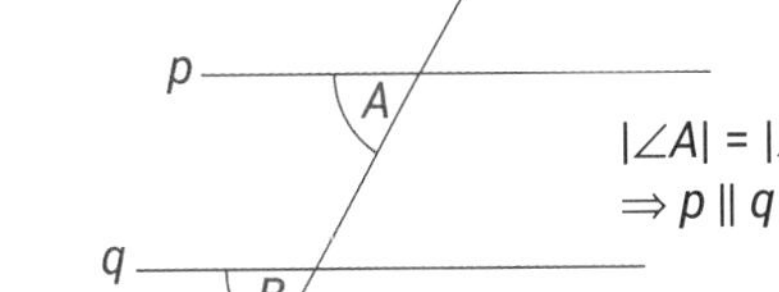

$|\angle A| = |\angle B|$
$\Rightarrow p \parallel q$

Interior angles between two parallel lines add up to 180°.

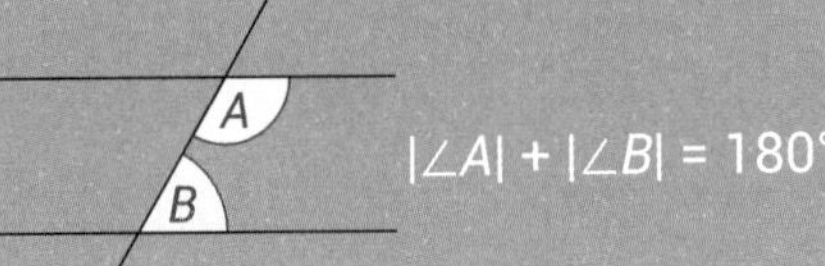

$|\angle A| + |\angle B| = 180°$

Worked Example 15.4

Without measuring, find the value of $|\angle A|$, $|\angle B|$, $|\angle C|$ and $|\angle D|$.

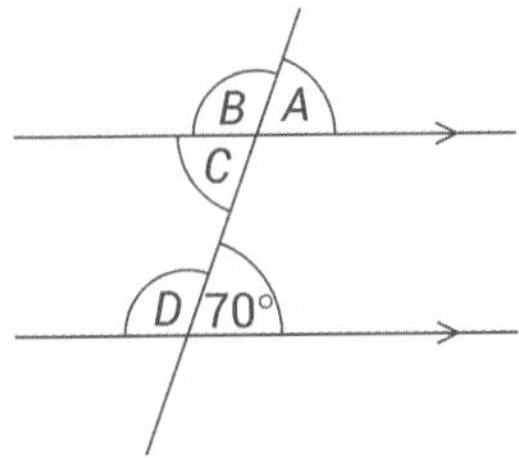

Solution

$|\angle D| = 180° - 70°$ (Straight angle)

$\therefore |\angle D| = 110°$

$|\angle C| = 70°$ (Equal alternate angle)

$|\angle A| = 70°$ (Equal corresponding angle or vertically opposite to C)

$|\angle B| = 110°$ (Equal corresponding angle to D)

Worked Example 15.5

Without measuring, find the value of $|\angle 1|$.

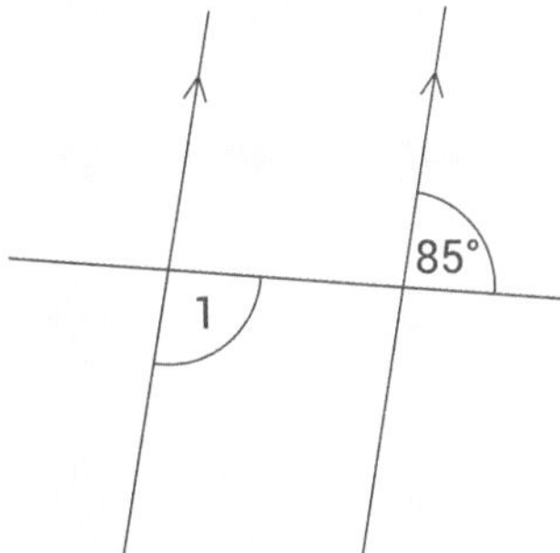

This question is more difficult, as we must determine ourselves which angles to use.

Solution

Fill in Angle 2.

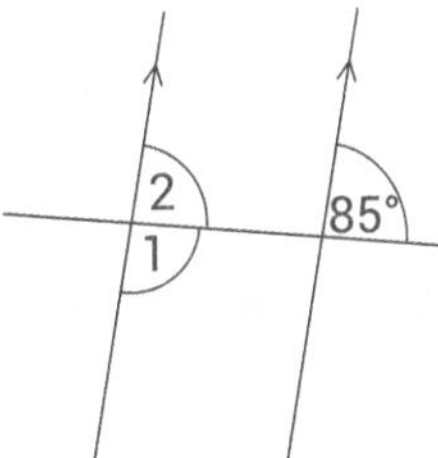

Remember: Many questions have more than one way in which to find the measure of the required angle.

$|\angle 2| = 85°$ (Equal corresponding angle)

$|\angle 1| = 180° - 85°$ (Straight angle)

$\therefore |\angle 1| = 95°$

Exercise 15.3

1. Find the measure of angle A in each of the following diagrams that show intersecting lines. Make sure to show all your work and give a reason for your answer. Do not use a protractor.

(i) (ii)

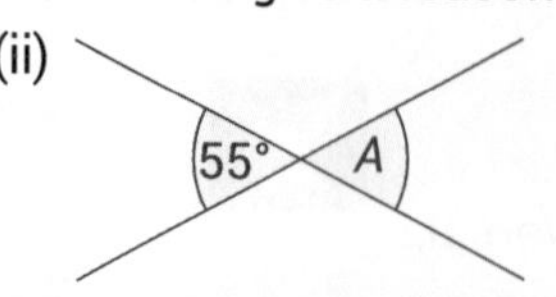

(iii)

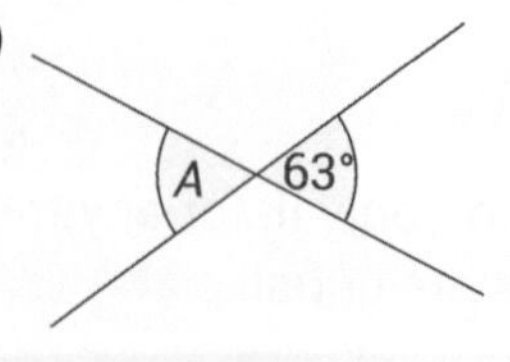

(iv)

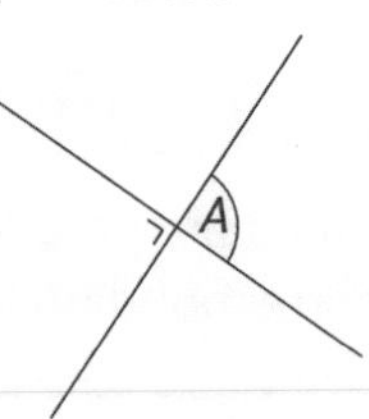

2. Find the value of B and C in each of the following diagrams that show intersecting lines. Make sure to show all your work. Do not use a protractor.

(i) (ii)

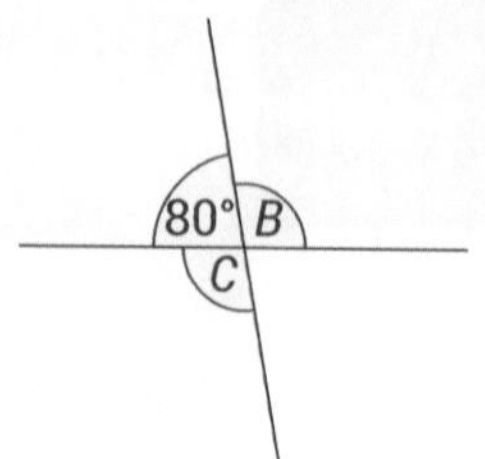

(iii)

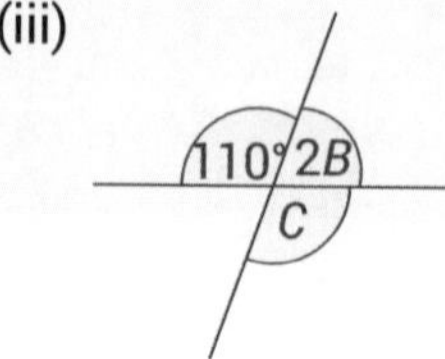

(iv)

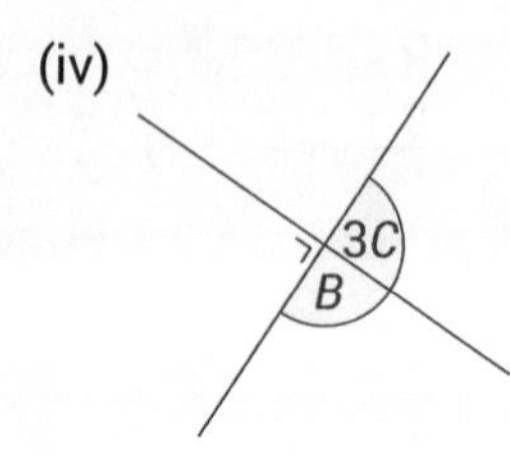

3. Find $|\angle 1|$ and $|\angle 2|$ in each of the following diagrams. Make sure to show all your work and give a reason for your answer.

(i)

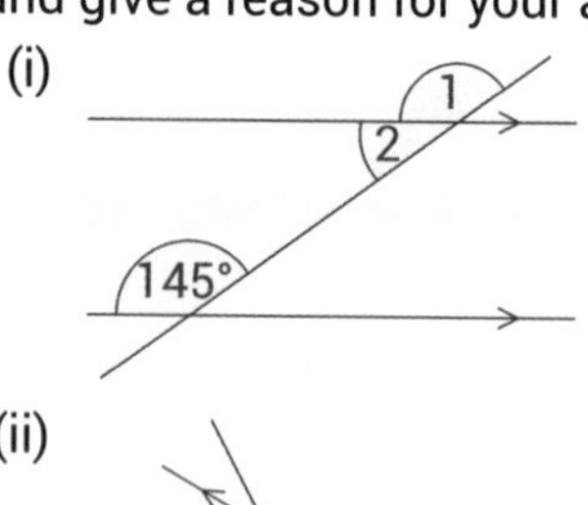

(ii)

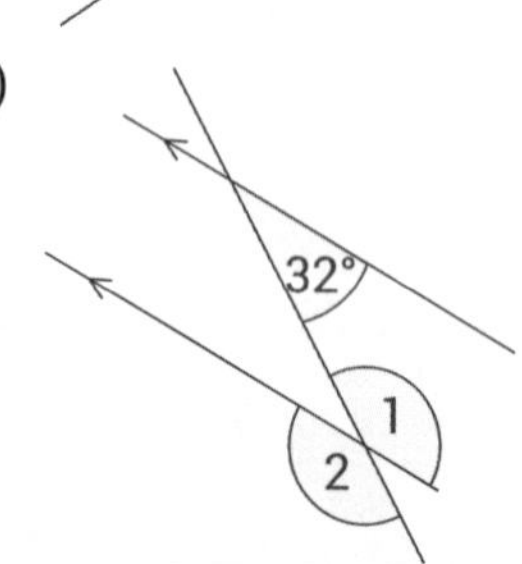

(iii)

(iv)

(v)

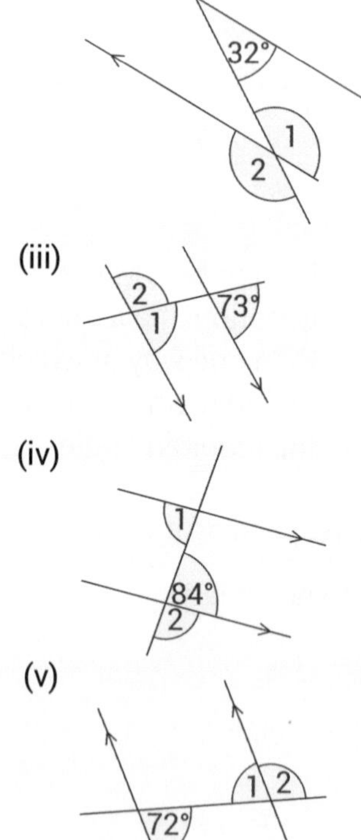

4. Investigate if each of the following pairs of lines are parallel. Explain your answer in each case.

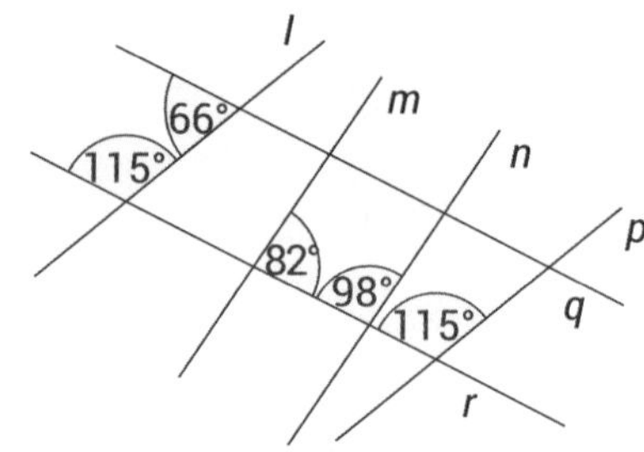

(i) m and n

(ii) p and l

(iii) r and q

5. Find the size of each of the unknown angles marked in each of the following diagrams. Make sure to show all your work and give a reason for your answer.

(i)

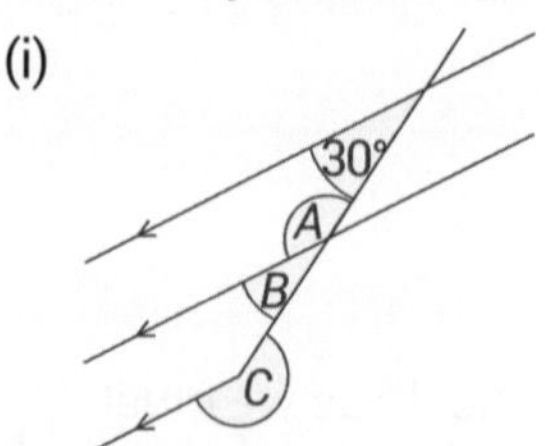

(ii)

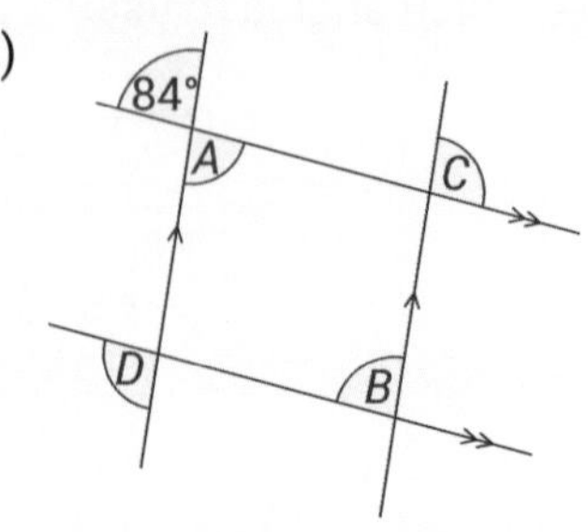

(iii)

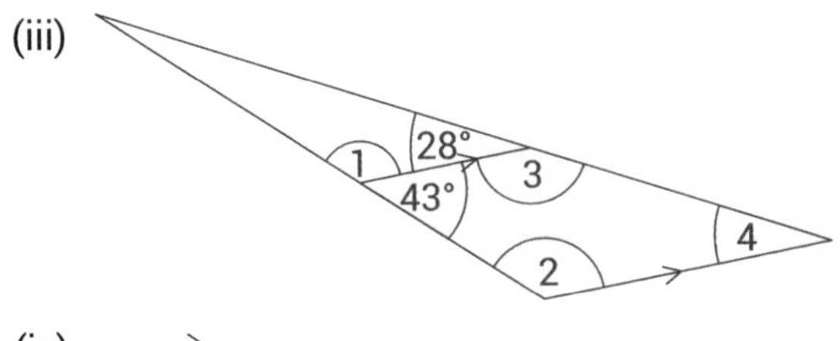

(iv)

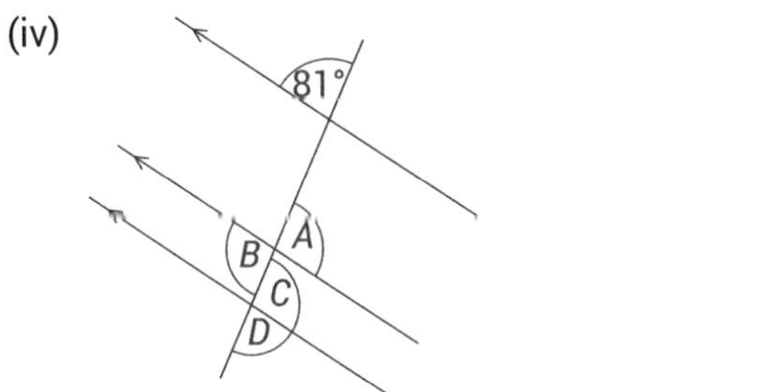

(v)

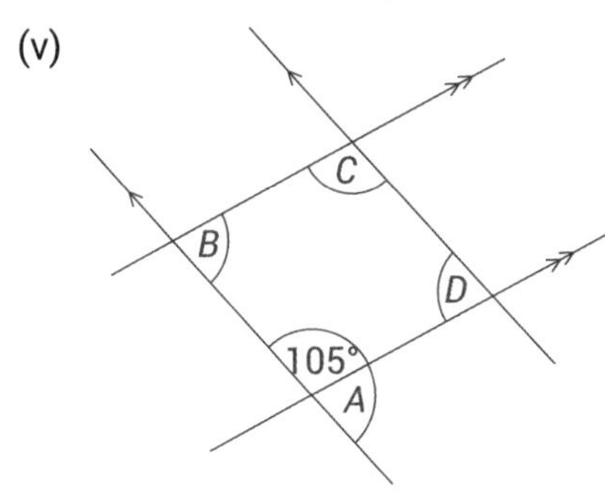

(vi)

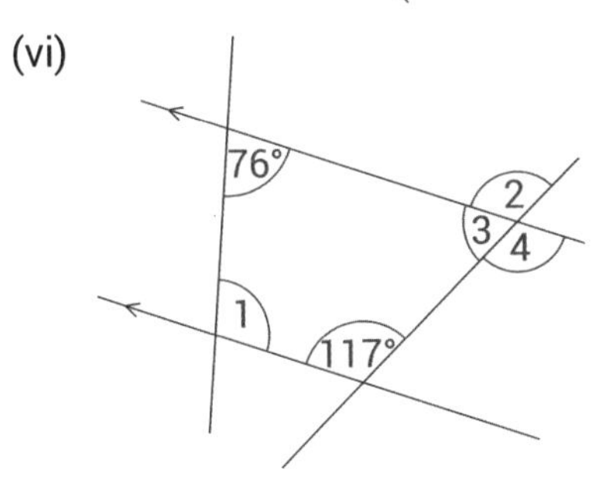

6. Find the value of x and y in each of the following diagrams. (Diagrams are not drawn to scale.)

(i)

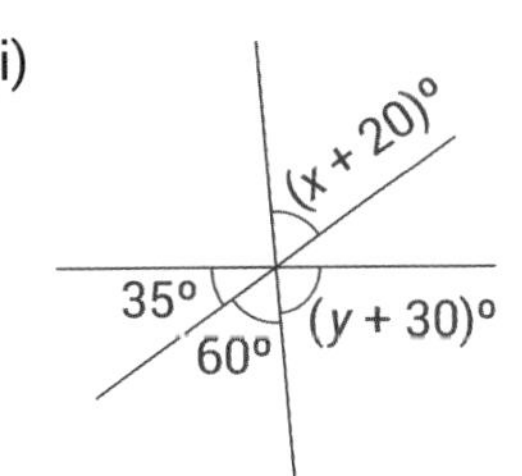

(ii)

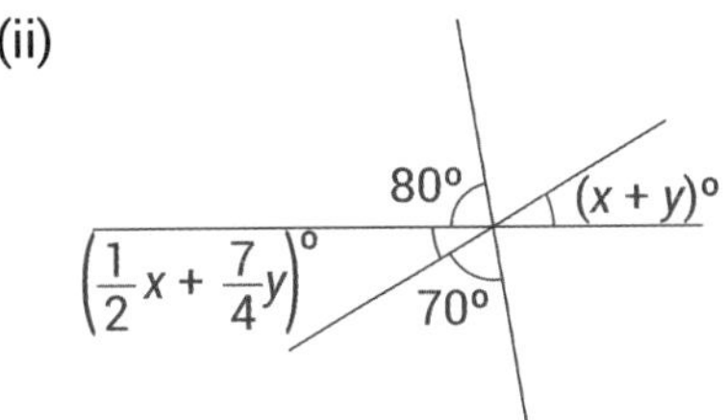

(iii)

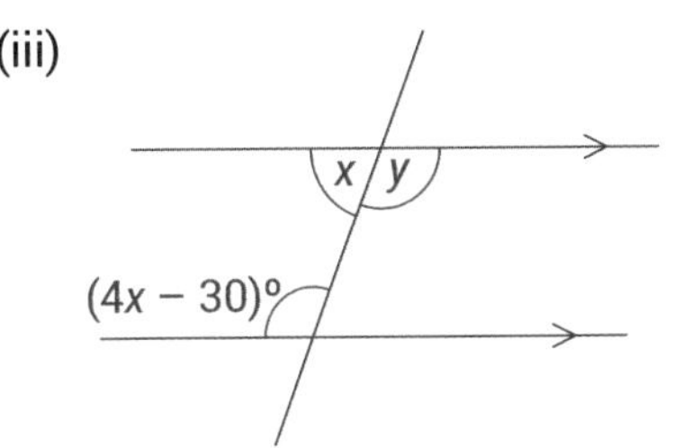

15.7 Triangles I: Angles and Sides

When investigating triangles, we must first be aware of the different types of triangles and the notation used to describe them.

Equilateral	Isosceles	Scalene
60° 60° 60°		
All sides the same length	At least two sides the same length	No sides the same length
All angles the same size (60°)	At least two angles the same size	No angles the same size

An equilateral triangle is also considered to be an isosceles triangle. This is because **at least two** sides or angles are equal.

Angles in Triangles

We can now investigate some theorems associated with triangles.

Theorem 2

In an isosceles triangle the angles opposite the equal sides are equal in measure. Conversely, if two angles in a triangle are equal in measure, then the triangle is isosceles.

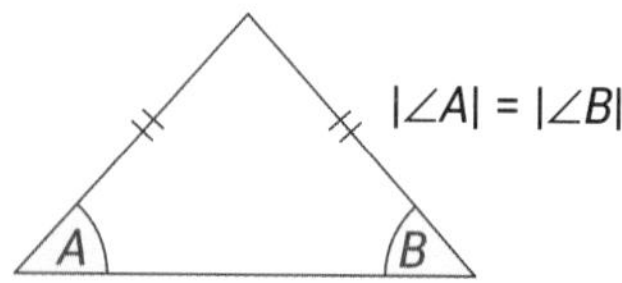

$|\angle A| = |\angle B|$

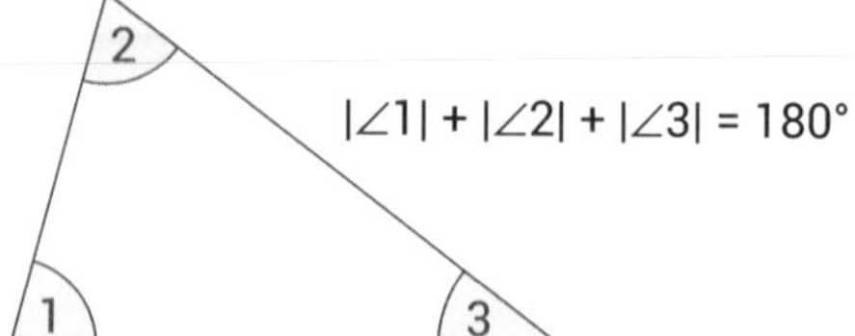

$|\angle 1| + |\angle 2| + |\angle 3| = 180°$

Theorem 4

The angles in any triangle add to 180°.

An **exterior angle** of a triangle is the angle between one side of the triangle and the extension of an adjacent side.

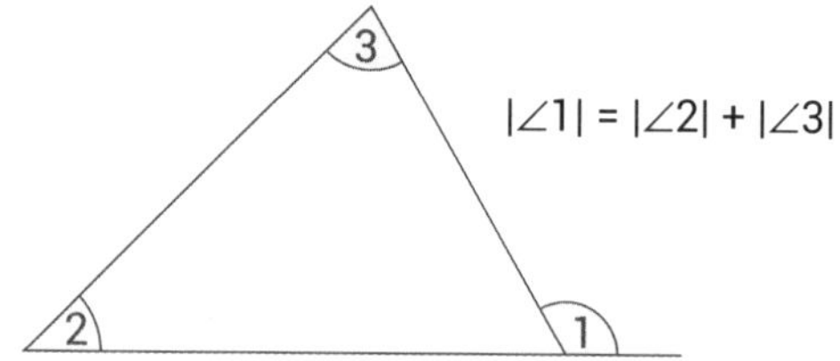

$|\angle 1| = |\angle 2| + |\angle 3|$

Theorem 6

Each exterior angle of a triangle is equal to the sum of the interior opposite angles.

Worked Example 15.6

Without measuring, find the value of $|\angle 1|$.

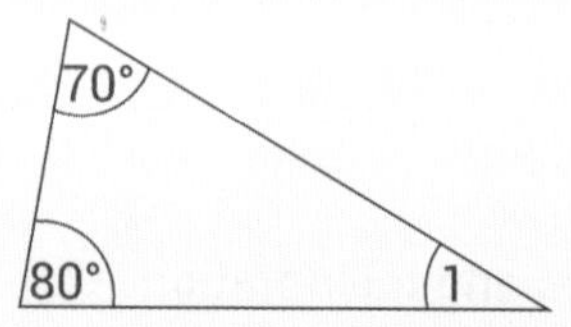

Solution

$|\angle 1| + 80° + 70° = 180°$ (180° in a triangle)

$\Rightarrow |\angle 1| = 180° - 80° - 70°$

$\therefore |\angle 1| = 30°$

Worked Example 15.7

Find $|\angle X|$.

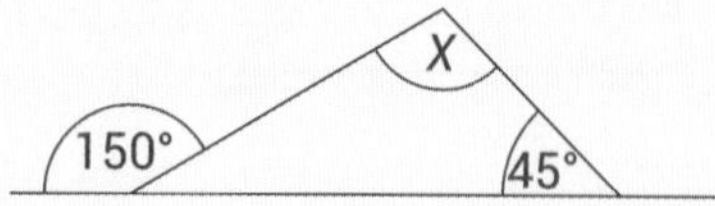

Solution

$|\angle X| + 45° = 150°$ (Exterior angle of a triangle)

$\Rightarrow |\angle X| = 150° - 45°$

$\therefore |\angle X| = 105°$

Worked Example 15.8

Find $|\angle A|$ and $|\angle B|$ without measuring the angles.

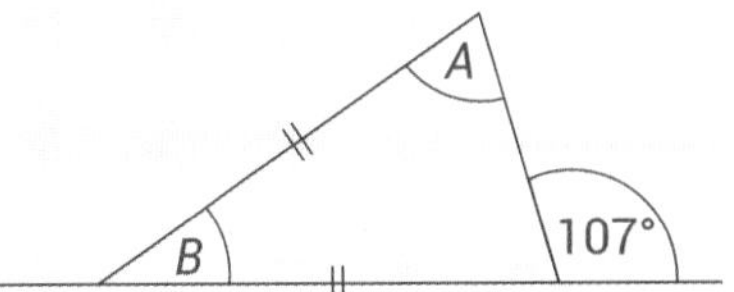

Solution

As the triangle is an isosceles triangle, we can fill in another angle A.

$|\angle A| = 180° - 107°$ (Straight angle)

$\therefore |\angle A| = 73°$

$|\angle B| + |\angle A| + |\angle A| = 180°$ (180° in a triangle)

$|\angle B| + 73° + 73° = 180°$

$\Rightarrow |\angle B| = 180° - 73° - 73°$

$\therefore |\angle B| = 34°$

OR $|\angle A| = 180° - 107°$ (Straight angle)

$\therefore |\angle A| = 73°$

$|\angle B| + |\angle A| = 107°$ (Exterior angle of a triangle)

$\Rightarrow |\angle B| + 73° = 107°$

$\Rightarrow |\angle B| = 107° - 73°$

$\therefore |\angle B| = 34°$

More Triangles

We will now deal with one property concerning the relationship between the angles and sides of triangles.

In any triangle:

- The largest angle is opposite the largest side.
- The smallest angle is opposite the smallest side.

The converse is also true.

In any triangle:

- The largest side is opposite the largest angle.
- The smallest side is opposite the smallest angle.

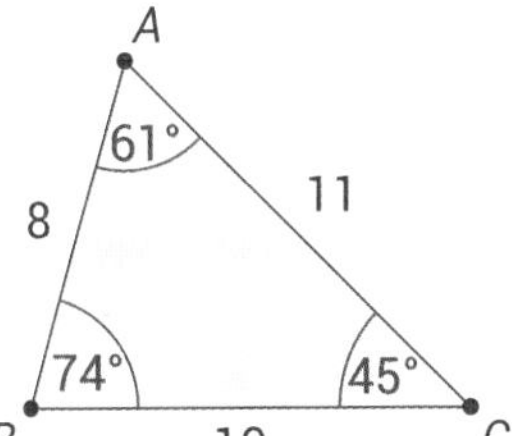

Theorem 7

The angle opposite the greater of two sides is greater than the angle opposite the lesser side. Conversely, the side opposite the greater of two angles is greater than the side opposite the lesser angle.

$|AC| > |BC|$,

$\therefore |\angle ABC| > |\angle BAC|$

Another property of triangles can help determine if three lengths can form the three sides of a triangle.

The sum of the lengths of any two sides of a triangle have to be greater than the length of the third side.

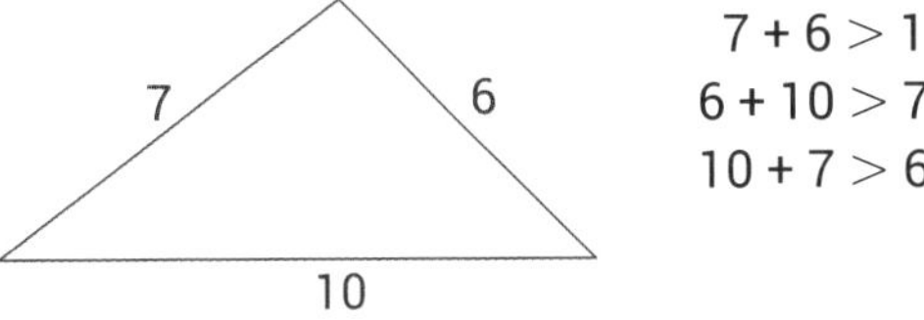

$7 + 6 > 10$
$6 + 10 > 7$
$10 + 7 > 6$

This allows us to state the following theorem:

Theorem 8

Two sides of a triangle are together greater than the third.
This theorem is sometimes referred to as the **triangle inequality theorem**.

$a + b > c$
$a + c > b$
$b + c > a$

This theorem implies that one side of a triangle must be smaller than the sum of the other two sides.

GEOMETRY

Worked Example 15.9

Consider ΔABC.

(i) Which is the smallest angle?

(ii) Which is the largest angle?

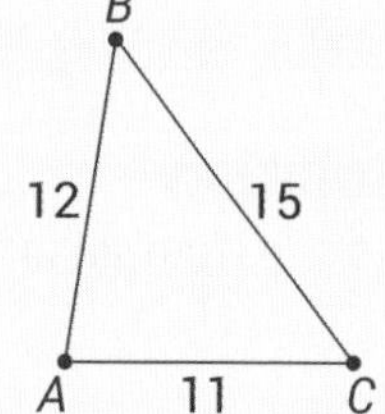

Solution

(i) $\angle ABC$ is the smallest angle (opposite smallest side).

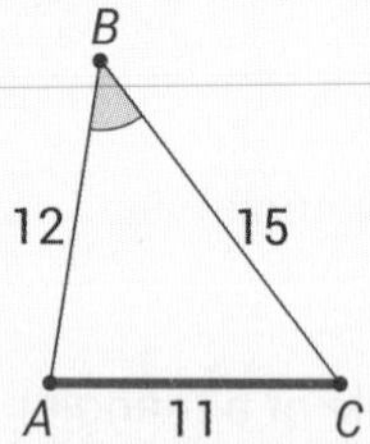

(ii) $\angle BAC$ is the largest angle (opposite largest side).

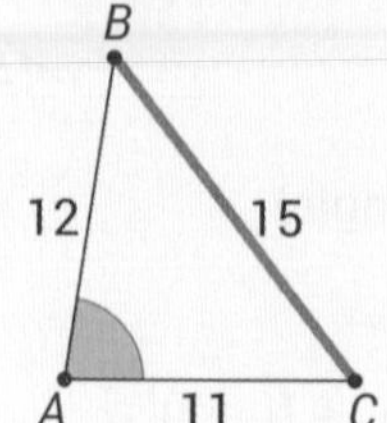

Worked Example 15.10

List the sides of the triangle DEF in ascending order of length.

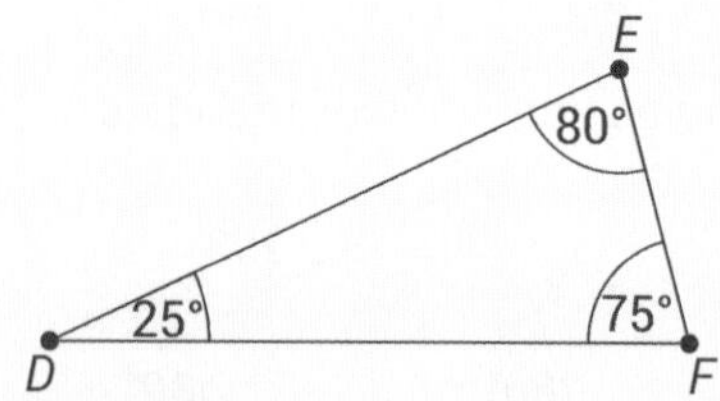

Solution

$[EF]$ is the smallest side (opposite the smallest angle).

$[DF]$ is the largest side (opposite the largest angle).

$\Rightarrow [DE]$ is the middle length side.

So the sides of the triangle DEF in ascending order (smallest to largest) are: $[EF]$, $[DE]$, $[DF]$.

Worked Example 15.11

Determine if a triangle can be constructed with the following side measurements:

(i) 3, 7 and 11 cm (ii) 3, 6 and 8 cm

Solution

(i) 3, 7 and 11 cm

It is a good idea to draw out a table and to start with the smaller sides first.

$3 + 7 = 10$	10 is not > 11	$\therefore$ Triangle can't be constructed.

(ii) 3, 6 and 8 cm

The two sides must add to a value greater than (and not equal to) the other side.

$3 + 6 = 9$	$9 > 8$	$\therefore$ Triangle can be constructed.
$3 + 8 = 11$	$11 > 6$	
$6 + 8 = 14$	$14 > 3$	

The Theorem of Pythagoras

One of the best-known theorems concerns the properties of right-angled triangles.

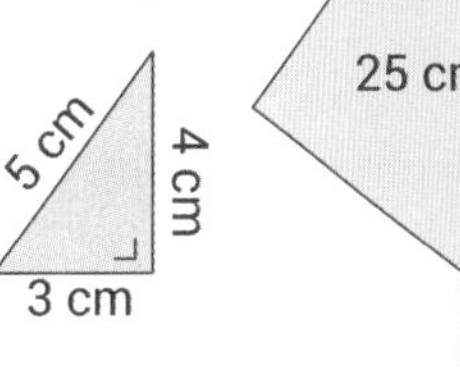

While this theorem is named after the Greek mathematician Pythagoras of Samos, who lived in the sixth century BC, it was widely known before then.

In the given right-angled triangle, it was noticed that $5^2 = 25$ and also that $3^2 + 4^2 = 25$.

We can show that:

Theorem 14: The Theorem of Pythagoras

In a right-angled triangle the square on the hypotenuse is equal to the sum of the squares on the other two sides.

This leads to the equation:

$c^2 = a^2 + b^2$

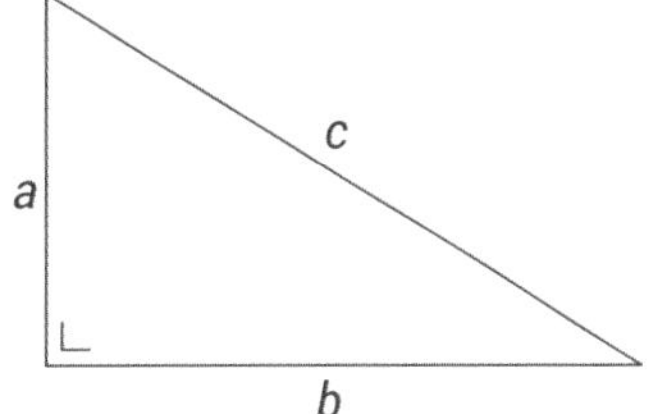

c is the hypotenuse: this is the longest side and also the side opposite the right angle.

The converse of Pythagoras' theorem can be used to investigate if a triangle is right-angled.

Theorem 15

If the square on one side of a triangle is equal to the sum of the squares on the other two sides, then the angle opposite the first side is a right angle.

Worked Example 15.12

Find $|AB|$.

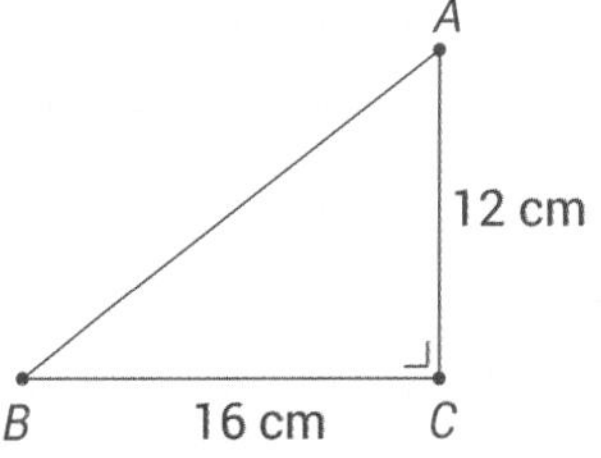

Solution

It is important to identify if we are trying to find the hypotenuse or another side. In this case we are trying to find the hypotenuse.

Write Pythagoras' theorem.	$c^2 = a^2 + b^2$
Write down the given values.	$a = 16, b = 12$
Put these values into the equation and solve.	$c^2 = 16^2 + 12^2$ $c^2 = 256 + 144$ $c^2 = 400$
Find the square root.	$c = \sqrt{400}$ $c = 20$ (As $c > 0$.)
State answer.	$\therefore |AB| = 20$ cm

GEOMETRY

Worked Example 15.13

Which of the following triangles are right-angled triangles? (Triangles are not drawn to scale.)

Triangle 1

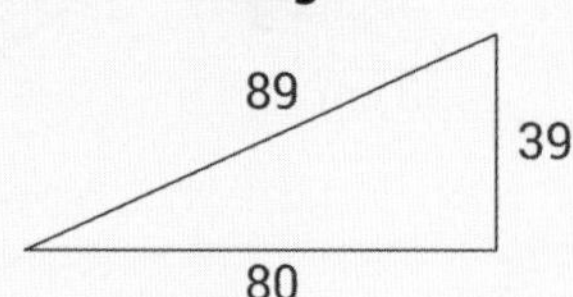

Triangle 2

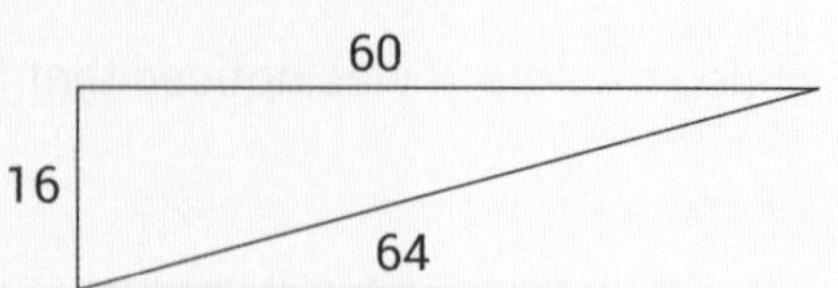

Solution

If a triangle is right-angled, then $c^2 = a^2 + b^2$.

We must first identify which side is the longest.

Once we have identified the largest side, we call the two other sides a and b.

Triangle 1	Triangle 2
$c = 89$ (longest side) $\therefore c^2 = (89)^2 = 7{,}921$	$c = 64$ (longest side) $\therefore c^2 = (64)^2 = 4{,}096$
If the triangle is right-angled, then $a^2 + b^2$ will also be equal to 7,921: $a = 80 \rightarrow a^2 = (80)^2 = 6{,}400$ $b = 39 \rightarrow b^2 = (39)^2 = 1{,}521$ $a^2 + b^2 = 6{,}400 + 1{,}521 = 7{,}921$	If the triangle is right-angled, then $a^2 + b^2$ will also be equal to 4,096: $a = 60 \rightarrow a^2 = (60)^2 = 3{,}600$ $b = 16 \rightarrow b^2 = (16)^2 = 256$ $a^2 + b^2 = 3{,}600 + 256 = 3{,}856$
$\therefore$ Triangle 1 is a right-angled triangle.	$3{,}856 \neq 4{,}096$ $\therefore$ Triangle 2 is **NOT** a right-angled triangle.

Worked Example 15.14

Find the value of x and y in the diagram, leaving your answer in surd form where necessary.

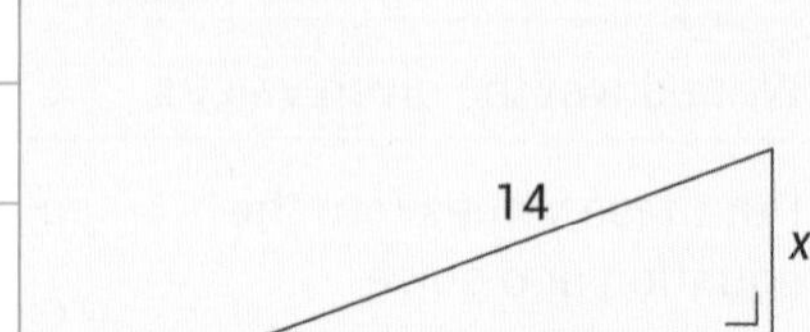

Solution

To find x:

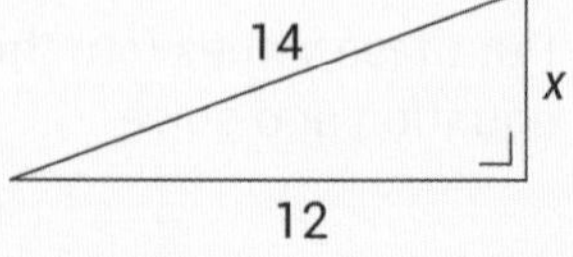

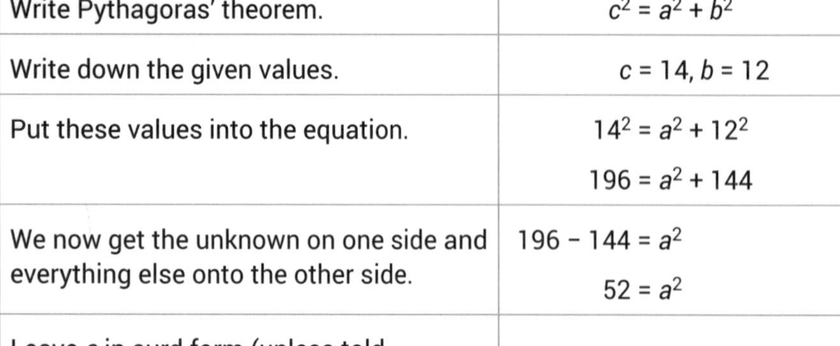

Write Pythagoras' theorem.	$c^2 = a^2 + b^2$
Write down the given values.	$c = 14, b = 12$
Put these values into the equation.	$14^2 = a^2 + 12^2$ $196 = a^2 + 144$
We now get the unknown on one side and everything else onto the other side.	$196 - 144 = a^2$ $52 = a^2$
Leave a in surd form (unless told otherwise).	$a = \sqrt{52}$
State answer.	$\therefore x = 2\sqrt{13}$

To find y:

Write Pythagoras' theorem.	$c^2 = a^2 + b^2$
Write down the given values.	$a = \sqrt{52}, b = \sqrt{12}$
Put these values into the equation and simplify.	$c^2 = (\sqrt{52})^2 + (\sqrt{12})^2$ $c^2 = 52 + 12$ $c^2 = 64$
Find the square root.	$c = \sqrt{64}$ $c = 8$
State answer.	$\therefore y = 8$

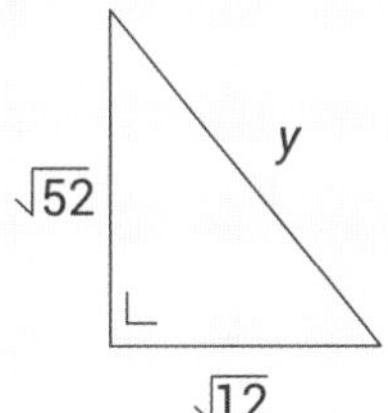

Worked Example 15.15

A ladder 3 m long is placed against a wall as shown.

The ladder is set 1.6 m from the bottom of the wall. Find, to the nearest cm, the height the ladder will reach up the wall.

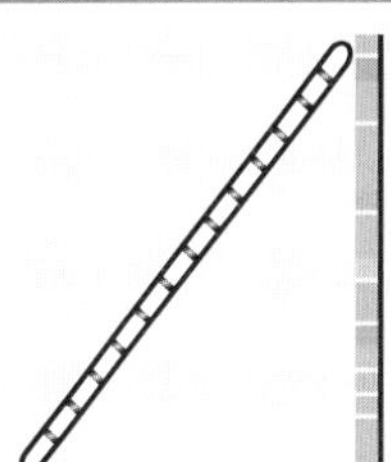

Solution

When faced with geometry problems dealing in real-life settings, it helps if we:

- Draw a digram to represent the problem.
- Fill in as much information on the diagram as possible, checking both the diagram and text given in the question.
- Identify and then label on the diagram what we are asked to find (in this case h).
- Identify which theorem(s) we will use.

The triangle drawn is a right-angled triangle. We are trying to find side h.

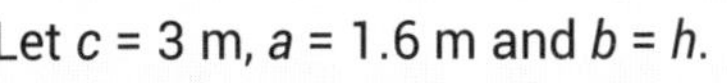

Theorem of Pythagoras: $c^2 = a^2 + b^2$

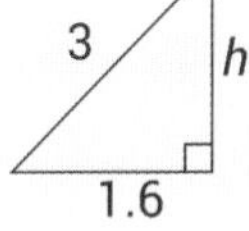

Let $c = 3$ m, $a = 1.6$ m and $b = h$.

$(3)^2 = (1.6)^2 + h^2$

$9 = 2.56 + h^2$

$9 - 2.56 = h^2$

$6.44 = h^2$

$h = \sqrt{6.44}$

$h \approx 2.54$ m

Exercise 15.4

1. Find the measure of the angles A and B in each of the following triangles. Do not use a protractor.

(i)

(ii)

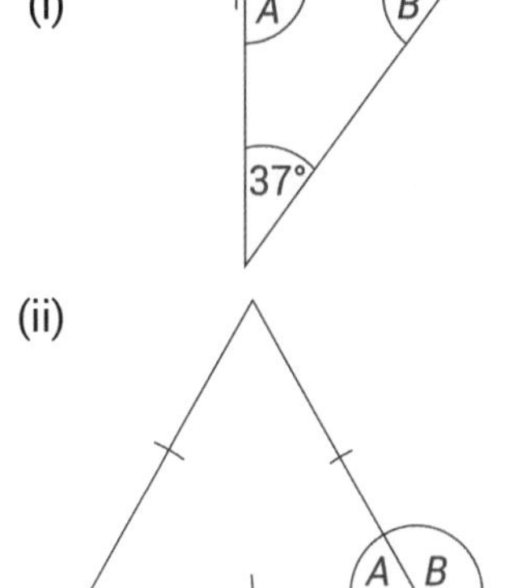

(iii)

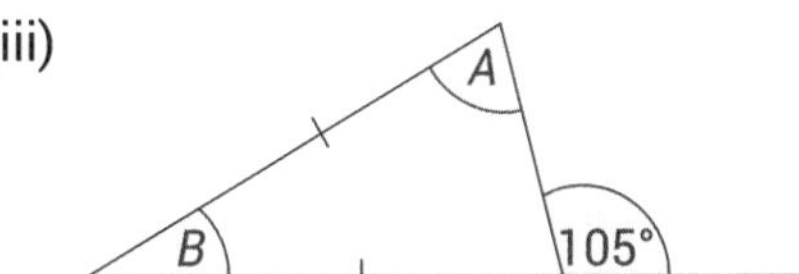

2. Find the size of the angles marked with letters in each of the following triangles:

(i)

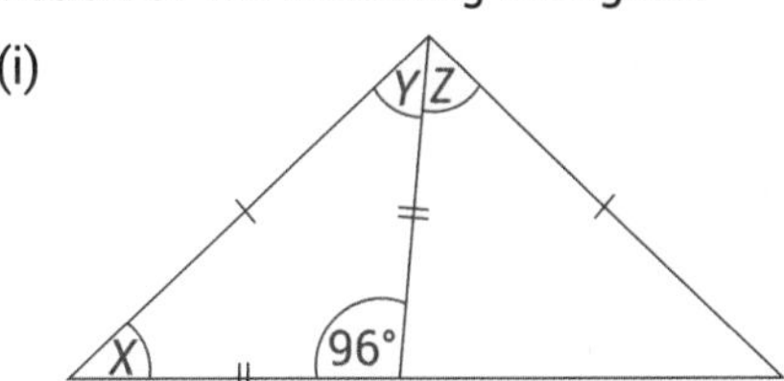

(ii)

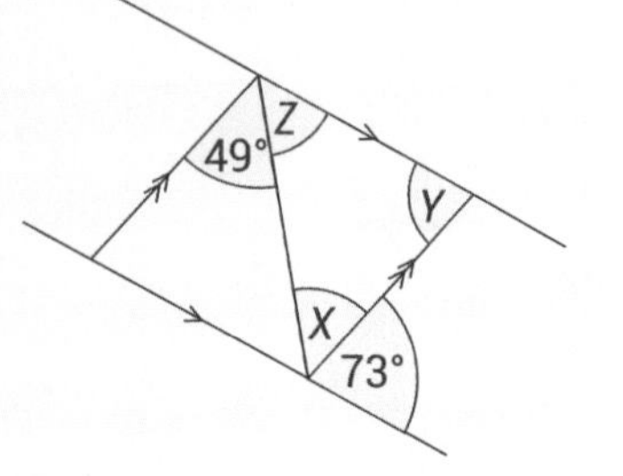

(iii)

Y X 72° Z

(iv)

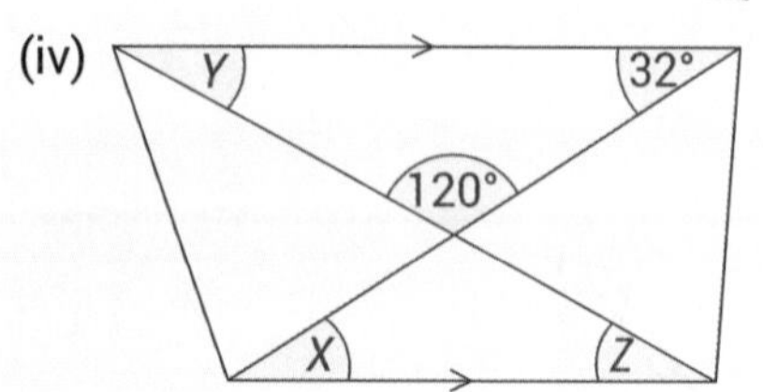

(v)

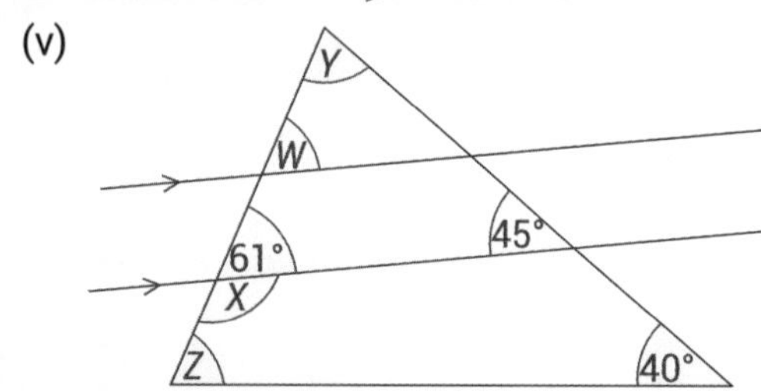

3. (i)

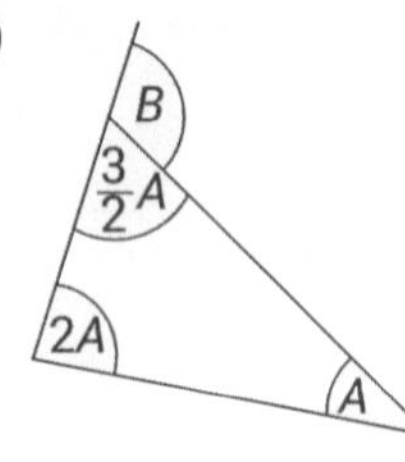

Find$|\angle A|$ and $|\angle B|$.

(ii)

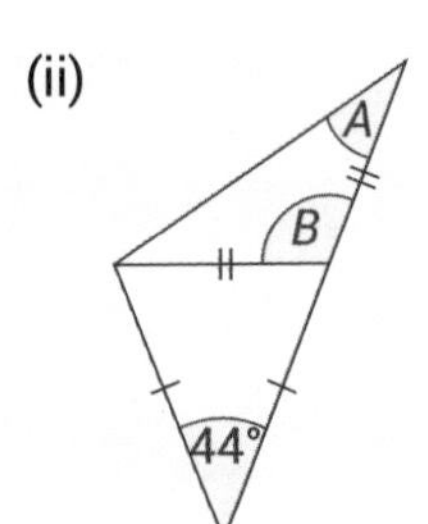

Find$|\angle A|$ and $|\angle B|$.

4. In each of the following triangles identify the smallest and largest angles:

(i)

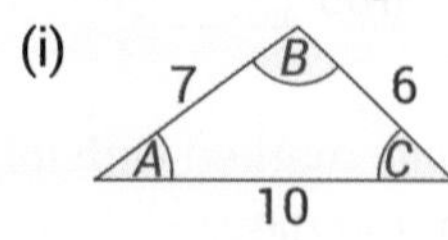

(ii)

10 2 9 1 3 11

(iii)

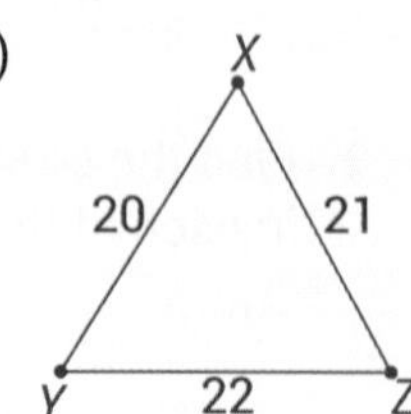

(iv)

A 17 18 B 19 C

(v)

1 7.3 7.2 2 3 8.5

5. In each of the following triangles identify the longest and shortest sides:

(i)

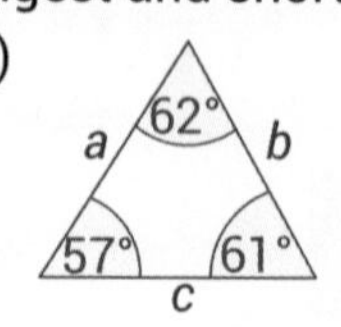

(ii)

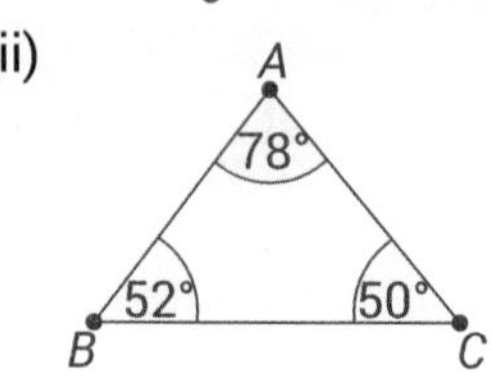

(iii)

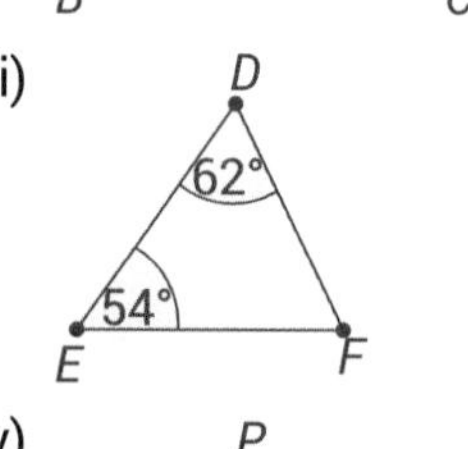

(iv)

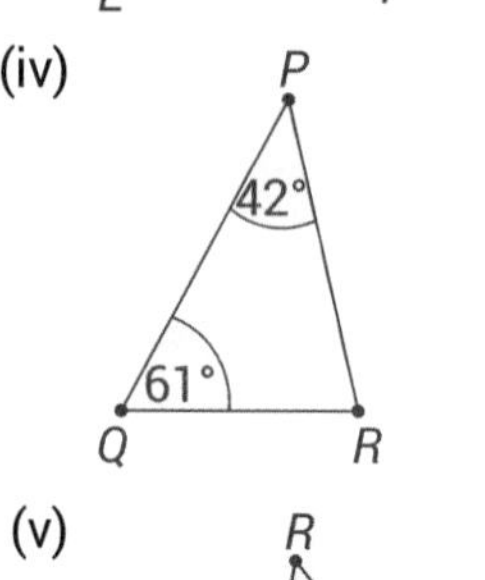

(v)

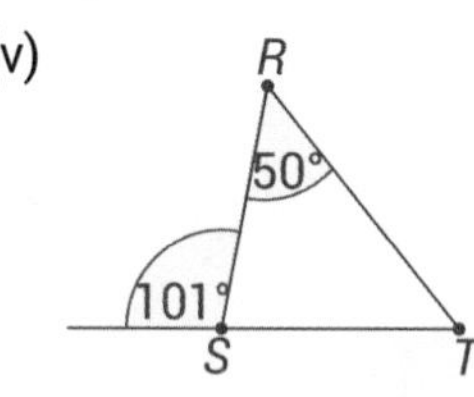

6. Explain, in each case, if it is possible to construct triangles with sides of the following lengths:

(i) 2, 3, 6

(ii) 17, 14, 26

(iii) 6, 2, 10

(iv) 11, 13, 24

(v) 52, 72, 95

(vi) 1.1, 0.8, 2

7. The sides of a triangle are of lengths 6.1, 7.2 and n, where $n \in N$. What is the:

(i) Smallest possible value of n

(ii) Largest possible value of n

8. The sides of a triangle are of lengths 11.7, 6.4 and a, where $a \in N$. What is the:

(i) Smallest possible value of a

(ii) Largest possible value of a

9. Find the value of x in each of the following triangles:

(i)

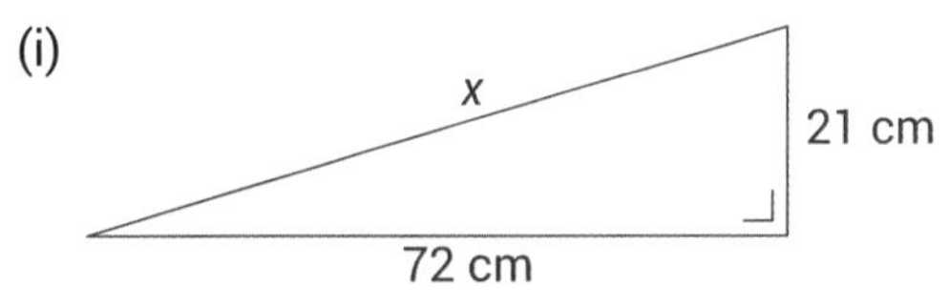

(ii)

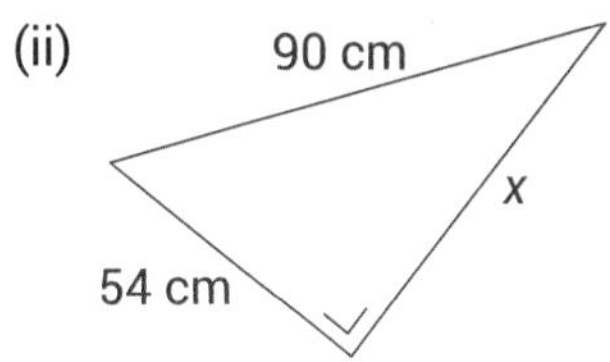

(iii)

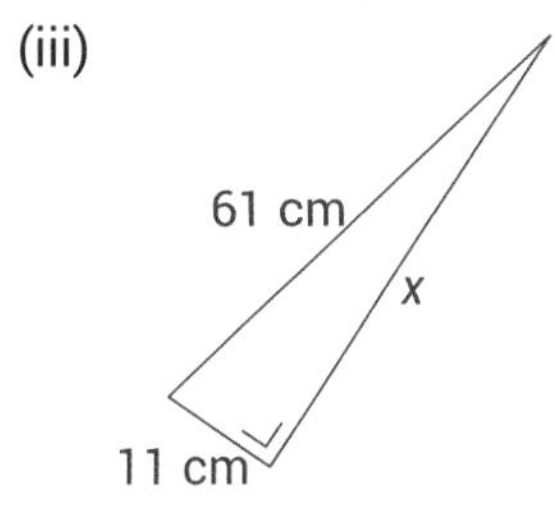

(iv)

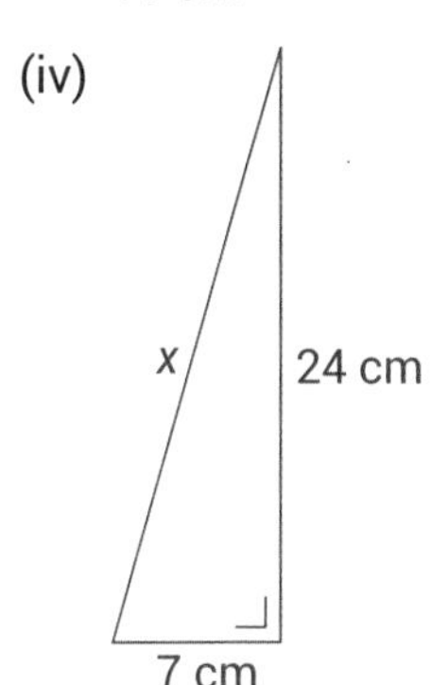

(v)

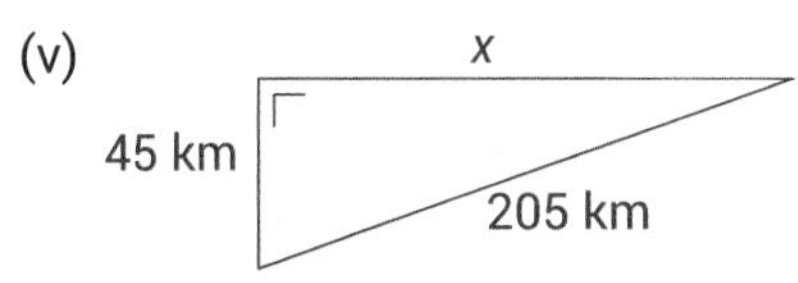

10. Find the value of y correct to two decimal places.

(i)

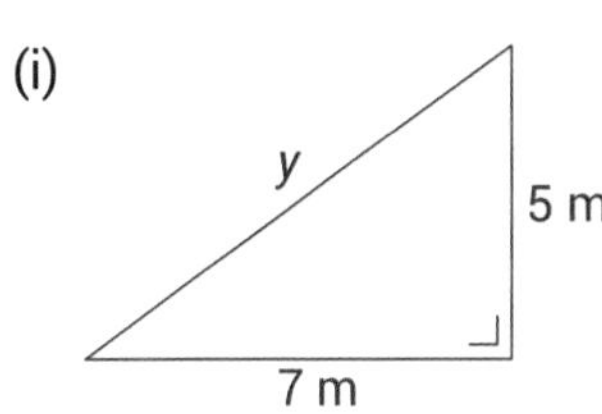

(ii)

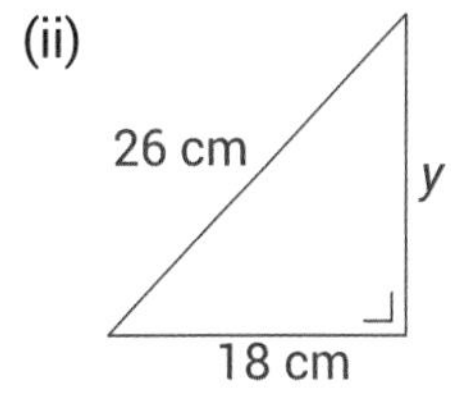

(iii)

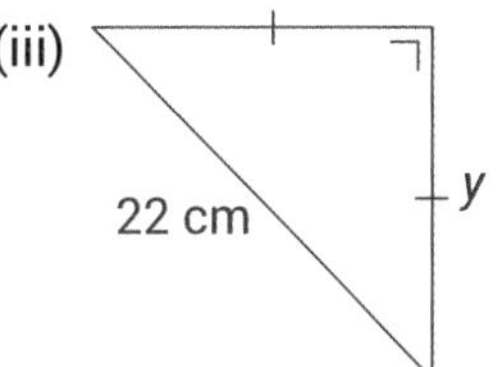

11. Find the length of the unknown side. Leave your answers in surd form where appropriate.

(i)

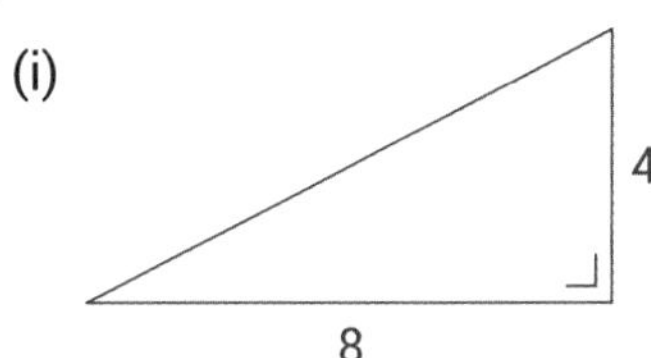

(ii)

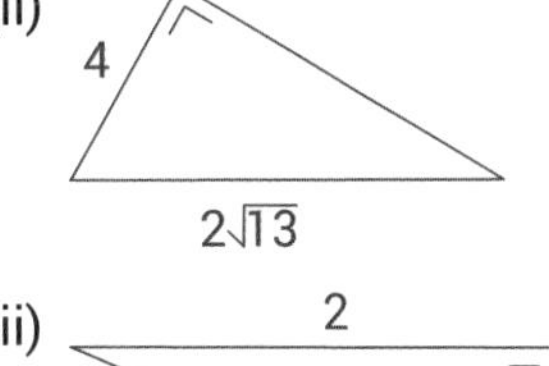

(iii)

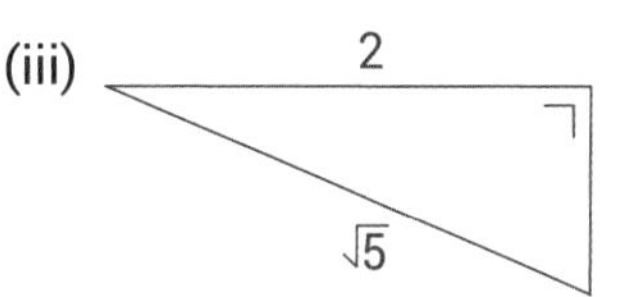

12. Identify which of these triangles are right-angled triangles. Show clearly how you arrived at your answer.

(i) (ii)

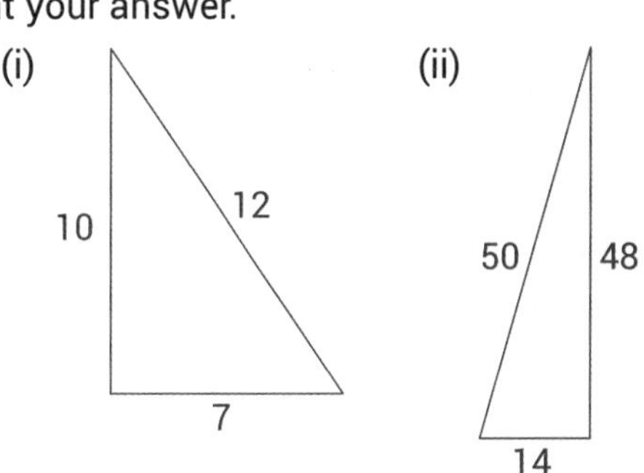

13. Find the length of x and y in each of the following triangles:

(i)

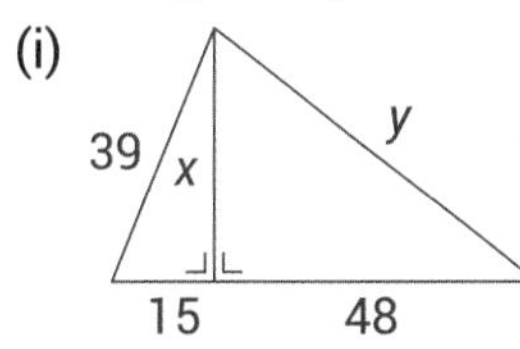

(ii)

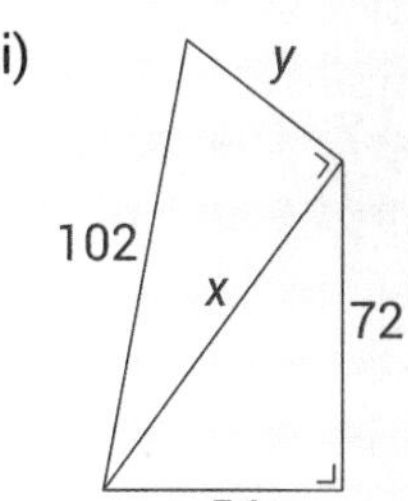

(iii)

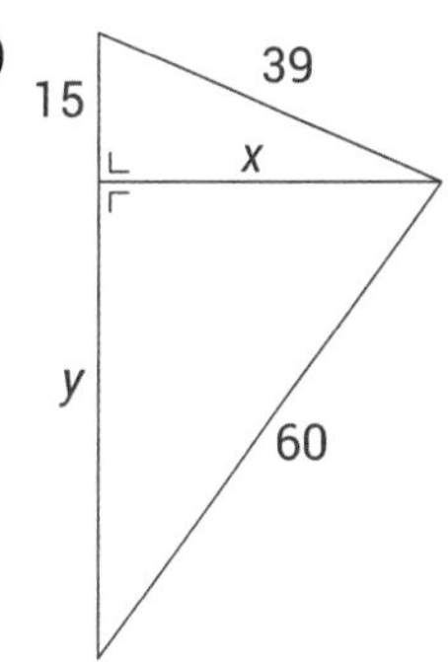

GEOMETRY

14. Danielle is building a triangular enclosure for her chicken coop. She decides that two of the sides of the pen must be 8 m and 10 m, respectively.
   (i) What is the smallest and the largest length the third side could be, to the nearest centimetre?
   (ii) If the fence costs €5 per metre, calculate the minimum and maximum cost of building this fence.
   (iii) Explain why Danielle may not want to pick the largest length for the third side.

15. In an exam, four answers are given for the possible sides of a scalene triangle. Which two answers are correct?
   A: (4, 6, 2) *B*: (3, 5, 4) *C*: (8, 7, 7) *D*: (4, 5, 6)

16. Jamie starts to set up the triangular front of his tent. He has four tent poles, from which he must choose three.
   Each pole has a different size: 1 m, 1.2 m, 2 m and 3 m.

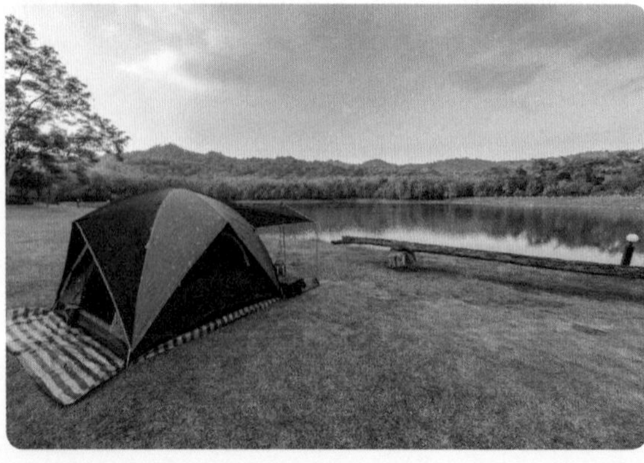

   In how many different ways can he build the front of his tent?

17. The sides of a triangle are of lengths 9, 14 and b, where $b \in N$. What is the:
   (i) Smallest possible value of b
   (ii) Largest possible value of b
   (iii) Range of possible values of b

18. The sides of a triangle are of lengths 10, 16 and c, where $c \in N$. What is the:
   (i) Smallest possible value of c
   (ii) Largest possible value of c
   (iii) Range of possible values of c

19. A ladder leans against a wall at a height of 2.5 m. The ladder's base is 0.75 m from the wall. The ladder slips down so that its base is now 90 cm away from the wall. How far down the wall did the ladder slip, to the nearest centimetre?

20. The side view of a barn is shown. All measurements are in metres.

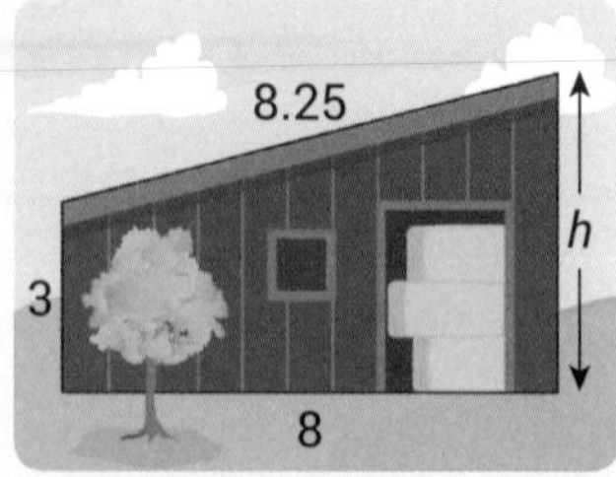

   Calculate the height (h) of the barn to the nearest centimetre.

21. A diagram of a roof is shown. Find the perpendicular height of this roof to the nearest centimetre. (All lengths are in metres.)

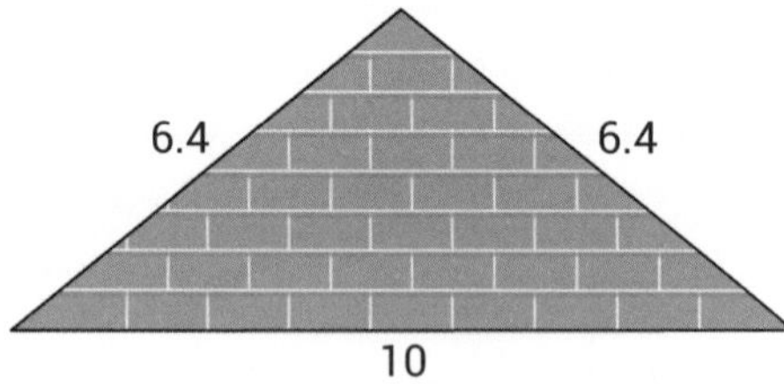

22. A builder is building rectangular frames 3.5 m by 5.2 m. To ensure that the sides are perpendicular to each other, what should the length of each diagonal measure, to the nearest centimetre?

23. A triangular end wall is shown.

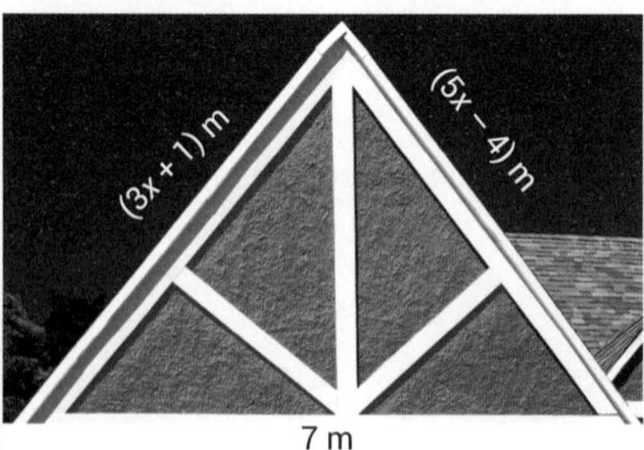

   Sheena works out the perimeter of the end wall to be 12 m. Elle works out the perimeter of the end wall to be 16 m.
   Which answer is correct?
   Give a reason for your answer.

24. Using the theorem of Pythagoras, find the value of x in each of the right-angled triangles:

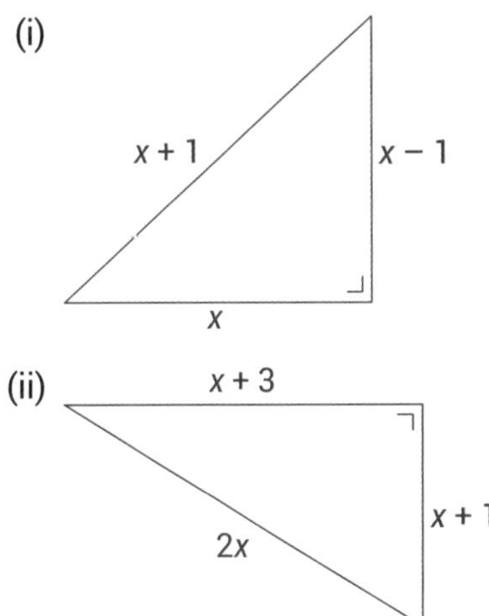

25. Rectangular blocks are to be packed as shown.

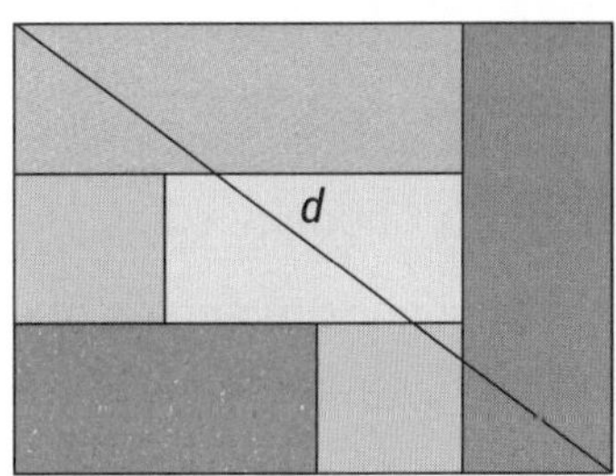

All blocks have the same width of x cm.
The medium size rectangular blocks are twice as long as the square orange blocks.

The diagonal length of the rectangle (d) formed by the packed blocks can be expressed as

$\sqrt{x^2 + 10x + 25}$.

Find the dimensions of each block.

15.8 Quadrilaterals

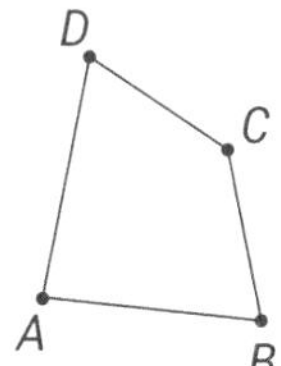

A **polygon** is a closed shape (without gaps or openings) with straight sides.
A polygon has at least three sides.

A **regular polygon** has equal sides and equal angles.

A **quadrilateral** is a four-sided polygon.

One type of **polygon** commonly encountered is the parallelogram.

Parallelograms

A **parallelogram** is a quadrilateral for which both pairs of opposite sides are parallel.

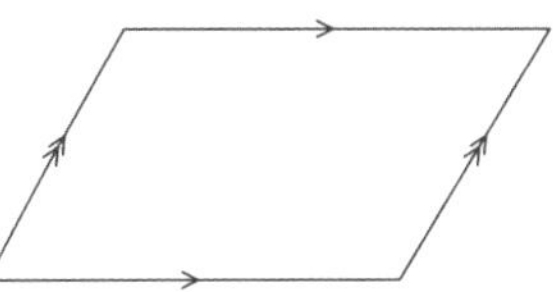

There are different types of parallelogram, each with their own properties.

Type of quadrilateral	Sides	Parallel sides	Angles	Diagonals
Parallelogram	Opposite sides are equal	Opposite sides are parallel	Opposite angles are equal	Bisect each other
Rhombus	Four equal sides	Opposite sides are parallel	Opposite angles are equal	Bisect each other – angle of 90° formed
Rectangle	Opposite sides are equal	Opposite sides are parallel	All angles the same size (90°)	Bisect each other
Square	Four equal sides	Opposite sides are parallel	All angles the same size (90°)	Bisect each other – angle of 90° formed

A square, rectangle and rhombus could all be described as being parallelograms.

We can now state specific theorems related to parallelograms.

Theorem 9

In a parallelogram, opposite sides are equal and opposite angles are equal.

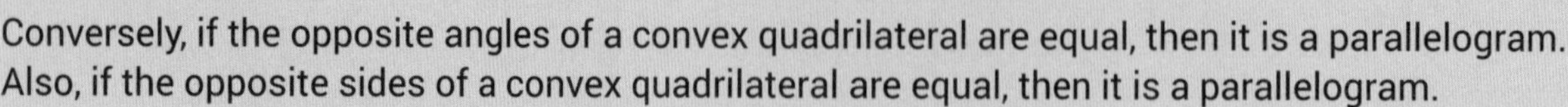

Conversely, if the opposite angles of a convex quadrilateral are equal, then it is a parallelogram. Also, if the opposite sides of a convex quadrilateral are equal, then it is a parallelogram.

A convex quadrilateral has both diagonals completely contained within the shape. Each interior angle is less than 180°.

Corollary 1

A diagonal divides a parallelogram into two congruent triangles.

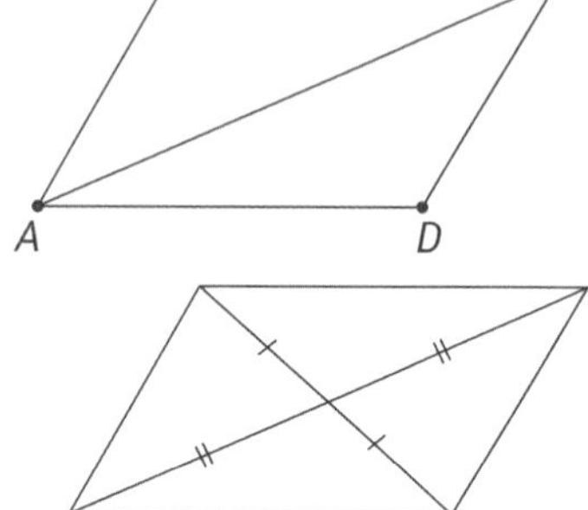

$\Delta ABC \equiv \Delta ADC$ (SAS)

Theorem 10

The diagonals of a parallelogram bisect each other.

The converse of this theorem is also true.

Converse to Theorem 10

If the diagonals of a quadrilateral bisect each other, then the quadrilateral is a parallelogram.

Worked Example 15.16

In the following parallelogram, find:

(i) $|AB|$

(ii) $|AC|$

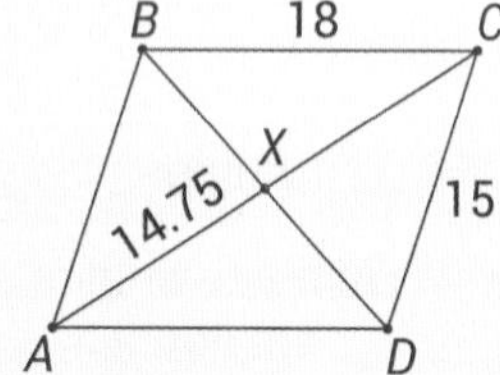

Solution

(i) $|AB| = 15$ (Opposite side to $[CD]$)

(ii) $|AC| = 2(14.75)$ Diagonals of a parallelogram bisect each other.

$\therefore |AC| = 29.5$

Worked Example 15.17

In the following parallelogram, find:

(i) $|\angle 1|$

(ii) $|\angle 2|$

(iii) $|\angle 3|$

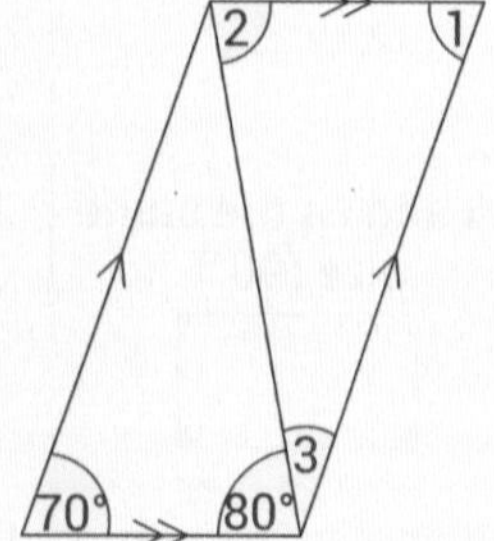

Solution

(i) $|\angle 1| = 70°$ (Opposite angles in a parallelogram)

(ii) $|\angle 2| = 80°$ (Equal alternate angles)

(iii) $|\angle 1| + |\angle 2| + |\angle 3| = 180°$ (180° in a triangle)

$\Rightarrow 70° + 80° + |\angle 3| = 180°$

$\Rightarrow |\angle 3| = 180° - 70° - 80°$

$\therefore |\angle 3| = 30°$

Worked Example 15.18

In the following rhombus, find:

(i) $|\angle A|$ (iii) $|\angle C|$

(ii) $|\angle B|$ (iv) $|\angle D|$

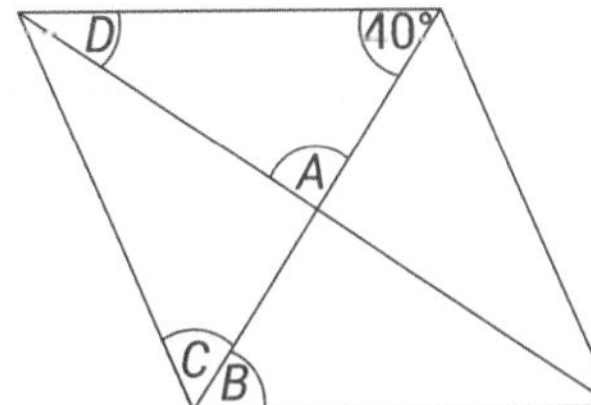

Solution

(i) $|\angle A| = 90°$ (Right angles at point of diagonals' intersection)

(ii) $|\angle B| = 40°$ (Equal alternate angles)

(iii) $|\angle C| = 40°$ (Diagonals in a rhombus bisect angle)

(iv) $|\angle D| + 40° + |\angle A| = 180°$ (180° in a triangle)

$|\angle D| + 40° + 90° = 180°$

$\therefore |\angle D| = 180° - 90° - 40°$

$\therefore |\angle D| = 50°$

15.9 Area of a Triangle and Area of a Parallelogram

Area of a Triangle

You should remember the formula for the area of a triangle:

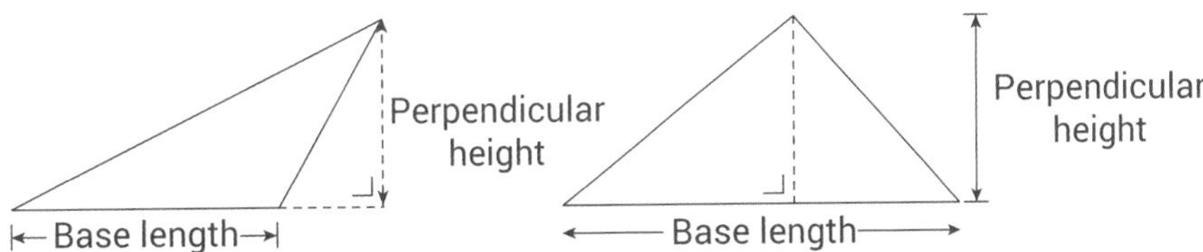

Area of a triangle = $\frac{1}{2}$ × base × perpendicular height

This formula is on page 9 of *Formulae and Tables*.

It is also clear that in calculating the area of a triangle:

It does not matter which base of the triangle we choose, as long as we know the perpendicular height from the corresponding base.

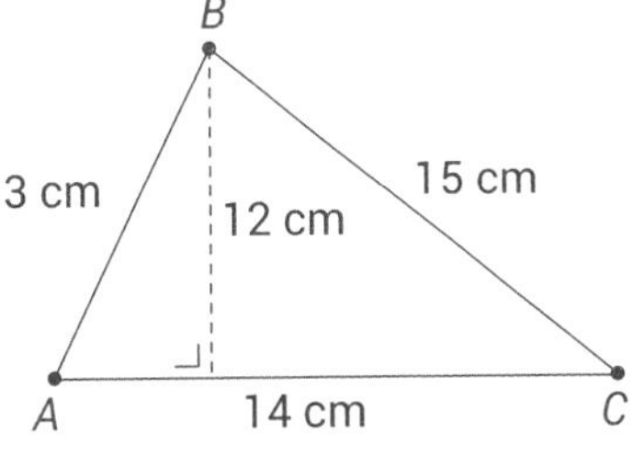
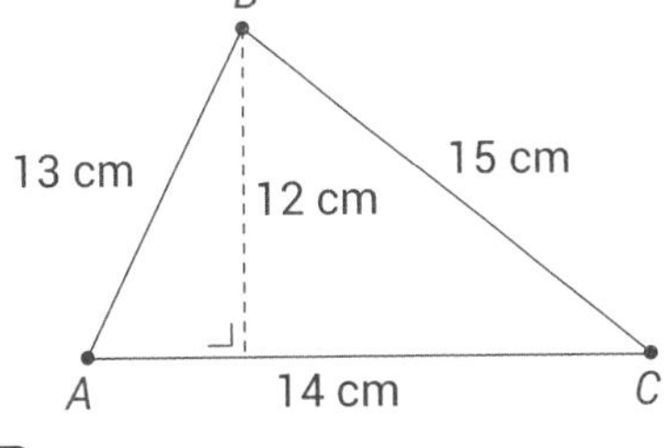

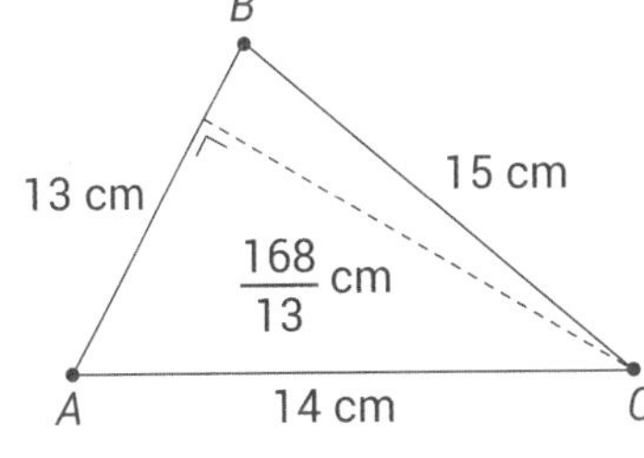

This is stated as:

Theorem 16

For a triangle, base times height does not depend on the choice of base.

Area ΔABC

$= \frac{1}{2}(14)(12)$

$= 84 \text{ cm}^2$

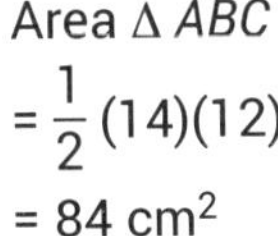

Area ΔABC

$= \frac{1}{2}(13)\left(\frac{168}{13}\right)$

$= 84 \text{ cm}^2$

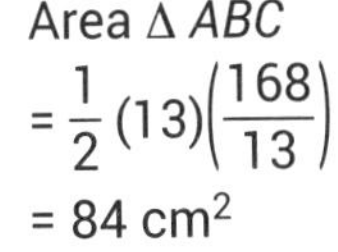

Area of a Parallelogram

We can now consider how to find the area of a parallelogram.

Theorem 17

A diagonal of a parallelogram bisects the area.

From Theorem 17, a parallelogram can be cut into two triangles of equal area.

Area triangle Ⓐ $= \frac{1}{2} \times \text{base} \times \text{height}$

$= \frac{1}{2} \times 8 \times 5 = 20 \text{ cm}^2$

Area triangle Ⓑ $= \frac{1}{2} \times \text{base} \times \text{height}$

$= \frac{1}{2} \times 8 \times 5 = 20 \text{ cm}^2$

Area of parallelogram = Area of triangles Ⓐ + Ⓑ

Area of parallelogram $= 20 \text{ cm}^2 + 20 \text{ cm}^2 = 40 \text{ cm}^2$ $(= 8 \times 5)$

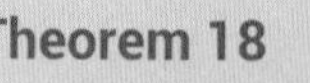

Theorem 18

The area of a parallelogram is the base times the height.

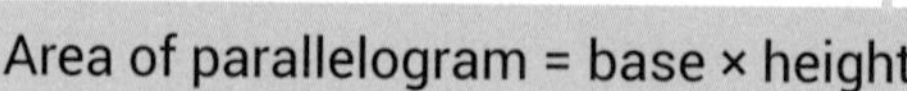

Area of parallelogram = base × height

This formula is on page 8 of *Formulae and Tables*.

Worked Example 15.19

Find the area of each of the following shapes:

(i)

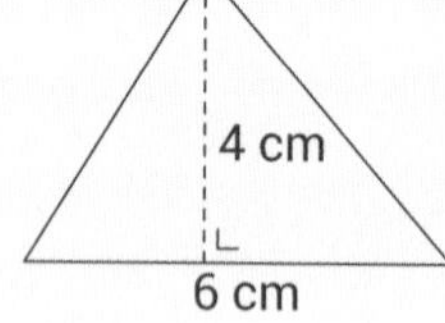

(ii)

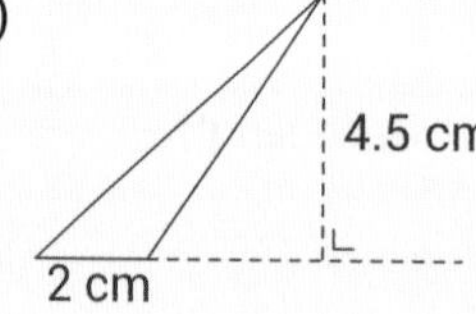

(iii)

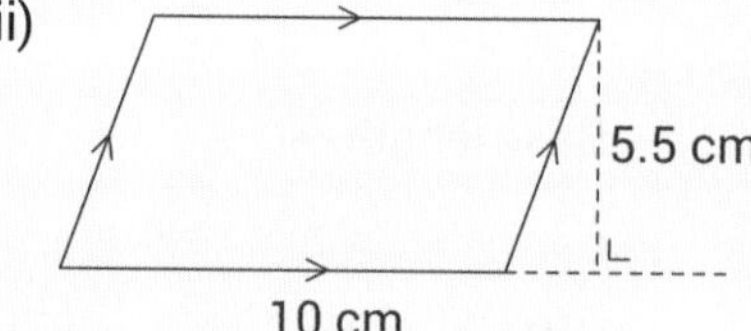

Solution

(i) Area $= \frac{1}{2} \times 6 \times 4 = 12 \text{ cm}^2$

(ii) Area $= \frac{1}{2} \times 2 \times 4.5 = 4.5 \text{ cm}^2$

(iii) Area $= 10 \times 5.5 = 55 \text{ cm}^2$

Worked Example 15.20

The area of the parallelogram *ABCD* is equal to the area of the triangle *PQR*. Find the value of x, the height of the parallelogram.

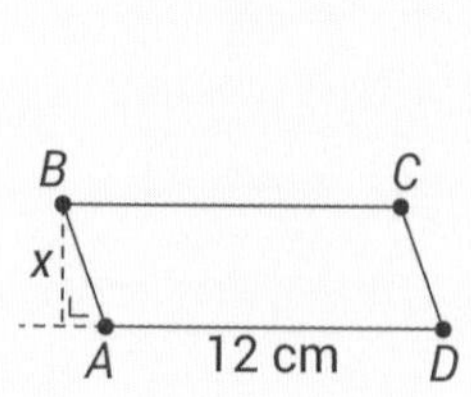

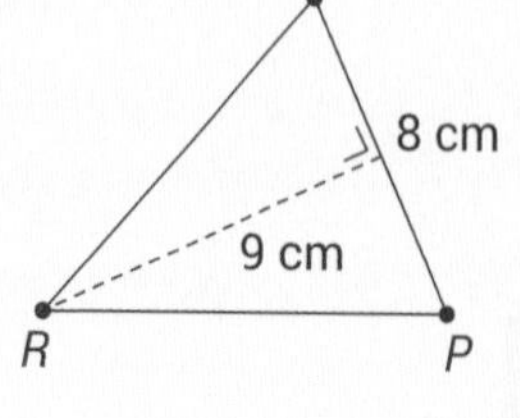

Solution

Area of parallelogram *ABCD*	Area of triangle *PQR*
= base × height	$= \frac{1}{2} \times \text{base} \times \text{height}$
$= 12(x)$	$= \frac{1}{2}(8)(9)$
$= 12x$	$= 36 \text{ cm}^2$

$\Rightarrow 12x = 36$

$\therefore x = 3 \text{ cm}$

Exercise 15.5

1. *ABCD* is a parallelogram.

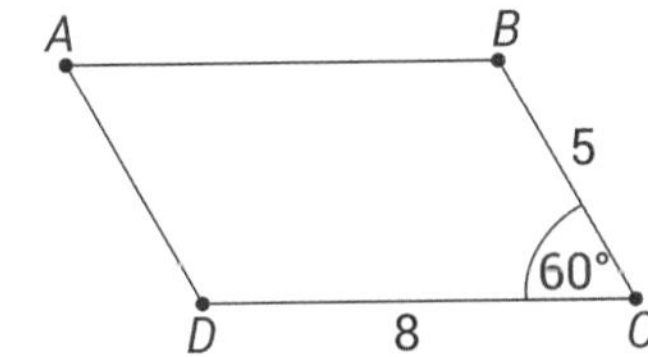

Find:

(i) $|\angle BAD|$ (ii) $|AB|$ (iii) $|\angle ADC|$

2. *DEFG* is a parallelogram.

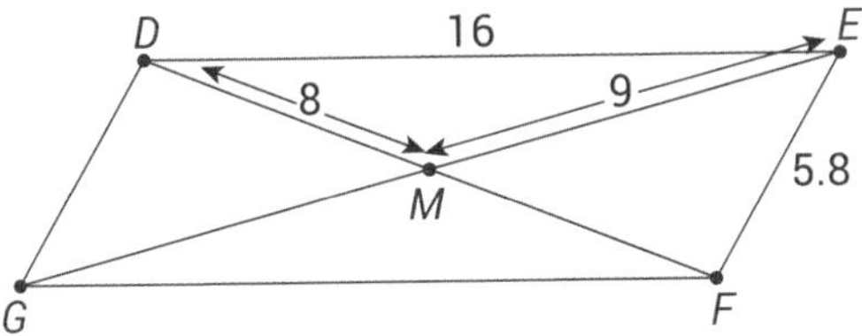

Find:

(i) $|GF|$ (iii) $|DF|$
(ii) $|EG|$ (iv) $|DG|$

3. Find the measure of the angles *A*, *B* and *C* in each of the following parallelograms:

(i)

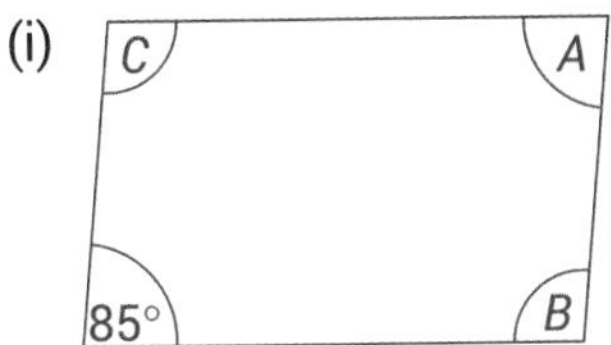

(ii)

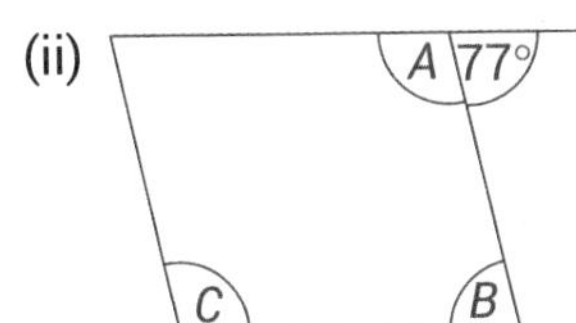

(iii)

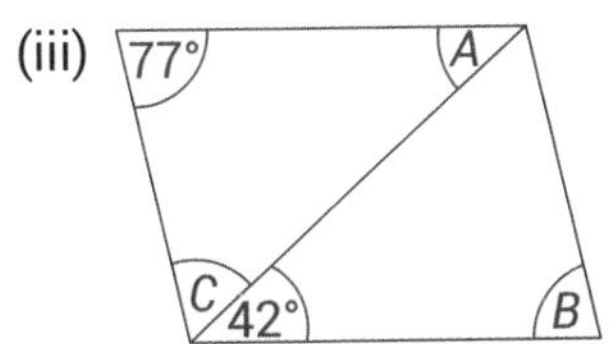

(iv)

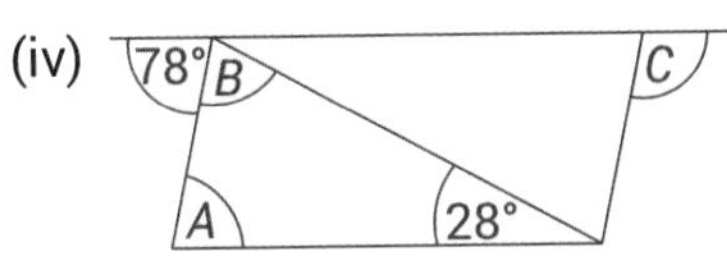

(v)

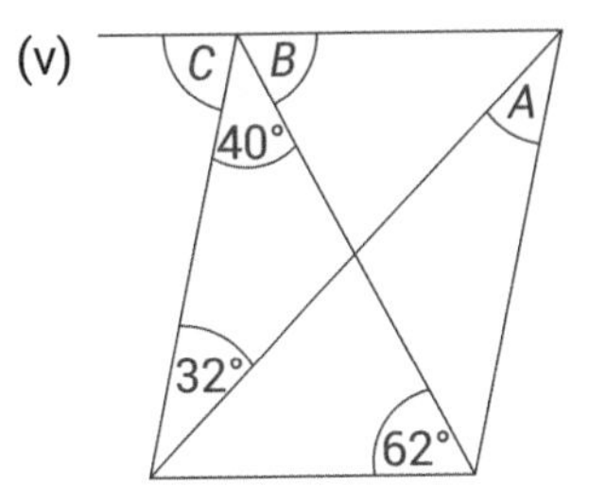

(vi)

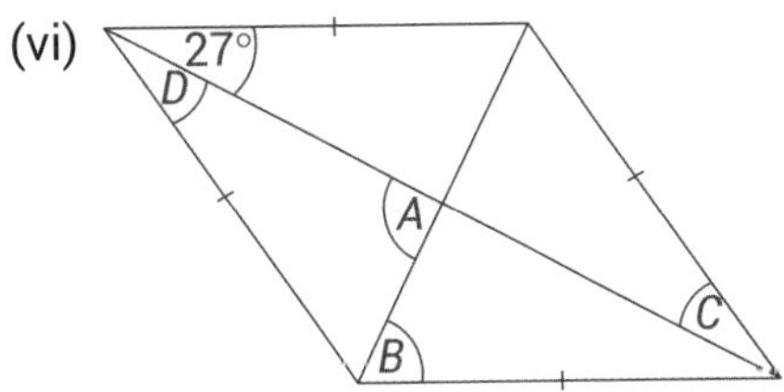

4. Find the area of each of the following triangles:

(i) (iv)

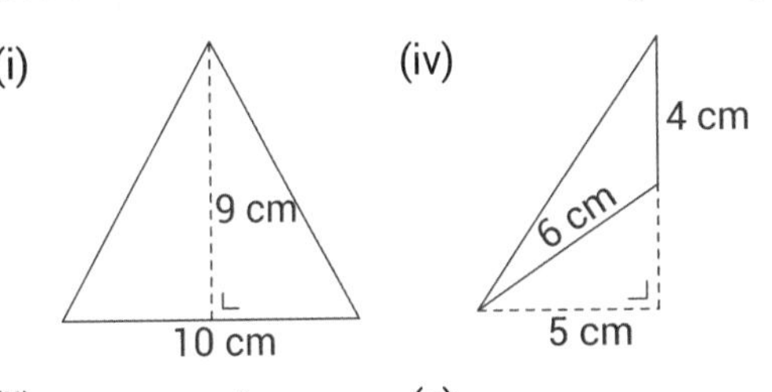

(ii) (v)

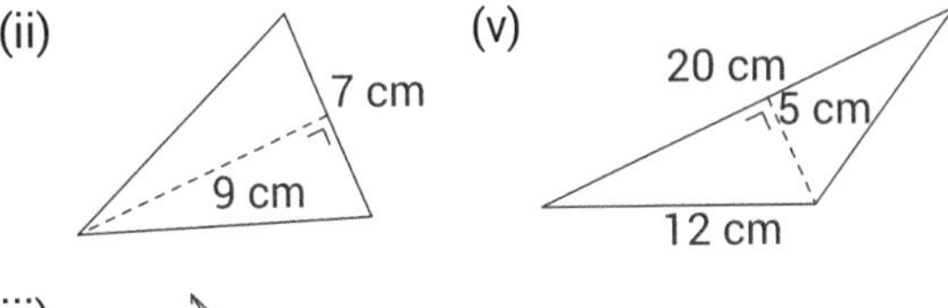

(iii)

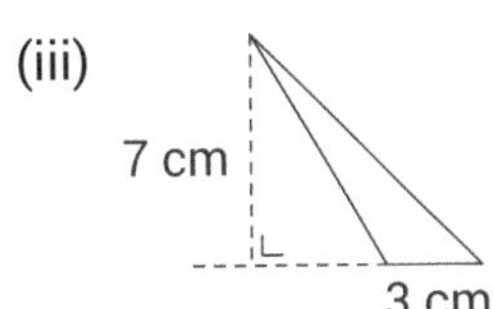

5. Find the area of each of the following parallelograms:

(i)

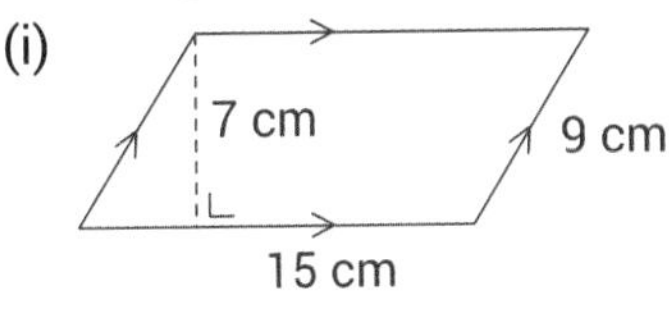

(ii)

(iii)

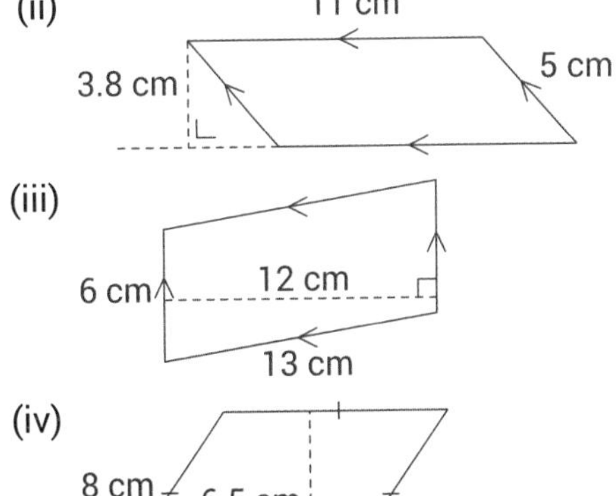

(iv)

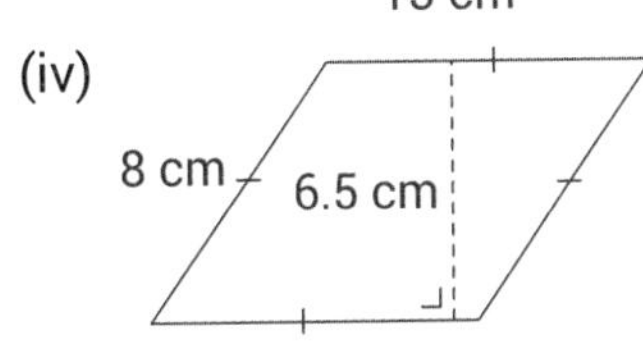

6. Find *h*, and hence find the area of the parallelogram.

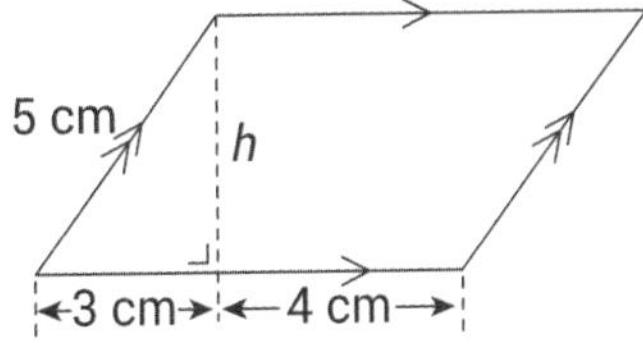

GEOMETRY

7. Consider the diagram below.

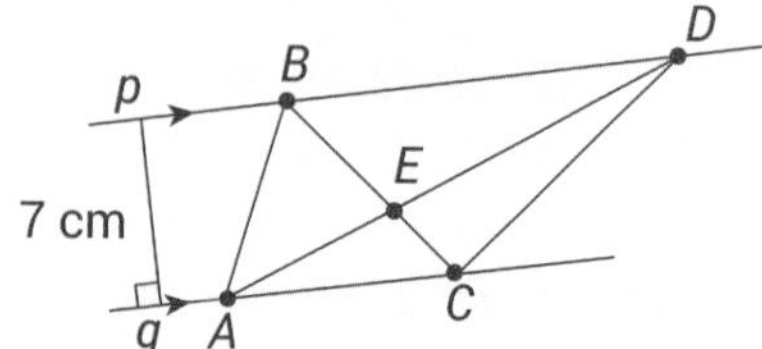

The lines p and q are parallel to each other and have a perpendicular distance of 7 cm between them as shown. $|AC| = 6.5$cm.

Find the area of:

(i) ΔABC

(ii) ΔADC

The point F is any point on the line p.

(iii) What is the area of the ΔAFC? Give a reason for your answer.

The point F is produced on the line p such that $ABFC$ is a parallelogram.

(iv) Find the area of the parallelogram $ABFC$.

The shortest distance between the point E and the line q is 2.5 cm.

Find the area of:

(v) ΔAEC

(vi) the polygon $ABEDC$

8. Find the value of x and y in each of the following polygons. (Diagrams are not drawn to scale.)

(i)

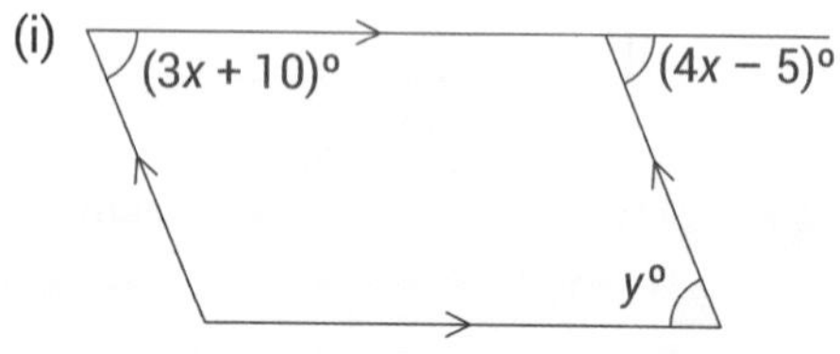

(ii)

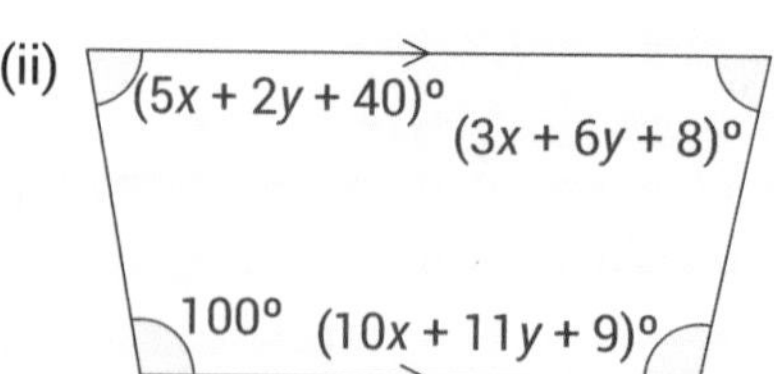

9. Find the value of x in each of the following triangles:

(i)

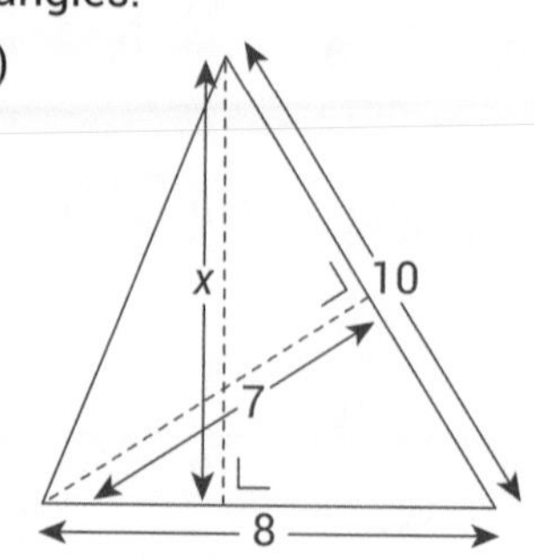

(ii)

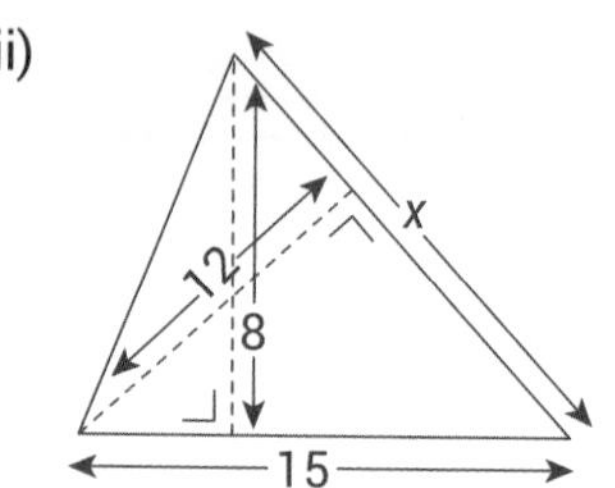

(iii)

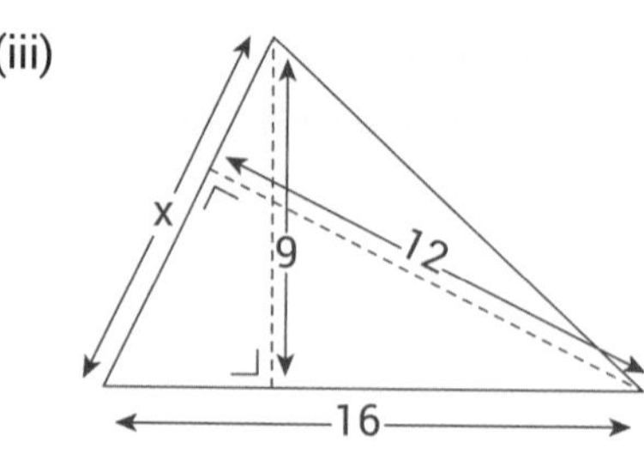

(iv)

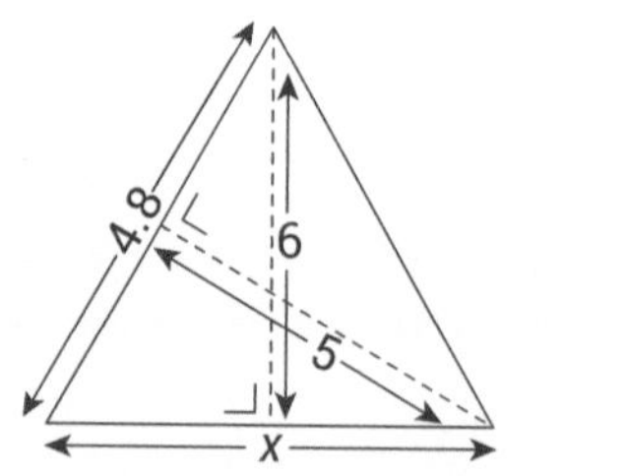

15.10 Triangles II: Congruent Triangles

If two triangles are identical to each other, they can also be described as being **congruent**.

Congruent triangles are triangles where all the corresponding sides and interior angles are equal in measure.

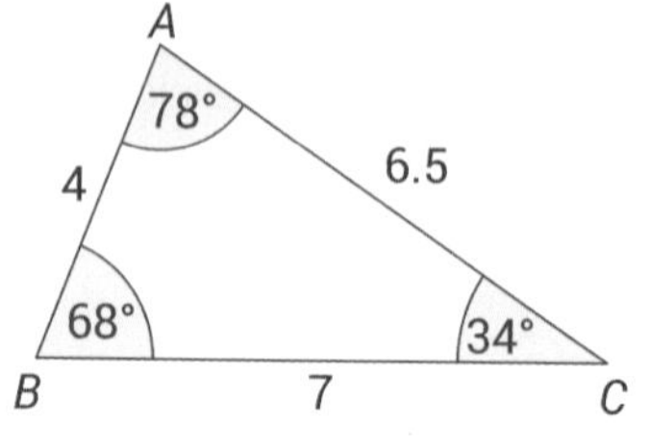

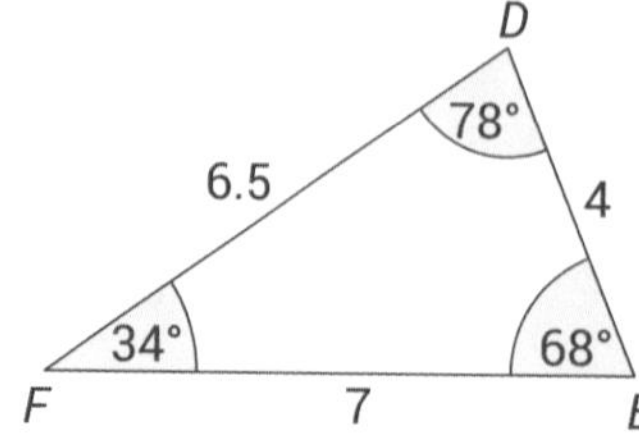

ΔABC is congruent to ΔDEF.
We write $\Delta ABC \equiv \Delta DEF$.

The symbol $\equiv$ is a shorthand way of describing two triangles as congruent.

GEOMETRY

There are four different methods or cases to show that two triangles are congruent. These methods are listed in Axiom 4:

Axiom 4
Congruent triangles (SSS, SAS, ASA and RHS).

Congruent Triangles: Side, Side, Side (SSS)

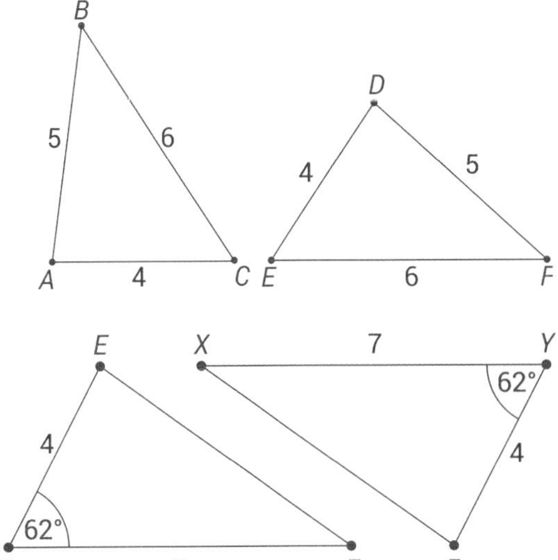

SSS means **Side, Side, Side**.

ΔABC is congruent to ΔDEF **or** $\Delta ABC \equiv \Delta DEF$.

The side lengths in ΔABC are the same as the side lengths in ΔDEF.

Congruent Triangles: Side, Angle, Side (SAS)

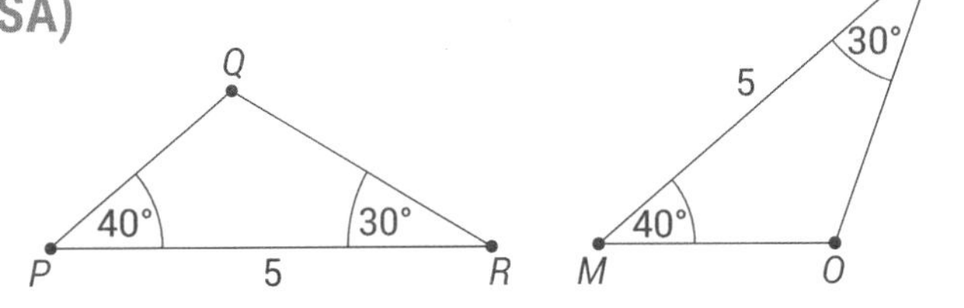

SAS means **Side, Angle, Side**.

ΔDEF is congruent to ΔXYZ **or** $\Delta DEF \equiv \Delta XYZ$.

Two sides and the angle in between them are equal.

The in-between angle can also be called the **included** angle.

Congruent Triangles: Angle, Side, Angle (ASA)

ASA means **Angle, Side, Angle**.

ΔPQR is congruent to ΔMNO or $\Delta PQR \equiv \Delta MNO$.

Two angles and the side in between them are equal.

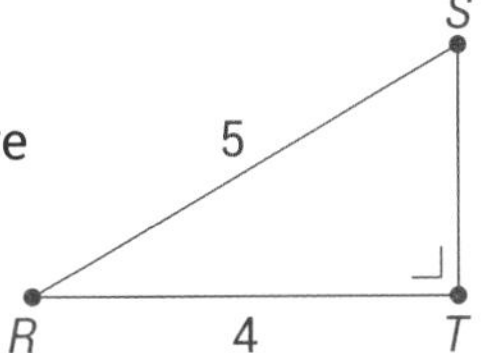

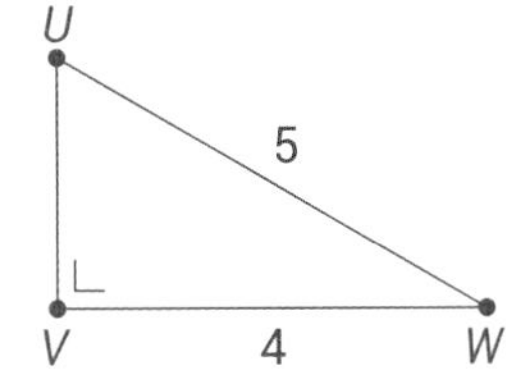

Congruent Triangles: Right Angle, Hypotenuse, One Other Side (RHS)

The hypotenuse is the side opposite the right angle; it is also the longest side in the right-angled triangle.

ΔRST is congruent to ΔUVW **or** $\Delta RST \equiv \Delta UVW$.

Both of these triangles are right-angled, their hypotenuses are of equal length, and they have one other side that is equal.

The areas of congruent triangles are equal as well.

S U 5 5 R 4 T V 4 W

Worked Example 15.21

Verify that the triangles ABC and ABD are congruent.

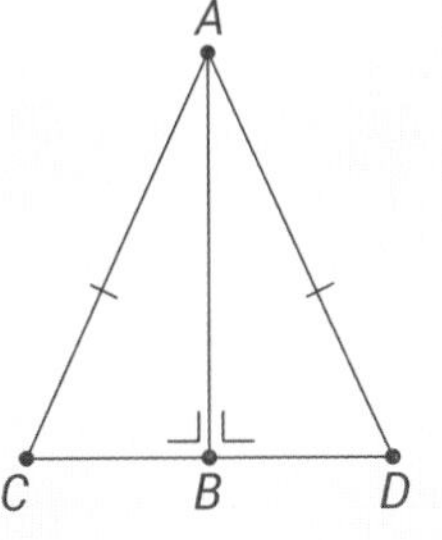

Solution

Statement	Reason
$\lvert\angle ABC\rvert = \lvert\angle ABD\rvert$	Both 90°
$\lvert AC\rvert = \lvert AD\rvert$	Given
$\lvert AB\rvert = \lvert AB\rvert$	Common

$\therefore \Delta ABC \equiv \Delta ABD$ (RHS) Q.E.D.

The same side, $[AB]$, is used in both triangles. This is known as the **common side**.

Always remember to state which case you used to show congruency.

GEOMETRY

Worked Example 15.22

Is $\Delta PQR \equiv \Delta RST$?

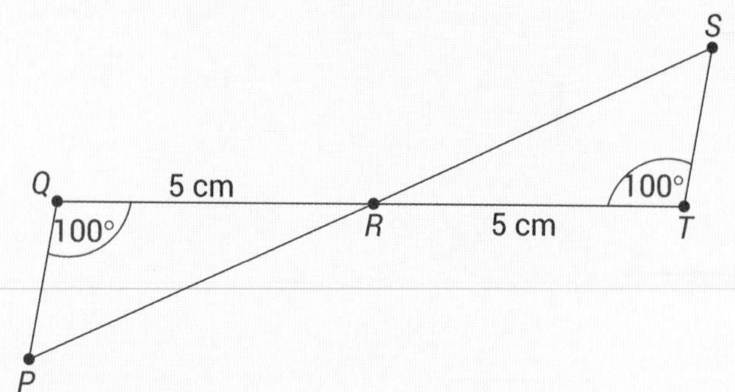

Solution

Statement	Reason
$\lvert\angle PQR\rvert = \lvert\angle RTS\rvert$	Both 100°
$\lvert QR\rvert = \lvert RT\rvert$	Both 5 cm
$\lvert\angle QRP\rvert = \lvert\angle SRT\rvert$	Vertically opposite

$\therefore \Delta PQR \equiv \Delta RST$ (ASA) Q.E.D.

We realise that these angles are equal, as they are vertically opposite to each other.

Exercise 15.6

1. State if any of the following triangles are congruent. Explain your answer fully.

(i)

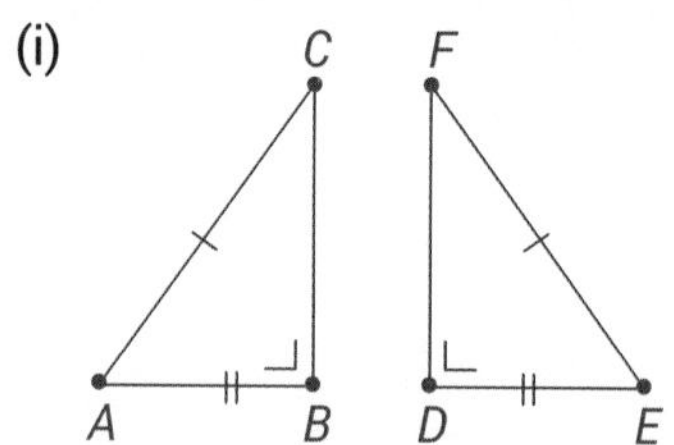

Is $\Delta ABC \equiv \Delta DEF$?

(ii)

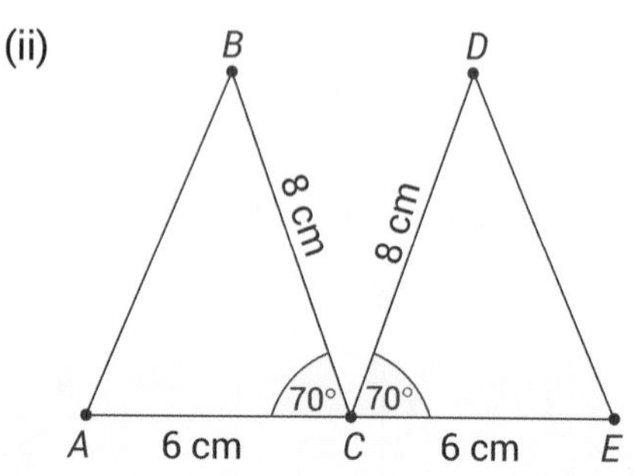

Is $\Delta ABC \equiv \Delta CDE$?

(iii)

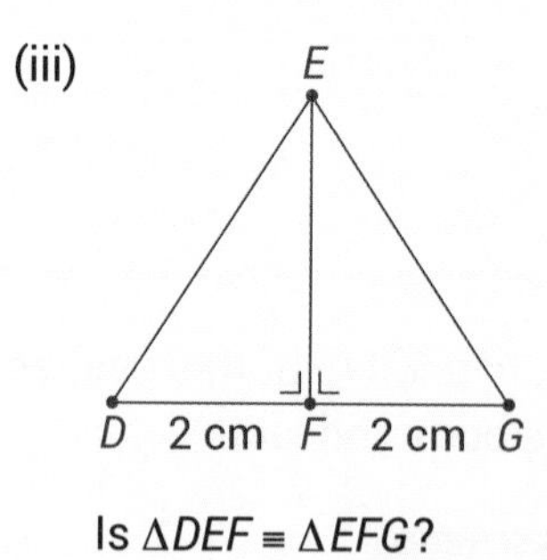

Is $\Delta DEF \equiv \Delta EFG$?

(iv)

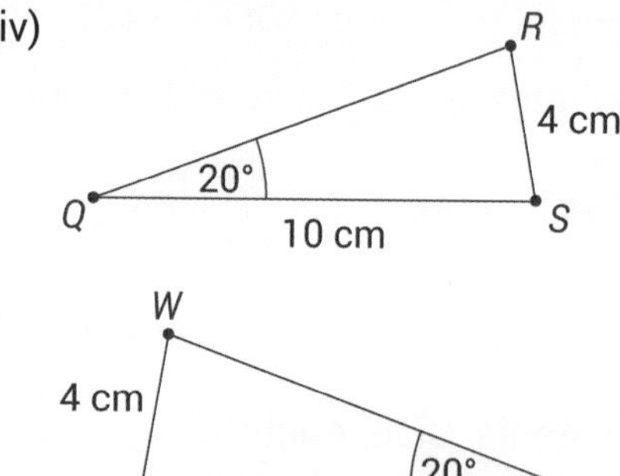

Is $\Delta QRS \equiv \Delta UVW$?

(v) A, C and D are collinear.

B, C and E are collinear.

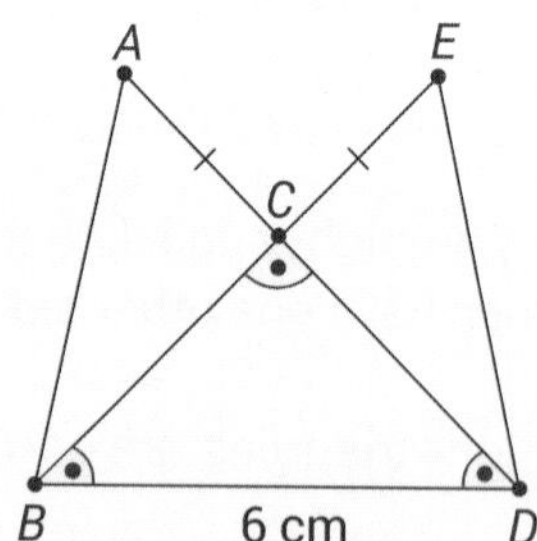

Is $\Delta ABC \equiv \Delta CDE$?

(vi) Note: $DEFG$ is a parallelogram.

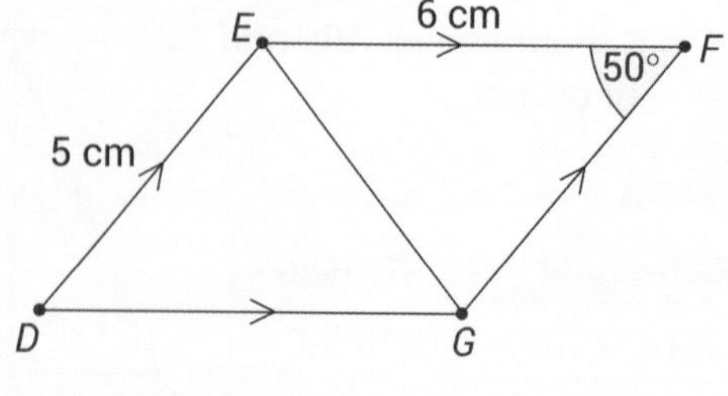

Is $\Delta DEG \equiv \Delta EFG$?

2. Consider the diagram below.

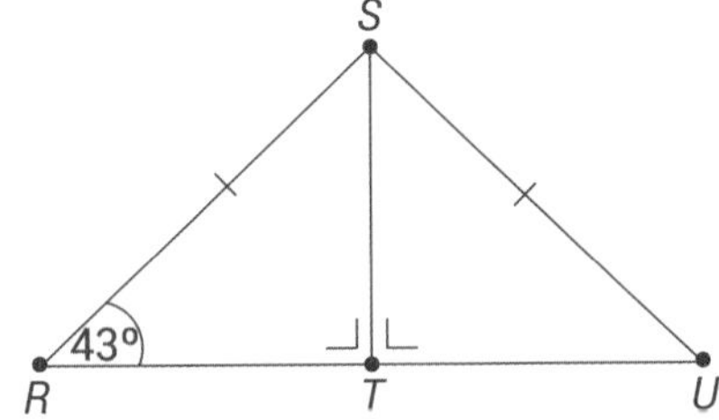

(i) Find $|\angle RST|$ and $|\angle SUT|$.

(ii) What type of triangle is ΔRSU?

(iii) Investigate if the triangle RST is congruent to the triangle STU.

3. In the diagram below, $ABCD$ is a parallelogram.

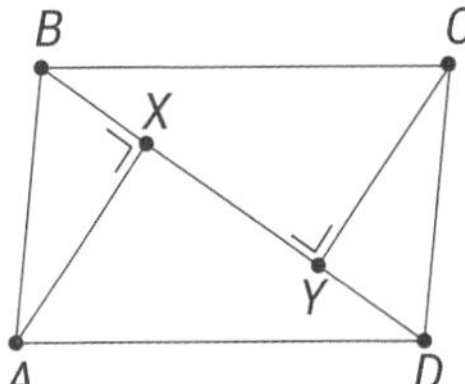

(i) Show that ΔABD is congruent to ΔBCD.

(ii) Show that ΔABX is congruent to ΔCYD.

15.11 Triangles III: Ratios

We will now study more properties associated with triangles.

Parallel Lines and Triangles

We will now consider:

(a) what happens when three parallel lines intersect a transversal and, specifically,

(b) what happens when that transversal is cut into two equal segments.

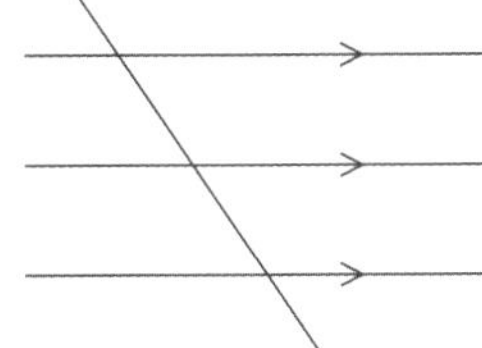

We can state that:

If a transversal is cut into two equal parts by three parallel lines, then any other transversal drawn between these parallel lines will also be cut into two equal parts.

We can now state this as a theorem.

Theorem 11

If three parallel lines cut off equal segments on some transversal line, then they will cut off equal segments on any other transversal.

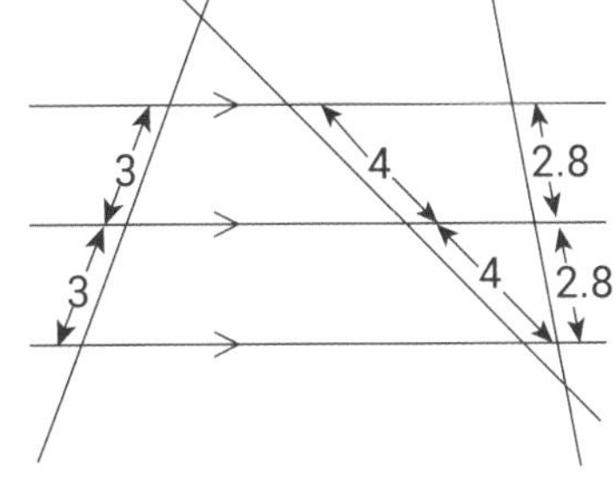

Worked Example 15.23

Find the value of x.

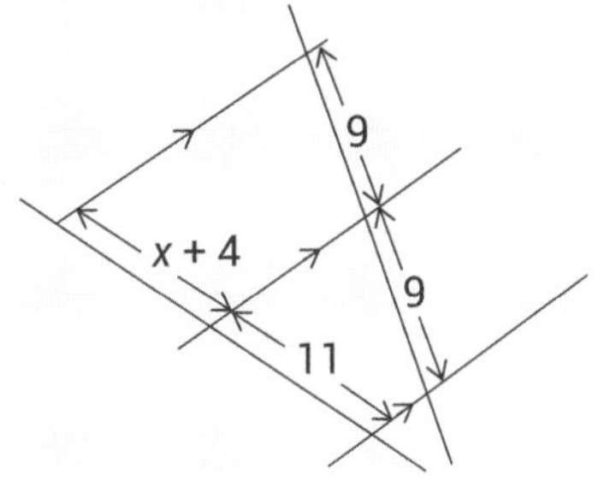

Solution

We can see that one transversal is cut into equal parts. Therefore, all the other transversals will be cut into equal parts as well.

$\Rightarrow x + 4 = 11$

$\therefore x = 7$

GEOMETRY

When a line is parallel to one side of a triangle, it divides another side of the triangle in a certain ratio.

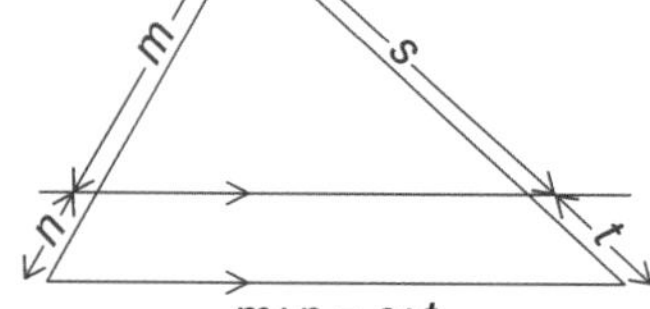

A line that is parallel to one side of a triangle cuts the other two sides of the triangle in the same ratio. This ratio is often referred to as **$m : n$**.

Consider the triangle shown on the right.

If the ratio $|AX| : |XB|$ is equal to $9 : 6 = 3 : 2$, then the ratio $|AY| : |YC|$ is also $3 : 2$.

This can be written more formally as:

Theorem 12

Let ABC be a triangle. If a line l is parallel to BC and cuts $[AB]$ in the ratio $m : n$, then it also cuts $[AC]$ in the same ratio.

Ratios can be written as fractions. So, this theorem can also be written as:

$$\frac{|AX|}{|XB|} = \frac{|AY|}{|YC|} \quad \text{or} \quad \frac{\text{Top length}}{\text{Bottom length}} = \frac{\text{Top length}}{\text{Bottom length}}$$

It is important to realise that all of these ratios can be inverted or turned upside down.

$$\frac{|XB|}{|AX|} = \frac{|YC|}{|AY|} \quad \text{or} \quad \frac{\text{Bottom length}}{\text{Top length}} = \frac{\text{Bottom length}}{\text{Top length}}$$

The theorem means that the following is also true:

$$\frac{|AB|}{|XB|} = \frac{|AC|}{|YC|} \quad \text{or} \quad \frac{\text{Overall length}}{\text{Bottom length}} = \frac{\text{Overall length}}{\text{Bottom length}}$$

And:

$$\frac{|AB|}{|AX|} = \frac{|AC|}{|AY|} \quad \text{or} \quad \frac{\text{Overall length}}{\text{Top length}} = \frac{\text{Overall length}}{\text{Top length}}$$

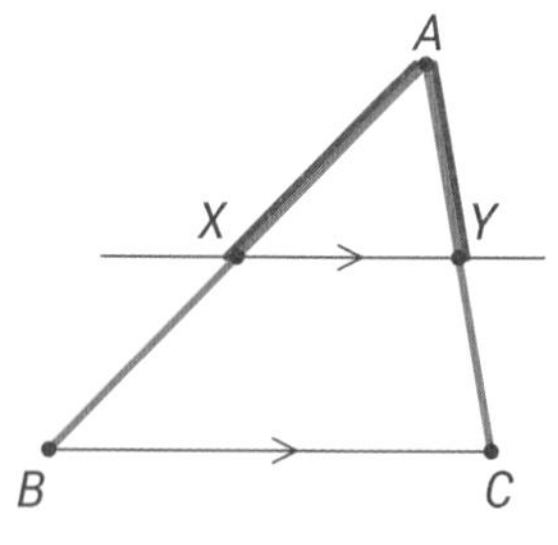

The converse of Theorem 12 can be used to show that two lines are parallel.

Converse to Theorem 12

If a line cuts two sides of a triangle in the same ratio, then the line is parallel to the side not cut by the line.

Worked Example 15.24

Find the length of $[AD]$, given that $DE \parallel BC$.

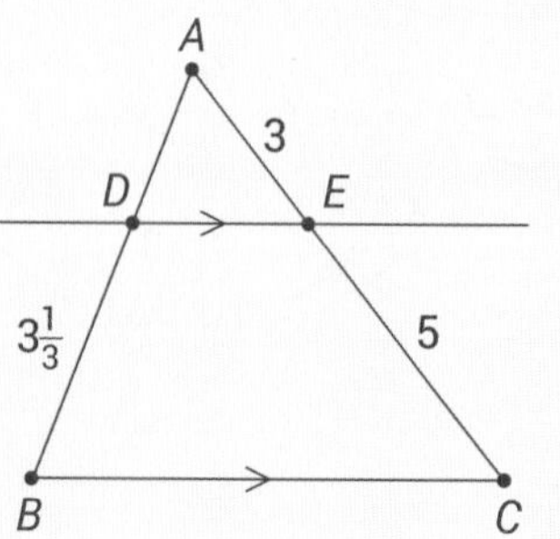

Solution

We need to find $|AD|$, so we first identify what ratio we will use.

We start with the side we are looking for when writing the ratio, as this makes our calculations much easier.

$$\frac{\text{Top length}}{\text{Bottom length}} = \frac{\text{Top length}}{\text{Bottom length}}$$

$$\frac{|AD|}{3\frac{1}{3}} = \frac{3}{5}$$

We cross-multiply to eliminate fractions:

$5|AD| = 3(3\tfrac{1}{3})$

$5|AD| = 10$

$\therefore |AD| = 2$

OR

$3\frac{1}{3} \times \left(\frac{|AD|}{3\frac{1}{3}}\right) = 3\frac{1}{3} \times \frac{3}{5}$

$\therefore |AD| = 2$

Worked Example 15.25

In the triangle PRT, $|RT| = 10.4$. Find the length of $[RS]$.

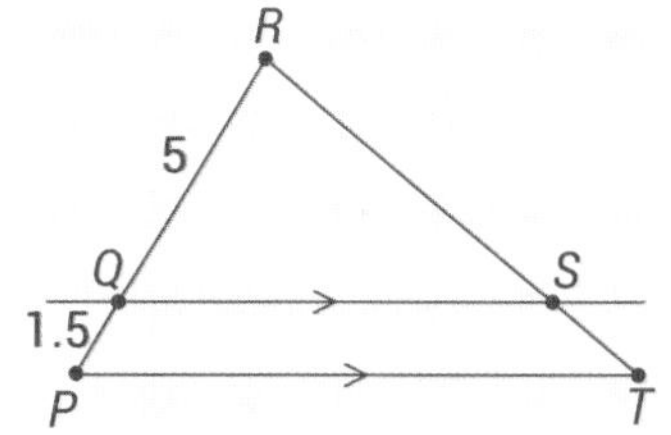

Solution

We need to find $|RS|$, so we again identify which ratio we are using.

We are looking for the top length, and we have been given the overall length of one side.

First, find $|RP|$.

$|RP| = |RQ| + |QP|$

$= 5 + 1.5$

$\therefore |RP| = 6.5$

$$\frac{\text{Top length}}{\text{Overall length}} = \frac{\text{Top length}}{\text{Overall length}}$$

$$\frac{|RS|}{10.4} = \frac{5}{6.5}$$

Cross-multiply:

$6.5|RS| = 5 \times 10.4$

$6.5|RS| = 52$

$\therefore |RS| = 8$

OR

$10.4\,\frac{|RS|}{10.4} = 10.4 \times \frac{5}{6.5}$

$\therefore |RS| = 8$

Similar Triangles

An important relationship that two triangles can have is that of similarity.

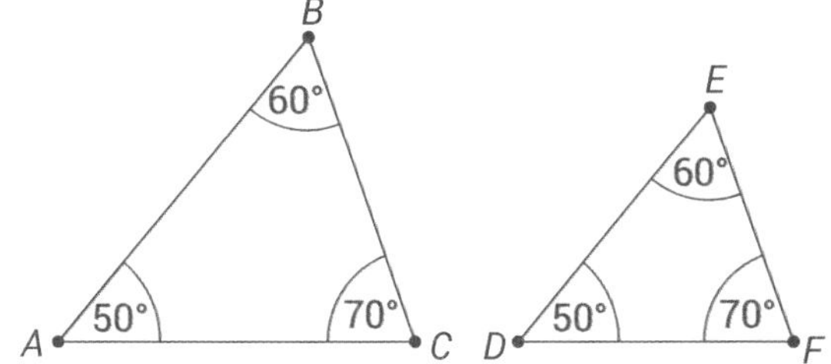

In **similar** or **equiangular** triangles, all three angles in one triangle have the same measure as the corresponding three angles in the other triangle.

Theorem 13

If two triangles are similar, then their sides are proportional, in order.

In **similar** triangles, the corresponding sides are proportional (in order):

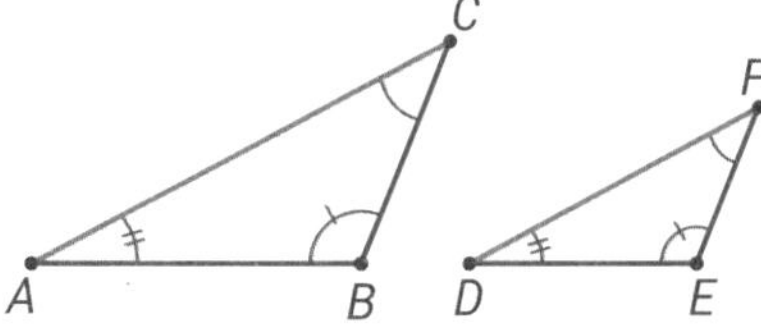

$$\frac{|AB|}{|DE|} = \frac{|AC|}{|DF|} = \frac{|BC|}{|EF|} \text{ or } \frac{|DE|}{|AB|} = \frac{|DF|}{|AC|} = \frac{|EF|}{|BC|}$$

Usually, we only need to use two of the ratios to determine the missing side.

The converse of Theorem 13 also applies.

Converse of Theorem 13

If, in any two triangles, the sides are proportional (in order), then the two triangles are similar to each other.

It is also apparent that:

If a triangle is cut by a line parallel to one of its sides, this line divides the triangle into two similar triangles.

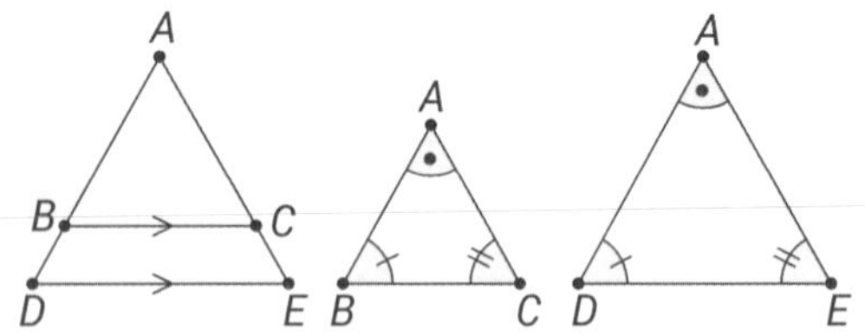

Worked Example 15.26

Find the value of y.

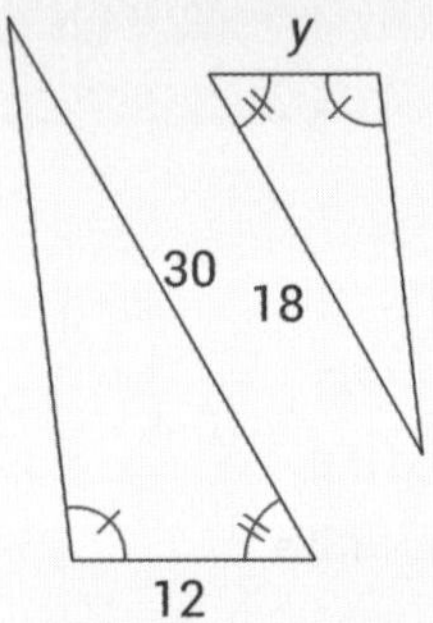

When dealing with similar triangles, it is always a good idea to redraw the triangles so that the corresponding sides match on the diagram.

Solution

These triangles are similar. If two pairs of angles are equal, then the third pair is equal as well (180° in a triangle).

Again, we start with the unknown side and put it over the corresponding side which we know:

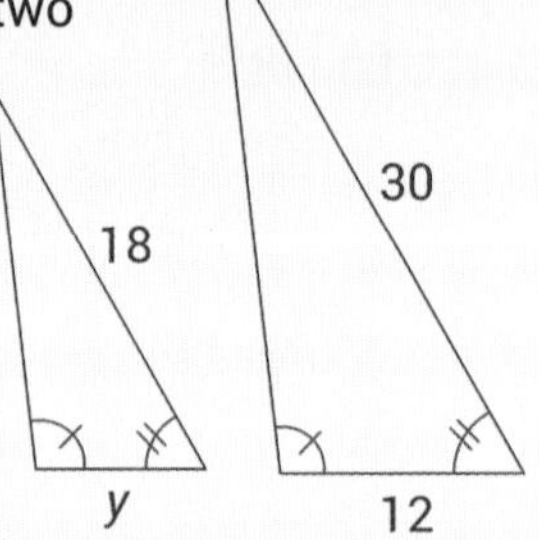

$$\frac{y}{12} = \frac{18}{30}$$

Cross-multiply: $30y = 18 \times 12$ **OR** $60\left(\frac{y}{12}\right) = 60\left(\frac{18}{30}\right)$

$30y = 216$ $\quad\quad$ $5y = 36$

$\therefore y = 7.2$ $\quad\quad$ $\therefore y = 7.2$

Worked Example 15.27

Find: (i) $|AE|$ (ii) $|DE|$

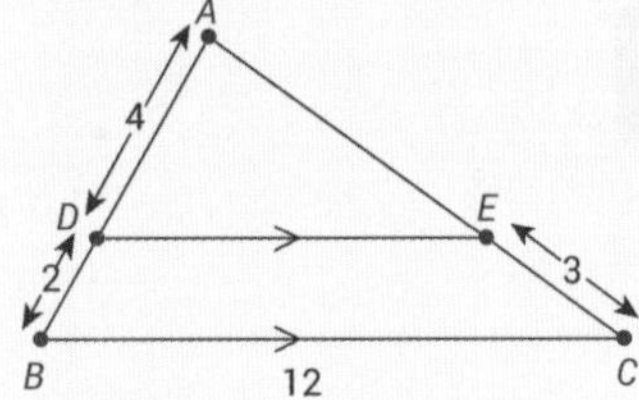

Solution

(i) To find $|AE|$:

$$\frac{|AE|}{3} = \frac{4}{2} \quad\quad 6\left(\frac{|AE|}{3}\right) = 6\left(\frac{4}{2}\right)$$

$\therefore \frac{|AE|}{3} = 2$ **OR** $2|AE| = 3(4)$

Cross-multiply: $\quad 2|AE| = 12$

$\therefore |AE| = 6$ $\quad\quad$ $|AE| = 6$

(ii) To find $|DE|$:

It is a good idea to redraw the triangles, but this time into two separate similar triangles.

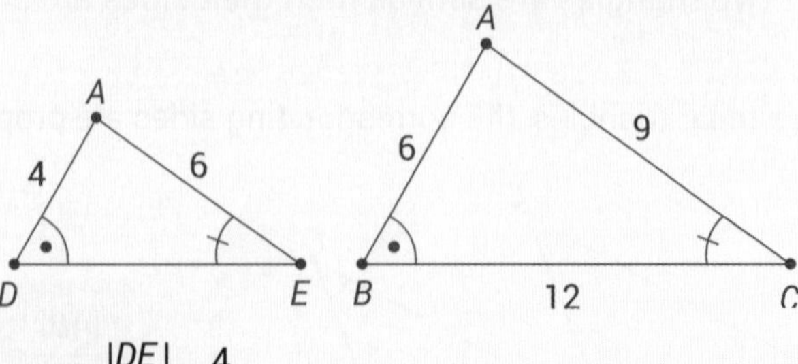

$$\frac{|DE|}{12} = \frac{4}{6}$$

$$\therefore \frac{|DE|}{12} = \frac{2}{3}$$

Cross-multiply:

$\therefore 3|DE| = 24$ **OR** $12\left(\frac{|DE|}{12}\right) = 12\left(\frac{2}{3}\right)$

$\therefore |DE| = 8$ $\quad\quad$ $\therefore |DE| = 8$

Worked Example 15.28

A pylon is placed 20 m away from a building as shown in the diagram.

Calculate the height of the building.

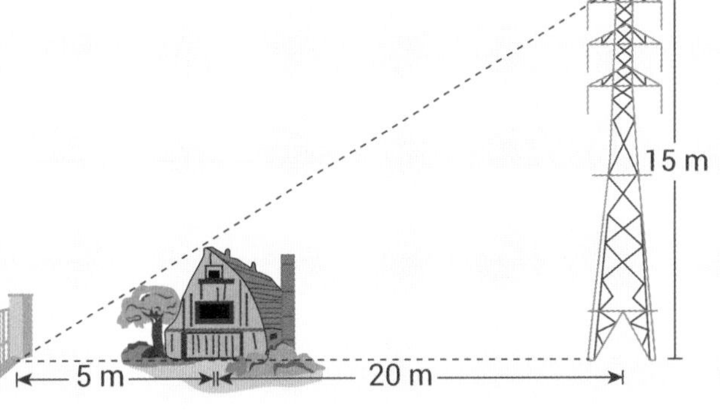

Solution

Again, when faced with geometry problems dealing in real-life settings, it helps if we:

- Draw a diagram to represent the problem.
- Fill in as much information on the diagram as possible, checking both the diagram and text given in the question.
- Identify and then label on the diagram what we are asked to find (in this case h).

Two pairs of angles are equal ⇒ triangles are similar.

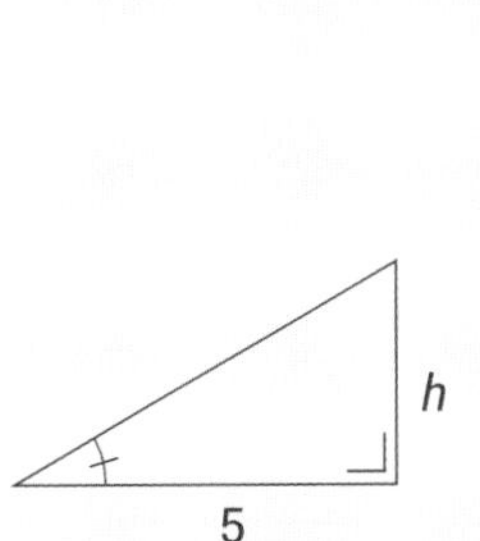

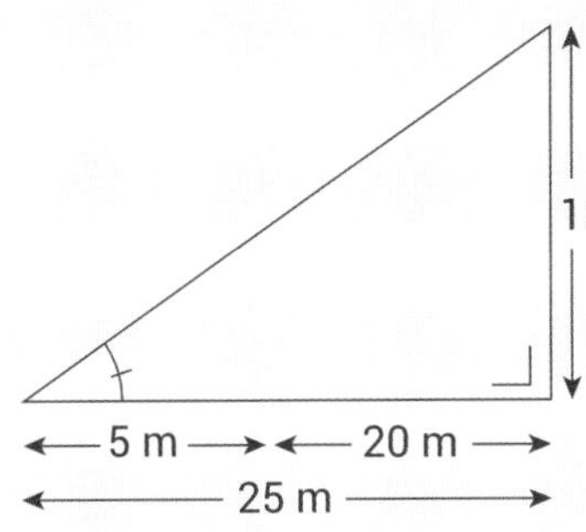

$$\frac{h}{15} = \frac{5}{25}$$

$$25h = 75$$

$$h = \frac{75}{25}$$

$$h = 3 \text{ m}$$

OR

$$75\left(\frac{h}{15}\right) = 75\left(\frac{5}{25}\right)$$

$$5h = 3(5)$$

$$5h = 15$$

$$h = 3 \text{ m}$$

Exercise 15.7

1. In each of the following diagrams, find the value of x:

(i)

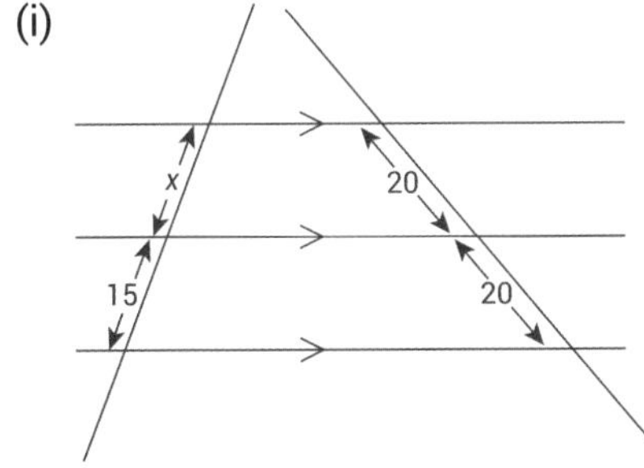

(ii)

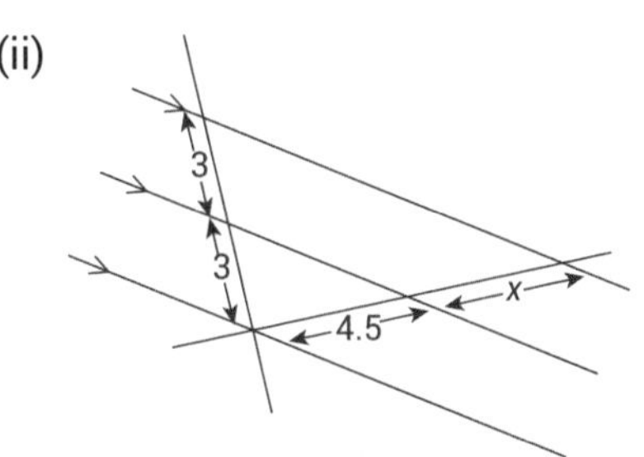

2. For each of the line segments below, find the following ratios (in their lowest terms):

(i) $|AB| : |BC|$ (ii) $|AC| : |AB|$ (iii) $|BC| : |AC|$

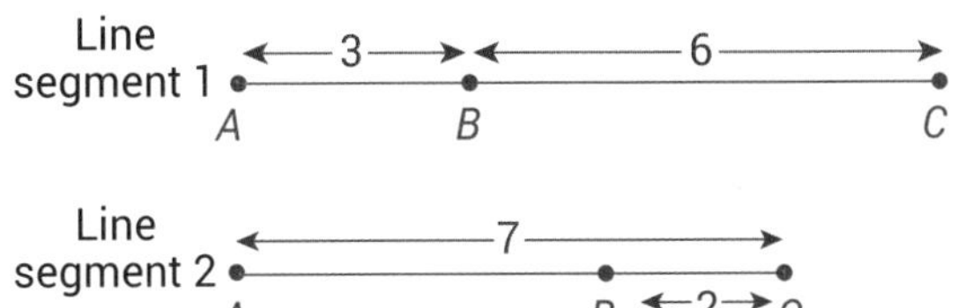

3. Find the value of x in each case:

(i)

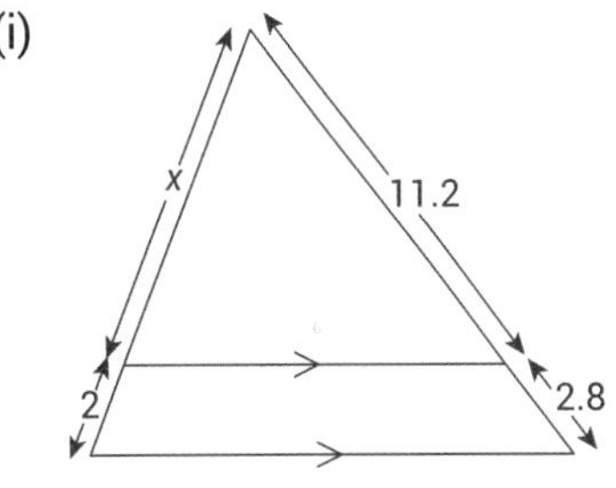

(ii)

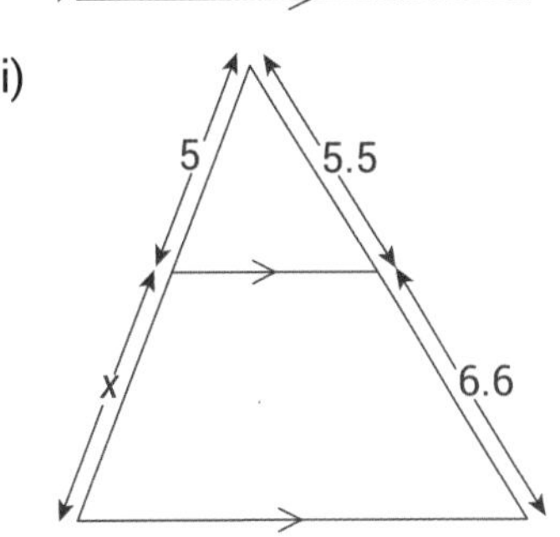

(iii)

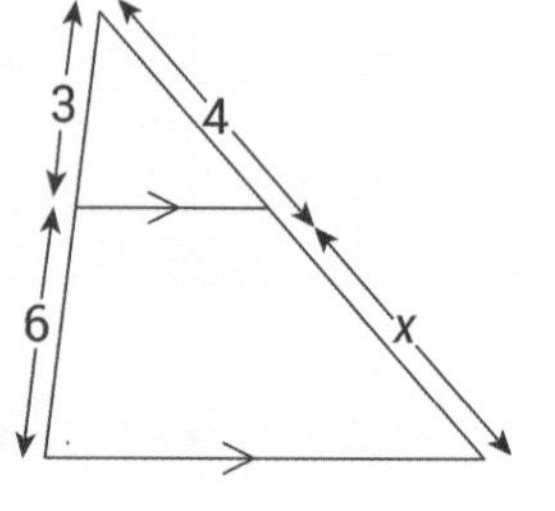

(iv)

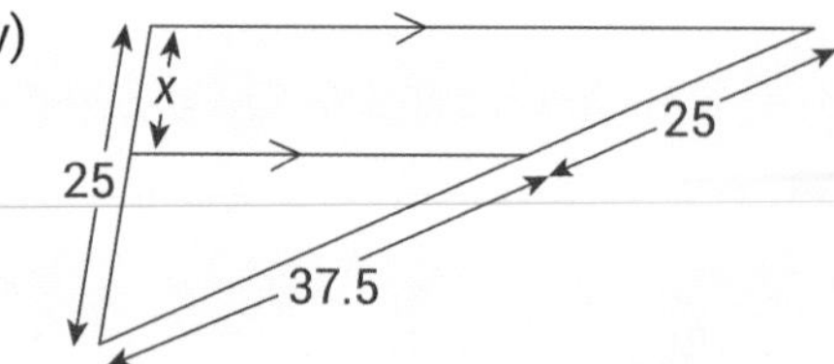

(v)

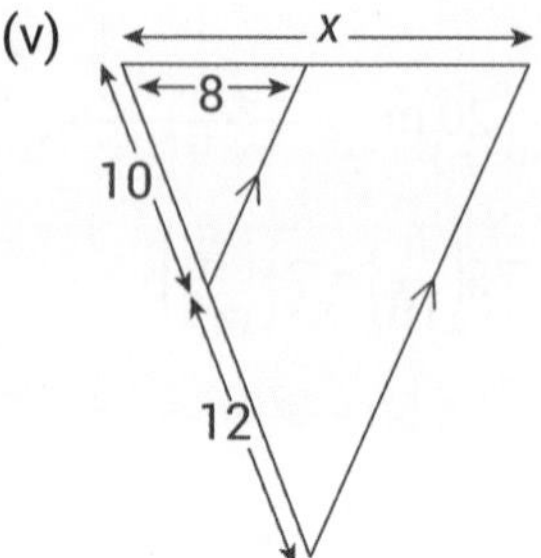

4. In the diagram $BD \parallel CE$.

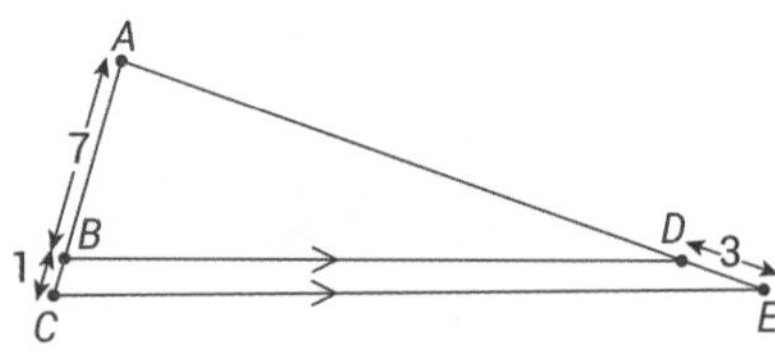

Find: (i) $|AD|$

(ii) $|AE|$

(iii) The ratio $|AB| : |AC|$

5. In the diagram $ST \parallel QR$. $|PS| : |SQ| = 5 : 2$.

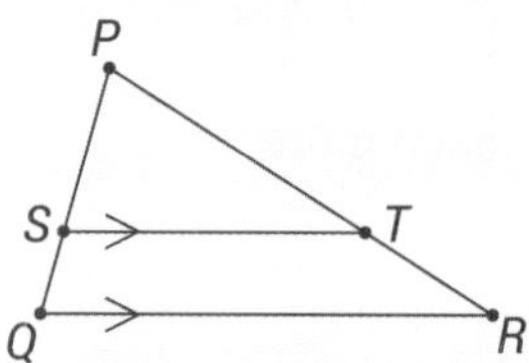

Find the following ratios:

(i) $|PT| : |TR|$

(ii) $|PR| : |PT|$

(iii) $|PQ| : |PS|$

(iv) Gemma writes, '$|SQ| = 2$'.

Could $[SQ]$ have a different length?

Give a reason for your answer.

6. In the diagram $XZ \parallel AB$. Also, $|XY| : |AY| = 7 : 3$.

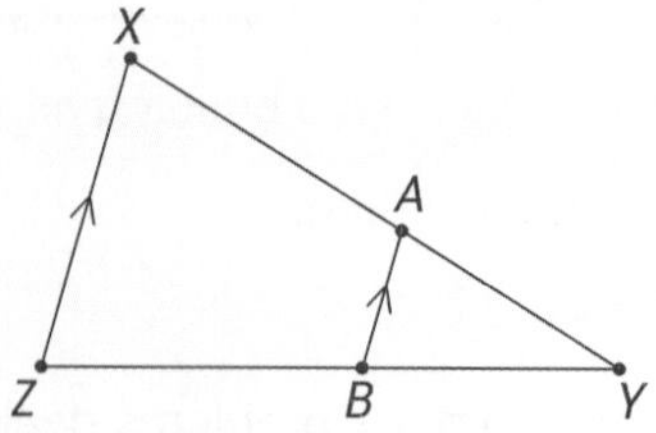

Write down the following ratios:

(i) $\frac{|XA|}{|AY|}$ (ii) $\frac{|ZB|}{|BY|}$ (iii) $\frac{|YZ|}{|BY|}$

If $|AX| = 8$ cm and $|ZB| = 7$ cm, find:

(iv) $|AY|$ (v) $|BY|$ (vi) $|ZY|$

7. Investigate if $XY \parallel PQ$.

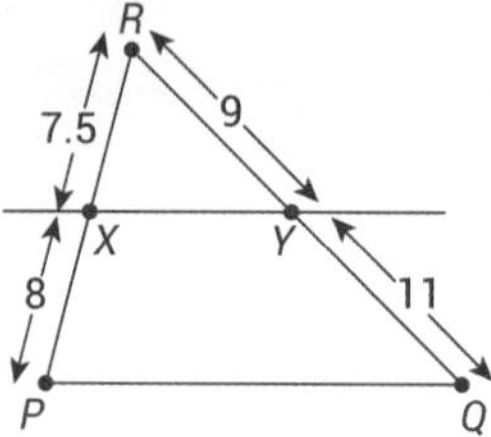

8. Investigate if $PQ \parallel AC$.

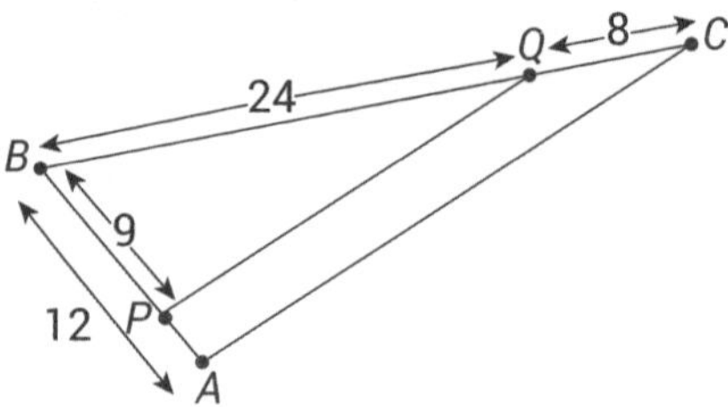

9. Identify the pairs of corresponding sides in each of the following similar triangles.

Part (i) has been done for you to show how to lay out your answer.

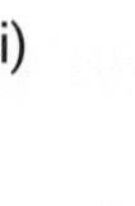

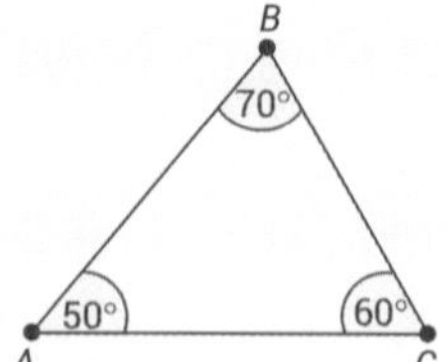

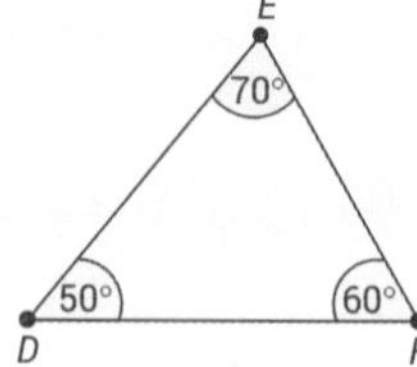

Answer:

$[AB]$ corresponds to $[DE]$.

$[AC]$ corresponds to $[DF]$.

$[BC]$ corresponds to $[EF]$.

(ii) 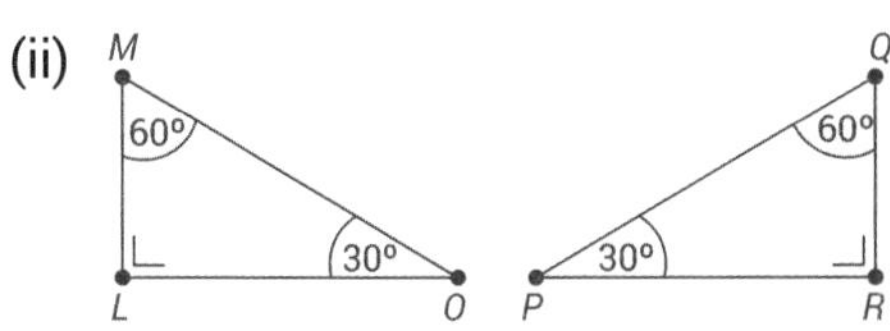

(iii) 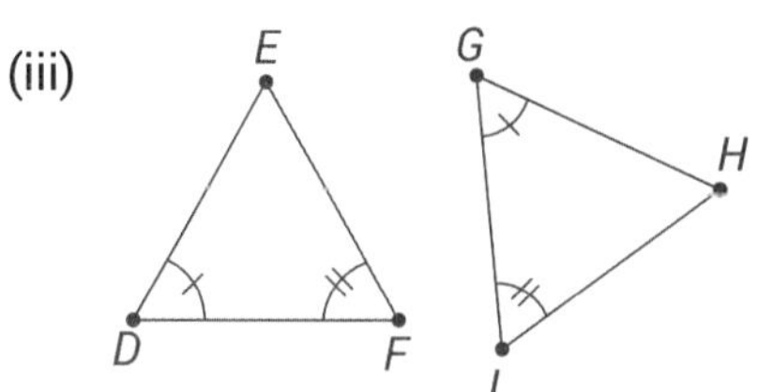

(iv) 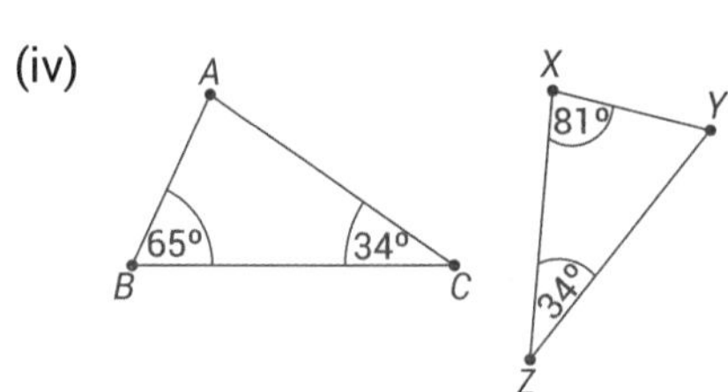

(v) 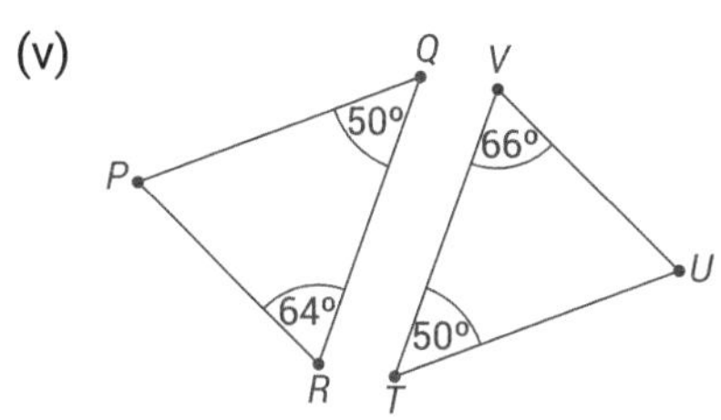

10. Find the value of x in each case:

(i) 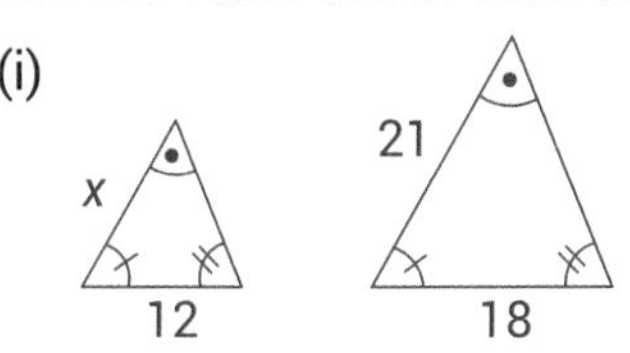

(ii) 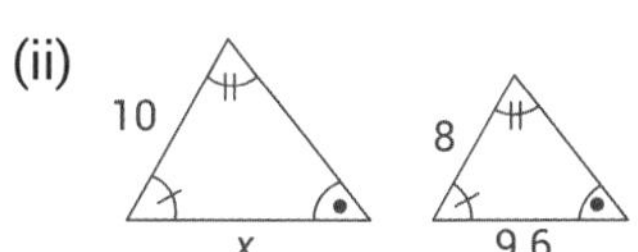

(iii) 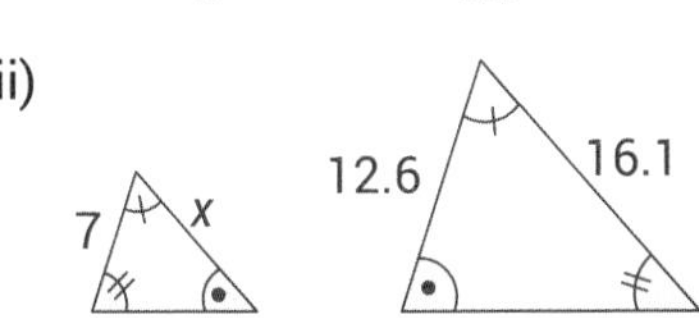

11. Find the value of x and y in each case:

(i) 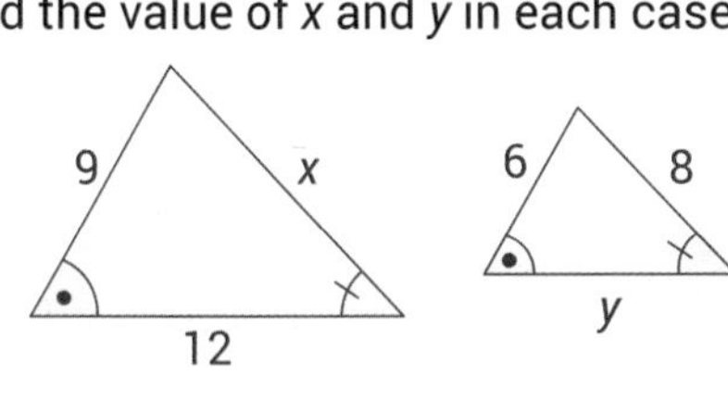

(ii) 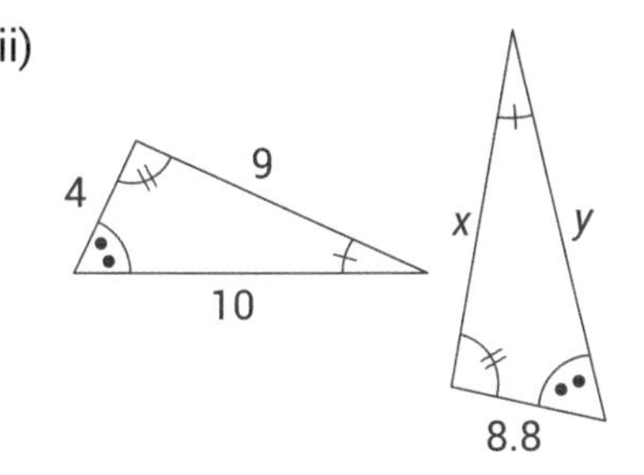

(iii) 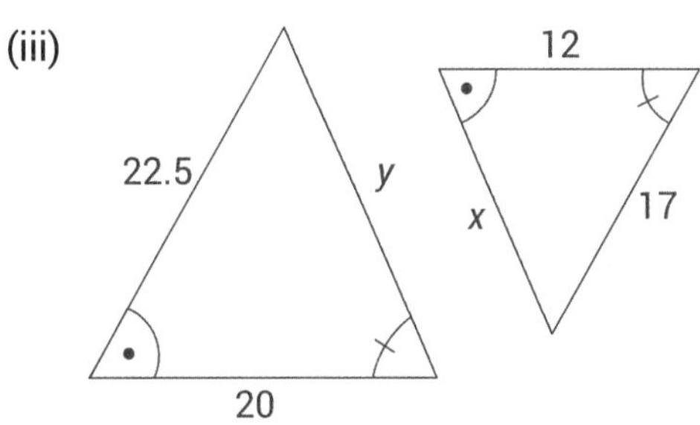

12. Investigate if the following pairs of triangles are similar to each other. Explain your answer.

(i) Is ΔPQR similar to ΔPST?

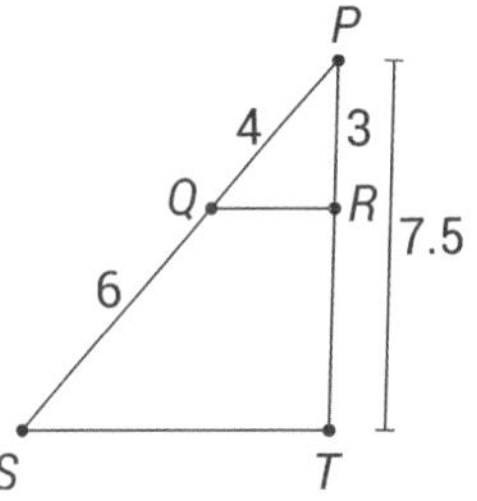

(ii) Is ΔDEF similar to ΔDGH?

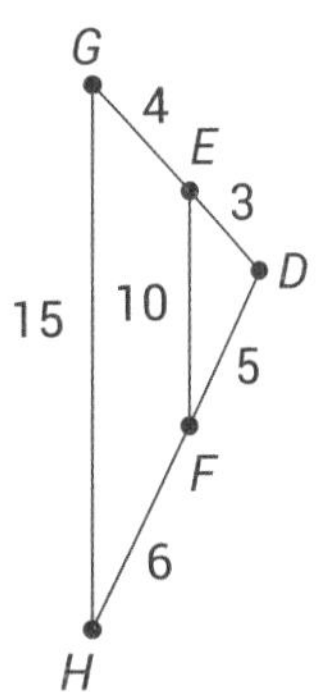

13. For each question, the triangles ABC and ADE are similar. Find the value of x and y in each case.

You can also use Theorem 12 to help find the required sides.

(i) 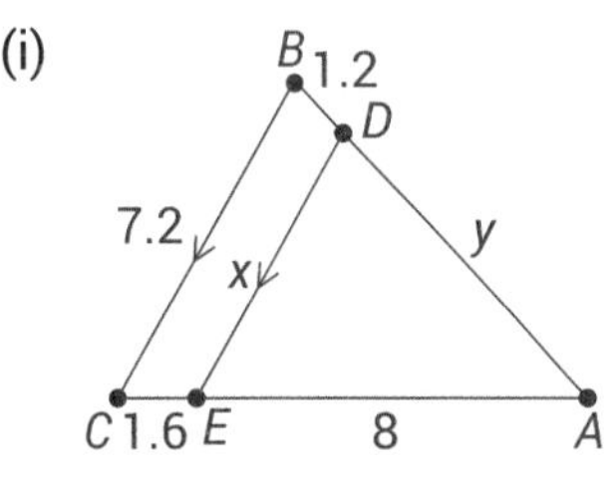

(ii) 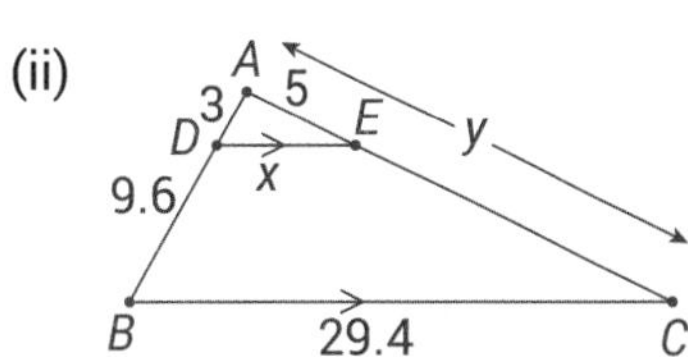

(iii) 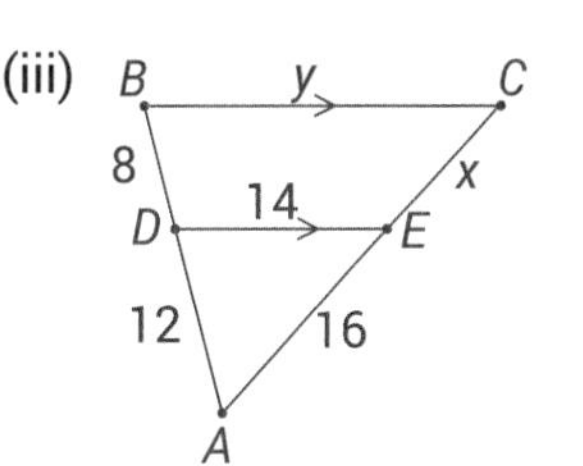

14. In the given diagram $AB \perp BC$ and $EC \perp ED$.

(i) Show that the two triangles ABC and EDC are similar.

Given that $|ED| = 3$, $|AB| = 6$ and $|DC| = 5$, find:

(ii) $|AC|$ (iii) $|BC|$ (iv) $|EC|$

15. In the triangle PQR, $ST \parallel QR$, and $|QS| = \frac{1}{3}|TR|$.

Find:

(i) $|TR|$ (ii) $|PS|$ (iii) $|PQ|$

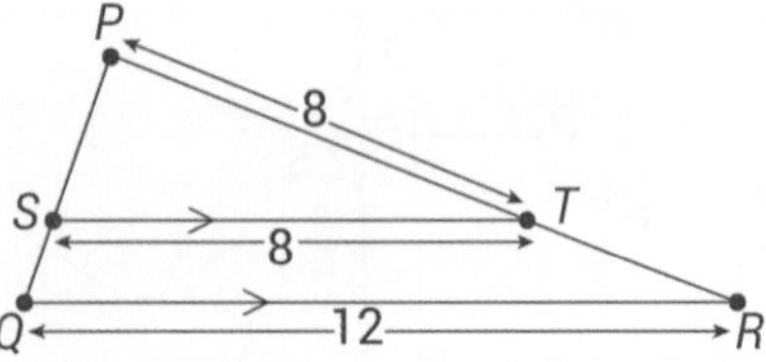

16. In the ΔXYZ, $AB \parallel YZ$.

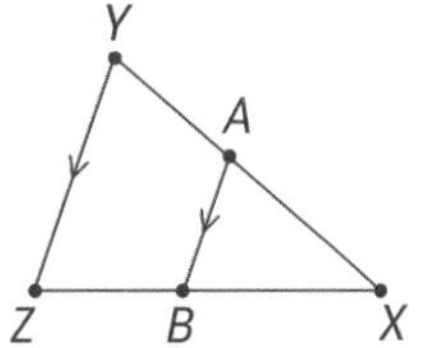

(i) In your own words explain why ΔXYZ and ΔXAB are similar.

If $|XB| : |XZ| = 3 : 5$, find the following ratios:

(ii) $|XB| : |BZ|$ (iii) $|XA| : |AY|$ (iv) $|XY| : |AY|$

17. Consider the triangles ABC and BEF, where $AC \parallel EF$.

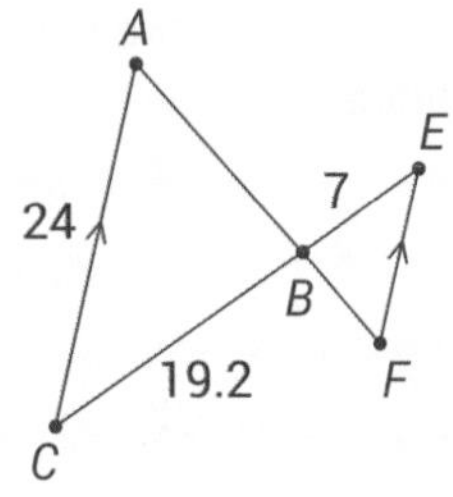

(i) Show that the two triangles ABC and BEF are similar.

(ii) Find $|EF|$.

18. A building casts a shadow of length 6.4 m. At the same time a 3 m high lamppost casts a shadow of length 2.5 m. How tall is the building? Diagram is not to scale.

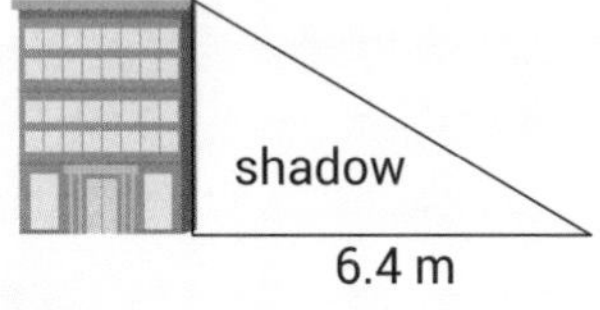

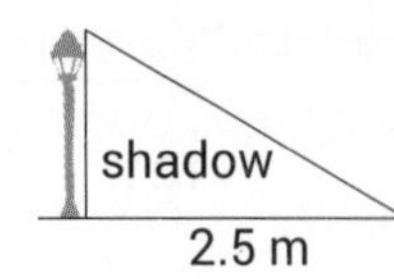

19. For a school project, students measure the lengths of their shadows on a sunny day. Student A's shadow was 3 m long and student B's shadow was 3.4 m long.

(i) Which student is taller?
Give a reason for your answer.

(ii) If student A is 1.6 m tall, how tall is student B? (Give your answer to two decimal places.)

(iii) A building close by has a height of 8.5 m. How long would its shadow be? (Give your answer to two decimal places.)

20. The diagram shows a person who is 1.74 m tall. Her shadow length is 4 m.

(i) Find the height of the nearby tree, if the person is standing 16.5 m away from the tree and the tip of her shadow and the tip of the tree's shadow coincide.

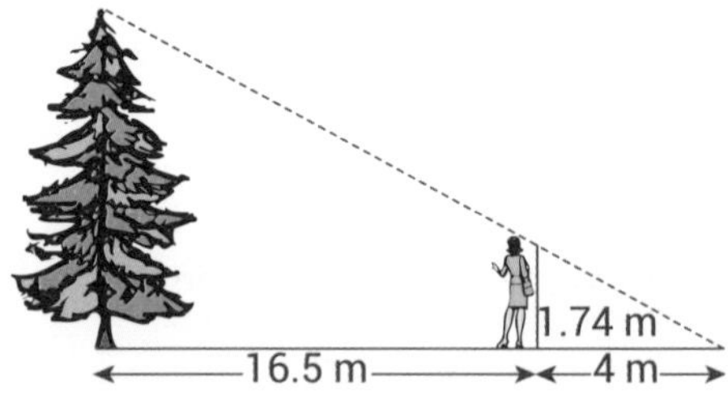

(ii) Another tree's shadow is 23 m in length. Find the height of this tree to the nearest metre.

21. A firework is fired from the ground at an angle. It travels in a straight line and hits a target at a height of 15 m, 55 m in a horizontal line away from where it was fired. Along its path it just passed over a stone wall which is a distance of 47.5 m from the target.

(i) Draw a diagram to show the above information.

(ii) Using a suitable theorem, find the approximate height of the wall to the nearest centimetre.

22. A rectangular field is shown adjoined by two triangular fields.

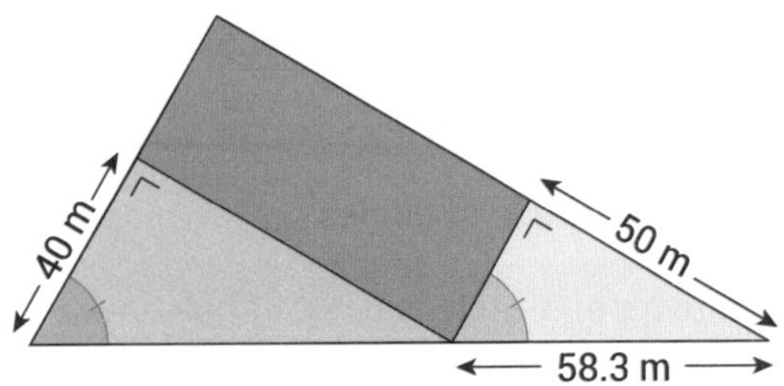

Find the combined area of the three fields to the nearest square metre.

23. Jane is 1.6 m tall. She stands in front of a lamppost which is 3 m high. When she stands 15 m away from the lamppost, she can see that the top of the lamppost just lines up with the top of her office block. The lamppost is 85 m away from the office block.

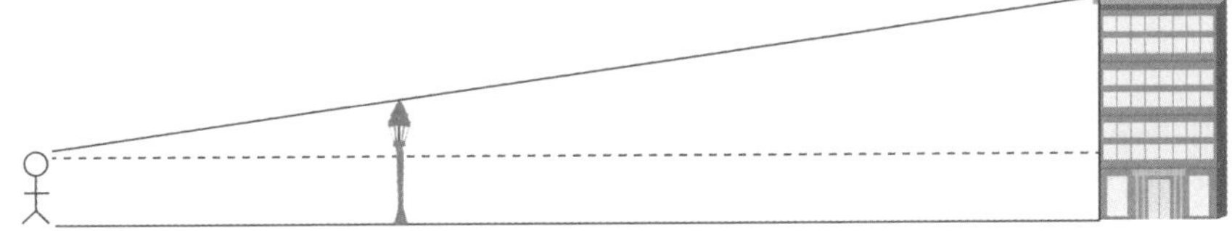

(i) Copy and fill in the diagram to show the above information.

(ii) Hence, find the height of the office block (to the nearest metre).

15.12 Circles

A **circle** is a very common shape found in all aspects of everyday life.

Some common terms associated with circles:

A **circle** is a set of points in a plane that are all equidistant from a fixed point, its centre.

Radius – the line segment from the centre of the circle to any point on the circle.

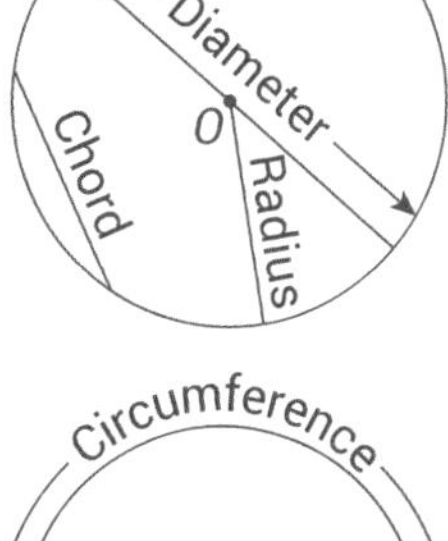

Note: The radius can often also be considered the measurement of the line segment.

The centre of a circle is usually marked with a dot and sometimes the letter O.

The plural of radius is **radii**.

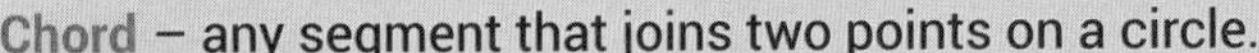

Chord – any segment that joins two points on a circle.

Diameter – a chord that passes through the centre of a circle. The diameter is twice the radius in length. The diameter is the longest chord of a circle.

Circumference
O
Arc

Circumference – the perimeter or length of the circle.

Arc – any part of the circumference of the circle.

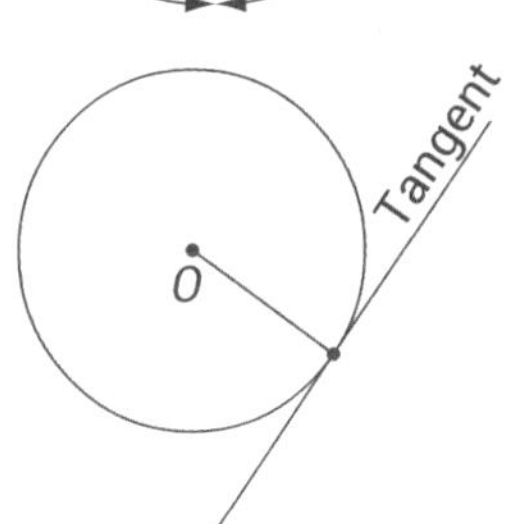

Tangent – a line that touches the circle at only one point. Where the tangent touches the circle is called the point of contact, or point of tangency.

GEOMETRY

Sector – the region of the circle enclosed by two radii and the arc between these radii.

Radius
Arc Sector
Radius

Circle Properties

We can now investigate some properties of circles.

The angle opposite the diameter in a circle is a right angle or 90°.

This can be stated as:

Corollary 3
Each angle in a semicircle is a right angle.

O
180°

From this corollary, we can also show another property of a circle:

Corollary 4
If the angle standing on a chord [*BC*] at some point of the circle is a right angle, then [*BC*] is a diameter.

This corollary could be considered the converse of Corollary 3.

Worked Example 15.29

Find: (i) |∠1| (ii) |∠2| (iii) |∠3| (iv) |∠4|
in the following diagram, where [*PQ*] is the diameter of the circle with centre *O*:

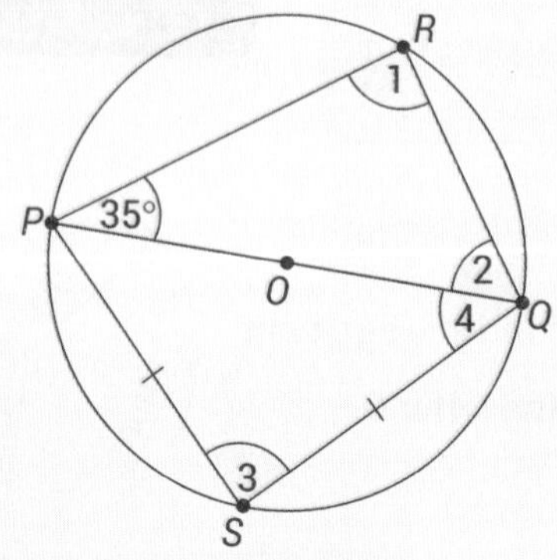

Solution

(i) |∠1| = 90° (Angle in a semicircle)

(ii) |∠2| = 180° – 90° – 35° (180° in a triangle)

∴ |∠2| = 55°

(iii) |∠3| = 90° (Angle in a semicircle)

(iv) |∠4| = (180° – 90°) ÷ 2 (Isosceles triangle and 180° in a triangle)

|∠4| = 90° ÷ 2

∴ |∠4| = 45°

Worked Example 15.30

Find: (i) |∠*OCA*| (ii) |∠*OBC*|
in the following diagram, where the points *A*, *O* and *B* are collinear and *O* is the centre of the circle:

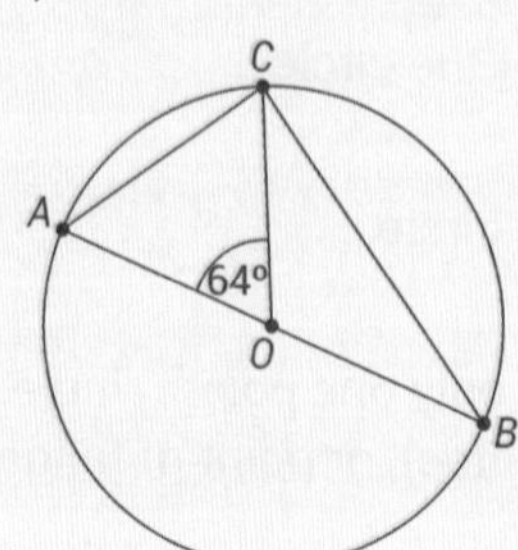

Solution

(i)

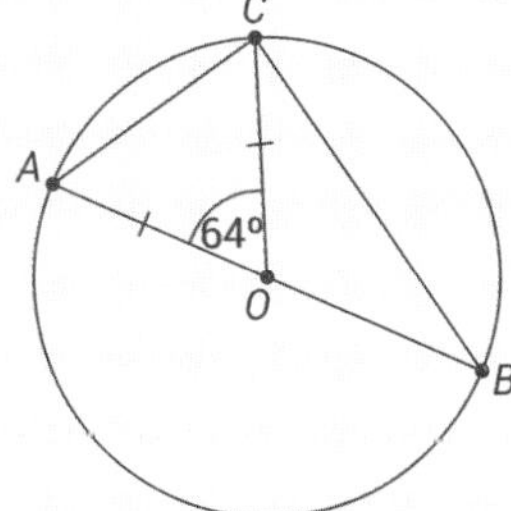

$|AO| = |CO|$ = radius

$\Rightarrow |\angle OAC| = |\angle OCA|$ (Isosceles triangle)

$\Rightarrow |\angle OCA| = (180° - 64°) \div 2$ (180° in a triangle)

$\Rightarrow |\angle OCA| = 116° \div 2$

$\therefore |\angle OCA| = 58°$

(ii)

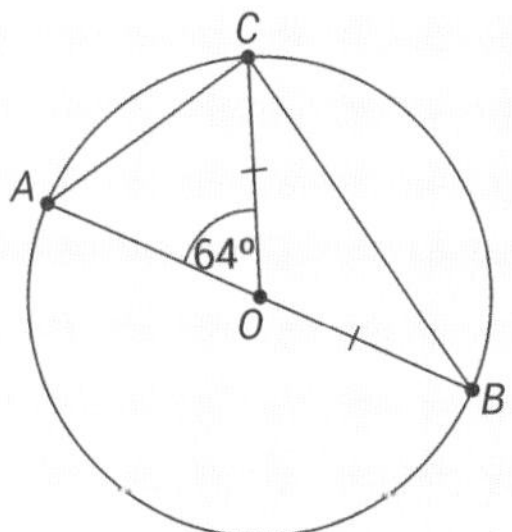

$|OC| = |OB|$ = radius

$\Rightarrow |\angle OCB| = |\angle OBC|$ (Isosceles triangle)

$\Rightarrow |\angle OBC| = (180° - 116°) \div 2$

$\Rightarrow |\angle OBC| = 64° \div 2$ (180° in a triangle)

$\therefore |\angle OBC| = 32°$

This question could also have been solved using the exterior angles of a triangle.

Exercise 15.8

1. In each of the following diagrams, identify and name the 90° angle. Also name the diameter of each of the circles.

   O is the centre in each case.

   (i)

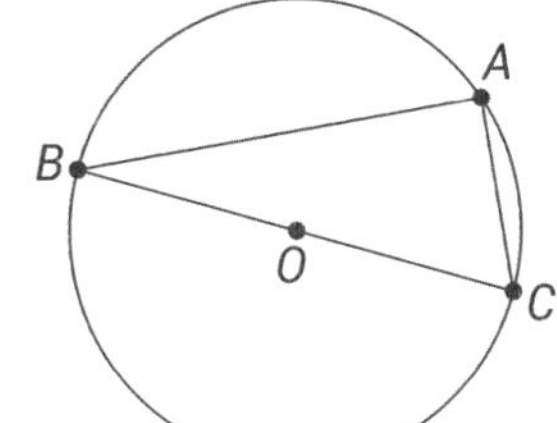

   (ii)

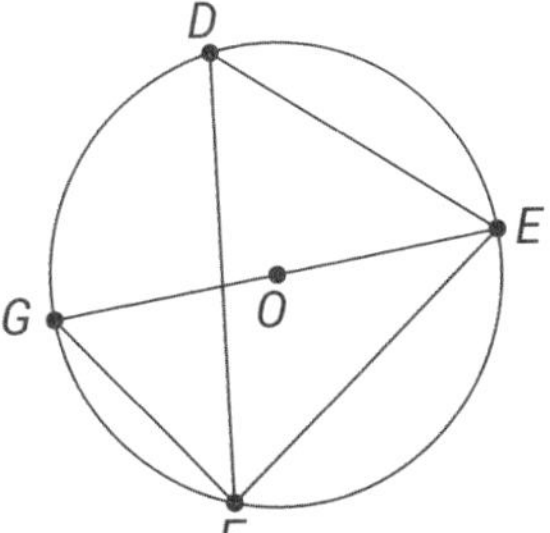

   (iii)

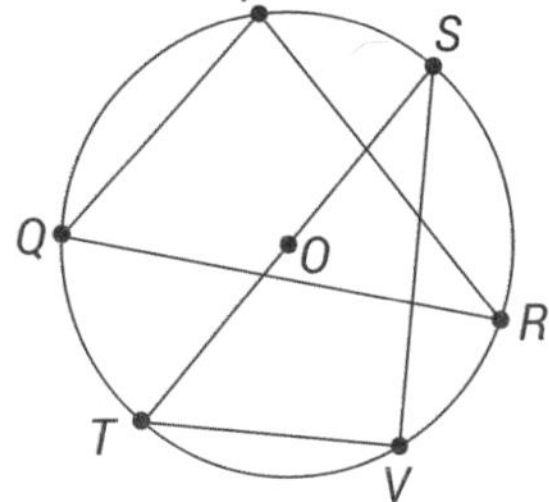

2. Find $|\angle 1|$ and $|\angle 2|$ in each of the following diagrams. Remember to show as much work as possible.

   O is the centre in each case.

   (i)

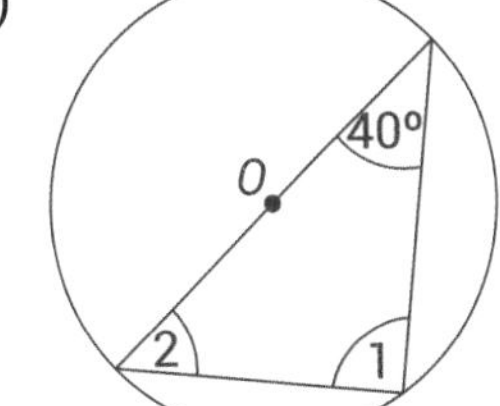

   (ii)

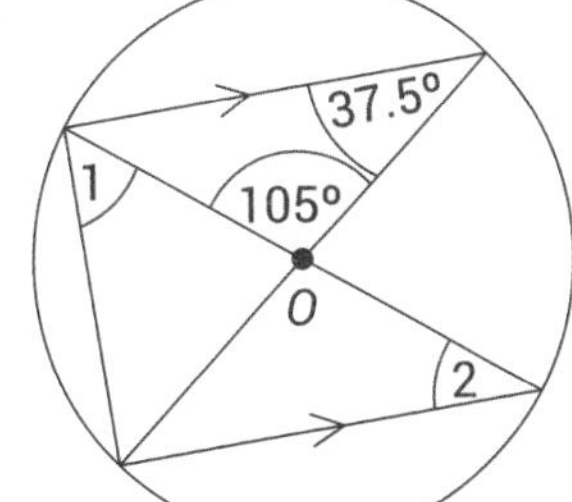

   (iii)

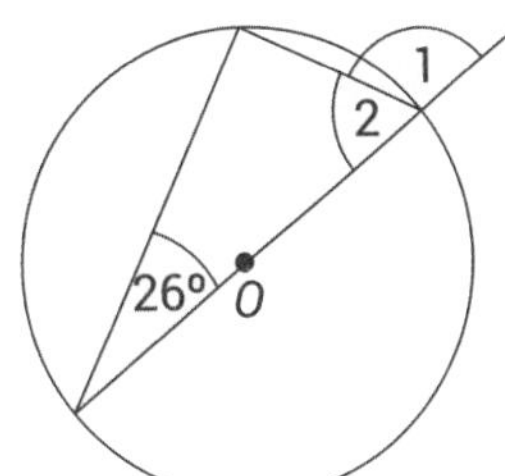

GEOMETRY

(iv)

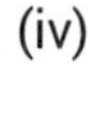

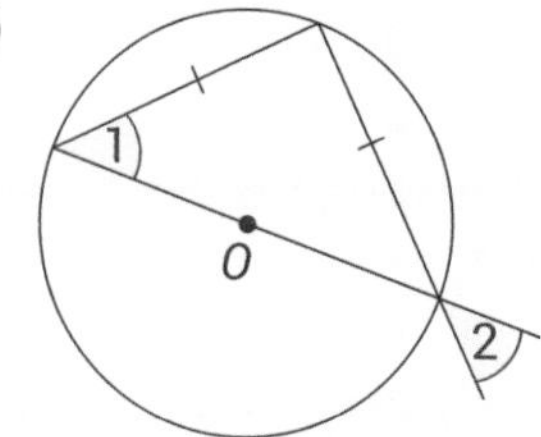

3. Find $|\angle A|$ and $|\angle B|$ in each of the following diagrams. Remember to show as much work as possible. O is the centre in each case.

(i)

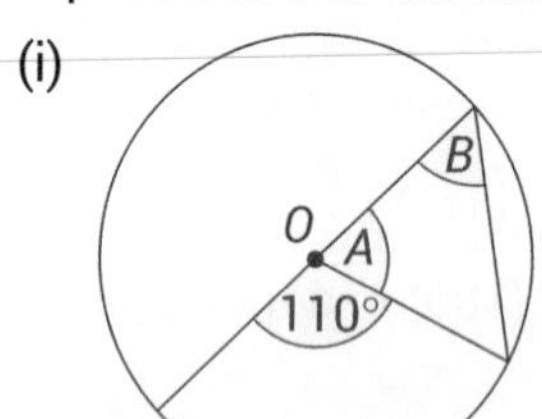

(ii)

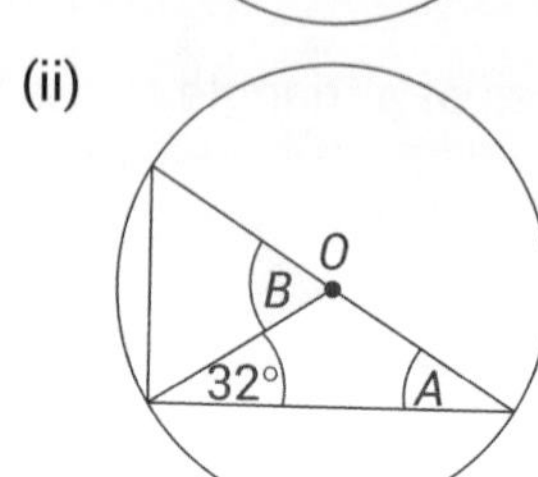

(iii)

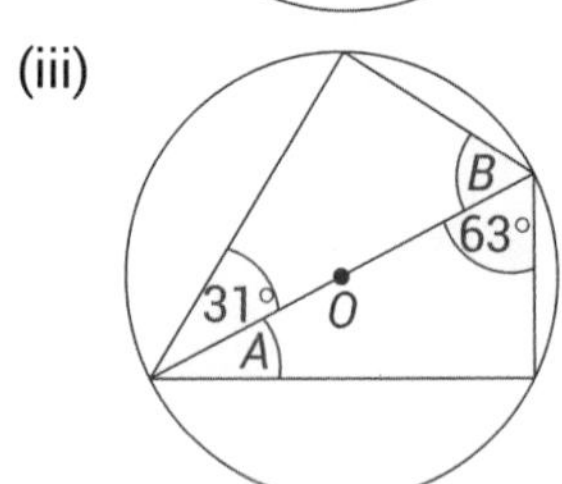

(iv)

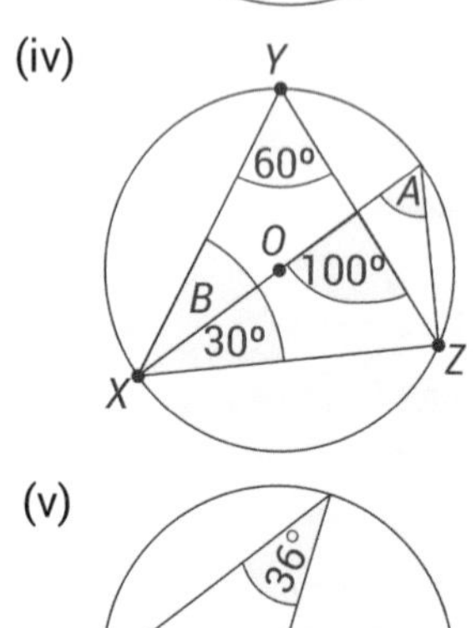

(v)

4. Find the length of the diameter of the given circles with centre O in each of the following diagrams.

(i)

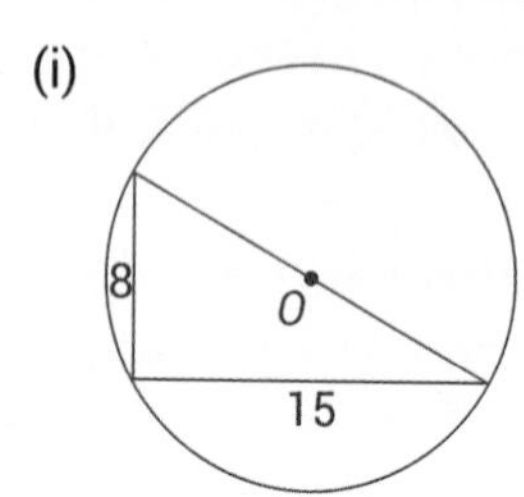

(ii)

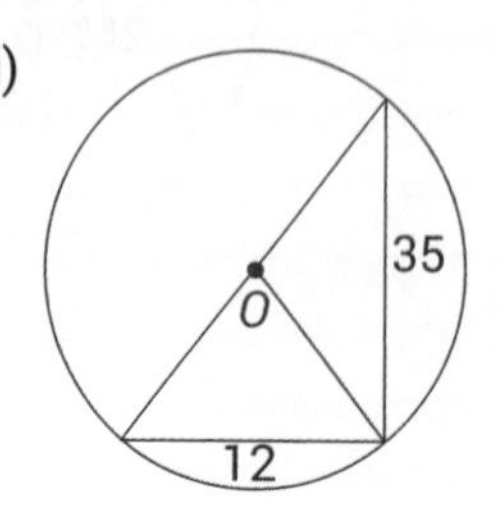

5. $[AD]$ is the diameter of the circle with centre O. $FE \parallel AD$.

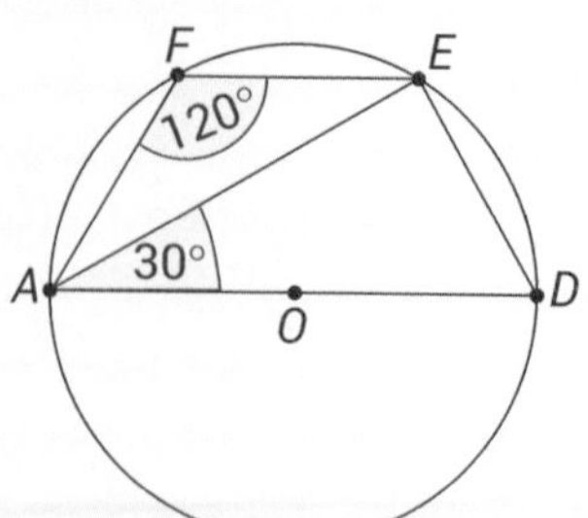

Find:

(i) $|\angle AED|$ (ii) $|\angle EDA|$

(iii) $|\angle FEA|$ (iv) Explain why $|AF| = |FE|$.

6. $[BD]$ is the diameter of the circle with centre O.

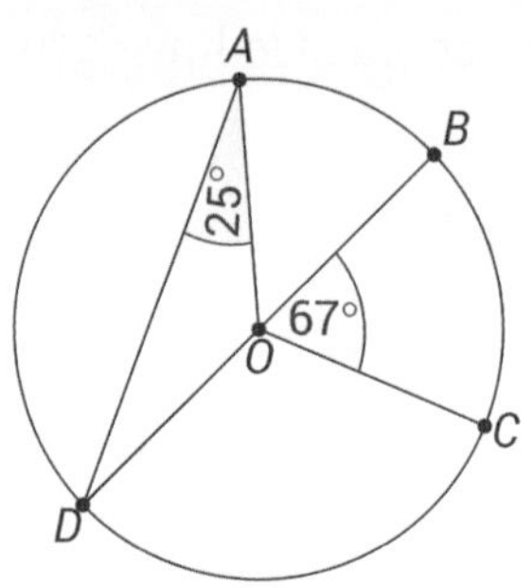

Find:

(i) $|\angle DOC|$ (ii) $|\angle DCO|$

(iii) $|\angle OBC|$ (iv) $|\angle BAO|$

7. The point P is on the circle c with centre O and diameter $[MN]$, as shown.

The length of the radius of c is $2\sqrt{5}$ cm.

$|MP| = x$ cm and $|PN| = 2x$ cm.

Find the value of x.

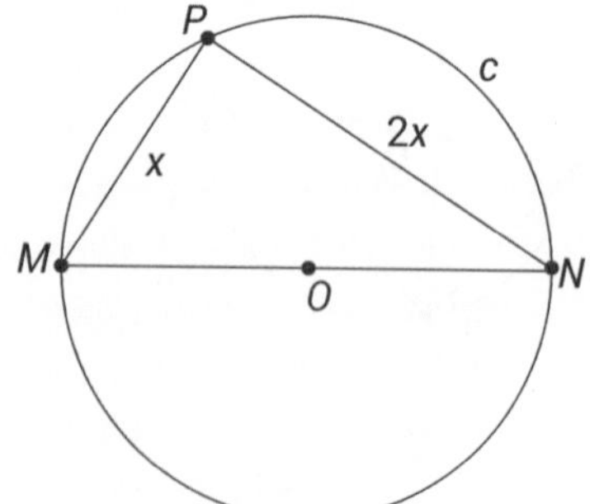

15.13 Further Circles

Another important theorem based on a circle concerns the properties of a **tangent** to the circle.

A **tangent** to a circle is at a right angle to the radius at the point of contact.

This is more formally stated as:

Theorem 20

Each tangent is perpendicular to the radius that goes to the point of contact.

The converse of Theorem 20 is:

If a point P lies on a circle s, and a line l that passes though the point P is perpendicular to the radius, then this line is a tangent to the circle at the point P.

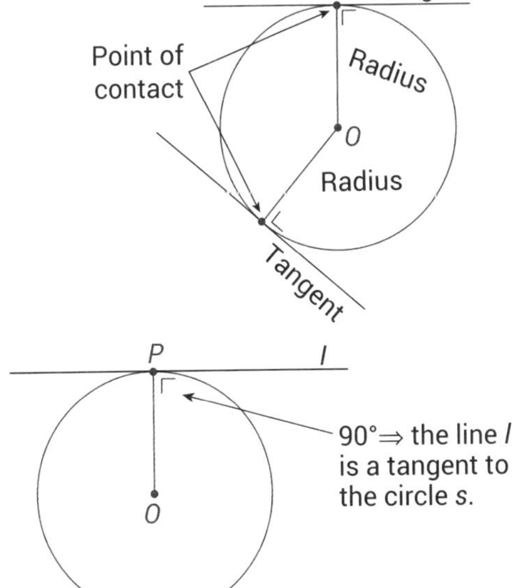

Worked Example 15.31

Consider the following circle with centre O and radius 5 cm. t is a tangent to the circle at the point P.

$|PS| = 12$ cm. Find $|RS|$.

O
5
R
5
t
P
12
S

Solution

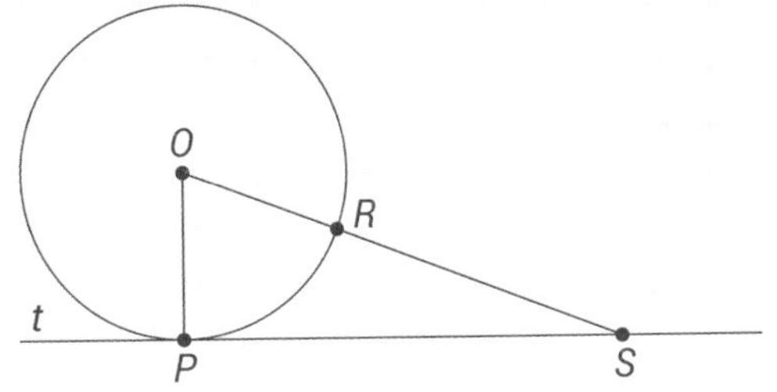

$|\angle OPS| = 90°$ (Tangent)

$|OP| = |OR|$ (Both radii)

Using the theorem of Pythagoras, we will find $|OS|$, the hypotenuse:

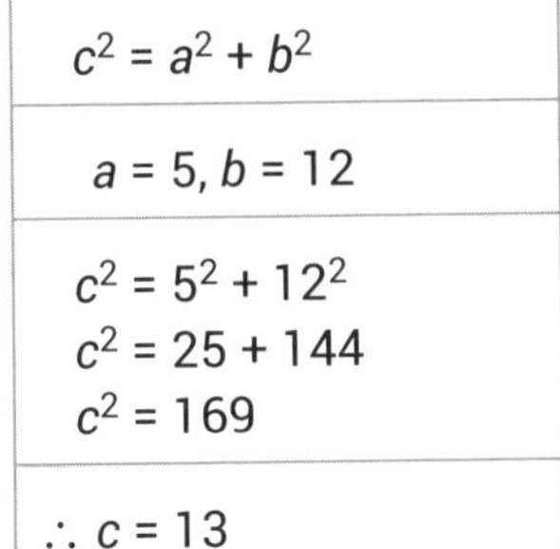

$c^2 = a^2 + b^2$
$a = 5, b = 12$
$c^2 = 5^2 + 12^2$ $c^2 = 25 + 144$ $c^2 = 169$
$\therefore c = 13$

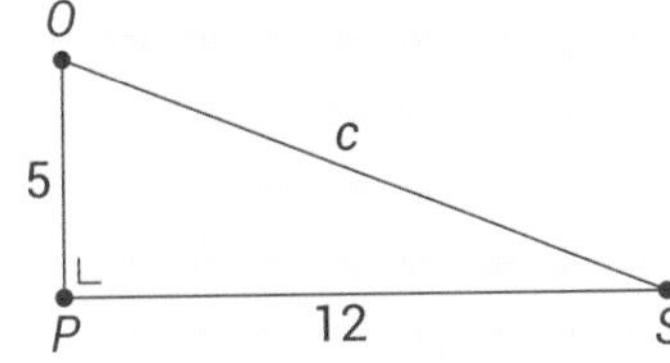

$|OS| = 13$ cm

$\Rightarrow |RS| = 13 - 5$

$\therefore |RS| = 8$ cm

GEOMETRY

Circles touch when they intersect at one point only. They therefore have a single point in common with each other. Circles can touch both externally and internally, as shown.

External:

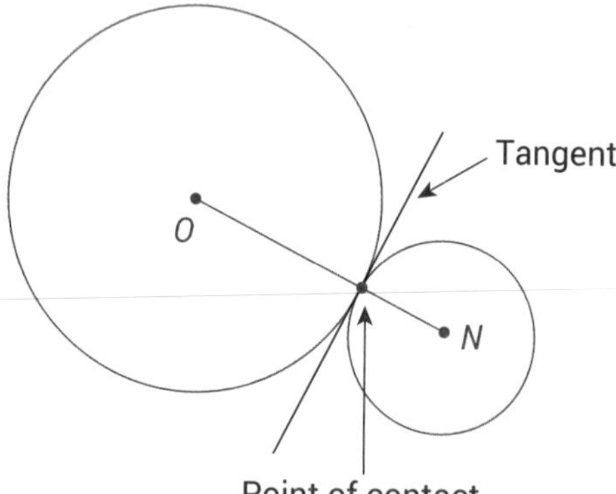

Internal:

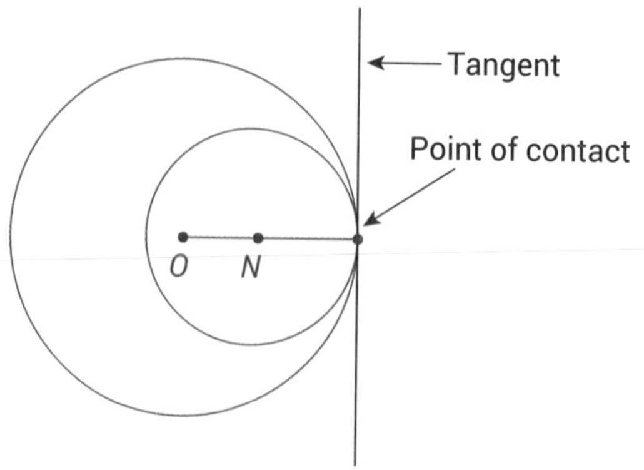

Tangents can also be found when two circles meet at one point only.

Corollary 6

If two circles intersect at one point only, then the two centres and the point of contact are collinear.

Perpendicular to a Chord

We can also consider the relationship between any chord of a circle and the centre of the circle.

If a line is drawn at right angles to a chord and this line goes through the centre of the circle, it will cut the chord into two equal segments.

This can more formally be written as:

Perpendicular bisector of [*AB*]

Centre

A *O* *B*

Theorem 21 Part (i)

The perpendicular from the centre to a chord bisects the chord.

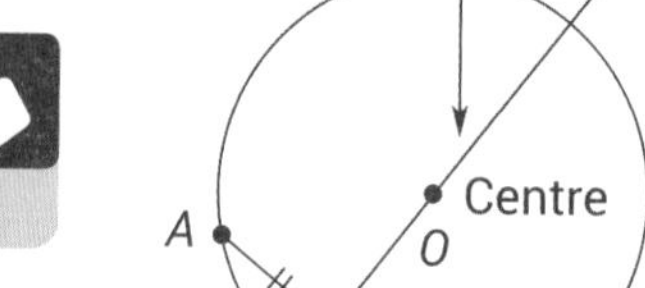

Theorem 21 Part (ii)

The perpendicular bisector of a chord passes through the centre.

By constructing the perpendicular bisectors of two chords, we can use this theorem to find the centre of a given circle.

Theorem 21 Part (ii) can be seen as the converse of Theorem 21 Part (i).

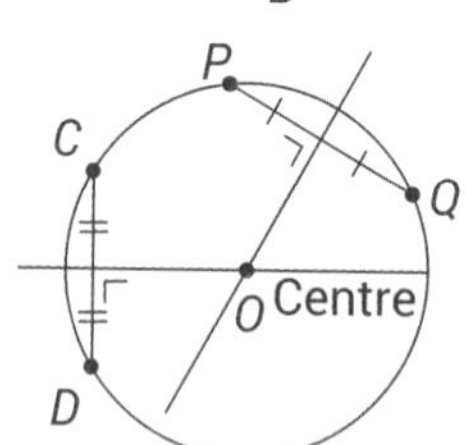

Worked Example 15.32

[*AB*] is the diameter of a circle with centre *O*.

[*CD*] is a chord with a midpoint *M*.

$AB \perp CD$

$|CD| = 64$ cm and $|OM| = 24$ cm.

Find:

(i) $|OC|$ (ii) $|BC|$ in simplest surd form

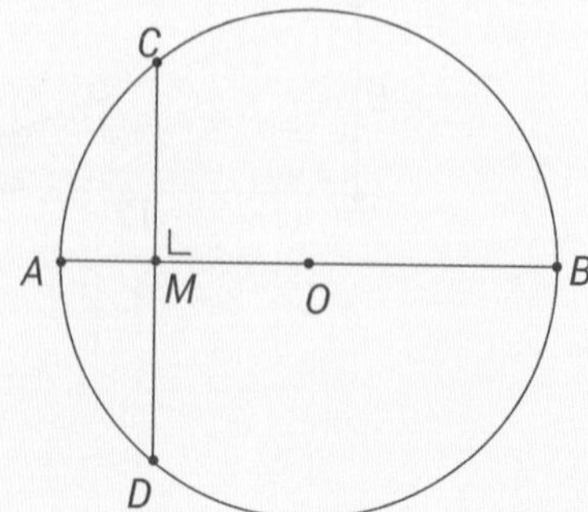

Solution

(i) To find $|OC|$:

$|CM| = 32$ cm The perpendicular from the centre to a chord bisects the chord.

ΔCMO is a right-angled triangle.

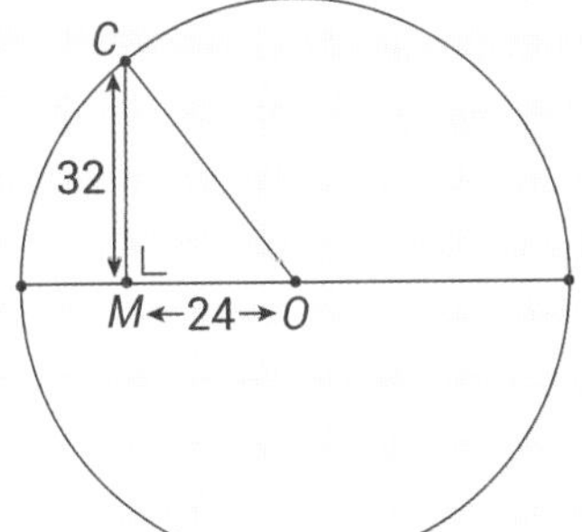

Using the theorem of Pythagoras:

$|OC|^2 = |CM|^2 + |OM|^2$

$= (32)^2 + (24)^2$

$= 1{,}600$

$\therefore |OC| = 40$ cm

(ii) To find $|BC|$:

ΔCMB is a right-angled triangle.

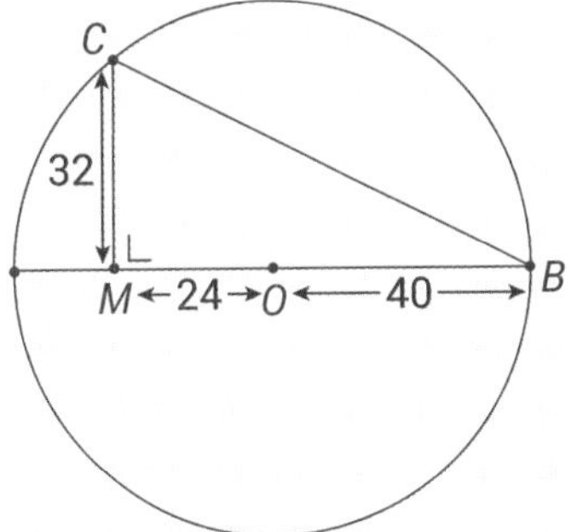

$|OB| = |OC| = 40$ cm (Radius)

$|CM| = 32$ cm and $|MB| = 64$ cm $(24 + 40)$

$|BC|^2 = |CM|^2 + |MB|^2$

$= (32)^2 + (64)^2$

$= 5{,}120$

$\therefore |BC| = 32\sqrt{5}$ cm

Exercise 15.9

1. O is the centre of the following circle. t is a tangent to the circle. Find:

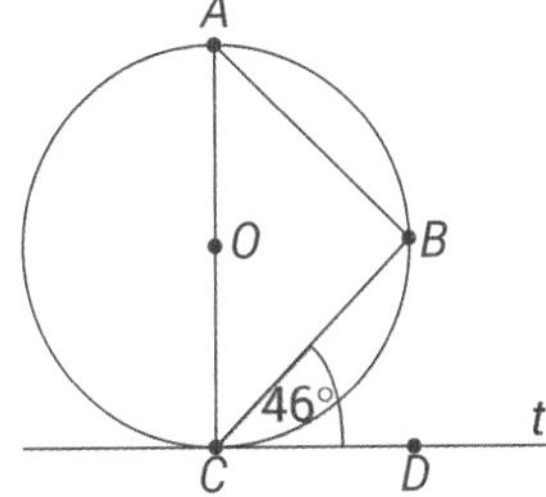

   (i) $|\angle ABC|$
   (ii) $|\angle ACD|$
   (iii) $|\angle ACB|$
   (iv) $|\angle CAB|$

2. O is the centre of the following circle. t is a tangent to the circle. Find:

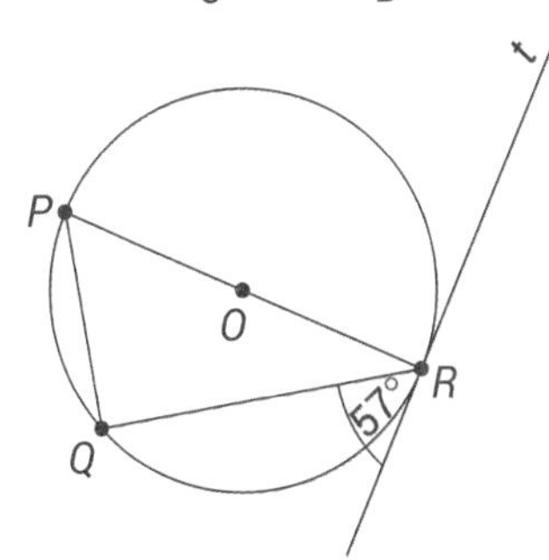

   (i) $|\angle PQR|$
   (ii) $|\angle PRQ|$
   (iii) $|\angle QPR|$

3. In each diagram, O is the centre of the circle. P is the point of contact between a tangent and the circle. Find the value of x in each case.

   (i)

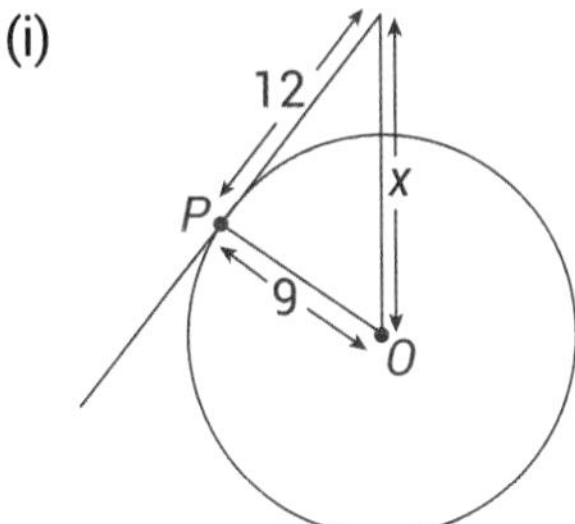

   (ii)

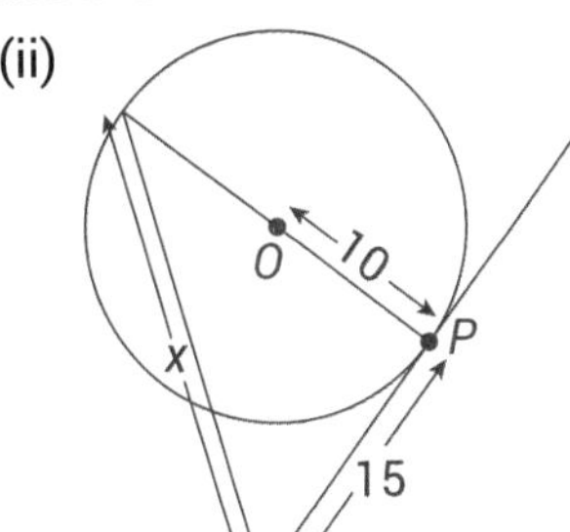

GEOMETRY

4. The circles p and q, with centres A and B respectively, touch at the point C. If the radius of p is 7 cm and the radius of q is 3 cm, find $|AB|$ in each of the following diagrams:

(i) 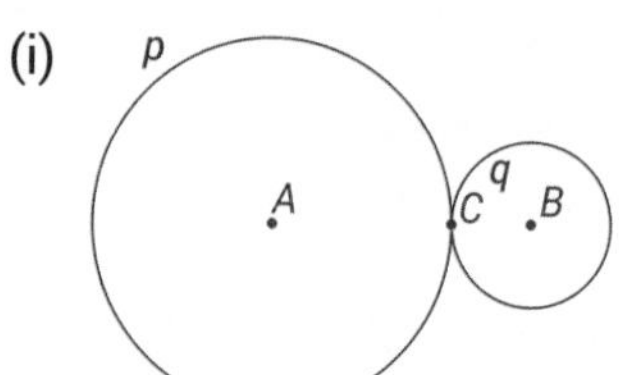

(ii) 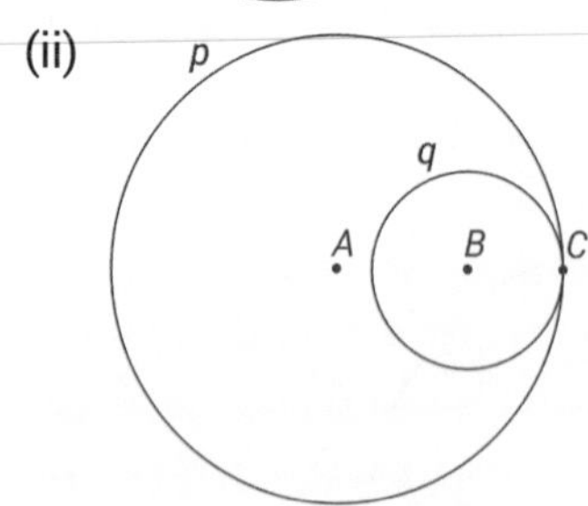

5. $[AB]$ is the diameter of a circle with centre O. $[CD]$ is a chord with a midpoint M. $AB \perp CD$.

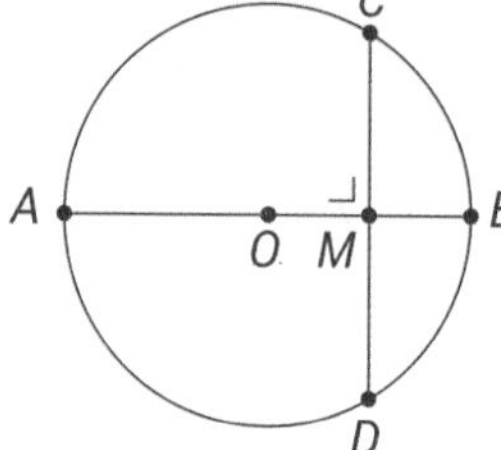

$|CD| = 8$ cm and $|OM| = 3$ cm. Find:

(i) $|OC|$ (ii) $|AM|$ (iii) $|MB|$ (iv) $|AC|$

6. $[EF]$ is the diameter of a circle with centre O. The length of the diameter is 10 cm.

$[QR]$ is a chord such that:

$|QM| = |MR| = 4$ cm and $|EM| = 2$ cm.

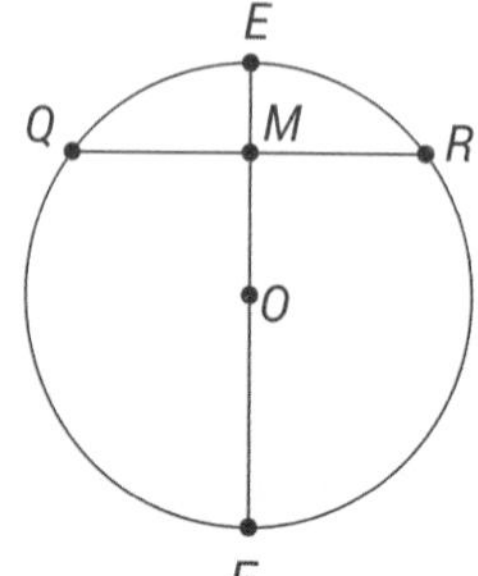

Find: (i) $|OM|$

(ii) $|QO|$

(iii) $|FM|$

7. The diagram shows a circle, with centre O and radius $[OK]$.

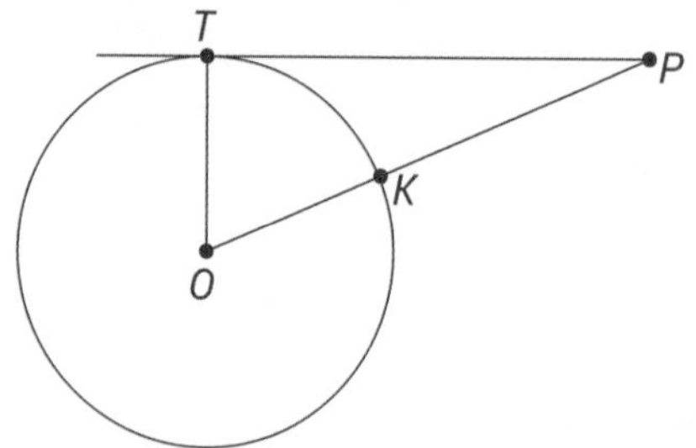

T is a point on the circle.

PT is a tangent to the circle such that $|PO| = 13$ cm and $|PT| = 12$ cm.

Find: (i) $|OK|$ (ii) $|PK|$

8. A circle with centre O has a radius of 17 cm. X is a point on the diameter $[PQ]$ such that $|OX| = 15$ cm. The chord $[RS]$ is perpendicular to the diameter $[PQ]$.

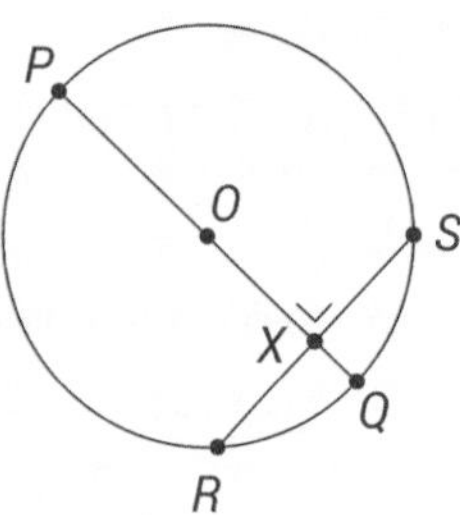

Find:

(i) $|XS|$

(ii) $|RS|$

(iii) $|XQ|$

(iv) $|PX|$

(v) $|PR|$ (in surd form)

9. A circle with centre O has two chords $[AB]$ and $[CD]$. It has a radius length of 20 cm.

$OM \perp AB$ and $ON \perp CD$.

$|OM| = 16$ cm and $|ON| = 12$ cm.

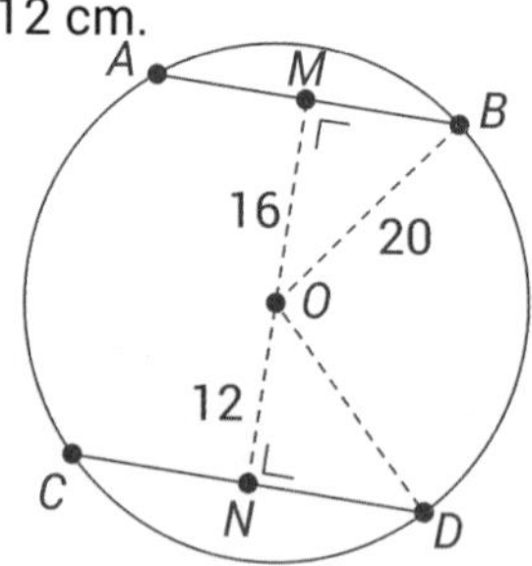

Find:

(i) $|AB|$

(ii) $|CD|$

(iii) Area of ΔMBO

(iv) Area of ΔNDO

10. A circle with centre O and radius $[OP]$ is shown. t is a tangent to the circle with a point of contact P.

$|OP| = 7$ cm and $|PS| = 4\sqrt{2}$ cm.

Find:

(i) $|OS|$

(ii) $|RS|$

(iii) Area of ΔOPS

11. The summit of a mountain is 8,900 m above sea level. Find the distance (nearest km) between the top of this mountain (T) and the horizon (point C) as shown on the diagram. Assume the earth is circular with a radius of approximately 6,300 km.

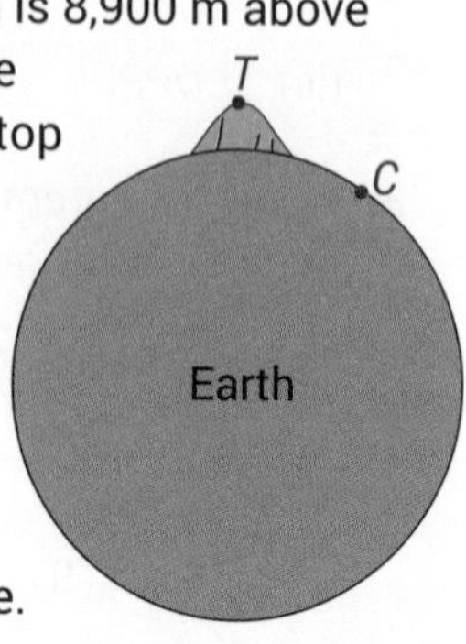

The diagram is not to scale.

12. A cylindrical tank of water is tipped on its side as shown. The diameter of the cylinder is 50 cm and the distance between the points A and B is 23 cm. Find, to the nearest mm, the depth of the water in the cylinder.

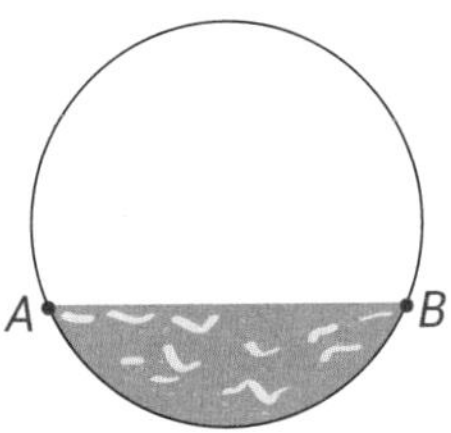

Revision Exercises

1. (a) Consider the following diagram:

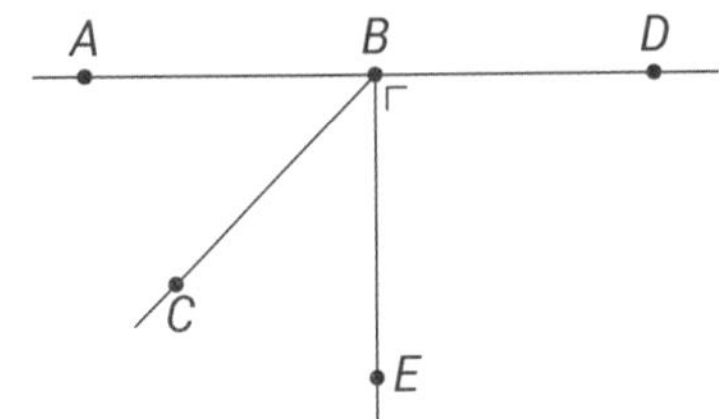

Identify and name:

(i) An acute angle

(ii) An obtuse angle

(iii) An ordinary angle

(iv) A right angle

(v) A ray

(vi) A line

(vii) The supplementary angles

(b) Consider the following diagram:

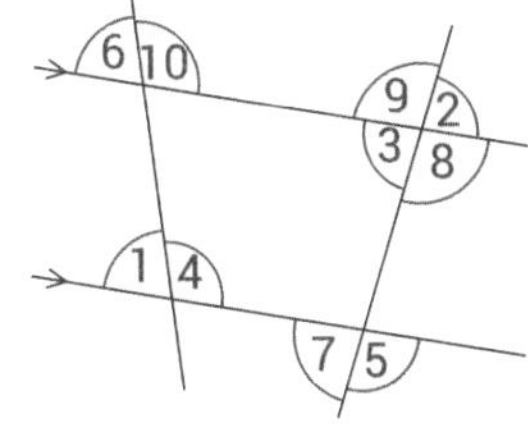

$|\angle 1| = 70°$ and $|\angle 2| = 85°$.
Find the measure of all the angles numbered below.

(i) $|\angle 3|$

(ii) $|\angle 4|$

(iii) $|\angle 5|$

(iv) $|\angle 6|$

(v) $|\angle 7|$

(vi) $|\angle 8|$

(vii) $|\angle 9|$

(viii) $|\angle 10|$

2. (a) In your own words, explain the difference between each of the following.

Use diagrams to help your explanations where necessary.

(i) A line and a line segment

(ii) A line and a ray

(iii) Coplanar and collinear

(iv) Perpendicular lines and parallel lines

(v) Theorem and corollary

(b) Investigate if:

(i) $p \parallel q$ (ii) $m \parallel n$

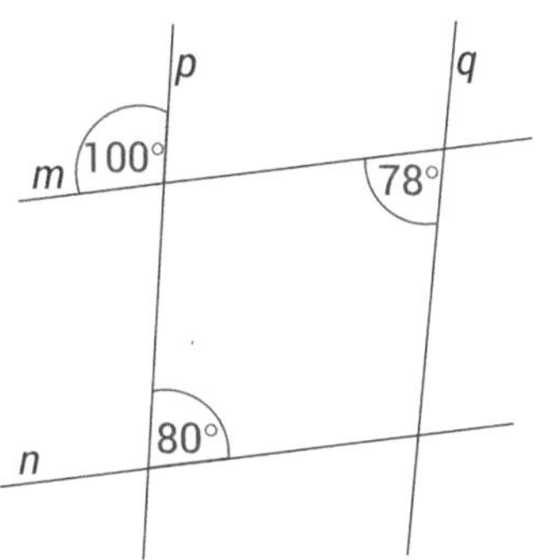

3. (a) Find the measure of the missing angles. Show as much work as possible.

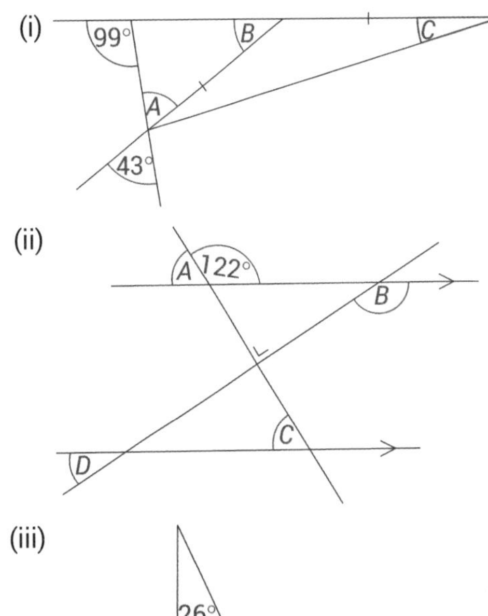

(iii)

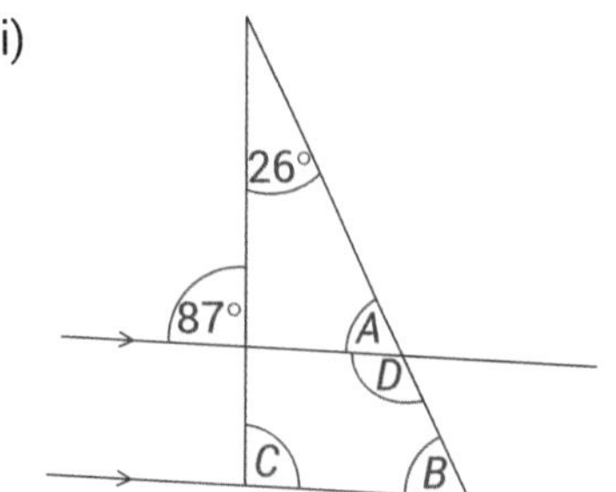

GEOMETRY

(b) Investigate if it is possible to construct a triangle using the three side lengths given:

(i) 2, 3 and 5

(ii) 10, 7 and 18

(iii) 15, 15 and 13

(iv) 8, 6.6 and 9

(v) $\sqrt{2}$, $\sqrt{5}$ and 6

4. (a) List the sides of each of the triangles below in ascending order of length.

(i)

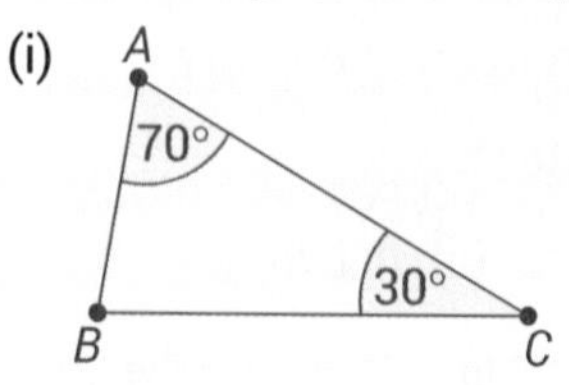

(ii)

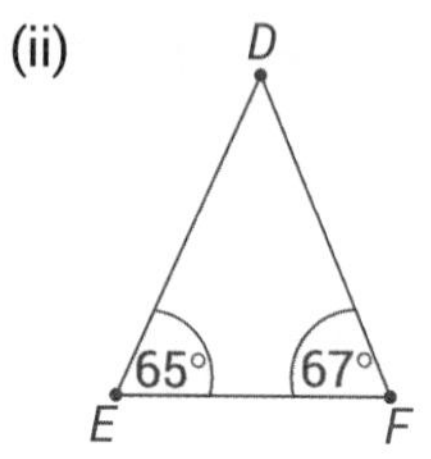

(iii)

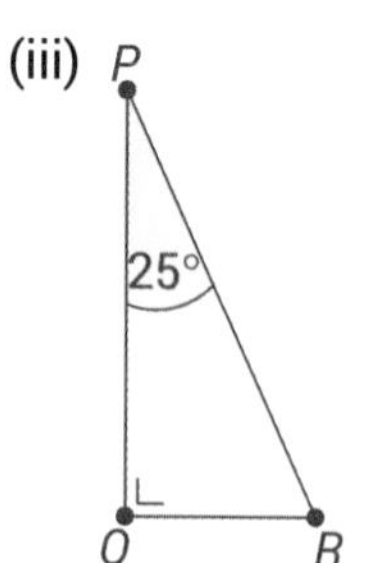

(b) A carpenter is given the dimensions of four different triangular roof beams that are to be constructed for use in a building:

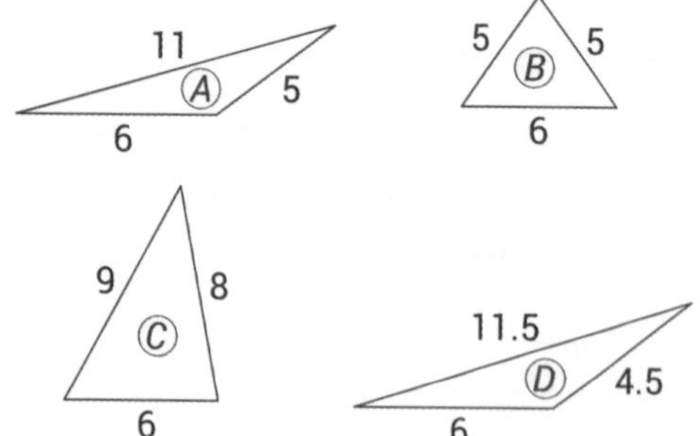

The carpenter complains that only two are actually possible to construct.

(i) Explain how the carpenter came to this decision.

(ii) Which two triangular roof beams could be constructed?

(c) Find the length of x and y in each of the following diagrams. Leave your answers in surd form where appropriate.

(i)

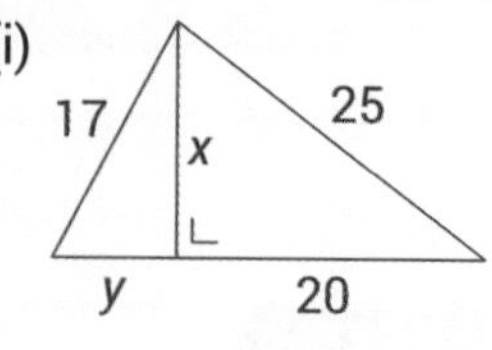

(ii)

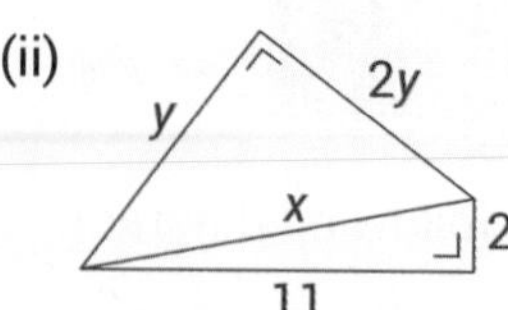

5. (a) Find the measure of the missing angles in each of the following parallelograms. Show as much work as possible.

(i)

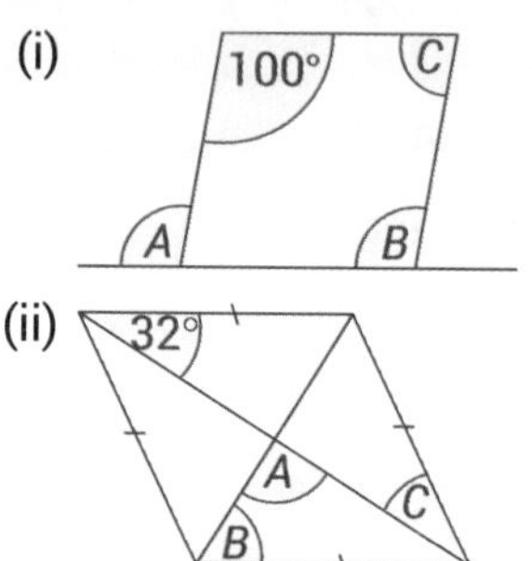

(ii)

(b) Consider the parallelogram $ABCD$, which is not a rectangle:

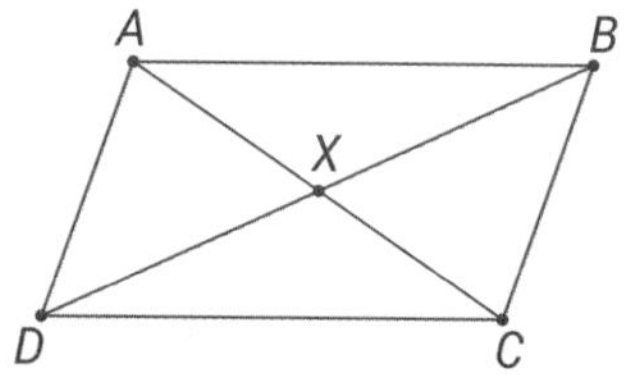

State if each of the following is true or false:

(i) $|AX| = |DX|$

(ii) $|DX| = |XC|$

(iii) $|AD| = |BC|$

(iv) $|\angle AXD| = |\angle BXC|$

(v) $|\angle DAX| = |\angle DBC|$

(c) State two properties of rectangles that are not properties of all parallelograms.

6. (a) Find the area of each of the following shapes:

(i)

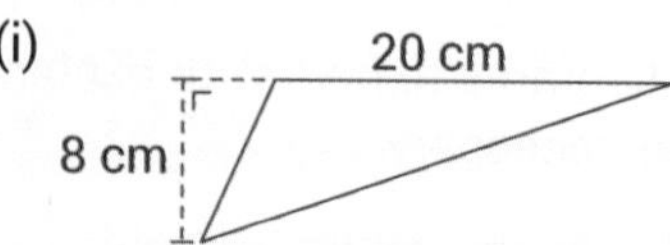

(ii)

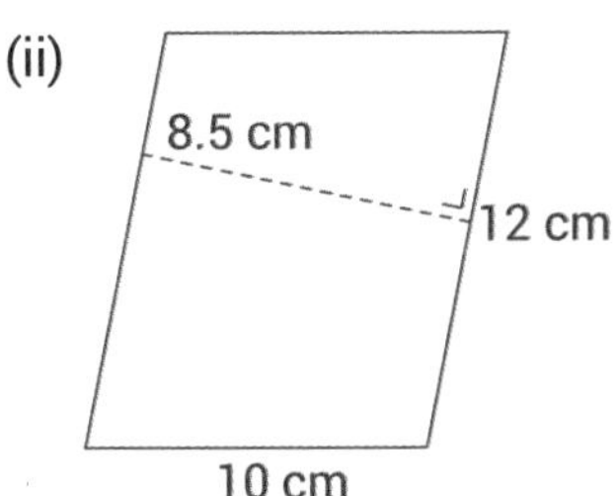

(iii)

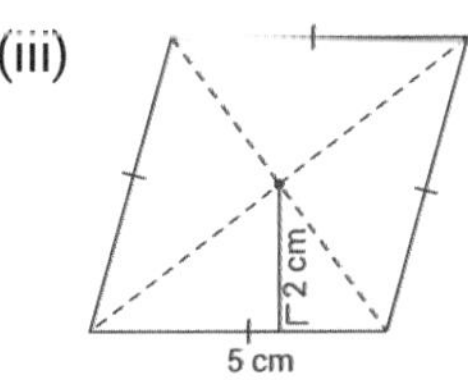

(b) Find the value of x in each of the following polygons, and hence, find the area of each polygon:

(i)

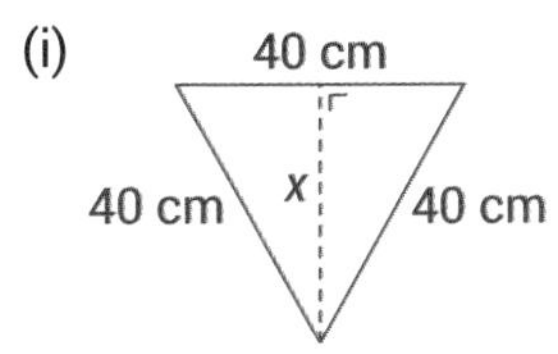

(ii)

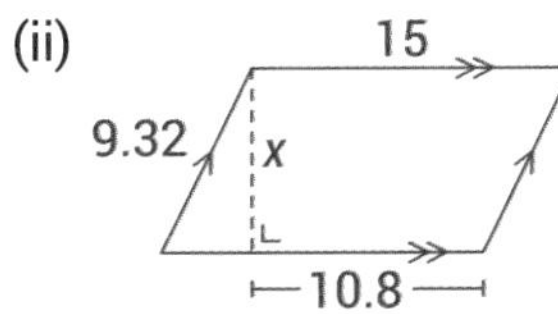

7. (a) State if each of the following pairs of triangles are congruent.
Explain how you reached your decision.

(i)

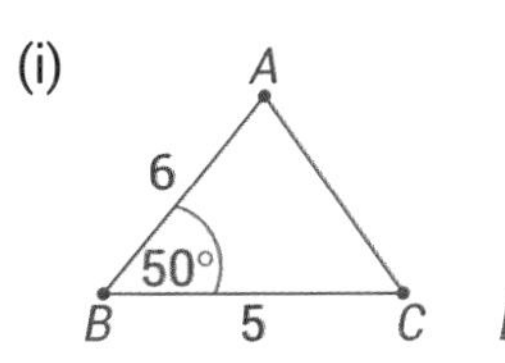

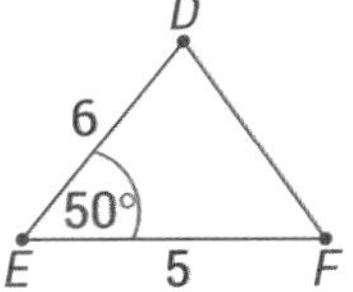

Is $\Delta ABC \equiv \Delta DEF$?

(ii)

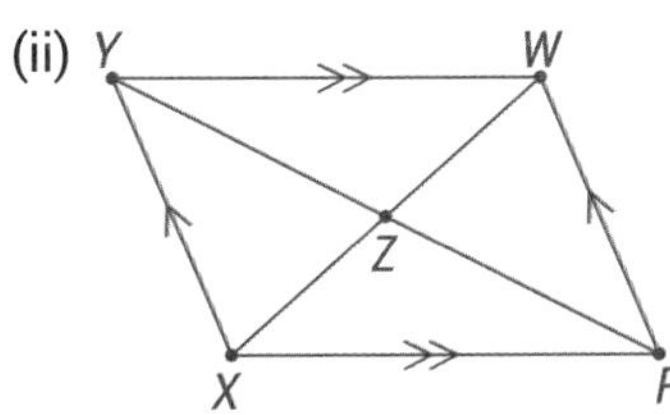

Is $\Delta XYZ \equiv \Delta WZR$?

(b) $ABCD$ is a quadrilateral.

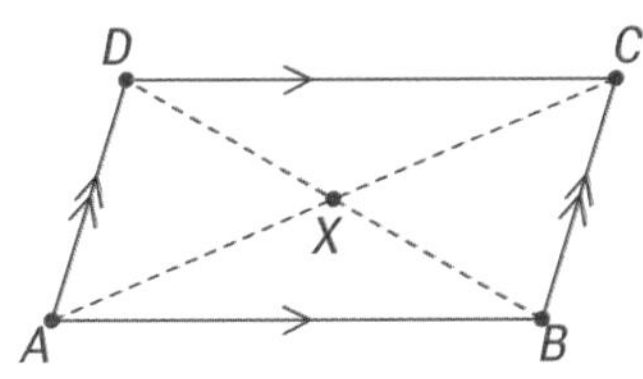

(i) What type of quadrilateral is $ABCD$?

(ii) Show that $\Delta AXD \equiv \Delta CXB$.

(iii) Is $\Delta DXC \equiv \Delta AXB$?
Give a reason for your answer.

(iv) If $|AB| = 15$ cm and the area of $ABCD = 90$ cm^2, find the perpendicular distance between $[AB]$ and $[DC]$.

8. (a) Find the value of x in the following diagrams:

(i)

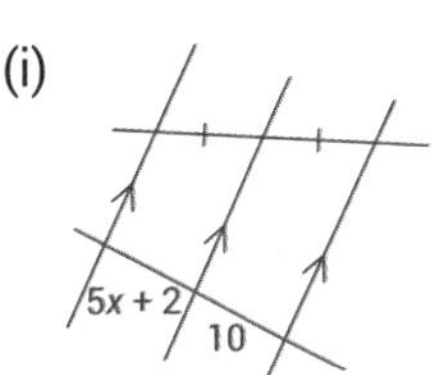

(ii)

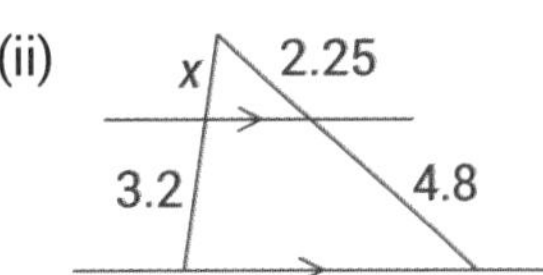

(iii)

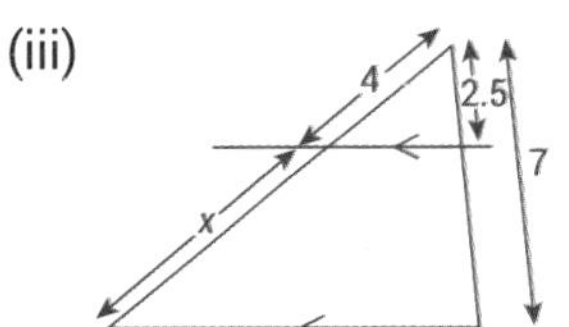

(b) Find the value of x and y in each case:

(i)

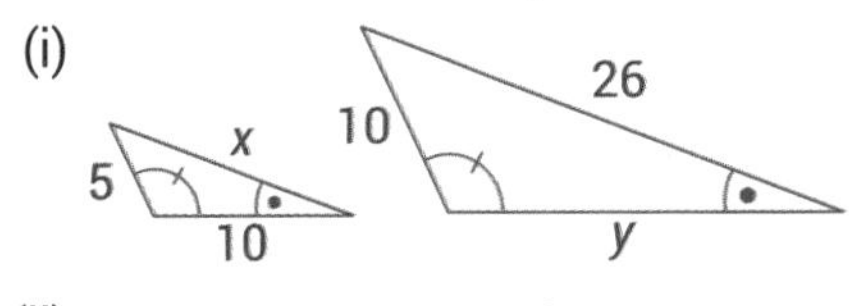

(ii)

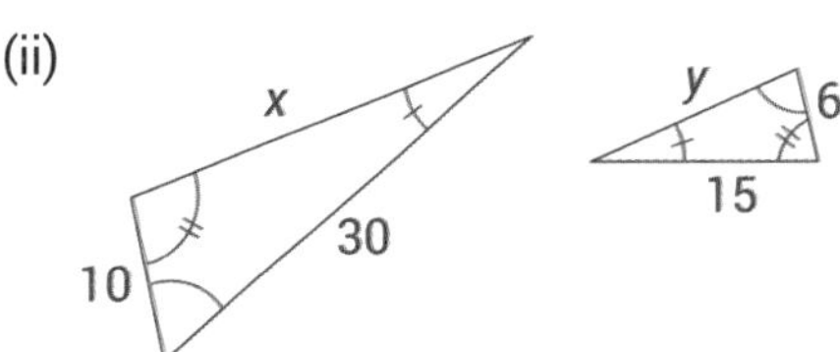

(iii)

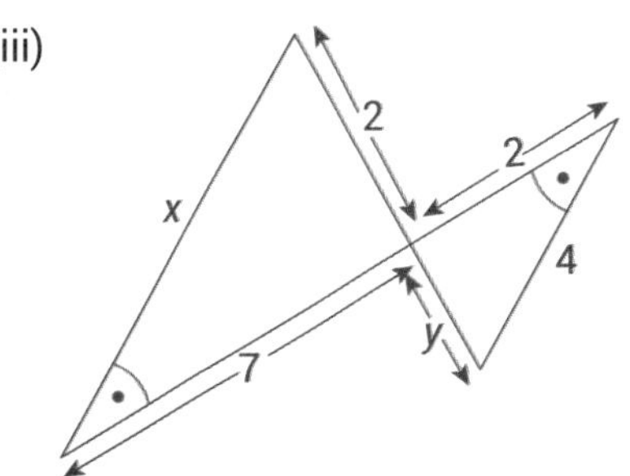

(c) In the triangle PQR, PR is parallel to ST.
$|QR| = 10$ cm, $|QS| = 4$ cm,
$|ST| = 8$ cm and $|PR| = 9$ cm.

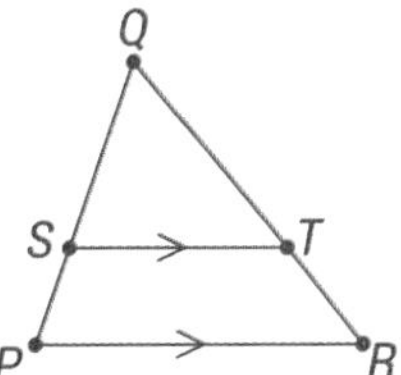

GEOMETRY

(i) Draw ΔPQR and ΔSQT separately.

(ii) Are ΔPQR and ΔSQT similar? Explain your answer.

(iii) Find $|QP|$.

(iv) Find $|QT|$.

(v) Find $|TR|$.

9. (a) Find the value of A and B in each of the following diagrams. Remember to show as much work as possible. O is the centre in each case.

(i)

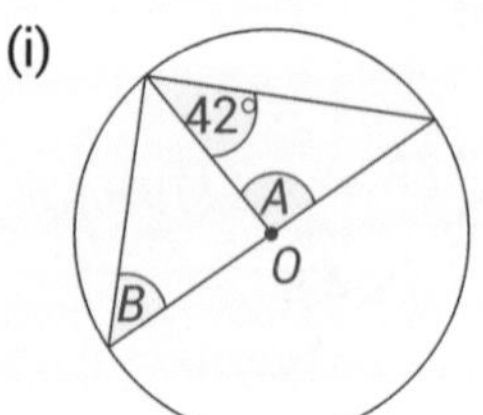

(ii)

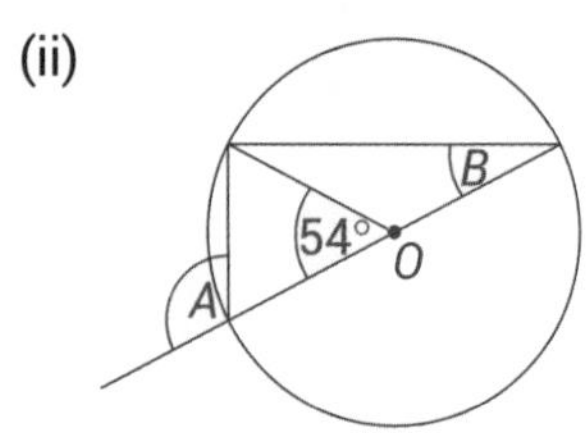

(b) In each diagram, O is the centre of the circle. P is the point of contact between a tangent and the circle. Find the value of x in each case:

(i)

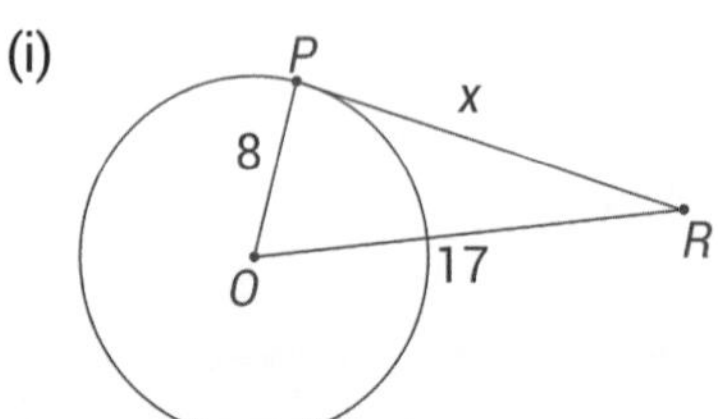

(ii)

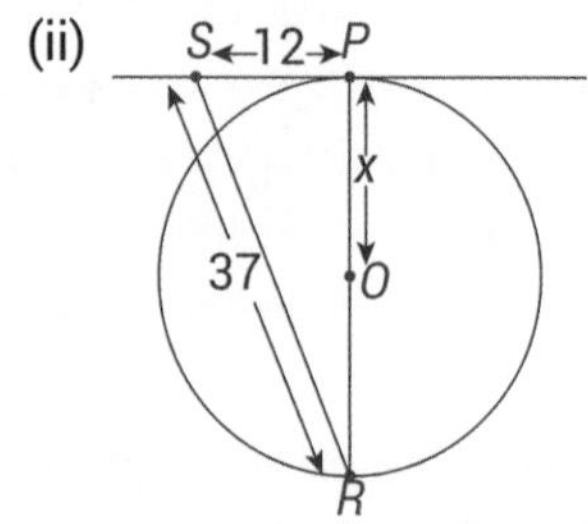

(iii)

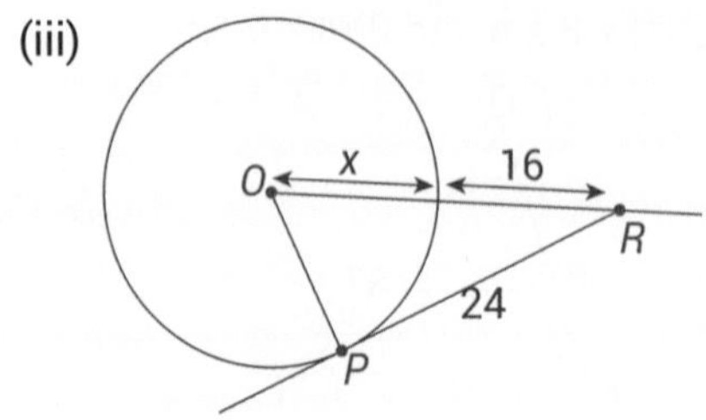

(c) Consider the following circle with centre O.

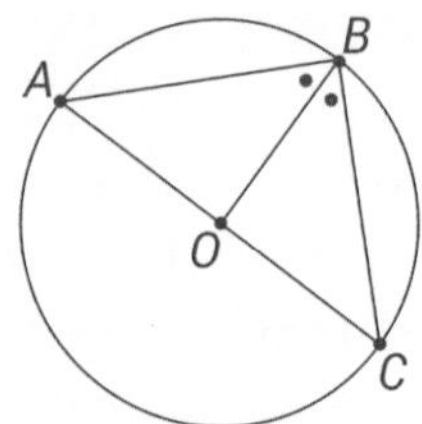

(i) What type of triangle is the ΔABC?

(ii) Show that $\Delta ABO \equiv \Delta BOC$.

(iii) Find $|\angle ABO|$.

(iv) If $|OB| = 15$ cm, find $|AB|$.

10. (a) State if each of the following statements is 'Always', 'Sometimes' or 'Never' true:

(i) A rectangle is a parallelogram.

(ii) A square is a rhombus.

(iii) A rhombus is a square.

(iv) A parallelogram is not a rectangle.

(v) A circle is a polygon.

(vi) A quadrilateral is any enclosed four-sided shape.

(vii) A parallelogram is a four-sided shape.

(b) An orienteering competition is run on a course as shown in the diagram below. Opposite sides are parallel.

The runners run from A to B to C to D and then back to A.

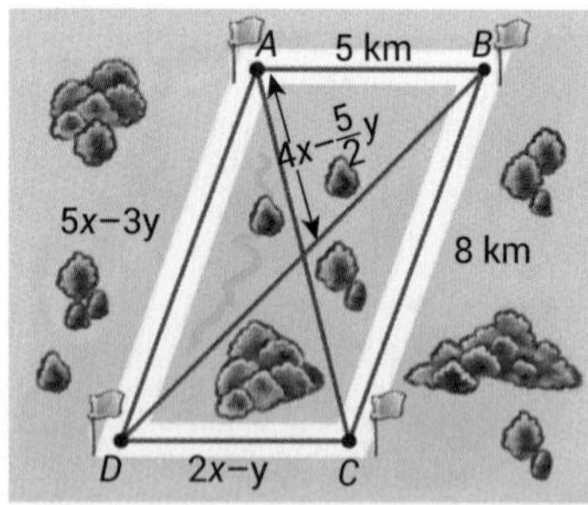

(i) How long is the course?

(ii) A runner cheats by running from A to C and then completes the course as normal.

What is the length of this route?

(c) The direct distance from town A to town B is 100 km.

The direct distance from town B to town C is 75 km.

(i) If the towns are collinear, what is the shortest possible distance and the longest possible distance from town B to town C?

(ii) If the towns are **not** collinear, write the range of distances that are possible from town B to town C.

11. (a) What is the measure of the ordinary angle formed by the two hands of the 12-hour clock at:

(i) 4.00 a.m. (ii) 12.30 a.m.

(b) Consider the following geometrical shape:

(i) How many sides does this shape have?

(ii) Name this shape.

(iii) Find the sum of all the interior angles in this shape. Explain your answer.

(c) A jeweller is asked to fix a brooch as shown below. One side of the brooch is 16 mm and the other side is 25 mm in length.

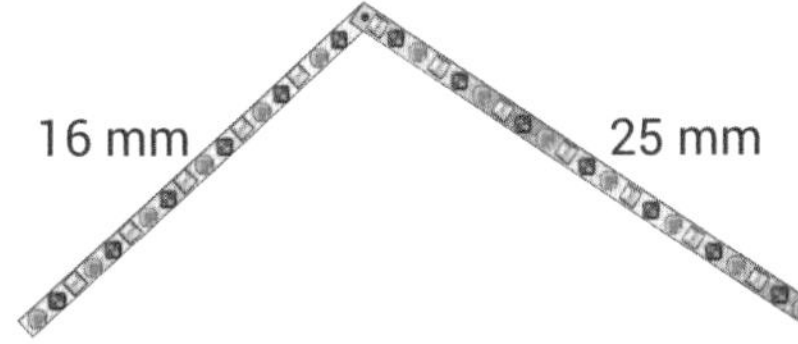

It is decided to connect the two ends of the brooch with a gold bar to form a triangle. This bar can be of different lengths.

- 1 cm of this gold bar costs \$25.
- The exchange rate is €1 = \$1.25.
- The jeweller charges €50 for labour.

Calculate to the nearest euro the highest and lowest price the jeweller could charge to fix this brooch.

12. (a) A rhombus $ABCD$ is shown.

$|AC| = 24$ mm and $|BD| = 10$ mm.

(i) Find $|AM|$ and $|DM|$.

(ii) Identify four right angles.

(iii) Find $|AD|$.

(iv) Is ΔADM congruent to ΔABM? Explain.

(v) Calculate the area of the rhombus.

(b) A barrel of oil is tipped onto its side as shown.

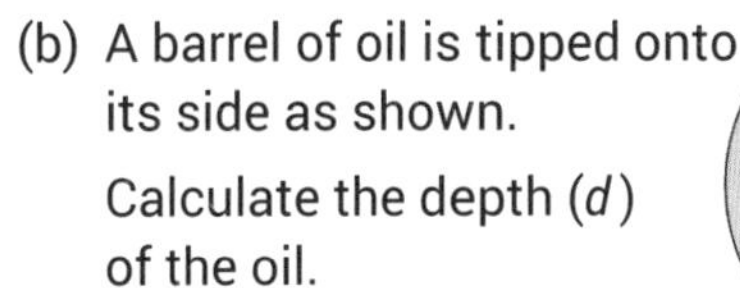

Calculate the depth (d) of the oil.

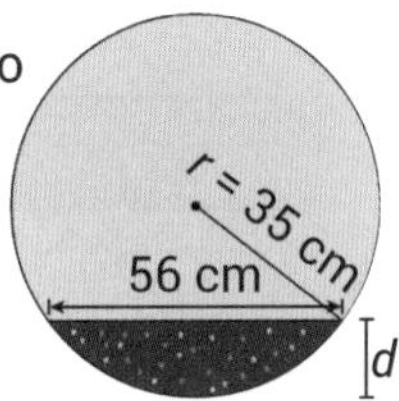

13. At a certain time, a group of students measure the length of the shadow of a building and the length of the shadow of a 1.5 m ranging pole.

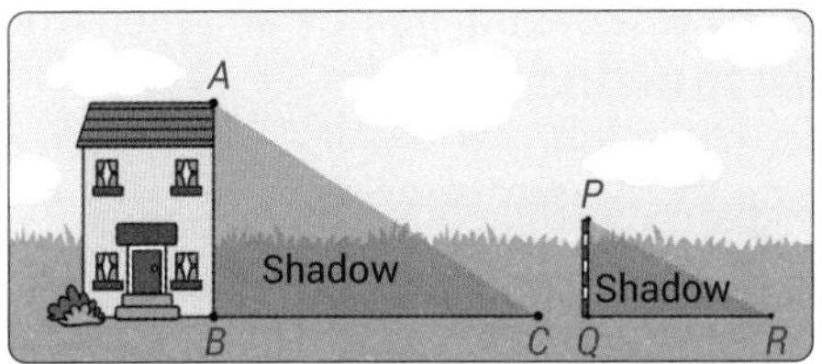

The shadow of the building is 5 m long, and that of the ranging pole is 2 m long.

The teacher explains that they can now calculate the height of the building. She states that the triangles ABC and PQR are similar.

(i) Give a reason for this statement.

(ii) Describe how you would check that the two triangles are similar.

The teacher asks the students to sketch the triangles ABC and PQR with all the measurements that were collected.

(iii) Sketch out the two triangles ABC and PQR with the measurements included.

(iv) Find the height of the building.

Megan measures the ranging pole and discovers that the pole is in fact 1.55 m long.

(v) Calculate the revised height of the building.

GEOMETRY

14. A new sewerage system is being laid in a housing estate as shown. It costs €20 per metre (including labour costs) to lay these pipes.

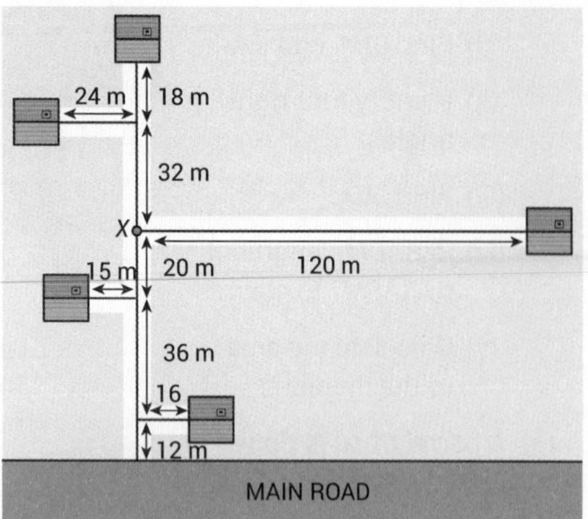

(i) Find the total length of pipe needed for this work.

(ii) Find the total cost to install this system.

An engineer suggests that it would be cheaper to connect all the sewer pipes from each house directly to a central point X and then from this point to the main road.

(iii) Find the total cost to install this new layout (to the nearest euro).

(iv) Which is the cheaper option and by how much?

15. A game is played in which the person who picks a point that is closest to the centre of a circle wins a prize. The circle has a radius length of 7 cm.

(i) State one theorem that could be used to locate the centre of the circle.

(ii) By drawing a circle of radius length 7 cm, demonstrate how the centre of the circle could be located using the theorem in part (i).

(iii) Describe another method that could be used to find the centre of a circle.

(iv) By drawing another circle of radius length 7 cm, demonstrate how the centre of this circle could be found using the method in part (iii).

GEOMETRY

Exam Questions

1. State which one of the following triangles can **not** be constructed.
Give a reason to support your answer.

Triangle 1	Triangle 2
Sides of lengths (cm) 3.2, 2.9, 5.4	Sides of lengths (cm) 6, 7, 15

SEC Leaving Certificate Ordinary Level, Paper 2, 2016

2. The lengths of the sides of a right-angled triangle are 5, x, and $x + 1$ as shown.

Use the theorem of Pythagoras to find the value of x.

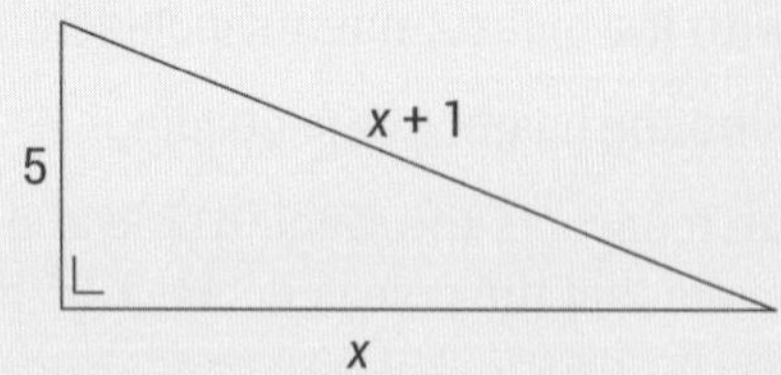

SEC Leaving Certificate Ordinary Level, Paper 2, 2016

3. The line p makes equal intercepts on the axes at A and at B, as shown. The line q is perpendicular to p and contains the point (0,0).

The lines p and q intersect at the point C.

Explain why the triangles OCA and OBC are congruent.

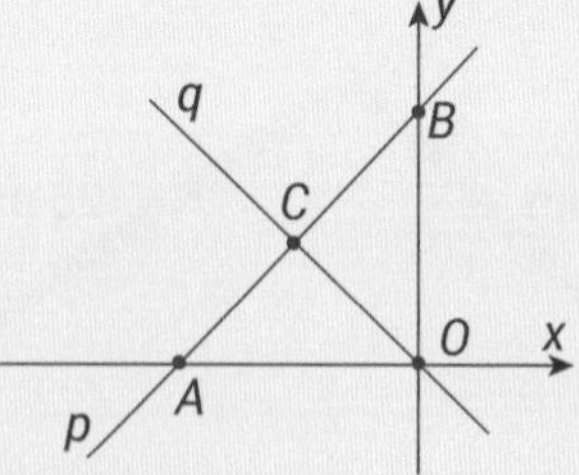

SEC Leaving Certificate Ordinary Level, Paper 2, 2015

4. (a) The diagram shows a parallelogram, with one side produced.
Use the data on the diagram to find the value of x, of y, and of z.
Give a reason for your answer in each case.

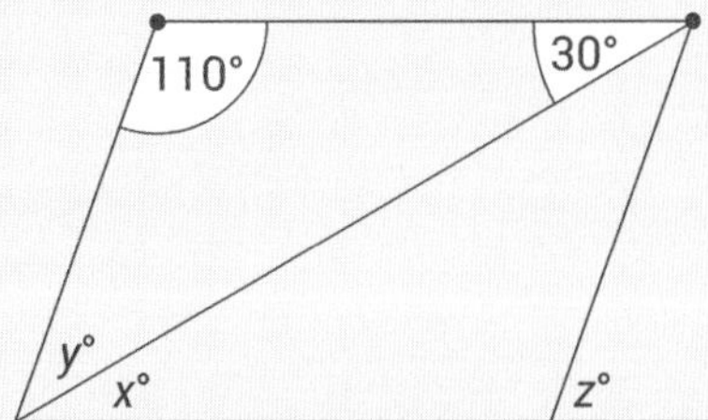

(b) The area of the parallelogram $ABCD$ is 480 m^2.

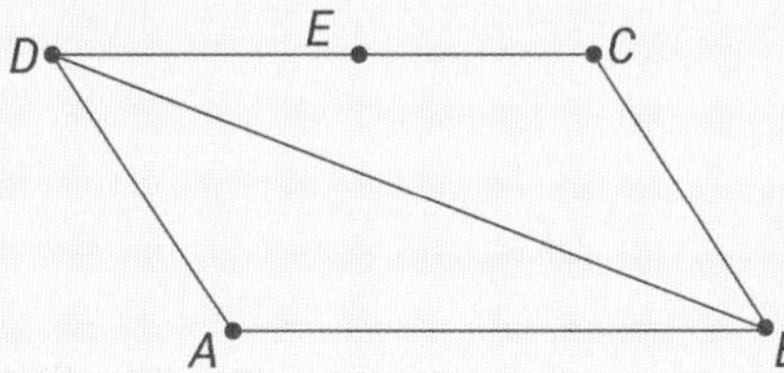

(i) Find the area of the triangle ABD.

(ii) E is the midpoint of $[CD]$. Find the area of the triangle BCE.

SEC Leaving Certificate Ordinary Level, Paper 2, 2015

5. The points $A(-9,3)$, $B(-4,3)$ and $C(-4,10)$ are the vertices of the triangle ABC, as shown.

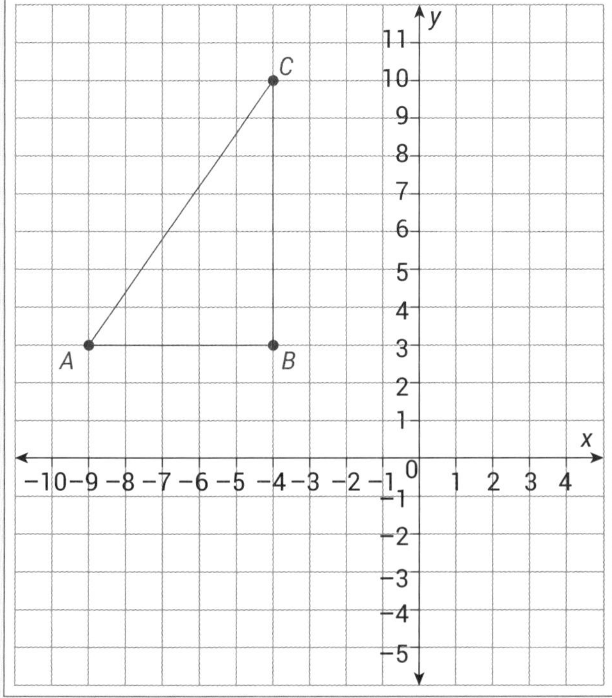

$X(2,-4)$ and $Y(2,1)$ are two points.

(a) Draw, on a copy of the diagram, a triangle, XYZ, which is congruent to the triangle ABC.

(b) Write down the co-ordinates of Z and explain why the triangle XYZ is congruent to the triangle ABC.

SEC Leaving Certificate Ordinary Level, Paper 2, 2014

6. Two circles, c_1 and c_2, intersect at the points B and X as shown.

The circle c_1 has diameter $[AB]$.

The circle c_2 has diameter $[BC]$.

The line CB is a tangent to c_1.

Prove that X is on the line AC.

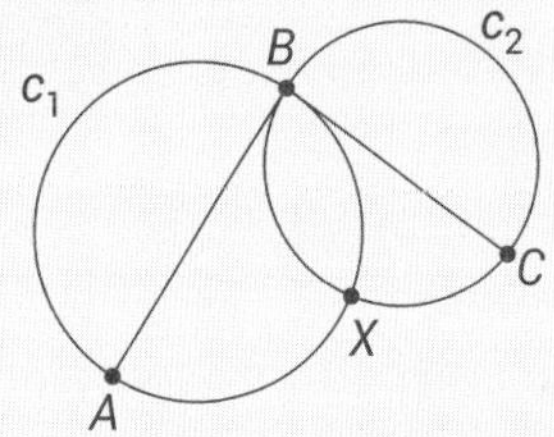

SEC Leaving Certificate Ordinary Level, Paper 2, 2014

7. (i) Explain what is meant by the *converse* of a theorem.

(ii) There are some geometric statements that are true, but have converses that are false. Give one such geometric statement, and state also the (false) converse.

SEC Leaving Certificate Ordinary Level, Sample Paper 2, 2014

8. A theorem on your course can be used to find $|\angle FDC|$.

Write down $|\angle FDC|$ and state the theorem.

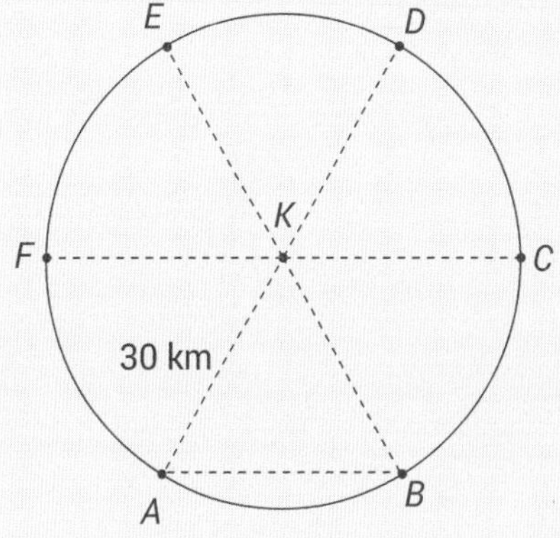

SEC Leaving Certificate Ordinary Level, Paper 2, 2013

9. $A(6, -1)$, $B(12, -3)$, $C(8, 5)$ and $D(2, 7)$ are four points.

(a) (i) Plot the four points.

(ii) Describe two different ways of showing, using co-ordinate geometric techniques, that the points form a parallelogram $ABCD$.

(b) Write down a geometrical result that can be used to construct a tangent to a circle at a point.

SEC Leaving Certificate Ordinary Level, Paper 2, 2012

10. (a) The photograph shows the *Dockland* building in Hamburg, Germany.

The diagram below is a side view of the building. It is a parallelogram.

The parallelogram is 29 metres high.

The top and bottom edges are 88 metres long.

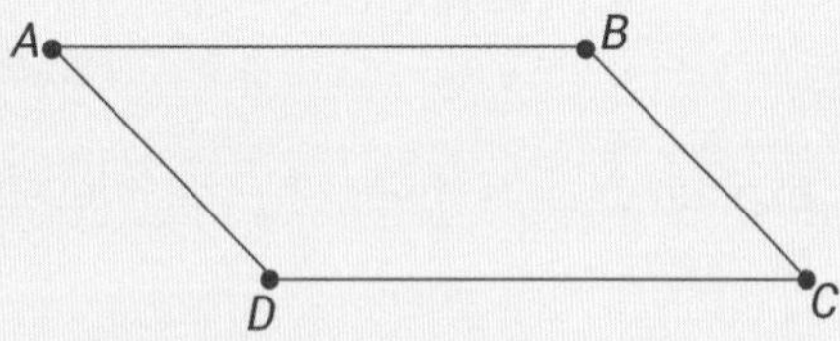

(i) Find the area of this side of the building.

(ii) If $|BD| = |AD|$, find $|BC|$.

(iii) The lines BC and AD are parallel. Find the distance between these parallel lines.

(b) There is a theorem on your geometry course that can be used to construct the tangent to a circle at a given point on the circle. State this theorem and use it to construct the tangent to the circle shown at the point P.

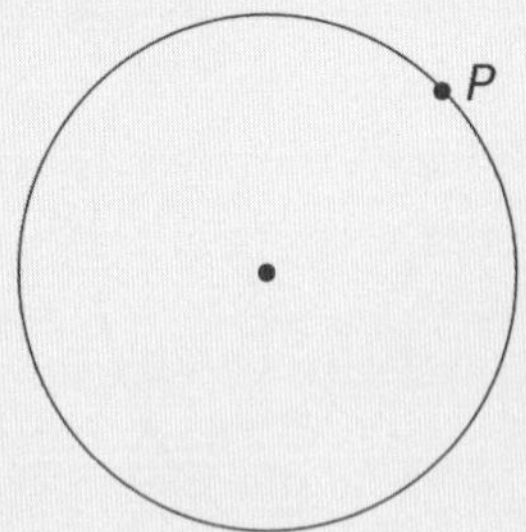

(c) In the diagram, the line l is a tangent to the circle.

Find the values of x, y and z.

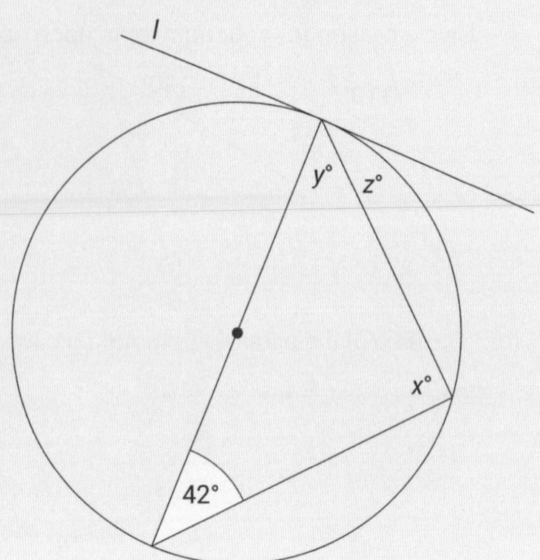

SEC Leaving Certificate Ordinary Level, Paper 2, 2010

11. In the diagram below, $ABCF$, $ABFE$, and $ACDE$ are parallelograms.

The area of the shaded triangle AFE is 15 square units.

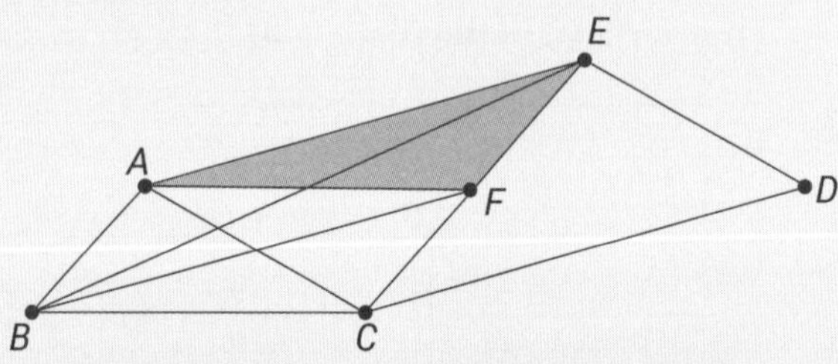

(i) State why the area of triangle AFB must also be 15 square units.

(ii) Find the area of the whole figure $ABCDE$.

Show your work.

(iii) If the perpendicular distance from D to the line EC is 6, find $|AB|$.

Show your work.

SEC Leaving Certificate Ordinary Level, Sample Paper 2, 2010

Solutions and chapter summary available online

16

Constructions, Transformations and Enlargements

In this chapter you will learn to:

- Perform constructions as specified on the Junior Certificate Ordinary Level Syllabus
- Construct the circumcentre and circumcircle of a given triangle, using only a straight edge and compass
- Construct the incentre and incircle of a given triangle, using only a straight edge and compass
- Construct an angle of 60°, without using a protractor or set square
- Construct a tangent to a given circle at a given point on it
- Construct a parallelogram, given the length of the sides and the measure of the angles
- Construct the centroid of a triangle
- Locate axes of symmetry in simple shapes
- Recognise images of points and objects under translation, central symmetry, axial symmetry and rotation
- Investigate enlargements and their effect on area, paying attention to
  - centre of enlargement
  - scale factor k, where $0 < k < 1$, $k > 1$, $k \in Q$
- Solve problems involving enlargements

You should remember...

- How to perform geometry constructions from the Junior Certificate course
- Geometry notation
- Transformations in geometry (translation, central symmetry, axial symmetry and rotation)

Key words

- Bisect
- Perpendicular bisector
- Parallelogram
- Tangent
- Circumcentre
- Circumcircle
- Incentre
- Incircle
- Centroid
- Median
- Symmetry
- Object
- Image
- Translation
- Central symmetry
- Rotation
- Enlargement
- Centre of enlargement
- Scale factor

16.1 Introduction

From the design of a new bridge to that of the next video game console, all new ideas, buildings or constructions start off on the drawing board.

Any engineer, architect or designer will first draw out a new design, and from these drawings a new invention is born.

One only has to remember that the Eiffel Tower and the Statue of Liberty (to name but two) were both designed without the aid of computers.

But how do you draw a circle or a triangle accurately?
This is where the knowledge and skills of constructions play a role.

16.2 Junior Certificate Constructions

The following constructions were studied at Junior Certificate Ordinary Level (numbered as defined in the syllabus). They must also be known at Leaving Certificate Ordinary Level.

1. Bisector of a given angle, using only compass and straight edge.
2. Perpendicular bisector of a line segment, using only compass and straight edge.
4. Line perpendicular to a given line *l*, passing through a given point on *l*.
5. Line parallel to a given line, through a given point.
6. Division of a line segment into two or three equal segments, without measuring it.
8. Line segment of given length on a given ray.
9. Angle of given number of degrees with a given ray as one arm.
10. Triangle, given lengths of three sides.
11. Triangle, given SAS data.
12. Triangle, given ASA data.
13. Right-angled triangle, given the length of the hypotenuse and one other side.
14. Right-angled triangle, given one side and one of the acute angles (several cases).
15. Rectangle, given side lengths.

Constructions 1 and 2 are used in several Leaving Certificate constructions and so are shown in detail here. All Junior Certificate Ordinary Level constructions are detailed in Active Maths 1. They are also reviewed in Exercise 16.1.

Construction 1 

Bisector of a Given Angle, Using Only Compass and Straight Edge

Worked Example 16.1

Construct the **bisector** of $\angle ABC$.

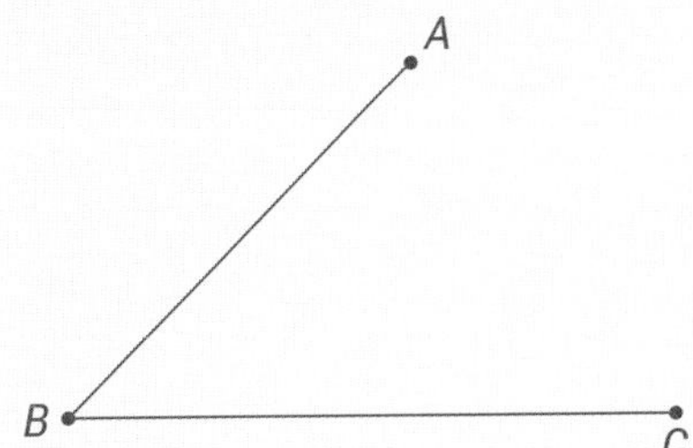

To **bisect** is to cut into two equal parts. The **bisector** of an angle is the line, line segment or ray that cuts the angle in two.

Solution

1 Place the compass needle point on the angle's **vertex** *B*.

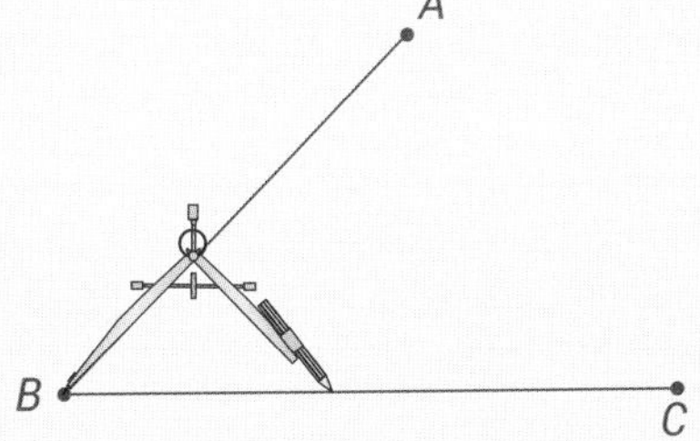

The **vertex** of an angle is the point where the two arms of the angle meet.

2 Draw an arc of the same width across each arm of the angle. Label *X*, *Y*.

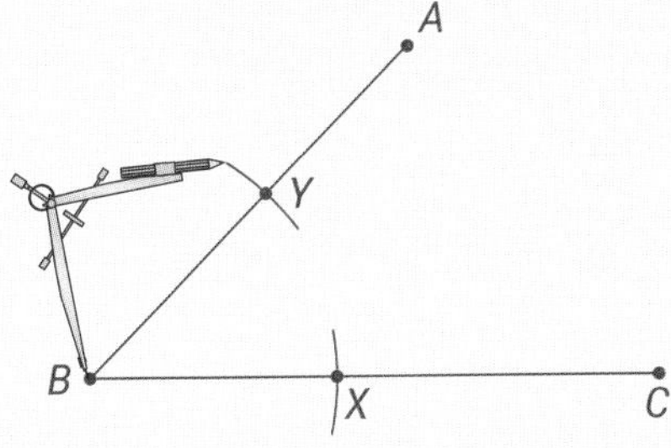

3 Place the compass needle point on the point *X* and draw an arc.

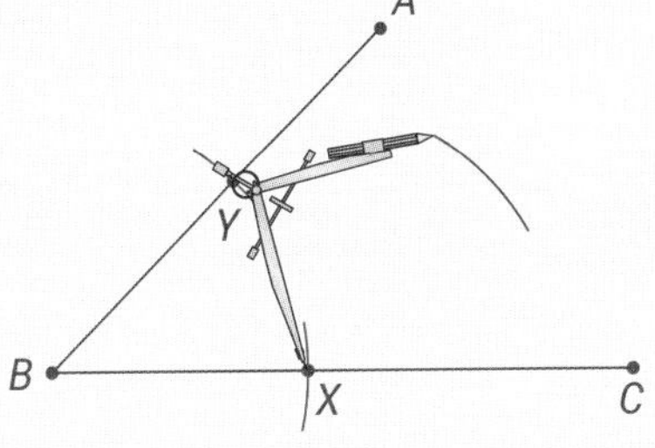

4 Without changing the compass width, place the compass needle point on the point *Y* and draw an overlapping arc.

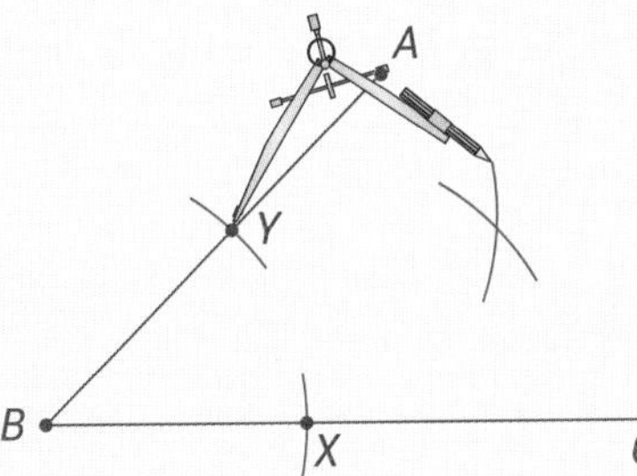

5 Mark the point where the two arcs intersect.

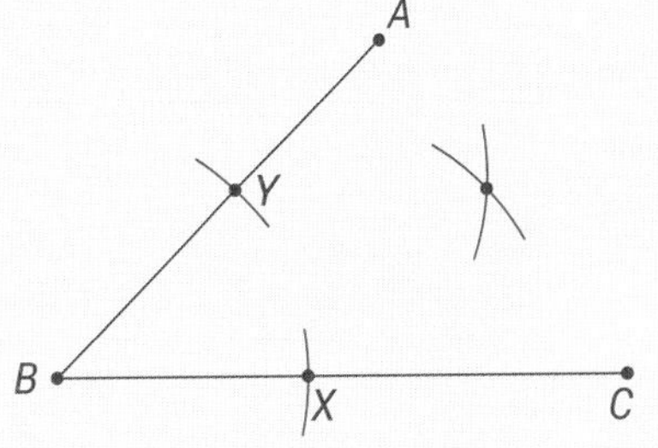

6 Using a straight edge, draw a line segment from this point to the vertex *B*.

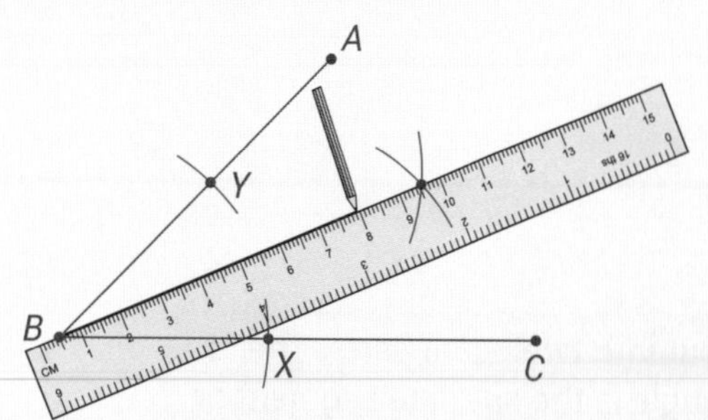

7 This line segment is the bisector of the angle *ABC*.

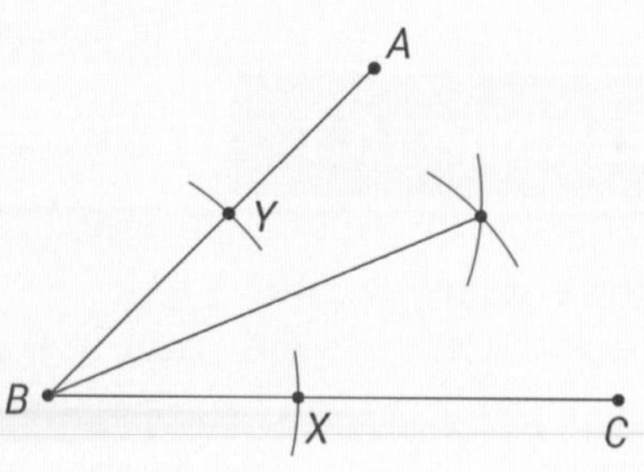

It is a good idea to check your construction using a protractor.

Construction 2

Perpendicular Bisector of a Line Segment, Using Only Compass and Straight Edge

Worked Example 16.2

Construct the **perpendicular bisector** of the line segment [*AB*].

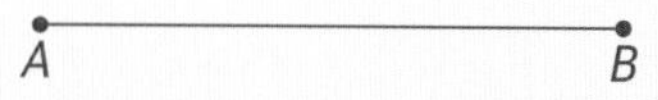

A **perpendicular bisector** cuts the line segment into two equal parts and meets the line segment at an angle of 90°.

Solution

1 Place the compass needle point on *A*.

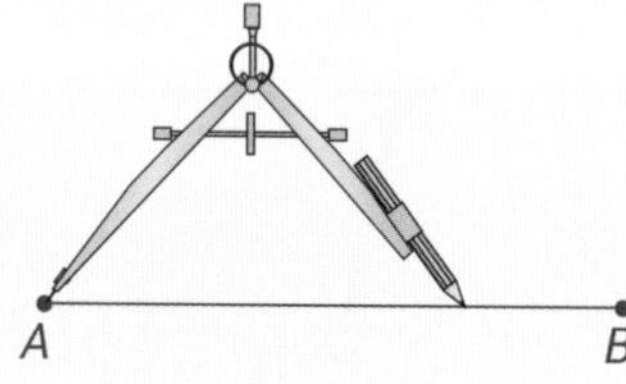

2 Set the compass width to **more than half** the length of [*AB*] and draw an arc.

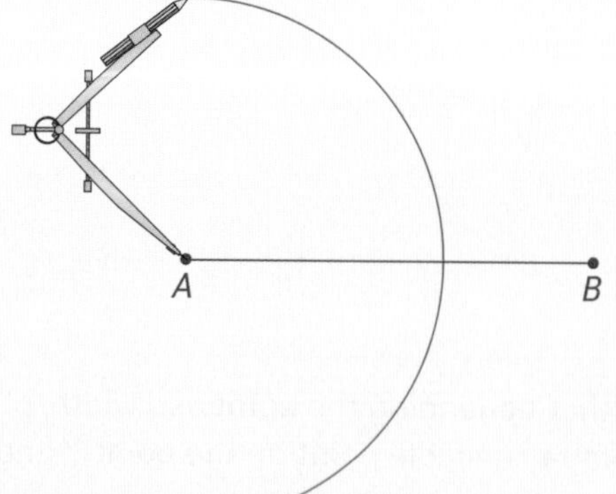

3 Without changing the compass width, place the compass needle point on *B* and draw an arc.

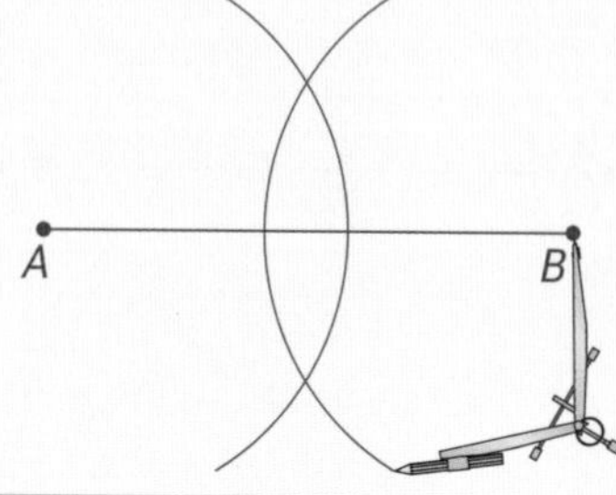

4 Mark the two points where the arcs intersect.

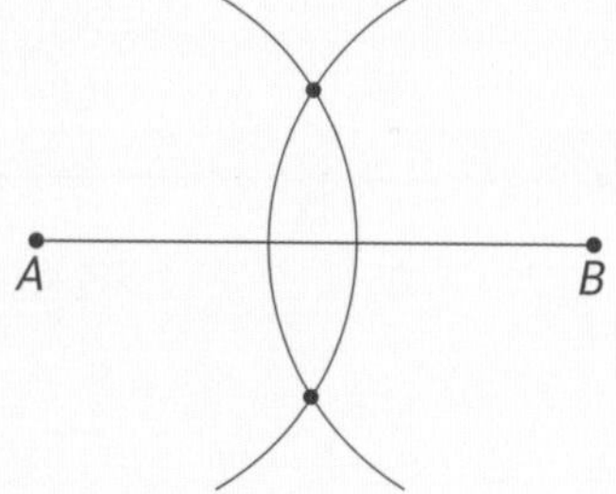

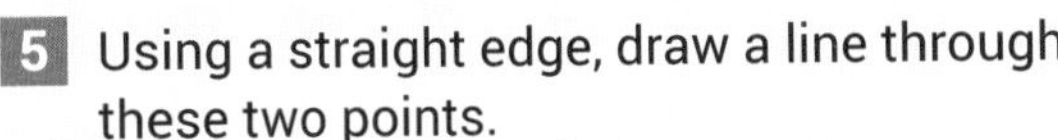

5 Using a straight edge, draw a line through these two points.

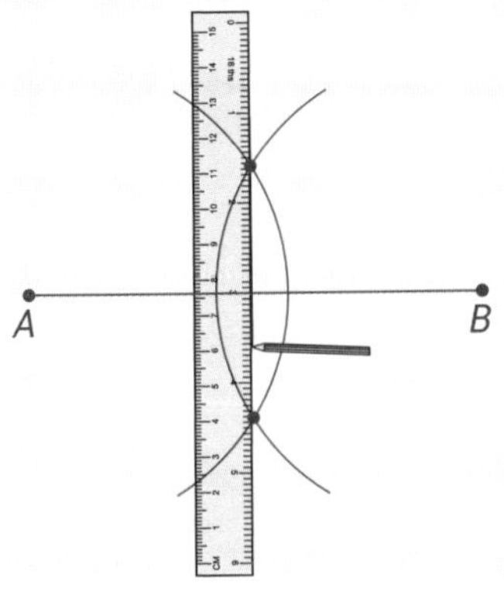

6 The line is the perpendicular bisector of the line segment [*AB*].

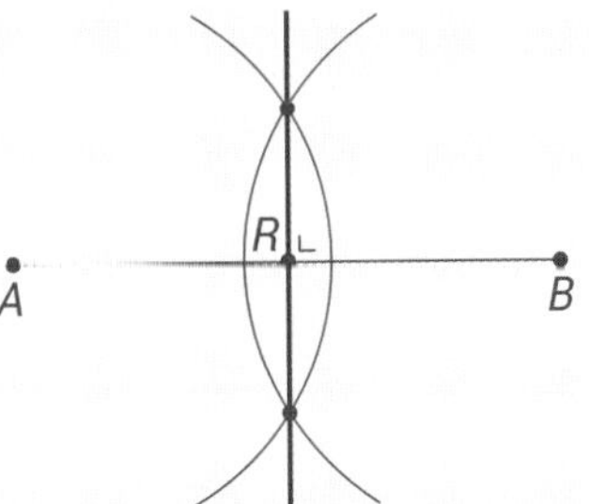

Constructing the perpendicular bisector of a line segment also finds the **midpoint** of the line segment. In this example, *R* is the midpoint of [*AB*].

Exercise 16.1

1. (a) Construct the following angles **using a protractor**:

   (i) 20° (iii) 70°

   (ii) 180° (iv) 330°

   (b) Bisect each of the constructed angles, **using only a compass and straight edge**.

2. Draw a line segment [*AB*] of length 9.5 cm. Construct the perpendicular bisector of [*AB*].

3. Draw a line segment [*CD*] of length 6.2 cm. Construct the perpendicular bisector of [*CD*].

4. Copy the following lines into your copybook. In each case, construct a line perpendicular to the given line passing through the given point.

   (i)

   (ii)

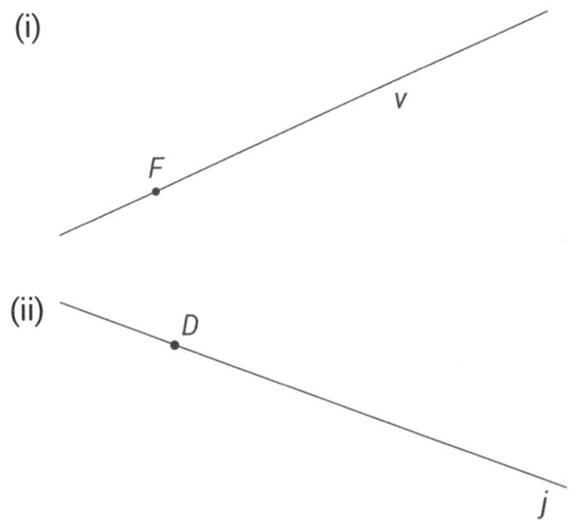

5. Copy the following figures into your copybook. In each case, construct a line parallel to the given line passing through the given point.

   (i)

   (ii)

   (iii)

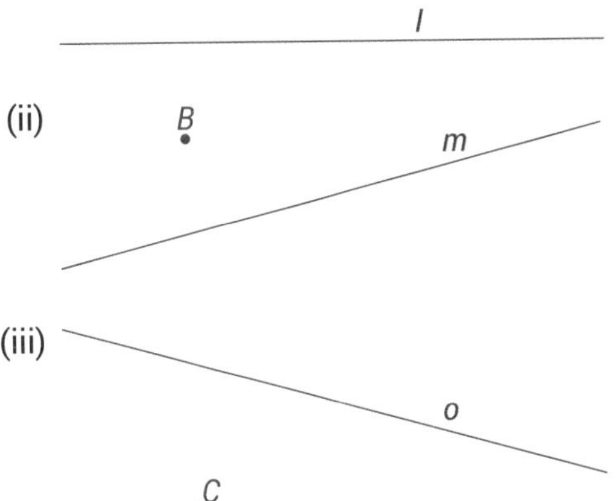

6. Draw a line segment [*CD*] of length 8.5 cm. Divide this line segment into three equal segments, without measuring it.

7. Draw a line segment [*KL*] of length 112 mm. Divide this line segment into three equal parts without measuring it.

8. Copy the following figures into your copybook. In each case, construct the given line segment on the given ray. Note that figures are not drawn to scale.

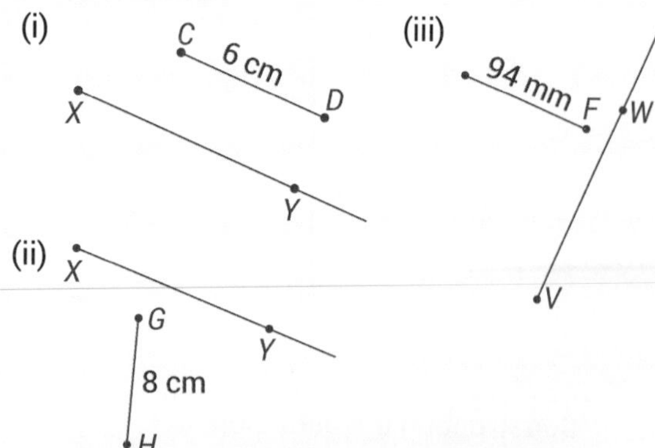

9. Construct the following angles with the given ray as one arm of the angle using a protractor.

(i) $|\angle PQR| = 70°$

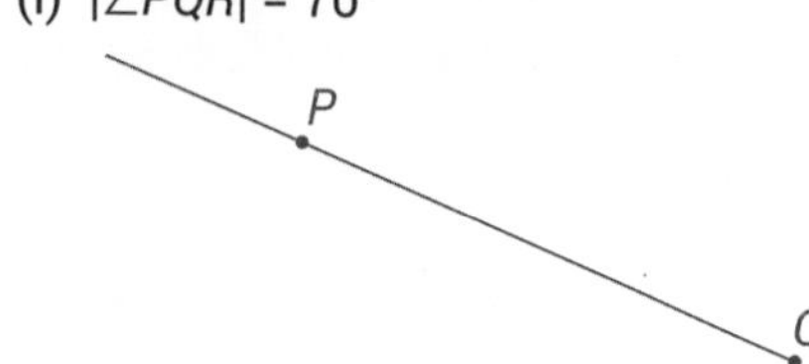

(ii) $|\angle STV| = 155°$

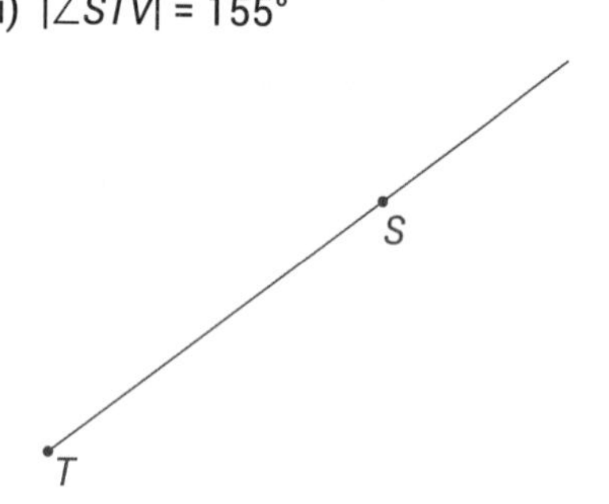

10. (i) Draw a line segment [*AB*] such that $|AB| = 8$ cm.

(ii) Find the midpoint of [*AB*], and label it point *C*.

(iii) Construct an angle of 45° at the point *C*.

(iv) Bisect this angle of 45° at the point *C*.

Construct the following triangles and rectangles. Don't forget to check to see if your construction has the correct dimensions. Diagrams are not to scale.

11. Triangle *ABC* where $|AB| = 8$ cm, $|BC| = 10$ cm and $|AC| = 9$ cm.

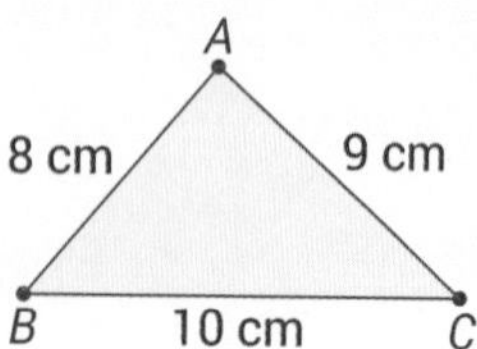

12. Triangle *GHI*, using the measurements shown in the diagram.

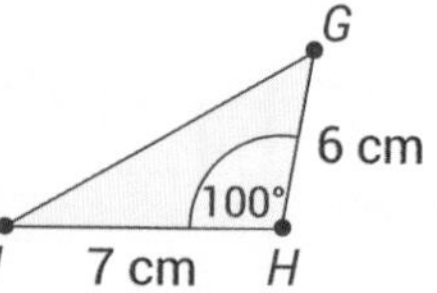

13. Triangle *ABC* where $|\angle BAC| = 40°$, $|AC| = 8$ cm and $|\angle BCA| = 55°$.

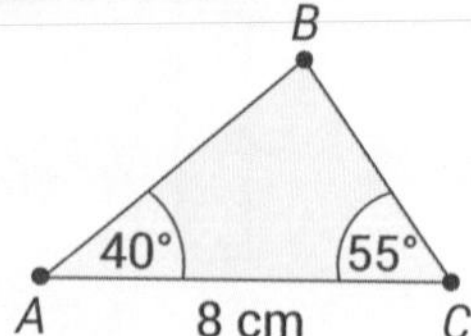

14. Triangle *JKL* where $|JK| = 6$ cm, $|KL| = 5$ cm and $|JL| = 8$ cm.

15. Triangle *PQR* where $|QR| = 6$ cm, $|PR| = 5$ cm and $|\angle QRP| = 140°$.

16. Triangle *PQR* where $|\angle QPR| = 100°$, $|PQ| = 7.5$ cm and $|\angle PQR| = 30°$.

17. Triangle *ABC* where $|\angle ACB| = 90°$, $|AC| = 5$ cm and $|AB| = 7$ cm.

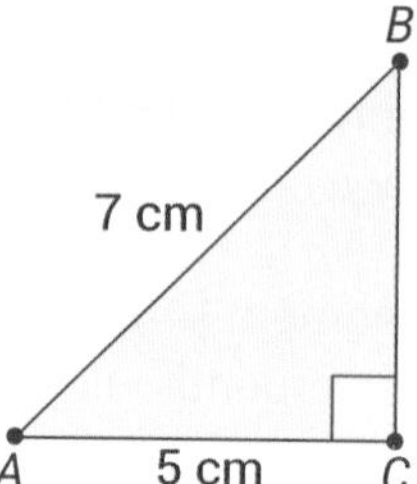

18. Triangle *GHI*, using the measurements shown in the diagram.

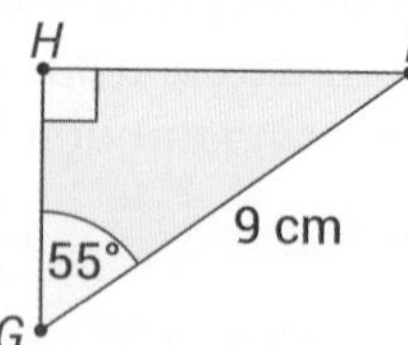

19. Triangle *MNO* where $|NO| = 4$ cm, $|\angle MNO| = 90°$ and $|MO| = 6.5$ cm.

20. Triangle *PQR* where $|\angle RPQ| = 90°$, $|QR| = 95$ mm and $|\angle QRP| = 35°$.

21. Rectangle *ABCD* where $|AB| = 8$ cm and $|BC| = 3$ cm.

22. Square *EFGH* whose perimeter is 240 mm.

23. Copy the following diagram into your copybook.

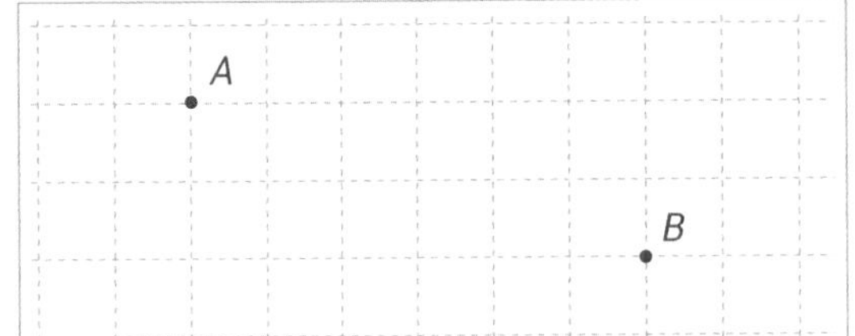

Using only a compass and a straight edge, construct a circle that passes through the points *A* and *B*.

24. A cable 13 m long joins the top of an antenna 12 m high as shown on the diagram.

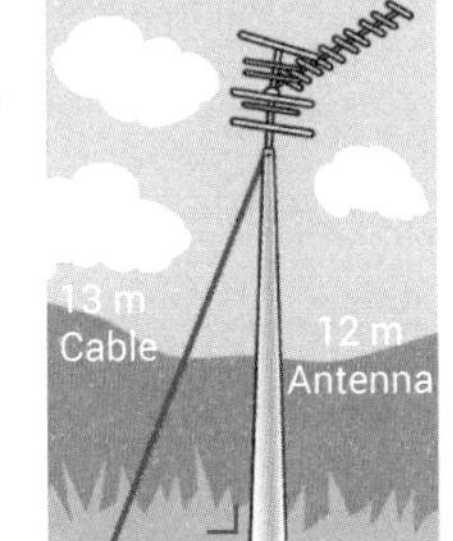

(i) Construct the triangle shown in the diagram using an appropriate scale.

(ii) Find the horizontal distance between the cable and the antenna, using a ruler.

(iii) What other method could you use to find this horizontal distance?

25. (i) A tree is 10 m high and casts a shadow of 4 m. Using a scale of 1 cm to represent 1 m, construct the triangle shown in the diagram.

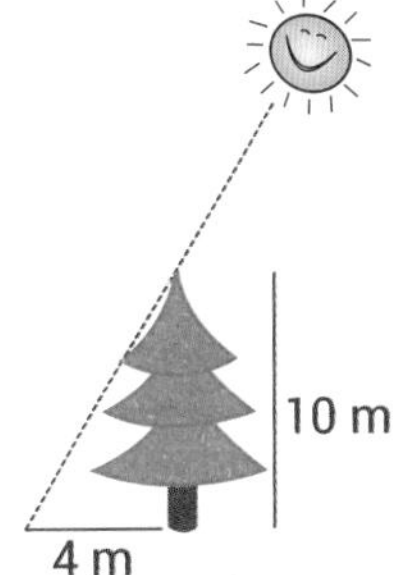

(ii) Use your protractor to measure the angle that the sun's rays make with the ground.

(iii) Write the scale you used as a ratio.

16.3 Leaving Certificate Ordinary Level Constructions

The following constructions were not studied at Junior Certificate Ordinary Level. Students at Leaving Certificate Ordinary Level are expected to be able to perform them.

Construction 18 

Angle of 60°, Without Using a Protractor or Set Square

Worked Example 16.3

Construct an angle of 60° without using a protractor or a set square.

Solution

1 Draw a line segment [*AB*].

A B

2 Place the compass needle point at *A* and draw an arc of radius length |*AB*|.

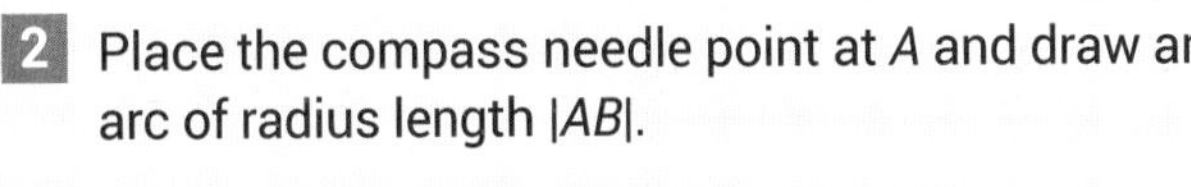

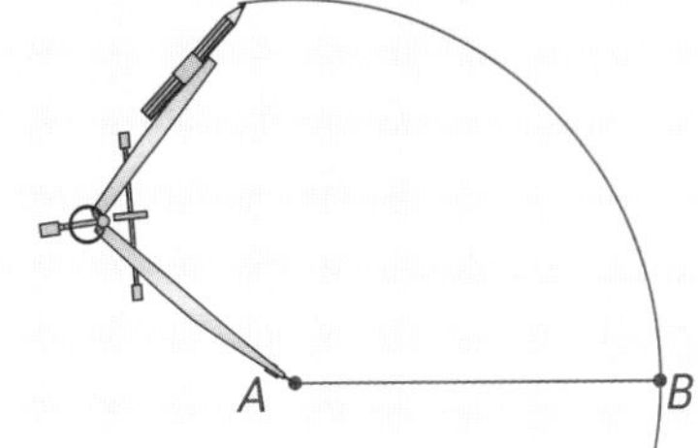

3 Place the compass needle point at B and draw an arc of radius length $|AB|$.

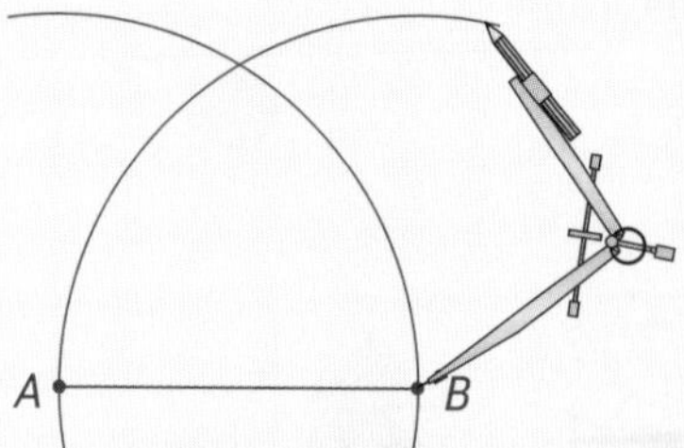

4 Mark the point of intersection of the arcs and label as point C.

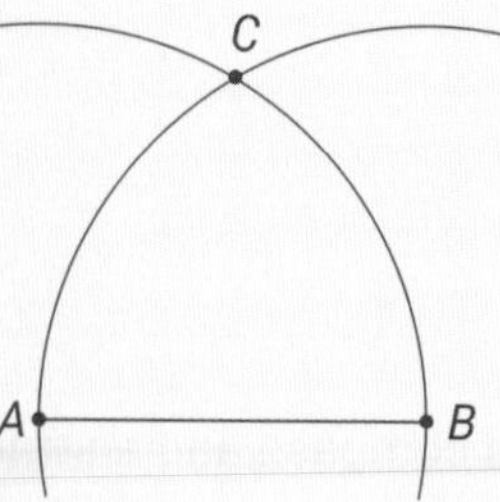

5 Join C to A using a straight edge.

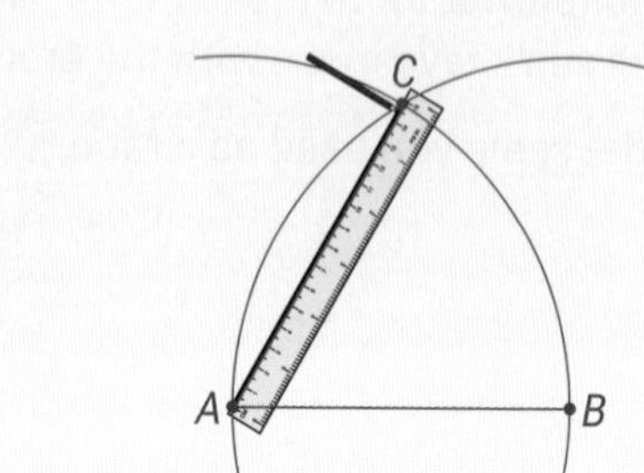

6 Label the measure of $\angle CAB$ as 60°.

$|\angle CAB| = 60°$ since ΔABC is equilateral.

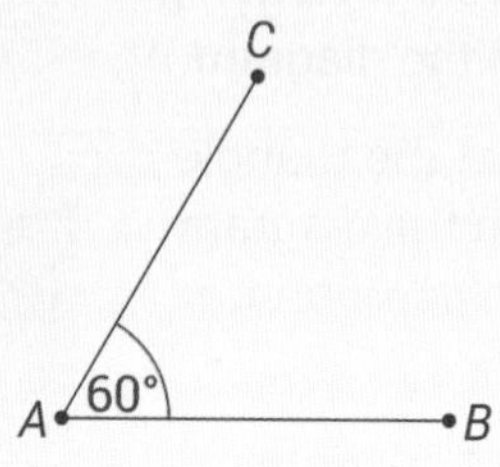

Construction 19 

Tangent to a Given Circle at a Given Point on it

Worked Example 16.4

Construct a **tangent** to the given circle at the point A.

A **tangent** is a line that touches the circle at a single point.

Solution

1 Draw a ray from the centre O of the circle through the given point A.

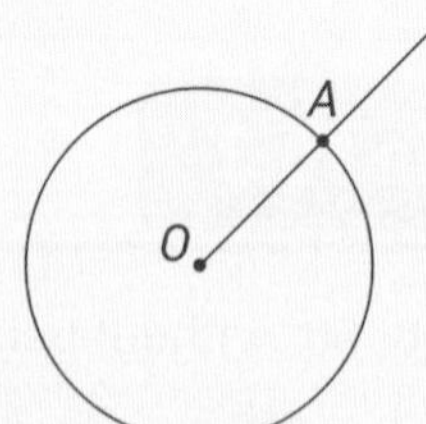

2 Construct a line perpendicular to the ray $[OA$ through the point A.

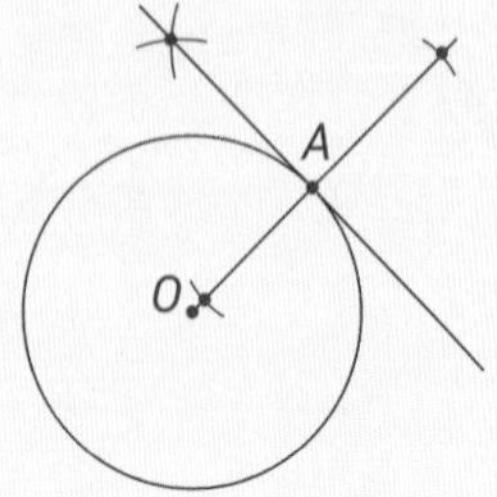

3 This is the tangent to the circle. Label the 90° angle at A.

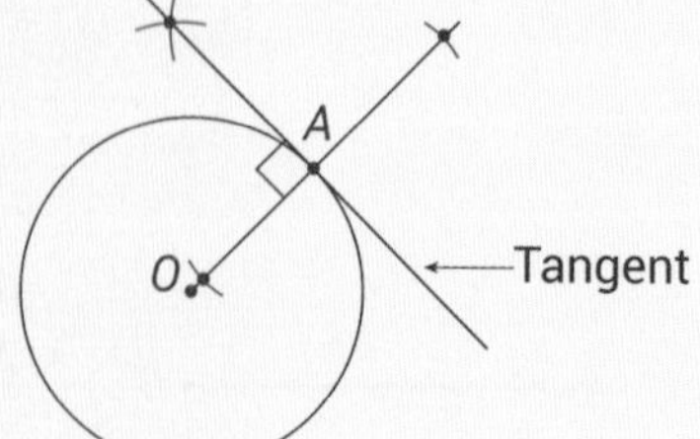

Construction 20

Parallelogram, Given the Length of the Sides and the Measure of the Angles

Worked Example 16.5

Construct a parallelogram *ABCD* where |*AB*| = 7 cm, |*BC*| = 4 cm and |∠*ABC*| = 60°.

Solution

1 Draw a rough sketch of the parallelogram.

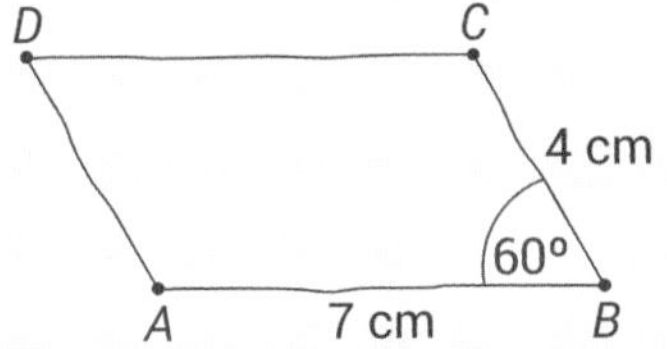

2 Construct the line segment [*AB*] where |*AB*| = 7 cm. Use your ruler to do this.

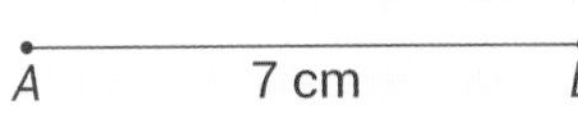

3 At point *B*, construct an angle of 60°, using the line segment [*AB*] as one arm of the angle.

Use your protractor for this angle.

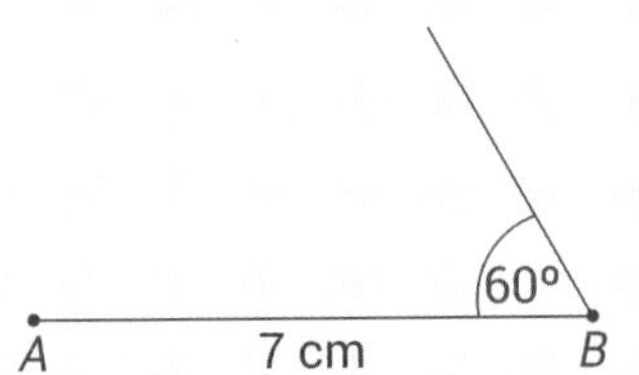

4 Mark the point *C* on this angle such that |*BC*| = 4 cm.

Use your compass (or ruler) for this measurement.

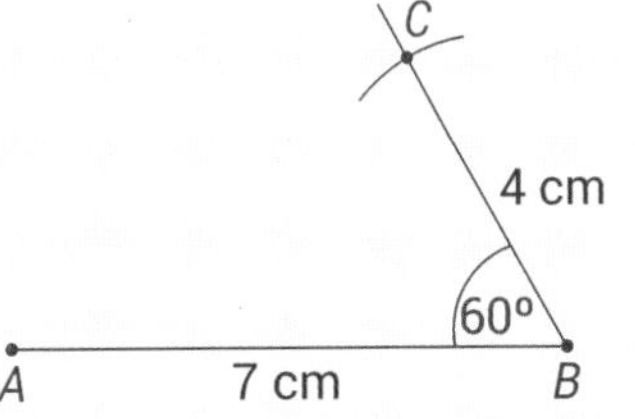

5 At point *A*, construct a ray parallel to *BC*.

Use your protractor to measure the correct angle.

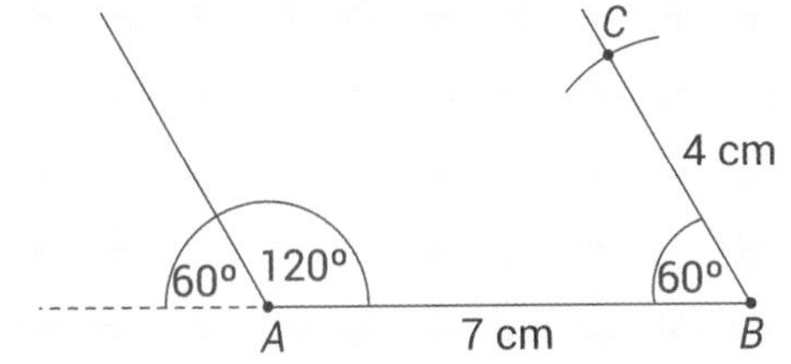

6 Mark the point *D* on this ray such that |*AD*| = 4 cm.

Use your compass (or ruler) for this measurement.

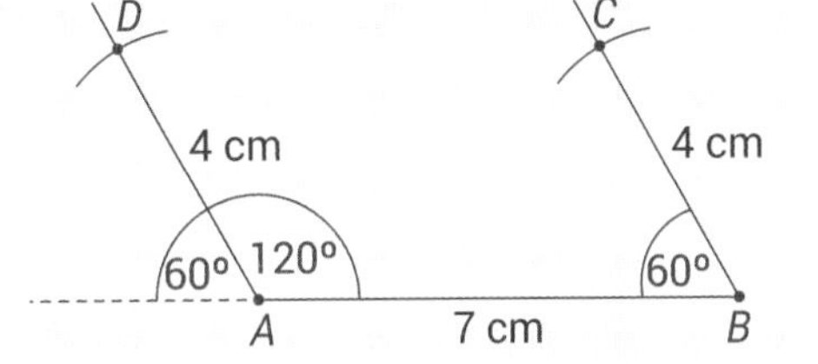

7 Using a straight edge, join *C* to *D*.

Label all given measurements.

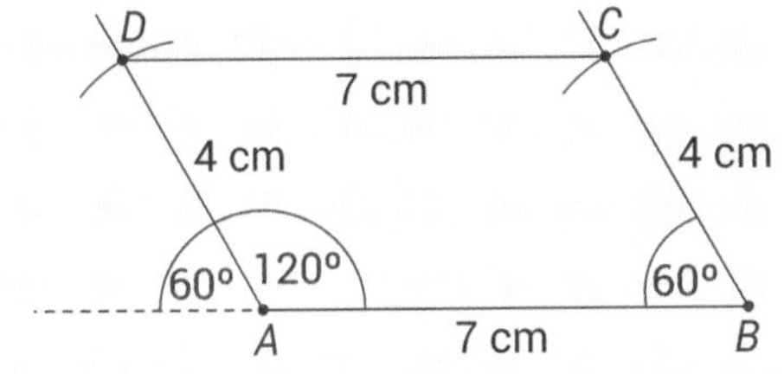

Exercise 16.2

1. Copy the following line segments into your copybook. Construct an angle of 60° on each line segment without using a protractor or set square.

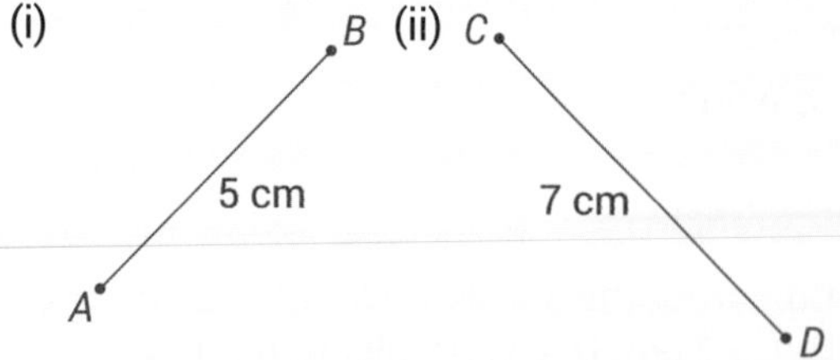

2. Construct an equilateral triangle of side length 6 cm using only a ruler and compass.

3. Using only a compass and straight edge, construct an angle of 30°. (*Hint:* First construct a 60° angle.)

4. Construct a circle of radius 5 cm, and draw a tangent to this circle at any point on the circle.

5. Construct a circle of diameter 12 cm, and draw a tangent to this circle at any point on the circle.

6. Construct the following circle with centre O in your copybook, and construct a tangent to the circle at the given point.

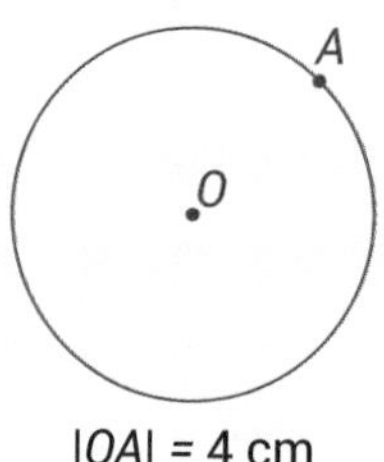

$|OA| = 4$ cm

Construct the following quadrilaterals:

7. Parallelogram $ABCD$ where $|AB| = 8$ cm, $|BC| = 4$ cm and $|\angle ABC| = 50°$.

8. Parallelogram $EFGH$ where $|EF| = 7$ cm, $|FG| = 3$ cm and $|\angle EFG| = 80°$.

9. Parallelogram $IJKL$ where $|IJ| = 9$ cm, $|JK| = 5$ cm and $|\angle IJK| = 110°$.

10. Rhombus $MNOP$ where $|MN| = 50$ mm and $|\angle MNO| = 40°$.

11. Parallelogram $QRST$ where $|QR| = 6.5$ cm, $|\angle QTS| = 135°$ and $|QT| = 5$ cm.

Construction 16

Circumcentre and Circumcircle of a Given Triangle, Using Only a Straight Edge and Compass

Worked Example 16.6

Construct the circumcentre and circumcircle of the triangle ABC.

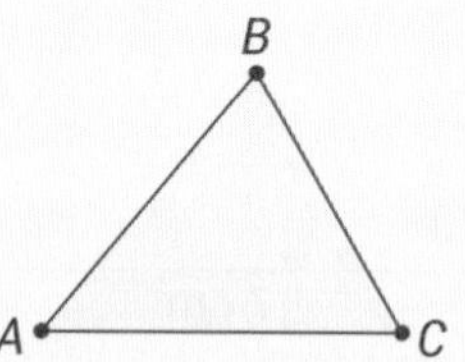

Solution

1 Construct the perpendicular bisector of $[AC]$.

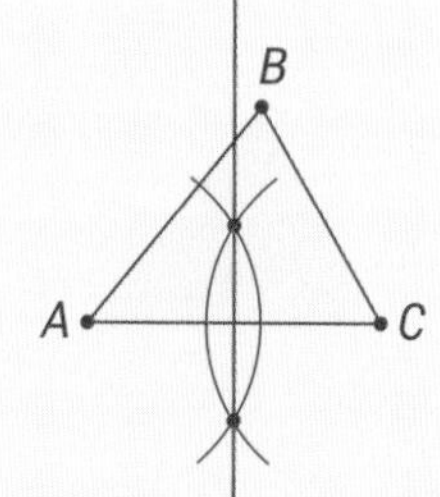

2 Construct the perpendicular bisector of any other side of the triangle – in this case the side $[BC]$.

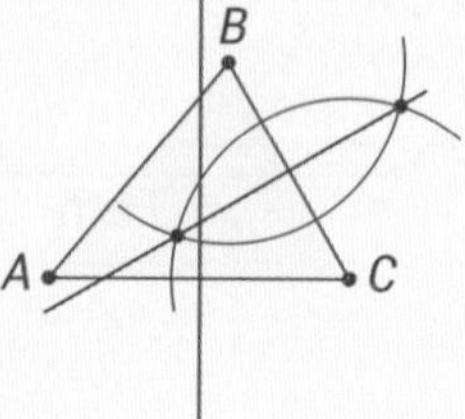

3 Mark the point of intersection of the perpendicular bisectors and label as point O.

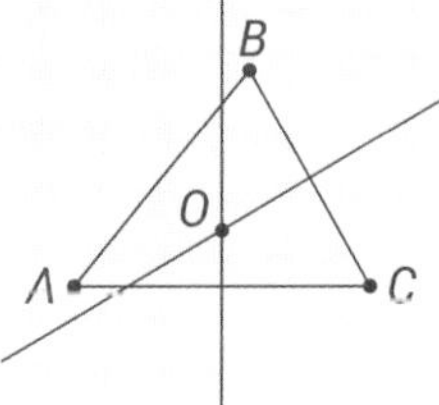

4 Point O is the **circumcentre** of the triangle ABC. Label this clearly.

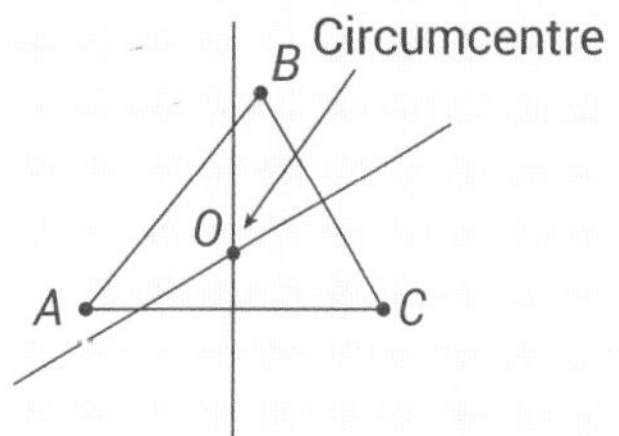

The **circumcentre** is the point where a triangle's three perpendicular bisectors meet.

5 Place the compass needle point on O and draw a circle of radius length $|OA|$.

This circle is the **circumcircle** of the triangle ABC. Label this clearly.

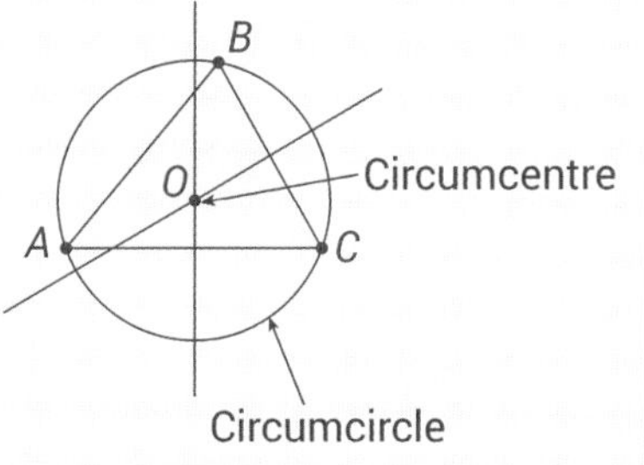

The **circumcircle** of a triangle is a circle that passes through all three vertices of the triangle, i.e. circumscribes the triangle.

$|AO| = |BO| = |CO| =$ radius

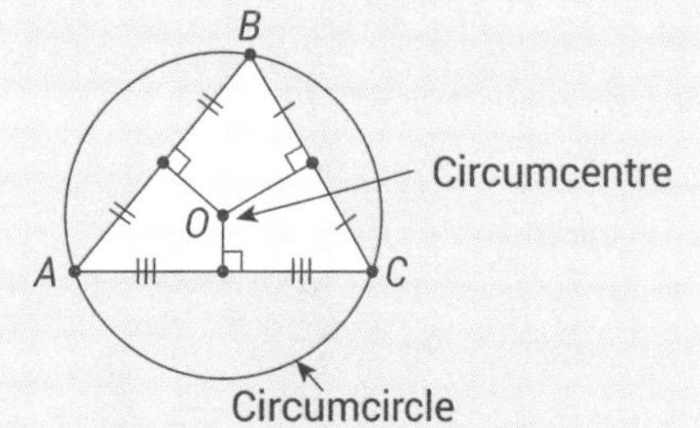

Always clearly label the circumcircle and the circumcentre.

Construction 17

Incentre and Incircle of a Given Triangle, Using Only a Straight Edge and Compass

Worked Example 16.7

Construct the incentre and incircle of the triangle PQR.

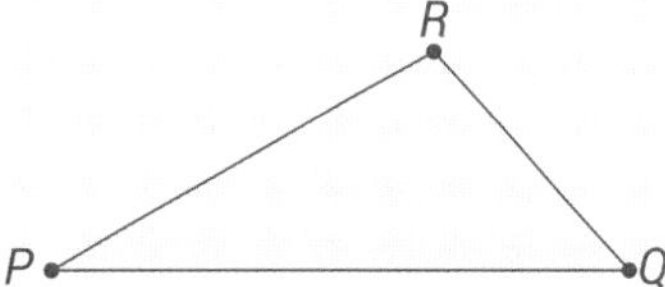

Solution

1 Construct the bisector of the angle PQR.

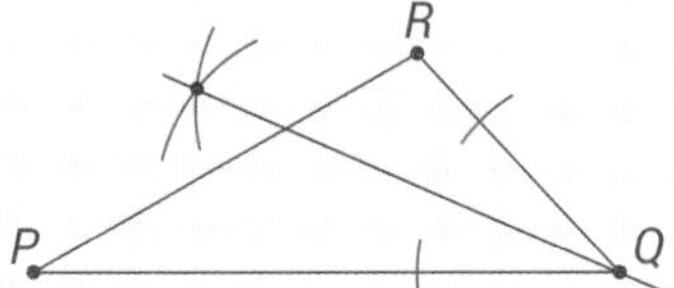

2 Construct the bisector of any other angle in the triangle, in this case $\angle RPQ$.

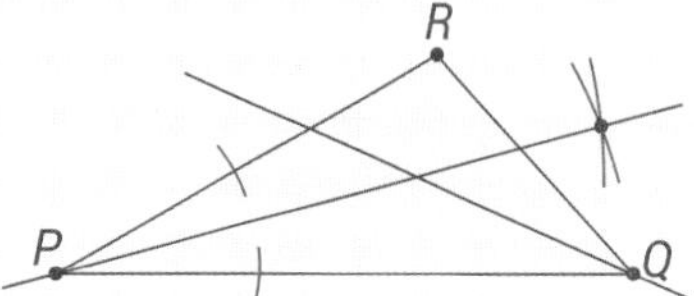

3 Mark the point of intersection of the angle bisectors, and label as point *O*.

Point *O* is the **incentre** of the triangle *PQR*.

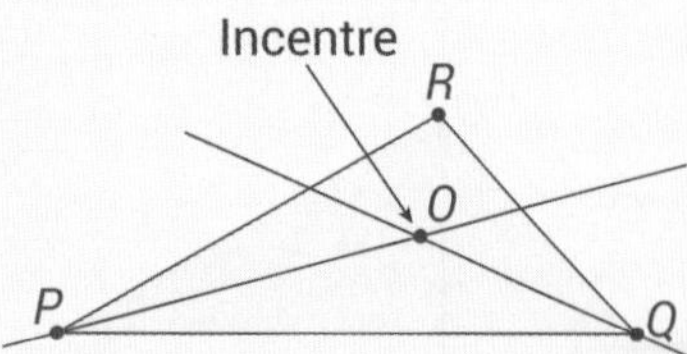

The **incentre** is the point where a triangle's three angle bisectors meet.

4 Using your set square, draw a perpendicular line segment from *O* to a side of the triangle. Label the point where it meets this side as *S*.

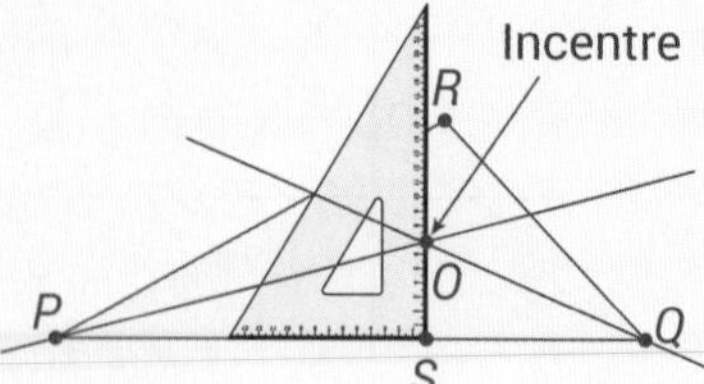

5 Place the compass needle point on *O* and draw a circle of radius |*OS*|. This circle should touch all three sides of the triangle.

This is the **incircle** of the triangle *PQR*. Label this clearly.

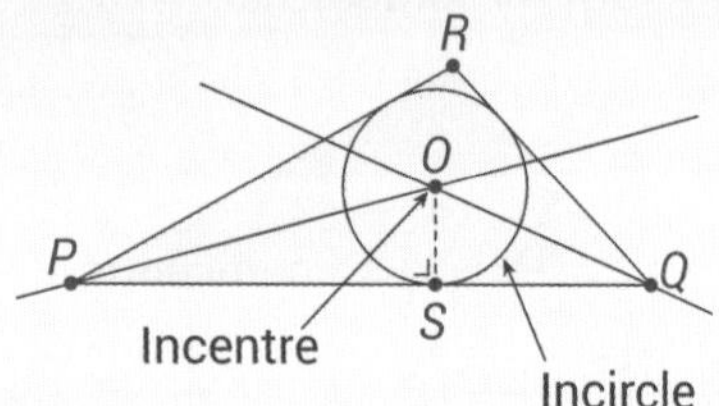

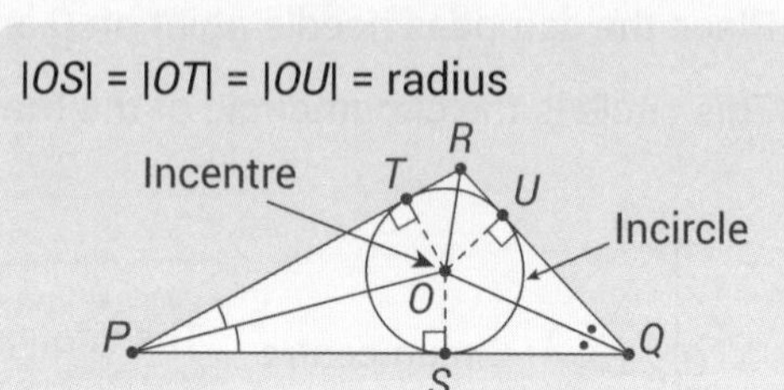

Always clearly label the incircle and the incentre.

The **incircle** of a triangle is the largest circle that will fit inside the triangle. Each of the triangle's three sides is a tangent to the circle.

Construction 21
Centroid of a Triangle

Worked Example 16.8

Construct the centroid of the triangle *PQR*.

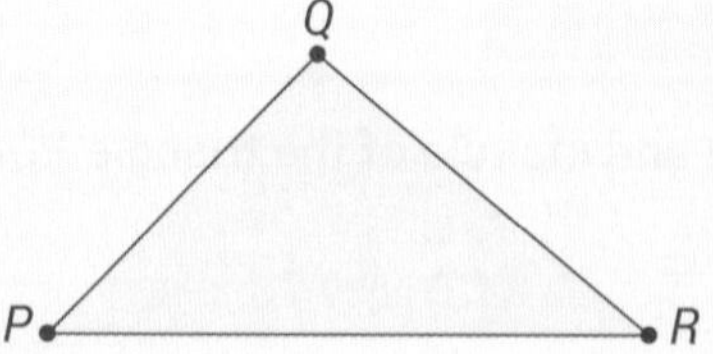

Solution

1 Construct the perpendicular bisector of the side [*PQ*].

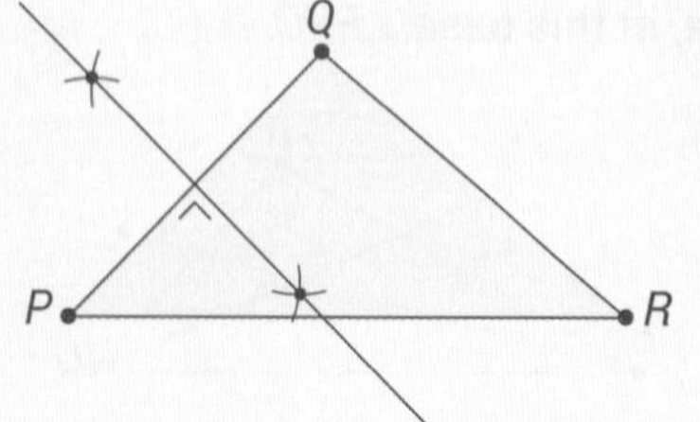

2 Label the midpoint of [*PQ*] as the point *X*.

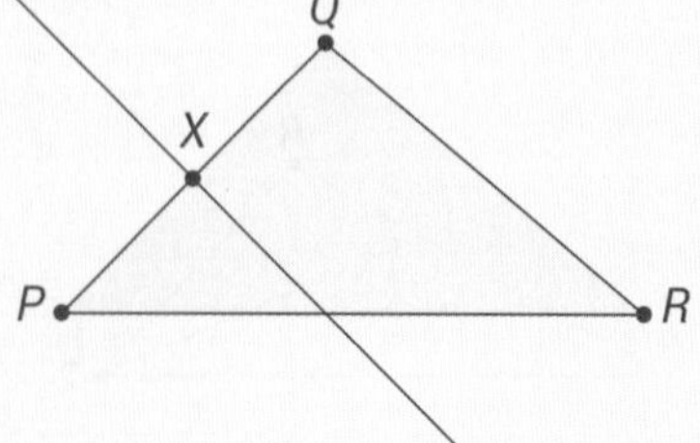

3 Using a straight edge, draw a line segment from X to R, the opposite vertex of the triangle.

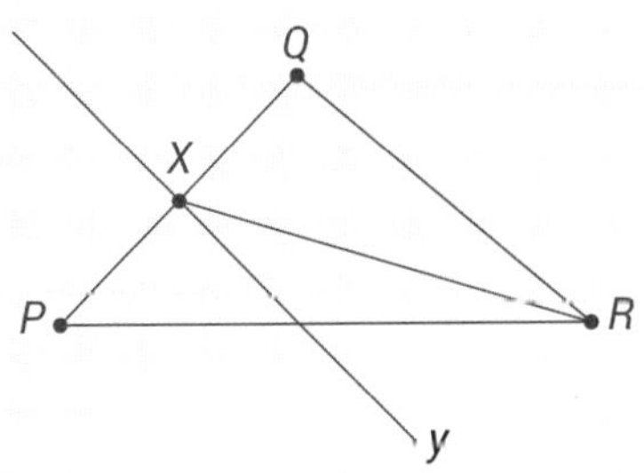

4 This line segment is a **median** of the triangle PQR.

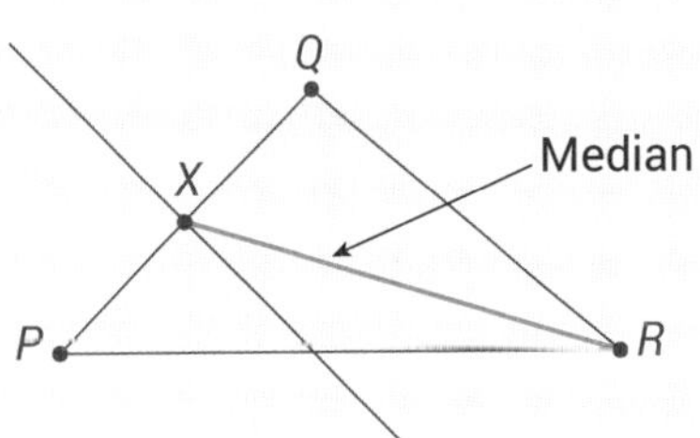

A **median** of a triangle is a segment that goes from one of the triangle's vertices to the midpoint of the opposite side.

5 Construct the perpendicular bisector of $[PR]$ and label the midpoint of $[PR]$ as Y.

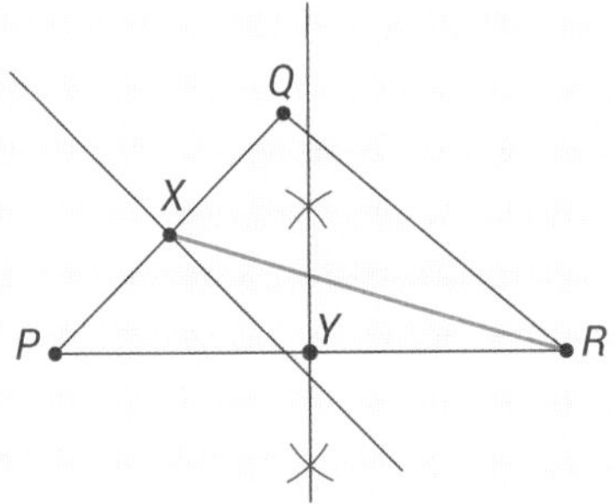

6 Using a straight edge, join Y to the opposite vertex, Q.

This is a second median.

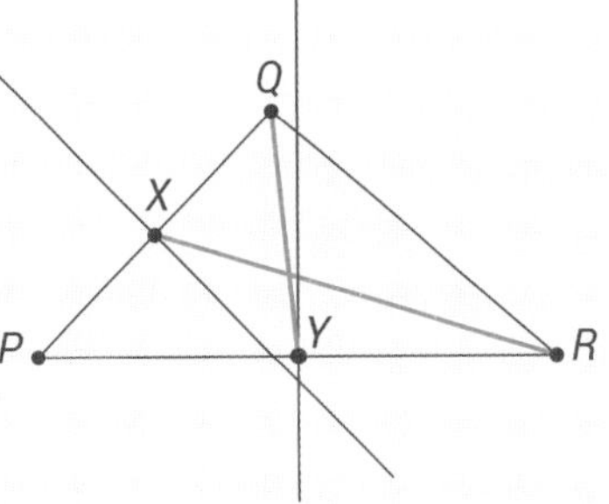

7 Where the medians intersect is the **centroid** of the triangle PQR. Label this clearly.

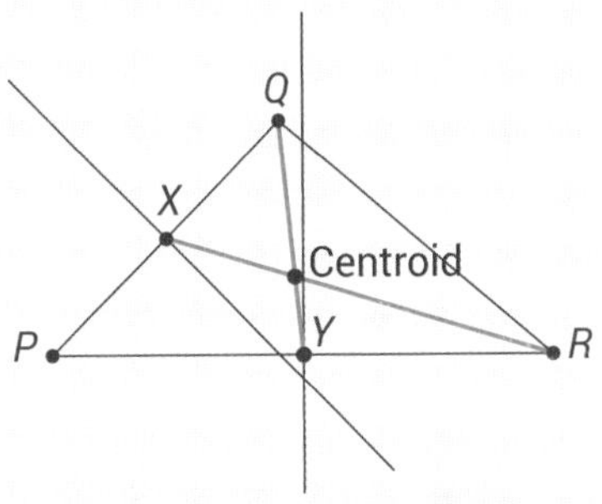

The centroid of a triangle divides each median in the ratio 2:1.

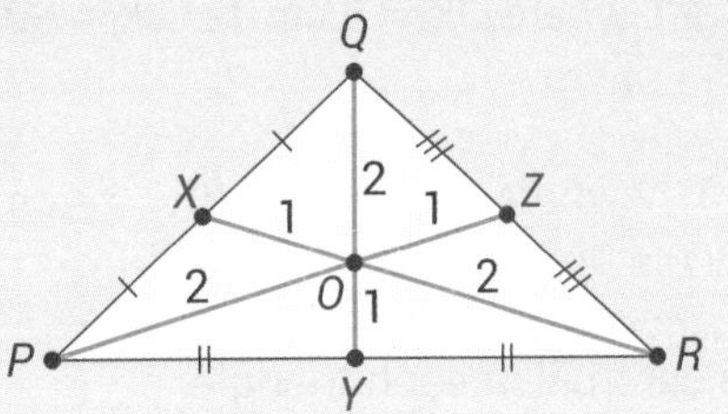

The **centroid** is the triangle's balance point or centre of gravity, i.e. the point on which you could balance the triangle on a pinpoint.

Exercise 16.3

Construct the following triangles in your copybook. Construct the circumcentre and circumcircle of each one.

1. Triangle ABC where $|AB| = 8$ cm, $|BC| = 6$ cm and $|AC| = 6$ cm.
2. Triangle EDF having $|ED| = 7$ cm, $|\angle FED| = 75°$ and $|EF| = 6$ cm.
3. Triangle JKL where $|JK| = 7$ cm, $|\angle JKL| = 90°$ and $|JL| = 10$ cm. What do you notice about the position of the circumcentre?
4. Triangle GHI where $|GH| = 6$ cm, $|\angle IGH| = 25°$ and $|\angle IHG| = 120°$. What do you notice about the position of the circumcentre?

5. The circumcentre of a triangle can be inside, on or outside the triangle, depending on the type of triangle given. Match the correct position of the circumcentre (inside, on, outside) with its corresponding triangle (right-angled, obtuse, acute) in the following table.

An obtuse triangle is a triangle that has one obtuse angle.

An acute triangle is a triangle in which all three angles are acute angles.

Position of circumcentre	Type of triangle
Inside	
On	
Outside	

Construct the following triangles in your copybook. Construct the incentre and incircle of each one.

6. Triangle *ABC* where |*AB*| = 7 cm, |*BC*| = 7 cm and |*AC*| = 9 cm.

7. Triangle *DEF* where |∠*EDF*| = 40°, |*DE*| = 8 cm and |*FD*| = 9.5 cm.

8. Triangle *GHI* where |*HI*| = 10 cm, |∠*GHI*| = 40° and |∠*GIH*| = 65°.

9. Triangle *JKL* where |*JK*| = 6 cm, |∠*LJK*| = 90° and |*JL*| = 7.5 cm.

10. Triangle *TUV* where |*TU*| = 9 cm, |*UV*| = 7 cm and |∠*UVT*| = 90°.

Construct the centroid of each triangle.

11. Triangle *ABC* where |*AB*| = 8 cm, |*BC*| = 6 cm and |*AC*| = 7 cm.

12. Triangle *DEF* where |∠*EDF*| = 75°, |*DE*| = 8 cm and |*FD*| = 6.5 cm.

13. Triangle *GHI* where |*HI*| = 6.5 cm, |∠*GHI*| = 30° and |∠*GIH*| = 110°.

14. Equilateral triangle *XYZ* where |*XY*| = 7.5 cm.

15. Triangle *JKL* where |*JK*| = 7 cm, |∠*LJK*| = 90° and |*JL*| = 7 cm. If *M* is the midpoint of [*LK*] and *C* the centroid, measure |*JC*| and |*CM*|. Verify that |*JC*| : |*CM*| = 2 : 1.

16. A town planner wishes to build a shopping centre that is the same distance from three towns.

(i) Show by construction, and using an appropriate scale, how this could be achieved. (Note: You can set your own figures for the distance between the towns.)

(ii) Using your construction, find the distance between the shopping centre and any one of these towns.

17. Two new houses are being built. A pipeline from a local well is to be laid to supply water to both houses. This pipe must always be the same distance from each house.

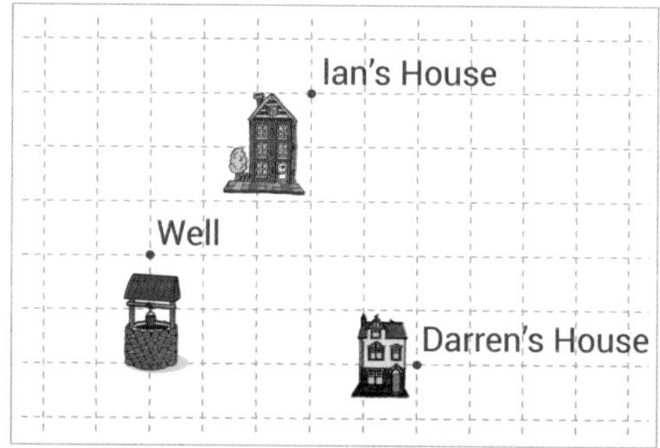

Show by construction, and using an appropriate scale, how this could be achieved.

18. A landscaper is given a design for a lawn. The lawn should be in the shape of a triangle and have dimensions of 6 m, 7.5 m and 5 m.

(i) Construct a scale drawing of this lawn.

(ii) The landscaper wishes to include a large circular flower-bed in the lawn as part of the design. Construct the largest flower-bed possible into your drawing in part (i).

(iii) Find the area of this flower-bed using the measurements from your construction.

16.4 Transformations

We see many examples of shapes being transformed in everyday life. In geometry, a transformation is when a shape's size or position is changed or **transformed**.

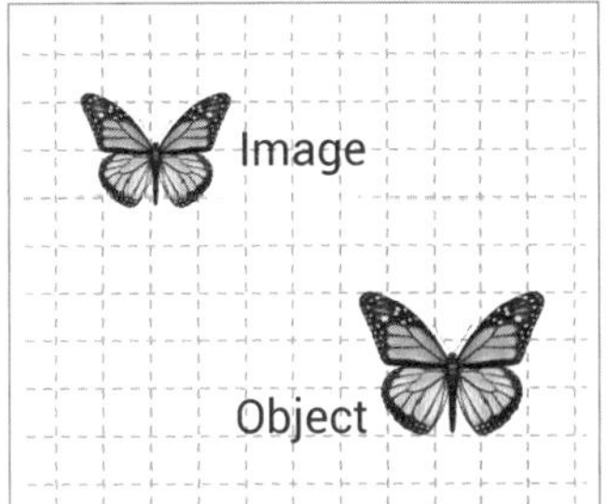

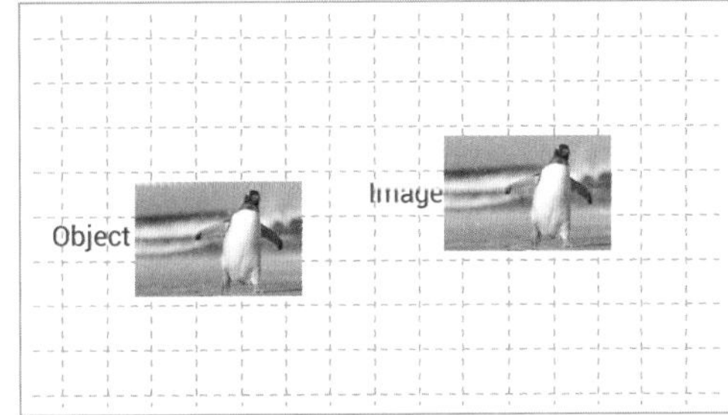

The point or shape we start with is called the **object**.
The transformed shape is called the **image**.

Translation

A **translation** is when a point or shape is moved in a straight line. A translation moves every point the same distance and in the same direction without changing the orientation of the shape or rotating it.

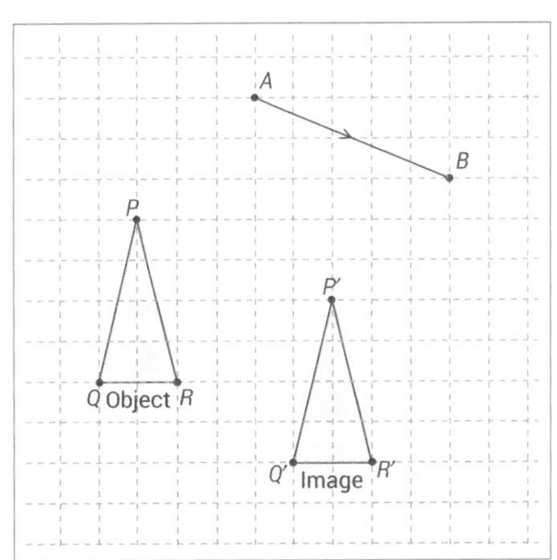

Each point in the object shape ΔPQR has been moved the same distance as $|AB|$, parallel to AB and in the direction of A to B.

This means that we are finding the image of ΔPQR under the translation AB, written $\overrightarrow{AB}$.

If ΔPQR is the object, then the image can be labelled as $\Delta P'Q'R'$.

$$\left.\begin{array}{l}|PQ| = |P'Q'| \\ |QR| = |Q'R'| \\ |PR| = |P'R'|\end{array}\right\} |PP'| = |QQ'| = |RR'|$$

In a translation, the image and the object are identical and face the same way.

Central Symmetry (in a Point)

A **central symmetry** is a reflection through a point.

For example, in the diagram shown, object DEF is transformed under a central symmetry in the point O to image $D'E'F'$.

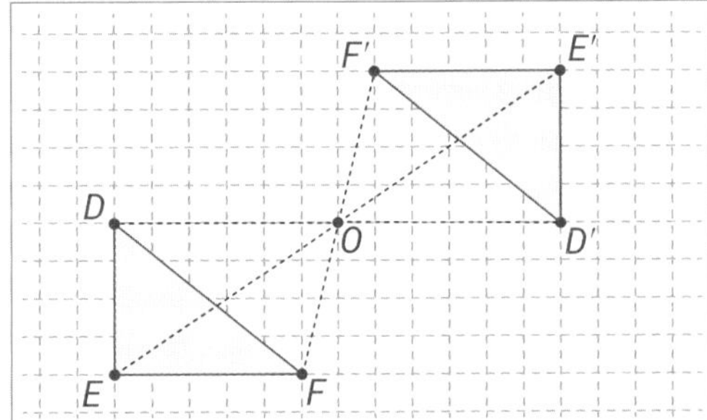

$|DO| = |OD'|$ and $\overrightarrow{DO} = \overrightarrow{OD'}$

$|EO| = |OE'|$ and $\overrightarrow{EO} = \overrightarrow{OE'}$

$|FO| = |OF'|$ and $\overrightarrow{FO} = \overrightarrow{OF'}$

In a **central symmetry**, each point is mapped through a specific point and reflected out the other side, the same distance in the same direction.

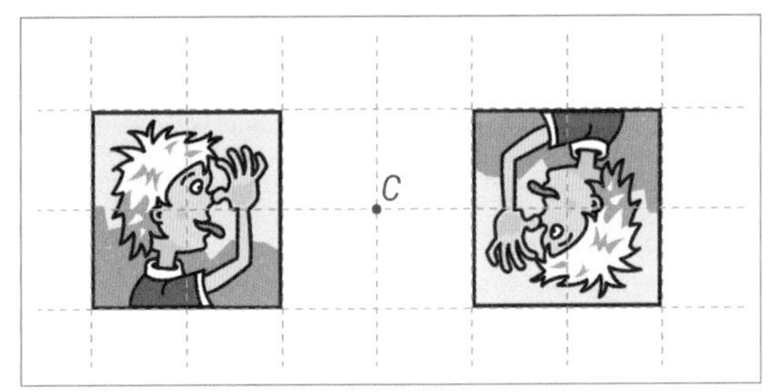

In a central symmetry, the image will be upside down and back to front.

Centre of Symmetry

If a shape can be mapped onto itself under a central symmetry in a point, this point is called a **centre of symmetry**.

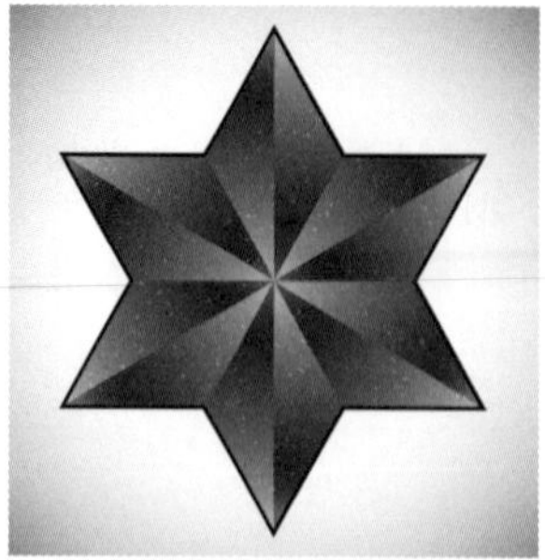

To check if an object has a **centre of symmetry**, we rotate the object around a fixed point exactly 180°. If the image lands exactly on the object, then the point used is a centre of symmetry.

Not all shapes have a centre of symmetry.

These shapes have a centre of symmetry. →

← These shapes do not have a centre of symmetry.

Axial Symmetry (in a Line)

An **axial symmetry** is a reflection in a line or axis. The line acts as a mirror. In an **axial symmetry**, each point is mapped through a line (axis) at right angles and reflected at right angles the same distance out the other side.

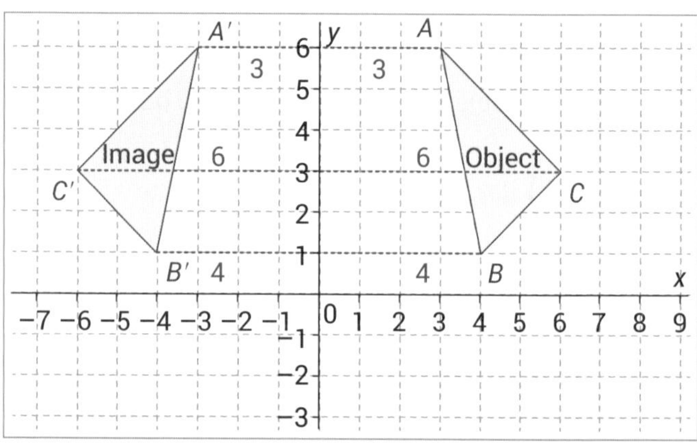

In the diagram, the object undergoes an **axial symmetry** in the y-axis. Note how each point in the image is the same distance (3, 6 and 4 units) away from the y-axis as each corresponding point in the object. The image is the same size as the object.

In an axial symmetry, each point is mapped through the line and reflected out the same distance on the other side.

In the diagram below $|AX| = |XA'|$, $|CY| = |YC'|$ and $|BZ| = |ZB'|$.

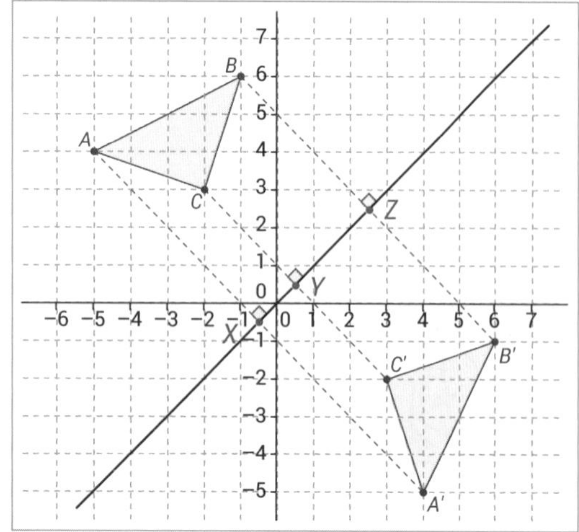

In an axial symmetry, the image and object are the same distance from the axis used, and one is a mirror image of the other.

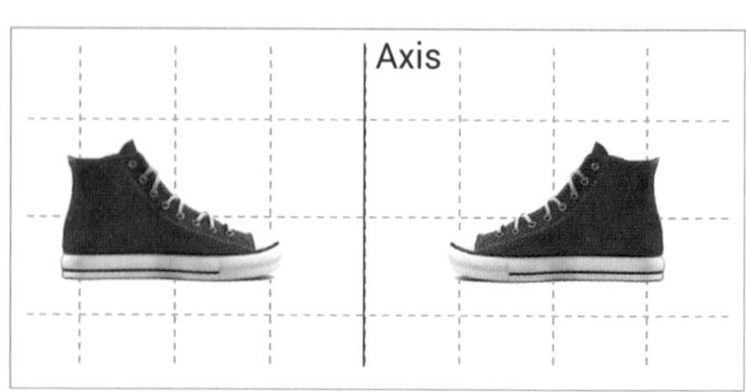

CONSTRUCTIONS, TRANSFORMATIONS AND ENLARGEMENTS

Rotations

Another type of transformation is a **rotation**.

The angle through which the shape rotates is called the angle of rotation.

> A rotation transforms a shape to a new position by turning it about a fixed point called the centre of rotation.

This is given either as an angle or as a fraction of a complete turn, for example, 270° or $\frac{3}{4}$ turn.

Rotations are assumed to be anti-clockwise. If we want to rotate an object in a clockwise direction through, say, 90°, we call this a rotation through −90°.

The fixed point about which the object is rotated is called the **point (centre) of rotation**.

Therefore, when describing the rotation of an object, we should include, if possible:

(i) The centre of rotation
(ii) The angle of rotation
(iii) The direction of rotation (positive or negative)

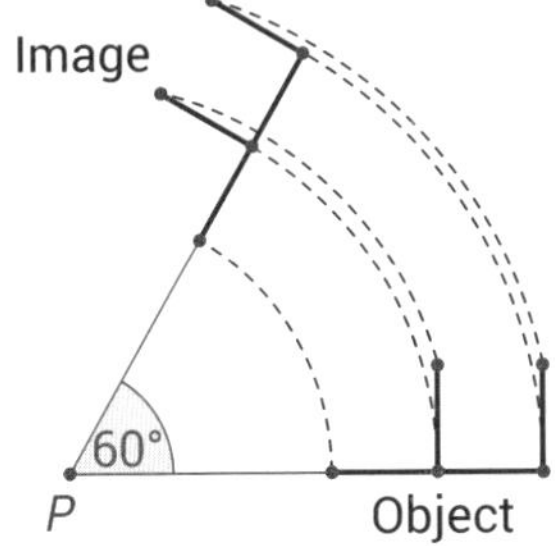

Every point on this object has been rotated anti-clockwise through an angle of 60° about the point *P*.

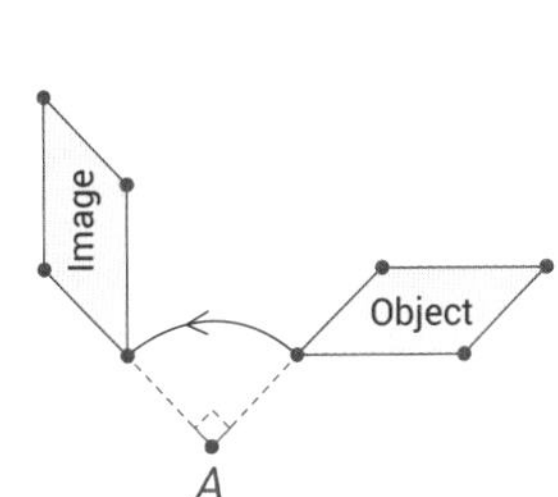

Positive (anti-clockwise) rotation of 90° about the point *A*. This is denoted as $R_{90°}$.

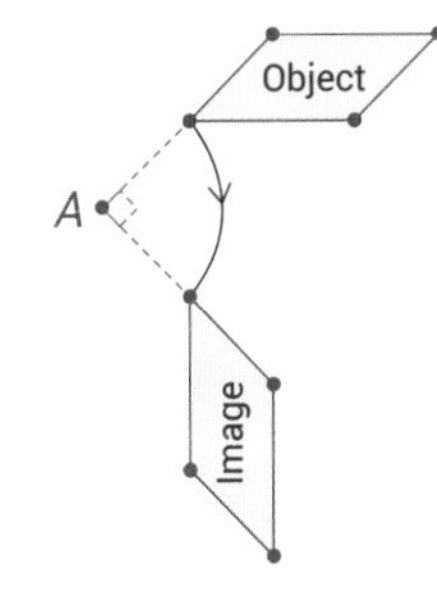

Negative (clockwise) rotation of 90° about the point *A*. This is denoted as $R_{-90°}$.

Worked Example 16.9

The following images are produced by a translation, an axial symmetry in the *x*-axis and a central symmetry in the origin. Match each image with the correct transformation.

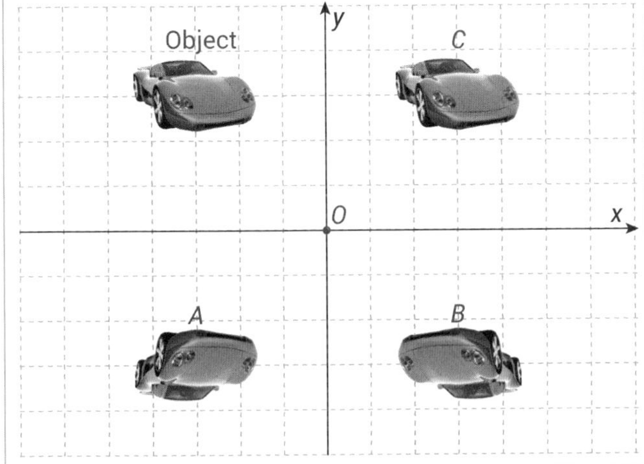

Solution

A: Axial symmetry in the *x*-axis (mirror image of the object)

B: Central symmetry (upside down and back to front, each point mapped through the point *O*)

C: Translation (facing in the same direction as the object, all points moved in a straight line, for the same distance)

Exercise 16.4

1. Identify in each diagram the image of the object under the translation $\overrightarrow{AB}$

(i)

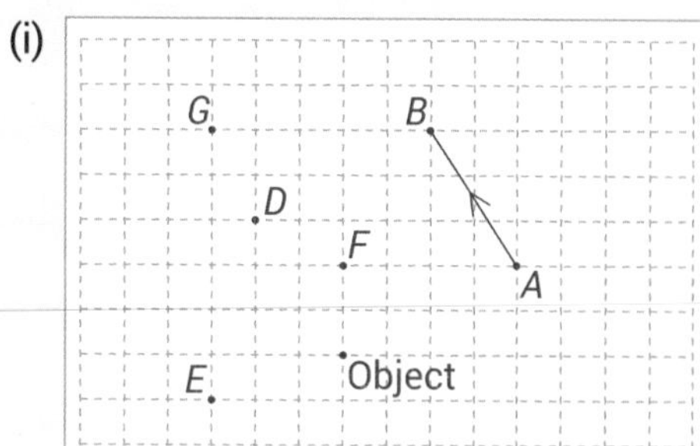

(ii)

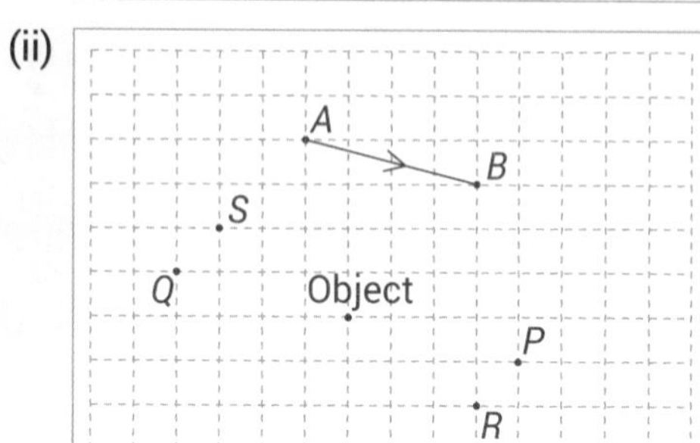

(iii)

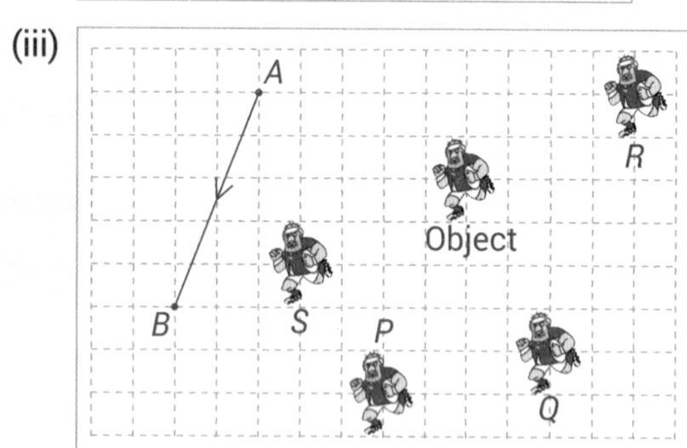

(iv)

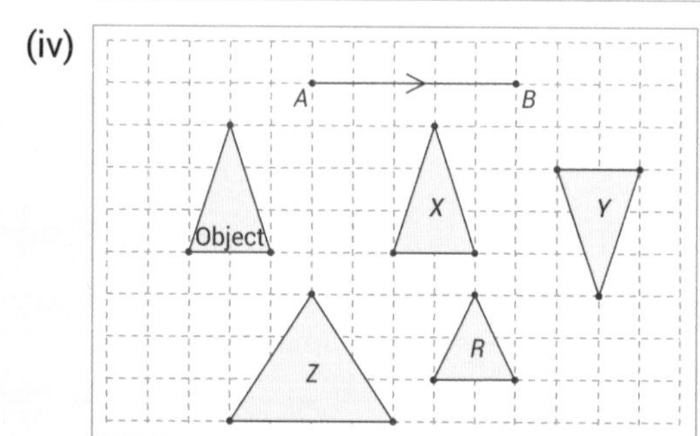

2. In each part identify the image of the pepper under a central symmetry in point O.

(i)

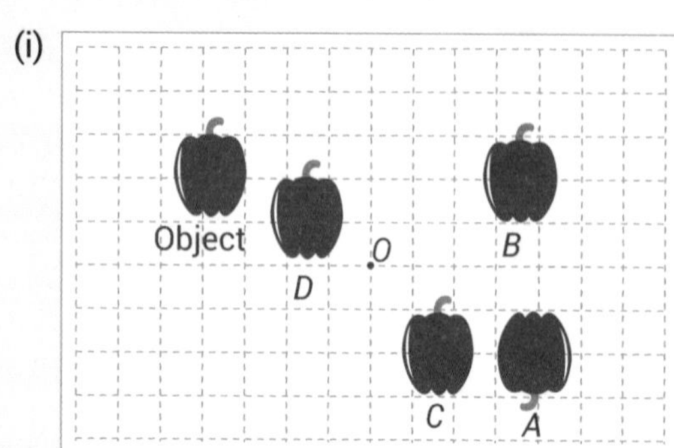

(ii)

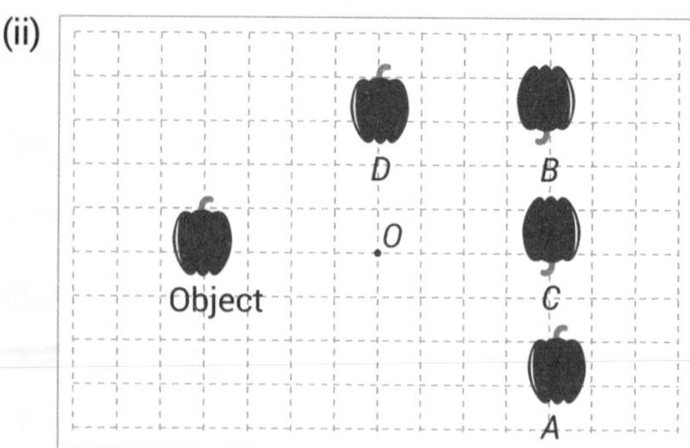

(iii)

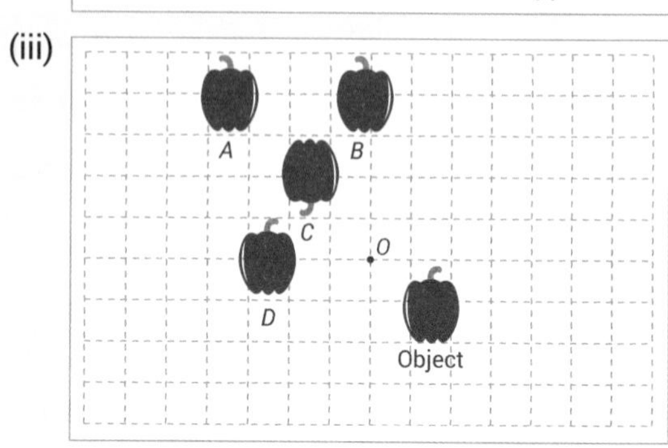

(iv)

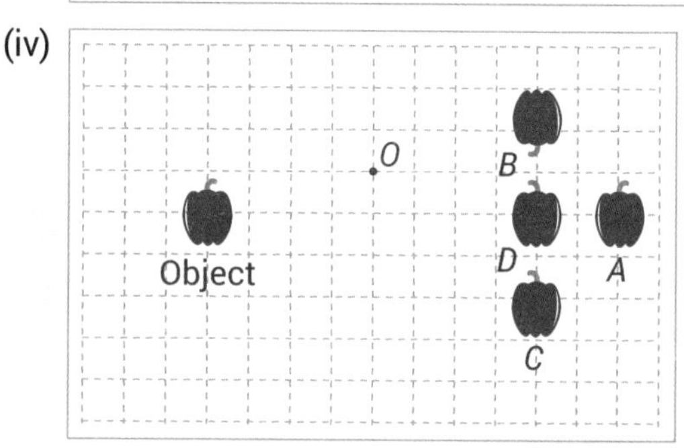

3. Identify in each diagram the image of the object under an axial symmetry in the named axis.

(i) Axial symmetry in the x-axis

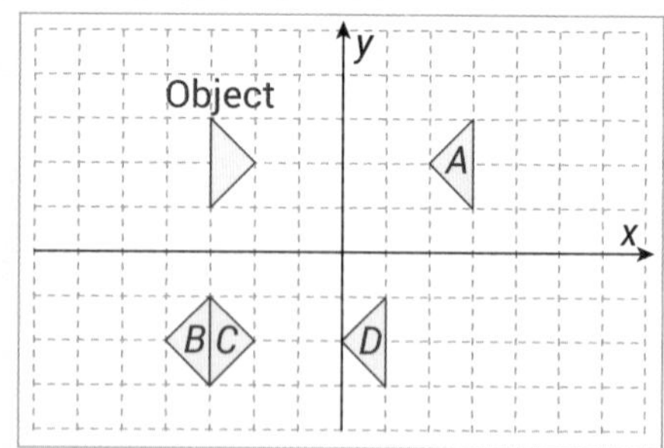

(ii) Axial symmetry in the x-axis

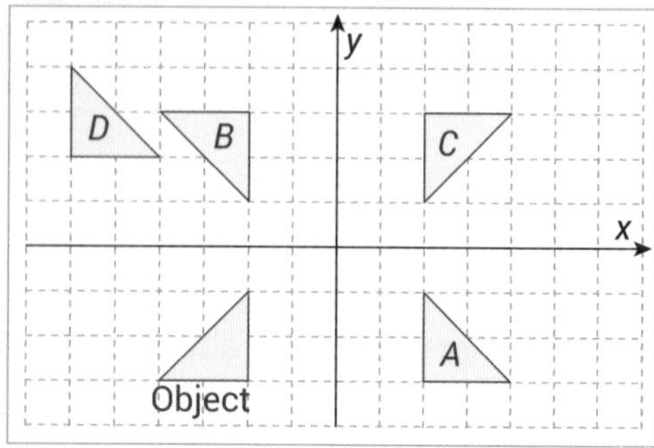

(iii) Axial symmetry in the y-axis

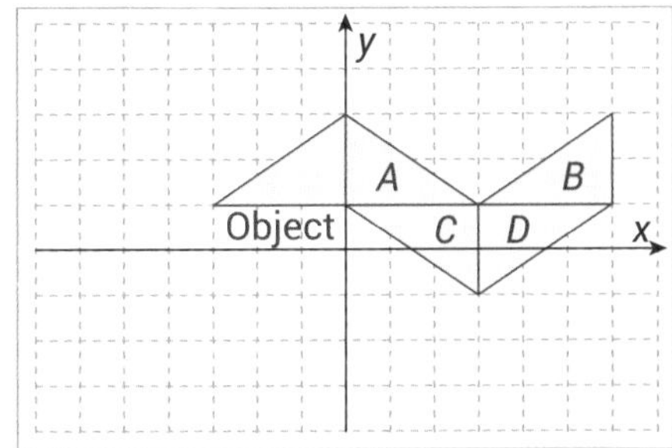

(iv) Axial symmetry in the y-axis

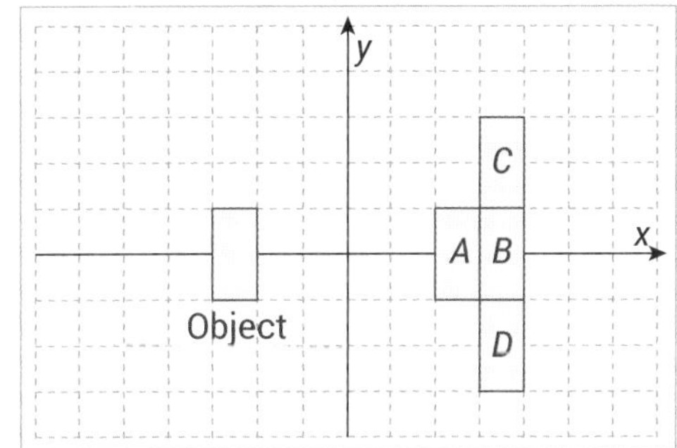

4. In each case, identify a rotation that maps:

(i) A onto B

(ii) C onto D

(iii) A onto D

(iv) A onto C

Make sure in your answer to include:

(a) The point of rotation

(b) The angle of rotation

(c) Whether the rotation is positive or negative

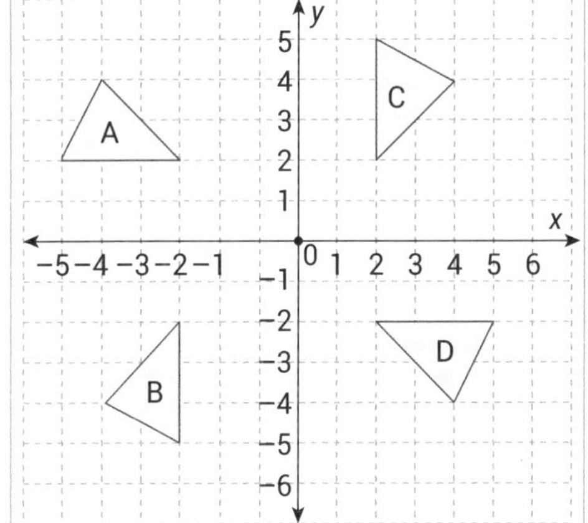

5. In each question below, three images labelled A, B and C are the images of the object under a transformation. The transformation could be a translation, an axial symmetry, a central symmetry or a rotation. For each image, state which transformation is used, and in the case of a rotation, state the angle and direction.

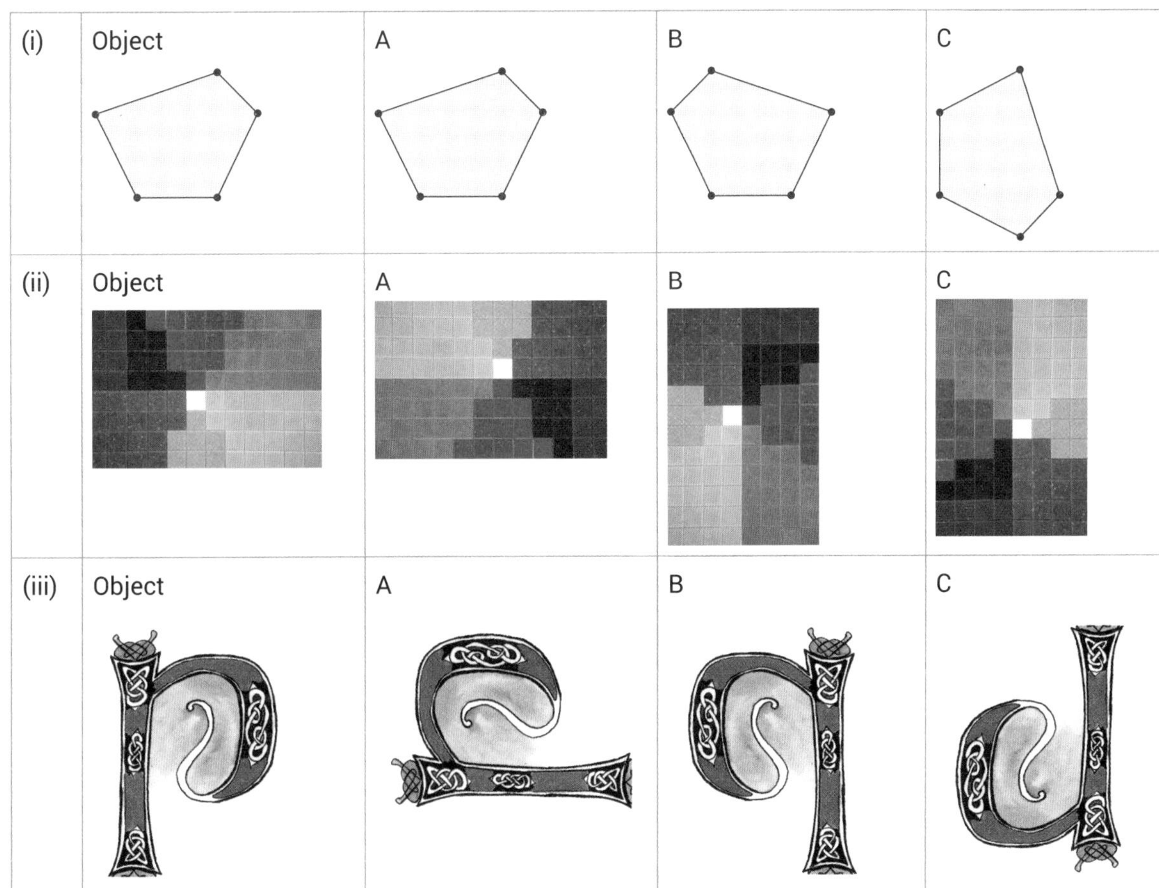

6. The diagram below shows the triangle ABC on the co-ordinate plane.

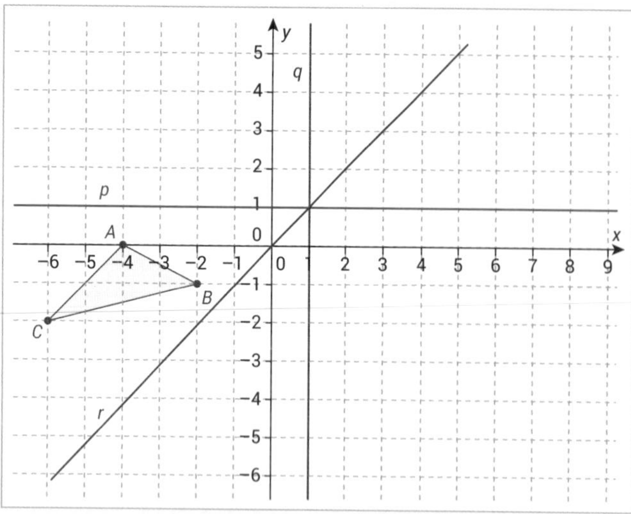

(a) Copy this diagram and draw the image of triangle ABC under a number of transformations.

(i) Axial symmetry in the line q

(ii) Axial symmetry in the line p

(iii) Axial symmetry in the line r

(b) Hence, write down the co-ordinates of the images of the vertices of the triangle ABC under each of the transformations.

Transformation	Co-ordinates of vertices
Axial symmetry in the line q	
Axial symmetry in the line p	
Axial symmetry in the line r	

16.5 Enlargements

We see many examples of **enlargements** in the modern world.

An **enlargement** is a transformation in which both the size and the position of a shape changes.

In geometry, when we enlarge a figure we need to know two things:

- The **centre of enlargement**
- The **scale factor**, k

The **centre of enlargement** is the point from which the enlargement is constructed.

The **scale factor**, k, is the number by which the object is enlarged.

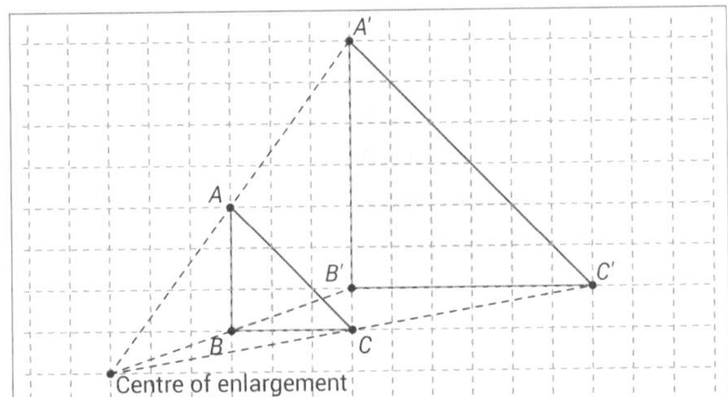

If we enlarge a shape by a scale factor of k, then each side of the image will be k times the length of the corresponding side of the object.

A scale factor of 2 means that the length of each image side will be twice the length of the corresponding object side.

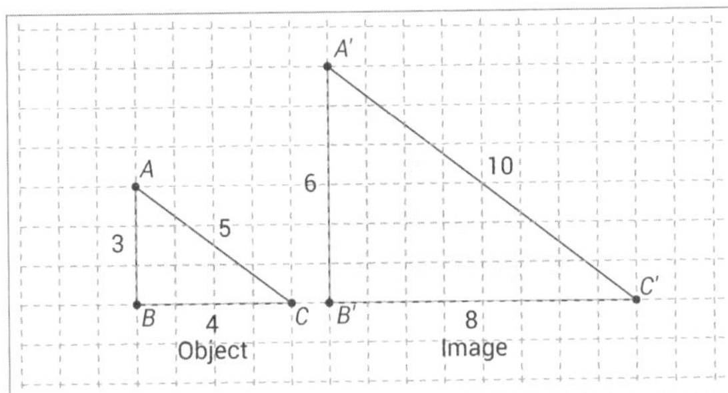

Any scale factor k which is greater than 1 will result in the image being bigger than the object.

A scale factor of $\frac{1}{2}$ means that the length of each image side will be $\frac{1}{2}$ the length of the corresponding object side.

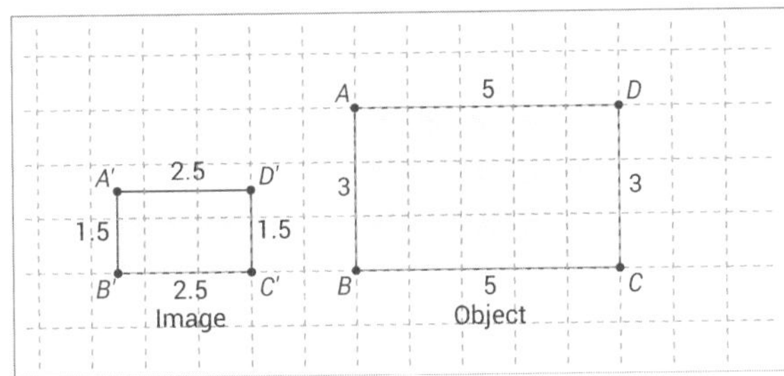

Any scale factor that is greater than 0 and less than 1 will result in the image being smaller than the object. This is still described as an enlargement.

If the scale factor is k, then:

(i) If $k > 1$, the figure is enlarged. (ii) If $0 < k < 1$, the figure is reduced.

Worked Example 16.10

Enlarge the triangle ABC by a scale factor of 3, with a centre of enlargement O.

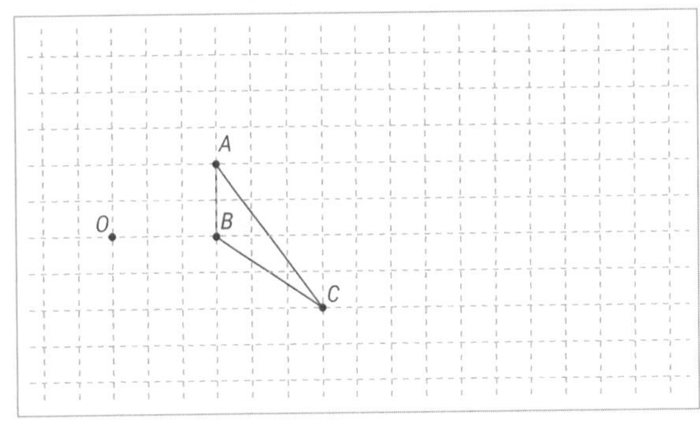

Solution

1 Draw rays from O, the centre of enlargement, though each of the vertices of the object shape.

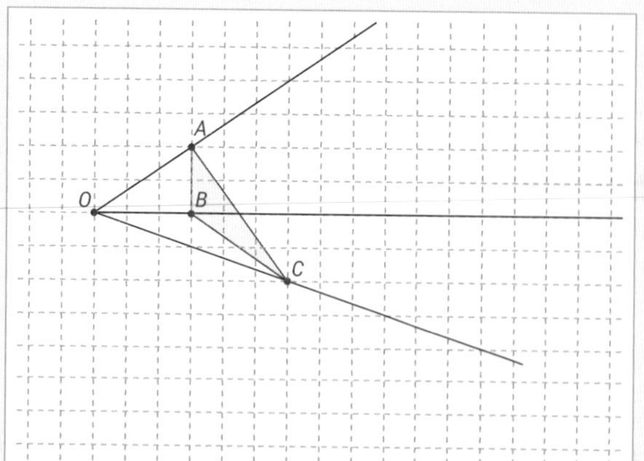

2 Using a ruler, measure the distance $|OA|$.

$|OA| = 1.4$ cm

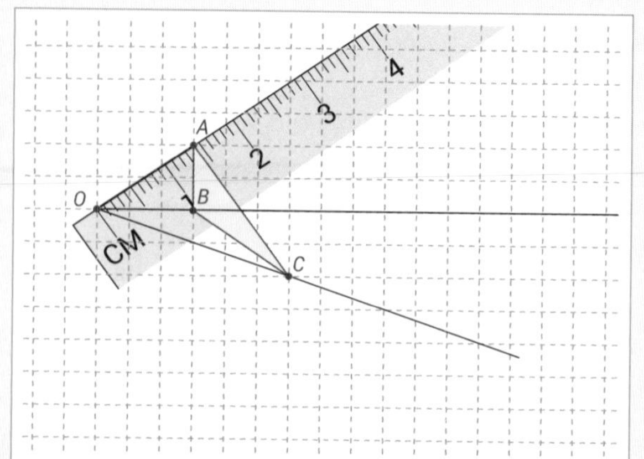

3 Using your ruler, mark off a new point A' such that $|OA'|$ is 3 times the distance $|OA|$.

$|OA'| = 3|OA|$

$= 1.4 \times 3$ Show your workings.

$|OA'| = 4.2$ cm

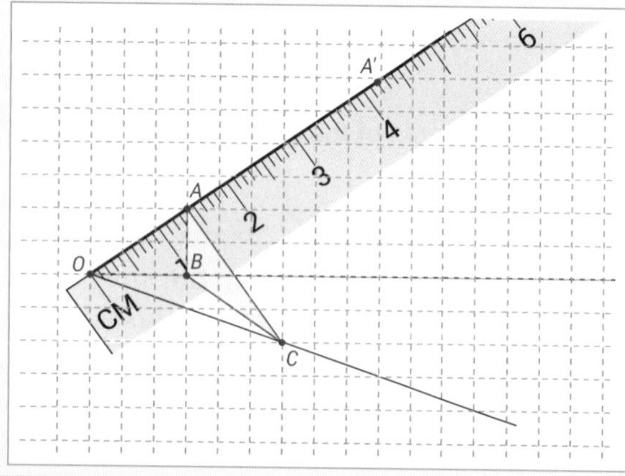

4 Measure $|OB|$.

Using a ruler, mark off a new point B' such that $|OB'|$ is 3 times the distance $|OB|$.

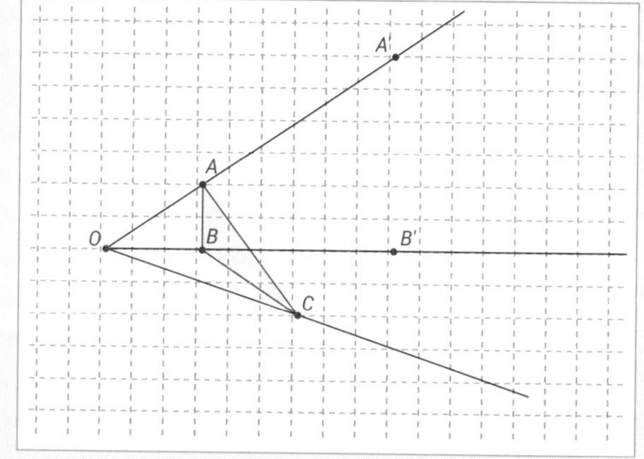

5 Measure $|OC|$.

Using a ruler, mark off a new point C' such that $|OC'|$ is 3 times the distance $|OC|$.

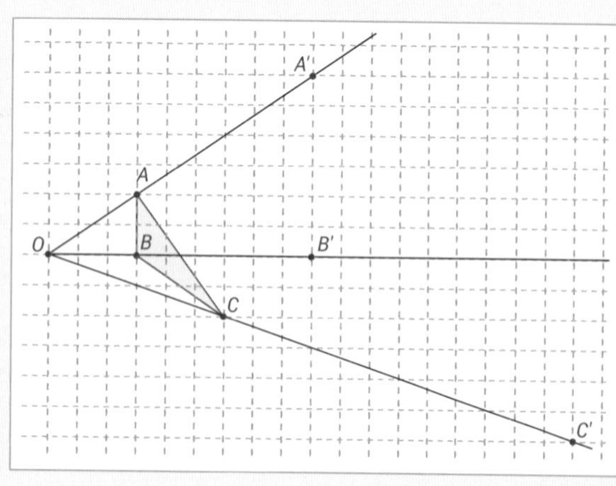

6 Draw the triangle $A'B'C'$.

The triangle $A'B'C'$ is the image of the triangle ABC under the required enlargement.

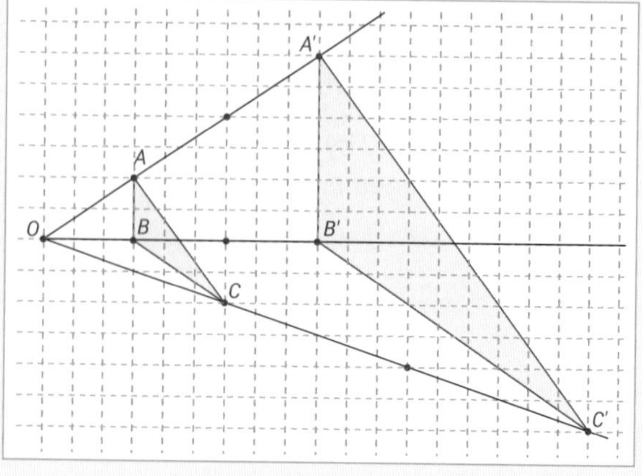

In cases where the scale factor of enlargement is a natural number (such as 2, 3, 4, etc.) it is possible to use a compass and straight edge to locate the image points.

Worked Example 16.11

Enlarge the triangle *ABC* by a scale factor of 3, with a centre of enlargement *O*.

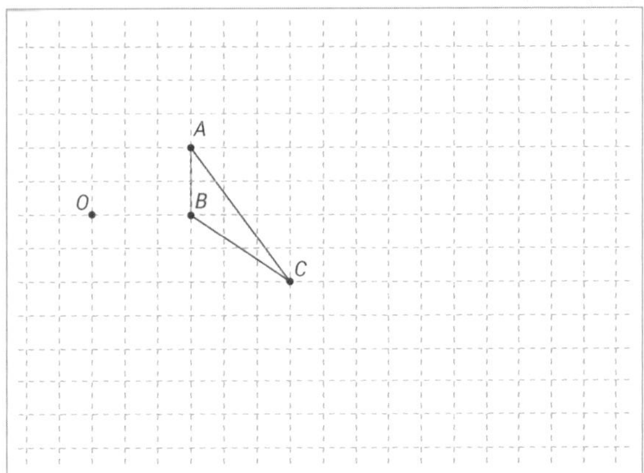

Solution

1 Draw rays from *O* though each of the vertices of the shape.

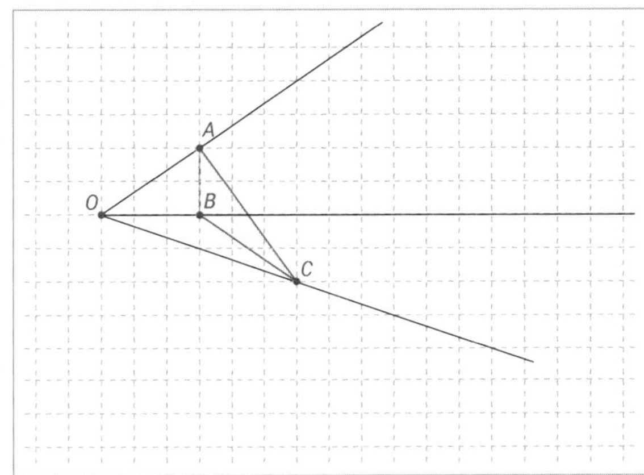

2 Using a compass, measure the distance |*OA*|.

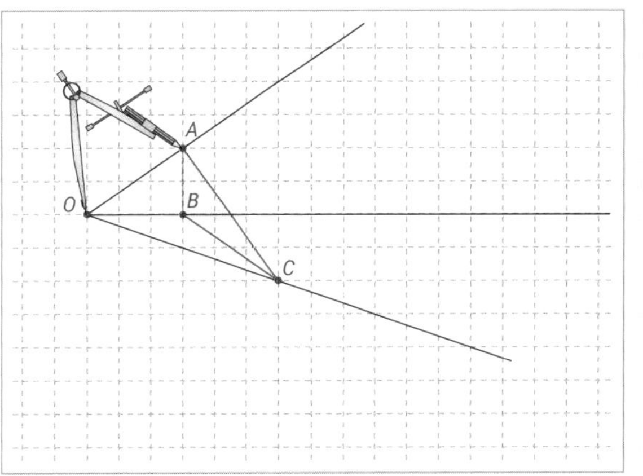

3 Mark off a new point *A*′ such that |*OA*′| = 3|*OA*|.

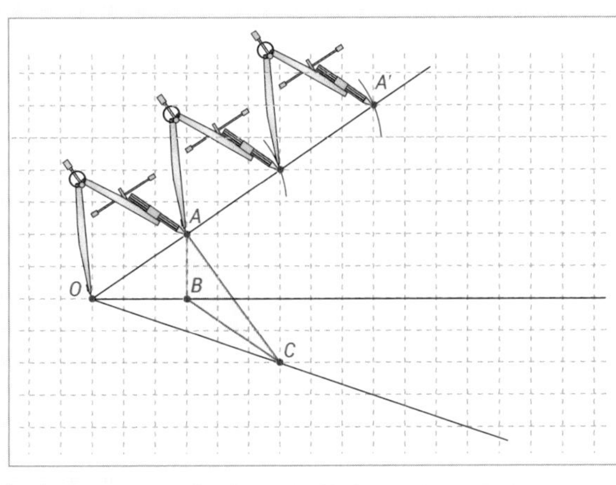

4 Using a compass, find |*OB*|. Mark off a new point *B*′ such that |*OB*′| = 3|*OB*|.

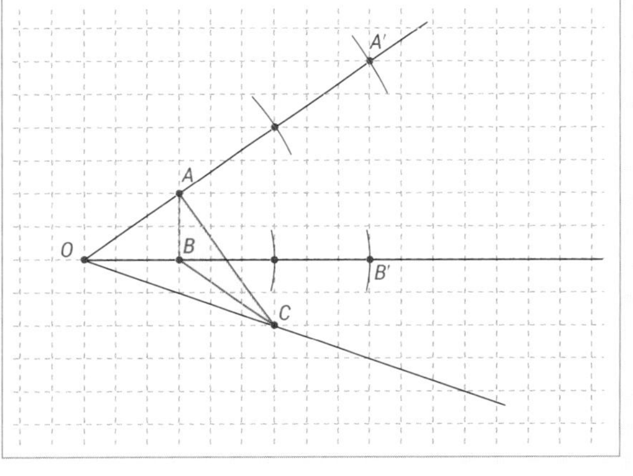

5 Using a compass, find $|OC|$. Mark off a new point C' such that $|OC'| = 3|OC|$.

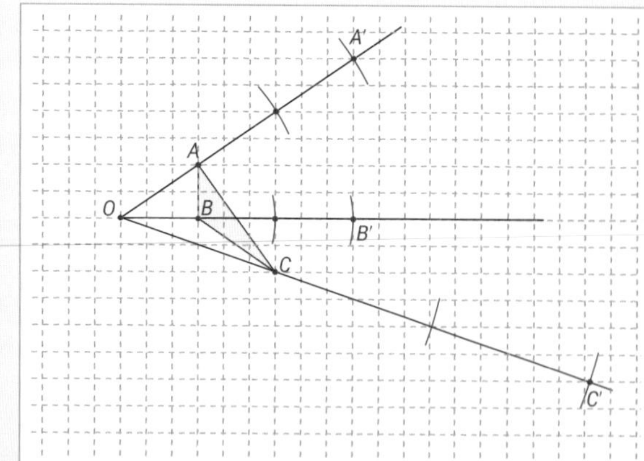

6 Draw the triangle $A'B'C'$.

The triangle $A'B'C'$ is the image of the triangle ABC under the required enlargement.

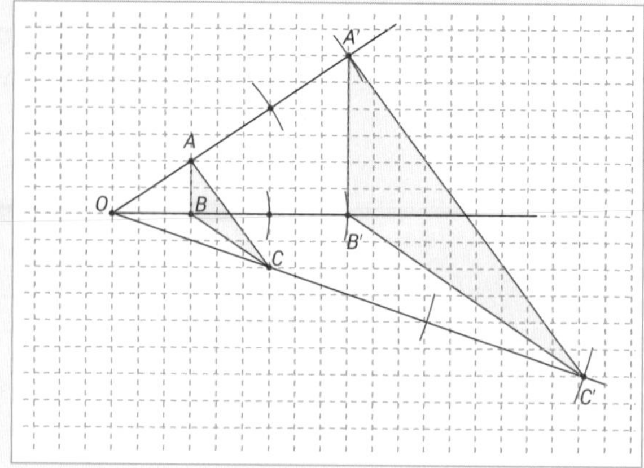

Worked Example 16.12

Enlarge the rectangle $PQRS$ by a scale factor of $\frac{1}{2}$ with a centre of enlargement O.

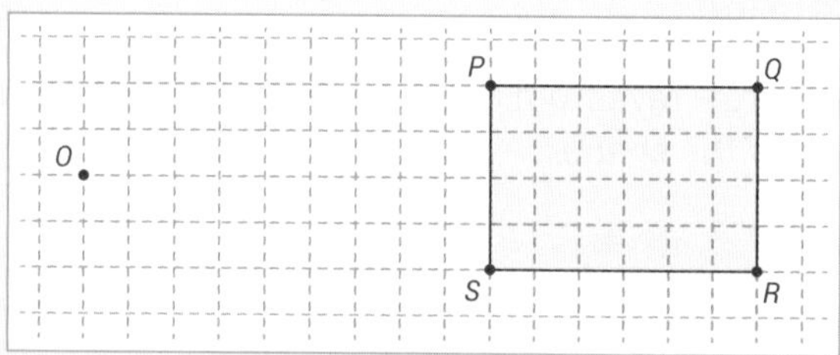

Solution

1 Draw rays from O though each of the vertices of the shape.

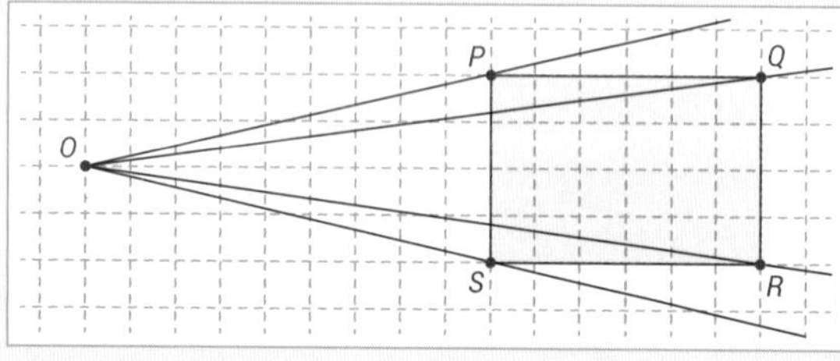

2 Using a compass or ruler, measure the distance $|OP|$.

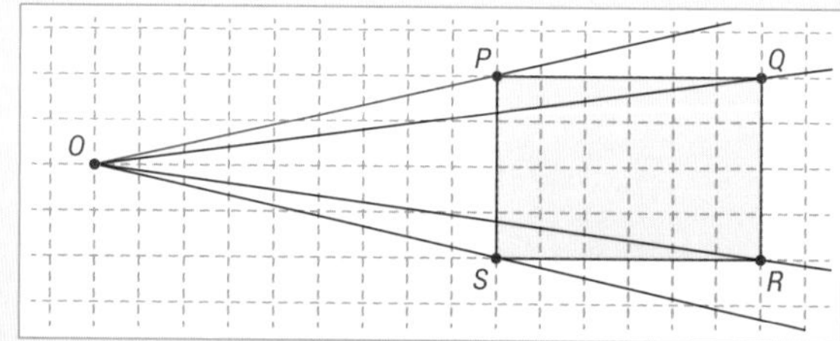

3 Mark off a new point P' such that $|OP'| = \frac{1}{2}|OP|$.

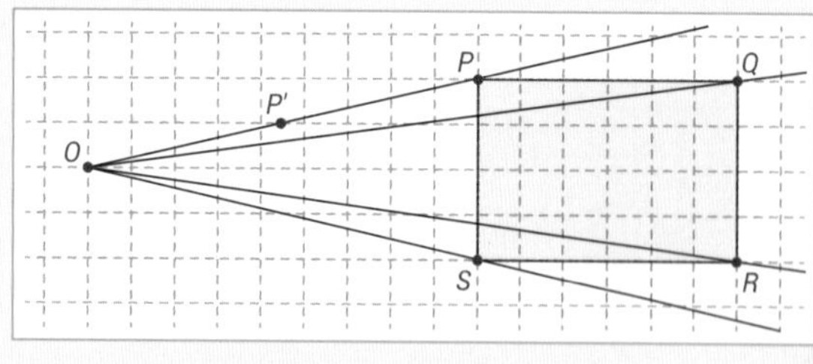

4 Repeat for the other vertices Q, R and S.

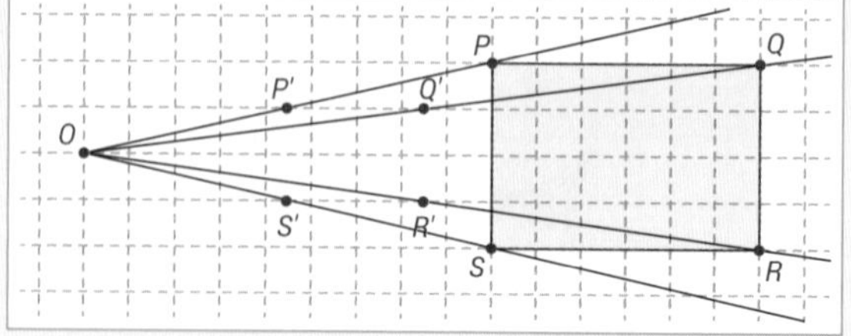

5 Draw the rectangle $P'Q'R'S'$.

The rectangle $P'Q'R'S'$ is the image of the rectangle $PQRS$ under the required enlargement.

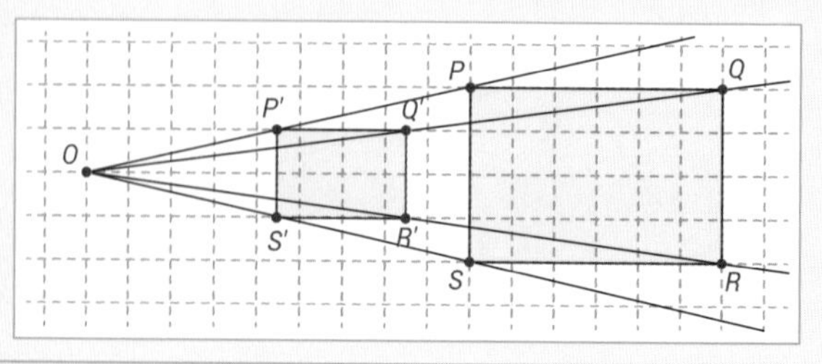

We sometimes encounter enlargements where the centre of enlargement is a point either on or inside the object.

Worked Example 16.13

Enlarge the triangle ABC by a scale factor of 2 with a centre of enlargement A.

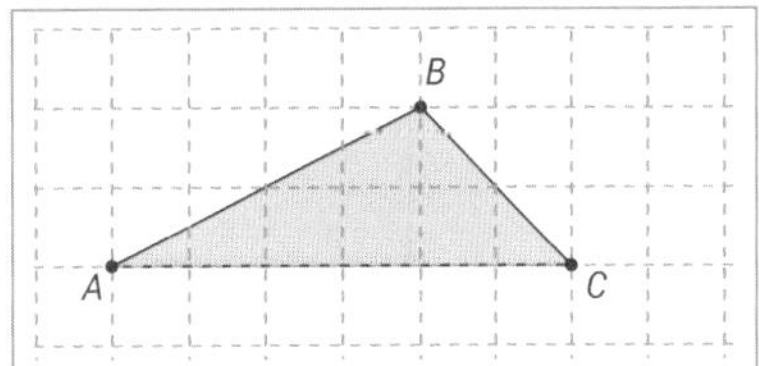

Solution

1 Draw rays from A through each of the remaining vertices.

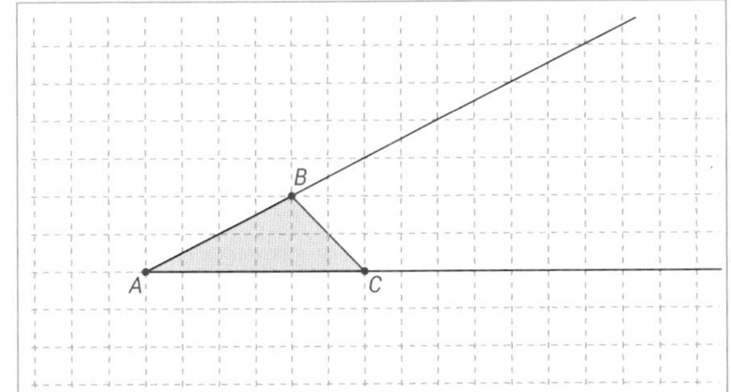

2 Using a compass or ruler, find $|AB|$.

Mark off a new point B' such that $|AB'| = 2|AB|$.

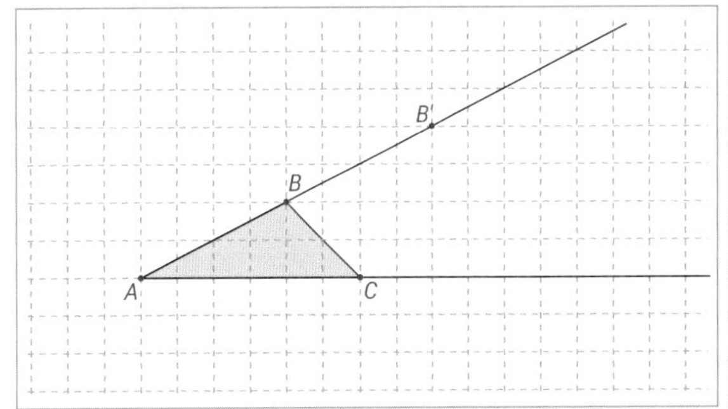

3 Find $|AC|$.

Mark off a new point C' such that $|AC'| = 2|AC|$.

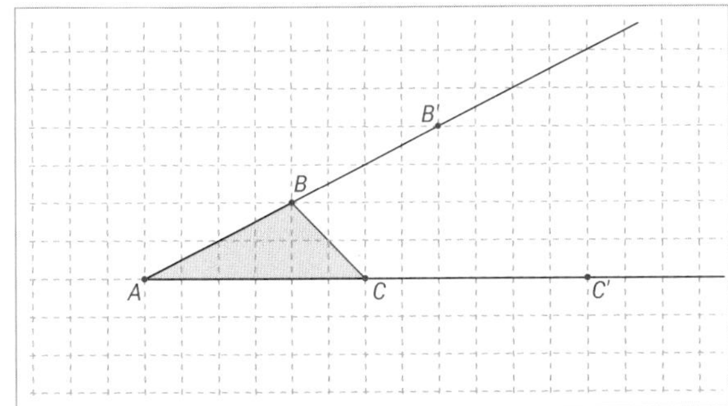

4 Draw the triangle $AB'C'$.

The triangle $AB'C'$ is the image of the triangle ABC under the required enlargement.

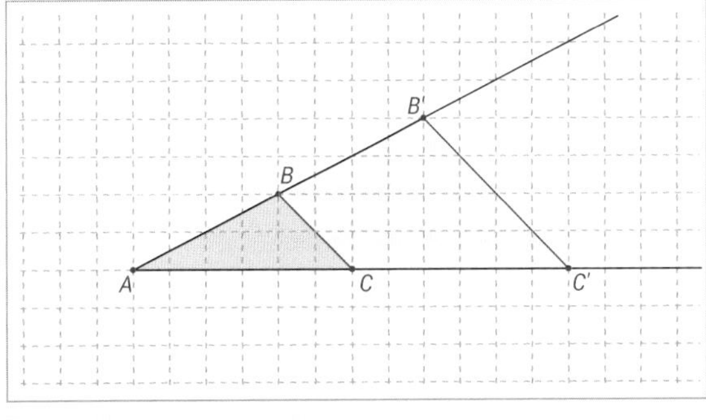

CONSTRUCTIONS, TRANSFORMATIONS AND ENLARGEMENTS

Exercise 16.5

1. Copy the following diagrams onto graph paper and show the image of each of the shapes under an enlargement with a scale factor of 2 and centre O:

(i)

(ii)

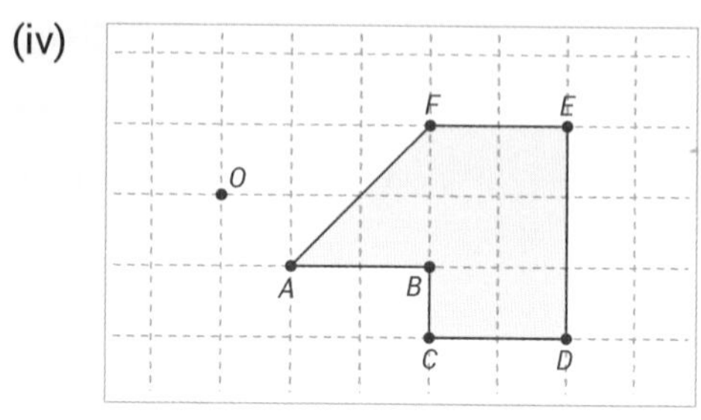

(iii)

(iv)

2. Copy the following diagrams onto graph paper, and show the image of each of the shapes under an enlargement with a scale factor of $\frac{1}{2}$ and centre P:

(i)

(ii)

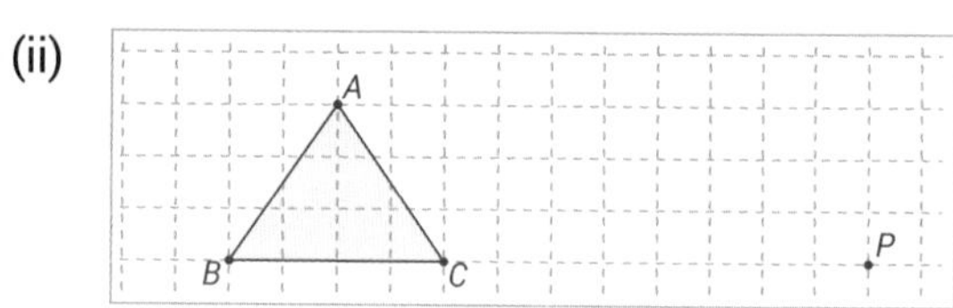

(iii)

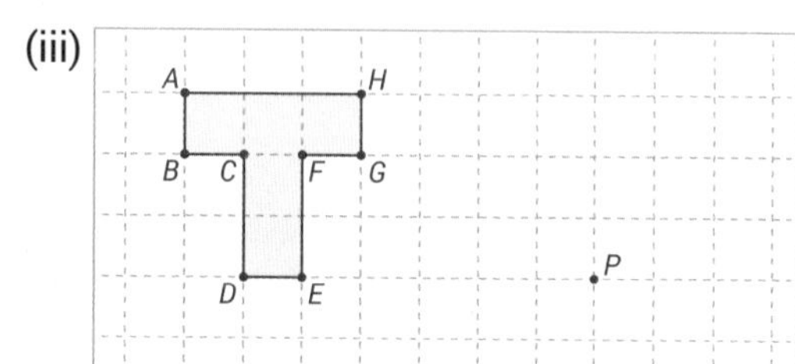

(iv)

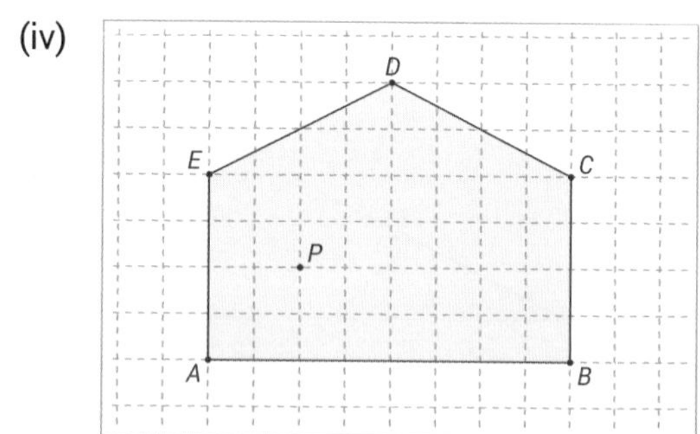

3. Copy the following diagrams onto graph paper, and show the image of each of the shapes under an enlargement with a scale factor of 1.5 and centre A:

(i)

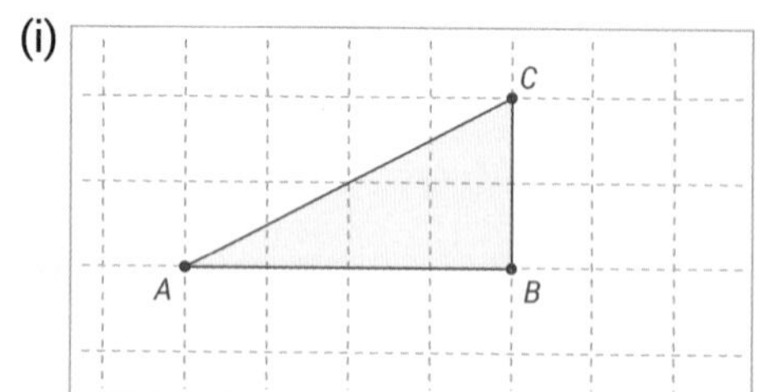

(ii)

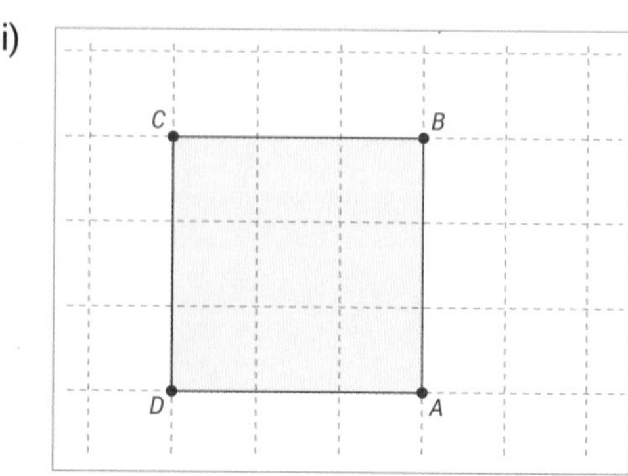

4. Copy the following diagrams onto graph paper, and show the image of each of the shapes under an enlargement with a scale factor of $\frac{1}{3}$ and centre Q:

(i)

(ii)

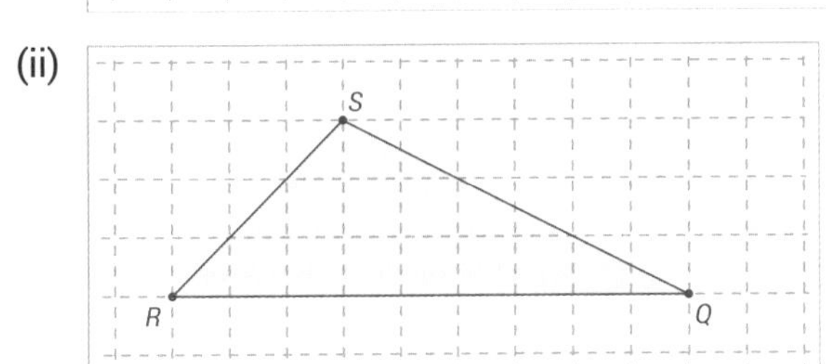

(iii)

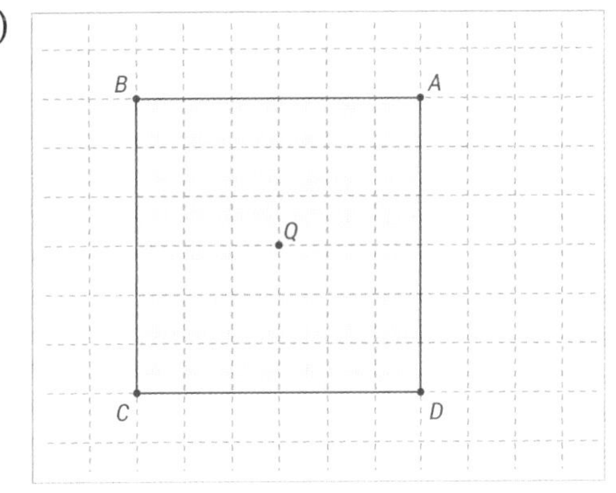

16.6 Properties of Enlargements

Now that we have explored how enlargements are constructed, we can investigate the various properties of enlargements.

From our investigations, we can determine the following characteristics of enlargements.

Similarity

Under an enlargement, **the object and image are similar to each other**.

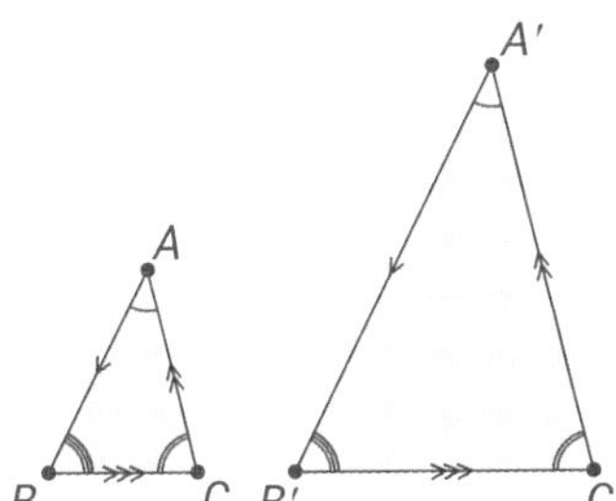

$|\angle ABC| = |\angle A'B'C'|$

$|\angle ACB| = |\angle A'C'B'|$

$|\angle BAC| = |\angle B'A'C'|$

$AB \parallel A'B'$

$AC \parallel A'C'$

$BC \parallel B'C'$

The corresponding sides of the object and image are in the same ratio:

$$\frac{|AB|}{|A'B'|} = \frac{|AC|}{|A'C'|} = \frac{|BC|}{|B'C'|}$$

OR

$$\frac{|A'B'|}{|AB|} = \frac{|A'C'|}{|AC|} = \frac{|B'C'|}{|BC|}$$

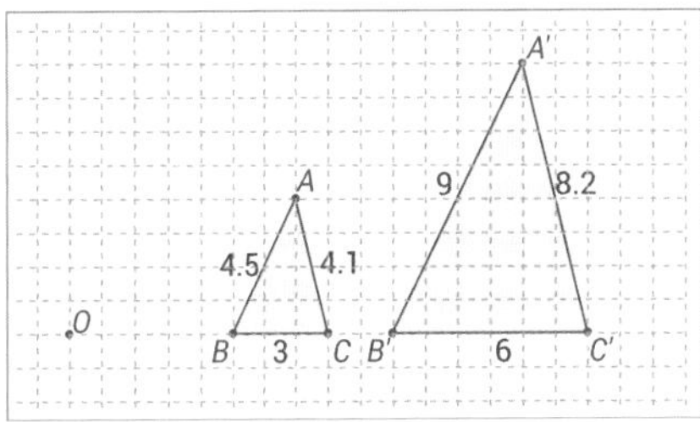

In this case:

$$\frac{|AB|}{|A'B'|} = \frac{4.5}{9} = \frac{1}{2} \qquad \frac{|AC|}{|A'C'|} = \frac{4.1}{8.2} = \frac{1}{2} \qquad \frac{|BC|}{|B'C'|} = \frac{3}{6} = \frac{1}{2}$$

We have encountered similar triangles and their properties in Chapter 15.

Find the Centre of Enlargement

To find the centre of enlargement, often labelled as the point O, we draw lines through the corresponding vertices of the object and image. The point where these lines intersect is called the **centre of enlargement**.

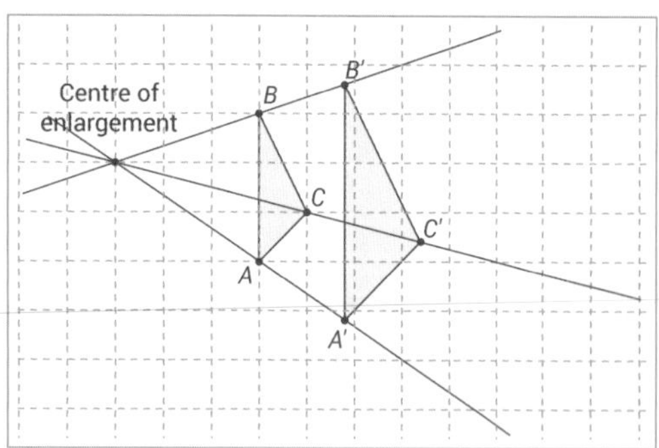

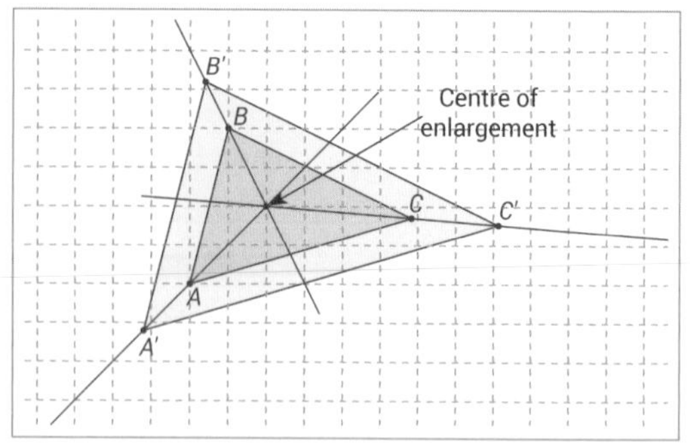

We need to connect only two pairs of corresponding vertices to find the centre of enlargement.

Find the Scale Factor

To find the scale factor, we measure the length of a side of the image and the length of the corresponding side of the object.

$$\text{Scale factor } (k) = \frac{\text{Image length}}{\text{Object length}}$$

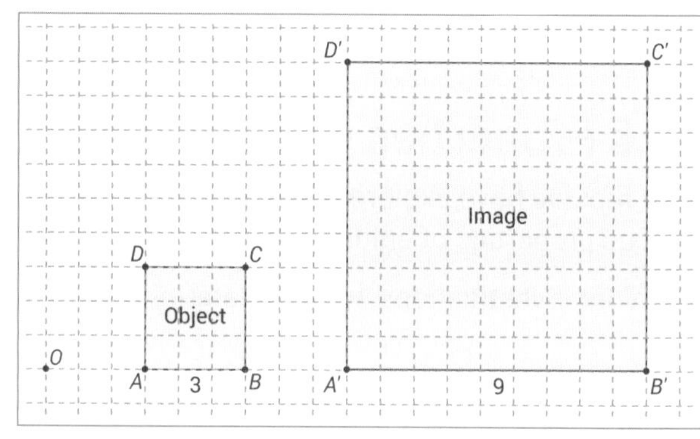

It is important to remember that it is **Image length ÷ Object length** that will give us the scale factor.

In this example:

Scale factor $k = \frac{9}{3}$

$\therefore k = 3$

Scale Factor and Area

If an object is enlarged by a scale factor of k, then the area of the image will be increased by a factor of k^2.

$$\text{Image area} = k^2 \times (\text{Object area}) \quad \textbf{OR} \quad \frac{\text{Image area}}{\text{Object area}} = k^2$$

Consider the following example where $ABCD$ is a rectangle and $k = 2$.

Area of object $= 6 \times 4 = 24$

Image area $= k^2 \times$ Object area

$= 2^2 \times 24$

$= 4 \times 24$

$= 96$ units^2

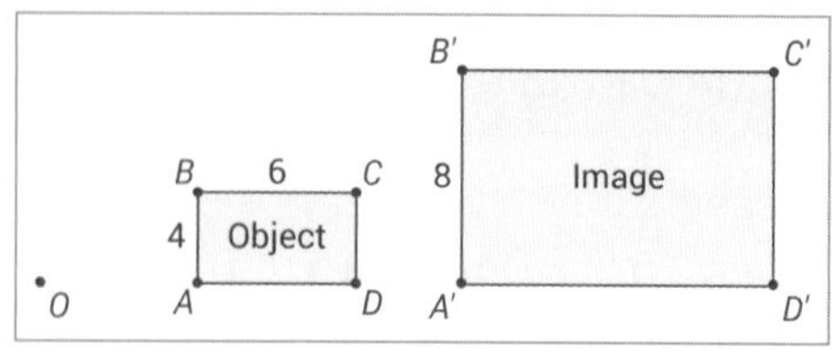

CONSTRUCTIONS, TRANSFORMATIONS AND ENLARGEMENTS

Worked Example 16.14

ΔABC is the image of ΔPQR under an enlargement of scale factor k and centre O.

(i) Find the value of k.

(ii) Find the length of $[AB]$.

(iii) Find the length of $[QR]$.

(iv) The area of ΔABC is 10 square units; find, correct to one decimal place, the area of ΔPQR.

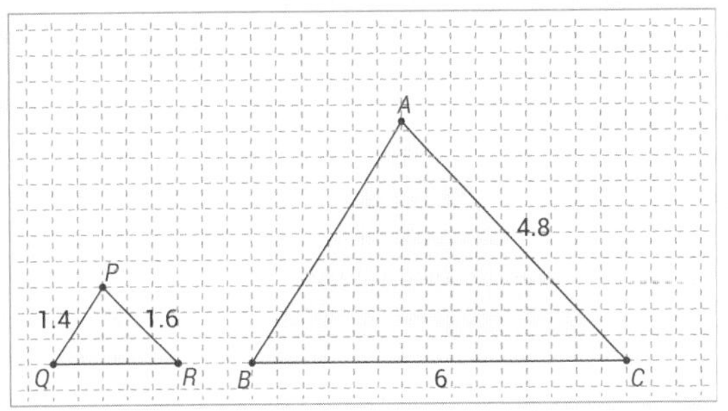

Solution

(i) $k = \frac{\text{Image length}}{\text{Object length}} = \frac{4.8}{1.6} = 3$

(ii) $k = 3$

$\therefore |AB| = 3 \times |PQ|$

$|AB| = 3 \times 1.4$

$|AB| = 4.2$ units

We could also have used the properties of similar triangles to find $|AB|$:

$\frac{|AB|}{|PQ|} = \frac{|AC|}{|PR|}$

$\frac{|AB|}{1.4} = \frac{4.8}{1.6} \Rightarrow \frac{|AB|}{1.4} = \frac{3}{1}$

$|AB| = 3 \times 1.4$

$|AB| = 4.2$ units

(iii) $k = 3$

$\therefore |BC| = 3 \times |QR|$

$\Rightarrow |QR| = \frac{|BC|}{3}$

$|QR| = \frac{6}{2}$

$\therefore |QR| = 2$ units

We are going from image to object here, so the scale factor is reversed.

Again, we could have used the properties of similar triangles to find $|QR|$:

$\frac{|QR|}{6} = \frac{1.6}{4.8}$

$\frac{|QR|}{6} = \frac{1}{3}$

$3|QR| = 6$

$|QR| = 2$ units

(iv) We remember that $\frac{\text{Image area}}{\text{Object area}} = k^2$, and let the area of $\Delta PQR = x$.

$\Rightarrow \frac{10}{x} = 3^2$

$\frac{10}{x} = 9$

$9x = 10$

$x = 1.1$ square units, to one decimal place

Exercise 16.6

1. Consider the following diagrams.

(a)

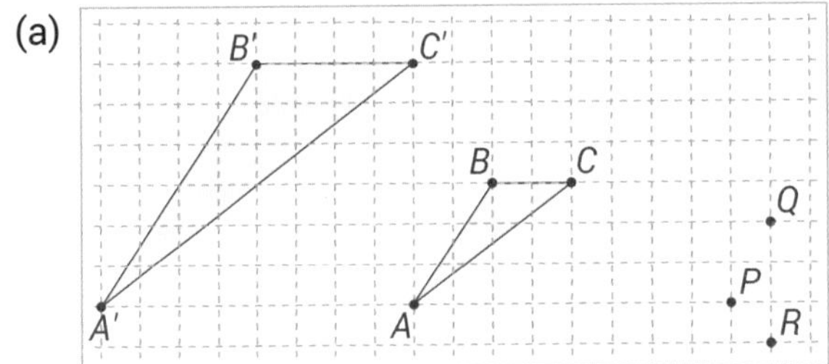

(b)

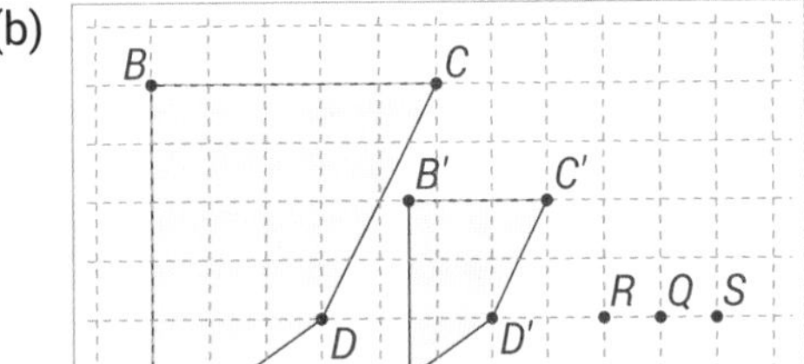

(i) Identify which point is the centre of enlargement.

(ii) Find the scale factor.

2. Copy the following diagram onto graph paper. $\Delta A'B'C'$ is an enlargement of ΔABC.

   (i) Find the centre of enlargement.

   (ii) Find the scale factor.

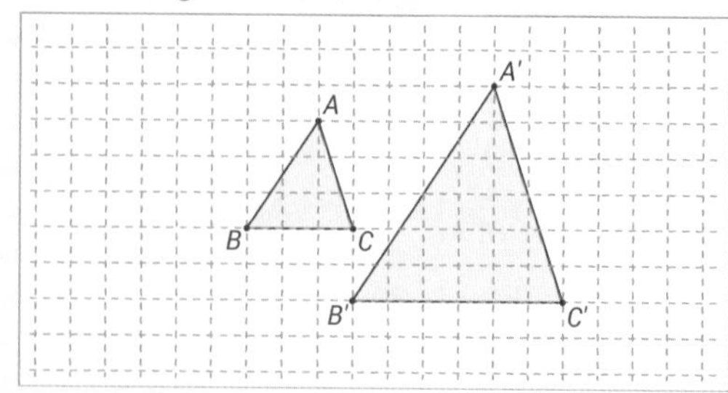

3. Copy this diagram of two rectangles onto graph paper. $A'B'C'D'$ is the image of the rectangle $ABCD$ under an enlargement.

   (i) Find the centre of enlargement.

   (ii) Find the scale factor, k.

   (iii) Show that the ratio
   Area of $A'B'C'D'$: Area of $ABCD = k^2 : 1$.

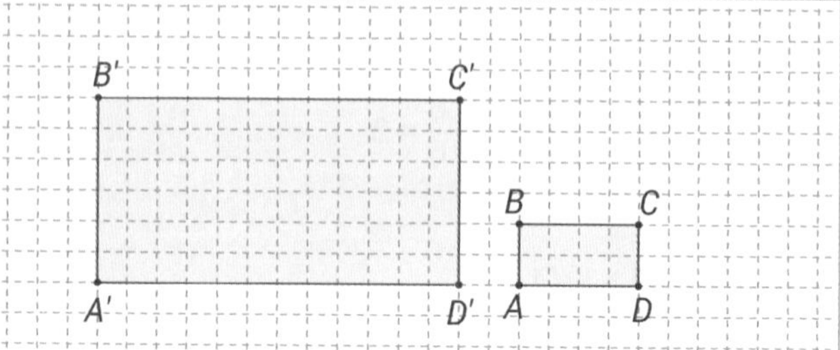

4. The regular pentagon $A'B'C'D'E'$ is the image of the polygon $ABCDE$ under an enlargement with a scale factor of 2.5 and with centre F.

   (i) If $|AB| = 2$ cm, find $|A'B'|$.

   (ii) If the area of the pentagon $ABCDE$ is 6.88 cm^2, find the area of the image $A'B'C'D'E'$.

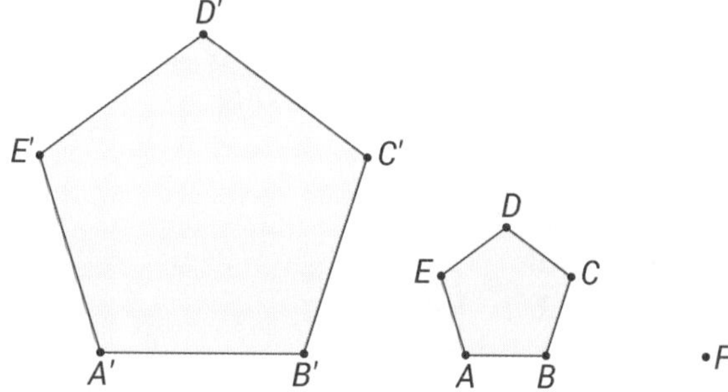

5. $O(0,0)$, $A(0,1)$, $B(2,0)$ are the vertices of ΔOAB.
   $P(-7,-1)$, $Q(-7,2)$, $R(-1,-1)$ are the vertices of ΔPQR.

   (i) Show these two triangles on the x–y co-ordinate plane.

   (ii) If ΔPQR is the image of ΔOAB under an enlargement, with centre C and of scale factor k, find the co-ordinates of C and the value of k.

6. The trapezoid $A'B'C'D'$ is the image of the trapezoid $ABCD$ under an enlargement.
   The scale of the graph paper is 1 square has an area of 4 cm^2.

   (i) Find the centre of enlargement.

   (ii) Find the scale factor.

   (iii) Find the ratio
   Area $ABCD$: Area $A'B'C'D'$.

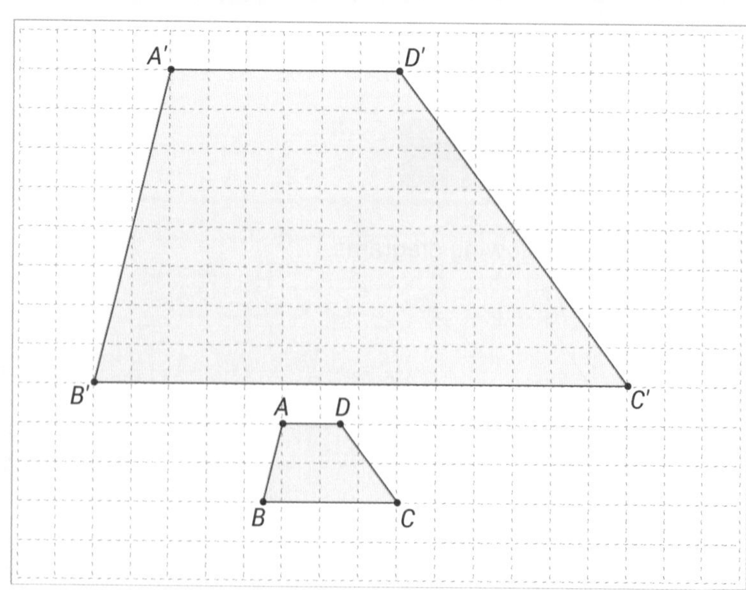

CONSTRUCTIONS, TRANSFORMATIONS AND ENLARGEMENTS

7. The rectangle $P'Q'R'S$ is an enlargement of the rectangle $PQRS$.

$|RS| = 5$ cm, $|PS| = 8$ cm and $|Q'P'| = 15$ cm.

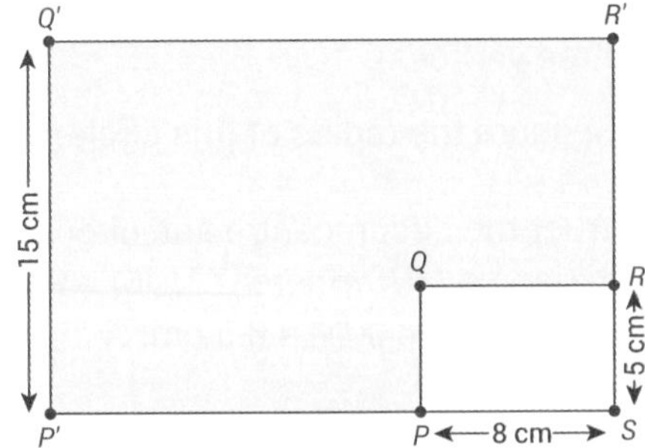

(i) Find the centre of enlargement.

(ii) Find the scale factor.

(iii) Find $|Q'R'|$.

(iv) Find $|PP'|$.

(v) Find the area of the region coloured yellow.

8. The cylinder shown is the image of a cylinder under an enlargement of scale factor 5.

If the surface area of the image is 50 cm^2, find the surface area of the object.

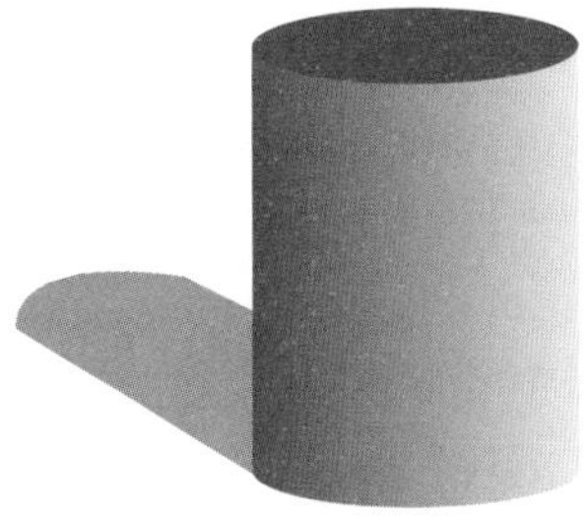

9. ΔPQR is an enlargement of ΔXYR.
Both triangles are right-angled, as shown.

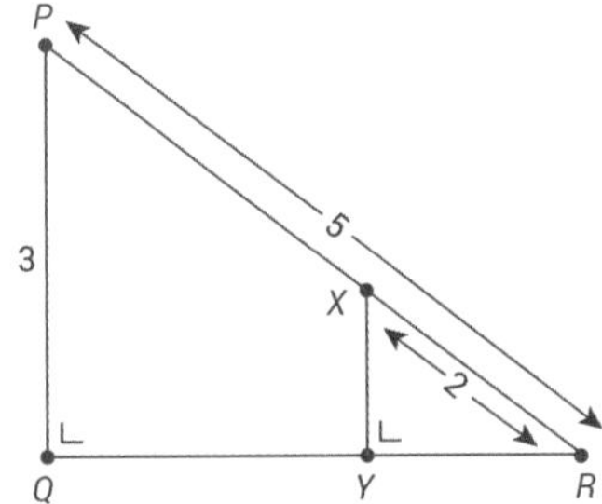

(i) Name the centre of enlargement.

(ii) Write down the value of k, the scale factor.

(iii) Find $|QR|$.

(iv) Find $|XY|$ and $|YR|$.

(v) Calculate the ratio Area ΔPQR : Area ΔXYR.

10. (i) Construct an equilateral triangle MNO of side 6 cm.

(ii) Construct the image of the triangle MNO under the enlargement of scale factor 1.75 and centre O.

(iii) Given that the area of the triangle MNO is $9\sqrt{3}$ cm^2, find the area of the image (of the triangle) to the nearest whole number.

11. The right-angled triangle ABC is the image of the triangle DEC under the enlargement of centre C and scale factor k.

A, D, 16.8, 18.2, B, 2, E, C

Find:

(i) $|EC|$

(ii) The scale factor, k

(iii) $|DE|$

(iv) The area of the triangle DEC

(v) The area of the figure $ADEB$

12. A cardboard model of the container shown is built with dimensions 24 cm long, 10 cm high and 10 cm wide.

(i) Calculate the surface area (external) of the cardboard container.

(ii) Calculate the volume of the cardboard container.

The actual container is to be built using a scale of 1 : 25 and will be made of metal.

(iii) Calculate the surface area (external) of the metal container.

(iv) Calculate the volume of the metal container.

(v) Find as a ratio, the surface area of the model : surface area of the container. What do you notice?

(vi) Find as a ratio, the volume of the model : volume of the container.

What do you notice?

Revision Exercises

1. (i) Using only a compass and a straight edge, construct an angle of 60°.
   (ii) Using only a compass and a straight edge, construct an angle of 120°. Explain how you constructed this angle.
2. (i) Draw a line segment $[AB]$ such that $|AB| = 5$ cm.
   (ii) Construct an equilateral triangle ABC of side length 5 cm using only a ruler and compass.
3. Construct a circle of radius 90 mm, and construct a tangent to this circle at any point on the circle.
4. (i) Construct a circle of radius 6 cm.
   (ii) Construct two tangents to this circle which are parallel to each other, using only a compass and ruler.
5. Construct the parallelogram $UVWX$ as shown in the diagram.

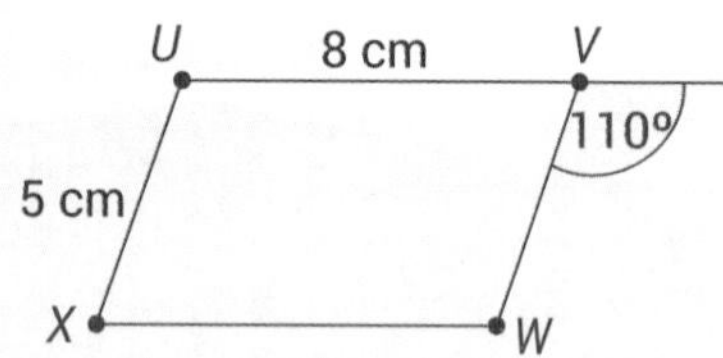

6. Construct a parallelogram $ABCD$ where $|AB| = 8$ cm, $|\angle ABC| = 130°$ and $|BC| = 5$ cm.
7. (i) Construct a triangle ABC as shown where $|AB| = 6$ cm, $|\angle ABC| = 80°$ and $|BC| = 6.5$ cm.

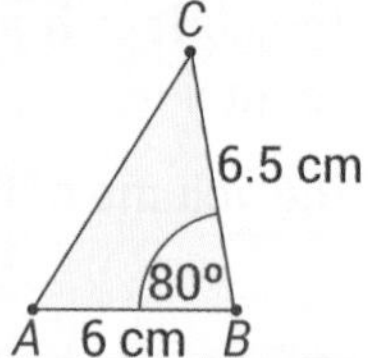

   (ii) Construct the circumcentre of the triangle ABC.
   (iii) Construct the circumcircle of the triangle ABC.
8. (i) Construct the triangle shown in the diagram.

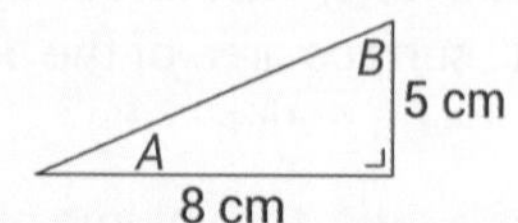

   (ii) Using a protractor, find the measure of angles A and B.
   (iii) Construct the circle that circumscribes the triangle (i.e. passes through the three vertices).
   (iv) Measure the radius of this circle.
9. Construct the circumcentre and circumcircle of the triangle MNO where $|\angle MON| = 90°$, $|\angle MNO| = 45°$ and $|MN| = 8.5$ cm.
10. (i) Construct a triangle PQR where $|PQ| = 6$ cm, $|\angle RPQ| = 110°$ and $|\angle RQP| = 35°$.
    (ii) Construct the incentre of the triangle PQR.
    (iii) Construct the incircle of the triangle PQR.
11. Construct the incentre and incircle of the triangle XYZ where $|XY| = 8$ cm, $|\angle XYZ| = 80°$ and $|\angle YXZ| = 45°$.
12. Construct the incentre and incircle of the triangle ABC where $|AB| = 6$ cm, $|BC| = 7.5$ cm and $|\angle ABC| = 90°$.
13. (i) Construct a triangle XYZ in which $|XY| = 10$ cm, $|XZ| = 5$ cm and $|YZ| = 8$ cm.
    (ii) Construct the centroid of the triangle. Label as the point P.
    (iii) Construct a line segment equal in length to $[XZ]$ on the ray $[PY$.
    (iv) If M is the midpoint of $[XY]$, verify, by measuring, that $|MP| : |PZ| = 1:2$.
14. Construct the centroid of the triangle TUV where $|TU| = 9$ cm, $|UV| = 6$ cm and $|\angle TUV| = 70°$.
15. Copy the following diagrams onto graph paper, and show the image of each of the shapes under an enlargement with the given scale factor and centre O.

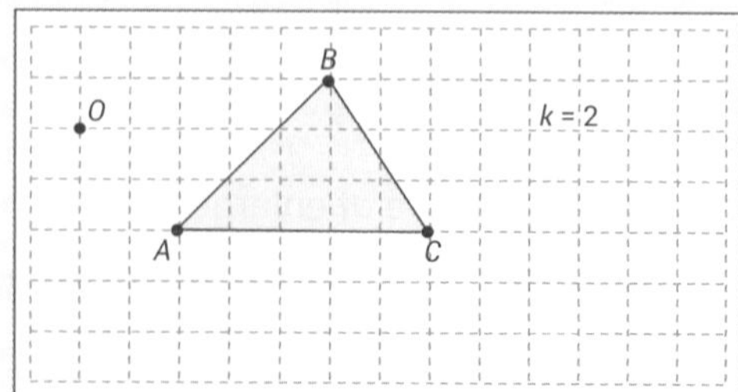

CONSTRUCTIONS, TRANSFORMATIONS AND ENLARGEMENTS

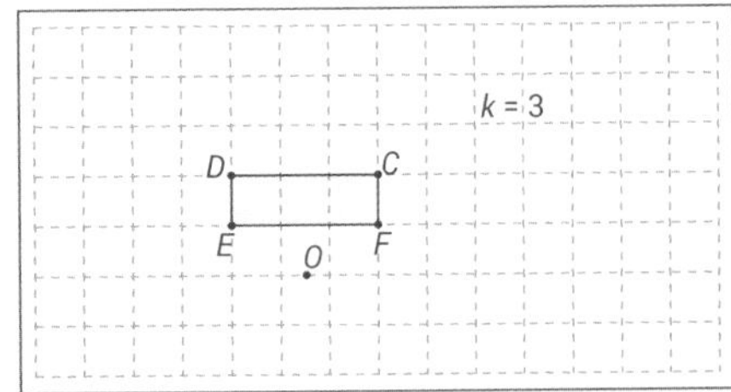

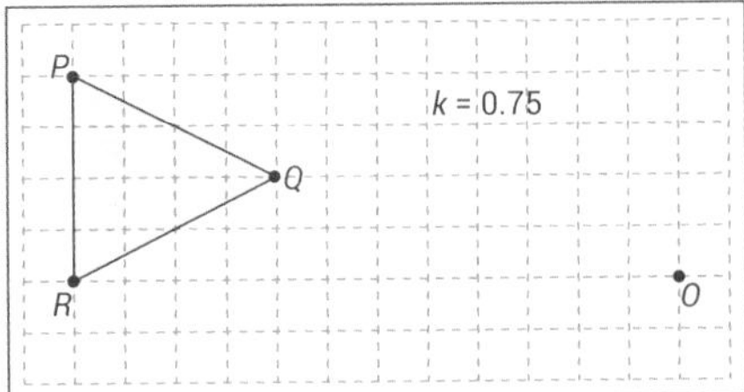

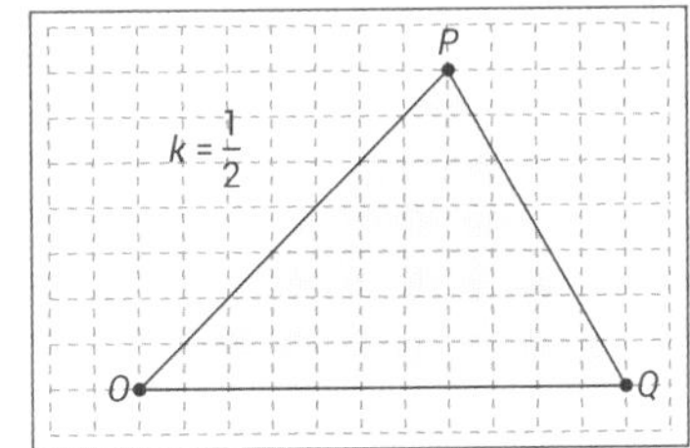

16. The rectangle *ABCD* is the image of *NMOS* under an enlargement.

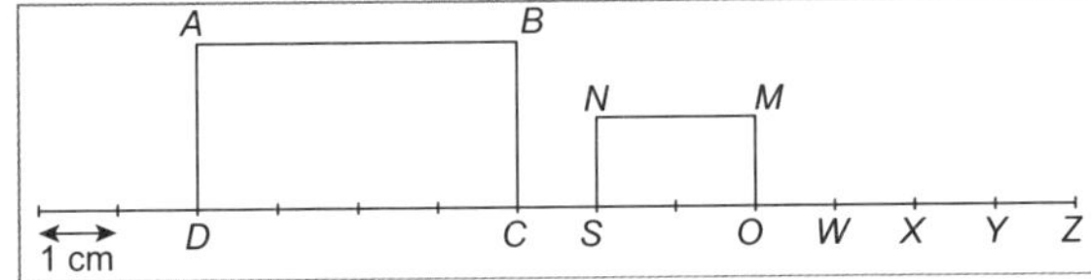

(i) Find the centre of enlargement.

(ii) Find the scale factor.

17.

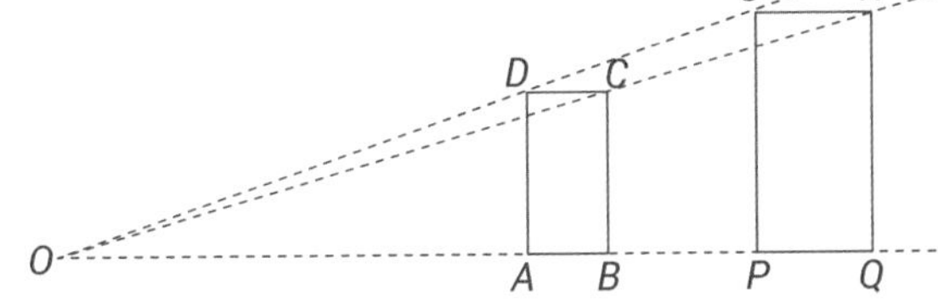

The rectangle *PQRS* is the image of the rectangle *ABCD* under an enlargement with centre *O*.

The scale factor is 1.5.

$|AB| = 3$ cm and $|QR| = 9$ cm.

(i) Calculate $|PQ|$.

(ii) Calculate $|BC|$.

(iii) Find the area of the rectangle *PQRS*.

18.

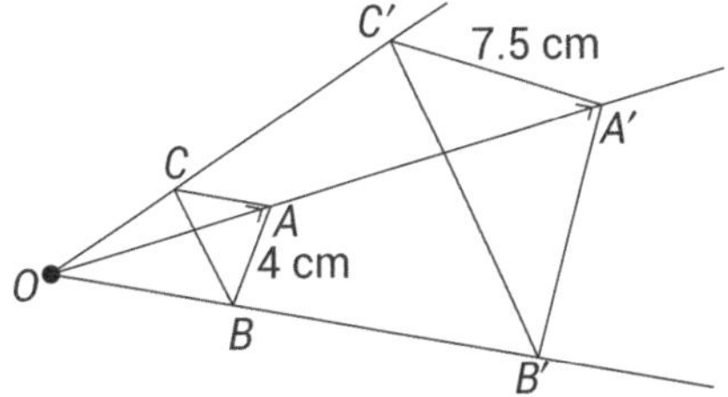

The right-angled triangle *A′B′C′* is the image of the right-angled triangle *ABC* under an enlargement with centre *O*.

The scale factor is 2.5.

(i) Find the length of [*AC*].

(ii) Find the length of [*A′B′*].

(iii) Find the area of the triangle *ABC*.

(iv) Find the area of the triangle *A′B′C′*.

19. (i) Draw a square *OABC* with side 4 cm and label the vertices.

(ii) Draw the image of the square under the enlargement with centre *O* and scale factor 2.5.

(iii) Calculate the ratio

Area of image square : Area of original square.

(iv) Another square, *OPQR*, is the image of the square *OABC* under a different enlargement with centre *O*.

The area of *OPQR* is 324 cm^2.

Calculate the scale factor of this enlargement.

20. The triangle *ADE* is the image of the triangle *ABC* under an enlargement of scale factor *k* and centre *A*.

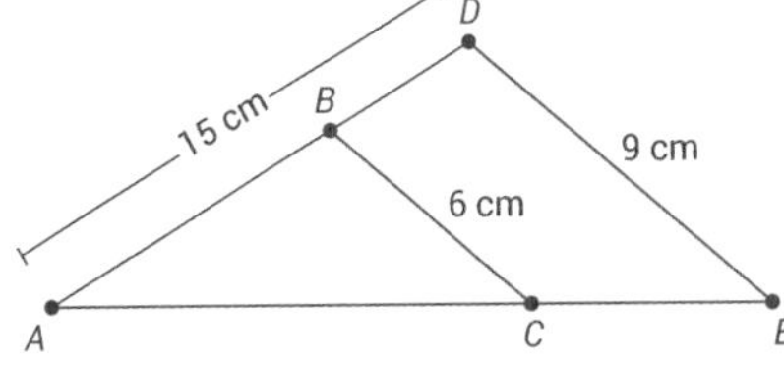

$|BC| = 6$ cm, $|AD| = 15$ cm and $|DE| = 9$ cm.

(i) Find the scale factor, *k*.

(ii) Find $|AB|$.

(iii) The area of the triangle *ADE* is 60.75 cm^2. Find the area of the triangle *ABC*.

(iv) Write down the area of the region *BCED*.

21. ΔADE is the enlargement of ΔABC, with centre A and of scale factor k.

(i) Write down the value of k.

(ii) If $|BC| = 1.5$, find $|DE|$.

(iii) If $|DB| = 3.5$, find $|AB|$.

(iv) Write down the ratio

Area ΔADE : Area ΔABC.

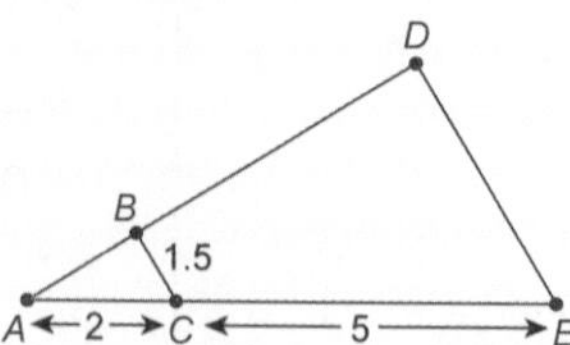

Exam Questions

1. (a) Construct a triangle ABC, where $|AB| = 7$ cm, $|\angle BAC| = 50°$ and $|AC| = 4.5$ cm.

(b) Measure the length of $[BC]$ and hence find the sum of the lengths of the sides $[AC]$ and $[BC]$, correct to one decimal place.

SEC Leaving Certificate Ordinary Level, Paper 2, 2016

2. The diagram below shows the right-angled triangle ABC, which is used in the logo for a company called *Deane Construction Limited (DCL)*. The triangle PQR is the image of ABC under an enlargement.

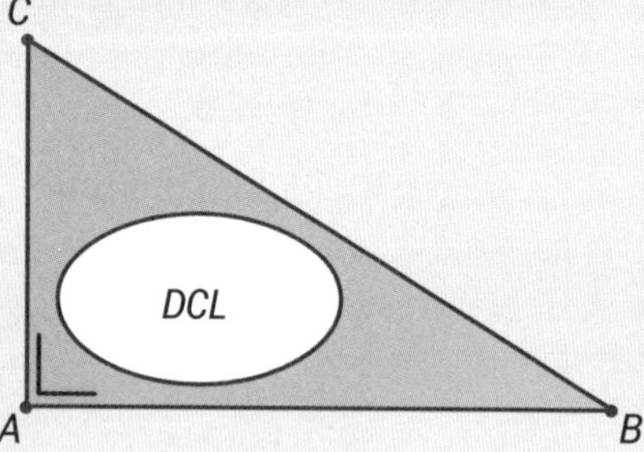

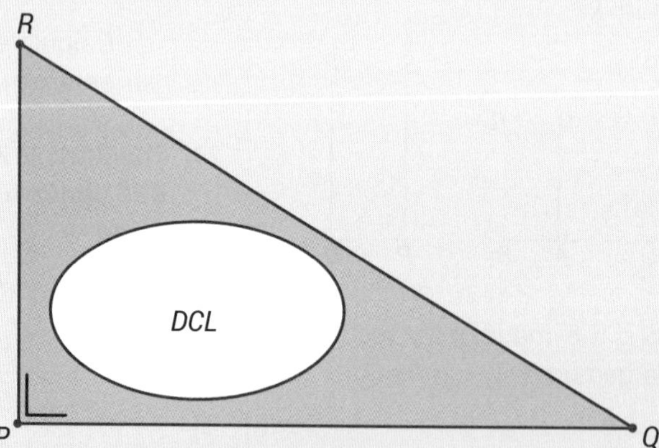

(a) (i) Construct the centre of enlargement and label it O.

(ii) Measure, in centimetres, $|OB|$ and $|OQ|$.

(iii) Use your measurements to find the scale factor of the enlargement, correct to one decimal place.

(b) The area of the triangle ABC is 7.5 cm^2. Use the scale factor to find the area of the image triangle PQR under the enlargement.

(c) (i) Given that $|AB| = 5$ cm, use the scale factor to find $|PQ|$.

(ii) Given that $|QR| = 8.7$ cm, use the scale factor to find $|BC|$.

SEC Leaving Certificate Ordinary Level, Paper 2, 2015

3. (a) Construct the incircle of the triangle *ABC* below. Show all your construction lines clearly.

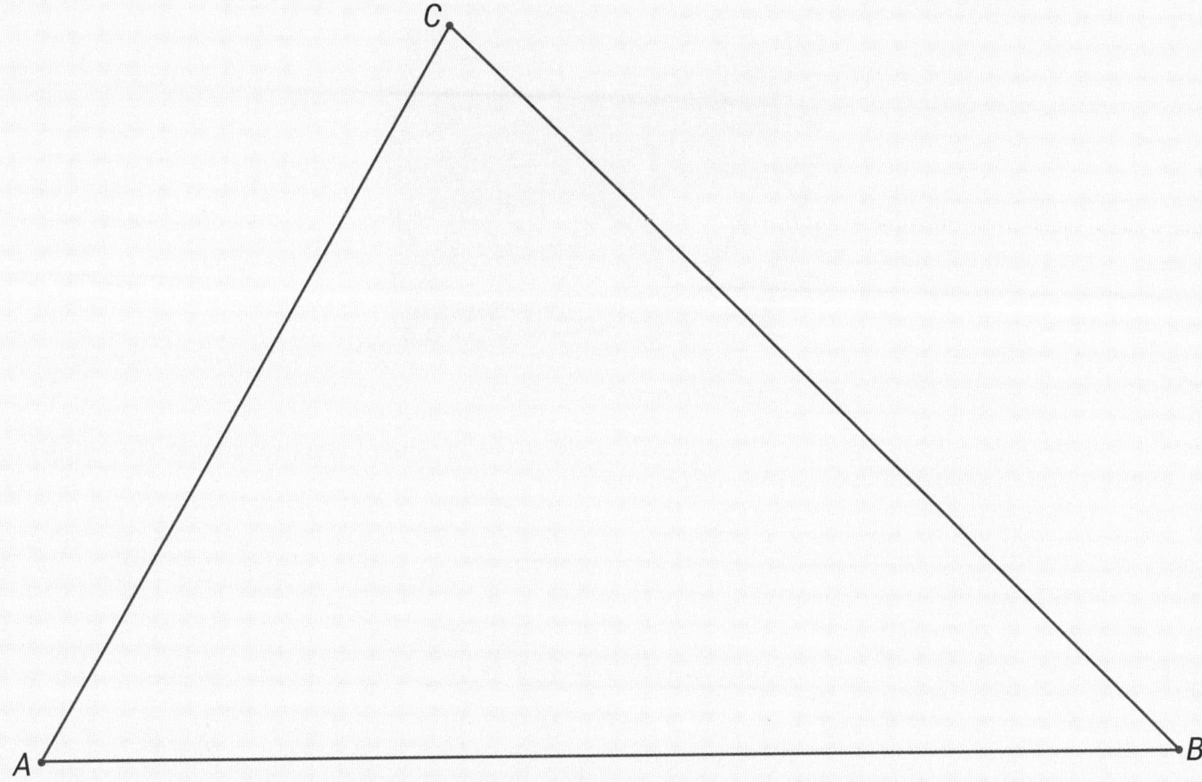

(b) Measure the length of the radius of the circle constructed in part **(a)**.

SEC Leaving Certificate Ordinary Level, Paper 2, 2014

4. (a) Construct the triangle *ABC* such that |*AB*| = 8 cm, |*BC*| = |*AC*| = 5 cm. The point *A* is given to you.

A

(b) On the same diagram, construct the image of the triangle *ABC* under the axial symmetry in *AB*.

SEC Leaving Certificate Ordinary Level, Paper 2, 2013

5. (a) (i) Write down a geometrical result that can be used to construct a tangent to a circle at a point.

(ii) On the diagram shown, construct the tangent to the circle at *A*.

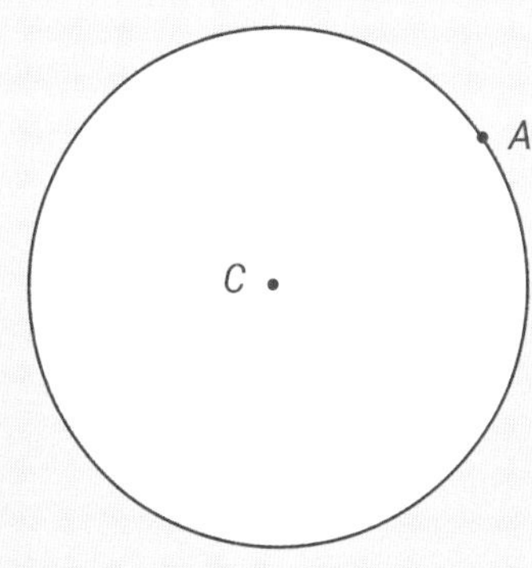

(b) Construct the circumcentre and circumcircle of the triangle below, using only a straight edge and compass. Show all construction marks clearly.

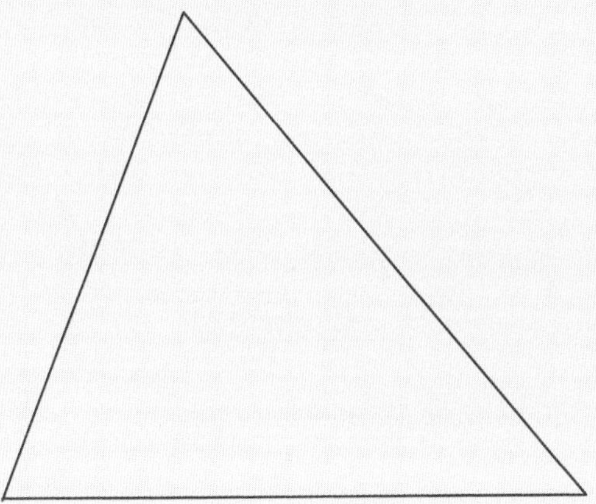

SEC Leaving Certificate Ordinary Level, Paper 2, 2012

6. The planned supports for the roof of a building form scalene triangles of different sizes.

(i) Explain what is meant by a **scalene triangle**.

The triangle *EFG* is the image of the triangle *CDE* under an enlargement and the triangle *CDE* is the image of the triangle *ABC* under the same enlargement.

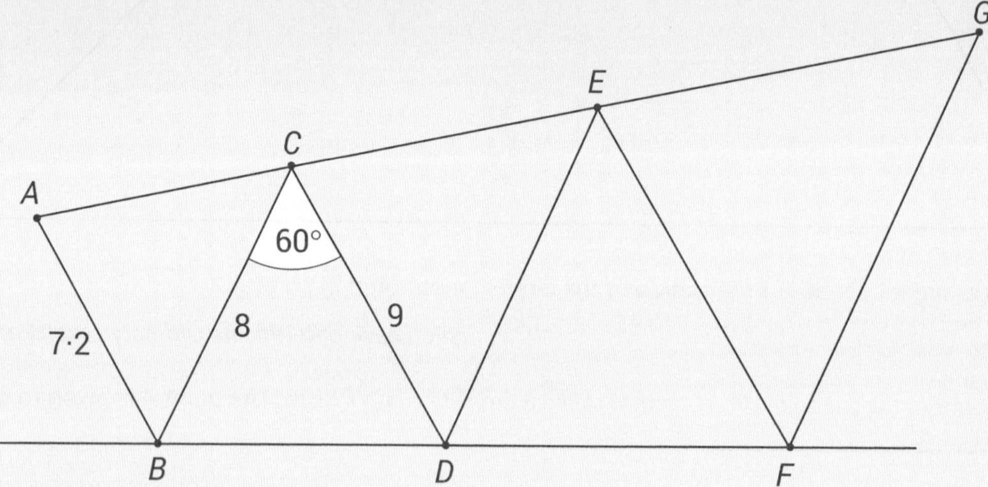

The proposed dimensions for the structure are $|AB| = 7.2$ m, $|BC| = 8$ m, $|CD| = 9$ m, and $|\angle DCB| = 60°$.

(ii) Find the length of $[FG]$.

(iii) Find the length of $[BD]$, correct to three decimal places.

(iv) The centre of the enlargement is O. Find the distance from O to the point B.

SEC Leaving Certificate Ordinary Level, Paper 2, 2012

7. Show clearly how to construct the centroid of the triangle shown. (Note: all instruments are permitted. If you are using measurements, show your measurements and calculations.)

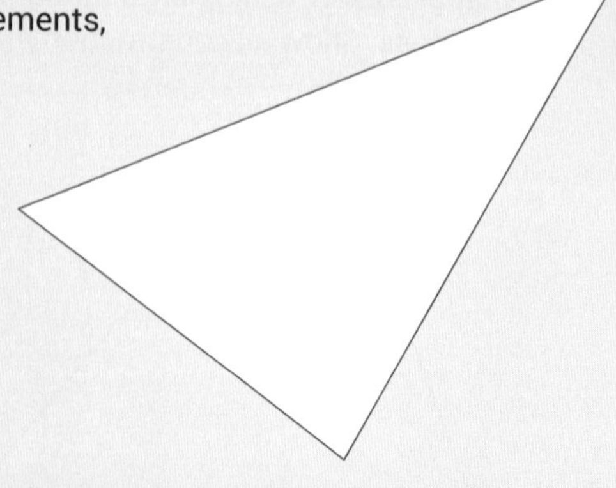

SEC Leaving Certificate Ordinary Level, Paper 2, 2011

Solutions and chapter summary available online

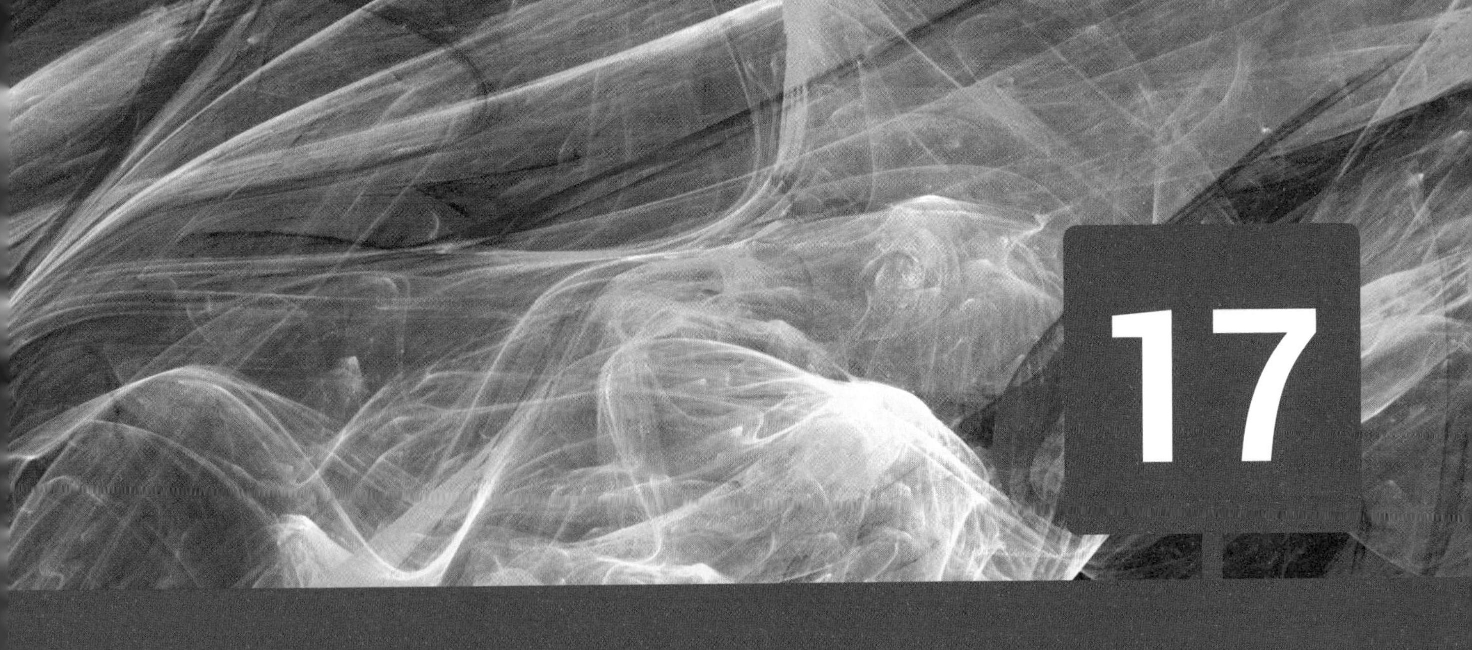

17 Trigonometry

In this chapter you will learn to:

- Use the theorem of Pythagoras to solve problems (2D only)
- Use the trigonometric ratios sin, cos and tan to solve problems
- Define sin θ and cos θ for all values of θ
- Define tan θ
- Work with trigonometric ratios in surd form
- Use trigonometry to calculate the area of a triangle
- Solve problems using the Sine and Cosine Rules (2D only)
- Solve problems involving the area of a sector of a circle and the length of an arc

You should remember...

- The angles in a triangle sum to 180°
- Angles at the base of an isosceles triangle are equal in measure
- All angles in an equilateral triangle measure 60°
- Distance = Speed × Time

Key words

- Right-angled triangle
- Pythagoras' theorem
- Opposite, adjacent, hypotenuse
- Sin, cos, tan
- Unit circle
- Reference angle
- Sine Rule
- Cosine Rule

Trigonometry is the study of triangles, their angles, areas and lengths. It is not the work of any one mathematician or nation. Its history dates back thousands of years.

Much of the technology that we use in today's highly developed world would not have been possible without trigonometry. Astronomers use trigonometry to calculate distances to nearby stars. Engineers use trigonometry to construct bridges and build giant skyscrapers. Seismologists use trigonometry to study earthquakes. The list goes on and on.

17.1 Right-Angled Triangles and Pythagoras' Theorem

Pythagoras, an ancient Greek mathematician, proved a very famous result that relates to right-angled triangles. Today, this result is known as **Pythagoras' theorem**.

In a right-angled triangle, the area of the square on the hypotenuse is equal to the sum of the areas of the squares on the other two sides.

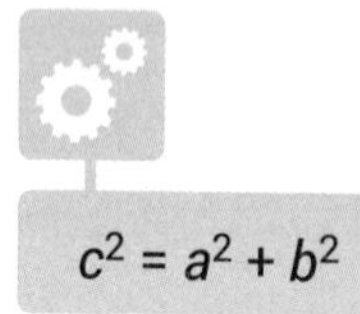

$c^2 = a^2 + b^2$

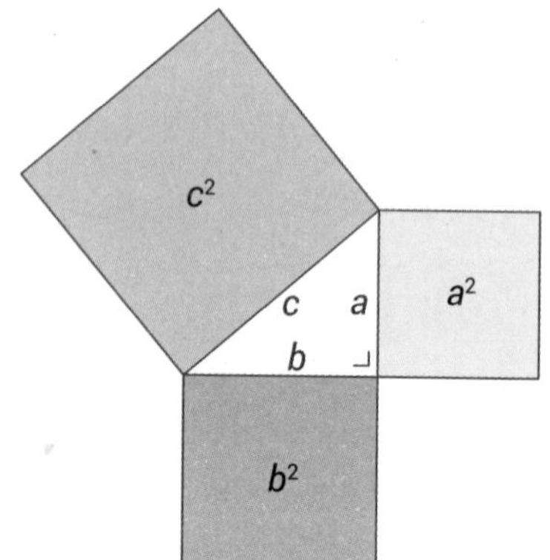

You can find this formula on page 16 of *Formulae and Tables*.

Worked Example 17.1

Use the theorem of Pythagoras to find the value of x.

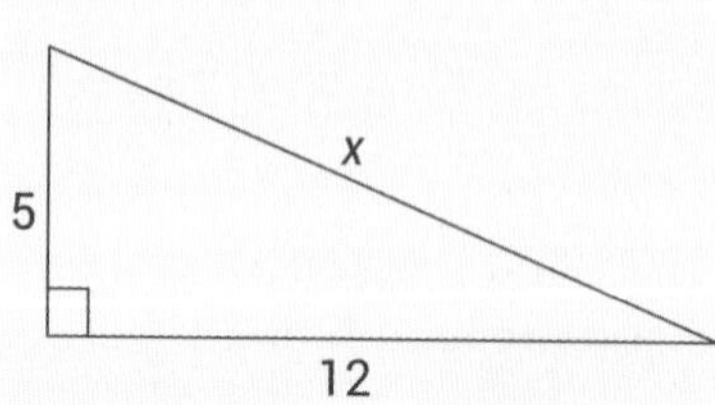

Solution

$x^2 = 12^2 + 5^2$ (Theorem of Pythagoras)

$x^2 = 144 + 25$

$x^2 = 169$

$x = \sqrt{169}$

$\therefore x = 13$

Worked Example 17.2

A vertical flagpole is 15 m high. It is held firm by a wire of length 17 m fixed to its top and to a point on the ground. How far is it from the foot of the flagpole to the point on the ground where the wire is secured?

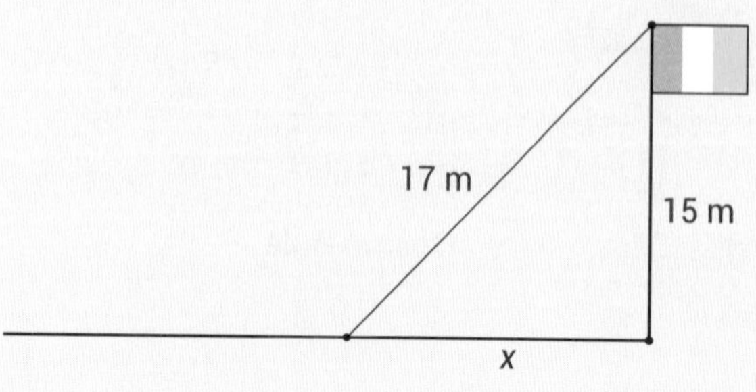

Solution

Let x be the distance from the foot of the flagpole to the point where the wire is secured.

$15^2 + x^2 = 17^2$ (Theorem of Pythagoras)

$225 + x^2 = 289$

$x^2 = 289 - 225$

$x^2 = 64$

$x = 8$

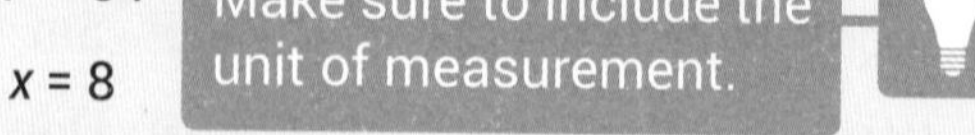

Make sure to include the unit of measurement.

$\therefore$ Distance = 8 m

Exercise 17.1

1. Find the value of x in each case:

(i)

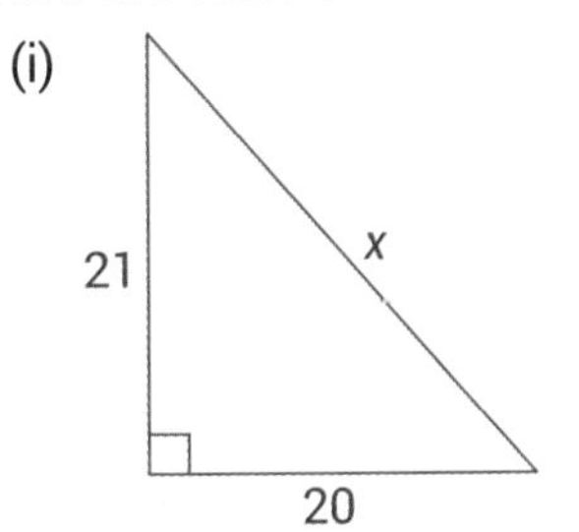

(ii)

13
x
84

(iii)

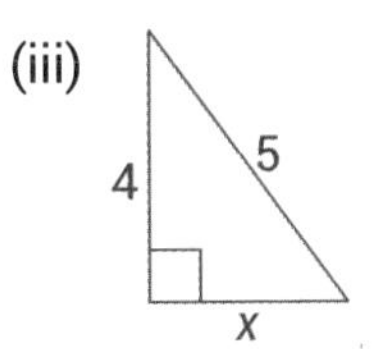

(iv)

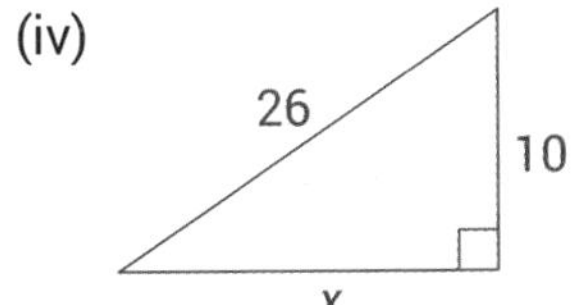

(v)

(vi)

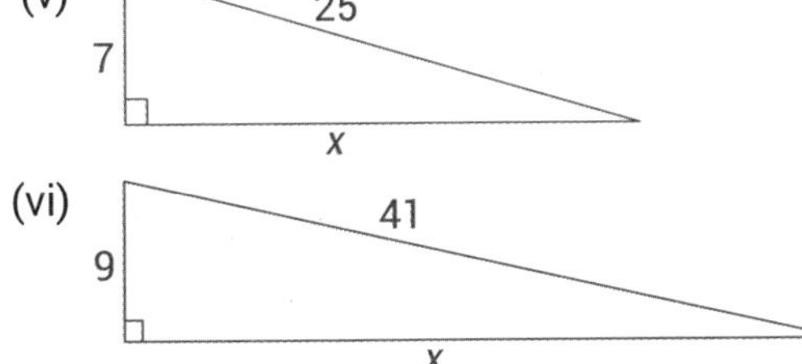

2. Find the value of x in each case (leave your answers in surd form):

(i)

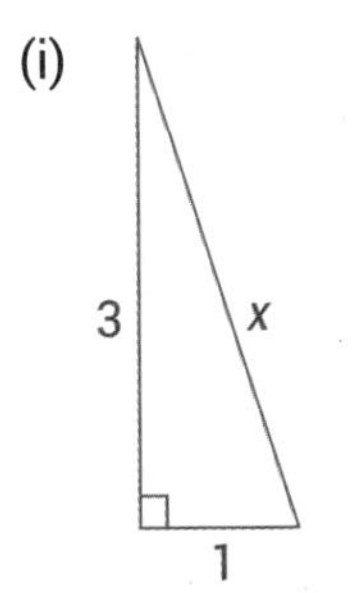

(ii)

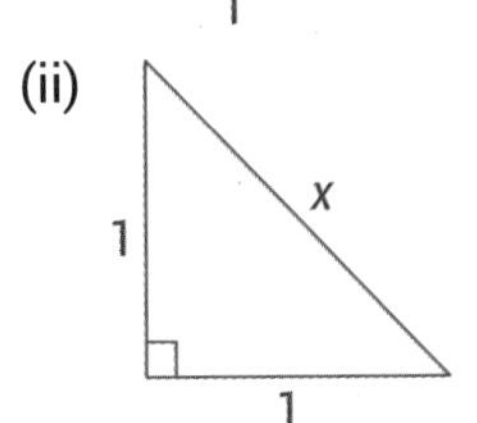

(iii)

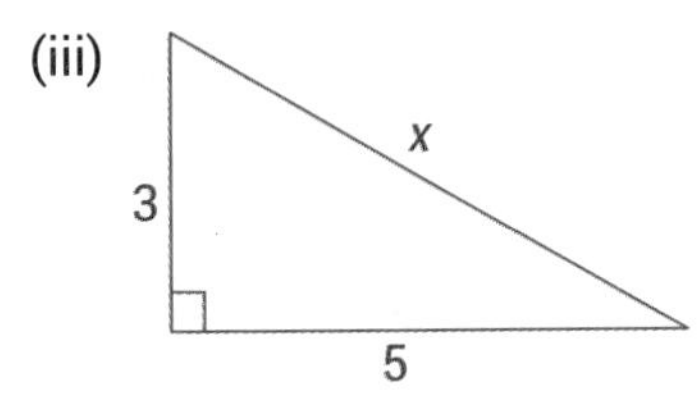

(iv)

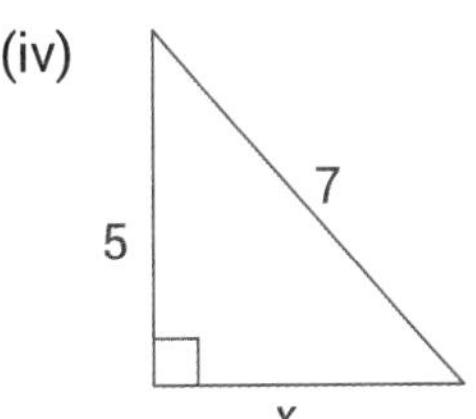

3. A ladder is 6.5 m long and rests against a vertical wall. The top of the ladder reaches a point on the wall that is 6 m above the ground. Find the distance from the wall to the foot of the ladder.

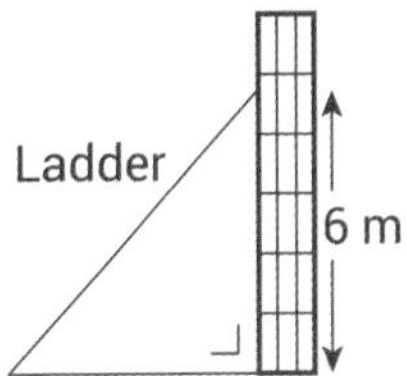

4. Find the value of x and y in each case:

(i)

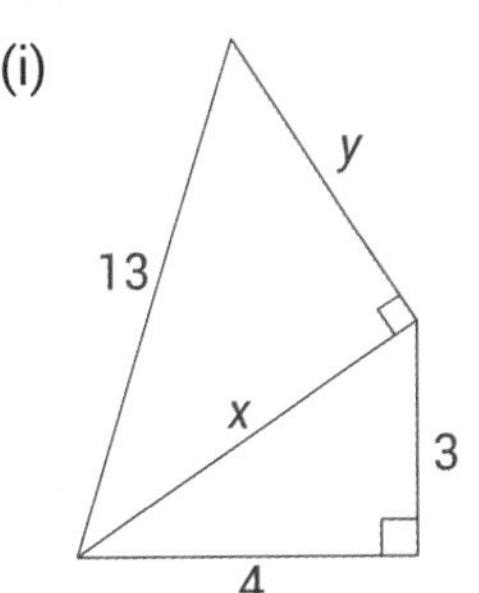

(ii)

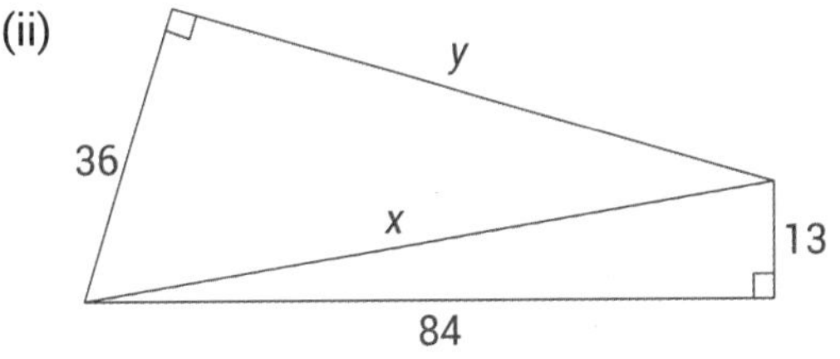

(iii)

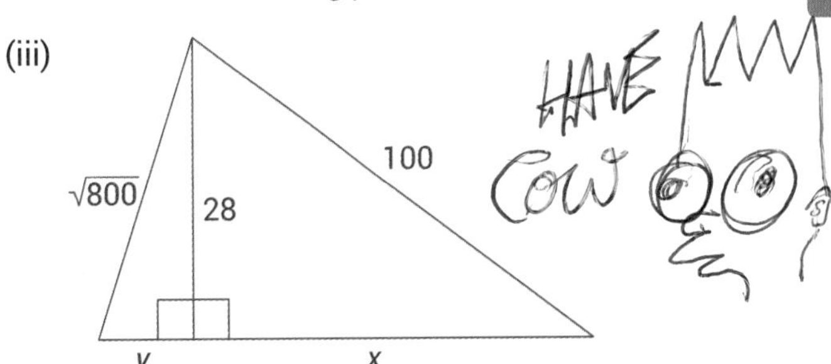

(iv)

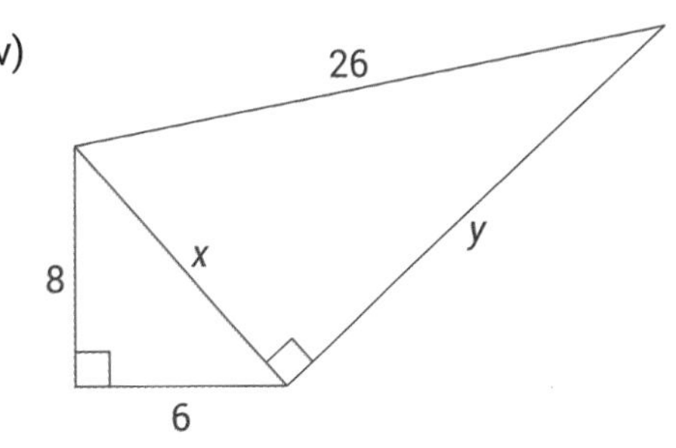

5. The perimeter of a rectangle is 280 cm. The length of the longest side is 80 cm. Find:
   (i) The length of the shortest side
   (ii) The length of a diagonal of the rectangle
   (iii) The area of the rectangle

6. The sides of a triangle are of lengths 85, 77 and 36.
   By applying the theorem of Pythagoras, investigate if the triangle is right-angled.

7. The sides of a triangle are of lengths 7, 24 and 25.
   By applying the theorem of Pythagoras, investigate if the triangle is right-angled.

8. The sides of a triangle are of lengths 11, 60 and 62.
   By applying the theorem of Pythagoras, investigate if the triangle is right-angled.

9. The width of a door frame is 84 cm and its height is 187 cm. What does x measure, if the door frame must have interior angles of 90°?

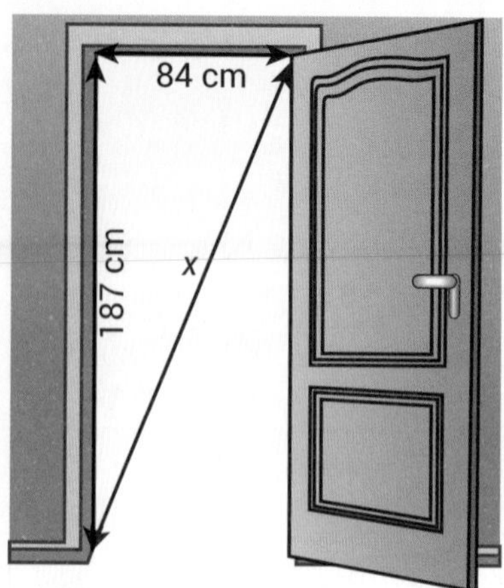

17.2 Right-Angled Triangles and the Trigonometric Ratios

In a right-angled triangle we have three special ratios connecting the angles and sides of the triangle.

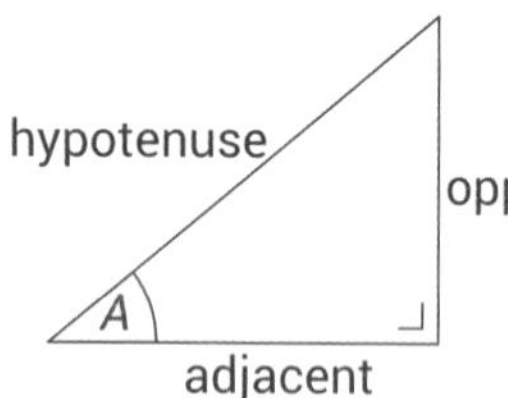

$\sin A = \dfrac{\text{opposite}}{\text{hypotenuse}}$ $\cos A = \dfrac{\text{adjacent}}{\text{hypotenuse}}$ $\tan A = \dfrac{\text{opposite}}{\text{adjacent}}$

These ratios can be found on page 16 of *Formulae and Tables*.

Worked Example 17.3

In the following right-angled triangle, write down the value of each of the following ratios:

(i) $\sin A$, $\cos A$ and $\tan A$ (ii) $\sin B$, $\cos B$ and $\tan B$

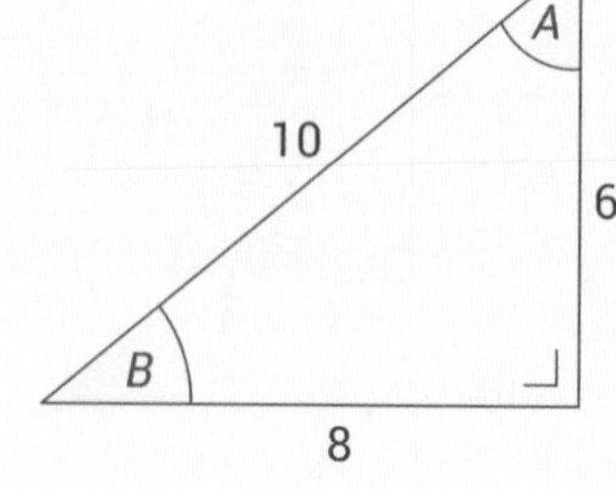

Solution

(i) $\sin A = \frac{8}{10} = \frac{4}{5}$

$\cos A = \frac{6}{10} = \frac{3}{5}$

$\tan A = \frac{8}{6} = \frac{4}{3}$

(ii) $\sin B = \frac{6}{10} = \frac{3}{5}$

$\cos B = \frac{8}{10} = \frac{4}{5}$

$\tan B = \frac{6}{8} = \frac{3}{4}$

Worked Example 17.4

Use your calculator to find the value of each of the following, correct to four decimal places:

(i) sin 32.4° (ii) cos 45.6° (iii) tan 22.5°

TRIGONOMETRY

Solution

Make sure your calculator is in degree mode.

(i) On the calculator, press:

The answer should be 0.5358 corrected to four decimal places.

(ii)

Answer = 0.6997

(iii)

Answer = 0.4142

Finding Angles

How can we find the measure of the angle *A*?

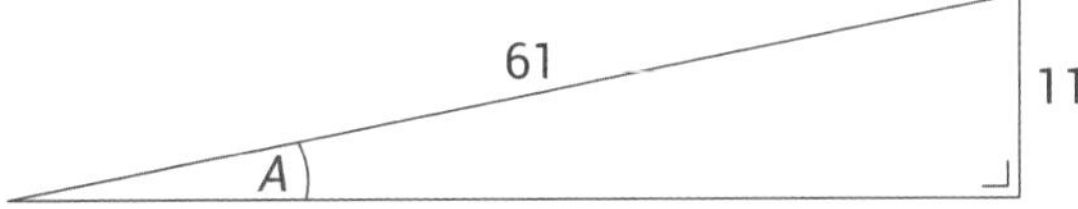

The side **opposite** the angle *A* measures 11 units and the **hypotenuse** measures 61 units.

As $\sin A = \frac{\text{opposite}}{\text{hypotenuse}}$, we have $\sin A = \frac{11}{61}$ $\therefore A = \sin^{-1}\left(\frac{11}{61}\right)$.

We can now use the calculator to find *A*. Key in the following:

$\therefore A = 10.39°$

Worked Example 17.5

Use your calculator to find the measure of the angle *X*, if $\sin X = 0.5469$.

Give your answer to the nearest degree.

Solution

$\sin X = 0.5469$

$\Rightarrow X = \sin^{-1} 0.5469$

The answer 33.15459885 is displayed.
Now convert this to the nearest degree.
$\therefore X = 33°$

Worked Example 17.6

Find, to the nearest degree, the measure of the angle *B* in each of the following triangles:

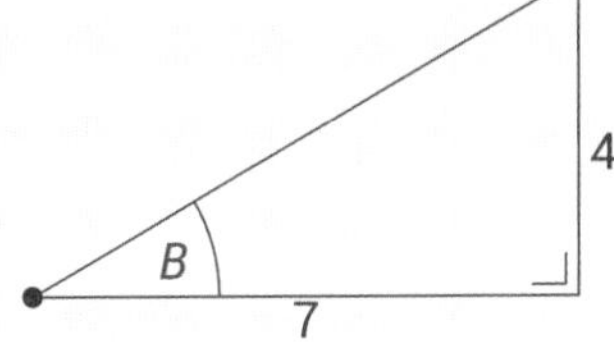

(ii)

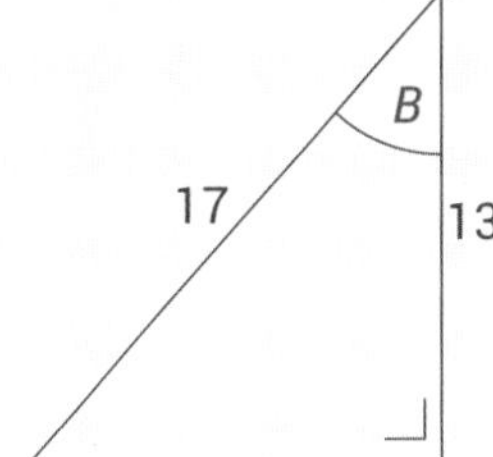

Solution

(i) The side **opposite** B in the triangle measures 4 units.

The side **adjacent** to B measures 7 units.

Since $\tan B = \frac{\text{opposite}}{\text{adjacent}}$, we have the following:

$\tan B = \frac{4}{7}$

$\therefore B = \tan^{-1} \frac{4}{7}$

Now key the following into the calculator:

$B = 29.7448813°$

$\therefore B = 30°$ (To nearest degree)

(ii) The side **adjacent** to B in the triangle measures 13 units.

The **hypotenuse** of the triangle measures 17 units.

Since $\cos B = \frac{\text{adjacent}}{\text{hypotenuse}}$, we have the following:

$\cos B = \frac{13}{17}$

$\therefore B = \cos^{-1} \frac{13}{17}$

Now key the following into the calculator:

$B = 40.1191669°$

$\therefore B = 40°$ (To nearest degree)

Exercise 17.2

1. In each of the following triangles, write down the values of sin A, cos A and tan A:

(i)

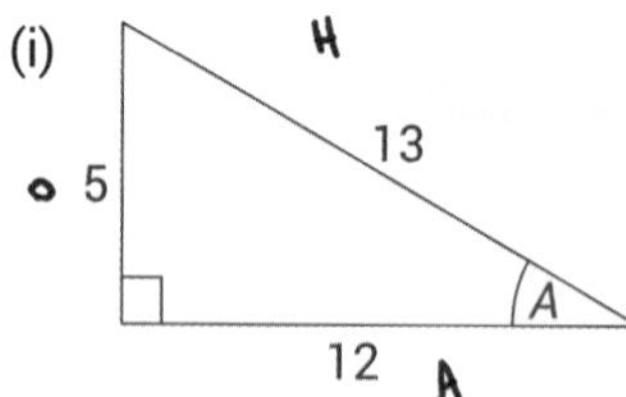

(ii)

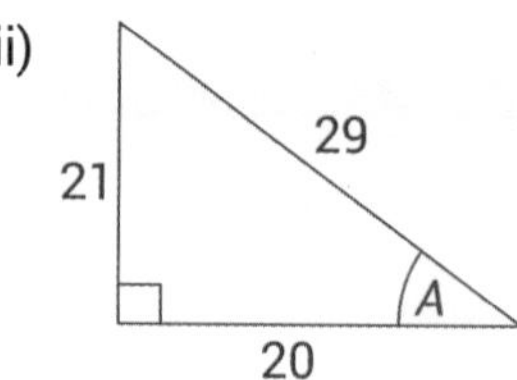

2. For each one of the following triangles, write down the values of sin A, cos A, tan A, sin B, cos B and tan B:

(i)

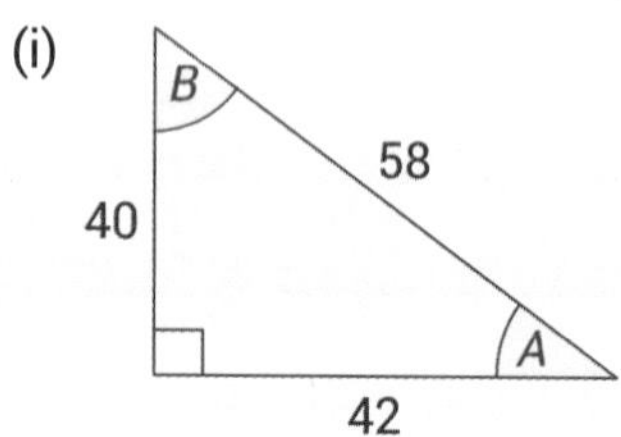

(ii)

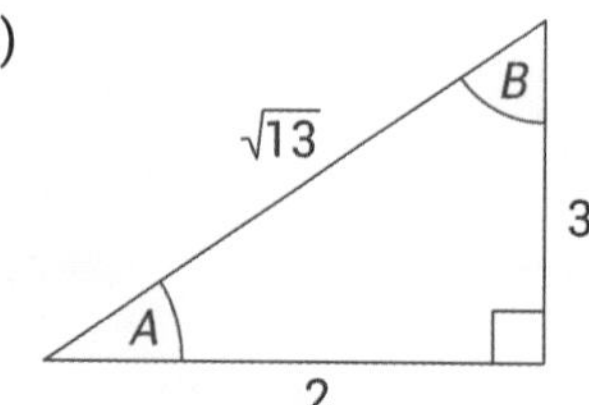

(iii)

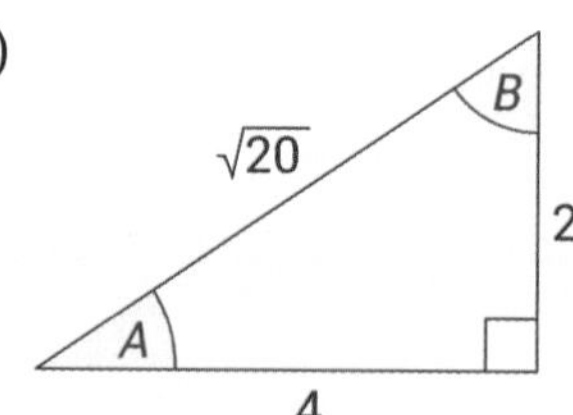

3. Use your calculator to find the value of each of the following, correct to four decimal places:

(i) sin 15° (ii) cos 30° (iii) tan 75° (iv) sin 14° (v) tan 42° (vi) cos 85° (vii) tan 12° (viii) sin 30° (ix) tan 80° (x) tan 25.6°

4. Use your calculator to find the measure of the angle A, $0° \leqslant A \leqslant 90°$. Give your answers correct to two decimal places.

(i) $\sin A = 0.6192$ (ii) $\cos A = 0.8694$ (iii) $\tan A = 0.3592$ (iv) $\sin A = 0.4375$ (v) $\tan A = 0.3762$ (vi) $\cos A = 0.1246$ (vii) $\tan A = 1.6347$ (viii) $\sin A = 0.7221$

5. Calculate, to the nearest degree, the value of the angle B.

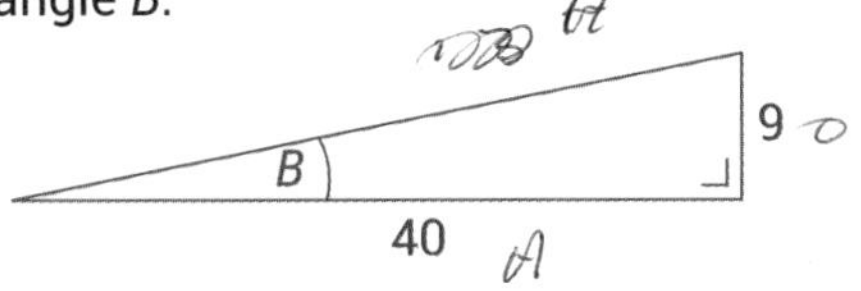

6. Calculate, to the nearest degree, the value of the angle C.

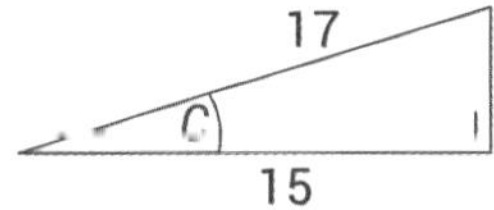

7. Calculate, to the nearest degree, the value of the angle A.

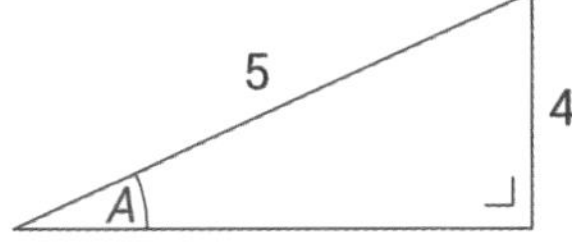

8. A tree 32 m high casts a shadow 63 m long. Calculate θ, the angle of elevation of the sun. Give your answer correct to the nearest degree.

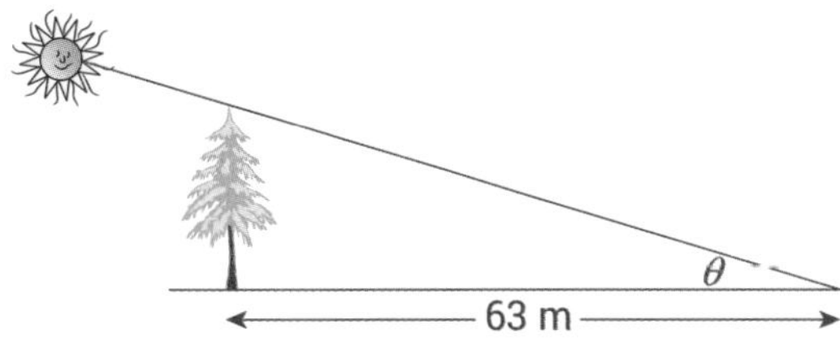

9. A right-angled triangle has sides of length 7 cm, 24 cm, and 25 cm. Find the size of the **smallest** angle in this triangle. Answer correct to one decimal place.

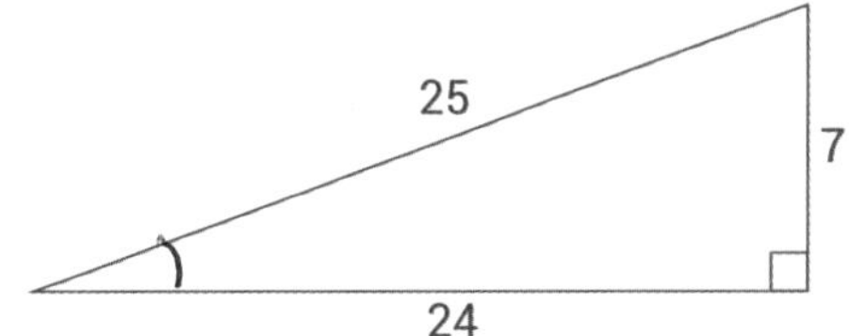

17.3 Finding the Length of a Side in a Right-Angled Triangle

If we know the measure of just one angle in a right-angled triangle (other than the right angle) and the length of one side, then we can find the lengths of the remaining two sides.

Worked Example 17.7

Consider the triangle ABC shown below.
If $|AB| = 8$ cm and $|\angle BAC| = 35°$, then find $|BC|$, correct to one decimal place.

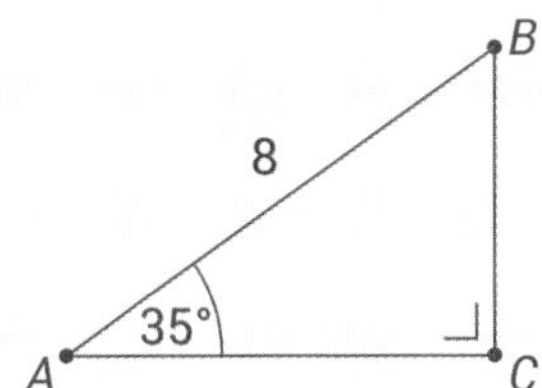

Solution

Let $|BC| = x$

$\sin 35° = \dfrac{x}{8}$

$8 \sin 35° = x$ (Cross-multiplying)

$4.588611491 = x$ (Calculator)

$\therefore\ |BC| = 4.6$ cm, to one decimal place

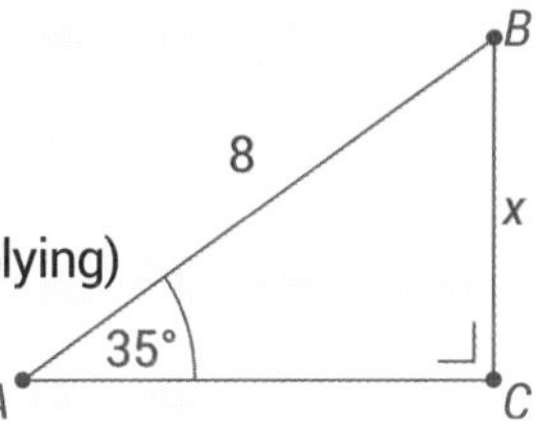

Worked Example 17.8

Find the values for x and y in the diagram below, correct to two decimal places.

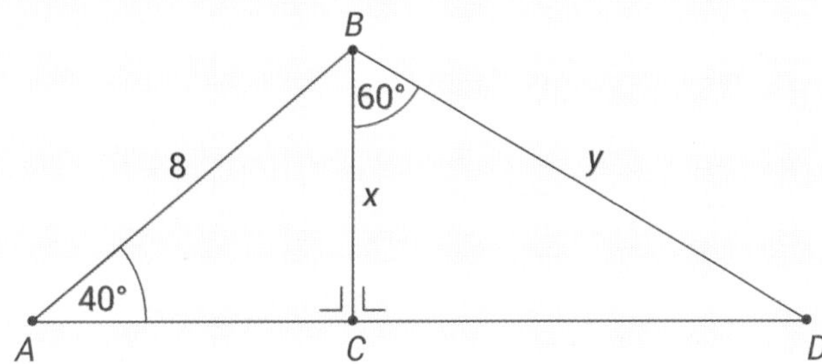

Solution

$\sin 40° = \frac{x}{8}$ $\left(\frac{\text{opposite}}{\text{adjacent}}\right)$

$\Rightarrow x = 8 \sin 40°$ (Cross-multiplying)

$x = 5.1423...$ (Calculator)

$x = 5.14$, to 2 decimal places

$\cos 60° = \frac{5.14}{y}$ $\left(\frac{\text{adjacent}}{\text{hypotenuse}}\right)$

$y \cos 60° = 5.14$ (Cross-multiplying)

$y = \frac{5.14}{\cos 60°}$

$y = 10.28$ (Calculator)

Exercise 17.3

1. Find the value of x in the following triangles (answer correct to two decimal places):

(i)

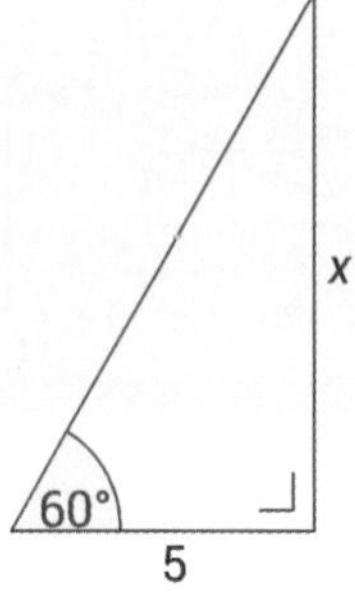

(ii)

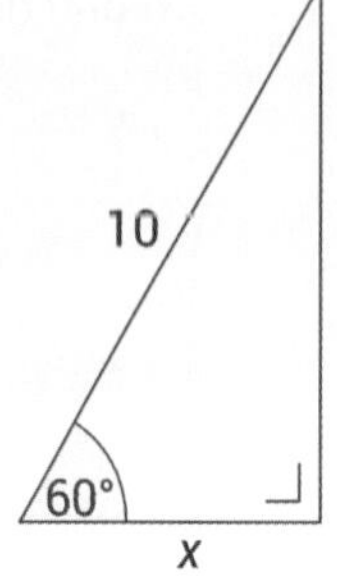

(iii)

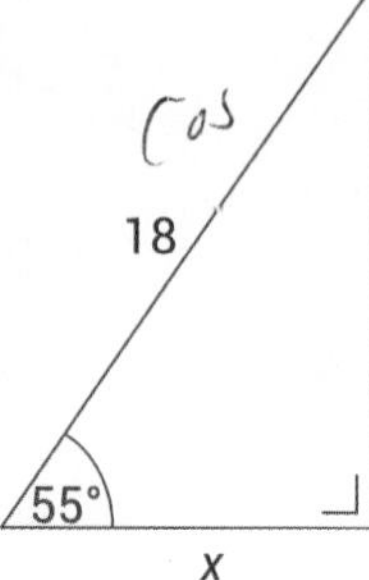

(iv)

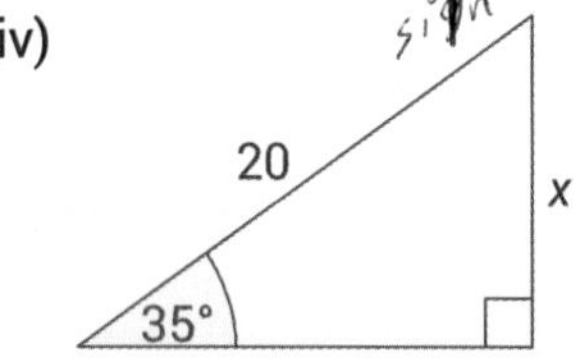

(v)

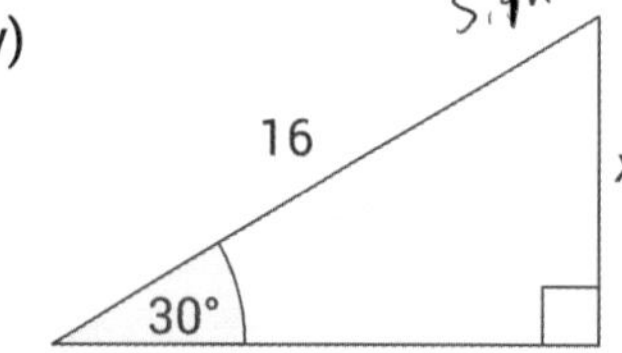

(vi)

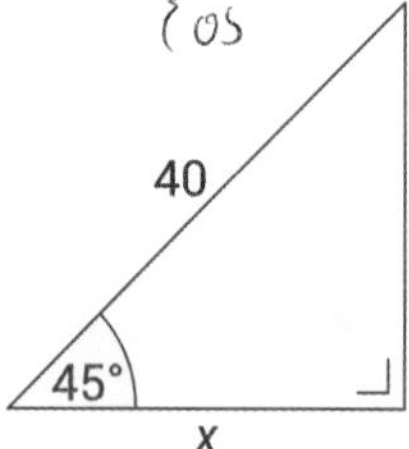

2. Find the value of y in the following triangles (answer correct to two decimal places):

(i)

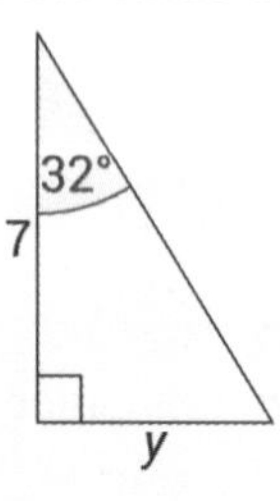

(ii)

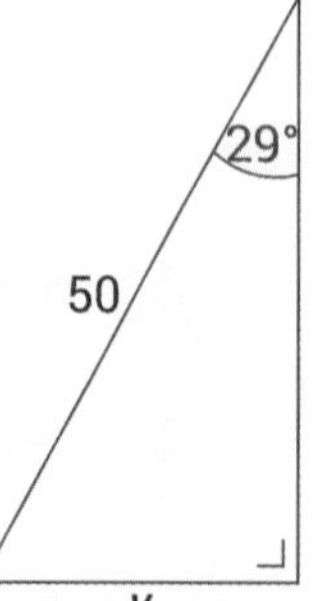

(iii)

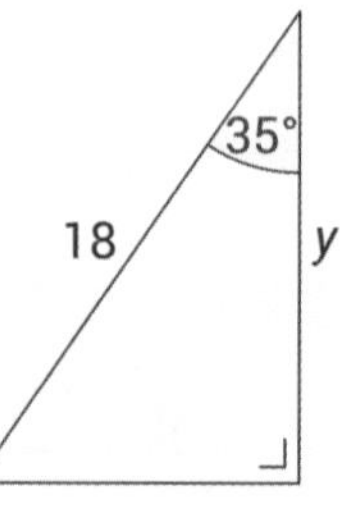

3. Find the value of y in each of the following triangles (answer correct to two decimal places):

(i)

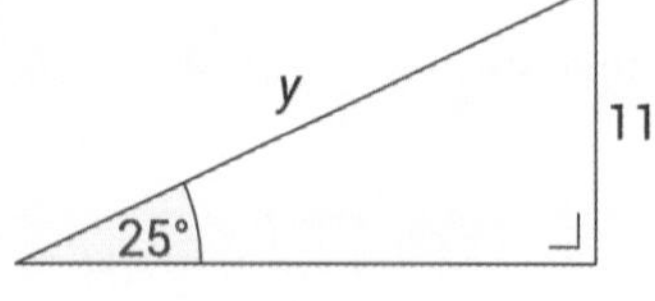

(ii)

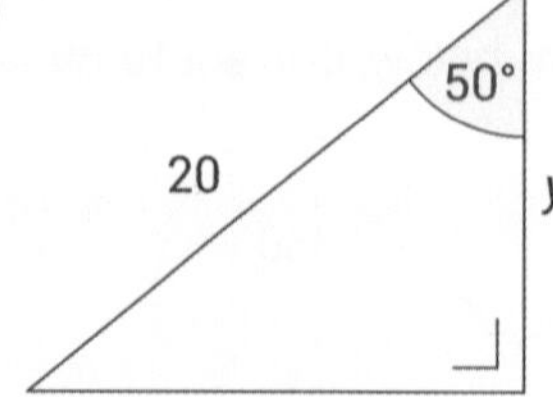

(iii)

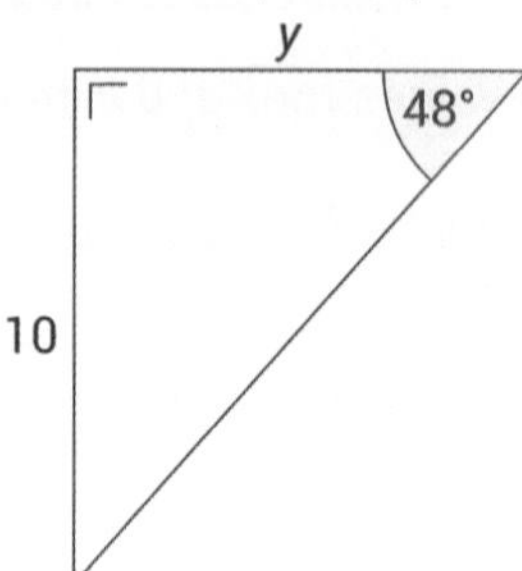

4. Find the measure of the angle A in each of the following (give your answer to the nearest degree):

(i)

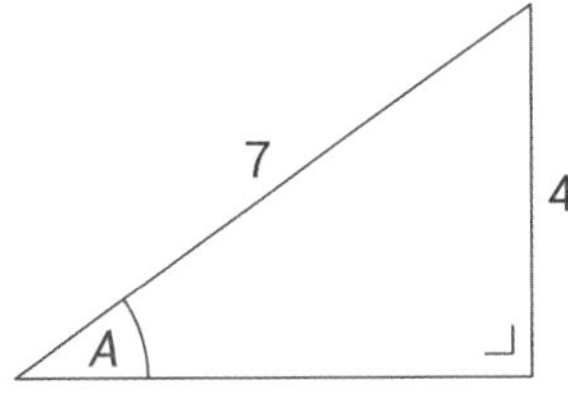

(ii)

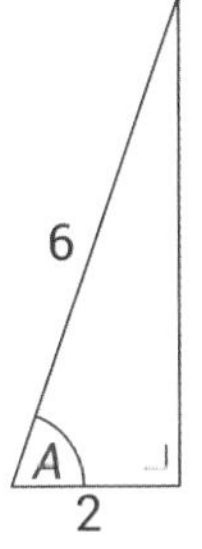

(iii)

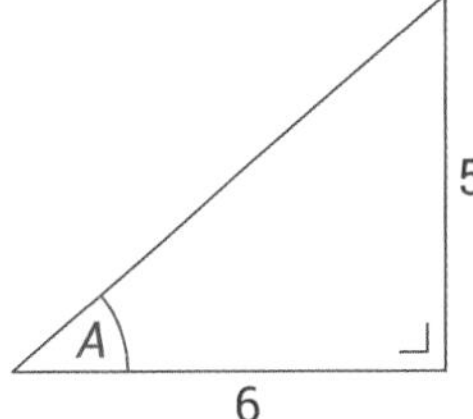

(iv)

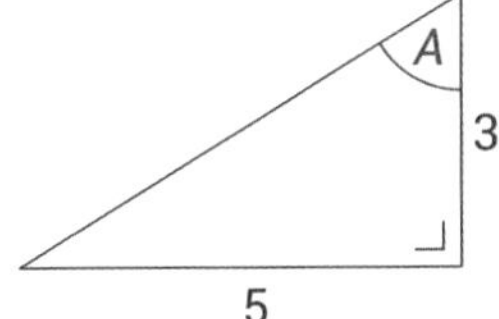

(v)

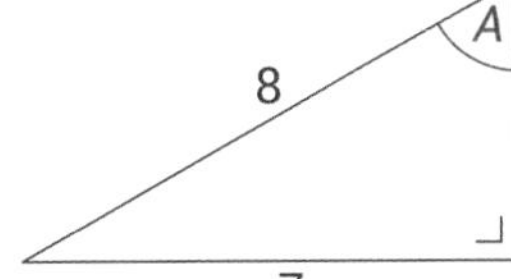

(vi)

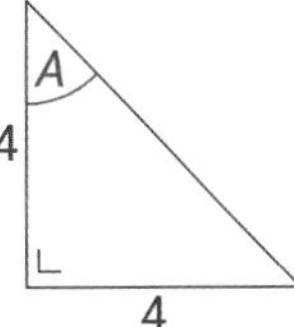

5. Solve for x and y to two decimal places.

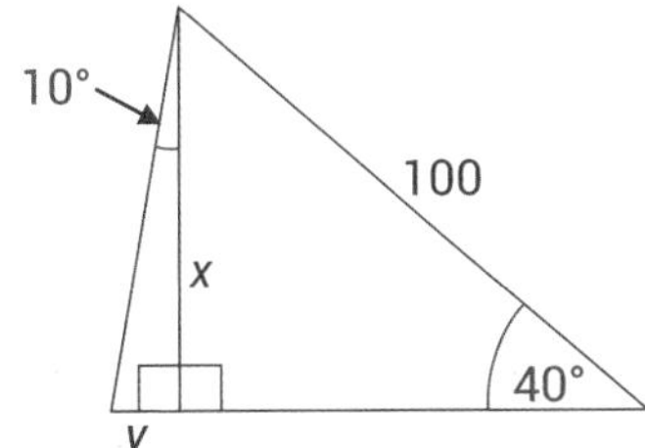

6. Solve for x, y and z to two significant figures.

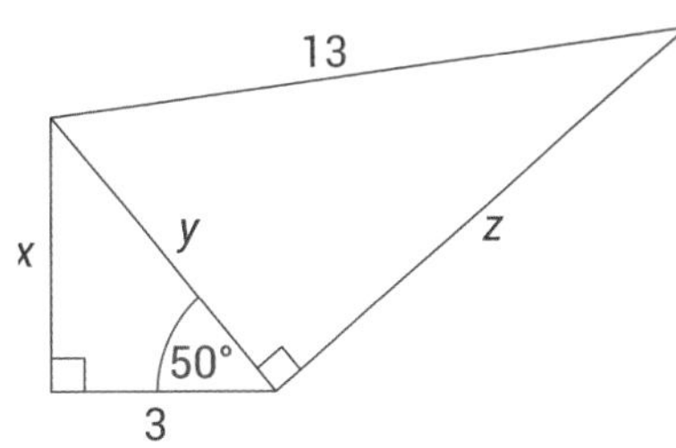

17.4 Using Trigonometry to Solve Practical Problems

Compass Directions

The diagram shows the four main compass directions: North, South, East and West.

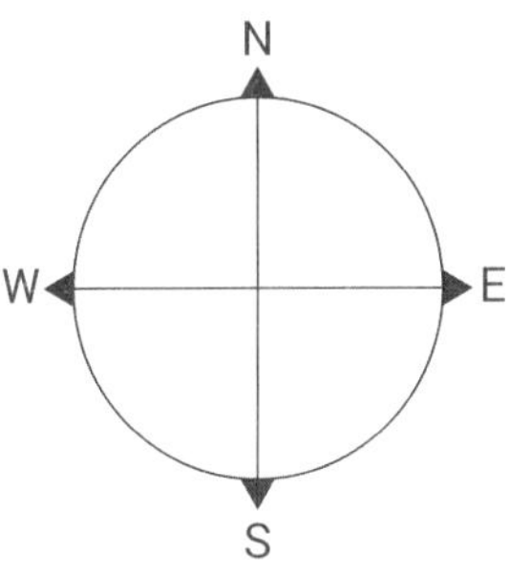

For all other compass directions, we can begin by looking North or South and then turning either East or West through the required number of degrees. This is shown in the diagrams below. One could also begin by looking East or West and then turning North or South through the required angle.

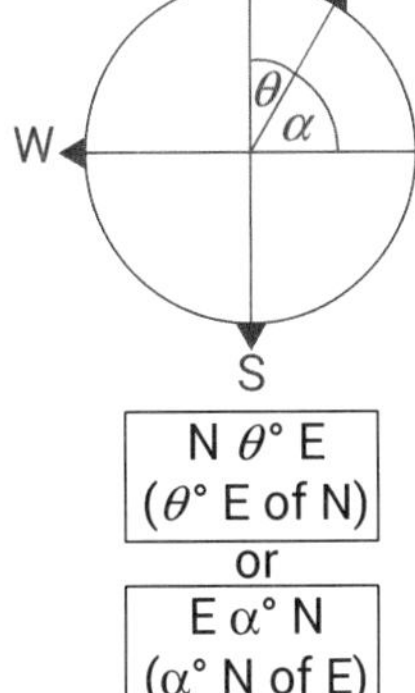

N $\theta°$ E
($\theta°$ E of N)
or
E $\alpha°$ N
($\alpha°$ N of E)

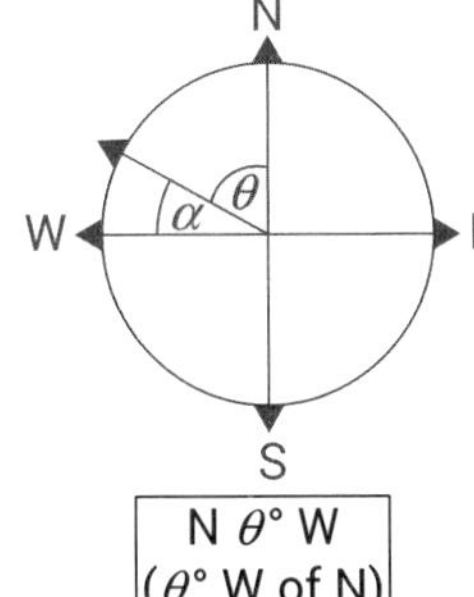

N $\theta°$ W
($\theta°$ W of N)
or
W $\alpha°$ N
($\alpha°$ N of W)

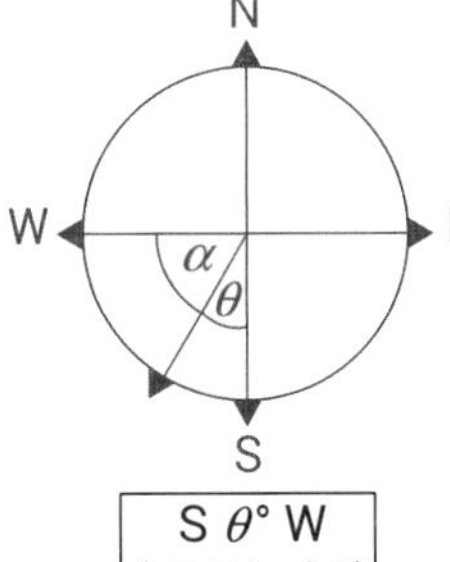

S $\theta°$ W
($\theta°$ W of S)
or
W $\alpha°$ S
($\alpha°$ S of W)

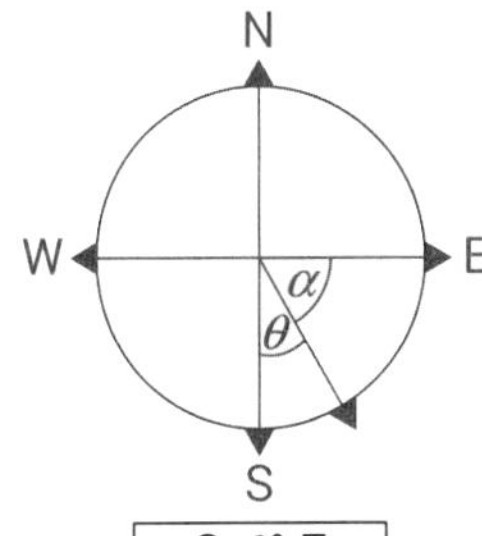

S $\theta°$ E
($\theta°$ E of S)
or
E $\alpha°$ S
($\alpha°$ S of E)

Angles of Elevation and Depression

If you look up at a tall building or object, the angle that your line of vision makes with the horizontal is called the **angle of elevation**.

The angle of elevation is the angle above the horizontal.

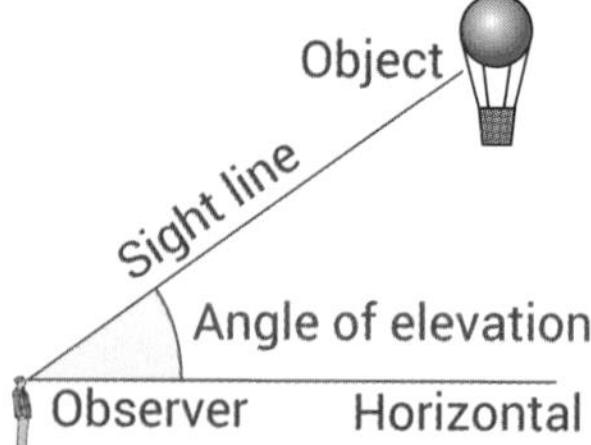

If you stand on top of a cliff and observe a swimmer out at sea, the angle that your line of vision makes with the horizontal is called the **angle of depression**.

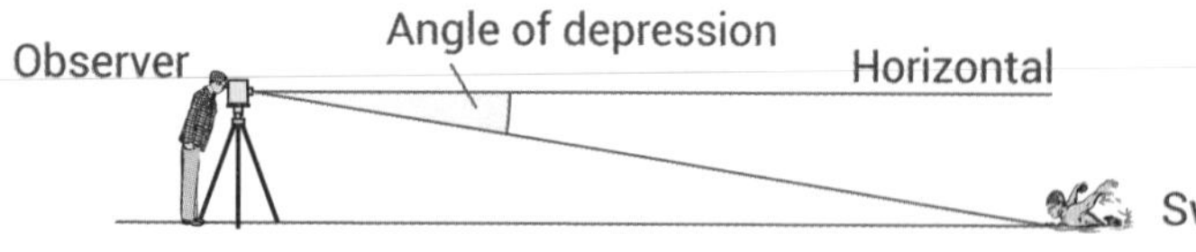

The angle of depression is the angle below the horizontal.

A clinometer is a device used to measure the angle of elevation and the angle of depression.

Worked Example 17.9

The Sears Tower in Chicago is one of the world's tallest structures. A tourist wishing to calculate the height of the tower makes the measurements shown in the diagram. Using these measurements, calculate the height of the tower.

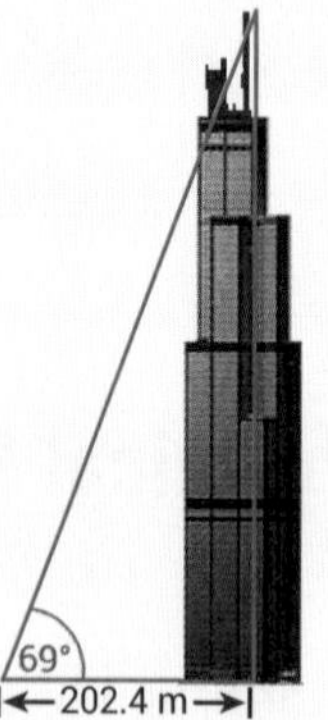

Solution

From the observer's position the angle of elevation of the top of the tower is 69°.

The length of the side **adjacent** to the angle of elevation measures 202.4 m.

Let h be the length of the side **opposite** the angle of elevation.

Since $\tan A = \dfrac{\text{opposite}}{\text{adjacent}}$,

we have the following:

$$\tan 69° = \frac{h}{202.4}$$

$$h = 202.4 \tan 69°$$

$$\therefore h = 527.27 \text{ m}$$

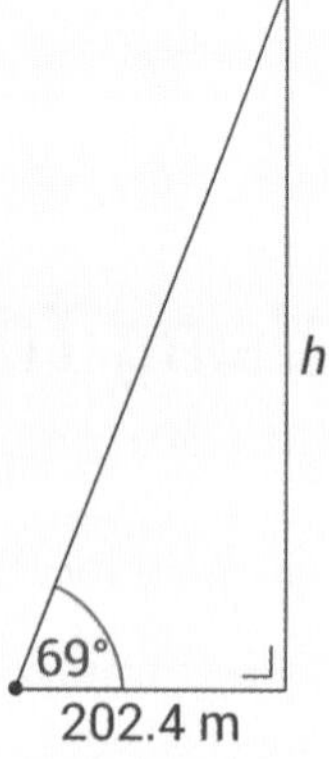

Worked Example 17.10

A ship leaves a port A and sails a distance of 4 km in the direction N 30° E to a point B (see diagram). The ship then changes direction and sails for a further 6 km in the direction S 60° E to a point C (see diagram).

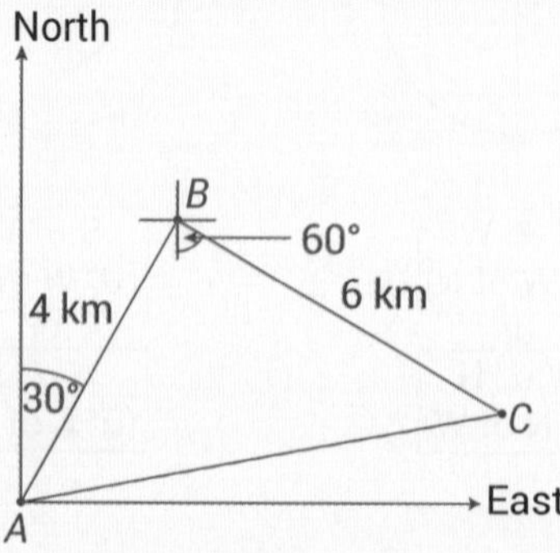

(i) Calculate the distance from the ship's present position at point C to port A. Give your answer to one decimal place.

(ii) Find $|\angle BCA|$, to the nearest degree.

(iii) Hence, find the direction of C **from** A.

Solution

(i)

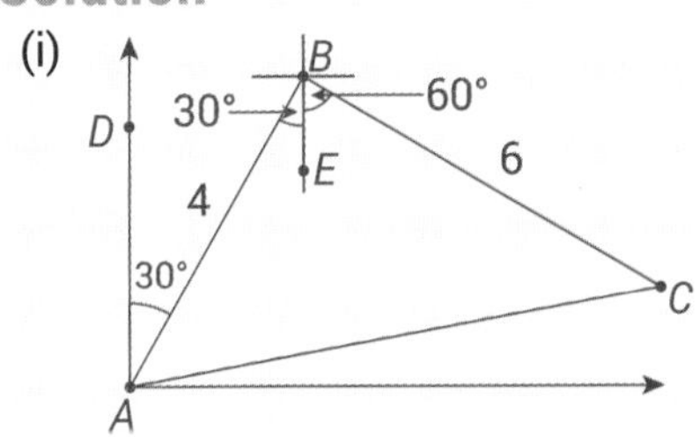

$|\angle DAB| = |\angle ABE| = 30°$ (Alternate angles)

$|\angle ABC| = 30° + 60° = 90°$

$|AC|^2 = 4^2 + 6^2$ (Theorem of Pythagoras)

$|AC|^2 = 52$

$|AC| = \sqrt{52}$

$\therefore |AC| = 7.2$ km, to 1 decimal place

(ii) Let $\angle BCA = \theta$.

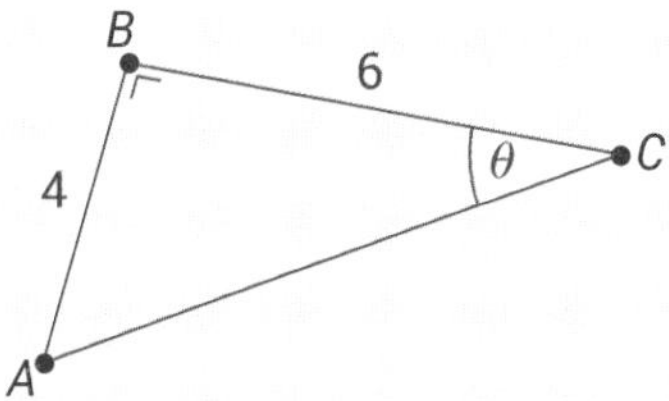

The side $[AB]$ is **opposite** θ and the side $[BC]$ is **adjacent** to θ.

Since $\tan\theta = \dfrac{\text{opposite}}{\text{adjacent}}$, we have

$$\tan\theta = \frac{4}{6} = \frac{2}{3}$$

$$\theta = \tan^{-1}\left(\frac{2}{3}\right)$$

$$\theta = 33.69006...°$$

$\therefore |\angle BCA| = 34°$, to nearest degree

(iii)

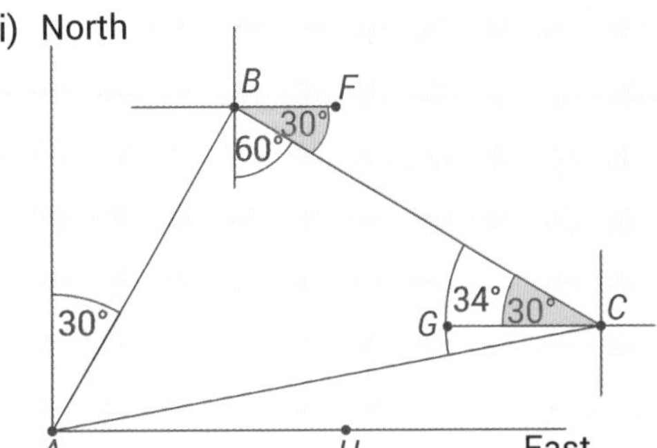

We need to find the direction of C from A, i.e. $|\angle CAH|$.

$|\angle FBC| = 90° - 60° = 30°$

$\therefore |\angle BCG| = 30°$ (Alternate to $\angle FBC$)

$|\angle GCA| = 34° - 30° = 4°$

$\therefore |\angle CAH| = 4°$ (Alternate to $\angle GCA$)

Hence, the direction of C from A is E 4° N.

17.5 Special Angles 30°, 45° and 60° 

Special Angles 30° and 60°

A 60° angle can be constructed as follows, with just a ruler and a compass:

1. Construct an equilateral triangle with sides of length 2 units.
2. Bisect one of the angles in the triangle.
3. Let x be the shortest distance from the vertex of the bisected angle to the opposite side.
4. Use the theorem of Pythagoras to find x.

$$x^2 + 1^2 = 2^2$$

$$x^2 + 1 = 4$$

$$x^2 = 4 - 1$$

$$x^2 = 3$$

$$x = \sqrt{3}$$

From the triangle, we have:

- $\sin 60° = \dfrac{\sqrt{3}}{2}$
- $\cos 60° = \dfrac{1}{2}$
- $\tan 60° = \sqrt{3}$

Also:

- $\sin 30° = \dfrac{1}{2}$
- $\cos 30° = \dfrac{\sqrt{3}}{2}$
- $\tan 30° = \dfrac{1}{\sqrt{3}}$

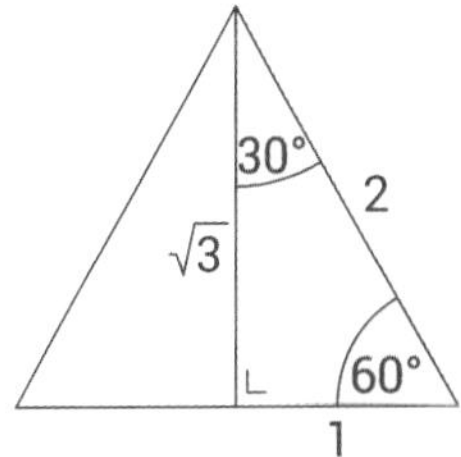

TRIGONOMETRY

Special Angle 45°

A 45° angle can also be constructed with just a ruler, a set square and a compass.

1. Construct a right-angled isosceles triangle with equal sides of 1 unit in length.
2. Let x be the length of the hypotenuse.
3. Use the theorem of Pythagoras to find x.

$$1^2 + 1^2 = x^2$$
$$2 = x^2$$
$$\sqrt{2} = x$$

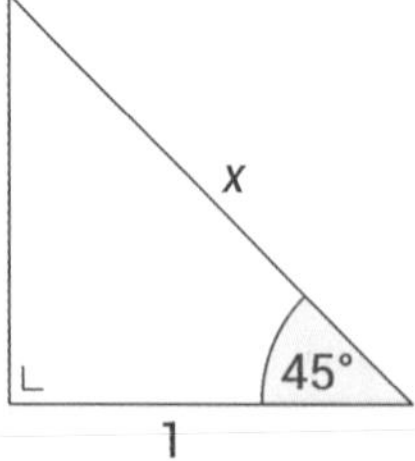

From the triangle, we have:

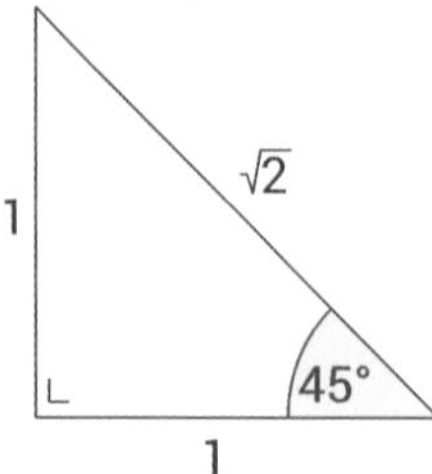

- $\sin 45° = \frac{1}{\sqrt{2}}$
- $\cos 45° = \frac{1}{\sqrt{2}}$
- $\tan 45° = \frac{1}{1} = 1$

These ratios for 30°, 45° and 60° appear on page 13 of *Formulae and Tables*.

Exercise 17.4

1. The Empire State Building pictured below is one of New York's tallest buildings. Using the information given, calculate the height of the building. Answer to the nearest metre.

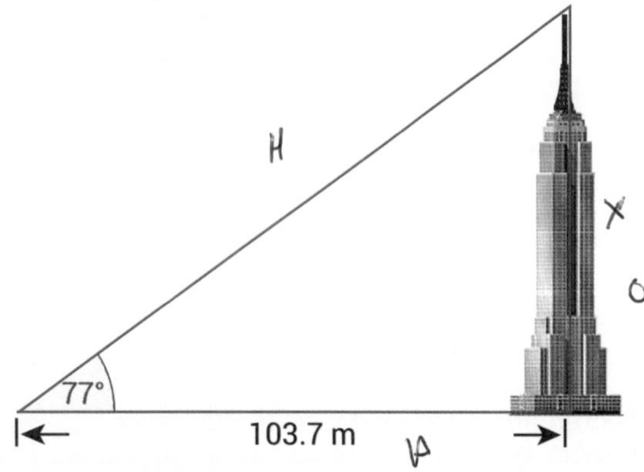

2. John is standing on a vertical cliff top and observes a boat drifting towards the base of the cliff. He decides to call the emergency services and give them the position of the boat. He measures the angle of depression of the boat from the cliff top to be 30°, and he knows the cliff top is 200 m above sea level. How far is the boat from the base of the cliff? Answer to the nearest metre.

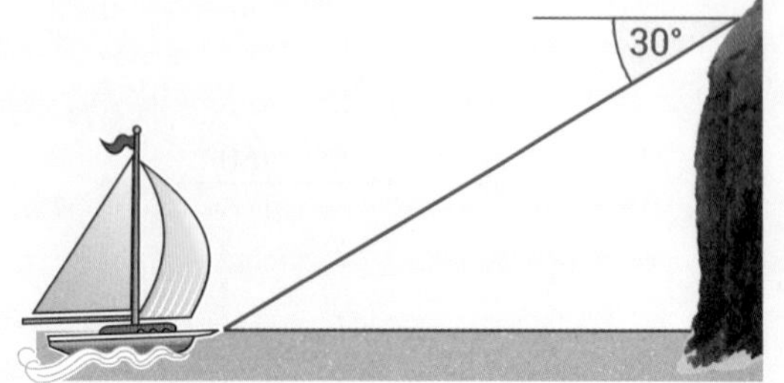

3. A vertical pole is tied to the horizontal ground by means of two wires. The longer wire is 22 m long and makes an angle of 47° with the ground. The shorter wire makes an angle of 63° with the ground.

   Find to the nearest metre:

   (i) The height of the pole

   (ii) The length of the shorter wire

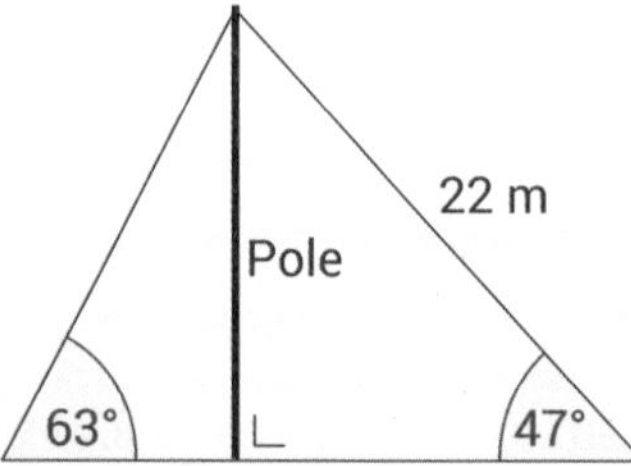

4. Two ships A and B leave the same harbour. Ship A travels due west and Ship B travels 67° south of west. After two hours, Ship A has travelled 46 km and is directly north of Ship B.

   (i) What is the distance (to the nearest km) travelled by Ship B in this time?

   (ii) Find the speed (to the nearest km h^{-1}) of Ship A.

   (iii) Find the speed (to the nearest km h^{-1}) of Ship B.

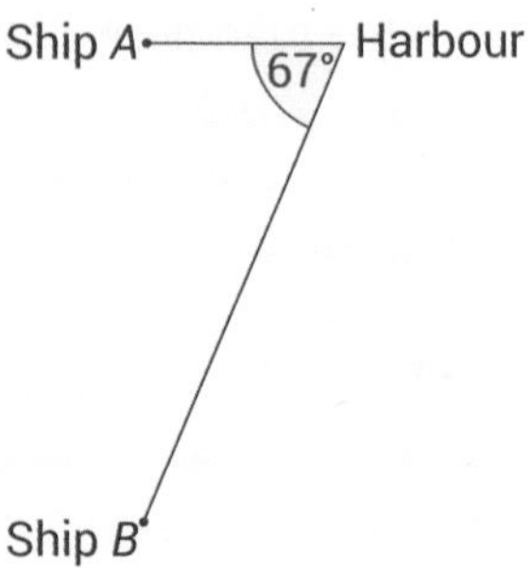

5. Liam wants to know the height of a tree in his back garden. Standing 5 m from the foot of the tree, and using a clinometer, he measures the angle of elevation of the top of the tree to be 33°. If Liam is 170 cm tall, find the height of the tree.

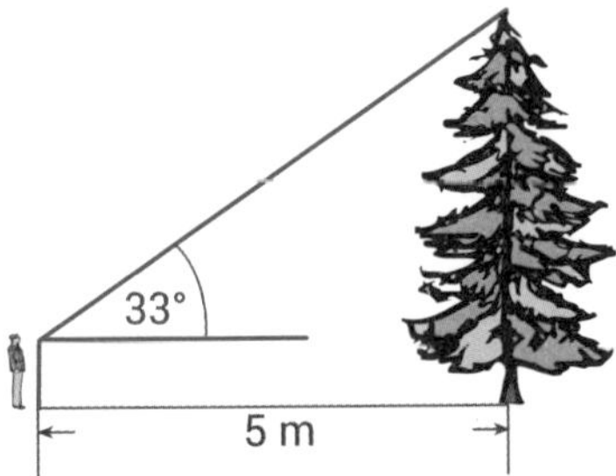

6. The Petronas Towers in Kuala Lumpur are among the world's tallest buildings. Using the information given in the diagram below, calculate the height, to the nearest metre, of the towers.

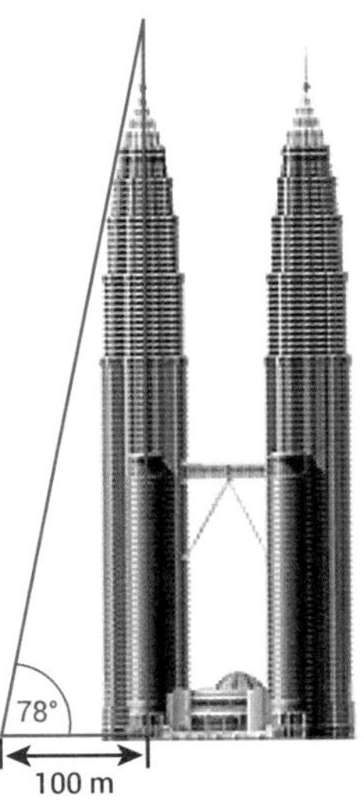

7. On a crane the structure between the point A and the point C is known as the jib of the crane. The structure between point B and point A is known as the counter jib. The cables connecting the jib and counter jib to the tower are known as jib ties.

$|AB| = 6$ m, $|AC| = 15$ m and the angle between counter jib and tie is 35°.

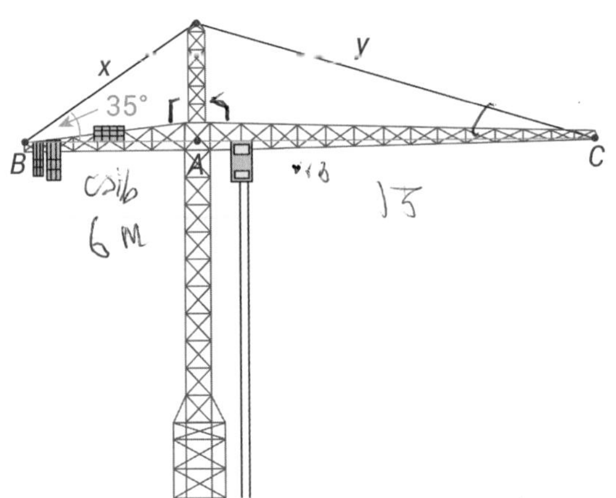

(i) Calculate the length of cable required to support the jib and counter jib on the crane shown. (Note: there are two strands of cable connected to each jib.)

(ii) Calculate the measure of each of the angles between the tower and the jib ties.

8. The diagram below is a plan of a triangular shaped dormer window. All measurements are in metres. All line segments represent the frame of the window.

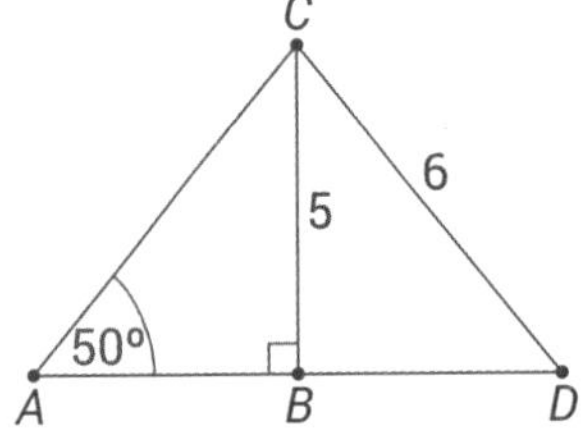

(i) Calculate $|BD|$ to the nearest centimetre.

(ii) Calculate the measure of $\angle CDB$ to the nearest degree.

(iii) Calculate the length of timber required to make this frame. Allow for 5% wastage.

9.

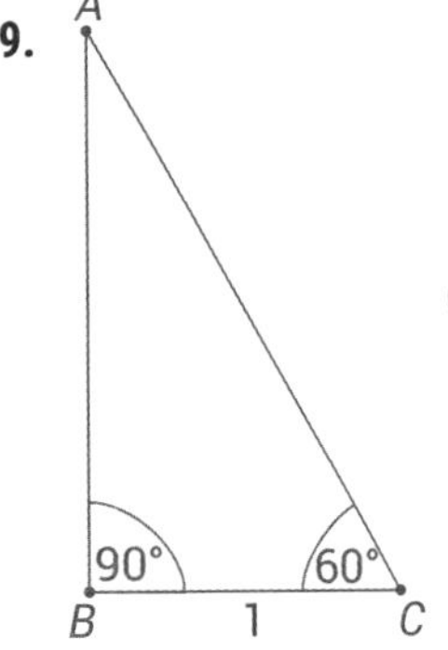

(i) What is the measure of $\angle BAC$?

(ii) Find $|AB|$ in surd form.

(iii) Use the theorem of Pythagoras to find $|AC|$.

10.

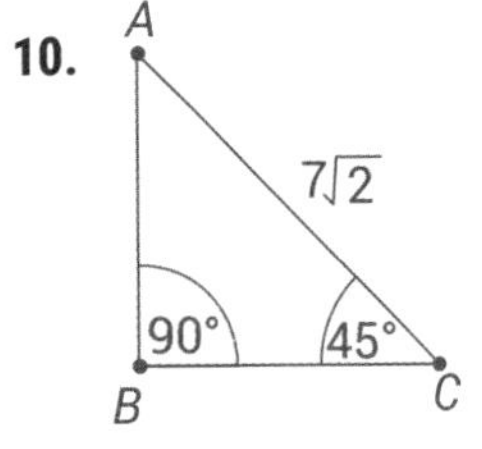

(i) Find the measure of $\angle BAC$.

(ii) Find $|BC|$.

11.

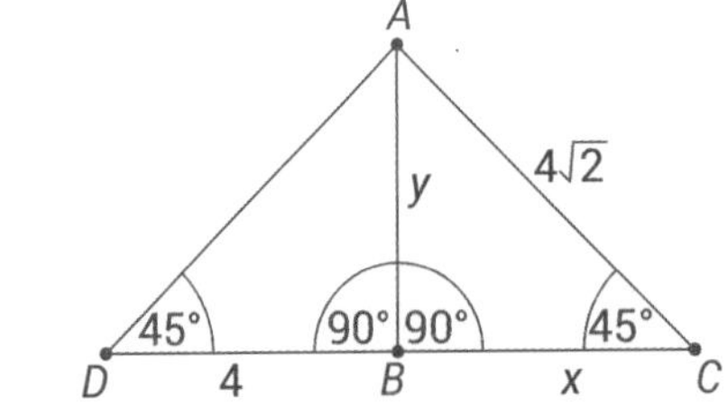

(i) Find the values of x and y.

(ii) What is the measure of $\angle DAB$?

TRIGONOMETRY

12. (a) *ABC* is a right-angled triangle.

$|\angle ACB| = 60°$ and $|AC| = 10$ cm.

Calculate the length of [*AB*], correct to two decimal places.

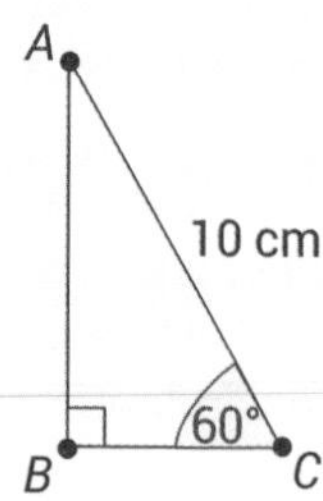

(b) In the diagram *MNO* is a triangle with [*OP*] perpendicular to [*MN*].

$|MP| = 10$ cm, $|ON| = 30$ cm and $|\angle PMO| = 65°$.

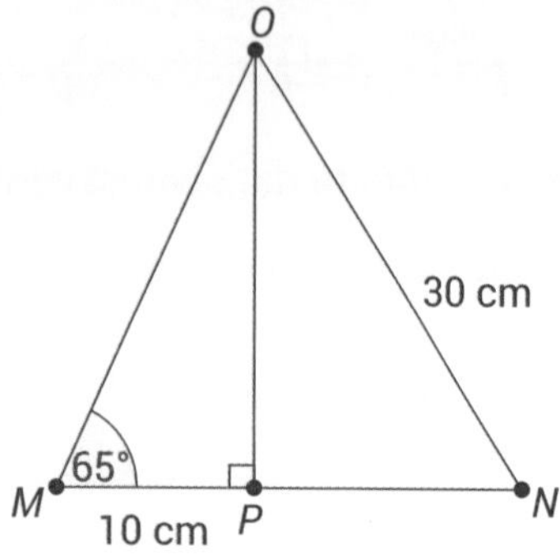

Calculate:

(i) $|OP|$, correct to one decimal place

(ii) $|\angle MON|$, correct to one decimal place

(c) A boat sails due east from the base *A* of a 30 m high lighthouse, [*AD*].

At the point *B*, the angle of depression of the boat from the top of the lighthouse is 68°.

Ten seconds later the boat is at the point *C* and the angle of depression is now 33°.

(i) Find $|BC|$, the distance the boat has travelled in this time.

(ii) Calculate the average speed at which the boat is sailing between *B* and *C*. Give your answer in metres per second, correct to one decimal place.

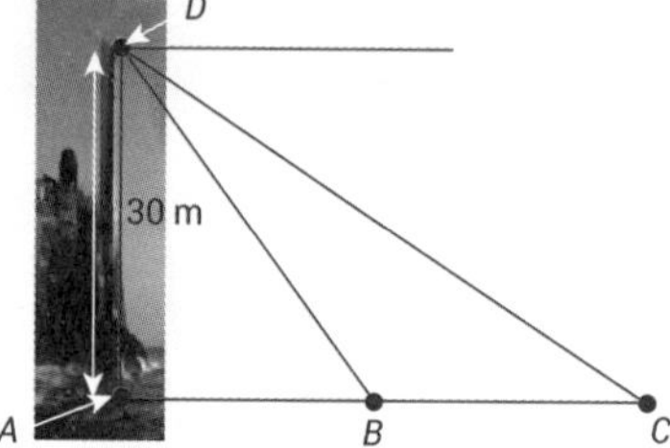

17.6 Area of a Triangle

Derivation of Area

The sine ratio can be used to derive a formula for the area of a triangle.

Step 1 Write down sin *C* in term of *a* and *h*.

$\sin C = \frac{h}{a}$

Step 2 Using the answer to step 1, write *h* in terms of *a* and sin *C*.

$h = a \sin C$

Step 3 Now, using the formula 'Area of a Triangle = $\frac{1}{2}$ Base × Perpendicular height', write down the area of the triangle in terms of *b* and *h*.

Area $= \frac{1}{2}bh$

Step 4 Using steps 2 and 3, write down the area of the triangle in terms of *a*, *b* and sin *C*.

$$\text{Area} = \frac{1}{2}bh = \frac{1}{2}(b)(a \sin C) = \frac{1}{2}ab \sin C$$

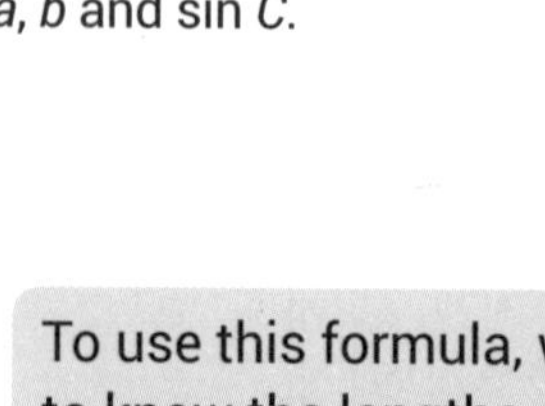

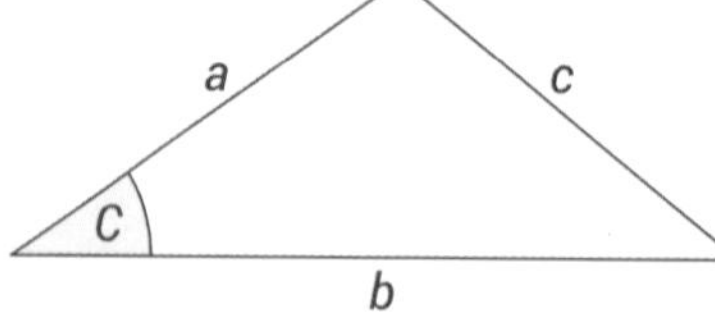

Area $= \frac{1}{2}ab \sin C$

To use this formula, we need to know the lengths of two sides of the triangle and the angle **between** these two sides.

This formula is given on page 16 of *Formulae and Tables*.

Worked Example 17.11

Find the area of the given triangle. Give your answer correct to two decimal places.

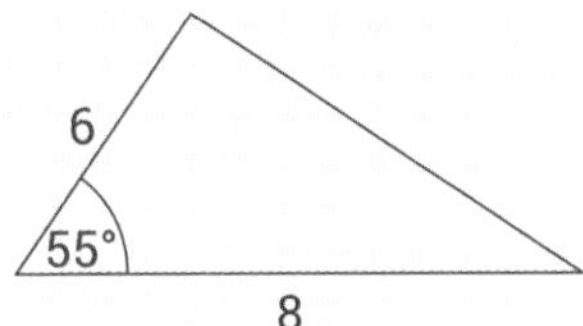

Solution

$$\text{Area} = \frac{1}{2}ab\sin C$$
$$= \frac{1}{2}(6)(8)(\sin 55°)$$
$$= 19.6596...$$
$= 19.66$ square units, to two decimal places

Worked Example 17.12

Find the measure of the angle A. Give your answer correct to the nearest degree.

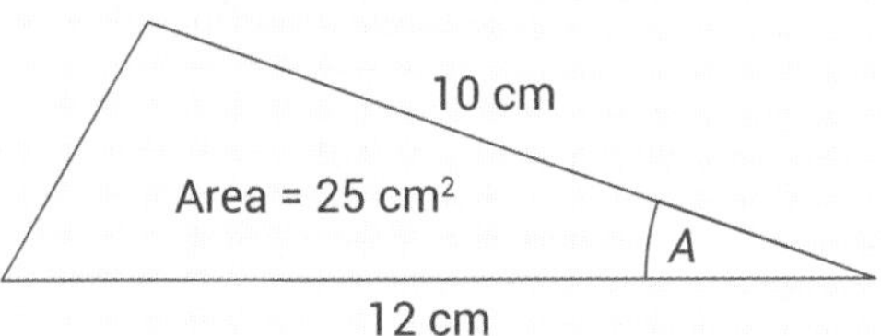

Solution

$$\frac{1}{2}ab\sin C = \text{Area}$$
$$\frac{1}{2}(12)(10)(\sin A) = 25$$
$$(60)(\sin A) = 25$$
$$\sin A = \frac{25}{60}$$
$$\sin A = \frac{5}{12}$$
$$A = \sin^{-1}\left(\frac{5}{12}\right)$$
$A = 25°$, to the nearest degree

We use angle A, as it is the angle between the two given sides.

Exercise 17.5

Find the area of each of the triangles in Questions 1 to 6 (answers correct to two decimal places).

1.

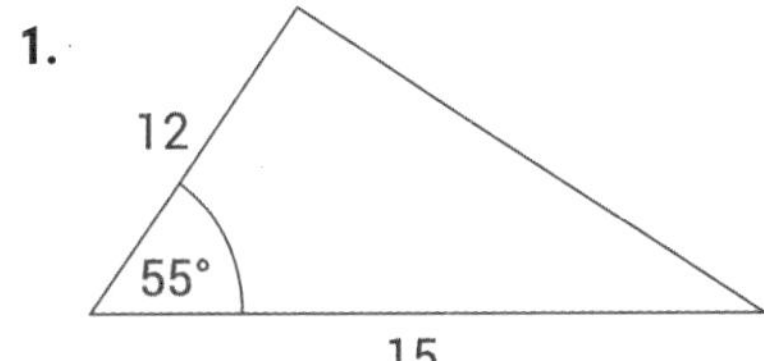

2.

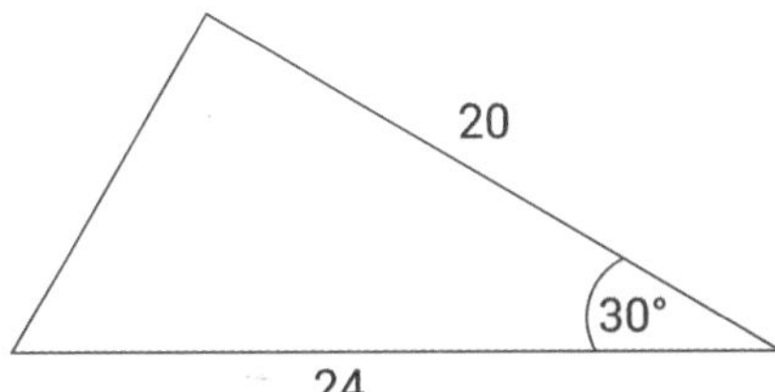

3.

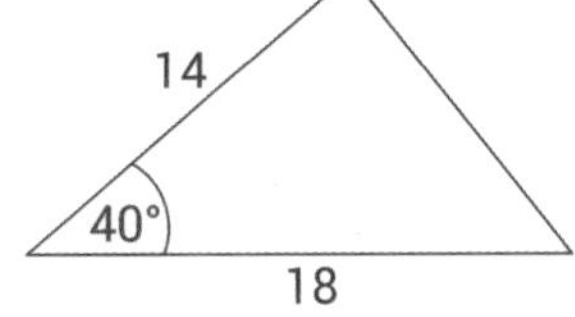

4.

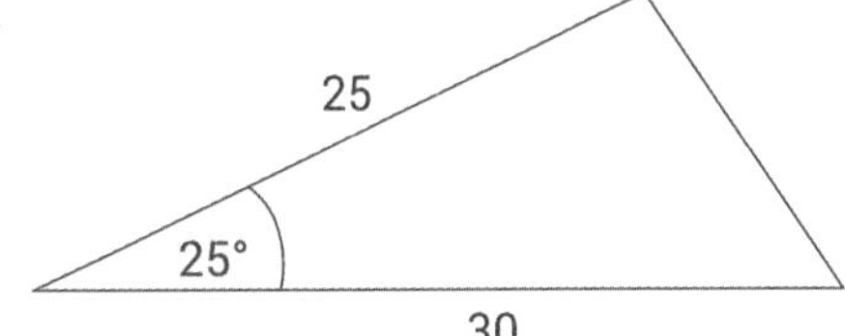

5.

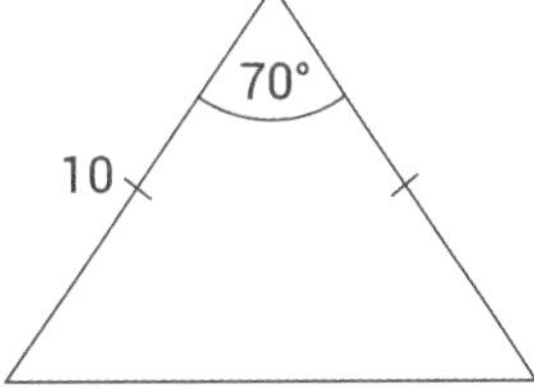

6. In a triangle ABC, $|AB| = 7$ cm, $|AC| = 8.4$ cm and $|\angle BAC| = 62°$.

Calculate, to the nearest square centimetre, the area of the triangle ABC.

7. In a triangle XYZ, $|XY| = 9$ cm, $|XZ| = 18.4$ cm and $|\angle YXZ| = 82°$.

Calculate, to the nearest square centimetre, the area of the triangle XYZ.

8. The area of each of the triangles shown is given. Find the measure of the angle A.

(i)

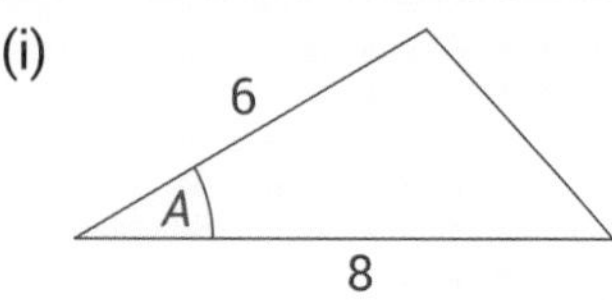

Area = 12 units²

(ii)

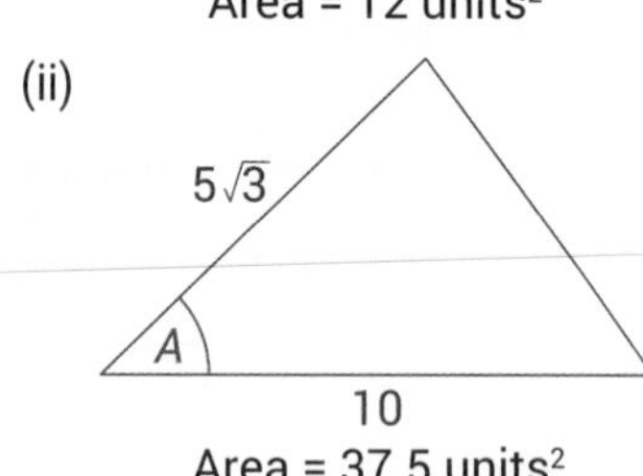

Area = 37.5 units²

9. A tile is in the shape of a parallelogram. The area of the parallelogram is 2227.18 mm². Other dimensions are shown on the diagram.

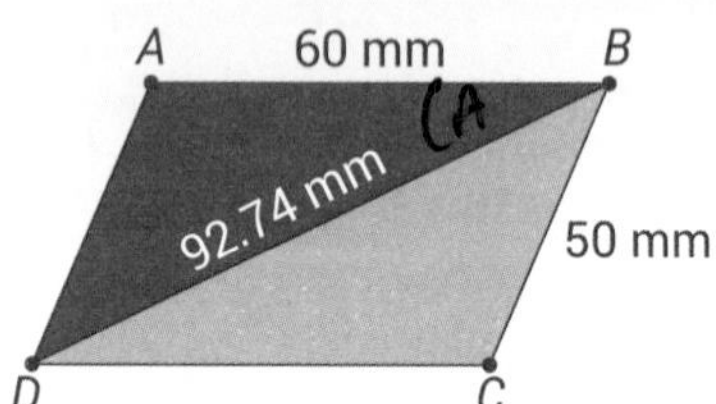

(i) Calculate $|\angle ABD|$ and $|\angle DBC|$.

(ii) Hence, find $|\angle DAB|$.

10. In the triangle XYZ, $\cos(\angle XYZ) = \frac{3}{5}$.

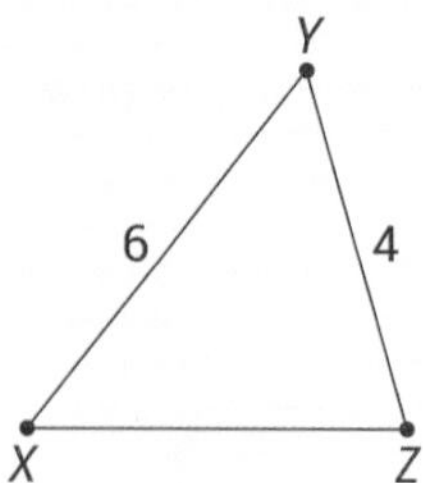

(i) By drawing a suitable triangle, find $\sin(\angle XYZ)$.

(ii) Hence, calculate the area of ΔXYZ.

11. In a triangle ABC, $|AB| = 10$ cm, $|BC| = 8$ cm and $\cos(\angle ABC) = \frac{5}{13}$.

(i) By drawing a suitable triangle, find $\sin(\angle ABC)$.

(ii) Hence, find the area of ΔABC.

17.7 The Unit Circle 

The unit circle has its centre at (0,0) and has a radius length of 1 unit.

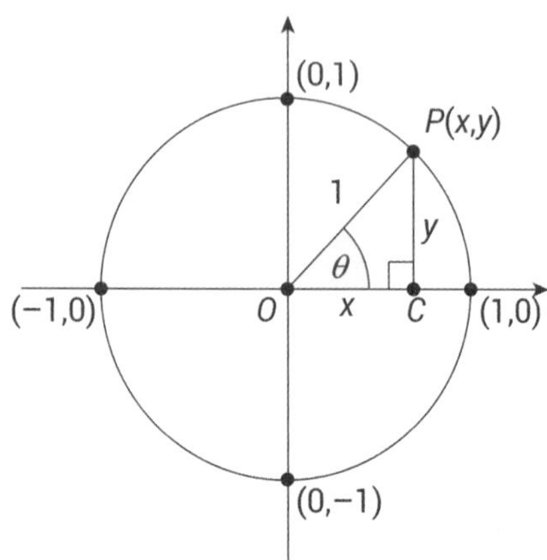

$\cos\theta = x$ co-ordinate

$\sin\theta = y$ co-ordinate

Also, $\tan\theta = \dfrac{\sin\theta}{\cos\theta}$

All of these definitions are on page 13 of *Formulae and Tables*.

Let $P(x,y)$ be any point on the unit circle, such that $|\angle POC| < 90°$.

From the triangle OPC we have,

$$\cos\theta = \frac{x}{1} \qquad \sin\theta = \frac{y}{1}$$

$$\therefore x = \cos\theta \qquad \therefore y = \sin\theta$$

So the co-ordinates of P can be written as $(\cos\theta, \sin\theta)$.

For $\theta \geqslant 90°$, we define $\cos\theta$ to be the x co-ordinate of P and $\sin\theta$ to be the y co-ordinate of P.

Worked Example 17.13

Use the unit circle to find cos 270° and sin 270°.

Solution

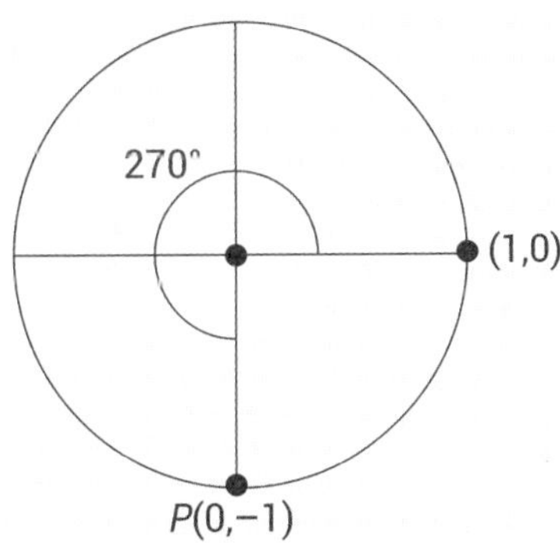

From the unit circle, cos 270° = 0 (x co-ordinate) and sin 270° = −1 (y co-ordinate).

17.8 Evaluating the Trigonometric Ratios of All Angles Between 0° and 360°

Reference Angles

Consider an angle AOB, where $|\angle AOB| = 140°$.

$\angle AOB$ will lie in the second quadrant of the unit circle.

$|\angle AOB| = 140°$

Reference angle

$= 180° - 140°$

$= 40°$

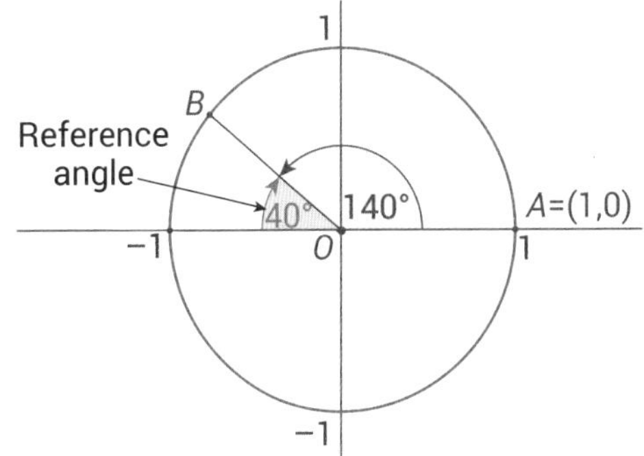

The acute angle formed by the terminal side of $\angle AOB$ (i.e. where the angle ends) and the **x-axis** is called the reference angle of $\angle AOB$.
In this case the reference angle measures 40°.

Here are similar examples for angles that lie in the third and fourth quadrants respectively.

$|\angle AOB| = 250°$

Reference angle

$= 250° - 180°$

$= 70°$

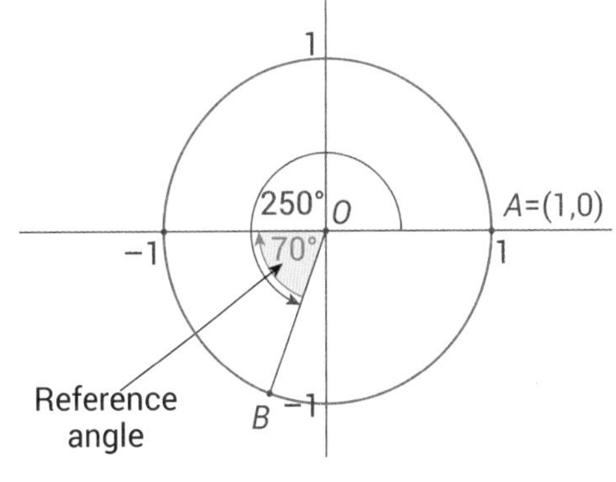

$|\angle AOB| = 330°$

Reference angle

$= 360° - 330°$

$= 30°$

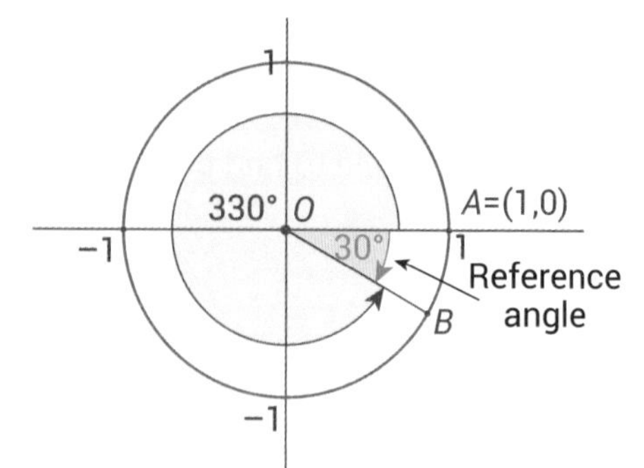

The Sign of the Ratios in Each Quadrant

First Quadrant (0° < θ < 90°)

In the first quadrant, all three ratios are positive.

- cos θ is positive, as its value lies on the positive *x*-axis.
- sin θ is positive, as its value lies on the positive *y*-axis.
- $\tan\theta = \frac{\sin\theta}{\cos\theta} = \frac{+}{+} = +$ Hence, tan θ is positive.

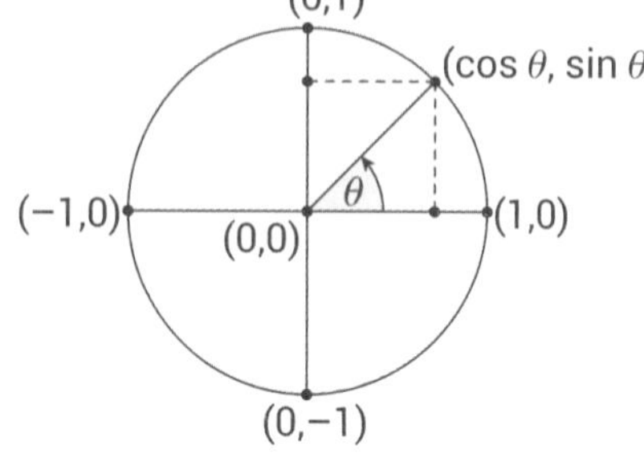

Second Quadrant (90° < θ < 180°)

In the second quadrant, sin is positive; cos and tan are negative.

- cos θ is negative, as its value lies on the negative *x*-axis.
- sin θ is positive, as its value lies on the positive *y*-axis.
- $\tan\theta = \frac{\sin\theta}{\cos\theta} = \frac{+}{-} = -$ Hence, tan θ is negative.

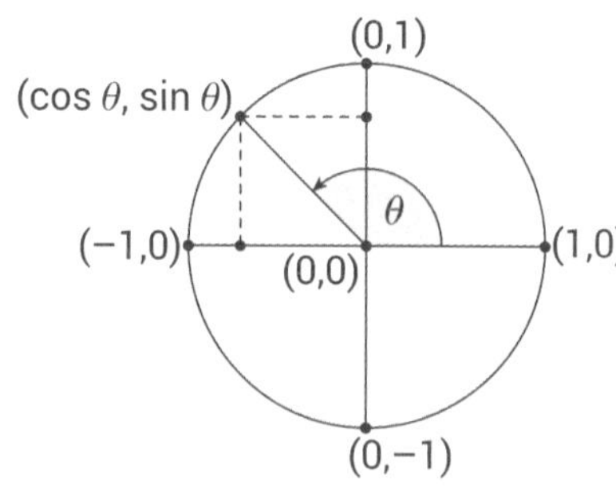

Third Quadrant (180° < θ < 270°)

In the third quadrant, tan is positive; sin and cos are negative.

- cos θ is negative, as its value lies on the negative *x*-axis.
- sin θ is negative, as its value lies on the negative *y*-axis.
- $\tan\theta = \frac{\sin\theta}{\cos\theta} = \frac{-}{-} = +$ Hence, tan θ is positive.

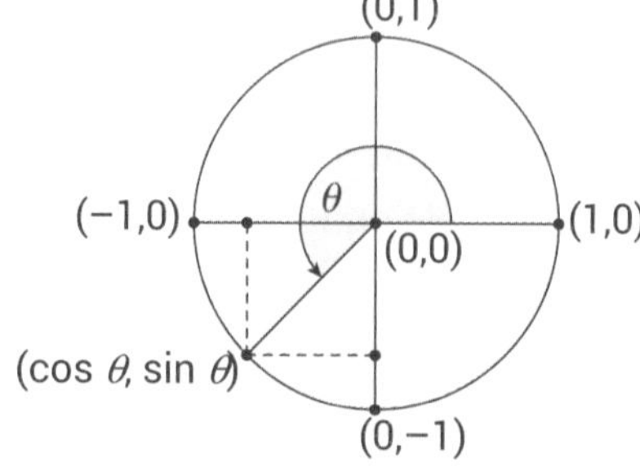

Fourth Quadrant (270° < θ < 360°)

In the fourth quadrant, cos is positive; sin and tan are negative.

- cos θ is positive, as its value lies on the positive *x*-axis.
- sin θ is negative, as its value lies on the negative *y*-axis.
- $\tan\theta = \frac{\sin\theta}{\cos\theta} = \frac{-}{+} = -$ Hence, tan θ is negative.

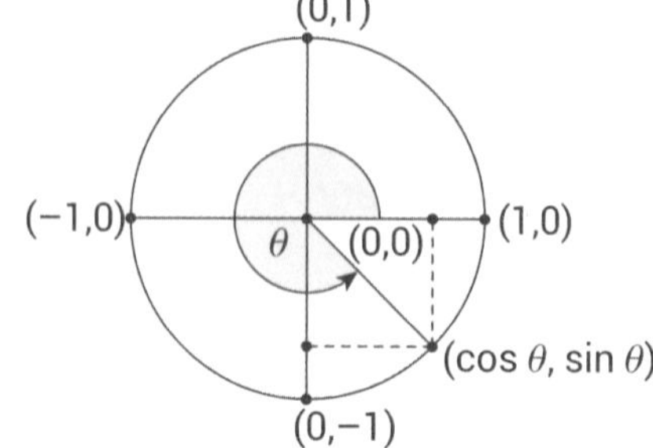

CAST

The diagram on the right summarises this section.

- In the first quadrant, all (A) are positive.
- In the second quadrant, only sin (S) is positive.
- In the third quadrant, only tan (T) is positive.
- In the fourth quadrant, only cos (C) is positive.

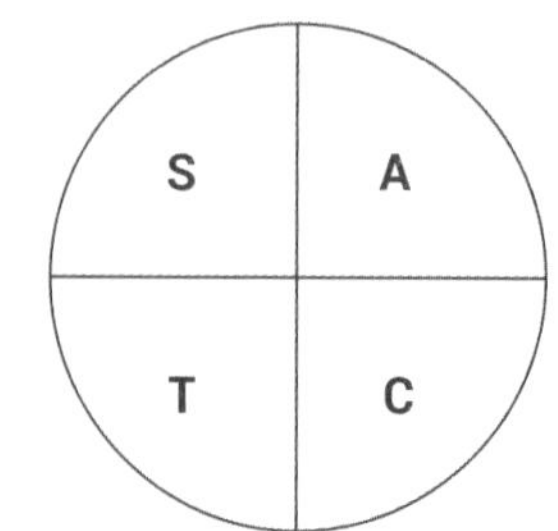

Worked Example 17.14

Write in surd form:

(i) cos 150° (ii) sin 330° (iii) tan 225°

Solution

(i) cos 150°

Step 1

Draw an angle of 150°.

Step 2

The angle is in the second quadrant; therefore, its cos is negative.

Step 3

The reference angle is 30° (180° − 150°).

$\cos 30° = \frac{\sqrt{3}}{2}$

Step 4

$\therefore \cos 150° = -\frac{\sqrt{3}}{2}$

(ii) sin 330°

Step 1

Draw an angle of 330°.

Step 2

The angle is in the fourth quadrant; therefore, its sin is negative.

Step 3

The reference angle is 30° (360° − 330°).

$\sin 30° = \frac{1}{2}$

Step 4

$\therefore \sin 330° = -\frac{1}{2}$

(iii) tan 225°

Step 1

Draw an angle of 225°.

Step 2

The angle is in the third quadrant; therefore, its tan is positive.

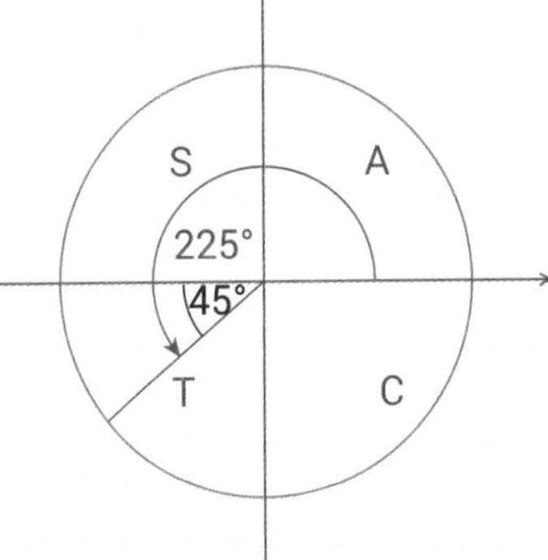

Step 3

The reference angle is 45° (225° − 180°).

$\tan 45° = 1$

Step 4

$\therefore \tan 225° = 1$

Worked Example 17.15

Given $\cos A = -\frac{1}{2}$ and $0° \leqslant A \leqslant 360°$, find two values of A that satisfy the equation.

Solution

Step 1 Locate the quadrants in which A lies. As cos A is negative, then A lies in the 2nd quadrant or in the 3rd quadrant.

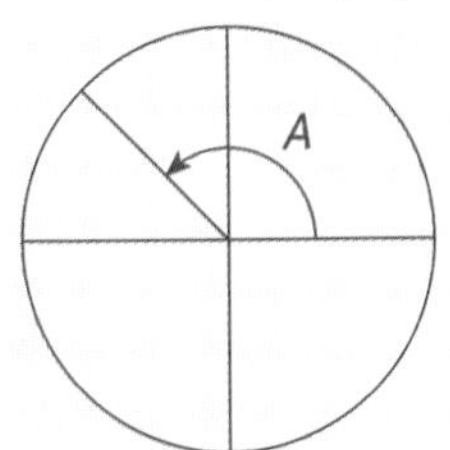

2nd quadrant

OR

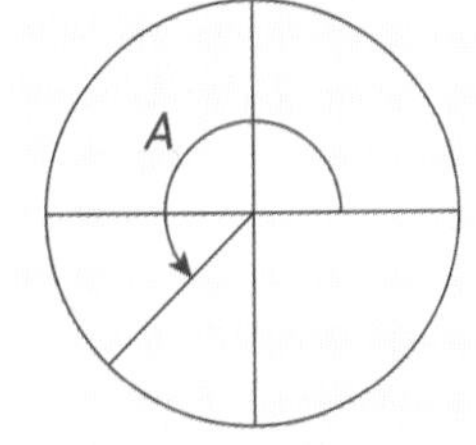

3rd quadrant

Step 2 Find the reference angle.

If A were acute,

$\cos A = \frac{1}{2}$

$A = 60°$

$\therefore$ Reference angle = 60°

Step 3 Find values for A.

2nd quadrant:

$A = 180° - 60°$

$= 120°$

OR

3rd quadrant:

$A = 180° + 60°$

$= 240°$

Exercise 17.6

In Questions 1 to 13, use the unit circle to evaluate the following:

1. cos 270°
2. sin 270°
3. cos 90°
4. sin 90°
5. tan 180°
6. cos 180°
7. sin 180°
8. cos 0°
9. sin 0°
10. tan 0°
11. cos 360°
12. sin 360°
13. tan 360°

For Questions 14 to 23, write your answer in surd form.

14. cos 135°
15. sin 150°
16. cos 240°
17. sin 330°
18. tan 210°
19. cos 315°
20. sin 120°
21. cos 210°
22. tan 300°
23. tan 60°

For Questions 24 to 33, use your calculator and give your answer correct to two decimal places.

24. cos 145°
25. sin 160°
26. cos 230°
27. sin 355°
28. tan 220°
29. cos 325°
30. sin 140°
31. cos 230°
32. tan 350°
33. tan 160°

34. If $\sin A = \frac{1}{2}$, find two values for A, if $0° \leqslant A \leqslant 360°$.
35. If $\cos A = \frac{1}{\sqrt{2}}$, find two values for A, if $0° \leqslant A \leqslant 360°$.
36. If $\tan A = \sqrt{3}$, find two values for A, if $0° \leqslant A \leqslant 360°$.

17.9 The Sine Rule

The Sine Rule enables us to find lengths of sides and measures of angles in any triangle, provided certain conditions are met.

Consider ΔXYZ.

Area $\Delta XYZ = \frac{1}{2} ab \sin C = \frac{1}{2} ac \sin B = \frac{1}{2} bc \sin A$

$\therefore ab \sin C = ac \sin B = bc \sin A$ (Multiplying by 2)

$$\frac{ab \sin C}{abc} = \frac{ac \sin B}{abc} = \frac{bc \sin A}{abc}$$ (Dividing by abc)

$$\therefore \frac{\sin A}{a} = \frac{\sin B}{b} = \frac{\sin C}{c}$$

or

$$\frac{a}{\sin A} = \frac{b}{\sin B} = \frac{c}{\sin C}$$

$$\frac{a}{\sin A} = \frac{b}{\sin B} = \frac{c}{\sin C}$$

OR

$$\frac{\sin A}{a} = \frac{\sin B}{b} = \frac{\sin C}{c}$$

You can find this formula on page 16 of *Formulae and Tables*.

To use the Sine Rule you need:

two angles and one side (opposite one of the angles)

OR

two sides and one angle (opposite one of the sides)

Worked Example 17.16

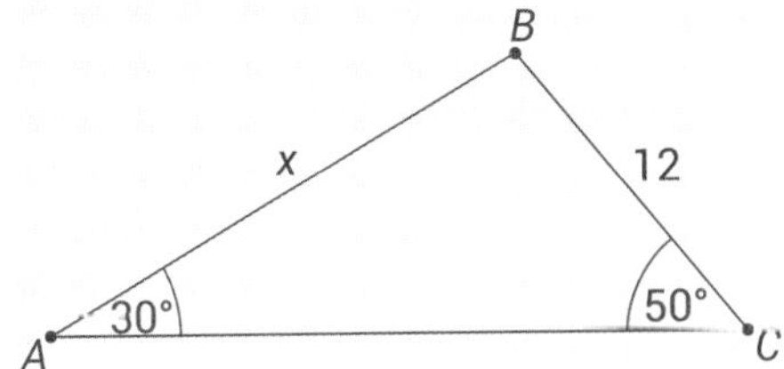

Find x, the distance from A to B.
Give your answer to two decimal places.

Solution

$$\frac{x}{\sin 50°} = \frac{12}{\sin 30°}$$

$$x = \frac{12 \sin 50°}{\sin 30°}$$

$x = 18.39$, to 2 decimal places

Use $\frac{a}{\sin A} = \frac{b}{\sin B}$ if calculating a side length.

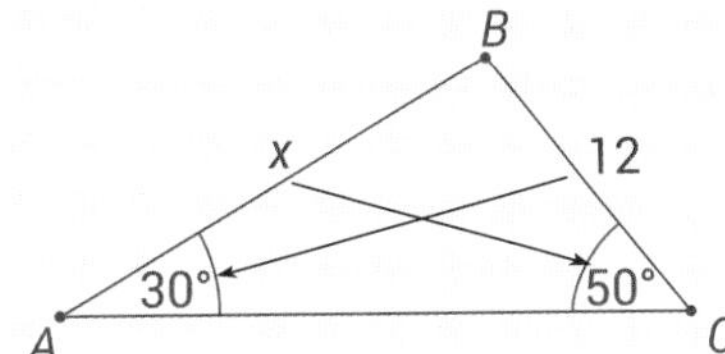

Worked Example 17.17

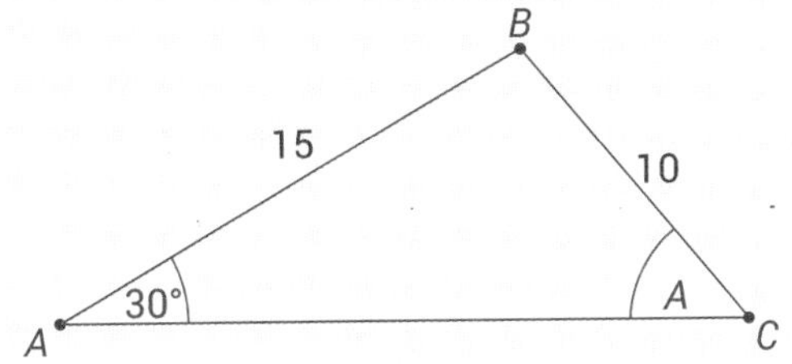

Find the value of A. Give your answer to the nearest degree.

Solution

$$\frac{\sin A}{15} = \frac{\sin 30°}{10}$$

$$\sin A = \frac{15(\sin 30°)}{10}$$

$\sin A = 0.75$

$A = \sin^{-1} 0.75$

$\therefore A = 49°$, to the nearest degree

Use $\frac{\sin A}{a} = \frac{\sin B}{b}$ if calculating an angle measurement.

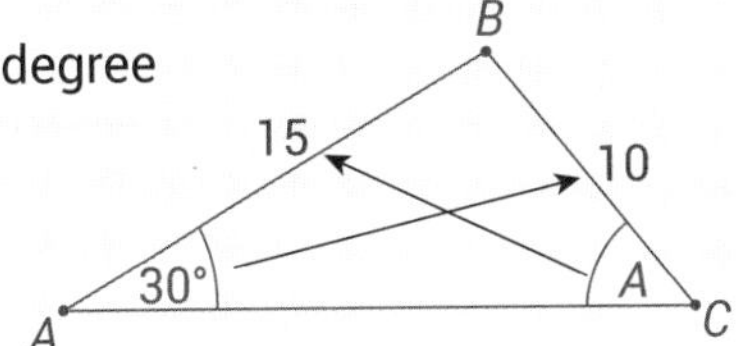

Exercise 17.7

In Questions 1 to 5, use the Sine Rule to find the value of x. Write each answer correct to two decimal places.

1.

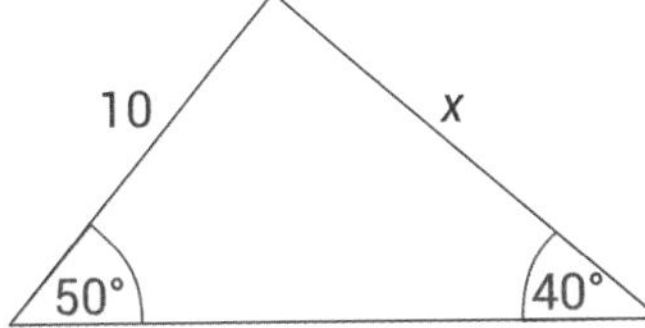

2.

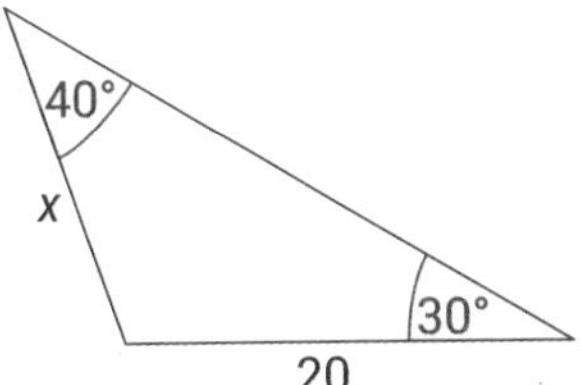

3.

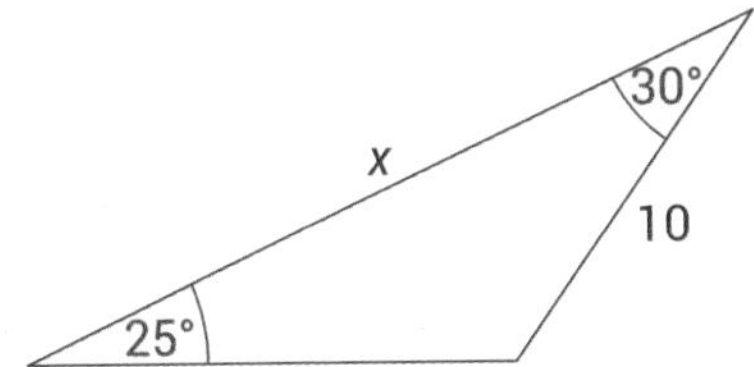

4.

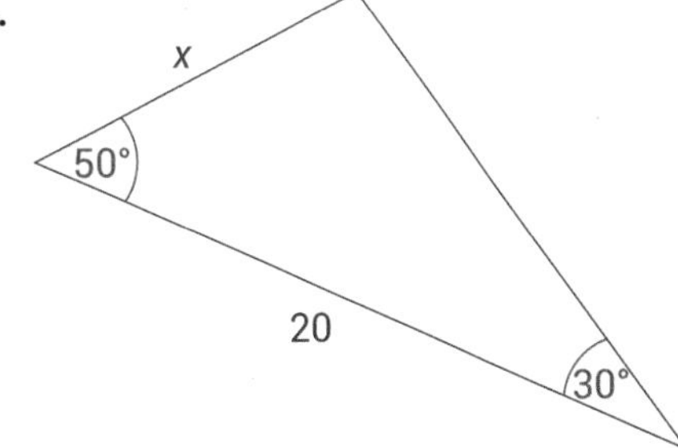

5.

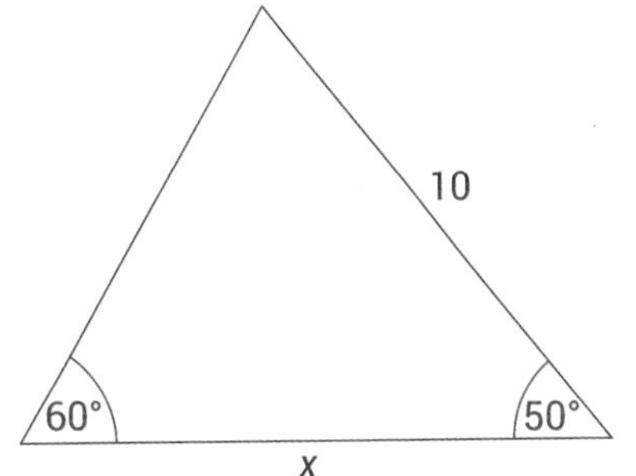

6. Find A, correct to the nearest degree.

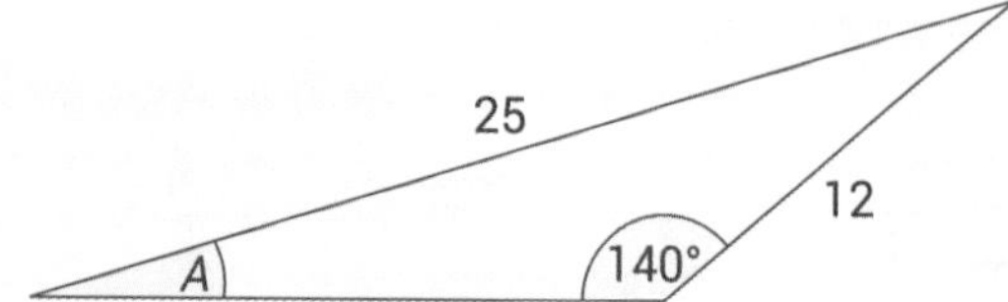

7. Find A, correct to the nearest degree.

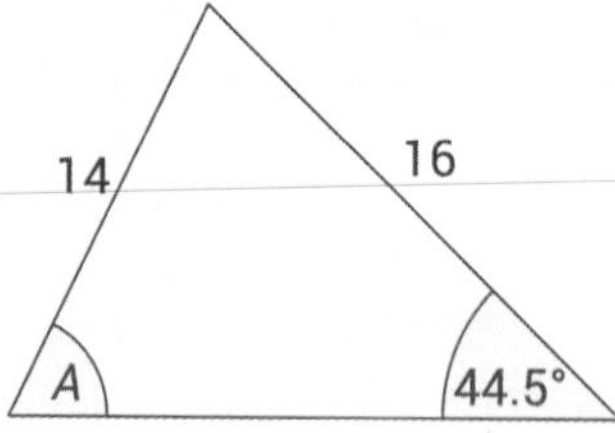

8. In the triangle shown, $a = 15$, $b = 25$ and $B = 50°$.

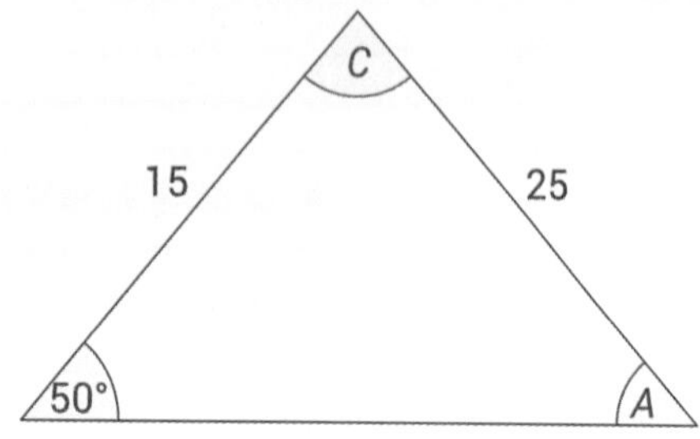

(i) Find A, correct to the nearest degree.

(ii) Hence, find the measure of the angle C.

(iii) Hence, find the area of the triangle, correct to one decimal place.

9. In the triangle shown, $B = 53°$, $b = 8$ and $a = 9.3$.

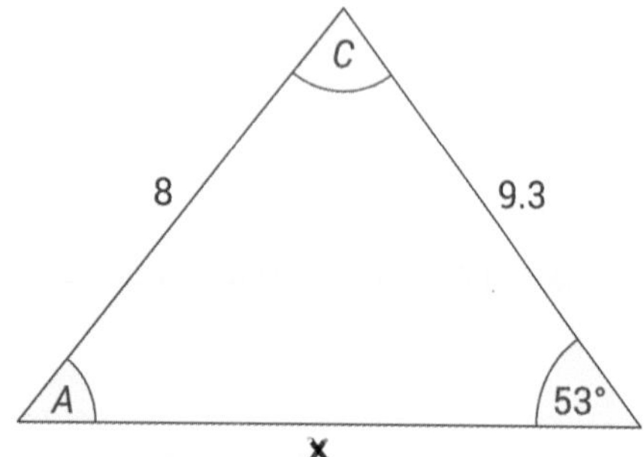

(i) Find A, correct to the nearest degree.

(ii) Hence, find the measure of the angle C.

(iii) Hence, find the area of the triangle, correct to one decimal place.

(iv) Using the area of the triangle, find the length of side c, to two decimal places.

10. In the diagram $a = 7$, $b = 12$ and $B = 45°$.

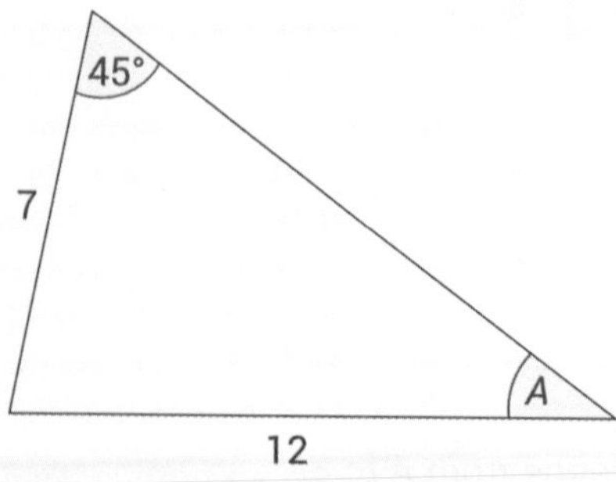

(i) Find A, correct to the nearest degree.

(ii) Hence, find the area of the triangle, correct to one decimal place.

(iii) Hence, find the length of side c, to two decimal places.

11. John is standing at a point P on the southern bank of a river. He wants to swim across to the northern bank. There are just two landing points, Q and R, on the northern bank. R is 80 m downstream from Q.

The path $[PQ]$ makes an angle of 50° with the bank, and the path $[PR]$ makes an angle of 60° with the bank. The situation is shown in the diagram below.

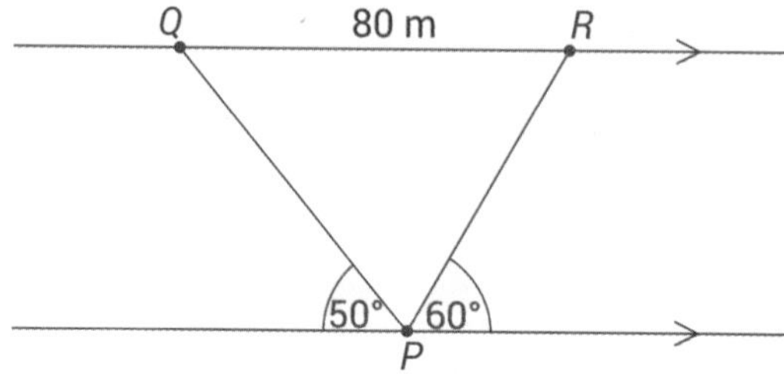

Using the Sine Rule, calculate $|PQ|$ and $|PR|$, to two decimal places.

12. A farmer needs to fertilise one of his fields. He must know the area of the field, so that he can order the correct quantity of fertiliser. A diagram of the field (including some measurements) is shown below.

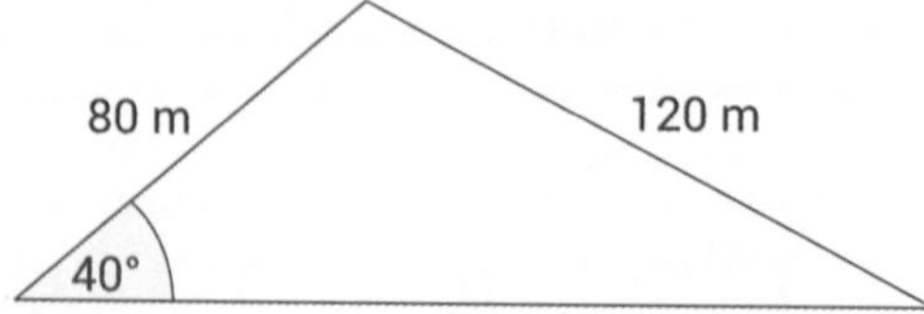

Calculate the area of the field to the nearest square metre.

(Hint: Find, using the Sine Rule, another angle in the triangle.)

17.10 The Cosine Rule

There are two cases in particular where the Sine Rule cannot be used to solve a triangle.

The first case arises when two sides of a triangle are known and the angle contained between the two sides is also known.

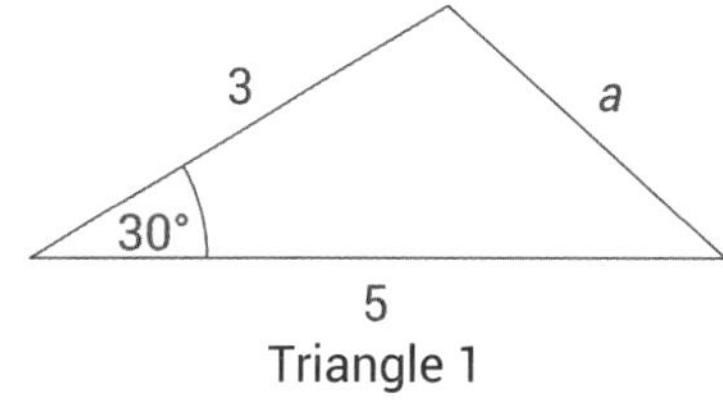

Triangle 1

In Triangle 1, we cannot find the length of the side *a* using the Sine Rule.

The second case arises when three sides of a triangle are known and we wish to find the measure of the angles in the triangle.

In Triangle 2, we cannot find the measure of any angle in the triangle.

Both cases can be solved using the Cosine Rule.

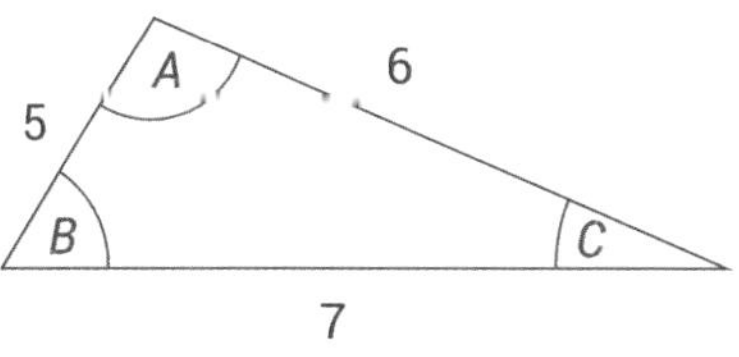

Triangle 2

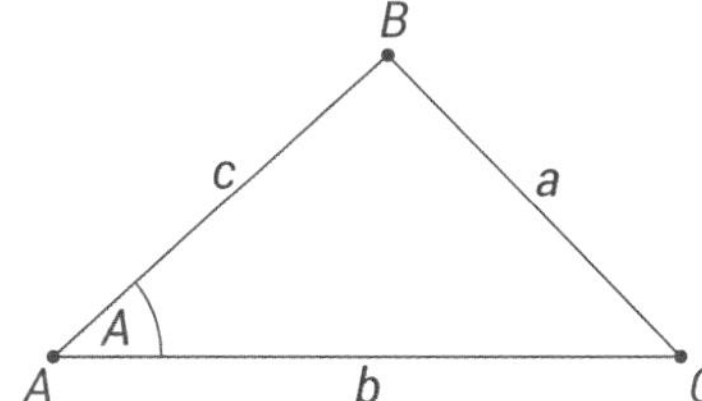

$$a^2 = b^2 + c^2 - 2bc \cos A$$

You can find this formula on page 16 of *Formulae and Tables*.

If the lengths of two sides of a triangle and the angle between these sides are known, then we can use the Cosine Rule to find the length of the third side in the triangle.

If we know the lengths of all three sides in a triangle, then we can use the Cosine Rule to find the measure of any angle in the triangle.

Worked Example 17.18

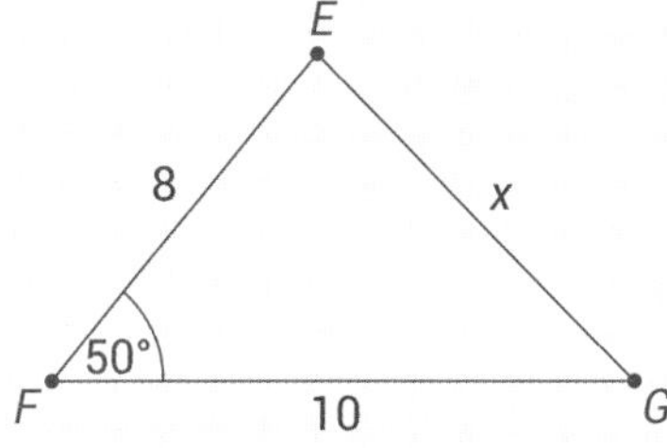

Find *x*, the distance from *E* to *G*. Give your answer to two decimal places.

Solution

$a^2 = b^2 + c^2 - 2bc \cos A$

$x^2 = 8^2 + 10^2 - 2(8)(10) \cos(50°)$

$x^2 = 61.15398...$ (Calculator)

$x = \sqrt{61.15398...}$

$\therefore x = 7.82$, to 2 decimal places

Worked Example 17.19

Find the measure of the angle θ.
Give your answer to the nearest degree.

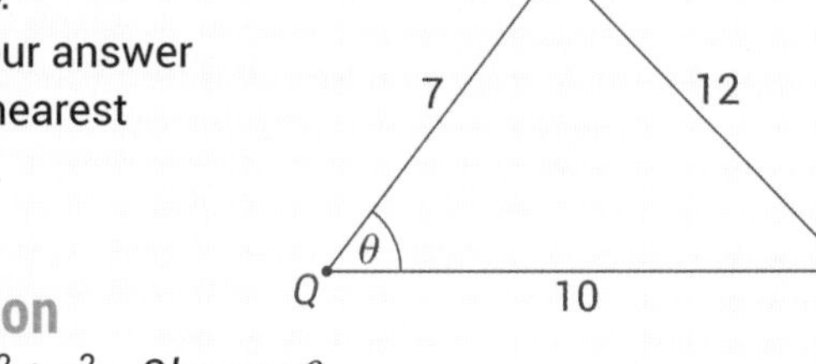

Solution

$a^2 = b^2 + c^2 - 2bc \cos\theta$

$12^2 = 7^2 + 10^2 - 2(7)(10) \cos\theta$

$144 = 49 + 100 - 140 \cos\theta$

$144 = 149 - 140 \cos\theta$

$140 \cos\theta = 149 - 144$

$140 \cos\theta = 5$

$\cos\theta = \frac{5}{140} = \frac{1}{28}$

$\theta = \cos^{-1}\left(\frac{1}{28}\right)$

$\therefore \theta = 88°$, to the nearest degree

Exercise 17.8

In Questions 1 to 5, use the Cosine Rule to find the value of *a*. Write each answer correct to two decimal places.

1.

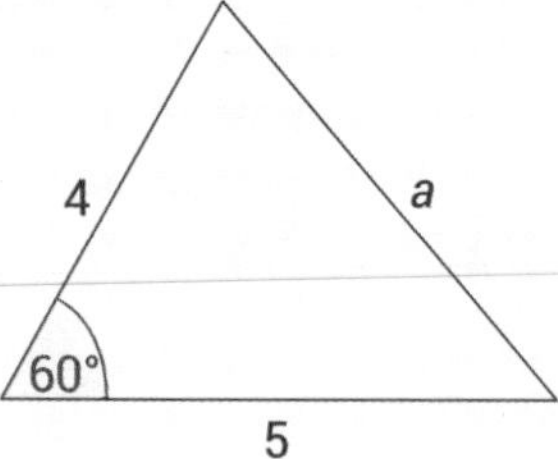

2.

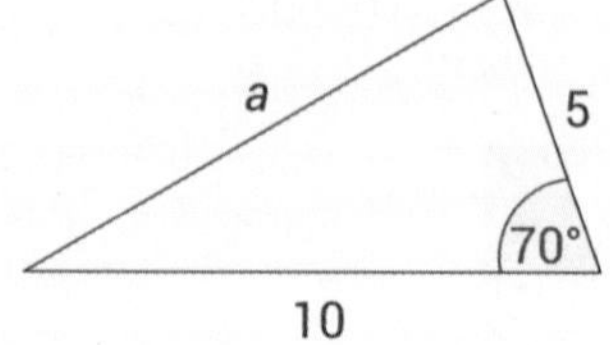

3.

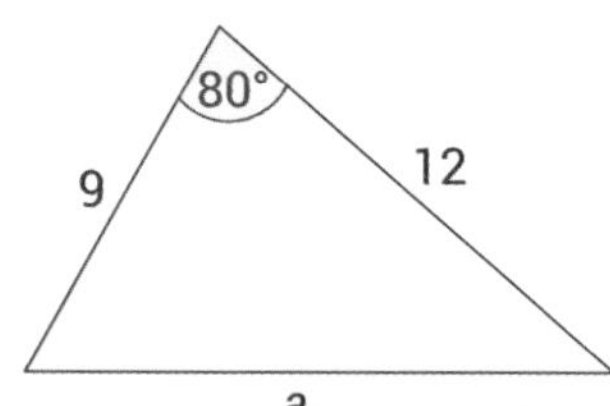

4.

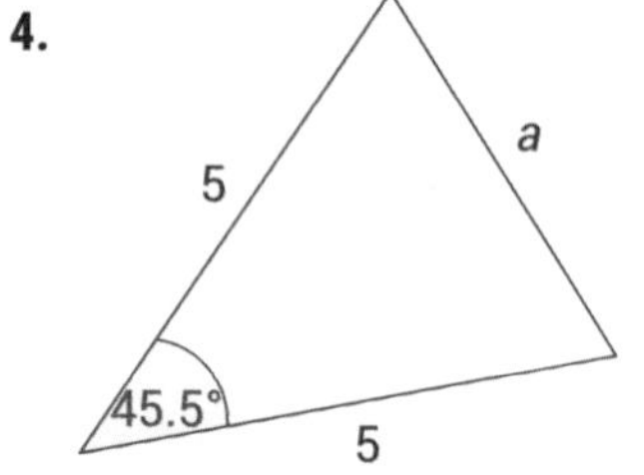

5.

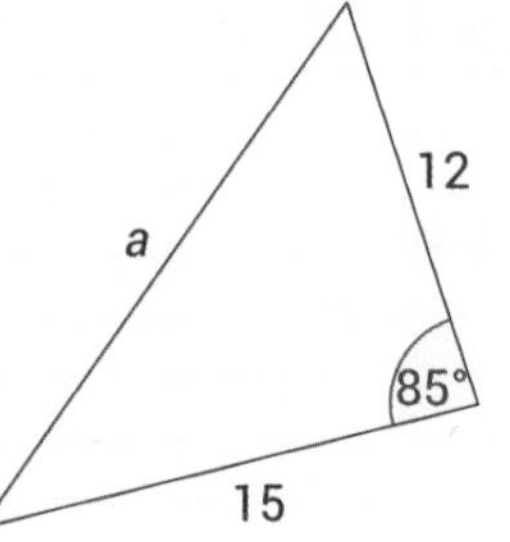

In Questions 6 to 9, use the Cosine Rule to find the value of *A*. Give your answers to the nearest degree.

6.

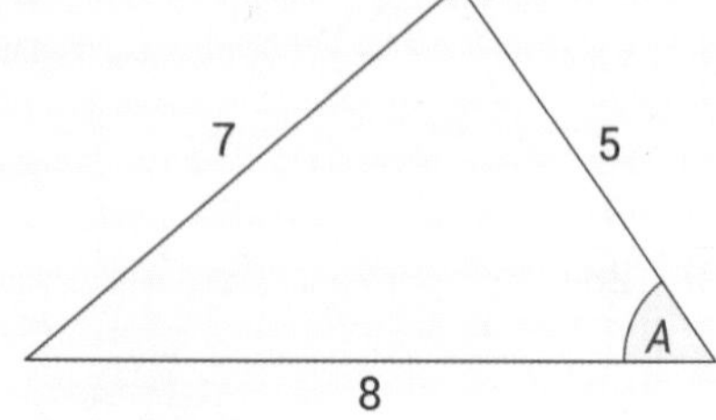

7.

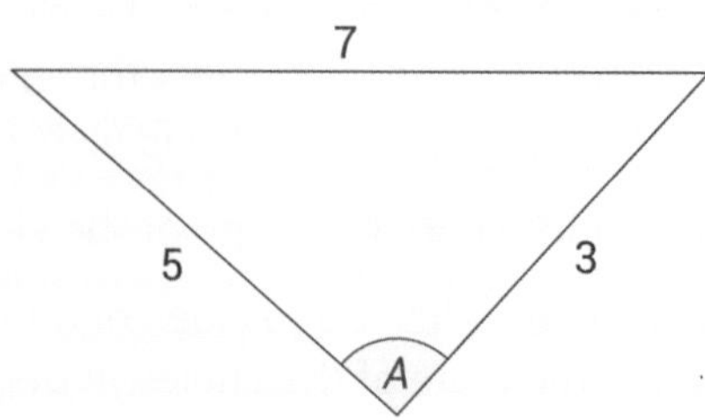

8.

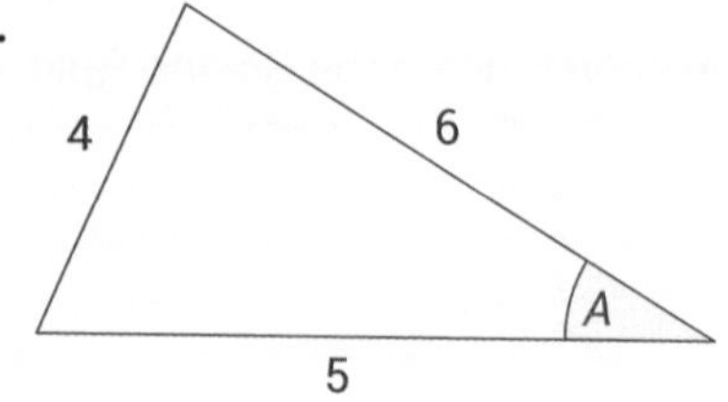

9.

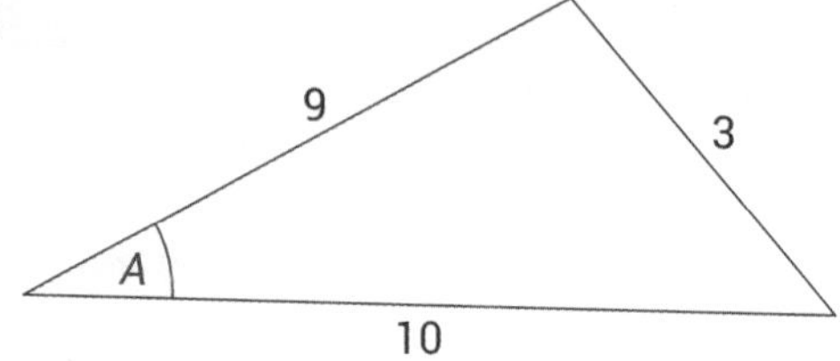

10.

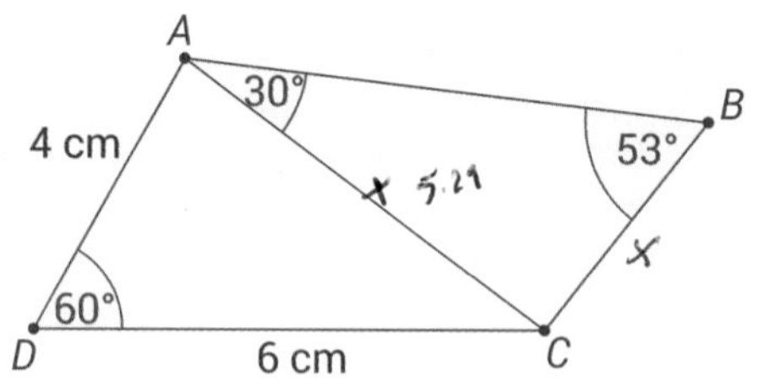

ABCD is a quadrilateral. $|AD| = 4$ cm and $|DC| = 6$ cm. $|\angle ADC| = 60°$, $|\angle CAB| = 30°$ and $|\angle ABC| = 53°$.

(a) Find, to two decimal places:

(i) $|AC|$

(ii) $|BC|$

(b) Hence, find the area of the quadrilateral *ABCD* to the nearest mm^2.

11. The sides of a triangle have lengths 9 cm, 5 cm and 7 cm.

(i) Construct the triangle.

(ii) Using a protractor, find the measure of the largest angle.

(iii) Confirm your answer by using the Cosine Rule to find (to the nearest degree) the measure of the largest angle.

(iv) Hence, find the area of the triangle to two decimal places.

12. The sides of a triangle have lengths 3 cm, 5 cm and 7 cm.

(i) Construct the triangle.

(ii) Using a protractor, find the measure of the smallest angle.

(iii) Confirm your answer by using the Cosine Rule to find (to the nearest degree) the measure of the smallest angle.

(iv) Find the area of the triangle.

13.

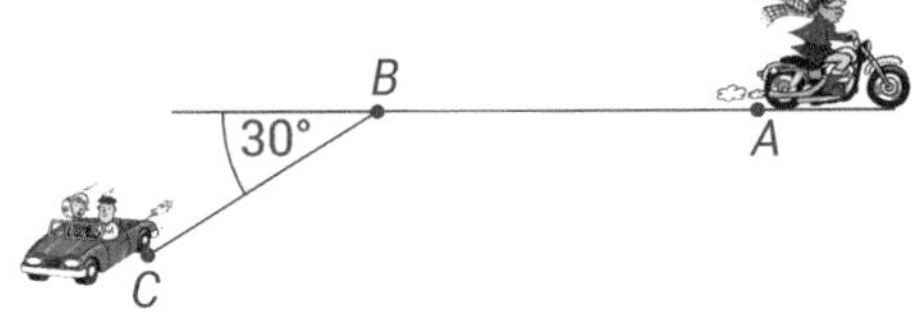

A motorcyclist and a car leave an intersection, *B*, at the same time. The motorcyclist drives east at a speed of 50 km h^{-1}. The car drives in a direction W 30° S at a speed of 60 km h^{-1}. After 15 minutes, the car stops.

(i) Find the distance travelled by the car in 15 minutes.

(ii) Find the distance travelled by the motorcyclist in 15 minutes.

(iii) Find the measure of $\angle ABC$.

(iv) Hence, find how far apart, to the nearest metre, the two vehicles are when the car stops.

14.

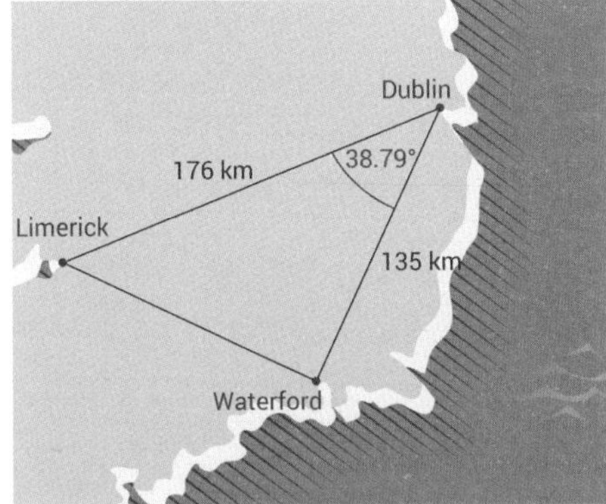

A helicopter pilot has plotted her route on a map. She plans to fly from Dublin to Limerick, from Limerick on to Waterford and, finally, from Waterford back to Dublin. She knows that the flying distance between Dublin and Limerick is 176 km and that the distance between Waterford and Dublin is 135 km. She also has the measure of one angle on the triangular route, as shown on the diagram.

(i) Find the flying distance between Limerick and Waterford.

(ii) If the helicopter has an average flying speed of 280 km h^{-1} and the pilot stops over in Limerick for 1 hour and in Waterford for 2 hours, find, to the nearest minute, the time taken for the pilot to complete the trip.

(iii) An Internet route planner gives the road distance between Limerick and Waterford as 127 km. As the helicopter takes off from Dublin, a driver begins his journey from Limerick to Waterford travelling at an average speed of 50 km h^{-1}. He has scheduled a meeting with the pilot. What is the maximum time the meeting can last if the pilot has to stick with the 2 hour stopover?

(iv) Suggest another method for finding the flying distance between Limerick and Waterford.

15.

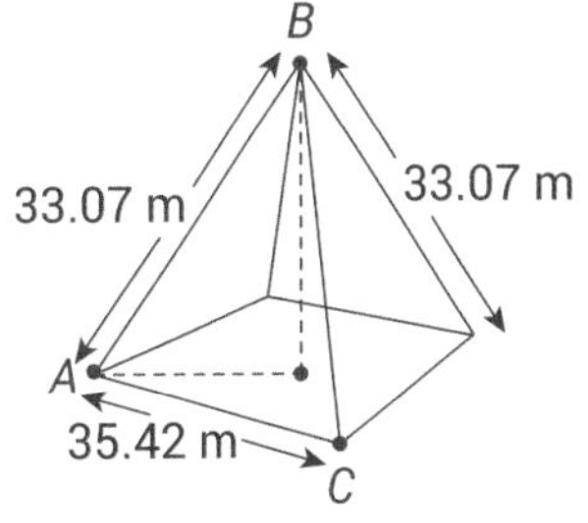

The Louvre Pyramid is a large glass pyramid in the main courtyard of the Louvre Palace in Paris. Some dimensions are given in the picture.

(i) Using the Cosine Rule, calculate to two decimal places the measure of $\angle ABC$.

(ii) Find the area of one face of the pyramid. Give your answer to two decimal places.

(iii) Hence, find the area of all four faces.

(iv) What is the area of the square base of the pyramid?

16. Rachel is training in her local soccer field. One of her training routines is a 10-lap run around the circuit shown in the diagram. $|AB| = 35$ m and $|BC| = 40$ m.

(i) Find $|AC|$.

(ii) What distance does Rachel cover in this routine?

(iii) What is the width of her local soccer field?

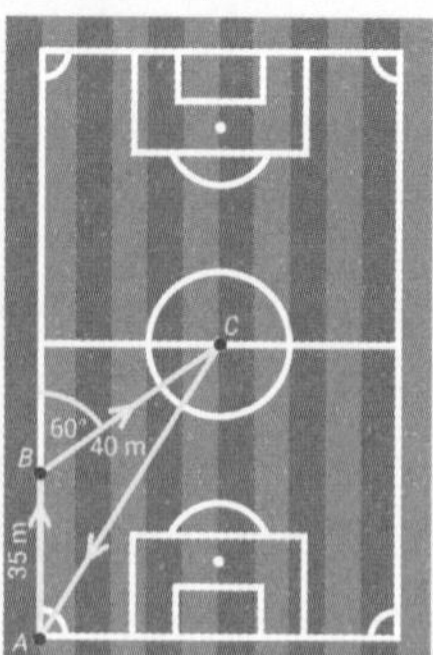

17.11 Length of an Arc and Area of a Sector

In this section we will learn how to find:

(i) The length of an arc of a circle

(ii) The area of a sector of a circle

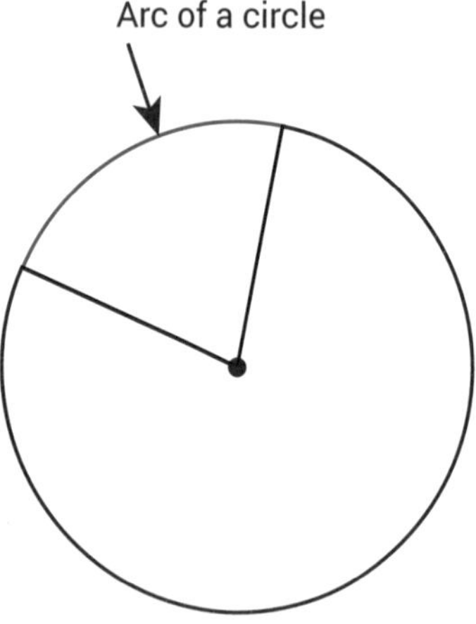

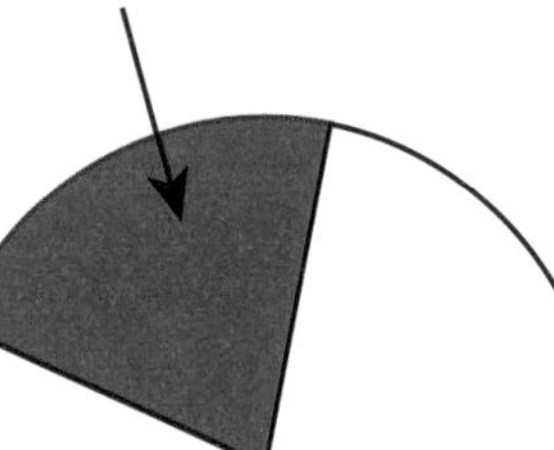

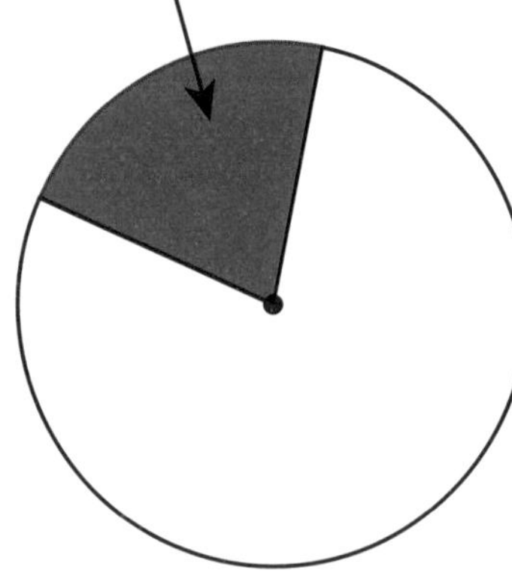

Length of an arc of a circle: $l = (2\pi r)\left(\frac{\theta}{360}\right)$, where θ is measured in degrees

Area of a sector of a circle: $A = (\pi r^2)\left(\frac{\theta}{360}\right)$, where θ is measured in degrees

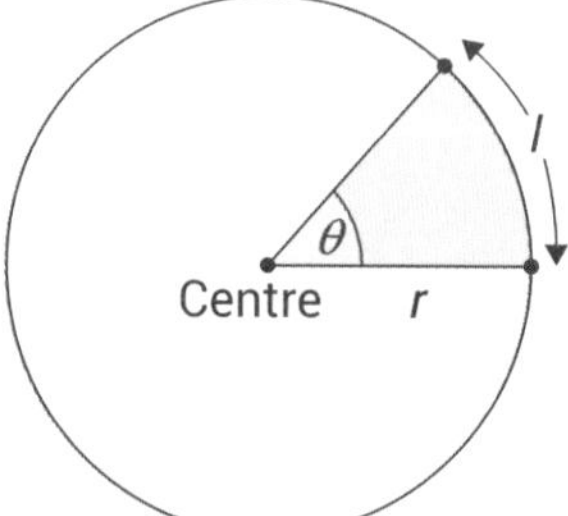

You can find these formulae on page 9 of *Formulae and Tables*.

Worked Example 17.20

Find:

(i) The area of the sector AOB

(ii) The length of the minor arc AB

Give your answers in terms of π.

The minor arc of a circle is the shorter arc joining two points on the circumference of the circle.

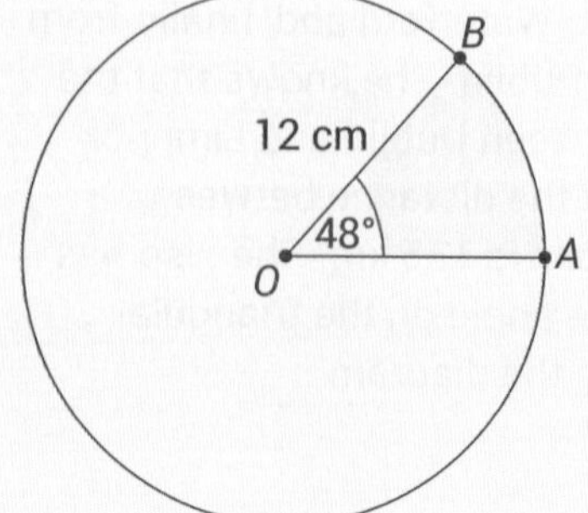

Solution

(i) Area of sector $= \pi r^2\left(\dfrac{\theta}{360}\right)$

$$\text{Area} = \pi(12)^2\left(\frac{48}{360}\right)$$
$$= 144\pi\left(\frac{2}{15}\right)$$
$$= \frac{96\pi}{5}\text{ cm}^2$$

(ii) Length of arc $= 2\pi r\left(\dfrac{\theta}{360}\right)$

$$\text{Length} = 2\pi(12)\left(\frac{48}{360}\right)$$
$$= 24\pi\left(\frac{2}{15}\right)$$
$$= \frac{16\pi}{5}\text{ cm}$$

Exercise 17.9

1. Find the area of each of the following shaded sectors.

Give your answers:

(a) In terms of π

(b) Correct to two decimal places

(i)

10 cm, 50°, O, A, B

(ii)

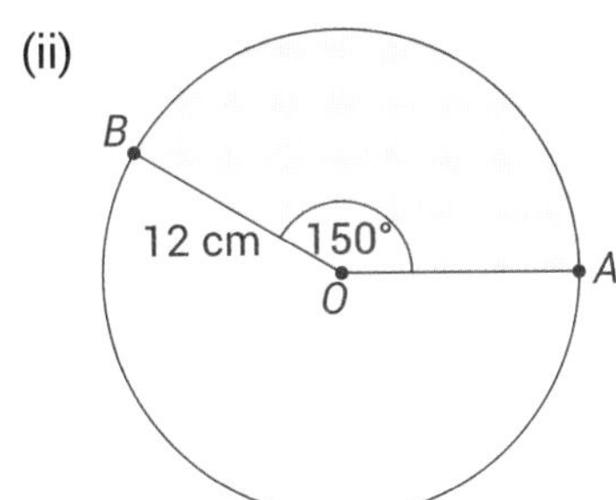

(iii)

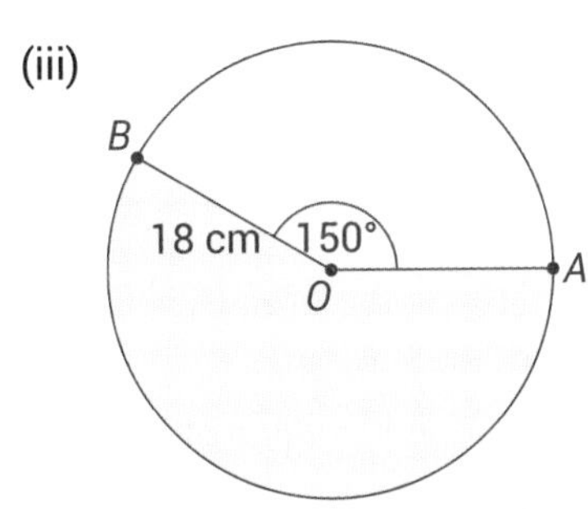

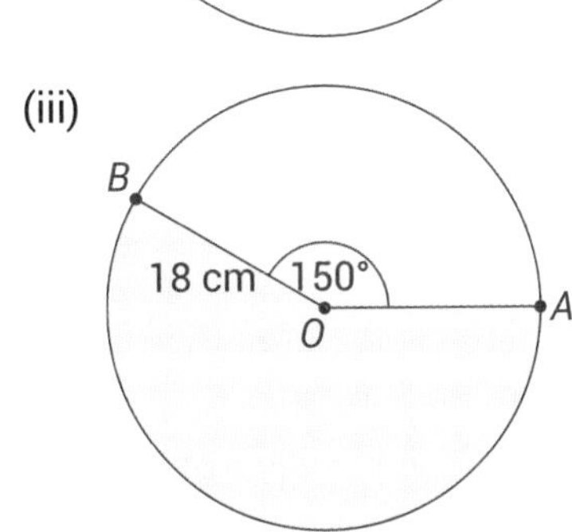

2. For each of the following, find the length of the minor arc AB.

Give your answers:

(a) In terms of π

(b) Correct to two decimal places

(i)

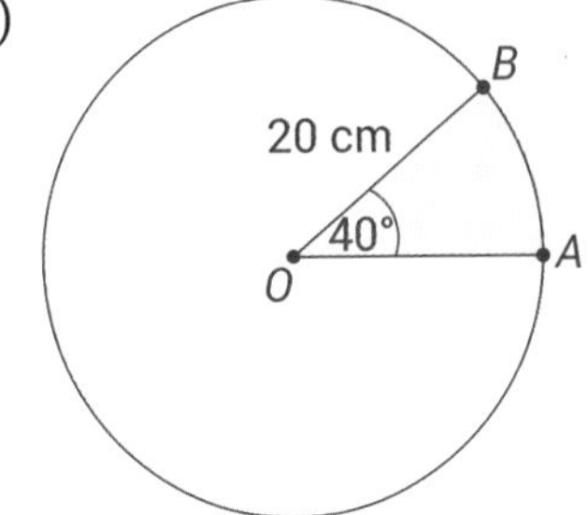

(ii)

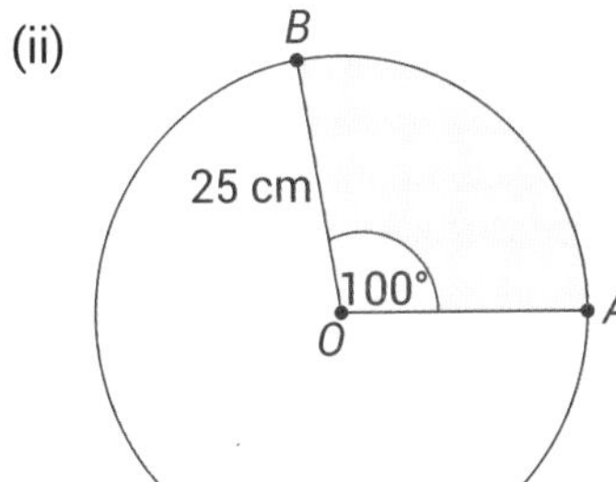

(iii)

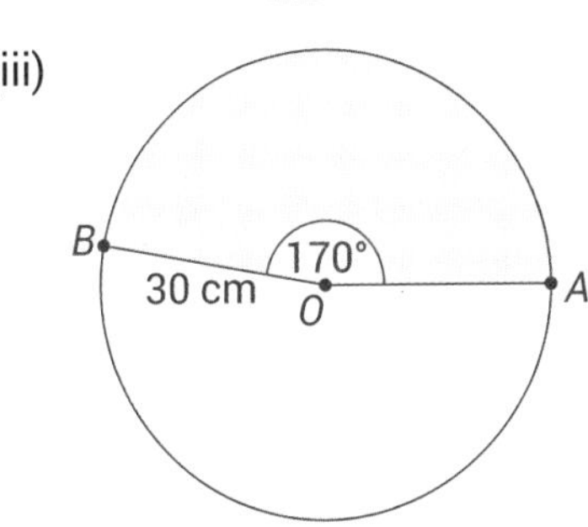

3. For each of the following, find the measure of the angle θ. θ is measured in degrees.

(i)

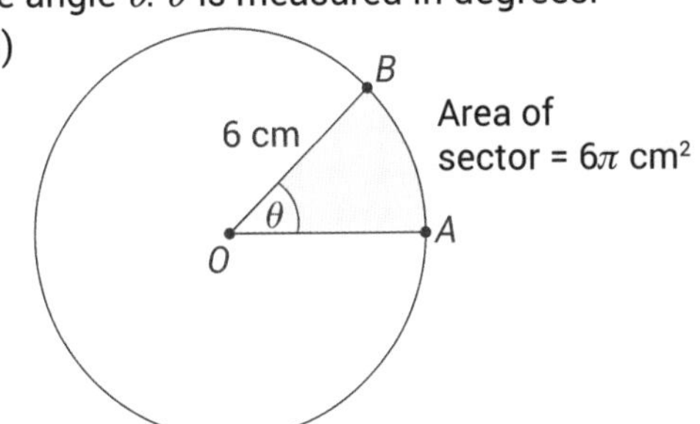

TRIGONOMETRY

(ii)

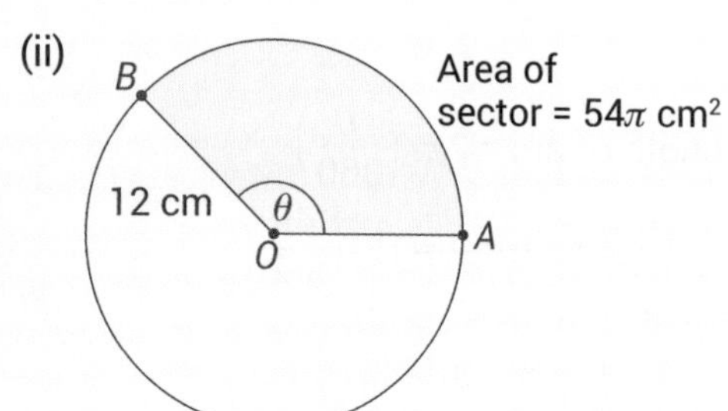

(iii)

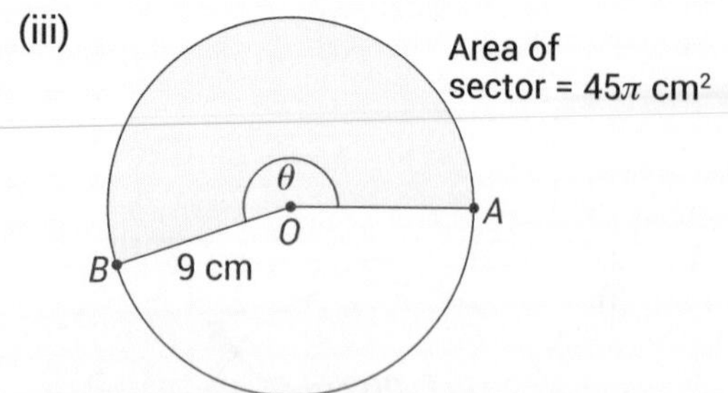

4. For each of the following, find the measure of the angle θ. θ is measured in degrees.

(i)

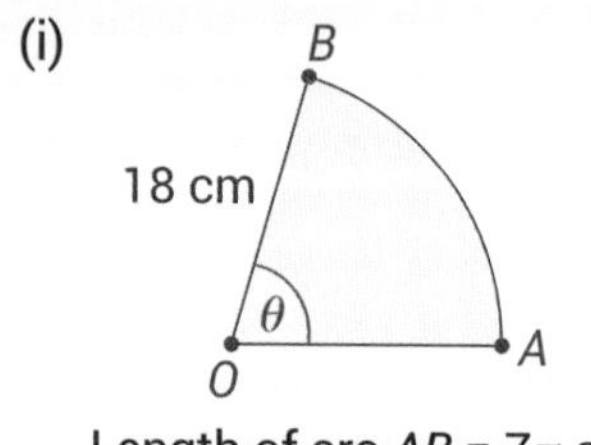

(ii)

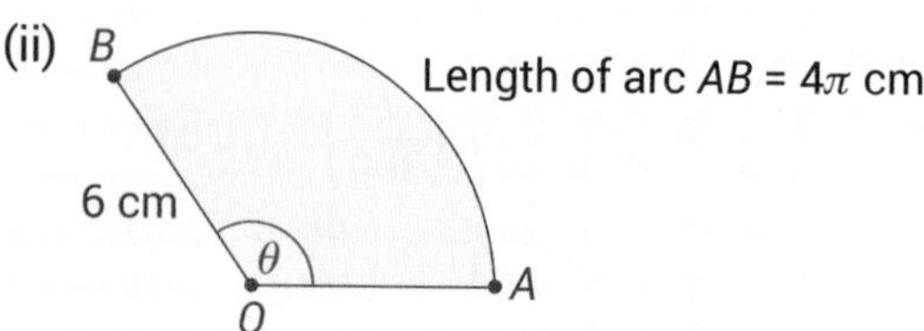

5. Find the area of the shaded region. Give your answer correct to three significant figures.

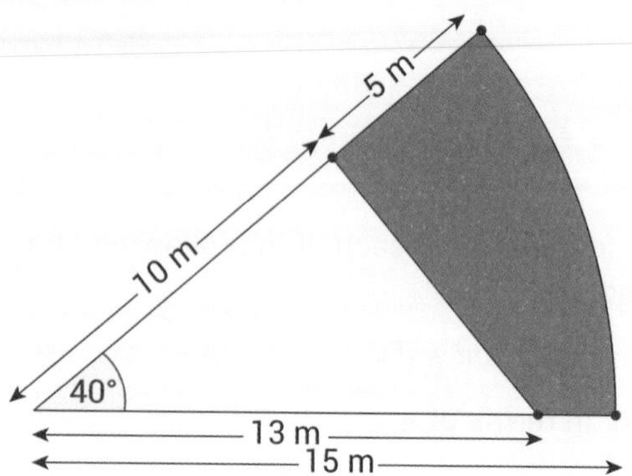

TRIGONOMETRY

Revision Exercises

1. (a)

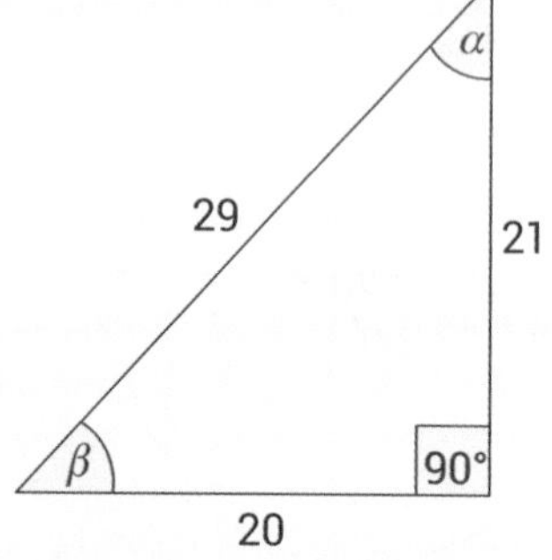

Copy and complete the tables below.

$\sin\alpha$	$\cos\alpha$	$\tan\alpha$

$\sin\beta$	$\cos\beta$	$\tan\beta$

(b)

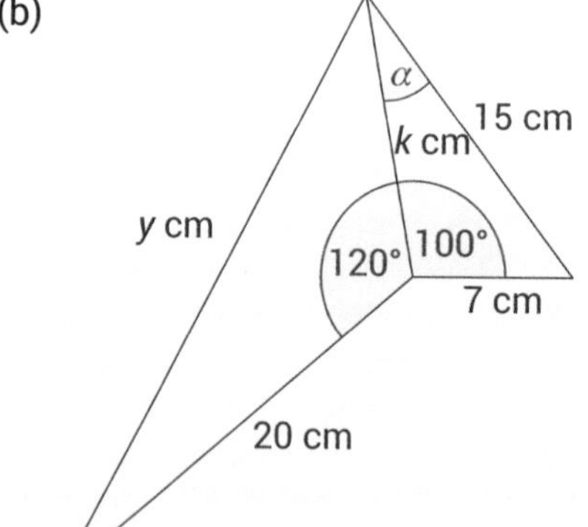

(i) Find the value of α. Give your answer to the nearest degree.

(ii) Hence, find the value of k, correct to two decimal places.

(iii) Using the Cosine Rule, evaluate y to two decimal places.

2. (a) Study the unit circle below. Then complete the table in terms of p and q.

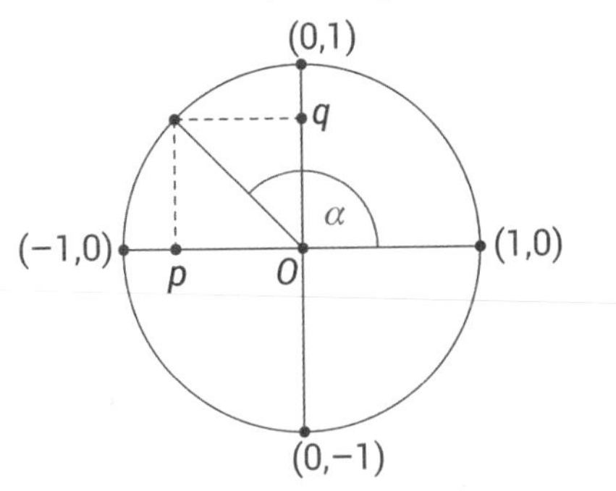

$\sin\alpha$	$\cos\alpha$	$\tan\alpha$

(b)

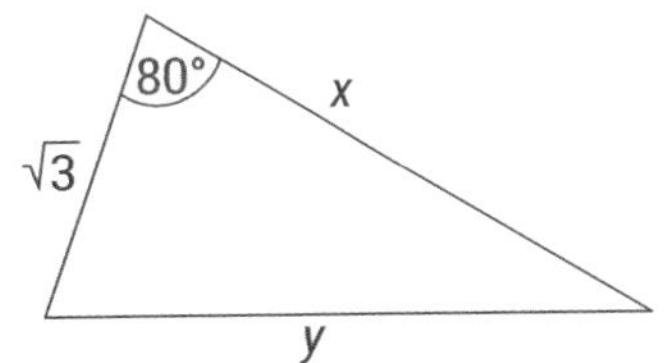

The area of the triangle shown above is 3 square units.

(i) Find the value of x, correct to two decimal places.

(ii) Using the Cosine Rule, find the value of y.

3.

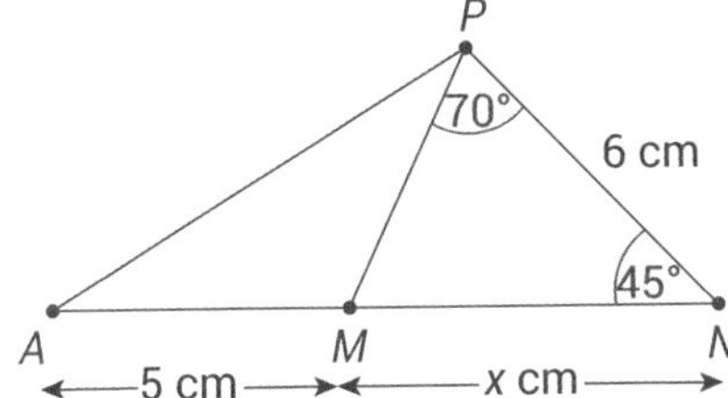

(i) Find the value of x, correct to two decimal places.

(ii) Hence, find the area of triangle PAN. Give your answer correct to two significant figures.

4. Copy and complete the table below (entries in surd form, where necessary).

A	30°	45°	60°
$\sin A$			
$\cos A$			
$\tan A$			

Using the given table, solve the following equations for A, B, C and D, where A, B, C and D are acute angles:

(i) $\sin A = \cos 60°$ (ii) $\tan B = 1$ (iii) $\sin C = \cos C$ (iv) $\sin D \cos 30° = \frac{3}{4}$

5. This is the new company logo for ABC Ltd. The logo is made by removing two equal sectors from an equilateral triangle. The sectors have their centres, respectively, on two vertices of the equilateral triangle. On the logo there are three straight edges, two measuring 10 cm and one measuring 6 cm.

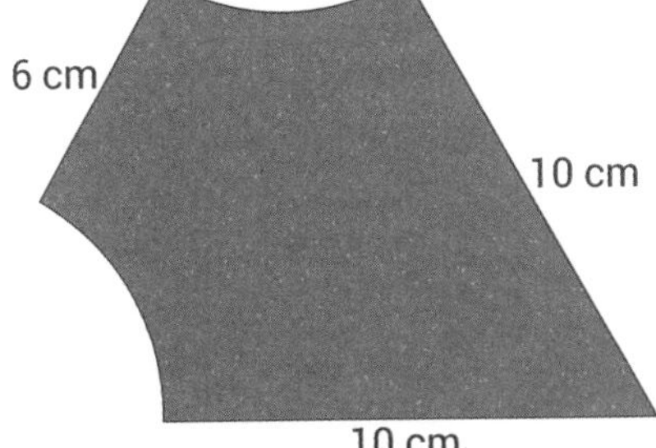

(i) Find the radius length of one of the sectors that have been removed.

(ii) Find the area of the sectors that were removed. Give your answer in terms of π.

(iii) Find the area of the equilateral triangle from which the logo has been taken. Give your answer in surd form.

(iv) Find the area of the logo. Give your answer correct to two decimal places.

6. John's Construction Studies teacher has asked him to construct a scaled model of any building in his town. The building John has chosen has a billboard mounted on one of its walls. He needs to know the height of the billboard and the height of its bottom edge above street level. He has a clinometer and a tape measure.

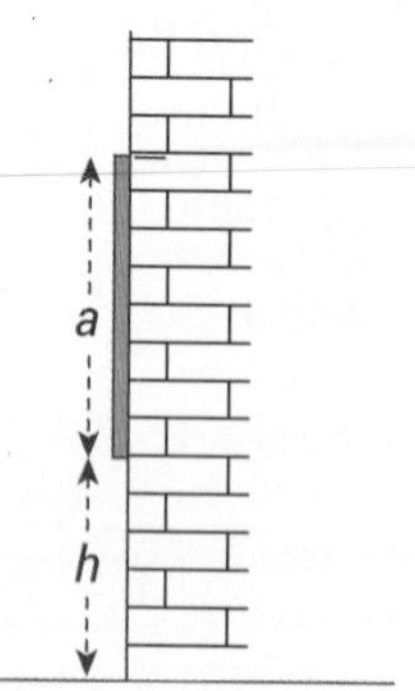

(i) Explain, with the aid of a diagram, how John could find the measurements he needs.

(ii)

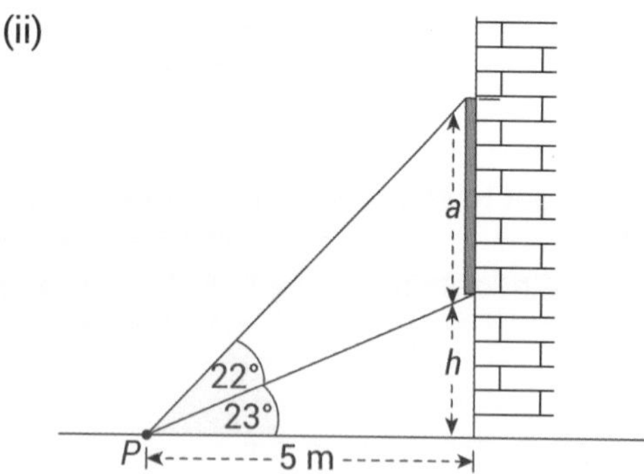

The diagram above shows the measurements John has taken with the help of the tape measure and clinometer. Calculate the value of a and the value of h, to the nearest centimetre.

(iii) John, using the clinometer and tape measure, has estimated the height of the building to be 8 m. The height of his scaled model of the building has to be 1 m. What will be the height of the billboard in the scaled model? Give your answer to the nearest centimetre.

7. A Fifth Year Maths class has been asked to find the width and height of a soccer goal. The students are equipped with just a clinometer. Any measurements have to be taken from the point P.

The teacher has already given the class the distance from P to the foot of both uprights and also the measure of the angle at P, formed by the two uprights and the point P. The students decide to measure the angle of elevation from P to the top of one of the uprights. They find the angle of elevation to be 22°.

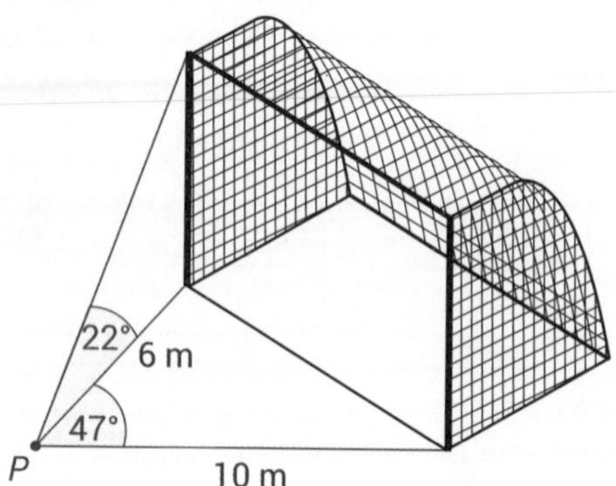

(i) Find the width of the goal. Give your answer in metres to two decimal places.

(ii) Find the height of the goal. Give your answer to the nearest centimetre.

(iii) If the class had chosen to measure the angle of elevation of the other upright from P, then what measurement should they have found? Give your answer to the nearest degree.

8. To find the height of a tower standing on a small hill, Aoife made some measurements.

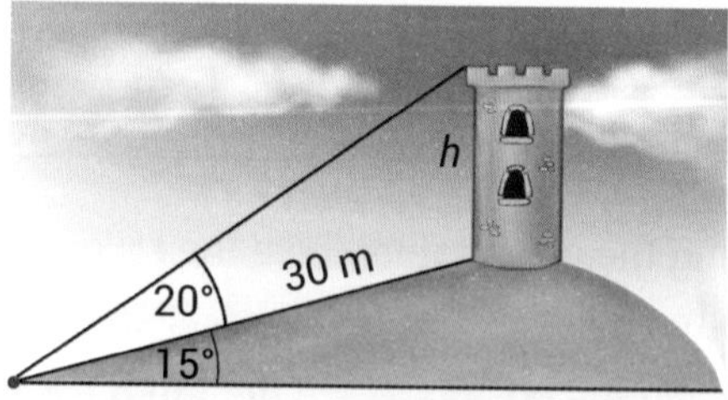

- She measured the angle of elevation to the top of the tower: 20°.
- She measured the angle at which the plane is inclined to the horizontal: 15°.
- She measured the distance from the base of the tower to the point where she took elevation measurements: 30 m.

(i) Represent this information on a diagram. The diagram should contain a right angle.

(ii) Find the height of the tower to the nearest metre.

Exam Questions

1. The diagram shows the triangles *BCD* and *ABD*, with some measurements given.

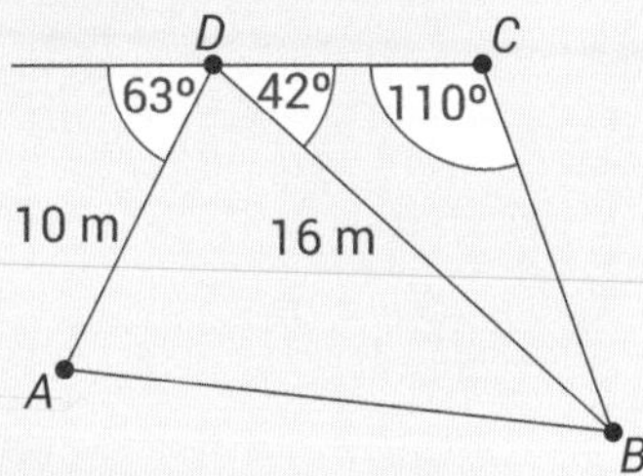

(a) (i) Find |*BC*|, correct to two decimal places.

(ii) Find the area of the triangle *BCD*, correct to two decimal places.

(b) Find |*AB*|, correct to two decimal places.

SEC Leaving Certificate Ordinary Level, Paper 2, 2015

2. (a) Find the area of the given triangle.

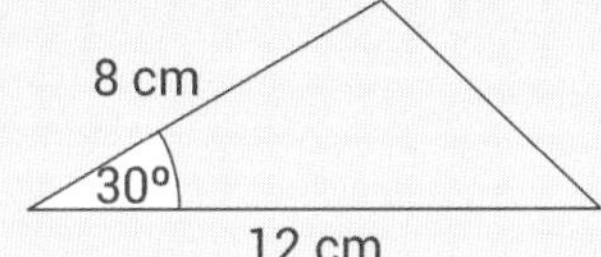

(b) A triangle has sides of length 3 cm, 5 cm and 7 cm.
Find the size of the largest angle in the triangle.

SEC Leaving Certificate Ordinary Level, Paper 2, 2016

3. At an activity centre a zip-line, [*BD*], runs between two vertical poles, [*AB*] and [*CD*], on level ground, as shown. The point *E* is on the ground, directly below the zip-line.
|*AE*| = 12 m, |*BE*| = 14 m, |*CD*| = 1.95 m, and |*EC*| = 10 m.

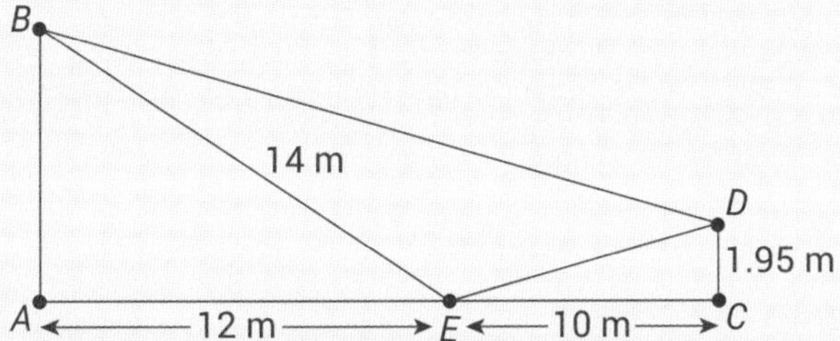

(a) (i) Find the distance |*ED*|, correct to one decimal place.

(ii) Find |∠*AEB*|, correct to the nearest degree.

(b) (i) Find |∠*DEB*|, given that |∠*CED*| = 11°, correct to the nearest degree.

(ii) Hence, or otherwise, find the distance |*DB*|. Give your answer correct to one decimal place.

SEC Leaving Certificate Ordinary Level, Paper 2, 2014

Solutions and chapter summary available online

TRIGONOMETRY

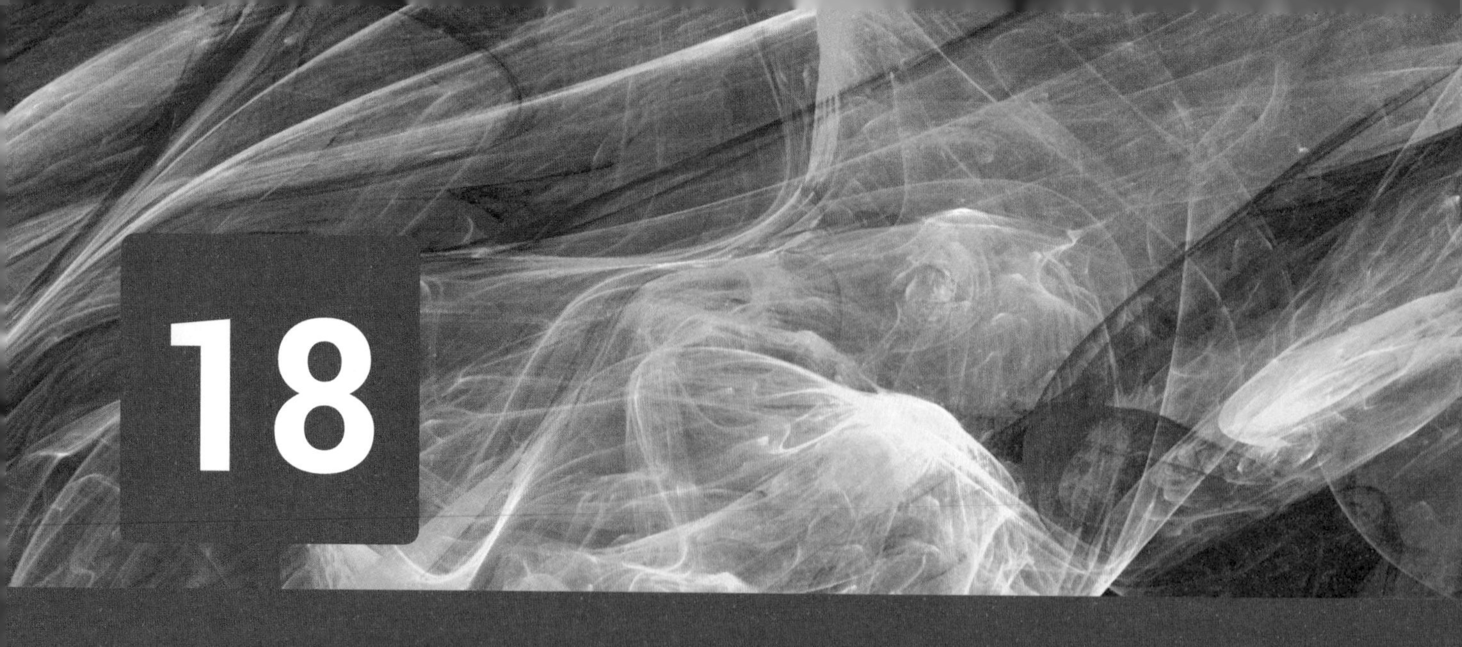

Co-ordinate Geometry: The Line

In this chapter you will learn to:

- Explore the properties of points, lines and line segments including the equation of a line
- Find the point of intersection of two lines
- Use slopes to show that two lines are
  - Parallel
  - Perpendicular
- Recognise the fact that the relationship $ax + by + c = 0$ is linear
- Solve problems involving slopes of lines
- Calculate the area of a triangle

You should remember...

- The theorem of Pythagoras
- How to find the area of a parallelogram
- How to find the area of a rectangle
- How to find the area of a triangle
- A circle is the set of all points that are a fixed distance from a given point
- Distance = Average speed × Time
- Junior Certificate Ordinary Level, Co-ordinate Geometry

Key words

- Distance
- Midpoint
- Slope of a line
- Equation of a line
- Parallel
- Perpendicular
- Collinear

The co-ordinate geometry we use today was invented by the French mathematician René Descartes (1596–1650). Descartes' co-ordinate system was much easier to work with than Euclid's geometry, and even today it is the foundation for many branches of modern mathematics.

René Descartes

Co-ordinate geometry has applications in such diverse areas as geography, astronomy, engineering and econozmics. In co-ordinate geometry, we refer to the plane on which we work as the *xy*-plane, or the Cartesian plane, after Descartes.

18.1 Distance Between Two Points on the *xy*-Plane

The *xy*-plane is the surface on which we do co-ordinate geometry.

The *x* and *y* axes divide the plane into four quadrants.

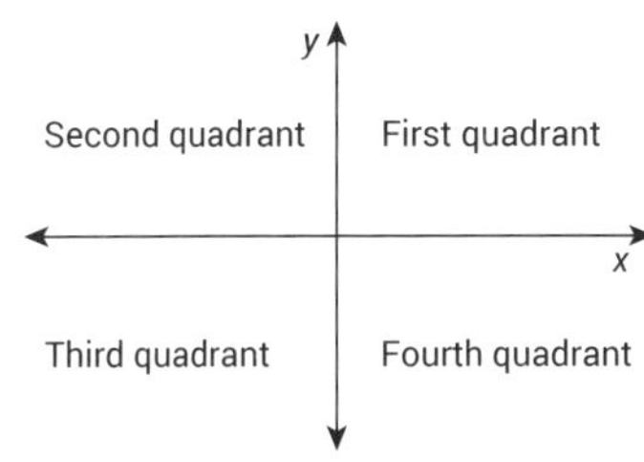

Worked Example 18.1

(i) Plot the following co-ordinates and say in which quadrant each point lies:

$A(-2,1)$ $B(5,2)$ $C(-3,-4)$ $D(5,-2)$

(ii) Plot the following co-ordinates and say on which axis each point lies:

$A(3,0)$ $B(0,4)$ $C(-2,0)$ $D(0,-1)$

Solution

(i)

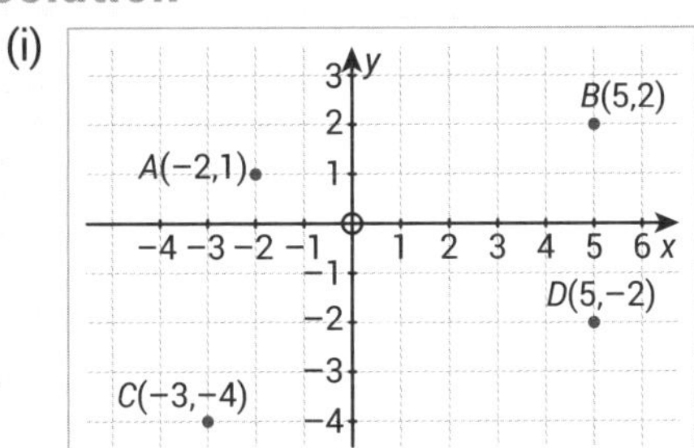

A lies in the second quadrant.

B lies in the first quadrant.

C lies in the third quadrant.

D lies in the fourth quadrant.

(ii)

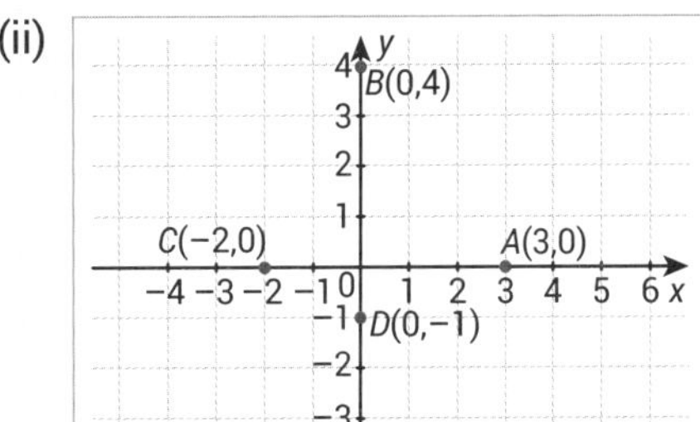

A lies on the *x*-axis.

B lies on the *y*-axis.

C lies on the *x*-axis.

D lies on the *y*-axis.

Finding the distance between two points *A* and *B* is the equivalent of finding the length of the line segment [*AB*].

Worked Example 18.2

Find the distance between $R(1,2)$ and $S(5,5)$.

Solution

Step 1 Plot the points $R(1,2)$ and $S(5,5)$. Draw a horizontal line through *R* and a vertical line through *S* to meet at the point *T*.

Step 2 Using the diagram, find $|RT|$ and $|ST|$.
$|RT| = 4$ units, since $T(5,2)$ lies 4 units to the right of $R(1,2)$.
$|ST| = 3$ units, since $S(5,5)$ lies 3 units above $T(5,2)$.

Step 3 Using the Theorem of Pythagoras, find $|RS|$.

$$|RS|^2 = |RT|^2 + |TS|^2$$
$$= 4^2 + 3^2$$
$$= 16 + 9$$
$$= 25$$
$$\therefore |RS| = \sqrt{25}$$
$$= 5 \text{ units}$$

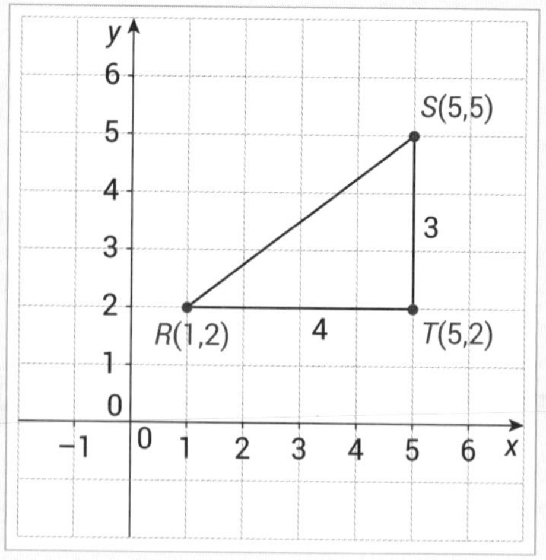

The formula for calculating the length of a line segment derives from Pythagoras' theorem.

Given a line segment $[AB]$, then
$|AB| = \sqrt{(x_2 - x_1)^2 + (y_2 - y_1)^2}$

This formula appears on page 18 of *Formulae and Tables*.

Worked Example 18.3

Find the distance between $A(-1,1)$ and $B(20,21)$.

Solution

$x_1 = -1$ $\quad y_1 = 1$

$x_2 = 20$ $\quad y_2 = 21$

Formula: $\sqrt{(x_2 - x_1)^2 + (y_2 - y_1)^2}$

$$|AB| = \sqrt{(20 - (-1))^2 + (21 - 1)^2}$$
$$= \sqrt{(20 + 1)^2 + (21 - 1)^2} \quad \text{(As } 20 - (-1) = 20 + 1\text{)}$$
$$= \sqrt{(21)^2 + (20)^2}$$
$$= \sqrt{441 + 400}$$
$$= \sqrt{841}$$
$$= 29$$
$$\therefore |AB| = 29 \text{ units}$$

Exercise 18.1

1. Write down the co-ordinates of the points that are plotted on the xy-plane, shown below.

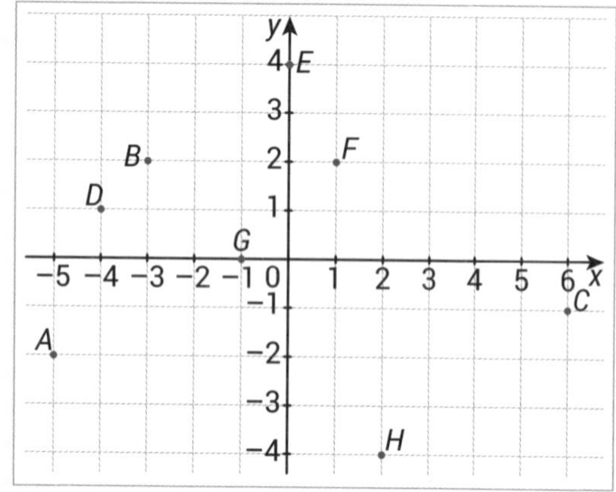

2. Name the quadrant in which each of the following points lies:

(i) (−4,2) (ii) (3,−8) (iii) (−3,6) (iv) (−2,−5) (v) (5,5) (vi) (3,2) (vii) (3,−4) (viii) (−5,−15) (ix) (2,20) (x) (−2,−8)

3. On which axis do the following points lie:

(i) (−5,0) (ii) (0,4) (iii) (0,−2) (iv) (5,0) (v) (100,0) (vi) (−300,0) (vii) (0,−100)

4. Find the value of x and the value of y for each of the following cases for the point A on the xy-plane:

(i) A lies on the positive x-axis a distance of 3 units from (0,0).

(ii) A lies on the negative x-axis a distance of 4 units from (0,0).

(iii) A lies on the positive y-axis a distance of 5 units from (0,−2).

(iv) A lies on the negative y-axis a distance of 4 units from (0,2).

5. Find the distance between the following pairs of points:

(i) (2,2) and (3,5)
(ii) (1,5) and (12,11)
(iii) (3,8) and (5,8)
(iv) (5,2) and (5,6)

6. Find the distance between the following pairs of points:

(i) (−1,3) and (5,6)
(ii) (4,−1) and (2,1)
(iii) (7,−4) and (0,0)
(iv) (5,2) and (2,−4)
(v) (−3,−2) and (3,−2)
(vi) (6,2) and (−2,1)

7. $A(0,0)$, $B(12,5)$, $C(17,-7)$ and $D(5,-12)$ are the vertices of the rhombus $ABCD$.

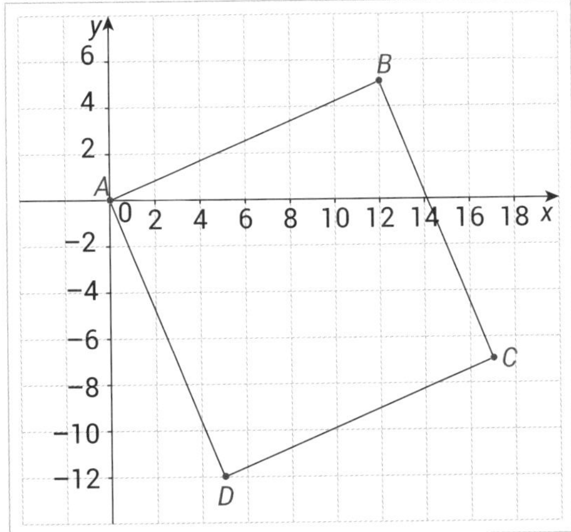

(i) Find the length of the side $[AB]$.

(ii) Find the length of the diagonal $[AC]$.

(iii) Investigate if $|BD| = |AC|$.

8. $A(-2,-2)$, $B(2,2)$, $C(3,0)$ and $D(-1,-4)$ are the vertices of a parallelogram $ABCD$.

(i) Plot the points A, B, C and D.

(ii) Show that $|AB| = |DC|$.

(iii) Find the length of the side $[BC]$.

(iv) Find the length of the diagonal $[AC]$.

(v) Are the diagonals of $ABCD$ equal in length? Explain your answer.

9. $A(0,-2)$, $B(3,2)$ and $C(6,6)$ are the co-ordinates of three points.

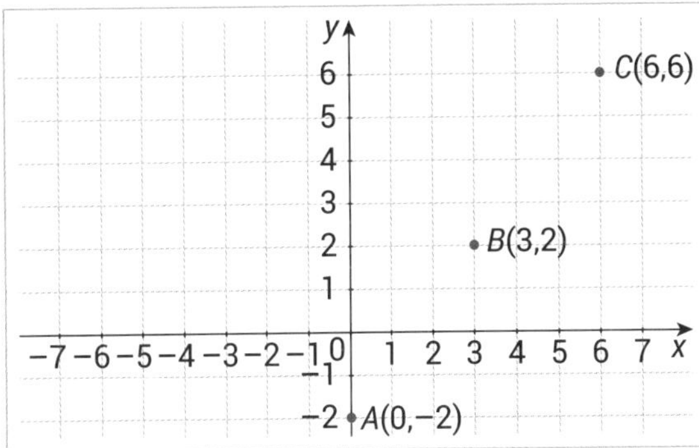

A, B and C will lie on a straight line if $|AB| + |BC| = |AC|$. Show that the points A, B and C are collinear (lie on a straight line).

10. Show that the triangle with vertices $A(1,3)$, $B(2,5)$ and $C(3,2)$ is an isosceles triangle.

11. Show that the triangle with vertices $W(0,0)$, $X(1,\sqrt{3})$, $Y(2,0)$ is an equilateral triangle.

12. If a circle is drawn with centre (0,0) and radius length 5, would (3,3) be inside or outside the circle? Explain your answer.

13. A circle has centre $C(3,4)$ and contains the point $A(-1,2)$.

Calculate $|CA|$, its radius length.

14. $A(5,0)$, $B(-4,3)$ and $C(4,4)$ are the co-ordinates of three points.

(i) Which of these points is furthest from the origin (0,0)?

(ii) On graph paper, plot the points A, B and C.

(iii) Explain why the points $A(5,0)$ and $B(-4,3)$ lie on the circle of radius length 5 and with its centre at the origin (0,0).

18.2 Midpoint of a Line Segment

Worked Example 18.4

Use the graph to find the midpoints of each of the horizontal and vertical line segments.

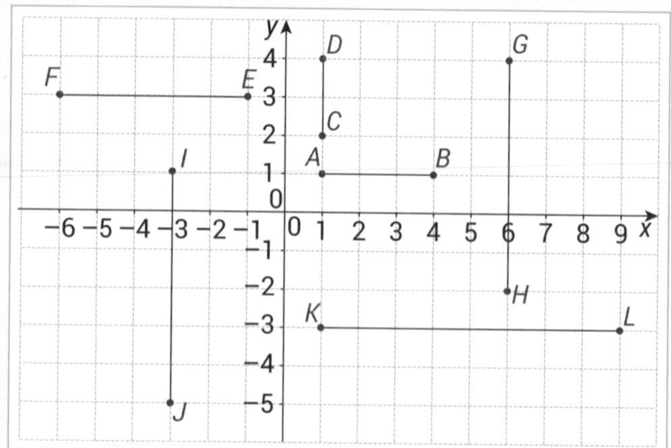

Solution

Midpoint of [AB] = (2.5,1)

Midpoint of [CD] = (1,3)

Midpoint of [EF] = (−3.5,3)

Midpoint of [GH] = (6,1)

Midpoint of [IJ] = (−3,−2)

Midpoint of [KL] = (5,−3)

The point that bisects a line segment is called the midpoint of the line segment.

If C is the midpoint of [AB], then $|AC| = |CB|$.

$$\text{Midpoint} = \left(\frac{x_1 + x_2}{2}, \frac{y_1 + y_2}{2}\right)$$

This formula appears on page 18 of *Formulae and Tables*.

Worked Example 18.5

$A(11,-2)$ and $B(-3,14)$ are two points. Find the midpoint of [AB].

Solution

$x_1 = 11 \quad x_2 = -3 \quad y_1 = -2 \quad y_2 = 14$

$$\text{Midpoint} = \left(\frac{x_1 + x_2}{2}, \frac{y_1 + y_2}{2}\right)$$

$$\text{Midpoint of } [AB] = \left(\frac{11 + (-3)}{2}, \frac{-2 + 14}{2}\right)$$

$$= \left(\frac{8}{2}, \frac{12}{2}\right)$$

$$= (4,6)$$

Worked Example 18.6

$A(11,-2)$ and $C(-3,14)$ are two points. Find the co-ordinates of B, if C is the midpoint of [AB].

Solution

Method 1

If (x_2, y_2) are the co-ordinates of the point B, then:

$$\left(\frac{11 + x_2}{2}, \frac{(-2) + y_2}{2}\right) = (-3,14)$$

(11,−2) A — (−3,14) C — (x_2,y_2) B

$$\therefore \frac{11 + x_2}{2} = -3 \quad \text{and} \quad \frac{-2 + y_2}{2} = 14$$

$11 + x_2 = -6 \qquad -2 + y_2 = 28$

$x_2 = -6 - 11 \qquad y_2 = 28 + 2$

$\therefore x_2 = -17 \qquad \therefore y_2 = 30$

The co-ordinates of the point B are (−17,30).

Method 2

The second method uses the translation $\overrightarrow{AC}$ to translate C to B.

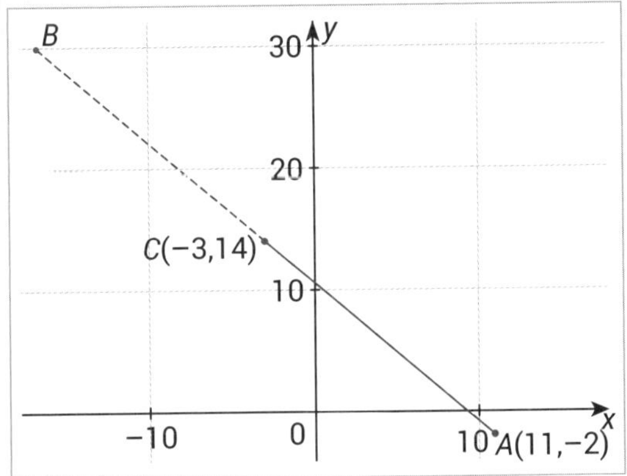

$$A(11,-2) \xrightarrow[y+16]{x-14} C(-3,14) \xrightarrow[y+16]{x-14} B(-17,30)$$

Subtract 14 from x.
Add 16 to y.

Exercise 18.2

1. Find the midpoints of the line segments joining the following pairs of points:
   (i) (4,2) and (6,4)
   (ii) (1,7) and (7,5)
   (iii) (3,7) and (9,9)
   (iv) (1,2) and (3,6)

2. Find the midpoints of the line segments joining the following pairs of points:
   (i) (−1,3) and (7,6)
   (ii) (4,−1) and (2,1)
   (iii) (7,−4) and (0,0)
   (iv) (−2,−2) and (3,−6)

3. Find the midpoint of $[AB]$ in each of the following:
   (i) $A(2,2)$ and $B(3,-5)$
   (ii) $A(1,-6)$ and $B(-3,-2)$
   (iii) $A(5,3)$ and $B(2,1)$
   (iv) $A(6,-7)$ and $B(-1,-5)$

4. The line k bisects the line segment $[AB]$.

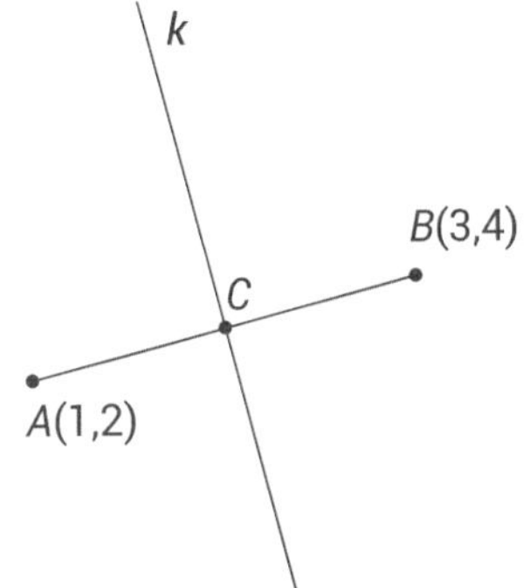

   Find the co-ordinates of the point C.

5. Show that the midpoint of $P(3,-7)$ and $Q(5,7)$ lies on the x-axis.

6. $[AB]$ is a diameter of the circle shown below.
   (i) Find the co-ordinates of C, the centre of the circle.
   (ii) Find the radius of the circle.

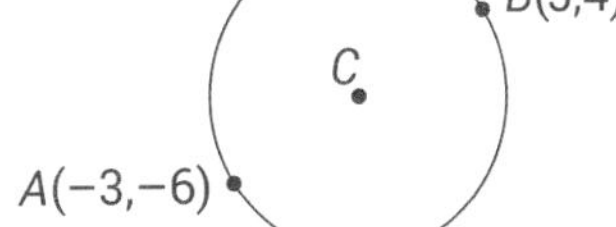

7. $A(1,3)$ and $B(5,-7)$ are the co-ordinates of two points.
   (i) Find M, the midpoint of $[AB]$.
   (ii) Verify that $|AM| = |MB|$.

8. $A(2,5)$, $B(5,-2)$ and $C(-2,2)$ are the vertices of a triangle.
   (i) Find the co-ordinates of M, the midpoint of $[AB]$.
   (ii) Find the co-ordinates of N, the midpoint of $[BC]$.
   (iii) Plot the points A, B, C, M and N.

9.

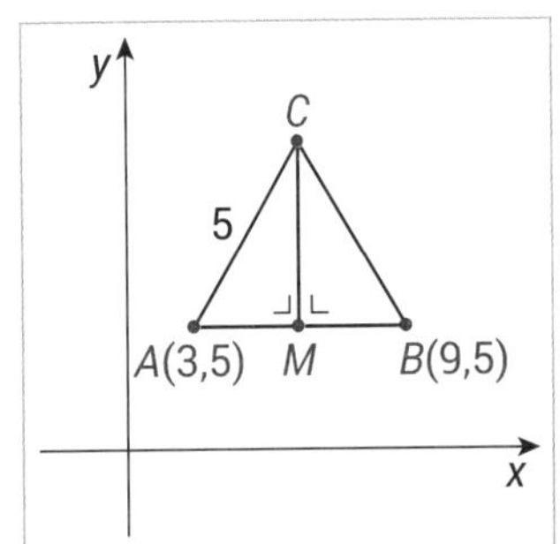

   ΔABC is isosceles with $|AC| = |BC| = 5$.

   M is the midpoint of $[AB]$ and $|\angle CMA| = |\angle CMB| = 90°$.

(i) Find M, the midpoint of $[AB]$.

(ii) Calculate $|AM|$.

(iii) Using the Theorem of Pythagoras, find $|CM|$.

(iv) Hence, find the co-ordinates of the point C.

10. $A(4,y)$ and $B(x,7)$ are two points.
If (3,5) is the midpoint of $[AB]$, find the value of x and the value of y.

11. For each of the following, find the co-ordinates of B, if C is the midpoint of $[AB]$:

(i) $A(2,2)$, $C(3,-5)$

(ii) $A(-1,-2)$, $C(4,-2)$

(iii) $A(6,3)$, $C(2,2)$

(iv) $A(6,7)$, $C(-1,-4)$

12. $A(-2,y)$ and $B(x,11)$ are two points. If $(-1,3)$ is the midpoint of $[AB]$, find the value of x and the value of y.

18.3 Slope of a Line

The slope of a line is a measure of the 'steepness' of the line. We measure the slope of a line by finding how much the line rises or falls as we move from left to right along it.

Consider the line l, which contains the points $A(1,1)$ and $B(4,3)$.

The horizontal difference between A and B is 3.
This number is called the **run**.

The vertical difference between A and B is 2.
This number is called the **rise**.

The slope of l is $\frac{\text{rise}}{\text{run}} = \frac{2}{3}$. We often use the letter m to represent the slope. Therefore, $m = \frac{2}{3}$ for our line l.

Consider the line k, which contains the points $C(-2,3)$ and $D(2,1)$.

The horizontal difference (the run) between C and D is 4. The vertical difference (the rise) between C and D is -2. The rise is negative here: we are dropping down from C to D, as we read from left to right.

The slope of k is: $m = \frac{\text{rise}}{\text{run}} = \frac{-2}{4} = -\frac{1}{2}$.

The slope is negative because the line goes down from left to right.

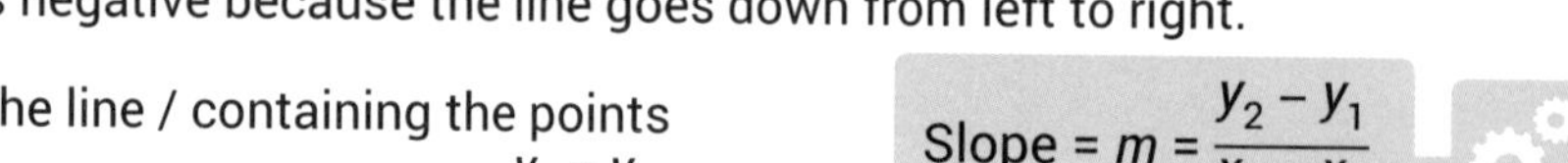

In general, the line l containing the points $A(x_1,y_1)$ and $B(x_2,y_2)$ has slope $m = \frac{y_2 - y_1}{x_2 - x_1}$.

Slope $= m = \frac{y_2 - y_1}{x_2 - x_1}$

This formula appears on page 18 of *Formulae and Tables*.

Worked Example 18.7

Find the slope of the line containing the points $G(-3,-5)$ and $H(3,4)$.

Solution

$x_1 = -3 \quad y_1 = -5$

$x_2 = 3 \quad y_2 = 4$

$$m = \frac{y_2 - y_1}{x_2 - x_1}$$

$$m = \frac{4-(-5)}{3-(-3)}$$

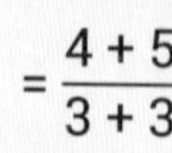

$$= \frac{4+5}{3+3}$$

$$= \frac{9}{6}$$

$$= \frac{3}{2}$$

A slope of $\frac{3}{2}$ means for every 2 steps to the right, the line rises 3 steps upwards.

Parallel and Perpendicular Lines

The two lines l_1 and l_2, shown in the diagram below, both have slope $\frac{1}{2}$. These lines are parallel.

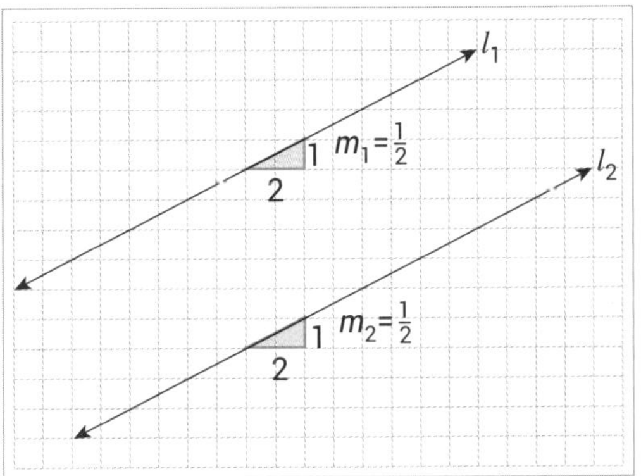

If two lines are parallel, then they have equal slopes, i.e. $m_1 = m_2$.

The two lines l_1 and l_2, shown in the diagram below, are perpendicular.

The slope of l_1 is $\frac{1}{2}$ and the slope of l_2 is $-\frac{2}{1}$.

You will notice that one slope is the negative of the reciprocal of the other. Also, if you multiply the slopes together, you get −1.

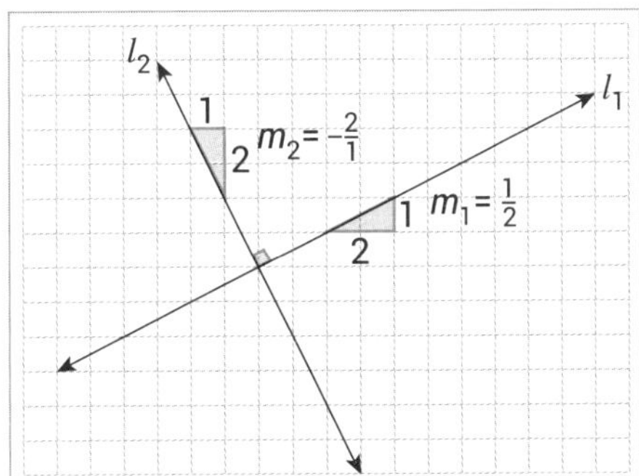

If two lines are perpendicular, then the product of their slopes is −1. (Except in the case where one line is vertical and the other horizontal.)

$l_1 \perp l_2 \Leftrightarrow m_1 \times m_2 = -1$

Worked Example 18.8

The line l_1 has a slope of $\frac{3}{8}$.

(i) Find the slope of l_2, if l_2 is parallel to l_1.

(ii) Find the slope of l_3, if l_3 is perpendicular to l_1.

Solution

(i) If l_1 is parallel to l_2, then l_1 and l_2 have equal slopes.

$\therefore$ Slope of l_2 is $\frac{3}{8}$.

(ii) If l_3 is perpendicular to l_1, then the slope of l_3 is the negative of the reciprocal of the slope of l_1.

$\therefore$ Slope of l_3 is $-\frac{8}{3}$.

Turn the given slope upside down and change the sign.

Exercise 18.3

1. Find the slope of the line which passes through each pair of points:

   (i) (3,3) and (4,6)

   (ii) (2,6) and (4,2)

   (iii) (5,8) and (6,8)

   (iv) (3,3) and (4,7)

2. Find the slope of the line which passes through each pair of points:

   (i) (0,6) and (5,7)

   (ii) (4,−2) and (1,0)

   (iii) (2,−4) and (0,0)

   (iv) (−6,−3) and (3,−5)

3. Find the slope of the line which passes through each pair of points:
   (i) $A(0,1)$ and $B(4,-3)$
   (ii) $A(-2,-3)$ and $B(4,-1)$
   (iii) $A(7,5)$ and $B(3,-2)$
   (iv) $A(5,8)$ and $B(-1,-3)$

4. Find the slope of each of the line segments shown below.

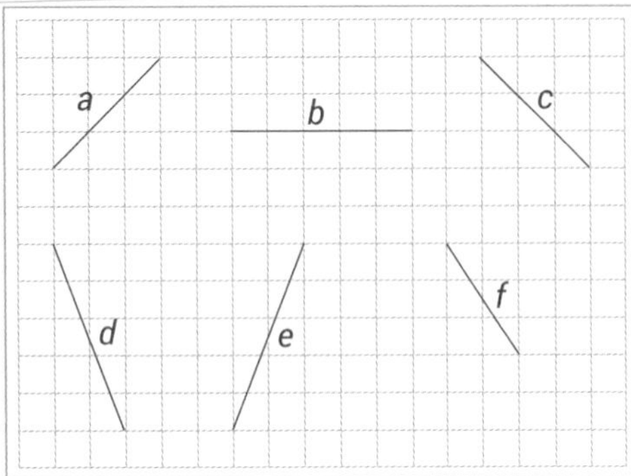

5. Match the correct line with the given slopes.

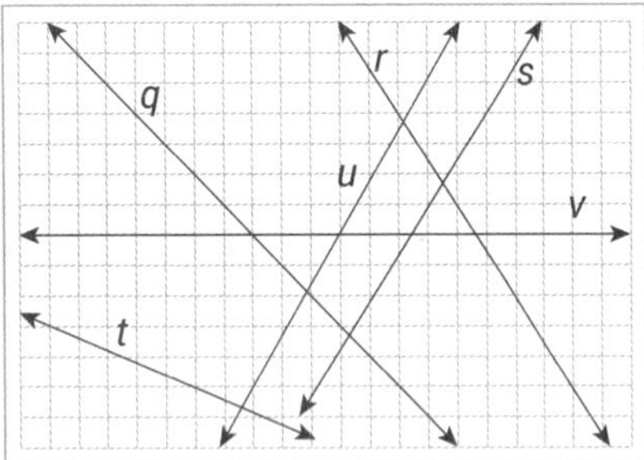

Slope	Line	Slope	Line
$\frac{5}{3}$		0	
$-\frac{2}{5}$		$\frac{3}{2}$	
-1		$-\frac{3}{2}$	

6.

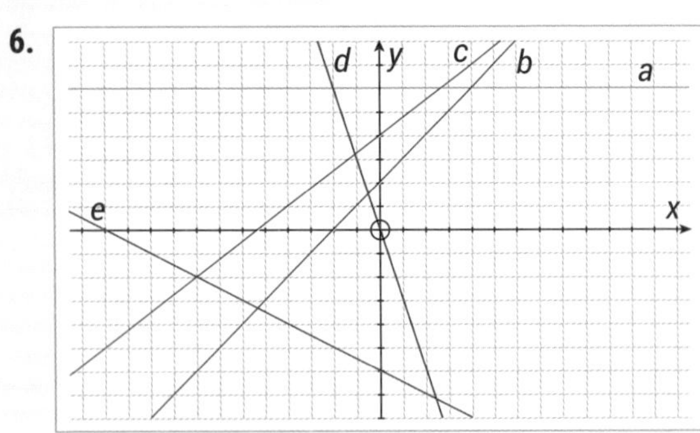

   (i) Which line has a slope of $\frac{3}{4}$?
   (ii) Find the slopes of the other lines on the diagram.

7. Using the same axes and scales, draw two lines with slope $\frac{5}{8}$.

   What do you notice about the two lines?

8. Using the same axes and scales, draw two lines, one line with slope $-\frac{3}{5}$ and another line with slope $\frac{5}{3}$.

   What do you notice about the two lines?

9. Copy and complete the table below.

Slope	Slope of parallel line	Slope of perpendicular line
$\frac{3}{4}$	$\frac{3}{4}$	$-\frac{4}{3}$
$\frac{5}{2}$		
-3		
$\frac{1}{2}$		
-2		
$-\frac{1}{4}$		
$-\frac{8}{11}$		

10. The line t has a slope of $\frac{5}{8}$.
    Find the slope of u, if $t \perp u$.

11. The line r has a slope of $\frac{1}{2}$.
    Find the slope of s, if $r \parallel s$.

12. The line m has a slope of $-\frac{3}{4}$.
    Find the slope of n, if $m \perp n$.

13. The line a has a slope of 4.
    Find the slope of b, if $a \parallel b$.

14. The line k has a slope of $\frac{4}{5}$.
    Find the slope of l, if $l \perp k$.

15. The line v has a slope of -5.
    Find the slope of w, if $v \perp w$.

16. You are given the following points: $P(1,3)$, $Q(5,3)$, $R(6,-4)$ and $S(2,-4)$.
    (i) Verify that $PQRS$ is a parallelogram by showing that opposite sides in the quadrilateral have the same slope.
    (ii) Show that $|PQ| = |RS|$ and $|PS| = |QR|$.
    (iii) Find M, the midpoint of $[PR]$.
    (iv) Verify that M is also the midpoint of $[QS]$.

18.4 The Equation of a Line

The equation of a line tells us how the x co-ordinate and the y co-ordinate of every point on the line are related to each other.

For example, consider the equation $x + y = 5$. This equation tells us that, for every point on this line, the x co-ordinate added to the y co-ordinate equals 5. Therefore, points on this line would include (0,5), (5,0), (1,4), (4,1), (2,3), (3,2), (6,−1), (−1,6) and so on.

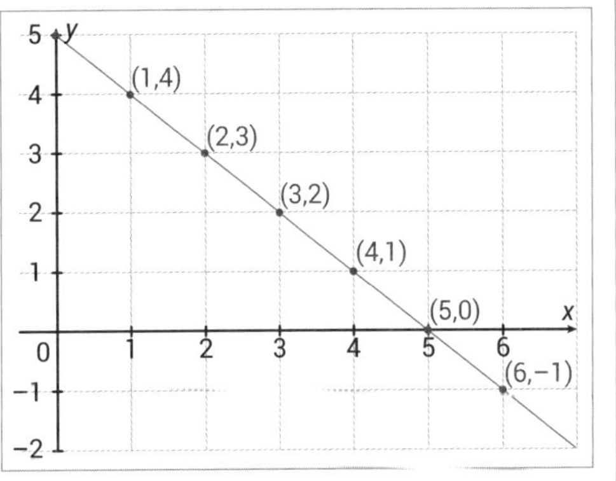

Worked Example 18.9

l is the line $2x + y = 8$.

(i) Find three points on l.

(ii) Draw the line l.

(iii) Find the slope of l.

(iv) Investigate if (58,−108) is on l.

Solution

(i) To find three points on l, we select values for x or y. Substitute into the given equation to find the corresponding ordinate.

l: $2x + y = 8$

Let $x = 3$.	Let $y = 0$.	Let $x = 5$.
$2(3) + y = 8$	$2x + (0) = 8$	$2(5) + y = 8$
$6 + y = 8$	$2x = 8$	$10 + y = 8$
$y = 2$	$x = 4$	$y = -2$
∴ Point (3,2)	∴ Point (4,0)	∴ Point (5,−2)

(ii)

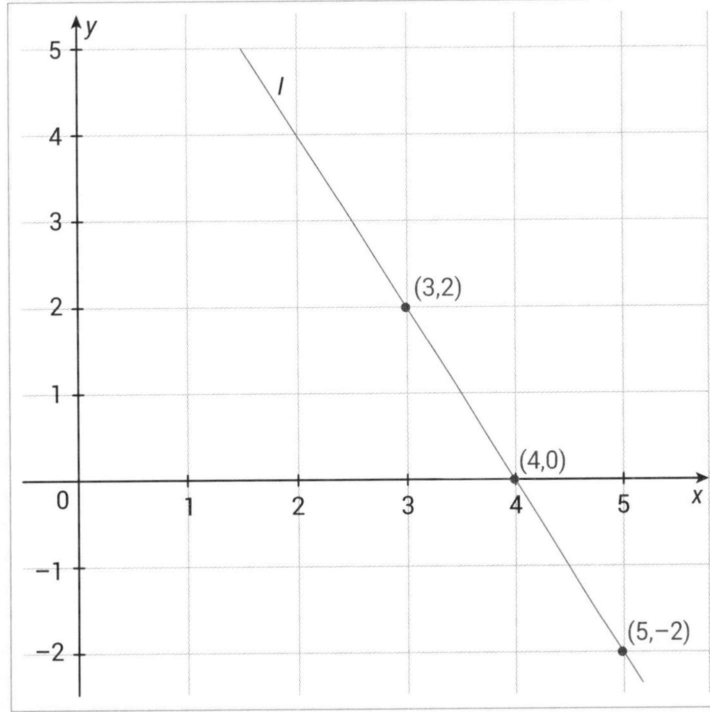

(iii) We can now use any two points on l to find the slope. Let's use (4,0) and (5,−2).

$x_1 = 4 \qquad y_1 = 0$

$x_2 = 5 \qquad y_2 = -2$

$m = \dfrac{y_2 - y_1}{x_2 - x_1}$

$m = \dfrac{-2 - 0}{5 - 4}$

$m = \dfrac{-2}{1} = -2$

(iv) Is (58, −108) on l?

Substitute 58 and −108 for x and y into l.

$l: 2x + y = 8$

$2(58) + (-108) = 8$

$116 - 108 = 8$

$8 = 8$ True

$\therefore$ (58, −108) is on l.

Equations of Horizontal and Vertical Lines

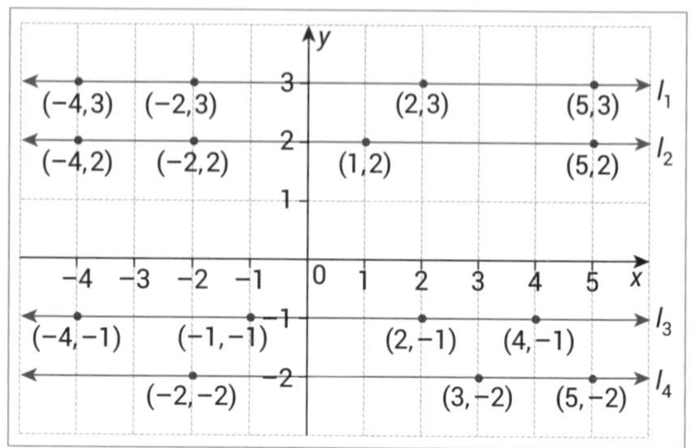

Consider the horizontal lines shown in the diagram. You will notice that the y ordinates of all points on a given line are equal. The line is completely defined by the common y ordinate of all its points. Therefore, all horizontal lines have an equation of the form $y = c$, where c is the common y ordinate of all the points. The following are the equations of the lines shown:

l_1: $y = 3$; l_2: $y = 2$; l_3: $y = -1$; l_4: $y = -2$.

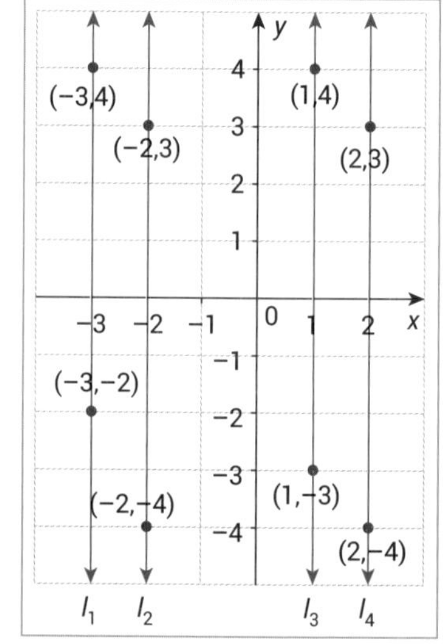

In the same way that a horizontal line is completely defined by the common y ordinate of all points on the line, a vertical line is completely defined by the common x ordinate of all points on the line. Therefore, all vertical lines have an equation of the form $x = c$, where c is the common x ordinate of all the points. The following are the equations of the lines shown:

l_1: $x = -3$; l_2: $x = -2$; l_3: $x = 1$; l_4: $x = 2$.

Worked Example 18.10

Find the equation of the line parallel to the y-axis containing the point (3,2).

Solution

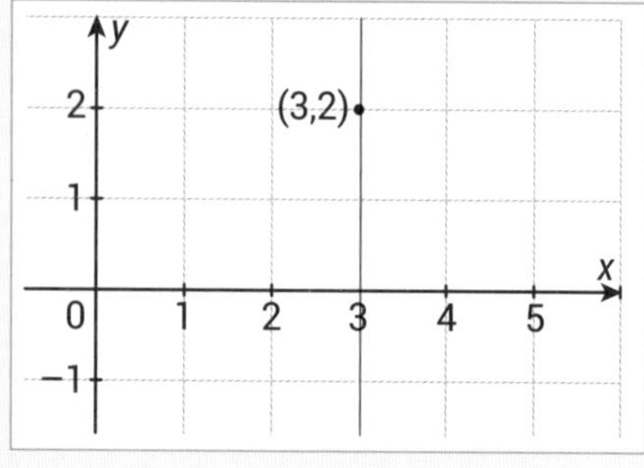

The co-ordinates of all points on the line have a common x ordinate (they are of the form $(3,k)$).

Therefore, the equation of the line is $x = 3$.

Exercise 18.4

1. Which of these lines passes through the point (3,2)?

Line	Insert ✓or ×
$2x + y = 8$	
$x + y = 5$	
$2x - y = 4$	
$x - y + 1 = 0$	
$3x + y = 11$	

2. Which of these lines passes through the point (−2,6)?

Line	Insert ✓or ×
$x + y = 2$	
$3x + y = 0$	
$2x + y = 2$	
$6{,}000x + 2{,}000y = 0$	
$x - y = 4$	

3. In each case, write down four points on the line and then draw the line.
   - (i) $x + y = 6$
   - (ii) $x + y = 9$
   - (iii) $x - y = 4$
   - (iv) $2x + y = 12$
   - (v) $x + 3y = 10$
   - (vi) $x + 2y = 6$
   - (vii) $2x + y = 9$
   - (viii) $x - y = 4$

4. Investigate if (11,−14) is on the line $2x + y - 8 = 0$.

5. Only one of the points (3,1), (−7,−7), (−1,−2), (8,5) is **not** on the line $4x - 5y = 7$. Which one? Justify your answer.

6. Investigate if (−31,17) is on the line $x + 2y = 2$.

7. k is the line $x + 3y = 6$.
   - (i) Find three points on k.
   - (ii) Draw the line.
   - (iii) Find the slope of k.
   - (iv) Investigate if (−54,20) is on k.

8. l is the line $2x - y = 8$.
   - (i) Find three points on l.
   - (ii) Draw the line.
   - (iii) Find the slope of l.
   - (iv) Investigate if (50,43) is on l.

9. (4,−1) is on the line $4x + 3y = k$. Find the value of k.

10. (−2,5) is on the line $2x - y + k = 0$. Find the value of k.

11. (2,−1) is on the line $5x + 3y = c$. Find the value of c.

12. The point (k,3) is on the line $3x + y = 15$. Find the value of k.

13. The point (c,−4) is on the line $2x + y = 10$. Find the value of c.

14. Find the equation of the line parallel to the y-axis and containing the point:
   - (i) (5,6)
   - (ii) (−2,3)
   - (iii) (−1,2)
   - (iv) (2,6)

15. Find the equation of the line parallel to the x-axis and containing the point:
   - (i) (2,3)
   - (ii) (5,−2)
   - (iii) (6,−3)
   - (iv) (7,5)

18.5 Equations of the Form $y = mx + c$

Many equations that model or represent real-life situtations are of the form $y = mx + c$. So, it makes sense to study equations of the form $y = mx + c$.

When we use equations to solve everyday problems, we usually refer to the equation as a **model** of the problem.

Given the equation $y = mx + c$, m is the slope and $(0,c)$ is the y-intercept, i.e. the point where the line crosses the y-axis.

For example, the equation that converts degrees Celsius (x) to degrees Fahrenheit (y) is:

$$y = \frac{9}{5}x + 32$$

The slope is $\frac{9}{5}$ and (0,32) is the y-intercept.

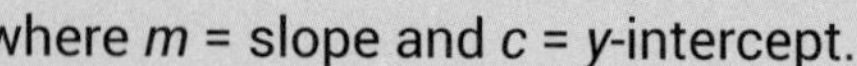

Equation of a line:

$$y = mx + c$$

where m = slope and c = y-intercept.

This formula appears on page 18 of *Formulae and Tables*.

Worked Example 18.11

k is the line $3x - 4y = 12$.

(i) Find the co-ordinates of the point where k cuts the x-axis.

(ii) Find the co-ordinates of the point where k cuts the y-axis.

(iii) Hence, draw the line k.

Solution

(i) The y co-ordinate of any point on the x-axis is 0. Let $y = 0$ in the equation of k and solve the equation to find x.

$$3x - 4(0) = 12$$
$$3x = 12$$
$$x = \frac{12}{3}$$
$$x = 4$$

$\therefore$ (4,0) are the co-ordinates of the point where k cuts the x-axis.

(ii) The x co-ordinate of any point on the y-axis is 0. Let $x = 0$ in the equation of k and solve the equation to find y.

$$3(0) - 4y = 12$$
$$-4y = 12$$
$$y = \frac{12}{-4}$$
$$y = -3$$

$\therefore$ (0,−3) are the co-ordinates of the point where k cuts the y-axis.

(iii)

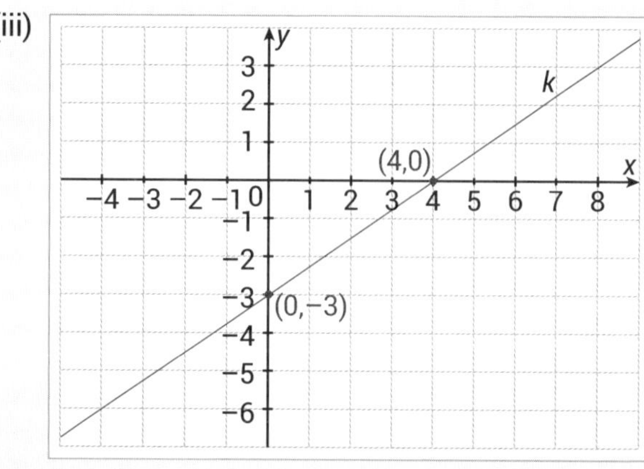

Worked Example 18.12

l is the line $y = \frac{3}{4}x - 9$.

(i) Write down the slope of l.

(ii) Write down the co-ordinates of the y-intercept of l.

(iii) Graph the line l.

(iv) Find the x-intercept of l.

Solution

(i) $m = \frac{3}{4}$

(ii) (0,−9)

(iii) (0,−9) is a point on l.

$$m = \frac{3}{4} = \frac{\text{Rise}}{\text{Run}}$$

Start at (0,−9), rise 3 and run 4.

This gives us a second point on l, (4,−6).

Alternatively, we could find a second point on l and then graph it.

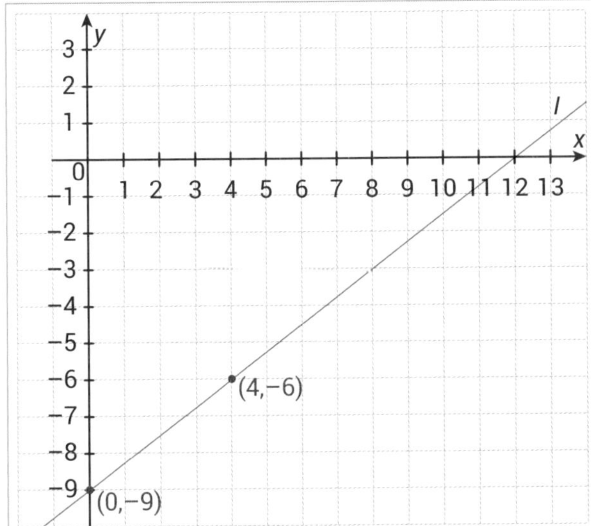

(iv) The y co-ordinate of any point on the x-axis is 0. Let $y = 0$ in the equation of l and solve the equation to find x.

$0 = \frac{3}{4}x - 9$

$0 = 3x - 36$ (Multiplying both sides by 4)

$3x = 36$

$x = 12$

$\therefore$ (12,0) is the x-intercept.

Exercise 18.5

1. Write down the slopes of the following lines:
   (i) $y = 2x + 6$ (iii) $y = 7x + 8$
   (ii) $y = 3x - 5$ (iv) $y = \frac{1}{2}x - 3$

2. Write down the slopes of the following lines:
   (i) $y = 2x - 8$ (iii) $y = -2x + 12$
   (ii) $y = \frac{2}{3}x - 6$ (iv) $y = -\frac{6}{5}x + 20$

3. Find the co-ordinates of the y-intercept of the following lines (i.e. the point where the lines cross the y-axis):
   (i) $y = \frac{4}{5}x - 8$ (iii) $y = \frac{1}{2}x + 3$
   (ii) $y = 5x - 4$ (iv) $y = -5x - \frac{1}{3}$

4. Find the co-ordinates of the y-intercept of the following lines (i.e. where the lines cross the y-axis):
   (i) $y = \frac{2}{3}x - 2$ (iii) $y = \frac{5}{2}x - 5$
   (ii) $y = 3x - 8$ (iv) $y = 2x - \frac{2}{5}$

5. Using graph paper, graph the following lines:
   (i) $y = \frac{1}{3}x + 5$ (v) $y = \frac{2}{3}x - 10$
   (ii) $y = 2x - 7$ (vi) $y = 2x - 5$
   (iii) $y = \frac{1}{2}x - 4$ (vii) $y = \frac{3}{2}x - 1$
   (iv) $y = -x - \frac{1}{3}$ (viii) $y = -\frac{5}{2}x + 10$

6. Using graph paper, graph the following lines:
   (i) $y = 3x + 1$ (ii) $y = 2x + 3$
   Using your graph, find the co-ordinates of the point where the two lines meet.

7. Using graph paper, graph the following lines:
   (i) $y = x + 3$ (ii) $y = 2x$
   Using your graph, find the co-ordinates of the point where the two lines meet.

8. Find the co-ordinates of the y-intercept of the following lines:
   (i) $y = 2x - 6$ (iii) $y = 4x + 8$
   (ii) $y = x + 2$ (iv) $y = 3x - 12$

9. Find the co-ordinates of the x-intercept of the following lines:
   (i) $y = 2x + 8$ (iii) $y = 2x - 18$
   (ii) $y = 2x - 12$ (iv) $y = 7x - 14$

10. Find the co-ordinates of the x-intercept and the y-intercept for each of the following lines and hence, graph the lines:
    (i) $x + y = 3$ (iv) $5x - y = 15$
    (ii) $x + 2y = 6$ (v) $5x + 3y = 30$
    (iii) $2x + y = 8$ (vi) $3x + 4y = 12$

18.6 Finding the Equation of a Line

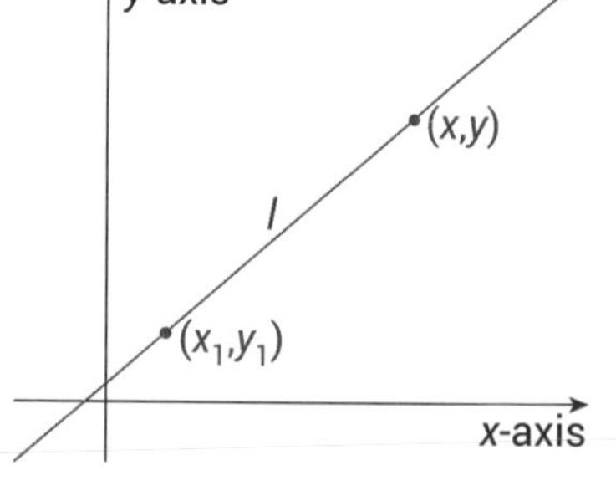

l is a line containing the point (x_1,y_1), and (x,y) is any other point on l.

Then, $\frac{y - y_1}{x - x_1} = m$, where m is the slope of the line l.

$\Rightarrow y - y_1 = m(x - x_1)$

This is the equation of the line. Therefore, to find the equation of a line, we need the slope of the line, m, and a point on the line, (x_1,y_1).

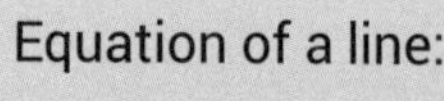
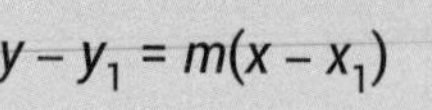

Equation of a line:
$y - y_1 = m(x - x_1)$

This formula appears on page 18 of *Formulae and Tables*.

Worked Example 18.13

Find the equation of the line which passes through the point $A(-3,4)$ and has a slope of $-\frac{1}{2}$.

Solution

$x_1 = -3 \quad y_1 = 4$

$m_1 = -\frac{1}{2}$

$y - y_1 = m_1(x - x_1)$

$y - 4 = -\frac{1}{2}(x + 3)$ Multiply both sides by 2.

$2(y - 4) = 2\left(-\frac{1}{2}\right)(x + 3)$

$2y - 8 = -1(x + 3)$

$2y - 8 = -x - 3$

$x + 2y - 5 = 0$ Bring all terms to the LHS.

Worked Example 18.14

Find the equation of the line which passes through the points (−1,5) and (2,6).

Solution

$x_1 = -1 \quad y_1 = 5$

$x_2 = 2 \quad y_2 = 6$

Step 1 Find the slope.

$m = \frac{y_2 - y_1}{x_2 - x_1}$

$m = \frac{6 - 5}{2 - (-1)}$

$m = \frac{1}{2 + 1} = \frac{1}{3}$

Step 2 Find the equation.

$m = \frac{1}{3}$ Point = (−1,5)

$y - y_1 = m(x - x_1)$

$y - 5 = \frac{1}{3}(x - (-1))$

$y - 5 = \frac{1}{3}(x + 1)$ Multiply both sides by 3.

$\therefore 3(y - 5) = 1(x + 1)$

$\therefore 3y - 15 = x + 1$

$\therefore x - 3y + 16 = 0$ is the equation. Bring all terms to the LHS.

Exercise 18.6

1. Find the equation of the line containing the point A and with slope m:
   (i) $A(1,1)$; $m = 2$
   (ii) $A(-3,2)$; $m = -1$
   (iii) $A(-6,-2)$; $m = -5$
   (iv) $A(-5,-4)$; $m = \frac{1}{2}$
   (v) $A(2,-8)$; $m = -\frac{1}{3}$
   (vi) $A(1,1)$; $m = 0$

2. Find the equations of the following lines containing the point B and with slope m:
   (i) $B(-3,2)$; $m = \frac{3}{2}$
   (ii) $B(-1,5)$; $m = -\frac{4}{3}$
   (iii) $B(-2,6)$; $m = \frac{2}{5}$
   (iv) $B(-2,6)$; $m = -\frac{1}{7}$
   (v) $B(4,-8)$; $m = -\frac{3}{5}$
   (vi) $B(-1,-1)$; $m = 0$

3. Find the equation of the line through the points A and B:

(i) $A(2,1)$; $B(3,2)$ (iv) $A(-3,6)$; $B(5,-2)$

(ii) $A(-1,3)$; $B(2,4)$ (v) $A(1,-3)$; $B(2,-10)$

(iii) $A(-5,-1)$; $B(-2,5)$ (vi) $A(2,3)$; $B(5,3)$

4. Find the equation of the line through the points A and B:

(i) $A(-2,2)$; $B(-5,3)$ (iv) $A(1,1)$; $B(-2,-1)$

(ii) $A(1,7)$; $B(-2,4)$ (v) $A(-3,4)$; $B(-2,-5)$

(iii) $A(6,-5)$; $B(-3,9)$ (vi) $A(1,1)$; $B(2,4)$

5. Find the equation of each line in the diagram below.

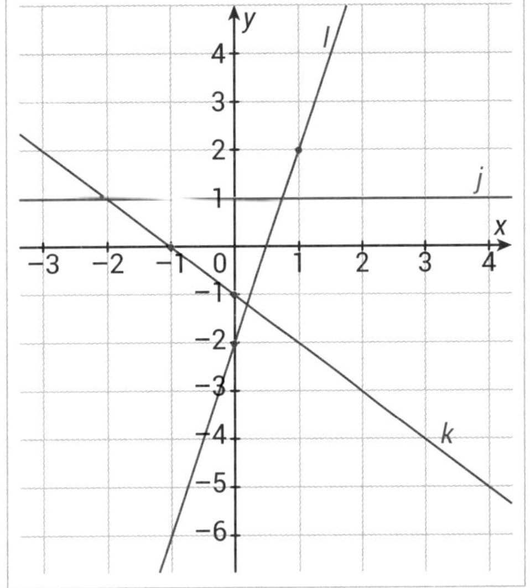

6. Find the equation of each line in the diagram below.

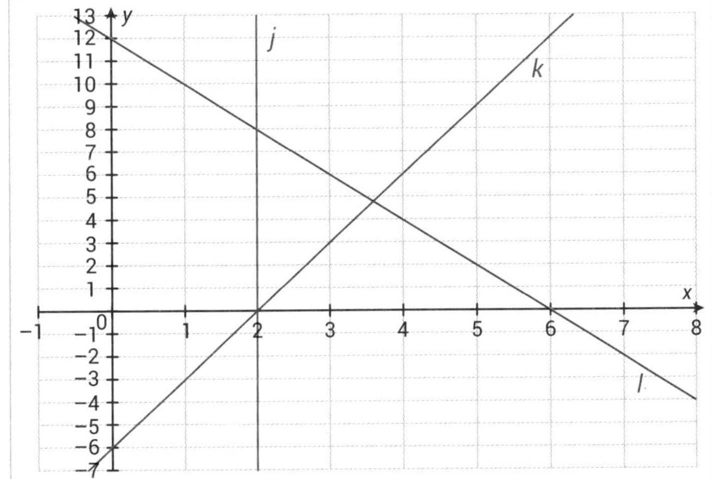

7. Plot the points A and B and hence, write down the equation of the line containing A and B.

(i) $A(1,1)$; $B(1,2)$ (iii) $A(-5,-6)$; $B(-5,4)$ (v) $A(1,3)$; $B(-2,3)$

(ii) $A(-1,3)$; $B(-1,4)$ (iv) $A(-1,4)$; $B(3,4)$ (vi) $A(2,5)$; $B(-1,5)$

8. Find the equation of the line through the points $A(3,1)$ and $B(-5,2)$. Show that the line contains $C(-13,3)$.

9. Find the equation of the line through the points $A(2,1)$ and $B(-1,-1)$. Show that the line contains $C(8,5)$.

10. Find the equation of the line through $C(3,1)$ that contains the midpoint of $A(3,1)$ and $B(-5,2)$.

18.7 Intersecting Lines

There are two methods for finding where two lines intersect.

1. Graph the two lines, and read the point of intersection from the graph.
2. Find the point that satisfies the equations of both lines. We do this by solving the equations simultaneously.

Worked Example 18.15

m is the line $x + 2y - 4 = 0$, and n is the line $x - y - 1 = 0$.

(i) Using the same axes and scales, draw the lines m and n.

(ii) Use your graphs to find the point of intersection of m and n.

(iii) Check your answer by solving the equations simultaneously.

Solution

(i) We graph the lines by finding the co-ordinates of the x-intercept and y-intercept for both lines.

Intercepts for m ($x + 2y - 4 = 0$)

Let $y = 0$

$\Rightarrow x - 4 = 0$

$x = 4$

$\therefore$ (4,0) are the co-ordinates of the x-intercept.

Let $x = 0$

$\Rightarrow 2y - 4 = 0$

$2y = 4$

$y = 2$

$\therefore$ (0,2) are the co-ordinates of the y-intercept.

Intercepts for n ($x - y - 1 = 0$)

Let $y = 0$

$\Rightarrow x - 1 = 0$

$x = 1$

$\therefore$ (1,0) are the co-ordinates of the x-intercept.

Let $x = 0$

$\Rightarrow -y - 1 = 0$

$-y = 1$

$y = -1$

$\therefore$ (0,−1) are the co-ordinates of the y-intercept.

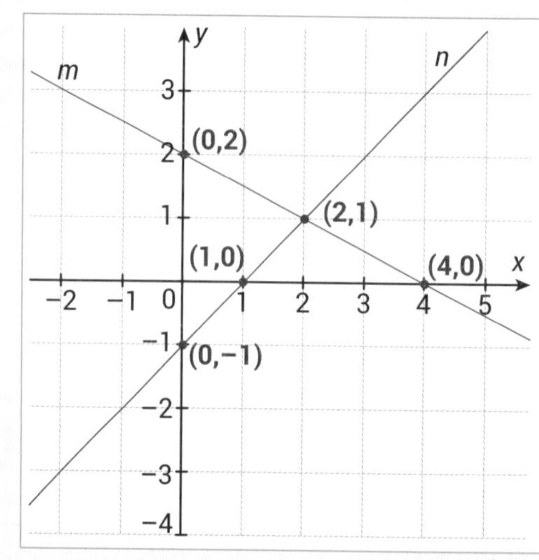

(ii) Using the graphs, the point of intersection is (2,1).

(iii) **Step 1**

Eliminate either x or y.

$x + 2y - 4 = 0$ **Eq. I**

$x - y - 1 = 0$ **Eq. II**

$x + 2y - 4 = 0$

$-x + y + 1 = 0$ (Eq. I − Eq. II)

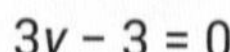

$3y - 3 = 0$

$3y = 3$

$\therefore y = 1$

See Solving simultaneous equations in Chapter 2.

Step 2

Find the value of x.

Put $y = 1$ into either equation to find the x ordinate of the point of intersection:

$x + 2(1) - 4 = 0$

$x + 2 - 4 = 0$

$x - 2 = 0$

$\therefore x = 2$

(2,1) are the co-ordinates of the point of intersection of m and n.

Exercise 18.7

1. l is the line $y - 3x = 9$, and k is the line $y = x - 3$.
   (i) Using the same axes and scales, draw the lines l and k.
   (ii) Use your graph to find the point of intersection of l and k. Scale the x-axis from −8 to 8 and the y-axis from −10 to 10.
   (iii) Check your answer by solving the equations simultaneously.

2. m is the line $x + 4y - 8 = 0$, and n is the line $x - y + 7 = 0$.
   (i) Using the same axes and scales, draw the lines m and n. Scale the x-axis from −8 to 8 and the y-axis from −2 to 8.
   (ii) Use your graph to find the point of intersection of m and n.
   (iii) Check your answer by solving the equations simultaneously.

3. r is the line $3x - y + 4 = 0$, and s is the line $5x + y - 10 = 0$.
   (i) Using the same axes and scales, draw the lines r and s. Scale the x-axis from −4 to 4 and the y-axis from −4 to 10.
   (ii) Use your graph to find the point of intersection of r and s.
   (iii) Check your answer by solving the equations simultaneously.

4. l is the line $x - y - 1 = 0$, and k is the line $x + 2y - 13 = 0$.
   (i) Using the same axes and scales, draw the lines l and k. Scale the x-axis from −2 to 14 and the y-axis from −2 to 8.
   (ii) Use your graph to find the point of intersection of l and k.
   (iii) Check your answer by solving the equations simultaneously.

5. p is the line $3x + 2y = 49$, and q is the line $y = 2x$.
   (i) Using the same axes and scales, draw the lines p and q. Scale the x-axis from −6 to 18 and the y-axis from −6 to 30.
   (ii) Use your graph to find the point of intersection of p and q.
   (iii) Check your answer by solving the equations simultaneously.

6. a is the line $x + y = 48$, and b is the line $y = 3x$.
   (i) Using the same axes and scales, draw the lines a and b. Scale the x-axis from −8 to 48 and the y-axis from −8 to 48.
   (ii) Use your graph to find the point of intersection of a and b.
   (iii) Check your answer by solving the equations simultaneously.

7. 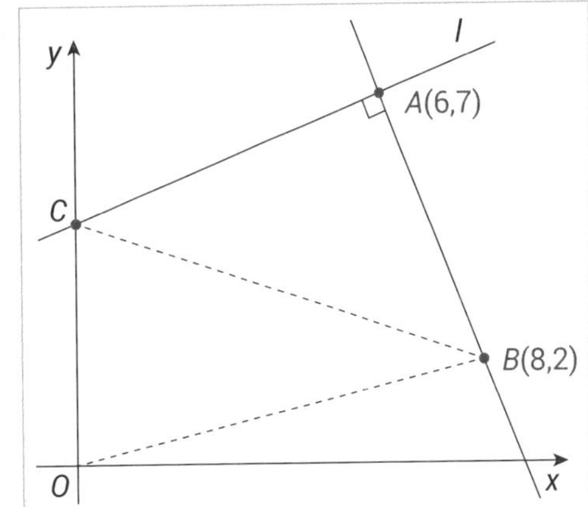

   The points A and B have co-ordinates (6,7) and (8,2) respectively.
   The line l passes through the point A and is perpendicular to the line AB, as shown in the diagram.
   (i) Find an equation for l in the form $ax + by + c = 0$, where a, b and c are integers.
   (ii) Given that l intersects the y-axis at the point C, find the co-ordinates of C.

8. The straight line l_1 passes through the points (−1,3) and (11,12).
   (i) Find an equation for l_1 in the form $ax + by + c = 0$, where a, b and c are integers.
   (ii) The line l_2 has equation $3y + 4x - 30 = 0$. Find the co-ordinates of the point of intersection of l_1 and l_2.

18.8 Further Equations

If we are given the equation of a line, l, in the form $ax + by + c = 0$, then we can find the slope of l by writing its equation in the form $y = mx + c$. This will helps us find the equations of lines that are either parallel or perpendicular to l.

Worked Example 18.16

l is the line $3x - 2y = 6$. The line k contains the point (1,1) and is perpendicular to l. Find the equation of k.

Solution

To find the equation of k, we need:

1. A point on k
2. The slope of k

We are told that k contains (1,1).

As $k \perp l$, we will be able to figure out the slope of k from the slope of l.

Slope of l

Write the equation of l in the form $y = mx + c$.

$$3x - 2y = 6$$
$$-2y = -3x + 6$$
$$2y = 3x - 6$$
$$y = \tfrac{3}{2}x - 3$$

The slope of l is $\frac{3}{2}$, so therefore, the slope of k is $-\frac{2}{3}$.

Equation of k

(1,1) is a point on k and the slope of k is $-\frac{2}{3}$.

Using the formula $y - y_1 = m(x - x_1)$, we can now find the equation of k:

$$y - 1 = -\tfrac{2}{3}(x - 1) \quad \text{Multiply both sides by 3.}$$
$$3(y - 1) = -2(x - 1)$$
$$3y - 3 = -2x + 2$$
$$k: 2x + 3y - 5 = 0$$

Worked Example 18.17

k is the line $y = 2x + 6$. Write down the equation of the line p that is perpendicular to k and has the same y-intercept as k.

Solution

The slope of k is 2, so the slope of p is $-\frac{1}{2}$.

Therefore, the equation of the line p is $y = -\frac{1}{2}x + 6$.

Exercise 18.8

1. A is the point (1,1) and B is the point (2,3).

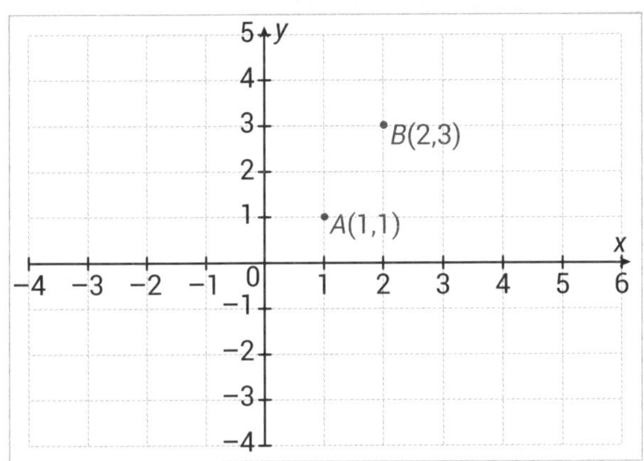

(i) Find the slope of the line AB.

(ii) Write down the slope of a line perpendicular to AB.

2. Write down the equation of the line that is perpendicular to each of the following lines and that passes through the same point on the y-axis:

(i) $y = \frac{3}{5}x - 2$
(ii) $y = 4x - 5$
(iii) $y = \frac{9}{8}x + 2$
(iv) $y = -2x + \frac{1}{3}$
(v) $y = \frac{5}{9}x - 8$
(vi) $y = 5x - 3$
(vii) $y = \frac{3}{2}x + 11$
(viii) $y = -5x + \frac{2}{5}$
(ix) $y = \frac{3}{7}x + 2$ v

3. Find the slopes of the following lines by first writing them in the form $y = mx + c$:

(i) $2x + y = 7$
(ii) $x - 3y = 5$
(iii) $5x - y = 4$
(iv) $2x - y = 12$
(v) $4x + 9y = 15$
(vi) $7x - 3y = -2$

4. l is the line $3x - 2y + 4 = 0$. The line k contains the point (2,−3) and is parallel to l. Find the equation of k.

5. m is the line $x - 6y + 12 = 0$. The line n contains the point (−3,2) and is perpendicular to m. Find the equation of n.

6. p is the line $2x - y + 14 = 0$. The line q contains the point (−1,2) and is parallel to p. Find the equation of q.

7. l is the line $x - y + 2 = 0$. The line k contains the point (2,2) and is perpendicular to l. Find the equation of k.

18.9 Area of a Triangle

Formula Approach

The diagram on the right shows a triangle with vertices (0,0), (x_1,y_1) and (x_2,y_2).

The area of this triangle is given by:

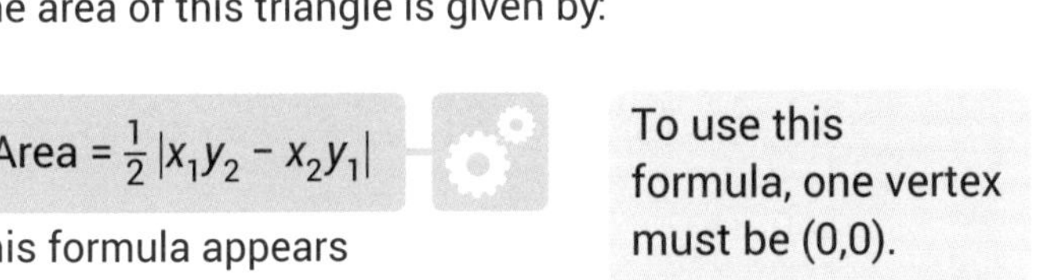

$$\text{Area} = \frac{1}{2}|x_1y_2 - x_2y_1|$$

This formula appears on page 18 of *Formulae and Tables*.

To use this formula, one vertex must be (0,0).

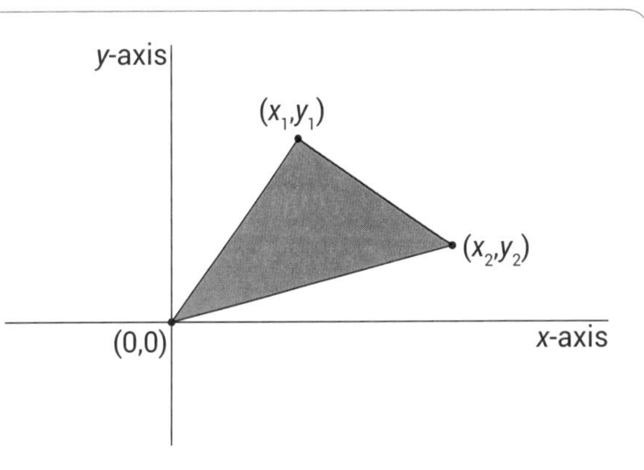

Worked Example 18.18

Find the area of the triangle with vertices (0,0), (7,3) and (15,0).

Solution

One of the vertices is at (0,0) so we can use the formula directly.

(0,0) (7,3) (15,0)

$\quad\quad\quad x_1 y_1 \quad x_2 y_2$

|−45| means a 'distance' of −45 from 0 on the number line.

∴ |−45| = 45

$$\text{Area} = \frac{1}{2}|x_1 y_2 - x_2 y_1|$$

$$= \frac{1}{2}|(7)(0) - (15)(3)|$$

$$= \frac{1}{2}|0 - 45|$$

$$= \frac{1}{2}|-45|$$

$$= \frac{1}{2}(45)$$

∴ Area = 22.5 units^2

Worked Example 18.19

Find the area of the triangle whose vertices are $A(3,6)$, $B(7,2)$ and $C(4,1)$.

Solution

Method 1

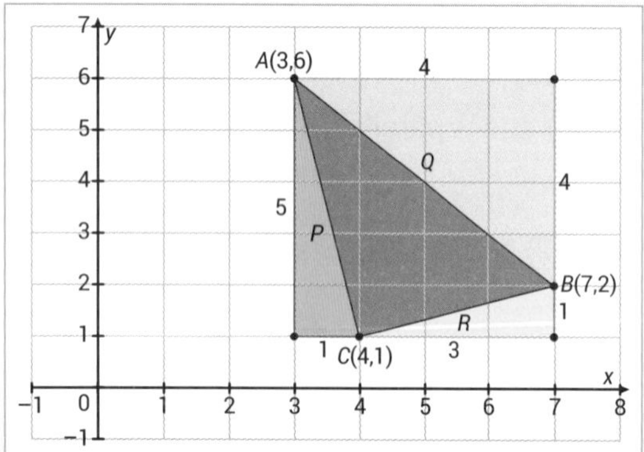

Step 1

Construct a rectangle around triangle ABC.

Area of rectangle = 5 × 4 = 20 units^2

Step 2

Area of ΔP + Area of ΔQ + Area of ΔR

$= \frac{1}{2}(1)(5) + \frac{1}{2}(4)(4) + \frac{1}{2}(3)(1) = 12$ units^2

Step 3

Area of ΔABC = 20 − 12 = 8 units^2

Method 2

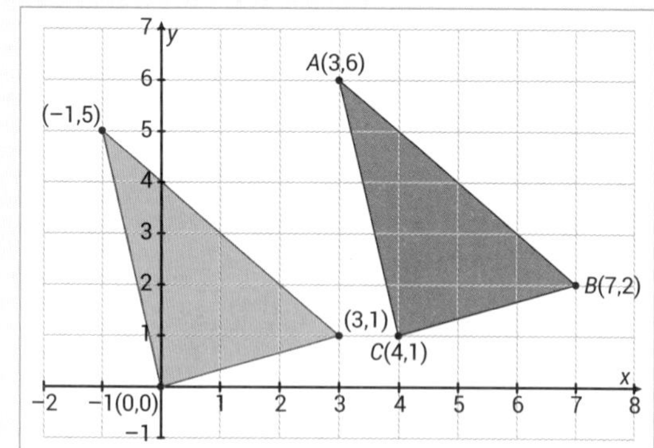

We can also use the formula to find the area of the triangle. We need to move (translate) the triangle until one of the vertices is (0,0).

(4,1) → (0,0)
(3,6) → (−1,5)
(7,2) → (3,1)

Here we take 4 from each x-value and 1 from each y-value for each of the three points.

$x_1 = -1 \quad y_1 = 5$

$x_2 = 3 \quad y_2 = 1$

$$\text{Area} = \frac{1}{2}|x_1 y_2 - x_2 y_1|$$

$$= \frac{1}{2}|(-1)(1) - (3)(5)|$$

$$= \frac{1}{2}|-1 - 15|$$

$$= \frac{1}{2}|-16|$$

$$= \frac{1}{2}(16)$$

= 8 units^2

Make sure to include the units of measurement.

Worked Example 18.20

$A(2,1)$ and $B(4,3)$ are two points.

C is the midpoint of $[AB]$, and k is the line through C perpendicular to AB.

(i) Find the co-ordinates of C.

(ii) What is the slope of AB?

(iii) Using your answers to parts (i) and (ii), find the equation of k.

(iv) Verify that $D(1,4)$ lies on k.

(v) Find $|AB|$ and $|CD|$.

(vi) Hence, find the area of ΔABD.

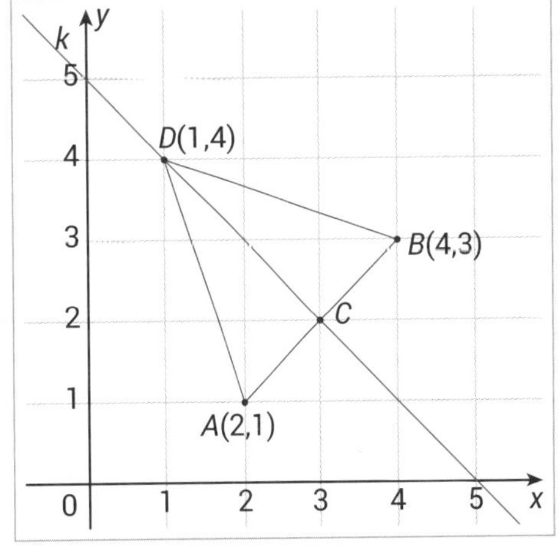

Solution

(i) $x_1 = 2 \quad y_1 = 1$

$x_2 = 4 \quad y_2 = 3$

$$\text{Midpoint} = \left(\frac{x_1 + x_2}{2}, \frac{y_1 + y_2}{2}\right)$$

$$C = \left(\frac{2+4}{2}, \frac{1+3}{2}\right) = \left(\frac{6}{2}, \frac{4}{2}\right) = (3,2)$$

(ii) $$m = \frac{y_2 - y_1}{x_2 - x_1}$$

$$m = \frac{3-1}{4-2} = \frac{2}{2} = 1$$

(iii) The slope of k is -1, as k is perpendicular to AB.

$C(3,2)$ is a point on k.

$$y - y_1 = m(x - x_1)$$

$$y - 2 = -1(x - 3)$$

$$y - 2 = -x + 3$$

$$k: x + y - 5 = 0$$

(iv) Substitute $D(1,4)$ into the equation of k.

$x + y - 5 = 0$

$\therefore 1 + 4 = 5$

$5 = 5$

$\therefore D(1,4)$ lies on k.

(v) $\text{Distance} = \sqrt{(x_2 - x_1)^2 + (y_2 - y_1)^2}$

$|AB| = \sqrt{(4-2)^2 + (3-1)^2}$ $\quad A(2,1) \quad B(4,3)$; $\quad x_1 y_1 \quad x_2 y_2$

$= \sqrt{(2)^2 + (2)^2}$

$= \sqrt{4+4}$

$= \sqrt{8}$

$|CD| = \sqrt{(1-3)^2 + (4-2)^2}$ $\quad C(3,2) \quad D(1,4)$; $\quad x_1 y_1 \quad x_2 y_2$

$= \sqrt{(-2)^2 + (2)^2}$

$= \sqrt{4+4}$

$= \sqrt{8}$

(vi) As k is perpendicular to AB, we can use the fact that the area of a triangle is **half the base length by the perpendicular height** to find the area of ΔABC.

Area of $\Delta ABC = \frac{1}{2}\sqrt{8}\sqrt{8} = 4$ units^2

Exercise 18.9

1. Use the formula $\frac{1}{2}|x_1 y_2 - x_2 y_1|$ to find the areas of the triangles with these vertices:

(i) $A(6,3), B(0,0), C(0,5)$

(ii) $A(2,4), B(3,8), C(0,0)$

(iii) $A(1,1), B(0,2), C(0,0)$

(iv) $A(5,3), B(2,2), C(0,0)$

2. Using a graphical approach, or by translating the triangle, find the areas of the triangles with these vertices:

(i) $X(5,3), Y(1,6), Z(3,5)$

(ii) $X(2,4), Y(1,1), Z(-5,6)$

(iii) $X(-1,-1), Y(3,2), Z(-1,8)$

(iv) $X(-1,3), Y(2,2), Z(6,-10)$

3. Find the areas of the triangles with these vertices:

(i) $P(3,8)$, $Q(2,-1)$, $R(3,0)$

(ii) $P(-1,3)$, $Q(1,2)$, $R(2,-7)$

(iii) $P(-5,6)$, $Q(-1,1)$, $R(5,0)$

(iv) $P(-1,-5)$, $Q(1,2)$, $R(-3,-2)$

4. If the area of a triangle is zero, then the vertices of the triangle are collinear, i.e. they lie on a straight line.

Show that the following points are collinear. Use the formula $\frac{1}{2}|x_1 y_2 - x_2 y_1|$.

(i) $T(5,4)$, $U(1,6)$, $V(3,5)$

(ii) $T(-3,1)$, $U(1,1)$, $V(-1,1)$

(iii) $T(-5,14)$, $U(3,2)$, $V(-1,8)$

(iv) $T(-1,3)$, $U(2,2)$, $V(5,1)$

5. $P(-3,1)$, $Q(1,3)$, $R(3,0)$ and $S(-1,-2)$ are the vertices of a parallelogram.

(i) Show *PQRS* on a diagram.

(ii) Find the area of *PQRS* by dividing it into two triangles.

6. $A(0,-4)$, $B(-1,-1)$, $C(5,4)$ and $D(8,0)$ are the vertices of a quadrilateral.

(i) Show *ABCD* on a diagram.

(ii) Find the area of *ABCD* by dividing it into two triangles.

7. The area of a triangle is half the base length by the perpendicular height. Use this fact to find the areas of the following triangles:

(i)

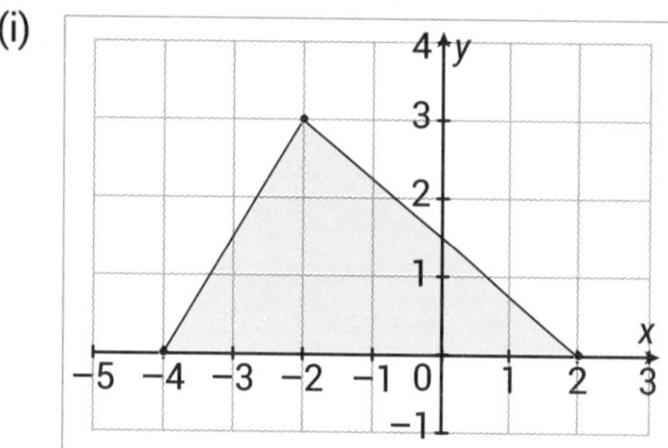

(ii)

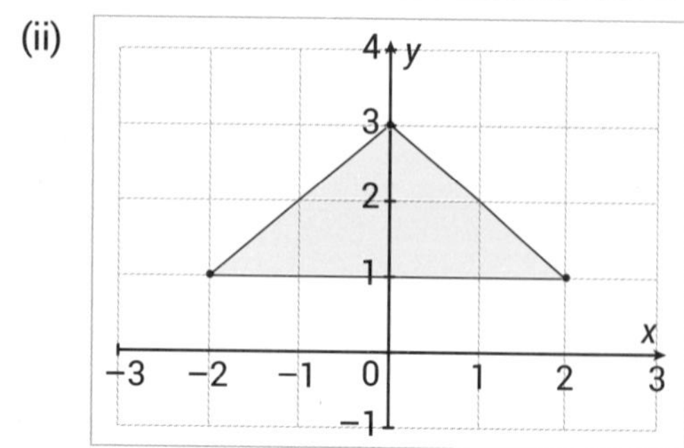

(iii)

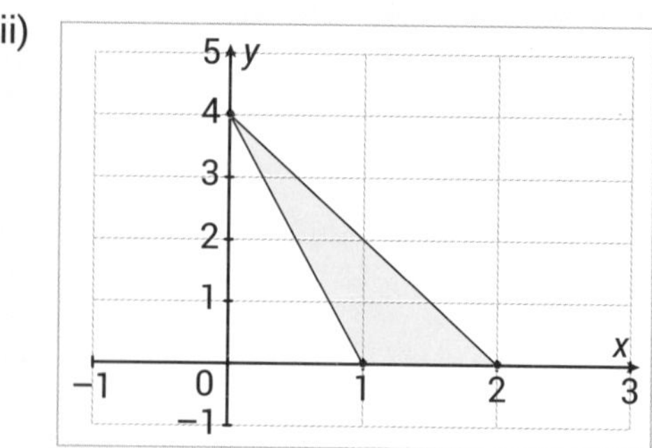

(iv)

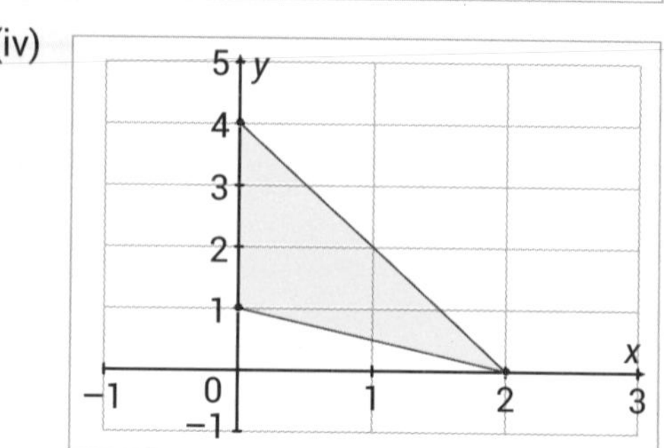

8. $A(-1,-6)$ and $B(3,-2)$ are two points. C is the midpoint of $[AB]$, and k is the line through C perpendicular to AB.

(i) Find the co-ordinates of C.

(ii) On graph paper, plot the points A, B and C.

(iii) What is the slope of AB?

(iv) Using your answers to parts (i) and (iii), find the equation of k.

(v) Verify that $D(-4,1)$ lies on k.

(vi) Show the line k on your graph.

(vii) Find $|AB|$ and $|CD|$.

(viii) Hence, find the area of ΔABD.

9. $W(0,-2)$ and $X(10,2)$ are two points. Y is the midpoint of $[WX]$, and l is the line through Y perpendicular to WX.

(i) Find the co-ordinates of Y.

(ii) On graph paper, plot the points W, X and Y.

(iii) What is the slope of WX?

(iv) Using your answers to parts (i) and (iii), find the equation of l.

(v) Verify that $Z(3,5)$ lies on l.

(vi) Show the line l on your graph.

(vii) Find $|WX|$ and $|YZ|$.

(viii) Hence, find the area of ΔWXZ.

10. $A(3,-2)$, $B(1,6)$ and $C(7,0)$ are the vertices of a triangle. Let M be the midpoint of $[BC]$.

(i) Find the co-ordinates of M.

(ii) Verify that area ΔABM = area ΔACM.

Revision Exercises

1. $A(-2,1)$ and $B(4,-5)$ are two points.
   (i) Plot the two points on graph paper.
   (ii) Find M, the midpoint of $[AB]$.
   (iii) Verify that $|AM| = |MB|$.
   (iv) Find the slope of AB.
   (v) Find the equation of AB.
   (vi) Find the co-ordinates of the point where AB cuts the x-axis.

2. Two points $A(0,-1)$ and $B(1,1)$ are shown on the diagram below.

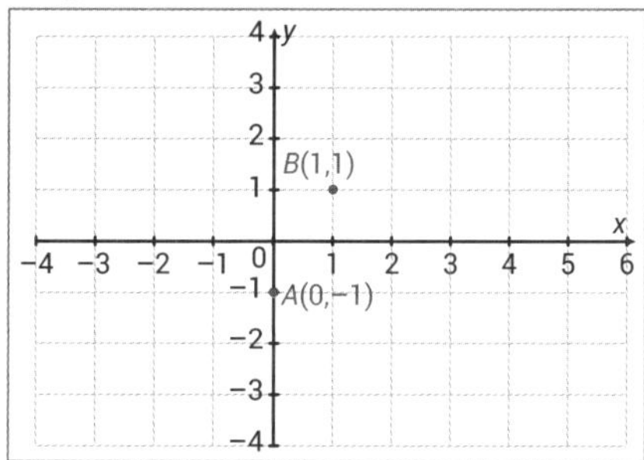

   (i) Plot two suitable points C and D such that $ABCD$ is a parallelogram.
   (ii) Write down the co-ordinates of C and D.
   (iii) By performing suitable calculations, verify that the points $ABCD$ do form a parallelogram.
   (iv) Show that the diagonal $[AC]$ bisects the area of the parallelogram.

3. $P(0,0)$, $Q(3,0)$ and $R(3,4)$ are three points.
   (i) Plot the three points.
   (ii) Find M, the midpoint of $[PQ]$.
   (iii) Find the slope of RM.
   (iv) Find the equation of RM.
   (v) Find the co-ordinates of the point where RM cuts the y-axis.
   (vi) Working from your graph, find the area of the triangle PQR.

4. $M(-5,1)$ and $N(2,6)$ are two points.
   (i) Plot the two points on graph paper.
   (ii) Find the slope of MN.
   (iii) Find the equation of MN.
   (iv) Find the co-ordinates of the point where MN cuts the y-axis.
   (v) Hence, write the equation of MN in the form $y = mx + c$.

5. l is the line $3x + y = 6$.
   (i) Verify that $(2,0)$ lies on l.
   (ii) If $(0,k)$ is a point on l, then find the value of k.
   (iii) Plot the line l.
   (iv) Find the slope of l using the slope formula.
   (v) Find the slope of l by writing the equation in the form $y = mx + c$.

6. (i) m is the line $16x - 8y + 12 = 0$. The line n contains the point $(1,1)$ and is parallel to m. Find the equation of n.
   (ii) l is the line $3x - 2y + 5 = 0$. The line n contains the point $(-3,-4)$ and is perpendicular to l. Find the equation of n.

7. (a) p is the line $3x - 9y + 4 = 0$. The line q contains the point $(-2,3)$ and is parallel to p. Find the equation of q.
   (b) l is the line $3x + 4y - 7 = 0$. The line k is perpendicular to l and contains the point $(7,9)$.
      (i) Find the equation of k.
      (ii) Find the point of intersection of l and k.

8. Find the areas of the triangles with these vertices:
   (i) $P(2,7)$, $Q(1,-2)$, $R(2,-1)$
   (ii) $P(-3,1)$, $Q(-1,0)$, $R(0,-9)$
   (iii) $P(-1,-4)$, $Q(1,1)$, $R(-3,-3)$

9.

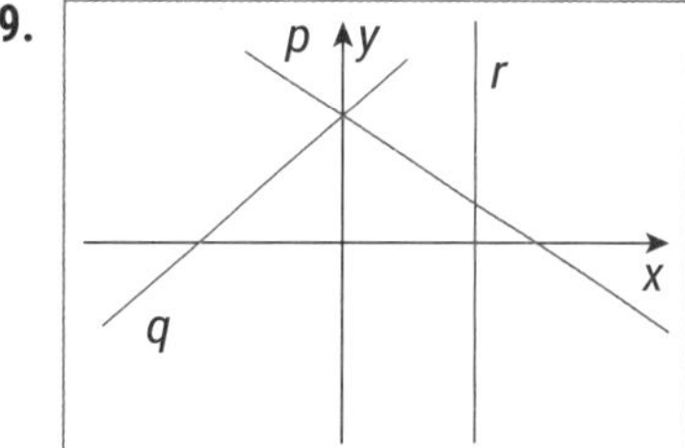

Copy and complete the table below.

Equation	Line
$x = 3$	
$x - y + 5 = 0$	
$y = -\frac{3}{4}x + 5$	

10. Find the slopes of each of the following lines:
   (i) $2x + 3y = 8$
   (ii) $x - 3y = 4$
   (iii) $y = 3x + 2$
   (iv) $5x - 8y = 9$

11. Find the point of intersection of the lines $2x + 3y = 5$ and $5x + 8y = 13$.

12. Find the point of intersection of the lines $5x + 2y = 1$ and $3x + y = 1$.

13. Graph each of the following lines:
(i) $x + y = 4$
(ii) $2x + 3y = 6$
(iii) $5x - 2y = 10$
(iv) $y = 3x + 2$

Exam Questions

1. (a) The line l contains the points $A(4,5)$ and $B(2,0)$. Find the equation of l.
Give your answer in the form $ax + by + c = 0$ where a, b, and $c \in Z$.
(b) Draw the line k: $x + 2y = 8$ on the axes below.

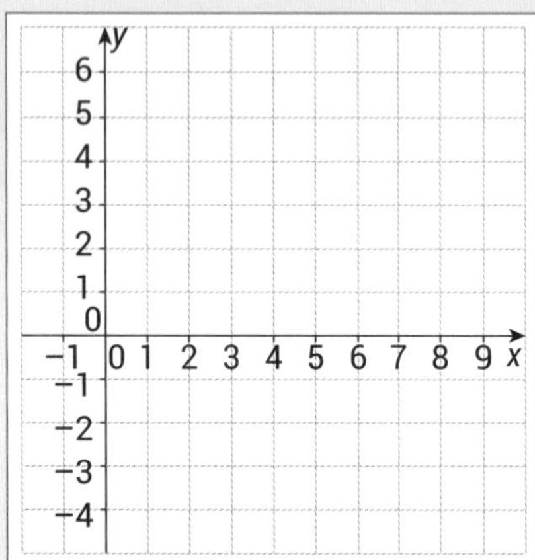

(c) Use a graphic, numeric or algebraic method to find the co-ordinates of $l \cap k$.

SEC Leaving Certificate Ordinary Level, Paper 2, 2016

2. Joe wants to draw a diagram of his farm. He uses axes and co-ordinates to plot his farmhouse at the point F on the diagram below.

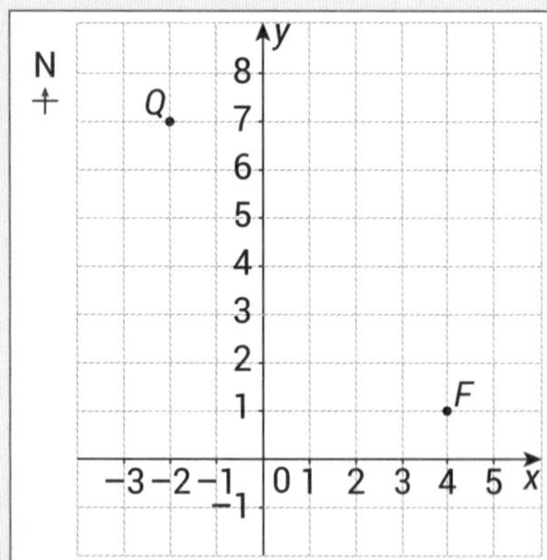

(a) (i) Write down the co-ordinates of the point F.
(ii) A barn is 5 units directly North of the farmhouse. Plot the point representing the position of the barn on the diagram. Label this point B.

(b) Joe's quad bike is marked with the point Q on the diagram.
Find the distance from the barn (B) to the quad (Q). Give your answer correct to 2 decimal places.

(c) Joe's tractor is at the point T, where $FBQT$ is a parallelogram.
Plot T on the diagram and write the co-ordinates of T.

(d) Joe wants to plough the land enclosed by the parallelogram $FBQT$.
Find the area of this parallelogram in square units.

SEC Leaving Certificate Ordinary Level, Paper 2, 2016

3. The line p makes equal intercepts on the axes at A and at B, as shown.

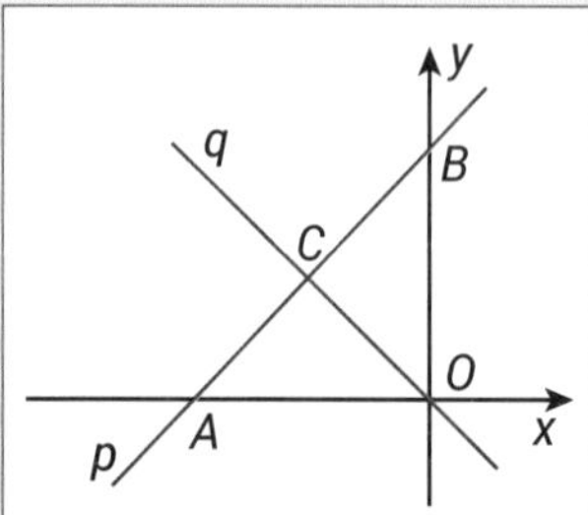

(a) (i) Write down the slope of p.
(ii) The point (1,5) is on p.
Find the equation of p.
Write your answer in the form $ax + by + c = 0$, where a, b, and $c \in Z$.

(b) The line q is perpendicular to p and contains the point $O(0,0)$.
Find the equation of q.

(c) The lines p and q intersect at the point C.
Explain why the triangles OCA and OBC are congruent.

SEC Leaving Certificate Ordinary Level, Paper 2, 2015

Solutions and chapter summary available online

19

Co-ordinate Geometry: The Circle

In this chapter you will learn to:

- Recognise that $(x - h)^2 + (y - k)^2 = r^2$ represents the relationship between the x and y co-ordinates of points on a circle with centre (h,k) and radius r
- Solve problems involving a line and a circle with centre (0,0)

You should remember...

- Chapter 18 Co-ordinate Geometry: The Line
- How to solve quadratic equations

Key words

- Equation of a circle
- Radius length
- Tangent

Since the earliest human civilisations arose, people have been fascinated by the mathematics of the **circle**. The ancient Greeks believed that the circle was the perfect form, because circular forms occurred so frequently in nature. They also thought that the stars and planets travelled in circular paths around the universe.

A circle is the set of all points in the plane that are equidistant from a fixed point, the centre. The distance from the centre to any point on the circle is called the radius length of the circle.

19.1 Circles with Centre (0,0) and Radius r

Consider the circle with centre $O(0,0)$ and radius r.

Let $P(x,y)$ be the co-ordinates of any point on the circle.

$$|OP| = \sqrt{(x-0)^2 + (y-0)^2} \quad \text{(Distance formula)}$$

$$\therefore |OP| = \sqrt{x^2 + y^2}$$

But $|OP| = r$

$$\therefore \sqrt{x^2 + y^2} = r$$

and hence, after squaring both sides,

$$x^2 + y^2 = r^2$$

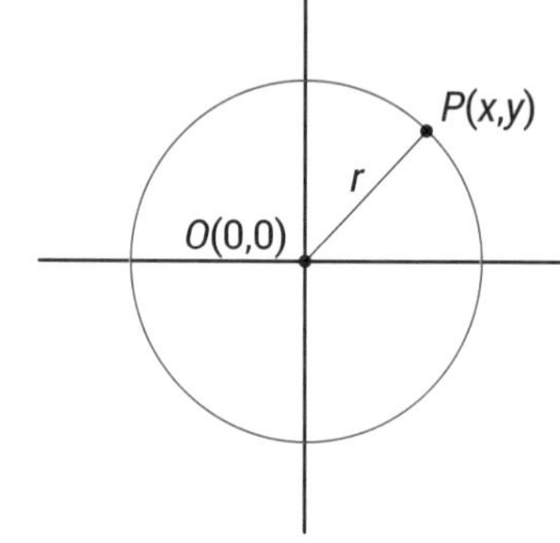

The equation of a circle with centre (0,0) and radius r is:

$$x^2 + y^2 = r^2$$

Worked Example 19.1

Find the equation of the circle with centre (0,0) and radius 7.

Solution

Equation: $x^2 + y^2 = r^2$

Given: $r = 7 \Rightarrow x^2 + y^2 = (7)^2$

$$\therefore x^2 + y^2 = 49$$

Worked Example 19.2

c is a circle with centre (0,0) and contains the point (5,12).

(i) Construct the circle c.

(ii) Calculate r, the radius of c.

(iii) Find the equation of c.

Solution

(i) • On graph paper, draw the x- and y-axes with a clearly marked common scale.

Remember: both axes must have the same scale.

• Plot the point (5,12).

• With the compass point at (0,0) and pencil point at (5,12), construct the circle.

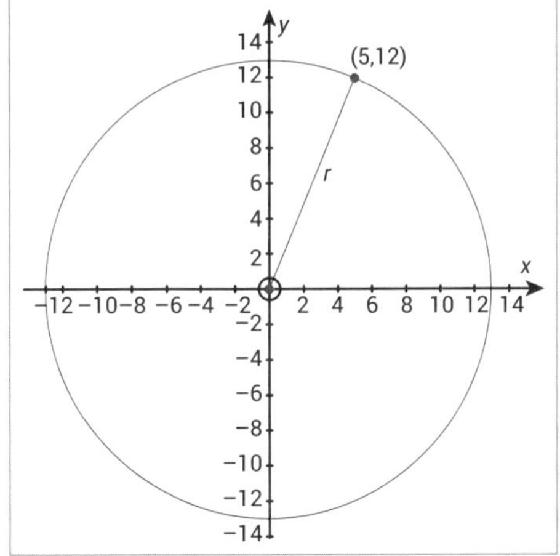

(ii) To calculate r, we get the distance from the centre, (0,0), to a point on the circle, (5,12).

$r = \sqrt{(5-0)^2 + (12-0)^2}$ (Distance formula)

$= \sqrt{(5)^2 + (12)^2}$

$= \sqrt{25 + 144}$

$= \sqrt{169}$

$\therefore r = 13$

(iii) $x^2 + y^2 = r^2$

$x^2 + y^2 = (13)^2$

$\therefore x^2 + y^2 = 169$

Worked Example 19.3

The equation of the circle t is $x^2 + y^2 = 9$.

(i) Find the centre of t.

(ii) Find the radius of t.

Solution

(i) Put the equation in the form $x^2 + y^2 = r^2$.

$x^2 + y^2 = 3^2$

The centre of t is (0,0).

(ii) $r^2 = 3^2$

$r = 3$, as $r > 0$

Worked Example 19.4

The equation of the circle s is $9x^2 + 9y^2 = 100$.

(i) Find the centre of s.

(ii) Find the radius of s.

Solution

(i) Dividing both sides of the equation s by 9 gives:

$x^2 + y^2 = \frac{100}{9}$

$x^2 + y^2 = \left(\frac{10}{3}\right)^2$

The equation is now in the form $x^2 + y^2 = r^2$.
The centre of s is (0,0).

(ii) $r^2 = \left(\frac{10}{3}\right)^2$

$\Rightarrow r = \frac{10}{3}$, as $r > 0$

Exercise 19.1

1. Write down the equation of each of the following circles with centre $O(0,0)$ and radius shown:

(i) 2 (iii) 1 (v) 5 (vii) $\sqrt{5}$ (ix) $\frac{1}{2}$

(ii) 3 (iv) 12 (vi) $\sqrt{2}$ (viii) $\frac{3}{4}$ (x) $2\frac{1}{3}$

2. Find the distance from $O(0,0)$ to $A(7,24)$.
Now write down the equation of the circle that has the centre O and that contains the point A.

3. Find the distance from $O(0,0)$ to $B(-6,-8)$.
Now write down the equation of the circle that has the centre O and that contains the point B.

4. Write down the equation of the circle that has the centre $O(0,0)$ and that contains the point $C(3,4)$.

5. Write down the centre and radius of each of these circles:

(i) $x^2 + y^2 = 25$ (v) $x^2 + y^2 = 2^2$ (ix) $4x^2 + 4y^2 = 9$

(ii) $x^2 + y^2 = 100$ (vi) $x^2 + y^2 = 7^2$ (x) $9x^2 + 9y^2 = 100$

(iii) $x^2 + y^2 = 64$ (vii) $x^2 + y^2 = 3$ (xi) $25x^2 + 25y^2 = 49$

(iv) $x^2 + y^2 = 81$ (viii) $x^2 + y^2 = 5$ (xii) $36x^2 + 36y^2 = 121$

6. Write down the radius of each of these circles and then construct the circles:

(i) $x^2 + y^2 = 49$ (iii) $x^2 + y^2 = 3^2$ (v) $4x^2 + 4y^2 = 1$

(ii) $x^2 + y^2 = 16$ (iv) $x^2 + y^2 = 5^2$ (vi) $16x^2 + 16y^2 = 1$

7. For each of the following circles, write down the co-ordinates of the four points A, B, C and D:

(i)

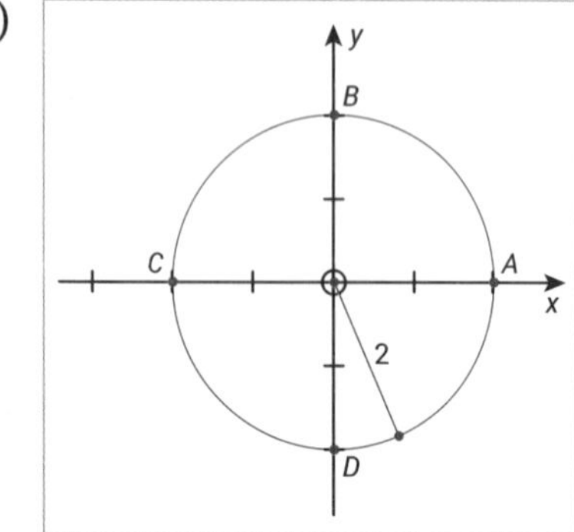

(ii)

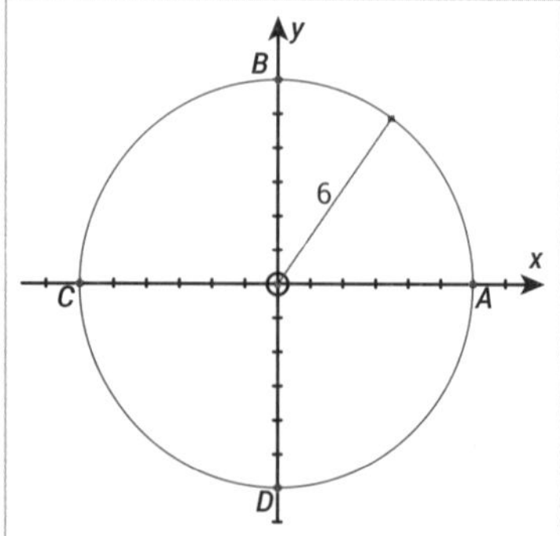

8. Find the equations of the following circles:

(i)

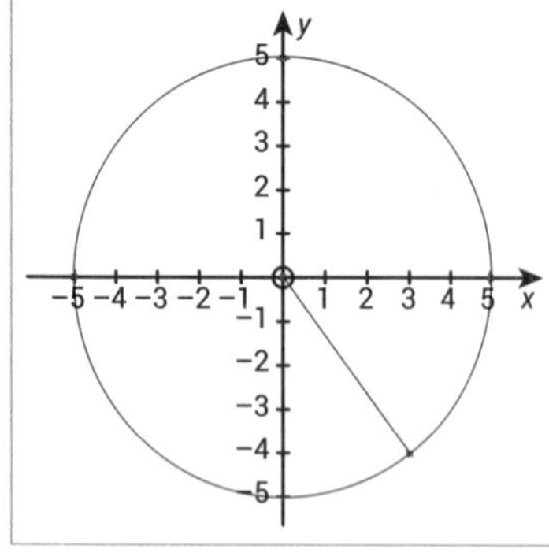

(ii)

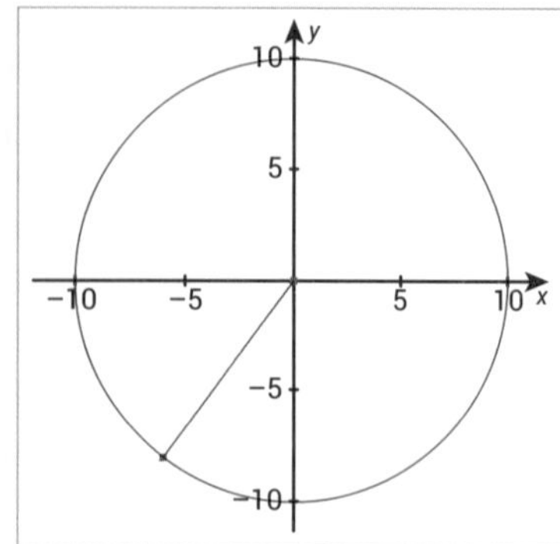

(iii)

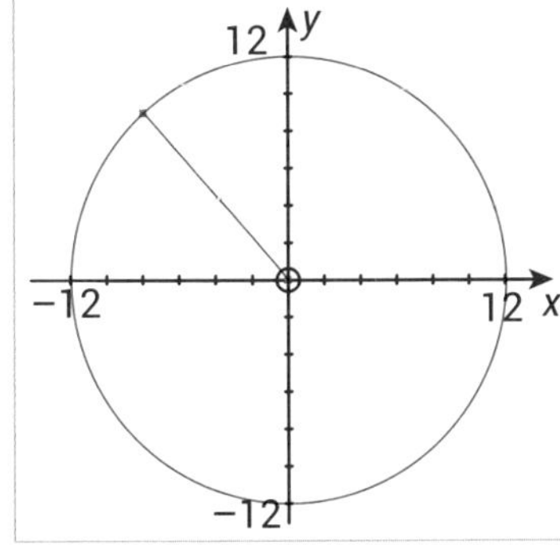

(iv)

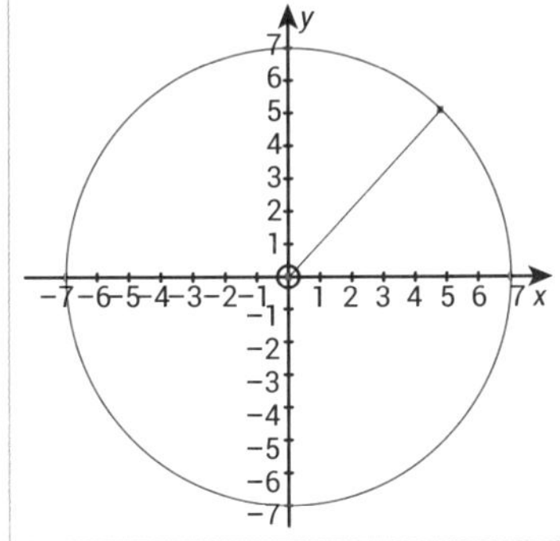

9. A circle has the equation $x^2 + y^2 = 4$.

(i) Write down the co-ordinates of the centre of the circle.

(ii) What is the radius of the circle?

(iii) Construct the circle.

(iv) Using the formula $C = 2\pi r$, find the length of the circle. Give your answer correct to two decimal places.

10. A circle has the equation $x^2 + y^2 = 36$.

(i) Write down the co-ordinates of the centre of the circle.

(ii) What is the radius of the circle?

(iii) Construct the circle.

(iv) Using the formula $C = 2\pi r$, find the length of the circle. Give your answer correct to two decimal places.

(v) Is the length of the line segment joining $O(0,0)$ and $A(36,15)$ greater than the length of the circle? Explain your answer.

11. The line segment joining $A(-3,4)$ and $B(3,-4)$ is the diameter of a circle.

(i) Find the centre of the circle.

(ii) Construct the circle.

(iii) Calculate the radius of the circle.

(iv) Write down the equation of the circle.

12. The line segment joining $A(-2,1)$ and $B(2,-1)$ is the diameter of a circle.

(i) Find the centre of the circle.

(ii) Construct the circle.

(iii) Calculate the radius of the circle.

(iv) Write down the equation of the circle.

(v) Using the formula $A = \pi r^2$, find the area of the circle. Give your answer correct to two decimal places.

13. The line segment joining $A(-5,1)$ and $B(5,-1)$ is the diameter of a circle.

(i) Find the centre of the circle.

(ii) Calculate the radius of the circle.

(iii) Write down the equation of the circle.

(iv) Using the formula $A = \pi r^2$, find the area of the circle. Give your answer correct to two decimal places.

(v) Is the area of the square with vertices $O(0,0)$, $A(9,0)$, $B(9,9)$ and $C(0,9)$ greater than the area of the circle? Explain your answer.

19.2 Lines and Circles

If a line and a circle are drawn on the plane, then the line and circle may meet at two points or at one point, or they may not meet at all. The diagrams below illustrate these three different situations.

Two points of intersection

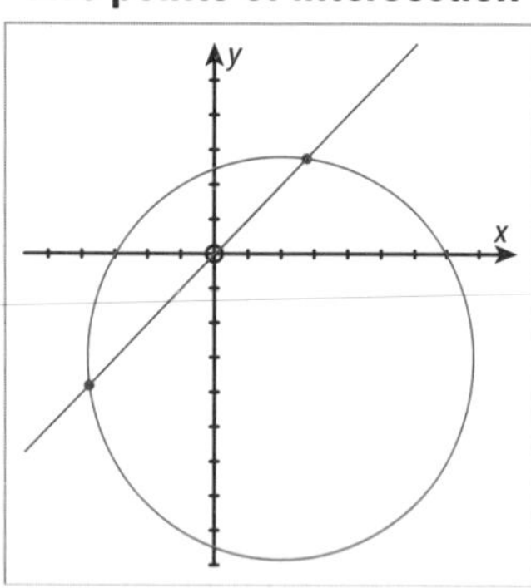

One point of intersection

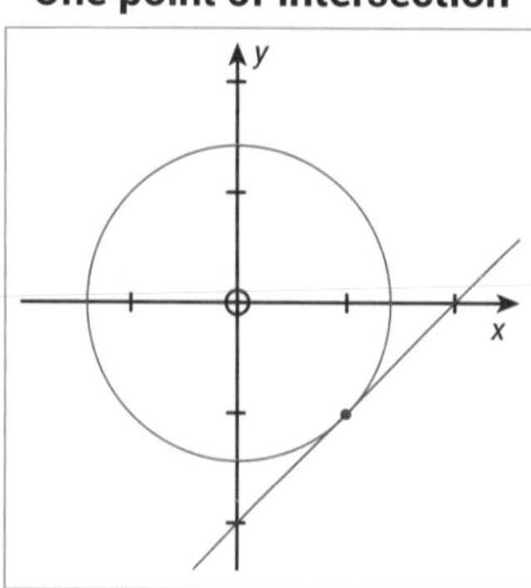

No points of intersection

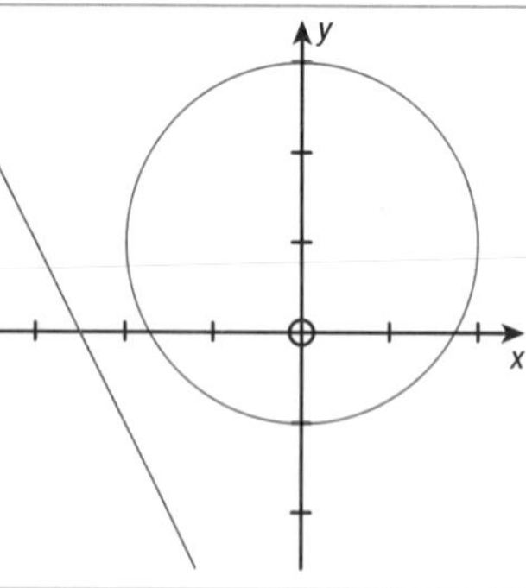

If the line meets the circle at one point only, then we say the line is a tangent to the circle.

In this section, we will be finding the co-ordinates of the points where lines and circles meet. In our course, we will not concern ourselves with the situation where a line and a circle do not meet.

Worked Example 19.5

Find the points of intersection of the line $x + 3y = 10$ and the circle $x^2 + y^2 = 50$.

See Chapter 5: Algebra II Solving simultaneous equations: one linear and one non-linear.

Solution

Step 1 Begin with the equation of the line. Write x in terms of y or write y in terms of x, whichever is the easier.

$$x + 3y = 10$$
$$x = 10 - 3y$$

Make the variable with the coefficient ±1 the subject.

Step 2 Now take the equation of the circle and substitute $10 - 3y$ for x.

$$x^2 + y^2 = 50$$
$$(10 - 3y)^2 + y^2 = 50$$
$$100 - 60y + 9y^2 + y^2 = 50$$
$$10y^2 - 60y + 50 = 0$$
$$y^2 - 6y + 5 = 0 \text{ (Dividing by 10)}$$
$$(y - 1)(y - 5) = 0$$
$$y - 1 = 0 \text{ or } y - 5 = 0$$
$$y = 1 \text{ or } y = 5$$

$$(10 - 3y)^2 = (10 - 3y)(10 - 3y)$$
$$= 10(10 - 3y) - 3y(10 - 3y)$$
$$= 100 - 30y - 30y + 9y^2$$
$$= 100 - 60y + 9y^2$$

Step 3 Now find the corresponding values of x, using the equation from Step 1.

$x = 10 - 3y$

$y = 1$	$y = 5$
$x = 10 - 3(1)$	$x = 10 - 3(5)$
$x = 10 - 3$	$x = 10 - 15$
$x = 7$	$x = -5$

∴ Two points of intersection: (7,1) and (−5,5).

Worked Example 19.6

Prove that the line l: $3x - y = -10$ is a tangent to the circle c: $x^2 + y^2 = 10$.

Solution

Step 1 $3x - y = -10$

$-y = -10 - 3x$

$\Rightarrow \quad y = 3x + 10$

Make the variable with the coefficient ±1 the subject.

Step 2 Now take the equation of the circle and substitute $3x + 10$ for y.

$$x^2 + y^2 = 10$$

$$x^2 + (3x + 10)^2 = 10$$

$$x^2 + 9x^2 + 60x + 100 = 10$$

$$10x^2 + 60x + 90 = 0$$

$$x^2 + 6x + 9 = 0 \quad \text{(Dividing by 10)}$$

$$(x + 3)(x + 3) = 0$$

$$\therefore x = -3$$

$$(3x + 10)^2 = (3x + 10)(3x + 10)$$
$$= 3x(3x + 10) + 10(3x + 10)$$
$$= 9x^2 + 30x + 30x + 100$$
$$= 9x^2 + 60x + 100$$

Step 3 Now find the corresponding value of y, using the equation from Step 1.

$y = 3x + 10$

If $x = -3$, then $y = 3(-3) + 10 = 1$.

Therefore, there is only one point of intersection, which is (−3,1).

Hence, we can conclude that the line is a tangent to the circle.

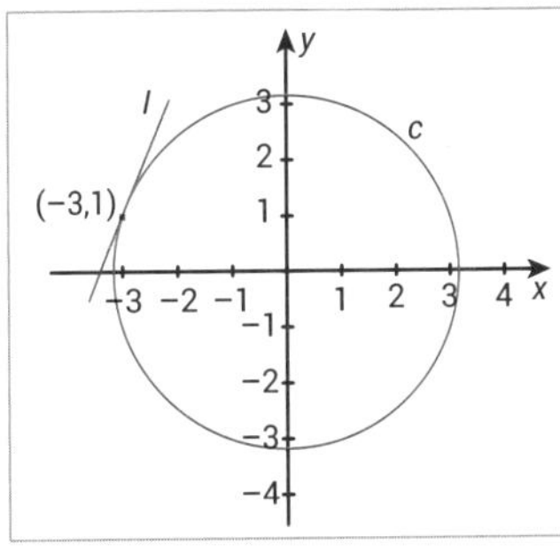

Exercise 19.2

1. Reading from each of the following graphs, write down the co-ordinates of the point(s) of intersection of the line and the circle:

(i)

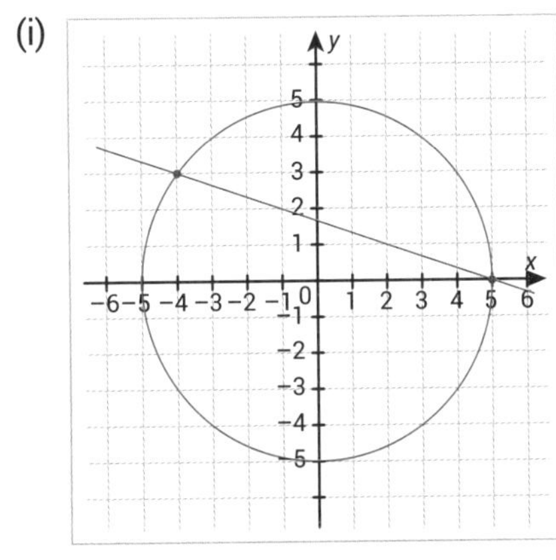

(ii)

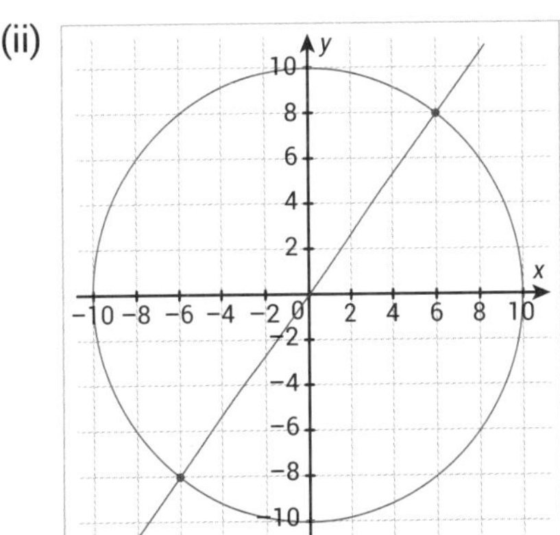

(iii)

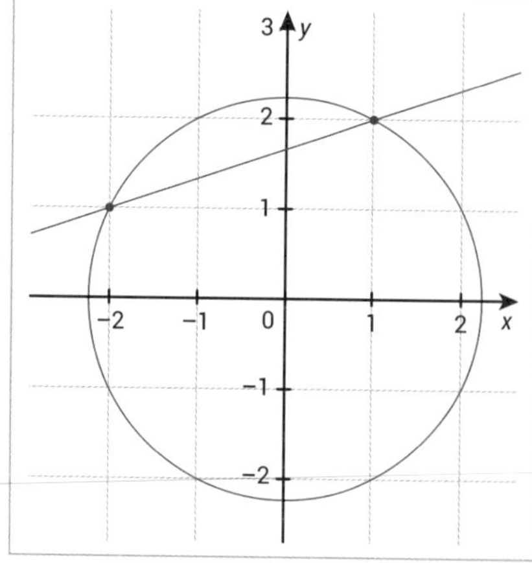

(iv)

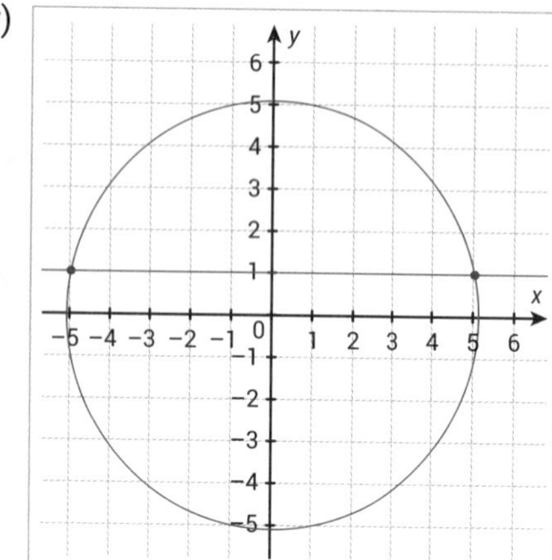

(v)

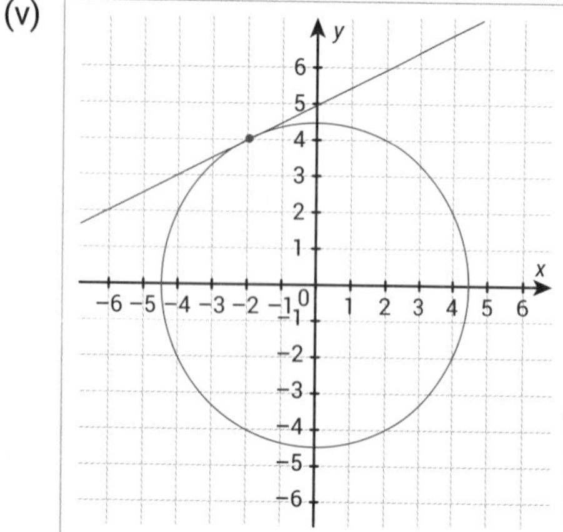

2.

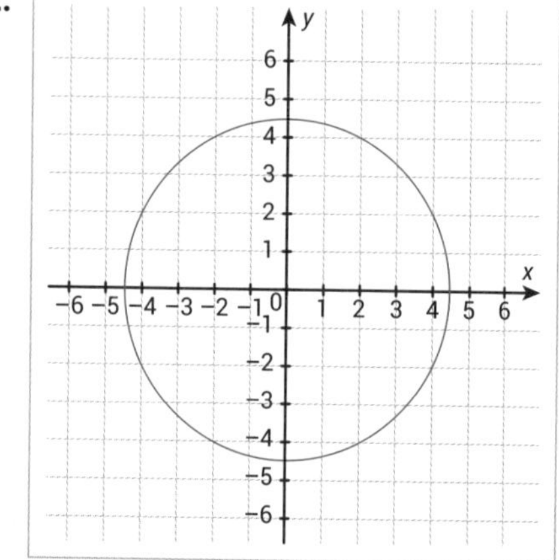

Using the graph, find the points of intersection of the above circle and the following lines:

(i) $x = 2$ (iii) $x = -2$

(ii) $y = 2$ (iv) $y = -2$

3. Solve the following pairs of simultaneous equations:

(i) $x^2 + y^2 = 20$, $x = 10 - 3y$

(ii) $x^2 + y^2 = 25$, $x - 2y = 5$

(iii) $x^2 + y^2 = 20$, $y = 2x$

(iv) $x^2 + y^2 = 40$, $y = -2$

4. Find the points of intersection of the line $x + y = 4$ and the circle $x^2 + y^2 = 10$.

5. Find the points of intersection of the line $x - y = 1$ and the circle $x^2 + y^2 = 13$.

6. l is the line $2x + y - 3 = 0$ and s is the circle $x^2 + y^2 = 26$. Find the points of intersection of l and s.

7. m is the line $x + 7y - 4 = 0$ and n is the circle $x^2 + y^2 = 10$. Find the points of intersection of m and n.

8. In each of the following, show that the line l is a tangent to the circle s and find the point of contact:

(i) s: $x^2 + y^2 = 2$, l: $x = y + 2$

(ii) s: $x^2 + y^2 = 25$, l: $x = 5$

(iii) s: $x^2 + y^2 = 20$, l: $x = 2y - 10$

(iv) s: $2x^2 + 2y^2 = 9$, l: $x + y = 3$

9. l is the line $y = x + 2$ and s is the circle $x^2 + y^2 = 10$.

(i) Write down the co-ordinates of O, the centre of s.

(ii) What is the radius of s?

(iii) The co-ordinates of the point A are (3,1). Find $|OA|$.

(iv) Is A on the circle s? Explain.

(v) Construct the circle s.

(vi) Draw the line l and from your graph find the points of intersection of s and l.

(vii) Verify your answers to part (vi) by solving the simultaneous equations:

$x^2 + y^2 = 10 \qquad y = x + 2$

19.3 Circles with Centre (h,k) and Radius Length r

We will now derive the equation of a circle centred at a point other than (0,0).

s is the circle with centre $Q(h,k)$.

Let $P(x,y)$ be any point on s.

Let r be the radius of s.

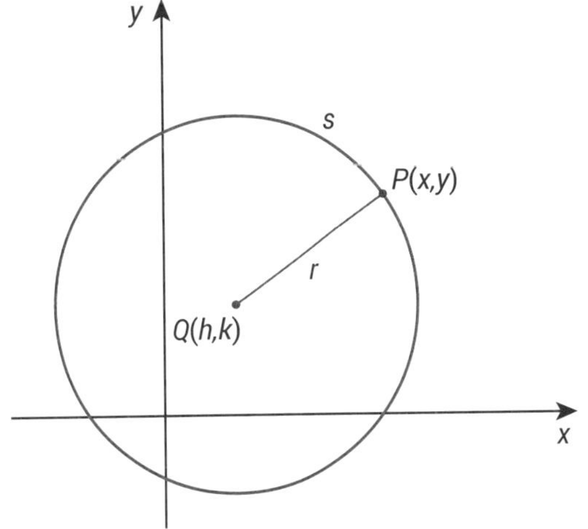

$|QP| = \sqrt{(x-h)^2 + (y-k)^2}$ (Distance formula)

But $|QP|$ = radius = r

Therefore, $\sqrt{(x-h)^2 + (y-k)^2} = r$

$(x-h)^2 + (y-k)^2 = r^2$ (Squaring both sides)

The equation of any circle with centre (h,k) and radius r is:

$(x-h)^2 + (y-k)^2 = r^2$

This equation is on page 19 of *Formulae and Tables*.

Worked Example 19.7

Find the equation of the circle with centre (1,−4) and radius 5.

Solution

$(x-h)^2 + (y-k)^2 = r^2$

$h = 1, k = -4, r = 5$

$(x-1)^2 + (y-(-4))^2 = (5)^2$

$(x-1)^2 + (y+4)^2 = (5)^2$

$\therefore (x-1)^2 + (y+4)^2 = 25$ is the equation of the circle.

There is no need to expand this equation. Always give the equation in the form:

$(x-h)^2 + (y-k)^2 = r^2$

Worked Example 19.8

Find the centre and radius of the circle $(x+2)^2 + (y-8)^2 = 49$.

Solution

Given equation: $(x+2)^2 + (y-8)^2 = 49$

General equation: $(x-h)^2 + (y-k)^2 = r^2$

Comparing: $-h = 2$, $-k = -8$, $r^2 = 49$

$\therefore h = -2, k = 8, r = \sqrt{49} = 7$

$\therefore$ The centre of the circle is (−2,8) and the radius is 7.

Worked Example 19.9

The circle shown has a diameter with endpoints (2,−3) and (6,−8).

Find:

(i) The centre of the circle

(ii) The radius of the circle in surd form

(iii) The equation of the circle

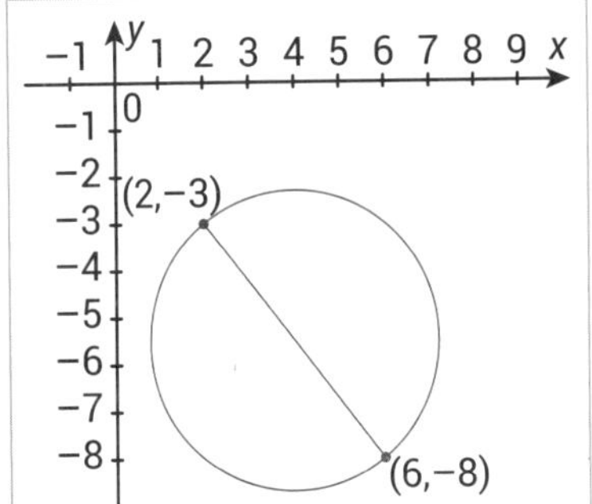

Solution

(i) The centre of the circle is the midpoint of the endpoints of the diameter.

$$\text{Midpoint} = \left(\frac{x_1 + x_2}{2}, \frac{y_1 + y_2}{2}\right)$$

$$\text{Centre} = \left(\frac{2+6}{2}, \frac{-3-8}{2}\right) = \left(\frac{8}{2}, \frac{-11}{2}\right) = \left(4, -\frac{11}{2}\right)$$

(ii) The radius of the circle is the distance from an endpoint of a diameter to the centre of the circle.

$$\text{Distance} = \sqrt{(x_2 - x_1)^2 + (y_2 - y_1)^2}$$

Points (2,–3) and $\left(4, -\frac{11}{2}\right)$

$\therefore x_1 = 2, y_1 = -3$ and $x_2 = 4, y_2 = -\frac{11}{2}$

$$r = \sqrt{(4-2)^2 + \left(-\frac{11}{2} + 3\right)^2}$$

$$r = \sqrt{(2)^2 + \left(-\frac{5}{2}\right)^2}$$

$$r = \sqrt{4 + \frac{25}{4}} = \sqrt{\frac{41}{4}}$$ Leave in surd form.

(iii) Equation: $(x - h)^2 + (y - k)^2 = r^2$

Centre = $\left(4, -\frac{11}{2}\right)$ $r = \sqrt{\frac{41}{4}}$

$$(x-4)^2 + \left(y + \frac{11}{2}\right)^2 = \frac{41}{4}$$

$(\sqrt{a})^2 = \sqrt{a}\sqrt{a} = a$ for $a \geqslant 0$

$\therefore \left(\sqrt{\frac{41}{4}}\right)^2 = \frac{41}{4}$

Worked Example 19.10

Find the equation of the tangent to the circle $(x - 1)^2 + (y + 2)^2 = 25$ at the point (–2,2).

Solution

Step 1 The centre of the circle is (1,–2) and the point on the circle is (–2,2).

$\therefore$ The slope of this radius is $\frac{2-(-2)}{-2-1} = -\frac{4}{3}$.

Step 2 $\therefore$ The slope of the tangent is $\frac{3}{4}$.
(tangent $\perp$ radius)

Step 3 Equation of the tangent:

$y - y_1 = m(x - x_1)$ Point (–2,2) $m = \frac{3}{4}$

$$y - 2 = \frac{3}{4}(x + 2)$$

$$4(y - 2) = 3(x + 2)$$

$$4y - 8 = 3x + 6$$

$$3x - 4y + 14 = 0$$

Exercise 19.3

1. Find the equations of the following circles:
   (i) Centre = (1,4) radius = 5
   (ii) Centre = (–2,3) radius = 3
   (iii) Centre = (6,–5) radius = 1
   (iv) Centre = (0,7) radius = 4
   (v) Centre = (–2,–1) radius = 2
   (vi) Centre = (–2,0) radius = 6

2. Find the equations of the following circles:
   (i) Centre = (0,0) radius = 8
   (ii) Centre = (8,1) radius = 6
   (iii) Centre = $\left(\frac{1}{2}, -\frac{1}{4}\right)$ radius = 9
   (iv) Centre = (1,1.5) radius = 7
   (v) Centre = (–3,–8) radius = $\frac{1}{2}$
   (vi) Centre = (3,0) radius = $\sqrt{3}$

3. A circle s that has centre (1,1) and that contains the point (5,6) is shown below.

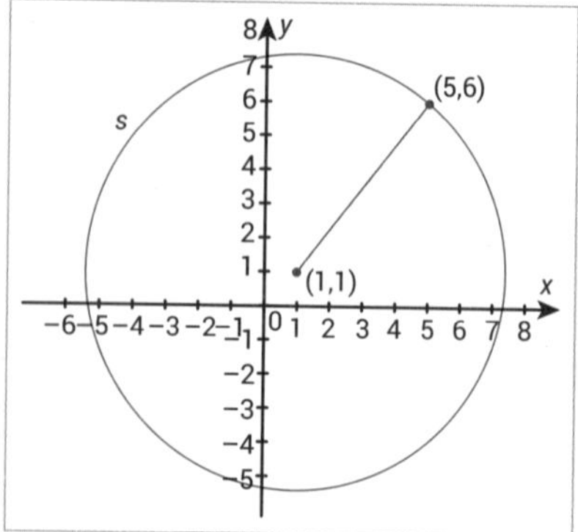

   (i) Calculate the radius of s.
   (ii) Write down the equation of s.

4. A circle t that has centre (−2,−1) and that contains the point (2,−3) is shown below.

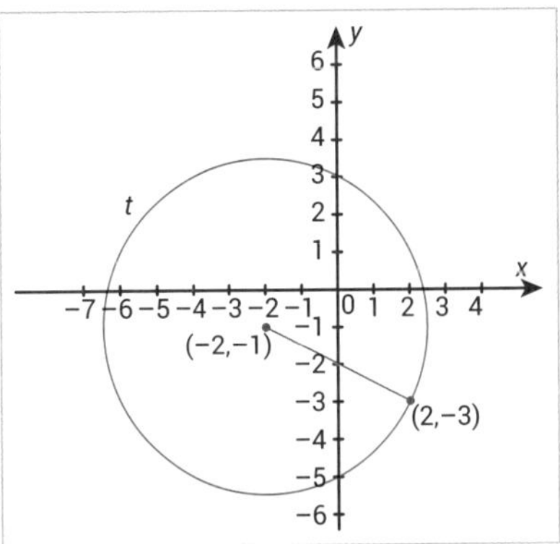

(i) Calculate the radius of t.

(ii) Write down the equation of t.

5. Find the centre and radius of each of the following circles:

(i) $(x - 2)^2 + (y - 3)^2 = 25$

(ii) $(x + 2)^2 + (y - 5)^2 = 36$

(iii) $(x - 1)^2 + (y + 3)^2 = 49$

(iv) $(x + 5)^2 + (y + 8)^2 = 1$

(v) $(x - 3)^2 + (y - 4)^2 = 64$

6. Find the centre and radius of each of the following circles:

(i) $x^2 + y^2 = 100$

(ii) $x^2 + (y - 8)^2 = 49$

(iii) $(x - 2)^2 + y^2 = 81$

(iv) $\left(x - \frac{1}{2}\right)^2 + \left(y - \frac{1}{3}\right)^2 = \frac{1}{9}$

(v) $(x - 2)^2 + (y - 3)^2 = 5$

7. The circle z shown in the diagram has a diameter with endpoints (−1,4) and (3,−2).

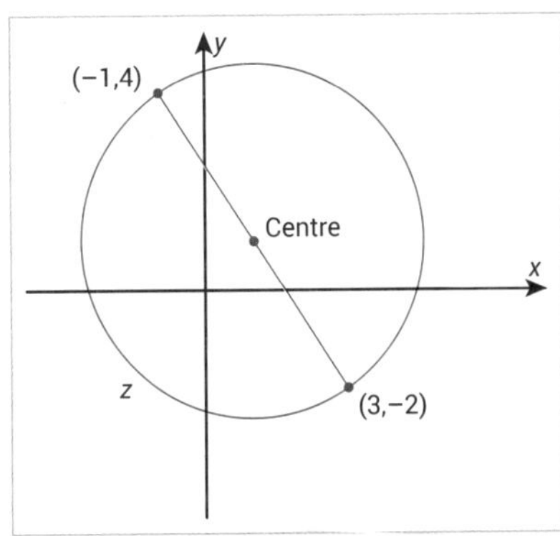

(i) Find the centre of z.

(ii) Calculate the radius of z.

(iii) Write down the equation of z.

8. The circle h shown in the diagram has a diameter with endpoints (−2,−3) and (4,7).

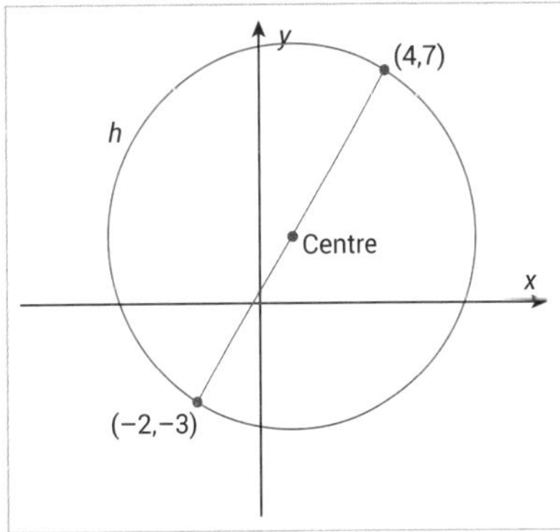

(i) Find the centre of h.

(ii) Calculate the radius of h.

(iii) Write down the equation of h.

9. A circle u with centre (2,4) is shown below. The x-axis is a tangent to the circle.

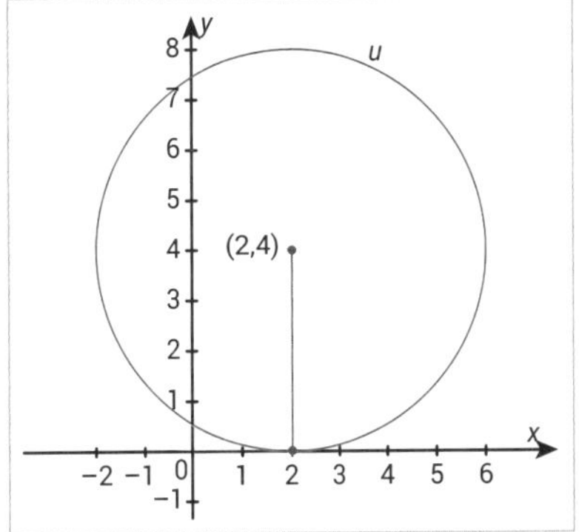

(i) Write down the radius of u.

(ii) Write down the equation of u.

10. A circle v with centre (3,−1) is shown below. The y-axis is a tangent to the circle.

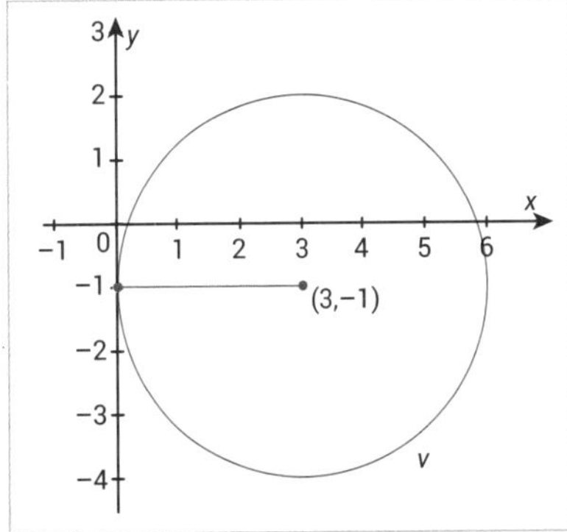

(i) Write down the radius of v.

(ii) Write down the equation of v.

11. The x-axis and the y-axis are both tangents to the circle w shown below.

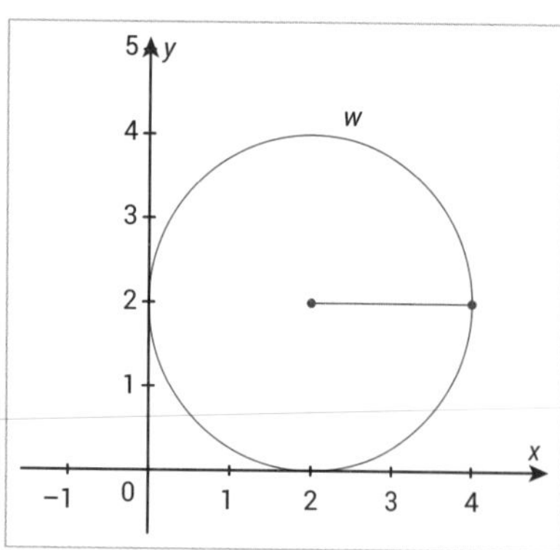

(i) Write down the co-ordinates of the centre of w.

(ii) Write down the radius of w.

(iii) Write down the equation of w.

12. The diagram below shows a circle s with centre $A(4,4)$. The circle touches the x-axis and the y-axis. m and n are tangents to the circle.

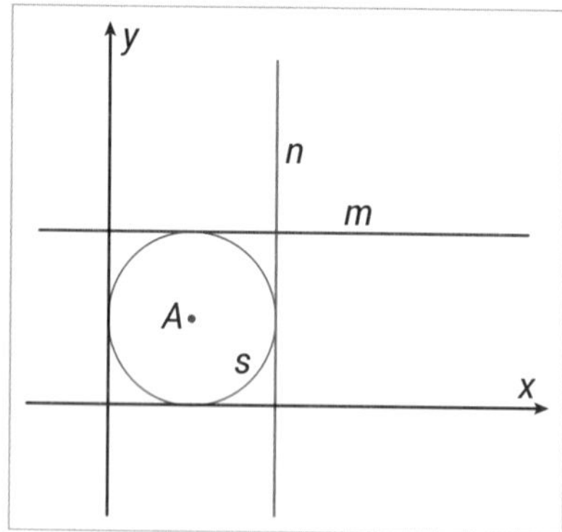

(i) Write down the radius of s.

(ii) What is the equation of each of the tangents, m and n?

(iii) Find the point of intersection of m and n.

(iv) Calculate the area of the square enclosed by m, n, the x-axis and the y-axis.

13. The centre of a circle is $(1,2)$ and the circle contains the point $(-2,3)$.

(i) Construct the circle.

(ii) Calculate the radius of the circle.

(iii) Calculate the equation of the circle.

14. A circle has a diameter with endpoints $A(5,3)$ and $B(-1,3)$. Find the equation of the circle.

15. (a) The circle c has equation $(x + 2)^2 + (y - 3)^2 = 100$.

(i) Write down the co-ordinates of A, the centre of c.

(ii) Write down r, the radius of c.

(iii) Show that the point $P(-8,11)$ is on the circle c.

(b) (i) Find the slope of the radius $[AP]$.

(ii) Hence, find the equation of t, the tangent to c at P.

(c) A second line k is a tangent to c at the point Q and $k \parallel t$. Find the co-ordinates of Q.

16. Find the equations of the tangents to the following circles at the given points:

(i) $x^2 + y^2 = 10$; $(3,1)$

(ii) $x^2 + y^2 = 20$; $(-4,2)$

(iii) $(x + 3)^2 + (y + 4)^2 = 25$; $(0,0)$

(iv) $(x - 6)^2 + (y + 3)^2 = 20$; $(2,1)$

(v) $(x - 1)^2 + (y + 2)^2 = 13$; $(3,1)$

19.4 Intercepts and Points Inside, Outside or On a Circle

Intercepts on the x-axis and y-axis

The points where a circle intersects the x-axis are called the x-intercepts of the circle and the points where a circle intersects the y-axis are called the y-intercepts of the circle.

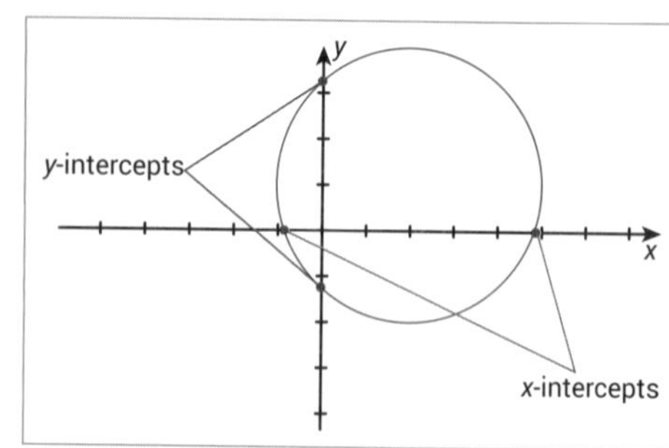

The co-ordinates of points on the x-axis are always of the form $(a,0)$ and the co-ordinates of points on the y-axis are always of the form $(0,b)$. Hence:

- We **let $y = 0$** in the equation of a circle and solve for x to find the co-ordinates of the **x-intercepts**.
- We **let $x = 0$** in the equation of a circle and solve for y to find the co-ordinates of the **y-intercepts**.

Worked Example 19.11

(a) Find the co-ordinates of the points at which:

(i) The circle s: $x^2 + y^2 = 25$ intersects the x-axis

(ii) The circle t: $(x + 1)^2 + (y - 9)^2 = 26$ intersects the y-axis

(b) Hence, sketch each circle showing these intercepts clearly.

Solution

(a) (i) $x^2 + y^2 = 25$ intersects the x-axis:

Let $y = 0$ in the equation of the circle.

$$x^2 + (0)^2 = 25$$
$$x^2 + 0 = 25$$
$$x^2 = 25$$
$$x = \pm 5$$

Therefore, the co-ordinates of the x-intercepts are $(-5,0)$ and $(5,0)$.

(ii) $(x + 1)^2 + (y - 9)^2 = 26$ intersects the y-axis:

Let $x = 0$ in the equation of the circle.

$$(0 + 1)^2 + (y - 9)^2 = 26$$
$$1^2 + (y - 9)^2 = 26$$
$$1 + (y - 9)^2 = 26$$
$$(y - 9)^2 = 26 - 1$$
$$(y - 9)^2 = 25$$
$$y - 9 = \pm 5$$
$$y - 9 = -5 \quad \textbf{or} \quad y - 9 = 5$$
$$y = 4 \quad \textbf{or} \quad y = 14$$

Therefore, the co-ordinates of the y-intercepts are $(0,4)$ and $(0,14)$.

(b) The centre of s is $(0,0)$ and it contains both $(-5,0)$ and $(5,0)$.

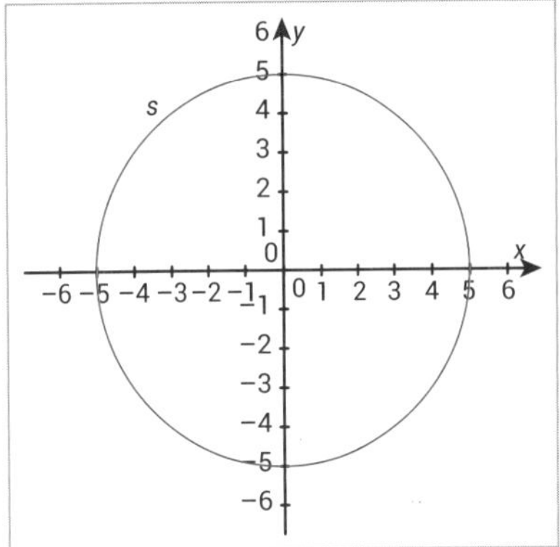

The centre of t is $(-1,9)$ and it contains both $(0,4)$ and $(0,14)$.

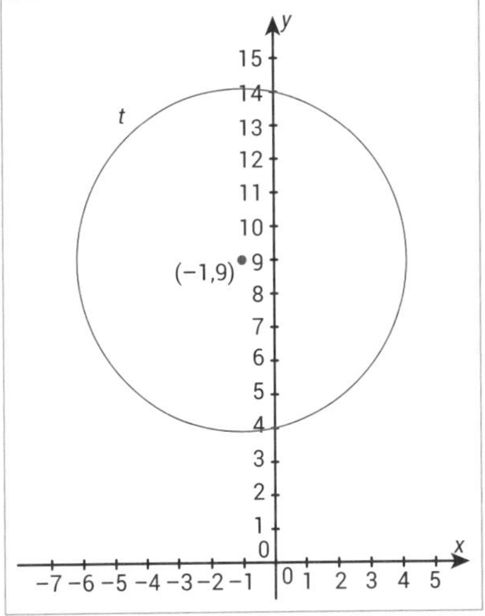

Points Inside, Outside or On a Circle

In a circle of the form $(x - h)^2 + (y - k)^2 = r^2$, a point (x_1,y_1) is:

- Inside the circle, if $(x_1 - h)^2 + (y_1 - k)^2 < r^2$
- Outside the circle, if $(x_1 - h)^2 + (y_1 - k)^2 > r^2$
- On the circle, if $(x_1 - h)^2 + (y_1 - k)^2 = r^2$

Worked Example 19.12

Investigate if the points (7,–5) and (8,–6) are outside, inside or on the following circle:

$(x - 4)^2 + (y + 1)^2 = 25$

Solution

Method 1

$(x - 4)^2 + (y + 1)^2 = 25$

Substitute (7,–5) into the left-hand side of the equation.

Is $(7 - 4)^2 + (-5 + 1)^2 = 25$?

$(3)^2 + (-4)^2 = 25$

$9 + 16 = 25$

$25 = 25$ True

Therefore, the point (7,–5) is **on** the circle.

Substitute (8,–6) into the left-hand side of the equation.

Is $(8 - 4)^2 + (-6 + 1)^2 = 25$?

$(4)^2 + (-5)^2 = 25$

$16 + 25 = 25$

$41 = 25$ False

$41 > 25$

Therefore, the point (8,–6) is **outside** the circle.

Method 2

An alternative approach is to find the distance from each point to the centre of the circle and compare to the radius.

$(x - 4)^2 + (y + 1)^2 = 25$

Step 1

Find the centre and radius of the circle.

Centre: $C(4,-1)$, $r = 5$

Step 2

Find the distance from the centre to the point.

(4,–1) (7,–5)

$x_1 = 4$ $x_2 = 7$

$y_1 = -1$ $y_2 = -5$

Distance $= \sqrt{(7 - 4)^2 + (-5 + 1)^2}$

$= \sqrt{(3)^2 + (-4)^2}$

$= \sqrt{9 + 16}$

$= \sqrt{25}$

$= 5$

5 is the radius length of the circle.

$\therefore$ (7,–5) is on the circle.

Similarly, check (8,–6).

(4,–1) (8,–6)

$x_1 = 4$ $x_2 = 8$

$y_1 = -1$ $y_2 = -6$

Distance $= \sqrt{(8 - 4)^2 + (-6 + 1)^2}$

$= \sqrt{(4)^2 + (-5)^2}$

$= \sqrt{16 + 25}$

$= \sqrt{41}$ which is greater than 5.

$\therefore$ (8,–6) is outside the circle.

Exercise 19.4

1. The circle shown has centre (0,0) and radius 4.
   (i) Find the values *a*, *b*, *c* and *d*.
   (ii) Write down the co-ordinates of *A* and *B*, the *x*-intercepts of the circle.
   (iii) Write down the co-ordinates of *C* and *D*, the *y*-intercepts of the circle.

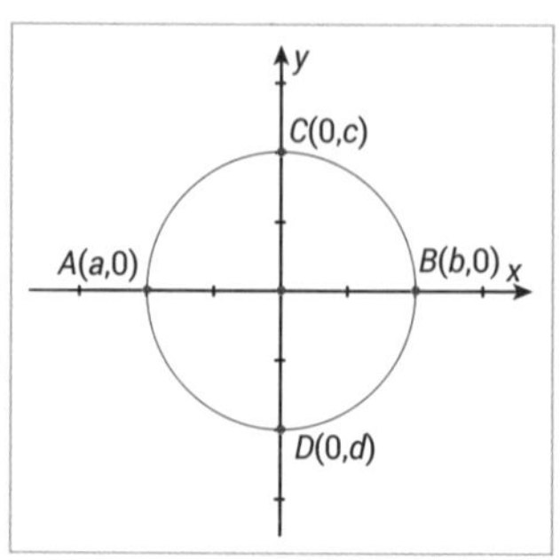

2. The circle shown below has centre (0,0) and radius 7.

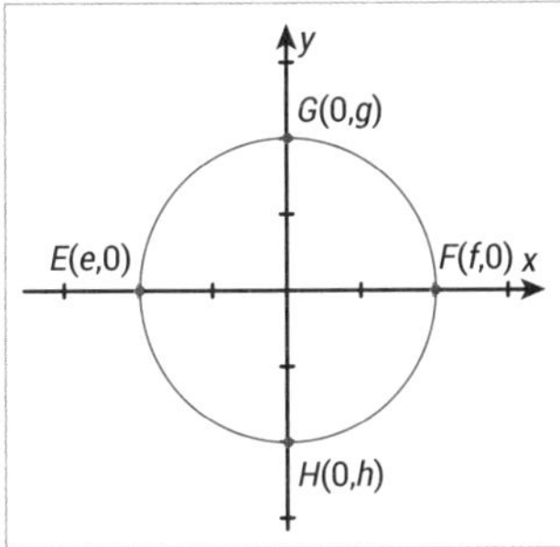

(i) Find the values e, f, g and h.

(ii) Write down the co-ordinates of E and F, the x-intercepts of the circle.

(iii) Write down the co-ordinates of G and H, the y-intercepts of the circle.

3. For each of the circles shown below, write down the co-ordinates of the x- and y-intercepts of the circle.

(i)

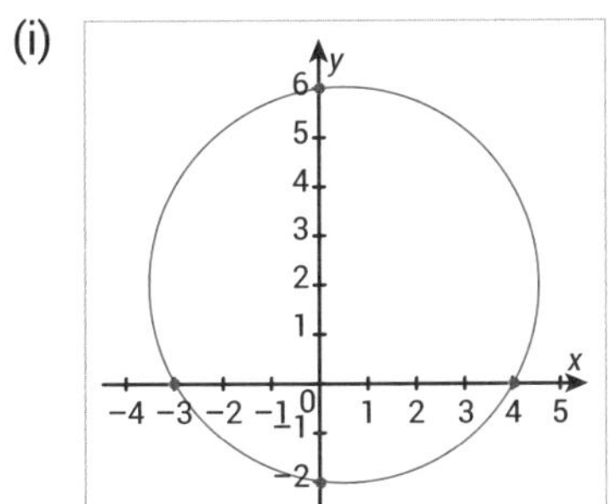

(ii)

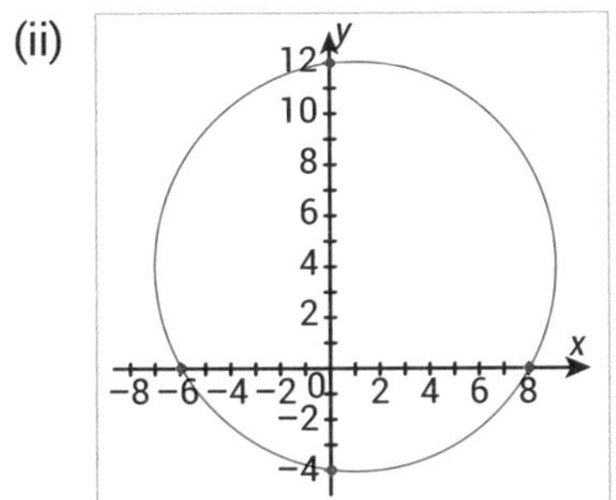

4. Find the x-intercepts and y-intercepts of each of the following circles:

(i) $x^2 + y^2 = 4$

(ii) $x^2 + y^2 = 9$

(iii) $x^2 + y^2 = 16$

(iv) $x^2 + y^2 = 36$

5. For each of the following circles, find the co-ordinates of the x-intercept:

(i) $(x - 2)^2 + (y + 3)^2 = 34$

(ii) $(x + 3)^2 + (y - 2)^2 = 40$

(iii) $(x + 5)^2 + (y - 8)^2 = 164$

6. For each of the following circles, find the co-ordinates of the y-intercept:

(i) $(x - 3)^2 + (y - 4)^2 = 90$

(ii) $(x + 2)^2 + (y - 5)^2 = 104$

(iii) $(x - 6)^2 + (y + 1)^2 = 72$

7. The equation of the circle c is $(x - 2)^2 + (y - 1)^2 = 13$.

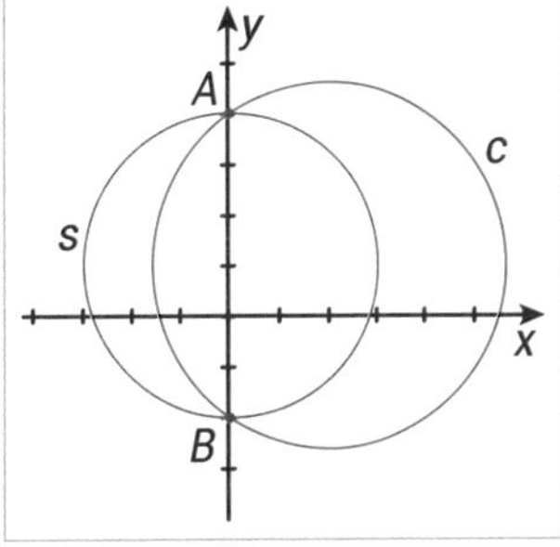

(i) Calculate the co-ordinates of A and B, the y-intercepts of c.

(ii) If A and B are the endpoints of a diameter of the circle s, then find the equation of s.

8. The equation of the circle m is $(x - 2)^2 + (y + 3)^2 = 34$.

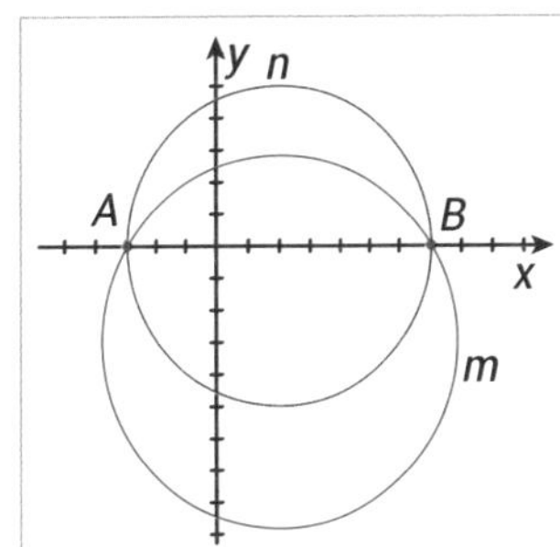

(i) Calculate the co-ordinates of A and B, the x-intercepts of m.

(ii) A and B are the endpoints of a diameter of the circle n. Find the equation of n.

9. Investigate if the point A is on the circle, inside the circle or outside the circle.

(i) $x^2 + y^2 = 36$ $A(7,4)$

(ii) $x^2 + (y - 2)^2 = 29$ $A(-5,4)$

(iii) $(x - 1)^2 + (y + 2)^2 = 36$ $A(1,1)$

10. Show that the point $A(-2,0)$ is inside the circle $(x + 4)^2 + (y - 1)^2 = 9$.

11. Show that the point $B(7,3)$ lies outside the circle $(x - 1)^2 + (y - 2)^2 = 9$.

12. For each of the circles c_1 to c_4, one and only one of the points A to D lies on the circle. Investigate which point is on which circle. Show all your workings.

Circle	Point
c_1: $x^2 + y^2 = 25$	$A(-5,4)$
c_2: $(x - 2)^2 + (y + 3)^2 = 65$	$B(3,5)$
c_3: $x^2 + (y - 2)^2 = 29$	$C(3,-4)$
c_4: $(x + 2)^2 + (y - 5)^2 = 58$	$D(1,-2)$

13. (i) The circle c has centre $(2,-3)$ and a radius of 4 cm.

    Write down the equation of c.

    (ii) Construct the circle c.

    (iii) Verify, using algebra, that the point $(3,1)$ is outside of c.

    (iv) Find the area of the smallest four-sided figure that will fit around the circle c.

Revision Exercises

1. Write down the centre and radius of each of these circles:

   (i) $x^2 + y^2 = 4$

   (ii) $x^2 + y^2 = 144$

   (iii) $64x^2 + 64y^2 = 25$

   (iv) $81x^2 + 81y^2 = 121$

2. Find the points of intersection of the line $x + y = 5$ and the circle $x^2 + y^2 = 13$.

3. Find the points of intersection of the line $x - 2y = 5$ and the circle $x^2 + y^2 = 10$.

4. Find the equations of the following circles:

   (i) Centre = $(0,0)$ radius = 3

   (ii) Centre = $(7,2)$ radius = 5

   (iii) Centre = $(-3,4)$ radius = 8

   (iv) Centre = $(-3,-2)$ radius = 1

5. Write down the centre and radius length of each of the following circles:

   (i) $(x - 3)^2 + (y + 2)^2 = 100$

   (ii) $(x + 1)^2 + (y - 3)^2 = 49$

   (iii) $x^2 + (y + 2)^2 = 64$

   (iv) $(x - 2)^2 + y^2 = 121$

6. $(-7,0)$ and $(1,0)$ are the endpoints of the diameter of the circle c.

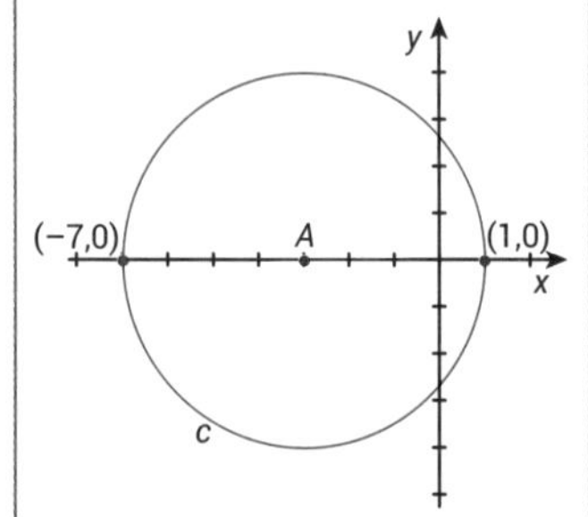

   (i) What are the co-ordinates of A, the centre of c?

   (ii) What is the radius of c?

   (iii) Write down the equation of c.

   (iv) Find the co-ordinates of the y-intercepts of c.

7. s is a circle with equation $(x + 1)^2 + (y - 1)^2 = 25$.

   (i) Write down the co-ordinates of R, the centre of s.

   (ii) What is the radius of s?

   (iii) Using graph paper, construct s.

   (iv) Show, using algebra methods, that the point $A(3,-2)$ is on the circle.

   (v) If $[AB]$ is a diameter of s, find the co-ordinates of B.

8. The three circles s, t and u shown below have their centres along the y-axis.

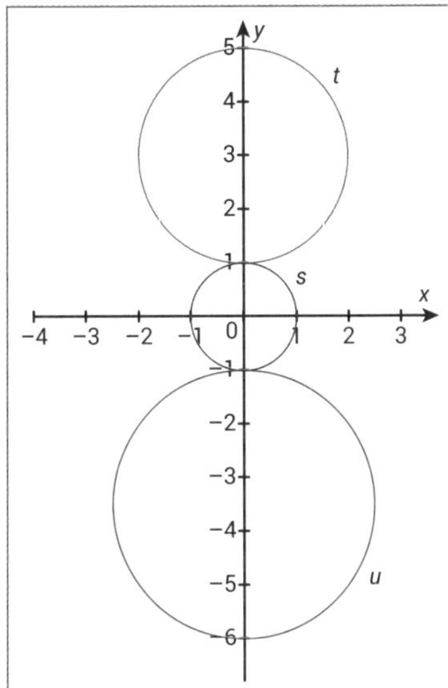

(i) Write down the co-ordinates of the centre and the radius of each circle.

(ii) Write down the equation of each circle.

(iii) What is the length of the circumference of s? Leave your answer in terms of π.

(iv) What is the length of the circumference of t? Leave your answer in terms of π.

(v) If C_t is the length of the circumference of t and C_s is the length of the circumference of s, then write down the ratio $C_t : C_s$.

(vi) Is $C_t : C_s = r_t : r_s$, where r_t and r_s are the radii of t and s, respectively?

9. The point (1,−7) is on a circle k, which has its centre at $O(0,0)$.

(i) Construct the circle k.

(ii) Find the equation of k.

(iii) If (p,p) is a point on k, find two possible values of p.

(iv) If the point $(3,n)$ is inside the circle k, find the greatest possible value of n, where $n \in N$.

10. A circle has centre (7,3). The line $y = 6$ and the x-axis are tangents to the circle.

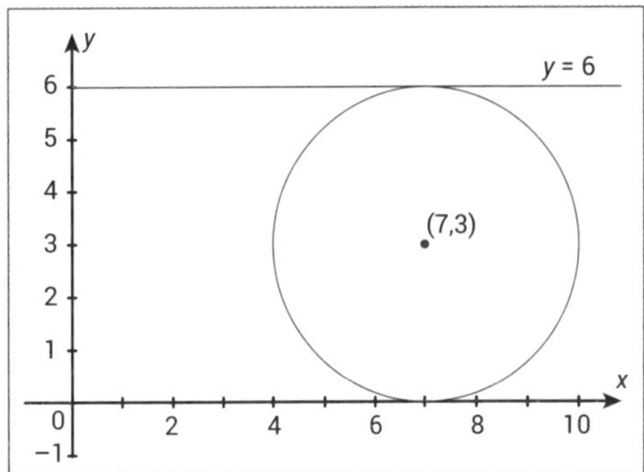

(i) Write down the radius of the circle.

(ii) Write down the equation of the circle.

(iii) Verify that the line $l: x - 2y - 1 = 0$ contains the centre of the circle.

(iv) Find the point of intersection of l and the tangent $y = 6$.

Exam Questions

1. The point A has co-ordinates (8,6) and O is the origin.

The diagram shows two circles c_1 and c_2.

c_1 has centre (0,0) and radius $|OA|$.

c_2 has a diameter of $[OA]$.

(a) Find the equation of c_1.

(b) Find the equation of c_2.

(c) The circle c_2 cuts the x-axis at the point P. Find the co-ordinates of P.

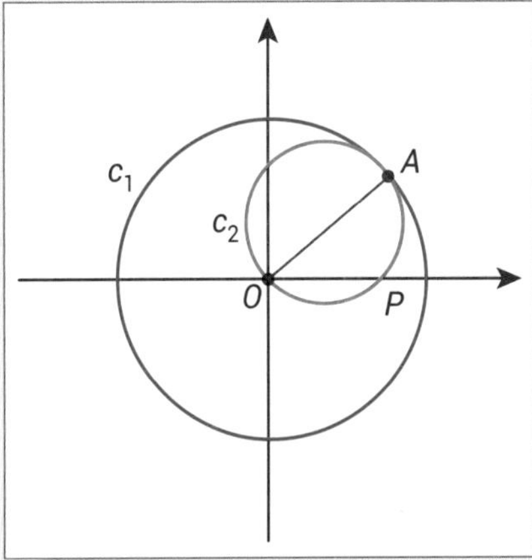

SEC Leaving Certificate Ordinary Level, Paper 2, 2013

2. (a) Draw the circle c: $x^2 + y^2 = 25$.
   (b) Verify, using algebra, that $A(-4,3)$ is on c.
   (c) Find the equation of the circle with centre $(-4,3)$ that passes through the point $(3,4)$.

SEC Leaving Certificate Ordinary Level, Paper 2, 2015

3. (a) (i) The circle c has equation $(x + 2)^2 + (y - 3)^2 = 100$.
   Write down the co-ordinates of A, the centre of c.
   Write down r, the length of the radius of c.
   (ii) Show that the point $P(-8,11)$ is on the circle c.
   (b) (i) Find the slope of the radius $[AP]$.
   (ii) Hence, find the equation of t, the tangent to c at P.
   (c) A second line k is a tangent to c at the point Q and $k \parallel t$. Find the co-ordinates of Q.

SEC Leaving Certificate Ordinary Level, Paper 2, 2014

4. The diagram shows two circles c_1 and c_2 of equal radius. c_1 has centre $(0,0)$ and it cuts the x-axis at $(5,0)$
   (a) Find the equation of c_1.
   (b) Show that the point $P(-3,4)$ is on c_1.
   (c) The two circles touch at $P(-3,4)$.
   P is on the line joining the two centres.
   Find the equation of c_2.
   (d) Find the equation of the common tangent at P.

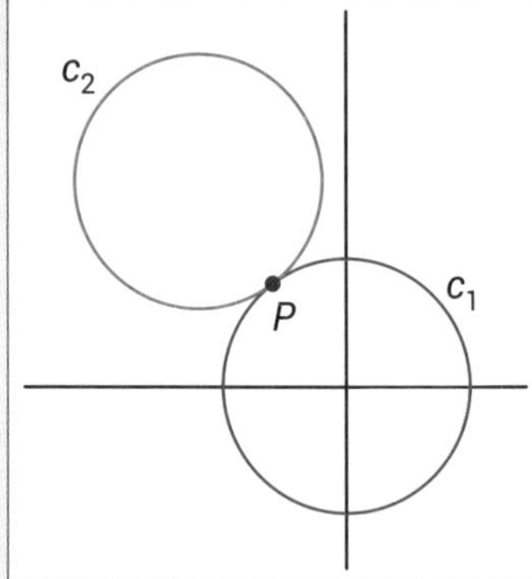

SEC Leaving Certificate Ordinary Level, Paper 2, 2012

5. A circle c_1 has centre $(0,0)$ and diameter 8 units.
   (a) Show c_1 on a co-ordinate diagram.
   (b) Find the equation of c_1.
   (c) Prove that the point $(3,2)$ is inside c_1 and that the point $(3,3)$ is outside it.
   (d) Another circle, c_2, has centre $(0,1)$ and just touches the circle c_1.
   Show c_2 on your diagram in part **(a)** above and find the equation of c_2.

SEC Leaving Certificate Ordinary Level, Paper 2, 2011

Solutions and chapter summary available online

Answers

Chapter 1

Exercise 1.1

1. (i) 1 : 2 (ii) 4 : 3 (iii) 3 : 5 (iv) 2 : 4 : 6 = 1 : 2 : 3 (v) 3 : 7 : 12 (vi) 2 : 3 (vii) 1 : 3 (viii) 2 : 1 : 8 (ix) 4 : 6 : 3 (x) 6 : 6 : 6 = 1 : 1 : 1 **2.** (i) $\frac{7}{9} \times 450 = 350$ g, $\frac{2}{9} \times 450 = 100$ g (ii) $132 \times \frac{7}{11} = €84$, $132 \times \frac{4}{11} = €48$ (iii) $169 \times \frac{9}{13} = 117$ cm, $169 \times \frac{4}{13} = 52$ cm (iv) $4{,}500 \times \frac{6}{15} = €1{,}800$, $4{,}500 \times \frac{9}{15} = €2{,}700$ (v) $156 \times \frac{8}{13} = 96$ kg, $156 \times \frac{5}{13} = 60$ kg (vi) $90 \times \frac{1}{6} = 15$ m, $90 \times \frac{2}{6} = 30$ m, $90 \times \frac{3}{6} = 45$ m (vii) $840 \times \frac{5}{7} = 600$ g, $840 \times \frac{1}{7} = 120$ g, $840 \times \frac{1}{7} = 120$ g (viii) $900 \times \frac{7}{18} = €350$, $900 \times \frac{8}{18} = €400$, $900 \times \frac{3}{18} = €150$ (ix) $221 \times \frac{8}{13} = 136$ g, $221 \times \frac{1}{13} = 17$ g, $221 \times \frac{4}{13} = 68$ g (x) $552 \times \frac{3}{12} = 138$ cm, $552 \times \frac{5}{12} = 230$ cm, $552 \times \frac{4}{12} = 184$ cm

3.

	Ratios	Answers
(i)	2 : 1	$450 \times \frac{2}{3} = 300$ g $450 \times \frac{1}{3} = 150$ g
(ii)	2 : 3	$150 \times \frac{2}{5} = €60$ $150 \times \frac{3}{5} = €90$
(iii)	1 : 3	$132 \times \frac{1}{4} = 33$ mm $132 \times \frac{3}{4} = 99$ mm
(iv)	2 : 1 : 8	$4400 \times \frac{2}{11} = 800$ g $4400 \times \frac{1}{11} = 400$ g $4400 \times \frac{8}{11} = 3{,}200$ g
(v)	4 : 6 : 3	$156 \times \frac{4}{13} = 48$ kg $156 \times \frac{6}{13} = 72$ kg $156 \times \frac{3}{13} = 36$ kg
(vi)	1 : 1 : 1	$900 \times \frac{1}{3} = 300$ m $900 \times \frac{1}{3} = 300$ m $900 \times \frac{1}{3} = 300$ m
(vii)	3 : 5 : 4	$444 \times \frac{3}{12} = 111$ g $444 \times \frac{5}{12} = 185$ g $444 \times \frac{4}{12} = 148$ g
(viii)	8 : 9 : 2	$1{,}425 \times \frac{8}{19} = €600$ $1{,}425 \times \frac{9}{19} = €675$ $1{,}425 \times \frac{2}{19} = €150$
(ix)	9 : 6 : 3 = 3 : 2 : 1	$222 \times \frac{3}{6} = 111$ g $222 \times \frac{2}{6} = 74$ g $222 \times \frac{1}{6} = 37$ g
(x)	3 : 2 = 1 : 4	$700 \times \frac{1}{5} = 140$ cm $700 \times \frac{4}{5} = 560$ cm

4. 50 ml **5.** Volley ball = €1,840, Soccer = €2,960
6. $\frac{94}{240} \times 24 = €9.40$, $\frac{83}{240} \times 24 = €8.30$, $\frac{63}{240} \times 24 = €6.30$
7. (i) €1,200 (ii) 30 cm (iii) €1105 (iv) 270 g (v) 600 cm (vi) €150 (vii) Bilal: 70 sweets, Cáit: 50 sweets **8.** $k = 5$
9. 256 pages **10.** First option is better for Niamh

Exercise 1.2

1.

	Error	Relative Error	% Error
(i)	$\lvert 150 - 149 \rvert = 1$	$\frac{1}{150}$	0.67%
(ii)	$\lvert 36 - 36.9 \rvert = 0.9$	$\frac{0.9}{36} = \frac{1}{40}$	2.5%
(iii)	$\lvert 180 - 183 \rvert = 3$	$\frac{3}{180} = \frac{1}{60}$	1.67%
(iv)	$\lvert 4.8 - 5 \rvert = 0.2$	$\frac{0.2}{4.8} = \frac{1}{24}$	4.17%
(v)	$\lvert 6.7 - 7 \rvert = 0.3$	$\frac{0.3}{6.7} = \frac{3}{67}$	4.48%
(vi)	$\lvert 54.15 - 55 \rvert = 0.85$	$\frac{0.85}{54.15} = \frac{17}{1083}$	1.57%
(vii)	$\lvert 1.36 - 1.5 \rvert = 0.14$	$\frac{0.14}{1.36} = \frac{7}{68}$	10.29%
(viii)	$\lvert 502 - 500 \rvert = 2$	$\frac{2}{502} = \frac{1}{251}$	0.40%
(ix)	$\lvert 360 - 359 \rvert = 1$	$\frac{1}{360}$	0.28%
(x)	$\lvert 58.6 - 60 \rvert = 1.4$	$\frac{1.4}{58.6} = \frac{7}{293}$	2.39%

2. 1.08% **3.** 1.29% **4.** 1% **5.** 2.6% **6.** (i) 0.0394 (ii) 0.8% **7.** (i) 0.05 (ii) 0.5% **8.** (i) €6,554 (ii) €6,555.6 (iii) €1.6

Exercise 1.3

1. €30,900 **2.** 21% **3.** (i) €7,600 (ii) 20% **4.** €73,500 **5.** (i) €28,550 (ii) €65,950 **6.** €44,190 **7.** €1,218.06 **8.** (i) €55.38 (ii) €148.85 (iii) €3,301.96 (iv) €899.59 **9.** (i) €8,800 (ii) €57,450 (iii) Eoin €2,452.81, Sorcha €1,768.06

Exercise 1.4

1. (i) €2.70 (ii) €1.89 (iii) €2.16 (iv) €1.69 **2.** (i) €544.50 (ii) €229.90 (iii) €968 (iv) €1,087.79 **3.** €18.15 **4.** €363 **5.** €36 **6.** €250 **7.** €1,800 **8.** €171.99 **9.** €450 **10.** €70 **11.** (i) €3,375 (ii) €4,083.75 **12.** (i) €791 (ii) €87.50 (iii) €787.50 (iv) €819 **13.** (i) €3693.09 (ii) €3678.75 **14.** €65.58 **15.** (i) Bill 1: 69, Bill 2: 1,451 (ii) Bill 1: €8.28, Bill 2: €174.12 (iii) Bill 1: €23.02, Bill 2: €211.25 **16.** (i) €9 (ii) €69 (iii) €83.49

Exercise 1.5

1. €11.25 **2.** (i) €138 (ii) 13%

3.

	Cost price (€)	Selling price (€)	Profit (€)	% Mark-up (2 d.p.)	% Margin (2 d.p.)
(i)	25.00	30.00	5.00	20.00	16.67
(ii)	31.00	36.00	5.00	16.13	13.89
(iii)	15.00	20.00	5.00	33.33	25.00
(iv)	14.00	28.00	14.00	100.00	50.00
(v)	12.00	18.00	6.00	50.00	33.33
(vi)	18.00	18.90	0.90	5.00	4.76
(vii)	1.00	4.00	3.00	300.00	75.00
(viii)	2.10	2.80	0.70	33.33	25.00
(ix)	10.00	12.00	2.00	20.00	16.67
(x)	11.00	15.50	4.50	40.91	29.03

4. (i) €157.50 (ii) €1,081.20 (iii) €2,520.00 (iv) €7,836.75 (v) €26,970.00 **5.** (i) €39.20 (ii) €80.75 (iii) €121.50 (iv) €99.50 (v) €1,518.05 **6.** (i) €47.50 (ii) €1,062.50 (iii) €25,500 (iv) €8,000 (v) €12,672 **7.** % Mark-up = 20%, % Margin = 16.67% **8.** (i) (a) €60 (b) €1,140 (ii) (a) €240 (b) €1,360 (iii) (a) €88 (b) €4,312 (iv) (a) €547.50 (b) €912.5 **9.** (i) 16.67% (ii) 8.33% (iii) 11.11% (iv) 7.88% (v) 12.00% **10.** (i) €79.86 (ii) €585.64 **11.** Cameras €250, Discount €37.50, Price paid €212.50 **12.** (i) €150 (ii) €31.25 **13.** €731.25

Exercise 1.6

1. €26,046.56 **2.** €310.48 **3.** €138,769.87 **4.** €8,735.48 **5.** €1,418,299.58 **6.** €791.35 **7.** A = €1,958.82 **8.** A = €1,400.27 **9.** €147,696 **10.** €16,177,050 **11.** €3,934.01 **12.** (i) €18,200 (ii) €231,065.97 (iii) €16,026.40 **13.** The first option is cheaper **14.** €9,563.09 **15.** 3.09% **16.** 3.23% **17.** 3.58%

Exercise 1.7

1. (i) €180,000 (ii) €783,009.38 (iii) €47,494.85 (iv) €19,555.73 **2.** (i) 15% (ii) €109, 724.07 (iii) 3.5% (iv) 25% **3.** €9,830.40 **4.** 150,859.81 m^3 **5.** A = €60,000 **6.** €979,100 **7.** 26% **8.** 20% **9.** 87.91%

Exercise 1.8

1. (i) $15\frac{3}{7}$ km/hr (ii) 100 km/hr (iii) 237.5 km (iv) 729 km **2.** $6\frac{74}{75}$ miles per hour **3.** ≈ 28 km/hr **4.** (i) 14:55 (ii) 09:30 (iii) 14:30 (iv) 09:08 **5.** (i) 68 km/hr (ii) ≈ 2 hrs 26 mins (iii) 3 hrs 41 mins **6.** (i) ≈ 83 km/hr (ii) 80 litres (iii) €97.85 **7.** €2,000 **8.** −€3 per month **9.** €241,200 **10.** (i) $59.50 (ii) No **11.** Niall: 93.75 km travelled per hour worked, John: 121.21 km travelled per hour worked

Exercise 1.9

2. (i) €67,500 (ii) €6.75 **3.** (i) 150 quiches (ii) €349 (iii) €2.63 (iv) €3.144 **4.** (i) 48,000 kg (ii) 45,000 kg (iii) €279,000 (iv) €305,000 **5.** (i) 40 m (ii) 120 m (iii) €1,540 (iv) €29.52 **6.** (i) 58,500 kg (ii) 78,000 hours (iii) €858,000 (iv) €1,778,000 (v) €397,000 (vi) €179,500

Exercise 1.10

1. (i) $828.80 (ii) ¥99.314 (iii) £356 (iv) €574.48 (v) €71.96 (vi) €3,700 **2.** Dublin O_2 tickets are more expensive **3.** (a) (i) £738 (ii) €903.75 (iii) 0.415% (b) (i) €54 (ii) bureau de change is better for Alison, by €0.25 **4.** $439.20 **5.** It's cheaper in the USA **6.** (i) €19.99 (ii) 2.5% **7.** €646.83

Exercise 1.11

1. 6 inches = 15.24 cm, 4.5 feet = 1.37 m, 5 miles = 8.05 km, 13 inches = 330.2 mm, 6 pints = 3.41 litres, 5 ounces = 141.75 grams, 6 lbs = 2.72 kg, 3.5 tonnes = 3556.18 kg, 22 yards = 20.12 m, 2.3 feet = 0.7 m **2.** 0.55 lb **3.** (i) 22.05 m (ii) 13.70 miles **4.** 10,200 kg of bricks is heavier **5.** Buy 7 metres **6.** Store B is cheaper

Revision Exercises

1. 9.6 cm **2.** 14.39 ounces **3.** €975 **4.** 9 years old **5.** (i) 0.7666 (ii) 4.4% **6.** (i) €2,816 (ii) €2,816.06 (iii) €0.06 **7.** €14,500 **8.** (i) €34.62 (ii) €93.03 (iii) €1,768.06 (iv) €623.69 **9.** (i) €26,450 (ii) €36,700 **10.** €3,986.12 **11.** (i) €283.12 (ii) €3.12 (iii) €26.88 (iv) €24.79 **12.** 181 minutes **13.** (i) 250 messages (ii) 150 messages (iii) Both networks cost the same. **14.** (i) €700 (ii) €700 (iii) 233.33% (iv) 70% **15.** (i) €510.75 (ii) €56.25 (iii) €506.25 (iv) €517.50 **16.** (i) €13,250 (ii) €169,009.36 (iii) €11,037.25 **17.** (i) Option 1: 1.41%, Option 2: 1.37%, Option 3: 1.74%, Option 4: 1.96% (ii) Option 2 **18.** €19,752.14 **19.** (i) €4,081.49 (ii) 7. 00% (iii) They are identical in terms of AER **20.** (i) €14,762.25 (ii) €47,123.51 (iii) €1,361,220.84 (iv) €181,623.47 (v) €115,492.97 **21.** €177,006.66 **22.** 20% **23.** (i) 37.00% **24.** (i) 552 Km/hr (ii) 285.84 miles **25.** (i) 306 (ii) ≈ 3,477 (iii) €121.69 (iv) €138.12 **26.** 1,730 litres **27.** (i) £769.50 (ii) €30.19 (iii) €179.07 (iv) €853.82 **28.** (i) 145,000 kg (ii) 95,000 kg (iii) 80,000 (hours) (iv) €600,000 (v) €1,449,000 (vi) €776,000 (vii) €998,500

Exam Questions

1. (a) 234 (b) 59·11 (c) (i) 311.11 (ii) 20.1% **2.** (a) 8,825.04 (b) 8,921.26 (d) 4% **3.** (a) $2580 (b) $1.40 (c) $1 = £0.67 **4.** (a) John: €10,000, Mary: €6,000, Eileen: €4,000 **5.** (a) €1,250 (b) €39.95 (c) 75.58% **6.** (a) €10,440 (b) (i) 1,552.50 (ii) €10,934.43

7. (a) €7,989.24 (b) $i = 2.305\%$ **8.** (b) ≈ €112.12
9. (a) €39 (b) €22.60 (c) €15.32

Chapter 2

Exercise 2.1

1. (i) 2 (ii) −6 (iii) −6 (iv) 17 (v) 1 (vi) 4 (vii) 27 (viii) −3 (ix) −3 (x) 9 (xi) −27 (xii) −27 **2.** (i) 10 (ii) −2 (iii) −10 (iv) 20 (v) 6 (vi) −1 (vii) 10 (viii) 2 **3.** (i) −48 (ii) 14 (iii) −44 (vi) −20 (vii) 2,304 (viii) −248 **4.** (i) 2 (ii) 32 (iii) −5 (iv) 110 **5.** (i) $\frac{2}{17}$ (ii) $-\frac{47}{10}$ (iii) 6 (iv) 1 (v) 1 **6.** (i) $261\frac{2}{3}$ cm^3 (ii) $83\frac{11}{15}$ m^3 (iii) $657{,}066\frac{2}{3}$ mm^3 **7.** (i) 32 m^2 (ii) 363 cm^2 (iii) 552 m^2 **8.** (i) ≈ 998 (ii) ≈ 937 (iii) ≈ 640 (iv) ≈ 1,051 (v) ≈ 957 (vi) ≈ 598 (vii) ≈ 942, Total points 6,123

Exercise 2.2

1. (i) $3a$ (ii) $11b$ (iii) $-2b$ (iv) $-6d$ (v) $-4a$ **2.** (i) $e - 5f$ (ii) $5g + 4h - 7$ (iii) $17j - 2k$ (iv) $8m - 7n$ (v) $-p - 2q$ **3.** (i) $6x + 5y + 12$ (ii) $4x + 2y + 8$ (iii) $7a - 5b - 7$ (iv) $-7p - 4q$ **4.** (i) $3x^2 + 7x + 5$ (ii) $4x^2 - 3x - 5$ (iii) $-a^2 + 4$ (iv) $-4p^2 - 5q - 3$

Exercise 2.3

1. (i) $3ab$ (ii) $12b$ (iii) $10a^2$ (iv) $8c^2$ (v) $-2bc$ (vi) $-d^2$ (vii) $10e^2$ (viii) e^2f **2.** (i) x^4 (ii) x^3y^2 (iii) $6x^7$ (iv) x^8 (v) $6a^{10}$ (vi) $-2y^5$ (vii) $20y^5$ (viii) $4b^{15}$ **3.** (i) a^2b (ii) a^2b^2 (iii) $6cd^2$ (iv) $-a^3b$ (v) $4x^2y^3$ (vi) a^3 (vii) $-3y^5$ (viii) $10y^2$ **4.** (i) $8x^3y^3$ (ii) $-9x^2y^3$ (iii) $50m^2n^2$ (iv) $-24a^8$ (v) $2x^3y^2$ (vi) $10p^4q^4$ (vii) $-8p^8q^3$ (viii) $10t^7p^4$ **5.** (i) b^2 (ii) $4b^2$ (iii) $9b^2$ (iv) $-27b^3$ (v) $64a^3b^3$ (vi) $4a^2b^2$ (vii) $16x^4y^2$ (viii) $-8x^6y^3$ **6.** (i) $5ab$ (ii) $10pq$ (iii) $3x^2y$ (iv) $a^2b - 11ab$ (v) $-x^2y^2 - 3x^2y$

Exercise 2.4

1. (i) $3a + 9$ (ii) $3b - 9$ (iii) $-4c + 16$ (iv) $5x - 15y - 5$
2. (i) $7x + 10$ (ii) $8a + 4$ (iii) $-3a - 3$ (iv) $9b + 6$
3. (i) $4a^2 + 8a + 10$ (ii) $-16a^2 - 2a + 8$ (iii) $7b^2 - 6b - 3$
4. (i) $4x + 9$ (ii) $5x^2 - 12x + 57$ (iii) $-a^2 - 15a + 4$
5. (i) $x^2 + 3x$ (ii) $y^2 - 6y$ (iii) $4a^2 + 2a$ (iv) $8b^2 - 8b$ (v) $2x^3 - 2x$ (vi) $-15x^3 + 35x$ **6.** (i) $2a^2 + 2a$ (ii) $4x^2 - 4x$ (iii) $9a^2 - 10a$ (iv) $8x^2 + 6x + 3$ (v) $4y^2 - 15y$

Exercise 2.5

1. $\frac{7x}{10}$ **2.** $\frac{3y}{8}$ **3.** $-\frac{2a}{15}$ **4.** $\frac{5c}{4}$ **5.** $\frac{26x}{21}$ **6.** $\frac{10a + 23}{12}$ **7.** $\frac{27a - 2}{15}$
8. $\frac{5x - 8}{8}$ **9.** $\frac{2x - 3}{9}$ **10.** $\frac{-23y + 37}{24}$ **11.** $\frac{7x - 18}{24}$ **12.** $\frac{-30x + 35}{6}$
13. $\frac{5x + 5}{3}$

Exercise 2.6

1. (i) $x^2 + 5x + 6$ (ii) $x^2 + 5x + 4$ (iii) $x^2 - 4x - 21$ (iv) $x^2 - 4x - 5$ (v) $y^2 - 12y + 32$ **2.** (i) $8x^2 + 6x + 1$ (ii) $6y^2 - 10y - 4$ (iii) $15x^2 - 21x + 6$ (iv) $12y^2 - 30y + 12$ (v) $-4b^2 + 6b - 2$ **3.** (i) $x^2 + 2xy + y^2$ (ii) $p^2 - q^2$ (iii) $m^2 - 2mn + n^2$ (iv) $4h^2 - 8hw + 3w^2$ **4.** (i) $x^2 + 2x + 1$ (ii) $x^2 + 6x + 9$ (iii) $x^2 - 4x + 4$ (iv) $x^2 - 10x + 25$ (v) $4y^2 - 4y + 1$ **5.** (i) $x^3 + 2x^2 + 2x + 1$ (ii) $2x^3 - 5x^2 - 4x + 3$ (iii) $16x^3 - 4x^2 - 14x - 3$ **6.** (i) $x^3 + 7x^2 + 12x$ (ii) $100h - 40h^2 + 40h^3$ (iii) $a^3 - ab^2$ **7.** (i) $8x^3 + 36x^2 + 54x + 27$ (ii) $y^3 - 6y^2 + 12y - 8$ **8.** (i) $6x^2 - x - 15$ (ii) $x^3 + 125$

Exercise 2.7

1. $x(x + 5)$ **2.** $x(x - 7)$ **3.** $x(x - 2)$ **4.** $x(x - 15)$ **5.** $a(a - 11)$
6. $x(x - 14)$ **7.** $(a + c)(d + e)$ **8.** $(a + b)(p + q)$
9. $(m + n)(p - q)$ **10.** $(c - d)(a - b)$ **11.** $(x - 1)(y - 4)$
12. $3p(2a - c) + a(2d - e)$ **13.** $(2x - s)(r - 5y)$
14. $(p + q)(m + n)$ **15.** $(x - 4)(x + 4)$ **16.** $(x - 3)(x + 3)$
17. $(x - 10)(x + 10)$ **18.** $(x - 2)(x + 2)$ **19.** $(b - 5)(b + 5)$
20. $(y - 11)(y + 11)$ **21.** $(x - 15)(x + 15)$ **22.** $(x + 3)^2$
23. $(x + 7)(x + 1)$ **24.** $(x + 9)(x + 4)$ **25.** $(x + 2)^2$
26. $(x - 3)(x - 9)$ **27.** $(x + 7)(x - 2)$ **28.** $(x - 7)(x + 2)$
29. $(x - 4)(x - 8)$ **30.** $(x - 8)^2$ **31.** $(x - 4)(x + 1)$
32. $(x + 9)(x - 2)$ **33.** $(x - 9)(x + 7)$ **34.** $(x - 6)(x + 4)$
35. $(x - 7)(x - 8)$ **36.** $(b - 19)(b + 19)$ **37.** $(p - b)(c - d)$
38. $(x + 10)(x - 7)$ **39.** $(x - 13)(x + 3)$ **40.** $(x + 7)(x + 8)$
41. $(x - 10)(x + 9)$ **42.** $(3 - x)(3 + x)$

Exercise 2.8

1. $2x(x + 3)$ **2.** $3x(x + 7)$ **3.** $5x(x - 5)$ **4.** $4x(x - 4)$
5. $3a(a - 13)$ **6.** $b(2b + 3)$ **7.** $a(2a - 15)$ **8.** $x(5x + 2)$
9. $x(3x + 7)$ **10.** $p(11p - 3)$ **11.** $4(x - 2)(x + 2)$
12. $(3b + 2)(3b - 2)$ **13.** $(8x - 7)(8x + 7)$ **14.** $25(a - 2)(a + 7)$
15. $(7x + 6)(7x - 6)$ **16.** $(11x - 5)(11x + 5)$ **17.** $(9y - 14)(9y + 14)$
18. $(13x + 18)(13x - 18)$ **19.** $(2x + 3)(x + 1)$ **20.** $(5x + 1)(x + 1)$
21. $(7p + 1)(p + 2)$ **22.** $(5x + 2)(x + 2)$ **23.** $(3q + 2)(q + 2)$
24. $(3x + 2)(x + 5)$ **25.** $(7x - 5)(x + 1)$ **26.** $(3y - 5)(y - 1)$
27. $(3x - 7)(x + 1)$ **28.** $(2x - 5)(x + 2)$ **29.** $(7a - 5)(a + 1)$
30. $(5x - 3)(x + 4)$ **31.** $(2b - 3)(b - 5)$ **32.** $(5x - 3)(x - 3)$
33. $(5p - 7)(p + 7)$ **34.** $(11x - 5)(x + 6)$ **35.** $(4x - 5)(x + 1)$
36. $(8q + 1)(q + 2)$ **37.** $(4x - 7)(x + 3)$ **38.** $4(15x - 7)(15x + 7)$
39. $2(3x + 2)(x + 1)$ **40.** $3(x - 4)(x - 2)$

Exercise 2.9

1. a^9 **2.** $8a$ **3.** $5a^2b$ **4.** $5a^5b$ **5.** $-3x^4$ **6.** $2xy$ **7.** $7x^4y^2$
8. $8xy^3z^2$ **9.** $a + 10$ **10.** $b + 1$ **11.** $p - 4$ **12.** $-2x + 1$
13. 1 **14.** $\frac{1}{5}$ **15.** $2x$ **16.** $7x$ **17.** $x^2 + 2x - 3$ **18.** x
19. $x + 5$ **20.** $x - 6$ **21.** $2x + 3$ **22.** $x - 2$ **23.** $2x - 5$
24. $\frac{1}{x^2 + 6x + 8}$ **25.** $\frac{1}{x + 8}$ **26.** $\frac{1}{x + 2}$ **27.** $\frac{1}{x + 3}$ **28.** $\frac{1}{3x + 1}$
29. $\frac{1}{2x - 3}$ **30.** $\frac{1}{12x - 5}$ **31.** $5x + 13$ **32.** $x + 6$ **33.** $-2x + 1$
34. $-5x - 13$

Exercise 2.10

1. $\frac{2x + 2}{x(x + 2)}$ **2.** $\frac{3x - 4}{x(x - 2)}$ **3.** $\frac{5x + 3}{x(2x - 1)}$ **4.** $\frac{6x - 8}{(x - 3)(x + 2)}$ **5.** $\frac{17 - x}{(2x + 1)(x + 4)}$
6. $\frac{32 - x}{(x - 8)(x + 4)}$ **7.** $\frac{1 - 10x}{(3x - 1)(2x - 3)}$ **8.** $\frac{8x + 10}{(2x - 1)(1 + 2x)}$ **9.** $\frac{19 - 2x}{3(2x + 5)}$
10. $\frac{14}{3x}$ **11.** $\frac{9}{4x}$ **12.** $\frac{1}{4x - 3}$

Exercise 2.11

1. $x = 3$ **2.** $y = 2$ **3.** $x = 4$ **4.** $a = 9$ **5.** $x = -1$ **6.** $x = -3$
7. $y = 4$ **8.** $x = 7$ **9.** $t = 3$ **10.** $x = \frac{5}{6}$ **11.** $x = -2$ **12.** $x = -\frac{5}{2}$
13. $x = -1$ **14.** $x = -6$ **15.** $y = \frac{3}{8}$ **16.** $x = -2$ **17.** $x = 4$
18. $x = -\frac{1}{3}$ **19.** $x = 2.3$ **20.** $x = -3$ **21.** $x = -\frac{5}{9}$ **22.** $a = -3$

23. $x = -12$ **24.** $x = -7$ **25.** $x = -1$ **26.** $x = \frac{1}{2}$ **27.** $y = -4$ **27.** $a = -1$ **29.** $b = -\frac{7}{3}$

Exercise 2.12

1. $x = 2$ **2.** $x = 12$ **3.** $x = 2$ **4.** $x = \frac{4}{3}$ **5.** $x = -15$ **6.** $x = 7$ **7.** $x = 11$ **8.** $y = 5$ **9.** $x = 2$ **10.** $x = \frac{38}{11}$ **11.** $t = \frac{15}{4}$ **12.** $x = 5$ **13.** $x = 4$ **14.** $x = -1$ **15.** $x = 36$ **16.** $x = 0$

Exercise 2.13

1. (i) $x = 3$ (ii) $y = 4$ (iii) $a = 1$ (iv) $b = 7$ (v) $y = \frac{16 - x}{4}$ (vi) $\frac{2b - 5}{3} = c$ (vii) $r = -2t$ (viii) $a = \frac{2}{3}$ **2.** $\frac{A}{l} = w$ **3.** $\frac{2K}{v^2} = m$ **4.** $\pm\sqrt{\frac{E}{m}} = c$ **5.** $\frac{b - a}{2} = c$ **6.** $\frac{Fr}{v^2} = m$ **7.** $3a - b = c$ **8.** $\frac{v^2}{2h} = g$ **9.** $2s - a - c = b$ **10.** $\frac{2(s - ut)}{t^2}$ **11.** $y = 6z - 3x$ **12.** $b = \frac{c}{a + c}$ **13.** $\frac{ac}{a - c} = b$ **14.** $q = \frac{c}{p - r}$ **15.** $b = \frac{x - a}{1 - x}$ **16.** $\frac{T^2 g}{4\pi^2} = l$ **17.** $\frac{ac}{c - a} = b$ **18.** (i) $V = \frac{M}{D}$ (ii) $41\frac{2}{3}$ cm³ **19.** (i) $3x - k(a + b) = y$ (ii) $x = \frac{k(a + b) + y}{3}$ **20.** (i) 1,570 cm³ (ii) 12 cm (iii) 24.5 cm **21.** (i) 2.84 seconds (ii) 2.24 metres

Exercise 2.14

1. $x = 4, y = 3$ **2.** $x = 8, y = 5$ **3.** $a = 7, b = -3$ **4.** $x = 1, y = 2$ **5.** $p = 3, q = 4$ **6.** $x = 2, y = 5$ **7.** $a = 0, b = -3$ **8.** $x = -1, y = 4$ **9.** $x = -4, y = 5$ **10.** $p = -3, q = -3$ **11.** $x = 5, y = 2$ **12.** $e = -4, f = -3$ **13.** $x = -2, y = -1$ **14.** $x = -5, y = -2$ **15.** $x = 3, y = 1$ **16.** $x = 14, y = 6$

Exercise 2.15

1. (i) $x = -\frac{2}{3}$ (ii) $x = 3$ (iii) $x = -5$ (iv) $x = 2$ (v) $x = -7$ **2.** (i) $x = 2, y = 2$ (ii) $x = 2\frac{6}{7}, y = -1\frac{5}{7}$ (iii) $x = -1, y = 3$ (iv) $x = 3, y = -1$ **3.** (a) (i) $x = 2, y = 2$ (ii) $x = 1, y = \frac{1}{2}$

Exercise 2.16

1. (i) 8, 9, 10 (ii) 6, 7, 8 (iii) −8, −7, −6 (iv) 1, 2, 3 (v) −4, −3, −2 **3.**(i) $x > 9, x \in N$ (ii) $x \geqslant -1, x \in Z$ (iii) $x \geqslant 5, x \in R$ (iv) $x < 3, x \in N$ or $x \leqslant 2, x \in N$ (v) $x \geqslant -2, x \in Z$ or $x > -3, x \in Z$ (vi) $x < 2, x \in R$ (vii) $x < 4, x \in Z$ or $x \leqslant 3, x \in Z$ (viii) $x \leqslant 19, x \in R$ **4.** (i) $x > 5$ or $x \geqslant 6, x \in N$ (ii) $x < -6$ or $x \leqslant -7, x \in Z$ (iii) $x > 5, x \in R$ (iv) $x \leqslant -3, x \in R$ (v) $x > 0, x \in R$

Exercise 2.17

1. $x > 2, x \in N$ **2.** $x \geqslant 3$ **3.** $x < 2$ **4.** $x \leqslant -1$ **5.** $x \leqslant -1$ **6.** $x > 4$ **7.** $x > -16$ **8.** $x \leqslant 2$ **9.** $x > -7, x \in Z$ **10.** $x \geqslant -1$ **11.** $x < 9$ **12.** $x \leqslant \frac{7}{2}$ **13.** $x > 7$ **14.** $x \geqslant 2$ **15.** $x > -4$ **16.** $x \geqslant \frac{1}{2}$ **17.** $x \geqslant 2$ **18.** $x \geqslant -\frac{1}{2}$

Exercise 2.18

1. (i) 35 (ii) 49 (iii) $7n$ **2.** (i) 60 (ii) 240 (iii) $60t$ **3.** (i) 19 (ii) $3x + y$ **4.** 26 (ii) $x + 4$ **5.** (i) $45l$ (ii) $\frac{3}{4}m$ **6.** $x + n$ **7.** (i) 5, 6, 7, 8, 9 (ii) $n + 1, n + 2, n + 3, n + 4, n + 5$ **8.** (i) 12, 14, 16, 18 (ii) $p + 2, p + 4, p + 6, p + 8$ **9.** (i) 33, 35, 37 (ii) $q + 2, q + 4, q + 6$ **10.** 37 (ii) $\frac{x}{2} - 3$ **11.** €50 (ii) €30 (iii) €$(100 - x)$ **12.** (i) 12 (ii) $29 - x$ **13.** $(28x - 2)$ m **14.** €$\left(\frac{1000 - x}{3}\right)$ for the three youngest €x for the eldest **15.** $C(€) = 90t + 60$ **16.** h (cm) $= 12 + 0.5d$ **17.** Option 1 is better if visiting gym 12 times in a year. **18.** (i) $t(\text{m}) = 40x + 20$ (ii) $t(\text{m}) = 50x + 20$ (iii) (i) $t(\text{m}) = 60x + 30$ **19.** $S(€) = (12x + 203)$ **20.** (i) 0.25 (ii) $Y(€) = 30{,}000 + 0.25x$

Exercise 2.19

1. (i) $2x + 17$ (ii) $2x + 17 = 35$ (iii) $x = 9$ **2.** (i) $3y - 7$ (ii) $3y - 7 = 26$ (iii) $y = 11$ **3.** (i) $8x + 60 = 180$ (ii) $5y - 20 = 180$ (iii) $x = 15$, 60°, 45°, 75°, $y = 40$, 65°, 30°, 85° **4.** (i) $4(x + 2)$ (ii) $6(x - 1)$ (iii) $4(x + 2) = 6(x - 1)$ (iv) Rectangle 1: 9, 4, Rectangle 2: 6, 6 **5.** (i) $n + 1$ (ii) $n + n + 1$ (iii) 41, 42 **6.** (i) $x + 37$ (ii) $x + 37 + x = 141$ (iii) $2x + 37 = 141$ (iv) Lower grade 52, High grade 89 **7.** (i) $2y$ (ii) $2y + 25$ (iii) $y + 2y + 2y + 25 = 80$ (iv) Annie is 11 years old **8.** (i) $100 - x$ (ii) $10(100 - x) + 5(x)$ (iii) 30 **9.** (i) $n + 2$ (ii) $7n = 5(n + 2) + 12$ (iii) 11, 13 **10.** (i) $4.5x$ (ii) $(4.5x + x) - 30$ (iii) 432 (iv) Arthur €42, Barry €189, Ciara €201 **11.** (i) $n + 1$ (ii) $n + n + 1 \geqslant -5$ (iii) −3, −2 **12.** (i) $\frac{3}{4}y$ (ii) $\frac{3}{4}y + y = 147$ (iii) 84 **13.** (i) $18{,}000 + 0.125x$ (ii) $18{,}000 + 0.125x \geqslant 60{,}000$ (iii) at least €336,000 **14.** (i) Per hour earns $12.50x$ (ii) $12.35x$ (iii) 194 **15.** 11 **16.** Amy: €100, Brenden: €300, Chloe: €150 **17.** €70 **18.** (i) Coach = $55t$ (ii) Car = $65t$ (iii) $65t + 55t = 180$ (iv) 1.5 hrs. (v) 18:30

Exercise 2.20

1. (i) $x + y = 25$ (ii) $2x + y = 35$ (iii) 10, 15 **2.** (i) $x + y = 20$ (ii) $x - y = 5$ (iii) $\frac{25}{2}, \frac{15}{2}$ **3.** (i) $3x + 2y = 11$ (ii) $5x + 2y = 11$ (iii) Soft Drink: €2, Burger: €0.50 **4.** (i) $x + y =$ €1 (ii) $4x + 2y =$ €3.40 (iii) Pen = €0.70, Pencil = €0.30 **5.** $x + y = 7, y = 2, x = 5$ **6.** (i) $x + y = 735$ (ii) $x - y = 105$ (iii) 420 ← Alan, 315 ← Carol **7.** (i) $x + y = 11$ (ii) $3x + y = 17$ (iii) 3 goals, 8 points **8.** $x = 20$ leather, $y = 30$ fabric **9.** 25 3 mk question, 10 5 mk question **10.** Coat: €60, Bag: €40 **11.** First: 30 m, Second: 120 m **12.** Karl: 40, Eddie: 25 **13.** (i) $2x - 2y = 3$ (ii) $3x + 3y = 25.5$ km (iii) Speed 3.5 km/hr, 5 km/hr.

Revision Exercises

1. (a) (i) $-2 + 3 = 1$ (ii) $-2 - 3 = -5$ (iii) $3 - (-2) = 3 + 2 = 5$ (iv) $-2(3) = -6$ (v) 0 (b) (i) 4 (ii) −6 (iii) $\frac{5}{4}$ (c) (i) 1: 2.47 seconds, 2: 24.73 seconds, 3: 28.56 seconds, 4: 14.28 seconds 5: 12.37 seconds (ii) 1.98 seconds (iii) $h \approx 19$ m **2.** (a) (i) $7x + 12xy$ (ii) $11a^2 + 3a$ (iii) $12x^2 + 11x$ (iv) $12y + 6$ (b) (i) $12x^2 + 11xy + 2$ (ii) $11x^2 + 3x - 13$ (iii) $2x^2 + 21x - 16$ (iv) $2x^2 + 7x - 2$ (c) (i) $14a^3$ (ii) $30c^3$ (iii) $20a^3b^2$ (iv) $12x^2y^3$ (v) $2a^2$ (vi) c^4 (d) (i) $121a^2$ (ii) $125c^3$ (iii) $-8b^3$ (iv) $27m^6$ (v) $-64b^3$ (vi) $4k^4$ **3.** (a) (i) $6a + 8b$ (ii) $12a + 30b$ (iii) $6x + 12y + 18z$ (iv) $-4x - 10y$ (b) (i) $2x + 6y + 6x + 3y = 8x + 9y$ (ii) $6m + 18n + 7m + 7n = 13m + 25n$ (iii) $x + 26y - 4$ (iv) $11x^2 - 10x - 15$ (v) $5x^2 - 13x + 11$ (c) (i) $2x^2 - 16x + x^2 - 7x = 3x^2 - 23x$ (ii) $3x^2 - x - 3x^2 + x + 11 = 11$ (iii) $4a^2 - 7ab - 4a^2 + 6ab = -ab$ (iv) $6x^3 + 2x^2 + 2x - 5x^3 - x^2 + 3x = x^3 + x^2 + 5x$

4. (a) (i) $\frac{5x+17}{(x+1)(x+7)}$ (ii) $\frac{3x+16}{(x+5)(x+6)}$ (iii) $\frac{4x-5}{(2x+1)(5x-1)}$
(iv) $\frac{-87}{(4x+1)(x-7)}$ or $-\frac{87}{(4x+1)(x-7)}$
(v) $\frac{-2x-7}{(2x+1)(2x-1)}$ or $-\frac{2x+7}{(2x+1)(2x-1)}$
(b) (i) x^2+6x+5 (ii) $y^2+9y+14$ (iii) k^2-6k-7
(iv) $x^2-11x+18$ (v) $6x^2+13x+5$ (vi) $4a^2+16a+16$
(viii) $9y^2+12y+4$ (ix) $16y^2-8y+1$ (x) $2x^3+12x^2+10x$
(c) (i) $(y-6)(y+6)$ (ii) $x(x-50)$ (iii) $(x-9)(x+9)$
(v) $(x-4)(x-3)$ (vi) $(x+5)(x-2)$ (vii) $(2x-1)(x-1)$
(viii) $(5x-2)(x+3)$ (ix) $16(2y-1)(2y+1)$ (x) $3x(4x+5)$
(xi) $x(8x-11)$ (xii) $(2x-5)(x-4)$ (xiii) $2(x-9)(x-6)$
(xiv) $(5x-1)(x+7)$ (xv) $5(2x-1)(x+1)$ (xvi) $(4x-13)(x-1)$
5. (a) (i) $12y^2$ (ii) $6x^2$ (iii) $6x^2y$ (iv) $6p^7q^2$
(b) (i) $\frac{(x+5)(x+3)}{x+5}=x+3$ (ii) $\frac{36x^3y}{6xy}=6x^2$
(iii) $2(x-2)$ or $2x-4$ (iv) $\frac{2x+5}{x}$ (v) $\frac{15(x-2)}{5(x-2)}=\frac{15}{5}=3$
6. (a) (i) $x=3, x=4$ (ii) $x=6$ (v) $9=x$ (iii) $x=3$ (vi) $x=4$
(v) $x=9$ (vi) $x=3$ (b) (i) $3=x$ (ii) $x=2$ (iii) $-1=x$ (iv) $2=x$
(v) $x=\frac{5}{2}$ **7.** (a) (i) $x=2$ (ii) $a=-1$ (iii) $x=-1$ (iv) $x=3$
(v) $x=10$ (b) (i) $\frac{y+t}{p}=q$ (ii) $\frac{p}{v}=t$ (iii) $a=\frac{-by-c}{x}$
(iv) $\frac{t-a}{n-1}=d$ (v) $\frac{A}{2\pi h}=r$ (c) (i) $x=\frac{c}{a+k}$ (ii) $r=\frac{1+c}{1+s}$
(iii) $a=\frac{b}{1-k}$ (iv) $\frac{a-c}{c+1}=b$ (v) $\frac{a-d}{d+5}=c$
8. (a) (ii) $x=5, y=-1$ (iii) $x=1, y=-1$ (iv) $x=\frac{1}{2}, y=\frac{1}{2}$
(b) (i) $y=0, x=1$ (ii) $x=7, y=\frac{3}{2}$ **9.** (i) $x \in \{1, 2, 3\}$
(ii) $x \in \{1, 2, 3, 4, 5\}$ (iii) $x \in \{1, 2, 3\}$ (b) (i) $x > 3, x \in Z$
(ii) $x \leqslant 7, x \in N$ (iii) $x < -2, x \in R$ (c) (i) $x < 4, x \in R$
(ii) $x \geqslant 5, x \in R$ (iii) $x > 4, x \in R$ (iv) $x \leqslant 1, x \in R$
10. (a) $44-n$ (b) $\frac{53-x}{2}$ (c) $\left(\frac{3}{5}n-200\right)$ (d) (i) $4x+37$
(ii) $4x+37=325$ (iii) $x=72$ (e) (i) $x+5$ (ii) $3(x+5)$
(iii) $x+(x+5)+3(x+5)=95$ (iv) Marie: 15 years old
11. (a) (i) $x+y=12$ (ii) $10x+50y=240$ (iii) 9 10 cent coins, 3 5 cent coins (b) $x=12, y=5$ (c) $y=3, x=7$

Exam Questions

1. (a) $x=7$ (b) $a=3, b=-5$ (c) $\{1, 2, 3\}$
2. (a) €9 per hour (b) $w=9h+2d$ (c) 8 **3.** (a) $2-3x$
(b) $x \in \{1, 2\}$ (c) $-5x+4$ **4.** (a) 144 cm^2
(b) Length of box $=12-2h$, width of box $=12-2h$
5. (i) $x=-5$ **6.** $x=2$ **7.** (a) 55 mg (b) (i) $C=\left(\frac{Y}{Y+12}\right)\times A$
(ii) $C=\frac{A}{\left(\frac{Y+12}{Y}\right)}$ (iii) $C=\frac{A\times Y}{Y+12}$ (c) $C=\frac{YA}{Y+12}$ (d) 50 mg per day
(e) The child is 3 years old (f) ≈110 mg. (g) Weight $29\frac{1}{7}$ kg, Height 142 cm (using chart) **8.** (a) $f=\frac{1}{2}, g=-3$ (b) $x \geqslant 3.5$

Chapter 3

Exercise 3.1

2. (i) {1, 2, 4, 5, 8, 10, 20, 40} (ii) {1, 2, 4, 8, 16, 32, 64}
(iii) {1, 2, 4, 7, 14, 28} (iv) {1, 5, 7, 35}
(v) {1, 2, 3, 4, 6, 8, 12, 16, 24, 32, 48, 96}
(vi) {1, 2, 3, 4, 6, 8, 12, 16, 24, 48} **3.** (i) {4, 8, 12, 16, 20, 24}
(ii) {6, 12, 18, 24, 30, 36} (iii) {8, 16, 24, 32, 40, 48},
(iv) {9, 18, 27, 36, 45, 54} (v) {12, 24, 36, 48, 60, 72}
(vi) {14, 28, 42, 56, 70, 84} **5.** (i) HCF = 2 (ii) HCF = 5
(iii) HCF = 12 (iv) HCF = 3 (v) HCF = 4 (vi) HCF = 3
6. (i) LCM = 12 (ii) LCM = 60 (iii) LCM = 80 (iv) LCM = 12
(v) LCM = 40 (iv) LCM = 90 **8.** (i) $64 = 2^6$
(ii) $2310 = 2 \times 3 \times 5 \times 7 \times 11$ (iii) $1870 = 2 \times 5 \times 11 \times 17$
(iv) $102 = 2 \times 3 \times 17$ (v) $368 = 2^4 \times 23$
(vi) $5250 = 2 \times 3 \times 5^3 \times 7$ **9.** (i) (b) HCF = 34, LCM = 408
(ii) (b) HCF = 13, LCM = 1,170 (iii) (b) HCF = 58, LCM = 174
(iv) (b) HCF = 34, LCM = 510 **10.** 42 **11.** Step 20 (20th step)
12.

n	$\frac{4n^2+1}{13}$
17	$\frac{4(17)^2+1}{13}=89$
19	$\frac{4(19)^2+1}{13}=111\frac{2}{13}$
21	$\frac{4(21)^2+1}{13}=135\frac{10}{13}$

Exercise 3.2

1. (i) −12 (ii) 7 (iii) −10 (iv) −15 (v) −60 (vi) −3
2. (i) 2 (ii) −7 (iii) 0 (iv) 2 (v) −18 (vi) 2 **3.** €1,000
4. Alice: 14, Bob: 35, Kylie: 25 **5.** (i) 40 (ii) −32 (iii) −56
(iv) 90 (v) 90 (vi) −150 **6.** (i) 3 (ii) −6 (iii) −12
(iv) 2 (v) −11 (vi) −8

Exercise 3.3

1. (i) $\frac{13}{12}\left(1\frac{1}{12}\right)$ (ii) $\frac{1}{2}$ (iii) $\frac{29}{36}$ (iv) $\frac{21}{8}\left(2\frac{5}{8}\right)$ (v) $\frac{277}{24}\left(11\frac{13}{24}\right)$
(vi) $\frac{7}{4}\left(1\frac{3}{4}\right)$ **2.** (i) $\frac{2}{15}$ (ii) $\frac{5}{24}$ (iii) $\frac{9}{20}$ (iv) $\frac{17}{15}$ (v) $\frac{15}{2}$ (vi) $\frac{49}{16}$
3. (i) $\frac{1}{4}$ (ii) $\frac{4}{3}$ (iii) $\frac{4}{15}$ (iv) 12 **4.** 28 **5.** (i) $78\frac{17}{28}$ kg
(ii) $5\frac{1}{2}$ weeks **6.** 21 bars **7.** 64 km each day **8.** 200 cm

Exercise 3.4

1. (i) 2.2361 (ii) 2.8284 (iii) 4.1231 (iv) 4.3589 **2.** (i) 2
(ii) 11 (iii) 3 (iv) 15 (v) 45 (vi) 52 **3.** (i) 4.414 (ii) 2.764
(iii) 5.292 (iv) 2.804 **4.** (i) 50 (ii) 8 (iii) 20,000 (iv) 7,000
(v) 6,000 (vi) 10,000 **5.** (i) 0.0089 (ii) 0.022 (iii) 0.0023
(iv) 0.00000085 (v) 2.0 (vi) 0.000048 (vii) 960,000
(viii) 0.24 (ix) 0.00091 (x) 0.000000080 **6.** (i) 5 (ii) 6
(iii) 10 (iv) 3 (v) 2.8699 **7.** (i) 9 (ii) 20 (iii) 1
8. (i) 9.9954 (ii) 16.7358 (iii) 1.0581 **9.** (i) 1.4, $\sqrt{2}$, 1.5
10. $\sqrt{2}, (1.19)^2, \frac{10}{7}, \frac{7}{2\sqrt{6}}$
11. (i)

Number/Set	N	Z	Q	$R\backslash Q$	R
$\sqrt{5}$	No	No	No	Yes	Yes
8	Yes	Yes	Yes	No	Yes
−4	No	Yes	Yes	No	Yes
$3\frac{1}{2}$	No	No	Yes	No	Yes
$\frac{3\pi}{4}$	No	No	No	Yes	Yes

Exercise 3.5

1. (i) 3.8×10^3 (ii) 7.5×10^4 (iii) 2.4×10^2 (iv) 8.48×10^5
(v) 5.376×10^6 (vi) 1×10^{-2} (vii) 1×10^{-3} (viii) 3.2×10^{-5}
(ix) 1×10^{-4} (x) 1.2×10^{-3} (xi) 3×10^{-5} (xii) 5.326×10^5
2. (i) 265 (ii) 0.00453 (iii) 7,200,000 (iv) 0.000017
(v) 300 (vi) 0.04 (vii) 26,400,000 (viii) 7612

(ix) 276,000,000 (x) 0.00000000302 **3.** (i) 3.6×10^{-5} (ii) 5.613×10^{-4} (iii) 3.45×10^{-2} (iv) 6.3×10^{-4} (v) 7.8×10^{-3} **4.** (i) 0.0015 (ii) 0.000254 (iii) 0.000035 (iv) 0.00000667 (v) 0.0815 **5.** 5×10^2 seconds **6.** 4.26 light years **7.** 1.53×10^{11} bits/sec **8.** 10^{13} (times)

Exercise 3.6

1. (i) 10 (ii) 0 (iii) 25 (iv) 1 (v) 125 **2.** (i) 313 (ii) 1,897 (iii) 365 (iv) 2 **3.** (i) 9 (ii) 100 (iii) 5 (iv) 60
4. (i) $\frac{2}{9}$ (ii) $8\left(\frac{125}{252}\right)$ (iii) $140\frac{1}{3}$ (iv) $14\frac{8}{27}$
5. (i) 1 (ii) 4 (iii) $16\frac{2}{3}$ (iv) $7\frac{3}{5}$

Revision Exercises

1. (a) (i) 5, 10, 15, 20, 25, 30 (ii) 2, 4, 6, 8, 10, 12 (iii) 12, 24, 36, 48, 60, 72 (iv) 13, 26, 39, 52, 65, 78 (b) (i) {1, 2, 5, 7, 10, 14, 35, 70} (ii) {1, 2, 4, 5, 8, 10, 16, 20, 40, 80} (iii) {1, 2, 4, 7, 8, 14, 28, 56} (iv) {1, 2, 4, 8, 16, 32, 64, 128} (c) (i) 2^7 (ii) $2^2 \times 3 \times 17$ (iii) $2^2 \times 11 \times 17$ (iv) $2^2 \times 3 \times 13 \times 17$
2. (i) LCM = 204, HCF = 34 (ii) LCM = 2829, HCF = 3 (iii) LCM = 2808, HCF = 13 (iv) LCM = 615, HCF = 41 × 3 = 123
3. (i) 0.9710 (ii) 1.7737 (iii) 0.9361 (iv) 0.9361
4. (i) 850,000 (ii) 0.13 (iii) 2.0 (iv) 0.000054 (v) 650,000 (vi) 0.00081 **5.** (i) 58,344 (ii) $\frac{1043}{6250}$ **6.** (a) (i) $p = 2, q = 17$ (ii) $m = 7, n = 19$ (iii) HCF = 2^3 = 8, LCM = 705,432 (b) 4×10^{-4} **7.** (ii) €35, €3,500

8. (i)

p	$6p + 1$	$6p + 5$
0	1	5
1	7	11
2	13	17
3	19	23
4	25	29
5	31	35

Exam Questions

1. (b) $2^2 \times 3 \times 13 \times 17$ (c) 2.3×10^{18} (d) 19

2. (a)

Number	Rational	Irrational
a		✓
$a - 1$		✓
$(-a)^2$	✓	
$(a - 2)^2$		✓
$1 + a^2$	✓	

3. (a) 1.5×10^8 km

(b) (i)

	A	B	C	D	E	F	G
Number	2.1	$\sqrt{5}$	$\frac{243}{85}$	tan 70°	$\frac{3\pi}{4}$	250%	$\left(1 + \frac{1}{10}\right)^{10}$
Decimal Number	2.10	2.24	2.86	2.75	2.36	2.50	2.59

Chapter 4

Exercise 4.1

1. (i) 25 (ii) 8 (iii) 25 (iv) −216 (v) 16 (vi) −3 (vii) 16 (viii) 1 **2.** (i) $b = 729$ (ii) $n = 6$ (iii) $a = 10$

3.

Column A	Column B
3^4	-4^4
$(-2)^8$	-6^8
$(-6)^8$	−125
$-(-4)^4$	27
$-(6)^8$	6^8
$(-4)^4$	16
$-(-3)^3$	81
$(-5)^3$	4^4
$(-2)^4$	256

4. (i)

Index notation	2	2^2	2^3	2^4	2^5	2^6	2^7
Whole number	2	4	8	16	32	64	128

(ii)

Index notation	3	3^2	3^3	3^4	3^5	3^6
Whole number	3	9	27	81	243	729

(iii)

Index notation	4	4^2	4^3	4^4	4^5	4^6
Whole number	4	16	64	256	1,024	4,096

(iv)

Index notation	9	9^2	9^3	9^4	9^5	9^6
Whole number	9	81	729	6,561	59,049	531,441

5. (i) 5^5 (ii) 8^{10} (iii) 6^3 (iv) 5^{10} (v) -2^9 (vi) $\left(\frac{1}{2}\right)^{12}$ (vii) $\left(\frac{1}{4}\right)^{11}$ (viii) $-\left(\frac{1}{6}\right)^5$ (ix) $(0.2)^5$ (x) $(2.4)^{13}$ (xi) $-(2.7)^7$ (xii) $-(3.2)^{15}$
6. (i) 3 (ii) 2^6 (iii) 10^3 (iv) 7^7 (v) -12^5 (vi) -2^3 (vii) 4^0 (viii) 8^{-6} (ix) 7^{-2} (x) $\left(\frac{1}{2}\right)^4$ (xi) $-\left(\frac{3}{5}\right)^{-7}$ **7.** (i) 3^{15} (ii) 6^{20} (iii) 10^{25} (iv) 4^{30} (v) 7^{42} (vi) 8^{15} (vii) 16^6 (viii) 10^{36} (ix) 2^4 (x) 13^{27} **8.** (i) 8^7 (ii) 7^3 (iii) 5^6 (iv) 6^{22} **9.** (i) 3^7 (ii) 4^6 (iii) 5^{15} (iv) 5

Exercise 4.2

1.

x	1	2	3	4	5	6	7	8	9	10
x^2	1	4	9	16	25	36	49	64	81	100

x	1	4	9	16	25	36	49	64	81	100
$\sqrt{x}$	1	2	3	4	5	6	7	8	9	10

2.

x	1	2	3	4	5	6	7	8	9	10
x^3	1	8	27	64	125	216	343	512	729	1,000

x	1	8	27	64	125	216	343	512	729	1,000
$\sqrt[3]{x}$	1	2	3	4	5	6	7	8	9	10

3. (i) 10 (ii) 8 (iii) 6 (iv) 8 (v) 4 (vi) 2 (vii) 3 (viii) 10 (ix) 4 (x) 6 **4.** (i) $\frac{1}{2^3} = \frac{1}{8}$ (ii) $\frac{1}{4^2} = \frac{1}{16}$ (iii) $\frac{1}{9^3} = \frac{1}{729}$ (iv) $\frac{1}{5^3} = \frac{1}{125}$ (v) $\frac{1}{6^2} = \frac{1}{36}$ (vi) $\frac{1}{7^2} = \frac{1}{49}$ (vii) $\frac{1}{3^4} = \frac{1}{81}$ (viii) $\frac{1}{8^2} = \frac{1}{64}$ (ix) $\frac{1}{4^3} = \frac{1}{64}$ (x) $\frac{1}{5^2} = \frac{1}{25}$ **5.** (i) $\frac{2}{125}$ (ii) $\frac{3}{64}$ (iii) $\frac{5}{16}$ (iv) $\frac{4}{81}$ (v) $\frac{2}{64} = \frac{1}{32}$ (vi) $\frac{3}{49}$ (vii) $\frac{1}{4}$ (viii) $\frac{1}{12}$ (ix) $\frac{1}{8}$ (x) $\frac{1}{200}$ **6.** (i) 5 (ii) 7 (iii) 3 (iv) 2 (v) 2 (vi) 1 (vii) 6 (viii) 3 (ix) 2 (x) 11 **7.** (i) 2 (ii) 9 (iii) 16 (iv) 8 (v) 1,000 (vi) 25 (vii) 32 (viii) 27 (ix) 27 (x) 256

8. (i) $27x^6y^3$ (ii) $\frac{t^6}{4}$ **9.** (i) $\frac{1}{10}$ (ii) $\frac{1}{6}$ (iii) $\frac{1}{2}$ (iv) $\frac{1}{27}$ (v) $\frac{1}{27}$ (vi) $\frac{1}{4}$ (vii) $\frac{1}{243}$ (viii) $\frac{1}{25}$ (ix) $\frac{1}{32}$ (x) $\frac{1}{100{,}000}$ **10.** (i) $\frac{1}{2}$ (ii) $\frac{1}{5}$ (iii) $\frac{2}{3}$ (iv) $\frac{9}{5}$ (v) $\frac{2}{3}$ (vi) $\frac{2}{5}$ (vii) $\frac{8}{27}$ (viii) $\frac{9}{16}$ **11.** (i) $\frac{5}{6}$ (ii) $\frac{11}{2}$ (iii) $\frac{5}{2}$ (iv) $\frac{100}{9}$ (v) $\frac{9}{25}$ (vi) $\frac{25}{4}$ (vii) $\frac{27}{8}$ (viii) $\frac{16}{9}$

12. (i) 4.39 (ii) 57.19 (iii) 3.04 (iv) 1.90 (v) 15.61 (vi) 0.02 (vii) 11.51 (viii) 0.04 (ix) 2.02 (x) 2.15

13. (i) 2^2 (ii) 2^3 (iii) 2^4 (iv) 2^5 (v) 2^{-1} (vi) 2^{-2} (vii) $2^{\frac{1}{2}}$ (viii) $2^{\frac{1}{3}}$ (ix) $2^{-\frac{1}{2}}$ **14.** (i) 3^0 (ii) 3^2 (iii) 3^3 (iv) 3^4 (v) 3^{-1} (vi) 3^{-2} (vii) $3^{\frac{1}{2}}$ (viii) $3^{\frac{3}{2}}$ (ix) $3^{-\frac{1}{2}}$ **15.** (i) 5^2 (ii) 5^3 (iii) 5^{-1} (iv) 5^0 (v) 5^{-2} (vi) 5^{-3} (vii) $5^{\frac{1}{2}}$ (viii) $5^{\frac{1}{5}}$ (ix) $5^{-\frac{1}{2}}$

16. (i) 10^2 (ii) 10^3 (iii) 10^{-2} (iv) 10^4 (v) 10^{-1} (vi) 10^{-3} (vii) $10^{\frac{1}{2}}$ (viii) $10^{\frac{1}{100}}$ (ix) $10^{-\frac{1}{2}}$ (x) $10^{\frac{1}{6}}$ (xi) $10^{\frac{3}{2}}$ (xii) $10^{\frac{3}{2}}$

17. (i) $5^4 \times 4^4$ (ii) $3^6 \times 5^6$ (iii) $9^{\frac{1}{2}} \times 4^{\frac{1}{2}}$ (iv) $8^{\frac{1}{3}} \times 27^{\frac{1}{3}}$

18. (i) $\left(\frac{3}{4}\right)^8$ (ii) $\left(\frac{3}{5}\right)^9$ (iii) $\left(\frac{9}{16}\right)^{\frac{1}{2}}$ (iv) $\left(\frac{25}{64}\right)^{-\frac{1}{2}}$

Exercise 4.3

1. (i) $x = 2$ (ii) $x = 3$ (iii) $x = 3$ (iv) $x = 3$ (v) $x = 3$ (vi) $x = 4$ (vii) $x = 4$ (viii) $x = 3$ (ix) $x = 2$ (x) $x = 6$ **2.** (i) $x = 2$ (ii) $x = 3$ (iii) $x = 4$ (iv) $x = 6$ (v) $x = 10$ (vi) $x = 20$ (vii) $x = \frac{9}{4}$ (viii) $x = 2$ (ix) $x = \frac{3}{2}$ (x) $x = 3$ **3.** (i) 2^4 (ii) 2^3 (iii) $(2^3)^{\frac{1}{2}} = 2^{\frac{3}{2}}$ (iv) $\frac{17}{4}$ **4.** (i) 3^3 (ii) $\frac{9}{2}$ **5.** (i) 5^2 (ii) $5^{\frac{3}{2}}$ (iii) 7

6. (i) 7^2 (ii) $7^{\frac{1}{3}}$ (iii) −24 **7.** (i) $8^{\frac{1}{3}} = \sqrt[3]{8} = 2$ (ii) $4^{\frac{1}{4}} = (2^2)^{\frac{1}{4}} = 2^{\frac{1}{2}}$ (iii) $\frac{7}{2}$ **8.** 4 **9.** (i) $7\frac{1}{2}$ (ii) 5 (iii) $2\frac{1}{2}$ (iv) $\frac{1}{2}$ (v) $1\frac{1}{2}$ (vi) $\frac{5}{3} = 1\frac{2}{3}$ (vii) $\frac{3}{4}$ (viii) $\frac{9}{4}$ **10.** (i) $\frac{10}{3}$ (ii) $\frac{10}{3}$

11. (i)

$2^2 - 2$	$2^3 - 2^2$	$2^4 - 2^3$	$2^5 - 2^4$	$2^6 - 2^5$	$2^7 - 2^6$
2	2^2	2^3	2^4	2^5	2^6

(ii) 2^p (iii) 8 **12.** (i) $-\frac{1}{4}$ (ii) 4

13.

Level	0	1	2	3	4	5	6	7
No. of message	1	10	100	1000	10,000	100,000	1,000,000	10,000,000

(i) 10,000,000 messages (ii) 10,000,000,000 messages

14. (i) 2400 ants (ii) After 7 months the population will exceed 50,000

Exercise 4.4

1. (i) 3 (ii) 6 (iii) 17 (iv) 19 (v) 30 (vi) 28 (vii) 250 (viii) 20 (ix) 200 (x) 135 **2.** (i) False (ii) False (iii) True (iv) True **3.** (i) 6 (ii) 10 (iii) 4 (iv) 8 (v) 10 (vi) 3 (vii) 5 (viii) 2 (ix) 3 (x) 5 **4.** (i) $2\sqrt{2}$ (ii) $3\sqrt{5}$ (iii) $10\sqrt{3}$ (iv) $2\sqrt{3}$ (v) $4\sqrt{2}$ (vi) $10\sqrt{5}$ (vii) $3\sqrt{3}$ (viii) $3\sqrt{6}$ (ix) $5\sqrt{3}$ (x) $7\sqrt{2}$ **5.** $7\sqrt{2}$ **6.** $5\sqrt{3}$ **7.** $7\sqrt{5}$ **8.** $5\sqrt{11}$

Revision Exercises

1. (i) 5^{11} (ii) $8^0 = 1$ (iii) 3^6 (iv) 16^4 **2.** (i) 7^{-5} (ii) $15^{\frac{1}{8}}$ (iii) $17^{\frac{3}{5}}$ (iv) $5^{\frac{1}{2}}$ **3.** (i) 2^{16} (ii) 7^{22} (iii) 2^{24} (iv) 5^{35} **4.** (i) $5\sqrt{5}$ (ii) $7\sqrt{3}$ (iii) $7\sqrt{3}$ (iv) $3\sqrt{2}$ **5.** (i) a^{10} (ii) a^{24} (iii) $a^{\frac{3}{2}}$ (iv) a^2 **6.** (i) $17\sqrt{2}$ (ii) $20\sqrt{5}$ **7.** (i) 5 (ii) $\frac{3}{2}$ (iii) 6

8. (i) $\frac{1}{8}$ (ii) $\frac{11}{4}$ **9.** (i) $\frac{9}{2}$ (ii) (a) 7^3 (b) $\frac{1}{4}$ **10.** (i) 3^7 (ii) 3^{11} (iii) 2^6 (iv) $2^{\frac{9}{4}}$ **11.** $y^{-2}, y^0, y^{\frac{1}{2}}, y, y^2$ **12.** (i) xy^3z^3 (ii) $\frac{y^{\frac{5}{12}}z^{\frac{2}{15}}}{x}$ (iii) $x^6y^{\frac{3}{2}}z^{15}$ (iv) $\frac{z^3}{x^2y^4}$

13.

n	$2^{\frac{1}{n}}$
1	2
2	1.41
5	1.15
10	1.07
100	1.01

n	$\left(\frac{1}{2}\right)^{\frac{1}{n}}$
1	0.5
2	0.71
5	0.87
10	0.93
100	0.99

Exam Questions

1. 2

Chapter 5

Exercise 5.1

1. $x = -3$ or $x = -4$ **2.** $x = -1$ or $x = -9$ **3.** $p = -8$ or $p = -9$ **4.** $b = -5$ or $b = 3$ **5.** $x = 4$ **6.** $x = 9$ or $x = -8$ **7.** $y = 0$ or $y = 5$ **8.** $x = \pm 9$ **9.** $x = -2$ or $x = -5$ **10.** $y = 0$ or $y = -\frac{3}{2}$ **11.** $x = 0$ or $x = -12$ **12.** $x = 12$ or $x = -12$

Exercise 5.2

1. $x = \frac{5}{2}$ or $x = -9$ **2.** $t = \frac{-3}{2}$ or $t = 3$ **3.** $x = -\frac{4}{5}$ or $x = -3$ **4.** $x = \frac{3}{7}$ or $x = 3$ **5.** $x = 0$ or $x = \frac{7}{10}$ **6.** $y = \pm\frac{15}{7}$ **7.** $x = 5$ or $x = -1$ **8.** $x = -\frac{2}{7}$ or $x = 6$ **9.** $x = \pm 1$ **10.** $x = 0$ or $x = 3$ **11.** $x = 0$ or $x = 11$ **12.** $x = \frac{1}{2}$ or $x = 2$ **13.** $x = \frac{3}{4}$ or $x = 3$ **14.** $y = 0$ or $y = \frac{1}{3}$ **15.** $x = \pm\frac{4}{12} = \pm\frac{1}{3}$ **16.** $x = \pm 2$ **17.** $q = \frac{1}{5}$ or $q = 6$ **18.** $x = -\frac{5}{3}$ or $x = 6$ **19.** $x = -\frac{1}{2}$ or $x = 4$ **20.** $y = -1$ or $y = 7$ **21.** $x = 7$ or $x = -2$ **22.** $x = \frac{4}{5}$ or $x = -\frac{1}{2}$ **23.** $x = -\frac{1}{6}$ or $x = -2$ **24.** $p = \frac{3}{7}$ or $p = -\frac{3}{2}$ **25.** $e = -\frac{7}{2}$ or $e = 3$ **26.** $x = -\frac{2}{5}$ or $x = -1$

Exercise 5.3

1. -1 or -5 **2.** 4 or 3 **3.** 3 or -4 **4.** -2 or $\frac{-7}{2}$ **5.** 1 or $-\frac{5}{3}$ **6.** 1 or $-\frac{2}{7}$ **7.** 9 or $-\frac{1}{3}$ **8.** 2 or $-\frac{13}{4}$ **9.** 4 or $-\frac{3}{5}$ **10.** $-\frac{5}{2}$ or -17 **11.** $-\frac{1}{14}$ or $-\frac{1}{2}$ **12.** $-\frac{1}{2}$ or $\frac{2}{15}$

Exercise 5.4

1. -0.6 or -3.4 **2.** -0.7 or -8.3 **3.** -0.11 or -4.39 **4.** 2.05 or -2.55 **5.** -0.333 **6.** $-3 \pm \sqrt{5}$ **7.** $4 \pm \sqrt{7}$ **8.** $\frac{-1 \pm 3\sqrt{14}}{5}$ **9.** $\frac{-2 \pm \sqrt{10}}{4}$ **10.** $\frac{-2 \pm 4\sqrt{2}}{7}$ **11.** 4.22 or -2.72 **12.** 1.6 or -0.7 **13.** 0.9 or -2.3 **14.** 2.25 or -1.92 **15.** 0.271 or -0.396 **16.** 1.106 or -1.356 **17.** $\pm$ 0.9428 **18.** $\frac{5 \pm 2\sqrt{5}}{15}$ **19.** $\frac{-3 \pm \sqrt{39}}{3}$ **20.** 1.15 or 0.72

Exercise 5.5

1. $x = 4$ or $x = -2$ **2.** $x = -\frac{15}{7}$ or $x = 2$ **3.** $x = -3$ or $x = 2$ **4.** $x = 1$ or $x = \frac{7}{3}$ **5.** $x = 1$ **6.** $x = \frac{2}{3}$ or $x = 1$ **7.** $x = -\frac{1}{2}$ or $x = 2$ **8.** $x = -\frac{21}{11}$ or $x = 2$ **9.** $x = \frac{26}{15}$ or $x = \frac{1}{2}$ **10.** $x = 0$ or $x = \frac{1}{2}$ **11.** $x = -2.29, -3.71$ **12.** $x \approx 0.94, 0.26$ **13.** $x = 16.08, -2.58$ **14.** $x = 1.62, 0.25$ **15.** $x = 6.70, 0.30$

Exercise 5.6

1. $x^2 - 7x + 12 = 0$ **2.** $x^2 - 7x + 10 = 0$ **3.** $x^2 - x - 2 = 0$ **4.** $x^2 - 10x - 11 = 0$ **5.** $x^2 + 6x + 9 = 0$ **6.** $x^2 - 7x = 0$ **7.** $x^2 - 64 = 0$ **8.** $x^2 + 4x = 0$ **9.** $x^2 - 9 = 0$ **10.** $x^2 - 3px + 2p^2 = 0$ **11.** $x^2 - p^2 = 0$ **12.** $x^2 - (p + q)x + pq = 0$ **13.** $b = -8, c = 15$ **14.** $c = 0, b = 6$ **15.** $r = (-4)^2 = 16$ **16.** $c = a^2 = 6^2 = 36$

Exercise 5.7

1. (4,1) or (1,4) **2.** (−3,−4) or (4,3) **3.** (0,4) or (4,0) **4.** (5,−1) or (1,−5) **5.** (1,3) or (−3,1) **6.** $\left(-\frac{3}{5},\frac{3}{5}\right)$ or (−1,−1) **7.** (−2,3) or (−3,−2) **8.** (5,1) or (1,3) **9.** (1,1) or (−1,−1) **10.** (−7,−7) or (5,5) **11.** (3,4) or (4,3) **12.** $\left(4,\frac{7}{2}\right)$ or (7,2) **13.** $\left(-4,-\frac{3}{2}\right)$ or (5,3) **14.** (2,−4) or (−2,4) **15.** (−9,−21) or (6,9)

Exercise 5.8

1. (i) x^2 (ii) $3x$ (iii) $x^2 + 3x = 18$ (iv) $x = -6$ or $x = 3$ **2.** (i) $4x$ (ii) $5x^2$ (iii) $5x^2 + 4x = 28$ (iv) $x = \frac{-14}{5}$ or $x = 2$ **3.** (i) $y + 3$ (ii) $y^2 + (y + 3)^2 = 65$ (iii) (−7,−4), (4,7) **4.** (i) $n + 1$ (ii) $\frac{n(n+1)}{n^2+n}$ (iii) $n^2 + n = 56$ (iv) 7, 8 **5.** (i) $3n + 2$ (ii) $9n^2 + 6n$ (iii) $9n^2 + 6n = 483$ (iv) 21, 23 **6.** (i) $x + 14$ (ii) $x^2 + 14$ (iii) $x^2 + 14 = 2.5(x + 14)$ (iv) Girl: 6 years old, Father: 36 years old **7.** (i) Amy: $x + 5$ (ii) Caroline: $2(x + 5) = 2x + 10$ (iii) Bridget = 14, Amy = 19, Caroline = 38 **8.** (i) $(x + 5)$ m (ii) $(x^2 + 5x)$ m^2 (iii) $x^2 + 5x = 234$ (iv) 13n, 18m **9.** (i) $12 + x + x = (2x + 12)$ m (ii) $10 + x + x = (2x + 10)$ m (iii) $(4x^2 + 44x + 120)$ m^2 (iv) 1 m **10.** (i) **Corners:** The area of these squares is $x \times x = x^2$ m^2, **Top and Bottom:** The area of these rectangles is $x \times 8 = 8x$ m^2, **Sides:** The area of these rectangles is $x \times 10 = 10x$ m^2, **Centre:** The area of this rectangle is $8 \times 10 = 80$ m^2 (ii) $4x^2 + 36x - 63 = 0$ (iii) The overall width of the plot is $8 + 2x$, The overall length of the plot is $10 + 2x$ (iv) $4x^2 + 36x - 63 = 0$ (v) 1.5 m (vi) $x = 1.5 \Rightarrow$ Area $= (8 + 3)(10 + 3) = 143$ m^2 (vii) Elaine's method is best. **11.** (i) $l = (40 - 2x)$ m (ii) $w = (30 - 2x)$ m (iii) $(1200 - 140x + 4x)$ m^2 (iv) 5 cm **12.** (i) $(7 - 2x)$ cm (ii) $(7 - 2x)(22)$ cm^2 or $(154 - 44x)$ cm^2 (iii) 110 (iv) 1 (v) 110 cm^3 **13.** 13, 5, 12

14. (i)

	A to B	B to C
Distance (km)	10	12
Speed (km/hr)	x	$x - 1$
Time (hrs)	$\frac{10}{x}$	$\frac{12}{x-1}$

(ii) $x = 5$

15. (i)

Total Prize	€400	€400
No of members	x	$x + 2$
Prize per member	$\frac{400}{x}$	$\frac{400}{x+2}$

(iii) 8

16. (i)

	Ben	Ann
Distance (km)	45	12
Speed (km/hr)	x	$x + 1$
Time	$\frac{45}{x}$	$\frac{45}{x+1}$

(ii) $\frac{45}{x} - \frac{45}{x+1} = \frac{1}{2}$ (iii) **Ben:** 9 km/hr, **Ann:** 10 km/hr **17.** (i) $2x + 2y = 264$ (ii) $2y = 264 - 2x$ (iii) $y = 132 - x + 6$ (v) $1656 + 126x - x^2 = 4400$ (vi) length = 98 m or length = 28 m, width = 34 m or width = 104 m **18.** (i) $2x + 2y = 32$ (ii) $2y = 32 - 2x$ (iii) $xy = 60$ (iv) Length = 10 m, width = 6 m or Length = 6 m, width = 10 m **19.** (i) $V = 0\%$ (ii) $A = 42\frac{6}{7}\%$ **20.** (i) 24 m (ii) 8 m (iii) 4 secs **21.** (i) (2,−5) or (−5,2) (ii) 2 km East, 5 km South, 5 km West, 2 km North (iii) $\sqrt{29}$ km (each) **22.** (i) Production cost: €20,000 (ii) €4,000 (iii) $P(x) = -5x^2 + 450x - 3{,}000$ (iv) €7,125 (v) 10 items

Revision Exercises

1. (a) (i) $x = 0$ or $x = -3$ (ii) $x = -2$ or $x = 4$ (iii) $x = 2$ or $x = 10$ (iv) $x = -3$ or $x = 2$ (v) 0 or $\frac{-7}{2}$ (vi) $x = 10$ or $x = -10$ (vii) $x = \frac{3}{2}$ (viii) $x = \frac{10}{7}$ or $x = -\frac{10}{7}$ (b) (i) $x = -1$ or $x = 6$ (ii) $x = \frac{1}{2}$ (iii) $x = \frac{3}{5}$ (iv) $x = \frac{-4}{3}$ or $x = \frac{-5}{2}$ (c) (i) $x = \pm 5$ (ii) $x = 0$ or $x = 2$ (iii) $x = \frac{2}{5}$ or $x = -\frac{3}{4}$ **2.** (a) (i) 1.45 or −3.45 (ii) 11.57 or 0.43 (iii) 2.70 or −3.70 (iv) 6.22 or −3.22 (v) 0.37 or −1.37 (b) (i) $x = \frac{3 \pm \sqrt{5}}{2}$ (ii) $\frac{12 \pm \sqrt{136}}{4} = \frac{6 \pm \sqrt{34}}{2}$ (iii) $\frac{14 \pm \sqrt{116}}{10} = \frac{7 \pm \sqrt{29}}{5}$ **3.** (a) (i) $x^2 - 8x + 12 = 0$ (ii) $x^2 - 9x - 22 = 0$ (iii) $x^2 + 4x = 0$ (iv) $x^2 - 12x - 35 = 0$ (b) (i) $p = 8$ or $q = 16$ (ii) $b = -20$ or $c = 100$ (iii) $k = 25$ **4.** (i) $x = 8$ or $x = -7$ (ii) $x = -6$ or $x = 3$ (iii) $x = \frac{3}{2}$ or $x = 5$ (iv) $x = \frac{1}{5}$ or $x = 3$ **5.** (a) (i) 5, 6 (ii) −4,7 or 7, 4 (b) (i) (−5,−8) or (4,1) (ii) (2,1) or (−2,−1) (iii) $\left(-\frac{3}{2}, -10\right)$ or (5,3) (iv) $\left(-4, -\frac{3}{2}\right)$ or (5,3) **6.** (b) (i) (−3,−4) and (3,4) (ii) (−5,−1) and (5,1) **7.** (a) (i) x^2 (ii) $6x$ (iii) $x^2 + 6x = 55$ (iv) 5,−11 (b) (i) $y - 3$ (ii) $y(y - 3)$ (iii) $y^2 - 3y = 378$ (iv) 21,18 (c) length = 5 m, width = 6 m **8.** (a) (i) 60 m (ii) 4 seconds (iii) 8 seconds

(b) (i)

	Journey A	Journey B
Distance (km)	30	20
Speed (km/hrs)	x	$x + 1$
Time	$\frac{30}{x}$	$\frac{20}{x+1}$

(ii) 3 (c) (i) $x + y = 27$ (ii) $x^2 - y^2 = 81$ (iii) 15 and 12

Exam Questions

1. $x = 5.2$; $x = 0.8$ **2.** (a) $x = 3 \pm 4\sqrt{2}$ (b) $r = 8$ or $r = 7$, $s = 6$, $s = 4$ **3.** $x = 3$, $x = 4$ **4.** (a) $x = -2$, $x = 3$, or $x = 3$, $x = -2$ (b) Graph D **5.** $x = 2.3$ or $x = -1.2$

Chapter 6

Exercise 6.1

1. All except (c) **2.** (a), (b) and (d) are functions, (c) is not since one input gets mapped to two outputs, (e) is not for the same reason and also because one input is not mapped to any output. **3.** $B = \{3, 7, 11, 15, 19, 23\}$ **4.** (i) {1, 4, 9, 25, 36} (ii) {4, 9, 25, 49, 121} (iii) {0, 1, 4, 9, 16}

5.

	Domain	Codomain	Range
(i)	{0, 1, 2, 3}	{0, 3, 4, 6, 9}	{0, 3, 6, 9}
(ii)	{2, 5, 7, 9}	{4, 6, 7, 8, 11}	{4, 7, 11}
(iii)	{−3, 3, 4}	{5, 8, 13, 20}	{13, 20}
(iv)	{1, 2, 4, 6}	{5, 6, 7, 8, 11, 15, 19}	{5, 6, 7}

6. (i) Each input is mapped to a unique output. (ii) Domain = {1, 2, 3, 4}, Range = {8, 9, 10, 11} (iii) $x \rightarrow x + 7$ (iv) 70

7.

Shape	Number of sides
Triangle	3
Hexagon	6
Pentagon	5
Rectangle	4
Square	4
Rhombus	4
Octagon	8

Range = {3, 4, 5, 6, 8}

8. (i) $f : x \mapsto \frac{x}{2} + 3$ (ii) 5, 12, 0 (iii) 12 **9.** (i) 10 (ii) 2 (iii) 6 (iv) 0 (v) 14 (vi) 13

10.

x	$2x^2 - 6x + 1$	y
0	2(0) + 0 + 1	1
−2	2(4) + 12 + 1	21
3	2(9) − 18 + 1	1
−3	2(9) + 18 + 1	37
4	2(16) − 24 + 1	9
$\frac{1}{2}$	$2\left(\frac{1}{4}\right) - 3 + 1$	$-1\frac{1}{2}$

(i) 1 (ii) 21 (iii) 1 (iv) 37 (v) 9 (vi) $-1\frac{1}{2}$ **11.** (i) 2 (ii) $\frac{1}{3}$ (iii) $-\frac{2}{3}$ (iv) 3 (v) $\frac{5}{6}$ (vi) $\frac{2}{3}$ **12.** (i) 3 (ii) 1 (iii) $\frac{5}{2}$ (iv) $\frac{1}{3}$ **13.** 8 **14.** 4 **15.** (i) $-\frac{1}{2}$ (ii) $-\frac{1}{2}$ (iii) $\frac{2}{11}$ (iv) $\frac{2x - 1}{4x^2 + 2}$ (v) $\frac{x - x^2}{1 + 2x^2}$ (vi) $\frac{x + h - 1}{x^2 + 2hx + h^2 + 2}$ **16.** 8 **17.** (i) 19 (ii) 12 (iii) $f(-3) = g(-3)$ (iv) 5 **18.** $a = 2$, $b = 3$ **19.** $a = -\frac{5}{2}$, $b = \frac{17}{2}$ **20.** $a = 2$, $b = 3$ **21.** (a) −3, (b) 2 **22.** (a) 5, (b) 2 **23.** (i) $4x$ (iii) 100 (iv) 25 **24.** (i) $200 - x^2$ (ii) $10\sqrt{2}$ minutes (iii) 10 minutes

Exercise 6.2

1. (i) 0 (ii) 18 (iii) 32 (iv) 72 (v) 2 (vi) 8 (vii) 18 (viii) 72 **2.** (i) 6 (ii) 24 (iii) 38 (iv) 78 (v) 8 (vi) 14 (vii) 24 (viii) 78 **3.** (i) 5 (ii) 1 (iii) 37 (iv) 2 (v) 10 (vi) 17 (vii) $\frac{41}{16}$ (viii) $\frac{5}{4}$ **4.** (i) 240 (ii) 38 **5.** (i) $3x^2 + 8$ (ii) $9x^2 + 12x + 6$ **6.** (i) $16x + 15$ (ii) −17

Exercise 6.3

1. (i)

x	$6x - 2$	y	(x,y)
−2	6(−2) − 2	−14	(−2,−14)
−1	6(−1) − 2	−8	(−1,−8)
2	6(2) − 2	10	(2,10)

(ii)

x	$2 - 4x$	y	(x,y)
−3	2 − 4(−3)	14	(−3,14)
−2	2 − 4(−2)	10	(−2,10)
1	2 − 4(1)	−2	(1,−2)

(iii)

x	$2 - 3x$	y	(x,y)
0	2 − 3(0)	2	(0,2)
1	2 − 3(1)	−1	(1,−1)
5	2 − 3(5)	−13	(5,−13)

(iv)

x	$x + 6$	y	(x,y)
6	6 + 6	12	(6,12)
7	7 + 6	13	(7,13)
12	12 + 6	18	(12,18)

(v)

x	$2x + \frac{3}{4}$	y	(x,y)
-8	$2(-8) + \frac{3}{4}$	$-15\frac{1}{4}$	$\left(-8,-15\frac{1}{4}\right)$
-7	$2(-7) + \frac{3}{4}$	$-13\frac{1}{4}$	$\left(-7,-13\frac{1}{4}\right)$
-2	$2(-2) + \frac{3}{4}$	$-3\frac{1}{4}$	$\left(-2,-3\frac{1}{4}\right)$

(vi)

x	$\frac{1}{5} - x$	y	(x,y)
-2	$\frac{1}{5} - (-2)$	$2\frac{1}{5}$	$\left(-2,2\frac{1}{5}\right)$
-1	$\frac{1}{5} - (-1)$	$1\frac{1}{5}$	$\left(-1,1\frac{1}{5}\right)$
2	$\frac{1}{5} - (2)$	$-1\frac{4}{5}$	$\left(2,-1\frac{4}{5}\right)$

(vii)

x	$\frac{x}{2} + \frac{3}{2}$	y	(x,y)
0	$\frac{0}{2} + \frac{3}{2}$	$\frac{3}{2}$	$\left(0,\frac{3}{2}\right)$
1	$\frac{1}{2} + \frac{3}{2}$	2	(1,2)
5	$\frac{5}{2} + \frac{3}{2}$	4	(5,4)

(viii)

x	$3x + \frac{1}{2}$	y	(x,y)
6	$3(6) + \frac{1}{2}$	$18\frac{1}{2}$	$\left(6,18\frac{1}{2}\right)$
7	$3(7) + \frac{1}{2}$	$21\frac{1}{2}$	$\left(7,21\frac{1}{2}\right)$
12	$3(12) + \frac{1}{2}$	$36\frac{1}{2}$	$\left(12,36\frac{1}{2}\right)$

(ix)

x	$\frac{4}{5}x + \frac{1}{5}$	y	(x,y)
-8	$\frac{4}{5}(-8) + \frac{1}{5}$	$-6\frac{1}{5}$	$\left(-8,-6\frac{1}{5}\right)$
-7	$\frac{4}{5}(-7) + \frac{1}{5}$	$-5\frac{2}{5}$	$\left(-7,-5\frac{2}{5}\right)$
-2	$\frac{4}{5}(-2) + \frac{1}{5}$	$-1\frac{2}{5}$	$\left(-2,-1\frac{2}{5}\right)$

(x)

x	$-0.2x$	y	(x,y)
-2	-0.2(-2)	0.4	(-2,0.4)
-1	-0.2(-1)	0.2	(-1,0.2)
2	-0.2(2)	-0.4	(2,-0.4)

2.

x	$3x - 1$	y	(x,y)
-3	3(-3) - 1	-10	(-3,-10)
-2	3(-2) - 1	-7	(-2,-7)
4	3(4) - 1	11	(4,11)

(i) 2.9 (ii) $-\frac{5}{3}$

3.

x	$4x - 3$	y	(x,y)
-3	4(-3) - 3	-15	(-3,-15)
-2	4(-2) - 3	-11	(-2,-11)
4	4(4) - 3	13	(4,13)

(i) 7 (ii) $\frac{9}{4}$ (iii) −1 (iv) $x \geq 1$

4.

x	$2x - 2$	y	(x,y)
-1	2(-1) - 2	-4	(-1,-4)
0	2(0) - 2	-2	(0,-2)
4	2(4) - 2	6	(4,6)

x	$8 - 4x$	y	(x,y)
-1	8 - 4(-1)	12	(-1,12)
0	8 - 4(0)	8	(0,8)
4	8 - 4(4)	-8	(4,-8)

Point of intersection is $\left(\frac{5}{3}, \frac{4}{3}\right)$

5.

t	$15 - 3t$	v	(t,v)
0	15 - 3(0)	15	(0,15)
1	15 - 3(1)	12	(1,12)
5	15 - 3(5)	0	(5,0)

(i) 8.1 m/s (ii) $\frac{5}{3}$ seconds (iii) 15 m/s (iv) 5 seconds

6. (i)

Miles	10	20	30	40	50	60	70	80	90	100
Kilometres	16	32	48	64	80	96	112	128	144	160

(ii) 120 km (iii) $87\frac{1}{2}$ miles (iv) [104 km, 120 km]

7. (i)

x	$5x$	y	(x, y)
0	5(0)	0	(0, 0)
10,000	5(10,000)	50,000	(10,000, 50,000)
50,000	5(50,000)	250,000	(50,000, 250,000)

(ii) Answer on graph in part (i).
(iii) Total Costs = $5x$ + 45,000 (in €)

(iv)

x	$5x$ + 45,000	y	(x,y)
0	0 + 45,000	45,000	(0, 45,000)
10,000	50,000 + 45,000	95,000	(10,000, 95,000)
50,000	250,000 + 45,000	295,000	(50,000, 295,000)

Answer on graph in part (i)
(v) Sales Revenue = $6x$ (in €)

(vi)

x	$6x$	y	(x,y)
0	6(0)	0	(0, 0)
10,000	6(10,000)	60,000	(10,000, 60,000)
50,000	6(50,000)	300,000	(50,000, 300,000)

Answer on graph in part (i) (vii) 45,000 units

Exercise 6.4

1.

1	$x^2 - x - 6$	A
2	$x^2 + 2x + 1$	C
3	$-x^2 + x + 6$	B
4	$4 - 2x - x^2$	D

2.

x	$x^2 + 2x + 3$	y	(x,y)
−3	$(-3)^2 + 2(-3) + 3$	6	(−3,6)
−2	$(-2)^2 + 2(-2) + 3$	3	(−2,3)
−1	$(-1)^2 + 2(-1) + 3$	2	(−1,2)
0	$(0)^2 + 2(0) + 3$	3	(0,3)
1	$(1)^2 + 2(1) + 3$	6	(1,6)
2	$(2)^2 + 2(2) + 3$	11	(2,11)

3. (i)

x	$x^2 + x + 2$	y	(x,y)
-3	$(-3)^2 + (-3) + 2$	8	(-3,8)
-2	$(-2)^2 + (-2) + 2$	4	(-2,4)
-1	$(-1)^2 + (-1) + 2$	2	(-1,2)
0	$(0)^2 + (0) + 2$	2	(0,2)
1	$(1)^2 + (1) + 2$	4	(1,4)

(ii)

x	$2x^2 + x - 2$	y	(x,y)
-3	$2(-3)^2 + (-3) - 2$	13	(-3,13)
-2	$2(-2)^2 + (-2) - 2$	4	(-2,4)
-1	$2(-1)^2 + (-1) - 2$	-1	(-1,-1)
0	$2(0)^2 + (0) - 2$	-2	(0,-2)
1	$2(1)^2 + (1) - 2$	1	(1,1)

(iii)

x	$14 - 3x - 4x^2$	y	(x,y)
-3	$14 - 3(-3) - 4(-3)^2$	-13	(-3,-13)
-2	$14 - 3(-2) - 4(-2)^2$	4	(-2,4)
-1	$14 - 3(-1) - 4(-1)^2$	13	(-1,13)
0	$14 - 3(0) - 4(0)^2$	14	(0,14)
1	$14 - 3(1) - 4(1)^2$	7	(1,7)

(iv)

x	$x^2 + 2x + 12$	y	(x,y)
-3	$(-3)^2 + 2(-3) + 12$	15	(-3,15)
-2	$(-2)^2 + 2(-2) + 12$	12	(-2,12)
-1	$(-1)^2 + 2(-1) + 12$	11	(-1,11)
0	$(0)^2 + 2(0) + 12$	12	(0,12)
1	$(1)^2 + 2(1) + 12$	15	(1,15)

(v)

x	$-x^2 + 3x + 7$	y	(x,y)
-3	$-(-3)^2 - 3(-3) + 7$	7	(-3,7)
-2	$-(-2)^2 - 3(-2) + 7$	9	(-2,9)
-1	$-(-1)^2 - 3(-1) + 7$	9	(-1,9)
0	$-(0)^2 - 3(0) + 7$	7	(0,7)
1	$-(1)^2 - 3(1) + 7$	3	(1,3)

4. (i)

x	$6x - x^2$	y	(x,y)
0	$6(0) - (0)^2$	0	(0,0)
1	$6(1) - (1)^2$	5	(1,5)
2	$6(2) - (2)^2$	8	(2,8)
3	$6(3) - (3)^2$	9	(3,9)
4	$6(4) - (4)^2$	8	(4,8)
5	$6(5) - (5)^2$	5	(5,5)
6	$6(6) - (6)^2$	0	(6,0)

(iii) 9 metres (iv) 0.35 metres or 5.65 metres **5.** (i) −4.5 (ii) −1.45 OR 3.45 (iii) $-1.45 \leqslant x \leqslant 3.45$ (iv) −6 **6.** (i) −9.75 (ii) −6.5 **OR** 0.5 (iii) −6.75 **OR** 0.75 (iv) −7.15 **OR** 1.15 (v) −12. **7.** (i) 6 (ii) $\frac{2}{3}$ (iii) 1 **8.** (i) 16 (ii) 0.6 **OR** 6.9 (iii) $0.6 \leqslant x \leqslant 6.9$ (iv) $0 \leqslant x \leqslant 0.6$ **OR** $6.9 \leqslant x \leqslant 8$ **9.** (i) −2 (ii) −1.3 **OR** 2.8 (iii) −0.7 **OR** 2.2 **10.** (i) $y = 8 - x$, $8x - x^2$ (m^2) (iii) 16 m^2 **11.** (i) 5.75 (ii) −3 **OR** 1 (iii) 6 (iv) $2 \leqslant k \leqslant 6$ **12.** (i) $x = -2.6$ OR $x = 0.6$ (ii) $-3 \leqslant x \leqslant -2.6$ **OR** $0.6 \leqslant x \leqslant 2$ **13.** (ii) 2 seconds or 4 seconds (iii) $j + 1 = 1 + 1.2x$ (See graph in part (i)) (iv) 0.2 seconds (v) 1.3 metres **14.** (ii) €2,500 (iii) 500 units (iv) 400 units or 600 units

Exercise 6.5

1. (i) (b) $x = -1$ $x = 2$ and $x = 3$ (ii) (b) $x = -3$ $x = -0.5$ and $x = 2$ (iii) (b) $x = -2$ $x = -1$ and $x = 3$ **2.** (i) $x = -1, 0$ **OR** 3 (ii) $x = -1.5, 0.8$ **OR** 2.7 (iii) $-0.5 < x < 1.85$ (b) (i) $x = -2, -1.5, 2$ (ii) $x = -2.6, -0.7, 1.75$ (iii) $-1.75 < x < 0.85$ (c) (i) $x = -1.5, 2$ (ii) $x = -1.2, 0.9, 2.9$ (iii) $-0.4 < x < 2$ **3.** (i) $x = -2, -0.5$ **OR** 2 (ii) $x = -1.65, -1$ **OR** 2.15 **4.** (i) $x = \frac{2}{3}$ (ii) $x = -2.8, -1.45$ **OR** 0.25 **5.** (i) $x = -3, -1$ **OR** 1 (ii) $-2.2 < x < 0.2$ (iii) $x = 1.45$ **6.** (i) 12,000 units (ii) 0.65 years (iii) At time = 0 years, and at time = 2 years (iv) 30,000 units **7.** (i) $x = 4.9$ (ii) $x = -0.45$ **OR** 0.6 (iii) $x = -0.4, 1.15$ **OR** 1.45 **8.** (i) 30 °C (ii) 1 minute and 4 minutes (iii) 13 °C (iv) [0.7 minutes, 1.3 minutes] **OR** [3.95 minutes, 4 minutes] **9.** (i) 1.85 years (ii) 0.4 years **OR** 3.8 years

Exercise 6.6

1.

x	2^x	y	(x,y)
-2	2^{-2}	$\frac{1}{4}$	$\left(-2,\frac{1}{4}\right)$
-1	2^{-1}	$\frac{1}{2}$	$\left(-1,\frac{1}{2}\right)$
0	2^0	1	(0,1)
1	2^1	2	(1,2)
2	2^2	4	(2,4)
3	2^3	8	(3,8)

2.

x	4^x	y	(x,y)
-2	4^{-2}	$\frac{1}{16}$	$\left(-2,\frac{1}{16}\right)$
-1	4^{-1}	$\frac{1}{4}$	$\left(-1,\frac{1}{4}\right)$
0	4^0	1	(0,1)
1	4^1	4	(1,4)
2	4^2	16	(2,16)
3	4^3	64	(3,64)

3.

x	3^x	y	(x,y)
-2	3^{-2}	$\frac{1}{9}$	$\left(-2,\frac{1}{9}\right)$
-1	3^{-1}	$\frac{1}{3}$	$\left(-1,\frac{1}{3}\right)$
0	3^0	1	(0,1)
1	3^1	3	(1,3)
2	3^2	9	(2,9)
3	3^3	27	(3,27)

4.

x	5^{-x}	y	(x,y)
-2	5^2	25	(-2,25)
-1	5^1	5	(-1,5)
0	5^0	1	(0,1)
1	5^{-1}	$\frac{1}{5}$	$\left(1,\frac{1}{5}\right)$
2	5^{-2}	$\frac{1}{25}$	$\left(2,\frac{1}{25}\right)$
3	5^{-3}	$\frac{1}{125}$	$\left(3,\frac{1}{125}\right)$

5.

x	3^{-x}	y	(x,y)
-2	3^2	9	(-2,9)
-1	3^1	3	(-1,3)
0	3^0	1	(0,1)
1	3^{-1}	$\frac{1}{3}$	$\left(1,\frac{1}{3}\right)$
2	3^{-2}	$\frac{1}{9}$	$\left(2,\frac{1}{9}\right)$
3	3^{-3}	$\frac{1}{27}$	$\left(3,\frac{1}{27}\right)$

6.

x	$3(3^x)$	y	(x,y)
-2	$3(3^{-2})$	$\frac{1}{3}$	$\left(-2,\frac{1}{3}\right)$
-1	$3(3^{-1})$	1	(-1,1)
0	$3(3^0)$	3	(0,3)
1	$3(3^1)$	9	(1,9)
2	$3(3^2)$	27	(2,27)

7.

x	$3(2^x)$	y	(x,y)
-2	$3(2^{-2})$	$\frac{3}{4}$	$-2,\frac{3}{4}$
-1	$3(2^{-1})$	$\frac{3}{2}$	$-1,\frac{3}{2}$
0	$3(2^0)$	3	(0,3)
1	$3(2^1)$	6	(1,6)
2	$3(2^2)$	12	(2,12)

8.

x	$4(2^x)$	y	(x,y)
-2	$4(2^{-2})$	1	(-2,1)
-1	$4(2^{-1})$	2	(-1,2)
0	$4(2^0)$	4	(0,4)
1	$4(2^1)$	8	(1,8)
2	$4(2^2)$	16	(2,16)

9.

x	$2(4^x)$	y	(x,y)
-2	$2(4^{-2})$	$\frac{1}{8}$	$\left(-2,\frac{1}{8}\right)$
-1	$2(4^{-1})$	$\frac{1}{2}$	$\left(-1,\frac{1}{2}\right)$
0	$2(4^0)$	2	(0,2)
1	$2(4^1)$	8	(1,8)
2	$2(4^2)$	32	(2,32)

13. $a = 6, b = 2$ **14.** $a = 3, b = 2$ **15.** $a = 2.5, b = 2$ **16.** $a = 4, b = \frac{1}{2}$ **17.** $a = 2, b = \frac{1}{3}$

18. (i)

x	y	(x,y)
0	10	(0,10)
1	20	(1,20)
2	40	(2,40)
3	80	(3,80)
4	160	(4,160)

x = time (hours), y = volume (cm^3) (iii) 60 cm^3 (iv) 3.3 hours **19.** (i) 720,500 is the initial population in 1980; 1.022 is the rate at which the population is increasing (ii) 895,660 (iii) 2015 **20.** (i) $800(1.05)x$ (ii) Approx 1181 beetles

21.

t	1	2	3	4	5	6
P1	89	162	223	266	285	274
P2	45	67.5	101.25	151.875	227.8125	341.71875

22. (i)

Year	Cost (€)/ NBV	Rate of depreciation	Depreciation (€)	NBV (€)
1	60,000.00	0.2	12,000.00	48,000.00
2	48,000.00	0.2	9,600.00	38,400.00
3	38,400.00	0.2	7,680.00	30,720.00
4	30,720.00	0.2	6,144.00	24,576.00
5	24,576.00	0.2	4,915.20	19,660.80

(ii) €19,660.80 (iii) $F = p(1 - i)^t \Rightarrow F = 60{,}000(0.8)^t$

23. (i) $F = P(1 - i)^t$, Base = $(1 - i)$, Exponent = t (ii) $5{,}000(0.9)^3$ = €3,645 (iv) €3,850 (v) €3,842.17

Revision Exercises

1. All except (c) and (e) **2.** (i) and (ii) **3.** (i) {1, 2, 4, 8} (ii) {2, 4, 8, 16} **4.** (i) $5x$ (ii) {0, 1, 2, 3, ..., 14, 15} (iii) €65 **5.** (i) 2 (ii) 26 (iii) 6 (iv) 46 (v) 32 **6.** (i) 3 (ii) 0 (iii) 15 (iv) ±2 **7.** 3 **8.** 3 **9.** (i) {0, 3, 8, 24, 35} (ii) {3, 8, 24, 48, 120} (iii) {−1, 0, 3, 8, 15} **10.** (i) 5 (ii) $x = 3$ **OR** −2 (iii) $f(x)$ is never equal to x **11.** (i) 4 (ii) 31 (iii) 52 (iv) 112 (v) 7 (vi) 16 (vii) 31 (viii) 112

12. (i)

x	$3x - 4$	y	(x,y)
−2	3(−2)−4	−10	(−2,−10)
−1	3(−1)−4	−7	(−1,−7)
0	3(0)−4	−4	(0,−4)
1	3(1) − 4	−1	(1,−1)
2	3(2) − 4	2	(2,2)

(ii)

x	$2 - 2.5x$	y	(x,y)
−3	2 − 2.5(−3)	9.5	(−3,9.5)
−2	2 − 2.5(−2)	7	(−2,7)
−1	2 − 2.5(−1)	4.5	(−1,4.5)
0	2 − 2.5(0)	2	(0,2)
1	2 − 2.5(1)	−0.5	(1,−0.5)

(iii)

x	$6 - 4x$	y	(x,y)
0	6 − 4(0)	6	(0,6)
1	6 − 4(1)	2	(1,2)
2	6 − 4(2)	−2	(2,−2)
3	6 − 4(3)	−6	(3,−6)
4	6 − 4(4)	−10	(4,−10)
5	6 − 4(5)	−14	(5,−14)

13. (i) $f(x) = 5.5$ (ii) $x = 2.7$ (iii) $x = -1$ (iv) $x \geqslant 0.1$

14. (3.2,1.6)

15. (i)

Income (€)	10	20	30	40	50	60	70	80	90	100
Number of times to go out	3	5	7	9	11	13	15	17	19	21

(ii) 12 times (iii) €70 (iv) ⩾ €35

16.

x	$x^2 - 3x - 4$	y	(x,y)
−2	$(-2)^2 - 3(-2) - 4$	6	(−2,6)
−1	$(-1)^2 - 3(-1) - 4$	0	(−1,0)
0	$(0)^2 - 3(0) - 4$	−4	(0,−4)
1	$(1)^2 - 3(1) - 4$	−6	(1,−6)
2	$(2)^2 - 3(2) - 4$	−6	(2,−6)
3	$(3)^2 - 3(3) - 4$	−4	(3,−4)
4	$(4)^2 - 3(4) - 4$	0	(4,0)

(i) −5.75 (ii) $-1 \leqslant x \leqslant 4$ (iii) −6.25 (iv) $x = -1.2$
17. (i) $-4 \leqslant k < 8.25$ (ii) 8.25 (iii) $x = -4$ **OR** $x = 1$ (iv) 8.25 **18.** (i) $x = -1$ **OR** $x = 1$ (ii) $x \leqslant -1$ **OR** $x \geqslant 1$ (iii) $-1 < x < 1$ **19.** $a = -1, b = -2, c = 4$ **20.** $a = 6, b = 8$ **21.** $a = -1, b = 8$ **22.** $a = 1, b = -10$ **23.** (i) 275 m (ii) 55 m/s (iii) $t = 4$ **OR** $t = 12$ (seconds) **24.**(i) $x = 1$ (ii) $x = 1.5$ (iii) 3 real roots **25.** (i) $\frac{2}{3}$ (ii) $x = -2, -1$ **OR** 0 (iii) One real root **26.** $x = 2.35$ **27.** $a = -6, b = 11$ **29.** (i) 2.75 (ii) $x = 3$ (iii) $x = -0.85$ **31.** $a = 6$ **32.** $a = 2, b = -\frac{1}{4}$

33. (i)

Year	1	2	3	4	5
Value (€)	448	501.76	561.97	629.41	704.94

(iii) Exponent = 5, Base = 1.12 (iv) €580 **34.** (i) €100,000

(ii)

Year	0	1	2	3	4	5
Value (€)	100,000	25,000	6,250	1,562.50	390.63	97.66

(iii) Roughly 0.5 years (6 months) (iv) No

36. (i)

x	0	0.5	1	1.5	2	2.5	3
$f(x)$	1	1.4	2	2.8	4	5.7	8
$g(x)$	−1	2.75	5	5.75	5	2.75	−1

(ii) $x = 0.25$ **OR** $x = 2.15$ (iii) 2.25

Exam Questions

1. (a) $y = 10.5 - x$

(b) (i)

x	0	1	2	3	4	5	6	7	8	9	10
y	10.5	9.5	8.5	7.5	6.5	5.5	4.5	3.5	2.5	1.5	0.5
A (m^2)	0	9.5	17	22.5	26	27.5	27	24.5	20	13.5	5

(c)

Maximum area	$27.5 \leq A \leq 28$
x value	$5 \leq X \leq 5.5$
y value	$5.5 \geq Y \geq 5$

2. (a) (i)

Time (hours)	0	1	2	3	4	5
Company A charge $A(h)$ (€)	30	39.5	49	58.5	68	77.5
Company B charge $B(h)$ (€)	10	17.4	30.28	52.68	91.66	159.49

(b) B is Cheaper (from graph) (c) $h \approx 3.2$ (d) 190.52
3. (a) $A(1, 4), B(3, 6)$ (b) (ii) 18 square units
4. (a) $x = -2, x = 3$ (b) Graph D

5. (a)

Time, t	0	1	2	3	4	5	6	7	8	9	10
Height, h	0	9	16	21	24	25	24	21	16	9	0

(c) (i) 19 m (ii) 7.5 s (iii) (5, 25) (d) (i) $m = -3$ (ii) $m = -5$

6. (a)

x	0	0.5	1	1.5	2	2.5	3
$f(x)$	1	1.414	2	2.828	4	5.657	8
$g(x)$	−1	2.75	5	5.75	5	2.75	−1

Chapter 7

Exercise 7.1

1. (i) ♦ (ii) ÷ (iii) ∠ (iv) ➢ (v) ⌖ **2.** (i) red, red, blue (ii) blue, blue, red (iii) blue, red, green (iv) brown, blue, green **4.** (i) hexagon (ii) triangle (iii) hexagon (iv) triangle **5.** (i) square (ii) triangle (iii) circle **6.** (i) triangle (ii) hexagon (iii) yellow

8. (i)

Pattern number	1	2	3	4	5	6
Number of sticks	2	3	5	7	11	13

Exercise 7.2

1. (i) Yes (ii) Yes (iii) No (iv) No (v) Yes (vi) Yes (vii) Yes (viii) No (ix) Yes (x) Yes **2.** (a) (i) 2 (ii) 5

(iii) 19 (iv) 100 (v) 13 (vi) −5 (vii) 5.5 (viii) 1 (ix) 72 (x) $\frac{1}{6}$ (b) (i) 4 (ii) 2 (iii) −3 (iv) −10 (v) 7 (vi) 2 (vii) 0.5 (viii) $\frac{1}{4}$ (ix) −11 (x) $\frac{1}{6}$ (c) (i) 14, 18, 22 (ii) 13, 15, 17 (iii) 10, 7, 4 (iv) 70, 60, 50 (v) 34, 41, 48 (vi) 1, 3, 5 (vii) 7, 7.5, 8 (viii) $1\frac{3}{4}, 2, 2\frac{1}{4}$ (ix) 39, 28, 17 (x) $\frac{2}{3}, \frac{5}{6}, 1$ **3.** (a) (i) −3 (ii) −50 (iii) 1.6 (iv) 4 (v) $2\frac{1}{2}$ (vi) $-1\frac{1}{2}$ (vii) $2\frac{3}{4}$ (viii) 4.4 (ix) $\frac{1}{10}$ (x) $-\frac{1}{8}$ (b) (i) −12, −15, −18 (ii) 60, 10, −40 (iii) 9.2, 10.8, 12.4 (iv) 4, 8, 12 (v) $-5, -2\frac{1}{2}, 0$ (vi) $12\frac{1}{2}, 11, 9\frac{1}{2}$ (vii) $19\frac{1}{4}, 22, 24\frac{3}{4}$ (viii) 3.4, 7.8, 12.2 (ix) $\frac{3}{10}, \frac{2}{5}, \frac{1}{2}$ (x) $\frac{5}{8}, \frac{1}{2}, \frac{3}{8}$ **4.** (a) (i) 1 (ii) 3 (iii) −5 (iv) 40 (v) −11 (b) (i) 5 (ii) 4 (iii) 4 (iv) −5 (v) 2 (c) (i) 16 (ii) 15 (iii) 7 (iv) 25 (v) −5

5. (ii)

Term	T_1	T_2	T_3	T_4	T_5
Number of dots	6	9	12	15	18

(iii) Arithmetic sequence (iv) 27

6. (ii)

T_1	T_2	T_3	T_4	T_5
4	7	10	13	16

(iii) Arithmetic sequence (iv) 28

7. (ii)

T_1	T_2	T_3	T_4	T_5
6	8	10	12	14

(iii) Arithmetic sequence (iv) 18 (v) 8

8. (ii)

T_1	T_2	T_3	T_4	T_5
6	9	12	15	18

(iii) Arithmetic sequence (iv) 24 **9.** (i) Sequence A: 2, 4, 8, Sequence B: 1, 4, 9, Sequence C: 5, 9, 13 (ii) Sequence C (iii) 4 **10.** (i) Sequence A: 3, 9, 27, Sequence B: 2, 5, 10, Sequence C: 3, 5, 7 (ii) Sequence C (iii) 2 **11.** (i) $d_A = 6$, $d_B = 2$, $d_C = 3$ (ii) $m_A = 6$, $m_B = 2$, $m_C = 3$ (iii) Slope = common difference **12.** 4 **13.** 3 **14.** (i) 7 (ii) −3 (iii) 14 **15.** (i) 7 (ii) −4 (iii) $T_4 = 7$, $T_5 = 3$

Exercise 7.3

1. (a) (i) 5 (ii) 4 (iii) 1 (iv) 13 (v) 59 (vi) −12 (vii) 43 (viii) −16 (ix) 75 (x) −20 (b) (i) 2 (ii) 3 (iii) 4 (iv) 7 (v) −2 (vi) 5 (vii) −3 (viii) −4 (ix) 9 (x) 3 (c) (i) $2n + 3$ (ii) $3n + 1$ (iii) $4n - 3$ (iv) $7n + 6$ (v) $-2n + 61$ (vi) $5n - 17$ (vii) $-3n + 46$ (viii) $-4n - 12$ (ix) $9n + 66$ (x) $3n - 23$ **2.** (i) $-4n - 7$ (ii) −227 **3.** (i) $12n - 2$ (ii) 766 **4.** (i) $7n - 7$ (ii) 588 **5.** (i) $6n + 1$ (ii) 199 **6.** (i) $8n - 5$ (ii) 763 **7.** (i) $-6n + 37$ (ii) −89 **8.** (i) $4n + 1$ (ii) 221 **9.** (i) $n = 35$ **10.** 46 **11.** 21 **12.** 34 **13.** (i) $T_n = 207 - 7n$ (ii) 29 terms are positive (iii) −3 **14.** (a) (i) 3, 5, 7, 9 (ii) 2, 5, 8, 11 (iii) 4, 7, 12, 19 (iv) 10, 8, 6, 4 (v) $1, \frac{1}{2}, \frac{1}{3}, \frac{1}{4}$ (b) (i) arithmetic (ii) arithmetic (iii) not arithmetic (iv) not arithmetic (v) not arithmetic **15.** (a) (i) 5, 9, 13, 17 (ii) 10, 7, 4, 1 (iii) 5, 11, 21, 35 (iv) 7, 4, 1, −2 (v) 4, 16, 64, 256 (b) (i) arithmetic (ii) arithmetic (iii) not arithmetic (iv) arithmetic (v) not arithmetic **16.** 8 **17.** (i) 2, −3 (ii) $2n - 5$ **18.** −502 **19.** (i) $a + d$ (ii) $a + 3d$ (iii) $a + 9d$ (iv) 3, 5

20. (i)

	A	B	C	D	E
Row 1			2	3	4
Row 2	7	6	5		
Row 3			8	9	10
Row 4	13	12	11		
Row 5			14	15	16
Row 6	19	18	17		
Row 7			20	21	22
Row 8	25	24	23		
Row 9			26	27	28

(ii) 301 (iii) 298 (iv) Row 670 of Column A

Exercise 7.4

1. (i) 2,310 (ii) 480 (iii) 290 (iv) 780 (v) 1,590 **2.** (i) 1,425 (ii) 2,265 (iii) 2,895 (iv) 180 (v) 165 **3.** (i) 430 (ii) 190 (iii) −230 (iv) −170 (v) 50 **4.** 3240 **5.** 900 **6.** 1640 **7.** (i) 280 (ii) 1,160 (iii) 880 **8.** (i) 1,560 (ii) 6,320 (iii) 4,760 **9.** (i) 737 (ii) 4,785 (iii) 1,968 (iv) 396 (v) 1,683 **10.** (i) $4n + 1$ (ii) 221 (iii) 5,150 **11.** (i) €395 (ii) €14,850 **12.** 13, Common difference = 4 **13.** (i) 5 (ii) 2 (iii) $2n + 3$ (iv) $n^2 + 4n$ (v) 43 (vi) 1020 **14.** (i) (a) 3 (b) 2 (c) 35 (ii) (a) −2 (b) 3 (c) 20 (iii) (a) 5 (b) 4 (c) 65 (a) 7 (b) 1 (c) 45 **15.** (i) 34, 30, 26 (ii) −2 (iii) 90 (iv) 18 **16.** (a)

Year	1	2	3	4	5	6
Eoin's salary	20,000	20,500	21,000	21,500	22,000	22,500
Peter's salary	17,000	18,250	19,500	20,750	22,000	23,250

(b) 2009 (d) $19{,}500 + 500n$ (e) €25,000 (f) $625n^2 + 16{,}375n$ (g) €2,55,750 (h) It should be represented as a series of dots and not dots joined with straight lines.

17.

Row number	1	3	5	7	9	11
No. of red seats	2	3	4	5	6	7

(i) 27 red seats

(ii)

T_2	T_4	T_6	...	T_{98}
2	3	4		

50 red seats in 98th row (iii) 2650

Exercise 7.5

1. (ii)

Term	1	2	3	4	5
No. of dots	1	3	6	10	15

(iii) Quadratic (iv) 28

2. (ii)

T_1	T_2	T_3	T_4	T_5
1	4	9	16	25

(iii) Quadratic (iv) 64 (v) $L_n = n$ (vi) $H_n = n$ (vii) n^2 **3.** (i) Quadratic (ii) Exponential (iii) Quadratic (iv) Quadratic (v) Linear (vi) Exponential (vii) Quadratic (viii) Linear (ix) Exponential (x) Exponential **4.** (a) (i) 8 (ii) 1 (iii) 7 (iv) 3 (v) 15 (vi) 8 (vii) 5 (viii) 1 (ix) 10 (b) 1st: (i) 6, 10, 14 (ii) 2, 3, 4 (iii) 9, 15, 21 (iv) 10, 14, 18 (v) 8, 16, 24 (vi) 4, 2, 0, −2 (vii) 2, −2, −6, −10 (viii) −3, 0, 3 (ix) −6, −3, 0, 3

2nd: (i) 4 (ii) 1 (iii) 6 (iv) 4 (v) 8 (vi) −2 (vii) −4 (viii) 3 (ix) 3 (c) (i) 56, 78, 104 (ii) 15, 21, 28 (iii) 79, 112, 151 (iv) 67, 93, 123 (v) 95, 135, 183 (vi) 8, 2, −6 (vii) −25, −43, −65 (viii) 7, 16, 28 (ix) 10, 19, 31 **5.** (a) (i) Doubles (ii) Triples (iii) Triples (iv) Doubles (v) Triples (b) (i) 256, 512, 1,024 (ii) 1,458, 4,374, 13122 (iii) 2,673, 8,019, 24,057 (iv) 416, 832, 1,664 (v) −1,215, −3,645, −10,935

6. (i)

Term		First difference	Second difference
u_1	3		
u_2	/	4	
u_3	13	6	2
u_4	21	8	2
u_5	31	10	2
u_6	43	12	2
u_7	57	14	2

(ii) $1 + b + c$, $4 + 2b + c$ (iii) $b + c = 2$, $2b + c = 3$ (iv) $n^2 + n + 1$ (v) = 241

7. (i)

Term		First difference	Second difference
u_1	6		
u_2	11	5	
u_3	18	7	2
u_4	27	9	2
u_5	38	11	2
u_6	51	13	2
u_7	66	15	2
u_8	83	17	2

(ii) $1 + p + q$, $4 + 2p + q$ (iii) $p + q = 5$, $2p + q = 7$ (iv) $n^2 + 2n + 3$ (v) 678

8. (ii)

1	2	3	4
1	6	15	28

(iii) 45, 66 (iv) Quadratic

Revision Exercises

1. (ii) $4n - 3$ (iii) $T_{50} = 197$ (iv) 60th term

2. (ii) $T_n = 2n + 1$ (iii) $T_{50} = 101$ (iv) 99

3. (ii)

Term	1	2	3	4	5
Number of dots	5	9	13	17	21

(iii) Linear (iv) $T_n = 4n + 1$ (v) $T_8 = 33$ **4.** (i) 6 (ii) 5 (iii) 31 (iv) 402 **5.** (i) Neither (ii) Arithmetic (iii) Arithmetic (iv) Geometric (v) Neither (vi) Arithmetic (vii) Geometric (viii) Neither **6.** (i) (a) 16 (b) First differences: 1, 2, 3, 4, 5, ..., Second difference: 1 (a constant) (c) 37 (ii) (a) 1 (b) First differences: 2, 3, 4, 5, 6, 7, ..., Second difference: 1 (a constant) (c) 28 (iii) (a) 12 (b) First differences: 2, 3, 4, 5, 6, 7, ..., Second difference: 1 (a constant) (c) 39 (iv) (a) 1 (b) First differences: 5, 9, 13, 17, ..., Second difference: 4 (a constant) (c) 91 (v) (a) 8 (b) First differences: 1, −1, −3, −5, −7, −9 ..., Second difference: −2 (a constant) (c) −16

7. (i) 1 7 21 35 35 21 7 1

1 8 28 56 70 56 28 8 1

(ii) Linear (iii) Quadratic

8. (i)

Term	u_1	u_2	u_3	u_4	u_5	u_6	u_7
Number	3	12	29	54	87	128	177

(ii) Second difference is a constant, 8, Therefore the pattern is quadratic (iii) −3, 2 (iv) 1542

Exam Questions

1. (b)

	Black	White	Total
P_1	3	1	$T_1 = 4$
P_2	6	3	$T_2 = 9$
P_3	10	6	$T_3 = 16$
P_4	15	10	$T_4 = 25$
P_5	21	15	$T_5 = 36$

(c) quadratic sequence (d) (i) 55 (ii) 45 (iii) 100 (e) $T_n = (n + 1)^2$ (f) c = 1 (g) $\frac{1}{2}n^2 + \frac{1}{2}n$

(h) 325 black triangles; 300 white triangles.

2. (b)

Row number n	Number of 1 cent coins	Number of 5 cent coins	Total number of coins in the row	Total value of the coins in the row
4	3	4	7	23
5	5	4	9	25
6	5	6	11	35
7	7	6	13	37

(c) (i) n, $(n - 1)$ (ii) $(n - 1)$, n (d) $T_{40} = 79$ (e) 239 cent (f) Row 57 has a total value of 337 cent (g) 4,800 cent

3. (a) (i) 13, 11, 9 (ii) −1 (b) (i) $S_n = 14n - n^2$ (ii) 14

4. (a)

	Day 1	Day 2	Day 3	Day 4	Day 5	Day 6	Day 7
Plant 1	16	20	24	28	32	36	40
Plant 2	24	27.5	31	34.5	38	41.5	45

(b) $4n + 12$, $3.5n + 20.5$ (d) (i) (17, 80) (ii) At day 17, both plants will be 80 cm tall (e) Both formulae tested + verified.

5. (a) (i)

Term	Number
U_6	43
U_7	55
U_8	69

(ii)

1st Difference	2nd Difference
2	2
4	2
6	2
8	2
10	2
12	2
14	2

(b) −1, 13

Chapter 8

Exercise 8.1

1. (i) $10i$ (ii) $9i$ (iii) $5i$ (iv) $6i$ (v) $11i$ (vi) $7i$ (vii) $8i$ (viii) $13i$ (ix) $12i$ (x) $4i$ **2.** (i) $\sqrt{17}i\ (= i\sqrt{17})$ (ii) $\sqrt{31}i\ (= i\sqrt{31})$ (iii) $\sqrt{14}i$ (iv) $\sqrt{19}i$ (v) $\sqrt{21}i$ (vi) $\sqrt{23}i$ (vii) $\sqrt{29}i$ (viii) $\sqrt{43}i$ (ix) $\sqrt{5}i$ (x) $\sqrt{3}i$ **3.** (i) $2\sqrt{2}i$ (ii) $7\sqrt{2}i$ (iii) $3\sqrt{5}i$ (iv) $10\sqrt{3}i$ (v) $2\sqrt{3}i$ (vi) $4\sqrt{2}i$ (vii) $10\sqrt{5}i$ (viii) $3\sqrt{6}i$ (ix) $3\sqrt{3}i$ (x) $5\sqrt{5}i$ **4.** (i) $7\sqrt{2}i$ (ii) $\sqrt{3}i$ (iii) $7\sqrt{5}i$ (iv) $5\sqrt{11}i$ **5.** (i) $-i$ (ii) -1 (iii) i (iv) 1 (v) i (vi) i
6. (i) $27(-i) = -27i$ (ii) $125(-i) = -125i$ (iii) $625(1) = 625$ (iv) $1024i$ (v) $128(-i) = -128i$ (vi) $256(1) = 256$

7.

A	B
i^4	$1 - i$
$2i^3$	-3
$i^8 + i^3$	$-128i$
i^{98}	$1 + i$
$3(i)^2$	0
$i^4 - i^8$	$-64i$
$(2i)^7$	1
$i^4 - i^7$	$9i$
$(4i)^3$	$-2i$
$5i + 4i$	-1

8. (i) $\frac{1}{8}$ (ii) $\frac{3}{8}$

Exercise 8.2

1. Parts: (i) Real $\frac{1}{2}$, Imag. $-\frac{3}{2}$ (ii) Real $\sqrt{2}$, Imag. -3 (iii) Real $\frac{22}{7}$, Imag. -3.14 (iv) Real 3, Imag. $-\frac{1}{\sqrt{3}}$ (v) Real $-\frac{5}{6}$, Imag. 3 **4.** (i) Real (ii) Imag. (iii) Imag. (iv) Real (v) Imag. (vi) Real (vii) Real (as $i^2 = -1$) (viii) Imag. (as $i^3 = -i$) (ix) Real (as $i^4 = 1$) (x) Real (as $(2i)^4 = 16$) **5.** (i) $3 + 2i$ (ii) $5 + 7i$ (iii) $-4 + 3i$ (iv) $8 - 5i$ (v) $10 - 6i$ (vi) $-2 + i$ (vii) $1 - 12i$ (viii) $-4 - i$ (viii) $7 - 9i$ **6.** $3 + 2i, 3 - 2i, 2 + i, 2 - i, -2 + i, -2 + 3i$
7. $0 + 3i, 4 + 3i, 0 - 4i$ $4 - 5i, 0 + 5i$ $-4 + 3i, 3 + 0i$ $-5 + 3i,$ $3 - 4i$ $-5 + 4i, 3 + 5i$ $-5 + 0i$

Exercise 8.3

1. (i) $9 + 6i$ (ii) $5 + 4i$ (iii) $21 + 15i + 4 + 2i = 25 + 17i$ (iv) $14 + 10i - 6 - 3i = 8 + 7i$ **2.** (i) $5 + 2i$ (ii) $1 - 6i$ (iii) $3 - 2i + 6 + 12i = 9 + 10i$ (iv) $6 - 4i - 10 - 20i = -4 - 24i$
3. (i) $-2 + 4i + 2 + 3i = 0 + 7i$ (ii) $-2 + 4i - 2 - 3i = -4 + i$ (iii) $4 + 6i + 3 - 6i = 7 + 0i$ (iv) $2 + 3i + 1 - 2i = 3 + i$
4. (i) $5 + i$ (ii) $2 + 4i$ (iii) $-2z = -2(2 + i) = -4 - 2i$ (iv) $7z = 7(2 + i) = 14 + 7i$ (v) $2(2 + i) + 3 - 3i = 4 + 2i + 3 - 3i = 7 - i$ **5.** (i) $5 - 3i$ (ii) $2(2 - 3i) + 6i = 4 - 6i + 6i = 4$ (iii) $1 - (2 - 3i) = -1 + 3i$ (iv) $\frac{1}{2}(2 - 2i) = 1 - i$
6. (a) (i) $1 + i$ (ii) $2 + 2i$ (iii) $3 + 3i$ (iv) $4 + 4i$ (v) $5 + 5i$ (b) (ii) Dilation of factor 2 (iii) Dilation of factor 3 (iv) Dilation of factor 4 (v) Dilation of factor 5 **7.** (a) (i) $-1 + i$ (ii) $-2 + 2i$ (iii) $-3 + 3i$ (iv) $-4 + 4i$ (v) $-5 + 5i$ (b) (ii) Dilation of factor 2 (iii) Dilation of factor 3 (iv) Dilation of factor 4 (v) Dilation of factor 5
8. (a) (i) $-24 + 48i$ (ii) $-12 + 24i$ (iii) $-8 + 16i$ (iv) $-6 + 12i$ (v) $-4 + 8i$ (b) (ii) Dilation of factor $\frac{1}{2}$ (iii) Dilation of factor $\frac{1}{3}$ (iv) Dilation of factor $\frac{1}{4}$ (v) Dilation of factor $\frac{1}{6}$
9. (ii) $3 + 4i = z_1 + \omega$, $-1 + 6i = z_2 + \omega$, $0 + 5i = z_3 + \omega$ (iv) All numbers are translated a distance of $\sqrt{2}$ units in the direction north-east. **10.** (ii) $4 + i = z_1 + \omega$, $0 + 3i = z_2 + \omega$, $-2 + 4i = z_3 + \omega$ (iv) All numbers are translated a distance of $\sqrt{2}$ units in the direction south-east.

Exercise 8.4

1. (i) 10 (ii) 13 (iii) 25 (iv) 17 (v) 41 (vi) 5 **2.** (i) 61 (ii) 5 (iii) 37 (iv) 85 (v) 65 (vi) 10 **3.** (i) $\sqrt{5}$ (ii) $2\sqrt{2}$ (iii) $\sqrt{10}$ (iv) $\sqrt{2}$ (v) $\sqrt{109}$ (vi) $\sqrt{58}$ **4.** (i) $\sqrt{11}$ (ii) 3 (iii) $\sqrt{43}$ (iv) 4 (v) 5 (vi) $\sqrt{69}$ **5.** (i) $|z_1 - z_2| = |z_2 - z_1|$ (ii) $2|z_1| = |2z_1|$ **6.** (i) $5|z_1| = |5z_1|$ (ii) $|z_1 - z_2| = |z_2 - z_1|$
7. $|z_1 + z_2|, < |z_1| + |z_2|$ **8.** $|3 + 4i| = |0 + 5i|$ **9.** (i) $\pm 5 = k$ **10.** $k = \pm 6$ **11.** $p = \pm 5$

Exercise 8.5

1. (i) $z_2 = i(3 + i) = 3i + i^2 = -1 + 3i$ (iii) 90° anti-clockwise rotation about the origin. **2.** (i) $z_2 = i(-3 + 2i) = -3i + 2i^2 = -2 - 3i$ (iii) 90° anti-clockwise rotation about the origin.
3. (i) $z_2 = -i(-3 + 4i) = 3i - 4i^2 = 4 + 3i$ (iii) 90° clockwise rotation about the origin. **4.** (i) $z_2 = -i(-2 - 3i) = 2i + 3i^2 = -3 + 2i$ (iii) 90° clockwise rotation about the origin.
5. (i) $21i + 35i^2 = -35 + 21i$ (ii) $3i - i^2 = 1 + 3i$ (iii) $14 + 2i$ (iv) $3 + 15i$ (v) $14 - 7i$ (vi) $-8 - 2i$ **6.** (i) $41 + 11i$ (ii) $-18 + 13i$ (iii) $-15 + 16i$ (iv) 13 (v) 25 (vi) $10 + 4i$ (vii) $(1)^2 - (i)^2 = 1 - i^2 = 1 + 1 = 2$ (viii) $(-2)^2 - (2i)^2 = 4 - 4i^2 = 4 + 4 = 8$ (ix) $9 + 17i$ (x) $14 + 21i$ **7.** (i) $\frac{5}{8} + \frac{5}{8}i$ (ii) $\frac{2}{5}$ (iii) $\frac{293}{1760} - \frac{23}{220}i$ (iv) 7 (v) 88 (vi) $7 + \sqrt{6}i$ **8.** (i) $126 - 32i$ (ii) 130 (iii) $|z_1||z_2| = 5(26) = 130 = |z_1z_2|$ **9.** (iii) Rotation 90° anti-clockwise about the origin. **10.** (iii) Rotation 90° clockwise about the origin.

Exercise 8.6

1. (i) $1 - 2i$ (ii) $3 - 6i$ (iii) $-2 - 7i$ (iv) $-10 - 3i$ (v) $-2 + 4i$ (vi) $-3 + 5i$ (vii) $-4 + i$ (viii) $3 + 2i$ (ix) $\frac{1}{2} + \frac{3}{4}i$ (x) $10 - 0i$ (xi) $3 - 0i = 3$ (xii) $0 - 3i$ (xiii) $4i$ (xiv) $-5i$ **2.** (i) $7 - 5i$ (ii) $2 - i$ (iii) $7 + 5i + 7 - 5i = 14$ (iv) $2 + i + 2 - i = 4$
3. (i) $5 - 2i$ (ii) $3 + 4i$ (iii) $8 + 2i$ (iv) $8 - 2i$ (v) $8 + 2i$
4. (i) $-1 - 2i$ (ii) $2 - 3i$ (iii) $1 - 5i$ (iv) $1 + 5i$ (v) $1 - 5i$
5. (i) $5 - 6i$ (ii) $3 + i$ (iii) $21 + 13i$ (v) $21 - 13i$

Exercise 8.7

1. (i) $3 + \frac{3}{2}i$ (ii) $3 - 4i$ (iii) $2 - i$ (iv) $\frac{5}{7} + \frac{12}{7}i$ **2.** (i) $3 - i$ (ii) $3 - 2i$ (iii) $1 - 2i$ (iv) $2 + i$ **3.** (i) $1 - 3i$ (ii) $3 + 3i$ (iii) $5 - i$ (iv) $4 - 3i$ (v) $3 + 4i$ **4.** (i) $\frac{1}{2} - \frac{1}{2}i$ (ii) $\frac{7}{10} - \frac{1}{10}i$ (iii) $\frac{-3}{5} + \frac{11}{5}i$ (iv) $2 - \frac{1}{2}i$ (v) $\frac{-9}{2} - \frac{1}{2}i$ **5.** (i) $1 - 2i$ (ii) $-2 - 4i$ (iii) $-6 - 9i$ (iv) $-12 - 4i$ (v) $\frac{1}{5} - \frac{1}{5}i$ **6.** (i) $0 - 16i$ (ii) $0 - 5i$ (iii) $-\frac{25i}{3}$ (iv) $\frac{-17}{5i}$ (v) $-\frac{11}{4}i$ **7.** $\frac{-8 + 6i}{10} = \frac{-4}{5} + \frac{3}{5}i$ **10.** (i) $2 - 3i$ (ii) $|z_1| = \sqrt{221}$, $|z_2| = \sqrt{17}$

Revision Exercises

1. (i) $7 - i$ (ii) $-1 + 3i$ (iii) $14 - 2i$ (iv) $4 + 2i$ (v) $\frac{1}{2} + \frac{1}{2}i$ (vi) $2\sqrt{5}$ **2.** (i) $2 - 3i$ (ii) $12 + 5i$ (iii) $-31 - 33i$ (iv) $-5 + 4i$ (v) $\frac{-39}{41} + \frac{23}{41}i$ (vi) $5\sqrt{82}$ **3.** (i) $-9 + 8i$ (ii) $\frac{31}{202} - \frac{7}{202}i$ (iii) $\sqrt{5}$ (iv) $\sqrt{202}$ (v) $\sqrt{\frac{1,010}{202}}$ (vi) $\overline{z_1 z_2} = 13 - 29i$ **4.** (i) $1,309 - 588i$ (ii) $1,309 + 588i$ (iii) $21 - 28i$ (iv) $9 + 40i$ (v) $1309 + 588i$ (vi) $45 + 164i$ **5.** (i) $800 + 3,150i$ (ii) 3,250 (iii) 50 (iv) 65 (v) 3,250 (vi) $3 + 140i$ **6.** (i) $\frac{-204}{325} - \frac{253}{325}i$ (ii) (i) $\frac{-204}{325} - \frac{253}{325}i$ (iii) 65 (iv) 65 (v) 1 (vi) 1 **7.** (iii) Each number is moved

a distance of $\sqrt{2}$ units in the direction south-east
8. (i) $-10 - 2i$ (ii) $1 + i$ (iii) $-1 - 2i$

Exam Questions

1. (a) (i) $1 - 4i$ (ii) $\sqrt{17}$ (b) $a = \frac{17}{26}$ and $b = \frac{19}{26}$
2. (c) $-2z$ is twice as far from the origin as z is
(d) $k = 2$ or $k = -4$ **3.** (b) Yes (d) $-1 - 2i$
4. (a) $z_3 = 1 + 3i + 2(2 - i)$, $z_3 = 5 + i$ (d) $-\frac{1}{5} + \frac{7}{5i}$

Chapter 9

Exercise 9.1

1. (i)

x	f(x)	x	f(x)
1.0	-2	3.0	2
1.5	-1	2.5	1
1.8	-0.4	2.2	0.4
1.9	-0.2	2.1	0.2
1.95	-0.1	2.05	0.1
1.99	-0.02	2.01	0.02
1.995	-0.01	2.005	0.01
1.999	-0.002	2.001	0.002

(ii) 0

2. (i)

x	g(x)	x	g(x)
4.0	28	6.0	68
4.5	36.5	5.5	56.5
4.8	42.08	5.2	50.08
4.9	44.02	5.1	48.02
4.95	45.005	5.05	47.005
4.99	45.8002	5.01	46.2002
4.995	45.90005	5.005	46.10005
4.999	45.980002	5.001	46.020002

(ii) 46 **3.** (i) 6 (ii) 6 (iii) 2 (iv) 6 (v) 12 (vi) 6 **4.** (i) 7 (ii) −1 (iii) 4 (iv) 3 (v) 125 (vi) 9 (vii) 5 (viii) 20 (ix) −2 (x) 26 **5.** (i) $x + 3$ (ii) $x + 3$, $3 + 3 = 6$ **6.** (i) $x - 4$ (ii) $x - 4$, $-4 - 4 = -8$ **7.** (i) $x + 2$ (ii) 6

Exercise 9.2

1. (i) 1 (ii) 0 (iii) $\frac{1}{2}$ (iv) $-\frac{4}{3}$ (v) −2 **2.** (i) $3x^2$ (ii) $6x$ (iii) $6x^2$ (iv) −8 (v) −16 (vi) x **3.** (i) 2 (ii) $6t$ (iii) $15t^2$ (iv) t^2 (v) t (vi) −15 **4.** (i) 0 (ii) 0 (iii) 0 (iv) 0 (v) 0 (vi) 0 **5.** (i) 3 (ii) −2 (iii) 17 (iv) −15 (v) −1 (vi) $2x - 3$
6. (i) $\frac{dy}{dx} = x$ (ii) $\frac{ds}{dt} = t^2$ (iii) $\frac{dA}{dr} = 2\pi r$ (iv) $\frac{dA}{dr} = \pi r$
(v) $\frac{dC}{dr} = 2\pi$ (vi) $\frac{dV}{dx} = 3x^2$ **7.** (i) $8x + 2$ (ii) $6x + 10$ (iii) $2x + 9$ (iv) $9x^2 + 8x - 3$ (v) $6x$ **8.** (i) $3x^2 + 2x + 1$ (ii) $3x^2 - 1$ (iii) $3x^2 + 1$ (iv) $30x^2 + 22x$ (v) $27x^2 - 16x$ (vi) $3x^2 + 12x - 3$
9. (i) $3x^2 + 2x - 1$ (ii) $9x^2 + 4x - 1$ **10.** (i) $2x - 2$ (ii) 198
11. (i) $3x^2 - 2x$ (ii) 85 **12.** (i) $3x^2 - 6x + 2$ (ii) 11
13. (i) $6x^2 + 6x - 2$ (ii) −2 **14.** (i) $15x^2 - 4x - 12$ (ii) −12
15. (i) $x^2 + x - 12$ (ii) $2x + 1$ (iii) −10 (iv) 3

Exercise 9.3

1. (i) 24 (ii) 16 (iii) 18 (iv) $138x + 4$ (v) 66 **2.** (i) −18 (ii) 2 (iii) −16 (iv) −158 (v) 162 **3.** (i) 9.8 (ii) −9.8 (iii) $6t + 2$ (iv) $12t^2 - 2$ **4.** (i) $6x$ (ii) $6x - 6$ (iii) −8 (iv) 2π **5.** (i) $18x$ (ii) 36 **6.** (i) $6x$ (ii) 1

Exercise 9.4

1. (i) $2x + 2$ (ii) 2 (iii) $2x + 1$ **2.** (i) $3 - 2x$ (ii) $-5x + 21$
3. 0 **4.** (4,19) **5.** (3,2) **6.** (i) 5 (ii) $8x - 16$
7. (i) $f'(x) = 2 + 6x - 3x^2$ (ii) 2 (iii) $2x + 1$
(iv) x-intercept: $\left(-\frac{1}{2}, 0\right)$, y-intercept: (0, 1) (v) $\frac{1}{4}$ units^2
(vi) (3, 7)

Exercise 9.5

1. (i) (a) $-2 < x < 0$ (b) $-3{\cdot}2 < x < -2$ or $0 < x < 1$
(ii) (a) $0 < x < 2$ (b) $-1{\cdot}5 < x < 0$ or $2 < x < 3{\cdot}2$ **2.** (i) $x > 1$
(ii) $x > -\frac{3}{2}$ (iii) $x < 1$ **or** $x > 2$ (iv) $x < -3$ or $x > 3$
(v) $x < -\frac{1}{\sqrt{3}}$ **or** $x > \frac{1}{\sqrt{3}}$ (vi) $-3 < x < \frac{1}{2}$ **3.** Diagram A is the graph of the derivative of h **4.** Diagram A is the graph of the derivative of g **5.** Diagram D is the graph of the derivative of f

Exercise 9.6

1. (i) ±1 (ii) $f'(x) = 0$ (iii) $g(-1,3)$, $H(1,-1)$ **2.** (i) (−1,−9)
3. $\left(4\frac{1}{2}, 6\frac{1}{4}\right)$ **4.** (3,−71) is local minimum, (−2, 54) is local maximum **5.** (5,110) is local maximum, (−1,2) is local minimum **6.** (i) $f(x) = -x^3 + 0x^2 + 3x + 2$ (ii) (1,4) is local maximum, (−1,0) is a local minimum (iii) (−1,0) and (2,0) on x-axis (v) $-1 < x < 1$ **7.** (i) (4, −80) is local min, (−2, 28) is local max (ii) Graph of $f(x)$ intersects x-axis at $x = 0$

Exercise 9.7

1. (i) $y = 20 - x$ (m) (ii) $20x - x^2$ (m^2) (iii) $x = 10$ (m) (iv) 100 m^2 **2.** (i) $y = 150 - x$ (m) (ii) $150x - x^2$ (iii) 75 (m) (iv) 5,625 m^2 **3.** (i) $50 - x$ (ii) $50x - x^2$ (iii) $x = 25$ m (iv) 625 m^2 **4.** (i) Length = $100 - 2x$ (ii) $100x - 2x^2$ (iii) 25 (iv) 1250 m^2 **5.** 54 km/hr **6.** (i) $y = 200 - 2x$ (m) (ii) $200x - 2x^2$ (m^2) (iii) 50 (m) (iv) 5,000 m^2
7. (i) $y = 150 - \frac{3}{2}x$ (ii) $150x - \frac{3}{2}x^2$ (iii) 50 (m) (iv) 7,500 m^2
8. (i) $2y + \pi x$ (ii) $700 - \frac{\pi x}{2} = y$ (iii) Length = 350.0 m, Width = 222.8 m **9.** (i) Length: $50 - 2x$, Width: $50 - 2x$
(ii) $4x^3 - 200x^2 + 2500x$ (iii) $x = \frac{25}{3}$ cm gives maximum volume
(iv) $V_{max} = 9{,}259.26$ cm^3 **10.** (i) $440x - 0.3x^2$
(ii) $-0.8x^2 + 440x - 6{,}000$ (iii) 275 (iv) €54,500
11. (i) Production cost: €20, 000, Total income: €24,000
(ii) €4,000 (iii) $-5x^2 + 450x - 3{,}000$ (iv) 45 (v) €7,125 (vi) 10

Exercise 9.8

1. (i) $f(5)$ is the temperature of the bread 5 minutes out of the oven (ii) $f'(t) < 0$ as the temperature drops with time (iii) °C/minute **2.** (i) $f'(m) > 0$ since infants get heavier with time (ii) At seven months the infant's weight is 7.65 kg (iii) kg/month **3.** (i) 16 m (ii) 25 m (iii) $2t$ (m/s) (iv) 8 m/s

4. (i) 35 m (ii) $h'(t)$ is the rate of change in displacement with respect to time. This is defined as the speed (iii) $h'(t) = 40 - 10t$ (m/s) (iv) 0 m/s (v) 4 seconds (vi) 80 m **5.** (i) $T'(t) = -1.2t + 0.67$ (°C/day) (ii) −2.93 °C/day (iii) 13 hours **6.** (i) 29.4 m/s (ii) 105.84 km/hour **7.** (i) 9200 kg/hectare (ii) 160 kg/hectare (iii) 9650 kg/hectare (iv) €304.6/hectare **8.** (i) $-33 + 24t - 3t^2$ (ii) $24 - 6t$ (iii) 1.765 or 6.245 (iv) 0 m/s^2 **9.** (i) 1,600 m (ii) $200 - 8t$ m/s (iii) 120 m/s (iv) 200 m/s (v) 25 seconds (vi) 2,500 m

Revision Exercises

1. (i) $4x + 12$ (ii) $30x + 10$ (iii) $3x^2 - 19$ (iv) $9x^2 - 24x - 4$ (v) $12x^2$ **2.** (i) $3t^2 + 4t - 1$ (ii) $3y^2 + 2y + 1$ (iii) $2x$ (iv) $5 - 9.8t$ **3.** (i) $3x^2 - 3$ (ii) 3.75 (iii) $3.75x - 4.75$ (iv) (1.26,0) on x-axis, (0,−4.75) on y-axis (v) 3.0083 units^2 **4.** (i) 17 (ii) 4 (iii) 0 (iv) 14 **5.** (i) $f'(x) = 3x^2 - 6x - 10$ (ii) 5.75 (iii) $5.75x - 25$ **6.** (i) −50 (ii) −90 (iii) 54 **7.** (i) (0,0) is max. point, (2,−4) is min. point (ii) (0,0) and (3,0) on x-axis, (0,0) on y-axis (iv) $x < 0$ or $x > 2$ **8.** (i) kg/month (ii) At 3 months, the monthly growth rate is 4 kg/month **9.** (i) ±1 (ii) 96 **10.** (i) 2 metres (ii) 5 m/s (iii) $\frac{1}{3}$ or $t = 1$ (seconds) **11.** (i) $9x^2 - 32x$ (ii) $x < 0$ or $x > \frac{32}{9}$ **12.** (iii) (a) 1.125 cm/s (b) 1 cm/s (c) 0.5 cm/s (d) 0.75 cm/s (iv) 0.8 cm/s (v) 0.8 cm/s **13.** (i) width = $6 - x$ (ii) $6x - x^2$ (iii) 3 (iv) 9 cm^2

Exam Questions

1. (a) 0, 7 (b) 7 (c) (i) $x = 1, m = 3$ (ii) $3x - y + 4 = 0$

2. (a)

Time, t	0	1	2	3	4	5	6	7	8	9	10
Height, h	**0**	**9**	**16**	**21**	**24**	25	24	21	16	**9**	**0**

(c) (i) 19 m (ii) 7.5 s (iii) (5,25) (d) (i) −3 (ii) Yes (e) (i) $10 - 2t$ (ii) 25 m (iii) 4 m/s (iv) (4,24)

3. (a) $2x + 2y = 21$ (b) (i)

x	y	$A(m^2)$
0	10.5	0
1	9.5	9.5
2	8.5	17
3	7.5	22.5
4	6.5	26
5	5.5	27.5
6	4.5	27
7	3.5	24.5
8	2.5	20
9	1.5	13.5
10	0.5	5

(c)

Maximum area	$27.5 \leq A \leq 28$
x value	$5 \leq X \leq 5.5$
y value	$5.5 \geq Y \geq 5$

(d) (i) $A = 10.5x - x^2$ (ii) $\frac{dA}{dx} = 10.5 - 2x$ (iii) $x = 5.25$ (iv) $A = 27.56$

Chapter 10

Exercise 10.1

1. (i) 9 cm^2 (ii) 45.5 cm^2 (iii) 90 cm^2 (iv) 100 cm^2 (v) 390 cm^2 (vi) 56 cm^2 (vii) 62.64 cm^2 (viii) 3,192 cm^2 (ix) 12 cm^2 (x) 120 cm^2 **2.** (i) Area = 210 cm^2, Perimeter = 100 cm (ii) Area = 1155 cm^2, Perimeter = 1064 cm (iii) Area = 236.5 cm^2, Perimeter = 54 cm (iv) Area = 338 mm^2, Perimeter = 82 mm (v) Area = 256 m^2, Perimeter = 67 m **3.** (i) 60 cm^2 (ii) 1,667 tiles (iii) 100,000 cm^2 or 10 m^2 **4.** (i) €56 (ii) 560 panels **5.** (i) 9,936 m^2 (ii) 1,314 m^2 (iii) €3,449.25 **6.** (a) (i) 216 m^2 (ii) 225 m^2 (b) ≈ €3,059

Exercise 10.2

1.

	Area	Circumference
(i)	314 cm^2	62.8 cm
(ii)	45,216 mm^2	753.6 mm
(iii)	80,384 cm^2	1,004.8 cm

2.

	Area	Circumference
(i)	61,600 cm^2	880 cm
(ii)	$24{,}894\frac{4}{7}$ cm^2	$559\frac{3}{7}$ cm
(iii)	98.56 cm^2	35.2 cm

3.

	Area	Circumference
(i)	100π cm^2	20π cm
(ii)	144π m^2	24π m
(iii)	0.0625π cm^2	0.5π cm

4.

	Area	Arc Length	Perimeter
(i)	31.4 cm^2	6.28 cm	26.28 cm
(ii)	235.5 cm^2	31.4 cm	61.4 cm
(iii)	79.86 cm^2	24.2 cm	37.4 cm
(iv)	$905\frac{1}{7}$ cm^2	$100\frac{4}{7}$ cm	$136\frac{4}{7}$ cm

5. (i) Area = 124.2325 cm^2, Perimeter = 47.99 cm (ii) Area = 2,582.3125 cm^2, Perimeter = 191.05 cm (iii) Area = 1,324.28 m^2, Perimeter = 151.96 m **6.** 54 minutes **7.** (i) 148.5 m^2 (ii) €816.75 **8.** (i) 1 : 4 (ii) 1 : 16 **9.** Red **10.** (i) 400 m (ii) 112 m **11.** (i) 346.185 cm^2 (ii) 238

Exercise 10.3

1. (i) 6 cm (ii) 10 cm (iii) 10 cm (iv) 12 cm (v) 40 cm (vi) 9 cm (vii) 4.3 cm

2.

π	r	Area	Circumference
π	7	49π	14π
3.14	7	153.86	43.96
$\frac{22}{7}$	28	2,464	176
π	35	$1{,}225\pi$	70π
3.14	16	803.84	100.48
$\frac{22}{7}$	16	$804\frac{4}{7}$	$100\frac{4}{7}$
3.14	3	28.26	18.84
π	$\frac{1}{9}$	$\frac{1}{81}\pi$	$\frac{2}{9}\pi$

3. (i) 21 cm (ii) 60 cm (iii) 90° (iv) 142.8° (v) 167.5°
4. (i) 3 m (ii) 5 m **5.** (i) 5 m (ii) 13 m **6.** 600 cm^2
7. (i) 49 cm (ii) 30.8 km **8.** (i) 15 m (ii) 94.2 m
9. 149.12 m **10.** (i) 50 cm (ii) ≈ 28.5 cm^2 **11.** (i) 8.5 m
(ii) 87.135 m^2 **12.** Area of pink is largest

Exercise 10.4

1.

	Volume	Surface Area
(i)	1,680 cm^3	856 cm^2
(ii)	16.875 m^3	43.5 m^2
(iii)	13,000 mm^3	3,820 mm^2
(iv)	125 mm^3	150 mm^2

2.

	Volume	Surface Area
(i)	105 cm^3	142 cm^2
(ii)	64 cm^3	96 cm^2
(iii)	450 m^3	300 m^2

4. (i) Figure 4 **5.** (i) 248 cm^2 (ii) 30 cubes **6.** (i) 9.9 litres
(ii) 3,800 cm^2

Exercise 10.5

1. (i) Volume = 48,750 cm^3, Surface Area = 8,950 cm^2
(ii) Volume = 3,220 cm^3, Surface Area = 1,636 cm^2
(iii) Volume = 101 m^3, Surface Area = 2.9

3.

	Volume	Surface Area
(i)	27 cm^3	54 cm^2
(ii)	420 cm^3	386 cm^2
(iii)	43,200 cm^3	20,160 cm^2

4. 16 cm^3 **5.** (i) 18 m^2 (ii) 144 m^3 **6.** (i) 0.54 m^3 (ii) €47.52

Exercise 10.6

1. (i) 3,140 cm^3 (ii) $18\frac{18}{175}$ cm^3 (iii) 648π m^3 (iv) 41,250 m^3
(v) 1,099 mm^3

2.

	CSA	TSA
(i)	3.14 m^2	3.5325 m^2
(ii)	30π cm^2	48π cm^2
(iii)	345.4 cm^2	502.4 cm^2
(iv)	$6{,}084\frac{4}{7}$ cm^2	$9{,}126\frac{6}{7}$ cm^2

3.

	Volume	TSA
(i)	1232 mm^3	1,408 mm^2
(ii)	25.3125π mm^3	32.625π mm^2

4. (i) 1519.76 m^2 (ii) $905\frac{1}{7}$ cm^2 **5.** (i) ≈ 13.54 litres
(ii) 3,165.12 cm^2 **6.** (i) $2{,}560\pi$ cm^3 (ii) 4 : 1 **7.** ≈ 260,000 L
(ii) 268.784 m^2 **8.** ≈ 1,569.75 kg

Exercise 10.7

1. (i) $\frac{16\pi}{3}$ cm^3 (ii) 35,200 mm^3 (iii) 5,024 cm^3
(iv) $5{,}887\frac{1}{2}$ cm^3 (v) $9{,}166\frac{2}{3}$ cm^3 (vi) $418\frac{2}{3}$ cm^3
2. (i) CSA 2,106.94 cm^2, TSA 2,486.88 cm^2
(ii) CSA 60π m^2, TSA 96π m^2 (iii) CSA 3,080 mm^2,
TSA 5,544 mm^2 (iv) CSA $1{,}500\pi$ cm^2, TSA $2{,}400\pi$ cm^2
3. (i) Vol 8377.58 cm^3, TSA 3033.79 cm^2 (ii) Vol 8.82 m^3,
TSA 28.06 m^2 **4.** (i) A: 3.12536 litres, B: $0.3349\dot{3}$ litres
(ii) A: TSA 1,808.64 m^2 B: TSA ≈ 306.415 m^2 **5.** (i) €9,231.60
6. 144π m^3 **7.** (a) (i) $11{,}250\pi$ cm^3 (ii) 3375π cm^3
(iii) $\frac{3}{10}$ (b) ≈ 7650 cm^2

Exercise 10.8

1. (i) 927π cm^3 (ii) $7{,}241\frac{1}{7}$ cm^3 (iii) $523\frac{1}{3}$ mm^3
(iv) 4,851 cm^3 **2.** (i) $4{,}603\frac{5}{21}$ cm^3 (ii) 0.000144 m^3
(iii) 7.605 m^3 (iv) $5333\frac{1}{3}\pi$ mm^3 **3.** (i) 324π cm^2
(ii) $1{,}810\frac{2}{7}$ m^2 **4.** (i) 235.5 mm^2 (ii) $94,285\frac{5}{7}$ km^2
5. (i) TSA 1600π mm^2 (ii) CSA 1,413 m^2, TSA 2,119.5 m^2
(iii) CSA 4,578.12 cm^2, TSA 6,867.18 cm^2
(iv) TSA $2{,}552\frac{11}{14}$ cm^2 **6.** (i) ≈ 1,465 cm^2 (ii) ≈ 5,274 cm^3
7. (i) $1{,}473\frac{1}{3}$ cm^3 (ii) 2,744 cm^3 (iii) ≈ 47.6%
8. (i) 1,584 cm^3 (ii) $381\frac{6}{7}$ cm^3 (iii) $1{,}202\frac{1}{7}$ cm^3
9. 167 cm^3 **10.** (i) 179.50 cm^3 (ii) 21 cm (iii) 3.5 cm
(iv) 807.765 cm^3 (v) $\frac{2}{3}$ **11.** ≈ €43,824.35

Exercise 10.9

1. (i)

L (cm)	B (cm)	H (cm)	V (cm^3)	SA (cm^2)
4	5	9	180	202
2	1	3	6	22
14	7.5	2	210	296
1			5	$19\frac{2}{3}$
	0.5		0.0625	

(ii)

π	r (cm)	h (cm)	V (cm^3)	CSA (cm^2)	TSA (cm^2)
π	5	4	100π	40π	90π
3.14	9	11	2,797.74	621.72	1,130.4
		1			
$\frac{22}{7}$	7	14	2,156	616	924
		9.5			

(iii)

π	r (cm)	h (cm)	l (cm)	V (cm^3)	CSA (cm^2)	TSA (cm^2)
π	4	3	5	16π	20π	36π
		24	25			
3.14	9	40	41	3,391.2	1,158.66	1,413
$\frac{22}{7}$	20	99	101	$41,485\frac{5}{7}$	$6,348\frac{4}{7}$	$7,605\frac{5}{7}$

(iv) (a) Spheres

π	r (cm)	V (cm^3)	TSA (cm^2)
π	5	$166\frac{2}{3}\pi$	100π
$\frac{22}{7}$	2	$33\frac{11}{21}$	$50\frac{2}{7}$
3.14	9	3,052.08	1017.36

(b) Hemispheres

π	r (cm)	V (cm^3)	TSA (cm^2)	CSA (cm^2)
π	5	$83\frac{1}{3}\pi$	75π	50π
$\frac{22}{7}$	2	$16\frac{16}{21}$	$37\frac{5}{7}$	$25\frac{1}{7}$
3.14	9	1526.04	763.02	508.68
π	13			

2. 18 cm **3.** 30 cm **4.** (i) 288π cm^3 (ii) 96 cm = h **5.** 6 cm = r **6.** $h \approx 38$ mm **7.** More than half **8.** 10 cm **9.** 12, 24, 36 (cm) **10.** h = 2 cm **11.** 0.25 cm **12.** (i) 81π cm^3 (ii) h = 9 cm **13.** ≈ 21 cm **14.** 50 seconds **15.** (i) 2.25π cm^3 (ii) 1.5 cm drop (iii) 40 ladlefuls

Exercise 10.10

1. (i) 73 m^2 (ii) 330 m^2 (iii) 2,260 m^2 (iv) 843.75 m^2 (v) 702 m^2 **2.** $3\frac{2}{3}$ **3.** $4\frac{1}{3}$ **4.** 15 m

Revision Exercises

1. (a) (i) 516 cm^2 (ii) 5,000 mm^2 (iii) 286 m^2

(b)

	Area	Perimeter
(i)	$\pi(25)^2 = 625\pi$ cm^2	$2(\pi)(25) = 50\pi$ cm
(ii)	$3.14(18)^2 = 1{,}017.36$ cm^2	$2(3.14)(18) = 113.04$ cm
(iii)	$\frac{22}{7}(0.25)^2 = \frac{11}{56}$ mm^2	$2\left(\frac{22}{7}\right)(0.25) = 1\frac{4}{7}$ mm

2. (a) (i) 67.1175 cm^2 (ii) 1,553.7575 mm^2 (b) (i) $5\frac{1}{3}$ m (ii) 13 m (iii) 42 mm (iv) 290° **3.** (a) (i) 8 cm (ii) 320π cm^3 (b) $r \approx 21.5$ m **4.** (a) (i) 912 m^2 (ii) 1,380 m^2 (iii) 302.5 m^2 (b) (i) 45 (ii) $6\frac{2}{3}$

5.

	Volume	Surface Area
(i)	113,408 m^3	16,176 m^2
(ii)	960 m^3	736 m^2

6. (i) 88.3125 cm^2 (ii) 4 cm = h **7.** (i) 1,100 cm^3 (ii) 2 m × 2.4 m × 1 m **8.** 2,240 cups **9.** (a) 18.84 cm^2 (Area), 18.28 cm (perimeter) (b) (i) 60.75π cm^3 (ii) 4.5 cm drop (iii) 32 ladlefuls **10.** (a) 27 : 1 (b) (i) 2,300 m^2 (ii) 16,100 m^3 (c) (i) 528 cm^3 (ii) 1.9 cm **11.** (a) 100 cm/s (b) (i) $\frac{1}{8}$ cm drop (ii) 1.5 cm = r **12.** (a) (i) 122.5π cm^3 (ii) 6 cm = h (iii) h = 9 cm (b) $13\frac{1}{3}$ minutes

Exam Questions

1. (a) (i) 9 m (ii) 3,053.63 m^3 (b) 9,161 m^2 (c) (i) 1,908 m^2 (ii) 29 (iii) €996, 730 **2.** (a) (i) 6 m (ii) 905 m^3 (b) (i) 452.4 m^2 (ii) 129 or 130 litres (iii) €1,080 (c) (i) 191 m^3 (ii) ≈ 8.2 m **3.** (a) 9 cm (b) (i) 63.6 cm^2 (ii) 46.2 cm^2 (c) 16.8 cm^2 **5.** (a) 1.8 metres tall (c) 5.112π cm^3 or 16.06 m^3 **6.** (a) (i) 2 cm (ii) 3.4 cm^2 (b) (i) 12 cm (ii) 972 cm^3 **7.** 61 cm^2

Chapter 11

Exercise 11.1

1. {20, 21, 22, 23, 24, 25, 26, 27, 28, 29} **2.** (i) 52 (ii) Clubs, Spades, Hearts, Clubs (iii) 13 (iv) King of Hearts (v) 12

3.

Number	Digits
55	2
692	3
10,841	5
1,000,005	7

4.

		Coin	
		H	T
Die	1	1H	1T
	2	2H	2T
	3	3H	3T
	4	4H	4T
	5	5H	5T
	6	6H	6T

12 possible outcomes

5.

	Medium	Large
C	CM	CL
H	HM	HL
V	VM	VL

7.

	1	2	3	4	5	6
1	1,1	1,2	1,3	1,4	1,5	1,6
2	2,1	2,2	2,3	2,4	2,5	2,6
3	3,1	3,2	3,3	3,4	3,5	3,6
4	4,1	4,2	4,3	4,4	4,5	4,6
5	5,1	5,2	5,3	5,4	5,5	5,6
6	6,1	6,2	6,3	6,4	6,5	6,6

(i) 36 (ii) 36 (iii) 6

8. (i)

		Second spinner				
		1	2	3	4	5
First spinner	A	A1	A2	A3	A4	A5
	B	B1	B2	B3	B4	B5
	C	C1	C2	C3	C4	C5
	D	D1	D2	D3	D4	D5

(ii) 20 (iii) 12 (iv) 8 (v) 2{*A*2, *A*4}

(vi) 5 + 6 = 11

{A1, A2, A3, A4, A5} {B2, C2, D2, B4, C4, D4}

10. (i)

	10	11
1	11	12
2	12	13
3	13	14

(ii) 3

11.

		Second die					
		1	2	3	4	5	6
First die	1	1 - 1 = 0	2 - 1 = 1	3 - 1 = 2	4 - 1 = 3	5 - 1 = 4	6 - 1 = 5
	2	2 - 1 = 1	2 - 2 = 0	3 - 2 = 1	4 - 2 = 2	5 - 2 = 3	6 - 2 = 4
	3	3 - 1 = 2	3 - 2 = 1	3 - 3 = 0	4 - 3 = 1	5 - 3 = 2	6 - 3 = 3
	4	4 - 1 = 3	4 - 2 = 2	4 - 3 = 1	4 - 4 = 0	5 - 4 = 1	6 - 4 = 2
	5	5 - 1 = 4	5 - 2 = 3	5 - 3 = 2	5 - 4 = 1	5 - 5 = 0	6 - 5 = 1
	6	6 - 1 = 5	6 - 2 = 4	6 - 3 = 3	6 - 4 = 2	6 - 5 = 1	6 - 6 = 0

12. (ii) (a) 1 (b) 3 (c) 4 (d) 7

13. (ii) 12 (iii) (a) 2 (b) 8 (c) 6 (d) 5

Exercise 11.2

1. 20 **2.** 20 **3.** 75 **4.** 120 **5.** 260 **6.** 15,600 **7.** (i) 624 (ii) {Ace of Hearts, Head, two} **8.** (i) 7,776 (ii) 65,112 **9.** 1,024 **10.** 16,777,216 **11.** 336 **12.** 358,800 **13.** 840 **14.** (i) 60 (ii) 45 (iii) 15 (iv) 240 **15.** (i) 650,000 (ii) 486,720 (iii) 468,000

Exercise 11.3

2. 1 2 3 4 2 1 3 4 3 1 2 4 4 1 2 3

1 2 4 3 2 1 4 3 3 1 4 2 4 1 3 2

1 3 2 4 2 3 1 4 3 2 1 4 4 2 1 3

1 3 4 2 2 3 4 1 3 2 4 1 4 2 3 1

1 4 2 3 2 4 1 3 3 4 1 2 4 3 1 2

1 4 3 2 2 4 3 1 3 4 2 1 4 3 2 1

(i) 24 (ii) 12 (iii) 12 (iv) 8 (v) 16 (vi) 6

3. A G M S E E G M S A

A G S M E E G S M A

A M G S E E M G S A

A M S G E E M S G A

A S M G E E S M G A

A S G M E E S G M A

(i) 12 (ii) 4 (iii) 6 (iv) 6 (v) 6 (vi) 8 (vii) 4 **4.** 20 **5.** 120 **6.** 116,280 **7.** 120 **8.** 151,200 **9.** (i) 720 (ii) 720 (iii) 360 **10.** 9,000 **11.** 2,520 **12.** (i) 120 ways (ii) 24 (iii) 96 (iv) 24 **13.** (i) 5,040 ways (ii) 720 (iii) 120 (iv) 840 **15.** (i) 24 (ii) 64 (iii) 12 (iv) 12 **16.** (i) 468,000 (ii) 1,800 **17.** (i) 24 (ii) 6 (iii) 18 (iv) 18 **18.** (i) 40,320 (ii) 5,040 (iii) 15,120 (iv) 720 **19.** (i) 120 ways (ii) 12 ways **20.** (i) 720 (ii) 240 ways (iii) 48 ways (iv) 48 ways (v) 240 (vi) 480 ways **21.** (i) 100 (ii) 52 even (iii) 48 odd (iv) 60 (v) 28 (vi) 40 **22.** (i) 85 (ii) 34

Revision Exercises

1. (i)

	L	M	S
P	PL	PM	PS
LCD	LCDL	LCDM	LCDS

(ii) 6 **3.** (ii) 2 (iii) 1

4. (i)

		Second die				
		1	2	3	4	5
First die	1	2	3	4	5	6
	2	3	4	5	6	7
	3	4	5	6	7	8

(ii) (a) 7 (b) 8 (c) 8 (d) 5 **5.** (ii) 12 (iii) 2 HH (iv) 8 **6.** 120 **7.** (ii) 72 **8.** (i) 30 (ii) 16 **9.** (i) 120 (ii) 360 (iii) 720 (iv) 30 **10.** (i) 5,040 (ii) 10,000 (iii) 2,016 **11.** (i) 720 (ii) 240 (iii) 48 **12.** (i) 120 ways (ii) 24 (iii) 48 (iv) 72 **13.** (i) (a) 24 (b) 256 (ii) 18 **14.** (i) 720 (ii) 240 (iii) 48 (iv) 48 (v) 240 **15.** (i) 120 (ii) 72 (iii) 36 (iv) 48 **16.** (i) 24 (ii) 6 (iii) 12 (iv) 6 (v) 2 **17.** (i) 360 (ii) 60 (iii) 300 (iv) 36 **18.** (i) 40,320 (ii) 5,040 (iii) 15,120 (iv) 720 (v) 4,320 **19.** (i) 362,880 (ii) 2,880 (iii) 288 **20.** (i) 120 (ii) 24 (iii) 72 (iv) 18

Exam Questions

1. $\frac{2}{12}$ or $\frac{1}{6}$ **2.** (a) 1,000,000 (b) (i) 531,441 (ii) 0.468559 (c) $\binom{6}{3} = 20$ **3.** (b) 120 (c) 1,440 **5.** (c) $\frac{1}{8}$ or 0.125 or 12.5% (d) $\frac{7}{8}$ or 0.875 or 87.5%

Chapter 12

Exercise 12.1

1. Evens **2.** Unlikely (1 in 6 chance) **3.** Certain **4.** Evens **5.** Likely **6.** Evens **7.** Unlikely **8.** Evens **9.** Evens **10.** Impossible **11.** (i) E (ii) G (iii) I (iv) F (v) H **15.** (i) Probability must lie between 0 and 1 (ii) Probability should be between 0 and 1 (iii) Incorrect – probability given should be $\frac{1}{6}$

Exercise 12.2

1. $\frac{1}{4}$ **2.** (i) $\frac{7}{20}$ (ii) $\frac{13}{20}$ **3.** $\frac{13}{15}$ **4.** $\frac{2}{3}$ **5.** $\frac{2}{11}$ **6.** A = 10%, B = 20% C = 24%, D = 20%, E = 26% **7.** (i) 0.25 (ii) 1 (iii) 6 (iv) 36 **8.** (i) M = $\frac{1}{2}$, A = $\frac{2}{7}$, J = 0 (ii) Megan (iii) Need to take into account the number of games played. **9.** (i) 7 (ii) 22 (iii) 32 (iv) No **10.** 150 times **11.** (i) 130 times (ii) 60 times (iii) 5 times (iv) $\frac{1}{26}$ **12.** (i) Fair (ii) Unfair (iii) Fair **13.** No **14.** (i) Yes (ii) 36 **15.** 168 **16.** 11 missed **17.** 25 faulty **18.** Jan ≈ 4.01%, Feb ≈ 5.03%, March ≈ 3.69% **19.** Phone B as its relative frequency exceeds 5% **20.** W = 1,000, C = 2,500, B = 1,500 **21.** (ii) A = $\frac{5}{12}$, B = $\frac{1}{12}$, C = $\frac{1}{6}$, D = $\frac{1}{3}$ (iii) No

Exercise 12.3

1. (i) $\frac{1}{2}$ (ii) $\frac{1}{2}$ **2.** (i) $\frac{8}{15}$ (ii) $\frac{7}{15}$ **3.** 0.25 **4.** (a) (i) $\frac{1}{10}$ (ii) $\frac{3}{5}$ (iii) $\frac{2}{5}$ (iv) $\frac{1}{2}$ (b) (i) $\frac{1}{6}$ (ii) $\frac{5}{6}$ (iii) $\frac{1}{6}$ (iv) $\frac{1}{2}$ (v) 0 **5.** (i) $\frac{1}{6}$ (ii) $\frac{1}{6}$ (iii) 0 (iv) 1 (v) $\frac{1}{2}$ (vi) $\frac{1}{2}$ (vii) $\frac{1}{2}$ **6.** (i) 60% (ii) 24% (iii) 16% (iv) 84% (v) 84% **7.** (i) $\frac{1}{2}$ (ii) $\frac{1}{2}$ (iii) $\frac{1}{52}$ (iv) $\frac{1}{26}$ (v) $\frac{1}{52}$ **8.** (i) $\frac{1}{20}$ (ii) $\frac{1}{20}$ (iii) $\frac{1}{20}$ (iv) $\frac{1}{2}$ (v) $\frac{2}{5}$ (vi) $\frac{11}{20}$ **9.** (i) $\frac{3}{8}$ (ii) $\frac{1}{8}$ (iii) $\frac{2}{8} = \frac{1}{4}$ (iv) $\frac{3}{8}$ **10.** (i) $\frac{1}{8}$ (ii) $\frac{1}{8}$ (iii) $\frac{2}{8} = \frac{1}{4}$ **11.** (i) $\frac{12}{20} = \frac{3}{5}$ (ii) $\frac{2}{5}$ (iii) $\frac{10}{20} = \frac{1}{2}$ (iv) $\frac{3}{20}$ (v) $\frac{3}{8}$ **12.** (i) $\frac{1}{7}$ (ii) $\frac{6}{7}$ (iii) $\frac{1}{7} + \frac{1}{7} = \frac{2}{7}$ (iv) $\frac{5}{7}$ (v) $\frac{2}{7}$ **13.** (i) $\frac{1}{10}$ (ii) $\frac{3}{5}$ (iii) $\frac{2}{5}$ (iv) $\frac{3}{5}$ **14.** (i) $\frac{3}{7}$ (ii) $\frac{1}{7}$ (iii) $\frac{4}{7}$ (iv) $\frac{3}{7}$ (v) $\frac{4}{7}$ **15.** (i) $\frac{1}{10}$ (ii) $\frac{2}{5}$ (iii) $\frac{1}{2}$ (iv) $\frac{1}{2}$ (v) $\frac{9}{10}$ (vi) $\frac{3}{5}$ **16.** (i) 0.625 (ii) $\theta = 207°$ **17.** (i) 0.06 (ii) 8 bowls **18.** (i) $\frac{4}{13}$ (ii) $\frac{9}{13}$ (iii) 11 tokens added

Exercise 12.4

1. (i) A = {1, 2, 3, 4} (ii) B = {5, 6, 7} (iii) $\frac{4}{7}$ (iv) $\frac{3}{7}$

2. (i) {a, e, i} (ii) {b, c} (iii) Mutually exclusive events (iv) $\frac{1}{2}$ (v) $\frac{1}{3}$ **3.** (i) 3 (ii) 3 (iii) $\frac{1}{2}$ (iv) $\frac{5}{6}$ (v) $\frac{1}{6}$ **4.** (i) $\frac{7}{20}$ (ii) $\frac{39}{40}$ (iii) $\frac{1}{10}$ **5.** (a) (i) $\frac{12}{13}$ (ii) $\frac{3}{13}$ (iii) $\frac{4}{13}$ (iv) $\frac{1}{13}$ (b) (i) $\frac{8}{13}$ (ii) 0 (iii) $\frac{1}{13}$ (iv) $\frac{5}{13}$ **6.** (i) $\frac{3}{8}$ (ii) $\frac{5}{8}$ (iii) $\frac{9}{40}$ **7.** (i) $\frac{14}{25}$ (ii) $\frac{3}{50}$ (iii) $\frac{24}{25}$ (iv) $\frac{1}{25}$ **8.** (ii) 0.25 (iii) 0.65 (iv) 0.05

9. (ii) 0.75 or (1 − 0.25) (iii) 0.45 **10.** (ii) $\frac{11}{30}$ (iii) $\frac{7}{10}$ (iv) $\frac{17}{30}$ (v) $\frac{8}{15}$ (vi) $\frac{9}{10}$ or $\left(1 - \frac{1}{10}\right)$ **11.** (i) $\frac{1}{20}$ (ii) $\frac{4}{5}$ (iii) $\frac{9}{20}$ **12.** (i) $\frac{8}{15}$ (ii) $\frac{1}{3}$ (iii) $\frac{23}{30}$ **13.** (i) $\frac{3}{10}$ (ii) $\frac{6}{25}$ (iii) $\frac{2}{5}$ **14.** (i) $\frac{3}{20}$ (ii) $\frac{2}{5}$ (iii) $\frac{17}{20}$ **15.** (i) 2 (ii) 38 (iii) $\frac{3}{5}$ **16.** (i) $\frac{1}{3}$ (ii) 0 (iii) $\frac{5}{6}$ **17.** (i) $\frac{1}{6}$ (ii) $\frac{1}{3}$ (iii) $\frac{1}{2}$ (iv) 1 (v) $\frac{1}{6}$ (vi) $\frac{2}{3}$ **18.** (i) $\frac{1}{10}$ (ii) $\frac{11}{20}$ (iii) $\frac{3}{4}$ (iv) $\frac{1}{5}$ (v) $\frac{11}{20}$ (vi) $\frac{1}{10}$ (vii) $\frac{3}{5}$

Exercise 12.5

1. (i) $\frac{1}{12}$ (ii) $\frac{1}{4}$ (iii) $\frac{1}{4}$ (iv) $\frac{3}{4}$ **2.** (i) $\frac{1}{4}$ (ii) $\frac{3}{4}$ **3.** (ii) $\frac{1}{4}$ (iii) $\frac{1}{4}$ (iv) $\frac{1}{2}$ (v) $\frac{3}{4}$ **4.** (i) $\frac{1}{4}$ (ii) $\frac{1}{4}$ (iii) $\frac{1}{6}$ (iv) $\frac{5}{6}$ **5.** (i) $\frac{1}{9}$ (ii) $\frac{1}{2}$ (iii) $\frac{11}{18}$ (iv) $\frac{1}{18}$ **6.** (i) $\frac{5}{36}$ (ii) $\frac{5}{12}$ (iii) 1 (iv) $\frac{5}{12}$ (v) 0 **7.** (ii) 8 (iii) 1 (iv) $\frac{1}{8}$ (v) 1 (vi) $\frac{1}{8}$ (vii) 7 (viii) $\frac{7}{8}$ (ix) $\frac{1}{4}$ (x) $\frac{3}{8}$ **8.** (i) $\frac{1}{27}$ (ii) $\frac{1}{27}$ (iii) $\frac{1}{9}$ (iv) $\frac{8}{27}$ (v) $\frac{4}{9}$

9. (a)

	Art	Biology	Tech. graphics	Total
Boy	13	12	8	33
Girl	17	35	15	67
Total	30	47	23	100

(b) (i) 0.33 (ii) 0.30 (iii) 0.35 (iv) 0.53 (v) $\frac{17}{67}$ (vi) $\frac{52}{67}$

10.

	1	2	3	4	5	6
1	1	2	3	4	5	6
2	2	4	6	8	10	12
3	3	6	9	12	15	18
4	4	8	12	16	20	24

(i) $\frac{3}{4}$ (ii) $\frac{5}{24}$ (iii) $\frac{1}{8}$ (iv) $\frac{1}{12}$ (v) $\frac{1}{3}$ **11.** (i) $\frac{1}{8}$ (ii) $\frac{3}{8}$ (iii) $\frac{1}{2}$ (iv) $\frac{1}{8}$ **12.** (b) (i) $\frac{2}{15}$ (ii) $\frac{13}{15}$ (iii) $\frac{13}{75}$ (iv) $\frac{41}{150}$ (v) $\frac{1}{2}$ (vi) $\frac{41}{90}$

13. (a)

	O	W	G
1	1O	1W	1G
1	1O	1W	1G
2	2O	2W	2G
2	2O	2W	2G
2	2O	2W	2G
6	6O	6W	6G

(b) (i) $\frac{1}{3}$ (ii) $\frac{2}{9}$ (iii) $\frac{1}{9}$

14. (i)

	Eric	Fred	Gerry	Holly
Alan	AE	AF	AG	AH
Barbara	BE	BF	BG	BH
Claire	CE	CF	CG	CH
Declan	DE	DF	DG	DH

(ii) $\frac{1}{16}$ (iii) $\frac{3}{4}$ (iv) $\frac{1}{4}$ (v) $\frac{1}{2}$

15. (a)

	Hardback	Paperback	Totals
Fiction	210	420	630
Non-fiction	230	200	430
Children's books	110	80	190
Total	550	700	1250

(b) (i) 0.344 (ii) 0.44 (iii) 0.064 (iv) 0.328 (c) 48

Exercise 12.6

1. (a) (i) 100 (ii) 25 (iii) 16 (b) (i) $\frac{1}{4}$ (ii) $\frac{4}{25}$ (iii) $\frac{1}{100}$ **2.** $\frac{60}{289}$ **3.** $\frac{1}{1{,}000}$ **4.** (i) $\frac{2}{15}$ (ii) $\frac{6}{15}$ (iii) $\frac{4}{15}$ (iv) $\frac{7}{15}$ (v) $\frac{13}{15}$

5. (i) $\frac{25}{121}$ (ii) $\frac{30}{121}$ (iii) $\frac{60}{121}$ **6.** (i) $\frac{1}{4}$ (ii) $\frac{1}{16}$ (iii) $\frac{1}{169}$ (iv) $\frac{2}{169}$ **7.** (i) $\frac{20}{81}$ (ii) $\frac{20}{81}$ (iii) $\frac{25}{81}$ (iv) $\frac{41}{81}$ (v) $\frac{40}{81}$ **8.** (i) 0.2625 (ii) 0.1625 (iii) $\frac{0.2625}{0.425}$ (iv) 0.5125 **9.** (i) $\frac{1}{144}$ (ii) $\frac{1}{12}$ (iii) $\frac{11}{12}$ **10.** (ii) 0.72 (iii) 0.07 (iv) 0.08 (v) 0.21 (vi) 0.93 **11.** (i) 0.015 (ii) 0.076 (iii) 0.091 (iv) 0.035 (v) 0.126 **12.** (i) 50.4% (ii) 0.6% (iii) 12.6% (iv) 0.126, 0.056, 0.216, 39.8% (v) 49% **13.** (ii) 0.1521 (iii) 0.0138 (iv) 0.1056 (v) 0.379 (vi) 0.621 (vii) 0.0591 **14.** (i) 24 (ii) 6 (iii) 4 (iv) 12 (v) $\frac{1}{4}$ (vi) $\frac{1}{6}$ (vii) $\frac{1}{2}$ **15.** (a) (i) 17, 558, 424 (ii) 15, 584, 400 (b) (i) $\frac{1}{26}$ (ii) $\frac{10}{999}$

Exercise 12.7

1. (i) Yes (ii) No (iii) Yes (iv) No (v) Yes (vi) No **2.** (i) 0.6 (ii) 0.24 (iii) 0.096 **3.** (i) 0.5 (ii) 0.25 (iii) 0.125 **4.** (i) $\frac{1}{6}$ (ii) $\frac{5}{36}$ (iii) $\frac{25}{216}$ Doesn't win = $\frac{125}{216}$ **5.** (i) $\frac{1}{13}$ (ii) $\frac{12}{169}$ (iii) $\frac{144}{2{,}197}$, Doesn't win = $\frac{1{,}728}{2{,}197}$ **6.** $\frac{25}{72}$ **7.** (i) 0.2475 (ii) 0.136125 (iii) 0.166375 **8.** (i) 8% (ii) 7% (iii) 57% **9.** (i) 0.096 (ii) 0.064 (iii) 0.432 **10.** (a) (i) 0.15 (ii) 0.1275 (iii) 0.108375 (b) x 33% **11.** 0.064 **12.** (i) 0.25 (ii) 0.24375 (iii) 0.04375 (iv) 0.24375. She would expect to stop 227 times **13.** (a) (i) $\frac{3}{16}$ (ii) $\frac{9}{64}$ (c) (i) $\frac{216}{1331}$ (ii) $\frac{243}{1331}$ **14.** (i) 0.512 (ii) 0.488

Exercise 12.8

1. (a) €7 **2.** 6 **3.** (i) −€0.50 **4.** (i) −€ 0.25 per game (ii) No **5.** €-0.31 **6.** No **7.** (i) €1 (ii) −€4 **8.** No **9.** −€0.42. This is not a fair game **10.** (i) €21.25 (ii) €11.50 **11.** −€0.83 **13.** (i) −€3.75 (ii) Not a fair game. (iii) €487.50 **14.** (i) 0.00030003 (ii) €0.13

Revision Exercises

1. (a)(i) B (ii) A (c) (i) $\frac{1}{52}$ (ii) $\frac{1}{13}$ (iii) $\frac{1}{13}$ (iv) $\frac{4}{13}$ **2.** (a) (i) $\frac{1}{10}$ Total 10 (ii) $\frac{1}{5}$ (iii) $\frac{2}{5}$ (iv) $\frac{3}{5}$ (v) $\frac{2}{5}$ (vi) $\frac{3}{5}$ (vii) $\frac{2}{5}$ (viii) 0

(b) (i)

	1	2	3	4	5	6
H	H1	H2	H3	H4	H5	H6
T	T1	T2	T3	T4	T5	T6

(ii) $\frac{1}{12}$ (iii) $\frac{1}{12}$ (iv) $\frac{1}{4}$ (v) $\frac{1}{4}$ **3.** (c) (i) Yes (ii) Yes (iii) No (iv) Yes **4.** (a) (ii) 0.15 (iii) 0.35

(b) (i)

	1	2	3	4	5	6
1	1,1	1,2	1,3	1,4	1,5	1,6
2	2,1	2,2	2,3	2,4	2,5	2,6
3	3,1	3,2	3,3	3,4	3,5	3,6
4	4,1	4,2	4,3	4,4	4,5	4,6
5	5,1	5,2	5,3	5,4	5,5	5,6
6	6,1	6,2	6,3	6,4	6,5	6,6

(ii) Unfair (iii) Various rules possible. **5.** (a) (i) €0.5. (ii) Not a fair game. (iii) Yes (b)(i) $\frac{1}{6}$ (ii) $\frac{25}{216}$ (iii) $\frac{125}{216}$ (iv) $\frac{2}{27}$ **6.** (a) (i) $\frac{1}{16}$ (ii) $\frac{1}{16}$ (iii) $\frac{15}{16}$ (iv) $\frac{100}{169}$ (v) $\frac{25}{169}$ (b) (iii) 0.64 (iv) 0.04 (v) 0.16 or $\frac{0.16}{0.32}$

7. (a) (i)

	1	2	3	4	5	6
1	2	3	4	5	6	7
2	3	4	5	6	7	8
3	4	5	6	7	8	9
4	5	6	7	8	9	10
5	6	7	8	9	10	11
6	7	8	9	10	11	12

(iii) various changes possible (b) (ii) 0.045125 (iii) 0.857375 (iv) 0.142625. We expect 9,500 out of 10,000 components would not have a fault.

8. (a) (i) $\frac{1}{7}$ (ii) $\frac{6}{7}$ (iii) $\frac{1}{49}$ (iv) $\frac{12}{49}$ (v) $\left(\frac{6}{7}\right)$ **9.** (a) (i) 0.016 (ii) 0.144 (iii) 0.576 (iv) 0.064, 0.144, $\frac{0.016}{0.224}$ (v) 0.984 (b) (i) 720 (ii) 120 (iii) 48 (iv) 240 (v) $\frac{1}{6}$ (vi) $\frac{1}{3}$

Exam Questions

1. (a)(i) $\frac{2}{5}$ (ii) RRR, RRG, RGR, GRR, RGG, GRG, GGR, GGG

(b)

Player wins	€0	€1	€2	€3
Required outcomes	RRR	RRG RGR GRR	RGG GRG GGR	GGG

(c) Yes **2.** (ii) $\frac{64}{168}$ or $\frac{8}{21}$ (iii) 50.6% **3.** (a) (i) $\frac{5}{24}$ (ii) $\frac{7}{12}$ (b) $\frac{2}{3}$ **4.** (a) $\frac{1}{4}$ (b) $\frac{9}{16}$ (c) $\frac{27}{64}$ (d) $\frac{3}{1024}$ **5.** (a) 2.9 (b) 3.5 **7.** (a) $\frac{1}{2}$ since there are two outcomes and both are equally likely.

(b) (i) *MMMM* *FFFF* *FMMF* *MFFM*
MMMF *MMFM* *MFMM* *FMMM*
MMFF *MFMF* *FMFM* *FFMM*
MFFF *FMFF* *FFMF* *FFFM*

(ii)

four males	three males; one female	two males; two females	one male; three females	four females
$\frac{1}{16}$	$\frac{4}{16}=\frac{1}{4}$	$\frac{6}{16}=\frac{3}{8}$	$\frac{4}{16}=\frac{1}{4}$	$\frac{1}{16}$

(c) No the statement is not correct. **8.** (b) (i) $\frac{1}{52}$ (ii) $\frac{11}{26}$ (iii) ≈ 0.33 **9.** (b) (i) Group B (ii) 406 times (iii) $\frac{482}{600}$ (≈0.8) **10.** (a) ≈ 0.101 (b) ≈ 0.086 (c) €616.91 (d) €520.39 (e) Male €1071.09, Female €503.61 (f) €448

Chapter 13

Exercise 13.1

13. (i)

Outcome	1	2	3	4	5	6
Tally	𝍸 𝍸	𝍸 𝍸	𝍸 II	𝍸	𝍸 III	𝍸 𝍸
Frequency	10	10	7	5	8	10

(ii) 10 (iii) 10 (iv) 10%

14. (i)

Mode	Walk	Bus	Car	Rail
Frequency	9	5	4	2

(ii) Walk (iii) Rail (iv) Categorical

15. (i)

Goals	0	1	2	3	4
Tally	𝍸 II	𝍸 IIII	𝍸 𝍸 I	III	𝍸
Frequency	7	9	11	3	5

(ii) Numerical (iii) 35 (iv) 7 (v) 23 (vi) 7

16. (i) Categorical data

(ii)

Result	3 Heads	2 Heads	1 Head	0 Heads
Tally	III	𝍸 𝍸 I	𝍸 III	II
Frequency	3	11	9	2

(iii) 36%

Exercise 13.2

1. (i)

Stem	Leaf
3	0
4	0, 5, 8
5	2, 4, 5, 7
6	0, 1, 2, 2, 9
7	0, 6, 7
8	6, 6, 6
9	0 Key: 9|0 = 90

(ii) 80%

2. (i)

Stem	Leaf
13	9
14	0, 5, 9
15	0, 3, 3, 4, 5, 6, 7, 8
16	0, 0, 0, 5, 5, 6, 8
17	0, 0, 5
18	0, 1, 3 Key: 16|0 = 160

(ii) 25 (iii) $\frac{7}{25}$ **3.** (ii) Tanya and Rachel **4.** (ii) 27 cm (iii) 49 cm (iv) $\frac{5}{15} = \frac{1}{3}$ **5.** (i) The diagram is unordered. (ii) There are only 11 students recorded. (Should be 12) (iii) No key.

6. (i)

No. of sports	0	1	2	3	4	5
Frequency	4	11	18	8	5	4

7. (i) 29 (ii) Bus **8.** (i) 25 (ii) 1

9. (i)

Men	Stem	Women
	14	8, 9
9	15	0, 1, 2, 3, 4, 5, 5, 7, 7, 8, 8
8, 6, 1, 0	16	1, 2, 3, 5, 6, 7, 9
9, 9, 8, 6, 5, 5, 4, 4, 1, 0, 0	17	1, 4, 8
6, 5, 4, 3, 3, 1	18	
Key: 1|18 = 181 cm 1	19	Key: 17|1 = 171 cm

10. (i)

No. of students	5	15
Gender	Girls	Boys

(ii) 75% (iv) Pie chart.

11.

%	78%	21%	1%
Gas	Nitrogen	Oxygen	Other

Exercise 13.3

1. (i) Symmetric (ii) Skewed right (iii) Skewed left (iv) Symmetric

2. (i)

Stem	Leaf
1	2, 3, 4, 5, 5, 6, 6
2	1, 2, 2, 3, 4
3	4, 5, 6, 7
4	1, 1, 2, 3, 4
5	2, 2, 4, 4, 5, 5, 6 Key: 1|2 = 12

Symmetric

(ii)

Stem	Leaf
3	1, 2, 3, 4, 6, 7, 7, 8
4	2, 3, 3, 4, 5
5	6, 8, 8, 8
6	1, 2, 3
7	1 Key: 3|1 = 31

Skewed right

(iii)

Stem	Leaf
1	9
2	8, 9
3	3, 4, 5, 6
4	2, 3, 4, 4, 5, 5
5	2, 2, 2, 3, 5, 7, 9, 9 Key: 1|9 = 19

Skewed left

(iv)

Stem	Leaf
4	2, 3
5	3, 4, 5
6	1, 2, 2, 3, 8, 9
7	7, 8, 9, 9
8	2, 3 Key: 4|2 = 42

Roughly symmetric

3. (i)

Distance	0–2	2–4	4–6	6–8	8–10
Number	20	11	12	5	2

(ii) Positively

5. (i)

Time	0–1	1–2	2–3	3–4	4–5
Number	2	3	5	2	1

(ii) 13 (iii) 10 (iv) 15.38% **6.** (ii) 35 (iii) 15

7. (i) Roughly symmetric

(ii)

Time (sec)	2–3	3–4	4–5	5–6	6–7
Number	3	4	5	2	1

8. (a) 24 (c) (ii) €378.74 (nearest euro) (iii) €429.87

(d) 123,827 Litres.

10. (a)

	Scores in a 6th year Maths Test.
1	2, 7
2	9,
3	6, 6, 7, 9
4	4, 4, 6, 7, 9
5	0, 0, 3, 5, 6, 9, 9
6	1, 1, 1, 7, 7, 7, 8, 9, 9, 9
7	1, 2, 4, 4, 7, 8, 8, 9, 9, 9
8	1, 1, 3, 5, 5, 8, 8
9	0, 0, 1, 3 Key: 2|9 = 29%

(c)

Grade	08	07	06	05	04	03	02	01
Frequency	3	4	5	7	10	10	7	4

11. (a) 20 (e) Continuous numeric data.

(f) (i)

2	3, 5, 9
3	4, 7
4	3, 6, 7, 8, 9, 9
5	1, 1, 3, 3, 7
6	0, 2, 5
7	1 Key: 5|1 = 5.1

(g)

Category	Background	Mild	Moderate	Severe
Frequency	3	3	12	2

(j)

Ireland	Stem	California
	0	
9, 6, 4, 3, 1	1	
9, 7, 7, 7, 5, 2, 0	2	3, 5, 9
9, 6, 3, 3, 1, 0	3	4, 7
0, 0	4	3, 6, 7, 8, 9, 9
	5	1, 1, 3, 3, 7
	6	0, 2 ,5
Key: 0|3 = 3.0	7	1 Key: 3|4 = 3.4

12. (a) (i) 1.71 million

(c) (i)

Valuation Band	Tax per property	Number of properties	Total tax due (€)
€0 – €100,000	€45	425,790	19,160,550
€100,001 – €150,000	€112	489,060	54,774,720
€150,001 – €200,000	€157	374,490	58,794,930
€200,001 – €250,000	€202	177,840	35,923,680
€250,001 – €300,000	€247	83,790	20,696,130
Over €300,000	NA	159,030	NA

NA = Not Available

(ii) €189,350,010 (iii) €51,649,990 (iv) €324.78
(iv) €4,401,540

Exercise 13.4

1. (i) *W* and *Z* (ii) *X* (iii) *Y* **2.** (i) *Z* (ii) *Y* (iii) *Z* **5.** (ii) -0.9 **6.** (i) Positive weak (ii) Negative strong (iii) No correlation (iv) Negative strong (v) No correlation (vi) Positive strong **8.** (ii) 3 (iii) 0 (iv) 6.8 cm (v) 0.96 **9.** (i) Strong positive correlation (ii) Strong negative correlation (iii) No correlation **10.** (a) (i) B (ii) 7

Revision Exercises

1. (i)

Mode of transport	Car	Bus	Bike	Walk
Number	40	20	15	15

(ii) Categorical (iii) 16.7% **6.** (i) 20

(ii)

Stem	Leaf
40	1, 2, 2, 9
41	2, 2
42	2, 4, 5, 6
43	0, 8
44	0
45	7, 8
46	4, 7
47	2, 2
48	2 Key: 41|2 = 412 songs

(iii) 65% **8.** (ii) 0.99 (iii) Strong positive correlation

9. (i)

Age	20–30	30–40	40–50	50–60	60–70
Frequency	8	9	15	10	5

(ii)

Age	20–30	30–40	40–50	50–60	60–70
Frequency	8	9	15	10	5

(iii) Symmetric distribution **10.** (a) Incorrect (c) Incorrect

Exam Questions

1. (b) (i)

Table 2 (Girls, %)								
Height (cm)	145–150	150–155	155–160	160–165	165–170	170–175	175–180	180–185
Percentage of girls	3	9.6	16	22.4	25	16.2	5.8	2

2. (a) (i) 27,098 (ii) 308,973

Chapter 14

Exercise 14.1

1. (i) 6.6 (ii) 10 (iii) 5 (iv) 8 (v) 0.5 (vi) −4.4
2. Median (i) 6 (ii) 5 (iii) 2 (iv) 7.5 (v) 0; Mode (i) 7 (ii) 3 (iii) 2 (iv) 6, 7, 8 (v) 0 **3.** (ii) 45 (iii) 25 (iv) 38 **4.** (i) 10.86° (ii) 10.38° **5.** (i) 43% (ii) 49% (iii) 10 **6.** (i) 25 (ii) 20, 22, 22, 22, 23, 23, 24, 24, 24, 25, 25, 25, 25, 25, 25, 26 (iii) 24 (iv) 23.75 **7.** (i) 4.8 kg (ii) 5.45 kg (iii) 5.41 **8.** (i) 2007 (ii) 2012 (iii) 211,680 (iv) 175,982 **9.** (i) 02 **10.** (i) 4.7 (ii) 6

11. (i)

Time	30–35	35–40	40–45	45–50	50–55
Frequency	13	13	24	20	4

(ii) 41.76 minutes (iii) 26 **12.** (i) 96 (ii) 33.90625 (iii) 25% **15.** (i) 168 (ii) 240 (iii) 40.8 (iv) No

Exercise 14.2

1. (i) Mean – numerical and continuous
(ii) Mode – categorical (iii) Mean – numerical
(iv) Mode – categorical (v) Median – numerical
3. (i) Nominal Categorical (ii) Mode **4.** (i) Median (iii) Mean **5.** Mean = $32\frac{8}{9}$, Median = 18 and Mode = 12
6. (i) continuous numerical data

(ii)

Hours	0–1	1–2	2–3	3–4	4–5	5–6	6–7
Tally	~~1111~~ 1	~~1111~~ ~~1111~~	1111	1111	11	111	1
Number of days	6	10	4	4	2	3	1

(vii) 2.38 **7.** (i) continuous numerical data
(ii)

Max temp	29–31	31–33	33–35	35–37	37–39	39–41
Tally	11	~~1111~~ 111	~~1111~~ 111	~~1111~~ 111	11	11
Number of days	2	8	8	8	2	2

(iv) Symmetric (v) 34.25 (vi) 34.4 (vii) 34.47 (viii) 0.2%

Exercise 14.3

1. (i) IQR = $Q_3 - Q_1$ = 5 (ii) IQR = $Q_3 - Q_1$ = 3 (iii) IQR = Q_3 − Q1 = 4 (iv) IQR = $Q_3 - Q_1$ = 3 (v) IQR = $Q_3 - Q_1$ = 4 (vi) IQR = $Q_3 - Q_1$ = 10 **2.** (i) 51 (ii) 17.5 (iii) 47.5 (iv) 30 **3.** (i) 47 (ii) 3.2 (iii) 4.7 (iv) 1.5 **4.** Boys: (i) Q_2 = 56 (ii) Q_1 = 39 (iii) Q_3 = 69 (iv) IQR = 30 Girls: (i) Q_2 = 46 (ii) Q_1 = 42 (iii) Q_3 = 79 (iv) IQR = 37
5. (i)

Stem	Leaf
8	7 8
9	3 7 9
10	0 2 3 6 8 9 9
11	0 0 3 5 6 6 7 9 9 9
12	1 3 5 6
13	0 0 2 2 Key: 8|7 = 87

(ii) Roughly Symmetric (iii) 45 (iv) 114
(v) IQR = $Q_3 - Q_1$ = 18

6. (i)

0	2 3 5 7 8 9
1	1 1 2 2 4 5 6 7 8 9
2	3 5 5 8
3	1 2 3
4	0 0 2
5	0 2 2
6	0 Key 5/0 = 5.00

(ii) Skewed right (iii) 5.8 (iv) 1.85 (v) 2.15 (3.25 - 1.1)

Exercise 14.4

1. (i) 1.9 (ii) 2.6 (iii) 1.9 (iv) 3.7 (v) 0.1 **3.** (ii) 2.1, 3.9 **4.** 1.26 **5.** 1.1 **6.** (i) 7.95 (ii) 2.8 **7.** (i) 4.16 (ii) 2.4 **8.** (i) 70 (ii) 27 **9.** (i) Set A:
This distribution is symmetric
Set B:
This distribution is skewed right. (ii) mean A = $38\frac{1}{3}$ median B = 32 (iv) IQR = 38 - 25 = 13 (v) 10.168

Exercise 14.5

1. (i) 68% (ii) 95% (iii) 99.7% **2.** (i) $\mu = 18.6$ (ii) 4.2 (iii) [14.4, 22.8] **3.** (i) [175, 225] (ii) [80, 120] (iii) [18, 22] (iv) [22.5, 27.5] **4.** (i) [210, 350] (ii) [60, 180] (iii) [21, 29] (iv) [24, 46] **5.** (i) [75, 225] (ii) [255, 345] (iii) [14, 26] (iv) [85, 115] **7.** 193.5 cm **9.** 68% **11.** $x = 186.6575$

Exercise 14.7

1. −0.0247, 0.0647 **2.** 0.6587, 0.8413 **3.** (i) 0.7084, 0.7716 (ii) Yes **4.** 0.2384, 0.3016 **5.** $n \geq 400$, Sample size must be at least 400 **6.** 50% is not in [54.5%, 56.5%]
7. 50% is in [47%, 67%] **8.** $0.1\dot{6}$ is in [0.1477, 0.2967]
9. 70% is in [68%, 76%]

Revision Exercises

1. (i) Discrete; only whole number counts of beats are possible.
(ii)

No. of beats	Frequency
56–59	5
60–63	3
64–67	8
68–71	1
72–75	6
76–79	1
80–83	0
84–87	6

(iv) 65 (v) 66 (vi) 68.97 (vii) 4.31% (viii) 10.19
2. (i) Numerical (ii) 26

(iii)

Stem	Leaf
2	1, 2
3	1, 6, 8
4	1, 3, 7, 8, 9
5	2, 3, 4, 6, 8, 8, 9
6	0, 4, 4, 6
7	5, 9, 9
8	3, 6

(iv) Symmetric (v) 55 (vi) 54.6923 (vii) 0.3077
3. (i) 37 (iii) Symmetric (iv) 7.73 (v) 4.17
4. (i) 41 (ii) 18 (iii) 53.5 (iv) 35.5 (v) 58 (vi) 37.8
5. (i) 6 hours 17 min
6. (i)

Salary	Number
2450–2500	3
2500–2550	5
2550–2600	5
2600–2650	2
2650–2700	4
2700–2750	1

(iii) skewed right (iv) 2587.5 (v) 2580 (vi) Q1 2535, Q3 2644.5, IQR = Q3 − Q1 = 109.5
7. (i)

Stem	Leaf
51	0
52	6 7 9 9
53	0 4 4 6 9
54	2 4 6 7
55	0 3 5 7 8
56	1 Key 51|0 = 5.10

(ii) Symmetric (iii) Mean 5.4035, Median 5.405 (iv) $Q_3 - Q_1 = 0.22$ **9.** (i) [140.25, 177.75], (ii) [152.75, 165.25], (iii) [146.5, 171.5]

Exam Questions

1. (i) 3.2% (ii) $50.8 \leq p \leq 57.2$
2. (a)

Marriage rate		Death rate
9 8 7 7 6 6 5 5 3 3	4	
2 2 2 2 2 1 1 1 0 0 0	5	
	6	1 3 3 4 7 8
	7	1 3 6 9
	8	3 5 6 6 7 7 7 9
	9	0 0 0
		Key: 6|1 = 61

(c) Median: 50, Interquartile range: 5.5 (d) (i) Mean = 78.3
(ii) 68, 71, 73, 76, 79, 83, 87, 85, 86, 87, 86, 87 (e) 4 556 000
(f) 27791 **3.** (a) Mode = 12, Median = 24.5 (b) 22.7

(c)

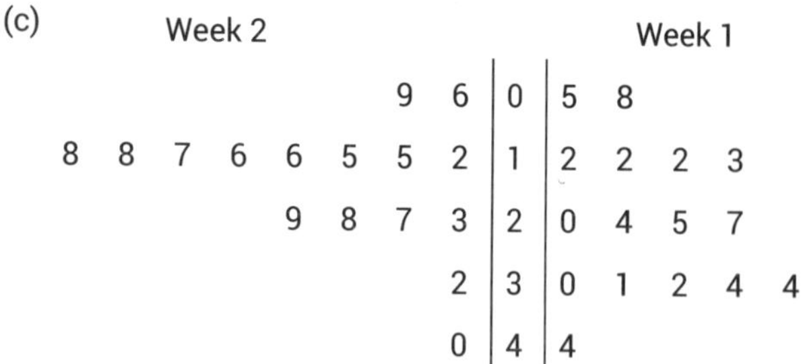

Week 2		Week 1
9 6	0	5 8
8 8 7 6 6 5 5 2	1	2 2 2 3
9 8 7 3	2	0 4 5 7
2	3	0 1 2 4 4
0	4	4

Key 1|3 = 13 minutes

Chapter 15

Exercise 15.1

1. (i) Any letter in question (ii) *PR*, *AC*, *AY*, etc. (iii) *FG* or another appropriate ray (iv) *RP*, *FE* (v) *XZ*, *XY* (vi) *A*, *C*, *Y*, *B* (vii) *X* OR *Y* **3.** (i) 70° acute (ii) 115° obtuse (iii) 45° acute (iv) 260° reflex (v) 120° obtuse **5.** (iv) No **6.** (i) 65° (ii) 27° (iii) 44° (iv) 63.5° (v) 120° (vi) 335° (vii) 65° **7.** (i) 10° (ii) 20° (iii) 6° (iv) 12° **8.** (i) $x = 22.5°$, $y = 45°$ (ii) $x = 15°$, $y = 8°$

Exercise 15.3

1. (i) 65° (ii) 55° (iii) 63° (iv) 90° **2.** (i) B = 25°, C = 155° (ii) *B* = 100°, *C* = 100° (iii) *B* = 35°, *C* = 110° (iv) *B* = 90°, *C* = 30° **3.** (i) $|\angle 1| = 145°$, $|\angle 2| = 35°$ (ii) $|\angle 1| = 148°$, $|\angle 2| = 148°$ (iii) $|\angle 1| = 73°$, $|\angle 2| = 107°$ (iv) $|\angle 1| = 84°$, $|\angle 2| = 96°$ (v) $|\angle 1| = 72°$, $|\angle 2| = 108°$ **4.** (i) Yes (ii) Yes (iii) No **5.** (i) *A* = 150°, *B* = 30°, *C* = 210° (ii) *A* = 84°, *B* = 84°, *C* = 96°, *D* = 96° (iii) $\angle 1 = 137°$, $\angle 2 = 137°$, $\angle 3 = 152°$, $\angle 4 = 28°$ (iv) *A* = 99°, *B* = 99°, *C* = 99°, *D* = 81° (v) *A* = 75°, *B* = 75°, *C* = 105°, *D* = 75° (vi) $\angle 1 = 104°$, $\angle 2 = 117°$, $\angle 3 = 63°$, $\angle 4 = 117°$ **6.** (i) $x = 40°$, $y = 55°$ (ii) $y = 12°$, $x = 18°$ (iii) $x = 42°$, $y = 138°$

Exercise 15.4

1. (i) *A* = 90°, *B* = 53° (ii) *A* = 60°, *B* = 120° (iii) *A* = 75°, *B* = 30° **2.** (i) *X* = 42°, *Y* = 42°, *Z* = 54° (ii) *X* = 49°, *Y* = 73° *Z* = 58° (iii) *X* = 60°, *Y* = 48°, *Z* = 84° (iv) *X* = 32°, *Y* = 28°, *Z* = 28° (v) *W* = 61°, *X* = 119°, *Y* = 74°, *Z* = 66° **3.** (i) $|\angle A| = 40°$, $|\angle B| = 120°$ (ii) $|\angle B| = 112°$, $|\angle A| = 34°$

4.

	Smallest	Largest
(i)	$\angle A$	$\angle B$
(ii)	$\angle 1$	$\angle 2$
(iii)	$\angle XZY$	$\angle YXZ$
(iv)	$\angle ACB$	$\angle BAC$
(v)	$\angle 2$	$\angle 1$

5.

	Longest	Shortest
(i)	*c*	*b*
(ii)	[*BC*]	[*AB*]
(iii)	[*DE*]	[*DF*]
(iv)	[*PQ*]	[*QR*]
(v)	[*RT*]	[*ST*]

6. (i) No (ii) Yes (iii) No (iv) No (v) Yes (vi) No **7.** (i) 2 (ii) 13 **8.** (i) 6 (ii) 18 **9.** (i) 75 cm (ii) 72 cm (iii) 60 cm (iv) 25 cm (v) 200 km **10.** (i) 8.60 m (ii) 18.76 cm (iii) 15.56 cm **11.** (i) $y = 4\sqrt{5}$ (ii) 6 (iii) $x = 1$ **12.** (i) No (ii) Yes **13.** (i) $x = 36$, $y = 60$ (ii) $x = 90$, $y = 48$ (iii) $x = 36$, $y = 48$ **14.** (i) Largest value = 17.99 m, Smallest value = 2.01 m (ii) Min = €100.05, Max = €179.95 **15.** *B* and *D* **16.** 2 **17.** (i) $b = 6$ (ii) $b = 22$ (iii) $6 \leq b \leq 22, b \in N$ **18.** (i) $c = 7$ (ii) $c = 25$ (iii) $7 \leq c \leq 25, c \in N$ **19.** 5 cm **20.** 5.02 m or 502 cm **21.** 3.99 m **22.** 6.27 m or 627 cm **23.** Elle is correct **24.** (i) $x = 4$ (ii) $x = 5$ **25.** Square blocks = 1.25 cm × 1.25 cm, Smaller rectangle blocks = 1.25 × 2.5 cm, Large rectangle blocks = 1.25 × 3.75 cm

Exercise 15.5

1. (i) 60° (ii) 8 (iii) 120° **2.** (i) 16 (ii) 18 (iii) 16 (iv) 5.8 **3.** (i) *A* = 85°, *B* = 95°, *C* = 95° (ii) *A* = 103°, *B* = 77°, *C* = 103° (iii) *A* = 42°, *B* = 77°, *C* = 61° (iv) *A* = 78°, *B* = 74°, *C* = 102° (v) *A* = 32°, *B* = 62°, *C* = 78° (vi) *A* = 90°, *B* = 63°, *C* = 27°, *D* = 27° **4.** (i) 45 cm^2 (ii) 31.5 cm^2 (iii) 10.5 cm^2 (iv) 10 cm^2 (v) 50 cm^2 **5.** (i) 105 cm^2 (ii) 41.8 cm^2 (iii) 72 cm^2 (iv) 52 cm^2 **6.** 28 cm^2 **7.** (i) 22.75 cm^2 (ii) 22.75 cm^2 (iii) 22.75 cm^2 (iv) 45.5 cm^2 (v) 8.125 cm^2 (vi) 37.375 cm^2 **8.** (i) $x = 15$, $y = 55°$ (ii) $x = 6$, $y = 5$ **9.** (i) 8.75 (ii) 10 (iii) 12 (iv) 4

Exercise 15.6

1. (i) Yes (ii) Yes (iii) Yes (iv) No (v) Yes (vi) Yes **2.** (i) $|\angle RST| = 47°$, $|\angle SUT| = 43°$ (ii) Isosceles (iii) Yes

Exercise 15.7

1. (i) 15 (ii) 4.5 **2.** (i) 3:6 = 1:2, 5:2 (ii) 9:3 = 3:1, 7:5 (iii) 6:9 = 2:3, 2:7 **3.** (i) 8 (ii) 6 (iii) 8 (iv) 10 (v) 17.6 **4.** (i) 21 (ii) 24 (iii) 7:8 **5.** (i) 5:2 (ii) 7:5 (iii) 7:5 (iv) Yes **6.** (i) $\frac{4}{3}$ (ii) $\frac{4}{3}$ (iii) $\frac{7}{3}$ (iv) 6 cm (v) 7 cm, 5.25 cm (vi) 12.25 cm **7.** Not parallel **8.** Parallel **9.** (ii) [*ML*] [*QR*], [*LO*] [*PR*], [*MO*] [*QP*] (iii) [*DF*] [*IG*], [*DE*] [*GH*], [*EF*] [*HI*] (iv) [*AC*] [*XZ*], [*AB*] [*XY*], [*BC*] [*YZ*] (v) [*QR*] [*UT*], [*PR*] [*VU*], [*QP*] [*VT*] **10.** (i) 14 (ii) 12 (iii) $5\frac{11}{23}$ **11.** (i) $x = 12$, $y = 8$ (ii) $x = 19.8$, $y = 22$ (iii) $x = 13\frac{1}{2}$, $y = 28\frac{1}{3}$ **12.** (i) Similar (ii) Not Similar **13.** (i) $x = 6$, $y = 6$ (ii) $x = 7$, $y = 21$ (iii) $x = 10\frac{2}{3}$, $y = 23\frac{1}{3}$ **14.** (ii) 10 (iii) 8 (iv) 4 **15.** (i) 4 (ii) $2\frac{2}{3}$ (iii) 4 **16.** (ii) 3:2 (iii) 3:2 (iv) 5:2 **17.** (ii) $|EF| = 8.75$ **18.** 7.68 m **19.** (i) Student B (ii) 1.81 m (iii) $x \approx 15.94$ m **20.** (i) 8.9175 m (ii) 10 m **21.** (ii) 2.05 m or 205 cm **22.** $x = 66.71$ m, $y = 29.98$ m, ≈ 4084 m^2 **23.** (ii) 11 m

Exercise 15.8

1. (i) $\angle BAC$ [*BC*] (ii) $\angle GFE$ [*GE*] (iii) $\angle TVS$ [*TS*]
2. (i) $|\angle 1| = 90°$, $|\angle 2| = 50°$ (ii) $\angle 1 = 52.5°$, $\angle 2$ = Alternate (iii) $|\angle 1| = 116°$, $|\angle 2| = 64°$ (iv) $|\angle 1| = 45°$, $|\angle 2| = 45°$
3. (i) *A* = 70°, *B* = 55° (ii) *A* = 32°, *B* = 64° (iii) *A* = 27°, *B* = 59° (iv) *A* = 60°, *B* = 40° (v) *A* = 72°, *B* = 54°
4. (i) $d = 17$ (ii) $d = 37$ **5.** (i) 90° (ii) 60° (iii) 30° (Alternate) (iv) isosceles **6.** (i) 113° (ii) 33.5° (iii) 56.5° (iv) 65°
7. $x = 4$ cm

Exercise 15.9

1. (i) 90° (ii) 90° (iii) 44° (iv) 46° **2.** (i) 90° (ii) 33° (iii) 57° **3.** (i) 15 (ii) $5\sqrt{13}$ **4.** (i) 10 cm (ii) 4 cm **5.** (i) 5 cm (ii) 8 cm (iii) 2 cm (iv) $4\sqrt{5}$ cm **6.** (i) 3 cm (ii) 5 cm (iii) 8 cm **7.** (i) 5 cm (ii) 8 cm **8.** (i) 8 cm (ii) 16 cm (iii) 2 cm (iv) 32 cm (v) $8\sqrt{17}$ cm **9.** (i) 24 cm (ii) 32 cm (iii) 96 cm^2 (iv) 96 cm^2 **10.** (i) 9 cm (ii) 2 cm (iii) $14\sqrt{2}$ cm^2 **11.** ≈ 335 km **12.** 2.8 cm **OR** 28 mm

Revision Exercises

1. (a) (i) $\angle ABC$ (ii) $\angle CBD$ (iii) $\angle CBE$ (iv) $\angle EBD$ (v) [*BE* (vi) *BD* (vii) $\angle ABE$, $\angle EBD$ (b) (i) 85° (ii) 110° (iii) 95° (iv) 70° (v) 85° (vi) 95° (vii) 95° (viii) 110°
2. (a) Opinion of students (b) (i) No (ii) Yes
3. (a) (i) $A = 43°$, $B = 56°$, $C = 28°$ (ii) $A = 58°$, $B = 148°$, $C = 58°$, $D = 32°$ (iii) $A = 61°$, $B = 61°$, $C = 93°$, $D = 119°$ (b) (i) No (ii) No (iii) Yes (iv) Yes (v) No
4. (a) (i) [*AB*], [*BC*], [*AC*] (ii) [*EF*], [*DF*], [*DE*] (iii) [*QR*], [*PQ*], [*PR*] (b) (ii) *B*, *C* (c) (i) $x = 15$, $y = 8$ (ii) $x = 5\sqrt{5}$, $y = 5$
5. (a) (i) $A = 100°$, $B = 100°$, $C = 80°$, (ii) $A = 90°$, $B = 58°$, $C = 32°$ (b) (i) F (ii) F (iii) T (iv) T (v) F **6.** (a) (i) 80 cm^2 (ii) 102 cm^2 (iii) 20 cm^2 (b) (i) $400\sqrt{3}$ cm^2 (ii) 124.8 sq units **7.** (a) (i) Yes (ii) No (b) (i) Parallelogram (iii) Yes (iv) 6 cm **8.** (a) (i) $x = \frac{8}{5}$ (ii) $x = 1.5$ (iii) $x = 7.2$ (b) (i) $x = 13$, $y = 20$ (ii) $x = 25$, $y = 18$ (iii) $x = 14$, $y = \frac{4}{7}$ (c) (iii) 4.5 cm (iv) $8\frac{8}{9}$ cm (v) $1\frac{1}{9}$ cm **9.** (a) (i) $A = 96°$, $B = 48°$ (ii) $A = 117°$, $B = 27°$ (b) (i) $x = 15$ (ii) $x = 17.5$ (iii) $x = 10$ (c) (i) Right angled (ii) ΔABC is isosceles (iii) 45° (iv) $15\sqrt{2}$ cm **10.** (a) (i) Always (ii) Always (iii) Sometimes (iv) Sometimes (v) Never (vi) Always (vii) Always (b) (i) 26 km (ii) 24 km (c) (i) 175 km longest, 25 km shortest (ii) 25 km $< x <$ 175 km
11. (a) (i) 120° (ii) 165° (b) (i) 6 (ii) Hexagon (iii) 720° [4 Triangles] (c) €70, €130 **12.** (a) (i) $|AM| = 12$ mm, $|DM| = 5$ mm (ii) $\angle AMD$, $\angle AMB$, $\angle DMC$, $\angle BMC$ (iii) 13 mm (v) 120 mm^2 (b) 14 cm **13.** (iv) 3.75 m (v) 3.875 m
14. (i) 293 m (ii) €5,860 (iii) ≈ €7,225 (iv) Original is cheapest by €1,365

Exam Questions

1. Triangle 2 **2.** $x = 12$ **4.** (a) $x = 30°$, $y = 40°$, $z = 70°$ (b) (i) 240 m^2 (ii) 120 m^2 **5.** (b) (−5, 1) **OR** (−5, −4) **10.** (a) (i) 2552 m^2 (ii) ≈ 52.697 m (iii) 48.427 m (c) $x = 90$, $y = 48$, $z = 42$

Chapter 16

Exercise 16.1

24. (ii) ≈ 5 cm (iii) Pythagoras theorem **25.** (ii) ≈ 68° (iii) 1 : 100

Exercise 16.3

5.

Point of Intersection	Type of triangle
Inside	acute
On	Right-angled
Outside	obtuse

Exercise 16.4

1. (i) *D* (ii) *P* (iii) *P* (iv) *X* **2.** (i) *A* (ii) *C* (iii) *C* (iv) *B*
3. (i) *C* (ii) *B* (iii) *A* (iv) *A* **4.** (i) Positive 90° (ii) Negative 90° (iii) Positive/negative 180° (iv) Negative 90° **6.** (b) *q*: (4, −1), (6, 0), (8, 2) *p*: (−2, 3), (−4, 2), (−6, 4) *r*: (−1, −2), (0, −4), (−2, −6)

Exercise 16.6

1. (a) (i) *P* (ii) 2 (b) (i) *Q* (ii) 0.5 **3.** (ii) $k = 3$ (iii) k^2
4. (i) 5 cm (ii) 43 cm^2 **6.** (ii) 4 (iii) 1 : 16
7. (i) *S* (ii) 3 (iii) 24 cm (iv) 16 cm (v) 320 cm^2 **8.** 2 cm^2 **9.** (i) *R* (ii) 2.5 (iii) 4 (iv) $|XY| = 1.2$, $|YR| = 1.6$ (v) 6.25 : 1 **10.** (iii) 48 cm^2 **11.** (i) 5 (ii) 1.4 (iii) 12 (iv) 30 sq units (v) 28.8 sq units **12.** (i) 1,160 cm^2 (ii) 2,400 cm^3 (iii) 725,000 cm^2 or 72.5 m^2 (iv) 37.5 m^3 (v) 1 : $(25)^2$ (vi) 1 : $(25)^3$

Revision Exercises

16. (i) *Z* (ii) 2 **17.** (i) 4.5 cm (ii) 6 cm (iii) 40.5 cm^2
18. (i) 3 cm (ii) 10 cm (iii) 6 cm^2 (iv) 37.5 cm^2
19. (iii) 100 : 16 or 25 : 4 (iv) 4.5 **20.** (i) 1.5 (ii) 10 cm (iii) 27 cm^2 (iv) 33.75 cm^2 **21.** (i) 3.5 (ii) 5.25 (iii) 1.4 (iv) 12.25 : 1

Exam Questions

1. (b) 9.9 cm **2.** (ii) $|OB| = 15$ cm, $|OQ| = 22.5$ cm (iii) 1.5 (b) 16.875 cm^2 (c) (i) 7.5 cm (ii) 5.8 cm **3.** (b) 3.6 cm
5. (a) (i) The tangent is perpendicular to the tangent at the point of contact **6.** (ii) 12.5 m (iii) 8.544 m (iv) 34.176 m

Chapter 17

Exercise 17.1

1. (i) 29 (ii) 85 (iii) 3 (iv) 24 (v) 24 (vi) 40 **2.** (i) $\sqrt{10}$ (ii) $\sqrt{2}$ (iii) $\sqrt{34}$ (iv) $\sqrt{24}$ **3.** 2.5 m **4.** (i) 12 (ii) 77 (iii) 4 (iv) 24 **5.** (i) 60 cm (ii) 100 (iii) 4,800 cm^2 **6.** Triangle is right-angled **7.** Triangle is right-angled **8.** Triangle is right-angled **9.** 205

Exercise 17.2

1. (i) $\sin A = \frac{5}{13}$ $\cos A = \frac{12}{13}$ $\tan A = \frac{5}{12}$ (ii) $\sin A = \frac{21}{29}$ $\cos A = \frac{20}{29}$ $\tan A = \frac{21}{20}$ **2.** (i) $\sin A = \frac{40}{58}$ $\cos A = \frac{42}{58}$ $\tan A = \frac{40}{42}$ $\sin B = \frac{42}{58}$ $\cos B = \frac{40}{58}$ $\tan B = \frac{42}{40}$ (ii) $\sin A = \frac{3}{\sqrt{13}}$ $\cos A = \frac{2}{\sqrt{13}}$ $\tan A = \frac{3}{2}$ $\sin B = \frac{2}{\sqrt{13}}$ $\cos B = \frac{3}{\sqrt{13}}$ $\tan B = \frac{2}{3}$ (iii) $\sin A = \frac{2}{\sqrt{20}}$ $\cos A = \frac{4}{\sqrt{20}}$ $\tan A = \frac{2}{4}$ $\sin B = \frac{4}{\sqrt{20}}$ $\cos B = \frac{2}{\sqrt{20}}$ $\tan B = \frac{4}{2}$ **3.** (i) 0.2588 (ii) 0.8660 (iii) 3.7321 (iv) 0.2419 (v) 0.9004 (vi) 0.0872 (vii) 0.2126 (viii) 0.5000 (ix) 5.6713 (x) 0.4791 **4.** (i) 38.26 (ii) 29.61 (iii) 19.76 (iv) 25.94 (v) 20.62 (vi) 82.84 (vii) 58.54 (viii) 46.23
5. ≅13° **6.** ≅28° **7.** 53° **8.** 27° **9.** 16.3°

Exercise 17.3

1. (i) 8.66 (ii) 5 (iii) 10.32 (iv) 10.45 (v) 8 (vi) 30.42 **2.** (i) 4.37 (ii) 24.24 (iii) 14.74 **3.** (i) 26.03 (ii) 12.86 (iii) 9.00 **4.** (i) 35° (ii)71° (iii) 40° (iv) 59° (v) 61° (vi) 45° **5.** 64.28, 11.33 **6.** ≅3.6, ≅4.7, ≅12

Exercise 17.4

1. 449 m **2.** 346 m **3.** (i) ≅16 metres (ii) 18 m **4.** (i) 118 km (ii) 23 km/hr (iii) 59 km/hr **5.** (i) 4.95 metres **6.** 470 m **7.** (i) 45.8 m (ii) $\angle ADB = 55°$, $\angle ADC = 74.36°$ **8.** (i) $|BD| = 3.3166$ m (ii) $\angle CDB = 56°$ (iii) $x = 4.2$ m, $y = 6.53$ m, 21.03 m **9.** (i) 30° (ii) $\sqrt{3} = |AB|$ (iii) $|AC| = 2$ **10.** (i) 45° (ii) $|BC| = 7$ **11.** (i) 4, 4 (ii) 45° **12.** (a) 8.66 cm (b) (i) 21.4 cm (ii) 69.5° (c) (i)12.12 m, 34.08 m (ii) 3.4 ms^{-1}

Exercise 17.5

1. 73.72 sq units **2.** 120 sq units **3.** 80.99 sq units **4.** 158.48 sq units **5.** 46.98 sq units **6.** 26 cm^2 **7.** 82 cm^2 **8.** (i) 30° (ii) 60° **9.** (i) $|\angle ABD| = 23.59°$, $|\angle DBC| = 28.71°$ (ii) 127.7° **10.** (i) $\frac{4}{5}$ (ii) 9.6 $units^2$

Exercise 17.6

1. 0 **2.** −1 **3.** 0 **4.** 1 **5.** 0 **6.** −1 **7.** 0 **8.** 1 **9.** 0 **10.** 0 **11.** 1 **12.** 0 **13.** 0 **14.** $-\frac{1}{\sqrt{2}}$ **15.** $\frac{1}{2}$ **16.** $-\frac{1}{2}$ **17.** $-\frac{1}{2}$ **18.** $\frac{1}{\sqrt{3}}$ **19.** $\frac{1}{\sqrt{2}}$ **20.** $\frac{\sqrt{3}}{2}$ **21.** $-\frac{\sqrt{3}}{2}$ **22.** $-\sqrt{3}$ **23.** $\sqrt{3}$ **24.** −0.82 **25.** 0.34 **26.** −0.64 **27.** −0.09 **28.** 0.84 **29.** 0.82 **30.** 0.64 **31.** −0.64 **32.** −0.18 **33.** −0.36 **34.** 30° **OR** 150° **35.** 45° **OR** 315° **36.** 60° **OR** 240°

Exercise 17.7

1. 11.92 **2.** 15.56 **3.** 19.38 **4.** 10.15 **5.** 10.85 **6.** 18° **7.** 53° **8.** (i) 27.3° (ii) 103 (iii) 182.7 **9.** (i) 68° (ii) 59° (iii) 31.9 $units^2$ (iv) 8.60 **10.** (i) 24° (ii) 39.2 $units^2$ (iii) 16.06 **11.** $|PQ| = 73.73$ m, $|PR| = 65.22$ m **12.** 4,350 $metres^2$

Exercise 17.8

1. 4.58 **2.** 9.53 **3.** 13.69 **4.** 3.87 **5.** 18.37 **6.** 60° **7.** 120° **8.** 41° **9.** 17° **10.** (a) (i) 5.29 (ii) 3.31 (b) 1908 mm^2 **11.** (ii) 96° (iii) 96° (iv) 17.40 cm^2 **12.** (ii) 22° (iii) 22° (iv) 6.5556 cm^2 **13.** (i) 15 km (ii) 12.5 km (iii) 150° (iv) 26, 571 m **14.** (i) ≅110 km (ii) 4.5 hrs (iii) 1 hr 29 mins **15.** (i) 64.76° (ii) 494.61 m^2 (iii) 1978.44 m^2 (iv) 1254.5764 m^2 16. (i) 65 m (ii) 140 m (iii) 34.64 m

Exercise 17.9

1. (i) 13.89π cm^2 (ii) 60π cm^2 (iii) 189π cm^2 **2.** (i) 4.44π cm (ii) 13.89π cm (iii) 28.33π cm **3.** (i) $\theta = 60°$ (ii) $\theta = 135°$ (iii) $\theta = 200°$ **4.** (i) $\theta = 70°$ (ii) $\theta = 120°$ **5.** 36.8 m^2

Revision Exercises

1. (a) $\sin\alpha = \frac{20}{29}$ $\cos\alpha = \frac{21}{29}$ $\tan\alpha = \frac{20}{21}$, $\sin\beta = \frac{21}{29}$ $\cos\beta = \frac{20}{29}$ $\tan\beta = \frac{21}{20}$ (b) (i) $\alpha = 27°$ (ii) 12.16 cm (iii) 28.13 cm **2.** (a)

sin α	cos α	tan α
p	$-q$	$\frac{-p}{q}$

(b) (i) 3.52 (ii) 3.64 **3.** (i) 6.22 cm (ii) 24 cm^2 **4.** (i) 30° (ii) 45° (iii) 45° (iv) 60° **5.** (i) 2 cm (ii) 2.09 cm^2 (iii) 43.30 cm^2 (iv) 39.12 cm^2 **6.** (ii) $h = 2$ m = 200 cm, $a = 3$ m = 300 cm (iii) 36 cm 7. (i) 7.36 m (ii) 242 cm (iii) 14° **8.** (ii) 13 m

Exam Questions

1. (a) (i) 11.39 m (ii) 42.75 m^2 (b) 16.53 m **2.** (a) 24 cm^2 (b) 120° **3.** (a) (i) 10.2 m (ii) 31° (b) (i) 138° (ii) 22.6 m

Chapter 18

Exercise 18.1

1. $A(-5,-2)$, $B(-3,2)$, $C(6,-1)$, $D(-4,1)$, $E(0,4)$, $F(1,2)$, $G(-1,0)$, $H(2,-4)$ **2.** (i) 2nd (ii) 4th (iii) 2nd (iv) 3rd (v) 1st (vi) 1st (vii) 4th (viii) 3rd (ix) 1st (x) 3rd **3.** (i) X (ii) Y (iii) Y (iv) X (v) X (vi) X (vii) Y **4.** (i) (3,0) (ii) (−4,0) (iii) (0,3) (iv) (0,−2) **5.** (i) $\sqrt{10}$ (ii) $\sqrt{157}$ (iii) 2 (iv) 4 **6.** (i) $\sqrt{45}$ (ii) $\sqrt{8}$ (iii) $\sqrt{65}$ (iv) $\sqrt{45}$ (v) 6 (vi) $\sqrt{65}$ **7.** (i) 13 (ii) $|AC|$ $\sqrt{338}$ (iii) Yes. **8.** (ii) $|AB| = \sqrt{32}$, $|DC| = \sqrt{32}$ (iii) $|BC| = \sqrt{5}$. (iv) $|AC| = \sqrt{29}$ (v) $|BC| = \sqrt{45}$ **9.** $|AB| = 5$, $|BC| = 5$, $|AC| = 10$, **10.** $|AB| = |AC|$, ΔABC is isosceles **11.** $|WX| = |WY| = |XY|$, ΔWXY is equilateral **12.** $\sqrt{18}$, Inside, as $\sqrt{18} < 5$ **13.** $\sqrt{20}$ **14.** (i) (4,4)

Exercise 18.2

1. (i) (5,3) (ii) (4,6) (iii) (6,8) (iv) (2,4) **2.** (i) (3,4.5) (ii) (3,0) (iii) (3.5,−2) (iv) (0.5,−4) **3.** (i) (2.5,−1.5) (ii) (−1,−4) (iii) (3.5,2) (iv) (2.5,−6) **4.** $C(2,3)$ **5.** Midpoint = (4,0) **6.** (i) $C(1,-1)$ (ii) $\sqrt{41}$ **7.** (i) $M(3,-2)$ (ii) $|AM| = \sqrt{29}$, $|MB| = \sqrt{29}$ **8.** (i) $M\left(3\frac{1}{2}, 1\frac{1}{2}\right)$ (ii) $N\left(1\frac{1}{2}, 0\right)$ **9.** (i) $M(6,5)$ (ii) 3 (iii) 4 (iv) $C(6,9)$ **10.** $x = 2$, $y = 3$ **11.** (i) $B(4,-12)$ (ii) $B(9,-2)$ (iii) $B(-2,1)$ (iv) $B(-8,-15)$ **12.** $x = 0$, $y = -5$

Exercise 18.3

1. (i) 3 (ii) −2 (iii) 0 (iv) 4 **2.** (i) $\frac{1}{5}$ (ii) $-\frac{2}{3}$ (iii) −2 (iv) $-\frac{2}{9}$ **3.** (i) −1 (ii) $\frac{1}{3}$ (iii) $\frac{7}{4}$ (iv) $\frac{11}{6}$ **4.** 1, 0, −1, $-\frac{5}{2}$, $\frac{5}{2}$, $-\frac{3}{2}$ **5.** $q = -1$ $r = -\frac{3}{2}$ $s = \frac{3}{2}$ $t = \frac{-2}{5}$ $u = \frac{5}{3}$ $v = 0$ **6.** (i) c (ii) slope $a = 0$, slope $b = 1$, slope $d = -3$, slope $e = -\frac{1}{2}$

7. The two lines are parallel
8. The two lines are perpendicular
9.

Slope	Slope of parallel line	Slope of perpendicular line
$\frac{3}{4}$	$\frac{3}{4}$	$\frac{-4}{3}$
$\frac{5}{2}$	$\frac{5}{2}$	$\frac{-2}{5}$
-3	-3	$\frac{1}{3}$
$\frac{1}{2}$	$\frac{1}{2}$	-2
-2	-2	$\frac{1}{2}$
$\frac{-1}{4}$	$\frac{-1}{4}$	4
$\frac{-8}{11}$	$\frac{-8}{11}$	$\frac{11}{8}$

10. $\frac{-8}{5}$ **11.** $\frac{1}{2}$ **12.** $\frac{4}{3}$ **13.** 4 **14.** $\frac{-5}{4}$ **15.** $\frac{1}{5}$ **16.** (iii) $\left(\frac{7}{2}, -\frac{1}{2}\right)$

Exercise 18.4

1.

Line	✓ or ×
$2x + y = 8$	✓
$x + y = 5$	✓
$2x - y = 4$	✓
$x - y + 1 = 0$	×
$3x + y = 11$	✓

2.

Line	✓ or ×
$x + y = 2$	×
$3x + y = 0$	✓
$2x + y = 2$	✓
$6000x + 2000y = 0$	✓
$x - y = 4$	×

3. (i) (0,6) (1,5) (2,4) (3,3) (ii) (0,9) (1,8) (2,7) (3,6) (iii) (8,4) (7,3) (6,2) (5,1) (iv) (0,12) (1,10) (2,8) (3,6) (v) (10,0) (7,1) (4,2) (1,3) (vi) (6,0) (4,1) (2,2) (0,3) (vii) (0,9) (1,7) (2,5) (3,3) (viii) (4,0) (5,1) (6,2) (7,3) **4.** On line **5.** Not on the line **6.** Not on the line **7.** (i) Any three points (0,2) (−3,3) (6,0) (iii) $\frac{-2}{6} = \frac{-1}{3}$ (iv) On line **8.** (i) (0,−8), (1,−6), (4,0) (iii) 2 (iv) Not on line **9.** $k = 13$ **10.** $k = 9$ **11.** $c = 7$ **12.** $k = 4$ **13.** $c = 7$ **14.** (i) $x = 5$ (ii) $x = -2$ (iii) $x = -1$ (iv) $x = 2$ **15.** (i) $y = 3$ (ii) $y = -2$ (iii) $y = -3$ (iv) $y = 5$

Exercise 18.5

1. (i) 2 (ii) 3 (iii) 7 (iv) $\frac{1}{2}$ **2.** (i) 2 (ii) $\frac{2}{3}$ (iii) −2 (iv) $\frac{-6}{5}$ **3.** (i) (0,−8) (ii) (0,−4) (iii) (0,3) (iv) $\left(0,\frac{-1}{3}\right)$ **4.** (i) (0,−2) (ii) (0,−8) (iii) (0,−5) (iv) $\left(0,\frac{-2}{5}\right)$ **6.** Point of intersection (2,7) **8.** (i) 0,−6) (ii) (0,2) (iii) (0,8) (iv) (0,−12) **9.** (i) (−4,0) (ii) (6,0) (iii) (9,0) (iv) (2,0) **10.** (i) (3,0), (0,3) (ii) (6,0), (0,3) (iii) (4,0) (iv) (3,0), (0,−15) (v) (6,0), (0,10) (vi) (4,0), (0,3)

Exercise 18.6

1. (i) $2x - y - 1 = 0$ (ii) $x + y + 1 = 0$ (iii) $5x + y + 32 = 0$ (iv) $x - 2y - 3 = 0$ (v) $x + 3y + 22 = 0$ (vi) $y - 1 = 0$ **2.** (i) $3x - 2y + 13 = 0$ (ii) $4x + 3y - 11 = 0$ (iii) $2x - 5y + 34 = 0$ (iv) $x + 7y - 40 = 0$ (v) $3x + 5y + 28 = 0$ (vi) $y + 1 = 0$ **3.** (i) $y = x - 1$ (ii) $x - 3y + 10 = 0$ (iii) $2x - y + 9 = 0$ (iv) $x + y - 3 = 0$ (v) $7x + y - 4 = 0$ (vi) $y - 1 = 0$ **4.** (i) $x + 3y - 4 = 0$ (ii) $x - y + 6 = 0$ (iii) $14x + 9y - 39 = 0$ (iv) $2x - 3y + 1 = 0$ (v) $9x + y + 23 = 0$ (vi) $3x - y - 2 = 0$ **5.** $4x - y - 2 = 0, y = 1$ **6.** $3x - y - 6 = 0, 2x + y - 12 = 0$ **7.** (i) $x = 1$ (ii) $x = -1$ (iii) $x = -5$ (iv) $y = 4$ (v) $y = 3$ (vi) $y = 5$ **8.** $0 = 0$ **9.** $0 = 0$ **10.** $x + 8y - 11 = 0$

Exercise 18.7

7. (i) The slope of l is $\frac{2}{5}$ $2x - 5y + 23 = 0$ (Equation by l) (ii) $C\left(0, \frac{23}{5}\right)$ **8.** (i) $3x - 4y + 15 = 0$ (Equation of l_1) (ii) (3,6) is the point of intersection of l_1 and l_2

Exercise 18.8

1. (i) $\frac{3-1}{2-1} = 2$ (ii) $\frac{-1}{2}$ **2.** (i) $y = \frac{-5}{3}x - 2$ (ii) $y = \frac{-1}{4}x - 5$ (iii) $y = \frac{-8}{9}x + 2$ (iv) $y = \frac{1}{2}x + \frac{1}{3}$ (v) $y = \frac{-9}{5}x - 8$ (vi) $y = \frac{-1}{5}x - 3$ (vii) $y = \frac{-2}{3}x + 11$ (viii) $y = \frac{1}{5}x + \frac{2}{5}$ (ix) $y = \frac{-7}{3}x + 2$ **3.** (i) −2 (ii) $\frac{1}{3}$ (iii) 5 (iv) 2 (v) $\frac{-4}{9}$ (vi) $\frac{7}{3}$ **4.** $3x - 2y - 12 = 0$ **5.** $6x + y + 16 = 0$ **6.** $2x - y + 4 = 0$ **7.** $x + y - 4 = 0$

Exercise 18.9

1. (i) 15 sq units (ii) 2 sq units (iii) 1 sq unit (iv) 2 sq units **2.** (i) 1 (ii) 11.5 (iii) 18 (iv) 16 **3.** (i) 4 sq units (ii) 8.5 sq units (iii) 13 sq units (iv) 10 sq units **4.** (i) $\frac{1}{2}|-4 + 4| = 0 \Rightarrow$ Collinear (ii) area $= \frac{1}{2}|4.0 - 2.0| = 0 \Rightarrow$ Collinear. (iii) $\frac{1}{2}|-48 + 48| = 0 \Rightarrow$ Collinear (iv) area $= \frac{1}{2}|3(-2) - 6(-1)| = 0 \Rightarrow$ Collinear. **5.** (ii) 16 sq units. **6.** (ii) 33.5 units^2 **7.** (i) 3 sq units (ii) 4 sq units (iii) 2 sq units (iv) 3 sq units. **8.** (i) $\left(\frac{-1+3}{2}, \frac{-6-2}{2}\right)$, $C(1,-4)$ (iii) $\frac{-2+6}{3+1} = \frac{4}{4} = 1$ (iv) $x + y + 3 = 0$ (vii) $|AB| = \sqrt{32}$, $|CD| = \sqrt{50}$ (viii) $ABD = 20$ units^2 **9.** (i) $Y(5,0)$ (iii) $\frac{4}{10} = \frac{2}{5}$ (iv) $5x + 2y = 25$ (vi) $\sqrt{116}$ (vii) $\sqrt{29}$ (viii) 29 sq units **10.** (i) $M(4,3)$

Revision Exercises

1. (ii) (1, −2) (iv) $\frac{-5-1}{4+2} = -1$ (v) $x + y + 1 = 0$ (vi) (−1,0) **2.** (ii) $D = (-1,-1)$, $C = (0,1)$ **3.** (ii) (1.5,0) (iii) $\frac{4}{1.5} = \frac{8}{3}$ (iv) $8x - 3y - 12 = 0$ (v) (0,−4) (vi) 6 sq units **4.** (ii) $\frac{5}{7}$ (iii) $7y = 5x + 32$ (iv) $\left(0, \frac{32}{7}\right)$ (v) $y = \frac{5}{7}x + \frac{32}{7}$ **5.** (ii) $k = 6$ (iv) $\frac{6-0}{0-2} = -3$ (v) $y = -3x + 6$ **6.** (i) $2x - y - 1 = 0$ (ii) $2x + 3y + 18 = 0$ **7.** (a) $x - 3y + 11 = 0$ (b) (i) $4x - 3y - 1 = 0$ (ii) point of intersection: (4,5) **8.** (i) 4 sq units (ii) 8.5 sq units (iii) 6 sq units

9.

Equation	Line
$x = 3$	r
$x - y + 5 = 0$	q
$y = -\frac{3}{4}x + 5$	p

10. (i) $m = -\frac{2}{3}$ (ii) $m = \frac{1}{3}$ (iii) $m = 3$ (iv) $m = \frac{5}{8}$ **11.** Point of intersection: (1,1) **12.** Point of intersection: (1,−2)

Exam Questions

1. (a) $5x - 2y - 10 = 0$ (c) **Numerical:** $l \cap k = \left(3, 2\frac{1}{2}\right)$ **Algebraic:** $\left(3, 2\frac{1}{2}\right)$ **2.** (a) (i) (4,1) (b) 6.08 (c) (−2, 2) (d) 30 **3.** (a) (i) 1 (ii) $x - y + 4 = 0$ (b) $x + y = 0$

Chapter 19

Exercise 19.1

1. (i) 4 (ii) 9 (iii) 1 (iv) 144 (v) 25 (vi) 2 (vii) 5 (viii) $\frac{9}{16}$ (ix) $\frac{1}{4}$ (x) $\left(\frac{7}{3}\right)^2, \frac{49}{9}$ **2.** 625 **3.** 100 **4.** 25 **5.** (i) 5 (ii) 10 (iii) 8 (iv) 9 (v) 2 (vi) 7 (vii) $\sqrt{3}$

(viii) $\sqrt{5}$ (ix) $\frac{3}{2}$ (x) $\frac{10}{3}$ (xi) $\frac{7}{5}$ (xii) $\frac{11}{6}$

7. (i) $A(2,0)$, $B(0,2)$, $C(-2,0)$, $D(0,-2)$ (ii) $A(6,0)$, $B(0,6)$, $C(-6,0)$ $D(0,-6)$ **8.** (i) 25 (ii) 100 (iii) 144 (iv) 49 **9.** (i) (0,0) (ii) $r = 2$ (iv) 12.57 **10.** (i) (0,0) (ii) $r = 6$ (iv) 37.70 (v) Yes **13.** (i) centre = (0,0) (ii) $\sqrt{26}$ (iii) 26 (iv) ≈ 81.68 square units (v) No

Exercise 19.2

1. (i) (−4,3) (5,0) (ii) (−6,−8) (6,8) (iii) (−2,1) (1,2) (iv) (−5,1) (5,1) (v) (−2,4) **2.** (i) (2,4) (2,−4) (ii) (−4,2) (4,2) (iii) (−2,4) (−2,−4) (iv) (−4,−2) (4,−2) **3.** (i) (4,2) and (−2,4) (ii) $y = 0$, $y = -4$, (5,0) and (−3,−4) (iii) (2,4) and (−2,−4) (iv) (6,−2) and (−6,−2) **4.** (1,3) and (3,1)

5. (3,2) and (−2,−3) **6.** $\left(\frac{17}{5}, -\frac{19}{5}\right)$ and (−1,5) **7.** $\left(\frac{78}{25}, \frac{6}{50}\right)$ and (−3,1) **8.** (i) (1,−1) is the point of contact ⇒ tangent (ii) (5,0) is the point of contact ⇒ tangent (iii) (−2,4) is the point of contact ⇒ tangent

(iv) $\left(\frac{3}{2}, \frac{3}{2}\right)$ is the point of contact⇒ tangent

9. (i) (0,0) (ii) $\sqrt{10}$ (iii) $\sqrt{10}$ (iv) yes (vii) (−3,−1)

Exercise 19.3

1. (i) 25 (ii) 9 (iii) 1 (iv) 16 (v) 4 (vi) 36 **2.** (i) 64 (ii) 36 (iii) 81 (iv) 49 (v) $\frac{1}{4}$ (vi) 3 **3.** (i) $\sqrt{41}$ (ii) 41

4. (i) $\sqrt{20}$ (ii) 20 **5.** (i) $r = 5$ (ii) $r = 6$ (iii) $r = 7$ (iv) $r = 1$ (v) $r = 8$ **6.** (i) $r = 10$ (ii) $r = 7$ (iii) $r = 9$ (iv) $r = \frac{1}{3}$ (v) $r = \sqrt{5}$ **7.** (i) (1,1) (ii) $\sqrt{13}$ (iii) 13 **Q. 8.** (i) (1,2) (ii) $\sqrt{34}$ (iii) 34 **9.** (i) 4 (ii) 16 **10.** (i) 3 (ii) 9 **11.** (i) (2,2) (ii) $r = 2$ (iii) 4 **12.** (i) 4 units (ii) m : $y = 8$, n : $x = 8$ (iv) (8,8) (v) 64 sq units **13.** (ii) $\sqrt{10}$ (iii) 10 **14.** $(x - 2)^2 + (y - 3)^2 = 9$ **15.** (a) (i) $A(-2,3)$ (ii) 10 (b) (i) $-\frac{4}{3}$ (ii) $3x - 4y + 68 = 0$ (c) Q (4,−5)

16. (i) $3x + y - 10 = 0$ (ii) $2x - y + 10 = 0$ (iii) $3x + 4y = 0$ (iv) $x - y - 1 = 0$ (v) $2x + 3y - 9 = 0$

Exercise 19.4

1. (i) $a = -4$, $b = 4$, $c = 4$, $d = -4$ (ii) $A(-4,0)$, $B(4,0)$ (iii) $C(0,4)$, $D(0,-4)$ **2.** (i) $e = -7$, $f = 7$, $g = 7$, $h = -7$ (ii) $E = (-7,0)$, $F = (7,0)$ (iii) $G = (0,7)$, $H = (0,-7)$ **5.** (i) (−3,0) and (7,0) (ii) (3,0) and (−9,0) (iii) (−15,0) and (5,0) **6.** (i) (0,−5) and (0,13) (ii) (0,−5) and (0,15) (iii) (0,−7) and (0,5) **7.** (i) B(0,−2) and A(0,4) (ii) $x^2 + (y - 1)^2 = 9$ **8.** (i) $A(-3,0)$ and $B(7,0)$ (ii) n: $(x - 2)^2 + y^2 = 25$ **9.** (i) (7,4) is outside the circle (ii) (−5,4) is on the circle (iii) (1,1) is inside the circle **10.** A is inside the circle **11.** $B(7,3)$ lies outside the circle **12.** D is on c4 **13.** (i) $(x - 2)^2 + (y + 3)^2 = 16$ (iv) 64 cm²

Revision Exercises

1. (i) $c(0, 0)$, $r = 2$ (ii) $c(0, 0)$, $r = 12$ (iii) $c(0, 0)$, $r = \frac{5}{8}$ (iv) $c(0, 0)$, $r = \frac{11}{9}$ **2.** (3, 2) (3, 2) **3.** (−1, −3) (3, −1)

4. (i) 9 (ii) 25 (iii) 64 (iv) 1 **5.** (i) $c(3, -2)$, $r = 10$ (ii) $c(-1, 3)$, $r = 7$ (iii) $c(0, -2)$, $r = 8$ (iv) $c(2, 0)$, $r = 11$ **6.** (i) A (−3,0) (ii) $r = 4$ (iii) 16 (iv) $(0,\sqrt{7})(0,-\sqrt{7})$ **7.** (i) R (−1,1) (ii) $r = 5$ (iv) A is on circle.

(v) $A(3,-2) \rightarrow R(-1,1) \rightarrow B(-5,4)$ **8.** (i) Centre t (0,3), Radius 2, Centre s (0,0), Radius 1, Centre $u\left(0,-\frac{7}{2}\right)$, Radius $\frac{5}{2}$ (ii) $\frac{25}{4}$ (iii) 2π (iv) 4π (v) 2 : 1 (vi) yes **9.** (ii) $x^2 + y^2 = 50$ (iii) $p = \pm 5$ (iv) $n = 6$ **10.** (i) 3 (ii) (x − 7) squared + (y − 3) squared = 9 (iv) (13,6)

Exam Questions

1. (a) $x^2 + y^2 = 100$ (b) $(x - 4)^2 + (y - 3)^2 = 25$ (c) P (8,0)

2. (c) 50 **3.** (a) (i) A (−2,3), 10 (b) (i) $-\frac{4}{3}$ (ii) $3x - 4y + 68 = 0$ (c) $Q(4, -5)$ **4.** (a) $x^2 + y^2 = 5^2 = 25$

(b) $x^2 + y^2 = (-3)^2 + 4^2 = 9 + 16 = 25 = r^2$

(c) $(x + 6)^2 + (y - 8)^2 = 25$ (d) $y - 4 = \frac{3}{4}(x + 3) \Rightarrow 3x - 4y + 25 = 0$

5. (b) $x^2 + y^2 = (4)^2$, $[\Rightarrow x^2 + y^2 = 16]$